PrincetonReview.com

THE BEST 368 COLLEGES

2009 Edition

**By Robert Franek,
Tom Meltzer, Christopher Maier, Erik Olson,
Julie Doherty, and Eric Owens**

Random House, Inc., New York
2009 Edition

The Princeton Review, Inc.
2315 Broadway
New York, NY 10024
E-mail: bookeditor@review.com

ISBN   978-0-375-42872-2

VP, Publisher: Robert Franek
Editors: Seamus Mullarkey, Adam Davis, Laura Braswell
Senior Production Editor: M. Tighe Wall
Executive Director, Print Production: Scott Harris
Director, Data Collection: Ben Zelevansky

Printed in the United States of America.

9 8 7 6 5 4 3 2 1

2009 Edition

FOREWORD

Every year, about two million high school graduates go to college. To make sure they end up at the *right* school, they spend several billion dollars on the admissions process. This money pays for countless admissions officers and counselors, a bunch of standardized tests (and preparation for them), and many books similar to—but not as good as—this one.

It's expensive because most admissions professionals have a thing about being in control. As a group, colleges resist almost every attempt to standardize or otherwise simplify the process. Admissions officers want you to believe that every admissions decision that they render occurs within systems of weights, measures, and deliberations that are far too complex for you to comprehend. They shudder at the notion of having to respond to students and their parents in down-to-earth language that might reveal the arbitrary nature of a huge percentage of the admissions and denials that they issue during each cycle. That would be admitting that good luck and circumstance play a major part in many successful applications. So, in flight from public accountability, they make the process a lot more mysterious than it needs to be.

Even the most straightforward colleges hide the information you would want to know about the way they'll evaluate your application: What grades and SATs are they looking for? Exactly how much do extracurricular activities count? What percentage of the aid that they give out is in loans and what percentage is in grants?

We couldn't get answers to these questions from many colleges. In fact, we couldn't get answers to *any* questions from some schools. Others who supplied this information to us for earlier editions of this guide have since decided that they never should have in the first place. After all, knowledge is power.

Colleges seem to have the time and money to create beautiful brochures that generally show that all college classes are held under a tree on a beautiful day. Why not just tell you what sort of students they're looking for and what factors they'll use to consider your application?

Until the schools demystify the admissions process, this book is your best bet. It's not a phone book containing every fact about every college in the country. And it's not a memoir written by a few graduates describing their favorite dining halls or professors. We've given you the facts you'll need to apply to the few hundred best schools in the country, and we offer enough information about them—which we gathered from more than 120,000 current college students—to help you make a smart decision about which school to attend.

As complicated and difficult as the admissions process is, we think you'll love college itself—especially at the schools listed in this book.

Good luck in your search.

John Katzman
June 2008

ACKNOWLEDGMENTS

Each year we assemble an awe-inspiringly talented group of colleagues who work together to produce our guidebooks; this year is no exception. Everyone involved in this effort—authors, editors, data collectors, production specialists, and designers—gives so much more than is required to make *The Best 368 Colleges* an exceptional student resource guide. This new edition yields the essentials of what prospective college students really want: The most honest, accessible, and pertinent information about the colleges they are considering attending for the next four years of their lives. My sincere thanks go to the many who contributed to this tremendous project. I am proud to note here that we have again successfully provided an uncompromising look into the true nature of each profiled college or university based on the opinions of each institution's current students. I know our readers will benefit from our collective efforts.

A special thank you goes to our authors, Tom Meltzer, Christopher Maier, Erik Olson, Julie Doherty, and Eric Owens, for their dedication in sifting through tens of thousands of surveys to produce the essence of each school profiled. Very special thanks go to Adrinda Kelly, Adam Davis, and Laura Braswell for their editorial commitment and vision. They met the challenges of this book head on; I am grateful for their thoughtful and careful reading.

A warm and special thank you goes to our Student Survey Manager Jen Adams, who works exceptionally well with school administrators and students alike. Jen is in the trenches every day, and her spirit never wavers.

My continued thanks go to our data collection pros, Ben Zelevansky and David Soto, for their successful efforts in collecting and accurately representing the statistical data that appear with each college profile. A sincere thank-you goes to Ben Zelevansky for all the detailed work he completed for data generation and presentation.

The enormousness of this project and its deadline constraints could not have been realized without the calm presence of our production team, Scott Harris, Executive Director of Print Production; and M. Tighe Wall, Senior Production Editor. Their unconditional dedication, focus, and most important, careful eyes, continue to inspire and impress me. They deserve great thanks for their flexible schedules and uncompromising efficiency.

Special thanks also go to Jeanne Krier, our Random House publicist, for the work she has done on this book and the overall series since its inception. Jeanne continues to be my trusted colleague, media advisor, and friend. I would also like to make special mention of Tom Russell and Nicole Benhabib, our Random House publishing team, for their continuous investment and faith in our ideas.

Last, I thank John Katzman, Mark Chernis, and Young Shin for their steadfast confidence in this book and our publishing department, and for always being the champions of student opinion. It is a pleasure to work with each of you.

Again, to all who contributed so much to this publication, thank you for your efforts; they do not go unnoticed.

Robert Franek
VP—Publisher
Lead Author—*The Best 368 Colleges*

CONTENTS

PART I INTRODUCTION

GETTING INTO SELECTIVE COLLEGES:
A GUIDE FOR HIGH SCHOOL STUDENTS

This is a guide to the nation's 368 most academically outstanding institutions, so it's no surprise that many of them may be selective in their admissions. If you're like any one of the 2,000,000 (and growing!) high school students who apply to college each year, you're probably wondering what admissions officers at these schools are looking for in an applicant. What exactly does it take to get into a selective college? To be sure, high grades in challenging courses are just the beginning. To get into most of the colleges in this book, you will need to:

- Earn high grades
- Enroll in challenging courses
- Prepare for the SAT or the ACT, and SAT Subject Tests
- Polish your writing skills
- Plan ahead for those letters of recommendation you'll need by establishing great relationships with your teachers and advisors
- Focus on activities, community service, and/or after-school or summer employment that show commitment over a long period of time and allow you to demonstrate leadership skills

Here's a brief primer in what you should be doing year by year in high school to prepare yourself for admission to *your* "Best" college. For a detailed guide on how you can make the most of your high school years and segue those experiences into a successful college application, check out our book: *The Road to College: The High School Student's Guide to Discovering Your Passion, Getting Involved, and Getting Admitted.* Pick it up at PrincetonReview.com/college/bookstore.asp.

Freshman Year

It's easier to finish well in high school if you start off that way. Concentrate on your studies and work hard to earn good grades. Get to know your teachers and ask for their help if you are having trouble in a subject (or even if you just really enjoy it and want to learn more). They'll most certainly want to help you do your best. Odds are, there is an honor roll at your school: Make it a goal to get on it. And if your grades are so good that you qualify for membership in the National Honor Society, pat yourself on the back and don't think twice about accepting the invitation to join.

Make it a point to meet your guidance counselor to begin thinking about colleges you may be interested in and courses and admission tests they require. Also work on building your vocabulary to get an early start on prepping for the SAT and ACT. Sign up for the Princeton Review's Vocab Minute on PrincetonReview.com. Consider participating in the National Vocabulary Championship (www.WinWithWords.com).

The Princeton Review is a proud partner of this contest with the Game Show Network, now in its second year. Last year, winners walked away with over $100,000 in prizes and Princeton Review services. To learn how you can enter, visit WinWithWords.com.

Read a Good Book!

Your vocabulary and reading skills are key to doing well on the SAT and ACT. You can do some early prep for both tests by reading good books. Here are some fiction and non-fiction books we love by great authors you may not have encountered before.

- *The Curious Incident of the Dog in the Night-Time: A Novel* by Mark Haddon
- *A Heartbreaking Work of Staggering Genius* by Dave Eggers
- *Life of Pi* by Yann Martel
- *Reading Lolita in Tehran* by Azar Nafisi
- *White Teeth* by Zadie Smith

For extra practice building your vocabulary, check out our *Word Smart* books. Full of mnemonic tricks, they make learning even the toughest vocabulary a breeze.

Sophomore Year

As a sophomore, you'll need to stay focused on your studies. You'll also want to choose one or more extracurriculars that interest you. Admissions Officers look favorably on involvement in student government, student newspaper, varsity sports, and community service. But don't overload your schedule with activities just to rack up a long list of extracurriculars that you hope will impress admissions officers. Colleges would much rather see you focus on a few worthwhile extracurriculars than divide your time among a bunch of different activities that you're not passionate about. If you didn't earn strong grades during your freshman year, start doing so this year. Scope out the Advanced Placement course offerings at your school. You'll want to sign up for as many AP courses as you can reasonably take, starting in your junior year. Our test-prep series, *Cracking the AP*, can help give you a leg up on passing the AP exams and gaining college credit while in high school, and Admissions Officers will want to see that you've earned high grades in challenging classes.

Your sophomore year is when you'll have an opportunity to take the PSAT. Given every October, the PSAT is a shortened version of the SAT. It is used to predict how well students may do on the SAT and it determines eligibility for National Merit Scholarships. While your PSAT scores won't count until you retake the test in your junior year, you should approach this as a test run for the real thing. Check out our book, *Cracking the PSAT /NMSQT* for more info. It has two full-length practice tests and tips on how to score your best on the test.

What Should You Do This Summer?

Ahhh, summer. The possibilities seem endless. You can get a job, intern, travel, study, volunteer, or do nothing at all. The Princeton Review book *500 Ways for Teens to Spend the Summer* offers plenty of suggestions of ways for you to get involved in summer activities. It's full of advice and features a directory of 500 summer programs for college-bound teens. Our other book, *The Road to College*, also has great suggestions for summer projects. Here are a few ideas to get you started:

- **Go to College**: No, not for real. However, you can participate in summer programs at colleges and universities at home and abroad. Programs can focus on anything from academics (stretch your brain by taking an intensive science or language course) to sports to admissions guidance. This is also a great opportunity to explore college life firsthand, especially if you get to stay in a dorm.
- **Prep for the PSAT, SAT, or ACT:** So maybe it's not quite as adventurous as trekking around Patagonia for the summer or as cool as learning to slam dunk at basketball camp, but hey, there's nothing adventurous or cool about being rejected from your top-choice college because of unimpressive test scores. Plus, you'll be ahead of the game if you can return to school with much of your PSAT, SAT, and ACT preparation behind you.
- **Research Scholarships:** College is expensive. While you should never rule out a school based on cost, the more scholarship money you can secure beforehand, the more college options you will have. You'll find loads of info on financial aid and scholarships (including a scholarship search tool) on our site, PrincetonReview.com.

Junior Year

You'll start the year off by taking the PSAT in October. High PSAT scores in junior year qualify you for the National Merit Scholarship competition. To become a finalist, you also need great grades and a recommendation from your school.

Make sure your grades are high this year. When colleges look at your transcripts they put a heavy emphasis on junior year grades. Decisions are made before admissions officers see your second-semester senior-year grades, and possibly before they see your first-semester senior-year grades! It's critical that your junior-year grades are solid.

During your junior year, you'll probably take the SAT or ACT test for the first time. Most colleges require scores from one of these tests for admission and/or scholarship award decisions. Plan to spend 3–12 weeks preparing for the tests. The SAT is comprised of Math, Critical Reading, and Writing sections. Colleges will see your individual section scores and your composite score, but generally they'll be most concerned with your composite score.

More and more students are opting to take the ACT in addition to, or instead of, the SAT. Most colleges accept the ACT in lieu of the SAT. The ACT has an English, Reading, Math, and Science section, plus the optional Writing section. (Some schools require the essay, so be sure to ask before you take the test.) One great advantage of the ACT is that you can take the test several times and choose what scores to send. If you take the SAT several times, all your scores are sent to the colleges. If you're not sure which test to take, first make sure that all the schools to which you're applying accept both tests. If they do, then take the test on which you do better. Visit PrincetonReview.com to take a free assessment test that will help you identify whether the ACT or SAT is better for you.

Most highly selective colleges also require you to take three SAT Subject Tests in addition to the SAT or ACT. If you have SAT Subject Tests to take, plan now. You can't take the SAT and SAT Subject Tests on the same day. It's worth noting that The Princeton Review can help with all the standardized tests you will need to take throughout high school. Log on to PrincetonReview.com/college/testprep/.

Also take time during your junior year to research colleges, and, if possible, visit schools high on your "hopes" list. When researching colleges, you'll want to consider a variety of factors besides whether or not you can get in, including location, school size, majors or programs offered that interest you, and cost and availability of financial aid. It helps to visit schools because it's the best way to learn whether a school may be right for you. If you can schedule an interview with an admissions officer during your visit, it may help him or her discover how right *you may be* for the school. The Princeton Review book, *Guide to College Visits*, offers plenty of tips on how you can make the most of your college visits, plus it has profiles of more than 370 popular colleges with tips on how to get there, where to stay, and what to do on campus.

Senior Year

It's time to get serious about pulling everything together on your applications. Deadlines will vary from school to school and you will have a lot to keep track of, so make checklists of what's due when. If you're not happy with your previous SAT scores, you should take the October SAT. If you still need to take any SAT Subject Tests, now's the time.

If you have found the school of your dreams and you're happy with your grades and test scores, consider filing an Early Decision application. Many selective colleges commit more than half of their admissions spots to Early Decision applicants. To take this route, you must file your application in early November. By mid-December, you'll find out whether you got in—but there's a catch. If you're accepted Early Decision to a college, you must withdraw all applications to other colleges. This means that your financial aid offer might be hard to negotiate, so be prepared to take what you get.

Regardless of which route you decide to take, have a backup plan. Make sure you apply to at least one safety school—one that you feel confident you can get into and afford. Another option is to apply Early Decision at one school, but apply to other colleges during the regular decision period in the event that you are rejected from the early decision college.

Financial Aid 101

All students applying for financial aid (including federal, state, and institutional need-based aid), need to complete the FAFSA (Free Application for Federal Student Aid) form. The form is available in high schools in December, but you can't submit it until January. You may also need to complete the CSS/PROFILE form, state aid forms, and any additional forms provided by the colleges. The Princeton Review's *Paying for College Without Going Broke* is the only annually-updated guide that explains how the financial aid process works and how to maximize your eligibility for aid. It gives line-by-line strategies for completing the FAFSA, which is particularly complicated and crucial. The FASFA is the need analysis document used to determine your "EFC" (Expected Family Contribution)—the amount of money the family is expected to ante up towards the cost of college.

When you ask teachers to write recommendations for you, give them everything they need. Tell them your application deadline and include a stamped, addressed envelope, or directions on how to submit the recommendation online, and be sure to send them a thank-you note after you know the recommendation was turned in. Your essay, on the other hand, is the one part of your application you have total control over. Don't repeat information from other parts of your application. And by all means, proofread! You'll find tips from admissions officers on what they look for (and what peeves them the most) about college applicants' essays in our book, *College Essays That Made a Difference*.

In March/April, colleges will send you a decision from the admissions office regarding your admission or rejection. If you are admitted (and you applied for financial aid) you'll also receive a decision from the financial aid office detailing your aid award package. The decision from the financial aid office can sometimes be appealed. The decision from the admissions office is almost always final. If you are wait-listed, don't lose hope. Write a letter to the college expressing how much you'd still like to attend the school and include an update on your recent activities. When colleges admit students from wait lists, they almost always give preference to students who have made it clear that they really want to attend.

It's important to wait until you've heard from all of the colleges you've applied to before making your final choice. May 1 is when you'll need to commit to the lucky college that will have you in its freshman class. We know how exciting but stressful that decision can be. If you're having a difficult time choosing between two colleges, try to visit each of them one more time. Can you imagine yourself walking around that campus, building a life in that community, and establishing friendships with those people? Finally, decide and be happy. Don't forget to thank your recommenders and tell them where you'll be going to school. Some of the best times of your life await!

GREAT SCHOOLS FOR 15 OF THE MOST POPULAR UNDERGRADUATE MAJORS

Worried about having to declare a major on your college application? Relax. Most colleges won't require you to declare a major until the end of your sophomore year, giving you plenty of time to explore your options. However, problems may arise if you are thinking about majoring in a program that limits its enrollment—meaning that if you don't declare that major early on, you might not get into that program at a later date. On the flip side, some students declare a major on their application because they believe it will boost their chances of gaining admission. This is a slippery slope to climb, however. If you later decide to change your major and it involves switching from one school within the college to another (from the school of arts and sciences to the school of business, for example), it can be tricky.

Never choose a college solely on the perceived prestige of a particular pro gram. College will expose you to new and exciting learning opportunities. To choose a school based on a major before you even know what else is out there would limit you in many ways. (Choosing a school based on program availability is a different story.) You may also want to investigate opportunities to design your own major. At the end of these lists, you'll find info on our other resources to help you choose a major and find colleges offering great programs in these and other fields.

How did we compile these lists?

Each year we collect data from more than a thousand colleges on the subject of—among many other things—undergraduate academic offerings. We ask colleges not only to report which undergraduate majors they offer, but also which of their majors have the highest enrollment. The list below identifies (in alphabetical order) fifteen of the forty "most popular" majors that the schools responding to our survey reported to us. We also conduct our own research on college majors. We look at institutional data and we consult with our in-house college admissions experts as well as our National College Counselor Advisory Panel (whom we list in our Index, p. 797) for their input on schools offering great programs in these majors. We thank them and all of the guidance counselors, college admissions counselors, and education experts across the country whose recommendations we considered in developing these lists.

Of the roughly 3,500 schools across the United States, those on these lists represent only a snapshot of the many offering great programs in these majors. Use our lists as a starting point for further research. Some schools on these lists may not appear in the Best 368 Colleges (these are marked with an asterisk*), but you can find profiles of them in our Complete Book of Colleges: 2009 Edition.

Great Schools for Accounting Majors

- Alfred University
- Auburn University
- Babson College
- Baylor University
- Birmingham—Southern College
- Boston College
- Boston University
- Brigham Young University
- Bucknell University
- Calvin College
- Claremont McKenna College
- Clemson University
- College of Charleston
- Cornell University
- DePaul University
- Drexel University
- Duquesne University
- Elon University
- Emory University
- Fordham University
- Georgetown University
- Indiana University—Bloomington
- Iowa State University
- James Madison University
- Lehigh University
- Michigan State University
- New York University
- Northeastern University
- Pennsylvania State University
- Pepperdine University
- Rider University
- Rochester Institute of Technology
- Seton Hall University
- Suffolk University
- Temple University
- Texas A&M University— College Station
- University of Illinois at Urbana- Champaign
- University of Michigan— Ann Arbor
- University of Pennsylvania
- University of Southern California
- The University of Texas at Austin

Great Schools for Biology Majors

- Agnes Scott College
- Albion College
- Austin College
- Baylor University
- Brandeis University
- Carleton College
- Colby College
- Cornell University
- Drexel University
- Duke University
- Guilford College
- Harvard College
- Haverford College
- Howard University
- Illinois Wesleyan University
- Indiana University—Bloomington
- Johns Hopkins University
- Louisiana State University
- Loyola University—Chicago
- Massachusetts Institute of Technology
- Mount Holyoke College
- The Ohio State University— Columbus
- Pomona College
- Reed College
- Rice University
- Siena College
- Swarthmore College
- Temple University
- Texas A&M University— College Station
- University of California—Davis
- The University of Chicago
- University of Dallas
- University of Delaware
- University of Denver
- University of New Mexico
- University of the Pacific
- Wofford College
- Xavier University of Louisiana

Great Schools for Business/Finance Majors

- Babson College
- Bentley College
- Boston College

Schools marked with an asterisk do not appear in the *Best 368 Colleges*.
You can find those school profiles in *Complete Book of Colleges, 2009 Edition*.

- Carnegie Mellon University
- City University of New York—Baruch College
- Cornell University
- DePaul University
- Emory University
- Florida State University
- Indiana University—Bloomington
- Iowa State University
- Lehigh University
- Massachusetts Institute of Technology
- Miami University
- Michigan State University
- New York University
- Northwestern University
- Ohio University—Athens
- Rice University
- Seattle University
- University of California—Berkeley
- University of California—Los Angeles
- University of Chicago
- University of Florida
- University of Illinois at Urbana-Champaign
- University of Michigan
- University of Pennsylvania
- University of Southern California
- The University of Texas at Austin
- University of Virginia
- Washington University in St. Louis
- Wharton University of Pennsylvania

Great Schools for Communications Majors
- Augsburg College*
- Baylor University
- Boise State University*
- Boston University
- Bradley University
- City University of New York—Hunter College
- Clemson University
- College of Charleston

- Cornell University
- Denison University
- DePaul University
- Duquesne University
- Eckerd College
- Emerson College
- Fairfield University
- Fordham University
- Gonzaga University
- Gustavus Adolphus College
- Hollins University
- Indiana University—Bloomington
- Iowa State University
- Ithaca College
- James Madison University
- Lake Forest College
- Loyola University—New Orleans
- Michigan State University
- Muhlenberg College
- New York University
- Northwestern University
- Pepperdine University
- Ripon College
- Salisbury University
- Seton Hall University
- St. John's University (NY)
- Stanford University
- Suffolk University
- Syracuse University
- University of California—San Diego
- University of California—Santa Barbara
- University of Iowa
- University of Maryland—College Park
- University of Southern California
- The University of Texas at Austin
- University of Utah

Great Schools for Computer Science/Computer Engineering Majors
- Auburn University
- Boston University
- Bradley University
- Brown University
- California Institute of Technology

Schools marked with an asterisk do not appear in the *Best 368 Colleges*.
You can find those school profiles in *Complete Book of Colleges, 2009 Edition*.

- Carnegie Mellon University
- Clemson University
- Drexel University
- Florida State University
- George Mason University
- Georgia Institute of Technology
- Gonzaga University
- Hampton University
- Harvey Mudd College
- Iowa State University
- Johns Hopkins University
- Lehigh University
- Massachusetts Institute of Technology
- Michigan State University
- New Jersey Institute of Technology
- Northeastern University
- Northwestern University
- Princeton University
- Rice University
- Rochester Institute of Technology
- Rose-Hulman Institute of Technology
- Seattle University
- Stanford University
- State University of New York at Binghamton
- State University of New York— University at Buffalo
- Texas A&M University— College Station
- United States Air Force Academy
- University of Arizona
- University of California— Berkeley
- University of California— Los Angeles
- University of California— Riverside
- University of Illinois at Urbana-Champaign
- University of Massachusetts— Amherst
- University of Michigan— Ann Arbor
- University of Washington

Great Schools for Criminology Majors

- American University
- Auburn University
- City University of New York— John Jay College of Criminal Justice*
- North Carolina State University
- The Ohio State University— Columbus
- Ohio University—Athens
- Quinnipiac University
- Sam Houston State University
- Suffolk University
- University of California—Irvine
- University of Delaware
- University of Denver
- University of Maryland— College Park
- University of Miami
- University of New Hampshire
- University of South Florida
- University of Utah
- Valparaiso University

Great Schools for Education Majors

- Adelphi University*
- Alma College*
- Arcadia University*
- Ashland University*
- Auburn University
- Augsburg College*
- Barnard College
- Bethany College (WV)*
- Bryn Athyn College of the New Church*
- Bucknell University
- California State University— Sacramento*
- Carthage College*
- City University of New York— Brooklyn College
- City University of New York— Hunter College
- Colgate University
- College of William & Mary
- Columbia College (MO)
- Columbia University

Schools marked with an asterisk do not appear in the *Best 368 Colleges*. You can find those school profiles in *Complete Book of Colleges, 2009 Edition*.

- Cornell College
- Cornell University
- Duquesne University
- Elon University
- Franklin Pierce College*
- Gonzaga University
- Goucher College
- Hardin-Simmons University*
- Hillsdale College
- Indiana University—Bloomington
- Jewish Theological Seminary— Albert A. List College*
- LaSalle University*
- Loyola Marymount University
- Marquette University
- McGill University
- Miami University
- Montana State University— Bozeman*
- Nazareth College of Rochester*
- New York Institute of Technology*
- New York University
- Northeastern University
- Northwestern University
- The Ohio State University— Columbus
- San Francisco State University*
- Simmons College
- Skidmore College
- Smith College
- State University of New York— New Paltz*
- Trinity University (Washington, DC)*
- Trinity University (San Antonio, TX)
- University of Maine
- The University of Montana
- University of St. Thomas (TX)
- University of Toledo*
- Vanderbilt University
- Villanova College
- Wagner College
- Wellesley College
- Xavier University (OH)

Great Schools for Engineering Majors

- California Institute of Technology
- California Polytechnic State University
- Carnegie Mellon University
- Columbia University
- Cooper Union
- Cornell University
- Drexel University
- Duke University
- Franklin W. Olin College of Engineering
- Georgia Institute of Technology
- Harvard College
- Harvey Mudd College
- Illinois Institute of Technology
- Johns Hopkins University
- Massachusetts Institute of Technology
- Pennsylvania State University
- Princeton University
- Purdue University— West Lafayette
- Rose-Hulman Institute of Technology
- Stanford University
- Texas A&M University— College Station
- University of California—Berkeley
- University of California— Los Angeles
- The University of Texas at Austin
- University of Wisconsin—Madison
- Worcester Polytechnic Institute

Great Schools for English Literature and Language Majors

- Amherst College
- Auburn University
- Bard College
- Barnard College
- Bennington College
- Boston College
- Brown University
- City University of New York— Hunter College
- Claremont McKenna College

Schools marked with an asterisk do not appear in the *Best 368 Colleges*.
You can find those school profiles in *Complete Book of Colleges, 2009 Edition*.

- Clemson University
- Colby College
- Colgate University
- Columbia University
- Cornell University
- Dartmouth College
- Denison University
- Duke University
- Emory University
- Fordham University
- George Mason University
- Gettysburg College
- Harvard College
- Johns Hopkins University
- Kenyon College
- The New School University
- Pitzer College
- Pomona College
- Princeton University
- Rice University
- Stanford University
- Syracuse University
- Tufts University
- University of California—Berkeley
- The University of Chicago
- University of Michigan—Ann Arbor
- University of Notre Dame
- University of Utah
- Vassar College
- Washington University in St. Louis
- Wellesley College
- Yale University

Great Schools for History Majors
- Bowdoin College
- Brown University
- Centre College
- Colgate University
- College of the Holy Cross
- Columbia University
- Drew University
- Furman University
- Georgetown University
- Grinnell College

- Hampden-Sydney College
- Harvard College
- Haverford College
- Hillsdale College
- Kenyon College
- Oberlin College
- Princeton University
- Trinity College (CT)
- Tulane University
- University of Virginia
- Wabash College
- Washington and Lee University
- Yale University

Great Schools for Journalism Majors
- American University
- Boston University
- Carleton College
- Columbia University
- Emerson College
- Hampton University
- Howard University
- Indiana University at Bloomington
- Loyola University—New Orleans
- Middle Tennessee State University
- Northwestern University
- Ohio University—Athens
- Pennsylvania State University
- Samford University
- St. Bonaventure University
- Syracuse University
- Temple University
- University of Florida
- University of Maryland—College Park
- University of Missouri—Columbia
- The University of North Carolina at Chapel Hill
- University of Oregon
- University of Southern California
- The University of Texas at Austin
- University of Wisconsin—Madison

Schools marked with an asterisk do not appear in the *Best 368 Colleges*.
You can find those school profiles in *Complete Book of Colleges, 2009 Edition*.

Great Schools for Marketing and Sales Majors

- Babson College
- Baylor University
- Bentley College
- Duquesne University
- Fairfield University
- Hofstra University
- Indiana University—Bloomington
- Iowa State University
- James Madison University
- Miami University
- Providence College
- Seattle University
- Siena College
- Syracuse University
- Texas A&M University
- University of Central Florida
- University of Michigan—Ann Arbor
- University of Mississippi
- University of Pennsylvania
- University of South Florida
- The University of Texas at Austin

Great Schools for Mechanical Engineering Majors

- Bradley University
- California Institute of Technology
- Clarkson University
- Colorado School of Mines*
- Drexel University
- Franklin W. Olin College of Engineering
- Georgia Institute of Technology
- Harvey Mudd College
- Iowa State University
- Lehigh University
- Massachusetts Institute of Technology
- New Jersey Institute of Technology
- North Carolina State University
- Purdue University—West Lafayette
- Rose-Hulman Institute of Technology

- Stanford University
- State University of New York—University at Buffalo
- Stevens Institute of Technology
- United States Military Academy
- University of California—Berkeley
- University of Illinois at Urbana-Champaign
- University of Michigan—Ann Arbor
- University of Missouri—Rolla
- Worcester Polytechnic Institute

Great Schools for Political Science/Government Majors

- American University
- Amherst College
- Bard College
- Bates College
- Bowdoin College
- Brigham Young University
- Bryn Mawr College
- Carleton College
- Claremont McKenna College
- College of the Holy Cross
- Columbia University
- Davidson College
- Dickinson College
- Drew University
- Furman University
- George Mason University
- George Washington University
- Georgetown University
- Gettysburg College
- Gonzaga University
- Harvard College
- Kenyon College
- Macalester College
- Princeton University
- Stanford University
- Swarthmore College
- Syracuse University
- University of Arizona
- University of California—Berkeley
- University of California—Los Angeles
- University of Washington

Schools marked with an asterisk do not appear in the *Best 368 Colleges*. You can find those school profiles in *Complete Book of Colleges, 2009 Edition*.

- Vassar College
- Yale University

Great Schools for Psychology Majors
- Albion College
- Bates College
- Carnegie Mellon University
- Clark University
- Colorado State University
- Columbia University
- Cornell University
- Dartmouth College
- Duke University
- George Mason University
- Gettysburg College
- Harvard College
- James Madison University
- Lewis & Clark College
- Loyola University—Chicago
- New York University
- Pitzer College
- Princeton University
- Smith College
- Stanford University
- University of California—Davis
- University of California—Los Angeles
- University of California—Riverside
- University of California—Santa Barbara
- University of California—Santa Cruz
- University of Michigan—Ann Arbor
- University of Southern California
- The University of Texas at Austin
- University of Utah
- Washington University in St. Louis
- Yale University

CHECK OUT OUR OTHER "MAJORLY" HELPFUL RESOURCES

Unsure about what you want to major in at college? Our *Guide to College Majors* profiles more than 400 undergraduate majors and covers high school preparation for them, college courses you'll likely take, career options and salary prospects.

Our *College Navigator: Find a School to Match Any Interest from Archery to Zoology* has hundreds of lists of colleges identifying everything from terrific schools for various majors to those with exceptional extracurriculars and more.

Our *Television, Film, and Digital Media Programs* profiles more than 500 media arts programs at top colleges and universities. We teamed up with the Academy of Television Arts and Sciences Foundation to create this guide for students exploring careers in entertainment or digital media.

If you're looking for a college with exceptional community involvement and service learning programs, pick up our *Colleges with a Conscience*. It profiles 81 great schools with outstanding citizenship track records. We developed it with Campus Compact (www.Compact.org), a coalition of college presidents committed to supporting the public services purposes of higher education.

You'll find these and all of our 200 college guidebooks at PrincetonReview.com/college/bookstore.asp. Also check out the "Majors & Careers" info in the "College" area of our site, www.PrincetonReview.com.

Good luck with your search!

Schools marked with an asterisk do not appear in the *Best 368 Colleges*.
You can find those school profiles in *Complete Book of Colleges, 2009 Edition*.

How and Why We Produce This Book

When we published the first edition of this book in 1992, there was a void in the world of college guides (hard to believe, but true!). No publication provided college applicants with statistical data from colleges that covered academics, admissions, financial aid, and student demographics along with narrative descriptions of the schools *based on comprehensive surveys of students attending them.* Of course, academic rankings of colleges had been around for some time. They named the best schools on hierarchical lists, from 1 to 200 and upwards, some in tiers. Their criteria factored in such matters as faculty salaries, alumni giving, and peer reviews (i.e. what college administrators thought of the schools that, in many cases, they competed with for students). But no one was polling students at these terrific colleges about their experiences on campus—both inside and outside the classroom. We created our first *Best Colleges* guide to address that void. It was born out of one very obvious omission in college guide publishing and two very deep convictions we held then and hold even more strongly today:

- **One:** The key question for students and parents researching colleges shouldn't be *"What college is best, academically?"* The thing is, it's not hard to find academically great schools in this country. (There are hundreds of them.) The key question—and one that is truly tough to answer—is *"What is the best college for me?"*

- **Two:** We believe the best way for students and parents to know if a school is right—and ultimately best—for them is to visit it. Travel to the campus, get inside a dorm, audit a class, browse the town and—most importantly—talk to students attending the school. In the end it's the school's customers—its students—who are the real experts about the college. Only they can give you the most candid and informed feedback on what life is really like on the campus.

Fueled by these convictions, we worked to create a guide that would help people who couldn't always get to the campus nonetheless get in-depth campus feedback to find the schools best for them. We culled an initial list of 250 academically great schools, based on our own college knowledge and input we got from 50 independent college counselors. We gathered institutional data from those schools and we surveyed 30,000 students attending them (about 120 per campus on average). We wrote the school profiles featured in the book, incorporating extensive quotes from surveyed students, and we included in the book over 60 ranking lists of top 20 schools in various categories based on our surveys of students at the schools. In short, we designed a college guide that did something no other guide had done: It brought the opinions of a huge number of students at the nation's top colleges to readers' doorsteps.

In the 16 years since, our *Best Colleges* guide has grown considerably. We've added over 100 colleges to the guide (and deleted several along the way). For this edition, we feature 368 "best" colleges at which we surveyed 120,000 students (about 320 per campus on average). How we choose the schools for the book, and how we produced it, however, has not changed significantly over the years (with the exception of how we conduct our student survey—more on this follows).

To determine which schools will be included in each edition, we don't use mathematical calculations or formulas. Instead we rely on a wide range of quantitative and qualitative input. Every year we collect data from nearly 2,000 colleges for our *Complete Book of Colleges* and our web-based profiles of schools. We visit colleges and meet with scores of admissions officers and college presidents. We talk with hundreds of high school counselors, parents, and students. Colleges also submit information to us requesting consideration for inclusion in the book. As a result, we are able to maintain a constantly evolving list of colleges to consider adding to each new edition of the book. Any college we add to the guide, however, must agree to allow its students to complete our anonymous student survey. (Sometimes a college's administrative protocols will not allow it to participate in our student survey; this has caused some academically outstanding schools to be absent from the guide.) Finally, we work to ensure that our book features a wide representation of colleges by region, character, and type. It includes public and private schools, historically black colleges and universities, men's and women's colleges, science- and technology-focused institutions, nontraditional colleges, highly selective schools, and some with virtually open-door admissions policies. We added four schools to the guide this year: City University of New York—Baruch College, Nazareth College, Prescott College, University of Alabama at Birmingham.

Our student survey for the book is a mammoth undertaking. In the early years, our surveys were conducted on campuses and on paper, but the launch several years ago of our online survey (http://survey.review.com), has made it possible for students to complete a survey anytime and anywhere. In fact, 90 percent of our student surveys are now completed online. Some schools prefer the old-fashioned paper survey route; in those instances we work with the administration to hire a campus representative (usually a student) to set up shop in one or more highly-trafficked areas of the campus where students can stop and fill out the survey.

Early on we surveyed all of the colleges and universities in the book on an annual basis. By the time we'd gone through a few editions, we found that unless there's been some grand upheaval or administrative change on campus, there's little change in student opinion from one year to the next, but that shifts tended to emerge in a third or fourth year (as surveyed students leave or matriculate). With this in mind, we switched to a three-year cycle for resurveying each campus. Thus, each year we target about 100 campuses for resurveying. We resurvey colleges more often than that if colleges request it (and we can accommodate the request) or if we believe it is warranted for one reason or another. Online surveys submitted by students outside of a school's normal survey cycle and independent of any solicitation on our part are factored into the subsequent year's rankings and ratings calculations. In that respect, our surveying is a continuous process.

All colleges and universities whose students we plan to survey are notified about the survey through our administrative contacts at the schools. We depend upon them for assistance either in notifying the student body about the availability of the online survey via email or, if the school opts for a paper version of the survey, in identifying common, high-traffic areas on campus at which to survey. The survey has more than 80 questions divided into four sections: "About Yourself," "Your School's Academics/Administration," "Students," and "Life at Your School." We ask about all sorts of things, from "How many out-of-class hours do you spend studying each day?" to "How do you rate your campus food?" Most questions offer students a five-point grid on which to indicate their answer choices (headers may range from "Excellent" to "Awful"). Eight questions offer students the opportunity to expand on their answers with narrative comment. These essay-type responses are the sources of the student quotations that appear in the school profiles.

Once the surveys have been completed and responses stored in our database, every college is given a score (similar to a grade point average) for its students' answers to each question. This score enables us to compare students' responses to a particular question from one college to the next. We use these scores as an underlying data point in our calculation of the ratings in the profile sidebars and the ranking lists in the section of the book titled "Schools Ranked by Category." Once we have the student survey information in hand, we write the college profiles. Student quotations in each profile are chosen because they represent the sentiments expressed by the majority of survey respondents from the college; or, they illustrate one side or another of a mixed bag of student opinion, in which case there will also appear a counterpoint within the text. We do not select quotes for their extreme nature, humor, or unique perspective. (Instead, we dedicate a section of this book titled, "Cow Tipping Is Definitely Passé Here," to these kinds of quotes—flip to the back to check them out!)

Our survey is qualitative and anecdotal rather than quantitative. In order to guard against producing a write-up that's off the mark for any particular college, we send our administrative contact at each school a copy of the profile we intend to publish prior to its publication date, with ample opportunity to respond with corrections, comments, and/or outright objections. In every case in which we receive requests for changes, we take careful measures to review the school's suggestions against the student survey data we collected and make appropriate changes when warranted.

For this year's edition, on average, we surveyed 320 students per campus, though that number varies depending on the size of the student population. We've surveyed anywhere from 20-odd men at Deep Springs College (100 percent of the student body) to over 1,000 collegians at such colleges as Drexel University, Clemson University, and the United States Military Academy. Whether the number of students we survey at a particular school is 100 or 1,000, on the whole we have found their opinions to be remarkably consistent over the years. What is most compelling to us about how representative our survey findings are is this: We ask students who take the survey—after they have completed it—to review the information we published about their school in the previous edition of our book and grade us on its accuracy and validity. Year after year we've gotten high marks: This year, 81 percent of students said we were *right on*.

All of the institutions in this guide are academically terrific in our opinion. The 368 schools featured—our picks of the cream of the crop colleges and universities—comprise only the top 10 percent of all colleges in the nation. Not every college will appeal to every student but that is the beauty of it. These are all very different schools with many different and wonderful things to offer.

We hope you will use this book as a starting point (it will certainly give you a snapshot of what life is like at these schools) but not as the final word on any one school. Check out other resources. Visit as many colleges as you can. Talk to students at those colleges—ask what they love and what bothers them most about their schools. Finally, *form your own opinions* about the colleges you are considering. At the end of the day, it's what YOU think about the schools that matters most, and that will enable you to answer that all-important question: *"Which college is best for me?"*

How This Book Is Organized

Each of the colleges and universities in this book has its own two-page profile. To make it easier to find and compare information about the schools, we've used the same profile format for every school. Look at the sample pages below:

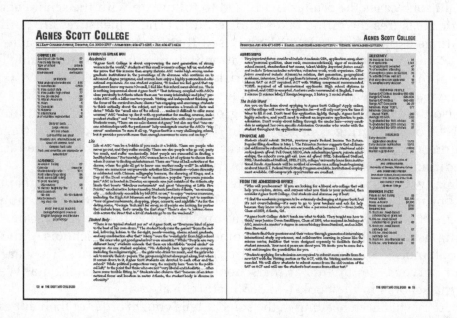

Each profile has nine major components. First, at the very top of the profile you will see the school's address, telephone, and fax numbers for the admissions office, the telephone number for the financial aid office, and the school's website and/or e-mail address. Second, there are two sidebars (the narrow columns on the outside of each page, which consist mainly of statistics) divided into the categories of Campus Life, Academics, Selectivity, and Financial Facts. Third, there are four headings in the narrative text: Students Say, Admissions, Financial Aid, and From the Admissions Office. Here's what you'll find in each part:

The Sidebars

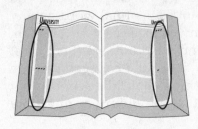

The sidebars contain various statistics culled from our surveys of students attending the school and from detailed questionnaires that school administrators complete at our request in the Fall of each year. Keep in mind that not every category will appear for every school—in some cases the information is not reported or not applicable.

We compile the eight ratings—Quality of Life, Fire Safety, Green Rating, Academic, Profs Interesting, Profs Accessible, Admissions Selectivity, and Financial Aid—listed in the sidebars based on the results from our student surveys and/or institutional data we collect from school administrators. These ratings are on a scale of 60–99 If a **60*** (60 with an asterisk) appears as any rating for any school, it means that the school reported so few of the rating's underlying data points by our deadline that we were unable to calculate an accurate rating for it. In such cases the reader is advised to follow up with the school about the specific measures the rating takes into account. (These measures are outlined in the ratings explanation below.) Be advised that because the Admissions Selectivity Rating is a factor in the computation that produces the Academic Rating, a school that has **60*** (60 with an asterisk) as its Admissions Selectivity Rating will have an Academic Rating that is lower than it should be.

Also bear in mind that each rating places each college on a continuum for purposes of comparing colleges within *this edition only*. Since our ratings computations may change from year to year, it is invalid to compare the ratings in this edition to those that appear in any prior or future edition.

Finally, these ratings are quite different from the ranking lists that appear in Part 2 of the book, "Schools Ranked by Category." The ratings are numerical measures that show how a school "sizes up," if you will, on a fixed scale. Our 62 ranking lists report the top 20 (or in some cases bottom 20) schools of the 368 in the book (not of all schools in the nation) in various categories. They are based on our surveys of students at the schools and/or institutional data. We don't rank the schools in the book 1 to 368 hierarchically.

Here is what each heading in the sidebar tells you, in order of their appearance:

Quality of Life Rating

On a scale of 60–99, this rating is a measure of how happy students are with their lives outside the classroom. To compile this rating, we weighed several factors, all based on students' answers to questions on our survey. They included the students' assessments of: their overall happiness; the beauty, safety, and location of the campus; comfort of dorms; quality of food; ease of getting around campus and dealing with administrators; friendliness of fellow students; and the interaction of different student types on campus and within the greater community.

Fire Safety Rating

On a scale of 60–99, this rating measures how well prepared a school is to prevent or respond to campus fires, specifically in residence halls.

We asked schools several questions about their efforts to ensure fire safety for campus residents. We developed the questions in consultation with the Center for

Campus Fire Safety (www.CampusFire.org). Each school's responses to eight questions were considered when calculating its Fire Safety Rating. They cover:

1. The percentage of student housing sleeping rooms protected by an automatic fire sprinkler system with a fire sprinkler head located in the individual sleeping rooms;
2. The percentage of student housing sleeping rooms equipped with a smoke detector connected to a supervised fire alarm system;
3. The number of malicious fire alarms that occur in student housing per year;
4. The number of unwanted fire alarms that occur in student housing per year;
5. The banning of certain hazardous items and activities in residence halls, like candles, smoking, halogen lamps, etc.;
6. The percentage of student housing fire alarm systems that, if activated, result in a signal being transmitted to a monitored location, where security investigates before notifying the fire department;
7. The percentage of student housing fire alarm systems that, if activated, result in a signal being transmitted immediately to a continuously monitored location which can then immediately notify the fire department to initiate a response;
8. How often fire safety rules-compliance inspections are conducted each year.

Schools that did not report answers to any of the questions receive a Fire Safety Rating of 60* (60 with an asterisk). The schools have an opportunity to update their fire safety data every year and will have their fire safety ratings recalculated and published annually. You can also find Fire Safety Ratings for the *Best 368 Colleges* (and several additional schools) in our *Complete Book of Colleges, 2009 Edition*. On p. 49 of this book, you'll find a list of the schools with 99 (the highest score) Fire Safety Ratings.

Green Rating

We asked all the schools we collect data from annually to answer a number of questions that evaluate the comprehensive measure of their performance as an environmentally aware and responsible institution. The questions were developed in consultation with ecoAmerica, a research and partnership-based environmental nonprofit that convened an expert committee to design this comprehensive rating system, and cover: 1) whether students have a campus quality of life that is both healthy and sustainable; 2) how well a school is preparing students not only for employment in the clean energy economy of the 21st century, but also for citizenship in a world now defined by environmental challenges; and 3) how environmentally responsible a school's policies are.

Each school's responses to ten questions were considered when calculating its Green Rating. They cover:

1. The percentage of food expenditures that go toward local, organic, or otherwise environmentally preferable food.
2. Whether the school offers programs including free bus passes, universal access transit passes, bike sharing/renting, car sharing, carpool parking, vanpooling, or guaranteed rides home to encourage alternatives to single-passenger automobile use for students.

3. Whether the school has a formal committee with participation from students that is devoted to advancing sustainability on campus.
4. Whether new buildings are required to be LEED Silver certified or comparable.
5. The schools overall waste diversion rate.
6. Whether the school has an environmental studies major, minor or concentration.
7. Whether the school has an 'environmental literacy' requirement.
8. Whether a school has produced a publicly available greenhouse gas emissions inventory and adopted a climate action plan consistent with 80% greenhouse gas reductions by 2050 targets.
9. What percentage of the school's energy consumption, including heating/cooling and electrical, is derived from renewable resources (this definition included 'green tags' but not nuclear or large scale hydro power)
10. Whether the school employs a dedicated full-time (or full-time equivalent) sustainability officer.

Colleges that did not supply answers to a sufficient number of the green campus questions for us to fairly compare them to other colleges receive a Green Rating of 60*. The schools have an opportunity to update their green data every year and will have their green ratings re-calculated and published annually. On p. 49 of this book, you'll find a list of the schools with 99 (the highest score) Green Ratings.

Type of school

Whether the school is public or private.

Affiliation

Any religious order with which the school is affiliated.

Environment

Whether the campus is located in an urban, suburban, or rural setting.

Total undergrad enrollment

The total number of degree-seeking undergraduates who attend the school.

"% male/female" through "# countries represented"

Demographic information about the full-time undergraduate student body, including male to female ratio, ethnicity, and the number of countries represented by the student body. Also included are the percentages of the student body who are from out of state, attended a public high school, live on campus, and belong to Greek organizations.

Survey Says

A snapshot of the key results of our student survey. This list shows what the students we surveyed felt unusually strongly about, both positively and negatively, at their schools (see the end of this section for a detailed explanation of items on the list).

Academic Rating

On a scale of 60–99, this rating is a measure of how hard students work at the school and how much they get back for their efforts. The rating is based on results from our surveys of students and institutional data we collect from administrators. Factors weighed included how many hours students reported that they study each day outside of class, and the quality of students the school attracts as measured by admissions statistics. We also considered students' assessments of their professors' teaching abilities and of their accessibility outside the classroom.

Calendar

The school's schedule of academic terms. A "semester" schedule has two long terms, usually starting in September and January. A "trimester" schedule has three terms, one usually beginning before Christmas and two after. A "quarterly" schedule has four terms, which go by very quickly: the entire term, including exams, usually lasts only nine or ten weeks. A "4-1-4" schedule is like a semester schedule, but with a month-long term in between the fall and spring semesters. (Similarly, a 4-4-1 has a short term following two longer semesters.) When a school's academic calendar doesn't match any of these traditional schedules, we note that by saying "other." For schools that have "other" as their calendar, it is best to call the admissions office for details.

Student/faculty ratio

The ratio of full-time undergraduate instructional faculty members to all undergraduates.

Profs interesting rating

On a scale of 60–99, this rating is based on levels of surveyed students' agreement or disagreement with the statement: "Your instructors are good teachers."

Profs accessible rating

On a scale of 60–99, this rating is based on levels of surveyed students' agreement or disagreement with the statement: "Your instructors are accessible outside the classroom."

% profs teaching UG courses

This category reports the percentage of professors who teach undergraduates and distinguishes between faculty who teach and faculty who focus solely on research.

% classes taught by TAs

This category reports the percentage of classes that are taught by TAs (teaching assistants) instead of regular faculty. Many universities that offer graduate programs use graduate students as teaching assistants. They teach undergraduate courses, primarily at the introductory level.

Most common lab size; Most common regular class size

Institutionally-reported figures of the most commonly occurring class size for regular courses and for labs/discussion sections.

Most Popular Majors

The three majors with the highest enrollments at the school.

Admissions Selectivity Rating

On a scale of 60–99, this rating is a measure of how competitive admission is at the school. This rating is determined by several factors, including the class rank of entering freshmen, test scores, and percentage of applicants accepted. By incorporating these factors (and a few others), our admissions selectivity rating adjusts for "self-selecting" applicant pools. The University of Chicago, for example, has a very high admissions selectivity rating, even though it admits a surprisingly large proportion of its applicants. This is because Chicago's applicant pool is self-selecting; that is, nearly all the school's applicants are exceptional students.

% of applicants accepted

The percentage of applicants to whom the school offered admission.

% of acceptees attending

The percentage of those who were accepted who eventually enrolled.

accepting a place on wait list

The number of students who decided to take a place on the wait list when offered this option.

% admitted from wait list

The percentage of applicants who opted to take a place on the wait list and were subsequently offered admission. These figures will vary tremendously from college to college, and should be a consideration when deciding whether to accept a place on a college's wait list.

of early decision applicants

The number of students who applied under the college's early decision or early action plan.

% accepted early decision

The percentage of early decision or early action applicants who were admitted under this plan. By the nature of these plans, the vast majority who are admitted ultimately enroll. (See the early decision/action description that follows in the Glossary section for more detail.)

Range/Average SAT Verbal, Range/Average SAT Math, Range/Average SAT Writing

The average and the middle 50 percent range of test scores for entering freshmen. Don't be discouraged from applying to the school of your choice even if your combined SAT scores are 80 or even 120 points below the average, because you may still have a chance of getting in. Remember that many schools value other aspects of your application (e.g., your grades, how good a match you make with the school) more heavily than test scores.

Minimum TOEFL

The minimum test score necessary for entering freshmen who are required to take the TOEFL (Test of English as a Foreign Language). Most schools will require all international students or non-native English speakers to take the TOEFL in order to be considered for admission.

Average HS GPA

The average grade point average of entering freshman. We report this on a scale of 1.0–4.0 (occasionally colleges report averages on a 100 scale, in which case we report those figures). This is one of the key factors in college admissions.

% graduated top 10%, top 25%, top 50% of class

Of those students for whom class rank was reported, the percentage of entering freshmen who ranked in the top tenth, quarter, and half of their high school classes.

Early decision/action deadlines

The deadline for submission of application materials under the early decision or early action plan.

Early decision, early action, priority, and regular admission deadlines

The dates by which all materials must be postmarked (we'd suggest "received in the office") in order to be considered for admission under each particular admissions option/cycle for matriculation in the fall term.

Early decision, early action, priority, and regular admission notification

The dates by which you can expect a decision on your application under each admissions option/cycle.

Nonfall registration

Some schools will allow incoming students to matriculate at times other than the fall term, which is the traditional beginning of the academic calendar year. Other schools will allow you to register for classes only if you can begin in the fall term. A simple "yes" or "no" in this category indicates the school's policy on nonfall registration.

Applicants also look at

These lists are based on information we receive directly from the colleges. Admissions officers are annually given the opportunity to review and suggest alterations to these lists for their schools, as most schools track as closely as they can other schools to which applicants they accepted applied, and whether the applicants chose their school over the other schools, or vice versa.

Financial Aid Rating

On a scale of 60–99, this rating is a measure of the financial aid the school awards and how satisfied students are with the aid they receive. It is based on school-reported data on financial aid and students' responses to the survey question, "If you receive financial aid, how satisfied are you with your financial aid package?"

Annual in-state tuition

The tuition at the school, or for public colleges, the cost of tuition for a resident of the school's state. Usually much lower than out-of-state tuition for state-supported public schools.

Annual out-of-state tuition

For public colleges, the tuition for a nonresident of the school's state. This entry appears only for public colleges, since tuition at private colleges is generally the same regardless of state of residence.

Required fees

Any additional costs students must pay beyond tuition in order to attend the school. These often include fitness center fees and the like. A few state schools may not officially charge in-state students tuition, but those students are still responsible for hefty fees.

Tuition and fees

In cases when schools do not report separate figures for tuition and required fees, we offer this total of the two.

Comprehensive fee

A few schools report one overall fee that reflects the total cost of tuition, room and board, and required fees. If you'd like to see how this figure breaks down, we recommend contacting the school.

Room & board

Estimated annual room and board costs.

Books and supplies

Estimated annual cost of necessary textbooks and/or supplies.

% frosh receiving need-based aid

The percentage of all degree-seeking freshmen who applied for financial aid, were determined to have financial need, and received any sort of aid, need-based or otherwise.

% UG receiving need-based aid

The percentage of all degree-seeking undergrads who applied for financial aid, were determined to have financial need, and received any sort of aid, need-based or otherwise.

Avg frosh grant

The average grant or scholarship given to freshmen who receive either or both.

Avg frosh loan

The average amount of loans disbursed to freshmen.

Nota Bene: The statistical data reported in this book, unless otherwise noted, was collected from the profiled colleges from the fall of 2007 through the summer of 2008. In some cases, we were unable to publish the most recent data because schools did not report the necessary statistics to us in time, despite our repeated outreach efforts. Because the enrollment and financial statistics, as well as application and financial aid deadlines, fluctuate from one year to another, we recommend that you check with the schools to make sure you have the most current information before applying.

Students Say

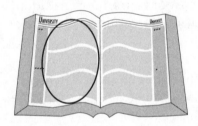

This section shares the straight-from-the-campus feedback we get from the school's most important customers: The students attending them. It summarizes the opinions of freshman through seniors we've surveyed and it includes direct quotes from scores of them. When appropriate, it also incorporates statistics provided by the schools. The Students Say section is divided into three subsections: Academics, Life, and Student Body. The Academics section describes how hard students work and how satisfied they are with the education they are getting. It also often tells you which programs or academic departments students rated most favorably and how professors interact with students. Student opinion regarding administrative departments also works its way into this section. The Life section describes life outside the classroom and addresses questions ranging from "How comfortable are the dorms?" to "How popular are fraternities and sororities?" In this section, students describe what they do for entertainment both on-campus and off, providing a clear picture of the social environment at their particular school. The Student Body section will give you the lowdown on the types of students the school attracts and how the students view the level of interaction among various groups, including those of different ethnic, socioeconomic, and religious backgrounds.

All quotations in these sections are from students' responses to open-ended questions on our survey. We select quotations based on the accuracy with which they reflect overall student opinion about the school as conveyed in the survey results. Entertaining but non-representative student responses about the Academics, Life, and Student Body at a school are featured in a special section in the back of this book titled "Cow Tipping Is Definitely Passé Here." Be sure to check it out for a good laugh.

Admissions

This section lets you know which aspects of your application are most important to the admissions officers at the school. It also lists the high school curricular prerequisites for applicants, which standardized tests (if any) are required, and special information about the school's admissions process (e.g., Do minority students and legacies, for ex-

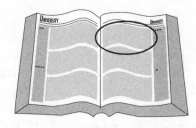

ample, receive special consideration? Are there any unusual application requirements for applicants to special programs?).

Financial Aid

Here you'll found out what you need to know about the financial aid process at the school, namely what forms you need and what types of merit-based aid and loans are available. Information about need-based aid is contained in the financial aid sidebar. This section includes specific deadline dates for submission of materials as reported by the colleges. We strongly encourage stu-

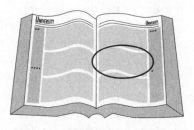

dents seeking financial aid to file all forms—federal, state, and institutional—carefully, fully, and on time. Check out our annually-updated book, *Paying for College Without Going Broke*, for advice on completing the forms and strategies for getting the most financial aid possible.

The Inside Word

This section gives you the inside scoop on what it takes to gain admission to the school. It reflects our own insights about each school's admissions process and acceptance trends. (We visit scores of colleges each year and talk with hundreds of admissions officers in order to glean this info.) It also incorporates information from institutional data we collect and our surveys over the years of students at the school.

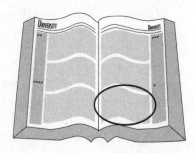

From the Admissions Office

This section is the school's chance to speak directly to you about the key things they would like you to know about their institution. For schools that did not respond to our invitation to supply text for this space, we excerpted an appropriate passage from the school's catalog, web site, or other admissions literature.

For this section, we also invited schools to submit a brief paragraph explaining their admissions policies regarding the SAT (especially the Writing portion of the exam) and the SAT Subject Tests. We are pleased that nearly every school took this opportunity to clarify its policies as we know there has been some student and parent confusion about how these scores are evaluated for admission.

Survey Says

Our Survey Says list, located in the Campus Life sidebar on each school's two-page spread, is based entirely on the results of our student survey. In other words, the items on this list are based on the opinions of the students we surveyed at those schools (*not* on any quantitative analysis of library size, endowment, etc.). These items reveal popular or unpopular trends on campus for the purpose of providing a snapshot of life on *that campus only*. The appearance of a Survey Says item in the sidebar for a particular school does *not* reflect the popularity of that item relative to its popularity amongst the student bodies at other schools. To ascertain the relative popularity of certain items/trends on campus, see the appropriate ranking (e.g., for the Survey Says item "Library needs improving," see the "This is a Library?" ranking). Some of the terms that appear on the Survey Says list are not entirely self-explanatory; these terms are defined below.

Different types of students interact: We asked students whether students from different class and ethnic backgrounds interacted frequently and easily. When students' collective response is "yes," the heading "Different types of students interact" appears on the list. When the collective student response indicates there are not many interactions between students from different class and ethnic backgrounds, the phrase "Students are cliquish" appears on the list.

No one cheats: We asked students how prevalent cheating is at their school. If students reported cheating to be rare, the term "No one cheats" shows up on the list.

Students are happy: This category reflects student responses to the question "Overall, how happy are you?"

Students are very religious *or* **Students aren't religious:** We asked students how religious students are at their school. Their responses are reflected in this category.

Diverse student types on campus: We asked students whether their student body is made up of a variety of ethnic groups. This category reflects their answers to this question. This heading shows up as "Diversity lacking on campus" or "Diverse student types on campus." It does not reflect any institutional data on this subject.

Students get along with local community: This category reflects student responses to a question concerning how well the student body gets along with residents of the college town or community.

Career services are great: New to the book this year, this category reflects student opinion on the quality of career/job placement services on campus. This heading shows up as "Career services are great."

Glossary

ACT: Like the SAT but less tricky—the ACT tests stuff you actually learned in the classroom. Most schools accept either SAT or ACT scores; if you consistently get blown away by the SAT, consider taking the ACT instead of (or in addition to) the SAT.

APs: Advanced Placement courses are essentially college-level courses offered in various high schools that culminate in the Advanced Placement Examinations each May. Students who obtain a minimum score on their AP exams may be awarded college credit or placement out of intro-level courses in the subject area. Excellent deal, no matter how you cut it!

College-prep curriculum: 16 to 18 academic credits (each credit equals a full year of a high school course), usually including: 4 years of English, 3 to 4 years of social studies, and at least 2 years each of science, mathematics, and foreign language.

Common Application: A general application form (available online and in a paper version) used by over 300 colleges and universities. Students who complete the Common Application save on time and mental frenzy, but may be required to submit application supplements to schools.

Core curriculum: Students at schools with core curricula must take a number of required courses, usually in such subjects as world history, western civilization, writing skills, and fundamental math and science.

CSS/Financial Aid PROFILE: The College Scholarship Service PROFILE, an optional financial aid form required by some colleges in addition to the FAFSA.

Direct Lender: Direct Lending schools participate in the federal Direct Loan Program. See "Direct Loan Program."

Direct Loan Program: With this federal educational loan program, funds are lent directly by the U.S. Government through the school's financial aid office, with no need of a private lender such as a bank. If the college only participates in the (William D. Ford) Direct Loan Program, the borrower must obtain any Stafford, PLUS, or GradPLUS loan through this program, though one can use a private alternative loan program for any additional non-federal funding.

Distribution or general education requirements: Students at schools with distribution requirements must take a number of courses in various subject areas, such as foreign language, humanities, natural science, and social science. Distribution requirements do not specify which courses you must take, only which types of courses.

Early Decision/Early Action: Early decision is generally for students for whom the school is a first choice. The applicant commits to attending the school if admitted; in return, the school renders an early decision, usually in December or January. Early action is similar to early decision, but less binding; applicants need not commit to attending the school and in some cases may apply early action to more than one school. Early decision and early action policies of a few of the most selective colleges in the country have changed quite dramatically recently. It's a good idea to call the school and get full details if you plan to pursue one of these options.

FAFSA: Stands for the Free Application for Federal Student Aid. This is a financial aid need analysis form written by the U.S. Department of Education. This form is required for virtually all students applying to colleges for financial aid. Some colleges also require that applicants complete other aid application forms (such as the CSS/Financial Aid PROFILE or the college's own form) to be considered for financial aid.

Greek system, Greeks: Fraternities and sororities.

Humanities: The branches of knowledge concerned with human art and culture. These include such disciplines as art history, drama, English, foreign languages, music, philosophy, and religion.

Merit-based grant: A scholarship (not necessarily covering the full cost of tuition) given to students because of some special talent or attribute. Artists, athletes, community leaders, and academically outstanding applicants are typical recipients.

Natural sciences: The branches of knowledge concerned with the rational study of the universe using the rules or laws of natural order. These include such disciplines as astronomy, biology, chemistry, genetics, geology, mathematics, physics, and zoology.

Need-based grant: A scholarship (not necessarily covering the full cost of tuition) given to students because they would otherwise be unable to afford college. Student need is determined on the basis of the FAFSA. Some schools also require the CSS PROFILE and/or institutional applications to determine a student's need.

Priority deadline: Some schools will list a deadline for admission and/or financial aid as a "priority deadline," meaning that while they will accept applications after that date, all applications received prior to the deadline are assured of getting the most thorough, and potentially more generous, appraisal possible.

RA: Residence assistant (or residential advisor). Someone, usually an upperclassman or graduate student, who supervises a floor or section of a dorm, usually in return for free room and board. RAs are responsible for enforcing the drinking and noise rules.

SAT: A college entrance exam required by many schools; most schools will accept either the ACT or the SAT.

SAT Subject Tests: Subject-specific exams administered by the Educational Testing Service (the same folks who do the SAT). These tests are required by some, but not all, colleges.

Social sciences: The branches of knowledge which emphasize the use of the scientific method in the study of the human aspects of the world. These include such disciplines as anthropology, economics, geography, history, international studies, political science, psychology, and sociology.

Work-study: A federally-funded financial aid program that provides assistance to students by subsidizing their wages for on-campus and off-campus jobs. Eligibility is based on need.

ABOUT THOSE COLLEGE RANKINGS

We've shed some light on how we publish our *Best Colleges*, how we select the schools featured in it, how we compile our school profiles, and how we conduct the student survey which is the centerpiece of the book.

But the part of our *Best Colleges* guide that many people turn to first is the section titled "Schools Ranked By Category." Here you won't find the colleges in the book ranked hierarchically, 1 to 368. We think such lists—particularly those driven by and perpetuating a "best academics" mania—are not useful for the people they are supposed to serve (college applicants). More and more college administrators—including several at schools ranked high on these lists—agree.

In fact, the primary reason we developed this book was to give applicants and parents better and broader information that will help them winnow a list of colleges right for them. Finding a college that has terrific academics is the easy part. There are hundreds of academically great colleges in this country. Their campus cultures, student bodies, and school offerings, however, differ widely. Finding the academically great school that is right for you is the tough part. Hence, we compile not one ranking list but 62 unique lists, each one reporting the top 20 (or in some cases bottom 20) schools from our *Best Colleges* book in a specific category.

None of the lists are based on what we think of the schools (though members of the media, the public and school administrators mistakenly credit or blame us for the results, saying "According to The Princeton Review, X school is the best in the nation for…" or "The Princeton Review ranks Y school the 10th most…."). In fact, the only thing *we* say is that all of the 368 colleges in this book are outstanding (hence, the "Best" designation). It's what students think of their schools—how they rate various aspects of their colleges' offerings and what they report to us about their campus experiences—that results in a school's appearance on our ranking lists. About 85 percent of the schools in our book end up on one or more of the lists in each edition. The students are the raters—we are simply the folks who compile the ranking lists based on their opinions. To college officials happy about the lists their schools are on, we say don't thank us, we're just the messengers. To college officials unhappy about the lists their schools are on (and unsurprisingly, it is mainly they who say our student survey has no validity whatsoever), we say don't blame us, we're just the messengers.

Sixty-one of these ranking lists are based entirely on students' answers to questions on our surveys (e.g. our "Best Campus Food" list and inverse list, "Is it Food?" are each based on the single survey question, "How do you rate your campus food?") or students' answers to a combination of survey questions (e.g. our "Party Schools" list and our inverse list, "Stone-cold Sober Schools" are each based on students' answers to survey questions concerning the use of alcohol and drugs on their campuses, the popularity of the frat/sorority scene on their campuses, and the number of hours they say they study each day outside of class time). Only one of our 62 ranking lists factors in statistical data from the colleges: "Toughest to Get Into."

Each list, even those with somewhat irreverent titles (such as "Dorms Like Dungeons"), covers one of many aspects of a college's character that can be helpful in deciding if it's the right or wrong place for an individual student. They report on a wide range of issues that may be important, either singly or, more likely, in combination. Our ranking lists cover: financial aid, campus facilities and amenities, extracurriculars, town-gown relations, the student body's political leanings, social life, race/class relations, gay-friendly (or not so friendly) atmosphere, and more. New in this edition is a ranking list category inspired by a parent who urged us to report on schools most likely to help his son find a job—thus, our "Best Career Services" ranking was born. Also new is our "Best Classroom Experience" list, based on students' answers to five survey questions concerning their professors, classroom/lab facilities, the percentage of class time devoted to discussion, and the percentage of classes they attend.

The ranking list category that media covers the most (though it appears 57th among the lists in our "Schools Ranked by Category" section, and is only referenced briefly in our press materials) is the "Party Schools" list. It's even been the subject of a *Doonesbury* cartoon (which appears on the frontispiece of this book) as well as a *USA Today* editorial in which the paper commended us for reporting the list, calling it "a public service." Our "Party Schools" list draws a wide range of reaction every year. Some students complain that their college didn't make the list, while others are irate because their college did. One reporter from the *Washington Post* whose alma mater was #1 on the list several years back wrote a column in which he argued that the ranking was grossly undeserved: He had recently visited his campus and pronounced the then current student body lame as "partiers" compared to the revelers of *his day*.

Many incorrectly assume that an institution that shows up on the "Party Schools" list is not an advisable college to attend. We recommend all 368 schools in this book as outstanding institutions at which to earn one's college degree. But just as the schools on our "Alternative Lifestyle Not an Alternative" (gay-unfriendly) list may not be ideal campuses for gay students, the schools on our "Party Schools" list may not be ideal for students seeking a campus at which the use of alcohol and drugs and the frat/sorority scene is, well, less exuberant.

On the other hand, no one should make the mistake of assuming that the colleges and universities that don't show up on our "Party Schools" list are in any way insulated from the influences of alcohol and drugs on their campuses. An oft-quoted Harvard University School of Public Health study a few years back found that 44 percent of undergraduates, in general, binge drink (consume five or more alcoholic beverages in one sitting for men, four drinks or more for women).[1] These facts are alarming, as they should be. College administrators face tremendous challenges in creating and enforcing campus alcohol and drug use/abuse policies. Many struggle with problems resulting from the prevalence of bars and liquor stores near their campuses; at some universities that have appeared on our "Party Schools" list there are more than 100 such establishments within a few miles from the campus. "Dry campus" policies often exacerbate the problem, driving drinking off-campus, making it even more dangerous for students.

1 Harvard University School of Public Health. "College Student Binge Drinking Rates Remain High Despite Efforts by School Administrations." www.hsph.harvard.edu/news/press-releases/2000-releases/press03142000.html.

Despite the claims of some administrators at colleges that have repeatedly made our "Party School" list that our reporting this list promotes drinking on campuses (a group of such administrators receiving funding through the American Medical Association to address their campus alcohol problems made the news several years back with this claim, after which *USA Today* published the editorial praising our ranking as a "public service"), we neither encourage nor discourage students who wish to drink. None of our lists promote behavior: They report on it, plain and simple. What we promote is information.

What we do say to college students—as we have said in this very section of this book for over 10 years—is this: If you're going to drink, do it safely, smartly, responsibly, and legally. If you're going off campus to drink, don't drive back drunk—get a designated driver. Don't let a peer situation (fraternity rush, etc.) put you in jeopardy—it's simply not worth it. Don't use alcohol or drugs as a badge of your coolness—there's not much of a fine line between someone who's socially engaging and someone who's totally disengaging because he or she has performed a chemical auto-lobotomy. Last, don't simply take responsibility for yourself; remember to keep an eye on your friends, and never leave them passed out and alone.

Finally, we'd like to thank all the college officials, college counselors, advisors, students, and parents, who have made this annual guide possible by supporting us these past fifteen years. Our ranking lists have, collectively, been based on surveys of more than 750,000 students whose input has been vital to our publication of this book. We know that it has helped students find great colleges perfect for them, and it has brought to the colleges in our book many outstanding students who otherwise may not have considered attending their institutions.

To all of our readers, we welcome your feedback on how we can continue to improve this guide. We hope you will share with us your comments, questions, and suggestions. Please contact us at Editorial Department, Princeton Review Books, 2315 Broadway, New York, NY 10024, or e-mail us at bookeditor@review.com. We welcome it.

To college applicants, we wish you all the best in your college search. And when you get to your campuses and settle in to your college life, come back to us online; participate in our survey for this book at http://survey.review.com. Let your honest comments about your schools guide prospective students who want your help answering the $64,000 question (goodness knows, the sticker price at some schools may be that high or even higher!): *"Which is the best college for me?"*

PART 2

Schools Ranked by Category

One of the great things about a multiple-choice survey administered to more than 120,000 college students is that the results give you lots of numbers. We wanted to present those numbers to you in a fun and informative way; hence, the following rankings of schools in 62 categories. In the following lists, the top 20 schools in each category appear in descending order. Remember, of course, that our survey included only students at *The Best 368 Colleges*, and that all schools appearing on what you might consider to be negative lists have many assets that counterbalance their various potential deficiencies.

Simply put, our ranking lists are unique. They can be used to help you clarify some of the choices you have to make in picking the right college. College-bound students, their parents, and counselors searching for substantive, easy-to-understand information will benefit from these kinds of rankings because they are based on the opinions of tens of thousands of in-the-trenches college experts—students. As you read through them, focus on those categories that are important to you: Do you want to go to a school where students tend to be liberal or conservative in their political views? Our ranking lists in these and more than 50 other categories will help you find great schools that may be ideal for you.

We've broken the rankings down into eight categories: Academics/Administration; Quality of Life; Politics; Demographics; Social Life; Extracurriculars; Parties; and Schools by Type. Under each list heading, we tell you the survey question or assessment that we used to tabulate the list. We tally student responses to several questions on our survey for our lists "Best Classroom Experience," "Best Quality of Life, " and the six lists in our Schools by Type rankings (including our "Party Schools" and "Stone-cold Sober Schools" lists).

Be aware that all of our 62 ranking lists are based entirely on our student surveys. They do not reflect our opinions of the schools. They are entirely the result of what students attending these schools tell us about them: it's how students rate their own schools and what they report to us about their campus experiences at them that makes our ranking lists so unusual. After all, what better way is there to judge a school than by what its customers - its students - say about it?

You will find more information on how we tally our ranking lists and conduct our survey for them in the introductory section of this book. In Part I, see "How and Why we Produce This Book" (p.14) and "About Those College Rankings" (p.28). There, you'll also find our recommended lists of "Great Schools for 15 of the Most Popular Undergraduate Majors" (p. 6). These are not ranking lists but lists of schools offering outstanding programs in various popular majors. We compile these lists based on data we collect from colleges, the opinions of our in-house college experts, and savvy suggestions from our National College Counselor Advisory Panel (p. x).

ACADEMICS/ADMINISTRATION

Best Classroom Experience
Based on a combination of survey questions concerning teachers, classroom/lab facilities, classes attended, and amount of in-class discussion

1. Stanford University
2. Reed College
3. Pomona College
4. Wabash College
5. Mount Holyoke College
6. Wellesley College
7. United States Military Academy
8. Middlebury College
9. Whitman College
10. Williams College
11. Hanover College
12. Kenyon College
13. Lawrence University
14. Princeton University
15. Claremont McKenna College
16. Colgate University
17. Sarah Lawrence College
18. Bowdoin College
19. Agnes Scott College
20. University of Richmond

Students Study the Most
How many out-of-class hours do you spend studying each day?

1. Massachusetts Institute of Technology
2. Franklin W. Olin College of Engineering
3. Reed College
4. California Institute of Technology
5. Harvey Mudd College
6. Bennington College
7. Harvard College
8. Middlebury College
9. University of Chicago
10. Swarthmore College
11. Grinnell College
12. College of the Holy Cross
13. Davidson College
14. United States Coast Guard Academy
15. Williams College
16. Haverford College
17. United States Military Academy
18. The Cooper Union for the Advancement of Science and Art
19. Bryn Mawr College
20. Princeton University

Students Study the Least
How many out-of-class hours do you spend studying each day?

1. University of Florida
2. University of Maryland—College Park
3. University of Georgia

4. University of Mississippi
5. West Virginia University
6. Flagler College
7. University of North Dakota
8. Louisiana State University
9. Auburn University
10. Florida State University
11. State University of New York—University at Albany
12. Florida Southern College
13. Monmouth University (NJ)
14. University of Central Florida
15. Arizona State University at the Tempe campus
16. The University of Texas at Austin
17. University of Alabama—Tuscaloosa
18. University of Illinois—Urbana Champaign
19. Penn State—University Park
20. Loyola University—New Orleans

Professors Get High Marks
Are your instructors good teachers?

1. Middlebury College
2. Franklin W. Olin College of Engineering
3. Ripon College
4. Wellesley College
5. Simon's Rock College of Bard
6. Reed College
7. Sweet Briar College
8. Harvey Mudd College
9. Kenyon College
10. Centre College
11. Prescott College
12. Davidson College
13. Hillsdale College
14. Hampden-Sydney College
15. Whitman College
16. Thomas Aquinas College
17. Carleton College
18. Sarah Lawrence College
19. Wabash College
20. Wofford College

Professors Get Low Marks
Are your instructors good teachers?

1. Stevens Institute of Technology
2. United States Merchant Marine Academy
3. California Institute of Technology
4. New Jersey Institute of Technology
5. State University of New York—University at Albany
6. Johns Hopkins University
7. Illinois Institute of Technology
8. Georgia Institute of Technology
9. Rensselaer Polytechnic Institute

10. Rutgers, The State University of New Jersey—New Brunswick
11. University of Rhode Island
12. State University of New York—Stony Brook University
13. Drexel University
14. University of New Mexico
15. University of California—Riverside
16. University of Toronto
17. Iowa State University
18. University of New Hampshire
19. State University of New York—University at Buffalo
20. University of California—San Diego

Most Accessible Professors
Are your instructors accessible outside the classroom?

1. United States Air Force Academy
2. Sweet Briar College
3. Wabash College
4. Lawrence University
5. United States Military Academy
6. Hampden-Sydney College
7. Williams College
8. Webb Institute
9. United States Naval Academy
10. College of the Atlantic
11. Claremont McKenna College
12. Wellesley College
13. Harvey Mudd College
14. Ripon College
15. Franklin W. Olin College of Engineering
16. Davidson College
17. University of Puget Sound
18. St. John's College (NM)
19. Centre College
20. Whitman College

Least Accessible Professors
Are your instructors accessible outside the classroom?

1. University of New Mexico
2. Illinois Institute of Technology
3. University of Utah
4. Georgia Institute of Technology
5. University of Toronto
6. Rutgers, The State University of New Jersey—New Brunswick
7. Tuskegee University
8. St. John's University of NY
9. State University of New York—University at Albany
10. State University of New York—Stony Brook University
11. New Jersey Institute of Technology
12. Stevens Institute of Technology

13. New York University
14. University of New Hampshire
15. Drexel University
16. Spelman College
17. University of Massachusetts Amherst
18. University of California—Berkeley
19. University of Rhode Island
20. City University of New York—Hunter College

Class Discussions Encouraged
How much of your overall class time is devoted to discussion as opposed to lectures?

1. Bennington College
2. Marlboro College
3. Sarah Lawrence College
4. Eugene Lang College—The New School for Liberal Arts
5. Simon's Rock College of Bard
6. Prescott College
7. Reed College
8. Hampshire College
9. Wesleyan College
10. College of the Atlantic
11. Sweet Briar College
12. Wells College
13. Stephens College
14. Colorado College
15. Hanover College
16. Bard College
17. United States Military Academy
18. Stanford University
19. Goucher College
20. Emerson College

Class Discussions Rare
How much of your overall class time is devoted to discussion as opposed to lectures?

1. California Institute of Technology
2. McGill University
3. Georgia Institute of Technology
4. University of Toronto
5. State University of New York—Stony Brook University
6. North Carolina State University
7. Colorado State University
8. Louisiana State University
9. Webb Institute
10. New Mexico Institute of Mining & Technology
11. Virginia Tech
12. Stevens Institute of Technology
13. Marquette University
14. Missouri University of Science and Technology
15. Rose-Hulman Institute of Technology

16. University of California—Davis
17. Montana Tech of the University of Montana
18. Rutgers, The State University of New Jersey—New Brunswick
19. Clarkson University
20. University of California—San Diego

Best Career/Job Placement Services
Based on students' rating of campus career/job placement services

1. Northeastern University
2. Claremont McKenna College
3. Wabash College
4. University of Texas—Austin
5. Penn State—University Park
6. Sweet Briar College
7. Rose-Hulman Institute of Technology
8. Clemson University
9. University of Virginia
10. Barnard College
11. University of Notre Dame
12. Yale University
13. University of Florida
14. Cornell University
15. Smith College
16. Middlebury College
17. Hampden-Sydney College
18. American University
19. Villanova University
20. Bentley College

Best College Library
Based on students' assessment of library facilities

1. Harvard College
2. Princeton University
3. Duke University
4. The College of New Jersey
5. Cornell University
6. Brigham Young University (UT)
7. Loyola University New Orleans
8. College of William and Mary
9. University of Chicago
10. Columbia University
11. Wesleyan University
12. Whitman College
13. Furman University
14. Mount Holyoke College
15. Emory University
16. The University of Texas at Austin
17. Case Western Reserve University
18. Colgate University
19. University of Virginia
20. West Virginia University

This is a Library?

Based on students' assessment of library facilities

1. Bennington College
2. United States Coast Guard Academy
3. Clarkson University
4. Bradley University
5. Spelman College
6. Bard College
7. University of Dallas
8. Duquesne University
9. Eugene Lang College—
   The New School for Liberal Arts
10. Tuskegee University
11. William Jewell College
12. Salisbury University
13. Centenary College of Louisiana
14. State University of New York—Purchase College
15. American University
16. Catawba College
17. Stevens Institute of Technology
18. Wagner College
19. The Catholic University of America
20. The Evergreen State College

Students Happy with Financial Aid

Based on students' assessments of how satisfied they are with their financial aid package.

1. Princeton University
2. Stanford University
3. Pomona College
4. Harvard College
5. New College of Florida
6. Thomas Aquinas College
7. Beloit College
8. College of the Atlantic
9. Wabash College
10. Claremont McKenna College
11. Washington University in St. Louis
12. Lake Forest College
13. Tulane University
14. Denison University
15. California Institute of Technology
16. Knox College
17. Truman State University
18. Ripon College
19. New Jersey Institute of Technology
20. Randolph College

Students Dissatisfied with Financial Aid

Based on students' assessments of how satisfied they are with their financial aid package.

1. New York University
2. Emerson College
3. Penn State—University Park

4. Rutgers, The State University of New Jersey—New Brunswick
5. University of Mary Washington
6. Hampton University
7. Amherst College
8. University of Colorado—Boulder
9. Spelman College
10. State University of New York—Purchase College
11. Hofstra University
12. City University of New York—Queens College
13. State University of New York—University at Albany
14. Quinnipiac University
15. George Mason University
16. College of the Holy Cross
17. Duquesne University
18. Dartmouth College
19. Villanova University
20. University of Delaware

School Runs Like Butter

Overall, how smoothly is your school run?

1. Pomona College
2. Princeton University
3. Stanford University
4. Middlebury College
5. Claremont McKenna College
6. Davidson College
7. Bowdoin College
8. Whitman College
9. Washington University in St. Louis
10. Rose-Hulman Institute of Technology
11. Wabash College
12. Carleton College
13. Furman University
14. University of Notre Dame
15. Amherst College
16. Elon University
17. Brigham Young University (UT)
18. Williams College
19. Yale University
20. Clemson University

Long Lines and Red Tape

Overall, how smoothly is your school run?

1. Eugene Lang College—
   The New School for Liberal Arts
2. Tuskegee University
3. Hampton University
4. State University of New York—Purchase College
5. Bennington College
6. New York University

7. Drexel University
8. State University of New York—University at Albany
9. Howard University
10. Hampshire College
11. Illinois Institute of Technology
12. State University of New York—Stony Brook University
13. Fisk University
14. The Cooper Union for the Advancement of Science and Art
15. United States Merchant Marine Academy
16. University of Mary Washington
17. New Jersey Institute of Technology
18. City University of New York—Hunter College
19. The Catholic University of America
20. Whittier College

QUALITY OF LIFE

Happiest Students
Overall, how happy are you?

1. Clemson University
2. Brown University
3. Princeton University
4. Claremont McKenna College
5. Franklin W. Olin College of Engineering
6. Stanford University
7. University of Dayton
8. Bowdoin College
9. The College of New Jersey
10. Tulane University
11. Yale University
12. Prescott College
13. University of North Carolina at Chapel Hill
14. Pomona College
15. Rice University
16. Brigham Young University (UT)
17. Whitman College
18. St. Mary's College of Maryland
19. Washington University in St. Louis
20. The George Washington University

Least Happy Students
Overall, how happy are you?

1. United States Merchant Marine Academy
2. New Jersey Institute of Technology
3. State University of New York—Stony Brook University
4. Fisk University
5. Tuskegee University
6. University of California—Riverside

7. United States Coast Guard Academy
8. New Mexico Institute of Mining & Technology
9. State University of New York—University at Albany
10. Illinois Institute of Technology
11. Albion College
12. Hanover College
13. New York University
14. Eugene Lang College— The New School for Liberal Arts
15. Clarkson University
16. Whittier College
17. United States Air Force Academy
18. University of Massachusetts Amherst
19. United States Military Academy
20. Alfred University

Most Beautiful Campus
Based on students' rating of campus beauty

1. Princeton University
2. Sweet Briar College
3. Colgate University
4. Wagner College
5. Mount Holyoke College
6. Scripps College
7. University of Notre Dame
8. University of Richmond
9. University of San Diego
10. College of the Holy Cross
11. Elon University
12. Wellesley College
13. University of California—Santa Cruz
14. Pepperdine University
15. Bennington College
16. Loyola Marymount University
17. Warren Wilson College
18. College of the Atlantic
19. Samford University
20. Sewanee—The University of the South

Least Beautiful Campus
Based on students' rating of campus beauty

1. State University of New York—Purchase College
2. State University of New York—University at Albany
3. Drexel University
4. New Jersey Institute of Technology
5. City University of New York—Hunter College
6. Harvey Mudd College
7. The Cooper Union for the Advancement of Science and Art
8. University of Massachusetts Amherst

9. North Carolina State University
10. University of Dallas
11. Illinois Institute of Technology
12. Clarkson University
13. Massachusetts Institute of Technology
14. University of Tennessee—Knoxville
15. University of New Orleans
16. Rutgers, The State University of New Jersey—New Brunswick
17. Eugene Lang College—The New School for Liberal Arts
18. Xavier University of Louisiana
19. State University of New York—Stony Brook University
20. Rochester Institute of Technology

Best Campus Food
Based on students' rating of campus food

1. Wheaton College (IL)
2. Bowdoin College
3. Virginia Tech
4. Saint Olaf College
5. James Madison University
6. Colby College
7. Franklin W. Olin College of Engineering
8. Washington University in St. Louis
9. University of Notre Dame
10. Gustavus Adolphus College
11. Cornell University
12. University of California—Los Angeles
13. Scripps College
14. Middlebury College
15. Claremont McKenna College
16. Bryn Mawr College
17. Miami University
18. College of the Atlantic
19. Bates College
20. University of Georgia

Is It Food?
Based on students' rating of campus food

1. Wells College
2. Catawba College
3. United States Merchant Marine Academy
4. Fisk University
5. Guilford College
6. State University of New York at Albany
7. Eugene Lang College—The New School for Liberal Arts
8. Hampton University
9. Missouri University of Science and Technology
10. United States Air Force Academy
11. Carnegie Mellon University
12. Centenary College of Louisiana
13. Flagler College

14. Grove City College
15. Hiram College
16. Fordham University
17. The Evergreen State College
18. Bard College
19. United States Naval Academy
20. Whittier College

Dorms Like Palaces
Based on students' rating of dorm comfort

1. Loyola College in Maryland
2. Franklin W. Olin College of Engineering
3. Smith College
4. Scripps College
5. Bryn Mawr College
6. The George Washington University
7. Washington University in St. Louis
8. Bowdoin College
9. Bennington College
10. Harvard College
11. Claremont McKenna College
12. Pomona College
13. Trinity University
14. Skidmore College
15. Mount Holyoke College
16. Thomas Aquinas College
17. Wellesley College
18. Pepperdine University
19. Stephens College
20. Whitman College

Dorms Like Dungeons
Based on students' rating of dorm comfort

1. University of Louisiana at Lafayette
2. United States Coast Guard Academy
3. United States Merchant Marine Academy
4. Tuskegee University
5. University of New Orleans
6. Hampton University
7. State University of New York—University at Albany
8. Hanover College
9. The Evergreen State College
10. University of Florida
11. University of Idaho
12. Xavier University of Louisiana
13. The University of South Dakota
14. Missouri University of Science and Technology
15. Eugene Lang College—The New School for Liberal Arts
16. Louisiana State University
17. Indiana University of Pennsylvania
18. Rider University
19. University of Washington
20. United States Military Academy

Best Quality of Life

Based on The Princeton Review's QUALITY OF LIFE RATING (page 20)

1. Washington University in St. Louis
2. Rice University
3. Princeton University
4. Bowdoin College
5. Claremont McKenna College
6. Clemson University
7. Macalester College
8. Middlebury College
9. Villanova University
10. Pomona College
11. Barnard College
12. Whitman College
13. American University
14. Saint Michael's College
15. Agnes Scott College
16. Brigham Young University (UT)
17. Saint Olaf College
18. Westminster College
19. Stanford University
20. Seattle University

POLITICS

Most Conservative Students

Based on students' assessment of their personal political views

1. Texas A&M University—College Station
2. Thomas Aquinas College
3. Southern Methodist University
4. Hillsdale College
5. United State Air Force Academy
6. University of Mississippi
7. The University of Alabama at Birmingham
8. Brigham Young University (UT)
9. Randolph-Macon College
10. Hampden-Sydney College
11. Pepperdine University
12. United States Naval Academy
13. Wofford College
14. College of the Ozarks
15. William Jewell College
16. Wheaton College (IL)
17. Texas Christian University
18. University of Dallas
19. Grove City College
20. University of Nebraska—Lincoln

Most Liberal Students

Based on students' assessment of their personal political views

1. Occidental College
2. Warren Wilson College
3. Hampshire College
4. New College of Florida
5. Bennington College
6. Prescott College
7. Clark University
8. Bard College
9. Brandeis University
10. Sarah Lawrence College
11. State University of New York—Purchase College
12. Marlboro College
13. Haverford College
14. Reed College
15. Eugene Lang College— The New School for Liberal Arts
16. Pitzer College
17. Grinnell College
18. The Evergreen State College
19. Kenyon College
20. Macalester College

Most Politically Active Students

How popular are political/activist groups?

1. American University
2. The George Washington University
3. Princeton University
4. New College of Florida
5. United States Military Academy
6. Warren Wilson College
7. Harvard College
8. George Mason University
9. Simon's Rock College of Bard
10. Georgetown University
11. Claremont McKenna College
12. Wesleyan University
13. The University of Texas at Austin
14. Macalester College
15. Bates College
16. Smith College
17. United States Air Force Academy
18. Lewis & Clark College
19. Bryn Mawr College
20. University of Oregon

Election? What Election?
How popular are political/activist groups?

1. The University of Scranton
2. Salisbury University
3. Sacred Heart University
4. Fisk University
5. Quinnipiac University
6. Ohio Northern University
7. Bradley University
8. University of Rhode Island
9. Washington State University
10. College of the Ozarks
11. Florida Southern College
12. St. Bonaventure University
13. Worcester Polytechnic Institute
14. Monmouth University (NJ)
15. State University of New York at Geneseo
16. Birmingham-Southern College
17. University of Connecticut
18. Moravian College
19. Westminster College (PA)
20. Rider University

DEMOGRAPHICS

Diverse Student Population
Is your student body made up of diverse social and ethnic types?

1. City University of New York—Baruch College
2. University of Maryland Baltimore County
3. City University of New York—Brooklyn College
4. The University of Alabama at Birmingham
5. Temple University
6. University of Miami
7. City University of New York—Hunter College
8. State University of New York—Stony Brook University
9. City University of New York—Queens College
10. DePaul University
11. George Mason University
12. Manhattanville College
13. Mount Holyoke College
14. Wellesley College
15. State University of New York—University at Buffalo
16. Stanford University
17. St. John's University of NY
18. Randolph College
19. University of Cincinnati
20. Wesleyan College

Homogeneous Student Population
Is your student body made up of diverse social and ethnic types?

1. Providence College
2. Fairfield University
3. Grove City College
4. Miami University
5. University of New Hampshire
6. Muhlenberg College
7. Bucknell University
8. University of Richmond
9. The University of Scranton
10. Saint Anselm College
11. Ohio Northern University
12. Hampden-Sydney College
13. Wake Forest University
14. Gettysburg College
15. University of Mary Washington
16. Flagler College
17. Thomas Aquinas College
18. Lehigh University
19. Samford University
20. The Catholic University of America

Lots of Race/Class Interaction
Do different types of students (Black/White, rich/poor) interact frequently and easily?

1. Pitzer College
2. Rice University
3. Franklin W. Olin College of Engineering
4. Wesleyan College
5. City University of New York—Baruch College
6. Stanford University
7. St. Mary's College of Maryland
8. The University of Alabama at Birmingham
9. Beloit College
10. Prescott College
11. Macalester College
12. Mount Holyoke College
13. Oglethorpe University
14. Webb Institute
15. Randolph College
16. University of Miami
17. Yale University
18. Claremont McKenna College
19. Brown University
20. The College of Idaho

Little Race/Class Interaction
Do different types of students (Black/White, rich/poor) interact frequently and easily?

1. Trinity College (CT)
2. Miami University
3. Fairfield University
4. University of New Hampshire
5. Wake Forest University
6. Providence College
7. University of Richmond
8. Syracuse University
9. Texas Christian University
10. Rollins College
11. University of California—San Diego
12. Lehigh University
13. Gettysburg College
14. Union College (NY)
15. University of Georgia
16. Boston College
17. Eugene Lang College—
    The New School for Liberal Arts
18. University of Mississippi
19. University of Virginia
20. Vanderbilt University

Gay Community Accepted
Is there very little discrimination against homosexuals?

1. Emerson College
2. New College of Florida
3. New York University
4. Stanford University
5. Prescott College
6. Macalester College
7. Simon's Rock College of Bard
8. College of the Atlantic
9. Wellesley College
10. Mount Holyoke College
11. Bennington College
12. Sarah Lawrence College
13. Bryn Mawr College
14. Marlboro College
15. Beloit College
16. Swarthmore College
17. St. Mary's College of Maryland
18. Hampshire College
19. Grinnell College
20. Reed College

Alternative Lifestyles Not an Alternative*
Is there very little discrimination against homosexuals?

1. University of Notre Dame
2. Thomas Aquinas College
3. Hampden-Sydney College
4. Trinity College (CT)
5. Wheaton College (IL)

6. Grove City College
7. College of the Ozarks
8. Baylor University
9. Seton Hall University
10. Brigham Young University (UT)
11. Miami University
12. Texas A&M University—College Station
13. Samford University
14. Southern Methodist University
15. Calvin College
16. University of Tennessee—Knoxville
17. Duquesne University
18. Mercer University—Macon
19. University of Mississippi
20. Hillsdale College

* Each of the five military academies was excluded from this list because of current, "Don't ask, don't tell" policies.

Most Religious Students
Are students very religious?

1. Brigham Young University (UT)
2. University of Notre Dame
3. Wheaton College (IL)
4. Grove City College
5. Hillsdale College
6. University of Dallas
7. Thomas Aquinas College
8. College of the Ozarks
9. Furman University
10. Samford University
11. Baylor University
12. Calvin College
13. Texas A&M University—College Station
14. United States Air Force Academy
15. Pepperdine University
16. The Catholic University of America
17. Auburn University
18. Brandeis University
19. Valparaiso University
20. University of Utah

Least Religious Students
Are students very religious?

1. Lewis & Clark College
2. Eugene Lang College—
   The New School for Liberal Arts
3. Reed College
4. Bennington College
5. Bard College
6. Emerson College
7. Simon's Rock College of Bard
8. Sarah Lawrence College
9. Vassar College
10. Hampshire College

11. Wesleyan University
12. Pitzer College
13. Skidmore College
14. Pomona College
15. New College of Florida
16. Macalester College
17. Marlboro College
18. Beloit College
19. Grinnell College
20. University of Puget Sound

SOCIAL LIFE

Great College Towns
Based on students' assessment of the surrounding city or town

1. DePaul University
2. New York University
3. The George Washington University
4. Barnard College
5. American University
6. Columbia University
7. Eugene Lang College—
   The New School for Liberal Arts
8. University of San Francisco
9. The University of Texas at Austin
10. Georgetown University
11. Northeastern University
12. McGill University
13. Tulane University
14. Emerson College
15. College of Charleston
16. University of Colorado—Boulder
17. Suffolk University
18. Boston College
19. Stevens Institute of Technology
20. Boston University

More to Do on Campus
Based on students' assessment of the surrounding city or town

1. Tuskegee University
2. Union College (NY)
3. United States Military Academy
4. Albion College
5. New Jersey Institute of Technology
6. Wheaton College (MA)
7. Wittenberg University
8. Hofstra University
9. United States Coast Guard Academy
10. Rensselaer Polytechnic Institute
11. Beloit College
12. Rose-Hulman Institute of Technology
13. Vassar College

14. DePauw University
15. College of the Holy Cross
16. Duke University
17. New Mexico Institute of Mining
    & Technology
18. Clark University
19. Trinity College (CT)
20. University of Notre Dame

Town-Gown Relations are Great
Do students get along well with members of the local community?

1. Wheaton College (IL)
2. Clemson University
3. Ripon College
4. Saint Michael's College
5. Stephens College
6. Franklin W. Olin College of Engineering
7. Davidson College
8. Saint Olaf College
9. College of the Ozarks
10. Brigham Young University (UT)
11. Agnes Scott College
12. Millsaps College
13. Samford University
14. Wesleyan College
15. William Jewell College
16. Loyola University New Orleans
17. University of Louisiana at Lafayette
18. Seattle University
19. Kansas State University
20. The University of Tulsa

Town-Gown Relations are Strained
Do students get along well with members of the local community?

1. Union College (NY)
2. Trinity College (CT)
3. Lehigh University
4. Sarah Lawrence College
5. Illinois Institute of Technology
6. University of New Hampshire
7. Duke University
8. Colorado College
9. DePauw University
10. Howard University
11. College of the Holy Cross
12. Vassar College
13. Bennington College
14. New Jersey Institute of Technology
15. Northwestern University
16. Bates College
17. Providence College
18. The College of Wooster
19. Franklin & Marshall College
20. University of Pennsylvania

EXTRACURRICULARS

Best Athletic Facilities
Based on students' rating of campus athletic facilities

1. University of Maryland—College Park
2. Texas A&M University—College Station
3. Wabash College
4. University of Florida
5. University of Tennessee—Knoxville
6. Georgia Institute of Technology
7. Clemson University
8. West Virginia University
9. Penn State—University Park
10. University of Georgia
11. University of Virginia
12. University of California—Los Angeles
13. University of Notre Dame
14. University of Alabama—Tuscaloosa
15. The University of Texas at Austin
16. Duke University
17. Gonzaga University
18. University of Miami
19. The Ohio State University—Columbus
20. St. Lawrence University

Students Pack the Stadiums
How popular are intercollegiate sports?

1. University of Florida
2. University of Maryland—College Park
3. University of Notre Dame
4. Penn State—University Park
5. University of North Carolina at Chapel Hill
6. University of Georgia
7. Clemson University
8. University of Michigan—Ann Arbor
9. The University of Texas at Austin
10. Duke University
11. University of California—Los Angeles
12. West Virginia University
13. Boston College
14. Wabash College
15. Gonzaga University
16. University of Wisconsin—Madison
17. University of Alabama—Tuscaloosa
18. University of Southern California
19. Virginia Tech
20. Indiana University at Bloomington

Intercollegiate Sports Unpopular or Nonexistent
How popular are intercollegiate sports?

1. Eugene Lang College The New School for Liberal Arts
2. St. John's College (NM)
3. New College of Florida
4. Bennington College
5. College of the Atlantic
6. Thomas Aquinas College
7. Prescott College
8. Franklin W. Olin College of Engineering
9. Marlboro College
10. Reed College
11. Hampshire College
12. Sarah Lawrence College
13. St. John's College (MD)
14. University of Chicago
15. New York University
16. State University of New York—Purchase College
17. Harvey Mudd College
18. Simon's Rock College of Bard
19. New Mexico Institute of Mining & Technology
20. Emerson College

Everyone Plays Intramural Sports
How popular are intramural sports?

1. University of Notre Dame
2. Whitman College
3. Penn State—University Park
4. Ripon College
5. Wabash College
6. University of Florida
7. Grove City College
8. Clemson University
9. Colorado College
10. Gonzaga University
11. University of Dayton
12. St. John's College (MD)
13. United States Air Force Academy
14. Carleton College
15. United States Naval Academy
16. United States Coast Guard Academy
17. University of Nebraska—Lincoln
18. Brigham Young University (UT)
19. University of Connecticut
20. Providence College

Nobody Plays Intramural Sports
How popular are intramural sports?

1. Eugene Lang College—
   The New School for Liberal Arts
2. Stephens College
3. College of the Atlantic
4. Sarah Lawrence College
5. Emerson College
6. New York University
7. Prescott College
8. New College of Florida
9. Hollins University
10. Suffolk University
11. Bennington College
12. Bryn Mawr College
13. The Cooper Union for the Advancement
    of Science and Art
14. Marlboro College
15. Hampshire College
16. Simon's Rock College of Bard
17. Randolph College
18. Spelman College
19. Barnard College
20. The Evergreen State College

Best College Radio Station
How popular is the radio station?

1. Emerson College
2. St. Bonaventure University
3. DePauw University
4. Stanford University
5. Ithaca College
6. Seton Hall University
7. Brown University
8. Guilford College
9. Knox College
10. Howard University
11. University of Puget Sound
12. Carleton College
13. Alfred University
14. Whitman College
15. Reed College
16. The Evergreen State College
17. Swarthmore College
18. Westminster College (PA)
19. Skidmore College
20. Bates College

Best College Newspaper
How popular is the newspaper?

1. Yale University
2. University of North Carolina at
   Chapel Hill
3. Howard University
4. Harvard College

5. University of Georgia
6. University of Maryland—College Park
7. University of Florida
8. Texas A&M University—College Station
9. Penn State—University Park
10. University of California—Los Angeles
11. Louisiana State University
12. Duke University
13. West Virginia University
14. University of Pennsylvania
15. The University of Texas at Austin
16. University of Mississippi
17. University of Kansas
18. Indiana University at Bloomington
19. Syracuse University
20. Northwestern University

Best College Theater
How popular are college theater productions?

1. Yale University
2. Wagner College
3. Emerson College
4. Bennington College
5. Drew University
6. Muhlenberg College
7. Stephens College
8. Vassar College
9. Nazareth College of Rochester
10. Catawba College
11. Ithaca College
12. Lawrence University
13. College of the Ozarks
14. Whitman College
15. Brown University
16. Simon's Rock College of Bard
17. Knox College
18. Carnegie Mellon University
19. Oglethorpe University
20. Manhattanville College

PARTIES

Lots of Beer
How widely used is beer?

1. DePauw University
2. Penn State—University Park
3. University of New Hampshire
4. Randolph-Macon College
5. Ohio University—Athens
6. University of Wisconsin—Madison
7. University of Florida
8. University of Mississippi
9. Hampden-Sydney College
10. Colgate University

11. University of Iowa
12. West Virginia University
13. Claremont McKenna College
14. The University of Texas at Austin
15. Union College (NY)
16. Trinity College (CT)
17. Hamilton College
18. James Madison University
19. Indiana University at Bloomington
20. Lehigh University

Got Milk?
How widely used is beer?

1. Brigham Young University (UT)
2. Wheaton College (IL)
3. College of the Ozarks
4. Grove City College
5. City University of New York—Queens College
6. Spelman College
7. City University of New York—Brooklyn College
8. Wesleyan College
9. Xavier University of Louisiana
10. United States Coast Guard Academy
11. City University of New York—Baruch College
12. Howard University
13. Wellesley College
14. Fisk University
15. City University of New York—Hunter College
16. Calvin College
17. Hampton University
18. Berea College
19. Samford University
20. Pepperdine University

Lots of Hard Liquor
How widely used is hard liquor?

1. Ohio University—Athens
2. Randolph-Macon College
3. University of Iowa
4. University of California—Santa Barbara
5. University of Mississippi
6. DePauw University
7. Providence College
8. Indiana University at Bloomington
9. University of Wisconsin—Madison
10. Trinity College (CT)
11. University of Georgia
12. The University of Texas at Austin
13. Florida State University
14. University of Colorado—Boulder
15. Sewanee: The University of the South

16. Tulane University
17. University of Florida
18. West Virginia University
19. Loyola University New Orleans
20. Penn State—University Park

Scotch and Soda, Hold the Scotch
How widely used is hard liquor?

1. Brigham Young University (UT)
2. Wheaton College (IL)
3. College of the Ozarks
4. Grove City College
5. City University of New York—Queens College
6. United States Coast Guard Academy
7. City University of New York—Brooklyn College
8. City University of New York—Baruch College
9. Wesleyan College
10. City University of New York—Hunter College
11. Calvin College
12. Samford University
13. Wellesley College
14. Spelman College
15. Thomas Aquinas College
16. Berea College
17. United States Air Force Academy
18. Xavier University of Louisiana
19. Pepperdine University
20. California State University—Stanislaus

Reefer Madness
How widely used is marijuana?

1. Bard College
2. Warren Wilson College
3. University of Colorado—Boulder
4. University of Vermont
5. New College of Florida
6. University of California—Santa Cruz
7. Colorado College
8. Hampshire College
9. Eugene Lang College—The New School for Liberal Arts
10. Sarah Lawrence College
11. Ithaca College
12. Pitzer College
13. Skidmore College
14. University of Oregon
15. Wesleyan University
16. Guilford College
17. West Virginia University
18. University of California—Santa Barbara
19. Eckerd College
20. University of New Hampshire

Don't Inhale
How widely used is marijuana?

1. United States Naval Academy
2. United States Coast Guard Academy
3. Brigham Young University (UT)
4. United States Air Force Academy
5. United States Military Academy
6. United States Merchant Marine Academy
7. Thomas Aquinas College
8. Wheaton College (IL)
9. College of the Ozarks
10. Webb Institute
11. Grove City College
12. University of Notre Dame
13. Hillsdale College
14. Samford University
15. Calvin College
16. Wesleyan College
17. City University of New York—Queens College
18. Franklin W. Olin College of Engineering
19. City University of New York—Baruch College
20. Agnes Scott College

Major Frat and Sorority Scene
How popular are fraternities/sororities?

1. Birmingham-Southern College
2. Wofford College
3. Bucknell University
4. Transylvania University
5. University of Mississippi
6. Penn State—University Park
7. DePauw University
8. Randolph-Macon College
9. Lehigh University
10. University of Florida
11. Vanderbilt University
12. University of Georgia
13. Wake Forest University
14. Wabash College
15. University of Tennessee—Knoxville
16. Gettysburg College
17. Millsaps College
18. University of Illinois—Urbana Champaign
19. Miami University
20. Albion College

Party Schools
Based on a combination of survey questions concerning the use of alcohol and drugs, hours of study each day, and the popularity of the Greek system

1. University of Florida
2. University of Mississippi
3. Penn State—University Park
4. West Virginia University
5. Ohio University—Athens
6. Randolph-Macon College
7. University of Georgia
8. The University of Texas at Austin
9. University of California—Santa Barbara
10. Florida State University
11. University of New Hampshire
12. University of Iowa
13. University of Colorado—Boulder
14. Indiana University at Bloomington
15. Tulane University
16. University of Illinois—Urbana Champaign
17. Arizona State University at the Tempe campus
18. University of Tennessee—Knoxville
19. University of Alabama—Tuscaloosa
20. Loyola University—New Orleans

Stone-Cold Sober Schools
Based on a combination of survey questions concerning the use of alcohol and drugs, hours of study each day, and the popularity of the Greek system

1. Brigham Young University (UT)
2. Wheaton College (IL)
3. United States Coast Guard Academy
4. College of the Ozarks
5. Grove City College
6. United States Air Force Academy
7. United States Naval Academy
8. Wellesley College
9. Thomas Aquinas College
10. Calvin College
11. United States Military Academy
12. Wesleyan College
13. Franklin W. Olin College of Engineering
14. City University of New York—Queens College
15. Webb Institute
16. Berea College
17. Agnes Scott College
18. City University of New York—Baruch College
19. Simmons College
20. Bryn Mawr College

Jock Schools

Based on a combination of survey questions concerning intercollegiate and intramural sports, the popularity of the Greek system

1. Clemson University
2. University of Florida
3. Wabash College
4. Penn State—University Park
5. University of Notre Dame
6. University of Nebraska—Lincoln
7. Wake Forest University
8. University of Michigan—Ann Arbor
9. Florida State University
10. Purdue University—West Lafayette
11. University of Georgia
12. Villanova University
13. University of North Carolina at Chapel Hill
14. University of California—Los Angeles
15. University of Virginia
16. University of Connecticut
17. Duke University
18. Texas A&M University—College Station
19. University of Tennessee—Knoxville
20. Kansas State University

Dodgeball Targets

Based on a combination of survey questions concerning intercollegiate and intramural sports, the popularity of the Greek system

1. New College of Florida
2. Bennington College
3. Eugene Lang College— The New School for Liberal Arts
4. College of the Atlantic
5. St. John's College (NM)
6. Marlboro College
7. Stephens College
8. Prescott College
9. Hampshire College
10. Sarah Lawrence College
11. Reed College
12. Emerson College
13. Simon's Rock College of Bard
14. New York University
15. Bard College
16. The Evergreen State College
17. Thomas Aquinas College
18. State University of New York— Purchase College
19. Suffolk University
20. Hollins University

Future Rotarians and Daughters of the American Revolution

Based on a combination of survey questions concerning political persuasion, the use of marijuana and hallucinogens, the prevalence of religion, the popularity of student government, and the students' level of acceptance of the gay community on campus

1. Brigham Young University (UT)
2. Grove City College
3. University of Dallas
4. United States Air Force Academy
5. University of Notre Dame
6. Wheaton College (IL)
7. United States Military Academy
8. Texas A&M University—College Station
9. Furman University
10. United States Merchant Marine Academy
11. College of the Ozarks
12. Thomas Aquinas College
13. Auburn University
14. United States Coast Guard Academy
15. Xavier University of Louisiana
16. William Jewell College
17. Calvin College
18. Samford University
19. Saint Olaf College
20. Baylor University

Birkenstock-Wearing, Tree-Hugging, Clove-Smoking Vegetarians

Based on a combination of survey questions concerning political persuasion, the use of marijuana and hallucinogens, the prevalence of religion, the popularity of student government, and the students' level of acceptance of the gay community on campus

1. Warren Wilson College
2. Hampshire College
3. Bard College
4. The Evergreen State College
5. Bennington College
6. Reed College
7. Sarah Lawrence College
8. Simon's Rock College of Bard
9. Vassar College
10. Wesleyan University
11. University of California—Santa Cruz
12. State University of New York— Purchase College
13. Colorado College
14. Oberlin College
15. University of Vermont
16. Skidmore College
17. Beloit College
18. Brown University
19. Grinnell College
20. Kenyon College

Deep Springs Honor Roll

Since Deep Springs is a two-year college—the only one of its kind in The Best 368 Colleges—we've decided to remove it from the body of our individual rankings in order to avoid comparing "apples and oranges." Instead we've created this "honor roll," which includes all categories in which Deep Springs ranks high (or low, as it were) among the best colleges.

Most Accessible Professors
Students Study the Most
Class Discussions Encouraged
This is a Library?
School Runs Like Butter
Most Beautiful Campus
Dorms Like Palaces
Best Quality of Life
Most Liberal Students
Lots of Race/Class Interaction
Gay Community Accepted
Least Religious Students
Great College Towns
Town-Gown Relations are Great
Intercollegiate Sports Unpopular or Nonexistent
Got Milk?
Scotch and Soda, Hold the Scotch
Don't Inhale
Stone-Cold Sober Schools
Dodgeball Targets

A Final Note

The following schools have been excluded from our ranking lists dealing with financial aid:

Berea College
College of the Ozarks
The Cooper Union for the Advancement
    of Science and Art
Franklin W. Olin College of Engineering
United States Air Force Academy
United States Coast Guard Academy
United States Merchant Marine Academy
United States Military Academy
United States Naval Academy
Webb Institute

The reason—they're free!
We would like to commend each of these schools on their ability to do the seemingly impossible—not charge tuition. However, we thought it less than fair to include each of these schools in our financial lists, since each would have an unfair advantage over schools that charged even a moderate tuition.

PRINCETON REVIEW "GREEN RATING"AND "FIRE SAFETY RATING" HONOR ROLLS

We salute these schools that received a 99 (the highest score) in the tallies for our new "Green Rating" and our "Fire Safety Rating"—two of eight ratings on some of the school profiles in this book as well as in our *Best Northeastern Colleges* and *Complete Book of Colleges*, 2009 Editions, and at www.PrincetonReview.com.

Our school ratings are numerical scores (note: they are not ranking lists) that show how a school "sizes up" on a fixed scale. They are comparable to grades and they are based primarily on institutional data we collect directly from the colleges.

"Green Rating" Honor Roll

Schools are listed in alphabetical order. See p. 19 for information on how our "Green Rating" is determined.

Arizona State University at the Tempe Campus
Bates College
College of the Atlantic
Emory University
Georgia Institute of Technology
Harvard College
State University of New York at Binghamton
University of New Hampshire
University of Oregon
University of Washington
Yale University

"Fire Safety Rating" Honor Roll

Schools are listed in alphabetical order. See p. 18 for information on how our "Fire Safety Rating" is determined.

Adelphi University*
Bay Path College*
Bentley College
California State University, Stanislaus
Cazenovia College*
College of Mount St. Joseph*
Kean University*
Mountain State University*
Neumann College*
Suffolk University
The College of Saint Rose*
University of Oklahoma

*Schools marked with an asterisk do not appear in Best 368 Colleges. You can find those school profiles in Complete Book of Colleges, 2009 Edition.

PART 3

THE BEST
368 COLLEGES

AGNES SCOTT COLLEGE

141 EAST COLLEGE AVENUE, DECATUR, GA 30030-3797 • ADMISSIONS: 404-471-6285 • FAX: 404-471-6414

STUDENTS SAY ". . ."

Academics

"Agnes Scott College is about empowering the next generation of strong women in the world," students at this small women's college tell us, and statistics prove that this is more than empty rhetoric. ASC ranks high among undergraduate institutions in the percentage of its alumnae who continue on to advanced degree programs, and women here enjoy a highly personalized educational experience. As one student explains, "It makes me feel good that my professors know my name! Overall, I feel like this school cares about me. There is nothing impersonal about Agnes Scott." That intimacy, coupled with ASC's close proximity to Atlanta where there are "so many internships and jobs," provides ASC with a killer one-two punch. Writing and independent thinking are the focus of the curriculum here; classes "are engaging and encourage students to think critically about the subject, not just memorize a bunch of facts and dates." While the "small size of the school . . . makes it difficult to offer some courses," ASC "makes up for it with opportunities for reading courses, independent studies," and "wonderful personal interaction with one's professors." Students warn, "There are no cake classes at Agnes," but also say that "one-on-one relationships with the professors" help undergrads master the ASC's "rigorous" academics. To sum it all up, "Agnes Scott is a very challenging school, but it provides you with more than enough resources to come out on top."

Life

Life at ASC "can be a bubble if you make it a bubble. There are people who never go out, and they suffer socially. There are also people who go out, party too much, and suffer academically. Most people are successful in finding a healthy balance." Fortunately, ASC women have a lot of options to choose from when it comes to finding entertainment. There are "tons of hall activities at the dorms, where the girls all get to know one another really well!" In addition, "There are numerous campus-wide activities like Diversifest—where diversity is celebrated with Chinese calligraphy banners, the showing of *Ringu*, and a Day of the Dead workshop"—not to mention a popular "pre-exam pancake jam." ASC is located in Decatur, an upscale area just outside of the Atlanta city limits that boasts "fabulous restaurants" and great "shopping at Little Five Points," an alternative hotspot nearby. Students head into Atlanta, "an amazing city . . . ridiculously accessible by MARTA or car," to enjoy "various museums, including the High Art Museum and the Georgia Aquarium," not to mention "tons of great restaurants, shopping, plays, concerts, and nightlife." As for the dating scene, "Georgia Tech isn't far away, so if people are looking for parties that include boys, that's usually the first stop."

Student Body

"There is no typical student per se" at Agnes Scott, as "Everyone kind of goes to the beat of her own drum." The student body runs the gamut "from the radical, left-wing lesbian to the far-right, pearls-wearing, charm school graduate, and any combination after that." Many "were the 'weird girls' from high school . . . the ones who got good grades but were eccentric." While "People are very different here," students concede that there are identifiable "social circles" on campus. As one student explains, "We definitely have 'groups' on campus, including the religious right, . . . the girls who drink too much, and the girls who ask to rewrite their A- papers. The groups might not always get along, but when it comes down to it, Agnes Scott students are devoted to each other and the school." While political perspectives vary, the majority here "lean to the political left," to the point that those who are not "very liberal and idealistic . . . often have some trouble fitting in." Students also observe that "because of an international focus and location in metro Atlanta, the student body is diverse in ethnicity."

FINANCIAL AID: 404-471-6395 • E-MAIL: ADMISSION@AGNESSCOTT.EDU • WEBSITE: WWW.AGNESSCOTT.EDU

THE PRINCETON REVIEW SAYS

Admissions

Very important factors considered include: Class rank, application essay, academic GPA, recommendation(s), rigor of secondary school record, standardized test scores, character/personal qualities, talent/ability. *Important factors considered include:* Extracurricular activities, volunteer work, work experience. *Other factors considered include:* Alumni/ae relation, first generation, geographical residence, interview, level of applicant's interest, racial/ethnic status, state residency, SAT or ACT required; ACT with Writing component required. TOEFL required of all international applicants. High school diploma is required and GED is accepted. *Academic units recommended:* 4 English, 3 mathematics, 2 science, (2 science labs), 2 foreign language, 2 social studies, 2 history.

Financial Aid

Students should submit: FAFSA. Provide previous year's tax return. Regular filing deadline is 5/1. The Princeton Review suggests that all financial aid forms be submitted as soon as possible after January 1. *Need-based scholarships/grants offered:* Federal Pell, SEOG, state scholarships/grants, private scholarships, the school's own gift aid. *Loan aid offered:* FFEL Subsidized Stafford, FFEL Unsubsidized Stafford, FFEL PLUS, college/university loans from institutional funds. Applicants will be notified of awards on a rolling basis beginning 3/1. Federal Work-Study Program available. Institutional employment available. Off-campus job opportunities are excellent.

The Inside Word

Are you on the fence about applying to Agnes Scott College? Apply online, and the college will waive the application fee—it will only cost you the time it takes to fill it out. Don't treat this application lightly, though; Agnes Scott is highly selective, and you'll need to submit an impressive application to gain admission. Don't worry about falling through the cracks here—every candidate is assigned her own specific Admission Counselor who works with the student throughout the application process.

THE SCHOOL SAYS "..."

From The Admissions Office

"Who will you become? If you are looking for a liberal arts college that will help you explore, strive, and surpass what you think is your potential, then consider Agnes Scott College. Our students and alumnae say it best:

"'I find the academic program to be extremely challenging at Agnes Scott; but it's not overwhelming—it's easy to go to your teachers and ask for help because they know who you are and take a personal interest.'—Evan Joslin, Class of 2008, Atlanta, GA.

"'Agnes Scott College didn't teach me what to think. They taught me how to think,' says Jessica Owen Sanfilippo, Class of 1998, who majored in biology at ASC, received a master's degree in cancer biology from Stanford, and an MBA from Harvard.

"Students find their passions and their voices through guaranteed internships, international study experiences, and collaborative learning in places like the science center, facilities that were designed expressly to facilitate faculty-student research. Your next 4 years are about you. We invite you to come for a visit and imagine the possibilities for you.

"Students applying for admission are required to submit score results from the SAT with the Writing section or the ACT, with the Writing section recommended."

SELECTIVITY

Admissions Rating	92
# of applicants	1,595
% of applicants accepted	45
% of acceptees attending	30
# accepting a place on wait list	4
% admitted from wait list	50
# of early decision applicants	49
% accepted early decision	39

FRESHMAN PROFILE

Range SAT Critical Reading	550–680
Range SAT Math	500–610
Range SAT Writing	550–660
Range ACT Composite	22–29
Minimum paper TOEFL	577
Minimum computer TOEFL	233
Minimum web-based TOEFL	90–91
Average HS GPA	3.65
% graduated top 10% of class	41
% graduated top 25% of class	73
% graduated top 50% of class	92

DEADLINES

Early decision	
Deadline	11/15
Notification	12/15
Regular	
Priority	3/1
Nonfall registration?	yes

APPLICANTS ALSO LOOK AT

AND OFTEN PREFER
Emory University
Oxford College

AND SOMETIMES PREFER
University of Georgia

AND RARELY PREFER
Spelman College

FINANCIAL FACTS

Financial Aid Rating	89
Annual tuition	$26,600
Room and board	$9,350
Required fees	$787
Books and supplies	$1,000
% frosh rec. need-based scholarship or grant aid	71
% UG rec. need-based scholarship or grant aid	70
% frosh rec. non-need-based scholarship or grant aid	54
% UG rec. non-need-based scholarship or grant aid	35
% frosh rec. need-based self-help aid	61
% UG rec. need-based self-help aid	61
% frosh rec. any financial aid	99
% UG rec. any financial aid	88
% UG borrow to pay for school	73
Average cumulative indebtedness	$24,070

ALBION COLLEGE

611 EAST PORTER, ALBION, MI 49224 • ADMISSIONS: 517-629-0321 • FAX: 517-629-0569

STUDENTS SAY ". . ."

Academics

Albion College, a small liberal arts school with "a great biology department" and "wonderful programs in the sciences and pre-law," has "an amazing ability to provide the 'small school' intimacy with peers and instructors while delivering world-class education that competes with major universities," according to its students. Albion boasts "professors that would make many bigger schools drool," and "Since it's strictly an undergraduate institution, Albion's services are all geared toward the students." Indeed, here "The entire faculty and staff always make time for students and even acknowledge you by name when you walk past them on campus," and "The professors seem to genuinely envision a greater academic career for all students and strongly encourage further schooling after attaining the four-year degree." Students also enjoy a "number of available opportunities, in class and out of class, for internships and studying abroad, and even after the students leave here," thanks to a strong alumni network. As one undergrad explains, "Albion is about connections. Even though it is a small school, everyone knows someone who goes to or has graduated from Albion. Even though it is out of the way we are very connected to the wider world." A solid selection of study abroad and research opportunities also "puts us on the cutting edge of this shrinking world." The Albion curriculum is flexible enough to "emphasize the freedom of choice for every individual. It allows students to express themselves in various ways and allows students to get hands-on experience of specific areas of work" while completing their studies.

Life

"There isn't a lot to do in the city of Albion itself," but students tell us that "There is always something happening on campus" to compensate. Greek life "is a very large part of Albion, and there are always things going on at the frats"; about one-third of all students join Greek organizations. Other options include "concerts, comedians, and other activities put on by Union Board, an event planning committee sponsored with student activity funds." The school works hard to draw big-name entertainment and in recent years has hosted performances by Dane Cook, Pablo Francisco, OAR, and Less Than Jake. While "A lot of people drink and party because they don't know what else to do," students insist that those who choose not to drink have plenty of options. Hometown Albion "is a small one-horse town where there isn't a whole bunch for the residents to do, let alone the student body." The town's one saving grace is the Bohm movie theatre, "where all students get in for free with ID."

Student Body

"I think one word can describe the Albion student: involved," one student writes, adding that "Nearly every Albion student is involved with multiple organizations that engage in community outreach, philosophical discussions, diversity awareness, hobby enthusiasts, and nearly every other aspect of a social organization you can think of." Most here "seem to come from either wealthy backgrounds or are from the surrounding town and are from low-income families," with the balance tilted firmly toward the former group. "There is not a dominant religion" on campus, "but Albion College was founded as a Christian school," meaning that "many of the students are Christian." Most "are white, and about half of those who aren't are foreign exchange students," and many "have always lived in Michigan" and "could be described as the attractive, popular, smart kid in school" who "came to Albion to be a big fish in a small pond."

FINANCIAL AID: 517-629-0440 • E-MAIL: ADMISSIONS@ALBION.EDU • WEBSITE: WWW.ALBION.EDU

THE PRINCETON REVIEW SAYS

Admissions

Very important factors considered include: Academic GPA, recommendation(s), rigor of secondary school record, character/personal qualities, interview, level of applicant's interest. *Important factors considered include:* Application essay, standardized test scores, extracurricular activities, talent/ability. *Other factors considered include:* Class rank, alumni/ae relation, first generation, geographical residence, racial/ethnic status, volunteer work, SAT or ACT required; SAT and SAT Subject Tests or ACT recommended; ACT with Writing component recommended. TOEFL required of all international applicants. High school diploma is required and GED is accepted. *Academic units required:* 4 English, 3 mathematics, 3 science, (1 science labs), 3 social studies, 3 academic electives. *Academic units recommended:* 4 English, 3 mathematics, 3 science, 3 foreign language, 3 social studies, 3 history.

Financial Aid

Students should submit: FAFSA. The Princeton Review suggests that all financial aid forms be submitted as soon as possible after January 1. *Need-based scholarships/grants offered:* Federal Pell, SEOG, state scholarships/grants, private scholarships, the school's own gift aid. *Loan aid offered:* FFEL Subsidized Stafford, FFEL Unsubsidized Stafford, FFEL PLUS, Federal Perkins, state loans Applicants will be notified of awards on a rolling basis beginning 3/15. Federal Work-Study Program available. Institutional employment available. Off-campus job opportunities are fair.

The Inside Word

Albion fills each incoming class with solid if not exceptional high school students. The average GPA for incoming students was 3.56 and the average SAT score 1200. Albion applicants are a self-selecting group, which explains the schools 80+ percent acceptance rate. Borderline candidates can improve their chances by presenting an impressive roster of extracurriculars and volunteer work, strong essays, and a strong interview. A campus visit is highly encouraged.

THE SCHOOL SAYS " . . ."

From The Admissions Office

"Albion offers a purposeful blend of a classical foundation in the liberal arts with a strong emphasis on professional development through highly selective institutes in environmental science, public policy and service, professional management, premedical and health care studies, honors and education, world-class internships, and study abroad opportunities. *Yahoo! Internet Life* ranks Albion the 'Seventh Most Wired College in America' for integrating technology into academic, professional, and cocurricular programs; and a recent study conducted by the Council on Undergraduate Research ranked Albion among the top four colleges in the nation for the percentage of students engaged in original, funded undergraduate research. Albion is among the top 85 private, liberal arts colleges for the number of alumni who are corporate executives, including top executives and CEOs of *Newsweek*, the Lahey Clinic (MA), the Wharton School (University of Pennsylvania), PricewaterhouseCoopers, Dow Corning, Avon, the NCAA, and the Federal Accounting Standards Board (FASB). Albion's places over 95 percent of graduates into law, dental, and medical schools including Harvard, Michigan, Columbia, Northwestern, Notre Dame, Vanderbilt, and Wisconsin. A full-service equestrian center opens August 2004 for all students, including the IHSA equestrian team. Campus organizations include Model United Nations, Fellowship of Christian Athletes, Canoe Club, Black Student Alliance, Equestrian Club, Ecological Awareness Club and Greek life. Of particular note are Albion's athletics (Britons), often dominating Division III football, women's basketball and soccer, and men's and women's golf and swimming. Five varsity teams have recently earned the highest grade point average in the MIAA conference, NCAA Division III, or any division nationwide. Submission of SAT or ACT test scores are optional. Students with weighted GPA above a 3.85 need not submit scores. Homeschooled students, learning disabled, and students with a GPA less than 3.85 should contact the Admission Office."

SELECTIVITY

Admissions Rating	84
# of applicants	2,204
% of applicants accepted	81
% of acceptees attending	28

FRESHMAN PROFILE

Range SAT Critical Reading	520–660
Range SAT Math	530–650
Range ACT Composite	23–28
Minimum paper TOEFL	550
Minimum computer TOEFL	270
Average HS GPA	3.55
% graduated top 10% of class	30
% graduated top 25% of class	64
% graduated top 50% of class	90

DEADLINES

Early action	
Deadline	12/1
Notification	1/1
Regular	
Priority	12/1
Deadline	3/1
Notification	rolling
Nonfall registration?	yes

APPLICANTS ALSO LOOK AT

AND OFTEN PREFER
University of Michigan—Ann Arbor
Grinnell College

AND SOMETIMES PREFER
Hope College
Kalamazoo College
Michigan State University
DePauw University
Kenyon College

AND RARELY PREFER
Alma College
Calvin College
Adrian College
Olivet College

FINANCIAL FACTS

Financial Aid Rating	89
Annual tuition	$27,054
Room and board	$7,806
Required fees	$476
Books and supplies	$700
% frosh rec. need-based scholarship or grant aid	65
% UG rec. need-based scholarship or grant aid	61
% frosh rec. non-need-based scholarship or grant aid	62
% UG rec. non-need-based scholarship or grant aid	57
% frosh rec. need-based self-help aid	48
% UG rec. need-based self-help aid	48
% frosh rec. any financial aid	95
% UG rec. any financial aid	94
% UG borrow to pay for school	65
Average cumulative indebtedness	$25,340

ALFRED UNIVERSITY

ALUMNI HALL, ONE SAXON DRIVE, ALFRED, NY 14802-1205 • ADMISSIONS: 607-871-2115 • FAX: 607-871-2198

CAMPUS LIFE

Quality of Life Rating	**78**
Fire Safety Rating	**60***
Green Rating	**60***
Type of school	private
Environment	rural

STUDENTS

Total undergrad enrollment	2,030
% male/female	49/51
% from out of state	35
% live on campus	67
% African American	4
% Asian	2
% Caucasian	63
% Hispanic	2.5
% international	1

SURVEY SAYS . . .

Large classes
Great library
Frats and sororities are unpopular
or nonexistent
Lots of beer drinking

ACADEMICS

Academic Rating	**82**
Calendar	semester
Student/faculty ratio	12:1
Profs interesting rating	85
Profs accessible rating	84
Most common reg class size	10–19 students
Most common lab size	fewer than 10 students

MOST POPULAR MAJORS

fine/studio arts
ceramic sciences and engineering
business/commerce

STUDENTS SAY ". . ."

Academics

Alfred University is best known for its unique and prestigious glass engineering, ceramic arts, and ceramic engineering programs ("the best in the nation," students insist). These programs' reputations are well earned, but they occasionally overshadow AU's many other assets, according to undergrads here; as one student points out, "Alfred offers tons of majors and minors within four different undergraduate schools (Art School, Engineering School, College of Liberal Arts and Sciences, and the College of Business)," and the school does a good job of "integrating the four very distinct schools into one cohesive whole, so you can make friends from absolutely every conceivable background while pursuing any course of study." Engineering is among the school's hallmark disciplines, attracting nearly one in seven undergraduates; business studies are nearly as popular. AU offers its breadth of academic options on an intimate scale; explains one undergrad, "The size of the school is a strength. Because the school is so small, students have chances that they might never have had at other schools. Some of the best friends I have made here are upperclassmen whom I probably would not have met had I gone to a larger school. In such a small school, everyone also has the chance to make his or her voice heard in a way that probably cannot happen at larger schools."

Life

Alfred University is located "in the middle of nowhere" in "the one-stoplight town" of Alfred, New York. "If the Student Activities Board does not provide it, it does not happen," warns one student. Undergrads fill their spare time with "over one hundred clubs and organizations" and "crazy stuff" like "snow sculptures and secret sledding (we have snow more often than not)." Students here "are very forward thinking," so many "try to get internships and co-ops during their undergraduate years." Otherwise, there's always the "multiple events and programs each week, especially on the weekends," sponsored by Student Activities, which are "very well-publicized and have great attendance." Such events include "movies, lectures, comedy acts, music shows, art shows, and plays." Low-key activities such as group dinners, watching DVDs, and video gaming are also quite popular. As one student sums up the situation, "Life is quiet for those who like it quiet, but it also offers something for everybody." Party nights "are pretty popular," and "a lot of students from both schools"—Alfred State College, located across the street, and Alfred University—"go out to a party and drink."

Student Body

"There really is no typical student at Alfred" because the "wide variety of majors and minors…attracts such a wide variety of students." The predominant note is "a mix of engineers and art students" (they make up about 40 percent of the student body) with "a smattering of other majors" across a broad range of disciplines, business and psychology most prominent among them. Students report that the population is "polarized among the art school, the liberal arts school, and the business school. Everybody seems to fit in somewhere, though." Engineers and artists tend toward the outer edges of the bell curve, so it's not surprising that "The school is made up of crazies of every variety. If you're a freak in high school, you will fit right in at Alfred. We have everything from people who will fall over themselves to discuss postmodernism to people who make chain mail bikinis." Most here "are from small towns, although there is also a proportionally high percentage of study abroad students."

ALFRED UNIVERSITY

FINANCIAL AID: 607-871-2159 • E-MAIL: ADMWWW@ALFRED.EDU • WEBSITE: WWW.ALFRED.EDU

THE PRINCETON REVIEW SAYS

Admissions

Very important factors considered include: Class rank, recommendation(s), rigor of secondary school record, character/personal qualities, extracurricular activities. *Important factors considered include:* Application essay, standardized test scores, volunteer work, work experience. *Other factors considered include:* Interview, talent/ability, SAT or ACT required; TOEFL required of all international applicants. High school diploma is required and GED is accepted. *Academic units required:* 4 English, 2 mathematics, 2 science, (2 science labs), 2 social studies. *Academic units recommended:* 4 mathematics, 3 science, (3 science labs), 3 social studies.

Financial Aid

Students should submit: FAFSA, institution's own financial aid form, state aid form, noncustodial PROFILE, business/farm supplement. Regular filing deadline is 3/15. The Princeton Review suggests that all financial aid forms be submitted as soon as possible after January 1. *Need-based scholarships/grants offered:* Federal Pell, SEOG, state scholarships/grants, private scholarships, the school's own gift aid. *Loan aid offered:* FFEL Subsidized Stafford, FFEL Unsubsidized Stafford, FFEL PLUS, Federal Perkins, college/university loans from institutional funds. Private alternative loans. Applicants will be notified of awards on a rolling basis beginning 2/15. Federal Work-Study Program available. Institutional employment available. Off-campus job opportunities are poor.

The Inside Word

Alfred is a fine university somewhat hampered by its location; it takes a special kind of student to want to spend four years in so remote a location, especially one in which winter can seem endless. Outdoorsy types comfortable in layered clothing are best suited to the challenge. The allure for arts students is obvious—Alfred's programs in the arts are especially well regarded—and as a result competition is fiercest among applicants for these programs. A killer portfolio, even more than great grades and standardized test scores, is your most likely ticket in.

THE SCHOOL SAYS "..."

From The Admissions Office

"The admissions process at Alfred University is the foundation for the personal attention each student can expect during their time at AU. Each applicant is evaluated individually and receives genuine, individual care and consideration.

"The best way to discover all Alfred University has to offer is to come to campus. We truly have something for everyone with over 60 courses of study, 22 intercollegiate athletic teams, and 100 clubs and organizations. You can tour campus; meet current students, faculty, coaches, and staff; attend a class; and eat in our dining hall—experience first hand what life at AU is like.

"Alfred University is a place where students are free to pursue their dreams and interests—all of them—no matter how varied or different. Academics, athletics, study abroad, special interests—they're all part of what makes you who you are and who you are going to become."

SELECTIVITY
Admissions Rating	78
# of applicants	2,355
% of applicants accepted	74
% of acceptees attending	30
# of early decision applicants	53
% accepted early decision	83

FRESHMAN PROFILE
Range SAT Critical Reading	490–610
Range SAT Math	500–620
Range ACT Composite	22–27
Minimum paper TOEFL	550
Minimum computer TOEFL	213
% graduated top 10% of class	18
% graduated top 25% of class	46
% graduated top 50% of class	85

DEADLINES
Early decision	
Deadline	12/1
Notification	12/15
Regular	
Priority	2/1
Notification	rolling
Nonfall registration?	yes

APPLICANTS ALSO LOOK AT
AND OFTEN PREFER
State University of New York at Geneseo
AND SOMETIMES PREFER
State University of New York—University at Buffalo
Syracuse University

FINANCIAL FACTS
Financial Aid Rating	86
Annual tuition	$23,428
Room and board	$10,796
Required fees	$850
Books and supplies	$900
% frosh rec. need-based scholarship or grant aid	74
% UG rec. need-based scholarship or grant aid	73
% frosh rec. non-need-based scholarship or grant aid	44
% UG rec. non-need-based scholarship or grant aid	39
% frosh rec. need-based self-help aid	66
% UG rec. need-based self-help aid	66
% frosh rec. any financial aid	92
% UG rec. any financial aid	90
% UG borrow to pay for school	82.5
Average cumulative indebtedness	$23,292

THE BEST 368 COLLEGES ■ 57

ALLEGHENY COLLEGE

Office of Admissions, Allegheny College, Meadville, PA 16335 • Admissions: 814-332-4351 • Fax: 814-337-0431

CAMPUS LIFE

Quality of Life Rating	75
Fire Safety Rating	79
Green Rating	93
Type of school	private
Environment	town

STUDENTS

Total undergrad enrollment	2,163
% male/female	44/56
% from out of state	37
% from public high school	83
% live on campus	77
% in (# of) fraternities	20 (5)
% in (# of) sororities	28 (4)
% African American	2
% Asian	3
% Caucasian	92
% Hispanic	2
% international	1
# of countries represented	32

SURVEY SAYS . . .
Small classes
Lab facilities are great
Athletic facilities are great
Career services are great
Students are friendly
Students are happy
Lots of beer drinking

ACADEMICS

Academic Rating	87
Calendar	semester
Student/faculty ratio	14:1
Profs interesting rating	91
Profs accessible rating	89
Most common reg class size	10–19 students
Most common lab size	10–19 students

MOST POPULAR MAJORS
psychology
biology/biological sciences
economics

STUDENTS SAY "..."

Academics

Allegheny College challenges students to expand their horizons by immersing themselves in "unusual combinations" of classes and resources. This theme, promoted heavily in the school's literature, isn't just rhetoric—students report that it is evidenced in every aspect of their academic experience. "Fostering students" personal interests even when they are unrelated to their major (e.g. a biology major in the orchestra)... Allegheny allows students to pursue their educations while continuing to develop themselves as strong people and contributors to society." Or, to put it more simply, "our school is about doing what you want to do and following your interests and passions." All students at Allegheny must complete both a major and a minor. In conjunction with a mandatory senior project and a battery of required communications classes, this means that "the academics are challenging; you spend a lot of time in class and even more time studying, but it's worth it," and though "there will be times, more often then not, that you may want to pull your hair out." That said, come graduation time, membership has its privileges. The school has "a very good reputation in western Pennsylvania and eastern Ohio and good alumni relations in those areas, so job placement and graduate school connections are excellent there." The curriculum is "very strong in writing (no matter what the major is) and speaking in public due to the large amounts of papers and presentations," and also "strong in research, whether for a thesis paper or in the lab, as we are exposed to it early and often."

Life

"Class work can dominate your life if you are not careful," so students here "need to find a balance among schoolwork, extra-curricular activities, and your social life." This balance is readily available through the bounty of opportunities the school offers. As one student explains, there are "more clubs then I can name, a slew of intramural sports, and the college always has some sort of programming going on," such as "comedians, paint-your-own-pottery, and other fun, non-alcoholic events." For those so inclined, "Weekends are the real 'party hard' time." However, students also spend their time off "doing community service, participating in athletic events, and raising awareness of global concerns." Hometown Meadville offers "good, small places to eat" along with "little shops," "a bowling alley," and "a movie theater," but it's hardly cosmopolitan, leading some to opine that "If Allegheny could pick itself up out of Meadville and relocate itself somewhere warmer and more exciting, this school could be perfect."

Student Body

The typical Allegheny student has "varied interests." "Each student interacts with a large number of groups each day, [for instance] they may be a political science major but also be involved in the theater program, all before attending their service fraternity at night." The fact that "seemingly everyone has different interests, beliefs, and personal backgrounds" helps offset the fact that Allegheny "is not an extremely ethnically diverse school." Students also tell us that Greek life "only makes up about 25 percent of the student population so anyone is free to have Greek or independent friends and not worry about one or the other dominating the social scene." While undergrads insist they're "not your cookie cutter students" and that "atypical is typical," you can still expect to see a lot of "North Face fleeces and Ugg boots" as you traverse the campus.

FINANCIAL AID: 800-835-7780 • E-MAIL: ADMISSIONS@ALLEGHENY.EDU • WEBSITE: WWW.ALLEGHENY.EDU

THE PRINCETON REVIEW SAYS

Admissions

Very important factors considered include: Class rank, academic GPA, rigor of secondary school record. *Important factors considered include:* Recommendation(s), standardized test scores, character/personal qualities, extracurricular activities, interview. *Other factors considered include:* Application essay, alumni/ae relation, first generation, geographical residence, level of applicant's interest, racial/ethnic status, talent/ability, volunteer work, work experience. SAT or ACT required; ACT with Writing component recommended. TOEFL required of all international applicants. High school diploma is required and GED is accepted. *Academic units required:* 4 English, 3 mathematics, 3 science, 2 foreign language, 3 social studies, 1 academic elective.

Financial Aid

Students should submit: FAFSA. The Princeton Review suggests that all financial aid forms be submitted as soon as possible after January 1. *Need-based scholarships/grants offered:* Federal Pell, SEOG, state scholarships/grants, private scholarships, the school's own gift aid, Federal Academic Competitiveness Grant, National SMART Grant, Veterans Educational Benefits. *Loan aid offered:* FFEL Subsidized Stafford, FFEL Unsubsidized Stafford, FFEL PLUS, Federal Perkins, Private loans from commercial lenders. Applicants will be notified of awards on a rolling basis beginning 3/1. Federal Work-Study Program available. Institutional employment available. Off-campus job opportunities are excellent.

The Inside Word

Academic promise plays a large role in the admissions process at Allegheny. The college looks for students who go beyond their high school's minimum requirements, particularly those who pursue honors and Advanced Placement courses. Admissions officers are known for their individualized approach. While standardized test scores and class rank factor significantly in their decisions, consideration is also given to personal character and extracurricular activities.

THE SCHOOL SAYS "..."

From The Admissions Office

"We're proud of Allegheny's beautiful campus and cutting-edge technologies,. and we know that our professors are leading scholars who pride themselves even more on being among the best teachers in the United States. Yet it's our students who make Allegheny the unique and special place that it is.

"Allegheny attracts students with unusual combinations of interests, skills, and talents. How do we characterize them? Although it's impossible to label our students, they do share some common characteristics. You'll find an abiding passion for learning and life, a spirit of camaraderie, and shared inquiry that spans across individuals as well as areas of study. You'll see over and over again such a variety of interests and passions and skills that, after a while, those unusual combinations don't seem so unusual at all.

"Allegheny is not for everybody. If you find labels reassuring, if you're looking for a narrow technical training, if you're in search of the shortest distance between point A and point B, then perhaps another college will be better for you.

"But, if you recognize that everything you experience between points A and B will make you appreciate point B that much more; if you've noticed that when life gives you a choice between two things, you're tempted to answer both or simply yes; if you start to get excited because you sense there is a college willing to echo the resounding *yes*, then we look forward to meeting you.

"Applicants for Fall 2008 are required to take either the new SAT or ACT (the new ACT Writing section is recommended but not required). If both tests are taken, we will use the better score of the two. The Writing score of both the SAT and ACT will be reviewed but will not be a major factor in admission decisions."

SELECTIVITY

Admissions Rating	91
# of applicants	4,354
% of applicants accepted	57
% of acceptees attending	23
# accepting a place on wait list	509
% admitted from wait list	4
# of early decision applicants	90
% accepted early decision	71

FRESHMAN PROFILE

Range SAT Critical Reading	560–660
Range SAT Math	555–650
Range ACT Composite	24–28
Minimum paper TOEFL	550
Minimum computer TOEFL	213
Average HS GPA	3.8
% graduated top 10% of class	46
% graduated top 25% of class	77
% graduated top 50% of class	97

DEADLINES

Early decision	
Deadline	11/15
Notification	12/15
Regular	
Deadline	2/15
Notification	4/1
Nonfall registration?	yes

APPLICANTS ALSO LOOK AT
AND OFTEN PREFER
Kenyon College
Bucknell University
University of Rochester
AND SOMETIMES PREFER
The College of Wooster
Denison University
Dickinson College
Gettysburg College
AND RARELY PREFER
Miami University
Washington & Jefferson College
Penn State—University Park

FINANCIAL FACTS

Financial Aid Rating	86
Annual tuition	$31,680
Room and board	$8,000
Required fees	$320
Books and supplies	$900
% frosh rec. need-based scholarship or grant aid	69
% UG rec. need-based scholarship or grant aid	68
% frosh rec. non-need-based scholarship or grant aid	13
% UG rec. non-need-based scholarship or grant aid	11
% frosh rec. need-based self-help aid	57
% UG rec. need-based self-help aid	58
% frosh rec. any financial aid	98
% UG rec. any financial aid	98

AMERICAN UNIVERSITY

4400 MASSACHUSETTS AVENUE, NORTHWEST, WASHINGTON, DC 20016-8001 • ADMISSIONS: 202-885-6000 • FAX: 202-885-1025

STUDENTS SAY "..."

Academics

American University in Washington, DC boasts a "rigorous" and "very challenging" academic experience that offers students all the benefits of its location close to the political center of the country. The School of Public Affairs is nationally renowned, and "The international studies program is one of the best in the world." There's a "strong business school" too. "Aside from its location," "The best thing about American University is its ability to offer the course catalog of a midsized university while maintaining the feel of a small liberal arts college." "Small classes" ensure that "discussion flows freely." "Extremely accessible" professors "love to teach" and "look forward to speaking with students and helping them in their academic careers." It's not uncommon for an AU faculty member to "have real-world experience with a major corporation, government agency, or international organization." The "amazing" Career Center helps students to find "good jobs" and brings big-time recruiters to campus. "Volunteering with a nonprofit organization" is also a common student activity. Though the AU campus is "completely wireless," "a few buildings are in need of repair," and many students think that the library could use some improvement. "The science facilities don't need any TLC," but only because "No one is using them," one student says.

Life

"The best thing about AU is if you want to do it, it's here for you; if not, it won't bother you." A club exists "for just about every type of person you can think of." Parties "are big on the weekends, but they don't dominate campus life," and "The nightlife on and off campus is always active." AU is located "a little ways outside of the downtown area," but virtually everything is "just a short Metro ride away." "There's so much to do for fun in DC, it's stunning," asserts a sophomore. "Midnight trips to the national monuments" are popular, as are "touring the Smithsonian Museums for free, sampling ethnic food in Adams Morgan, and visiting trendy coffee shops" near Dupont Circle. Attending "protests" is big, too, if that's your bag. Back on campus, AU provides a plethora of speakers. Recent invitees have included Bob Dole, John Kerry, and "former presidents of several countries." Of course, because of the school's location, politics "infect the campus": "Watching CNN" and "working on the Hill" are everyday activities for many students. "Social justice and community-service groups" are also "very popular." "This school lives, breathes, eats, and sleeps politics," explains one student. "When William Rehnquist died, I was at a fraternity party, and when we heard about it over half the party left to go watch the news."

Student Body

American is not really a place for the "college-y college experience," asserts one undergrad, though "It can be if that's what you want." "The atypical student is the norm": The "passionate" and highly "eclectic" student population here runs the gamut from "hippies to hard-core young Republicans." There are "pretty-boy frat guys looking for their next keg to conquer" and "political enthusiasts who love to debate the hottest issues." There are "bookish students" and "pseudo-serious intellectuals." You'll find students of every socioeconomic level and "a good number of minorities." One student says that "for every person who pops his collar, there is someone with blue hair." AU boasts a throng of international students, "a large gay population," and lots of women: "Our female/male ratio is 60/40. I would not complain if we had more guys on campus," laments a frustrated female. Not surprisingly, the biggest differences among students involve politics. "There is a huge amount of contention between the liberals and conservatives on campus," observes a sophomore. "The conservatives walk around like high and mighty warriors of truth, and the liberals walk around like they're saving the world from the conservatives."

FINANCIAL AID: 202-885-6100 • E-MAIL: AFA@AMERICAN.EDU • WEBSITE: WWW.AMERICAN.EDU

THE PRINCETON REVIEW SAYS

Admissions

Very important factors considered include: Rigor of secondary school record, standardized test scores, level of applicant's interest. *Important factors considered include:* Application essay, academic GPA, recommendation(s), extracurricular activities, volunteer work. *Other factors considered include:* Class rank, alumni/ae relation, character/personal qualities, first generation, geographical residence, racial/ethnic status, talent/ability, work experience. SAT Subject Tests recommended; SAT or ACT required; ACT with Writing component required. TOEFL required of all international applicants. High school diploma is required and GED is accepted. *Academic units required:* 4 English, 3 mathematics, 3 science, (2 science labs), 2 foreign language, 2 social studies, 3 academic electives. *Academic units recommended:* 4 English, 4 mathematics, 4 science, 3 foreign language, 4 social studies, 4 academic electives.

Financial Aid

Students should submit: FAFSA, institution's own financial aid form. Regular filing deadline is 2/15. The Princeton Review suggests that all financial aid forms be submitted as soon as possible after January 1. *Need-based scholarships/grants offered:* Federal Pell, SEOG, state scholarships/grants, private scholarships, the school's own gift aid, Academic merit scholarships: Presidential Scholarships, Dean's Scholarships, Leadership Scholarships, Phi Theta Kappa Scholarships (transfers only), Tuition Exchange Scholarships, United Methodist Scholarships, and other private/restricted scholarships are awarded by the Undergraduate Admissions Office. Most scholarships do not require a separate application and are renewable for up to three years if certain criteria are met. *Loan aid offered:* Direct Subsidized Stafford, Direct Unsubsidized Stafford, Direct PLUS, FFEL PLUS, Federal Perkins, college/university loans from institutional funds. Applicants will be notified of awards on or about 4/1. Federal Work-Study Program available. Institutional employment available. Off-campus job opportunities are excellent.

The Inside Word

While DC is a popular locale for undergrads, it also has its fair share of top-notch universities. For that reason, American must compete for students with a number of area schools, so its admissions stats are relatively relaxed for applicants who have strong academic records. Nonetheless, American is a solid option, especially for those interested in government and international relations. Candidates with leadership experience are particularly appealing to Admissions Officers at AU.

THE SCHOOL SAYS "..."

From The Admissions Office

"Ideas, action, and service—at AU, you interact regularly with decision makers and leaders in every profession and corner of the globe. You'll be academically challenged in a rich multicultural environment. Our expert teaching faculty provide a strong liberal arts education, characterized by small classes, the use of cutting-edge technology, and an interdisciplinary curriculum in the arts, education, humanities, social sciences, and sciences. Not just a political town, Washington, DC offers a variety of research, internship, and community-service opportunities in every field. Our AU Abroad Program, with over 80 international locations, lets you expand your studies into international settings. The Princeton Review selected AU for the 2005 edition of *America's Best Value Colleges.* AU was one of 77 schools, and the only one from DC, selected as a 'best value' for its combination of outstanding academics, moderate tuition, and financial aid packages.

"AU requires all applicants graduating from high school in, or after, 2006 to take the new SAT or the ACT with the Writing section. Fall 2008 applicants are allowed to submit scores from the old versions of both tests as their best scores will be used in making admissions decisions."

SELECTIVITY

Admissions Rating	93
# of applicants	15,847
% of applicants accepted	53
% of acceptees attending	15
# of early decision applicants	370
% accepted early decision	55

FRESHMAN PROFILE

Range SAT Critical Reading	590–690
Range SAT Math	580–670
Range SAT Writing	580–690
Range ACT Composite	25–30
Minimum paper TOEFL	610
Minimum computer TOEFL	263
Minimum web-based TOEFL	101
% graduated top 10% of class	50
% graduated top 25% of class	83
% graduated top 50% of class	99

DEADLINES

Early decision	
Deadline	11/15
Notification	12/31
Regular	
Deadline	1/15
Notification	4/1
Nonfall registration?	yes

APPLICANTS ALSO LOOK AT

AND OFTEN PREFER
The George Washington University
New York University
Georgetown University
Boston University

AND SOMETIMES PREFER
Northeastern University
Boston College
Tufts University

AND RARELY PREFER
Fordham University
University of Pennsylvania

FINANCIAL FACTS

Financial Aid Rating	83
Annual tuition	$32,816
Room and board	$12,418
Required fees	$467
Books and supplies	$600
% frosh rec. need-based scholarship or grant aid	34
% UG rec. need-based scholarship or grant aid	34
% frosh rec. non-need-based scholarship or grant aid	14
% UG rec. non-need-based scholarship or grant aid	11
% frosh rec. need-based self-help aid	39
% UG rec. need-based self-help aid	40
% frosh rec. athletic scholarships	3
% UG rec. athletic scholarships	2
% frosh rec. any financial aid	82
% UG rec. any financial aid	69
% UG borrow to pay for school	50

AMHERST COLLEGE

CAMPUS BOX 2231, PO BOX 5000, AMHERST, MA 01002 • ADMISSIONS: 413-542-2328 • FAX: 413-542-2040

CAMPUS LIFE

Quality of Life Rating	94
Fire Safety Rating	60*
Green Rating	60*
Type of school	private
Environment	town

STUDENTS

Total undergrad enrollment	1,683
% male/female	50/50
% from out of state	88
% live on campus	98
% African American	10
% Asian	12
% Caucasian	44
% Hispanic	32
% Native American	3
% international	7
# of countries represented	39

SURVEY SAYS . . .

Large classes
No one cheats
Campus feels safe
Students are happy

ACADEMICS

Academic Rating	94
Calendar	semester
Student/faculty ratio	8:1
Profs interesting rating	86
Profs accessible rating	93
Most common reg class size	10–19 students
Most common lab size	fewer than 10 students

MOST POPULAR MAJORS

political science and government
psychology
biology/biological sciences

STUDENTS SAY ". . ."

Academics

At Amherst College, a small, elite liberal arts school in western Massachusetts, "The academic experience is well balanced, comprehensive, and tailored to the desires and needs of each individual student." Students truly get exactly what they want because "There are no core requirements. Every person in every class . . . is enthusiastic about the subject and wants to learn." Students love this set-up, telling us that "the open curriculum guarantees that every student in every class really wants to be there, which makes a huge difference in the liveliness of discussion." Academics "are extremely challenging without being overly burdensome," in part because support networks are so strong. Students "really develop personal relationships with professors, which makes classes that much more enjoyable." Students also appreciate that they "get all the things [they] need and want (services, advice, etc.) when [they] need and want them." As one student puts it, "Amherst College is a small family. Everyone here wants you to succeed; however, it's up to you to reach out for that guidance. If you knock, Amherst shall respond." Professors "all have a great sense of humor" and "are engaging and eclectic." As one student writes, "Even in introductory courses, professors literally bounce off the walls with enthusiasm for the subject." The results tell the story: Nearly three-quarters of all Amherst alumni proceed to postgraduate study within 5 years of graduation.

Life

"Life is usually busy" at Amherst, where "People are generally pretty involved." Academics are demanding, but fortunately "Everyone is here for the same reason: to learn. We learn as much from each other as we do in the classroom because everyone is just so different and has a story to tell. I stay up till the wee hours of the morning with some of my dorm-mates sharing stories and ordering Antonio's Pizza." When they're not working, students "are often playing sports" or "engaging in some other activity." Undergrads "love the academic culture of the Five Colleges area. You can go to music performances, plays, or poetry readings any night of the week." As one student reports, "Events are happening all the time, and there is always something going on . . . concerts, talks about Brazilian economics, West African dance shows, etc. Life here is comfortable and exciting." A "free bus to get to other colleges and towns" makes it easy to access these events, even without a car. It's not only about personal enrichment here, though; while students "work hard throughout the week," they "party on Thursday and Saturday." Why not on Friday? "Because nearly one-third of the student body [are] athletes, parties are often thrown by various teams, but open to all. As a result, Friday nights are pretty dead, since all the athletes are resting up for their games."

Student Body

"It seems like there are many of your typical White, private school students from the New England area" at Amherst, but "Then there are [also] students from all over the United States and from other countries who are so diverse." Most of these "typically well-rounded and motivated" undergraduates "played some sort of sport in high school, and a very large percentage play club or varsity sports at college." These students are "witty, friendly, thoughtful, non-competitive, self-effacing, and know how to have a good time."

Nearly everyone agrees that "Amherst is amazing because of its small size. It's a really close-knit community where everyone is extremely open-minded and considerate." According to another student, "I love that [Amherst's] students are politically aware and serious students but also willing to have a good time. The first thing that struck me about my school is how nice everyone is. The school has a reputation for being stuck-up, but I have not experienced that in the least."

FINANCIAL AID: 413-542-2296 • E-MAIL: ADMISSION@AMHERST.EDU • WEBSITE: WWW.AMHERST.EDU

THE PRINCETON REVIEW SAYS

Admissions

Very important factors considered include: Application essay, academic GPA, recommendation(s), rigor of secondary school record, standardized test scores, character/personal qualities, extracurricular activities, first generation, talent/ability. *Important factors considered include:* Class rank, alumni/ae relation, volunteer work. *Other factors considered include:* Geographical residence, state residency, work experience. SAT and SAT Subject Tests or ACT required; ACT with Writing component recommended. High school diploma or equivalent is not required. *Academic units recommended:* 4 English, 4 mathematics, 3 science, (1 science labs), 4 foreign language, 2 social studies, 2 history.

Financial Aid

Students should submit: FAFSA, CSS/Financial Aid PROFILE, noncustodial PROFILE, business/farm supplement. Income documentation submitted through College. The Princeton Review suggests that all financial aid forms be submitted as soon as possible after January 1. *Need-based scholarships/grants offered:* Federal Pell, SEOG, state scholarships/grants, private scholarships, the school's own gift aid. *Loan aid offered:* Direct Subsidized Stafford, Direct Unsubsidized Stafford, Direct PLUS, Federal Perkins, college/university loans from institutional funds. Applicants will be notified of awards on or about 4/5. Federal Work-Study Program available. Institutional employment available. Off-campus job opportunities are excellent.

The Inside Word

A $1 billion endowment allows Amherst to provide admitted students with generous financial aid packages. The school is deeply committed to economic diversity in the student body, increasing the number of working-class and low-income students in the Class of 2010 from 15 percent to 20 percent (*New York Times*, September 19, 2006). The school is also considering scaling back, or even doing away with, early decision admissions, which are believed to favor upper-income students.

THE SCHOOL SAYS "..."

From The Admissions Office

"Amherst College looks, above all, for men and women of intellectual promise who have demonstrated qualities of mind and character that will enable them to take full advantage of the college's curriculum. . . . Admission decisions aim to select from among the many qualified applicants those possessing the intellectual talent, mental discipline, and imagination that will allow them most fully to benefit from the curriculum and contribute to the life of the college and of society. Whatever the form of academic experience—lecture course, seminar, conference, studio, laboratory, independent study at various levels—intellectual competence and awareness of problems and methods are the goals of the Amherst program, rather than the direct preparation for a profession.

"Applicants must submit scores from the new SAT plus two SAT Subject Tests, or the old SAT plus three SAT Subject Tests. Students may substitute the ACT with the Writing component (as of Spring 2005) or without Writing if the test was taken prior to Spring 2005."

SELECTIVITY

Admissions Rating	**98**
# of applicants	6,680
% of applicants accepted	18
% of acceptees attending	40
# accepting a place on wait list	574
# of early decision applicants	350
% accepted early decision	39

FRESHMAN PROFILE

Range SAT Critical Reading	670–770
Range SAT Math	660–760
Range SAT Writing	670–760
Range ACT Composite	29–34
% graduated top 10% of class	85
% graduated top 25% of class	95
% graduated top 50% of class	100

DEADLINES

Early decision	
Deadline	11/15
Notification	12/15
Regular	
Deadline	1/1
Notification	4/5
Nonfall registration?	no

FINANCIAL FACTS

Financial Aid Rating	**92**
Annual tuition	$35,580
Room and board	$9,420
Required fees	$652
Books and supplies	$1,000
% frosh rec. need-based scholarship or grant aid	51
% UG rec. need-based scholarship or grant aid	52
% frosh rec. need-based self-help aid	45
% UG rec. need-based self-help aid	46
% frosh rec. any financial aid	53
% UG rec. any financial aid	51
% UG borrow to pay for school	43
Average cumulative indebtedness	$11,655

Arizona State University

PO Box 870112, Tempe, AZ 85287-0112 • Admissions: 480-965-7788 • Fax: 480-965-3610

CAMPUS LIFE

Quality of Life Rating	**71**
Fire Safety Rating	**87**
Green Rating	**99**
Type of school	public
Environment	metropolis

STUDENTS

Total undergrad enrollment	38,597
% male/female	51/49
% from out of state	27
% live on campus	17
% in (# of) fraternities	7 (29)
% in (# of) sororities	6 (21)
% African American	4
% Asian	6
% Caucasian	68
% Hispanic	14
% Native American	2
% international	3
# of countries represented	119

SURVEY SAYS . . .

Great computer facilities
Great library
Great off-campus food
Everyone loves the Sun Devils
Student publications are popular
Lots of beer drinking
Hard liquor is popular
(Almost) everyone smokes

ACADEMICS

Academic Rating	**71**
Calendar	semester
Student/faculty ratio	23:1
Profs interesting rating	63
Profs accessible rating	68

MOST POPULAR MAJORS

psychology
multi-/interdisciplinary studies
journalism

STUDENTS SAY ". . ."

Academics

"A great academic environment" and "perfect weather, cheaper tuition," bring many students to Arizona State University. With over 38,000 undergraduates on the Tempe campus, any description of ASU has to begin with its sheer size. As one student sums up, "Arizona State University is an enormous institution," and that means "Variety is inevitable." There are 250 undergraduate majors to choose from in more than 20 colleges and schools, so students have access to "tons of resources, and you can study whatever you want." Variety also comes in the form of teacher quality; "Some professors are fantastic and some are ridiculous—it's luck of the draw." That said, students generally agree that "professors are always available and willing to listen, as long as students make the effort to meet with them." Getting one-on-one time with professors isn't the only sphere where a little student initiative goes a long way. The secret to overall success at ASU seems to be "tak[ing] charge of your own education." Because of the school's size, administrators have to "run ASU like a business," which means "Some of the personal touch is lost." But if students "feel like just a number [when dealing with the bureaucracy] at the university level," at the college/school level, administrators "are very easy to meet." When it comes to gripes, many students list the fact that "academic advisors are not very helpful" at the very top.

Life

Students note that "the administration is doing [its] all to diminish the party school image ASU has been known for," although many are skeptical of the success of these efforts. One student echoes the feelings of many of his fellow undergraduates when he states, "Partying is a big part of the ASU experience." Intercollegiate sporting events are "very popular with students," and while only a small minority of students joins frats and sororities, the Greek scene on campus is very visible and "active." But parties aren't all ASU has to offer. There is also "excellent nightlife in the valley," including Mill Avenue, with its movie theaters and "easy access to bars, shopping, and eating places"; College Avenue, offering "many campus stores and more food options"; and Old Town Scottsdale, "which also has shopping, clubs, [and] fine dining." "Friendly, diverse, and inexpensive . . . Tempe is a great place to go to college," but it can be "difficult to go places off campus if you don't have a car." Perhaps one of the nicest benefits of ASU's Tempe location is that "most of the school year it is pool weather."

Student Body

If there's consensus on what the typical ASU student is like, it's worth stating the obvious: "This campus is so big [that] if you can't find someone to fit in with here, you're not going to anywhere." Simply put, ASU is "a school overflowing with beautiful people." It's "Barbie and Ken go to college" at ASU. The campus' numerous "California types" are "concerned with material things," but are "normally very friendly" and "basically good-hearted." Students say they value "fashion and the virtue of exercising," and they "like to party." While many students are "not religious," there is a "mutual respect of individuals among everyone." Sprinkled amongst these bronzed gods and goddesses are a "lot of international students, and the usual mix of people who live like monks," as well as a few "students over the age of 30." However you categorize them, most of ASU's students are "open-minded and polite." "Racial, ethnic, and sexual orientation [are] not taboo subject[s] here."

ARIZONA STATE UNIVERSITY

FINANCIAL AID: 480-965-3355 • E-MAIL: ASKASU@ASU.EDU • WEBSITE: WWW.ASU.EDU

THE PRINCETON REVIEW SAYS

Admissions

Very important factors considered include: Class rank, academic GPA, standardized test scores. *Important factors considered include:* State residency, SAT or ACT required; ACT with Writing component recommended. TOEFL required of all international applicants. High school diploma is required and GED is accepted. *Academic units required:* 4 English, 4 mathematics, 3 science, (3 science labs), 2 foreign language, 1 social studies, 1 history, 1 Fine Arts.

Financial Aid

Students should submit: FAFSA. The Princeton Review suggests that all financial aid forms be submitted as soon as possible after January 1. *Need-based scholarships/grants offered:* Federal Pell, SEOG, state scholarships/grants, private scholarships, the school's own gift aid, Federal Nursing Scholarships. *Loan aid offered:* Direct Subsidized Stafford, Direct Unsubsidized Stafford, Direct PLUS, FFEL PLUS, Federal Perkins Federal Work-Study Program available. Institutional employment available. Off-campus job opportunities are good.

The Inside Word

Numbers count for a lot at ASU. You have excellent odds of acceptance if you meet the minimum curriculum, GPA, and standardized test requirements. These minimums are slightly higher for out-of-state students. Additionally, three of the undergraduate colleges at ASU (business, engineering, and journalism and mass communications) have additional admission requirements; we suggest visiting ASU's website to find out what they are. ASU awards a great many merit-based scholarships. To be eligible for many of them, you must be an Arizona resident and apply for admission to the school by December 1.

THE SCHOOL SAYS "..."

From The Admissions Office

"ASU is a place where students from all 50 states and abroad come together to live and study in one of the nation's premier collegiate environments. Situated in metropolitan Phoenix, ASU boasts a physical setting and climate second to none. ASU offers more than 250 academic programs of study leading to the BS and BA in 19 undergraduate colleges and schools. Many of these programs have received national recognition for their quality of teaching, innovative curricula, and outstanding facilities. Barrett, the Honors College at Arizona State University, the only honors college in the Southwest that spans all academic disciplines, provides unique and challenging experiences for its students and was recently named as one of three honors colleges that offer "an Ivy League–style education minus the sticker shock" by Reader's Digest.

"In addition to ASU's Tempe campus, ASU offers comprehensive undergraduate and graduate programs at campuses throughout the metropolitan Phoenix area: the Polytechnic campus in the East Valley, the West campus in northwest Phoenix, and the Downtown Phoenix campus.

"ASU does not require the submission of either ACT of SAT scores in order to be reviewed for undergraduate admission, however, test scores are needed for merit scholarship consideration and class placement. Presently, the essay portions of either exam are not required in order to be admitted."

SELECTIVITY

Admissions Rating	78
# of applicants	20,290
% of applicants accepted	95
% of acceptees attending	40

FRESHMAN PROFILE

Range SAT Critical Reading	470–600
Range SAT Math	490–620
Range ACT Composite	20–26
Minimum paper TOEFL	500
Minimum computer TOEFL	173
Minimum web-based TOEFL	61
Average HS GPA	3.34
% graduated top 10% of class	27
% graduated top 25% of class	52
% graduated top 50% of class	81

DEADLINES

Priority	2/1
Nonfall registration?	yes

FINANCIAL FACTS

Financial Aid Rating	74
Annual in-state tuition	$5,063
Annual out-of-state tuition	$17,697
Room and board	$8,797
Required fees	$252
Books and supplies	$1,130
% frosh rec. need-based scholarship or grant aid	34
% UG rec. need-based scholarship or grant aid	33
% frosh rec. non-need-based scholarship or grant aid	6
% UG rec. non-need-based scholarship or grant aid	3
% frosh rec. need-based self-help aid	19
% UG rec. need-based self-help aid	27
% frosh rec. athletic scholarships	1
% UG rec. athletic scholarships	1
% frosh rec. any financial aid	73
% UG rec. any financial aid	66
% UG borrow to pay for school	43
Average cumulative indebtedness	$16,856

AUBURN UNIVERSITY

202 MARY MARTIN HALL, AUBURN, AL 36849-5149 • ADMISSIONS: 334-844-4080 • FAX: 334-844-6179

CAMPUS LIFE

Quality of Life Rating	87
Fire Safety Rating	60*
Green Rating	60*
Type of school	public
Environment	town

STUDENTS

Total undergrad enrollment	19,812
% male/female	51/49
% from out of state	31
% live on campus	14
% in (# of) fraternities	22 (30)
% in (# of) sororities	31 (19)
% African American	9
% Asian	2
% Caucasian	85
% Hispanic	2
% Native American	1
% international	1
# of countries represented	88

SURVEY SAYS . . .

Great library
Students are friendly
Great off-campus food
Students are happy
Everyone loves the Tigers
Lots of beer drinking

ACADEMICS

Academic Rating	70
Calendar	semester
Student/faculty ratio	18:1
Profs interesting rating	64
Profs accessible rating	64
% classes taught by TAs	14
Most common reg class size	20–29 students
Most common lab size	10–19 students

MOST POPULAR MAJORS

education
engineering
business administration and
management

STUDENTS SAY "..."

Academics

Auburn University, a school that "is about family, traditions, and education," is the sort of place that inspires "a strong sense of pride in the past and future of [the school]." In fact, Auburn's "traditions and sense of family continue even after graduation." These traditions are numerous, beloved, and often involve football. The education isn't half bad here, either; Auburn numbers among its many academic assets "a good business school, one of the best vet schools, and one of the best architecture schools in the nation." The school also excels in engineering, education, and communications. Students enrolled in Auburn's honors program enjoy "priority registration [and] smaller classes" that are almost always taught by professors—not TAs. Speaking of Auburn's professors, students appreciate that they are "readily available," "super friendly," and "always willing to help no matter what size the class." They are "concerned with each student's progress," and "always willing to work with [students] to teach the curriculum and how it applies to [their] life." Academically, "As with any school, you get out of it what you put into it. You can put in the bare minimum and be happy with your C, or you can go to class every day, study hard, and make an A. No one here is going to baby you. You won't get reminders not to miss class, and teachers won't hunt you down for make-ups."

Life

Auburn is "an ideal college town" with "enough bars and such to keep one occupied but small enough to where there is a definite sense of community." The town also offers "movies, bowling, a park," and the attractions of Birmingham, which "isn't that far away." Auburn might not be a good fit for the sort of big-city types who "lament about how few options we have for entertainment, and how food consists [solely] of pizza, chicken tenders (on every corner), and subs," but everyone else seems to love it. They also love that the campus is "beautiful" and "life is slow paced—full of sweet tea and Southern food." Be warned, though: Auburn "is a drinking town with a football problem." "Football seems to dominate the Fall semester here. It's a huge deal, and it's when most big parties and events [take place]. If you hate football, this might not be the place for you." In the off-season, students take advantage of Auburn's "very popular" outdoor activities, and when they want to head off-campus, nearby Atlanta is a "great stop for city life and entertainment."

Student Body

Auburn students share "an incredible sense of pride" that "most who have never been here will never comprehend. Ask any Auburn student or alumn[us], and they'll generally tell you that Auburn ranks among God, country, family, and the South as things most beloved." Many students "love how Auburn is deeply Republican when most colleges are quite banal in their liberalism," and "prides itself in not being politically correct, and this is not due to ignorance." Not everyone at this large university fits this description—"At a school this large, there are people from all walks of life"—but a significant number of students do, and they set the tone for the campus. While "slightly conservative," Southern," "White, Protestant" students may dominate the student body here, there are also "Black, Asian, and also a lot of foreign exchange students [at Auburn]." Whatever their background, Auburn students across the board "are very open-minded, and accept everyone for who they are."

FINANCIAL AID: 334-844-4367 • E-MAIL: ADMISSIONS@AUBURN.EDU • WEBSITE: WWW.AUBURN.EDU

THE PRINCETON REVIEW SAYS

Admissions

Very important factors considered include: Application essay, academic GPA, standardized test scores. *Other factors considered include:* Class rank, recommendation(s), rigor of secondary school record, alumni/ae relation, character/personal qualities, extracurricular activities, first generation, geographical residence, state residency, talent/ability, volunteer work, work experience. SAT or ACT required; High school diploma is required and GED is accepted. *Academic units required:* 4 English, 3 mathematics, 2 science, 3 social studies. *Academic units recommended:* 4 English, 3 mathematics, 3 science, 1 foreign language, 4 social studies.

Financial Aid

Students should submit: FAFSA, institution's own financial aid form. The Princeton Review suggests that all financial aid forms be submitted as soon as possible after January 1. *Need-based scholarships/grants offered:* Federal Pell, SEOG, state scholarships/grants, private scholarships, the school's own gift aid. *Loan aid offered:* FFEL Subsidized Stafford, FFEL Unsubsidized Stafford, FFEL PLUS, Federal Perkins, college/university loans from institutional funds. Off-campus job opportunities are good.

The Inside Word

Auburn Admissions Officers crunch the numbers, sorting students according to high school GPA and standardized test scores, then offering admission to all who qualify from the top of the list on down. The school also looks at "fit" and the student's potential to make contributions to the Auburn community, but with an 69 percent admit rate, it's safe to say that these factors only come into play for marginal candidates, and then only to mitigate poor grades or test scores.

THE SCHOOL SAYS "..."

From The Admissions Office

"Auburn University is a comprehensive land-grant university serving Alabama and the nation. The university is especially charged with the responsibility of enhancing the economic, social, and cultural development of the state through its instruction, research, and extension programs. In all of these programs, the university is committed to the pursuit of excellence. The university assumes an obligation to provide an environment of learning in which the individual and society are enriched by the discovery, preservation, transmission, and application of knowledge; in which students grow intellectually as they study and do research under the guidance of competent faculty, and in which the faculty develop professionally and contribute fully to the intellectual life of the institution, community, and state. This obligation unites Auburn University's continuing commitment to its land-grant traditions and the institution's role as a dynamic and complex, comprehensive university.

"Applicants for Fall 2009 must submit scores from the SAT or ACT (with the Writing components from either test)."

SELECTIVITY

Admissions Rating	85
# of applicants	17,798
% of applicants accepted	69
% of acceptees attending	34

FRESHMAN PROFILE

Range SAT Critical Reading	500–610
Range SAT Math	520–630
Range ACT Composite	22–27
Average HS GPA	3.61
% graduated top 10% of class	27
% graduated top 25% of class	57
% graduated top 50% of class	87

DEADLINES

Regular	
Priority	2/1
Notification	rolling
Nonfall registration?	yes

FINANCIAL FACTS

Financial Aid Rating	62
Annual in-state tuition	$5,250
Annual out-of-state tuition	$15,750
Room and board	$7,466
Required fees	$344
Books and supplies	$1,100
% frosh rec. need-based scholarship or grant aid	22
% UG rec. need-based scholarship or grant aid	20
% frosh rec. non-need-based scholarship or grant aid	14
% UG rec. non-need-based scholarship or grant aid	11
% frosh rec. need-based self-help aid	23
% UG rec. need-based self-help aid	27
% frosh rec. athletic scholarships	3
% UG rec. athletic scholarships	2
% frosh rec. any financial aid	57
% UG rec. any financial aid	54
% UG borrow to pay for school	65
Average cumulative indebtedness	$25,176

AUSTIN COLLEGE

900 NORTH GRAND AVENUE, SUITE 6N, SHERMAN, TX 75090-4400 • ADMISSIONS: 903-813-3000 • FAX: 903-813-3198

STUDENTS SAY "..."

Academics

Whether they are biochemists-in-training or budding musicians, "challenging" is the word most undergraduates use to describe the academics at Austin College. Among all of the demanding disciplines at this small liberal arts school in way-north Texas, the premed curriculum has a rep for being especially so. (Nearly 10 percent of this school's graduates attend medical school after graduation.) The work here may be tough, but "Class sizes are small, the teachers are extremely well qualified (no TAs), and people really care about you as a person." When push comes to shove in the academic arena, the "Academic Skills Center is an excellent resource, and other students will often volunteer their assistance on school matters." Alternatively, students can seek help from their professors, who "are more like really wise friends" than aloof academics. Students can stop by during office hours or wait until they're invited over for a meal, which, students tell us, happens from time to time. Other unique attributes of an AC education include an Academic Integrity Policy that students pledge to follow before classes begin. Fans like it because they "don't have to worry about other students cheating. As a matter of fact, my teachers sometimes leave the room after handing out quizzes with no reaction from the class." As far as the administration goes, "Oscar Page (the school's president, affectionately known as 'O Page') is the most down-to-earth guy ever; he's often in the cafeteria eating with students."

Life

"We go to Starbucks and Wal-Mart a lot because there's not much to do in Sherman." According to students, "Sherman is a boring city with little shopping, no fine dining, and no outdoor parks worth exploring." To make things worse, "There is no night life." This does not mean, however, that the resourceful students at AC do not find ways to divert themselves from their studies when they need a little R&R. They mainly line up for two kinds of fun: The kind offered by the Greeks, which usually means partying, and the kind offered by groups like Christian Intervarsity, which usually means something a little more wholesome. On the one hand, "Greek parties are fun and a popular weekend activity. Ninety-nine percent of them are open to the entire student body." On the other, activities sponsored by Intervarsity include "boxsledding [down a snow-covered hill], Ultimate Frisbee, video scavenger hunts, and community service projects." In addition, a "local dance hall, Calhoun's; local parties; free movies on campus; art exhibitions; choral and music recitals; guest musicians every Thursday; varsity athletic events to watch; or intramural games to compete in" round out the busy scene on campus. Fun further afield can be found in Dallas, an hour-and-a-half drive away, or at "the lake campus [recreational property owned by the college] out at Lake Texoma." Be mindful that "a car is required to get anywhere, because nothing useful is within walking distance of the school."

Student Body

The typical undergraduate at AC is often "one who started off premed but ended up doing something else." He or she is "open-minded, casual, cares about the community around them, works hard for [his or her] grades, and is overly involved in school organizations and committees." "Many are religious." Contrary to what such devoutness might suggest, AC undergrads mainly feel that "for a Texas school, it is very liberal." "There are not that many students who are from states other than Texas and Oklahoma," and while "Most students here are White and middle-class," minorities are in no way excluded. Indian students are well-represented, as "The Indian Cultural Association is the largest group on campus, made up of more than Indian students, followed by the Muslim Students Association, and then by Los Amigos and Black Expressions."

THE PRINCETON REVIEW SAYS

Admissions

Very important factors considered include: Academic GPA, rigor of secondary school record. *Important factors considered include:* Class rank, application essay, recommendation(s), standardized test scores, character/personal qualities, extracurricular activities, talent/ability. *Other factors considered include:* Alumni/ae relation, first generation, geographical residence, interview, racial/ethnic status, religious affiliation/commitment, state residency, volunteer work, work experience. SAT or ACT required; ACT with Writing component required. TOEFL required of all international applicants. High school diploma is required and GED is accepted. *Academic units required:* 4 English, 3 mathematics, 3 science, (2 science labs), 2 foreign language, 2 social studies, 1 visual/performing arts, 1 academic elective. *Academic units recommended:* 4 English, 4 mathematics, 4 science, (3 science labs), 3 foreign language, 3 social studies, 2 visual/performing arts.

Financial Aid

Students should submit: FAFSA, institution's own financial aid form. The Princeton Review suggests that all financial aid forms be submitted as soon as possible after January 1. *Need-based scholarships/grants offered:* Federal Pell, SEOG, state scholarships/grants, private scholarships, the school's own gift aid. *Loan aid offered:* FFEL Subsidized Stafford, FFEL Unsubsidized Stafford, FFEL PLUS, Federal Perkins, state loans, college/university loans from institutional funds. Alternative loans through various sources. Applicants will be notified of awards on a rolling basis beginning 3/1. Federal Work-Study Program available. Institutional employment available. Off-campus job opportunities are good.

The Inside Word

Candidates hoping for an acceptance letter from Austin should keep a rigorous academic schedule. The college covets students who challenge themselves and Admissions Officers are prone to prefer students who have slightly lower GPAs but have proven themselves in difficult courses. Of course, applicants are more than just statistics and counselors are also looking for caring, committed students who want to contribute to the Austin community. An interview is strongly encouraged.

THE SCHOOL SAYS "..."

From The Admissions Office

"Students visiting Austin College immediately sense something different about the campus community. People look you in the eye. They call you by name. They want to see you succeed.

"That success comes from a strong academic foundation in the liberal arts and sciences, plus added opportunities like international study, January Term, and close involvement with committed faculty who become your partners in learning.

"The comments on these pages from students make it clear that there is no 'typical' student at Austin College. Students can retain their individuality and still fit in. Our students value and respect differences of background, style, and belief. Campus organizations offer activities for all interests.

"Austin College prepares you to do more than make a living. It prepares you to make a difference in the place you work, in the community you call home, in the friends you make, and in the way you live. Service to others is an important part of campus life.

"Visit and discover Austin College's legacy of learning, leadership, and lasting values for yourself.

"Applicants for Fall 2008 must submit Writing scores from the new SAT or ACT."

SELECTIVITY

Admissions Rating	83
# of applicants	1,678
% of applicants accepted	71
% of acceptees attending	28
# accepting a place on wait list	27
% admitted from wait list	70

FRESHMAN PROFILE

Range SAT Critical Reading	560–670
Range SAT Math	560–660
Range SAT Writing	530–660
Range ACT Composite	23–28
Minimum paper TOEFL	550
Minimum computer TOEFL	213
% graduated top 10% of class	38.01
% graduated top 25% of class	73.06
% graduated top 50% of class	95.2

DEADLINES

Early action	
Deadline	1/15
Notification	3/1
Regular	
Priority	1/15
Deadline	5/1
Nonfall registration?	yes

APPLICANTS ALSO LOOK AT

AND OFTEN PREFER
Trinity University
Southwestern University

AND SOMETIMES PREFER
Southern Methodist University
Baylor University
Texas A&M University—College Station
The University of Texas at Austin
Texas Christian University
Rice University

AND RARELY PREFER
University of Dallas
Hendrix College

FINANCIAL FACTS

Financial Aid Rating	97
Annual tuition	$24,192
Room and board	$4,030
Required fees	$160
Books and supplies	$1,000
% frosh rec. need-based scholarship or grant aid	60
% UG rec. need-based scholarship or grant aid	57
% frosh rec. non-need-based scholarship or grant aid	22
% UG rec. non-need-based scholarship or grant aid	14
% frosh rec. need-based self-help aid	48
% UG rec. need-based self-help aid	45
% frosh rec. any financial aid	97
% UG rec. any financial aid	96

BABSON COLLEGE

LUTHER UNDERGRADUATE ADMISSION CENTER, BABSON PARK, MA 02457 • ADMISSIONS: 781-239-5522 • FAX: 781-239-4135

CAMPUS LIFE

Quality of Life Rating	**82**
Fire Safety Rating	**86**
Green Rating	**60***
Type of school	private
Environment	village

STUDENTS

Total undergrad enrollment	1,799
% male/female	59/41
% from out of state	46
% from public high school	50
% live on campus	84
% in (# of) fraternities	13 (4)
% in (# of) sororities	15 (3)
% African American	4
% Asian	11
% Caucasian	44
% Hispanic	8
% international	18
# of countries represented	60

SURVEY SAYS . . .
Small classes
Great computer facilities
Great library
Career services are great
Diverse student types on campus
Campus feels safe
Lots of beer drinking

ACADEMICS

Academic Rating	**88**
Calendar	semester
Student/faculty ratio	16:1
Profs interesting rating	88
Profs accessible rating	87
Most common	
reg class size	30–39 students

MOST POPULAR MAJORS
accounting
entrepreneurial and small business
operations
finance

STUDENTS SAY ". . ."

Academics

If you already know anything about Babson, you probably know that at this small school in the suburbs of Boston, "everything is related to business. So if you don't like business, you should not even think about coming here." Indeed, Babson has one of the best known and most respected undergraduate business programs in the country. It begins with the Foundations of Management and Entrepreneurship (FME) freshman year, during which students work in groups to conceive and launch a (hopefully) profitable small business. This segues into the sophomore year in which students participate in an integrated experience that includes instruction in core business disciplines like accounting, marketing, and finance, among others. By nearly all accounts the curriculum is extremely challenging, and the severe grade curve based on an average of 2.7 comes as a shock to some. But most students feel that although "the homework tends to be a lot compared to most of my friends at other business schools . . . we receive a better education." In large part that's because "Many of the professors have started or still run very successful companies," and they share their invaluable "industry experience" in the classroom. At least business professors do. "The liberal arts teachers vary a lot more in quality." By and large, the administration receives average marks, but most students don't focus on any administrative shortcomings. "At the end of the day, if you want to be a successful entrepreneur or business person, Babson is the best place for you."

Life

The "business boot camp" that is Babson is not known for its social life. During the week, "People are consumed by work, and are constantly concentrating on their future. On the weekends people socialize a lot because they need a break from the stress of the week." The student body splinters into distinct factions when it's time to unwind: "American kids typically party on campus more often, the athletes will party together, frats do their thing, and the international rich kids go in town and are scarce on the weekends since they live at the clubs in Boston." Some undergrads cross-pollinate groups, of course, but these are generally where the lines are drawn. Students who choose to party on campus, however, are well aware that "the campus police [referred to locally as 'Babo'] and Office of Campus Life take a strong stance against parties and alcohol" and that Babo is quite adept at breaking up unauthorized get-togethers. School-sanctioned on-campus activities include "'Knight Parties' on one Saturday night during each month (a club-like atmosphere with a DJ, dancing, and lots of free food and drinks, and beer for 21-year-olds)." Additionally, "The on-campus pub is fun and a common hangout for upperclassmen." For those who feel the lure of Boston, a car definitely makes getting there easier, but "The school also offers a bus that runs into Boston on the weekends for students."

Student Body

At this small business school where "Professionalism is a part of your grade," a "typical student is pretty well off, dressed well no matter what their style is, and pretty intelligent on business and similar subjects." Given its business focus, some students speculate that "Babson is probably the only school in Massachusetts where Republicans are in the majority." Noticeable cliques include the BISOs (Babson International Students), the athletes, and the Greeks, but regardless of the groups students fall into, nearly all of them "constantly think about the next great business idea, internship, or great job at firms like Lehman Brothers, KPMG, Ernst & Young, etc." It should come as no surprise, then, that "we are short on hippies, punks, and extreme liberals. If you fall into those categories, people will still accept you, but eventually you'll probably want to strangle the rest of us and will transfer." No matter what you start out as, the consensus seems to be that 4 years of "Babson will transform you from a driven/motivated individual into a lethal business machine."

FINANCIAL AID: 781-239-4219 • E-MAIL: UGRADADMISSION@BABSON.EDU • WEBSITE: WWW.BABSON.EDU

THE PRINCETON REVIEW SAYS

Admissions

Very important factors considered include: Application essay, academic GPA, recommendation(s), rigor of secondary school record, standardized test scores, character/personal qualities. *Important factors considered include:* Class rank, extracurricular activities. *Other factors considered include:* Alumni/ae relation, first generation, geographical residence, interview, level of applicant's interest, racial/ethnic status, state residency, talent/ability, volunteer work, work experience. SAT or ACT required; SAT and SAT Subject Tests or ACT recommended; ACT with Writing component required. TOEFL required of all international applicants. High school diploma is required and GED is accepted. *Academic units recommended:* 4 English, 4 mathematics, 4 science, (3 science labs), 4 foreign language, 2 social studies, 2 history, 1 Pre-Calculus.

Financial Aid

Students should submit: FAFSA, CSS/Financial Aid PROFILE, noncustodial PROFILE, business/farm supplement. Federal tax returns, W-2s, and Verification Worksheet. Regular filing deadline is 2/15. The Princeton Review suggests that all financial aid forms be submitted as soon as possible after January 1. *Need-based scholarships/grants offered:* Federal Pell, SEOG, state scholarships/grants, the school's own gift aid. *Loan aid offered:* FFEL Subsidized Stafford, FFEL Unsubsidized Stafford, FFEL PLUS, Federal Perkins, state loans Applicants will be notified of awards on or about 4/1. Federal Work-Study Program available. Institutional employment available. Off-campus job opportunities are good.

The Inside Word

Though Babson offers a unique educational opportunity, their admissions practices are as traditional as they come. Personal qualities and extracurricular activities are taken into consideration, but the best way to impress a Babson Admissions Officer is through strong academic performance. Both scholastic rigor and the demonstration of intellectual curiosity are extremely important. Additionally, applicants will want to focus on their essay—writing ability is viewed as vital at Babson.

THE SCHOOL SAYS "..."

From The Admissions Office

"In addition to theoretical knowledge, Babson College is dedicated to providing its students with hands-on business experience. The Foundations of Management and Entrepreneurship (FME) and Management Consulting Field Experience (MCFE) are two prime examples of this commitment. During the FME, all freshmen are placed into groups of 30 and actually create their own businesses that they operate until the end of the academic year. The profits of each FME business are then donated to the charity of each group's choice.

"MCFE offers upperclassmen the unique and exciting opportunity to work as actual consultants for private companies and/or nonprofit organizations in small groups of three to five. Students receive academic credit for their work as well as invaluable experience in the field of consulting. FME and MCFE are just two of the ways Babson strives to produce business leaders with both theoretical knowledge and practical experience.

"Babson College requires freshmen applicants to submit scores from either the new SAT or the ACT with Writing component. The school recommends that students also submit results from SAT Subject Tests."

SELECTIVITY

Admissions Rating	93
# of applicants	3,530
% of applicants accepted	38
% of acceptees attending	34
# accepting a place on wait list	159
% admitted from wait list	13
# of early decision applicants	235
% accepted early decision	55

FRESHMAN PROFILE

Range SAT Critical Reading	560–640
Range SAT Math	590–680
Range SAT Writing	570–650
Range ACT Composite	25–29
Minimum paper TOEFL	600
Minimum computer TOEFL	250
Minimum web-based TOEFL	100
% graduated top 10% of class	22
% graduated top 25% of class	17
% graduated top 50% of class	99

DEADLINES

Early decision	
Deadline	11/15
Notification	12/15
Early action	
Deadline	11/15
Notification	1/1
Regular	
Priority	11/15
Deadline	1/15
Notification	4/1
Nonfall registration?	no

FINANCIAL FACTS

Financial Aid Rating	87
Annual tuition	$36,096
% frosh rec. need-based scholarship or grant aid	40
% UG rec. need-based scholarship or grant aid	38
% frosh rec. non-need-based scholarship or grant aid	6
% UG rec. non-need-based scholarship or grant aid	6
% frosh rec. need-based self-help aid	44
% UG rec. need-based self-help aid	41
% frosh rec. any financial aid	44
% UG rec. any financial aid	42
% UG borrow to pay for school	51
Average cumulative indebtedness	$28,902

BARD COLLEGE

OFFICE OF ADMISSIONS, ANNANDALE-ON-HUDSON, NY 12504 • ADMISSIONS: 845-758-7472 • FAX: 845-758-5208

CAMPUS LIFE

Quality of Life Rating	66
Fire Safety Rating	78
Green Rating	90
Type of school	private
Environment	rural

STUDENTS

Total undergrad enrollment	1,737
% male/female	44/56
% from out of state	70
% from public high school	64
% live on campus	77
% African American	2
% Asian	3
% Caucasian	75
% Hispanic	3
% Native American	1
% international	9
# of countries represented	48

SURVEY SAYS . . .

Lots of liberal students
Small classes
No one cheats
Students aren't religious
Campus feels safe
Frats and sororities are unpopular
or nonexistent
Political activism is popular
Lots of beer drinking
(Almost) everyone smokes

ACADEMICS

Academic Rating	92
Calendar	semester
Student/faculty ratio	9:1
Profs interesting rating	88
Profs accessible rating	86
Most common reg class size	10–19 students

MOST POPULAR MAJORS

English language and literature
social sciences
visual and performing arts

STUDENTS SAY ". . ."

Academics

Bard College, a small school that excels in the liberal and fine arts, takes a "progressive approach" to academics, allowing students "the opportunity to control your own education and learn more than you would at most other academic institutions." It doesn't make for a walk in the park, though; students claim that the workload can get heavy, "But if you're passionate about your classes, as most people here are, time often goes quickly as you study. This is not the place for anyone who is not intellectually motivated." A "relaxed, pressure-free environment" makes Bard "a great place to learn" and takes some of the stress out of the hard work, as do the "great professors, who are passionate about the subjects they teach and have often just written a book about the material in a class they are currently teaching." Bard doesn't do as much hand-holding as do comparable liberal arts schools; here "The academics rely heavily on the motivation of the individual student," although "Once you begin coming up with your own special projects and supplementing the required reading, professors bend over backward to help you." The relaxed atmosphere does have its downside, though; students claim that "things are extremely disorganized, and you can easily find yourself being told five different things from five different people."

Life

"People are really involved, both inside and outside of the classroom" at Bard, where "There is a really active club life. We have everything from the International Student Organization to the Surrealist Training Circus and the Children's Expressive Arts Project. There are always dance, theater, music, and art events every weekend," and "The shows are really popular, both those that are student-run and those put on by professionals." Bard undergrads also indulge in "a lot of after-hours discussion about what we're all doing in classes. My friends and I talk about experiments, theories, literature, and various artistic/scientific installations." The Bard campus "is gorgeous, so some people take advantage of amazing hiking and outdoor sports. Other people enjoy Blithewood, a hill that overlooks the Catskills, in a more passive fashion, sunbathing or lounging with friends." Students tell us that they "always feel safe here, even walking in the middle of the night." Bard's party scene is primarily confined to weekends; one student explains, "People party a lot on the weekends but during the week everyone seems to be working." The quaint towns that surround Bard appeal to some, but many prefer "the 2-hour train ride to New York City. It's convenient when you have nothing else to do on the weekend."

Student Body

"Hippies, hipsters, and geek chic" are common sights on the Bard campus, as are "people who have that 'I'm on the cutting edge of underground fashion' look." However, while Bard might appear to be "all about tight designer jeans, indie rock, and everything else NYC or LA," the reality is "There are really a lot of normal college kids here—people seem to think everyone here was a social outcast in high school, but most people here are friendly, social, and pretty normal (although certainly a bit cerebral)." Undergrads tend to be "politically conscious and left-wing-activist types." One student notes, "If you're uncreative or conservative you probably wouldn't fit in. Other than that, just about anything works." Another agrees, "A large percentage of people are extremely talented and creative and express themselves best through creative writing, music, art, dance, or theater." In short, Bard is about "a lot of kids being different together."

FINANCIAL AID: 845-758-7526 • E-MAIL: ADMISSION@BARD.EDU • WEBSITE: WWW.BARD.EDU

THE PRINCETON REVIEW SAYS

Admissions

Very important factors considered include: Application essay, academic GPA, recommendation(s), rigor of secondary school record, character/personal qualities, extracurricular activities, talent/ability. *Important factors considered include:* Volunteer work, work experience. *Other factors considered include:* Class rank, standardized test scores, alumni/ae relation, first generation, geographical residence, interview, level of applicant's interest, racial/ethnic status, religious affiliation/commitment, state residency, TOEFL required of all international applicants. High school diploma is required and GED is accepted. *Academic units recommended:* 4 English, 4 mathematics, 4 science, (3 science labs), 4 foreign language, 4 social studies, 4 history.

Financial Aid

Students should submit: FAFSA, CSS/Financial Aid PROFILE, state aid form, noncustodial PROFILE, business/farm supplement. Regular filing deadline is 2/15. The Princeton Review suggests that all financial aid forms be submitted as soon as possible after January 1. *Need-based scholarships/grants offered:* Federal Pell, SEOG, state scholarships/grants, private scholarships, the school's own gift aid. *Loan aid offered:* FFEL Subsidized Stafford, FFEL Unsubsidized Stafford, FFEL PLUS, Federal Perkins, Loans from institutional funds (for international students only). Applicants will be notified of awards on or about 4/1. Federal Work-Study Program available. Institutional employment available. Off-campus job opportunities are good.

The Inside Word

Because Bard boasts healthy application numbers, it is in a position to concentrate on matchmaking. To that end, Admissions Officers seek students with independent and inquisitive spirits. Applicants who exhibit academic ambition while extending their intellectual curiosity beyond the realm of the classroom are particularly appealing. Successful candidates typically have several honors and Advanced Placement courses on their transcripts, as well as strong letters of recommendation and well-written personal statements.

THE SCHOOL SAYS "..."

From The Admissions Office

"An alliance with Rockefeller University, the renowned graduate scientific research institution, gives Bardians access to Rockefeller's professors and laboratories and to places in Rockefeller's Summer Research Fellows Program. Almost all our math and science graduates pursue graduate or professional studies; 90 percent of our applicants to medical and health professional schools are accepted.

"The Globalization and International Affairs (BGIA) Program is a residential program in the heart of New York City that offers undergraduates a unique opportunity to undertake specialized study with leading practitioners and scholars in international affairs and to gain internship experience with international-affairs organizations. Topics in the curriculum include human rights, international economics, global environmental issues, international justice, managing international risk, and writing on international affairs, among others. Internships/tutorials are tailored to students' particular fields of study.

"Student dormitory and classroom facilities are in Bard Hall, 410 West Fifty-eighth Street, a newly renovated 11-story building near the Lincoln Center District in New York City.

"Bard College does not require SAT scores, new or old, to be submitted for admissions consideration. Students may choose to submit scores, and, if submitted, we will consider them in the context of the overall application. "

SELECTIVITY

Admissions Rating	96
# of applicants	4,980
% of applicants accepted	27
% of acceptees attending	36
# accepting a place on wait list	279
% admitted from wait list	8

FRESHMAN PROFILE

Range SAT Critical Reading	680–740
Range SAT Math	640–690
Minimum paper TOEFL	600
Minimum computer TOEFL	250
Average HS GPA	3.5
% graduated top 10% of class	63
% graduated top 25% of class	85
% graduated top 50% of class	100

DEADLINES

Early action	
Deadline	11/1
Notification	1/1
Regular	
Deadline	1/15
Notification	4/1
Nonfall registration?	no

APPLICANTS ALSO LOOK AT

AND OFTEN PREFER
Harvard College
Yale University
Brown University
Amherst College

AND SOMETIMES PREFER
Oberlin College
New York University
Reed College
Vassar College
Boston University

AND RARELY PREFER
Macalester College
Hampshire College
Ithaca College
Skidmore College
Sarah Lawrence College

FINANCIAL FACTS

Financial Aid Rating	87
Annual tuition	$37,574
Books and supplies	$850
% frosh rec. need-based scholarship or grant aid	56
% UG rec. need-based scholarship or grant aid	53
% frosh rec. need-based self-help aid	52
% UG rec. need-based self-help aid	49
% frosh rec. any financial aid	64
% UG rec. any financial aid	65
% UG borrow to pay for school	65
Average cumulative indebtedness	$19,507

BARNARD COLLEGE

3009 BROADWAY, NEW YORK, NY 10027 • ADMISSIONS: 212-854-2014 • FAX: 212-854-6220

STUDENTS SAY "..."

Academics

Life is lived in the fast lane at Barnard, an all-women's liberal arts college affiliated with Columbia University that incorporates "a small school feel with big school resources and incorporates both campus and city life." Nestled in the Morningside Heights neighborhood of Manhattan on a gated (main) campus, the school maintains an "independent spirit" while providing a "nurturing environment," and its partnership with a larger research university gives it the "best of both worlds" and affords its students the opportunities, course options, and resources that many colleges don't have.

The academic experience at Barnard is simply "wonderful," according to the students. Teachers here are "experts in their field" and "value their positions as both teachers and mentors," to the point where "they make you want to stay on Barnard's campus for class and not take classes at Columbia." "I've never been in an environment where there is such a reciprocal relationship between students wanting to learn and be challenged and professors wanting to teach and help," says a junior. Though underclassmen typically aren't able to get into as many of the small classes (the process of which "is a nightmare"), one student claims that "some of the best classes I've had have been in large lecture halls." The administration gets thumbs up (nearly) across the board for their accessibility and compassion for students; says one, "Every time there is an issue on campus that students care about or an event that has happened, we get e-mails and town-hall meetings devoted to discussing the issues." Deans are always available to students wanting to meet, and the alumni network and career services are singled out for their efficacy. "Barnard is New York—busy, exciting, full of opportunity, and impersonal," says one student symbolically.

Life

Not much goes on around campus, to the chagrin of a few, but as one freshman puts it, "Why stay on campus when you're in New York?" Students take good advantage of the resources available to them in New York City, from Broadway shows and Central Park to museums and restaurants; "the possibilities are endless," and "make it impossible to stick to a budget." People go out a fair amount, either to campus parties at Columbia or the local bar scene (if they have a fake ID, which many do), and "dancing is huge." Theater and a capella are also very big here, and many students are involved with clubs and organizations at Columbia, sometimes even dominating them. There are some complaints that facilities and dorms are "crumbling," but the new student activities building (called the Nexus) should help alleviate building woes when it's completed in August of 2009. According to one junior, "Life at Barnard is probably 60–75% academic, and around 25–40% free."

Student Body

Even though it's all women here, Barnard is "the anti-women's college," as "very, very few students are here for the single-sex education"—they're here for the academics and New York. There's a definite liberal slant on campus, and these "usually politically savvy," "very cultured," "energetic and motivated" girls are "ambitious and opinionated" and have career goals and leadership at the top of their agenda. "Barnard students are not lazy" and have no problems booking their days full of study and activities; most here learn to "fit into the mad rush" very quickly and take advantage of their four short years. Although quite a few students are from the tri-state area and the majority are white, "there is still a sense of diversity" thanks to a variety of different backgrounds, both cultural and geographical; there's also a "tiny gay community" that is easily accepted.

THE PRINCETON REVIEW SAYS

Admissions

Very important factors considered include: Application essay, academic GPA, recommendation(s), rigor of secondary school record, character/personal qualities, extracurricular activities. *Important factors considered include:* Class rank, standardized test scores, talent/ability, volunteer work. *Other factors considered include:* Alumni/ae relation, first generation, geographical residence, interview, level of applicant's interest, racial/ethnic status, work experience. SAT and SAT Subject Tests or ACT required; ACT with Writing component required. High school diploma or equivalent is not required. *Academic units recommended:* 4 English, 3 mathematics, 3 science, (2 science labs), 3 foreign language.

Financial Aid

Students should submit: FAFSA, institution's own financial aid form, CSS/Financial Aid PROFILE, state aid form, noncustodial PROFILE, business/farm supplement, federal income tax returns. Regular filing deadline is 2/1. The Princeton Review suggests that all financial aid forms be submitted as soon as possible after January 1. *Need-based scholarships/grants offered:* Federal Pell, SEOG, state scholarships/grants, private scholarships, the school's own gift aid. *Loan aid offered:* FFEL Subsidized Stafford, FFEL Unsubsidized Stafford, FFEL PLUS, Federal Perkins, state loans, college/university loans from institutional funds. Applicants will be notified of awards on or about 3/31. Federal Work-Study Program available. Institutional employment available. Off-campus job opportunities are excellent.

The Inside Word

As at many top colleges, early decision applications have increased at Barnard—although the admissions standards are virtually the same as for their regular admissions cycle. The college's Admissions Staff is open and accessible, which is not always the case at highly selective colleges with as long and impressive a tradition of excellence. The Admissions Committee's expectations are high, but their attitude reflects a true interest in who you are and what's on your mind. Students have a much better experience throughout the admissions process when treated with sincerity and respect—perhaps this is why Barnard continues to attract and enroll some of the best students in the country.

THE SCHOOL SAYS " . . . "

From The Admissions Office

"Barnard College is a small, distinguished liberal arts college for women that is affiliated with Columbia University and located in the heart of New York City. The college enrolls women from all over the United States, Puerto Rico, and the Caribbean. More than 30 countries, including France, England, Hong Kong, and Greece, are also represented in the student body. Students pursue their academic studies in over 40 majors and are able to cross register at Columbia University.

"Applicants for the Fall 2008 entering class must submit scores from the SAT Reasoning Test and two SAT Subject Tests of their choice, or the ACT with the Writing component."

SELECTIVITY

Admissions Rating	97
# of applicants	4,574
% of applicants accepted	29
% of acceptees attending	43
# accepting a place on wait list	457
% admitted from wait list	3
# of early decision applicants	432
% accepted early decision	42

FRESHMAN PROFILE

Range SAT Critical Reading	640–740
Range SAT Math	620–700
Range SAT Writing	650–730
Range ACT Composite	29–31
Average HS GPA	3.91
% graduated top 10% of class	75
% graduated top 25% of class	94
% graduated top 50% of class	100

DEADLINES

Early decision	
Deadline	11/15
Notification	12/15
Regular	
Deadline	1/1
Notification	4/1
Nonfall registration?	no

FINANCIAL FACTS

Financial Aid Rating	94
Annual tuition	$35,972
% frosh rec. need-based scholarship or grant aid	41
% UG rec. need-based scholarship or grant aid	42
% frosh rec. need-based self-help aid	44
% UG rec. need-based self-help aid	44
% frosh rec. any financial aid	44
% UG rec. any financial aid	43
% UG borrow to pay for school	44
Average cumulative indebtedness	$17,630

BATES COLLEGE

23 CAMPUS AVENUE, LINDHOLM HOUSE, LEWISTON, ME 04240 • ADMISSIONS: 207-786-6000 • FAX: 207-786-6025

CAMPUS LIFE

Quality of Life Rating	86
Fire Safety Rating	93
Green Rating	99
Type of school	private
Environment	town

STUDENTS

Total undergrad enrollment	1,660
% male/female	48/52
% from out of state	89
% from public high school	56
% live on campus	92
% African American	3
% Asian	6
% Caucasian	81
% Hispanic	2
% international	5
# of countries represented	70

SURVEY SAYS . . .

Small classes
Great library
Students are friendly
Frats and sororities are unpopular
or nonexistent
Lots of beer drinking

ACADEMICS

Academic Rating	94
Calendar	4-4-1
Student/faculty ratio	10:1
Profs interesting rating	89
Profs accessible rating	94
Most common reg class size	10–19 students
Most common lab size	10–19 students

MOST POPULAR MAJORS

political science and government
economics
psychology

STUDENTS SAY "..."

Academics

"You will not find it hard to gain access to resources" at Bates College, a small school in Maine that "tries to be unique in the homogeneous world of New England's small liberal arts colleges by weaving together academics with real world experience." First-year seminars, mandatory senior theses, service-learning, and a range of interdisciplinary majors are part of the academic experience. About two-thirds of the students here study abroad at some point before graduation. "Research and internship opportunities" are absurdly abundant. A fairly unusual 4-4-1 calendar includes two traditional semesters and an "incredible" five-week spring term that provides really cool opportunities. Examples include studying marine biology on the Maine coast, Shakespearean drama in England, or economics in China and Taiwan. The "brilliant, accessible, and friendly" faculty does "whatever it takes to actually teach you the material instead of just lecturing and leaving." "The professors at Bates are here because they are passionate about their field and want to be teaching," explains a politics major. "I have never met so many professors who are willing to dedicate endless time outside of class to their students," gushes a psychology major. Course selection can be sparse but the "regularly available" administration is "responsive to student concerns" as well.

Life

"The library is the place to be during the week because everyone is there." The academic workload is reportedly substantial but "it is entirely manageable and does not restrict you from participating in athletics, clubs, or just having some down time." Parties are common on the weekends and students "stand mashed up against everyone else in the keg line." There's a great college radio station—91.5 on your FM dial—and many students get involved. "Bates also has a lot of traditions that students get excited about." In the winter during Puddle Jump, just for instance, Batesies who feel especially courageous can take the plunge into the frigid water of Lake Andrews. Otherwise, "dances, comedians, and trivia challenges are shockingly well attended because there's not a whole lot else to do." The biggest social complaint here centers on the surrounding area. It's the kind of place where "you wouldn't want to be walking alone at three in the morning." Also, relations between Batesies and local residents are reportedly strained. "The interaction between the town and college is relatively minimal," relates a junior. When students feel they just have to get away, they can "hit up the nearby ski slopes." The great outdoors is another option. Bates rents "tents, sleeping bags, kayaks, climbing gear, stoves, vans—really anything you want for outdoor fun." Also, Boston and some smaller cities such as Freeport and Portland are easily accessible.

Student Body

Students tell us that "Bates needs to improve its ethnic diversity." Most of the students here are white. "Your typical Batesie owns at least two flannel shirts" and "likes to have fun on the weekends." There are "a lot of jocks" and some "take the sports teams here way too seriously." Students here call themselves "down to earth" yet "intellectually driven." They enjoy "participating in academics, sports, and clubs." They "love the outdoors." However, this campus is "eclectic" and "Bates students are by no means monolithic in character." "We have everyone from the prep-school spoiled brat to the hippie environmentalist, from people with all different gender and sexual preferences and orientations to the former or current goth," observes a junior. "There are dorks and brains and goof-offs and class clowns." There are "plenty of kids who apparently haven't found the dorm showers," too. "There are few, if any, cliques on campus." "Crossing boundaries" is quite common. "There are different groups but none of them are exclusive in any way." "Even those who do not fit into any specific social group are widely accepted" (with the possible exception of the people who "plain suck").

FINANCIAL AID: 207-786-6096 • E-MAIL: ADMISSIONS@BATES.EDU • WEBSITE: WWW.BATES.EDU

THE PRINCETON REVIEW SAYS

Admissions

Very important factors considered include: Class rank, application essay, academic GPA, recommendation(s), rigor of secondary school record, character/personal qualities, extracurricular activities, interview, level of applicant's interest, talent/ability. *Other factors considered include:* Standardized test scores, alumni/ae relation, first generation, geographical residence, racial/ethnic status, state residency, volunteer work, work experience. TOEFL required of all international applicants. High school diploma is required and GED is not accepted. *Academic units required:* 4 English, 3 mathematics, 3 science, (2 science labs), 2 foreign language, 3 social studies. *Academic units recommended:* 4 English, 4 mathematics, 4 science, (3 science labs), 4 foreign language, 4 social studies.

Financial Aid

Students should submit: FAFSA, CSS/Financial Aid PROFILE, noncustodial PROFILE, business/farm supplement. Regular filing deadline is 2/1. The Princeton Review suggests that all financial aid forms be submitted as soon as possible after January 1. *Need-based scholarships/grants offered:* Federal Pell, SEOG, state scholarships/grants, private scholarships, the school's own gift aid. *Loan aid offered:* FFEL Subsidized Stafford, FFEL Unsubsidized Stafford, FFEL PLUS, Federal Perkins, state loans Applicants will be notified of awards on or about 4/1. Federal Work-Study Program available. Institutional employment available. Off-campus job opportunities are good.

The Inside Word

While holding its applicants to lofty standards, Bates strives to adopt a personal approach to the admissions process. Officers favor qualitative information and focus more on academic rigor, essays, and recommendations than GPA and test scores. They seek students who look for challenges and take advantage of opportunities in the classroom and beyond. Interviews are strongly encouraged—candidates who opt out may place themselves at a disadvantage.

THE SCHOOL SAYS "..."

From The Admissions Office

"Bates College is widely recognized as one of the finest liberal arts colleges in the nation. The curriculum and faculty challenge students to develop the essential skills of critical assessment, analysis, expression, aesthetic sensibility, and independent thought. Founded by abolitionists in 1855, Bates graduates have always included men and women from diverse ethnic and religious backgrounds. Bates highly values its study abroad programs, unique calendar (4-4-1), and the many opportunities available for one-on-one collaboration with faculty through seminars, research, service-learning, and the capstone experience of senior thesis.

"Co-curricular life at Bates is rich; most students participate in club or varsity sports; many participate in performing arts; and almost all students participate in one of more than 100 student-run clubs and organizations. More than two-thirds of alumni enroll in graduate study within 10 years.

"The Bates College Admissions Staff reads applications very carefully; the high school record and the quality of writing are of particular importance. Applicants are strongly encouraged to have a personal interview, either on campus or with an alumni representative. Students who choose not to interview may place themselves at a disadvantage in the selection process. Bates offers tours, interviews and information sessions throughout the summer and fall. Drop-ins are welcome for tours and information sessions. Please call ahead to schedule an interview.

"At Bates, the submission of standardized testing (the SAT, SAT Subject Tests, and the ACT) is not required for admission. After two decades of optional testing, our research shows no differences in academic performance and graduation rates between submitters and nonsubmitters."

SELECTIVITY
Admissions Rating	95
# of applicants	4,434
% of applicants accepted	30
% of acceptees attending	34

FRESHMAN PROFILE
Range SAT Critical Reading	635–710
Range SAT Math	630–700
% graduated top 10% of class	55
% graduated top 25% of class	86
% graduated top 50% of class	99

DEADLINES
Early decision	
Deadline	11/15
Notification	12/20
Regular	
Deadline	1/1
Notification	3/31
Nonfall registration?	yes

APPLICANTS ALSO LOOK AT
AND OFTEN PREFER
Dartmouth College
Williams College
Brown University
AND SOMETIMES PREFER
Middlebury College
Colby College
Bowdoin College
AND RARELY PREFER
Connecticut College
Bucknell University
Trinity College (CT)

FINANCIAL FACTS
Financial Aid Rating	92
Comprehensive fee	$46,800
Books and supplies	$1,150
% frosh rec. need-based scholarship or grant aid	41
% UG rec. need-based scholarship or grant aid	38
% frosh rec. need-based self-help aid	39
% UG rec. need-based self-help aid	38
% frosh rec. any financial aid	43
% UG rec. any financial aid	40
% UG borrow to pay for school	48.1
Average cumulative indebtedness	$13,947

BAYLOR UNIVERSITY

ONE BEAR PLACE #97056, WACO, TX 76798-7056 • ADMISSIONS: 254-710-3435 • FAX: 254-710-3436

CAMPUS LIFE

Quality of Life Rating	**77**
Fire Safety Rating	**79**
Green Rating	**78**
Type of school	private
Affiliation	Baptist
Environment	city

STUDENTS

Total undergrad enrollment	11,786
% male/female	41/59
% from out of state	17
% live on campus	32
% in (# of) fraternities	13 (24)
% in (# of) sororities	17 (19)
% African American	8
% Asian	7
% Caucasian	72
% Hispanic	10
% Native American	1
% international	2
# of countries represented	70

SURVEY SAYS . . .

Lab facilities are great
Great computer facilities
Great library
Athletic facilities are great
Students are friendly
Intramural sports are popular
Frats and sororities dominate
social scene

ACADEMICS

Academic Rating	**79**
Calendar	semester
Student/faculty ratio	16:1
Profs interesting rating	76
Profs accessible rating	78
Most common reg class size	20–29 students
Most common lab size	10–19 students

MOST POPULAR MAJORS
biology/biological sciences
psychology
nursing/registered nurse
(RN, ASN, BSN, MSN)

STUDENTS SAY " . . ."

Academics

Baylor University, the largest Baptist school on the planet, "provides a great education and a wholesome Christian atmosphere where the professors seem to genuinely care about their students." "There is quite a bit of studying" for everyone, and "most professors are very involved with the students," exudes a nursing major. "I cannot say enough good things about my professors and about my academic experience at Baylor." Other students are more moderate in their praise. "There are some great professors and some not-so-great ones," sagely counsels a senior. "You just have to pick the right ones." Also, freshmen and sophomore classes can be sizeable, and "all the tests are multiple choice" in these larger courses. There is a "fantastic" Honors College. Other outstanding programs here include engineering, the entrepreneurship program, and "strong science programs." The rather conservative administration receives mixed reviews. There is "what can only be described as a profound disconnect between the student population and the administrative personnel," says one student. Others say that management "keeps things running smoothly most of the time."

Life

The surrounding town of Waco offers "absolutely nothing to do." Consequently, life at Baylor is centered on campus. Students call it "the Baylor Bubble." "Baylor is not small and lonely, but it is also not overwhelming like most public universities." Intramural sports are big, and the student recreation center is an athletic paradise. School spirit is "outrageous." Here, "you become a Baylor Bear, and you are really part of the family." "Traditions are crazy." Homecoming is a huge deal and features a tremendous parade. On Diadeloso in the spring, classes are cancelled and students are treated to athletic events, live shows, and a campuswide party. Given Baylor's Baptist affiliation, it's not surprising that "rules are very strict." It's a gravely dry campus, and you can't have anyone of the opposite sex in your dorm room after midnight. "Required chapel sessions" for freshmen involve "lectures about how people found Christ" as well as discussion about time management and study techniques. "There is a large sect of students who do not do anything besides church and religious activities." These students also participate in mission trips around the world and go forth to "serve the city of Waco"—mentoring disadvantaged kids, taking care of the elderly, and building houses. "There is a party scene at Baylor" too, and it's dominated by a large Greek system. "Most people think of Baylor as an innocent Baptist school, which is semi-correct, but it for sure has its wild partiers," explains a sophomore. Still, "it is not the normal thing to go get drunk every night."

Student Body

Baylor's undergrads are overwhelmingly female and "the bounty of beautiful Baptist babes is unmatched." Sadly though, at least according to one female, "Baylor boys aren't the greatest." Ethnic diversity isn't bad, and students swear it's getting better. "Gays or lesbians are almost nonexistent or do not identify themselves." Baylor is generally "conservative" and "very Christian." "It is an expensive private university, so you have plenty of students here that are very financially well off." While some students are "preppy, rich types who drive a Lexus and have a 2.0 GPA," "the vast majority of students seek out Baylor for the Christian environment and strong academic reputation." "The stereotype of Bobby and Betty Baylor… actually does not fit nearly as many students as I thought," reckons a freshman. "Many of us work hard to get the money to come here through scholarships and jobs." "There are good people at Baylor, and there are many of them." Virtually everyone is "super nice." There are "radical Pentecostals" and "the kids who have never committed a sin in their lives and are somewhat naïve." There are others "who become obsessed with Greek Life" or "who party and drink all night." If you don't embrace religion, chances are you'll fit in fine. "As an atheist at a Christian school it might be expected that I would find myself isolated from the broader population, but this simply wasn't the case," reflects a senior.

FINANCIAL AID: 254-710-2611 • E-MAIL: ADMISSIONS_SERV_OFFICE@BAYLOR.EDU • WEBSITE: WWW.BAYLOR.EDU

THE PRINCETON REVIEW SAYS

Admissions

Very important factors considered include: Class rank, rigor of secondary school record, standardized test scores. *Important factors considered include:* Academic GPA, recommendation(s). *Other factors considered include:* Application essay, alumni/ae relation, character/personal qualities, extracurricular activities, first generation, geographical residence, interview, level of applicant's interest, religious affiliation/commitment, talent/ability, volunteer work, SAT or ACT required; ACT with Writing component required. High school diploma is required and GED is accepted. *Academic units required:* 4 English, 3 mathematics, 2 science, (2 science labs), 2 foreign language, 1 social studies, 1 history, 3 academic electives.

Financial Aid

Students should submit: FAFSA, State Residency Affirmation. The Princeton Review suggests that all financial aid forms be submitted as soon as possible after January 1. *Need-based scholarships/grants offered:* Federal Pell, SEOG, state scholarships/grants, the school's own gift aid. *Loan aid offered:* FFEL Subsidized Stafford, FFEL Unsubsidized Stafford, FFEL PLUS, Federal Perkins, state loans Applicants will be notified of awards on a rolling basis beginning 3/5. Federal Work-Study Program available. Institutional employment available. Off-campus job opportunities are good.

The Inside Word

Baylor's pool of largely self-selected applicants faces a straightforward admissions process. If your values reflect those of the community here and you have good grades in a solidly college-prep high school curriculum and decently high standardized test scores, you'll be admitted.

THE SCHOOL SAYS "..."

From The Admissions Office

"Baylor University is a Christian university in the Baptist tradition and is affiliated with the Baptist General Convention of Texas. As the oldest institution of higher learning in the state, Baylor's founders sought to establish a college dedicated to Christian principles, superior academics, and a shared sense of community. Students come from all 50 states and some 90 foreign countries. Baylor's nationally recognized academic divisions offer 141 undergraduate degree programs, 71 master's degree programs, and 20 doctoral degree programs. Baylor ranks in the top 15 percent of colleges and universities participating in the National Merit Scholarship program. Baylor is one of the select 11 percent of U.S. colleges and universities with a Phi Beta Kappa chapter. The Templeton Foundation repeatedly names Baylor as one of America's top character-building colleges. Baylor's undergraduate programs emphasize the central importance of vocation (calling) and service in students' lives, helping them explore their value and role in society. Baylor is a charter member of the Independent 529 Tuition Plan, a prepaid college tuition plan. Baylor's tuition is one of the lowest of any major private university in the Southwest and one of the least expensive in the nation. Approximately 75 percent of Baylor students receive student financial assistance. The 508-acre main campus adjoins the Brazos River near downtown Waco, a Central Texas city of 110,000 people. By 2012, Baylor intends to enter the top tier of American universities while reaffirming its distinctive Christian mission. This bold 10-year vision, Baylor 2012, is well underway, benefiting students entering Baylor now.

"Baylor University requires applicants for admission into the Fall 2008 freshman class to take the new version of the SAT or the ACT with the Writing section. Students may also choose to submit scores from the old version of the SAT or ACT (prior to March 2005) as their best scores (old/new) will be used when making admissions decisions."

SELECTIVITY

Admissions Rating	88
# of applicants	21,393
% of applicants accepted	43
% of acceptees attending	31

FRESHMAN PROFILE

Range SAT Critical Reading	540–650
Range SAT Math	560–660
Range SAT Writing	530–640
Range ACT Composite	23–28
% graduated top 10% of class	40
% graduated top 25% of class	70
% graduated top 50% of class	93

DEADLINES

Early action	
Deadline	12/1
Notification	1/15
Regular	
Deadline	2/1
Nonfall registration?	yes

FINANCIAL FACTS

Financial Aid Rating	71
Annual tuition	$22,220
Room and board	$7,526
Required fees	$2,270
Books and supplies	$1,548
% frosh rec. need-based scholarship or grant aid	47
% UG rec. need-based scholarship or grant aid	46
% frosh rec. non-need-based scholarship or grant aid	44
% UG rec. non-need-based scholarship or grant aid	37
% frosh rec. need-based self-help aid	38
% UG rec. need-based self-help aid	38
% frosh rec. athletic scholarships	3
% UG rec. athletic scholarships	3
% frosh rec. any financial aid	93
% UG rec. any financial aid	84

BELLARMINE UNIVERSITY

2001 NEWBURG ROAD, LOUISVILLE, KY 40205 • ADMISSIONS: 502-452-8131 • FAX: 502-452-8002

STUDENTS SAY "..."

Academics

Perched atop a hill in the storied city of Louisville, Bellarmine University's "beautiful campus" earns student praise for being a "sheltering creative community." Students also laud their "entertaining and passionate educators," who "bend over backward to help students." Professors here are like "big brothers and sisters: They harass you, but they're there when you need a helping hand." They are more than just buddies, though: "Each has a strong professional and academic background" and challenges students to strive for success, both inside the classroom and out. Particularly "popular professors," however, teach courses that are sometimes "hard to get into." It's not just the professors who are accessible at Bellarmine; the "administration has an open-door policy that actually means open door!" There "seems to be no administrative 'red tape'; administrators know what's going on and do their jobs very well." Students looking for support praise the "Academic Resource Center that aids students with tutoring, editing essays, and presentations," and appreciate the fact that the school helps them "find internships and co-op programs" for experiential learning outside the classroom.

Life

"Bellarmine is located in the center of the Highlands, Kentucky's cultural mecca. There's everything from sushi to Rasta stores, skate shops to thrift malls" to be found, as well as "many coffee shops in this area, most locally owned. There is a great music scene here, and many bars and venues offer live music." Louisville's "downtown is growing and flourishing. There are gallery hops twice a month, and trolley hops every Friday." Housing off-campus is "awesome and pretty cheap in this area for what you get." With such terrific off-campus amenities, it's no wonder that so few people opt to live on campus, though Bellarmine has added two residence halls in the past two years and the campus is becoming increasingly residential. Still, students report that they stay connected with on-campus life, especially during the week; one writes: "Our school provides a lot of activities throughout the week," such as guest lecturers and intercollegiate sporting events, "but lacks events during the weekend." "Greek life at Bellarmine is [also] almost nonexistent," though students claim that "they are working on that" problem. As a result of a tame Greek scene and relatively quiet weekend campus life, "A lot of people go home during the weekend or to parties off campus," including "the University of Louisville's frat/sorority parties."

Student Body

"The typical student at Bellarmine comes from a private Catholic high school in and around Louisville, and is therefore usually cut from the same political, moral, and educational mold." While the perception is that there are many "high-middle-class White people" at the school, students stress the fact that "our student body does have diversity"; as one student puts it, "The student body at Bellarmine definitely gets more and more diverse each year. The administration is working hard to emphasize the importance of diversity. The only area [in which] they do not seem to be focusing is religious background diversity. I do not know one student at Bellarmine who is not Christian, whether it be Catholic, Baptist, Methodist," or other Christian faiths. The small size of the school creates a close "community atmosphere": "Most of the campus knows who you are." This closeness can be a benefit or a drawback, depending on how you look at it; one respondent remarks: "If you do something stupid, the whole campus has heard about it by lunch."

FINANCIAL AID: 502-452-8124 • E-MAIL: ADMISSIONS@BELLARMINE.EDU • WEBSITE: WWW.BELLARMINE.EDU

THE PRINCETON REVIEW SAYS

Admissions

Very important factors considered include: Academic GPA, recommendation(s), rigor of secondary school record, standardized test scores, character/personal qualities, level of applicant's interest. *Important factors considered include:* Class rank, extracurricular activities. *Other factors considered include:* Application essay, alumni/ae relation, first generation, geographical residence, interview, racial/ethnic status, state residency, talent/ability, volunteer work, work experience. SAT or ACT required; High school diploma is required and GED is accepted. *Academic units required:* 4 English, 3 mathematics, 3 science, (2 science labs), 2 foreign language, 2 social studies, 1 history, 5 academic electives. *Academic units recommended:* 4 English, 4 mathematics, 4 science, (2 science labs), 2 foreign language, 3 social studies, 2 history, 7 academic electives.

Financial Aid

Students should submit: FAFSA. The Princeton Review suggests that all financial aid forms be submitted as soon as possible after January 1. *Need-based scholarships/grants offered:* Federal Pell, SEOG, state scholarships/grants, private scholarships, the school's own gift aid. *Loan aid offered:* FFEL Subsidized Stafford, FFEL Unsubsidized Stafford, FFEL PLUS, Federal Perkins, state loans, college/university loans from institutional funds. Applicants will be notified of awards on a rolling basis beginning 4/1. Federal Work-Study Program available. Institutional employment available. Off-campus job opportunities are excellent.

The Inside Word

Bellarmine views applicants as more than the sum total of their GPA and test scores. Aspects of the application, such as recommendations and personal statements, which present a more complete picture of the students seeking admission, hold significant weight. Candidates with solid grades and diverse interests are likely to earn acceptance.

THE SCHOOL SAYS "..."

From The Admissions Office

"Bellarmine University is known for providing students with outstanding personal attention in the classroom. For many out-of-town students, however, Bellarmine's location makes the difference. Just five miles from downtown Louisville, Bellarmine is at the heart of the cultural and recreational offerings of the nation's sixteenth-largest city. The 135-acre campus is set in a safe, historic neighborhood that features an executive golf course, indoor and outdoor tennis courts, a fitness center, sand volleyball court, and athletic fields.

"Recent additions to the campus reflect the university's academic emphasis on a liberal arts core curriculum surrounded by competitive graduate and professional schools. The state-of-the-art Norton Health Sciences Center and a Service Learning Clinic offer real-life, hands-on experience for nursing and physical therapy students, while the campus library houses the largest collection of works by and about internationally renowned author and Trappist monk Thomas Merton.

"With over 50 clubs and organizations on campus and 18 NCAA Division II athletic teams, and Division I men's lacrosse, Bellarmine offers a variety of recreational opportunities for all students. Countless internships and study abroad programs offer additional opportunities for students to expand their horizons outside the classroom.

"Students who live on campus will also find a Bellarmine difference, namely the living arrangements. From the traditional college residence hall layout to apartment-style and suite living arrangements, students have many housing options. All residence halls offer amenities such as laundry facilities, computer labs, study rooms, and air conditioning.

"As of this book's publication, Bellarmine University did not have information available about their policy regarding the new SAT."

SELECTIVITY

Admissions Rating	80
# of applicants	3,481
% of applicants accepted	63
% of acceptees attending	26

FRESHMAN PROFILE

Range SAT Critical Reading	500–620
Range SAT Math	510–610
Range ACT Composite	22–27
Average HS GPA	3.5
% graduated top 10% of class	22
% graduated top 25% of class	50
% graduated top 50% of class	80

DEADLINES

Early action	
Deadline	11/1
Notification	12/1
Regular	
Priority	2/1
Deadline	8/15
Notification	rolling
Nonfall registration?	yes

FINANCIAL FACTS

Financial Aid Rating	78
Annual tuition	$27,000
Room and board	$8,406
Required fees	$1,030
% frosh rec. need-based scholarship or grant aid	79
% UG rec. need-based scholarship or grant aid	65
% frosh rec. non-need-based scholarship or grant aid	15
% UG rec. non-need-based scholarship or grant aid	8
% frosh rec. need-based self-help aid	52
% UG rec. need-based self-help aid	49
% frosh rec. athletic scholarships	1
% UG rec. athletic scholarships	7
% frosh rec. any financial aid	100
% UG rec. any financial aid	97
% UG borrow to pay for school	65
Average cumulative indebtedness	$18,112

BELOIT COLLEGE

700 COLLEGE STREET, BELOIT, WI 53511 • ADMISSIONS: 608-363-2500 • FAX: 608-363-2075

STUDENTS SAY "..."

Academics

"It feels like a big family here" at Beloit College. Professors "are on a first-name basis with students (you never hear someone say 'Professor _____')." "The Dean of Students will sit and eat with students," and at least one student has "e-mailed a comment to the president, and . . . received a reply e-mail the very next day." The professors here "love what they're doing, and it shows in how they manage their class." They each have a very distinctive teaching style that students either love or hate. It's important to do some research before signing up for any class," advises one sophomore. Even though professors have a range of teaching styles, "Classes are very interdisciplinary and often unintentionally work well in conjunction with other courses." When it comes to curricula, the college affords undergrads a generous dose of independence "with the freedom for students to explore what it is that they want to do . . . [including] the opportunity students have to create their own interdisciplinary major." Students tell us that the faculty and administration here recognize that not every student's interests fit neatly into a few categories, which is why the interdisciplinary major program is an excellent way for students to pursue multiple interests. If there is one complaint that some students have about such a self-directed academic experience, it's that the "Classes are not as challenging as I hoped they would be."

Life

Beloit is the kind of place where "Cultural relativism is very popular," and where special interest houses throw parties that serve as foils (or supplements, perhaps) to the Greek parties that go down nearly every weekend. Students generally praise "a liberal alcohol policy [that] is nice and does lower the overall abuse among the student body." Most of the drinking seems to happen on the weekends at Beloit; "During the week, there are all sorts of presentations, [and] lectures by guests, etc.," that capture the interest of many undergrads. In addition, there's the "[the] Coughy Haus Hause (a type of 'bar' run by the college) where they often have live bands." On the quiet side of the spectrum, some "People like to go to the Java Joint, the campus coffee shop, and play chess, board games, or do a puzzle." And "Almost everyone hangs out at 'The Wall' [a catch-all meeting place in the middle of campus] at some point in their time at Beloit." Also on campus, "movies [are] shown almost every weekend—sometimes very good ones." When they need a change of scenery, students find a friend with a car and road trip to Madison, Milwaukee, or Chicago to go out on the town. When they're not relaxing, "People are very politically active; they encourage voting and the signing of a ridiculous amount of petitions."

Student Body

"Atypical at other schools is typical here—being genderless, atheist/agnostic, liberal, and 'weird' is a 'normal' Beloit student." Since everyone at Beloit is at least partially weird, lines have to be drawn somewhere. On one end of the spectrum are the conservative kids (who are considered unusual at Beloit). On the other end, on the very outer limit of weirdness, are the folks who make up the "Beloit Science Fiction and Fantasy Association (BSFFA), who like Dungeons & Dragons, and who pretend to be wizards, etc." All other Beloiters exist somewhere between these two extremes. But no matter how they are weird, Beloiters are good at their weirdness: "A Beloit student is the kid in high school who played Ping-Pong even though it wasn't cool, and just because it wasn't considered cool, became state Ping-Pong champion to prove a point," explains one freshman. As far as diversity in its traditional sense is concerned, "There are lots of rich kids, but the school does a good job recruiting (and financing) students from lower socioeconomic classes." Students are eager, however, to see the fruits of the Office of Admissions' efforts to recruit more minority students.

FINANCIAL AID: 608-363-2500 • E-MAIL: ADMISS@BELOIT.EDU • WEBSITE: WWW.BELOIT.EDU

THE PRINCETON REVIEW SAYS

Admissions

Very important factors considered include: Application essay, academic GPA, recommendation(s), rigor of secondary school record. *Important factors considered include:* Class rank, standardized test scores, interview. *Other factors considered include:* Alumni/ae relation, character/personal qualities, extracurricular activities, first generation, level of applicant's interest, racial/ethnic status, talent/ability, volunteer work, work experience. SAT or ACT required; High school diploma is required and GED is accepted. *Academic units recommended:* 4 English, 4 mathematics, 3 science, 2 foreign language, 4 social studies.

Financial Aid

Students should submit: FAFSA, institution's own financial aid form, state aid form Regular filing deadline is 3/1. The Princeton Review suggests that all financial aid forms be submitted as soon as possible after January 1. *Need-based scholarships/grants offered:* Federal Pell, SEOG, state scholarships/grants, private scholarships, the school's own gift aid. *Loan aid offered:* FFEL Subsidized Stafford, FFEL Unsubsidized Stafford, FFEL PLUS, Federal Perkins, college/university loans from institutional funds. Applicants will be notified of awards on a rolling basis beginning 4/1. Federal Work-Study Program available. Institutional employment available. Off-campus job opportunities are good.

The Inside Word

Beloit takes a well-rounded approach to the admissions game. Realizing that applicants are more than statistics on a page, the college works diligently to assess the total package. While most weight is given to a candidate's secondary school transcript, which is evaluated not only for grades but for academic rigor, significant attention is also paid to his or her essay and recommendations. Counselors strive to find students who not only demonstrate success in the classroom but also display strong character and leadership skills.

THE SCHOOL SAYS "..."

From The Admissions Office

"While Beloit students clearly understand the connection between college and career, they are more apt to value learning for its own sake than for the competitive advantage that it will afford them in the workplace. As a result, Beloit students adhere strongly to the concept that an educational institution, in order to be true to its own nature, must imply and provide a context in which a free exchange of ideas can take place. This precept is embodied in the mentoring relationship that takes place between professor and student and the dynamic, participatory nature of the classroom experience.

"Beloit College requires that students applying for the Fall of 2009 submit scores from the ACT or SAT. The writing exam from either test is not evaluated for purposes of admission. Beloit offers a nonbinding early action plan with a December 1 deadline. The preferred deadline for regular decision applicants is January 15."

SELECTIVITY

Admissions Rating	89
# of applicants	2,157
% of applicants accepted	60
% of acceptees attending	25
# accepting a place on wait list	85
% admitted from wait list	6

FRESHMAN PROFILE

Range SAT Critical Reading	620–710
Range SAT Math	590–670
Range ACT Composite	25–29
Average HS GPA	3.4
% graduated top 10% of class	31
% graduated top 25% of class	68
% graduated top 50% of class	97

DEADLINES

Early action	
Deadline	12/1
Notification	1/1
Regular	
Priority	1/15
Notification	rolling
Nonfall registration?	yes

FINANCIAL FACTS

Financial Aid Rating	97
Annual tuition	$31,316
Room and board	$6,696
Required fees	$230
Books and supplies	$400
% frosh rec. need-based scholarship or grant aid	63
% UG rec. need-based scholarship or grant aid	64
% frosh rec. non-need-based scholarship or grant aid	37
% UG rec. non-need-based scholarship or grant aid	35
% frosh rec. need-based self-help aid	63
% UG rec. need-based self-help aid	65
% frosh rec. any financial aid	90
% UG rec. any financial aid	90
% UG borrow to pay for school	70
Average cumulative indebtedness	$23,214

BENNINGTON COLLEGE

OFFICE OF ADMISSIONS, BENNINGTON, VT 05201 • ADMISSIONS: 800-833-6845 • FAX: 802-440-4320

CAMPUS LIFE

Quality of Life Rating	78
Fire Safety Rating	81
Green Rating	88
Type of school	private
Environment	town

STUDENTS

Total undergrad enrollment	583
% male/female	32/68
% from out of state	96
% live on campus	99
% African American	2
% Asian	2
% Caucasian	84
% Hispanic	2
% international	3
# of countries represented	15

SURVEY SAYS . . .

Class discussions encouraged
Small classes
No one cheats
Students aren't religious
Dorms are like palaces
Campus feels safe
Intercollegiate sports are unpopular
or nonexistent
Frats and sororities are unpopular
or nonexistent
Theater is popular

ACADEMICS

Academic Rating	95
Calendar	15 Wk Fall Spring, 7 Wk Winter Work Term
Student/faculty ratio	8:1
Profs interesting rating	97
Profs accessible rating	96
% classes taught by TAs	0
Most common reg class size	10–19 students

MOST POPULAR MAJORS

visual and performing arts
English language and literature
drama and dramatics/theatre arts

STUDENTS SAY "..."

Academics

"I chose Bennington because it was everything high school wasn't," one undergrad writes, neatly summing up what makes this small school with a no distribution-requirements curriculum so appealing to many. Bennington students don't declare majors; rather, they formulate an interdisciplinary academic plan in consultation with faculty advisors. The system makes Bennington a great place "for motivated self-starters who may not know exactly what they want from school but who will thrive if they have control of their education." Prospective students should be forewarned that "it is truly up to the student to decide whether they wish to make their education demanding. Although no one will be allowed to slip by through our plan process, motivation is a must to be extremely successful." Bennington is strongest in the arts; students love their work in writing, visual arts, and theater. In these and all disciplines, professors "are all active participants in their fields, so literature classes are taught by writers, painting classes by painters, dancing classes by dancers, and so on. This ensures that all faculty members are knowledgeable and have personal experiences that are of use to students. As an added bonus, it is not infrequent that a professor will ask for the help of students in big, exciting projects." Bennington is a small school, and that naturally creates some limitations. Several students in our survey wished for an Art History Department, for example.

Life

Undergraduates at Bennington "work really, really hard and play with the same intensity. In fact, if you were going to describe Bennington in one word, you would call it 'intense.'" Daily life consists of "a mix of independent work and cooperative work. Everyone is working on a project that they are excited about, stressed out about, etc." As one student explains, "A Bennington student reflects the passion that burns in their interests, and the way that they express these interests is by not creating boundaries between work and play. Our lives are our passions. You will be living, working, and playing with dedicated students, supportive and motivated faculty, and a diverse curriculum." When they take a work break, "People here like to hang out a lot, watch movies or just chill and talk, or attend on-campus activities, bands, sponsored parties, theater events, and art openings." The school organizes a lot of "extracurricular opportunities. The campus activities board tries really hard to have things going on all the time for students, and if there isn't something to your liking it isn't very hard to get away to New York or Boston for the weekend." The ease of visiting these cities is a good thing, because there's not much happening immediately off campus; Bennington "is so secluded" that "it's possible to be completely cut off from the world outside if you don't make an attempt to watch/read the news. The closest big city is Albany (a 40- to 50-minute drive), and that's not saying much."

Student Body

"Most of the students enjoy going against the grain" at Bennington. These "really interesting, crazy, creative, brilliant people . . . try to 'out-different' each other: Who can be the most eccentric? Everyone, no matter how nerdy, will not only be super cool here, but have a group of friends just like them." Although they insist that "there is no typical Bennington student," most students would concede that their peers "are usually creative, self-motivated, smart, and hilarious. The only students who don't feel like they fit in are those unwilling to work or take charge of their own college experience." Bennington "is racially very homogenous," but, one student says, "Racial diversity doesn't guarantee diversity of experience or ideals, anyway. Among students here, there is a wide variety of social backgrounds, religious upbringings, intended academic concentrations, and motivations. Politically, though, we are quite limited—the vast majority of students are very liberal."

FINANCIAL AID: 802-440-4325 • E-MAIL: ADMISSIONS@BENNINGTON.EDU • WEBSITE: WWW.BENNINGTON.EDU

THE PRINCETON REVIEW SAYS

Admissions

Very important factors considered include: Class rank, application essay, academic GPA, recommendation(s), rigor of secondary school record, character/personal qualities, extracurricular activities, interview, talent/ability. *Other factors considered include:* Standardized test scores, alumni/ae relation, first generation, geographical residence, level of applicant's interest, racial/ethnic status, volunteer work, work experience. TOEFL required of all international applicants. High school diploma is required and GED is accepted. *Academic units recommended:* 4 English, 4 mathematics, 3 science, 2 foreign language, 4 social studies, 4 history.

Financial Aid

Students should submit: FAFSA, institution's own financial aid form, CSS/Financial Aid PROFILE, noncustodial PROFILE, Student and Parent Federal Tax Returns and W-2s. The Princeton Review suggests that all financial aid forms be submitted as soon as possible after January 1. *Need-based scholarships/grants offered:* Federal Pell, SEOG, state scholarships/grants, private scholarships, the school's own gift aid. *Loan aid offered:* FFEL Subsidized Stafford, FFEL Unsubsidized Stafford, FFEL PLUS, college/university loans from institutional funds. NOTE: College/university loans from institutional funds for International students only. Applicants will be notified of awards on or about 4/1. Federal Work-Study Program available. Institutional employment available. Off-campus job opportunities are good.

The Inside Word

Given the freedom and flexibility inherent in a Bennington education, ideal prospective applicants tend to be motivated and independent students. The college hopes to learn as much about each applicant as possible in the admissions process and tries to have a conversation with each applicant in person or via telephone or email. Applicants may (and should!) use their personal statements and interviews to distinguish themselves.

THE SCHOOL SAYS "..."

From The Admissions Office

"The educational philosophy of Bennington is rooted in an abiding faith in the talent, imagination, and responsibility of the individual; thus, the principle of learning by practice underlies every major feature of a Bennington education. We believe that a college education should not merely provide preparation for graduate school or a career, but should be an experience valuable in itself and the model for lifelong learning. Faculty, staff, and students at Bennington work together in a collaborative environment based upon respect for each other and the power of ideas to make a difference in the world. We are looking for intellectually curious students who have a passion for learning, are willing to take risks, and are open to making connections.

"Submission of standardized test scores (the SAT, SAT Subject Tests, or the ACT) is recommended, but not required."

SELECTIVITY

Admissions Rating	88
# of applicants	1,011
% of applicants accepted	63
% of acceptees attending	32
# accepting a place on wait list	10
# of early decision applicants	73
% accepted early decision	73

FRESHMAN PROFILE

Range SAT Critical Reading	580–700
Range SAT Math	540–630
Range SAT Writing	580–690
Range ACT Composite	24–30
Minimum paper TOEFL	577
Minimum computer TOEFL	233
Minimum web-based TOEFL	90–91
Average HS GPA	3.4
% graduated top 10% of class	28
% graduated top 25% of class	70
% graduated top 50% of class	95

DEADLINES

Early decision	
Deadline	11/15
Notification	12/15
Regular	
Deadline	1/3
Notification	4/1
Nonfall registration?	yes

APPLICANTS ALSO LOOK AT

AND OFTEN PREFER
New York University
Bard College

AND SOMETIMES PREFER
Eugene Lang
Sarah Lawrence College
Vassar College

AND RARELY PREFER
Hampshire College
Skidmore College

FINANCIAL FACTS

Financial Aid Rating	73
Annual tuition	$37,280
Room and board	$10,680
Books and supplies	$800
Required Fees	$990
% frosh rec. need-based scholarship or grant aid	71
% UG rec. need-based scholarship or grant aid	67
% frosh rec. non-need-based scholarship or grant aid	4
% UG rec. non-need-based scholarship or grant aid	2
% frosh rec. need-based self-help aid	64
% UG rec. need-based self-help aid	64
% frosh rec. any financial aid	81
% UG rec. any financial aid	77
% UG borrow to pay for school	72
Average cumulative indebtedness	$20,936

BENTLEY COLLEGE

175 FOREST STREET, WALTHAM, MA 02452-4705 • ADMISSIONS: 781-891-2244 • FAX: 781-891-3414

STUDENTS SAY "..."

Academics

Bentley College, an institution dedicated to creating "business and business-technical leaders," combines a winning location with an intense focus on technology to produce "the business moguls of tomorrow." Students say that the "Resources here are second to none, if you need help scheduling classes, choosing a major, creating a resume . . . anything at all, then there is an entire office of people ready and willing to help you in any way possible." Some of Bentley's perks include "a state-of-the-art trading room that would be used in the case of an emergency on Wall Street," a "superbly wired campus," and a brand-new library that "has all the resources a student could need, with quite a few significant, (not so necessary) extras" (such as a "large flat-panel TV monitors in each of its 20-some odd study rooms"). Bentley doesn't just flash the hardware, though; it also teaches students how to "integrate the newest technological resources into the business environment" by "embedding them into [your] courses. This is important, because technology "is key to success in the business world, whatever profession you are interested in." Bentley's proximity to Boston "makes this a very special place," helping students find meaningful internships and, after graduation, meaningful jobs. Academics here "are challenging but not overwhelming," and most of the classes "weigh class participation in the overall grade, which motivates [you] to complete the readings and assignments in a timely manner." Professors typically have "previous real-life experience in the business world. They like to incorporate that in the classroom."

Life

Life is "very hectic" at Bentley, where "Students tend to crack down during the weekdays and really get their work done. By Thursday [we're] ready for the weekend to start." Bentley's "beautiful campus" has "tons to offer" when it comes to finding activities outside of class, including "Greek life, sports organizations" and "tons of bars, restaurants, sports events, and concerts" so that "it's hard to be bored." Intramural sports "are also very popular, as is exercising in general. Being fit and working out are definitely the 'in' things to do." There are also plenty of parties; "Registered parties are allowed (with regulations) where of-age students can have keg parties in their room," but "There is also substance-free housing available if that's not your fancy." Students across the board agree that "Boston is Bentley's main attraction." Fortunately the city "is easily accessible via the school's shuttle service." Students love to head for Cambridge, the North End, Quincy Market, and other city destinations on the weekend "just to see a show, eat at a restaurant, shop, or just walk around," although some prefer to hang out on campus because the city can be "pretty expensive."

Students

The typical Bentley undergrad is "rich, foreign, and smart." Check that, they're "usually two out of the three: rich and foreign, rich and smart, or smart and foreign." Internationals make up a conspicuous subpopulation, "which is interesting" because you get to "learn from other cultures." One student writes, "Venture through any apartment complex to be greeted to the smells of Indian, Creole, Chinese, South American, and European foods. Diversity is greatly appreciated, as is evidenced by the fact that one of the events with the largest attendance each year is the Festival of Colors, an international extravaganza." The exception to the rule, we're told, is that students from Europe "hail from very big money" and "very rarely interact with domestic students." Most here, unsurprisingly, "are typical business students, usually quite driven and business oriented. They are fairly fun loving as well," the sort who are "studious during the week, rowdy on weekends." Overall, students tend to be "preppy collar-poppin' kids" who can "talk the talk" and "take pride [in] attending Bentley."

FINANCIAL AID: 781-891-3441 • E-MAIL: UGADMISSION@BENTLEY.EDU • WEBSITE: WWW.BENTLEY.EDU

THE PRINCETON REVIEW SAYS

Admissions

Very important factors considered include: Academic GPA, rigor of secondary school record, standardized test scores. *Important factors considered include:* Class rank, application essay, recommendation(s), character/personal qualities, extracurricular activities, volunteer work, work experience. *Other factors considered include:* Alumni/ae relation, first generation, geographical residence, interview, level of applicant's interest, racial/ethnic status, state residency, talent/ability, SAT or ACT required; ACT with Writing component required. TOEFL required of all international applicants. High school diploma is required and GED is accepted. *Academic units recommended:* 4 English, 4 mathematics, 3 science, (3 science labs), 3 foreign language, 3 history, 2 additional English, mathematics, social or lab science, foreign language, speech.

Financial Aid

Students should submit: FAFSA, CSS/Financial Aid PROFILE, noncustodial PROFILE, business/farm supplement. Federal Tax Returns, including all schedules for parents and student. Regular filing deadline is 2/1. The Princeton Review suggests that all financial aid forms be submitted as soon as possible after January 1. *Need-based scholarships/grants offered:* Federal Pell, SEOG, state scholarships/grants, private scholarships, the school's own gift aid. *Loan aid offered:* FFEL Subsidized Stafford, FFEL Unsubsidized Stafford, FFEL PLUS, Federal Perkins, state loans Applicants will be notified of awards on a rolling basis beginning 3/25. Federal Work-Study Program available. Institutional employment available. Off-campus job opportunities are good.

The Inside Word

If you've got a bunch of electives available to you senior year, you may think that choosing business classes is the best way to impress the Bentley Admissions Office. Not so; the school would prefer you take a broad range of challenging classes—preferably at the AP level—in English, history/social sciences, math, lab sciences, and foreign language. The school enjoys a sizable applicant pool, so you'll need solid grades and test scores to gain admission.

THE SCHOOL SAYS ". . ."

From The Admissions Office

"Bentley is a national leader in business education. Centered on education and research in business and related professions, Bentley blends the breadth and technological strength of a university with the values and student focus of a small college. A Bentley education combines an unparalleled array of business courses with hands-on technology experience, and a strong foundation in liberal arts. Half of all required courses are in the arts and sciences. In addition, students have the opportunity to pursue a double major in business and liberal studies. The result is that students gain expertise for a competitive edge in today's economy and broad-based skills essential for success in all areas of life. An average class size of 25 students and a student/faculty ratio of 12:1 allow for personal attention and meaningful class discussion. Concepts and theories that students learn in the classroom come alive in several hands-on, high-tech learning laboratories like the Financial Trading Room, Center for Marketing Technology, and Media and Culture Labs and Studio. Outside the classroom, students choose from a number of athletic, social, and cultural opportunities." Ethics and social responsibility are woven throughout the school's curriculum; the Bentley Service-Learning Program is ranked among the top in the United States. Students also choose from 27 countries to study abroad. Students develop skills and build their resume thanks to internships with leading companies." State-of-the-art athletic and recreation facilities complement the 23 varsity teams in Division I and II, and the extensive intramural and recreational sports programs. Boston and Cambridge, just minutes from campus, are accessible via the school's free shuttle. Both cities are great resources for internships, job opportunities, cultural events, and social life. Students applying for freshman admission are required to take the SAT or the ACT with the Writing section. SAT Subject Tests are not required."

SELECTIVITY

Admissions Rating	91
# of applicants	6,689
% of applicants accepted	38
% of acceptees attending	37
# accepting a place on wait list	425
# of early decision applicants	210
% accepted early decision	60

FRESHMAN PROFILE

Range SAT Critical Reading	550–630
Range SAT Math	600–680
Range SAT Writing	550–640
Range ACT Composite	24–29
Minimum paper TOEFL	550
Minimum computer TOEFL	213
Minimum web-based TOEFL	80
% graduated top 10% of class	42.1
% graduated top 25% of class	80.5
% graduated top 50% of class	97.4

DEADLINES

Early decision	
Deadline	11/15
Notification	12/15
Early action	
Deadline	11/15
Notification	1/15
Regular	
Deadline	1/15
Notification	4/1
Nonfall registration?	yes

APPLICANTS ALSO LOOK AT AND SOMETIMES PREFER

Northeastern University
Villanova University
Boston College
Boston University
Babson College

FINANCIAL FACTS

Financial Aid Rating	80
Annual tuition	$31,450
Room and board	$10,940
Required fees	$1,446
Books and supplies	$1,000
% frosh rec. need-based scholarship or grant aid	46
% UG rec. need-based scholarship or grant aid	42
% frosh rec. non-need-based scholarship or grant aid	26
% UG rec. non-need-based scholarship or grant aid	13
% frosh rec. need-based self-help aid	49
% UG rec. need-based self-help aid	47
% frosh rec. athletic scholarships	1
% UG rec. athletic scholarships	1
% frosh rec. any financial aid	79
% UG rec. any financial aid	73
% UG borrow to pay for school	63
Average cumulative indebtedness	$31,665

BEREA COLLEGE

CPO 2220, BEREA, KY 40404 • ADMISSIONS: 859-985-3500 • FAX: 859-985-3512

CAMPUS LIFE

Quality of Life Rating	**75**
Fire Safety Rating	**85**
Green Rating	**89**
Type of school	private
Environment	village

STUDENTS

Total undergrad enrollment	1,528
% male/female	40/60
% from out of state	57
% live on campus	87
% African American	18
% Asian	2
% Caucasian	69
% Hispanic	2
% Native American	1
% international	7
# of countries represented	64

SURVEY SAYS . . .

Large classes
Great computer facilities
Great library
Diverse student types on campus
Low cost of living
*Frats and sororities are unpopular
or nonexistent*

ACADEMICS

Academic Rating	**88**
Calendar	4/1/4
Student/faculty ratio	11:1
Profs interesting rating	82
Profs accessible rating	80
Most common	
reg class size	10–19 students

MOST POPULAR MAJORS

business/commerce
manufacturing technology/techni-
cian
human development and family
studies

STUDENTS SAY "..."

Academics

Berea College in central Kentucky is "about bringing underprivileged high school graduates from the Appalachian region and beyond together for a chance at a higher education, a career, and a better life." Thanks to a labor program that requires all students to work 10 to 15 hours each week and a ton of donated cash, tuition here is "free." "Each student receives a laptop to use while in school" as well. "No tuition does not mean a full ride," though. "Extra costs such as technology fees, insurance, food plans, etc. add up quickly," advises a business major. About two-thirds of the students receive additional financial aid. Berea's administration is efficient but it "tends to be too parental in nature" can be overly concerned with image. "Donors hear a story of poor kids who are getting help from a school that sometimes styles itself as a charity," explains a junior. In addition to a decent range of liberal arts and sciences majors, there are several career-oriented programs. The academic atmosphere is "rigorous." Class attendance is mandatory. A few "hardcore" professors "abuse the idea of homework." Others "need refresher courses on how to deal with people." On the whole, though, faculty members are "witty" and they "have a strong passion for what they are teaching." "Everyone who I've had has been completely accessible outside of class," describes a nursing major. "Students are able to get so much more one-on-one time than at larger colleges."

Life

"Buildings, facilities, and technology are not always the newest, nicest, or most expensive" on this "tiny campus." There's no cable television in the dorm rooms and the "crazy" visitation policy for members of the opposite sex is "borderline 19th century." Academics take up a lot of time and "every student is required to have an on-campus job." Some students make stoneware pottery. Others "feed sheep and goats" on the college farm. However, "janitorial work," computer support, and similarly mundane jobs are more typical. "With work, classes, and studying, there's not much time left for anything else." "There are many clubs" and several religious groups. "Movie marathons" and "dances" are common. "Pick-up games" and intramurals are popular. "Some of us go camping when it's nice out, that kind of thing," says a first-year student. Otherwise, "life at Berea is generally regarded as boring." "If it weren't for videogames, I'd go nuts," speculates a junior. The surrounding town is "very small." "There is not even a movie theater." "Someone from a big city would be in for a shock." Freshmen can't bring cars at all and, generally, only students who live far away can ever have vehicles. The county is dry and there are no bars. Berea's alcohol polices are theoretically harsh but more lenient in practice. "If you can hide it, you can drink it." However, alcohol and drug usage is "very low." "We're not a party school," says a junior. "Basically, our weekends consist of walking down to Wal-Mart," explains a sophomore," and that's if we're really ready for a crazy night."

Student Body

"The typical student at Berea College is broke" but "has big dreams." "Most people are from working-class families." They were "raised in backwoods hollows" around "the Appalachian area." "We are all here because we have no money but are equipped with the hope for a bright future and a desire to learn," declares a senior. Students at Berea are "sleep deprived" and "too busy to really have the time to slack off (though there are some that still manage it)." They're "bright, hardworking," and "studious." "Most of us are nerds," admits a senior. There are "quite a few Bible thumpers." At the same time, Berea is "probably more liberal than conservative" and this is something of "a hippie school." "People are really big about recycling, sustainability, and the environment." Students tell us that Berea has "more diversity than most schools." "There is a very large homeschool population." There are quite a few "young married students." There's also a noticeable contingent of international students and "a large population of African Americans." Some students claim that minorities "blend in well." Others say the campus is "widely segregated."

BEREA **C**OLLEGE

FINANCIAL AID: 859-985-3310 • E-MAIL: ADMISSIONS@BEREA.EDU • WEBSITE: WWW.BEREA.EDU

THE PRINCETON REVIEW SAYS

Admissions

Very important factors considered include: Class rank, academic GPA, rigor of secondary school record, standardized test scores, geographical residence. *Important factors considered include:* Application essay, character/personal qualities, extracurricular activities, interview, racial/ethnic status, talent/ability, volunteer work. *Other factors considered include:* Recommendation(s), first generation, level of applicant's interest, state residency, work experience. SAT or ACT required; TOEFL required of all international applicants. High school diploma is required and GED is accepted. *Academic units recommended:* 4 English, 3 mathematics, 2 science, (2 science labs), 2 foreign language, 1 social studies, 1 history.

Financial Aid

Students should submit: FAFSA The Princeton Review suggests that all financial aid forms be submitted as soon as possible after January 1. *Need-based scholarships/grants offered:* Federal Pell, SEOG, state scholarships/grants, private scholarships, the school's own gift aid, United Negro College Fund. *Loan aid offered:* FFEL Subsidized Stafford, FFEL Unsubsidized Stafford, FFEL PLUS, Federal Perkins, college/university loans from institutional funds. Applicants will be notified of awards on a rolling basis beginning 5/1.

Inside Word

The full-tuition scholarship that every student receives understandably attracts a lot of applicants. Competition among candidates is intense. To make matters worse, you may be too wealthy to get admitted here. Berea won't admit students whose parents can afford to send them elsewhere. Financially qualified applicants should apply as early as possible.

THE SCHOOL SAYS "..."

From The Admissions Office

"Founded in 1855 by ardent abolitionists, Berea College was the first racially integrated coeducational college in the South. Over the past 150 years, Berea's has evolved into one of the most distinctive colleges in the United States. Serving students primarily from the Appalachian region, Berea College seeks to serve students who possess great academic promise but have access to limited financial resources. Berea provides an inviting and personal educational experience, evidenced in part by an 11:1 student/faculty ratio and extensive, faculty-led advising and orientation programs.

"In support of students with limited financial resources, every enrolling student receives a full-tuition scholarship, a laptop computer, as well as a paid on-campus job. Students pay room, board, and fee charges to the extent that they are able as determined by their FAFSA results. Any remaining room, board, and fee charges are covered through scholarships and grant-based aid. Students may use earnings from their job to assist with their portion of room, board, and fee charges; books and supplies; and other personal expenses.

"As a result of this combination of academic reputation and generous financial assistance, Berea attracts many more applicants than are able to be accepted and thus admission is competitive. The best means of improving the chances for admission is to complete the application process as early as possible, preferably by November 30 of the senior year.

"Applicants for Fall 2008 must submit scores from the SAT or ACT (with or without the Writing components from either test)."

SELECTIVITY
Admissions Rating	92
# of applicants	2,083
% of applicants accepted	29
% of acceptees attending	71

FRESHMAN PROFILE
Range SAT Critical Reading	480–593
Range SAT Math	478–600
Range SAT Writing	470–563
Range ACT Composite	21–25
Minimum paper TOEFL	500
Minimum computer TOEFL	173
Average HS GPA	3.42
% graduated top 10% of class	26
% graduated top 25% of class	67
% graduated top 50% of class	96

DEADLINES
Regular	
Priority	11/30
Deadline	4/30
Notification	rolling
Nonfall registration?	yes

FINANCIAL FACTS
Financial Aid Rating	82
Annual tuition	$24,500
% frosh rec. need-based scholarship or grant aid	100
% UG rec. need-based scholarship or grant aid	100
% frosh rec. non-need-based scholarship or grant aid	100
% UG rec. non-need-based scholarship or grant aid	100
% frosh rec. need-based self-help aid	100
% UG rec. need-based self-help aid	100
% frosh rec. any financial aid	100
% UG rec. any financial aid	100
% UG borrow to pay for school	79
Average cumulative indebtedness	$7,705

THE BEST 368 COLLEGES ■ 89

BIRMINGHAM-SOUTHERN COLLEGE

900 ARKADELPHIA ROAD, BIRMINGHAM, AL 35254 • ADMISSIONS: 205-226-4696 • FAX: 205-226-3074

STUDENTS SAY " . . ."

Academics

"Birmingham-Southern college is the best school in Alabama" students at this small, academically intense college in the state's largest city insist. Undergrads praise how the school achieves a "happy medium between well-rounded education and focused concentration on one's major," reporting that "BSC does a great job of preparing students for graduate, law, and medical schools." It also has "a good education program . . . and an excellent dance department that offers a top-notch dance faculty with a focus on ballet." Students tell us that "the overall academic experience is challenging, yet very rewarding," and that "classroom discussion is not only encouraged, but is a necessity, since much of the grades are derived from participation." Experiential learning is paramount; one student reports, "I have not had a class yet that didn't provide some sort of hands-on experience. I have participated in everything from labs at the Cahaba River in my population ecosystem course to observations at a local Montessori school in my human growth and development class." The small classes mean "Teachers get to know you by name, and many are willing to spend countless hours working with you individually on school matters and helping you plan [your] future. They take an interest in you as a person, not just as a student." Some here point out that "while being small is a benefit, it is also sometimes a downfall. Most classes are available every year, but you must be careful to schedule courses that only occur every other year or once a year carefully in order to graduate on time."

Life

"Most people live on campus because BSC is a smaller college," students here tell us, and "This allows for an attractive community-like atmosphere." Campus life includes "many student organizations, a very strong Greek system, [and] many different shows throughout the year, from dance to theater to music to art, all produced by the performing arts departments." Youth groups and religious organizations "are also big at the school. Many people attend chapel services." There's fun to be had off campus as well, as "Birmingham is a rockin' city. There is always a concert or something off campus." Exploring Birmingham "is very easy [because] the school is located downtown, although it doesn't feel that way. You can go out to the middle of the academic quad at 11:00 P.M. and feel safe." There's "plenty to do off campus, including shopping, visiting the zoo, or going to see a show at one of the many theaters in town." One student sums up, "Fun is either a night out in Birmingham—that's what you do if you have money: You go out to eat, then to the bars, a movie, or a small off-campus party at someone's apartment—or, if you're broke and you want to have fun, you usually end up on Fraternity Row. At least one of the fraternities is usually having a party, and there are always people down there."

Student Body

BSC undergrads "typically come from the Alabama, Mississippi, Tennessee, and Georgia areas," although "there are some students here from elsewhere." Many "are involved in Greek life, probably about 50 percent. Many more girls go Greek than guys, and the independents are still like their own Greek group," as they "find their own groups in which to socialize, such as the Ultimate Frisbee team or service clubs such as Students Offering Support." Most here agree that "the school could do better at attracting minorities and people of color," but point out that "with the size of our school you can only expect so much."

FINANCIAL AID: 205-226-4688 • E-MAIL: ADMISSION@BSC.EDU • WEBSITE: WWW.BSC.EDU

THE PRINCETON REVIEW SAYS

Admissions

Very important factors considered include: Application essay, academic GPA, recommendation(s), rigor of secondary school record, standardized test scores. *Important factors considered include:* Character/personal qualities, level of applicant's interest. *Other factors considered include:* Extracurricular activities, interview, talent/ability, volunteer work, work experience. SAT or ACT required; ACT with Writing component recommended. TOEFL required of all international applicants. High school diploma is required but GED is also accepted. *Academic units required:* 4 English. *Academic units recommended:* 4 mathematics, 4 science, (2 science labs), 2 foreign language, 2 social studies, 2 history.

Financial Aid

Students should submit: FAFSA. The Princeton Review suggests that all financial aid forms be submitted as soon as possible after January 1. *Need-based scholarships/grants offered:* Federal Pell, SEOG, private scholarships, the school's own gift aid, United Negro College Fund. *Loan aid offered:* FFEL Subsidized Stafford, FFEL Unsubsidized Stafford, FFEL PLUS, Federal Perkins Applicants will be notified of awards on a rolling basis beginning 3/1. Federal Work-Study Program available. Institutional employment available. Off-campus job opportunities are excellent.

The Inside Word

Birmingham-Southern's lack of widespread national recognition by students and parents results in a small applicant pool, the majority of whom are admitted. Most of the admits are looking for a quality Southern college, recognize a good situation here, and decide to enroll. Our impression is that few regret their decision. In a reflection of the entire administration, the Admissions Staff is truly personal and very helpful to prospective students.

THE SCHOOL SAYS "..."

From The Admissions Office

"Respected publishers continue to recognize Birmingham-Southern College as one of the top-ranked liberal arts colleges in the nation. One guide highlights our small classes and the fact that we still assign each student a 'faculty-mentor,' to assure individualized attention to our students. One notable aspect of our academic calendar is our January interim term, a 4-week period in which students can participate in special projects in close collaboration with faculty members, either on or off campus. One dimension of Birmingham-Southern's civic focus is the commitment to volunteerism. The Center for Leadership Studies assists students in realizing their leadership potential by combining the academic study of leadership with significant community service.

"Freshman applicants must present acceptable scores on the SAT or the ACT; they must also submit an original essay and a satisfactory recommendation from the high school."

SELECTIVITY

Admissions Rating	88
# of applicants	2,292
% of applicants accepted	67
% of acceptees attending	30

FRESHMAN PROFILE

Range SAT Critical Reading	530–660
Range SAT Math	520–630
Range SAT Writing	520–650
Range ACT Composite	23–28
Minimum paper TOEFL	500
Minimum computer TOEFL	173
Minimum web-based TOEFL	61
Average HS GPA	3.34
% graduated top 10% of class	34
% graduated top 25% of class	64
% graduated top 50% of class	84

DEADLINES

Regular	
Priority	1/1
Notification	rolling
Nonfall registration?	yes

APPLICANTS ALSO LOOK AT

AND OFTEN PREFER
Rhodes College
Vanderbilt University

AND SOMETIMES PREFER
Samford University
Sewanee: The University of the South
Furman University
University of Alabama—Tuscaloosa
Auburn University

AND RARELY PREFER
Tulane University
Louisiana State University

FINANCIAL FACTS

Financial Aid Rating	82
Annual tuition	$23,600
Room and board	$8,273
Required fees	$700
Books and supplies	$1,000
% frosh rec. need-based scholarship or grant aid	34
% UG rec. need-based scholarship or grant aid	26
% frosh rec. non-need-based scholarship or grant aid	37
% UG rec. non-need-based scholarship or grant aid	29
% frosh rec. need-based self-help aid	34
% UG rec. need-based self-help aid	28
% frosh rec. athletic scholarships	0
% UG rec. athletic scholarships	0
% frosh rec. any financial aid	98
% UG rec. any financial aid	97
% UG borrow to pay for school	60
Average cumulative indebtedness	$19,800

BOSTON COLLEGE

140 COMMONWEALTH AVENUE, DEVLIN HALL 208, CHESTNUT HILL, MA 02467-3809 • ADMISSIONS: 617-552-3100

STUDENTS SAY "..."

Academics

Students praise the strong academics, the competitive athletic teams, the lively social scene, and the premium location that all combine to create a remarkable all-around college experience at Boston College. For many, though, BC's greatest asset is the "strong spiritual presence [that] shows how positive an influence religion can have on one's life." Don't worry; "They don't try to make anybody be Catholic" here. Rather, the school "simply reflects the Jesuit ideals of community, spirituality, and social justice," and these ideals pervade both the curriculum and the academic community. True to the Jesuit ideal of "educating the entire person," BC requires a thorough core curriculum "including philosophy, theology, and language requirements," rounded out by "strong [but optional] programs, such as internships and studying abroad." Beyond the core curriculum, "BC offers something for everyone. If you go here, you are with business students, nursing students, education majors, and arts and science majors." Even though this is a fairly large school, students insist that "you never feel like a number here. Yes, you have to be independent and seek out your professors. But when you do seek them out, you get incredible individualized attention." One undergrad sums it up like this: "BC's strength is a mix of everything. It may not be an Ivy League school in academics or win national championships everywhere in NCAA athletics, but it is a 'jack of all trades' when it comes to academics, athletics, art, and social activity."

Life

There is a "real spirit of volunteerism and giving back to the community [that] is one of BC's greatest strengths," many students here tell us, reporting that "there are about a million volunteer groups on campus, as well as a bunch of immersion trips to different places, the most renowned of which is the Appalachia group trip." Students here "really care about the world outside of Chestnut Hill. In a way, even the notion of studying abroad has turned into a question of 'How can I help people while there?' BC's Jesuit mission is contagious." Not all extracurricular life at BC is so altruistic, however; students here love to have fun in "the greatest location of any college ever! We are on the T [train], so we can get into the city of Boston whenever we like, but we are in suburbia so we can relax without all of the gimmicks of city life." Undergrads love to explore Boston, a city with "tons of great museums, historical sights, restaurants, and a lot of great concerts," that also happens to be "such a big college town. It's easy to meet kids that go to BU, Harvard, Emerson, Northeastern, or any of the other universities in the area." Closer to campus, BC has "great sports. Our football team has won six bowl games in a row and basketball is, at this writing, playing Georgetown in the men's NCAA Tournament. The ice hockey team is consistently ranked high nationally," and students turn out to support their Eagles in both men's and women's athletics.

Student Body

Boston magazine once described the BC student body as "a J. Crew catalogue with a slight hangover," and while students protest that "there are a number of students who do not conform to such a vision of the student body," they also admit that "there are a lot of preppy people at our school. Girls usually wear skirts and Uggs (unless it's freezing out, but it has to be very, very cold), and boys usually wear jeans and t-shirts or collared cotton shirts." And yes, "the typical BC student is White, Catholic, usually from the Northeast, who probably had family who went to BC," but with 9,000 undergrads, "We have students from all sorts of backgrounds, religions, sexual orientations." BC students tend to be extremely ambitious; they are "those super-involved people in high school who were three-season team captains, class president, and straight-A students. [They] have carried over that focus and determination into college."

FAX: 617-552-0798 • FINANCIAL AID: 800-294-0294 • E-MAIL: UGADMIS@BC.EDU • WEBSITE: WWW.BC.EDU

THE PRINCETON REVIEW SAYS

Admissions

Very important factors considered include: Academic GPA, rigor of secondary school record, standardized test scores. *Important factors considered include:* Class rank, application essay, recommendation(s), alumni/ae relation, character/personal qualities, religious affiliation/commitment, talent/ability, volunteer work. *Other factors considered include:* Extracurricular activities, first generation, racial/ethnic status, work experience. SAT and SAT Subject Tests or ACT required; ACT with Writing component required. TOEFL required of all international applicants. High school diploma is required and GED is accepted. *Academic units recommended:* 4 English, 4 mathematics, 4 science, (4 science labs), 4 foreign language, 4 social studies.

Financial Aid

The Princeton Review suggests that all financial aid forms be submitted as soon as possible after January 1. Federal Work-Study Program available. Institutional employment available. Off-campus job opportunities are excellent.

The Inside Word

BC is one of many selective schools that eschew set admissions formulae. While a challenging high school curriculum and strong test scores are essential for any serious candidate, the college seeks students who are passionate and make connections between academic pursuits and extracurricular activities. The application process should reveal a distinct, mature voice and a student whose interest in education goes beyond the simple desire to earn an A.

THE SCHOOL SAYS "..."

From The Admissions Office

"Boston College students achieve at the highest levels with honors including two Rhodes scholarship winners, nine Fulbrights, and one each for Marshall, Goldwater, Madison, and Truman Postgraduate Fellowship Programs. Junior Year Abroad and Scholar of the College Program offer students flexibility within the curriculum. Facilities opened in the past 10 years include: the Merkert Chemistry Center, Higgins Hall (housing the Biology and Physics departments), three new residence halls, the Yawkey Athletics Center, the Vanderslice Commons Dining Hall, the Hillside Cafe, and a state-of-the-art library. Students enjoy the vibrant location in Chestnut Hill with easy access to the cultural and historical richness of Boston.

"Boston College requires freshman applicants to take the SAT with writing (or the ACT with the writing exam required). Two SAT Subject Tests are required; students are encouraged to take Subject Tests in fields in which they excel."

SELECTIVITY

Admissions Rating	97
# of applicants	28,850
% of applicants accepted	27
% of acceptees attending	29
# accepting a place on wait list	2,000
% admitted from wait list	5

FRESHMAN PROFILE

Range SAT Critical Reading	610–710
Range SAT Math	630–720
Range SAT Writing	620–710
Minimum paper TOEFL	600
Minimum computer TOEFL	250
% graduated top 10% of class	80
% graduated top 25% of class	95
% graduated top 50% of class	99

DEADLINES

Early action	
Deadline	11/1
Notification	12/25
Regular	
Deadline	1/1
Notification	4/15
Nonfall registration?	yes

APPLICANTS ALSO LOOK AT
AND OFTEN PREFER
Harvard College
Georgetown University
University of Pennsylvania
AND SOMETIMES PREFER
New York University
University of Michigan—Ann Arbor
University of Southern California
University of California—Los Angeles
Tufts University
AND RARELY PREFER
Boston University

FINANCIAL FACTS

Financial Aid Rating	93
Annual tuition	$37,410
Room and board	$11,610
Required fees	$540
Books and supplies	$750
% frosh rec. any financial aid	70
% UG rec. any financial aid	70

BOSTON UNIVERSITY

121 BAY STATE ROAD, BOSTON, MA 02215 • ADMISSIONS: 617-353-2300 • FAX: 617-353-9695

STUDENTS SAY ". . ."

Academics

Boston University's greatest strengths, students tell us, lie in "the choices students are granted. Do you want to be an alterna-teen or a jock? Do you want to drink or go to shows? Do you want to study ballet, bio, or film? Do you want a scenic riverside location or an energetic urban one? You can have all of the above at BU, which is both overwhelming and exciting." A "top-notch educational institution in the middle of one of the best college cities in the world," BU is the perfect place for independent students anxious to explore all options. As one student puts it, "BU not only allowed me access to over 65 majors in my school, the College of Arts and Sciences (I tried out astronomy, international relations, psychology, and anthropology before deciding on anthro/religion and French), but also majors in other schools (I took two drama classes in the College of Fine Arts)." Many are drawn here by the "top-notch pre-professional programs" that include "an excellent communications program," a "great management program," and "a great biology program." Students note that "BU fosters independence: Students can do whatever they want; they just have to have the motivation." Academics "are very, very rigorous," with more than a few students hypothesizing the existence of an unwritten "grade deflation" policy, which, understandably, they regard as unfair.

Life

BU "doesn't have a campus in a traditional sense, and that takes some getting used to. It also means that most of your social life isn't centered on the university," but more on the city itself. To many here, "Boston is the perfect city. Easy to walk around; not as big and crazy as NYC; and plenty to do on the weekends besides party," such as "walking all the way downtown, passing through all the big entertainment areas, or walking over to Cambridge and Central Square or down the river and over the footbridge to Harvard Square . . . A short T-ride puts you in the North End with its Italian food heaven. If you can't find what you're looking for within 20 minutes of campus, you just haven't looked hard enough." Parties typically occur off campus "since the university has a fairly strict alcohol and drug policy which RAs monitor closely. The off-campus parties are typically big (100-plus) and, of course, have beer and cheap liquor more than accessible. The bar and club scene is also big, with Lansdowne Street only a few blocks away, so going out to drink and dance on the weekends is also pretty common. . . . Because cabs are everywhere, getting around the city, even when [you are] drunk and [it is] late at night, is pretty simple." For those who prefer to stick with school activities, "The school makes a real effort to get students involved and to provide activities for us, albeit through our yearly undergraduate student fee. They have comedy clubs, student concerts, several interesting lectures for every interest imaginable, etc."

Student Body

The undergraduate student body at BU is 16,000 strong, so "there is no 'typical' BU student." Students here "tend to be liberal and politically aware, but other than that, one of the most desirable aspects of BU is that there are no 'types.' Because BU has strong athletics, as well as strong programs in the arts, there is a nice mix . . . and everyone seems to get along well enough. This diversity . . . adds an amazing dynamic to class discussions. This is one of the most valuable aspects of a BU education." That said, many here tell us that "a solid majority of people are very rich, well dressed, and reasonably snobby." New England prep-school grads are well represented, but so, too, are a broad array of states and nations.

FINANCIAL AID: 617-353-2965 • E-MAIL: ADMISSIONS@BU.EDU • WEBSITE: WWW.BU.EDU

THE PRINCETON REVIEW SAYS

Admissions

Very important factors considered include: Rigor of secondary school record. *Important factors considered include:* Class rank, application essay, academic GPA, recommendation(s), standardized test scores. *Other factors considered include:* Alumni/ae relation, character/personal qualities, extracurricular activities, first generation, geographical residence, level of applicant's interest, racial/ethnic status, state residency, volunteer work, work experience. SAT and SAT Subject Tests or ACT required; ACT with Writing component required. TOEFL required of all international applicants. High school diploma is required and GED is accepted. *Academic units required:* 4 English, 3 mathematics, 3 science, (3 science labs), 2 foreign language, 3 social studies. *Academic units recommended:* 4 English, 4 mathematics, 4 science, (4 science labs), 4 foreign language, 4 social studies.

Financial Aid

Students should submit: FAFSA, CSS/Financial Aid PROFILE, state aid form, noncustodial PROFILE, business/farm supplement. Regular filing deadline is 2/15. The Princeton Review suggests that all financial aid forms be submitted as soon as possible after January 1. *Need-based scholarships/grants offered:* Federal Pell, SEOG, state scholarships/grants, private scholarships, the school's own gift aid. *Loan aid offered:* Direct Subsidized Stafford, Direct Unsubsidized Stafford, Direct PLUS, Federal Perkins, state loans Applicants will be notified of awards on a rolling basis beginning in early April.

The Inside Word

BU has grown more selective over the years; the school added SAT subject exams to its admissions requirements in 2005, a solid indicator that the school is now looking for more ways to eliminate applicants from its pool. Requirements and admissions standards are somewhat more lenient for the College of General Studies, a 2-year program that takes students right up to the point at which they declare a major and enter one of the university's 8 other undergraduate schools. Students in the College of General Studies are admitted as four-year degree candidates and continue as juniors in one of the other schools or colleges, with no new application required.

THE SCHOOL SAYS "..."

From The Admissions Office

"Boston University (BU) is a private teaching and research institution with a strong emphasis on undergraduate education. We are committed to providing the highest level of teaching excellence, and fulfillment of this pledge is our highest priority. Boston University has 10 undergraduate schools and colleges offering more than 250 major and minor areas of concentration. Students may choose from programs of study in areas as diverse as biochemistry, theater, physical therapy, elementary education, broadcast journalism, international relations, business, and computer engineering. BU has an international student body, with students from every state and more than 100 countries. In addition, opportunities to study abroad exist through over 70 semester-long programs, spanning 33 cities and 22 countries on six continents.

"BU requires freshman applicants for Fall 2008 to take the SAT, and two SAT Subject Tests. Students are encouraged to take subject tests in fields in which they excel. Students may submit the results of the ACT (with the Writing section) in lieu of the SAT and SAT Subject Tests."

SELECTIVITY

Admissions Rating	94
# of applicants	33,390
% of applicants accepted	56
% of acceptees attending	22
# accepting a place on wait list	1,944
% admitted from wait list	59
# of early decision applicants	1,074
% accepted early decision	37

FRESHMAN PROFILE

Range SAT Critical Reading	580–680
Range SAT Math	590–690
Range SAT Writing	590–670
Range ACT Composite	25–30
Minimum paper TOEFL	550
Minimum computer TOEFL	215
Average HS GPA	3.45
% graduated top 10% of class	51
% graduated top 25% of class	85
% graduated top 50% of class	100

DEADLINES

Early decision	
Deadline	11/1
Notification	12/15
Regular	
Deadline	1/1
Nonfall registration?	yes

APPLICANTS ALSO LOOK AT

AND OFTEN PREFER
The George Washington University
New York University
University of Southern California

AND SOMETIMES PREFER
Cornell University
Boston College

AND RARELY PREFER
Northeastern University
University of Massachusetts—Amherst

FINANCIAL FACTS

Financial Aid Rating	82
Annual tuition	$36,450
Room and board	$11,418
Required fees	$510
Books and supplies	$860
% frosh rec. need-based scholarship or grant aid	41
% UG rec. need-based scholarship or grant aid	39
% frosh rec. non-need-based scholarship or grant aid	17
% UG rec. non-need-based scholarship or grant aid	11
% frosh rec. need-based self-help aid	40
% UG rec. need-based self-help aid	38
% frosh rec. athletic scholarships	2
% UG rec. athletic scholarships	2
% frosh rec. any financial aid	46
% UG rec. any financial aid	42
% UG borrow to pay for school	60
Average cumulative indebtedness	$24,939

BOWDOIN COLLEGE

5000 COLLEGE STATION, BOWDOIN COLLEGE, BRUNSWICK, ME 04011-8441 • ADMISSIONS: 207-725-3100 • FAX: 207-725-3101

STUDENTS SAY "..."

Academics

Highly selective Bowdoin College is all about providing an "excellent liberal arts education in a supportive, small community" in "a beautiful part of the country." Undergrads cite Bowdoin's "intelligent" and "diverse" student body, "absolutely top-notch" professors, and "challenging, fascinating academic program that allows you to explore all your areas of interest" as particularly deserving of praise. Students here reap the benefits of "a close-knit community of learners, teachers, and leaders pursuing academics, athletics, music, art, clubs, and fun with relentless positive enthusiasm" in "a very nurturing and safe environment, [where] you can develop without worrying about stuff you don't need to worry about, such as money, food, housing, etc." Standout programs include environmental studies, neuroscience, foreign language, and the English and education departments which students describe as "excellent, bar none." The workload at Bowdoin "is just a few steps shy from unmanageable, which is good" because it forces you to "not only do your work," but "to do it carefully." Students also appreciate a faculty that is "truly interested in learning everyone's name," and "will stay hours after review sessions" until the students grasp the concepts. "They challenge you, and push you to go beyond just the books." Great facilities include the Career Planning Center, Writing Center, Baldwin Center for Academic Development, Counseling Center, and administrative offices. The cherry on the sundae? "Excellent alumni networking."

Life

Students love how Bowdoin "embraces the intellectual experience in a balanced, healthy way, so that its students are generally very happy. There is an awareness that in college, learning comes from everywhere, so there is a real effort by the Bowdoin administration as well as Bowdoin students to bring speakers, events, and entertainment to the campus so that students can learn in every way possible." Extracurriculars are part of the constant learning; students here "are always doing at least one if not 10 things at a time." Physical activity is part of the mix; many students participate in Outing Club events, hiking, whitewater kayaking, and rafting at nearby parks, and "It seems like almost everyone is on a sports team, so during the week most people find a release there." Students tell us that "on the weekends, there is a lot of partying (and with that comes a lot of alcohol)," but "It's not excessive." Plus, the "alcohol policies are also pretty sweet—as long as everyone can be responsible and things are not out of control, security does not want to get anyone in trouble," and "a safe ride system" provides free rides home to intoxicated students for free. Those who don't drink tell us "There is plenty of music at night" and "Brunswick is great for a concert, coffee shop, or bowling." Gourmands, take note: "Bowdoin food is the best!"

Student Body

While "a fair amount of preppy kids" congregate on Bowdoin's campus, "There are all types of people here, providing an interesting mix of personalities, backgrounds, and interactions." Personality types "range from typical straight-out-of-prep-school preppy individuals to crusty hippies to jocks to artsy kids." "Bowdoin students either wear Chacos or Polos with their collars popped. Some even alternate between these two personalities." They also tend to be "multifaceted and multilayered; they are great intellectuals, as well as athletes, political activists, dancers, and community leaders. No one here is involved in just academic activities." Students say everyone here is "down to earth and very passionate about something—the environment, politics, science, the welfare of goats in Chile, etc." Despite being "extremely intelligent" and "highly motivated," Bowdoin undergrads "are not fiercely competitive or grade-grubby," and "Everyone gets along well."

FINANCIAL AID: 207-725-3273 • E-MAIL: ADMISSIONS@BOWDOIN.EDU • WEBSITE: WWW.BOWDOIN.EDU

THE PRINCETON REVIEW SAYS

Admissions

Very important factors considered include: Class rank, application essay, academic GPA, recommendation(s), rigor of secondary school record, character/personal qualities, extracurricular activities, talent/ability. *Important factors considered include:* Standardized test scores, alumni/ae relation, first generation. *Other factors considered include:* Geographical residence, interview, racial/ethnic status, state residency, High school diploma is required and GED is not accepted. *Academic units recommended:* 4 English, 4 mathematics, 4 science, (3 science labs), 4 foreign language, 4 social studies.

Financial Aid

Students should submit: FAFSA, CSS/Financial Aid PROFILE, noncustodial PROFILE, business/farm supplement. Regular filing deadline is 2/15. The Princeton Review suggests that all financial aid forms be submitted as soon as possible after January 1. *Need-based scholarships/grants offered:* Federal Pell, SEOG, state scholarships/grants, private scholarships, the school's own gift aid. *Loan aid offered:* FFEL Subsidized Stafford, FFEL Unsubsidized Stafford, FFEL PLUS, Federal Perkins, state loans. Bowdoin will replace loans with grants for all students beginning in Fall 2008. Applicants will be notified of awards on or about 4/5. Federal Work-Study Program available. Institutional employment available. Off-campus job opportunities are good.

The Inside Word

Standardized test scores are optional at Bowdoin, but if you aced the SAT or ACT you should definitely report your scores. The school will almost certainly look at them; in the spring of 2006, the Dean of Admissions at Bowdoin said as much to *The New York Times*, explaining that he considers test scores helpful. He noted that high school transcripts are difficult to compare, especially in light of grade inflation at many schools, and that the provenance of student essays is often uncertain.

THE SCHOOL SAYS "..."

From The Admissions Office

"A liberal arts education at Bowdoin isn't about being small and safe—it's about having the support to take surprising risks. That means caring more about the questions than giving the right answers. Discovering you're good at something you didn't think was your strength. Making connections where none appears to exist. Bowdoin's curriculum offers a bold blueprint for liberal education designed to inspire students to become world citizens with acute sensitivity to the social and natural worlds. Its interdisciplinary focus encourages students to make connections among subjects, to discover disciplines that excite their imaginations, and to develop keen skills for addressing the challenges of a changing world.

"A Bowdoin education is best summed up by 'The Offer of The College':"
    To be at home in all lands and all ages;
    To count Nature a familiar acquaintance,
    And Art an intimate friend;
    To gain a standard for the appreciation of others' work
    And the criticism of your own;
    To carry the keys of the world's library in your pocket,
    And feel its resources behind you in whatever task you undertake;
    To make hosts of friends...
    Who are to be leaders in all walks of life;
    To lose yourself in generous enthusiasms
    And cooperate with others for common ends —
    This is the offer of the college for the best four years of your life."
                    Adapted from the original 'Offer of the College'
                        by William DeWitt Hyde
            President of Bowdoin College 1885–1917"

SELECTIVITY

Admissions Rating	99
# of applicants	5,961
% of applicants accepted	19
% of acceptees attending	42
# of early decision applicants	710
% accepted early decision	30

FRESHMAN PROFILE

Range SAT Critical Reading	650–740
Range SAT Math	650–730
Range SAT Writing	650–730
Range ACT Composite	29–33
Average HS GPA	3.8
% graduated top 10% of class	85
% graduated top 25% of class	99
% graduated top 50% of class	100

DEADLINES

Early decision	
Deadline	11/15
Notification	12/31
Regular	
Deadline	1/1
Notification	4/5
Nonfall registration?	no

FINANCIAL FACTS

Financial Aid Rating	98
Annual tuition	$35,990
Room and board	$9,890
Required fees	$380
Books and supplies	$800
% frosh rec. need-based scholarship or grant aid	41
% UG rec. need-based scholarship or grant aid	43
% frosh rec. need-based self-help aid	38
% UG rec. need-based self-help aid	39
% frosh rec. any financial aid	45
% UG rec. any financial aid	46
% UG borrow to pay for school	48
Average cumulative indebtedness	$18,300

BRADLEY UNIVERSITY

1501 WEST BRADLEY AVENUE, PEORIA, IL 61625 • ADMISSIONS: 309-677-1000 • FAX: 309-677-2797

STUDENTS SAY ". . ."

Academics

Offering "the variety and opportunities of a large school with the personal interaction that only a small university can offer," Bradley University is "the perfect size," a place "large enough to provide students with a variety of choices but small enough that there is not much difficulty getting into the classes that you want to take." Small class sizes "allow the students to get to know the professors on a personal as well as professional level," creating a "family environment" reinforced by the fact that "the faculty is more focused on teaching and less focused on research," and that "all classes are taught by professors" and not by teaching assistants. The Bradley approach yields some impressive results: The school boasts excellent placement rates for its graduates in medical, dental, and natural science graduate programs. Students tell us that Bradley also has a "good graphic design program," "a great engineering school," and is "an excellent school for education majors." Bradley's "strong College of Communications" benefits from top-notch facilities at its Global Communications Center, which is "quite high-tech with good computers and even their own studio." Academic demands at Bradley "are pretty straightforward"; professors "are demanding and expect students to do a lot of work and work hard," in return for which students receive "lots of academic opportunities . . . as long as you take the time to discover them." Bradley's administration "is extremely open to student suggestions. Although not all suggestions are adopted, the administration will listen to any and all concerns."

Life

For many at Bradley, "Social life is focused on fraternities and sororities, but these groups are far more open here than at other places." Others find different social outlets; students report that "some split exists between the three major social groups on campus (Greeks, residence hall staff, and athletes) but each offers its own unique opportunities. Any student wanting to get involved on campus will not struggle for opportunities." The Bradley campus "always has things going on, as do our student organizations. We go to concerts (like Black Eyed Peas, Emerson Drive, etc.), listen to comedians, participate in all-school philanthropies (like Relay for Life, Dance Marathon, Habitat for Humanity,, etc.), on campus. Those are always well attended and usually really cheap." While "Drinking plays a big role in the campus social life . . . students can find sober social opportunities if they want them." Men's basketball is popular. Overall, "People do a pretty good job balancing social life and school life" here. Students give hometown Peoria middling grades, warning that "if you go very far from the 'Bradley streets,' you'll find yourself in a tough neighborhood."

Student Body

The typical Bradley student "is from the Chicago/St. Louis suburbs or from a small town in Central Illinois. . . . Students tend to be upper-middle class, but there are many exceptions. Many students seem to identify as Catholics but don't practice, and there are also large numbers of Jewish and Protestant students. The campus is very White, although the university is taking steps to attempt to change that." Most "are very intelligent. They worked hard in high school and they have a drive and ambition to be here." Yet, despite that drive, they are generally "jeans and t-shirt-wearing people, very relaxed, and not super-stressed out." They tend to be "friendly, outgoing, and active in organizations or Greek life."

FINANCIAL AID: 309-677-3089 • E-MAIL: ADMISSIONS@BRADLEY.EDU • WEBSITE: WWW.BRADLEY.EDU

THE PRINCETON REVIEW SAYS

Admissions

Very important factors considered include: Academic GPA, rigor of secondary school record. *Important factors considered include:* Class rank, standardized test scores. *Other factors considered include:* Application essay, recommendation(s), alumni/ae relation, character/personal qualities, extracurricular activities, geographical residence, interview, level of applicant's interest, racial/ethnic status, talent/ability, volunteer work, work experience. SAT or ACT required; TOEFL required of all international applicants. High school diploma is required and GED is accepted. *Academic units required:* 4 English, 3 mathematics, 2 science, (2 science labs), 2 social studies. *Academic units recommended:* 5 English, 4 mathematics, 3 science, (3 science labs), 2 foreign language, 3 social studies, 2 history.

Financial Aid

Students should submit: FAFSA The Princeton Review suggests that all financial aid forms be submitted as soon as possible after January 1. *Need-based scholarships/grants offered:* Federal Pell, SEOG, state scholarships/grants, private scholarships, the school's own gift aid. *Loan aid offered:* Direct Subsidized Stafford, Direct Unsubsidized Stafford, Direct PLUS, FFEL PLUS, Federal Perkins, Federal Nursing Federal Work-Study Program available.

The Inside Word

Bradley continues to be a regional school, with the vast majority of students originating from Illinois. It would undoubtedly love to broaden its geographic demographics, so the school presents an opportunity for out-of-staters seeking to attend an excellent university without having to endure a grueling admissions process. Above average students should find that gaining admission here is a relatively painless experience.

THE SCHOOL SAYS " . . ."

From The Admissions Office

"Unlike many smaller private colleges, Bradley offers the academic variety of more than 100 undergraduate and 30 graduate programs of study. In addition to the traditional liberal arts and sciences, academic programs include business, communications, education, engineering, fine and performing arts, and health sciences. Unique programs include entrepreneurship, multimedia, and a doctorate program in physical therapy. While students have the academic choices of a larger university, they also have the guidance and mentoring of faculty. Unlike many larger institutions, the Bradley academic experience happens in faculty-taught classes that average just 23 students. One-on-one interaction with professionals is the expectation at Bradley.

"Beyond a great academic experience, what really makes Bradley exceptional is campus life. Bradley students are involved in more than 220 student organizations, including more than 50 dedicated to student leadership and community service. Integration of career development is central to the Bradley experience. One measurable outcome of this career development integration is that 96 percent of graduates begin work, graduate school, or other postgraduate experiences within 6 months of graduation.

"The Peoria area is the largest metropolitan region in Illinois south of Chicago and is home to more than 360,000 residents. The sizeable city provides ample opportunities for internships, practicums, cooperative education, and volunteer experiences.

"In summary, the Bradley experience is unlike most other universities. A Bradley student will experience a blend of quality academics, focused career preparation, extensive activities, and leadership opportunities.

"Bradley requires freshman applicants to submit scores from either the old or the new SAT. Students may also choose to submit scores from the ACT, with or without the Writing component, in lieu of the SAT."

SELECTIVITY

Admissions Rating	77
# of applicants	4,612
% of applicants accepted	83
% of acceptees attending	28
# accepting a place on wait list	36
% admitted from wait list	53

FRESHMAN PROFILE

Range SAT Critical Reading	510–610
Range SAT Math	530–610
Range ACT Composite	23–27
Minimum paper TOEFL	550
Minimum computer TOEFL	213
% graduated top 10% of class	28
% graduated top 25% of class	65
% graduated top 50% of class	93

DEADLINES

Priority	3/1
Notification	rolling
Nonfall registration?	yes

APPLICANTS ALSO LOOK AT

AND OFTEN PREFER
Purdue University—West Lafayette
Illinois Wesleyan University
University of Illinois at Urbana—Champaign

AND SOMETIMES PREFER
Marquette University
Loyola University of Chicago
Augustana College (SD)

AND RARELY PREFER
University of Illinois at Chicago
Illinois State University
Northern Illinois University

FINANCIAL FACTS

Financial Aid Rating	73
Annual tuition	$21,200
Room and board	$7,050
Required fees	$178
Books and supplies	$500
% frosh rec. need-based scholarship or grant aid	63
% UG rec. need-based scholarship or grant aid	67
% frosh rec. non-need-based scholarship or grant aid	11
% UG rec. non-need-based scholarship or grant aid	8
% frosh rec. need-based self-help aid	55
% UG rec. need-based self-help aid	51
% frosh rec. athletic scholarships	1
% UG rec. athletic scholarships	1
% frosh rec. any financial aid	96
% UG rec. any financial aid	92
Average cumulative indebtedness	$15,209

BRANDEIS UNIVERSITY

415 South Street, MS003, Waltham, MA 02454 • Admissions: 781-736-3500 • Fax: 781-736-3536

CAMPUS LIFE
Quality of Life Rating	80
Fire Safety Rating	60*
Green Rating	60*
Type of school	private
Environment	city

STUDENTS
Total undergrad enrollment	3,203
% male/female	44/56
% from out of state	75
% from public high school	72
% live on campus	77
% African American	3
% Asian	9
% Caucasian	57
% Hispanic	4
% international	7
# of countries represented	55

SURVEY SAYS . . .
No one cheats
Great library
Students are friendly
Campus feels safe
Student publications are popular
Political activism is popular

ACADEMICS
Academic Rating	88
Calendar	semester
Student/faculty ratio	8:1
Profs interesting rating	82
Profs accessible rating	82
Most common reg class size	10–19 students

MOST POPULAR MAJORS
biology/biological sciences
psychology
economics

STUDENTS SAY ". . ."

Academics

Home to "lots of 'pre-somethings' trying to figure out if that 'something' is right for them," Brandeis University is "a good jumping-off point for those looking to go into medicine or law." Boasting "a very good liberal arts education," Brandeis also provides plenty of alternatives to those who start down the "pre-something" path only to find that it's not for them. Even those who stay the course appreciate the "large variety of options"; as one student explains, "Brandeis is very academically stimulating and has many interesting courses, professors who make themselves available outside of class, and teaching assistants who are very helpful." Aspiring doctors are drawn here by a "stellar" neuroscience department that gives undergraduates "the experience of graduate students as far as research is concerned," in addition to "a very high acceptance rate at medical schools." Other strong programs include psychology, music, economics, political science, and history. Students agree that most professors are "passionate about what they teach." Classes "are generally small, which puts pressure on you to come prepared," and there is "a fair amount of class discussion, which can be great or awful." Students are ready to be engaged in class, as they are typically "friendly and talkative. An intense philosophical discussion is more common at Brandeis than drunken boorishness."

Life

Brandeis boasts "plenty of performance-based clubs (theater, musical, improv comedy, sketch comedy, dance), community-service organizations, activist clubs, ethnic clubs, religious clubs, political clubs, independent sports clubs, and also clubs just for fun, like the hookah club. There are so many opportunities to be involved here," and students "take [their] extracurriculars just as seriously as [their] studies, and tend to excel in both." Students also love their access to Boston, noting that "a free shuttle runs us to and from the city Thursdays through Sundays, and the commuter rail stop on campus." The proximity of Boston helps offset the fact that "there is really nothing to do in Waltham. There is a movie theater, and some restaurants, and bars, but that is about it. Proximity to [Boston College] and Bentley is nice, however." Students say the social scene at Brandeis "is somewhat lacking. If you are looking for big sporting events with lots of spirit or parties with lots of people, you won't like Brandeis." Parties "don't ever fall into your lap at Brandeis; you have to look for them." For some, this is a plus; as one student writes, "I like the school because if you want a quiet Friday night with board games and old movies, it's very easy to do. People won't judge you or pressure you into drinking. But on Saturday when you're ready for some fun, you have to do a little digging."

Student Body

Brandeis has long been a popular destination for Jewish students. About 40 percent of the student population (undergrad and grad) is Jewish, and undergrads tell us that "there are a lot of orthodox Jews here, more than at your average college. Yet, there are also a lot of non-religious students, observant Muslims, and Christians. So the school just teaches us to recognize each others' religions," and "You never feel like your fellow students are judging you." A "nice-sized international community" also "helps diversify the school." Many here tend to be "pretty socially awkward, and kind of an overachiever, but generally well-intentioned and sweet." One student told us that students tend to be "quirky, prone to traditionally nerdy pursuits, and very friendly. At Brandeis, weird is normal." Everyone works hard here "because they want to do well," and students "spend most of their time studying."

FINANCIAL AID: 781-736-3700 • E-MAIL: SENDINFO@BRANDEIS.EDU • WEBSITE: WWW.BRANDEIS.EDU

THE PRINCETON REVIEW SAYS

Admissions

Very important factors considered include: Class rank, academic GPA, rigor of secondary school record, standardized test scores, character/personal qualities, level of applicant's interest. *Important factors considered include:* Application essay, recommendation(s), extracurricular activities, first generation, talent/ability, volunteer work, work experience. *Other factors considered include:* alumni/ae relation, geographical residence, interview, racial/ethnic status, SAT or ACT required; ACT with Writing component required. TOEFL required of all international applicants. High school diploma is required and GED is accepted. *Academic units recommended:* 4 English, 3 mathematics, 1 science, (1 science labs), 3 foreign language, 1 history, 4 academic electives.

Financial Aid

Students should submit: CSS/Financial Aid PROFILE, FAFSA, noncustodial PROFILE, business/farm supplement. The Princeton Review suggests that all financial aid forms be submitted as soon as possible after January 1. *Need-based scholarships/grants offered:* Federal Pell, SEOG, state scholarships/grants, private scholarships, the school's own gift aid. *Loan aid offered:* Direct Subsidized Stafford, Direct Unsubsidized Stafford, Direct PLUS, Federal Perkins, state loans, college/university loans from institutional funds. Federal Work-Study Program available. Off-campus job opportunities are fair.

The Inside Word

Brandeis requires one of two combinations of standardized test scores: the SAT or the ACT with Writing component. Most students choose the ACT with Writing option, but if you've already taken all your SATs and aced them, submit those scores instead. Brandeis is often looked at as a safety school for students applying to Ivies; as the Ivies now routinely reject many highly qualified applicants, admission to Brandeis is extremely competitive despite its safety school reputation.

THE SCHOOL SAYS ". . ."

From The Admissions Office

"Education at Brandeis is personal, combining the intimacy of a small liberal arts college and the intellectual power of a large research university. Classes are small and are taught by professors, 98 percent of whom hold the highest degree in their fields. They give students personal attention in state-of-the-art resources, giving them the tools to succeed in a variety of postgraduate endeavors.

"This vibrant, freethinking, intellectual university was founded in 1948. Brandeis University reflects the values of the first Jewish Supreme Court Justice Louis Brandeis, which are passion for learning, commitment to social justice, respect for creativity and diversity, and concern for the world.

"Brandeis has an ideal location on the commuter rail nine miles west of Boston; state-of-the-art sports facilities; and internships that complement interests in law, medicine, government, finance, business, and the arts. Brandeis offers generous university scholarships and need-based financial aid that can be renewed for 4 years.

"Brandeis requires that students send official scores for the new SAT or ACT with Writing in place of all SATs. Students for whom English is not their first language should take the TOEFL (Test of English as a Foreign Language)."

SELECTIVITY

Admissions Rating	**97**
# of applicants	7,562
% of applicants accepted	34
% of acceptees attending	27
# accepting a place on wait list	414
% admitted from wait list	25
# of early decision applicants	359
% accepted early decision	57

FRESHMAN PROFILE

Range SAT Critical Reading	630–720
Range SAT Math	650–740
Range ACT Composite	28–32
Minimum paper TOEFL	600
Minimum computer TOEFL	250
Minimum web-based TOEFL	100
Average HS GPA	3.8
% graduated top 10% of class	71
% graduated top 25% of class	96
% graduated top 50% of class	100

DEADLINES

Early decision I	
Deadline	11/15
Notification	12/15
Early decision II	
Deadline	1/1
Notification	2/1
Regular	
Deadline	1/15
Notification	4/1
Nonfall registration?	yes

FINANCIAL FACTS

Financial Aid Rating	**81**
Annual tuition	$34,566
Room and board	$9,908
Required fees	$1,136
Books and supplies	$700
% frosh rec. need-based scholarship or grant aid	52
% UG rec. need-based scholarship or grant aid	45
% frosh rec. non-need-based scholarship or grant aid	8
% UG rec. non-need-based scholarship or grant aid	5
% frosh rec. need-based self-help aid	41
% UG rec. need-based self-help aid	40
% frosh rec. any financial aid	53
% UG rec. any financial aid	47
% UG borrow to pay for school	74
Average cumulative indebtedness	$22,381

BRIGHAM YOUNG UNIVERSITY (UT)

A-153 ASB, Provo, UT 84602-1110 • Admissions: 801-422-2507 • Fax: 801-422-0005

CAMPUS LIFE

Quality of Life Rating	**98**
Fire Safety Rating	**63**
Green Rating	**60***
Type of school	private
Affiliation	Church of Jesus Christ
	of Latter-day Saints
Environment	city

STUDENTS

Total undergrad enrollment	30,873
% male/female	51/49
% from out of state	61
% live on campus	11
% Asian	3
% Caucasian	86
% Hispanic	3
% Native American	1
% international	4
# of countries represented	121

SURVEY SAYS . . .

Students are very religious
Very little hard liquor
(Almost) no one smokes
Very little drug use

ACADEMICS

Academic Rating	**83**
Calendar	semester
Student/faculty ratio	21:1
Profs interesting rating	83
Profs accessible rating	76
Most common	
reg class size	10–19 students

MOST POPULAR MAJORS

English language and literature
psychology
political science and government

STUDENTS SAY ". . ."

Academics

Brigham Young University is the academic epicenter of the Church of Jesus Christ of Latter Day Saints, more familiarly known as the Mormons, and as such it is "a place where academics and worldly knowledge are presented not from the viewpoint of the liberal world, but rather in the light of the gospel of Jesus Christ. Materials are taught with a conservative view; often the doctrine of the Church of Jesus Christ is discussed (even in classes like political science), and many classes begin with an opening prayer, while the professor is addressed as 'Brother' or 'Sister.'" The coupling of this unique worldview with tremendous resources results in "an awesome place for people of similar values and morals to be together." "The school is the bottomless toolbox that holds every tool for every task, from finding a beautiful spouse to providing the faculties and facilities to be successful in any pursuit," students say. Beyond that, you also "get a great education" that "mixes secular and religious edification all in one swoop." Many here rave about the foreign language programs (an essential component of LDS education, as nearly half of all students perform a two-year mission, many serving overseas), the business school, pre-law programs, and the engineering program. The school has "many programs in place to enhance campus learning through off-campus experiences, such as field studies, semesters abroad, and grant monies for research." A highly regarded honor code "ensures that everyone sticks to very high morals and really improves the quality of character of every person, as well as provides tons of opportunities (sports, parties, dances, games, etc.) to have fun within morally acceptable boundaries."

Life

With over 30,000 students, the BYU campus would constitute a decent-sized town even without the surrounding community of Provo. Accordingly, the campus provides many of the diversions one finds in such communities; with the caveat, of course, that the environment is "stone-cold sober, no drugs, and no caffeinated sodas on campus." It's hard not to think of the word "wholesome" when describing BYU campus life; "Intramural sports are big and playing sports just for fun like Frisbee, volleyball, and basketball are very popular." Students "go watch plays/concerts at the Fine Arts Center on campus, watch a movie at a dollar theater, go dancing off-campus on weekends, or attend club activities on Tuesdays," and "there is always some kind of church social. It is hard to be doing nothing." Most of all, "Everyone dates. Everyone is trying to get married, so single dates are very common. They usually consist of bowling, going out to eat, seeing a movie, or doing goofy free stuff—rolling down grass hills, playing board games, making cookies, etc." BYU "really emphasizes service," so students "really try to go out of their way and help others," and "many students at BYU participate in international volunteer programs and go on missions." What'd we tell you? Wholesome, right?

Student Body

"Because of the nature of BYU as a private institution run by a religious group, the school typically attracts a lot of Latter Day Saint (Mormon) individuals," most of whom are "friendly, clean-cut, and religious," with an "emphasis placed on education and social interaction." They "never drink or smoke, work part-time, and spend weekends either at the library or trying to find someone to marry." As one student explains, "Because of our religion, many students are very preoccupied with marriage and finding their special someone. This also is hard for those of us who are not yet ready to look for a marriage partner or who don't want to start a family right away." In fact, atypical students—there are some, "usually distinguishable by the way they dress (they try to stand out)"—can find it "hard to be around this culture." Writes one, "Sometimes I get really frustrated and don't like how close minded and judgmental a lot of the students can be."

BRIGHAM YOUNG UNIVERSITY (UT)

FINANCIAL AID: 801-422-4104 • E-MAIL: ADMISSIONS@BYU.EDU • WEBSITE: WWW.BYU.EDU

THE PRINCETON REVIEW SAYS

Admissions

Very important factors considered include: Academic GPA, rigor of secondary school record, standardized test scores, character/personal qualities, interview, religious affiliation/commitment. *Important factors considered include:* Application essay, recommendation(s), extracurricular activities, racial/ethnic status, volunteer work. *Other factors considered include:* Talent/ability, work experience. ACT required; ACT with Writing component recommended. High school diploma is required and GED is accepted. *Academic units required:* 4 English, 3 mathematics, 2 science, (2 science labs), 2 foreign language, 2 history, 2 Literature or Writing. *Academic units recommended:* 4 English, 4 mathematics, 3 science, (3 science labs), 4 foreign language.

Financial Aid

Students should submit: FAFSA. The Princeton Review suggests that all financial aid forms be submitted as soon as possible after January 1. *Need-based scholarships/grants offered:* Federal Pell, state scholarships/grants, private scholarships, the school's own gift aid. *Loan aid offered:* FFEL Subsidized Stafford, FFEL Unsubsidized Stafford, FFEL PLUS, college/university loans from institutional funds. Applicants will be notified of awards on a rolling basis beginning 4/1.

The Inside Word

An applicant pool of 9,000 necessitates a reliance on numbers, especially during the first round of cuts. Much of the matchmaking done at other schools isn't necessary here, as a highly self-selecting applicant pool typically precludes those who'd make a poor fit. Still, admissions officers want to see at least respect (if not reverence) for LDS principles, without which survival here would be difficult indeed.

THE SCHOOL SAYS " . . ."

From The Admissions Office

"The mission of Brigham Young University—founded, supported, and guided by the Church of Jesus Christ of Latter-day Saints—is to assist individuals in their quest for perfection and eternal life. That assistance should provide a period of intensive learning in a stimulating setting where a commitment to excellence is expected and the full realization of human potential is pursued. All instruction, programs, and services at BYU, including a wide variety of extracurricular experiences, should make their own contribution toward the balanced development of the total person. Such a broadly prepared individual will not only be capable of meeting personal challenge and change but will also bring strength to others in the tasks of home and family life, social relationships, civic duty, and service to mankind.

"Freshman applicants for Fall 2008 classes are required to take either the new ACT (with or without the optional Writing section) or the new version of the SAT. Students may also submit scores from the old (prior to the March 2005) version of either test. Their highest composite score will be used in admissions decisions."

SELECTIVITY

Admissions Rating	91
# of applicants	9,979
% of applicants accepted	74
% of acceptees attending	77

FRESHMAN PROFILE

Range SAT Critical Reading	550–670
Range SAT Math	570–680
Range ACT Composite	25–30
Average HS GPA	3.76
% graduated top 10% of class	49
% graduated top 25% of class	83
% graduated top 50% of class	98

DEADLINES

Regular	
Deadline	2/1
Nonfall registration?	yes

FINANCIAL FACTS

Financial Aid Rating	80
Annual tuition	$3,840
Room and board	$6,460
Books and supplies	$1,170
% frosh rec. need-based scholarship or grant aid	11
% UG rec. need-based scholarship or grant aid	28
% frosh rec. non-need-based scholarship or grant aid	11
% UG rec. non-need-based scholarship or grant aid	16
% frosh rec. need-based self-help aid	6
% UG rec. need-based self-help aid	15
% frosh rec. athletic scholarships	3
% UG rec. athletic scholarships	2
% frosh rec. any financial aid	20
% UG rec. any financial aid	36
% UG borrow to pay for school	34
Average cumulative indebtedness	$13,245

BROWN UNIVERSITY

PO Box 1876, 45 Prospect Street, Providence, RI 02912 • Admissions: 401-863-2378 • Fax: 401-863-9300

CAMPUS LIFE

Quality of Life Rating	97
Fire Safety Rating	86
Green Rating	93
Type of school	private
Environment	city

STUDENTS

Total undergrad enrollment	5,813
% male/female	48/52
% from out of state	95
% from public high school	60
% live on campus	80
% in (# of) fraternities	10 (8)
% in (# of) sororities	7 (2)
% African American	7
% Asian	15
% Caucasian	49
% Hispanic	8
% Native American	1
% international	7
# of countries represented	93

SURVEY SAYS . . .
No one cheats
Students are friendly
Great off-campus food
Students are happy

ACADEMICS

Academic Rating	91
Calendar	semester
Student/faculty ratio	9:1
Profs interesting rating	88
Profs accessible rating	89
Most common	
reg class size	10–19 students

MOST POPULAR MAJORS
biology/biological sciences
history
international relations and affairs

STUDENTS SAY ". . ."

Academics

Known for its somewhat unconventional (but still highly-regarded) approaches to life and learning, Brown University remains the slightly odd man out of the Ivy League, and wouldn't have it any other way. The school's willingness to employ and support different, untested methods such as the shopping period, the first two weeks of the semester where anyone can drop into any class in order to "find out if it's something they're interested in enrolling in," or the Critical Review, a student publication that produces reviews of courses based on evaluations from students who have completed the course, is designed to treat students "like an adult" through "freedom and choice." This open-minded environment allows them "to practice passion without shame or fear of judgment," the hallmark of a Brown education. Even if a student does find themselves exploring the wrong off-the-beaten path, "there are multitudes of built-in support measures to help you succeed despite any odds." Even grades are a non-issue here, "except amongst paranoid premeds."

Professors are mostly hit with a few misses, but there are "amazing professors in every department, and they're not hard to find," it's just "up to students to find the teaching styles that work for them." "Academics at Brown are what you make of them," and even though students are diligent in their academic pursuits and feel assured they're "getting a wonderful education with the professors," most agree that their education is "really more about the unique student body and learning through active participation in other activities." The administration gets cautiously decent reviews for their accessibility and general running of the school, but scolded for getting "distracted by the long term." The president, however, is absolutely loved by students for being "an incredible person with a great vision for the school."

Life

Thinking—yes, thinking—and discussing take up a great deal of time of time at Brown. "People think about life, politics, society at large, global affairs, the state of the economy, developing countries, animals, plants, rocket science, math, poker, each other, sex, sexuality, the human experience, gender studies, what to do with our lives, etc.," says a senior anthropology major. "Most people here don't go home that often," and like any school, "there are people who go out five nights a week and people who go out five nights a semester." "Alcohol and weed are pretty embedded in campus life," and most parties are dorm room events, even though partying "never gets in the way of academics or friendship. If you don't drink/smoke, that's totally cool." There's also plenty of cultural activities, such as indie bands, student performances, jazz, swing dancing, and speakers. Themed housing (Art House, Tech House, Interfaith House) and co-ops are also popular social mediators.

Student Body

It's a pretty unique crowd here, where "athletes, preps, nerds, and everyone in between come together" because they "love learning for the sake of learning, and love Brown equally as much." "The 'mainstream' is full of people who are atypical in sense of fashion, taste in music, and academic interests," says a junior. Unsurprisingly, everyone here's "very smart," as well as "very quirky and often funny," and "a great amount are brilliant and passionate about their interests"; "Most have interesting stories to tell." People here are "curious and open about many things," which is perhaps why sexual diversity is a "strong theme" among Brown interactions and events. The overall culture "is pretty laid-back and casual" and "most of the students are friendly and mesh well with everyone."

FINANCIAL AID: 401-863-2721 • E-MAIL: ADMISSION_UNDERGRADUATE@BROWN.EDU • WEBSITE: WWW.BROWN.EDU

THE PRINCETON REVIEW SAYS

Admissions

Very important factors considered include: Rigor of secondary school record, character/personal qualities, level of applicant's interest, talent/ability. *Important factors considered include:* Class rank, application essay, academic GPA, recommendation(s), standardized test scores, extracurricular activities. *Other factors considered include:* Alumni/ae relation, first generation, geographical residence, interview, racial/ethnic status, state residency, volunteer work, work experience. SAT and SAT Subject Tests or ACT required; ACT with Writing component required. TOEFL required of all international applicants. High school diploma is required and GED is not accepted. *Academic units required:* 4 English, 3 mathematics, 3 science, (2 science labs), 3 foreign language, 2 history, 1 academic elective. *Academic units recommended:* 4 English, 4 mathematics, 4 science, (3 science labs), 4 foreign language, 2 history, 1 visual/performing arts, 1 academic elective.

Financial Aid

Students should submit: FAFSA, CSS/Financial Aid PROFILE, noncustodial PROFILE, business/farm supplement. Regular filing deadline is 2/1. The Princeton Review suggests that all financial aid forms be submitted as soon as possible after January 1. *Need-based scholarships/grants offered:* Federal Pell, SEOG, state scholarships/grants, private scholarships, the school's own gift aid. *Loan aid offered:* Direct Subsidized Stafford, Direct Unsubsidized Stafford, Direct PLUS, Federal Perkins, college/university loans from institutional funds. Applicants will be notified of awards on or about 4/1. Federal Work-Study Program available. Institutional employment available. Off-campus job opportunities are excellent.

The Inside Word

The cream of just about every crop applies to Brown. Gaining admission requires more than just a superior academic profile from high school. Some candidates, such as the sons and daughters of Brown graduates (who are admitted at virtually double the usual acceptance rate), have a better chance for admission than most others. Minority students benefit from some courtship, particularly once admitted. Ivies like to share the wealth and distribute offers of admission across a wide range of constituencies. Candidates from states that are overrepresented in the applicant pool, such as New York, have to be particularly distinguished in order to have the best chance at admission. So do those who attend high schools with many seniors applying to Brown, as it is rare for several students from any one school to be offered admission.

THE SCHOOL SAYS "..."

From The Admissions Office

"Founded in 1764, Brown is a private, coeducational, Ivy League university in which the intellectual development of undergraduate students is fostered by a dedicated faculty on a traditional New England campus.

"Applicants will be required to submit results of the SAT Reasoning Test and any two SAT Subject Tests (except for the SAT Subject Test Writing). Students may substitute any SAT tests with the ACT with the Writing component."

SELECTIVITY

Admissions Rating	99
# of applicants	19,097
% of applicants accepted	14
% of acceptees attending	56
# accepting a place on wait list	450
% admitted from wait list	16
# of early decision applicants	2,324
% accepted early decision	23

FRESHMAN PROFILE

Range SAT Critical Reading	660–760
Range SAT Math	670–770
Range SAT Writing	660–760
Range ACT Composite	28–33
Minimum paper TOEFL	600
Minimum computer TOEFL	250
Minimum web-based TOEFL	100
% graduated top 10% of class	92
% graduated top 25% of class	99
% graduated top 50% of class	100

DEADLINES

Early decision	
Deadline	11/1
Notification	12/1
Regular	
Deadline	1/1
Notification	4/1
Nonfall registration?	no

APPLICANTS ALSO LOOK AT

AND OFTEN PREFER
Harvard College
Stanford University
Yale University
Princeton University

AND SOMETIMES PREFER
Massachusetts Institute of Technology
Williams College
Smith College
Amherst College

AND RARELY PREFER
Oberlin College
Georgetown University
Tufts University
Bowdoin College

FINANCIAL FACTS

Financial Aid Rating	95
Annual tuition	$35,584
% frosh rec. need-based scholarship or grant aid	44
% UG rec. need-based scholarship or grant aid	42
% frosh rec. need-based self-help aid	35
% UG rec. need-based self-help aid	39
% frosh rec. any financial aid	45
% UG rec. any financial aid	44
% UG borrow to pay for school	46
Average cumulative indebtedness	$18,610

BRYANT UNIVERSITY

1150 DOUGLAS PIKE, SMITHFIELD, RI 02917 • ADMISSIONS: 401-232-6100 • FAX: 401-232-6741

STUDENTS SAY ". . ."

Academics

There are liberal arts programs at Bryant University, but business is the top draw here. A wealth of programs in accounting, finance, marketing, and management has earned Bryant a reputation far and wide as "a business-driven institution that blends the academic and the real world." The placement rate for internships and meaningful jobs after graduation is "very high," thanks to a loyal alumni base and an "excellent" career center that offers a ton of personalized services. "During interview season, I had interviews every day, which led to second interviews, which led to multiple job offers," boasts an accounting major. Students also rave about their cutting-edge campus technology. Academically, we hear students complain about "too many PowerPoint presentations" and "an excessive amount of group work" but "classes are always small" and professors are "always available." Many professors are "obsessed with their jobs" and "pride themselves on seeing their students succeed." They are "good at teaching but even better at providing real working knowledge and examples." Others, however, could definitely improve "when it comes to the fundamentals of teaching and being able to effectively communicate the subject matter." The part-time faculty is especially "hit or miss." Despite some complaints about registration and limited course offerings, Bryant's "very friendly" and "approachable" administration generally ensures that things "flow smoothly." Red tape is rare.

Life

"Life at Bryant is the typical college experience." Most undergrads choose to live on this clean, "beautiful," and modern campus "all four years" and there's "a great sense of community." The "intense" academic workload means that weekdays can be "stressful." Nevertheless, students at Bryant are "very involved" in "massive amounts of extracurriculars." "The athletic facilities are great" and many students participate in both intramurals and varsity sports. Students are in charge of most of the activities on campus and they put on a lot of events. The "fun social scene" typically begins on Thursday. "Parties are generally all on campus" and "most people get really drunk on the weekends." An assortment of harder stimulants is also popular. "If you want to do drugs, you will be able to find them," suggests one student. "At the same time, if you want nothing to do with drugs, you will never see them." The surrounding town of Smithfield "has nothing to do" but "a short drive into Providence" leads to "great food, bars, clubs, and shopping." For more serious urban life, students can always head up to Boston as well.

Student Body

"Students at Bryant are very similar, with similar goals and objectives in mind." There's kind of a "common mold" here of "health-conscious" suburbanites "from the Northeast" who have "aspirations to make good sums of money after entering the job market." "The administrators and teachers are pretty much the most liberal people on campus," explains a senior. "We are a relatively conservative school." During the week, these "competitive" (occasionally "cutthroat") "business leaders of tomorrow" are "hardworking and diligent." Preppy attire dominates and "clothes often seem to be a big deal." "It is not unusual to see students in suits," but only "when they have presentations or interviews, not just for the hell of it." On the weekends, students tend to be "typical party kids." "There definitely are students who deviate" from the norm but there aren't many and they "don't fit in as well." Some students contend that this place is "diverse economically." Others tell us that "the typical student is white, middle to upper middle class." Ethnic diversity is "rather low" and minority students "tend to stick together." International students do, too. In fact, the whole campus is "very cliquey." "If you're not involved in a sport, or Greek life, or another huge group, then your social life will be limited to your small group of friends."

FINANCIAL AID: 401-232-6020 • E-MAIL: ADMISSION@BRYANT.EDU • WEBSITE: ADMISSION.BRYANT.EDU

THE PRINCETON REVIEW SAYS

Admissions

Very important factors considered include: Academic GPA, rigor of secondary school record. *Important factors considered include:* Class rank, application essay, recommendation(s), standardized test scores. *Other factors considered include:* Alumni/ae relation, character/personal qualities, extracurricular activities, first generation, geographical residence, interview, level of applicant's interest, racial/ethnic status, state residency, talent/ability, volunteer work, work experience. SAT or ACT required; TOEFL required of all international applicants. High school diploma is required and GED is accepted. *Academic units required:* 4 English, 4 mathematics, 2 science, (2 science labs), 2 foreign language, 2 history. *Academic units recommended:* 4 English, 4 mathematics, 3 science, (2 science labs), 3 foreign language, 3 history.

Financial Aid

Students should submit: FAFSA Regular filing deadline is 2/15. The Princeton Review suggests that all financial aid forms be submitted as soon as possible after January 1. *Need-based scholarships/grants offered:* Federal Pell, SEOG, state scholarships/grants, private scholarships, the school's own gift aid. *Loan aid offered:* Direct Subsidized Stafford, Direct Unsubsidized Stafford, FFEL PLUS, Federal Perkins Applicants will be notified of awards on or about 3/24. Federal Work-Study Program available. Institutional employment available. Off-campus job opportunities are fair.

The Inside Word

If you're a solid student you should meet little trouble getting into Bryant. The university's admissions effort has brought in qualified applicants from across the country, but the heaviest draw remains from New England. Students attending Bryant will receive a solid business education as well as precious connections in the corporate worlds of Providence and Boston.

THE SCHOOL SAYS "..."

From The Admissions Office

"Bryant is a four-year, private university in New England where students build knowledge, develop character, and achieve success—as they define it. In addition to a first-class faculty, state-of-the-art facilities, and advanced technology, Bryant offers stimulating classroom dynamics; internship opportunities at more than 350 companies; 70-plus student clubs and organizations; varsity, intramural, and club sports for men and women; and many opportunities for community service and leadership development. Bryant is the choice for individuals seeking the best integration of business and liberal arts, utilizing state-of-the-art technology. Bryant offers degrees in actuarial mathematics, applied mathematics and statistics, applied economics, applied psychology, business administration, communication, global studies, history, information technology, international business, literary and cultural studies, politics and law, and sociology.

"A cross-disciplinary academic approach teaches students the skills they need to successfully compete in a complex, global environment. Students can pursue one of 27 minors in business and liberal arts, and 80 areas of study. Bryant's rigorous academic standards have been recognized and accredited by NEASC and AACSB International. Bryant's international business program is a member of CUIBE, the Consortium for Undergraduate International Business Education. Technology is a fundamental component of the learning process at Bryant. Every entering freshman is provided with a Thinkpad® laptop for personal use. Students exchange their laptop for a new one in their junior year, which they will own upon graduation.

"Bryant University is situated on a beautiful 420-acre campus in Smithfield, Rhode Island. The campus is only 15 minutes away from the state capital, Providence; 45 minutes from Boston; and 3 hours from New York City.

"Bryant requires that students enrolling in Fall 2008 take the new SAT with the Writing component, or the ACT (writing section not required)."

SELECTIVITY

Admissions Rating	90
# of applicants	5,649
% of applicants accepted	44
% of acceptees attending	35
# accepting a place on wait list	563
% admitted from wait list	12
# of early decision applicants	190
% accepted early decision	55

FRESHMAN PROFILE

Range SAT Critical Reading	520–600
Range SAT Math	550–630
Range SAT Writing	520–600
Range ACT Composite	22–26
Minimum paper TOEFL	550
Minimum computer TOEFL	213
Minimum web-based TOEFL	80
Average HS GPA	3.42
% graduated top 10% of class	25
% graduated top 25% of class	64
% graduated top 50% of class	95

DEADLINES

Early decision	
Deadline	11/15
Notification	12/15
Regular	
Deadline	2/1
Notification	3/21
Nonfall registration?	yes

APPLICANTS ALSO LOOK AT
AND OFTEN PREFER
University of Massachusetts—Amherst
Providence College

AND SOMETIMES PREFER
University of New Hampshire
University of Connecticut

AND RARELY PREFER
Merrimack College
University of Rhode Island

FINANCIAL FACTS

Financial Aid Rating	93
Annual tuition	$27,639
Room and board	$10,715
Books and supplies	$1,200
% frosh rec. need-based scholarship or grant aid	53
% UG rec. need-based scholarship or grant aid	56
% frosh rec. non-need-based scholarship or grant aid	51
% UG rec. non-need-based scholarship or grant aid	32
% frosh rec. need-based self-help aid	60
% UG rec. need-based self-help aid	60
% frosh rec. athletic scholarships	2
% UG rec. athletic scholarships	2
% frosh rec. any financial aid	67
% UG rec. any financial aid	66
% UG borrow to pay for school	48
Average cumulative indebtedness	$29,128

BRYN MAWR COLLEGE

101 NORTH MERION AVENUE, BRYN MAWR, PA 19010-2859 • ADMISSIONS: 610-526-5152 • FAX: 610-526-7471

CAMPUS LIFE

Quality of Life Rating	**96**
Fire Safety Rating	**74**
Green Rating	**85**
Type of school	private
Environment	metropolis

STUDENTS

Total undergrad enrollment	1,275
% male/female	/100
% from out of state	82
% from public high school	66
% live on campus	95
% African American	6
% Asian	12
% Caucasian	47
% Hispanic	3
% international	7
# of countries represented	43

SURVEY SAYS . . .
Small classes
Dorms are like palaces
Frats and sororities are unpopular
or nonexistent

ACADEMICS

Academic Rating	**94**
Calendar	semester
Student/faculty ratio	8:1
Profs interesting rating	91
Profs accessible rating	91
Most common	
reg class size	10–19 students

MOST POPULAR MAJORS
mathematics
English language and literature
psychology

STUDENTS SAY " . . . "

Academics

Tiny Bryn Mawr College is "a community of women scholars" that offers "an amazing, intense, multifaceted," and "pretty tough" academic experience. Coursework "can be stressful, especially around midterms and final times, but in the end it's worth it." The faculty is mostly stellar. "One of the main things I love about Bryn Mawr is the personal relationships formed over the years with the professors," boasts a chemistry major. "Anywhere you go to school you will have some bad teachers and some boring classes, and Bryn Mawr is no exception," relates a junior, "but overall I have been extremely impressed with and challenged by the classes I have taken at my college." The highly popular administration is "here for the students' success." "Bryn Mawr is an extremely autonomous place where students are given a lot of freedom to do as they please." "If you need something and you go to the right people, you can pretty much make it happen." Additionally, students can take courses at nearby Haverford, Swarthmore, and Penn. And upon graduation, Mawrters can take advantage of a loyal network of alumnae who "are doing amazing things and have a really strong connection to the school."

Life

Bryn Mawr's "absolutely beautiful" campus is "ensconced in collegiate Gothic arches." The dorms are gorgeous and the food is "delicious." It's all a little slice of heaven—except for the "bleak" athletic facilities. Neat traditions at Bryn Mawr include Hell Week, which allows first-year students to bond with everyone else, and May Day, an entire day of catered picnics, live music, and hanging out on the greens, which always involves a Maypole dance, a Robin Hood play, and a late-night screening of *The Philadelphia Story* (starring BMC alum Katherine Hepburn). "These traditions are unique, intimate experiences that bring the whole school together and make you feel proud to be a Mawrter," explains a junior. When students aren't basking in the warm glow of ritual, they "love to study, study, study," but other activities are plentiful. "There is always something to do on campus, whether it's a student theatre production, an a cappella concert, an improv group show, movies being shown, outside groups coming to perform, speakers coming to campus, you name it," says a senior. Sports and dance are big extracurricular activities, too. Mawrters drink "more than you'd think for an allegedly quiet, nerdy women's college," but "Bryn Mawr's party scene is more of an intimate-friends-over-to-your-room type of deal." Trips to Swarthmore, Villanova, or Haverford provide "plenty of chances to interact with the opposite sex, if that's what you're after." "There are tons of great restaurants, music venues, galleries, and shopping all within minutes of campus" as well, and nearby Philadelphia offers more urban recreation.

Student Body

Many students say that diversity "is one of the things that makes Bryn Mawr stand out." Others say that students looking for diversity "may not find it here." Whatever the case, "Bryn Mawr is a bunch of brilliant women." They are "nerdy, ambitious, driven, talented" people who "can occasionally be over-competitive" and are "swamped with work yet thriving on it." "We all came into Bryn Mawr with a background in leadership, and all intend to leave Bryn Mawr as future leaders in our respective fields," asserts a junior. It's definitely a left-leaning crowd. "A lot of students at Bryn Mawr are adamant about being politically correct to the point that it begins to become annoying." "Contrary to popular belief, Bryn Mawr isn't a haven for lesbians," though "homosexuality is common and visible." Socially, "the campus is very stratified along group lines." "There is a variety of types of people at the school—from awkward, socially uncomfortable people to very outgoing, social butterflies" to "mud-splattered" rugby players. "Some of us fly that freak flag high and proud," declares a senior. However, "there are plenty of average girls who look at *Cosmo*," too.

FINANCIAL AID: 610-526-5245 • E-MAIL: ADMISSIONS@BRYNMAWR.EDU • WEBSITE: WWW.BRYNMAWR.EDU

THE PRINCETON REVIEW SAYS

Admissions

Very important factors considered include: Recommendation(s), rigor of secondary school record. *Important factors considered include:* Application essay, academic GPA, character/personal qualities, extracurricular activities. *Other factors considered include:* Class rank, standardized test scores, alumni/ae relation, first generation, geographical residence, interview, racial/ethnic status, talent/ability, volunteer work, work experience. SAT and SAT Subject Tests or ACT required; TOEFL is required of international applicants unless: a) English has been the primary language of instruction for the past four years or, b) if student's first language is English. High school diploma or its equivalent is accepted. *Academic units required:* 2 academic electives. *Academic units recommended:* 4 English, 3 mathematics, 2 science, (1 science labs), 3 foreign language, 2 social studies, 2 history.

Financial Aid

Students should submit: FAFSA, CSS PROFILE, signed copies of parents' and students' federal income tax information with all forms and schedules attached. Additional forms may be requested. International Students should submit: International Students Financial Aid Form and a statement of earnings from each parent's employer. Bryn Mawr strongly encourages students to file by 2/5. All forms and information must be received no later than 3/1. The Princeton Review suggests that all financial aid forms be submitted as soon as possible after January 1. *Need-based scholarships/grants offered:* Federal Pell, SEOG, state scholarships/grants, the school's own gift aid. Federal Academic Competitiveness Grant (ACG), Federal National Science and Mathematics to Retain Talent Grant (SMART). *Loan aid offered:* FFEL Subsidized Stafford, FFEL Unsubsidized Stafford, FFEL PLUS, Federal Perkins Applicants will be notified of awards on or about 3/23.

The Inside Word

Do not be deceived by Bryn Mawr's admission rate; its student body is among the academically best in the nation. Outstanding preparation for graduate study draws an applicant pool that is well prepared and intellectually curious. The Admissions Committee includes eight faculty members and four seniors. Each applicant is reviewed by four readers, including at least one faculty member and one student.

THE SCHOOL SAYS ". . ."

From The Admissions Office

"Bryn Mawr is one of the nation's most distinctive, distinguished colleges. Every year 1,300 women from around the world gather on the College's historic campus to study with leading scholars, conduct advanced research, and expand the boundaries of what's possible. A Bryn Mawr woman is defined by a rare combination of personal characteristics: an intense intellectual commitment; a purposeful vision of her life; and a desire to make a meaningful contribution to the world. Consistently producing outstanding scholars, Bryn Mawr is ranked among the top ten of all colleges and universities in percentage of graduates who go on to earn a Ph.D., and is considered excellent preparation for the nation's top law, medical and business schools. More than 500 students collaborate with faculty on independent projects every year; and to augment an already strong curriculum, students may choose from more than 5,000 courses offered through nearby Haverford and Swarthmore Colleges, as well as the University of Pennsylvania. Committed to recruiting a diverse student body, more than a third of Bryn Mawr students are women of color and international students. Furthermore, more than 33% of all students opt to study overseas. Minutes outside of Philadelphia and only two hours by train from New York City and Washington, D.C., Bryn Mawr is recognized by many as one of the most stunning college campuses in the United States. Its mixture of collegiate Gothic architecture and post-modern buildings owe much of their beauty to the original campus plan that was created and executed by Fredrick Law Olmsted and Calvert Vaux, landscape architects and the designers of New York's Central Park."

SELECTIVITY

Admissions Rating	95
# of applicants	2,106
% of applicants accepted	45
% of acceptees attending	37
# accepting a place on wait list	200
% admitted from wait list	10
# of early decision applicants	146
% accepted early decision	52

FRESHMAN PROFILE

Range SAT Critical Reading	620–730
Range SAT Math	580–690
Range SAT Writing	620–720
Range ACT Composite	26–30
Minimum paper TOEFL	600
Minimum computer TOEFL	250
Minimum web-based TOEFL	100
% graduated top 10% of class	62
% graduated top 25% of class	91
% graduated top 50% of class	100

DEADLINES

Early decision I	
Deadline	11/15
Notification	12/15
Early decision II	
Deadline	1/1
Notification	2/1
Regular	
Deadline	1/15
Notification	4/15
Nonfall registration?	no

APPLICANTS ALSO LOOK AT

AND OFTEN PREFER
Harvard College, Brown University, University of Pennsylvania

AND SOMETIMES PREFER
Haverford College, Scripps College, Mount Holyoke College

AND RARELY PREFER
Oberlin College, Vassar College

FINANCIAL FACTS

Financial Aid Rating	97
Annual tuition	$35,700
% frosh rec. need-based scholarship or grant aid	50
% UG rec. need-based scholarship or grant aid	53
% frosh rec. non-need-based scholarship or grant aid	11
% UG rec. non-need-based scholarship or grant aid	6
% frosh rec. need-based self-help aid	45
% UG rec. need-based self-help aid	51
% frosh rec. any financial aid	50
% UG rec. any financial aid	59
% UG borrow to pay for school	61
Average cumulative indebtedness	$19,049

BUCKNELL UNIVERSITY

FREAS HALL, BUCKNELL UNIVERSITY, LEWISBURG, PA 17837 • ADMISSIONS: 570-577-1101 • FAX: 570-577-3538

CAMPUS LIFE

Quality of Life Rating	81
Fire Safety Rating	87
Green Rating	83
Type of school	private
Environment	village

STUDENTS

Total undergrad enrollment	3,495
% male/female	49/51
% from out of state	73
% from public high school	70
% live on campus	87
% in (# of) fraternities	39 (13)
% in (# of) sororities	40 (6)
% African American	3
% Asian	7
% Caucasian	80
% Hispanic	3
% international	3
# of countries represented	42

SURVEY SAYS . . .

Small classes
Great library
Athletic facilities are great
Campus feels safe
Frats and sororities dominate
social scene
Lots of beer drinking

ACADEMICS

Academic Rating	91
Calendar	semester
Student/faculty ratio	11:1
Profs interesting rating	88
Profs accessible rating	89
Most common reg class size	10–19 students
Most common lab size	10–19 students

MOST POPULAR MAJORS

business administration and
management
economics
English language and literature

STUDENTS SAY ". . ."

Academics

Bucknell University, "a liberal arts school with a top engineering program," is "a typical Patriot League school where students somehow find a way to balance studying and partying" while remaining "ambitious about their studies, extremely friendly and caring in nature, and bound to succeed." "Small class sizes, a beautiful campus, friendly students and faculty, and amazing facilities" all conspire to justify the premium price tag on a Bucknell education; $31 million in annual financial aid means about half the students don't have to foot the entire bill. "The courses are tough, and the workload is heavy" here, "but the academic experience is a wonderful one," with professors who "are passionate and energetic and convey their love for their field to their students. They give us their home phone numbers and e-mail addresses and tell us to come to their offices just to say hello. They want to teach us, but also want to be our friends." Bucknell offers more than 50 majors and 60 minors, an impressive array for a school of this size; business and engineering majors are most popular, while premeds benefit from numerous opportunities to get involved in research. It's the kind of school that inspires lifelong loyalty; as one undergrad sums up, "Bucknell boasts a tight-knit community where most people are friends with most other people and 99 percent of varsity athletes graduate in four years. Bucknell is a community of scholars as well as social [beings], with many students possessing both qualities. Few students regret their choice and remain involved in campus affairs for lifetimes."

Life

"Life at Bucknell is centered on a social structure," and "While students do work hard at their academics, they party equally as hard." Indeed, according to some, "On weekends, you have a few choices: dorms or downtown, beer or hard liquor, drugs or alcohol. Partying is it, though." This perception is reinforced by the fact that hometown Lewisburg is very small and very quiet. Greek organizations play a huge role on campus; one reluctant fraternity member writes, "I never thought I would join a fraternity, and the prevalence of Greek life was one of the downsides of coming here originally, but I found a group of guys where I fit in quite well, so I spend a lot of time on fraternity activities. But that's really my choice because I enjoy it." Many here will tell you that there are options "that do not revolve around the party scene, such as the outing club, the nationally known Conservatives Club," and a number of religious- and service-related organizations such as Catholic Campus Ministry and Student Emergency Response Volunteers. Bucknell competes in the Patriot League against the likes of Army, Navy, Lehigh, and Lafayette; "The basketball team has been very good lately, so they're a lot of fun."

Student Body

"A lot of people are preppy—super preppy" on the Bucknell campus, many students tell us, observing that "the sheer number of student-owned luxury cars on this campus is astounding." An adamant minority insists that "Bucknell has a reputation for being a preppy school, but in my experience that reputation is overblown." Most everyone agrees that 'preppy' doesn't have to mean boring; the student body includes "plenty of interesting and different people to hang out with if you look for them." Undergrads tend to be "energetic" and "involved in many things on campus. Students try their best at everything they do." Students typically "come from Pennsylvania, New Jersey, or New York. There are a lot from New England also, and Maryland's probably next."

FINANCIAL AID: 570-577-1331 • E-MAIL: ADMISSIONS@BUCKNELL.EDU • WEBSITE: WWW.BUCKNELL.EDU

THE PRINCETON REVIEW SAYS

Admissions

*Very important factors considered include:*Academic GPA, rigor of secondary school record, standardized test scores, character/personal qualities, talent/ability, application essay. *Important factors considered include:* Recommendation(s), extracurricular activities, level of applicant's interest, volunteer work, work experience. *Other factors considered include:* Alumni/ae relation, first generation, geographical residence, interview, racial/ethnic status, religious affiliation/commitment, SAT or ACT with Writing component required. TOEFL required of all international applicants. High school diploma is required and GED is accepted. *Academic units required:* 4 English, 3 mathematics, 2 science, 2 foreign language, 2 social studies, 2 history, 1 academic elective. *Academic units recommended:* 4 English, 4 mathematics, 3 science, 4 foreign language, 2 social studies, 2 history, 1 academic elective.

Financial Aid

Students should submit: FAFSA, CSS/Financial Aid PROFILE, noncustodial PROFILE. Regular filing deadline is 1/1. The Princeton Review suggests that all financial aid forms be submitted as soon as possible after January 1. *Need-based scholarships/grants offered:* Federal Pell, SEOG, state scholarships/grants, private scholarships, the school's own gift aid, Federal ACG Grant, Federal SMART. *Loan aid offered:* FFEL Subsidized Stafford, FFEL Unsubsidized Stafford, FFEL PLUS, Federal Perkins Applicants will be notified of awards on or about 4/1. Federal Work-Study Program available. Institutional employment available. Off-campus job opportunities are poor.

The Inside Word

Admissions rates vary by intended major at Bucknell. The school receives applications from more prospective business majors than the school can handle; as a result, only about 23 percent were admitted to the class of 2010. Admit rates are higher among populations that tend to be self-selecting, including science majors, computer science majors, and engineers. Those listing "undecided" as prospective major made up about 17 percent of admitted applicants; 33 percent of such applicants were admitted. You certainly don't hurt yourself by listing "undecided" as your intended major.

THE SCHOOL SAYS "..."

From The Admissions Office

"Bucknell combines the personal experience of a small liberal arts college with the breadth and opportunity typically found at larger research universities. With a low student/faculty ratio, students gain exceptional hands-on experience, working closely with faculty in an environment enhanced by first-class academic, residential, and athletic facilities. Together, the College of Arts and Sciences and the College of Engineering offer 53 majors and 64 minors. Learning opportunities permeate campus life in and out of the classroom and across the disciplines. For example, engineering students participate in music ensembles, theater productions, and poetry readings, while arts and sciences students take engineering courses, conduct scientific research in the field, and produce distinctive creative works. Students also pursue their interests in more than 150 organizations and through athletic competition in the prestigious Division I Patriot League. These activities constitute a comprehensive approach to learning that teaches students how to think critically and develop their leadership skills so that they are prepared to make a difference locally, nationally, and globally."

SELECTIVITY

Admissions Rating	96
# of applicants	8,943
% of applicants accepted	30
% of acceptees attending	33
# accepting a place on wait list	1,046
% admitted from wait list	1
# of early decision applicants	639
% accepted early decision	56

FRESHMAN PROFILE

Range SAT Critical Reading	600–690
Range SAT Math	630–710
Range SAT Writing	600–690
Range ACT Composite	27–31
Minimum paper TOEFL	550
Minimum computer TOEFL	213
% graduated top 10% of class	72
% graduated top 25% of class	93
% graduated top 50% of class	100

DEADLINES

Early decision	
Deadline	11/15
Notification	12/15
Regular	
Deadline	1/15
Notification	4/1
Nonfall registration?	no

FINANCIAL FACTS

Financial Aid Rating	96
Annual tuition	$39,434
Room and board	$8,728
Required fees	$218
Books and supplies	$870
% frosh rec. need-based scholarship or grant aid	48
% UG rec. need-based scholarship or grant aid	45
% frosh rec. non-need-based scholarship or grant aid	6
% UG rec. non-need-based scholarship or grant aid	3
% frosh rec. need-based self-help aid	48
% UG rec. need-based self-help aid	47
% frosh rec. athletic scholarships	1
% UG rec. athletic scholarships	1
% frosh rec. any financial aid	62
% UG rec. any financial aid	64
% UG borrow to pay for school	64
Average cumulative indebtedness	$17,700

CALIFORNIA INSTITUTE OF TECHNOLOGY

1200 EAST CALIFORNIA BOULEVARD, MAIL CODE 328-87, PASADENA, CA 91125 • ADMISSIONS: 626-395-6341 • FAX: 626-683-3026

CAMPUS LIFE
Quality of Life Rating	**82**
Fire Safety Rating	**60***
Green Rating	**60***
Type of school	private
Environment	metropolis

STUDENTS
Total undergrad enrollment	913
% male/female	70/30
% from out of state	65
% from public high school	70
% live on campus	95
% African American	1
% Asian	38
% Caucasian	43
% Hispanic	5
% international	9
# of countries represented	30

SURVEY SAYS . . .
Small classes
No one cheats
Lab facilities are great
Great library
Students are friendly
Campus feels safe
Frats and sororities are unpopular
or nonexistent

ACADEMICS
Academic Rating	**87**
Calendar	quarter
Student/faculty ratio	3:1
Profs interesting rating	61
Profs accessible rating	67

MOST POPULAR MAJORS
physics
mechanical engineering
biology

STUDENTS SAY "..."

Academics
Nestled in sunny Pasadena, this world-renowned research university makes no concessions to students expecting to coast on natural ability alone. As one student explains, "Every day is a new challenge, and sometimes I find it miraculous that I'm able to keep up." Achieving success at this school is due in large part to "a tremendous amount of determination and will," as well as a collaborative atmosphere that encourages "students to learn to work together to solve problems." Chalk this kind of support up to a test-taking policy that "allows you to take your exams whenever you want, wherever you want" and a much-respected honor code that stipulates, "No member of the Caltech community shall take unfair advantage of any other member of the Caltech community." Students note they "have a closer relationship to [the administration] than [they might at] many other larger schools" and the administration "does appear to be taking steps to improve communication." Students love that they have the opportunity to "come into close contact with Nobel Laureates and other famed scientists, as they all teach courses and accept students into their labs for research." As one student sums up, "The amount of information each student is expected to digest in the course of the year is daunting, but once achieved makes a Caltech grad ready for anything."

Life
Despite the proximity of Los Angeles and all the forms of entertainment it provides, most students "work—a lot." As one student explains, "We live in our own little bubble of problem sets and lectures. The academics here are intense, probably the most intense you could hope to find. Not for the faint of heart." In this high-stakes environment the need to blow off steam is equally pressing, often involving "whatever crazy spontaneous stuff happens to pop up." "Athletics, movies, and video games" are also popular. Caltech students have a reputation for pranks, thanks to inventive minds and a housing system "which is very unique and a big part of the social life. The houses combine the feel and purpose of a dorm with the pride and spirit of a fraternity." "Each house plans social events" and "provides the main social community" for students who find it to be "Caltech's greatest feature." According to one student, the house system ensures that "everyone has a place in a tight-knit community with people who share their interests and personality." That said, if you ever want to get away from it all to hit the bar, club, stadium, or beach, "The key is to know someone with a car."

Student Body
As you might expect from such an academically rigorous university, at Caltech "Your worth is determined by your work ethic and your intelligence, not your appearance." As one student explains, most students "have an interest in what are conventionally considered nerdy topics." It is in this embrace of difference that Caltech students find themselves united, since "All together we form a very atypical, brainy, hardworking but fun group." Consider it a meeting of the minds as, "The typical student is smarter than you, no matter how smart you are." While the notion that "more than one person in your class will win the Nobel prize someday" may seem intimidating at first, being in such close proximity to brilliance is very useful "when you need help with problem sets." The student population is mostly male and not hugely diverse, but "The student body makes up for its lack of physical diversity with personality diversity." All in all, it's an "accepting" campus where "everyone finds a place."

CALIFORNIA INSTITUTE OF TECHNOLOGY

FINANCIAL AID: 626-395-6280 • E-MAIL: UGADMISSIONS@CALTECH.EDU • WEBSITE: ADMISSIONS.CALTECH.EDU

THE PRINCETON REVIEW SAYS

Admissions

Very important factors considered include: Rigor of secondary school record. *Important factors considered include:* Class rank, application essay, academic GPA, recommendation(s), standardized test scores, character/personal qualities, extracurricular activities. *Other factors considered include:* Alumni/ae relation, first generation, racial/ethnic status, talent/ability, volunteer work, work experience. SAT Subject Tests required; SAT or ACT required; High school diploma or equivalent is not required. *Academic units required:* 3 English, 4 mathematics, 2 science, (1 science labs), 1 social studies, 1 history. *Academic units recommended:* 4 English, 4 science.

Financial Aid

Students should submit: FAFSA, CSS/Financial Aid PROFILE, state aid form, noncustodial PROFILE, business/farm supplement. Noncustodial Parent's Statement and Business/Farm Supplement forms are required only when applicable. Regular filing deadline is 1/15. The Princeton Review suggests that all financial aid forms be submitted as soon as possible after January 1. *Need-based scholarships/grants offered:* Federal Pell, SEOG, state scholarships/grants, private scholarships, the school's own gift aid. *Loan aid offered:* Direct Subsidized Stafford, Direct Unsubsidized Stafford, Direct PLUS, Federal Perkins, college/university loans from institutional funds. Applicants will be notified of awards on or about 4/15.

The Inside Word

Each Caltech application receives three independent reads before it is presented to the Admissions Committee. This ensures that all candidates receive a thorough evaluation. The school values the unique drive and energy of its current students and desires applicants whom display a similar combination of creativity and intellect. Stellar academic credentials are a must, and prospective students must display an aptitude for math and science.

THE SCHOOL SAYS "..."

From The Admissions Office

"Admission to the freshman class is based on many factors—some quantifiable, some not. What you say in your application is important! Because we don't interview students for admission, your letters of recommendation are weighed heavily. High school academic performance is very important, as is a demonstrated interest in math, science, and/or engineering. We are also interested in your character, maturity, and motivation. We are very proud of the process we use to select each freshman class. It's very individual, it has great integrity, and we believe it serves all the students who apply. If you have any questions about the process or about Caltech in general, write us a letter or give us a call. We'd like to hear from you!

"Freshman applicants must submit scores from either the new or old SAT (or ACT, Writing section optional). In addition, students must submit the results of two SAT Subject Tests: Mathematics IIC and one of the following: Biology (Ecological or Molecular), Chemistry, or Physics. "

SELECTIVITY

Admissions Rating	99
# of applicants	3,597
% of applicants accepted	17
% of acceptees attending	38
# accepting a place on wait list	164
% admitted from wait list	18

FRESHMAN PROFILE

Range SAT Critical Reading	700–780
Range SAT Math	770–800
Range SAT Writing	680–770
% graduated top 10% of class	99
% graduated top 25% of class	100
% graduated top 50% of class	100

DEADLINES

Early action	
Deadline	11/1
Notification	12/15
Regular	
Deadline	1/1
Notification	4/1
Nonfall registration?	no

APPLICANTS ALSO LOOK AT

AND OFTEN PREFER
Harvard College
Stanford University
Princeton University

AND SOMETIMES PREFER
University of California—Berkeley
Harvey Mudd College
Massachusetts Institute of Technology

AND RARELY PREFER
Carnegie Mellon University
Cornell University

FINANCIAL FACTS

Financial Aid Rating	99
Annual tuition	$31,437
Room and board	$10,146
Required fees	$3,000
Books and supplies	$1,194
% frosh rec. need-based scholarship or grant aid	51
% UG rec. need-based scholarship or grant aid	47
% frosh rec. non-need-based scholarship or grant aid	10
% UG rec. non-need-based scholarship or grant aid	4
% frosh rec. need-based self-help aid	36
% UG rec. need-based self-help aid	38
% frosh rec. any financial aid	56
% UG rec. any financial aid	56
% UG borrow to pay for school	43
Average cumulative indebtedness	$6,268

CALIFORNIA STATE UNIVERSITY—STANISLAUS

801 WEST MONTE VISTA AVENUE, TURLOCK, CA 95382 • ADMISSIONS: 209-667-3070 OR 800-300-7420 (CA ONLY) • FAX: 209-667-3394

CAMPUS LIFE
Quality of Life Rating	**80**
Fire Safety Rating	**99**
Green Rating	**94**
Type of school	public
Environment	town

STUDENTS
Total undergrad enrollment	6,883
% male/female	35/65
% live on campus	8
% in (# of) fraternities	4 (5)
% in (# of) sororities	2 (7)
% African American	4
% Asian	12
% Caucasian	40
% Hispanic	30
% Native American	1
% international	1
# of countries represented	35

SURVEY SAYS . . .
Small classes
Great computer facilities
Great library
Students are friendly
Diverse student types on campus
Great off-campus food
Campus feels safe
Students are happy

ACADEMICS
Academic Rating	**76**
Calendar	4/1/4
Student/faculty ratio	19:1
Profs interesting rating	75
Profs accessible rating	72

MOST POPULAR MAJORS
business/commerce
liberal arts and sciences/
liberal studies
psychology

STUDENTS SAY "..."

Academics
"California State University—Stanislaus is all about getting an education that's useful in the real world," students at this state university in California's Central Valley tell us. CSUS boasts a "great nursing program" that "only has 80 students each year, so you get great personal attention," a College of Business that "is one of the strongest pieces to the CSUS puzzle," and solid programs in psychology, social work, criminal justice, and biology. That's not a bad selection for a school that is "small enough to make a true commitment to accommodate its students. It's also a school that does not forget its students once they graduate." One student quotes CSU Stanislaus president Hamid Shirvani who says, "We are small enough to foster the formation of lifelong relationships inside the classroom and out, yet big enough to offer a wide range of courses and activities to encourage you to stretch yourself and to make the most of some of the most precious years of your life: your college years." Students appreciate their school's dedication to "bringing every student the highest quality education in the Central Valley by providing up-to-speed technology in the classrooms, high diversity of classes, and most importantly, excellent professors who personally care for their students."

Campus Life
The CSUS campus is "a very tranquil place to study, very quiet, and with beautiful scenery." It's not a wild social hub, though, in large part because there are relatively few resident students on campus. As one commuter notes, "There aren't many fun organized activities on campus, especially not for commuters; this is because the activities that are fun are usually late at night after classes have ended." Those who stick around after class report that "we have Late Night Stanislaus every Friday night with a wide range of activities ranging from comedy to crafts, and there is always free food!" They also point out that "the RAs plan fun things for the students living on the campus to do, from camping to rock climbing to special events during the holidays." Recreational facilities include "two game rooms, one on campus and one on the villa, tennis courts, basketball courts, and a soccer field with access to equipment." Hometown Turlock "is a small town so there is not much to do," but fortunately "Modesto is close and San Francisco is not that far. Plays, dinner, movies, and sporting events are all within reach."

Student Body
With fewer than 1,000 students residing on campus, CSUS "can be best described as a 'commuter' school" with "different ages, ethnicities, and social groups on campus" though the school has been steadily losing its commuter population in recent years. Hispanic and Asian students constitute the largest minority groups at this "rural college in an agrarian area." The typical undergrad, we're told, is "very Abercrombie & Fitch." There aren't "a lot of outcasts," and "atypical students seem to fit in just fine." Some students observe that "CSUS is divided into two sections: Serious students who enjoy the small school size, and casual students who are just there for the ride."

CALIFORNIA STATE UNIVERSITY—STANISLAUS

FINANCIAL AID: 209-667-3336 • E-MAIL: OUTREACH_HELP_DESK@CSUSTAN.EDU • WEBSITE: WWW.CSUSTAN.EDU

THE PRINCETON REVIEW SAYS

Admissions

Very important factors considered include: Academic GPA, rigor of secondary school record, standardized test scores. *Important factors considered include:* Class rank, High school diploma is required and GED is accepted. *Academic units required:* 4 English, 3 mathematics, 2 science, (2 science labs), 2 foreign language, 1 social studies, 1 history, 1 visual/performing arts, 1 academic elective.

Financial Aid

Students should submit: FAFSA The Princeton Review suggests that all financial aid forms be submitted as soon as possible after January 1. *Need-based scholarships/grants offered:* Federal Pell, SEOG, state scholarships/grants, private scholarships, the school's own gift aid, Federal Nursing Scholarships. *Loan aid offered:* FFEL Subsidized Stafford, FFEL Unsubsidized Stafford, FFEL PLUS, Federal Perkins, college/university loans from institutional funds. Applicants will be notified of awards on a rolling basis beginning 3/15. Federal Work-Study Program available. Institutional employment available. Off-campus job opportunities are good.

The Inside Word

Typical of most state schools, CSUS's admissions practices are fairly straightforward. The university adheres to the eligibility index as defined by the California state system. Therefore, applicants who meet GPA and standardized test score minimums are automatically granted admission. Out-of-state candidates do face more stringent requirements as do those applying for certain majors/programs such as the Pre-Licensure Nursing Program. If you are a student applying from out-of-state, make sure your GPA, test scores, and application package are in top form.

THE SCHOOL SAYS "..."

From The Admissions Office

"CSUS was recognized by the American Association of State Colleges and Universities as one of 12 public universities nationwide that demonstrate exceptional performance in retention and graduation rates. Student success is facilitated by a dense network of on-campus resources including consistent advising, a strong first-year program, frequent and meaningful contact with professors, and supportive staff and administrators.

"CSUS has 10 nationally accredited programs widely recognized for its quality academics. A new state-of-the-art science building opened in 2007 along with a new bookstore and student recreation complex in 2008. The campus is widely known as the most beautiful and friendly of the CSU campuses, blending modern facilities with the pastoral charm of the countryside. The campus enjoys an ideal location in the heart of California's Central Valley, a short distance from the San Francisco Bay Area, Monterey, the Sierra Nevada mountains, and Yosemite National Park. The proximity allows for hiking, skiing, snowboarding, kayaking, surfing, and other outdoors sports and activities.

"CSUS awarded more than $16.9 million in merit- and need-based grants and scholarships for the 2006–2007 school year. Approximately 68 percent of freshmen received need-based aid and the average gift aid for the group was $6,116. Scholarships range from full tuition, board, and books through the President's Scholarship to hundreds of other scholarships ranging from $100 to $5,000 per school year. The CSUS experience can be summed up as providing a small private school atmosphere at a public school price.

"CSU—Stanislaus considers only the Critical Reading and Math portions of the new SAT for admission eligibility and accepts the Math, Verbal, and total of the old SAT."

SELECTIVITY

Admissions Rating	60*
# of applicants	4,689
% of applicants accepted	65
% of acceptees attending	32

FRESHMAN PROFILE

Range SAT Critical Reading	420–530
Range SAT Math	430–540
Range ACT Composite	18–23
Average HS GPA	3.2

DEADLINES

Early action	
Deadline	11/30
Notification	3/1
Regular	
Priority	11/30
Deadline	8/30
Notification	rolling
Nonfall registration?	yes

FINANCIAL FACTS

Financial Aid Rating	63
Annual out-of-state tuition	$10,170
Room and board	$7,707
Required fees	$3,307
Books and supplies	$1,386
% frosh rec. need-based scholarship or grant aid	54
% UG rec. need-based scholarship or grant aid	62
% frosh rec. non-need-based scholarship or grant aid	3
% UG rec. non-need-based scholarship or grant aid	2
% frosh rec. need-based self-help aid	26
% UG rec. need-based self-help aid	35
% frosh rec. athletic scholarships	3
% UG rec. athletic scholarships	3
% frosh rec. any financial aid	68
% UG rec. any financial aid	57
% UG borrow to pay for school	24
Average cumulative indebtedness	$16,500

CALVIN COLLEGE

3201 BURTON STREET SOUTHEAST, GRAND RAPIDS, MI 49546 • ADMISSIONS: 616-526-6106 • FAX: 616-526-6777

CAMPUS LIFE
Quality of Life Rating	**84**
Fire Safety Rating	**67**
Green Rating	**60***
Type of school	private
Affiliation	Christian Reformed
Environment	metropolis

STUDENTS
Total undergrad enrollment	4,078
% male/female	46/54
% from out of state	44
% from public high school	38
% live on campus	59
% African American	1
% Asian	3
% Caucasian	84
% Hispanic	2
% international	7
# of countries represented	54

SURVEY SAYS . . .
Large classes
Great library
Frats and sororities are unpopular
or nonexistent

ACADEMICS
Academic Rating	**80**
Calendar	4/1/4
Student/faculty ratio	12:1
Profs interesting rating	85
Profs accessible rating	87
Most common reg class size	20–29 students
Most common lab size	20–29 students

MOST POPULAR MAJORS
business/commerce
nursing/registered nurse
(RN, ASN, BSN, MSN)
engineering

STUDENTS SAY "..."

Academics
Calvin College, a small, liberal arts school affiliated with the Christian Reformed Church, is "not just a college with a Christian label, it is a Christian community that challenges academically as well as spiritually." Indeed, while Calvin "integrates faith with learning" throughout its curriculum, students are adamant that they are not simply being spoon fed dogma here; on the contrary, they "are encouraged to have open discussions about the hard issues. One cannot come to Calvin and not be challenged." The result is "serious academics from a Christian perspective" capable of "training students to engage thoughtfully with the world around them and examine what it means to be a reformed Christian living in a secular world." Despite the school's relatively small size, "The resources available to students at Calvin are phenomenal. We have spectacular research facilities as well as a career development office that is very willing to engage with students." Biotech labs feature "many types of instrumentation that even bigger schools lack." Study abroad opportunities are "'sweet' and accessible," as are internships. Best of all, Calvin students receive all these perks without forfeiting the personal attention students understandably expect at a small private school. "Professors actually care about their students and want them to learn" and "are so willing to give help outside the classroom. They are very approachable." No wonder one student sums up: "I think many students come to Calvin with only moderate excitement about the school, but almost everyone leaves the school a proud Knight."

Life
The Calvin community "is incredibly strong. There are always people studying together and living life together. Support is easy to find from dorm leadership or just the people on your floor. It's easy to get involved in a club or within the dorm." Students "are very focused on faith, so many of them go to church, LOFT (evening worship on Sundays), and many of the weekday chapel breaks." In addition, "many of the students are extremely involved in sports," and "evening lectures are well attended. Student-run talent showcases like Dance Guild, Airband, and Rangeela performances are extremely popular. The Improv and Calvin Theater Company are top-notch. Hockey games attract hundreds of students. And, the library is always full." In short, "If you think college should be more than drinking and partying, come here. If that idea scares the hell out of you, then avoid this place at all costs." That's not to say a party scene doesn't exist; however, "Nearly all parties are 5 to 10 minutes away (where most off-campus students live)." One student points out that "There is a lot to do at Calvin, but most of it requires a drive off campus." "Restaurants are either on several major streets 5 minutes away, or downtown (10 to 15 minutes)." Downtown Grand Rapids provides "a number of things to do," including ice skating, shopping, and restaurants."

Student Body
"Many of the students here are from a Christian Reformed Church background, and many are Dutch," but "there are exceptions. The atypical students fit in well." "Tall, blond, and blue eyed" is the standard look here; "moderate to conservative" is the mainstream political perspective. "It is a strange dynamic to be at a college where the professors are more liberal than the student body as a whole," one student explains. However, the times are changing here, as one student reports: "The typical Calvin student is not the typical Calvin student from 20 years ago." The student body is "becoming increasingly diverse, [with] many students from Korea, Africa," and other places. "Students also represent many faith backgrounds and ethnicities within the United States. Students are very open to people of differing backgrounds and beliefs."

FINANCIAL AID: 616-957-6134 • E-MAIL: ADMISSIONS@CALVIN.EDU • WEBSITE: WWW.CALVIN.EDU

THE PRINCETON REVIEW SAYS

Admissions

Very important factors considered include: Academic GPA, rigor of secondary school record, standardized test scores, religious affiliation/commitment. *Important factors considered include:* Application essay, recommendation(s), character/personal qualities, extracurricular activities. *Other factors considered include:* Class rank, level of applicant's interest, volunteer work, work experience. SAT or ACT required; TOEFL required of all international applicants. High school diploma is required and GED is accepted. *Academic units required:* 3 English, 3 mathematics, 2 science, 2 social studies, 3 academic electives. *Academic units recommended:* 4 English, 3 mathematics, 2 science, (1 science labs), 2 foreign language, 3 social studies, 3 academic electives.

Financial Aid

Students should submit: FAFSA The Princeton Review suggests that all financial aid forms be submitted as soon as possible after January 1. *Need-based scholarships/grants offered:* Federal Pell, SEOG, state scholarships/grants, private scholarships, the school's own gift aid. *Loan aid offered:* Direct Subsidized Stafford, Direct Unsubsidized Stafford, Direct PLUS, Federal Perkins, state loans, college/university loans from institutional funds, Private Alternative. Applicants will be notified of awards on a rolling basis beginning 3/15. Federal Work-Study Program available. Institutional employment available. Off-campus job opportunities are excellent.

The Inside Word

Calvin's applicant pool is highly self-selected and small. Nearly all candidates get in, and nearly half choose to enroll. The freshman academic profile is fairly solid, but making a good match with the college philosophically is by far the most important factor for gaining admission.

THE SCHOOL SAYS "..."

From The Admissions Office

"Calvin's well-respected faculty, innovative core curriculum, and inquiring student body come together in an environment that links intellectual freedom with a heart for service. Calvin's 400-acre campus is home to 4,200 students and 400 professors who chose Calvin because of its national reputation for academic excellence and faith-shaped thinking. Calvin encourages students to explore all things and offers over 100 academic options to choose from, including accredited professional programs.

"Quality teaching and accessibility to students are considered top priorities by faculty members. More than 80 percent of Calvin professors hold the highest degree in their field, the student/faculty ratio is 12:1, and the average class size is 22. The college's 4-1-4 calendar offers opportunities for off-campus and international study, while service-learning projects draw Calvin students into the local community. Internships allow students to try their individual gifts in the workplace while gaining professional experience. In a recent survey, 96 percent of Calvin graduates reported that they had either secured a job or begun graduate school within 6 months of graduation. Calvin is among the top 3 percent of 4-year private colleges in the number of graduates who go on to earn a PhD.

"Students applying for admission are required to submit scores from either the SAT or the ACT college entrance exam. Calvin does not require the Writing section of either test."

SELECTIVITY

Admissions Rating	80
# of applicants	2,277
% of applicants accepted	95
% of acceptees attending	48
# accepting a place on wait list	50
% admitted from wait list	60

FRESHMAN PROFILE

Range SAT Critical Reading	530–650
Range SAT Math	540–650
Range ACT Composite	23–28
Minimum paper TOEFL	550
Minimum computer TOEFL	213
Average HS GPA	3.59
% graduated top 10% of class	26
% graduated top 25% of class	51
% graduated top 50% of class	80

DEADLINES

Regular	
Deadline	8/15
Notification	rolling
Nonfall registration?	yes

APPLICANTS ALSO LOOK AT

AND OFTEN PREFER
Hope College

AND SOMETIMES PREFER
Wheaton College (IL)
Grand Valley State University
University of Michigan—Ann Arbor

AND RARELY PREFER
Michigan Technological University
Michigan State University

FINANCIAL FACTS

Financial Aid Rating	78
Annual tuition	$21,460
Room and board	$7,460
Required fees	$225
Books and supplies	$810
% frosh rec. need-based scholarship or grant aid	65
% UG rec. need-based scholarship or grant aid	63
% frosh rec. non-need-based scholarship or grant aid	21
% UG rec. non-need-based scholarship or grant aid	17
% frosh rec. need-based self-help aid	54
% UG rec. need-based self-help aid	57
% frosh rec. any financial aid	92
% UG rec. any financial aid	93
% UG borrow to pay for school	66
Average cumulative indebtedness	$21,600

CARLETON COLLEGE

100 SOUTH COLLEGE STREET, NORTHFIELD, MN 55057 • ADMISSIONS: 507-646-4190 AND 800-995-2275 • FAX: 507-646-4526

CAMPUS LIFE
Quality of Life Rating	93
Fire Safety Rating	60*
Green Rating	60*
Type of school	private
Environment	village

STUDENTS
Total undergrad enrollment	1,986
% male/female	48/52
% from out of state	74
% from public high school	73
% live on campus	89
% African American	5
% Asian	10
% Caucasian	73
% Hispanic	5
% Native American	1
% international	6
# of countries represented	30

SURVEY SAYS . . .
Small classes
No one cheats
Frats and sororities are unpopular
or nonexistent

ACADEMICS
Academic Rating	96
Calendar	trimester
Student/faculty ratio	9:1
Profs interesting rating	98
Profs accessible rating	96
Most common reg class size	10–19 students
Most common lab size	20–29 students

MOST POPULAR MAJORS
biology/biological sciences
economics
political science and government

STUDENTS SAY "..."

Academics

"There is a sense of community that's hard to find elsewhere" at Carleton College, a small, liberal arts school "well known for its all-around academic rigor." One undergraduate explains, "You'll find yourself striking up conversations with complete strangers at the post office, in town, and along sidewalks in the middle of a snowy night. New friends are found everywhere." This is true even among the faculty; "Carleton is not a research college, so while professors do some research, they are much more focused on students." One student adds, "Know those special teachers you had in high school, the ones you will actually remember after graduation? That's what Carleton professors are like." Carleton operates on a trimester calendar, which students endorse. "It's nice to be only taking three classes, though more intensely, rather than spreading yourself over four or five." Students also love the "great Study Abroad Office," which has provided students here with "opportunities to travel to Hong Kong, China, Thailand, Spain, and, soon, Africa." But most of all, they love this Midwestern school's "intellectually stimulating environment. People are not afraid to work hard and get engrossed in what they study. At the same time, no one takes themselves too seriously, and we're always ready for a good time."

Life

"Small and quaint" are two words Carleton students frequently use to describe their school's hometown. "Northfield is not that exciting," cedes a freshman, "but I'm not sure anyone wants to change that." Most students are content simply to find "nice restaurants" and "locals [who] are darn helpful in [just] about any situation" in town. This might be because things are much livelier on campus. "An evening doesn't go by without some kind of event, whether it be musical, artistic, theatrical, or political," a sophomore writes. The notoriously heavy workload can make students a little wacky, to the point that "eventually some people lose it. This comes more in the form of weird, creative outlets than it does self-destructive behavior, though. There are a lot of Naked Winter Olympics, pranks, tradition[s], and general goofing off." Students are proud of this "little bit of eccentricity [that] makes everything fun." Intramurals "are really hot at Carleton; the people who aren't playing them are much fewer and far between than the people who are." Ultimate Frisbee and broomball are the games of choice. "Don't know how to play broomball?" queries one student. "It's easy to pick up. And if you're really horrible at it, don't worry. That doesn't stop anyone from playing." There are also "plenty of parties," and while "a third of the student body will be drunk on a typical weekend," there is "absolutely no pressure to drink if you don't want to." One freshman told us that for fun she "makes a smoothie run to the Sayles-Hill Student Center," then later stops by "Dacie Moses House, a place where students gather to bake cookies."

Student Body

The "creative, warm, compassionate, and helpful" undergrads of Carleton are "super smart and nerdy, but fun-nerdy, not scary-nerdy." Notably, they "don't form cliques based on [conventional] criteria" such as "socioeconomic background, race, gender, [or] sexual orientation"—students report they're more "interested in each other's quirks." An upbeat studio art major writes, "We have a wonderful mix of people that reach[es] from nerds to jocks, people who dye their hair to [those] who swear by Abercrombie, people who are Republican to those who are Democrat to those who are Independent to those who don't care; we have vegetarians and we have people who would live on steak if you let them. We have a truly rich mix of all sorts of people and we all enjoy each other and end up with the most amazing groups of friends." Basically, you'll find the campus to be "a place where energy, creativity, and a good sense of humor get you really far."

FINANCIAL AID: 507-646-4138 • E-MAIL: ADMISSIONS@ACS.CARLETON.EDU • WEBSITE: WWW.CARLETON.EDU

THE PRINCETON REVIEW SAYS

Admissions

Very important factors considered include: Class rank, academic GPA, rigor of secondary school record. *Important factors considered include:* Application essay, recommendation(s), standardized test scores, alumni/ae relation, character/personal qualities, extracurricular activities, racial/ethnic status, talent/ability, volunteer work, work experience. *Other factors considered include:* First generation, geographical residence, interview, state residency, SAT Subject Tests recommended; SAT or ACT required; ACT with Writing component required. TOEFL required of all international applicants. High school diploma is required and GED is accepted. *Academic units recommended:* 4 English, 3 mathematics, 3 science, (1 science labs), 3 foreign language, 3 Social Studies and History.

Financial Aid

Students should submit: FAFSA, CSS/Financial Aid PROFILE, noncustodial PROFILE, business/farm supplement, prior year tax forms. Regular filing deadline is 2/15. The Princeton Review suggests that all financial aid forms be submitted as soon as possible after January 1. *Need-based scholarships/grants offered:* Federal Pell, SEOG, state scholarships/grants, private scholarships, the school's own gift aid. *Loan aid offered:* FFEL Subsidized Stafford, FFEL Unsubsidized Stafford, FFEL PLUS, Federal Perkins, state loans, college/university loans from institutional funds, Minnesota SELF Loan program. Applicants will be notified of awards on or about 4/1.

The Inside Word

Admission to Carleton would be even more difficult if the college had more name recognition. Current applicants should be grateful for this because standards are already rigorous. Only intense competition with the best liberal arts colleges in the country prevents an even lower admit rate.

THE SCHOOL SAYS "..."

From The Admissions Office

"In an annual college freshmen survey, Carleton students identify themselves as everything from conservatives to liberals, with a majority of them falling in the moderate to liberal range. Although individualistic and energetic Carls take their academics seriously, they don't take themselves seriously. Participation in athletics, theater, or music, religious events, or dining hall discussion over hearty fare marks the Carleton experience. Cool fact: More snow fell in the Northeast than did here in the past 5 years. Since the year 2000, Carleton has opened a new recreation center with indoor track and fitness center, a new language and dining center, and nine townhouse complexes, providing some apartment-style living for students.

"With nearly three-fifths of the student body receiving need-based grant aid, there is a broad socioeconomic representation across the student body. Five percent of all students are international, and nearly 20 percent come from traditionally underrepresented groups. A look at majors in the past decade shows that graduates cover all areas, with about one-third of them in each of the following: math/science, humanities and arts, and social sciences. Typically, over two-thirds of all students will spend time studying off campus; Carleton participates in programs worldwide from Asia to Africa. You can scuba dive off the Greater Barrier Reef or walk the Great Wall of China.

"Five years after graduating, between 65 percent and 75 percent of alumni pursue graduate or professional degrees. More Carleton graduates have pursued their doctorates in the sciences in the past 20 years than have graduates of other small, comparable liberal arts colleges.

"2008 high school graduates must take the new SAT or ACT with Writing component. Carleton will not accept results from the old SAT format for 2008 application. SAT Subject Tests are not required, though it is recommended that a student submit these if they have taken any."

SELECTIVITY

Admissions Rating	97
# of applicants	4,840
% of applicants accepted	30
% of acceptees attending	35
# accepting a place on wait list	306
% admitted from wait list	2
# of early decision applicants	414
% accepted early decision	44

FRESHMAN PROFILE

Range SAT Critical Reading	650–750
Range SAT Math	660–740
Range SAT Writing	650–730
Range ACT Composite	29–33
Minimum paper TOEFL	600
Minimum computer TOEFL	250
% graduated top 10% of class	74
% graduated top 25% of class	92
% graduated top 50% of class	100

DEADLINES

Early decision	
Deadline	11/15
Notification	12/15
Regular	
Deadline	1/15
Notification	4/15
Nonfall registration?	no

APPLICANTS ALSO LOOK AT

AND OFTEN PREFER
Williams College
Yale University

AND SOMETIMES PREFER
Washington University in St. Louis
Wesleyan College
Grinnell College
Bowdoin College

AND RARELY PREFER
Oberlin College
Macalester College

FINANCIAL FACTS

Financial Aid Rating	97
Annual tuition	$37,860
Room and board	$9,978
Required fees	$204
Books and supplies	$629
% frosh rec. need-based scholarship or grant aid	50
% UG rec. need-based scholarship or grant aid	54
% frosh rec. non-need-based scholarship or grant aid	7
% UG rec. non-need-based scholarship or grant aid	10
% frosh rec. need-based self-help aid	48
% UG rec. need-based self-help aid	53
% UG borrow to pay for school	55
Average cumulative indebtedness	$19,185

CARNEGIE MELLON UNIVERSITY

5000 FORBES AVENUE, PITTSBURGH, PA 15213 • ADMISSIONS: 412-268-2082 • FAX: 412-268-7838

STUDENTS SAY ". . ."

Academics

Carnegie Mellon University is "all about technology. Whether it be engineering, music, theater, robotics, science, or psychology; it's about learning by breaking things down to find out how they work." With nearly half the students engaged in computer- and engineering-related disciplines, Carnegie Mellon can seem to be the domain of number-crunchers, but in fact the school also excels in music, theater, design, architecture, all the hard sciences, business, and economics; it is truly "a place where nerds of all kinds can thrive." One student observes, "Carnegie Mellon is strong in so many different fields. I wasn't sure what I wanted to do, but I wanted to be in a place where I could find out early in a hands-on way, and switch to an equally great program if I wanted." Those who choose Carnegie Mellon should prepare for academic demands that can "overwhelm you with work and stress in order to weed out the weak from the strong." To help students cope, the school offers "tons of academic resources to get extra help, from peer tutoring to office hours to student-led review sessions. Still, it's incredibly important to stay on top of assignments, or they really pile up." Hard work "prepares Carnegie Mellon students for post-undergraduate success," students agree, and when you reach that stage you'll be assisted by "a great career center" that draws "constant job recruiting on campus" and maintains "fantastic alumni connections," though this is somewhat dependent on a student's major.

Life

"Work hard, then work harder" might be the mantra of some Carnegie Mellon students; among them is the undergrad who tells us: "I go to class, I study in the library, and I work out. The day is so long that generally by the time I get home, I eat and am ready for bed because most of the time it's 11:00 or 12:00 at night already." Others tell us, however, that "if you are a social person, you can and will find other social people that you can have fun with." The weekend, or Friday night and Saturday—"Sunday will of course be spent doing work"—is the time to cut loose. Greek life and movies are the big on-campus draws: "Every Friday, Saturday, and Sunday night a just-released movie from the main theaters plays on campus; you can get a ticket, popcorn, and a drink for under three dollars." A good deal of students, though, prefer to have their fun in the city. Pittsburgh "offers a wide variety of things to do off-campus and the Port Authority bus system (free with a Carnegie Mellon ID) does a decent job of transporting students wherever they want to go." There's "always a gallery show to go see" in Pittsburgh, and professional sports, "great restaurants, shopping centers, and malls" are also a draw. The city "has a pretty big bar and club scene, but you must be 21." One student writes, "You can do virtually anything within a reasonable distance, including a trip to a ski mountain."

Student Body

The workload at Carnegie Mellon can be pretty daunting, so it's no surprise that the typical undergrad here "is extremely studious and serious about academics." In terms of priorities, "Extracurricular activities and a social life are far behind academics. Socially, people can be awkward." Even so, "For every recluse or extroverted musical theater major that you'd expect at Carnegie Mellon, there is a polar opposite. People here feel a need to define themselves some way, to defy established stereotypes." Carnegie Mellon draws "a very diverse student body where most people, regardless of race, ethnicity, or gender, tend to get along. Occasionally some cliques form on campus (for example, a certain set of international students, or students from a particular major), but most of the time everyone is friendly."

FINANCIAL AID: 412-268-2068 • E-MAIL: UNDERGRADUATE-ADMISSIONS@ANDREW.CMU.EDU • WEBSITE: WWW.CMU.EDU

THE PRINCETON REVIEW SAYS

Admissions

Very important factors considered include: Academic GPA, rigor of secondary school record. *Important factors considered include:* Class rank, application essay, recommendation(s), standardized test scores. *Other factors considered include:* Alumni/ae relation, character/personal qualities, extracurricular activities, first generation, geographical residence, interview, racial/ethnic status, talent/ability, volunteer work, work experience. SAT or ACT required; ACT with Writing component required. High school diploma is required and GED is accepted. *Academic units required:* 4 English, 4 mathematics, 3 science, (3 science labs), 2 foreign language, 3 academic electives. *Academic units recommended:* 4 English, 4 mathematics, 3 science, (3 science labs), 2 foreign language, 4 academic electives.

Financial Aid

Students should submit: FAFSA, institution's own financial aid form, Parent and student Federal Tax Returns. Parent W2 Forms. Regular filing deadline is 5/1. The Princeton Review suggests that all financial aid forms be submitted as soon as possible after January 1. *Need-based scholarships/grants offered:* Federal Pell, SEOG, state scholarships/grants, private scholarships, the school's own gift aid. *Loan aid offered:* FFEL Subsidized Stafford, FFEL Unsubsidized Stafford, FFEL PLUS, Federal Perkins, Gate Student Loan. Applicants will be notified of awards on or about 3/15. Federal Work-Study Program available. Institutional employment available. Off-campus job opportunities are good.

The Inside Word

Don't be misled by Carnegie Mellon's acceptance rate. Although relatively high for a university of this caliber, the applicant pool is fairly self-selecting. If you haven't loaded up on demanding courses in high school, you are not likely to be a serious contender. The Admissions Office explicitly states that it doesn't use formulas in making admissions decisions. That said, a record of strong academic performance in the area of your intended major is key.

THE SCHOOL SAYS "..."

From The Admissions Office

"Carnegie Mellon is a private, coeducational university with approximately 5,300 undergraduates; 4,400 graduate students; and 1,200 full-time faculty members. The university's 144-acre campus is located in the Oakland area of Pittsburgh, five miles from downtown. The university is composed of seven colleges: the Carnegie Institute of Technology (engineering), the College of Fine Arts, the College of Humanities and Social Sciences (combining liberal arts education with professional specializations), the Tepper School of Business (undergraduate business and industrial management), the Mellon College of Science, the School of Computer Science, and the H. John Heinz III School of Public Policy and Management.

"Freshman applicants for Fall 2008 must take the SAT plus two SAT Subject Tests, depending on their major interest. Students may take the ACT with Writing in lieu of the SAT. An applicant's best scores will be used in admissions decision-making.

"Carnegie Mellon has campuses in the Silicon Valley, California, and Qatar in the Arabian Gulf."

SELECTIVITY

Admissions Rating	97
# of applicants	18,864
% of applicants accepted	34
% of acceptees attending	22
# accepting a place on wait list	319
% admitted from wait list	18
# of early decision applicants	813
% accepted early decision	35

FRESHMAN PROFILE

Range SAT Critical Reading	610–710
Range SAT Math	690–780
Range SAT Writing	610–700
Range ACT Composite	28–32
Average HS GPA	3.61
% graduated top 10% of class	75
% graduated top 25% of class	95
% graduated top 50% of class	100

DEADLINES

Early decision	
Deadline	11/1
Notification	12/15
Regular	
Deadline	1/1
Notification	4/15
Nonfall registration?	no

FINANCIAL FACTS

Financial Aid Rating	78
Annual tuition	$35,580
Room and board	$9,350
Required fees	$404
Books and supplies	$966
% frosh rec. need-based scholarship or grant aid	49
% UG rec. need-based scholarship or grant aid	46
% frosh rec. non-need-based scholarship or grant aid	18
% UG rec. non-need-based scholarship or grant aid	22
% frosh rec. need-based self-help aid	49
% UG rec. need-based self-help aid	47
% frosh rec. any financial aid	68
% UG rec. any financial aid	66
% UG borrow to pay for school	52
Average cumulative indebtedness	$27,395

CASE WESTERN RESERVE UNIVERSITY

103 TOMLINSON HALL, 10900 EUCLID AVENUE, CLEVELAND, OH 44106-7055 • ADMISSIONS: 216-368-4450 • FAX: 216-368-5111

CAMPUS LIFE

Quality of Life Rating	69
Fire Safety Rating	68
Green Rating	80
Type of school	private
Environment	metropolis

STUDENTS

Total undergrad enrollment	4,120
% male/female	58/42
% from out of state	46
% live on campus	82
% in (# of) fraternities	29 (17)
% in (# of) sororities	23 (7)
% African American	5
% Asian	16
% Caucasian	60
% Hispanic	2
% international	3
# of countries represented	26

SURVEY SAYS . . .
Lab facilities are great
Great computer facilities
Great library
Great off-campus food

ACADEMICS

Academic Rating	83
Calendar	semester
Student/faculty ratio	9:1
Profs interesting rating	68
Profs accessible rating	71
% classes taught by TAs	5
Most common reg class size	10–19 students
Most common lab size	fewer than 10 students

MOST POPULAR MAJORS
biomedical/medical engineering
biology/biological sciences
psychology

STUDENTS SAY ". . ."

Academics

With over half its students in the labor-intensive disciplines of engineering and the sciences, it's no wonder students tell us that "Case is about hard work." Undergrads here tell us that "a 9-to-5 job will be exceptionally easy after a Case undergraduate education (which is 9-to-5 classes, then 5-to-2 homework)." And while some complain that Case Western "is designed to beat students down [and they] attempt to compete with better schools by giving more homework," others counter that "You can choose to complain about it all the time or you can take advantage of everything that's offered here—enjoy yourself and get a great education." For those who know where to look, Case offers "great means for student development outside of the classroom. The Emerging Leaders Program for first-year students…holds leadership conferences—largely planned and organized by students for students—every semester." It's also "incredibly easy to get involved" in the "groundbreaking research" that occurs on this campus daily. Some here acknowledge that Case "could improve on diversifying its non-engineering and non-science offerings," a matter of significance to all since the school introduced mandatory interdisciplinary seminars (called the SAGE program, which students tell us "is still a work in progress"). Most agree that while the administration "has done a better job at getting to know the students," most would like to see an increase in "their willingness to cater to students' interests, especially when these differ from the beaten path."

Life

"Many students feel that Case Western students do much more work than a typical student and thus miss out on more chances for socializing, even during the weekend," but others tell us that despite the "ton of hard work," there is "still plenty of time in the day for extracurricular activities." "Actually, that's part of the reason why people are so busy in the first place," says one student. Case offers "a wide range of on- and off-campus activities to choose from. Events such as Drag Ball, a local sorority's Mr. CWRU, and our University Program Board's major concerts pull hundreds of students out to bond and have a great time. Smaller events are always going on through one of our officially recognized student organizations, be they guest lecturers brought in by the Case Democrats, choral showcases featuring one or many of our a cappella groups, or simply smaller events." Cleveland provides further diversion; the school is located in University Circle, home to "a number of museums, the Cleveland Orchestra, the Botanical Gardens, and much more. This is a great resource of our school, which we are encouraged to take advantage of." The party scene here is "more mellow" than other colleges. "If you want to party, you can. If you'd rather stay away from the "sex, drugs, and rock 'n roll" scene, you can. There's no pressure to conform to either group."

Student Body

A typical Case student is "heartily dedicated to classes and tries to figure out what else can fit into his schedule." Because the school is "so academically focused, there are plenty of the overstressing pre-medical students" along with similarly disposed engineers ("mostly male") and nursing students ("mostly female"). While "many Case students are primarily gamers" who "may not leave their rooms" very often, students "who are incredibly involved and busy joining and leading numerous organizations" are "increasingly more common" on campus. There is also "a vibrant musical community" as well as an active group of intramural sports enthusiasts. One student sums it up, "The greatest strengths of Case are the diversity of the student body, the studious character of the student body, the professors, and the tolerance students have toward different students."

FINANCIAL AID: 216-368-4530 • E-MAIL: ADMISSION@CASE.EDU • WEBSITE: WWW.CASE.EDU

THE PRINCETON REVIEW SAYS

Admissions

Very important factors considered include: Class rank, academic GPA, rigor of secondary school record, standardized test scores, extracurricular activities. *Important factors considered include:* Application essay, recommendation(s), character/personal qualities, interview, talent/ability, volunteer work, work experience. *Other factors considered include:* Alumni/ae relation, first generation, level of applicant's interest, racial/ethnic status, SAT or ACT required; ACT with Writing component required. High school diploma is required and GED is accepted. *Academic units required:* 4 English, 3 mathematics, 3 science, (2 science labs), 2 foreign language, 3 social studies. *Academic units recommended:* 4 mathematics, (3 science labs), 3 foreign language, 4 social studies.

Financial Aid

Students should submit: FAFSA, institution's own financial aid form, business/farm supplement, parent and student income tax returns and W-2 forms. The Princeton Review suggests that all financial aid forms be submitted as soon as possible after January 1. *Need-based scholarships/grants offered:* Federal Pell, SEOG, state scholarships/grants, private scholarships, the school's own gift aid. *Loan aid offered:* FFEL Subsidized Stafford, FFEL Unsubsidized Stafford, FFEL PLUS, Federal Perkins, Federal Nursing, state loans, college/university loans from institutional funds. Applicants will be notified of awards on a rolling basis beginning 2/15. Federal Work-Study Program available. Institutional employment available. Off-campus job opportunities are good.

The Inside Word

Case faces tough competition from similar schools and handles it well as both the number of overall applications and out-of-state applications has increased substantially over the past decade, indicating an improving national profile. As a result, Case grows ever more selective. Case uses a 'single door' admissions policy, meaning that once you are admitted you can change your intended major without having to reapply, even if it means switching schools (e.g. switching from the School of Engineering to the School of Management).

THE SCHOOL SAYS "..."

From The Admissions Office

"Challenging and innovative academic programs, next-level technology, experiential learning, real-world environments, and faculty mentors are at the core of the Case Western Reserve University experience. Case's faculty challenges and supports motivated students, and its partnerships with world-class cultural, educational, and scientific institutions ensure that your education extends beyond the classroom.

"Case offers more than 75 majors and minors and a single-door admission policy; once admitted to Case, you can major in any of our programs, or double and even triple major in several of them. Our student/faculty ratio, among the best in the nation, allows students to have close interaction with professors. Co-ops, internships, study abroad and other opportunities bring theory to life in amazing settings, and 66 percent of students participate in research and independent study. SAGES, Case's 4-year undergraduate core curriculum, connects students with faculty, peers and the community through small seminars that explore effective communication and analytical skills, and culminates in a Senior Capstone project.

"With 85 percent of students living on campus, Case has a residential feel unique to urban universities. First-year students live together in one of three themed residential colleges that involve resources from across Northeast Ohio: Cedar (arts), Juniper (world culture) or Mistletoe (leadership through service).

"Admission Counselors consider all sections of the SAT, taking the best score for each section from multiple dates. The SAT (or ACT with writing) is used for evaluating applications for admission (and not used for course placement purposes)."

SELECTIVITY	
Admissions Rating	92
# of applicants	7,297
% of applicants accepted	75
% of acceptees attending	21
# accepting a place on wait list	101

FRESHMAN PROFILE	
Range SAT Critical Reading	580–690
Range SAT Math	620–720
Range SAT Writing	580–680
Range ACT Composite	26–31
% graduated top 10% of class	67
% graduated top 25% of class	92
% graduated top 50% of class	99

DEADLINES	
Early action	
Deadline	11/1
Notification	1/1
Regular	
Deadline	1/15
Notification	4/1
Nonfall registration?	yes

FINANCIAL FACTS	
Financial Aid Rating	95
Annual tuition	$33,500
Room and board	$10,590
Required fees	$752
Books and supplies	$1,100
% frosh rec. need-based scholarship or grant aid	70
% UG rec. need-based scholarship or grant aid	62
% frosh rec. non-need-based scholarship or grant aid	58
% UG rec. non-need-based scholarship or grant aid	51
% frosh rec. need-based self-help aid	57
% UG rec. need-based self-help aid	53
% frosh rec. any financial aid	91
% UG rec. any financial aid	84
% UG borrow to pay for school	59
Average cumulative indebtedness	$32,195

CATAWBA COLLEGE

2300 WEST INNES STREET, SALISBURY, NC 28144 • ADMISSIONS: 704-637-4402 • FAX: 704-637-4222

CAMPUS LIFE
Quality of Life Rating	**86**
Fire Safety Rating	**64**
Green Rating	**60***
Type of school	private
Affiliation	United Church of Christ
Environment	town

STUDENTS
Total undergrad enrollment	291
% male/female	50/50
% from out of state	26
% from public high school	80
% live on campus	48
% African American	16
% Asian	1
% Caucasian	80
% Hispanic	1
% Native American	1
% international	1
# of countries represented	14

SURVEY SAYS . . .
Large classes
Students are happy
Everyone loves the Catawba Indians
Theater is popular

ACADEMICS
Academic Rating	**79**
Calendar	semester
Student/faculty ratio	15:1
Profs interesting rating	91
Profs accessible rating	86
Most common reg class size	10–19 students
Most common lab size	fewer than 10 students

MOST POPULAR MAJORS
sport and fitness administration/management
drama and dramatics/theatre arts
business/commerce

STUDENTS SAY "..."

Academics

Catawba College, a "small school with a student body of fewer than three thousand" "known for its environmental science and theatre programs," is the sort of place where students meet "people who make a big difference in your life, whether it be your caring admissions counselor, easily accessible professor, friendly department head, or large group of friends," all of whom boast a "diverse range of interests. At Catawba, it's the people who define the school." An "atmosphere of creativity and curiosity" envelops a "learning community focused on involvement in academics, athletics, campus clubs, and volunteer work." This is abetted by faculty who "are generally very willing to work with and help you if you are confused," not to mention "a good tutoring system." An honors program "is top notch, but underappreciated," providing participants with courses specifically designed to facilitate "discussion and interaction." Besides the aforementioned theatre department ("which comprises one-fifth of the student population" and "puts a lot of effort into productions and regularly wins awards") and the environmental science program standout offerings include music and history. The school is undergoing a growth spurt these days and the administration "is continuing to change and update the buildings." Although "construction could go faster," students love the direction in which their school is headed, telling us that the college is "constantly improving and growing."

Life

Catawba's administration imposes some moderately strict regulations—students must be twenty-three years old in order to live off campus, for example—leading some to complain that the school "runs on a high school mindset." "It's as if the administration didn't get the memo that Catawba is a college, not a boarding school." Not all students mind the restrictions; some happily report that "for the most part people love Catawba" and that "there is almost always something going on around campus that you can get into. Everyone goes to the same places—movies, dinner, bars, clubs, on-campus events—and hangs out and has fun." As one student puts it, "Life at school is dependent upon how many activities you are involved with. The more activities that you participate in, the more fun you will have on campus. We have outdoor movies, Casino nights, late night campus-sponsored events, intramurals, athletics, and much more." Some undergrads demur, reporting that "There are very few activities or facilities for us to enjoy on campus. After dark, there is nothing to do." All agree that sports "are a very big thing." "People come from all over to see the Indians play. Tailgate parties are a regular thing." "There's not much to do as far as social events" in hometown Salisbury. "The music scene in Salisbury is nonexistent which is frustrating, so parties tend to be kind of exclusive (theatre majors tend to stick together, etc.). There is a lot drinking on Saturday nights." It's possible some drink to forget the school dining service. Student reviews range from "getting better but still not great" to "needs some help" to "really dreadful."

Student Body

Catawba "is a very diverse school with all different people and majors, but it's very divided into sects: the theater kids, the e-sci kids, the sports kids, etc. Catawba's nickname—Catawba High—sums us up." The theatre group is further divided into "the more 'bohemian' set and the musical theatre set." While these groups don't actively socialize with one another, the campus is hardly Balkanized; "The athletes go to the plays and music events, and the theater people support the athletes in their events." Catawba undergrads "tend to be from within two hundred miles of the school. This is reflected in the 'southern values' mindset of the school. Being from New York, I find it to be a refreshing change." Students activities tend not to be "limited to the classroom; instead, they are athletes, actors, and club presidents. You would be hard-pressed to find anyone on campus who isn't involved in something else other than just going to class. This involvement in school really makes Catawba as great as it is."

FINANCIAL AID: 704-637-4416 • E-MAIL: ADMISSION@CATAWBA.EDU • WEBSITE: WWW.CATAWBA.EDU

THE PRINCETON REVIEW SAYS

Admissions

Very important factors considered include: Class rank, application essay, academic GPA, recommendation(s), standardized test scores. *Important factors considered include:* rigor of secondary school record, character/personal qualities, extracurricular activities, interview, level of applicant's interest, talent/ability. *Other factors considered include:* Volunteer work, SAT or ACT required; ACT with Writing component recommended. TOEFL required of all international applicants. High school diploma is required and GED is accepted. *Academic units required:* 4 English, 2 mathematics, 2 science, 2 social studies, 6 academic electives. *Academic units recommended:* 4 English, 3 mathematics, 3 science, (3 science labs), 2 foreign language, 3 social studies, 2 academic electives.

Financial Aid

Students should submit: FAFSA, state aid form The Princeton Review suggests that all financial aid forms be submitted as soon as possible after January 1. *Need-based scholarships/grants offered:* Federal Pell, SEOG, state scholarships/grants, private scholarships, the school's own gift aid. *Loan aid offered:* FFEL Subsidized Stafford, FFEL Unsubsidized Stafford, FFEL PLUS, Federal Perkins, college/university loans from institutional funds, TERI Loans, Nellie Mae Loans, Advantage Loans, Alternative Loans. Applicants will be notified of awards on a rolling basis beginning 2/15.

The Inside Word

Because it competes with so many top schools for regional students, Catawba is willing to take a chance on some applicants who may not make the cut at Davidson, Duke, or Chapel Hill. High school underachievers who are ready to excel at the college level will find a great opportunity to do just that at Catawba. Such students may well benefit from the close attention administrators and professors lavish on Catawba undergrads.

THE SCHOOL SAYS "..."

From The Admissions Office

"Catawba College prepares students for rewarding lives and careers in the liberal arts tradition. This attractive campus is centrally located in Salisbury, North Carolina, a short drive away from the mountains and Atlantic beaches. The community possesses a rich past and commitment to preserving its cultural and historic charm. In contrast, just 45 minutes away is the much faster pace of Charlotte, North Carolina where shopping, transportation, and entertainment of all kinds are readily available.

"On campus, students study and socialize in a small college setting that offers strong traditions, excellent facilities, and beautiful surroundings. The high standards of quality set by Catawba's academic programs are matched by equally demanding sports and co-curricular programs. Students describe the community as caring and personable. They also exhibit a high rate of involvement in campus activities ranging form the performing arts to homecoming and travel abroad. Faculty and staff are described by students as being important mentors. Whether in a state-of-the-art environmental science facility, attractive music and theatrical performance center, classroom, or one of the college's first-class athletic facilities, students report they feel as if they are among family when on campus.

"Perhaps the most important testimony to the attractiveness of Catawba is found in the words of its graduates who report numerous successful careers and rich memories of their time at school.

"Students applying for admissions to Catawba College are required submit to scores from the SAT, including the Writing test. In lieu of SAT scores, Catawba will accept student scores on the ACT when they include scores on the ACT Writing test. Catawba will use the student's best scores from either test in making admissions decisions."

SELECTIVITY

Admissions Rating	79
# of applicants	822
% of applicants accepted	75
% of acceptees attending	43

FRESHMAN PROFILE

Range SAT Critical Reading	450–570
Range SAT Math	470–580
Range ACT Composite	18–25
Minimum paper TOEFL	525
Minimum computer TOEFL	197
Average HS GPA	3.366
% graduated top 10% of class	13
% graduated top 25% of class	45
% graduated top 50% of class	70

DEADLINES

Notification	rolling
Nonfall registration?	yes

APPLICANTS ALSO LOOK AT AND SOMETIMES PREFER

Appalachian State University
University of North Carolina at Chapel Hill
University of North Carolina—Charlotte

AND RARELY PREFER

North Carolina State University
University of North Carolina—Greensboro
University of North Carolina—Wilmington

FINANCIAL FACTS

Financial Aid Rating	84
Annual tuition	$22,290
Room and board	$7,700
Books and supplies	$800
% frosh rec. need-based scholarship or grant aid	49
% UG rec. need-based scholarship or grant aid	42
% frosh rec. non-need-based scholarship or grant aid	76
% UG rec. non-need-based scholarship or grant aid	66
% frosh rec. need-based self-help aid	57
% UG rec. need-based self-help aid	50
% frosh rec. athletic scholarships	29
% UG rec. athletic scholarships	24
% frosh rec. any financial aid	96
% UG rec. any financial aid	96
% UG borrow to pay for school	70
Average cumulative indebtedness	$21,726

THE CATHOLIC UNIVERSITY OF AMERICA

OFFICE OF ENROLLMENT SERVICES, WASHINGTON, DC 20064 • ADMISSIONS: 202-319-5305 • FAX: 202-319-6533

CAMPUS LIFE

Quality of Life Rating	67
Fire Safety Rating	85
Green Rating	69
Type of school	private
Affiliation	Roman Catholic
Environment	metropolis

STUDENTS

Total undergrad enrollment	3,245
% male/female	46/54
% from out of state	94
% from public high school	49
% live on campus	68
% in (# of) fraternities	1 (1)
% in (# of) sororities	1 (1)
% African American	5
% Asian	3
% Caucasian	69
% Hispanic	6
% international	2
# of countries represented	76

SURVEY SAYS . . .

Large classes
Students are friendly
Frats and sororities are unpopular
or nonexistent
Political activism is popular
Lots of beer drinking
Hard liquor is popular

ACADEMICS

Academic Rating	75
Calendar	semester
Student/faculty ratio	10:1
Profs interesting rating	73
Profs accessible rating	75
% classes taught by TAs	9
Most common reg class size	10–19 students
Most common lab size	10–19 students

MOST POPULAR MAJORS

political science and government
architecture (barch, ba/bs, march,
ma/ms, phd)
nursing/registered nurse
(RN, ASN, BSN, MSN)

STUDENTS SAY ". . ."

Academics

You'll receive "an education heavy in philosophy and theology" at the Catholic University of America, "a beautiful college campus located in the heart of our nation's capital." That's because every student at CUA completes a core curriculum with an "emphasis on philosophy and religion. Students are required to take a series of both. Unless you are planning on making a career out of either, when else in life will you study these in depth than college?" For a school of just over 3,000 students, CUA has a remarkable number of strong disciplines. Undergrads laud the "incredibly strong" nursing program, a "wonderful music program" that's ideal for students who "don't want conservatory straight out of high school but still want a challenging program," "the best education in architecture in the DC area," and a "very strong" drama department. While liberal arts and science programs aren't as highly regarded, students appreciate that "Professors are helpful and always available," and point out that political studies are greatly abetted by the school's location. Of DC, one student observes that the school's location in the nation's provides, "easy access to internships, government, and seemingly endless other political opportunities." The school also offers an honors program that "challenges students to push [to] the edge of their abilities."

Life

CUA's Washington, DC address "is absolutely one of the great strengths of the school. A student can get on the Metro and go basically wherever they want, and get whatever it is that they need." Indeed, students "have DC, a storied and cosmopolitan city," at their fingertips, "with plenty of concert venues, movie theaters, play houses, shopping districts, landmarks, and museums to visit on the weekends." Undergrads "go to Starbucks and have study sessions . . . on Sundays, or go and visit friends at George Washington or Georgetown on the weekends." "Chinatown, Dupont Circle, and Union Station" are also popular destinations for "fun times." As one student sums up, "We are in the nation's capital, we have plenty to do." Students tell us that "almost everyone on this campus likes to drink," and while "The school tries really hard to offer nonalcoholic alternatives on the weekends," their efforts "aren't quite enticing enough to lure us away from the neighborhood bars." Drinking generally takes place in the bars, as "House parties are almost nonexistent" on campus. However, students also tell us that "if you don't feel like drinking on the weekends, there is always some option for you" including campus ministry events which provide "students [with] a healthy environment and people to be around as an alternative to drinking."

Student Body

The typical student at CUA "is from the Mid-Atlantic states, White, and went to a Catholic high school"; "fairly conservative," and looks like a "page out of an Abercrombie & Fitch ad." "Everyone wears flip-flops, polo shirts, and khakis. People only wear jeans during the wintertime." Exceptions to the rule include "the very vocal minority groups" who work to make sure "Diversity is highlighted" on campus, "people of other religious backgrounds," and the many "musical theater students" including a large number of "gay men, which is pretty surprising at a Catholic university." Many students are devout and "very open about their faith," but "Very few people will force religion down your throat." Atypical students are "generally welcomed and accepted by these 'typical' students with little or no friction due to religion, sexual orientation, race, socioeconomic class."

FINANCIAL AID: 202-319-5307 • E-MAIL: CUA-ADMISSIONS@CUA.EDU • WEBSITE: WWW.CUA.EDU

THE PRINCETON REVIEW SAYS

Admissions

Very important factors considered include: Academic GPA, recommendation(s), rigor of secondary school record, standardized test scores, character/personal qualities, level of applicant's interest, volunteer work. *Important factors considered include:* Application essay, extracurricular activities, first generation, interview, talent/ability. *Other factors considered include:* Class rank, alumni/ae relation, racial/ethnic status, work experience. SAT Subject Tests recommended; SAT or ACT required; ACT with Writing component required. TOEFL required of all international applicants. High school diploma is required and GED is accepted. *Academic units recommended:* 4 English, 3 mathematics, 3 science, (1 science labs), 2 foreign language, 4 social studies, 1 fine arts or humanities.

Financial Aid

Students should submit: FAFSA, Alumni and Parish Scholarship Applications if appropriate. The Princeton Review suggests that all financial aid forms be submitted as soon as possible after January 1. *Need-based scholarships/grants offered:* Federal Pell, SEOG, state scholarships/grants, private scholarships, the school's own gift aid, Federal Nursing Scholarships. *Loan aid offered:* FFEL Subsidized Stafford, FFEL Unsubsidized Stafford, FFEL PLUS, Federal Perkins, Federal Nursing, college/university loans from institutional funds, commericial Loans. Applicants will be notified of awards on or about 4/1. Federal Work-Study Program available. Institutional employment available. Off-campus job opportunities are good.

The Inside Word

The Catholic University of America is a conservative school that adopts a very traditional approach to higher education. Your application should demonstrate an appreciation for the school's unique qualities and educational philosophy. Present your strongest case by showing solid grades in a demanding curriculum, backed by above average test scores, and you should have little trouble gaining admission. CUA now accepts the Common Application.

THE SCHOOL SAYS "..."

From The Admissions Office

"The Catholic University of America's friendly atmosphere, rigorous academic programs, and emphasis on time-honored values attract students from all 50 states and more than 95 foreign countries. Its 193-acre, tree-lined campus is only 10 minutes from the nation's capital. Distinguished as the national university of the Catholic Church in the United States, CUA is the only institution of higher education established by the U.S. Catholic bishops; however, students from all religious traditions are welcome.

"CUA offers undergraduate degrees in more than 80 major areas in seven schools of study. Students enroll into the School of Arts and Sciences, Architecture, Nursing, Engineering, Metropolitan College, Music, or Philosophy. Additionally, CUA students can concentrate in areas of preprofessional study including law, dentistry, medicine, or veterinary studies.

"With Capitol Hill, the Smithsonian Institution, NASA, the Kennedy Center, and the National Institutes of Health among the places students obtain internships, firsthand experience is a valuable piece of the experience that CUA offers. Numerous students also take the opportunity in their junior year to study abroad at one of Catholic's 17 country program sites. Political science majors even have the opportunity to do a Parliamentary Internship in either England or Ireland. With the campus just minutes away from downtown via the Metrorail rapid transit system, students enjoy a residential campus in an exciting city of historical monuments, theaters, festivals, ethnic restaurants, and parks.

"Freshman applicants for Fall 2008 must take the new SAT or ACT. Additionally, students may submit scores from the old SAT, and the best scores from either test will be used. Matriculating students should submit the SAT Subject Test: Foreign Language exam if they plan to continue studying that language at CUA."

SELECTIVITY

Admissions Rating	84
# of applicants	4,911
% of applicants accepted	80
% of acceptees attending	22

FRESHMAN PROFILE

Range SAT Critical Reading	520–620
Range SAT Math	510–610
Range SAT Writing	520–610
Range ACT Composite	22–26
Minimum paper TOEFL	560
Minimum computer TOEFL	220
Minimum web-based TOEFL	80
Average HS GPA	3.26
% graduated top 10% of class	18
% graduated top 25% of class	57
% graduated top 50% of class	87

DEADLINES

Early action	
Deadline	11/15
Notification	12/15
Regular	
Deadline	2/15
Notification	3/15
Nonfall registration?	yes

APPLICANTS ALSO LOOK AT

AND OFTEN PREFER
University of Maryland University College
University of Notre Dame
Boston College

AND SOMETIMES PREFER
University of Virginia

AND RARELY PREFER
The George Washington University
Fordham University
American University
Saint Joseph's University (PA)

FINANCIAL FACTS

Financial Aid Rating	85
Annual tuition	$30,520
% frosh rec. need-based scholarship or grant aid	58
% UG rec. need-based scholarship or grant aid	50
% frosh rec. need-based self-help aid	54
% UG rec. need-based self-help aid	45
% frosh rec. any financial aid	99
% UG rec. any financial aid	92

CENTENARY COLLEGE OF LOUISIANA

2911 CENTENARY BOULEVARD, SHREVEPORT, LA 71104 • ADMISSIONS: 318-869-5131 • FAX: 318-869-5005

CAMPUS LIFE

Quality of Life Rating	**75**
Fire Safety Rating	**80**
Green Rating	**60***
Type of school	private
Affiliation	Methodist
Environment	metropolis

STUDENTS

Total undergrad enrollment	891
% male/female	41/59
% from out of state	43
% from public high school	72
% live on campus	66
% in (# of) fraternities	28 (5)
% in (# of) sororities	35 (2)
% African American	8
% Asian	2
% Caucasian	82
% Hispanic	4
% international	2
# of countries represented	12

SURVEY SAYS . . .
Large classes
Registration is a breeze
Students are friendly
Musical organizations are popular

ACADEMICS

Academic Rating	**83**
Calendar	semester
Student/faculty ratio	12:1
Profs interesting rating	88
Profs accessible rating	87
Most common reg class size	10–19 students

MOST POPULAR MAJORS
biology/biological sciences
business/commerce
mass communication/media studies

STUDENTS SAY ". . ."

Academics

With fewer than 1,000 undergraduates, Centenary College of Louisiana certainly qualifies as a small school. In fact, there are only a handful of elite undergraduate institutions smaller. That said, smallness has its virtues. As one student notes, "The small size of the student body gives students the opportunity to receive individual attention in class and be involved in many organizations and hold leadership positions outside of class." It also fosters "a community atmosphere" in which "professors really care about you emotionally and academically," along with providing "a lot of one-on-one help and projects." Premedical sciences are said to be excellent (nearly 20 percent of all students major in life sciences), as are business studies, music, and communications. Academics are "extremely rigorous and thorough," so much so that "No one graduates without expanding their knowledge base." As at many small schools, "The professors are absolutely wonderful. They're engaging, knowledgeable, and really care about what they're teaching and about their students." The school places a premium on such high-caliber teaching skill. "Bad teachers do not last long around here," one undergrad assures us. The downside of a small school, of course, is that certain limitations are an unavoidable fact of life. Some "miss the perks a bigger school [has to offer] like more classes and a better cafeteria."

Life

"Campus life is centers around athletics, clubs, and Greek life" at Centenary, where "The real trick is finding that one thing that you love (be it sororities, radio, theatre, whatever) and excelling at it. The school has a lot of opportunities for responsible individuals." There's the "awesome" radio station, for one, and lots of lectures, internships, and mentoring opportunities. And while "There are occasional events on weekdays, including sports games," when it comes time for fun "Life at Centenary revolves around the weekend" and "includes going to some of the local attractions, to a movie, to dinner, or to either one of the sport teams house or a fraternity house." Because the campus is officially dry, "those unwilling to hide their contraband alcohol…normally just hang out in residence hall lobbies and watch movies" or they "go down to the fraternity houses (which allow alcohol)." Hometown Shreveport "doesn't offer many options for students, especially students under 21. It's definitely not a 'college town.'" Another student explains, "There is not a lot to do in Shreveport besides shopping, but there are many opportunities to do so in the surrounding area. There are not too many local music shows but the Shreveport Opera and community theaters are worth the time."

Student Body

For such a small school, Centenary does a good job of drawing a diverse mix of interests and backgrounds. Here "You can find everything from far right-wing ministry majors to highly liberal individuals actively involved in campus organizations promoting gay rights" as well as "a large and diverse number of international students most notably from Europe and Hong Kong." What you won't find is a lot of minority students; "There are very few minorities on this campus," one student observes. Most students here "are overachievers or hard workers, whether it is in an academic sense or in an extracurricular sense." Though many note that the student body is "generally white, middle-class, and religious," they are also quick to point out that it also accommodates "a lot of gay and lesbian students, and overall, the campus is very accepting and supportive of these students."

CENTENARY COLLEGE OF LOUISIANA

FINANCIAL AID: 318-869-5137 • E-MAIL: ADMISSIONS@CENTENARY.EDU • WEBSITE: WWW.CENTENARY.EDU

THE PRINCETON REVIEW SAYS

Admissions

Very important factors considered include: Academic GPA, rigor of secondary school record. *Important factors considered include:* Class rank, application essay, recommendation(s), standardized test scores, alumni/ae relation, character/personal qualities, extracurricular activities, interview, level of applicant's interest, talent/ability, volunteer work, work experience. *Other factors considered include:* Geographical residence, racial/ethnic status, religious affiliation/commitment, SAT or ACT required; TOEFL required of all international applicants. High school diploma is required and GED is accepted. *Academic units recommended:* 4 English, 3 mathematics, 3 science, (2 science labs), 2 foreign language, 3 social studies.

Financial Aid

Students should submit: FAFSA, institution's own financial aid form The Princeton Review suggests that all financial aid forms be submitted as soon as possible after January 1. *Need-based scholarships/grants offered:* Federal Pell, SEOG, state scholarships/grants, private scholarships, the school's own gift aid. *Loan aid offered:* FFEL Subsidized Stafford, FFEL Unsubsidized Stafford, FFEL PLUS, Federal Perkins Applicants will be notified of awards on or about 3/15. Federal Work-Study Program available. Institutional employment available. Off-campus job opportunities are good.

The Inside Word

Centenary's applicant pool has grown substantially over the past decade, allowing the school to become more selective in its admissions process. The school's reputation, though regional, is quite solid, and the college does a good job of enrolling those it admits—a sign that the school is tops on more than a few applicants' lists. No doubt a very friendly and efficient admissions office also contributes to this success.

THE SCHOOL SAYS "..."

From The Admissions Office

"Just as a student's 4-year experience at Centenary will be very personalized, so too is the application process. We pride ourselves on treating each applicant as an individual. We encourage all interested students to visit us—not only so they can see our campus and get a sense of the atmosphere, but also to provide us the opportunity to meet and get to know them.

"Consider Centenary for a life-changing experience. Our professors value your ideas and contributions and are passionate about teaching. We consider the Centenary Experience to be more than just a degree. You will live in a comprehensive learning environment that features connections to your academic, social, personal, and residential lives.

"Our students work and live within a strong community to create personalized, distinctive experiences. Our students enjoy a vibrant college life and graduate from Centenary prepared for their professional and personal lives.

"First-year applicants for Fall 2007 must submit either ACT or SAT examination scores. If either exam was taken before the recently revised version (February 2005 for ACT and March 2005 for the SAT), those scores can be submitted. We recommend, but do not require, the ACT Writing exam."

SELECTIVITY

Admissions Rating	83
# of applicants	1,069
% of applicants accepted	65
% of acceptees attending	34
# of early decision applicants	35
% accepted early decision	80

FRESHMAN PROFILE

Range SAT Critical Reading	500–620
Range SAT Math	510–620
Range ACT Composite	23–28
Minimum paper TOEFL	550
Minimum computer TOEFL	213
Minimum web-based TOEFL	79–80
% graduated top 10% of class	35
% graduated top 25% of class	62
% graduated top 50% of class	83

DEADLINES

Early decision	
Deadline	12/1
Notification	12/15
Early action	
Deadline	1/15
Notification	1/15
Regular	
Priority	2/15
Deadline	8/1
Notification	rolling
Nonfall registration?	yes

FINANCIAL FACTS

Financial Aid Rating	85
Annual tuition	$19,850
Room and board	$7,050
Required fees	$1,100
Books and supplies	$1,000
% frosh rec. need-based scholarship or grant aid	60
% UG rec. need-based scholarship or grant aid	56
% frosh rec. non-need-based scholarship or grant aid	18
% UG rec. non-need-based scholarship or grant aid	16
% frosh rec. need-based self-help aid	32
% UG rec. need-based self-help aid	31
% frosh rec. athletic scholarships	12
% UG rec. athletic scholarships	13
% frosh rec. any financial aid	97
% UG rec. any financial aid	95
% UG borrow to pay for school	64
Average cumulative indebtedness	$19,206

THE BEST 368 COLLEGES ■ 129

Centre College

600 West Walnut Street, Danville, KY 40422 • Admissions: 800-423-6236 • Fax: 859-238-5373

CAMPUS LIFE

Quality of Life Rating	**86**
Fire Safety Rating	**60***
Green Rating	**81**
Type of school	private
Affiliation	Presbyterian
Environment	village

STUDENTS

Total undergrad enrollment	1,184
% male/female	46/54
% from out of state	36
% from public high school	79
% live on campus	93
% in (# of) fraternities	34 (4)
% in (# of) sororities	37 (4)
% African American	3
% Asian	2
% Caucasian	90
% Hispanic	2
% international	2
# of countries represented	12

SURVEY SAYS . . .

Small classes
No one cheats
Great library
Students are friendly
Students are happy
Frats and sororities dominate
social scene
Lots of beer drinking
Hard liquor is popular

ACADEMICS

Academic Rating	**91**
Calendar	4/1/4
Student/faculty ratio	11:1
Profs interesting rating	99
Profs accessible rating	97
Most common reg class size	10–19 students
Most common lab size	10–19 students

MOST POPULAR MAJORS

English language and literature
economics
history

STUDENTS SAY ". . ."

Academics

Many schools offer opportunities for major-related internships and study abroad. Few, however, guarantee both. Centre College, a small liberal arts school in Kentucky, does. Under "The Centre Commitment," Centre not only ensures an internship and international study, it also guarantees graduation in 4 years and offers up to an additional year of tuition-free study to those who cannot graduate on time. Undergrads here praise the "awesome study abroad programs," reporting that "a wide variety of CentreTerm (i.e., January term) and long-term programs promises that there is something to study abroad that everyone will enjoy. It's a great way to get a break from campus and to see the world (and it really isn't that expensive)." They are even more impressed, however, with the amount of personal attention lavished on each student by faculty and administration. "Centre's greatest strength is that no one can slip through the figurative cracks, since nearly every person at Centre seems genuinely concerned about the students," writes one student. "Even the president of the college tries to get to know each student by name." Not only that, but "Where else would your college president have you over for a BBQ, teach a class, and perform in a concert? Only at Centre." All this support helps students handle Centre's "strong academic program" that requires that "either you work hard or you flunk out." As one student puts it, "Classes, as a rule, are difficult, but we learn to push ourselves and achieve more." The entire experience leaves many here concluding that "Centre is just perfect. The small school environment lends itself so well to the liberal arts education platform, and Centre excels at everything it does."

Life

Centre "is academics-driven during the week, but on the weekend the school knows how to have fun," with a lively Greek scene occupying center (no pun intended) stage. One student writes, "The 'Centre Experience' is all about being a part of the Centre community. We all work hard but we all know how to party hard as well. Weekends are filled with frat parties, the 'running of the flame' (streaking from a dorm to the statue in front of the library and back to the dorm), and playing pool at the Warehouse (i.e., the Student Center)." Students must devote some extracurricular time to fulfilling Centre's convocation requirement, which mandates attendance at 30 convocation-designated events per year; such events typically include lectures and performances. Many fulfill their obligations at the Norton Center for the Arts, which "brings in many musicals, operas, ballets, plays, speakers, orchestras, etc., that would normally cost quite a bit to go see, but students get to go for free." Because "There isn't much to do in Danville," a lot of free time is spent "hanging out in each other's rooms, listening to music, or watching shows." Students have discovered that "although Danville is a small town, Centre is a revitalizing, dynamic force in this community." And "The occasional jaunt to Lexington or Louisville helps to throw in some variety."

Student Body

"Most Centre students are from upper-middle-class families in the South" and are "quite friendly and usually willing to go to great extents to help out other students." They tend to be "Christian, moderately conservative, and very enthusiastic about Greek life." One student writes, "The boys have that Southern gentleman quality about them, and the girls are pretty and outgoing." Beyond the mainstream crowd, "There is a fair amount of atypical students. For example, there are many active liberals on campus as well as conservatives, and Greek life is big but you can have fun without it. Since everyone is pretty well acquainted with everyone else on such a small campus, it's easy to fit in." Most everyone "works very hard but leaves room in their schedule to participate in sports and clubs and to just hang out with friends."

FINANCIAL AID: 859-238-5365 • E-MAIL: ADMISSION@CENTRE.EDU • WEBSITE: WWW.CENTRE.EDU

THE PRINCETON REVIEW SAYS

Admissions

Very important factors considered include: Academic GPA, rigor of secondary school record. *Important factors considered include:* Class rank, application essay, standardized test scores. *Other factors considered include:* Recommendation(s), alumni/ae relation, character/personal qualities, extracurricular activities, first generation, geographical residence, interview, racial/ethnic status, talent/ability, volunteer work, work experience. SAT or ACT required; ACT with Writing component recommended. TOEFL required of all international applicants. High school diploma or equivalent is not required. *Academic units required:* 4 English, 4 mathematics, 2 science, (2 science labs), 2 foreign language, 2 history. *Academic units recommended:* 4 English, 4 mathematics, 4 science, (3 science labs), 4 foreign language, 2 social studies, 2 history, 1 visual/performing arts.

Financial Aid

Students should submit: FAFSA, institution's own financial aid form Regular filing deadline is 3/1. The Princeton Review suggests that all financial aid forms be submitted as soon as possible after January 1. *Need-based scholarships/grants offered:* Federal Pell, SEOG, state scholarships/grants, private scholarships, the school's own gift aid, Federal ACG Federal SMART. *Loan aid offered:* FFEL Subsidized Stafford, FFEL Unsubsidized Stafford, FFEL PLUS, Federal Perkins, college/university loans from institutional funds. Applicants will be notified of awards on or about 3/25. Federal Work-Study Program available. Institutional employment available. Off-campus job opportunities are fair.

The Inside Word

Centre's small but very capable student body reflects solid academic preparation from high school, and it's no surprise that this is exactly what the Admissions Committee expects from applicants. If you're ranked in the top quarter of your graduating class and have taken challenging courses throughout your high school career, you should have smooth sailing through the admissions process. Those who rank below the top quarter or who have inconsistent academic backgrounds will find entrance here more difficult, and may benefit from an interview.

THE SCHOOL SAYS "..."

From The Admissions Office

"Centre provides its students with a personal education that enables them to achieve extraordinary success in advanced study and their careers. Centre Professors, virtually all of whom hold the highest degree available in their field, challenge their students and give them the individual attention and support they need to meet those challenges. The end result is highly capable graduates with a can-do attitude and the ability to accomplish their goals.

"Centre offers a multitude of advantages, such as a national top-50 academic reputation, 'majors' options, and exposure to the internationally known artists and scholars; benefits like these produce extraordinary success. For example, entrance to top graduate and professional schools; the most prestigious postgraduate scholarships (Rhodes, Fulbright, Goldwater); interesting, rewarding jobs (96 percent of graduates are either employed or engaged in advance study within nine months of graduation).

"How do alumni respond? They have expressed their customer satisfaction by leading the United States in their percentage of annual financial support over the last 20 years. How much does all this cost? Because of our nation-leading alumni support, Centre is the most affordable of America's top 50 national liberal arts colleges.

"Centre's admissions policies have not been affected by the new SAT, and we will not consider a student's scores from the new Writing section."

SELECTIVITY

Admissions Rating	93
# of applicants	2,159
% of applicants accepted	61
% of acceptees attending	24
# accepting a place on wait list	35
% admitted from wait list	54

FRESHMAN PROFILE

Range SAT Critical Reading	570–690
Range SAT Math	570–650
Range ACT Composite	26–30
Minimum paper TOEFL	580
Average HS GPA	3.6
% graduated top 10% of class	58
% graduated top 25% of class	84
% graduated top 50% of class	98

DEADLINES

Early action	
Deadline	12/1
Notification	1/15
Regular	
Deadline	2/1
Notification	3/15
Nonfall registration?	no

APPLICANTS ALSO LOOK AT
AND OFTEN PREFER
Washington and Lee University
Davidson College
AND SOMETIMES PREFER
Rhodes College
Furman University
Kenyon College
AND RARELY PREFER
University of Kentucky
Transylvania University
University of Louisville

FINANCIAL FACTS

Financial Aid Rating	85
Annual tuition	$28,000
Room and board	$7,000
Books and supplies	$900
% frosh rec. need-based scholarship or grant aid	58
% UG rec. need-based scholarship or grant aid	57
% frosh rec. need-based self-help aid	38
% UG rec. need-based self-help aid	41
% UG borrow to pay for school	55
Average cumulative indebtedness	$17,600

CHAPMAN UNIVERSITY

ONE UNIVERSITY DRIVE, ORANGE, CA 92866 • ADMISSIONS: 714-997-6711 • FAX: 714-997-6713

STUDENTS SAY ". . ."

Academics

"A great small school dedicated to personalized education," Chapman University has lately been making a concerted effort to grow in size, particularly in its popular film production department. Most students see expansion as a good thing—"Our school is doing a good job at building up its reputation"—but growth does come at a cost. For some, the school isn't big enough: "Because the school is so small, there aren't enough classes offered," so students with "obscure majors" sometimes feel that they are forced to "take what they can get." Students praise professors who "are excellent scholars in their fields," but admit that "the growing enrollment and courses of studies" sometimes necessitates hiring "part-time professors" who are at times "not the greatest." Most students recognize that this problem is "a necessary evil in order to accommodate" the school's expansion. For the most part, however, "Professors are fastidious in keeping office hours, and great advising is easy to come across. On the whole, GE [general education] classes are challenging, interesting, and inspiring." Administrators also receive generally high marks: "The president of our school even takes the time to teach classes here, as well [as] get to know the students at his school. I even run with him once a month, and then we get breakfast together."

Life

Most social life at Chapman is an off-campus occurrence: "A great deal of students live off-campus at the La Veta Grand Apartments, which have pretty much become the off-campus dorms. La Veta is always the party place." Not far from campus, a popular student hangout is "the Block, which is an amazing outdoor shopping mall that has a bowling alley, laser tag, a 30-screen AMC theater, and a skate park." More "stores and restaurants" can be found at the nearby Orange Circle. Since Disneyland is "right down the street," many students "have Disneyland annual passes, and people go there a lot." Disneyland's theme park competition, Knotts Berry Farm, is also only "minutes away. Newport Beach is only about 15 minutes away. LA is only a half an hour away." Ambitious students who have the means "can even go to Vegas for a weekend." All these distances, however, are calculated in driving minutes; for many excursions from Chapman, "You will need a car, since Southern California public transportation is awful." Students who don't have cars can rest assured that there's also "a constant stream of things to do on campus."

Student Body

Life seems to imitate art at Chapman; the school is located in the real "OC" (Orange County), and "If you have ever seen *The OC* on Fox, then you have seen a sample of the students who attend Chapman University. The students in general are very wealthy, and personal appearance and designer clothes are pretty important to the average student," writes one typical respondent. Not everyone agrees, however: "If you want warm weather and friendly smiles along with a good education, Chapman is the place to come. Just please don't bring any obsessions with *The OC* or *Laguna Beach* with you—when you live in the OC, you find out that it is not really like that here." Another oft-stereotyped demographic at Chapman is "the film majors, who can tend to be moody and brooding" but also "artistic and fun." Politically, "Even though Chapman is located in the middle of conservative Orange County, there is an equal mix of liberal, conservative, and moderate students at the school." While ethnic diversity is described by some as "pretty thin," the school has a lot of "social diversity"; in particular, students praise the "very strong and welcoming GLBT community," who are "well accepted" by peers. This fact is not surprising; according to many students, "Chapman is all about community."

FINANCIAL AID: 714-997-6741 • E-MAIL: ADMIT@CHAPMAN.EDU • WEBSITE: WWW.CHAPMAN.EDU

THE PRINCETON REVIEW SAYS

Admissions

Very important factors considered include: Class rank, application essay, academic GPA, rigor of secondary school record, standardized test scores, character/personal qualities. *Important factors considered include:* Extracurricular activities, interview, talent/ability, volunteer work. *Other factors considered include:* Recommendation(s), alumni/ae relation, first generation, geographical residence, racial/ethnic status, state residency, work experience. SAT Subject Tests recommended; SAT or ACT required; ACT with Writing component required. TOEFL required of all international applicants. High school diploma is required and GED is accepted. *Academic units required:* 2 English, 2 mathematics, 2 science, (1 science labs), 2 foreign language, 3 social studies. *Academic units recommended:* 4 English, 4 mathematics, 3 science, (1 science labs), 3 foreign language, 3 social studies.

Financial Aid

Students should submit: FAFSA, state aid form The Princeton Review suggests that all financial aid forms be submitted as soon as possible after January 1. *Need-based scholarships/grants offered:* Federal Pell, SEOG, state scholarships/grants, private scholarships, the school's own gift aid, Academic Competitiveness Grants. *Loan aid offered:* FFEL Subsidized Stafford, FFEL Unsubsidized Stafford, FFEL PLUS, Federal Perkins Applicants will be notified of awards on a rolling basis beginning 3/15. Federal Work-Study Program available. Institutional employment available. Off-campus job opportunities are excellent.

Inside Word

Despite a plethora of California schools, Chapman continues to receive a steady stream of applications. Rather than work with formulas or cut-offs, Admissions Officers here prefer to take many factors into account. Well-rounded students are likely to make the most impact. Applicants who are service oriented are also apt to do well, particularly given Chapman's "global responsibility" program.

THE SCHOOL SAYS "..."

From The Admissions Office

"During our 144-year history, Chapman has evolved from a small, church-related liberal arts college into a vibrant and comprehensive midsized liberal arts and sciences university distinguished for an eclectic group of nationally recognized programs including athletic training, film and television production, business and economics, dance, music, theater, writing, and teacher education. Our Orange County, California location was recently rated by *Places Rated Almanac* as "the number-one place to live in North America" citing superior climate, cultural, recreational, educational, and career entry opportunities.

"Chapman's environment is involving, and we seek students who are willing to enter an atmosphere of healthy competition where their talents will be nurtured and manifest to the fullest—whether in the classroom, on the stage, or the athletic field. We challenge prospective students to thoroughly investigate our fine balance of liberal and professional learning so they may make a fully informed decision about 'fit' with regard to their personalities and that of the university.

"Applicants for freshman admission to Chapman University will be required to submit scores from either the new SAT or the ACT including the ACT Writing section. Transfer applicants, if requested, will be allowed to submit scores from either the old or new SAT, or ACT with or without the Writing section."

SELECTIVITY

Admissions Rating	94
# of applicants	4,861
% of applicants accepted	49
% of acceptees attending	39
# accepting a place on wait list	128
% admitted from wait list	58

FRESHMAN PROFILE

Range SAT Critical Reading	552–665
Range SAT Math	553–669
Range SAT Writing	555–667
Range ACT Composite	25–29
Minimum paper TOEFL	550
Minimum computer TOEFL	213
Average HS GPA	3.67
% graduated top 10% of class	55
% graduated top 25% of class	91
% graduated top 50% of class	98

DEADLINES

Early action	
Deadline	11/15
Notification	1/15
Regular	
Deadline	1/15
Notification	rolling
Nonfall registration?	yes

APPLICANTS ALSO LOOK AT

AND OFTEN PREFER
New York University
University of Southern California
University of California—Los Angeles
University of San Diego
Loyola Marymount University

AND SOMETIMES PREFER
University of Redlands
Ithaca College
Santa Clara University
University of California—Irvine

FINANCIAL FACTS

Financial Aid Rating	97
Annual tuition	$33,760
Room and board	$11,315
Required fees	$940
Books and supplies	$1,100
% frosh rec. need-based scholarship or grant aid	56
% UG rec. need-based scholarship or grant aid	57
% frosh rec. need-based self-help aid	46
% UG rec. need-based self-help aid	48
% frosh rec. any financial aid	78
% UG rec. any financial aid	81
% UG borrow to pay for school	67
Average cumulative indebtedness	$22,956

CITY UNIVERSITY OF NEW YORK—BARUCH COLLEGE

ONE BERNARD BARUCH WAY, NEW YORK, NY 10010 • ADMISSIONS: 646-312-1400 • FAX: 646-312-1361

CAMPUS LIFE
Quality of Life Rating	74
Fire Safety Rating	60*
Green Rating	66
Type of school	public
Environment	metropolis

STUDENTS
Total undergrad enrollment	12,626
% male/female	48/52
% from out of state	3
% in (# of) fraternities	10 (9)
% in (# of) sororities	10 (7)
% African American	11
% Asian	30
% Caucasian	30
% Hispanic	17
% international	13
# of countries represented	151

SURVEY SAYS . . .
Great computer facilities
Great library
Diverse student types on campus
Students love New York, NY
Very little drug use

ACADEMICS
Academic Rating	73
Calendar	semester
Student/faculty ratio	19:1
Profs interesting rating	64
Profs accessible rating	64
Most common reg class size	20–29 students
Most common lab size	10–19 students

MOST POPULAR MAJORS
accounting
finance

STUDENTS SAY "..."

Academics

Baruch College consists of three schools, and although its School of Arts and Sciences and School of Public Affairs are both fine, it's the Zicklin School of Business that garners nearly all the attention here (as well over three-quarters of the student body). Zicklin offers a "very demanding business-oriented program that provides a great education in an overcrowded environment" where "it's very easy to get lost," but just as easy for go-getters to access "unparalleled internships, career, and networking opportunities to major global companies' headquarters." Because New York City is a worldwide finance capital, Baruch's connections and internships provide "a gateway to the world of finance," and it is for this reason—as well as for the fact that "tuition is about one-fourth what it is at NYU," making it "the best college value in New York City"—that students flock to Baruch. Students warn that you must be willing to "put 110 percent into your studies and take advantage of the NYC network and Starr Career Development Center" to reap all available benefits here. Those who make the effort will discover a career office that "works tirelessly to prepare its students for the working world. Not only do they offer workshops on how to make yourself an attractive candidate, they also offer counseling and even resume reviews to make sure your resume is perfect, as well as mock interviews that help you analyze your strengths and weaknesses as an interviewer."

Life

Baruch has no campus, just a collection of six buildings scattered over four city blocks. Most of the action centers around the 17-story Newman Vertical Campus facility, which is "beautiful" but "does not offer a lot of things to do" between classes. Furthermore, the mostly residential area surrounding the school offers "few places you can hang out at, especially when you have huge breaks between classes." Although the building is fairly new, "the escalators almost never work" and the elevators "are always as packed as the commute on the train." Many here grumpily opt for the stairway. School-related extracurriculars are hampered by the lack of a "real campus" and by the fact that many students are commuters who work part-time. Some get involved in community service and/or major-related clubs and organizations, but anyone coming here for a traditional college experience will be sorely disappointed. Access to New York City, for most, more than compensates for this drawback.

Student Body

The "hard-working" student body at Baruch could well be "the most diverse university in the country." It's the sort of place where "You can eat samosas on Tuesday, mooncakes on Wednesday, and falafel on Thursdays for free because of all the cultural events that are held." Students brag that "hundreds of countries are represented in our student body" and note that "The one common thread would be we are mostly business-oriented and have jobs/internships outside of school." While students get along well in class, outside the classroom they can be "very cliquey." One student explains, "If you know people from your high school, you stick with them; if you're a foreign student you stick with others from your home country. Otherwise you get the cold shoulder." Because "the school puts tremendous pressure on grades," most here are "extremely stressed."

CITY UNIVERSITY OF NEW YORK—BARUCH COLLEGE

FINANCIAL AID: 646-312-1360 • E-MAIL: ADMISSIONS@BARUCH.CUNY.EDU • WEBSITE: WWW.BARUCH.CUNY.EDU

THE PRINCETON REVIEW SAYS

Admissions

Very important factors considered include: Rigor of secondary school record, Academic GPA, Standardized test scores. *Important factors considered include:* Application Essay, Recommendation(s). *Other factors considered include:* Class rank, Interview, Extracurricular activities, Talent/ability, Character/personal qualities, Alumni/ae relation, Work experience. SAT or ACT required. TOEFL required of all international applicants. High school diploma is required and GED is accepted. *Academic units required:* 4 English, 3 mathematics, 2 science, (2 science labs), 2 foreign language, 4 social studies. *Academic units recommended:* 4 mathematics, 3 foreign language, 1 academic elective.

Financial Aid

Students should submit: FAFSA. The Princeton Review suggests that all financial aid forms be submitted as soon as possible after January 1. *Need-based scholarships/grants offered:* Federal Pell, SEOG, state scholarships/grants, private scholarships, the school's own gift aid, City merit scholarships. *Loan aid offered:* Federal Perkins. Applicants will be notified of awards on a rolling basis beginning 4/30. Federal Work-Study Program available. Institutional employment available. Off-campus job opportunities are excellent.

The Inside Word

In 2001, Baruch opened its new state-of-the-art business school building, greatly upgrading the school's profile in its hallmark academic field. Admissions have grown steadily more competitive since, especially for students seeking undergraduate business degrees. Today, Baruch receives nearly 10 applications for every slot in its freshman class. Your math scores on standardized tests count more heavily here than verbal scores.

THE SCHOOL SAYS "..."

From The Admissions Office

"Baruch College is in the heart of New York City. As an undergraduate, you will join a vibrant learning community of students and scholars in the middle of an exhilarating city full of possibilities. Baruch is a place where theory meets practice. You can network with city leaders; secure business, cultural, and nonprofit internships; access the music, art, and business scene; and meet experts who visit our campus. You will take classes that bridge business, arts, science, and social policy, learning from professors who are among the best in their fields.

"Baruch offers 23 majors and 62 minors in three schools: the School of Public Affairs, the Weissman School of Arts and Science and the Zicklin School of Business. Highly qualified undergraduates may apply to the Baruch College Honors program, which offers scholarships, small seminars and honors courses. Students may also study abroad through programs in 100 countries.

"Our seventeen-floor Newman Vertical Campus serves as the college's hub. Here you will find the atmosphere and resources of a traditional college campus, but in a lively urban setting. Our classrooms have state-of-the-art technology, and our library was named the top college library in the nation. Baruch also has a simulated trading floor for students who are interested in Wall Street. You can also enjoy a three-level Athletics and Recreation Complex, which features a 25 meter indoor pool as well as a performing arts complex.

"Baruch's selective admission standards, strong academic programs, and top national honors make it an exceptional educational value."

SELECTIVITY

Admissions Rating	88
# of applicants	17,114
% of applicants accepted	26
% of acceptees attending	34

FRESHMAN PROFILE

Range SAT Critical Reading	480–580
Range SAT Math	540–650
Minimum paper TOEFL	620
Minimum computer TOEFL	260
Average HS GPA	3.0
% graduated top 10% of class	37
% graduated top 25% of class	67
% graduated top 50% of class	93

DEADLINES

Regular	
Deadline	2/1
Notification	rolling
Nonfall registration?	yes

APPLICANTS ALSO LOOK AT AND OFTEN PREFER

City University of New York—Hunter College

FINANCIAL FACTS

Financial Aid Rating	70
Annual in-state tuition	$4,000
Annual out-of-state tuition	$8,640
Required fees	$320
Books and supplies	$1,016
% frosh rec. need-based scholarship or grant aid	50
% UG rec. need-based scholarship or grant aid	59
% frosh rec. non-need-based scholarship or grant aid	69
% UG rec. non-need-based scholarship or grant aid	18
% frosh rec. need-based self-help aid	21
% UG rec. need-based self-help aid	20
% frosh rec. any financial aid	72
% UG rec. any financial aid	57
% UG borrow to pay for school	19
Average cumulative indebtedness	$14,159

CITY UNIVERSITY OF NEW YORK—BROOKLYN COLLEGE

2900 BEDFORD AVENUE, BROOKLYN, NY 11210-2889 • ADMISSIONS: 718-951-5001 • FAX: 718-951-4506

CAMPUS LIFE

Quality of Life Rating	64
Fire Safety Rating	60*
Green Rating	77
Type of school	public
Environment	metropolis

STUDENTS

Total undergrad enrollment	11,923
% male/female	40/60
% from out of state	2
% in (# of) fraternities	2 (NR)
% in (# of) sororities	2 (NR)
% African American	27
% Asian	14
% Caucasian	41
% Hispanic	12
% international	6

SURVEY SAYS . . .

Small classes
Great computer facilities
Great library
Diverse student types on campus
Very little drug use

ACADEMICS

Academic Rating	64
Calendar	semester
Student/faculty ratio	16:1
Profs interesting rating	63
Profs accessible rating	63
Most common reg class size	20–29 students

STUDENTS SAY "..."

Academics

Brooklyn College of the City University of New York, "the poor people's Harvard," provides "a great education for an unbelievable cost." Students here can take advantage of more than 70 undergraduate programs as well as "the infinite resources" of the CUNY system. "Brooklyn College is the kind of place where anything you want is at your finger tips should you choose to seek it out." The "technologically advanced" library "is a great place to study and do research," and there are enough sections of courses in most majors "for even the most time-limited student." All students must complete a broad core curriculum that consists of about a dozen arts and sciences courses and a foreign language requirement. Some students tell us the core is "challenging and engaging." Others disagree. "Many of the core courses—though they have lots of potential—are organized and conducted in a completely uninspired and un-ambitious manner," argues one less-than-thrilled student. "The faculty here seems really invested in the idea of providing quality higher education to students who otherwise might not be able to afford it" but professors are a mixed bag in the classroom. There are "dedicated and knowledgeable professors." And then there are other profs who "are nuts" or "severely lacking" in teaching skills. The administration is generally "uncoordinated and disorganized." "The staff in the offices has the worst attitude ever," grouses an irate first-year student.

Life

Brooklyn College's "clean" and "very beautiful" urban campus boasts sprawling lawns and some gorgeous buildings. It's a "very serene, New England-looking place to escape to and learn." "There are no dorms," though, which is something of an inconvenience according to many, and the expensive cafeteria food is "average at best." BC is home to hoards of clubs and organizations, and the school tries hard to get people involved, but students here "aren't really that into social life." "Students often have long commutes to the school from other boroughs" and once classes end, many "rush to get home or to work." "There is no school pride or engagement with others in any constructive way," observes a sophomore. "Few involve themselves in any activities, and those who do are unenthusiastic." On the other hand, why bother with this campus or any campus when the whole of the Big Apple is at your feet? Brooklyn and all of New York City "is in many ways a part of the experience." The immediate neighborhood of Midwood is quiet and unhip, but "tons of places to eat and cool places to shop" are minutes away, and, of course, the even brighter lights of Manhattan are always available.

Student Body

Politically, it's fair to say that BC leans left, but you'll find "conservative political thinkers" as well. Students here are "serious about learning." They are "mostly working students, which means that they are not stuck-up and take nothing for granted." Diversity at Brooklyn College is fabulous. "Students at Brooklyn College are as diverse as the New York City population," proudly boasts a senior. You'll find students of many, many ethnicities, religions, and cultures here. There are people of all ages, too. You've got your "child prodigies." "You have your baby-faced freshman straight from high school and then your older gentleman who could pass for a history professor with his suit and tie." "Brooklyn College is about opportunity for students of all ages, for whenever they have the time, to be able to get their degrees and feel accomplished, without the burden of any kind of community on campus." Students largely lead their own lives in the city, though, and they "don't seem to really mix with each other." There are "many iPod holders who keep to themselves."

CITY UNIVERSITY OF NEW YORK—BROOKLYN COLLEGE

FINANCIAL AID: 718-951-5051 • E-MAIL: ADMINQRY@BROOKLYN.CUNY.EDU • WEBSITE: WWW.BROOKLYN.CUNY.EDU

THE PRINCETON REVIEW SAYS

Admissions

Very important factors considered include: Academic GPA, rigor of secondary school record, standardized test scores. *Other factors considered include:* Recommendation(s), SAT or ACT required; TOEFL required of all international applicants. High school diploma is required and GED is accepted. *Academic units recommended:* 4 English, 3 mathematics, 3 science, 3 foreign language, 4 social studies, 4 academic electives.

Financial Aid

Students should submit: FAFSA, state aid form The Princeton Review suggests that all financial aid forms be submitted as soon as possible after January 1. *Need-based scholarships/grants offered:* Federal Pell, SEOG, state scholarships/grants, private scholarships, the school's own gift aid. *Loan aid offered:* Direct Subsidized Stafford, Direct Unsubsidized Stafford, Direct PLUS, Federal Perkins Applicants will be notified of awards on a rolling basis beginning 5/1. Federal Work-Study Program available. Institutional employment available. Off-campus job opportunities are excellent.

The Inside Word

Like other CUNY schools, Brooklyn College provides easy access to a college education for students who want one. Brooklyn raises the bar, however, with superior offerings in the arts and sciences. You don't have to have a spotless academic record to get into Brooklyn College, but once there you will receive a solid and respected education.

THE SCHOOL SAYS "..."

From The Admissions Office

"Brooklyn College, a premier public liberal arts college founded in 1930, ranked sixth this year in The Princeton Review's *America's Best Value Colleges*. In the 2003 edition of The Princeton Review's *The Best 351 Colleges* the college ranked first in the country for its "Beautiful Campus" and fifth for providing the "Best Academic Bang for Your Buck" and for its friendly diversity on the "Students from Different Backgrounds Interact" list. It again placed among the top five in the guide's 2004 edition.

"Brooklyn College's 15,000 undergraduate and graduate students represent the ethnic and cultural diversity of the borough. And the college's accessibility by subway or bus allows students to further enrich their educational experience through New York City's many cultural events and institutions.

"The college continues on an ambitious program of expansion and renewal. The dazzling new library is the most technologically advanced educational and research facility in the CUNY system. A state-of-the-art student services and physical education building, currently under construction, is scheduled to be completed in 2009.

"Respected nationally for its rigorous academic standards, the college takes pride in such innovative programs as its award-winning Freshman Year College; the Honors Academy, which houses nine programs for high achievers; and the core curriculum. Brooklyn College's strong academic reputation has attracted an outstanding faculty of nationally renowned teachers and scholars. Among the awards they have won are Pulitzers, Guggenheims, Fulbrights, and National Institutes of Health grants. Brooklyn College students also receive such prestigious honors as Fulbright Scholarships, the Beinecke Memorial Scholarship, and the Paul and Daisy Soros Fellowships for New Americans.

"Brooklyn College only factors in the Critical Reading and Math components of the current SAT."

SELECTIVITY

Admissions Rating	80
# of applicants	14,754
% of applicants accepted	40
% of acceptees attending	22

FRESHMAN PROFILE

Range SAT Critical Reading	450–560
Range SAT Math	490–590
Minimum paper TOEFL	509
Minimum computer TOEFL	545
% graduated top 10% of class	14
% graduated top 25% of class	48
% graduated top 50% of class	77

DEADLINES

Regular	
Priority	3/1
Notification	rolling
Nonfall registration?	yes

FINANCIAL FACTS

Financial Aid Rating	93
Annual in-state tuition	$4,000
Annual out-of-state tuition	$10,800
Required fees	$381
% frosh rec. need-based scholarship or grant aid	76
% UG rec. need-based scholarship or grant aid	67
% frosh rec. non-need-based scholarship or grant aid	24
% UG rec. non-need-based scholarship or grant aid	21
% frosh rec. need-based self-help aid	71
% UG rec. need-based self-help aid	70
% frosh rec. any financial aid	80
% UG rec. any financial aid	64
% UG borrow to pay for school	36
Average cumulative indebtedness	$15,500

CITY UNIVERSITY OF NEW YORK—HUNTER COLLEGE

695 PARK AVENUE, NEW YORK, NY 10021 • ADMISSIONS: 212-772-4490 • FAX: 212-650-3336

STUDENTS SAY ". . ."

Academics

Prospective students for looking for an academic "bang for the buck" in New York City should take a long look at Hunter College, the largest (in terms of enrollment) and most selective of the CUNY colleges. Physically, Hunter is a reflection of its hometown; with nearly 16,000 undergraduates attending classes in four buildings on three blocks of the Upper East Side, the "halls of Hunter College are extremely crowded." There are figurative similarities to the city, too. Like the Big Apple itself, Hunter has a ton to offer academically, but it's not just handed to you: "The academic experience can be inspiring or painfully dull, depending on one's interests, motivation, and desire to be challenged intellectually, as well as luck." Take professors, for example. "Many professors are accomplished and respected," are "often winners of the highest awards in their chosen profession[s], work as professionals in New York City, and are excellent contacts for further academic pursuits or for work after college." Others are "graduate students with limited experience or time" for students. Moreover, "Dealing with administrative matters at this school is not for the faint of heart," and "run of the mill transactions (processing of financial aid paperwork, registering for classes)" can "devour hours of your life." But students assure us that "if you are self-motivated you'll be fine." Registration is tough "because everyone is competing against each other for classes," but on the upside, "Hunter's class schedule is very accommodating to people who work either part- or full-time" and "Evening classes are abundant."

Life

As a commuter school, "There isn't as much campus life as you would find in other schools." Only about 600 of Hunter's 16,000 undergraduates live in the college's lone residence hall, and of the vast majority of students who are commuters, many simply "have too much going on outside of school to try to experience all that college life has to offer." But that's not to say that school unity is totally lacking. In lieu of residence life bonding experiences, "Clubs are very good at connecting people with similar interests." Plus, during the school day, "There's plenty of places [around campus] to just lounge with friends." Off campus—the question is, what *isn't* there? For those who like to unwind outside, "The school is close to Central Park." For the more urban-minded, "There are concerts, Broadway plays, and comedy shows." There are "movies," "great restaurants, bars, nightclubs, and shopping." And let's not forget that this is New York City; "just walking down the street can be a very entertaining experience."

Student Body

The typical Hunter student "is from one of the five boroughs and commutes to school every day." That's pretty much where generalizations of the student body end. Hunter College has made repeated appearances on this publication's "Diverse Student Population" top 20 ranking list, and for good reason. "In terms of socioeconomic status, immigrants, languages, cultures, religion, race, ethnicity, age . . . Hunter has it all." "Students range in age from newly graduated high schoolers to retirees." And "There really doesn't seem to be [a] dominant ethnic group." It's the kind of place where "nothing seems too out of the ordinary," "everyone fits in fine," and where it won't surprise you to see a "White punk rock girl having a friendly conversation with a Muslim girl in the full head-to-toe [garb]." If you must generalize, it's easier to say what most Hunter students are not. This list is short: "out-of-state students" who are "not liberal."

CITY UNIVERSITY OF NEW YORK—HUNTER COLLEGE

FINANCIAL AID: 212-772-4820 • E-MAIL: ADMISSIONS@HUNTER.CUNY.EDU • WEBSITE: WWW.HUNTER.CUNY.EDU

THE PRINCETON REVIEW SAYS

Admissions

Very important factors considered include: Application essay, academic GPA, rigor of secondary school record, standardized test scores, SAT or ACT required; High school diploma is required and GED is accepted. *Academic units required:* 2 English, 2 mathematics, 1 science, (1 science labs). *Academic units recommended:* 4 English, 3 mathematics, 2 science, 2 foreign language, 4 social studies, 1 visual/performing arts, 1 academic elective.

Financial Aid

Students should submit: FAFSA, state aid form The Princeton Review suggests that all financial aid forms be submitted as soon as possible after January 1. *Need-based scholarships/grants offered:* Federal Pell, state scholarships/grants, the school's own gift aid. *Loan aid offered:* Direct Subsidized Stafford, Direct Unsubsidized Stafford, Direct PLUS, Federal Perkins, state loans, college/university loans from institutional funds. , CUNY Student Assistance Program(CUSTA), Aide for Part-Time-Study (APTS), SEEK . Applicants will be notified of awards on a rolling basis beginning 5/15.

The Inside Word

In terms of statistics, Hunter College is the most selective of the CUNY undergraduate colleges, but this doesn't mean that you have to be an academic superstar in high school to be admitted. Hunter is, after all, first and foremost a CUNY, dedicated to educating the citizens of New York City. But given an applicant pool comprised mainly of New York City residents, high school grades and test scores are the main factors separating those admitted from those who are not. If you are planning to apply to Hunter's Honors College, note that applications are due December 15, rather than on the regular application deadline of March 15.

THE SCHOOL SAYS "..."

From The Admissions Office

"Located in the heart of Manhattan, Hunter offers students the stimulating learning environment and career-building opportunities you might expect from a college that's been a part of the world's most exciting city since 1870. The largest college in the City University of New York, Hunter pulses with energy. Hunter's vitality stems from a large, highly diverse faculty and student body. Its schools—Arts and Sciences, Education, the Health Professions, and Social Work—provide an affordable first-rate education. Undergraduates have extraordinary opportunities to conduct high-level research under renowned faculty, and many opt for credit-bearing internships in such exciting fields as media, the arts, and government. The college's high standards and special programs ensure a challenging education. The Block Program for first-year students keeps classmates together as they pursue courses in the liberal arts, pre-health science, pre-nursing, premed, or honors. A range of honors programs is available for students with strong academic records, including the highly competitive tuition-free Hunter CUNY Honors College for entering freshmen and the Thomas Hunter Honors Program, which emphasizes small classes with personalized mentoring by outstanding faculty. Qualified students also benefit from Hunter's participation in minority science research and training programs, the prestigious Andrew W. Mellon Minority Undergraduate Program, and many other passports to professional success.

"Applicants for the Fall 2008 entering class are required to take either the SAT or the ACT. We will accept scores from the new SAT and scores from the old (prior to March 2005) version of the SAT. We will use the student's best scores from any of these tests."

SELECTIVITY

Admissions Rating	85
# of applicants	24,701
% of applicants accepted	30
% of acceptees attending	26

FRESHMAN PROFILE

Range SAT Critical Reading	480–550
Range SAT Math	490–560

DEADLINES

Regular	
Deadline	3/15
Notification	rolling
Nonfall registration?	yes

FINANCIAL FACTS

Financial Aid Rating	84
Annual in-state tuition	$4,000
Annual out-of-state tuition	$10,800
Room and board	$3,276
Required fees	$329
% frosh rec. need-based scholarship or grant aid	60
% UG rec. need-based scholarship or grant aid	6
% frosh rec. non-need-based scholarship or grant aid	43
% UG rec. non-need-based scholarship or grant aid	2
% frosh rec. need-based self-help aid	13
% UG rec. need-based self-help aid	2
% UG borrow to pay for school	38
Average cumulative indebtedness	$7,124

CITY UNIVERSITY OF NEW YORK—QUEENS COLLEGE

65-30 KISSENA BOULEVARD, FLUSHING, NY 11367 • ADMISSIONS: 718-997-5000 • FAX: 718-997-5617

CAMPUS LIFE

Quality of Life Rating	67
Fire Safety Rating	60*
Green Rating	60*
Type of school	public
Environment	metropolis

STUDENTS

Total undergrad enrollment	14,610
% male/female	40/60
% from out of state	1
% from public high school	55
% in (# of) fraternities	1 (4)
% in (# of) sororities	1 (3)
% African American	9
% Asian	20
% Caucasian	46
% Hispanic	18
% international	7
# of countries represented	140

SURVEY SAYS . . .

Large classes
Great library
Diverse student types on campus
Students love Flushing, NY
Dorms are like dungeons
Students are happy
Very little drug use

ACADEMICS

Academic Rating	72
Calendar	semester
Student/faculty ratio	17:1
Profs interesting rating	65
Profs accessible rating	63
% classes taught by TAs	1
Most common	
reg class size	20–29 students

MOST POPULAR MAJORS

accounting
psychology
sociology

STUDENTS SAY ". . ."

Academics

New York state residents can get "a great education for a cheap price" at Queens College, one of the premier campuses of the City University of New York system. The school's affordable tuition "gives many students a chance to get a higher education." Some here go so far as to call QC "the Harvard of the CUNY system," although students at Baruch, Hunter, City College, and Brooklyn College would probably beg to differ. Regardless of its relative status in the CUNY system, QC undoubtedly provides "great and challenging programs" that are "unique and comprehensive, and are compatible [with one's objectives]." With no residence halls on or near the campus, QC serves a commuter population focused on "building career opportunities" by "getting an education in service of your future profession (and maybe having some fun)." Accounting, psychology, health sciences, and sociology are among the most popular majors here; QC is also home to a competitive school of music. Students at QC tell us that "the administration is okay—comparable to any other out there," and that teachers here are surprisingly "easy to talk to and very helpful, not at all intimidating. You're not afraid to express yourself in class." Students say "smaller classes" and "more students in campus involvement" would be nice, but overall they are satisfied with the college's "multicultural feast sprinkled with a quasi-intellectual environment."

Life

Queens College "is a commuter school, so campus life is not very lively." Its students "are primarily education- and career-oriented." Many "Students work part-time jobs so they really do not have much time left for other activities." Even so, "Queens has a strong community that is diverse and conducive to positive social interactions and communication." The campus is home to tons of "clubs and organizations," and those with the time to do so report that "joining a club helps make the experience at Queens College worthwhile." One student writes, "Political clubs are pretty popular. A lot of times there are club fairs on the grass. Also, anyone can play club sports. The girls could join the soccer club with the boys if they wanted to." While few students stick around campus once their final classes for the day are done, "Between classes students lounge around in the cafeterias or Student Union to talk with friends." Undergrads tell us that there are events to go to "almost every day of the week," in part because the school's New York City location allows it to attract some prominent speakers. The QC campus is surprisingly large and sports a surprisingly large expanse of green for an urban campus. Hometown Queens is a truly international borough and the area surrounding QC is no exception; right outside the campus gates students will find restaurants serving everything from kosher to Korean, from pizza to pita sandwiches.

Student Body

"There is no typical student at Queens College, and that's what's great about the student body," say the students who belong to this "diverse and dedicated community." "Every racial background imaginable is represented and has a group [on campus], and every religious background is apparent." QC is a place where "Everywhere you turn people are able to speak more than one language." There's also plenty of diversity in personality types, although all students tend to be "very focused." Expect "some very religious students" and some nonbelievers as well; "Most students are very different and that makes it easy for everybody to fit in." In short, "Everyone is unique" here, but students across the board "work hard, and are eager to learn," and "This is something that bonds people together."

FINANCIAL AID: 718-997-5101 • E-MAIL: ADMISSIONS@QC.EDU • WEBSITE: WWW.QC.EDU

THE PRINCETON REVIEW SAYS

Admissions

Very important factors considered include: Academic GPA, rigor of secondary school record, standardized test scores, SAT or ACT required; TOEFL required of all international applicants. High school diploma is required and GED is accepted. *Academic units required:* 4 English, 3 mathematics, 2 science, (2 science labs), 3 foreign language, 4 social studies. *Academic units recommended:* 3 science, (3 science labs).

Financial Aid

Students should submit: FAFSA, and New York state application The Princeton Review suggests that all financial aid forms be submitted as soon as possible after January 1. *Need-based scholarships/grants offered:* Federal Pell, SEOG, ACG and SMART grants, state and city scholarships/grants, private scholarships, the school's own gift aid. *Loan aid offered:* Direct Subsidized Stafford, Direct Unsubsidized Stafford, Direct PLUS, Federal Perkins, and Graduate PLUS. Applicants will be notified of awards on a rolling basis beginning 3/1. Federal Work-Study Program available. Institutional employment available. Off-campus job opportunities are good.

The Inside Word

Minority enrollment has declined at CUNY in the past 7 years, partially as a result of changes to admissions criteria and stiffer competition for minority applicants. The school would love to boost its numbers, meaning that qualified minority students could be able to finagle a pretty sweet financial aid package here, making an already economical education even more affordable.

THE SCHOOL SAYS "..."

From The Admissions Office

"Often called "the jewel of the City University of New York," Queens College boasts an award-winning faculty committed to scholarship and teaching, as well as students from more than 140 nations. Combined with our fast-growing student-life program, this creates an exceptionally dynamic learning environment.

"Queens expects to open the doors of its first on-campus residence hall in time for the fall '098 semester. The college boasts a beautifully landscaped, 77-acre campus and a traditional quad facing the Manhattan skyline. Powdermaker Hall, our major classroom building, features state-of-the-art technology throughout. Queens College is also the only CUNY college to participate in Division II sports.

"Consistently included in the Princeton Review America's Best Value Colleges, Queens College offers nationally recognized programs in many fields, including the Aaron Copland School of Music. Recently added degrees include a Bachelor of Business Administration with majors in finance, international business, and actuarial studies, and a Bachelor of Science in Graphic Design. Queens College is the ideal choice for aspiring teachers, preparing more educators than any college in the tristate area through its innovative programs. Would-be teachers admitted to the University Teacher Academy receive free tuition while working towards a degree in math or science. The college also participates in the Macaulay Honors College and offers qualified students its own honors programs in the arts and humanities, sciences, and social sciences.

"Applicants for Fall 2008 should submit the SAT comprising Critical Reading, Writing, and Math. Pending further research on the merits of the Writing section, students will continue to be assessed based on their highest Math and Critical Reading scores."

SELECTIVITY

Admissions Rating	60*
# of applicants	14,436
% of applicants accepted	40
% of acceptees attending	30

FRESHMAN PROFILE

Range SAT Critical Reading	450–550
Range SAT Math	480–580
Range SAT Writing	490–550
Minimum paper TOEFL	500
Minimum computer TOEFL	173
Minimum web-based TOEFL	62

DEADLINES

Regular	
Priority	1/1
Notification	rolling
Nonfall registration?	yes

FINANCIAL FACTS

Financial Aid Rating	64
Annual in-state tuition	$4,000
Annual out-of-state tuition	$8,640
Required fees	$377
% frosh rec. need-based scholarship or grant aid	34
% UG rec. need-based scholarship or grant aid	45
% frosh rec. non-need-based scholarship or grant aid	25
% UG rec. non-need-based scholarship or grant aid	10
% frosh rec. need-based self-help aid	20
% UG rec. need-based self-help aid	15
% frosh rec. athletic scholarships	2
% UG rec. athletic scholarships	1
% frosh rec. any financial aid	55
% UG rec. any financial aid	58
% UG borrow to pay for school	41
Average cumulative indebtedness	$18,000

CLAREMONT McKENNA COLLEGE

890 COLUMBIA AVENUE, CLAREMONT, CA 91711 • ADMISSIONS: 909-621-8088 • FAX: 909-621-8516

CAMPUS LIFE
Quality of Life Rating	**99**
Fire Safety Rating	**87**
Green Rating	**93**
Type of school	private
Environment	town

STUDENTS
Total undergrad enrollment	1,135
% male/female	54/46
% from out of state	56
% live on campus	98
% African American	3
% Asian	11
% Caucasian	41
% Hispanic	10
% international	4
# of countries represented	23

SURVEY SAYS . . .
Large classes
*Frats and sororities are unpopular
or nonexistent*
Lots of beer drinking

ACADEMICS
Academic Rating	**96**
Calendar	semester
Student/faculty ratio	9:1
Profs interesting rating	96
Profs accessible rating	98
Most common	
reg class size	10–19 students

MOST POPULAR MAJORS
economics
international relations and affairs
political science and government

STUDENTS SAY "..."

Academics

It's almost awkward the way students at Claremont McKenna College gush about their "pragmatic" little liberal arts school. "There is no better place to come to college," promises a sophomore. CMC offers small classes, and a "challenging academic environment." "Classes kick my butt, but I keep coming back for more," admits a biology major. Courses also tend toward discussion and CMCers report that "your beliefs and ideologies will be challenged whether you like it or not." There are "super boring" profs but, generally, "professors are here because they want to teach and love students. Their enthusiasm is palpable." The faculty is "on a completely different level of accessibility" as well. Administratively, CMC is among "the best-run" anywhere. Even the folks in financial aid are "amazing." The broad core curriculum includes a mandatory senior thesis. Resources are "vast." "Students have the opportunity to get involved with nearly anything they can think of, and mostly with the college footing the bill." A wealth of institutes allows undergrads to participate in research. Internships and study abroad (and internships abroad) are readily available. The Claremont Colleges Consortium allows students to supplement their curricula with classes at four other schools. The Athenaeum brings a slew of "prominent speakers" to campus (e.g., Bill Clinton, Antonin Scalia, and Bono). Great programs here include many in the hard sciences and some students loathe the notion that CMC is purely based on economics and government. However, the fact is that "the school is incredibly focused on those fields."

Life

CMC's campus is "constantly abuzz with activity." There are so many events around the Claremont campuses "that you constantly have to sacrifice one for another." Intramural and varsity sports enjoy tremendous popularity even though CMC's athletics facilities "*really* need improvement." "Food is good and healthy, dorms are big and spacious, and the campus is always green and sunny." "People are always outside." There's also a "vibrant" political atmosphere. These students "debate politics 24/7." "It's common to overhear very complex political discussion as you walk by people who appear to be casually conversing." The level of debauchery is solid if not outstanding. If you don't drink, "it doesn't make you uncool." On the whole, though, "people at CMC party." They also "know how to manage their time well" because, in addition to all the diversions, there are "bundles of work." "Learn to balance them," warns one student, "or you will be screwed." "The school is very academic from Sunday till Thursday. Then everyone parties Thursday, Friday, and Saturday." The festivities "are open to everyone, as there are no frats." There are many "big, school-sponsored outdoor parties that are generally themed." "The student government buys us alcohol and that's important," notes a junior. The other Five C's throw a lot of bashes, too. "There will always be a big party somewhere, and there will usually be free drinks."

Student Body

"People here are smart, and they have a pretty good idea of what they want to do in their life and what has to get done in order for them to be able to do it." CMCers are "driven," "extremely career oriented," and "incredibly ambitious." More than two-thirds end up with advanced degrees. The typical student "drinks a lot but studies like a slave." Some "would trade their soul for a keg or an internship." "CMC students are all closet nerds," reflects a senior. "They look like normal people, work out a lot, love to go outside on sunny days and throw footballs around, play some video games, and drink a lot of beer. On the other hand, they talk about politics, investment strategy and economics, philosophy, and science while doing all those things." Many students are "relatively rich" but others come "from less affluent backgrounds" thanks to generous financial aid packages. "Very few students can be described as reclusive." "You won't see too many students with dyed hair," either. Politically, CMC has a conservative reputation but liberalism flourishes just fine here. "I think the number of Democrats outweigh the number of Republicans, but only slightly," estimates a junior.

FINANCIAL AID: 909-621-8356 • E-MAIL: ADMISSION@CLAREMONTMCKENNA.EDU • WEBSITE: WWW.CLAREMONTMCKENNA.EDU

THE PRINCETON REVIEW SAYS

Admissions

Very important factors considered include: Rigor of secondary school record, standardized test scores, extracurricular activities. *Important factors considered include:* Application essay, recommendation(s), volunteer work. *Other factors considered include:* Class rank, academic GPA, alumni/ae relation, character/personal qualities, first generation, geographical residence, interview, racial/ethnic status, state residency, talent/ability, work experience. SAT or ACT required; ACT with Writing component required. High school diploma is required and GED is accepted. *Academic units required:* 4 English, 3 mathematics, 2 science, (2 science labs), 3 foreign language, 1 social studies, 1 history. *Academic units recommended:* 4 English, 4 mathematics, 3 science, (2 science labs), 4 foreign language, 1 social studies, 1 history.

Financial Aid

Students should submit: FAFSA, CSS/Financial Aid PROFILE, noncustodial PROFILE, business/farm supplement. Regular filing deadline is 2/1. The Princeton Review suggests that all financial aid forms be submitted as soon as possible after January 1. *Need-based scholarships/grants offered:* Federal Pell, SEOG, state scholarships/grants, private scholarships, the school's own gift aid, United Negro College Fund. *Loan aid offered:* Direct Subsidized Stafford, Direct Unsubsidized Stafford, Direct PLUS, FFEL Subsidized Stafford, FFEL Unsubsidized Stafford, FFEL PLUS, Federal Perkins, college/university loans from institutional funds. Applicants will be notified of awards on or about 4/1. Federal Work-Study Program available. Institutional employment available. Off-campus job opportunities are excellent.

The Inside Word

Although applicants have to possess exemplary academic qualifications to gain admission to Claremont McKenna, the importance of making a good match should not be underestimated. Colleges of such small size and selectivity devote much more energy to determining whether the candidate as an individual fits than they do to whether a candidate has the appropriate test scores.

THE SCHOOL SAYS ". . ."

From The Admissions Office

"CMC's mission is clear: To educate students for meaningful lives and responsible leadership in business, government, and the professions. While many other colleges champion either a traditional liberal arts education with emphasis on intellectual breadth or training that stresses acquisition of technical skills, CMC offers a clear alternative. Instead of dividing the liberal arts and working world into separate realms, education at CMC is rooted in the interplay between the world of ideas and the world of events. By combining the intellectual breadth of liberal arts with the more pragmatic concerns of public affairs, CMC students gain the vision, skills, and values necessary for leadership in all sectors of society.

"Applicants for Fall 2008 must take the new SAT Reasoning Test or ACT with Writing. Scores from the old SAT Reasoning Test (before March 2005) or ACT without the Writing section will not be accepted for application purposes. We will use the highest scores from the SAT or ACT. SAT Subject Tests are recommended, but not required."

SELECTIVITY

Admissions Rating	**98**
# of applicants	3,778
% of applicants accepted	18
% of acceptees attending	40
# accepting a place on wait list	344
# of early decision applicants	288
% accepted early decision	32

FRESHMAN PROFILE

Range SAT Critical Reading	620–730
Range SAT Math	630–740
% graduated top 10% of class	84
% graduated top 25% of class	99
% graduated top 50% of class	100

DEADLINES

Early decision	
Deadline	11/15
Notification	12/15
Regular	
Deadline	1/2
Notification	4/1
Nonfall registration?	no

FINANCIAL FACTS

Financial Aid Rating	**99**
Annual tuition	$34,980
Books and supplies	$1,850
% frosh rec. need-based scholarship or grant aid	48
% UG rec. need-based scholarship or grant aid	45
% frosh rec. non-need-based scholarship or grant aid	14
% UG rec. non-need-based scholarship or grant aid	10
% frosh rec. need-based self-help aid	28
% UG rec. need-based self-help aid	28
% frosh rec. any financial aid	62
% UG rec. any financial aid	56

CLARK UNIVERSITY

950 MAIN STREET, WORCESTER, MA 01610-1477 • ADMISSIONS: 508-793-7431 • FAX: 508-793-8821

STUDENTS SAY ". . ."

Academics

Clark University is a "vibrant," "left-wing" liberal arts school in Worcester, Massachusetts. There are "good research opportunities" and standout offerings in psychology, geography, and the hard sciences. Clark also offers an accelerated, one-year Master's program in several majors at no extra charge. Coursework is "hard but doable." "I am challenged but not burned out," reports an English major. "Overall, you'll get a lot out of Clark if you're willing to work for it." "The small size is very comfortable and welcoming" and "Class discussions are often interesting and enlightening." Professors are generally "committed to facilitating their students' education." "Most get very enthusiastic when teaching." "I've never had a class here with a sage on a stage who just stands behind a lectern and reads from their lecture notes without making eye contact," reports a government major. "My professors have always been available outside of class for help," adds a business major. However, there are also some "utter bores" who "really don't seem to know what they are teaching." The range of classes is "limited" as well. "There is not much variety" and popular courses "fill up fast." Views of the administration are very mixed. Some students call management "nondescript." Others contend that Clark's bureaucracy "rivals some small countries." Still others insist that the brass is "very visible and accessible" and "tries to listen to what the students want."

Life

Some buildings on Clark's "pretty compact" campus are "falling apart." Some classrooms are "kind of crappy." "The food leaves something to be desired," too. "Please send frozen dinners," begs a sophomore. Socially, there's a community feel. Many students are involved in community service and various kinds of activism. "Politics play a huge role." "Every student here believes strongly in something, which makes for an interesting campus." "There aren't big turnouts" at athletic events. "Students are actually more likely to attend a lecture on refugees from Rwanda than a basketball game," predicts a senior. "Many students hang out in small groups in their dorms, suites, or apartments." "There's a substance-free scene." There's also "plenty of weed and alcohol with dabbles here and there into harder drugs." "There is the huge kegger like once a month." "Clark isn't a major party school," though. "People here like to be mellow." "The area around the school isn't the greatest" but some students tell us that Worcester is "a perfectly good place to go to school." "Nightlife off campus is fun," they say, and "there are so many restaurants, it's ridiculous." Also, the "extremely active" Colleges of Worcester Consortium allows students to attend classes and events at several nearby schools. Others students complain that "the city of Worcester is depressing and gloomy at best." "It's unfortunate that Clark is where it is," laments one Clarkie. When students want to escape, Boston isn't too far.

Student Body

"If you couldn't find your niche in high school, you will probably find it at Clark," advises a junior. "It is kind of a haven for the awkward and slightly awkward." Clarkies are an "eclectic" "collection of independent minds." "There's a little of everything." "You can carve your own path here without being a loner." Conservatives are "accepted with curiosity" but most students are "socially conscious" types who "scream their bleeding liberal hearts out at any given cause of the week." Clark also "has an artsy feel." "Hipsteresque" "groovy people" who "dress sloppily in expensive clothes" are numerous. Jocks are here but they are "in the vast minority." "The closet-rich hippie" is not uncommon. However, many students tell us that Clark's flower-power reputation is unwarranted. "Sure, there are maybe a token five students who don't wear shoes, don't shower as often as most people would like, and own bongos," asserts a sophomore, "but three of them are posers anyway." You'll find "various sexual orientations" at Clark but ethnic diversity is pretty paltry. There is a strong contingent of Jewish students and a large population of "filthy rich" international students but little in the way of traditionally underrepresented minorities.

FINANCIAL AID: 508-793-7478 • E-MAIL: ADMISSIONS@CLARKU.EDU • WEBSITE: WWW.CLARKU.EDU

THE PRINCETON REVIEW SAYS

Admissions

Very important factors considered include: Academic GPA, recommendation(s), rigor of secondary school record, standardized test scores, character/personal qualities. *Important factors considered include:* Application essay, extracurricular activities, talent/ability, volunteer work. *Other factors considered include:* Class rank, alumni/ae relation, first generation, geographical residence, interview, level of applicant's interest, racial/ethnic status, work experience. SAT or ACT required; TOEFL required of all international applicants. High school diploma is required and GED is accepted. *Academic units recommended:* 4 English, 3 mathematics, 3 science, (2 science labs), 2 foreign language, 2 social studies, 2 history.

Financial Aid

Students should submit: FAFSA, CSS/Financial Aid PROFILE Regular filing deadline is 2/1. The Princeton Review suggests that all financial aid forms be submitted as soon as possible after January 1. *Need-based scholarships/grants offered:* Federal Pell, SEOG, state scholarships/grants, the school's own gift aid. *Loan aid offered:* FFEL Subsidized Stafford, FFEL Unsubsidized Stafford, FFEL PLUS, Federal Perkins, state loans Applicants will be notified of awards on or about 3/31. Federal Work-Study Program available. Institutional employment available. Off-campus job opportunities are good.

The Inside Word

Clark is surrounded by formidable competitors, and its selectivity suffers because of it. Most B students will encounter little difficulty gaining admission. Given the university's solid academic environment and access to other member colleges in the Worcester Consortium, it can be a terrific choice for students who are not up to the ultra-competitive admission expectations of "top-tier" universities.

THE SCHOOL SAYS "..."

From The Admissions Office

"Challenge Convention, Change Our World" isn't just a motto at Clark University. It's a long tradition that our students and faculty continue in their work—inside and outside the classroom—every day. At Clark, students and faculty are encouraged to follow their intellectual curiosity, seek innovative solutions to real-world problems and create positive change in the world.

"Clark's vibrant intellectual environment is built upon learning through inquiry, making a difference and experiencing diverse cultures. These key elements of a Clark education permeate campus life through courses, independent projects, internships, and other learning opportunities; through research and social action, both locally and globally; through the diverse, urban campus community; through interactions with members of the Clark community, and study-abroad experiences.

"Clark as an institution and its faculty and students have an obligation and a rare opportunity to make our world a better place. Whether in science and technology, international development or business, students who apply to Clark want to be in an environment that will challenge their assumptions and encourage them to understand the ways in which their work as adults will make a difference.

"Clark requires that students submit scores from the SAT. Students will be judged by their performance in Critical Reading and Math. Pending further analysis of the new Writing section, writing aptitude is evaluated as part of the application review process."

SELECTIVITY

Admissions Rating	89
# of applicants	5,201
% of applicants accepted	56
% of acceptees attending	20
# accepting a place on wait list	28
% admitted from wait list	25
# of early decision applicants	90
% accepted early decision	84

FRESHMAN PROFILE

Range SAT Critical Reading	553–660
Range SAT Math	543–650
Range ACT Composite	24–28
Minimum paper TOEFL	577
Minimum computer TOEFL	233
Minimum web-based TOEFL	90–91
Average HS GPA	3.47
% graduated top 10% of class	32
% graduated top 25% of class	74
% graduated top 50% of class	98

DEADLINES

Early decision	
Deadline	11/15
Notification	12/15
Regular	
Deadline	1/15
Notification	4/1
Nonfall registration?	yes

APPLICANTS ALSO LOOK AT

AND OFTEN PREFER
New York University
Bard College

AND SOMETIMES PREFER
Eugene Lang College The New School for Liberal Arts

AND RARELY PREFER
Hampshire College
Skidmore College

FINANCIAL FACTS

Financial Aid Rating	90
Annual tuition	$33,900
Room and board	$6,650
Required fees	$320
Books and supplies	$800
% frosh rec. need-based scholarship or grant aid	52
% UG rec. need-based scholarship or grant aid	52
% frosh rec. non-need-based scholarship or grant aid	31
% UG rec. non-need-based scholarship or grant aid	31
% frosh rec. need-based self-help aid	45
% UG rec. need-based self-help aid	45
% frosh rec. any financial aid	78
% UG rec. any financial aid	81
% UG borrow to pay for school	99
Average cumulative indebtedness	$21,100

CLARKSON UNIVERSITY

PO Box 5605, Potsdam, NY 13699 • Admissions: 315-268-6479 • Fax: 315-268-7647

CAMPUS LIFE

Quality of Life Rating	62
Fire Safety Rating	76
Green Rating	95
Type of school	private
Environment	village

STUDENTS

Total undergrad enrollment	2,521
% male/female	74/26
% from out of state	28
% live on campus	83
% in (# of) fraternities	13 (10)
% in (# of) sororities	14 (3)
% African American	3
% Asian	3
% Caucasian	90
% Hispanic	2
% international	2
# of countries represented	43

SURVEY SAYS . . .

Career services are great
Students are friendly
Low cost of living
Everyone loves the Golden Knights
Lots of beer drinking
Hard liquor is popular

ACADEMICS

Academic Rating	70
Calendar	semester
Student/faculty ratio	15:1
Profs interesting rating	64
Profs accessible rating	72
% classes taught by TAs	1
Most common reg class size	fewer than 10 students
Most common lab size	20–29 students

MOST POPULAR MAJORS
engineering
biology/biological sciences
business/commerce

STUDENTS SAY ". . ."

Academics

A "demanding," "hands-on," and "absolutely innovative" academic environment is the big draw at tech-heavy Clarkson University in the "frozen wasteland" of northern New York. Opportunities "for co-ops, internships, and jobs" are another great feature. "Companies love to hire future employees" here. The hard sciences and other fields "are growing," but Clarkson basically remains an "engineering school with some business classes." For engineers, "Clarkson is all about preparing you for the ridiculous amount of work you will get in the real world by giving you an even more ridiculous amount of work." Outstanding programs for business majors include entrepreneurship and supply chain management. Classroom discussion is generally rare here and the faculty gets wildly mixed reviews, which is pretty normal wherever techies congregate. Some professors are "super friendly," and "willing to meet outside of their office hours." "Others couldn't teach at elementary schools" and are "more interested in their own research than their classes." Opinions concerning the administration also vary. Some students call management "very visible" and "truly concerned about student life." Others strongly disagree. "I feel like they market to get students in," vents a senior, "and then really drop the ball." We would be remiss if we did not also add that Clarkson's library is "worthless."

Life

"There's nothing to do" in "extremely rural" Potsdam. "Don't come here if you like the city," advises a senior. "There is a bittersweet relationship between the students and Clarkson," adds a freshman. The "dreary" campus is full of "atrocious" "concrete buildings." The food is "horrible." The "overcrowded" dorms "could use some updating." Winters are "cold and desolate." On the plus side, the students here are "fairly tight knit." "It's a small campus with small classes in a small town" explains a junior, "so people get a chance to develop meaningful relationships." Also, the Adirondack Mountains are "very close" and "a lot of the students" are into the outdoors. If you like ice hockey, it's "the most popular thing on campus." The team here is a Division I powerhouse and home games "bring the whole school together" "We show so much school spirit it's like the other team's fans aren't there," vaunts a first-year student. Business majors (and others) reportedly have "copious amounts of free time." For the engineers, though, grading can be "merciless" and "downtime is a luxury." It's "very hard to achieve good grades but rewarding when you do." Weekend life at Clarkson "gets rowdy." "Greek life is pretty popular" and "stoners and drunks" are abundant. However students "just stay in their dorms" "all day and night" playing "way too many videogames."

Student Body

"It's mostly white males and Asians" "looking to get managerial and high-end engineering jobs" here. "There are many athletes" and plenty of business majors with "gelled hair." Overall, though, Clarkson students are "something of a nerdy crowd." "The typical student is a nerdy white guy," observes a senior. "The only people I have my nerdy classes with are other nerdy white guys." "Pretty much everyone looks the same from an outsider's view," agrees a sophomore. "Diversity has a different meaning at Clarkson," adds a junior. "What type of a techie are you?" Students describe themselves as "very smart," "hardworking," and "generally ambitious." A large contingent is "friendly" and outgoing. The "socially awkward" "quiet kid in high school" who "doesn't understand hygiene" is also here in spades. Clarkson's "horrible ratio of men to women" makes for a "miserable sausage fest," at least according to many males. Meanwhile, women have their own complaints. "It's hard to find a good looking guy," laments a senior. "There is a saying: 'although the odds are good, the goods are odd.'" "If you take out most of the antisocial engineering boys, the ratio becomes closer to 50:50." Other students claim that the ratio is "improving" and note that "SUNY Potsdam isn't far."

FINANCIAL AID: 315-268-7699 • E-MAIL: ADMISSION@CLARKSON.EDU • WEBSITE: WWW.CLARKSON.EDU

THE PRINCETON REVIEW SAYS

Admissions

Very important factors considered include: Academic GPA, rigor of secondary school record, interview. *Important factors considered include:* Class rank, recommendation(s), standardized test scores, extracurricular activities, volunteer work. *Other factors considered include:* Application essay, alumni/ae relation, character/personal qualities, first generation, level of applicant's interest, talent/ability, work experience. SAT Subject Tests recommended; SAT or ACT required; TOEFL required of all international applicants. High school diploma is required and GED is accepted. *Academic units required:* 4 English, 3 mathematics, 2 science. *Academic units recommended:* 4 mathematics, 3 science.

Financial Aid

Students should submit: FAFSA, institution's own financial aid form, state aid form. The Princeton Review suggests that all financial aid forms be submitted as soon as possible after January 1. *Need-based scholarships/grants offered:* Federal Pell, SEOG, state scholarships/grants, private scholarships, the school's own gift aid, HEOP. *Loan aid offered:* Direct Subsidized Stafford, Direct Unsubsidized Stafford, Direct PLUS, FFEL Subsidized Stafford, FFEL Unsubsidized Stafford, FFEL PLUS, Federal Perkins, college/university loans from institutional funds. , Private/alternative loans. Applicants will be notified of awards on or about 3/19. Federal Work-Study Program available. Institutional employment available. Off-campus job opportunities are excellent.

The Inside Word

Clarkson's acceptance rate is too high for solid applicants to lose much sleep about gaining admission. Serious candidates should interview anyway. If you are particularly solid and really want to come here, it could help you get some scholarship money. Women and minorities will encounter an especially friendly Admissions Committee.

THE SCHOOL SAYS "..."

From The Admissions Office

"Clarkson University, a private, nationally ranked research university located in Potsdam, New York, is the institution of choice for 3,000 enterprising, high-ability scholars from diverse backgrounds who embrace challenge and thrive in a rigorous, highly collaborative learning environment.

"Clarkson's programs in engineering, business, the sciences, liberal arts, and health sciences emphasize team-based learning as well as creative problem solving and leadership skills. Clarkson is also on the leading edge of today's emerging technologies and fields of study offering innovative, boundary-spanning degree programs in engineering and management, digital arts and sciences, and environmental science and policy, among others.

"At Clarkson, students and faculty work closely together in a supportive, friendly environment. Students are encouraged to participate in faculty-mentored research projects from their first year, and to take advantage of co-ops and study abroad programs. Our collaborative approach to education translates into graduates in high demand; our placement rates are among the highest in the country. Alumni experience accelerated career growth. One in seven alumni is already a CEO, president, or vice president of a company.

"Recent awards and honors include: Among the Top 100 engineering schools (*U.S. News & World Report* 2007); ranked number 10 in the nation in 'Supply Chain Management' (*U.S. News & World Report* 2007); top 25 in the nation in Innovation and Entrepreneurship' (*The Princeton Review/Entrepreneur* magazine); and among the 'Top 20 Most Wired Colleges' (*The Princeton Review/PC* magazine 2007). Applicants for Fall 2008 are required to take the ACT with Writing section optional, or the new version of the SAT. We will allow students to submit scores from the old (prior to March 2005) version of the SAT (or ACT) as well, and will use the student's best scores from either test. SAT Subject Tests are recommended but not required."

SELECTIVITY

Admissions Rating	86
# of applicants	2,983
% of applicants accepted	81
% of acceptees attending	28
# accepting a place on wait list	23
% admitted from wait list	83
# of early decision applicants	98
% accepted early decision	97

FRESHMAN PROFILE

Range SAT Critical Reading	510–610
Range SAT Math	560–670
Range SAT Writing	500–630
Range ACT Composite	23–29
Minimum paper TOEFL	550
Minimum computer TOEFL	213
Average HS GPA	3.52
% graduated top 10% of class	39.5
% graduated top 25% of class	73
% graduated top 50% of class	96

DEADLINES

Early decision	
Deadline	12/1
Notification	1/1
Regular	
Deadline	1/15
Nonfall registration?	yes

APPLICANTS ALSO LOOK AT

AND OFTEN PREFER
State University of New York at Geneseo

AND SOMETIMES PREFER
State University of New York—University at Buffalo
Syracuse University

FINANCIAL FACTS

Financial Aid Rating	63
Annual tuition	$30,320
Room and board	$10,612
Required fees	$690
Books and supplies	$1,100
% frosh rec. need-based scholarship or grant aid	61
% UG rec. need-based scholarship or grant aid	64
% frosh rec. non-need-based scholarship or grant aid	11
% UG rec. non-need-based scholarship or grant aid	9
% frosh rec. need-based self-help aid	53
% UG rec. need-based self-help aid	69
% frosh rec. athletic scholarships	2
% UG rec. athletic scholarships	1
% frosh rec. any financial aid	95
% UG rec. any financial aid	91
% UG borrow to pay for school	87
Average cumulative indebtedness	$33,774

CLEMSON UNIVERSITY

106 SIKES HALL, BOX 345124, CLEMSON, SC 29634-5124 • ADMISSIONS: 864-656-2287 • FAX: 864-656-2464

STUDENTS SAY ". . ."

Academics

Clemson University, a tradition-rich Southern school "that focuses on engineering, agriculture, science, and football," draws students who want to experience "a true community where everyone shares the same passion for education, friendship, kindness, and cheering on the Tigers." Students here speak lovingly of "the spirit of 'the Clemson family,'" and "bleeding orange" (if you don't understand what that means, perhaps Clemson isn't the right school for you). They're almost as enthusiastic about their school's academics, lauding their beloved president's efforts "to transform Clemson into a top 20 university." Clemson is already an engineering powerhouse, with "a great program for civil engineering" and "a well-organized and challenging industrial engineering program." The school's nursing program, education department, and hard sciences also earn raves from undergrads. The legendary family spirit here pervades student-faculty relations: professors "are very approachable and truly care about their students. If a faculty member is working on a research project and you stop by with a question from class, they will stop what they're doing and work with you as long as it takes until you understand the subject matter." Administrators are also "surprisingly helpful and available," and they make an effort to show that they are people, too: "Even the school president has been seen at the late night 'Cookie Break' sponsored by the dining hall, talking with students and getting their opinions on the school," says one undergrad. For those "who enjoy a cozy life in a rural area," Clemson offers "a big-university feel on a slightly smaller scale, and a solid education."

Life

"Clemson football and tailgating are the most amazing experiences of college," most Clemson undergrads agree, noting that "Saturdays in the fall there is no question where everyone is, and that's Death Valley [the nickname of the stadium, so dubbed because it's such a hostile environment for the opposing team]. We don't just show up, either; everyone is tailgating at least 3 to 4 hours before the game, and I mean everyone." The city of Clemson, "a town completely devoted to the school," "comes to a complete stop for games, which is great." Aside from their intensity for football, "Clemson students approach life 'Southern style': We're pretty laid-back, we like to have a good time, we work hard, and we have pride." The surrounding area offers plenty in the way of outdoor activity, as "Lake Hartwell borders the campus. We're about a half hour from great hiking and mountain biking, and the weather is great most of the time, so we spend a lot of time outdoors." Undergrads tell us that "Clemson is a typical college in that there is definitely a party scene" that often centers on Greek life, "which is very big." They also point out that "there are abundant activities for those who aren't into partying. There are movies, sporting events and intramural sports, and plenty of places to eat." Hometown Clemson is small, but "With Greenville, Anderson, and Atlanta reasonably close by, you can do all of the shopping you need within driving distance."

Student Body

While "the typical student is White, from South Carolina, somewhat religious, and preppy" at Clemson, "there are plenty of students who do not fit that profile" among the school's nearly 14,000 undergraduates. Students tell us that "Clemson has become more diverse as its reputation has grown. Even in the 2 years since I got here," says one, "I would say that there are more students of different cultures, ethnicities, and especially religions other than Christianity; many, many more students not from the South; and also plenty of students who are not conservative." Even so, the student body tends to be "very conservative." Of course, regardless of students' political views, football is a unifying force: Almost all undergrads here are "smart but laid-back, and huge football fans."

CLEMSON UNIVERSITY

FINANCIAL AID: 864-656-2280 • E-MAIL: CUADMISSIONS@CLEMSON.EDU • WEBSITE: WWW.CLEMSON.EDU

THE PRINCETON REVIEW SAYS

Admissions

Very important factors considered include: Class rank, academic GPA, rigor of secondary school record, standardized test scores, state residency. *Important factors considered include:* Alumni/ae relation. *Other factors considered include:* Application essay, recommendation(s), extracurricular activities, talent/ability, SAT or ACT required; ACT with Writing component required. TOEFL required of all international applicants. High school diploma is required and GED is accepted. *Academic units required:* 4 English, 3 mathematics, 3 science, (3 science labs), 3 foreign language, 3 social studies, 1 history, 2 academic electives, 1 PE or ROTC. *Academic units recommended:* 4 mathematics, (4 science labs).

Financial Aid

Students should submit: FAFSA The Princeton Review suggests that all financial aid forms be submitted as soon as possible after January 1. *Need-based scholarships/grants offered:* Federal Pell, SEOG, state scholarships/grants, private scholarships, the school's own gift aid, Federal Nursing Scholarships. *Loan aid offered:* FFEL Subsidized Stafford, FFEL Unsubsidized Stafford, FFEL PLUS, Federal Perkins, state loans, college/university loans from institutional funds. Applicants will be notified of awards on a rolling basis beginning 4/1. Federal Work-Study Program available. Institutional employment available. Off-campus job opportunities are fair.

The Inside Word

Clemson's admissions decisions are based largely on academic credentials. As is typically the case at sizeable public institutions, if you fit the formula, you're in. A straightforward admissions philosophy doesn't come with any guarantees, though. The university has seen its popularity grow steadily, and as a result, it's become increasingly selective.

THE SCHOOL SAYS "..."

From The Admissions Office

"One of the country's most selective public research universities, Clemson University was founded with a mission to be a high seminary of learning dedicated to teaching, research, and service. Nearly 120 years later, these three concepts remain at the heart of this university and provide the framework for an exceptional educational experience for Clemson students.

"At Clemson, professors take the time to get to know students and to explore innovative ways of teaching. Exceptional teaching is one reason Clemson's retention and graduation rates rank among the highest in the country among public universities. Exceptional teaching is also why Clemson continues to attract an increasingly talented student body. The class rank and SAT scores of Clemson's incoming freshman are among the highest of the nation's public research universities.

"Clemson offers over 250 student clubs and organizations; the spirit that students show for this university is unparalleled.

"Midway between Charlotte, North Carolina, and Atlanta, Georgia, Clemson University is located on 1,400 acres of beautiful rolling hills within the foothills of the Blue Ridge Mountains and along the shores of Lake Hartwell.

"Applicants are required to take either the new version of the SAT or the ACT with the Writing section. Scores from the old version of the SAT (prior to March 2005) will be accepted as well, and the best combined scores from either SAT test will be used in the admission process. We do not however, combine sub scores from the ACT in order to create a new composite score."

SELECTIVITY
Admissions Rating	92
# accepting a place on wait list	162
% admitted from wait list	22

FRESHMAN PROFILE
Range SAT Critical Reading	550–640
Range SAT Math	580–680
Range ACT Composite	25–30
Minimum paper TOEFL	550
Minimum computer TOEFL	213
Average HS GPA	4.13
% graduated top 10% of class	52
% graduated top 25% of class	75
% graduated top 50% of class	97

DEADLINES
Regular	
Priority	12/1
Deadline	5/1
Notification	rolling
Nonfall registration?	yes

APPLICANTS ALSO LOOK AT
AND OFTEN PREFER
Duke University
University of Georgia
University of North Carolina at Chapel Hill
AND SOMETIMES PREFER
Wake Forest University
Furman University
Georgia Institute of Technology
AND RARELY PREFER
University of South Carolina—Columbia
North Carolina State University
Auburn University

FINANCIAL FACTS
Financial Aid Rating	70
Annual in-state tuition	$9,868
Annual out-of-state tuition	$20,292
Room and board	$5,874
Required fees	$122
Books and supplies	$820
% frosh rec. need-based scholarship or grant aid	15
% UG rec. need-based scholarship or grant aid	18
% frosh rec. non-need-based scholarship or grant aid	38
% UG rec. non-need-based scholarship or grant aid	22
% frosh rec. need-based self-help aid	24
% UG rec. need-based self-help aid	28
% frosh rec. athletic scholarships	3
% UG rec. athletic scholarships	3
% frosh rec. any financial aid	87
% UG rec. any financial aid	71
% UG borrow to pay for school	44
Average cumulative indebtedness	$17,882

THE BEST 368 COLLEGES ■ 149

COE COLLEGE

1220 FIRST AVENUE NORTHEAST, CEDAR RAPIDS, IA 52402 • ADMISSIONS: 319-399-8500 • FAX: 319-399-8816

STUDENTS SAY ". . ."

Academics

Coe College, a small liberal arts school in Iowa's second-largest city, is "an institution that fosters community, political awareness, active student involvement, and the broadening of minds through multiple venues not expressed at other colleges and especially universities." Coe's distinctiveness results in part from the Coe Plan, with integrated curricular and experiential components, including service learning requirements, campus engagement activities, opportunities to participate in job-search workshops, and an academic practicum, completed in their junior or senior year. The school also offers "fantastic research opportunities for undergraduate students" that "allow them to interact with professors on more of a colleague level" and provide "experiences that most students don't get until graduate school." Academic offerings here feature "special attention to the natural sciences" as well as strengths in nursing, fine arts, and math. The school's Writing Center is one of the only writing centers in the country to allow freshmen to become consultants; students call it "a great strength" of the school. As at most small schools, "The availability of the professors is astounding. Many professors provide students with their home phone numbers, allowing students to become more comfortable with conversing and asking questions rather than trying to interpret the assignment on their own."

Life

Life on the Coe campus "is very relaxing but at the same time involved." Students tell us that "there always seems to be something going on at Coe: late night movies on Fridays, musicians in the Pub, Bible study groups, Blindspot [an open mic/experimental theatre event], visiting speakers, the list goes on. People are always welcoming to a new person joining the group." Greek organizations "are very popular for men and women," and "athletics are important, including intramural sports and general fitness in our two fitness centers." Coe "still has a wet campus," so while students hit the books hard during the week, "on the weekends we do make up for our good behavior" and "party hard." Students add that "While there is a heavy drinking culture at Coe, it is very possible to have fun and find things to do if you choose not to drink." Hometown Cedar Rapids offers "lots of restaurants, bars, and shopping venues for students to go to" and "also hosts environmental or cultural events that students can walk to and participate in."

Student Body

Coe students "know they are here for an education and study accordingly, but they also know that there is a time and place to get involved, have fun, and interact with faculty students, and the surrounding community." They are "able to balance athletics, class, and free time," and "have time to be social and time to study." Coe students "cannot be pinned down as being a jock, or a geek, or any other stereotype. The vast majority of students at Coe are involved in multiple activities on a very diverse scale." While "most students at Coe are from small towns in Iowa" and "many of us may be Caucasian, there are also plenty of foreign exchange students who really add to the mix. We embrace cultural differences through multiple clubs, as well as our Annual Cultural Show."

FINANCIAL AID: 319-399-8540 • E-MAIL: ADMISSION@COE.EDU • WEBSITE: WWW.COE.EDU

THE PRINCETON REVIEW SAYS

Admissions

Very important factors considered include: Rigor of secondary school record, standardized test scores. *Important factors considered include:* Class rank, application essay, recommendation(s). *Other factors considered include:* Alumni/ae relation, character/personal qualities, extracurricular activities, interview, racial/ethnic status, talent/ability, volunteer work, SAT or ACT required; TOEFL required of all international applicants. High school diploma is required and GED is accepted. *Academic units recommended:* 4 English, 3 mathematics, 3 science, (1 science labs), 2 foreign language, 3 social studies, 2 academic electives.

Financial Aid

Students should submit: FAFSA The Princeton Review suggests that all financial aid forms be submitted as soon as possible after January 1. *Need-based scholarships/grants offered:* Federal Pell, SEOG, state scholarships/grants, private scholarships, the school's own gift aid. *Loan aid offered:* Direct Subsidized Stafford, Direct Unsubsidized Stafford, Direct PLUS, Federal Perkins, college/university loans from institutional funds. Applicants will be notified of awards on a rolling basis beginning 3/15. Federal Work-Study Program available. Institutional employment available. Off-campus job opportunities are excellent.

The Inside Word

Coe's small incoming classes allow the school to be extremely selective in admissions. Your application will get a very close review here, so take the time to make it distinctive. Don't be afraid to contact the school and plead your case; a firm commitment to attending Coe may tip the balance for marginal applicants. Even so, no one gets in here without at least decent academic credentials; most admitted students, in fact, excelled at the high school level.

THE SCHOOL SAYS "..."

From The Admissions Office

"A Coe education begins to pay off right away. In fact, 98 percent of last year's graduating class was either working or in graduate school within 6 months of graduation. One reason our graduates do so well is the Coe Plan—a step-by-step sequence of activities designed to prepare our students for life after Coe. This required sequence stretches from the first-year seminar to community service, issue dinners, career planning seminars, and the required hands-on experience. The hands-on component may be satisfied through an internship, research, practicum, or study abroad. One student lived with a Costa Rican family while she studied the effects of selective logging on rain forest organisms. Others have interned at places like Warner Brothers in Los Angeles and the Chicago Board of Trade. Still others combine travel with an internship or student teaching for an unforgettable off-campus experience. Coe College is one of the few liberal arts institutions in the country to require hands-on learning for graduation.

"For Fall 2008, Coe will continue to focus on the Critical Reading/Verbal and Math subsections of the SAT. Coe Admission Counselors believe it is best to learn about the new Writing component at the same time as students and parents, and we want to know more before deciding to use them in our admission decision-making."

SELECTIVITY

Admissions Rating	88
# of applicants	1,177
% of applicants accepted	72
% of acceptees attending	37

FRESHMAN PROFILE

Range SAT Critical Reading	550–650
Range SAT Math	540–650
Range ACT Composite	22–28
Minimum paper TOEFL	500
Minimum computer TOEFL	173
Average HS GPA	3.58
% graduated top 10% of class	25
% graduated top 25% of class	57
% graduated top 50% of class	93

DEADLINES

Early action	
Deadline	12/10
Notification	1/20
Regular	
Priority	12/10
Deadline	3/1
Notification	3/15
Nonfall registration?	yes

APPLICANTS ALSO LOOK AT AND SOMETIMES PREFER

University of Iowa
Cornell College
Beloit College
Grinnell College
Knox College

FINANCIAL FACTS

Financial Aid Rating	82
Annual tuition	$26,100
Room and board	$6,600
Required fees	$290
Books and supplies	$800
% frosh rec. need-based scholarship or grant aid	84
% UG rec. need-based scholarship or grant aid	80
% frosh rec. non-need-based scholarship or grant aid	16
% UG rec. non-need-based scholarship or grant aid	11
% frosh rec. need-based self-help aid	69
% UG rec. need-based self-help aid	71
% frosh rec. any financial aid	98
% UG rec. any financial aid	96
% UG borrow to pay for school	78
Average cumulative indebtedness	$23,159

COLBY COLLEGE

4000 MAYFLOWER HILL, WATERVILLE, ME 04901-8848 • ADMISSIONS: 800-723-3032 • FAX: 207-859-4828

CAMPUS LIFE

Quality of Life Rating	83
Fire Safety Rating	95
Green Rating	95
Type of school	private
Environment	village

STUDENTS

Total undergrad enrollment	1,867
% male/female	45/55
% from out of state	90
% from public high school	54
% live on campus	94
% African American	2
% Asian	8
% Caucasian	75
% Hispanic	3
% international	6
# of countries represented	50

SURVEY SAYS . . .

Small classes
Great food on campus
Frats and sororities are unpopular
or nonexistent
Lots of beer drinking

ACADEMICS

Academic Rating	91
Calendar	4/1/4
Student/faculty ratio	10:1
Profs interesting rating	91
Profs accessible rating	87
Most common reg class size	10–19 students
Most common lab size	10–19 students

MOST POPULAR MAJORS

Biology/biological sciences
economics
government

STUDENTS SAY ". . ."

Academics

This small, close-knit liberal arts college draws praise from students for its rigorous but caring approach to academics. It's a place where devoted professors "invite students to dinner" and learning happens "for learning's sake." Small classes are one of Colby's biggest draws. "Professors are always willing to go the extra mile," one student says. A senior adds, "Over the course of my time at Colby I've been to at least six different professors' houses for departmental events, class dinners, and group discussions." Professors get high grades for their teaching and accessibility, which together foster a "love for learning" in undergraduates. As one student dryly notes, "Waterville, Maine is not the country's academic capital, so the professors that choose to be at Colby are here to teach, not to use the facilities." This dedication to academics can make Colby an intense place to go to school, and students here aren't "afraid to work hard and study." In addition, students must not only complete their major requirements but also fulfill a hefty load of distribution requirements to graduate. The popular "Jan Plan" lets students take an extra month-long term of focused or independent study in January, sometimes accompanied by an internship. While the administration "works hard to keep students happy and entertained," some feel that their needs are "occasionally ignored in favor of the everlasting quest to turn Colby into a small Ivy."

Life

"Friends and a sense of community drive life at Colby," one senior writes. Students live together in coed, mixed-class dorms. Everything centers around the campus, which is "constructed on a gorgeous wooded hill near the Kennebec River in Central Maine." Since "There isn't a ridiculous amount to do" in these self-contained environs, "Colby works hard to fill the day with countless events, lectures, discussions, and concerts. People can study hard, party, take advantage of the beautiful outdoors, and most do all three." A student notes that "the size of the school is perfect: On any given day, I could see five friends or acquaintances (and countless familiar faces!) on my way to class." This makes for a friendly atmosphere as "it's easy to start up a conversation with pretty much anyone. When the great outdoors beckons, students answer the call by hiking in autumn and spring, skiing in winter, and participating in traditional outdoor sports like football. A senior explains, "People like to unwind after our incredibly stressful weeks with movies, skiing, and partying." The "alcohol-centered social scene" usually takes place at small dorm parties or at the few local pubs.

Student Body

While the prototypical Colby student may be "White and from 20 minutes outside of Boston," undergrads are quick to point out that their "campus is very open to diversity and ready to embrace it." Students single out the administration for "doing a great job of bringing in a more diverse student population." One student explains that "more and more international students and urban kids are coming through programs like the Posse Scholarship." A junior adds, "We have students here that dress in business suits and bow ties while others walk around in capes." Most students, however, settle for the more general description of "preppy students who enjoy the outdoors and enjoy having a good time." That said, students report that "there's pretty much a place for everyone somewhere at Colby; chances are you'll find people both very similar to you in interests, background, etc. and people who are completely the opposite." One student elaborates, explaining that despite all differences, "The one word I'd use to describe a Colby student is friendly."

FINANCIAL AID: 800-723-3032 • E-MAIL: ADMISSIONS@COLBY.EDU • WEBSITE: WWW.COLBY.EDU

THE PRINCETON REVIEW SAYS

Admissions

Very important factors considered include: Rigor of secondary school record, character/personal qualities. *Important factors considered include:* Class rank, application essay, academic GPA, recommendation(s), standardized test scores, extracurricular activities, interview, racial/ethnic status, talent/ability. *Other factors considered include:* Alumni/ae relation, first generation, geographical residence, level of applicant's interest, state residency, volunteer work, work experience. SAT or ACT required; TOEFL required of all international applicants. High school diploma or equivalent is not required. *Academic units recommended:* 4 English, 3 mathematics, 2 science, (2 science labs), 3 foreign language, 2 social studies, 2 academic electives.

Financial Aid

Students should submit: FAFSA and CSS Profile. Regular filing deadline is 2/1. The Princeton Review suggests that all financial aid forms be submitted as soon as possible after January 1. *Need-based scholarships/grants offered:* Federal Pell, SEOG, state scholarships/grants, private scholarships, the school's own gift aid. *Loan aid offered:* Direct Subsidized Stafford, Direct Unsubsidized Stafford, Direct PLUS, FFEL Subsidized Stafford, FFEL Unsubsidized Stafford, FFEL PLUS, Federal Perkins, state loans, college/university loans from institutional funds, alternative loans. Applicants will be notified of awards on or about 4/1. Federal Work-Study Program available. Institutional employment available. Off-campus job opportunities are poor. Colby does not include loans in any of its financial aid packages.

The Inside Word

Colby continues to be both very selective and successful in converting admits to enrollees, which makes for a perpetually challenging admissions process. Currently, only 33 percent of applicants are accepted, so hit those books and ace those exams to stand a fighting chance. One thing that could set you apart from the pack? An interest in travel. Two-thirds of Colby students study abroad—in fact, for some degrees it's required.

THE SCHOOL SAYS "..."

From The Admissions Office

"Colby is one of only a handful of liberal arts colleges that offer world-class academic programs, leadership in internationalism, an active community life, and rich opportunities after graduation. Set in Maine on one of the nation's most beautiful campuses, Colby provides students a host of opportunities for active engagement, in Waterville or around the world. The Goldfarb Center for Public Affairs and Civic Engagement connects teaching and research with current political, economic, and social issues at home and abroad. Beginning in 2008-09 Colby replaced loans in its financial aid packages with grants, which don't have to be repaid, making it possible for students to graduate without college-loan debt.

"Students' access to Colby's outstanding faculty is extraordinary, and the college is a leader in undergraduate research and project-based learning. The college has won awards for sustainable environmental practices as well as one of the first Senator Paul Simon Awards for Internationalizing the Campus.

"The challenging academic experience at the heart of Colby's programs is complemented by a vibrant community life and campus atmosphere featuring more than 100 student-run organizations, more than 50 athletic and recreational choices, and numerous leadership and volunteer opportunities.

"Colby graduates succeed, finding their places at the finest medical and other graduate schools, top Wall Street firms, and in the arts, government service, social service, education, and nonprofit organizations.

"Applicants must submit scores from the SAT or the ACT. The optional ACT Writing Test is recommended."

SELECTIVITY

Admissions Rating	96
# of applicants	4,679
% of applicants accepted	32
% of acceptees attending	31
# accepting a place on wait list	397
% admitted from wait list	11
# of early decision applicants	453
% accepted early decision	42

FRESHMAN PROFILE

Range SAT Critical Reading	640–720
Range SAT Math	640–720
Range SAT Writing	630–710
Range ACT Composite	28–31
Minimum paper TOEFL	600
Minimum computer TOEFL	240
% graduated top 10% of class	60
% graduated top 25% of class	90
% graduated top 50% of class	98

DEADLINES

Early decision	
Deadline	1/1
Notification	2/1
Regular	
Deadline	1/1
Notification	4/1
Nonfall registration?	yes

APPLICANTS ALSO LOOK AT

AND OFTEN PREFER
Dartmouth College
Middlebury College
Williams College
Amherst College

AND SOMETIMES PREFER
Colgate University
Tufts University
Bowdoin College

AND RARELY PREFER
Connecticut College
Hamilton College
Wellesley College
Trinity College (CT)
Bates College

FINANCIAL FACTS

Financial Aid Rating	94
Comprehensive fee	$48/520
Books and supplies	$700
% frosh rec. need-based scholarship or grant aid	39
% UG rec. need-based scholarship or grant aid	39
% frosh rec. need-based self-help aid	34
% UG rec. need-based self-help aid	33
% frosh rec. any financial aid	41
% UG rec. any financial aid	37
% UG borrow to pay for school	44
Average cumulative indebtedness	$19,222

COLGATE UNIVERSITY

13 OAK DRIVE, HAMILTON, NY 13346 • ADMISSIONS: 315-228-7401 • FAX: 315-228-7544

CAMPUS LIFE

Quality of Life Rating	**89**
Fire Safety Rating	**78**
Green Rating	**86**
Type of school	private
Environment	rural

STUDENTS

Total undergrad enrollment	2,750
% male/female	47/53
% from out of state	71
% from public high school	65
% live on campus	93
% in (# of) fraternities	28 (6)
% in (# of) sororities	34 (4)
% African American	5
% Asian	7
% Caucasian	75
% Hispanic	5
% Native American	1
% international	5
# of countries represented	36

SURVEY SAYS . . .

Large classes
Lab facilities are great
Great computer facilities
Great library
Students are happy
Lots of beer drinking
Hard liquor is popular

ACADEMICS

Academic Rating	**92**
Calendar	semester
Student/faculty ratio	10:1
Profs interesting rating	94
Profs accessible rating	97
Most common reg class size	10–19 students
Most common lab size	10–19 students

MOST POPULAR MAJORS
English language and literature
economics
history

STUDENTS SAY ". . ."

Academics

Colgate University, "the epitome of a work hard, play hard school," provides "a rigorous academic environment, an outstanding student and faculty population, and an abundance of social opportunities" to its "preppy," "intelligent-but-not-nerdy" student body. Students report that "Colgate is academically strong in the humanities, such as political science, English, psychology, and economics" and "also has good natural sciences programs that are enhanced by the new science building," a $56.3 million structure that houses 40 research labs, 13 teaching labs, and a teaching/research greenhouse. All students here must complete a set of general education requirements that "force you to look beyond your major work," sometimes leading to discovery of new, unanticipated areas of interest. "It is not uncommon for students to double major in two vastly different departments" as a result of their gen-ed experiences, students tell us. Colgate's size and location foster community-building; the "administration and faculty don't just work at Colgate, but live Colgate. In this way, they are dedicated to your education and create a passionate, hands-on, and inspiring place to learn," translating into "great opportunities to research with great professors and be in leadership positions." The workload is tough here; "At the end of a semester you may have four final exams and 80 pages of writing to do, but that absolutely won't stop you from going out on Friday night. (Saturday night too. And Wednesday night. Maybe Monday also.)"

Life

Colgate University, "the epitome of a work hard, play hard school," provides "a rigorous academic environment, an outstanding student and faculty population, and an abundance of social opportunities" to its "preppy," "intelligent-but-not-nerdy" student body. Students report that "Colgate is academically strong in the humanities, such as political science, English, psychology, and economics" and "also has good natural sciences programs that are enhanced by the new science building," a $56.3 million structure that houses 40 research labs, 13 teaching labs, and a teaching/research greenhouse. All students here must complete a set of general education requirements that "force you to look beyond your major work," sometimes leading to discovery of new, unanticipated areas of interest. "It is not uncommon for students to double major in two vastly different departments" as a result of their gen-ed experiences, students tell us. Colgate's size and location foster community-building; the "administration and faculty don't just work at Colgate, but live Colgate. In this way, they are dedicated to your education and create a passionate, hands-on, and inspiring place to learn," translating into "great opportunities to research with great professors and be in leadership positions." The workload is tough here; "At the end of a semester you may have four final exams and 80 pages of writing to do, but that absolutely won't stop you from going out on Friday night. (Saturday night too. And Wednesday night. Maybe Monday also.)"

Student Body

"When looking from the surface, Colgate students don't appear diverse" because of the "undeniable majority of white students all in Uggs and Oxfords," but "Although most students dress alike, there are great discussions in and out of the classroom because each Colgate student is actually very different from the next once you have the opportunity to talk to them." Even so, just about everyone here concedes that "This is a very preppy campus." Students tend to be "very laid back, but in that perfectly groomed, 'I just rolled out of bed looking this good' kind of way." They are also "passionate about something. Everyone has her own thing to enjoy. It could be a recreational club, a dance group, a community service group, an academic or research project, a student club, etc. You find that a lot of Colgate students are active members in one way or another."

COLGATE UNIVERSITY

FINANCIAL AID: 315-228-7431 • E-MAIL: ADMISSION@MAIL.COLGATE.EDU • WEBSITE: WWW.COLGATE.EDU

THE PRINCETON REVIEW SAYS

Admissions

Very important factors considered include: Class rank, academic GPA, rigor of secondary school record. *Important factors considered include:* Application essay, recommendation(s), standardized test scores, character/personal qualities, extracurricular activities, talent/ability. *Other factors considered include:* Alumni/ae relation, first generation, geographical residence, racial/ethnic status, volunteer work, work experience. SAT or ACT required; TOEFL required of all international applicants. High school diploma is required and GED is accepted. *Academic units required:* 4 English, 3 mathematics, 3 science, (2 science labs), 3 foreign language, 3 social studies. *Academic units recommended:* 4 English, 4 mathematics, 4 science, (3 science labs), 4 foreign language, 4 social studies.

Financial Aid

Students should submit: FAFSA, CSS/Financial Aid PROFILE, noncustodial PROFILE, business/farm supplement. Regular filing deadline is 1/15. The Princeton Review suggests that all financial aid forms be submitted as soon as possible after January 1. *Need-based scholarships/grants offered:* Federal Pell, SEOG, state scholarships/grants, the school's own gift aid. *Loan aid offered:* FFEL Subsidized Stafford, FFEL Unsubsidized Stafford, FFEL PLUS, Federal Perkins Applicants will be notified of awards on or about 4/1. Federal Work-Study Program available. Institutional employment available. Off-campus job opportunities are fair.

The Inside Word

As at many colleges, Colgate admissions caters to some long-established special interests. Athletes, minorities, and legacies (children of alumni) are among those who benefit from more favorable review. Wait-listed students, take note—less than one percent of students on the waitlist wind up admitted to the school.

THE SCHOOL SAYS "..."

From The Admissions Office

"Students and faculty alike are drawn to Colgate by the quality of its academic programs. Faculty initiative has given the university a rich mix of learning opportunities that includes a liberal arts core, 51 academic concentrations, and a wealth of Colgate faculty-led, off-campus study programs in the United States and abroad. But there is more to Colgate than academic life, including more than 160 student organizations, athletics and recreation at all levels, and a full complement of living options set within a campus described as one of the most beautiful in the country. A new center for community service builds upon the tradition of Colgate students interacting with the surrounding community in meaningful ways. Colgate students become extraordinarily devoted alumni, contributing significantly to career networking and exploration programs on and off campus. For students in search of a busy and varied campus life, Colgate is a place to learn and grow."

SELECTIVITY

Admissions Rating	96
# of applicants	8,759
% of applicants accepted	26
% of acceptees attending	33
# accepting a place on wait list	469
% admitted from wait list	44
# of early decision applicants	730
% accepted early decision	50

FRESHMAN PROFILE

Range SAT Critical Reading	620–720
Range SAT Math	630–710
Range ACT Composite	29–32
Average HS GPA	3.7
% graduated top 10% of class	64
% graduated top 25% of class	83
% graduated top 50% of class	100

DEADLINES

Early decision	
Deadline	11/15
Notification	12/15
Regular	
Deadline	1/15
Notification	4/1
Nonfall registration?	no

APPLICANTS ALSO LOOK AT

AND OFTEN PREFER
Dartmouth College
Cornell University
Georgetown University
Middlebury College
Tufts University

AND SOMETIMES PREFER
College of William and Mary
Colby College
Boston College
Bowdoin College

AND RARELY PREFER
Hamilton College
Lafayette College
Bucknell University

FINANCIAL FACTS

Financial Aid Rating	98
Annual tuition	$37,405
Room and board	$9,170
Required fees	$255
Books and supplies	$1,880
% frosh rec. need-based scholarship or grant aid	29
% UG rec. need-based scholarship or grant aid	33
% frosh rec. need-based self-help aid	23
% UG rec. need-based self-help aid	28
% frosh rec. athletic scholarships	5
% UG rec. athletic scholarships	6
% frosh rec. any financial aid	35
% UG rec. any financial aid	46
% UG borrow to pay for school	36
Average cumulative indebtedness	$16,666

College of the Atlantic

105 Eden Street, Bar Harbor, ME 04609 • Admissions: 207-288-5015 • Fax: 207-288-4126

CAMPUS LIFE
Quality of Life Rating	**93**
Fire Safety Rating	**88**
Green Rating	**99**
Type of school	private
Environment	rural

STUDENTS
Total undergrad enrollment	327
% male/female	36/64
% from out of state	80
% from public high school	71
% live on campus	40
% Asian	1
% Caucasian	24
% Hispanic	1
% international	13
# of countries represented	36

SURVEY SAYS . . .
Small classes
No one cheats
Campus feels safe
Intercollegiate sports are unpopular or nonexistent
Frats and sororities are unpopular or nonexistent

ACADEMICS
Academic Rating	**93**
Calendar	trimester
Student/faculty ratio	11:1
Profs interesting rating	95
Profs accessible rating	98
Most common reg class size	10–19 students
Most common lab size	fewer than 10 students

MOST POPULAR MAJORS
education
biology/biological sciences
ecology

STUDENTS SAY "..."

Academics

Every undergraduate at the tiny College of the Atlantic majors in human ecology. More than a course of study, human ecology is an approach to education that is interdisciplinary, in which all areas of study are seen in relationship to each other. In choosing an area of concentration, students can opt for one of the traditional sub-disciplines such as marine biology or public policy, or they can design their own concentration in another area working on an extensive collection of poetry that incorporates ornithological fieldwork, a book-length piece of creative non-fiction that features a student's pre-veterinary internship, or writing a full-fledged green business plan. This leaves students—bonded by a common major—stoked that they still "have the opportunity to shape their own educations. Students who are self-motivated and enthusiastic can have an awesome experience here." Whereas some schools offer a more prescribed program, COA calls on students to arrive inspired to take an active part in carving their own path to graduation. Also setting the school apart is the fact that it doesn't offer tenure to its teachers. Consequently, you'll find only the most dedicated professors at the head of these classrooms. "The professors at our school take a pay cut to work here. They truly love what it is they do, and their classes are incredible." With only 320 students total, it's no wonder that "by the end of your first year, most professors know you even if you haven't taken their classes." Concerning the "optional grades" policy, one sophomore warns prospective students that "just because we have optional grades doesn't mean that you can slack in a class. Evaluations are given at the end of each class. The evaluations give you a whole lot more feedback than a letter grade and make the academic experience a whole lot more personal."

Life

Bar Harbor, Maine, is "a small tourist town, [that's] beautiful in spring and summer, extremely cold and boring in winter." To fill the hole left by the closing of the seasonal Bar Harbor shops and restaurants, students take advantage of a variety of alternative activities. "There are coffeehouses, open mics, guest speakers, dance presentations, puppet shows, talent shows, bands, traveling drama performances, etc. It's wonderful! There will also be discussion groups that will get together. Professors will have their students over for meals. Students living off campus will always cook food together." In town, there's "a great movie theater" called Reel Pizza that serves pizza and beer. For outdoor enthusiasts, COA is a paradise, as it is located literally across the street from Acadia National Park. What's more, the college caters to activities that such a situation lends itself to, with "kayaks and canoes to take out. Many of us share the common passion for hiking. During the snow season, we throw a winter carnival and we also go skiing" and snowshoeing. Since only about a third of the student body resides on campus, "off-campus parties are popular, though there aren't many good ones." That's because "At COA, six people is a big party." In the fall of 2008, COA will open its new Kathryn W. Davis Student Residence Village, green housing with ocean views.

Student Body

"The typical COA student is very self-driven. (You have to be in a curriculum that is so open.) We are also very environmentally friendly. There is a lot of emphasis put on sustainability at the school. We take pride in our organic produce and our hippie ways." If you aren't a hippie when you come to COA, there is a pretty good chance that you'll start developing some of those tendencies before too long, just from pure exposure to the culture. Carnivores can take heart that "there are still meat eaters among our vegetarian population," though "it would be hard to find a right-wing Republican here." While leaning decidedly left on matters political, "People here tend to be accepting, curious, and open-minded, so I think it's hard to be an outcast." For such a small school, COA's student body includes a remarkably high percentage of international students; foreigners account for about one-fifth of the school's undergraduate population, "probably making it one the most diverse places in Maine."

FINANCIAL AID: 207-288-5015 • E-MAIL: INQUIRY@ECOLOGY.COA.EDU • WEBSITE: WWW.COA.EDU

THE PRINCETON REVIEW SAYS

Admissions

Very important factors considered include: Application essay, recommendation(s), rigor of secondary school record. *Important factors considered include:* Class rank, academic GPA, character/personal qualities, extracurricular activities, interview, talent/ability, volunteer work, work experience. *Other factors considered include:* Standardized test scores, alumni/ae relation, first generation, geographical residence, level of applicant's interest, racial/ethnic status, state residency, TOEFL required of all international applicants. High school diploma is required and GED is accepted. *Academic units required:* 4 English, 3 mathematics, 2 science, (2 science labs), 2 social studies. *Academic units recommended:* 4 mathematics, 3 science, 2 foreign language, 2 history, 1 academic elective.

Financial Aid

Students should submit: FAFSA, institution's own financial aid form, noncustodial PROFILE, business/farm supplement. Regular filing deadline is 2/15. The Princeton Review suggests that all financial aid forms be submitted as soon as possible after January 1. *Need-based scholarships/grants offered:* Federal Pell, SEOG, state scholarships/grants, private scholarships, the school's own gift aid. *Loan aid offered:* FFEL Subsidized Stafford, FFEL Unsubsidized Stafford, FFEL PLUS, Federal Perkins Applicants will be notified of awards on or about 4/1. Federal Work-Study Program available. Off-campus job opportunities are good.

The Inside Word

As applicants might expect, admissions standards at College of the Atlantic are somewhat atypical. The school covets students who carve their own intellectual course rather than follow a conventional academic path. Students at COA are expected to bring strong ideas and values to the classroom and applicants are assessed accordingly. Essays and interviews are where candidates make their mark. Of course, the college's integrated approach also means that applicants should have a well-rounded secondary school record. Candidates should also demonstrate a kinship with the philosophy of human ecology.

THE SCHOOL SAYS "..."

From The Admissions Office

"College of the Atlantic is a small, intellectually challenging college on Mount Desert Island, Maine. We look for students seeking a rigorous, hands-on, self-directed academic experience. Come for a visit and you will begin to understand that COA's unique approach to education, governance and community life extends throughout its structure. . Resolutely value centered and interdisciplinary—there are no departments and no majors, COA sees its mission as preparing people to become independent thinkers, to challenge conventional wisdom, to deal with pressing global change—both environmental and social—and to be passionately engaged in transforming the world around them into a better place.

"College of the Atlantic does not require standardized testing as part of the application process. Learning and intelligence can be gauged in many ways; standardized test scores are just one of many measures. If an applicant chooses to submit standardized test scores for consideration, the SAT (either version), SAT Subject Tests, or ACT scores are all acceptable."

SELECTIVITY

Admissions Rating	88
# of applicants	305
% of applicants accepted	77
% of acceptees attending	36
# of early decision applicants	31
% accepted early decision	90

FRESHMAN PROFILE

Range SAT Critical Reading	590–690
Range SAT Math	540–640
Range SAT Writing	570–670
Range ACT Composite	24–30
Minimum paper TOEFL	567
Minimum computer TOEFL	227
Average HS GPA	3.49
% graduated top 10% of class	33
% graduated top 25% of class	52
% graduated top 50% of class	89

DEADLINES

Early decision	
Deadline	12/1
Notification	12/15
Regular	
Priority	2/15
Deadline	2/15
Notification	4/1
Nonfall registration?	yes

APPLICANTS ALSO LOOK AT

AND OFTEN PREFER
Colby College
Bowdoin College

AND SOMETIMES PREFER
Hampshire College
Bard College

AND RARELY PREFER
Oberlin College
Warren Wilson College
University of Maine

FINANCIAL FACTS

Financial Aid Rating	84
Annual tuition	$30,990
Room and board	$8,490
Required fees	$480
Books and supplies	$600
% frosh rec. need-based scholarship or grant aid	79
% UG rec. need-based scholarship or grant aid	78
% frosh rec. need-based self-help aid	81
% UG rec. need-based self-help aid	81
% frosh rec. any financial aid	85
% UG rec. any financial aid	87
% UG borrow to pay for school	63
Average cumulative indebtedness	$19,692

COLLEGE OF CHARLESTON

66 GEORGE STREET, CHARLESTON, SC 29424 • ADMISSIONS: 843-953-5670 • FAX: 843-953-6322

CAMPUS LIFE
Quality of Life Rating	91
Fire Safety Rating	92
Green Rating	73
Type of school	public
Environment	city

STUDENTS
Total undergrad enrollment	9,499
% male/female	36/64
% from out of state	37
% from public high school	83
% live on campus	34
% in (# of) fraternities	14 (14)
% in (# of) sororities	18 (11)
% African American	6
% Asian	2
% Caucasian	84
% Hispanic	2
% international	1
# of countries represented	74

SURVEY SAYS . . .
Small classes
Great library
Students love Charleston, SC
Great off-campus food
Students are happy
Lots of beer drinking
Hard liquor is popular
(Almost) everyone smokes

ACADEMICS
Academic Rating	78
Calendar	semester
Student/faculty ratio	13:1
Profs interesting rating	80
Profs accessible rating	82
% classes taught by TAs	3
Most common reg class size	20–29 students
Most common lab size	20–29 students

MOST POPULAR MAJORS
psychology
biology/biological sciences
business administration and management

STUDENTS SAY ". . ."

Academics

It's satisfaction guaranteed at the College of Charleston, where one enters "the gateway to southern charm, grace, and hospitality" and gets "a private school atmosphere with a public school cost." Though the almost Siren-like appeal of the South Carolina location seems to have been the deciding factor for a fair number of students, the great value of the education (particularly for in-state residents) is cited by many as a definite perk to an already-perky school.

As for the learning part of the easy living, the "very high faculty to student ratio makes it easy to get help when you need it," and the class sizes "are just a little bigger than in high school," which is "conducive to learning." Science and pre-med programs are singled out as being particularly solid, and strong academics also abound in the "challenging courses, especially upper level classes" (which is good, because it can be "sort of hard as an underclassman to get into the classes and sections you want"). Registration can be hit or miss, but professors are "totally available and oftentimes brilliant" and offer "many opportunities to help, whether it be office hours, meetings or review sessions." Those enrolled here are satisfied with the "enthusiastic" administration as well, who are trying to counteract the school's very apparent homogeneity by "really trying to expand the school."

Life

Students just love, love, love Charleston, and it's not often you find most students using the phrase "Elysian backdrop" outside of a term paper. "When I tell people that I go to school in Charleston, they say, 'You are not going to school, you are going on vacation!'" says one. "The water is a five minute walk; the beach is a five minute drive," says another. "You read on the greenest grass in a scene from a movie. You walk around in 70 degree weather with smiling friends and class-mates during November and December," says yet another starry-eyed student. The campus is located in the center of the city, so campus housing options can be somewhat limited. The food has been universally panned, but a new cafeteria, opened in August 2007, will likely improve the culinary quality. Most students walk rather than drive, and having a car "is actually a hindrance," which comes in handy for resisting the temptation on the weekends, since the school "has great parties and an atmosphere to support them." Not that this means students shirk their work, they just learn to allocate their time (upperclassmen usually manage this better than the party-happy freshmen). "The real issue at hand is deciding: bar or library?" The arts are also big here—"theatre and music mostly" —and the historic sites even get a fair amount of patronage, such as the popular walk along the "battery where the Civil War started."

Student Body

The almost sickeningly happy student body is "upbeat and positive about being at CofC," and this collective group of "Southern belles, hard-core northerners, surfers, nerds and party animals" are "all united by the beach," though the sim-pler split is between preppy or the "the artsy/hippy type." It's interesting to note that there's a significantly larger number of women than men, and though the diversity is pretty low, students note that it is growing, even if right now they have "mostly your typical sorority and frat type students." Politically, "it's defi-nitely the most liberal school in South Carolina," and "most people are very open to other cultures and lifestyles." "For example, I had pink hair one time and everybody loved it!" says a sophomore. "It is highly implausible that you won't find your niche within the first weeks of school."

FINANCIAL AID: 843-953-5540 • E-MAIL: ADMISSIONS@COFC.EDU • WEBSITE: WWW.COFC.EDU

THE PRINCETON REVIEW SAYS

Admissions

Very important factors considered include: Academic GPA, rigor of secondary school record, standardized test scores, state residency. *Important factors considered include:* Class rank, character/personal qualities, first generation, talent/ability. *Other factors considered include:* Application essay, recommendation(s), extracurricular activities, racial/ethnic status, work experience. SAT or ACT required; TOEFL required of all international applicants. High school diploma is required and GED is accepted. *Academic units required:* 4 English, 3 mathematics, 3 science, (3 science labs), 3 foreign language, 3 social studies, 4 academic electives. *Academic units recommended:* 4 English, 4 mathematics, 2 history.

Financial Aid

Students should submit: FAFSA. The Princeton Review suggests that all financial aid forms be submitted as soon as possible after January 1. *Need-based scholarships/grants offered:* Federal Pell, SEOG, state scholarships/grants, private scholarships, the school's own gift aid. *Loan aid offered:* Direct Subsidized Stafford, Direct Unsubsidized Stafford, Direct PLUS, Federal Perkins Applicants will be notified of awards on a rolling basis beginning 4/10. Federal Work-Study Program available. Institutional employment available. Off-campus job opportunities are excellent.

The Inside Word

Prime location and relatively low tuition make admissions at College of Charleston quite competitive, and standards are a bit higher still for out-of-state applicants. High school grades and standardized test scores play a significant role in admissions decisions, but the school also takes the time to consider the "complete" student. Expect more personalized treatment here than you would receive from Clemson or the University of South Carolina.

THE SCHOOL SAYS "..."

From The Admissions Office

"To succeed in our increasingly complex world, college graduates must be able to think creatively, explore new ideas, compete, collaborate, and meet the challenges of our global society. At the College of Charleston, students find out about themselves, their lives and the lives of others. They discover how to shape their future, and they prepare to create change and opportunity.

"Founded in 1770, the College of Charleston's mission is to provide students with a first-class education in the arts and sciences, education and business. Students have 126 majors and minors from which to choose – and they often choose to combine several – and complement their academic courses with overseas study, research and internships for a truly customized education.

"Nearly 10,000 undergraduates choose the College for its small-college feel blended with the advantages and diversity of an urban, mid-sized university. The College, home to students from all 50 states and 74 countries, provides a creative and intellectually stimulating environment where students are challenged and guided by a committed and caring faculty of 500 distinguished teacher-scholars, all in an incomparable historic setting.

"The city of Charleston serves as a living and learning laboratory for student experiences in business, science, teaching, the humanities, languages and the arts. At the same time, students and faculty are engaged with the community in partnerships to improve education, enhance the business community and enrich the overall quality of life in the region.

"In the great liberal arts tradition, a College of Charleston education focuses on discovery and personal growth, as well as preparation for life, work and service to our society.

SELECTIVITY
Admissions Rating	88
# of applicants	8,941
% of applicants accepted	65
% of acceptees attending	36
# accepting a place on wait list	256
% admitted from wait list	31

FRESHMAN PROFILE
Range SAT Critical Reading	570–650
Range SAT Math	570–650
Range ACT Composite	23–26
Minimum paper TOEFL	550
Minimum computer TOEFL	213
Minimum web-based TOEFL	80
Average HS GPA	3.82
% graduated top 10% of class	26.7
% graduated top 25% of class	60.2
% graduated top 50% of class	91.5

DEADLINES
Early action	
Deadline	11/1
Notification	12/15
Regular	
Priority	11/1
Deadline	4/1
Nonfall registration?	yes

APPLICANTS ALSO LOOK AT
AND OFTEN PREFER
University of Georgia
University of North Carolina at Chapel Hill
AND SOMETIMES PREFER
University of South Carolina—Columbia
Clemson University
Furman University
James Madison University
AND RARELY PREFER
Coastal Carolina University
Winthrop University
Wofford College

FINANCIAL FACTS
Financial Aid Rating	75
Annual tuition	$7,778
% frosh rec. need-based scholarship or grant aid	29
% UG rec. need-based scholarship or grant aid	24
% frosh rec. non-need-based scholarship or grant aid	30
% UG rec. non-need-based scholarship or grant aid	16
% frosh rec. need-based self-help aid	28
% UG rec. need-based self-help aid	30
% frosh rec. athletic scholarships	2
% UG rec. athletic scholarships	2
% frosh rec. any financial aid	39
% UG rec. any financial aid	36
% UG borrow to pay for school	45.8
Average cumulative indebtedness	$17,118

COLLEGE OF THE HOLY CROSS

ADMISSIONS OFFICE, ONE COLLEGE STREET, WORCESTER, MA 01610-2395 • ADMISSIONS: 508-793-2443 • FAX: 508-793-3888

CAMPUS LIFE

Quality of Life Rating	**70**
Fire Safety Rating	**95**
Green Rating	**94**
Type of school	private
Affiliation	Roman Catholic
Environment	city

STUDENTS

Total undergrad enrollment	2,817
% male/female	44/56
% from out of state	61
% from public high school	51
% live on campus	90
% African American	4
% Asian	5
% Caucasian	71
% Hispanic	5
% international	1
# of countries represented	13

SURVEY SAYS . . .
Small classes
Great library
Frats and sororities are unpopular
or nonexistent
Lots of beer drinking
Hard liquor is popular

ACADEMICS

Academic Rating	**98**
Calendar	semester
Student/faculty ratio	11:1
Profs interesting rating	92
Profs accessible rating	92
Most common reg class size	10–19 students
Most common lab size	fewer than 10 students

MOST POPULAR MAJORS
economics
psychology
history

STUDENTS SAY ". . ."

Academics

Located in Worcester, the second-largest city in Massachusetts, Holy Cross offers an academic atmosphere that is "always challenging, never boring" thanks to professors who are "genuinely interested in getting their students to think critically about the world." Many students agree that "while it is hard to do well, the professors and overall state of mind here will push you to your maximum potential in every way." With an administration dedicated to making sure that "students are represented on virtually every administrative council at the college," and a system of departmental "student advisory councils which voice student opinion on professors who are up for tenure," it's no wonder the administration "is widely appreciated for its awesome accessibility." This accessibility carries over to the classroom where small class sizes allow for "a lot of faculty-student interaction." As one student explains, "There are no TAs at Holy Cross," which makes it easier for "students who are trying to form relationships" with their "accessible and interested professors." Be warned, however, that if you ever miss a class "Your professor will call to see where you were." Students here enjoy many opportunities for "independent research, study abroad, and intellectual enrichment," including "great internship programs" with "successful Holy Cross alumni" all designed to help them "learn and succeed."

Life

The mantra you might hear repeated often among students at Holy Cross is "work hard, party hard." As one student explains, "Based on all the partying that is done here, you can imagine how hard we work." The school's rigorous academic standards are offset by a lively social scene where the most popular relaxation activities come with a bar tab: "Beer is huge, particularly because our workload here is so intense." Some students boast that they "have a bar for each day of the week" and "theme parties" each weekend. Everyone here is "always active," taking time off from studying to participate in "a varsity team, intramurals, student government, clubs, the newspaper, theater, or music." Holy Cross goes out of its way to "create many on-campus opportunities as well as encourage students to explore off-campus opportunities." "Countless restaurants and bars in Worcester" as well as in nearby Boston and Providence, create "a lively social scene off campus." Physically getting off campus, however, can prove difficult, as "Students cannot have cars until their third year."

Student Body

The typical Holy Cross student is "hardworking, and loves to have fun." With a "general atmosphere of friendliness and acceptance" on campus, most students find it hard to "feel lonely or bored." While the majority of Holy Cross students are "White, Irish Catholics" from "upper-middle-class families," the school's administration has "done a lot of work toward becoming a more diverse and inclusive place." As one student explains, "Most all faculty and administrators are exceptionally welcoming of diversity." Although a Jesuit college, "Religion is not a major issue" here. "Most students do not go to mass though they consider themselves Catholic," and non-Catholics can, if they wish, attend "nondenominational masses" offered on campus. Regardless of their beliefs, Holy Cross students are "very conscious about affairs outside of the college" and "involved in working to better the community." "Devoted to excellence in academics" first and foremost, the typical Holy Cross student "is not afraid to meet new people, go out on the weekends, and have a great time."

FINANCIAL AID: 508-793-2265 • E-MAIL: ADMISSIONS@HOLYCROSS.EDU • WEBSITE: WWW.HOLYCROSS.EDU

THE PRINCETON REVIEW SAYS

Admissions

Very important factors considered include: Class rank, academic GPA, rigor of secondary school record. *Important factors considered include:* Application essay, recommendation(s), alumni/ae relation, character/personal qualities, extracurricular activities, interview. *Other factors considered include:* Standardized test scores, first generation, geographical residence, level of applicant's interest, racial/ethnic status, talent/ability, volunteer work, work experience. TOEFL required of all international applicants. High school diploma is required and GED is accepted. *Academic units recommended:* 4 English, 4 mathematics, 4 science, 3 foreign language, 2 social studies, 2 history, 1 academic elective.

Financial Aid

Students should submit: FAFSA, CSS/Financial Aid PROFILE, noncustodial PROFILE, business/farm supplement, parent and student federal tax returns. Regular filing deadline is 2/1. The Princeton Review suggests that all financial aid forms be submitted as soon as possible after January 1. *Need-based scholarships/grants offered:* Federal Pell, SEOG, state scholarships/grants, private scholarships, the school's own gift aid. *Loan aid offered:* FFEL Subsidized Stafford, FFEL Unsubsidized Stafford, FFEL PLUS, Federal Perkins, MDFA. Applicants will be notified of awards on or about 4/1. Federal Work-Study Program available. Institutional employment available. Off-campus job opportunities are fair.

The Inside Word

Admission to Holy Cross is competitive; therefore, a demanding high school course load is required to be a viable candidate. The college values effective communication skills—it thoroughly evaluates each applicant's personal statement and short essay responses. Interviews are important, especially for those applying early decision. Students who graduate from a Catholic high school might find themselves at a slight advantage.

THE SCHOOL SAYS "..."

From The Admissions Office

"When applying to Holy Cross, two areas deserve particular attention. First, the essay should be developed thoughtfully, with correct language and syntax in mind. That essay reflects for the Board of Admissions how you think and how you can express yourself. Second, activity beyond the classroom should be clearly defined. Since Holy Cross [has only] 2,800 students, the chance for involvement/participation is exceptional. The board reviews many applications for academically qualified students. A key difference in being accepted is the extent to which a candidate participates in-depth beyond the classroom—don't be modest; define who you are.

"Standardized test scores (i.e., SAT, SAT Subject Tests, and ACT) are optional. Students may submit their scores if they believe the results paint a fuller picture of their achievements and potential, but those who don't submit scores will not be at a disadvantage in admissions decisions."

SELECTIVITY

Admissions Rating	96
# of applicants	7,066
% of applicants accepted	33
% of acceptees attending	31
# accepting a place on wait list	296
% admitted from wait list	15
# of early decision applicants	469
% accepted early decision	54

FRESHMAN PROFILE

Range SAT Critical Reading	590–690
Range SAT Math	620–690
Minimum paper TOEFL	550
Minimum computer TOEFL	213
Minimum web-based TOEFL	79
% graduated top 10% of class	65
% graduated top 25% of class	97
% graduated top 50% of class	100

DEADLINES

Early decision	
Deadline	12/15
Notification	1/15
Regular	
Deadline	1/15
Notification	4/1
Nonfall registration?	yes

APPLICANTS ALSO LOOK AT

AND OFTEN PREFER
University of Notre Dame
Georgetown University
Boston College
Tufts University

AND SOMETIMES PREFER
Fairfield University
Fordham University
Loyola College in Maryland
Villanova University
Boston University

FINANCIAL FACTS

Financial Aid Rating	92
Annual tuition	$36,710
Room and board	$10,260
Required fees	$532
Books and supplies	$700
% frosh rec. need-based scholarship or grant aid	46
% UG rec. need-based scholarship or grant aid	46
% frosh rec. non-need-based scholarship or grant aid	1
% UG rec. non-need-based scholarship or grant aid	2
% frosh rec. need-based self-help aid	43
% UG rec. need-based self-help aid	42
% frosh rec. athletic scholarships	1
% UG rec. athletic scholarships	1
% frosh rec. any financial aid	61
% UG rec. any financial aid	58
Average cumulative indebtedness	$17,000

THE COLLEGE OF IDAHO

2112 CLEVELAND BOULEVARD, CALDWELL, ID 83605 • ADMISSIONS: 208-459-5305 • FAX: 208-459-5757

CAMPUS LIFE
Quality of Life Rating	79
Fire Safety Rating	66
Green Rating	81
Type of school	private
Environment	town

STUDENTS
Total undergrad enrollment	813
% male/female	39/61
% from out of state	28
% live on campus	59
% in (# of) fraternities	18 (3)
% in (# of) sororities	18 (4)
% African American	1
% Asian	3
% Caucasian	67
% Hispanic	7
% international	3
# of countries represented	16

SURVEY SAYS . . .
Small classes
Students are friendly
Lots of beer drinking

ACADEMICS
Academic Rating	86
Calendar	13-6-13
Student/faculty ratio	9:1
Profs interesting rating	92
Profs accessible rating	89
Most common reg class size	fewer than 10 students

MOST POPULAR MAJORS
biology/biological sciences
psychology
business/commerce

STUDENTS SAY ". . ."

Academics

With only about 800 undergraduates, the College of Idaho provides "a close, personal, friendly learning environment" to students seeking a "balanced liberal arts education." All students must complete the liberal arts core curriculum that "integrates disciplines to produce a better understanding of the world, how it works, and how people come together to make it work"; the graduates, as a result, are a well-rounded bunch. One undergrad explains, "A class from just about every major is required before you graduate; [this] gives you the opportunity to enjoy [things] you never knew you even liked." The core also "teaches you how to write," a facet of the curriculum that students appreciate, if sometimes grudgingly. Top offerings at C of I include a "really great premedical program," a "very good psychology department," science programs that "offer many research opportunities you can't find anywhere else," and music program that offers instruction from professionals: "With the Langroise Trio in residence at the college, you are guaranteed get great instruction and good small ensemble experience." The Gipson Honors Program here "allows students to choose concentrations rather than majors and work on a final thesis-like project," an excellent option for those who know exactly what they want from their bachelor's degree. Students overwhelmingly praise the school's small size and the individual attention they receive. In all areas, "The professors are absolutely amazing. They genuinely care about your progress and are willing to go out of their way to assist you in any way possible."

Life

C of I "is the type of school academics dream of and the type of community that party-goers and the quiet type can both enjoy." Schoolwork keeps students busy here—but not so busy that they can't take advantage of the "huge amount of opportunities for involvement in athletics, clubs, and other extracurricular activities." Undergrads "consistently obligate themselves to volunteer activities, student government, extracurriculars, sports, and so on. They really keep the atmosphere at Albertson dynamic and constantly on the move, so there's never a dull moment." Students especially love to take advantage of the school's location. While some note that hometown Caldwell "is not the best," Boise is "only about 20 minutes away, and it has good shopping and cultural events, so that's where a lot of students spend their time." Students who like the outdoors find great resources for "tour kayaking, backpacking, hiking, camping, rock climbing, canyoneering, road tripping, caving, scuba diving . . . and even skydiving." On weekends, "The party scene is very active, but there are always things to do if you don't want to drink. Most fraternities are very accepting of nondrinkers. Parties are a big part of campus life, but all activities have some place on the campus."

Student Body

"The stereotype is that C of I is mostly a bunch of white, affluent Republicans from around the state," but that reputation is changing: "As the population diversifies, political views are becoming less homogeneous." Political differences, students point out, tend to be less important than common interests: "How you orient yourself politically isn't really of any consequence on campus. For example, the debate team is extremely cohesive despite a wide array of varying political views. We all seem to get along." Above all, the students here immerse themselves in the things they do. This is particularly the case with school spirit. One remarks, "The student fans are becoming known as 'Coyote Crazies' because they are so loud at sporting events." Energetic C of I students "work hard at studies and at extracurricular activities. Due in part to the limited student population on campus, [students are] likely to be involved in many clubs and organizations outside of class."

FINANCIAL AID: 208-459-5308 • E-MAIL: ADMISSION@COLLEGEOFIDAHO.EDU • WEBSITE: WWW.COLLEGEOFIDAHO.EDU

THE PRINCETON REVIEW SAYS

Admissions

Very important factors considered include: Application essay, academic GPA, recommendation(s), rigor of secondary school record, standardized test scores, character/personal qualities, extracurricular activities, level of applicant's interest, work experience. *Important factors considered include:* Class rank, interview. *Other factors considered include:* Alumni/ae relation, first generation, geographical residence, talent/ability, volunteer work, SAT or ACT required; ACT with Writing component required. TOEFL required of all international applicants. High school diploma is required and GED is accepted. *Academic units required:* 4 English, 2 mathematics, 3 social studies, 3 history, 3 academic electives. *Academic units recommended:* 4 English, 4 mathematics, (4 science labs), 2 foreign language, 3 social studies, 3 history, 3 academic electives.

Financial Aid

Students should submit: FAFSA, institution's own financial aid form. The Princeton Review suggests that all financial aid forms be submitted as soon as possible after January 1. *Need-based scholarships/grants offered:* Federal Pell, SEOG, state scholarships/grants, private scholarships, the school's own gift aid. *Loan aid offered:* FFEL Subsidized Stafford, FFEL Unsubsidized Stafford, FFEL PLUS, Federal Perkins Applicants will be notified of awards on a rolling basis beginning 1/31. Federal Work-Study Program available. Off-campus job opportunities are good.

The Inside Word

Despite its high acceptance rate, the College of Idaho offers a quality academic program. Students who have thrived in the classroom and actively participated in extracurriculars will be the handed the keys to a unique college experience, one which stresses self-confidence and social responsibility.

THE SCHOOL SAYS "..."

From The Admissions Office

"While the mission of the College of Idaho is traditional in that it remains committed to the teaching of the liberal arts, many of the approaches to accomplishing this goal are unique. Within the campus community is the creativity to create classroom opportunities for students that span the globe—both technologically and geographically. Here, students are just as apt to attend a biology class on campus as they are to hike in the nearby Owyhee or Sawtooth Mountains to carry out field research. During the college's 6-week winter term, more than 30 percent of the students are emailing friends and family from such locales as Australia, Israel, France, Ireland, England, Peru, or Mexico while taking part in faculty-led, multidisciplinary trips. Students are invited to visit the campus and the Admissions Counselors, either in person or through the website at www.collegeofidaho.edu.

"C of I requires all admission candidates (who have not reached sophomore status in college) to submit either the new SAT or the ACT with the Writing component as of October 2005. ACI will consider all scores, including the old SAT without Writing. There is no SAT Subject Test requirement, but scores will be considered as part of a holistic evaluation."

SELECTIVITY

Admissions Rating	**86**
# of applicants	911
% of applicants accepted	81
% of acceptees attending	33

FRESHMAN PROFILE

Range SAT Critical Reading	488–640
Range SAT Math	498–633
Range SAT Writing	470–618
Range ACT Composite	21–27
Minimum paper TOEFL	550
Minimum computer TOEFL	213
Minimum web-based TOEFL	79
Average HS GPA	3.62
% graduated top 10% of class	33
% graduated top 25% of class	67
% graduated top 50% of class	92

DEADLINES

Early action	
Deadline	12/15
Notification	1/15
Regular	
Priority	6/1
Deadline	8/1
Notification	rolling
Nonfall registration?	yes

APPLICANTS ALSO LOOK AT

AND OFTEN PREFER
University of Puget Sound
Willamette University
Linfield College
Gonzaga University

AND SOMETIMES PREFER
Boise State University
University of Idaho

AND RARELY PREFER
Northwest Nazarene University

FINANCIAL FACTS

Financial Aid Rating	**79**
Annual tuition	$18,300
Room and board	$6,631
Required fees	$690
Books and supplies	$900
% frosh rec. need-based scholarship or grant aid	44
% UG rec. need-based scholarship or grant aid	39
% frosh rec. non-need-based scholarship or grant aid	55
% UG rec. non-need-based scholarship or grant aid	58
% frosh rec. need-based self-help aid	44
% UG rec. need-based self-help aid	44
% frosh rec. athletic scholarships	36
% UG rec. athletic scholarships	35
% frosh rec. any financial aid	95
% UG rec. any financial aid	96
% UG borrow to pay for school	56
Average cumulative indebtedness	$26,170

THE COLLEGE OF NEW JERSEY

PO Box 7718, Ewing, NJ 08628-0718 • Admissions: 609-771-2131 • Fax: 609-637-5174

CAMPUS LIFE

Quality of Life Rating	94
Fire Safety Rating	96
Green Rating	91
Type of school	public
Environment	village

STUDENTS

Total undergrad enrollment	6,164
% male/female	42/58
% from out of state	5
% from public high school	65
% live on campus	48
% in (# of) fraternities	12 (11)
% in (# of) sororities	11 (15)
% African American	6
% Asian	8
% Caucasian	73
% Hispanic	8
# of countries represented	20

SURVEY SAYS . . .
Small classes
Lab facilities are great
Great computer facilities
Great library
Students are friendly
Campus feels safe
Students are happy

ACADEMICS

Academic Rating	87
Calendar	semester
Student/faculty ratio	13:1
Profs interesting rating	89
Profs accessible rating	86
Most common reg class size	20–29 students
Most common lab size	10–19 students

MOST POPULAR MAJORS
business administration and management
elementary education and teaching
psychology

STUDENTS SAY " . . ."

Academics

Students at The College of New Jersey believe they've found "the best way to get private school education for public school cost." To hear them tell it, The College of New Jersey "is the total package," with "a beautiful campus, great location, top-notch faculty, the newest technology, an interested student body, and competitive sports teams." TCNJ students benefit from their small-school setting, which makes for lots of "interaction between students and professors. The classes are generally 15 to 20 students, enabling greater relationships between students and their professors." Those relationships yield substantial dividends "when it comes to getting recommendations, taking advantage of internship opportunities, and landing jobs in the 'real world,'" we're told. Of course, first they have to graduate, no small task given that "the classes aren't a joke. They're difficult and a lot of work, but at the end of your 4 years you'll be prepared because the professors know what they're talking about and want to make sure that you do well." Students appreciate that "professors and advisors will go out of their way to help you, whether it is with your schoolwork, your resume, or your career plans. Not only is the caliber of students high, but the professors are willing to work hard for you so you are willing to work hard for them, too!" What students appreciate most is "the affordable price" of a TCNJ education: "You get a great education and it will cost less than $20,000 a year for in-state residents and only a little over for out-of-state students."

Life

The TCNJ campus "is gorgeous, with tree-lined paths and brick buildings in the Georgian Colonial style," though some students wonder whether construction will ever end. Extracurricular options are varied here. Those involved in the Greek scene say it's "always available and fun"; the Greeks and the sports houses are the location of many off-campus parties, we're told. Tuesday, aka "Tuesday Booze Day," is one of the big party nights here, by the way—that's because "The school doesn't offer a lot of classes on Wednesday." There's "always something planned by the college that is announced in the newspaper (e.g., concerts, art exhibits, guest speakers)," and the school's proximity to New York and Philadelphia helps it draw some big names, including, recently, "John Leguizamo, Blessid Union of Souls, the cast of *Whose Line is it Anyway?*, and Wynton Marsalis." Of course, location also allows for "constant trips running to New York City and other off-campus destinations. Honestly, sometimes it's hard to say no to some of the stuff going on in order to get some work done." Students note that "on [any] given weekend, about half of the population empties out. Most of these students go home, to work, or to visit friends at other schools," but add that "people think everyone goes home on the weekends, and some people do, but for those of us who stay there are fun parties, bars, things to do."

Student Body

TCNJ draws primarily "from New Jersey middle-class suburbia," which "makes for fun 'arguments,' such as: Which is better, North or South Jersey? Is it 'jimmies' or 'sprinkles'? A 'hoagie' or a 'sub'?" A "decent number of students from other backgrounds, states, and countries" supplements the population and adds diversity. Students tend to be "hardworking, diligent, and very bright," and they are "able to balance their 18-credit workload and still have time to blow some steam off on the weekends. They're leaders, both in and out of the classrooms. Our 150-plus student organizations are a testament to that." The school attracts a reasonable cross-section of personality types; one student explains, "There are many different groups at TCNJ. There are athletes, artists, Greeks, and the few who are found playing with swords on Medieval Day out on the lawn. Everyone basically does their own thing, and it's generally just accepted."

FINANCIAL AID: 609-771-2211 • E-MAIL: ADMISS@VM.TCNJ.EDU • WEBSITE: WWW.TCNJ.EDU

THE PRINCETON REVIEW SAYS

Admissions

Very important factors considered include: Class rank, application essay, rigor of secondary school record, standardized test scores, character/personal qualities, extracurricular activities, talent/ability. *Important factors considered include:* Recommendation(s), volunteer work. *Other factors considered include:* Academic GPA, alumni/ae relation, first generation, geographical residence, interview, racial/ethnic status, state residency, work experience. SAT or ACT required; TOEFL required of all international applicants. High school diploma is required and GED is accepted. *Academic units required:* 4 English, 3 mathematics, 3 science, (2 science labs), 2 foreign language, 2 social studies. *Academic units recommended:* 4 English, 3 mathematics, 3 science, (3 science labs), 3 foreign language, 3 social studies.

Financial Aid

Students should submit: FAFSA. The Princeton Review suggests that all financial aid forms be submitted as soon as possible after January 1. *Need-based scholarships/grants offered:* Federal Pell, SEOG, state scholarships/grants, private scholarships, the school's own gift aid. *Loan aid offered:* FFEL Subsidized Stafford, FFEL Unsubsidized Stafford, FFEL PLUS, Federal Perkins, Federal Nursing Applicants will be notified of awards on a rolling basis beginning 6/1. Federal Work-Study Program available. Institutional employment available. Off-campus job opportunities are excellent.

The Inside Word

Don't be deceived by the relatively high acceptance rate at The College of New Jersey. The school boasts a number of rigorous and respected academic programs. Applicants cannot slack off in high school and expect to be handed an acceptance letter—or a favorable first-semester transcript. Those who have succeeded in demanding classes will have the opportunity to receive a stellar education at this lovely public institution and at bargain prices no less.

THE SCHOOL SAYS "..."

From The Admissions Office

"The College of New Jersey is one of the United States' great higher education success stories. With a long history as New Jersey's preeminent teacher of teachers, the college has grown into a new role as educator of the state's best students in a wide range of fields. The College of New Jersey has created a culture of constant questioning—a place where knowledge is not merely received but reconfigured. In small classes, students and faculty members collaborate in a rewarding process: As they seek to understand fundamental principles, apply key concepts, reveal new problems, and pursue new lines of inquiry, students gain a fluency of thought in their disciplines. The college's 289-acre tree-lined campus is a union of vision, engineering, beauty, and functionality. Neoclassical Georgian Colonial architecture, meticulous landscaping, and thoughtful design merge in a dynamic system, constantly evolving to meet the needs of TCNJ students. About 50 percent of TCNJ's 2004 entering class will be academic scholars, with large numbers of National Merit finalists and semifinalists. More than 400 students in the class received awards from New Jersey's Outstanding Student Recruitment Program. The College of New Jersey is bringing together the best ideas from around the nation and building a new model for public undergraduate education on one campus . . . in New Jersey!

"The College of New Jersey will accept both the new and old SAT (administered prior to March 2005 and without a Writing component), as well as the ACT with or without the Writing component."

SELECTIVITY

Admissions Rating	93
# of applicants	8,607
% of applicants accepted	47
% of acceptees attending	32
# accepting a place on wait list	547
% admitted from wait list	27
# of early decision applicants	532
% accepted early decision	42

FRESHMAN PROFILE

Range SAT Critical Reading	560–650
Range SAT Math	580–680
Range SAT Writing	560–660
Minimum paper TOEFL	550
Minimum computer TOEFL	213
% graduated top 10% of class	66
% graduated top 25% of class	87
% graduated top 50% of class	99

DEADLINES

Early decision	
Deadline	11/15
Notification	12/15
Regular	
Deadline	2/15
Notification	rolling
Nonfall registration?	yes

APPLICANTS ALSO LOOK AT

AND OFTEN PREFER
University of Delaware
New York University
Rowan University
Lehigh University

AND SOMETIMES PREFER
University of Maryland—College Park
Drexel University
Boston College

AND RARELY PREFER
Fordham University
Loyola College in Maryland

FINANCIAL FACTS

Financial Aid Rating	71
Annual in-state tuition	$8,072
Annual out-of-state tuition	$15,295
Room and board	$9,242
Required fees	$3,235
Books and supplies	$1,000
% frosh rec. need-based scholarship or grant aid	17
% UG rec. need-based scholarship or grant aid	16
% frosh rec. non-need-based scholarship or grant aid	16
% UG rec. non-need-based scholarship or grant aid	16
% frosh rec. need-based self-help aid	28
% UG rec. need-based self-help aid	31
% UG borrow to pay for school	55
Average cumulative indebtedness	$20,056

COLLEGE OF THE OZARKS

OFFICE OF ADMISSIONS, POINT LOOKOUT, MO 65726 • ADMISSIONS: 417-334-6411 • FAX: 417-335-2618

CAMPUS LIFE

Quality of Life Rating	**92**
Fire Safety Rating	**63**
Green Rating	**67**
Type of school	private
Environment	rural

STUDENTS

Total undergrad enrollment	1,336
% male/female	44/56
% from out of state	33
% from public high school	77
% live on campus	84
% African American	1
% Asian	1
% Caucasian	93
% Hispanic	1
% Native American	1
% international	1
# of countries represented	14

SURVEY SAYS . . .
Large classes
Frats and sororities are unpopular
or nonexistent
Very little drug use

ACADEMICS

Academic Rating	**80**
Calendar	semester
Student/faculty ratio	13:1
Profs interesting rating	78
Profs accessible rating	80
Most common	
reg class size	10–19 students
Most common	
lab size	10–19 students

MOST POPULAR MAJORS
business/commerce
elementary education and teaching
criminal justice/police science

STUDENTS SAY ". . ."
Academics
Tiny College of the Ozarks provides a very pre-professional liberal arts education and allows many students to graduate "debt-free" through four years of "honest, old-fashioned, hard work." You still need to cover books, room and board, and some fees but there are no tuition costs. Instead of paying tuition, students here are required to work 15 hours a week during school and two 40-hour weeks each year during breaks. "Students work in all offices and areas of the college." There are pedestrian jobs such as computer support and custodial work but there are cooler jobs, too. You might work for the campus fire department, or at the hog farm, or as a jelly cook in the jelly kitchen. Academically, the nursing and business programs are reportedly "excellent." There are "extraordinary, passionate" professors here and there are others who "just stand up there and read from PowerPoint." "The teachers aren't Einsteins," reflects an English major, "but most are very good teachers and are there for their students if needed." Without question, the administration at C of O is very good at soliciting all the donated money that is required to keep tuition free and it "seems to genuinely care about the students." However, campus rules are very, very strict.

Life
Some dorms and academic buildings at C of O "are in need of repair." ("Hello mold!") "Because the college runs on donations, some renovations simply can't be done until someone wants their name on a building," notes a junior. There is "a surplus" of spiritual events and a "Christian atmosphere" is pervasive. Men's and women's basketball and intramural sports in general are favorite pastimes. "We have movie nights and dances that are pretty cool," comments a sophomore. Mudfest is a campus-wide tug of war. "If you participate, the only part of your body left clean would be your eyes and teeth." "Outdoorsy activities are highly popular" and the Ozark area offers virtually everything. Just down the road, the "big tourist trap" of Branson offers "a lot of entertainment resources." In many ways, though, "life down here is pretty quiet" and "not necessarily a real world experience." Attendance at Chapel ("fondly called Crapel") is required a few times each semester. "Most C of O students are not interested in partying" but there is "a zero-tolerance policy" just in case. Caffeine is the stimulant of choice. Drugs and alcohol are "strictly prohibited." You can't smoke cigarettes, either. Other rules include a 1:00 A.M. curfew and restricted dorm visits by members of the opposite sex. "Weekly room checks" thwart clutter. Students "aren't allowed to dress outrageously." Everyone must maintain "natural-looking hair color." Pretty clearly, this environment is not for everyone. It's really a question of priorities. "What's more important," asks one student, "being able to look trashy or getting out of college without huge amounts of debt?"

Student Body
Ethnic diversity and diversity in general are paltry at College of the Ozarks. "The typical student here is a white, middle to lower class, conservative Christian," and almost certainly "from the Midwest." "There are a lot of home-school students." "For the most part, we come from families who could not afford a 'normal' school and so we are here," asserts one student. "Stuck." "At C of O, you have the Crispies (those who are so Christian and religious that it's bad), the normal Christians who enjoy life but aren't hung up on reciting Bible verses to each other, and the partiers," describes a senior. "That's about all there is to it." The population overwhelmingly falls into the first two groups, though; partiers are a rare and exotic species. These "well-rounded, good Christian kids" are "extremely helpful," "friendly," "down to earth," and "used to earning every penny they have." They typically are involved in extracurricular activities and they enjoy each other's company. "At C of O, most students are personable and enjoy community. Students who seem to be loners or who don't enjoy a close-knit community would probably not enjoy things here."

FINANCIAL AID: 417-334-6411 • E-MAIL: ADMISS4@COFO.EDU • WEBSITE: WWW.COFO.EDU

THE PRINCETON REVIEW SAYS

Admissions

Very important factors considered include: Class rank, rigor of secondary school record, character/personal qualities, interview. *Important factors considered include:* Academic GPA, recommendation(s), standardized test scores, geographical residence, level of applicant's interest, racial/ethnic status, volunteer work, work experience. *Other factors considered include:* Alumni/ae relation, extracurricular activities, first generation, religious affiliation/commitment, state residency, talent/ability, SAT or ACT required; ACT recommended; TOEFL required of all international applicants. High school diploma is required and GED is accepted. *Academic units recommended:* 4 English, 3 mathematics, 2 science, (1 science labs), 2 foreign language, 3 social studies, 1 Visual/Peforming Arts/Public Speaking.

Financial Aid

Students should submit: FAFSA The Princeton Review suggests that all financial aid forms be submitted as soon as possible after January 1. *Need-based scholarships/grants offered:* Federal Pell, SEOG, state scholarships/grants, private scholarships, the school's own gift aid. Applicants will be notified of awards on a rolling basis beginning 2/1. Federal Work-Study Program available. Off-campus job opportunities are excellent.

The Inside Word

The highly unusual nature of the College of the Ozarks translates directly into its admissions process. Because of the school's very purpose, providing educational opportunities to those with great financial need, one of the main qualifiers for admission is exactly that—demonstrated financial need. Despite not being a household name, Ozarks attracts enough interest to keep its admit rate consistently low from year to year. To be sure, the admissions process is competitive, but it's more important to be a good fit for the college philosophically and financially than it is to be an academic wizard. If you're a hard worker all around, you're just what they're looking for.

THE SCHOOL SAYS "..."

From The Admissions Office

"College of the Ozarks is unique because of its no-tuition, work-study program, but also because it strives to educate the head, the heart, and the hands. At C of O, there are high expectations of students—the college stresses character development as well as study and work. An education from 'Hard Work U.' offers many opportunities, not the least of which is the chance to graduate debt-free. Life at C of O isn't all hard work and no play, however. There are many opportunities for fun. The nearby resort town of Branson, Missouri, offers ample opportunities for recreation and summer employment, and Table Rock Lake, only a few miles away, is a terrific spot to swim, sun, and relax. Numerous on-campus activities such as Mudfest, Luau Night, dances, and holiday parties give students lots of chances for fun without leaving the college. At 'Hard Work U.,' we work hard, but we know how to have fun, too.

"Applicants for Fall 2008 are required to submit scores from the ACT or the new SAT. We will allow students to submit scores from the old (prior to March 2005) version of the SAT (or ACT) as well, and will use the student's best scores from either test. Writing scores are not required."

SELECTIVITY
Admissions Rating	89
# of applicants	2,709
% of applicants accepted	12
% of acceptees attending	88
# accepting a place on wait list	425
% admitted from wait list	4

FRESHMAN PROFILE
Range ACT Composite	21–26
Minimum paper TOEFL	550
Minimum computer TOEFL	213
Average HS GPA	3.48
% graduated top 10% of class	14
% graduated top 25% of class	52
% graduated top 50% of class	92

DEADLINES
Regular	
Priority	2/15
Deadline	3/15
Notification	rolling
Nonfall registration?	yes

APPLICANTS ALSO LOOK AT
AND OFTEN PREFER
Missouri State University
AND SOMETIMES PREFER
Southwest Baptist University

FINANCIAL FACTS
Financial Aid Rating	89
Annual tuition	$15,900
Room and board	$4,700
Required fees	$390
Books and supplies	$800
% frosh rec. need-based scholarship or grant aid	87
% UG rec. need-based scholarship or grant aid	91
% frosh rec. non-need-based scholarship or grant aid	12
% UG rec. non-need-based scholarship or grant aid	20
% frosh rec. need-based self-help aid	75
% UG rec. need-based self-help aid	71
% frosh rec. athletic scholarships	3
% UG rec. athletic scholarships	3
% frosh rec. any financial aid	100
% UG rec. any financial aid	100
% UG borrow to pay for school	14
Average cumulative indebtedness	$6,770

THE COLLEGE OF WILLIAM & MARY

PO Box 8795, Williamsburg, VA 23187-8795 • Admissions: 757-221-4223 • Fax: 757-221-1242

STUDENTS SAY "..."

Academics

The College of William and Mary is "the second oldest school in the country" and it has an Honor code "that was started here by Thomas Jefferson." "Registration can be a lesson in disappointment" but the administration "is very in touch with the student body" and "openly asks for and is responsive to criticism." The faculty is generally tremendous. "Professors are better than I could have imagined," reflects a geology major. "They are the best teachers I have ever had. They are passionate about what they teach." "I am in classes that range from a large lecture of 300 people to a small seminar of 15," adds a first-year student. "I find that all of the teachers teach in the exact same manner, so it seems like all of my classes are in an intimate setting." "Professors are always available outside of class" as well. Be warned, though, that "the academic scene is definitely intense" at W&M. "The amount of work is often unbearable." "You're not going to get a 4.0," cautions an international relations major. "It's absolutely unheard of." Instead, professor "will give you a 'B–,' smiling." "This school is incredibly challenging," concludes a public policy major, "but at the end of the semester, when you reflect back on just how much you've learned, you realize that the sleepless nights of study and stressful weekends spent cramming instead of relaxing were worth it."

Life

William and Mary is "small enough where you don't feel like you're swallowed up into a crowd of 30,000 people, but it's also large enough to allow you some anonymity." Food is "greasy and not very good" and parking is really bad but "the sheer number and variety of organizations is a huge strength." "Most students juggle numerous activities in addition to their school work." "I write for the newspaper, sing, and volunteer with a food kitchen," illustrates a sophomore. "That's pretty representative of the student body." "Fun at William and Mary is not completely orthodox." "A capella groups are more popular on campus than sports teams." "Big traditions" include a campus wide convocation ceremony in the fall; Yule Log in December, when the school president reads *The Grinch Who Stole Christmas*; and the well-attended King & Queens Ball in the spring. W&M "can be draconian toward drinking" but there's "a pretty decent nightlife." "If you want to drink, you won't have a problem finding alcohol and, if you don't drink, the parties are still social and lively, without any pressure." "The Greek scene is visible, but is not huge." Fraternities have dance parties every weekend "and no one is turned away." "Off campus parties are popular but they get busted a lot." Students also hang out a lot at a few delis. They're "pretty much bars, but since Williamsburg doesn't allow the title 'bars,' they call them delis." Surrounding Williamsburg is "a town full of people who are old or like to dress up as colonial people." It's "a historical haven," though, and "a pleasant detour from life's stresses" "after tourist season is over."

Student Body

There are certainly rich kids here but William and Mary is a state school and "a lot of people come from more modest backgrounds." Many students come from Northern Virginia "but it's not an epidemic." Students tell us that ethnic diversity could improve. "Minorities feel outnumbered," they say. "Dumb people stand out," too. This is a pretty "intelligent and well read" crowd. "It's not unheard of to get into a theoretical discussion of politics or history or literature while drunk at a party." "The typical student is dorky and slightly awkward but nonetheless very friendly," though there are "never-come-out-of-the-library people" and a few "complete social rejects." On the whole, students at W&M are "crazy perfectionists" who are "involved in different things." They're "eclectic and quirky." "They're warm and welcoming." "Everyone at William and Mary is in touch with their inner nerd and happy with it." "It's mainly people being themselves, unabashed and proud." "That guy who sits next to you in your 300-level science class is a starting linebacker on the football team."

THE COLLEGE OF WILLIAM & MARY

FINANCIAL AID: 757-221-2420 • E-MAIL: ADMISS@WM.EDU • WEBSITE: WWW.WM.EDU

THE PRINCETON REVIEW SAYS

Admissions

Very important factors considered include: Class rank, application essay, academic GPA, recommendation(s), rigor of secondary school record, standardized test scores, character/personal qualities, extracurricular activities, state residency, talent/ability. *Other factors considered include:* Alumni/ae relation, first generation, geographical residence, interview, racial/ethnic status, volunteer work, work experience. SAT or ACT required; TOEFL required of all international applicants. High school diploma is required and GED is not accepted for freshman applicants, only transfer admission. *Academic units recommended:* 4 English, 4 mathematics, 4 science, (3 science labs), 4 foreign language, 4 social studies.

Financial Aid

Students should submit: FAFSA The Princeton Review suggests that all financial aid forms be submitted as soon as possible after January 1. *Need-based scholarships/grants offered:* Federal Pell, SEOG, state scholarships/grants, private scholarships, the school's own gift aid. *Loan aid offered:* FFEL Subsidized Stafford, FFEL Unsubsidized Stafford, FFEL PLUS, Federal Perkins Applicants will be notified of awards on a rolling basis beginning 3/15. Federal Work-Study Program available. Institutional employment available. Off-campus job opportunities are excellent.

The Inside Word

The volume of applications at William & Mary is extremely high; thus admission is ultra-competitive. Only very strong students from out of state should apply. The large applicant pool necessitates a rapid-fire candidate evaluation process; each Admissions Officer reads roughly 100 application folders per day during the peak review season. But this is one Admissions Committee that moves fast without sacrificing a thorough review. There probably isn't a tougher public college Admissions Committee in the country.

THE SCHOOL SAYS "..."

From The Admissions Office

"William & Mary is the nation's second-oldest college and preeminent small public university. Yes, we have the lowest student/faculty ratio (11:1) of any public university. We're also known for having one of the most successful undergraduate business programs in the United States, a model United Nations team that perennially vies for the world championship, and alumni who wrote everything from the revolutionary Declaration of Independence (Thomas Jefferson, Class of 1762) to the hilarious *Naked Pictures of Famous People* (Comedy Central's Jon Stewart, Class of 1984). In short, William & Mary offers a top-rated educational experience at a comparatively low cost and in the company of interesting people from a broad variety of backgrounds. If you are an academically strong, involved student looking for a challenge in a great campus community, William & Mary may well be the place for you.

SELECTIVITY

Admissions Rating	97
# of applicants	10,853
% of applicants accepted	34
% of acceptees attending	37
# accepting a place on wait list	1,101
% admitted from wait list	6
# of early decision applicants	898
% accepted early decision	46

FRESHMAN PROFILE

Range SAT Critical Reading	630–740
Range SAT Math	620–710
Range SAT Writing	620–710
Range ACT Composite	27–32
Minimum paper TOEFL	600
Minimum computer TOEFL	250
Average HS GPA	4
% graduated top 10% of class	79
% graduated top 25% of class	97
% graduated top 50% of class	100

DEADLINES

Early decision	
Deadline	11/1
Notification	12/1
Regular	
Deadline	1/1
Notification	4/1
Nonfall registration?	no

APPLICANTS ALSO LOOK AT

AND OFTEN PREFER
University of Virginia
Duke University
Georgetown University

AND SOMETIMES PREFER
Vanderbilt University
Washington and Lee University
Johns Hopkins University
Dartmouth College
Notre Dame de Namur University
Yale University

FINANCIAL FACTS

Financial Aid Rating	84
Annual in-state tuition	$2,774.50
% frosh rec. need-based scholarship or grant aid	22
% UG rec. need-based scholarship or grant aid	23
% frosh rec. non-need-based scholarship or grant aid	14
% UG rec. non-need-based scholarship or grant aid	9
% frosh rec. need-based self-help aid	23
% UG rec. need-based self-help aid	24
% frosh rec. athletic scholarships	5
% UG rec. athletic scholarships	6
% frosh rec. any financial aid	30
% UG rec. any financial aid	28
% UG borrow to pay for school	32
Average cumulative indebtedness	$15,602

THE COLLEGE OF WOOSTER

847 COLLEGE AVENUE, WOOSTER, OH 44691 • ADMISSIONS: 330-263-2322 • FAX: 330-263-2621

CAMPUS LIFE

Quality of Life Rating	**76**
Fire Safety Rating	**60***
Green Rating	**73**
Type of school	private
Environment	town

STUDENTS

Total undergrad enrollment	1,792
% male/female	49/51
% from out of state	54
% from public high school	73
% live on campus	98
% in (# of) fraternities	13 (NR)
% in (# of) sororities	17 (NR)
% African American	4
% Asian	2
% Caucasian	75
% Hispanic	2
% international	5
# of countries represented	30

SURVEY SAYS . . .
Large classes
No one cheats
Lab facilities are great
Great library
Students are friendly
Low cost of living
Lots of beer drinking

ACADEMICS

Academic Rating	**87**
Calendar	semester
Student/faculty ratio	11:1
Profs interesting rating	90
Profs accessible rating	87
Most common reg class size	fewer than 10 students
Most common lab size	10–19 students

MOST POPULAR MAJORS
English language and literature
psychology
history

STUDENTS SAY " . . . "

Academics

Undergrads here maintain that The College of Wooster "is about developing the autonomy of its students in all areas" from "their academic achievement and extracurricular activities to their self-awareness and ability to help others." Nowhere is this more evident than in the curriculum's "nationally renowned senior Independent Study (IS) project," which is where, students say, the "gold of Wooster lies." One student explains, "The Independent Study allowed me to customize and focus my interests into a thoroughly challenging, yet enjoyable, year-long project. Being able to organize and approach my own selected topic was an invaluable experience that has prepared me for the prospect of graduate school." A junior states that she chose Wooster "because it seemed to me that if students were expected to create such an intensive project then the classes must also be at a high caliber. I have certainly found this to be the case." Physics, chemistry, business and management, music, and history are among the standout disciplines here. Like most top-notch liberal arts schools, Wooster features "a small, closely knit campus and accessible, genuinely interested professors, making it the ideal setting to branch out, both in and out of the classroom." Academics here involve "a lot of homework and reading," but students tell us that they get a good overall experience, one that "incorporat[es] relatively healthy doses of student activities, good dining halls, and a beautiful campus populated by (in general) great people."

Life

Wooster "is a tradition[s]-based school with awesome activities, from the kilt-wearing marching band to the many sports teams, varsity and intramural," and students embrace these traditions with gusto. "The school is good at providing activities on weekends," students say, which include "bands and outside entertainment" as well as showcases of "students' talents." This is a good thing given that the town of Wooster "is very small [and] has little to offer in terms of activities besides restaurants and movies." Big-city entertainment can be found in Cleveland and Columbus, but both are an hour's drive away, so they're only an option if you have a car or are chummy with someone who has wheels. The on-campus party scene is robust; on "Wooster Wednesday" "people drink like it's Friday" (on actual Fridays "Many students go to the college bar/club called the Underground") and the "fraternity and sorority houses" are known for their "themed parties (Beach Party, Funk Party, Heaven and Hell, Stop and Go)." For students in search of weekend options that don't involve alcohol, the school "sponsors events to substitute [for] partying for those of us who do not participate." Have we mentioned that Wooster also has "lots of student organizations"? Word on campus is that the average student "participates in a vast array" of them.

Student Body

"There are a lot of different types of students" at Wooster, including "people who seem to be at school just to have a good time," and many more people who "seem to be here to get as much as possible out of the[ir] education." Many are "from Ohio or the Midwest," but there are also "many international students on campus, and they fit in with the rest of the student population as much as anyone else." The typical undergrad is "liberal, but rather apathetic to politics and religion." Socially, the school "is divided into countless little social groups," many of which form "based on first-year experiences, athletic involvement, or extracurricular interests." Indeed, you'll find "a lot of athletes" among the student population, and many who "are involved in a wide array of extracurricular activities"; these activities prompt "students from different backgrounds and social groups [to] interact and work together."

FINANCIAL AID: 800-877-3688 • E-MAIL: ADMISSIONS@WOOSTER.EDU • WEBSITE: WWW.WOOSTER.EDU

THE PRINCETON REVIEW SAYS

Admissions

Very important factors considered include: Class rank, academic GPA, rigor of secondary school record. *Important factors considered include:* Application essay, recommendation(s), standardized test scores, character/personal qualities, talent/ability. *Other factors considered include:* Alumni/ae relation, extracurricular activities, geographical residence, interview, racial/ethnic status, state residency, volunteer work, work experience. SAT or ACT required; ACT with Writing component required. TOEFL required of all international applicants. High school diploma is required and GED is accepted. *Academic units required:* 4 English, 3 mathematics, 3 science, 2 foreign language, 3 social studies, 2 academic electives. *Academic units recommended:* 4 mathematics, 4 science, 3 foreign language, 4 social studies.

Financial Aid

Students should submit: FAFSA, institution's own financial aid form, CSS/Financial Aid PROFILE. Regular filing deadline is 9/1. The Princeton Review suggests that all financial aid forms be submitted as soon as possible after January 1. *Need-based scholarships/grants offered:* Federal Pell, SEOG, state scholarships/grants, private scholarships, the school's own gift aid. *Loan aid offered:* Direct Subsidized Stafford, Direct Unsubsidized Stafford, Direct PLUS, Federal Perkins, college/university loans from institutional funds. Applicants will be notified of awards on or about 4/1. Federal Work-Study Program available. Institutional employment available.

The Inside Word

The College of Wooster is a small, selective liberal arts school. Stiff competition from similarly situated institutions means the school occasionally admits students who may not be up to the challenges of the curriculum, but, by and large, only solid students get past the gatekeepers here. Expect a thorough review of your entire application.

THE SCHOOL SAYS "..."

From The Admissions Office

"At The College of Wooster, our mission is to graduate educated, not merely trained, people; to produce responsible, independent thinkers, rather than specialists in any given field. Our commitment to independence is especially evident in IS, the college's distinctive program in which every senior works one-to-one with a faculty mentor to complete a project in the major. IS comes from 'independent study,' but, in reality, it is an intellectual collaboration of the highest order and permits every student the freedom to pursue something in which he or she is passionately interested. IS is the centerpiece of an innovative curriculum. More than just the project itself, the culture that sustains IS—and, in turn, is sustained by IS—is an extraordinary college culture. The same attitudes of student initiative, openness, flexibility, and individual support enrich every aspect of Wooster's vital residential college life.

"College of Wooster requires freshman applicants to submit scores from the old or new SAT. Students may also choose to submit scores from the ACT (with the Writing component) in lieu of the SAT."

SELECTIVITY

Admissions Rating	**86**
# of applicants	2,218
% of applicants accepted	91
% of acceptees attending	25
# accepting a place on wait list	25
% admitted from wait list	100
# of early decision applicants	66
% accepted early decision	91

FRESHMAN PROFILE

Range SAT Critical Reading	540–670
Range SAT Math	560–650
Range SAT Writing	550–650
Range ACT Composite	23–29
Minimum paper TOEFL	550
Minimum computer TOEFL	213
Average HS GPA	3.55
% graduated top 10% of class	27
% graduated top 25% of class	61
% graduated top 50% of class	92

DEADLINES

Early decision	
Deadline	12/1
Notification	12/15
Regular	
Deadline	2/15
Notification	4/1
Nonfall registration?	yes

FINANCIAL FACTS

Financial Aid Rating	**93**
Comprehensive fee	$42,420
% frosh rec. need-based scholarship or grant aid	58
% UG rec. need-based scholarship or grant aid	55
% frosh rec. non-need-based scholarship or grant aid	9
% UG rec. non-need-based scholarship or grant aid	7
% frosh rec. need-based self-help aid	59
% UG rec. need-based self-help aid	55
% frosh rec. any financial aid	100
% UG rec. any financial aid	100
% UG borrow to pay for school	58
Average cumulative indebtedness	$23,527

COLORADO COLLEGE

14 East Cache la Poudre Street, Colorado Springs, CO 80903 • Admissions: 719-389-6344 • Fax: 719-389-6816

STUDENTS SAY ". . ."

Academics

"Block Plan": These two words sum up a key aspect of the Colorado College experience for most students. The plan, which breaks the school year into eight 3.5 week chunks, allows students and professors to take and teach one class at a time. Students "either love or hate" the Block Plan; its supporters feel that "the block system provides a unique learning experience because we get to give our full attention to one class at a time." They love the way professors "make use of the block system to take field trips so that learning happens both inside and outside of the classroom." Inside the classroom, "the discussions rock." Students with complaints about the Block Plan gripe about visiting professors who "don't seem to understand how the system works and tend to either give way too much work or hardly any at all. They also have trouble making their classes last for the expected 3 hours each day." In addition, students report, the shortened time frame for each course means that students "can forget about getting sick, even for a day, because then they will most likely have to drop the class." Given all this pressure, undergrads appreciate the fact that professors "are available to students in and out of the classroom and care if the students succeed." For students seeking international experience, Colorado College is a great option, since "so many students study abroad." Some classes "even spend a whole block in another city or country." An "exceptionally accessible" administration gets the thumbs-up from students. The president in particular earns kudos; students report that he "is extremely open to suggestions and ideas. He has open office hours every week."

Life

The Block Plan gives life at Colorado College an unusual tempo. "Because of the Block Plan, studying is always in the forefront and intense," and "people joke that they can't plan beyond the increment of 3.5 weeks because they have no idea what the next block will be like." But at the end of each block comes a 4-day break, and students plan for that by "organizing outdoor trips or other road trips to see what Colorado has to offer." In the thick of any given block, "a lot of kids do intramural sports and party hard on the weekends. Hiking, camping, backpacking, and mountain biking are also huge activities." So are "the hockey games. People go crazy for Tiger hockey. Even the city of Colorado Springs is behind the team." Of course, "skiing is a big part of Colorado College life in the winter." Many students comment on the school's "hippie" culture, but respondents were quick to note that "almost all students are extremely accepting [of] cultural, sexual, racial, and class differences."

Student Body

One student characterizes the typical student thus: "The typical Colorado College student is White and from an upper-middle-class home in a metropolitan suburb, but wishes this weren't true and acts accordingly. He or she is relatively aware politically, socially, and environmentally, and cares enough to be motivated and take advantage of what Colorado College has to offer, but won't let this interfere with his or her skiing plans." Visitors to Colorado College, another writes, will probably find "three major demographics. First and largest: outdoor enthusiasts with a little bit of hippie in them. Second: classic frat type. The Greek scene is small, but there are plenty of folks sporting American Eagle clothes and hanging out in the gyms. Third: outright hippies. This is a smaller demographic than you'd think." Many students feel like "liberals in a conservative town." Students also admit that "there is not a whole lot of diversity at Colorado College in terms of race, sexual orientation, class, or background," but add that "there are numerous clubs and groups that support all types of minorities."

FINANCIAL AID: 719-389-6651 • E-MAIL: ADMISSION@COLORADOCOLLEGE.EDU • WEBSITE: WWW.COLORADOCOLLEGE.EDU

THE PRINCETON REVIEW SAYS

Admissions

Very important factors considered include: Rigor of secondary school record. *Important factors considered include:* Class rank, application essay, academic GPA, recommendation(s), standardized test scores, extracurricular activities, interview. *Other factors considered include:* Alumni/ae relation, character/personal qualities, first generation, level of applicant's interest, racial/ethnic status, religious affiliation/commitment, talent/ability, volunteer work, work experience. SAT or ACT required; TOEFL required of all international applicants. High school diploma or equivalent is not required. *Academic units required:* 4 English. *Academic units recommended:* 4 English.

Financial Aid

Students should submit: FAFSA, CSS/Financial Aid PROFILE, noncustodial PROFILE, Federal 1040 parent and student tax returns and parent W-2 forms. Regular filing deadline is 2/15. The Princeton Review suggests that all financial aid forms be submitted as soon as possible after January 1. *Need-based scholarships/grants offered:* Federal Pell, SEOG, state scholarships/grants, private scholarships, the school's own gift aid, Federal ACG and SMART grants. *Loan aid offered:* FFEL Subsidized Stafford, FFEL Unsubsidized Stafford, FFEL PLUS, Federal Perkins Applicants will be notified of awards on or about 3/20. Federal Work-Study Program available. Institutional employment available. Off-campus job opportunities are good.

The Inside Word

Colorado College works to identify those students who will most benefit from its distinct academic environment. Because the block program requires focus and demands that students become active participants in their education, Admissions Officers value applicants who take on a rigorous course load in high school and engage in activities that complement their intellectual achievements. All candidates should take the application essay seriously—strong writing skills are seen as critical to success at CC.

THE SCHOOL SAYS "..."

From The Admissions Office

"Students enter Colorado College for the opportunity to study intensely in small learning communities. Groups of students work closely with one another and faculty in discussion-based classes and hands-on labs. CC encourages a well-rounded education, combining the academic rigor of an honors college with rich programs in athletics, community service, student government, the arts, and more. The college encourages students to push themselves academically, and many continue their studies at the best graduate and professional schools in the nation. CC is a great choice for field study and for international study (CC ranks fourth nationally in the number of students studying abroad). CC also takes advantage of its location, using its Baca campus in the San Luis Valley and the mountain cabin for a variety of classes. Its location at the base of the Rockies makes CC a great choice for students who enjoy backpacking, hiking, climbing, and skiing.

"Colorado College requires students to submit either the SAT or ACT. Scores are accepted for both with or without Writing component. CC uses the highest sub score on the SAT and the highest ACT composite. SAT Subject Tests are accepted for review, but are not required."

SELECTIVITY

Admissions Rating	95
# of applicants	4,826
% of applicants accepted	32
% of acceptees attending	34
# accepting a place on wait list	342
% admitted from wait list	12
# of early decision applicants	331
% accepted early decision	43

FRESHMAN PROFILE

Range SAT Critical Reading	610–700
Range SAT Math	620–690
Range SAT Writing	600–700
Range ACT Composite	27–31
Minimum paper TOEFL	550
Minimum computer TOEFL	213
Minimum web-based TOEFL	79
% graduated top 10% of class	60
% graduated top 25% of class	92
% graduated top 50% of class	100

DEADLINES

Early decision	
Deadline	11/15
Notification	12/20
Early action	
Deadline	11/15
Notification	1/15
Regular	
Priority	1/15
Deadline	1/15
Notification	4/1
Nonfall registration?	yes

FINANCIAL FACTS

Financial Aid Rating	88
Annual tuition	$33,972
Room and board	$8,498
Books and supplies	$936
% frosh rec. need-based scholarship or grant aid	35
% UG rec. need-based scholarship or grant aid	38
% frosh rec. non-need-based scholarship or grant aid	8
% UG rec. non-need-based scholarship or grant aid	7
% frosh rec. need-based self-help aid	31
% UG rec. need-based self-help aid	33
% frosh rec. athletic scholarships	1
% UG rec. athletic scholarships	2
% frosh rec. any financial aid	36
% UG rec. any financial aid	40
% UG borrow to pay for school	9
Average cumulative indebtedness	$16,503

COLORADO STATE UNIVERSITY

SPRUCE HALL, FORT COLLINS, CO 80523 • ADMISSIONS: 970-491-6909 • FAX: 970-491-7799

CAMPUS LIFE

Quality of Life Rating	**82**
Fire Safety Rating	**72**
Green Rating	**89**
Type of school	public
Environment	city

STUDENTS

Total undergrad enrollment	20,765
% male/female	48/52
% from out of state	17
% live on campus	27
% in (# of) fraternities	2 (19)
% in (# of) sororities	4 (15)
% African American	2
% Asian	3
% Caucasian	80
% Hispanic	7
% Native American	2
% international	2
# of countries represented	79

SURVEY SAYS . . .

Great computer facilities
Great library
Athletic facilities are great
Students love Fort Collins, CO
Great off-campus food
Campus feels safe
Student publications are popular
Lots of beer drinking

ACADEMICS

Academic Rating	**71**
Calendar	semester
Student/faculty ratio	17:1
Profs interesting rating	75
Profs accessible rating	72
% classes taught by TAs	8
Most common reg class size	20–29 students
Most common lab size	20–29 students

MOST POPULAR MAJORS

psychology
construction engineering
technology/technician
biology/biological sciences

STUDENTS SAY ". . ."

Academics

With a variety of majors and strong science programs available to them, students at Colorado State University find a lot to get excited about: "I want to go to every single one of my classes, and I love looking at all the other ones I get to take later," says one junior. Regardless of the large size of the student body, students get a lot of individual attention. Professors are "very approachable and willing to help you anytime, and they love knowing the students in their classes by name." For those who are looking for an even more personalized experience, the honors program is a great option; participants claim that "it's a huge benefit to you for only a bit more effort" because "The classes are small," "The professors are approachable," and best of all, "Honors students register first." This last benefit is particularly important, since "A lot of interesting classes described in the General Catalog are rarely offered." While students enjoy classes as a whole, claiming that they "just keep getting better" as the years go on, many are discontent the larger size of the introductory classes: One undergrad was "shocked by how many TAs teach undergraduate classes."

Life

Let's just say that CSU students didn't come to Colorado to spend their days indoors. "The amount of outdoor activities is insane, and there is always something to do outside," one senior writes; local al fresco distractions include "biking, hiking, Horsetooth Reservoir, Poudre Canyon, camping, and skiing/snowboarding." "It's not unusual for students to skip class to head to the ski slopes (naturally!)," says one snow bunny. Indoor activities include "quite a bit of drinking and the typical party scene," but "The majority of students drink responsibly," and "Everyone seems to do a fairly good job of balancing school and work and other activities." Students speak highly of hometown Fort Collins, claiming that "the community feeling in the town is really great." One sophomore writes, "Town is an incredibly popular hangout for students on evenings and weekends, with its wide array of stores, restaurants, and bars." With "multiple extracurricular activities" on campus available to them, including "a lot of religious groups," CSU is "definitely not a 'suitcase campus.' People stay through the weekend because there are things to do on and off campus."

Student Body

CSU Rams are a generally harmonious bunch, typically composed of students who are "White, middle-class," "athletic," and "typically Coloradoan." "People here are pretty laid-back," says one student. "Atypical students are few and far between, but they find their own niche," probably because "A large student body provides a large pool of social groups or cliques to fit into." The 25,000-strong student body can prove a bit daunting for some freshmen, who could "feel overwhelmed with the size and amount of people." Students claim that diversity is "lacking in some areas," but the campus still appears to have "a student body that is representative of the population of Colorado," and "The minorities we do have on campus seem to fit in just fine." As one senior puts it, "It's hard not to make friends at CSU."

FINANCIAL AID: 970-491-6321 • E-MAIL: ADMISSIONS@COLOSTATE.EDU • WEBSITE: WWW.COLOSTATE.EDU

THE PRINCETON REVIEW SAYS

Admissions

Very important factors considered include: Class rank, application essay, academic GPA, recommendation(s), rigor of secondary school record, standardized test scores. *Other factors considered include:* Alumni/ae relation, character/personal qualities, extracurricular activities, first generation, geographical residence, interview, level of applicant's interest, racial/ethnic status, state residency, talent/ability, volunteer work, work experience. SAT or ACT required; TOEFL required of all international applicants. High school diploma is required and GED is accepted. *Academic units required:* 4 English, 3 mathematics, 3 science, (2 science labs), 2 social studies, 1 history, 2 academic electives. *Academic units recommended:* 4 English, 4 mathematics, 3 science, (2 science labs), 2 foreign language, 2 social studies, 1 history, 2 academic electives.

Financial Aid

Students should submit: FAFSA The Princeton Review suggests that all financial aid forms be submitted as soon as possible after January 1. *Need-based scholarships/grants offered:* Federal Pell, SEOG, state scholarships/grants, private scholarships, the school's own gift aid. *Loan aid offered:* Direct Subsidized Stafford, Direct Unsubsidized Stafford, Direct PLUS, Federal Perkins, college/university loans from institutional funds, alternative loans. Applicants will be notified of awards on a rolling basis beginning 3/1. Federal Work-Study Program available. Institutional employment available. Off-campus job opportunities are excellent.

The Inside Word

Following the lead of other public schools, Colorado State uses GPA and standardized test scores as its chief admissions criteria. That said, the Admissions Team is interested in promoting and maintaining a campus of diverse student interests and backgrounds. Applicants interested in more competitive majors such as landscape architecture and engineering will face stricter requirements.

THE SCHOOL SAYS " . . ."

From The Admissions Office

"As one of the nation's premier research universities, Colorado State offers more than 150 undergraduate programs of study in eight colleges. Students come here from 50 states and 86 countries, and they appreciate the quality and breadth of the university's academic offerings. But Colorado State is more than just a place where students can take their scholarship to the highest level. It's also a place where they can gain invaluable experience in the fields of their choice, whether they're immersing themselves in professional internships, studying on the other side of the globe or teaming up with faculty on groundbreaking research projects. In addition to an outstanding experiential learning environment, Colorado State students enjoy a sense of community that's unusual for a large university. They develop meaningful relationships with faculty members who bring out their best work, and they live and learn with diverse peers who value their ideas and expand their perspectives. These types of connections lead to countless opportunities for social networking and professional accomplishments. By the time our students graduate from Colorado State, they have the knowledge, practical experience and interpersonal skills they need to make a significant contribution to their world.

"Although academic performance is a primary factor in admission decisions, Colorado State's holistic review process also recognizes personal qualities and experiences that have the potential to enrich the university and the Fort Collins community. To apply, students may submit the Common Application or the Colorado State University Application for Admission."

SELECTIVITY

Admissions Rating	78
# of applicants	11,727
% of applicants accepted	86
% of acceptees attending	44

FRESHMAN PROFILE

Range SAT Critical Reading	490–610
Range SAT Math	510–630
Range SAT Writing	480–590
Range ACT Composite	22–26
Minimum paper TOEFL	450
Minimum computer TOEFL	130
Minimum web-based TOEFL	45
Average HS GPA	3.53
% graduated top 10% of class	18.93
% graduated top 25% of class	48.33
% graduated top 50% of class	86.17

DEADLINES

Regular	
Priority	2/1
Deadline	7/1
Notification	rolling
Nonfall registration?	yes

APPLICANTS ALSO LOOK AT AND OFTEN PREFER

University of Colorado—Boulder
Arizona State University at the Tempe campus
Cornell University
Colorado College
University of Denver
Colorado School of Mines

FINANCIAL FACTS

Financial Aid Rating	80
Annual in-state tuition	$4,040
Annual out-of-state tuition	$17,480
Room and board	$7,382
Required fees	$1,379
Books and supplies	$990
% frosh rec. need-based scholarship or grant aid	23
% UG rec. need-based scholarship or grant aid	24
% frosh rec. need-based self-help aid	22
% UG rec. need-based self-help aid	29
% frosh rec. athletic scholarships	1
% UG rec. athletic scholarships	1
% frosh rec. any financial aid	62
% UG rec. any financial aid	65
% UG borrow to pay for school	55
Average cumulative indebtedness	$18,912

COLUMBIA UNIVERSITY

212 HAMILTON HALL MC 2807, 1130 AMSTERDAM AVENUE, NY, NY 10027 • ADMISSIONS: 212-854-2522 • FAX: 212-894-1209

CAMPUS LIFE
Quality of Life Rating	93
Fire Safety Rating	60*
Green Rating	60*
Type of school	private
Environment	metropolis

STUDENTS
Total undergrad enrollment	5,602
% male/female	53/47
% from out of state	75
% from public high school	59
% live on campus	95
% in (# of) fraternities	15 (17)
% in (# of) sororities	10 (11)
% African American	9
% Asian	18
% Caucasian	42
% Hispanic	10
% Native American	1
% international	9
# of countries represented	87

SURVEY SAYS . . .
Great library
Diverse student types on campus
Students love New York, NY
Great off-campus food
Campus feels safe
Students are happy

ACADEMICS
Academic Rating	96
Calendar	semester
Student/faculty ratio	6:1
Profs interesting rating	77
Profs accessible rating	74
Most common reg class size	10–19 students

MOST POPULAR MAJORS
political science
English
engineering

STUDENTS SAY ". . ."

Academics

Located on the upper west side of Manhattan, "Columbia University provides an exceptional education, fusing the chaos of New York City" with "the rigors of the Ivy League." The course work here "can be tremendously grueling." Expect to do a lot of studying and "thinking about the world in ways that are new and occasionally uncomfortable." Columbia's "inspiring" professors are "leaders in their fields" who are "brilliant (and don't hide the fact that they, too, think so)." They are "obsessed with what they study" and their "Enthusiasm is contagious." A few professors "have that certain scholarly air of arrogance" and can be tough graders. However, "The professors who are known to grade harshly and give hard tests are usually the ones who teach the best." Central to the academic experience here is the "eye-opening, thought-provoking" core curriculum, a sequence that immerses students in Western philosophy, literature, and fine arts. "Columbia's core prepares you to excel in any field," explains one first-year student. Taking core classes also helps "when you're first trying to make new friends" because "Everyone is dealing with the same classes." Most students feel that the administration here "listens to students" and "generally gets the job done," but can be "bureaucratic" at times. Be warned, however, that "advising is definitely not the strong point of Columbia." It's easy to feel "alone in the big city" on occasion. The resources are there, of course, but "People here don't treat you like a baby."

Life

Students on this "beautiful" campus "in the middle of Manhattan" say that they "study really hard during the week and party really hard on weekends." There's always something to do in the "chic, cultured city of opportunity" that is their home. "It's New York City," boasts one student, "the greatest city in the universe," where "Everything is only a subway ride away." As another student explains, "There is no one activity that dominates the social scene. Instead, everything is at our disposal." Options range from "a trip to the Met [and] shopping on Fifth Avenue" to "movies, clubs, theater, ice skating, and restaurants." Students can go to "art museums, comedy clubs, [and] jazz clubs." The bar scene is also popular. As one student explains, "[Lots of students get] a fake ID the first semester of their freshman year to give them access to New York City's nightlife." Students who plan on experiencing all the "glitzy things you hear about in NYC" should "make sure [they] have money to shell out," advises one cost-conscious student. "Even student tickets can add up and dining out is expensive." Students on a budget can do "plenty of other things around town that don't cost more than the subway fare." While Columbia students are "hardly bound by the campus gates," the university offers "as much of a campus life," including "frat parties or dorm parties," "various activity groups," and a popular "annual musical theater production" that "everyone goes to see."

Student Body

"Columbia is a microcosm of New York," sums up one student. The people here are a "mix of everything." Columbia's "very well-rounded" students "are very passionate about their interests." As one student explains, "You can find conversations about everything from the relationship between gods and mortals in Virgil's *Aeneid* to the latest hipster music group." On campus, you'll find "a great mix of ethnicities" as well as ample diversity of "religions, socioeconomic backgrounds, national heritage, sexual orientations, political beliefs, and geographic roots." These "smart, motivated, independent, and intellectually curious" students describe themselves as "hardworking, continuously busy," and "not very religious." One student warns, however, that "many students are book smart but not very worldly" and can be "very full of" themselves. Politically, left-liberalism is "raging" on campus, though Columbia is "not as crazy liberal as it used to be."

COLUMBIA UNIVERSITY

THE PRINCETON REVIEW SAYS

Admissions

Very important factors considered include: Rigor of secondary school record, class rank, application essay, academic GPA, recommendation (s), standardized test scores, extracurricular activities, talent/ability, character/personal qualities. *Other factors considered include:* Alumni/ae relation, geographical residence, interview, racial/ethnic status, volunteer work, work experience. SAT or ACT and SAT Subject Tests required; ACT with Writing component required. TOEFL required of some international applicants. High school diploma is required and GED is accepted. *Academic units recommended:* 4 English, 4 mathematics, 4 science, (4 science labs), 4 foreign language, 4 history, 4 academic electives.

Financial Aid

Students should submit: FAFSA, CSS/Financial Aid PROFILE, noncustodial PROFILE, Parent and student income tax forms. Regular filing deadline is 3/1. The Princeton Review suggests that all financial aid forms be submitted as soon as possible after January 1. *Need-based scholarships/grants offered:* Federal Pell, SEOG, state scholarships/grants, private scholarships, the school's own gift aid. *Loan aid offered:* FFEL Subsidized Stafford, FFEL Unsubsidized Stafford, FFEL PLUS, Federal Perkins, Alternative loans. Applicants will be notified of awards on or about 4/1. Federal Work-Study Program available. Institutional employment available. Off-campus job opportunities are excellent.

The Inside Word

Earning an acceptance letter from Columbia is no easy feat. Applications to the university continue to rise and many great candidates are rejected each year. Admissions officers take a holistic approach to evaluating applications; there's no magic formula or pattern to guide students seeking admission. One common denominator among applicants is stellar grades in rigorous classes and personal accomplishments in non-academic activities. Admissions Officers are looking to build a diverse class that will greatly contribute to the university.

THE SCHOOL SAYS "..."

From The Admissions Office

"Columbia maintains an intimate college campus within one of the world's most vibrant cities. After a day exploring New York City you come home to a traditional college campus within an intimate neighborhood. Nobel Prize–winning professors will challenge you in class discussions and meet one-on-one afterward. The core curriculum attracts intensely free-minded scholars, and connects all undergraduates. Science and engineering students pursue cutting-edge research in world-class laboratories with faculty members at the forefront of scientific discovery. Classroom discussions are only the beginning of your education. Ideas spill out from the classrooms, electrifying the campus and Morningside Heights. Friendships formed in the residence halls solidify during a game of Frisbee on the South Lawn or over bagels on the steps of Low Library. From your first day on campus, you will be part of our diverse community.

"Columbia offers extensive need-based financial aid and meets the full need of every student admitted as a first-year with grants instead of loans. Parents with calculated incomes below $60,000 are not expected to contribute any income or assets to tuition, room, board and mandatory fees and families with calculated incomes between $60,000 and $100,000 and with typical assets have a significantly reduced contribution. To support students pursuing study abroad, research, internships and community service opportunities, Columbia offers additional funding and exemptions from academic year and summer work expectations. A commitment to diversity—of every kind—is a long-standing Columbia hallmark. We believe cost should not be a barrier to pursuing your educational dreams."

SELECTIVITY
Admissions Rating	99
# of applicants	21,342
% of applicants accepted	10
% of acceptees attending	64
# of early decision applicants	2,429
% accepted early decision	24

FRESHMAN PROFILE
Range SAT Critical Reading	680–760
Range SAT Math	680–780
Range SAT Writing	670–760
Range ACT Composite	28–33
Minimum paper TOEFL	600
Minimum computer TOEFL	250
Average HS GPA	3.9
% graduated top 10% of class	94
% graduated top 25% of class	98
% graduated top 50% of class	99

DEADLINES
Early decision	
Deadline	11/1
Notification	12/15
Regular	
Deadline	1/2
Notification	4/1
Nonfall registration?	no

APPLICANTS ALSO LOOK AT
AND OFTEN PREFER
Harvard College
Stanford University
Massachusetts Institute of Technology
Yale University
AND SOMETIMES PREFER
University of Pennsylvania
Princeton University
AND RARELY PREFER
New York University
Dartmouth College
Cornell University
Brown University

FINANCIAL FACTS
Financial Aid Rating	96
Annual tuition	$35,516
% frosh rec. need-based scholarship or grant aid	49
% UG rec. need-based scholarship or grant aid	46
% frosh rec. need-based self-help aid	43
% UG rec. need-based self-help aid	43
% frosh rec. any financial aid	61
% UG rec. any financial aid	56

CONNECTICUT COLLEGE

270 MOHEGAN AVENUE, NEW LONDON, CT 06320 • ADMISSIONS: 860-439-2200 • FAX: 860-439-4301

STUDENTS SAY ". . ."

Academics

A "small liberal arts school with excellent academic standards" and an "interdisciplinary focus," Connecticut College provides its students with "a wide range of academic programs." The "enthusiastic," "approachable and involved" professors here are "great teachers" who regularly "meet with students outside of class to address any concerns." One student gushes, "I can honestly tell you that my professors have been some of the most inspiring, thought-provoking people I've ever met." Perhaps most important, "There are no teaching assistants, ever." The administration "can get a little exasperating," but most of the top brass is "readily available" and dedicated to "making the college run smoothly." Top programs include dance, chemistry, biological sciences, psychology, and international relations. Over half of all students study abroad during their 4 years here. The Career Center and internship programs receive solid praise as well: "A paid internship during the summer" after junior year is yours for the taking "if you complete all career services workshops," says one student. The "student-adjudicated" honor code "is also huge." "We wrote it; we enforce it," explains one student. "It applies to noise in the dorms, cheating on tests, self-scheduled exams, and tolerance of sexual orientations."

Life

Connecticut College's attractive and "very social" campus is its own little "close-knit" universe, complete with "a wide range of activities" and "a beautiful view of Long Island Sound and the ocean." Without question, students here "have a lot of fun." "Keg parties" are abundant, and "Small room parties are also popular." Dances "are quite popular" as well. "Thursday and Saturday nights are the big going-out nights," and there are "live bands every Friday." "If you aren't a party person, you can feel like an outsider," observes a first-year student. "But at the same time, academics are extremely important" to Connecticut College students. Because the school doesn't have Greek organizations, "It's important to make friends and be involved" in students organizations like "activism groups" and intramural and intercollegiate sports. Students tell us that athletics could use "more money," though, and "The fitness center and dorms need to be updated," which the college is planning to complete by fall 2009. As far as off-campus life goes, the surrounding town of New London is not particularly accessible. "It's hard or at least inconvenient to get off campus if you don't have a car," advises one student. If you do have a car—or if you take the train—"You can go to Boston or Providence or New York City for the weekend."

Student Body

Students here describe themselves as "open-minded, active, optimistic," and "not overly competitive." There is "a wide range of personalities" and "a good mix of hippies, jocks, book nerds, gamers, and conservatives." A notable international student population exists as well. "Conn says that it has a very diverse campus, but that's only if you've lived in a small New England town your whole life," asserts a jaded first-year student. "There is some diversity and the diversity that exists is fully embraced, but there isn't a huge variety of backgrounds." "A 'typical' student at Conn is involved in three to four extracurricular activities," including an intercollegiate athletic team. The typical student might also be "very rich," "preppy," and "from New England." Such students "look like they walked off the pages of a J. Crew catalog," comments one undergrad. Students are quick to emphasize, however, that stereotypes are often inaccurate: "We are not all trust-fund babies," a sophomore explains. "More students are on financial aid than it may seem." "There is a lot of wealth on this campus," another student asserts, "but one thing I like about this college is that people don't show their wealth off and everyone is able to get along with each other." "Atypical students" do "tend to stick together," though.

FINANCIAL AID: 860-439-2200 • E-MAIL: ADMISSION@CONNCOLL.EDU • WEBSITE: WWW.CONNCOLL.EDU

THE PRINCETON REVIEW SAYS

Admissions

TOEFL required of all international applicants. High school diploma is required and GED is accepted.

Financial Aid

Students should submit: FAFSA, CSS/Financial Aid PROFILE, noncustodial PROFILE, business/farm supplement, federal tax returns; personal, partnership, Federal W2 statements. Regular filing deadline is 2/1. The Princeton Review suggests that all financial aid forms be submitted as soon as possible after January 1. *Need-based scholarships/grants offered:* Federal Pell, SEOG, state scholarships/grants, ACG, SMART, the school's own gift aid. *Loan aid offered:* FFEL Subsidized Stafford, FFEL Unsubsidized Stafford, FFEL PLUS, Federal Perkins Federal Work-Study Program available. Institutional employment available. Off-campus job opportunities are good.

The Inside Word

Connecticut College is the archetypal selective New England college, and Admissions Officers are judicious in their decisions. Competitive applicants will have pursued a demanding course load in high school. Admissions Officers look for students who are curious and who thrive in challenging academic environments. Since Connecticut College has a close-knit community, personal qualities are also closely evaluated, and interviews are important.

THE SCHOOL SAYS " . . ."

From The Admissions Office

"Distinguishing characteristics of the diverse student body at this small, highly selective college are honor and tolerance. Student leadership is pronounced in all aspects of the college's administration from exclusive jurisdiction of the honor code and dorm life to active representation on the president's academic and administrative cabinets. Differences of opinion are respected and celebrated as legitimate avenues to new understanding. Students come to Connecticut College seeking opportunities for independence and initiative and find them in abundance.

"Applicants must submit the results of either two SAT Subject Tests or the ACT. For candidates who choose to submit an ACT score, we will accept either the old or the new version, with or without the optional Writing component. Submission of SAT scores in addition to the required testing is optional."

SELECTIVITY

Admissions Rating	95
# of applicants	4,742
% of applicants accepted	35
% of acceptees attending	30
# accepting a place on wait list	433
% admitted from wait list	7
# of early decision applicants	313
% accepted early decision	67

FRESHMAN PROFILE

Range SAT Critical Reading	630–720
Range SAT Math	610–690
Range SAT Writing	630–720
Range ACT Composite	25–29
Minimum paper TOEFL	600
Minimum computer TOEFL	250
Minimum web-based TOEFL	100
% graduated top 10% of class	60
% graduated top 25% of class	93
% graduated top 50% of class	100

DEADLINES

Early decision	
Deadline	11/15
Notification	12/15
Regular	
Deadline	1/1
Notification	3/31
Nonfall registration?	no

APPLICANTS ALSO LOOK AT

AND OFTEN PREFER
Hamilton College
Vassar College
Wesleyan University
Middlebury College
Colby College
Boston College
Tufts University
Bates College
Bowdoin College

AND SOMETIMES PREFER
Trinity College (CT)

AND RARELY PREFER
Brown University
Skidmore College

FINANCIAL FACTS

Financial Aid Rating	94
Comprehensive fee	$49,385
Books and supplies	$1,000
% frosh rec. need-based scholarship or grant aid	39
% UG rec. need-based scholarship or grant aid	38
% frosh rec. need-based self-help aid	37
% UG rec. need-based self-help aid	37
% frosh rec. any financial aid	45
% UG borrow to pay for school	38
Average cumulative indebtedness	$23,488

THE COOPER UNION FOR THE ADVANCEMENT OF SCIENCE AND ART

30 COOPER SQUARE, NEW YORK, NY 10003 • ADMISSIONS: 212-353-4120 • FAX: 212-353-4342

STUDENTS SAY "..."

Academics

One of the coolest things about The Copper Union is that there is no tuition. The school "offers a full-tuition scholarship to everyone who is accepted." We hasten to add, though, that room and board (in New York City), books and supplies, and various fees add up to quite a bit each year. There is a mandatory core curriculum here in the humanities but, so far as majors go, programs in engineering, art, and architecture are the only options on the menu. Cooper is "one of the best schools for what it does in the country." "It is a school where the students can really go crazy and learn a lot." "Classes are small" and "professors are more than willing to give extra help outside of class." However, it's "not for the weak of heart." The "very visceral and involving" academic experience is "hell." It's "exhaustive and murderous." "Cooper Union: where your best just isn't good enough," muses a civil engineering major. Cooper is about "hours of study, neglect of personal life," and generally "working your ass off." And "the work you put in does not necessarily reflect in your grades." "I have never worked so hard in my life and probably never will," speculates a junior. All of this "kind of sucks at times" but "as long as you can get through it, you're set for life." Complaints among students here include "worthless" adjunct professors. Some lab equipment "could be upgraded," too. "The administration is sometimes difficult to approach" and "scheduling is always weird." Nonetheless, management "mostly meets the students' needs, with minor mishaps."

Life

"There is no meal plan" at Cooper and the lodging situation is harsh. "There is only housing guaranteed for first-year students and since Manhattan is a very expensive place to live, it becomes a problem after freshman year." "Everyone is extraordinarily busy," comments a fine art major. "School is life and there's no way around it." For the architecture students, life is "nothing except architecture in radical explorations and expressions." For engineers, "Cooper is about selling your soul for four years." Art students sometimes "take time off because it's hard to be creative every minute." "The intense workload gives little break for fun." There are "many extracurricular programs" but the urban fare of New York City consumes most free time. The surrounding East Village is full of funky shops, cheap eateries, theaters, bars, and live music venues; subways can whisk students throughout the five boroughs at any time of day. "Drinking with friends is a great and sometimes necessary way to decompress" but for most students, "ruthlessly sucking on booze" is a very occasional thing. "We are not a party school," says a sophomore. "We get to campus in the morning, and leave late night." "Cooper isn't for everybody," advises a senior. "If you need excessive guidance, or prefer an exclusive, well-defined campus structure, you won't be happy here."

Student Body

Diversity here is simply dreamy. Cooper's overwhelming male population is exceptionally ethnically diverse and "everyone is very different from everyone else." "The student body is teeming with sensitive and excitable minds, which caters to an unbridled sense of adventure and exploration." These "really ridiculously smart" students have "incredible, raw talent." Personalities "range from your seemingly typical frat jock to your genius who knows everything but how to socialize." Cooper students are very often "hardcore" and come in three stereotypes. "The art kids all wear the same 'unique' clothing and smoke a lot." They're "definitely more free-spirit, social people." "The engineers are either playing video games or saying sad jokes that only other engineers would understand." And "the architecture students can be a mixture of both, or anywhere in between, but they are hard to catch because all they do is work all the time." These three groups of students "don't mix so much" and sometimes there are rivalries. "The battle is like the Cold War, mostly sent in written messages on bathroom walls but no direct actions. It's benign in nature and just for amusement."

THE COOPER UNION FOR THE ADVANCEMENT OF SCIENCE AND ART

FINANCIAL AID: 212-353-4130 • E-MAIL: ADMISSIONS@COOPER.EDU • WEBSITE: WWW.COOPER.EDU

THE PRINCETON REVIEW SAYS

Admissions

Very important factors considered include: Academic GPA, rigor of secondary school record, standardized test scores, level of applicant's interest, talent/ability. *Important factors considered include:* Application essay, character/personal qualities, extracurricular activities. *Other factors considered include:* Class rank, recommendation(s), first generation, interview, racial/ethnic status, volunteer work, work experience. SAT or ACT required; ACT with Writing component recommended. TOEFL required of all international applicants. High school diploma is required and GED is accepted. *Academic units required:* 4 English, 1 mathematics, 1 science, 1 social studies, 1 history, 8 academic electives. *Academic units recommended:* 4 English, 4 mathematics, 4 science, (3 science labs), 2 foreign language, 4 social studies.

Financial Aid

Students should submit: FAFSA, CSS/Financial Aid PROFILE Regular filing deadline is 6/1. The Princeton Review suggests that all financial aid forms be submitted as soon as possible after January 1. *Need-based scholarships/grants offered:* Federal Pell, SEOG, state scholarships/grants, private scholarships, the school's own gift aid. *Loan aid offered:* FFEL Subsidized Stafford, FFEL Unsubsidized Stafford, FFEL PLUS, Federal Perkins, college/university loans from institutional funds. Applicants will be notified of awards on or about 6/1. Federal Work-Study Program available. Institutional employment available. Off-campus job opportunities are excellent.

The Inside Word

It's ultra-tough to get into The Cooper Union. There are typically over 2500 applicants vying for fewer than 300 slots. Not only do students need to have top academic accomplishments, but also they need to be a good fit for Cooper's offbeat milieu.

THE SCHOOL SAYS " . . ."

From The Admissions Office

"Each of Cooper Union's three schools, architecture, art, and engineering, adheres strongly to preparation for its profession and is committed to a problem-solving philosophy of education in a unique, scholarly environment. A rigorous curriculum and group projects reinforce this unique atmosphere in higher education and contribute to a strong sense of community and identity in each school. With McSorley's Ale House and the Joseph Papp Public Theatre nearby, Cooper Union remains at the heart of the city's tradition of free speech, enlightenment, and entertainment. Cooper's Great Hall has hosted national leaders, from Abraham Lincoln to Booker T. Washington, from Mark Twain to Samuel Gompers, from Susan B. Anthony to Betty Friedan, and more recently, President Bill Clinton and Senator Barack Obama

"In addition, we eagerly await the arrival of our new academic building slated to open in 2009. Designed by Pritzker Prize–winning architect, Thom Mayne, the new building is expected to enhance and encourage more interaction between students in all three schools.

"We're seeking students who have a passion to study our professional programs. Cooper Union students are independent thinkers, following the beat of their own drum. Many of our graduates become world-class leaders in the disciplines of architecture, fine arts, design, and engineering.

"For art and architecture applicants, SAT scores are considered after the home test and portfolio work. For engineering applicants than high school grades, the SAT and SAT Subject Test scores are the most important factors considered in admissions decisions. Currently, we do not use the Writing section of the SAT to assist in making admissions decisions. We expect to reconsider that policy as more data is available in the near future."

SELECTIVITY

Admissions Rating	98
# of applicants	2,551
% of applicants accepted	11
% of acceptees attending	74
# accepting a place on wait list	60
% admitted from wait list	5
# of early decision applicants	380
% accepted early decision	20

FRESHMAN PROFILE

Range SAT Critical Reading	610–700
Range SAT Math	640–770
Range ACT Composite	29–33
Minimum paper TOEFL	600
Minimum computer TOEFL	250
Minimum web-based TOEFL	100
Average HS GPA	3.6
% graduated top 10% of class	93
% graduated top 25% of class	98
% graduated top 50% of class	99

DEADLINES

Early decision	
Deadline	12/1
Notification	12/23
Regular	
Priority	12/1
Deadline	1/1
Notification	4/1
Nonfall registration?	no

APPLICANTS ALSO LOOK AT
AND OFTEN PREFER
Cornell University
Massachusetts Institute of Technology
University of Pennsylvania
AND SOMETIMES PREFER
Carnegie Mellon University
AND RARELY PREFER
Rochester Institute of Technology

FINANCIAL FACTS

Financial Aid Rating	92
Annual tuition	$31,500
Room and board	$13,500
Required fees	$1,600
Books and supplies	$1,800
% frosh rec. need-based scholarship or grant aid	35
% UG rec. need-based scholarship or grant aid	31
% frosh rec. non-need-based scholarship or grant aid	35
% UG rec. non-need-based scholarship or grant aid	31
% frosh rec. need-based self-help aid	22
% UG rec. need-based self-help aid	22
% frosh rec. any financial aid	100
% UG rec. any financial aid	100
% UG borrow to pay for school	29

CORNELL COLLEGE

600 FIRST STREET WEST, MOUNT VERNON, IA 52314-1098 • ADMISSIONS: 319-895-4477 • FAX: 319-895-4451

CAMPUS LIFE

Quality of Life Rating	**80**
Fire Safety Rating	**62**
Green Rating	**60***
Type of school	private
Affiliation	Methodist
Environment	rural

STUDENTS

Total undergrad enrollment	1,075
% male/female	49/51
% from out of state	71
% from public high school	84
% live on campus	91
% in (# of) fraternities	20 (8)
% in (# of) sororities	21 (7)
% African American	3
% Asian	2
% Caucasian	83
% Hispanic	3
% Native American	1
% international	3
# of countries represented	20

SURVEY SAYS . . .

Large classes
No one cheats
Great library
Students are friendly
Low cost of living
Lots of beer drinking

ACADEMICS

Academic Rating	**87**
Calendar	
Student/faculty ratio	11:1
Profs interesting rating	94
Profs accessible rating	94
Most common	
reg class size	10–19 students

MOST POPULAR MAJORS

English language and literature
psychology
economics

STUDENTS SAY " . . . "

Academics

Welcome to Cornell College, a tiny liberal arts school in Iowa that employs a unique One-Course-At-A-Time program, allowing students to focus on just one course (or "block") each month and providing an "intense, thorough, complete immersion." Though students agree that this "series of experiences" makes for "three crazy weeks," it also increases the quality and amount of knowledge gained and gives them a better chance to throw themselves into their extracurriculars. "You either are overloaded or underloaded with your class; there's no mixing," says a freshman. It's true that some classes lean toward the unchallenging side, but "upper-level courses are very engaging and fulfilling." The block plan also makes it very easy to gain off-campus field experience or do international study, and "it's really nice that they can bring in professionals and outside experts to teach class for a block." Administration is generally well-liked here for their accessibility and their devotion to the institution, but "there is not much transparency at the administrative level, which frequently results in a high level of frustration," and it can be "out of touch" at times. The registrar is "the most dreaded office on campus," with Residence Life a close second. On the classroom side, professors "are incredibly helpful and really want students to succeed," and though "you may get a bad apple maybe once a year," they are "very supportive of students in their academic endeavors." "I could not possibly imagine being closer to my profs. Not a single one has asked us to call him/her by anything other than her/his first name, and generally by the end of a block I feel I know my prof as a person," says a student. All in all, students love the block structure and the sense of community it creates, as "no matter what it is you may want to do, you can find someone to do it with you." One student claims he "cannot imagine learning any other way."

Life

Since Cornell is very campus-focused ("there is very little to do in the surrounding area"), the school makes sure there is "a large variety of campus organizations to fit everyone's personality and interest." Cedar Rapids and Iowa City are both only a 20 minute drive away for those seeking shopping, bowling, and movies, and "ice climbing, rock climbing, paddling and hiking" are popular outdoor pastimes. The cold weather can cause problems here, in both a locked-in feel and the possibility for accidents, and a few students wish the school did a better job of clearing the snow and ice on the sidewalks. Many here tend to have a love-hate relationship with sports; some claim that the athletics are a huge boon, while others think there is an "unfortunately high number of jocks." Much like the curriculum, lunchtimes are pretty unique, and students all eat in a common cafeteria, naturally falling into a somewhat "high school" habit of eating at the same tables every day. The meals themselves are another matter. One student sums up the feelings of all: "Cornell needs to work on the food. There, I said it." People just hate, hate, hate the food here, both in quality and options. Parties do take place on weekends, as do long, cold walks to the bars, but "it is entirely possible to not be involved with substance use at Cornell."

Student Body

There is "a great spectrum" of people that attend Cornell, and students have a hard time defining a common characteristic than the fact that almost all are driven and involved. Some division into typical groups does occur—the "jocks, nerds, and the 'artsy' students"—but "even group to group there is always mingling because you never know who will be in your next class." Since the classes are so small and "you see the same people 4 hours a day for 3 1/2 weeks," students "get to know the people under the stereotypes, and most everyone is very accepting." As one freshman says, "The only intolerance I've seen is towards the consistently indolent."

FINANCIAL AID: 319-895-4216 • E-MAIL: ADMISSIONS@CORNELLCOLLEGE.EDU • WEBSITE: WWW.CORNELLCOLLEGE.EDU

THE PRINCETON REVIEW SAYS

Admissions

Very important factors considered include: Application essay, academic GPA, recommendation(s), rigor of secondary school record. *Important factors considered include:* Class rank, standardized test scores, character/personal qualities, extracurricular activities, first generation, level of applicant's interest, talent/ability, volunteer work, work experience. *Other factors considered include:* Alumni/ae relation, geographical residence, interview, racial/ethnic status, state residency, SAT or ACT required; TOEFL required of all international applicants. High school diploma is required and GED is accepted. *Academic units recommended:* 4 English, 3 mathematics, 3 science, 2 foreign language, 3 social studies.

Financial Aid

Students should submit: FAFSA, institution's own financial aid form, Noncustodial (Divorced/Separated) Parent's Statement. Regular filing deadline is 3/1. The Princeton Review suggests that all financial aid forms be submitted as soon as possible after January 1. *Need-based scholarships/grants offered:* Federal Pell, SEOG, state scholarships/grants, private scholarships, the school's own gift aid, AC and SMART Grants. *Loan aid offered:* FFEL Subsidized Stafford, FFEL Unsubsidized Stafford, FFEL PLUS, Federal Perkins, McElroy Loan, Sherman Loan, United Methodist Loan. Applicants will be notified of awards on a rolling basis beginning 3/1. Federal Work-Study Program available. Institutional employment available. Off-campus job opportunities are fair.

The Inside Word

Given Cornell's relatively unique approach to study, it's no surprise that the Admissions Committee here focuses attention on both academic and personal strengths. Cornell's small, highly self-selected applicant pool is chock-full of students with solid self-awareness, motivation, and discipline. Pay particular attention to offering evidence of challenging academic course work and solid achievement on your high school record. Strong writers can do much for themselves under admissions circumstances such as these.

THE SCHOOL SAYS ". . ."

From The Admissions Office

"Very few colleges are truly distinctive like Cornell College. Founded in 1853, Cornell is recognized as one of the nation's finest colleges of the liberal arts and sciences. It is Cornell's combination of special features, however, that distinguishes it. An attractively diverse, caring residential college, Cornell places special emphasis on service and leadership. Foremost, it is a place where theory and practice are brought together in exciting ways through the college's One-Course-at-a-Time academic calendar. Here, students enjoy learning as they immerse themselves in a single subject for a 3.5-week term. They and their professor devote all of their efforts to that course in an engagingly interactive learning environment. This academic system also offers wonderful enrichment experiences through field-based-study, travel abroad, student research, and meaningful internship opportunities. Nine terms are offered each year; 32 course credits are required for graduation with each course equal to 4 credit hours. Since all classes are on a standard schedule, students are able to pursue their extracurricular interests, whether in the performing arts, athletics, or interest groups, with the same passion with which they pursue their course work. Typically, each year applicants from all 50 states and more than 40 countries apply for admission. Cornell graduates are in demand, with more than two-thirds eventually earning advanced degrees. The college's beautiful hilltop campus is one of only two campuses nationwide listed on the National Register of Historic Places. Located in the charming town of Mount Vernon, Cornell is also within commuting distance of Iowa City (home of the University of Iowa) and Cedar Rapids (the second largest city in the state).

"Freshman applicants for Fall 2008 are required to submit their SAT Reasoning or ACT results (the Writing component is optional for the ACT as students are required to submit an essay as part of the application for admission). In addition, for students submitting multiple score reports their best scores from either exam will be used in the application review process. SAT Subject tests are not required."

SELECTIVITY

Admissions Rating	87
# of applicants	2,659
% of applicants accepted	45
% of acceptees attending	26
# accepting a place on wait list	131
% admitted from wait list	35
# of early decision applicants	49
% accepted early decision	78

FRESHMAN PROFILE

Range SAT Critical Reading	540–680
Range SAT Math	530–650
Range ACT Composite	24–29
Minimum paper TOEFL	550
Minimum computer TOEFL	213
Average HS GPA	3.44
% graduated top 10% of class	25
% graduated top 25% of class	51
% graduated top 50% of class	79

DEADLINES

Early decision	
Deadline	11/1
Notification	1/15
Early action	
Deadline	12/1
Notification	2/1
Regular	
Priority	2/1
Deadline	3/1
Nonfall registration?	yes

APPLICANTS ALSO LOOK AT

AND OFTEN PREFER
Macalester College
Carleton College
Grinnell College

AND SOMETIMES PREFER
Coe College
Beloit College
Knox College

FINANCIAL FACTS

Financial Aid Rating	88
Annual tuition	$26,100
Room and board	$6,970
Required fees	$180
Books and supplies	$720
% frosh rec. need-based scholarship or grant aid	68
% UG rec. need-based scholarship or grant aid	69
% frosh rec. non-need-based scholarship or grant aid	49
% UG rec. non-need-based scholarship or grant aid	57
% frosh rec. need-based self-help aid	68
% UG rec. need-based self-help aid	69
% frosh rec. any financial aid	93
% UG rec. any financial aid	95
% UG borrow to pay for school	79
Average cumulative indebtedness	$26,115

CORNELL UNIVERSITY

UNDERGRADUATE ADMISSIONS, 410 THURSTON AVENUE, ITHACA, NY 14850 • ADMISSIONS: 607-255-5241 • FAX: 607-255-0659

CAMPUS LIFE
Quality of Life Rating	88
Fire Safety Rating	72
Green Rating	92
Type of school	private
Environment	town

STUDENTS
Total undergrad enrollment	13,455
% male/female	51/49
% from out of state	62
% live on campus	44
% in (# of) fraternities	NR (49)
% in (# of) sororities	NR (22)
% African American	5
% Asian	16
% Caucasian	50
% Hispanic	6
% Native American	1
% international	8
# of countries represented	76

SURVEY SAYS . . .
Great computer facilities
Great library
Great food on campus
Frats and sororities dominate
social scene
Student publications are popular
Lots of beer drinking

ACADEMICS
Academic Rating	89
Calendar	semester
Student/faculty ratio	9:1
Profs interesting rating	74
Profs accessible rating	78
Most common reg class size	10–19 students
Most common lab size	10–19 students

MOST POPULAR MAJORS
labor and industrial relations
biology/biological sciences
agribusiness/agricultural business
operations

STUDENTS SAY ". . ."

Academics

"A large, diverse university offering a huge variety of courses and majors," Cornell University seems intent on putting the "universe" in "university." Students tell us that "all the academic programs are strong, so no matter what you want to study, Cornell has the resources." But just in case Cornell's standout undergraduate departments in engineering, business, biology, industrial and labor relations, hotel administration, food science, animal science, and natural resources don't get you going, "You can [always] design your own major." Cornell offers "a mix of anything and everything, with more opportunities than you could ever want." Undergrads point out that "Cornell is a great place for people who know what they want to do in life and want to get things done sooner rather than later, because each major program is very focused and concentrated right from the beginning." Academics here "are hard, extremely tough." "We don't all have 4.0s, but we work harder than students at the other Ivy League schools. Cornell is the easiest Ivy to get into, and the hardest to graduate from. Grade inflation doesn't exist here." The school does its best to help students navigate the academic challenges, offering "enough help so that even the most lost student can find his/her way to a good, deserving grade." Professors "are available anytime you need them and are more than happy to lend you a helping hand," while both your "peer advisor and faculty advisor" are "easily accessible." The administration does a great job "running the school smoothly" and "makes the effort to keep lines of communication open." Students tell us that "undergraduates are offered unbelievable research opportunities and instruction from those who are at the top of their respective fields." And when it's time to find a job, "Cornell has a really good alumni network" and a "helpful Career Services" Office.

Life

Cornell is located in remote Ithaca, "on the top of a hill in the middle of a beautiful and cold nowhere." "Beautiful gorges" and "unrivaled" outdoor activities—"Everything from kayaking to pumpkin picking is just a small trip away either by foot or by bus." "There really isn't anything you can't do when it comes to nature at Cornell," but there is not much in the way of urban diversion. As a result, many "Students exist strictly within the Cornell bubble." They "have no escape from the stress of school and everything they do revolves around school." For many, weekend options consist of "bars in Collegetown and house parties," along with some on-campus "concerts, activities, and student-led initiatives." Lots of students "participate in intramural sports or one of the many clubs." One student observes, "Being in a small town like Ithaca means that most people do one thing for fun: drink. At the same time, some of the dorms—i.e. the ones with fewer drinkers—are still up on the weekends playing poker or GameCube or something like that. Nevertheless, the lack of a big city around you means that sometimes you can get pretty bored"—but then, there is always schoolwork to attend to.

Student Body

Cornell's student body "is diverse, and not just in the racial or ethnic sense. There are so many different courses of study at Cornell that a wide range of personalities and interests are represented. Every day, architects, engineers, hotel school students, and dairy farm majors sit down to lunch together." Furthermore, "Because Cornell is half private and half public, the students come from diverse economic backgrounds." Pressed to provide a general description of their peers, students tell us that "the student body is divided into about three groups: The well-off, stylish-if-conservatively dressed 'practical majors' (most frat members, premeds, pre-laws, sorority girls, hoteLies, aggies); the study-a-holics (engineers, applied sciences, some of the premeds); and the Euro-acting, blazer-and-hoodie wearing, always-thin hipsters (English, comparative literature, philosophy, film, theater, etc.)."

FINANCIAL AID: 607-255-5145 • E-MAIL: ADMISSIONS@CORNELL.EDU • WEBSITE: WWW.CORNELL.EDU

THE PRINCETON REVIEW SAYS

Admissions

Very important factors considered include: Application essay, academic GPA, recommendation(s), rigor of secondary school record, standardized test scores, extracurricular activities, talent/ability. *Important factors considered include:* Class rank. *Other factors considered include:* alumni/ae relation, character/personal qualities, first generation, geographical residence, interview, racial/ethnic status, state residency, volunteer work, work experience. SAT or ACT required; ACT with Writing component required. High school diploma or equivalent is not required. *Academic units required:* 4 English, 3 mathematics. *Academic units recommended:* 3 science, (3 science labs), 3 foreign language, 3 social studies, 3 history.

Financial Aid

Students should submit: FAFSA, institution's own financial aid form, CSS/Financial Aid PROFILE, noncustodial PROFILE, business/farm supplement, prior year tax returns. Regular filing deadline is 2/11. The Princeton Review suggests that all financial aid forms be submitted as soon as possible after January 1. *Need-based scholarships/grants offered:* Federal Pell, SEOG, state scholarships/grants, private scholarships, the school's own gift aid. *Loan aid offered:* Direct Subsidized Stafford, Direct Unsubsidized Stafford, Direct PLUS, FFEL Subsidized Stafford, FFEL Unsubsidized Stafford, FFEL PLUS, Federal Perkins, college/university loans from institutional funds. , Key Bank Alternative Loan.. Applicants will be notified of awards on or about 4/1. Federal Work-Study Program available. Institutional employment available. Off-campus job opportunities are fair.

The Inside Word

Gaining admission to Cornell is a tough coup regardless of your intended field of study, but some of the university's seven schools are more competitive than others. If you're thinking of trying to 'backdoor' your way into one of the most competitive schools—by gaining admission to one, then transferring after one year—be aware that you will have to resubmit the entire application and provide a statement outlining your academic plans. It's not impossible to accomplish, but Cornell works hard to discourage this sort of maneuvering.

THE SCHOOL SAYS " . . ."

From The Admissions Office

"Cornell University, an Ivy League school and land-grant college located in the scenic Finger Lakes region of central New York, provides an outstanding education to students in seven small to midsize undergraduate colleges: Agriculture and Life Sciences; Architecture, Art, and Planning; Arts and Sciences; Engineering; Hotel Administration; Human Ecology; and Industrial and Labor Relations. Cornellians come from all 50 states and more than 100 countries, and they pursue their academic goals in more than 100 departments. The College of Arts and Sciences, one of the smallest liberal arts schools in the Ivy League, offers more than 40 majors, most of which rank near the top nationwide. Applied programs in the other six colleges also rank among the best in the world.

"Other special features of the university include a world-renowned faculty; 4,000 courses available to all students; an extensive undergraduate research program; superb research, teaching, and library facilities; a large, diverse study abroad program; and more than 700 student organizations and 36 varsity sports. Cornell's campus is one of the most beautiful in the country; students pass streams, rocky gorges, and waterfalls on their way to class. First-year students make their home on North Campus, a living-learning community that features a special advising center, faculty-in-residence, a fitness center, and traditional residence halls as well as theme-centered buildings such as Ecology House. Cornell University invites applications from all interested students and uses the Common Application exclusively with a short required Cornell Supplement. Students applying for admissions will submit scores from the SAT or ACT (with writing). We also require SAT Subject Tests. Subject test requirements are college-specific."

SELECTIVITY

Admissions Rating	98
# of applicants	30,383
% of applicants accepted	21
% of acceptees attending	47
# accepting a place on wait list	1,976
% admitted from wait list	14
# of early decision applicants	3,015
% accepted early decision	37

FRESHMAN PROFILE

Range SAT Critical Reading	630–770
Range SAT Math	660–730
Range ACT Composite	28–32
% graduated top 10% of class	87
% graduated top 25% of class	98
% graduated top 50% of class	100

DEADLINES

Early decision	
Deadline	11/1
Notification	12/15
Regular	
Deadline	1/1
Notification	4/1
Nonfall registration?	no

FINANCIAL FACTS

Financial Aid Rating	95
Annual tuition	$34,600
Room and board	$11,190
Required fees	$181
Books and supplies	$720
% frosh rec. need-based scholarship or grant aid	40
% UG rec. need-based scholarship or grant aid	38
% frosh rec. need-based self-help aid	39
% UG rec. need-based self-help aid	39
% frosh rec. any financial aid	44
% UG rec. any financial aid	42
% UG borrow to pay for school	54
Average cumulative indebtedness	$23,936

CREIGHTON UNIVERSITY

2500 CALIFORNIA PLAZA, OMAHA, NE 68178 • ADMISSIONS: 402-280-2703 • FAX: 402-280-2685

STUDENTS SAY ". . ."

Academics

Creighton University is a Jesuit school, and it "expects students to live out the Jesuit values in every aspect of their lives, from community service to being men and women for and with others to believing in themselves to never settling for less than the best to becoming strong individuals with well balanced lives," and a desire to "strive for social justice." As one student puts it, "It's about combining a strong academic education with an education of the whole person: service, faith, and justice." Premedical and pre-pharmacological studies are among CU's strong suits, evidenced in the school's solid reputation among medical schools. Business studies are also popular, but regardless of one's major, students experience "a heavy liberal arts focus, relatively small classes, and generally very good teachers," although some here warn that there are "some not-so-great teachers for general education classes" (instructors "get better as you get into upper-level courses," the same students inform us). Undergrads here also benefit from "lots of study abroad programs, internships, and extracurriculars." Some here complain that career services is "so focused on Omaha jobs when most people want to leave after they graduate. It doesn't make sense." They also feel that "alumni connections" could be better exploited.

Life

"Omaha is a nice town" and "Creighton is really close to downtown," so students get to enjoy the perks of the city, which include shopping ("the Old Market area with the eccentric little book shops, jewelry stores, family-owned restaurants and so much more" are popular), parks, and "a lot of great bars." Students report that "Omaha is the indie capital of the world, so it attracts lots of artists and bands, the only drawback with that being that concerts can get to be expensive." Creighton undergrads "are serious students during the week, but know how to party on the weekends," reporting that "fraternity and sorority parties are open to all and a focal point of weekend fun," or at least until students reach 21 and can get into bars legally. On campus, "The student government operates a program board that organizes concerts (such as Black Eyed Peas), BBQ tailgates before games, and other events on campus." In addition, "Creighton's NCAA Division I basketball team draws a huge crowd during its season," so much so that "students plan their schedules around the games."

Student Body

"Most students are of the same mold" at Creighton. They're "religious" "white Christians" who "work hard at school" and "volunteer." They "tend to be middle- to upper-class and focused on education and their futures," but are "also involved in extracurricular activities like community service or intramurals." Geography limits Creighton's draw somewhat. One student explains, "We are a Midwestern school that attracts many students from the area, so our student body reflects this." With about one in five students in biology or physical science programs, "The typical student is someone whose intent is to be admitted to an excellent medical professions program." An equal number study business, further augmenting the pre-professional vibe here. Politically, the student body has "its left wing/liberal streak mixed in with a lot of conservatives to live up to the Jesuit status." Overall, "It's not near as conservative as the Midwest area values that surround it."

CREIGHTON UNIVERSITY

FINANCIAL AID: 402-280-2731 • E-MAIL: ADMISSIONS@CREIGHTON.EDU • WEBSITE: WWW.ADMISSION.CREIGHTON.EDU

THE PRINCETON REVIEW SAYS

Admissions

Very important factors considered include: Academic GPA, rigor of secondary school record. *Important factors considered include:* Application essay, standardized test scores. *Other factors considered include:* Class rank, recommendation(s), character/personal qualities, extracurricular activities, first generation, level of applicant's interest, racial/ethnic status, talent/ability, volunteer work, SAT or ACT required; TOEFL required of all international applicants. High school diploma is required and GED is accepted. *Academic units required:* 4 English, 3 mathematics, 2 science, 2 foreign language, 2 social studies, 3 academic electives. *Academic units recommended:* 4 English, 4 mathematics, 3 science, 3 foreign language, 3 social studies, 1 history, 3 academic electives.

Financial Aid

Students should submit: FAFSA, institution's own financial aid form The Princeton Review suggests that all financial aid forms be submitted as soon as possible after January 1. *Need-based scholarships/grants offered:* Federal Pell, SEOG, state scholarships/grants, private scholarships, the school's own gift aid. *Loan aid offered:* FFEL Subsidized Stafford, FFEL Unsubsidized Stafford, FFEL PLUS, Federal Perkins, Federal Nursing, college/university loans from institutional funds. Applicants will be notified of awards on a rolling basis beginning 3/15. Federal Work-Study Program available. Institutional employment available. Off-campus job opportunities are excellent.

The Inside Word

Creighton's lack of name recognition and its location can handicap its search for quality students, occasionally forcing the school to lower the bar to fill its incoming classes, so their loss could well be your gain. For those comfortable in a Jesuit school, Creighton offers bright, hardworking students a great opportunity at a quality education.

THE SCHOOL SAYS "..."

From The Admissions Office

"Creighton University is committed to being one of the leading Jesuit, Catholic universities in the United States. Here, students from across the nation and around the world come to study in a wide range of disciplines – with an emphasis on developing the whole person: academically, socially and spiritually. Creighton is moving forward, with $200 million in new construction and renovations over the past five years – including a new integrated science building, junior/senior town homes, a nationally recognized soccer stadium and campus mall, and a unique student living-learning center. With about 7,000 students, about 4,000 of whom are undergraduates, and more than 50 undergraduate majors and more than 20 graduate and professional programs, Creighton University combines small, personal class sizes with a wide range of opportunities for undergraduate and advanced studies. Our students leave here professionally proficient, civically engaged and ethically competent—with a global perspective and a disposition for service. It's an education that not only prepares students to succeed in their chosen fields, but one that challenges them to go out and shape a more just world. While here, our students join faculty in leading research. In 2008, Creighton was one of just eight universities to have four students nationally recognized as Goldwater Scholars. Typically, about 40 percent of our students go immediately into medical, dental, pharmacy, physical or occupational therapy, graduate or law school, upon graduation – one of the highest placement rates for any university nationally."

SELECTIVITY
Admissions Rating	88
# of applicants	4,274
% of applicants accepted	81
% of acceptees attending	27
# accepting a place on wait list	101
% admitted from wait list	17

FRESHMAN PROFILE
Range SAT Critical Reading	530–640
Range SAT Math	550–660
Range SAT Writing	520–640
Range ACT Composite	24–30
Minimum paper TOEFL	550
Minimum computer TOEFL	213
Average HS GPA	3.78
% graduated top 10% of class	43
% graduated top 25% of class	74
% graduated top 50% of class	96

DEADLINES
Regular	
Priority	12/1
Deadline	2/15
Notification	rolling
Nonfall registration?	yes

APPLICANTS ALSO LOOK AT
AND OFTEN PREFER
University of Missouri—Columbia
University of Notre Dame
AND SOMETIMES PREFER
Saint Louis University
University of Colorado—Boulder
Marquette University
University of Kansas
AND RARELY PREFER
University of Saint Thomas (MN)
University of Iowa
Iowa State University

FINANCIAL FACTS
Financial Aid Rating	83
Annual tuition	$25,820
Room and board	$8,736
Required fees	$1,260
Books and supplies	$1,000
% frosh rec. need-based scholarship or grant aid	59
% UG rec. need-based scholarship or grant aid	53
% frosh rec. non-need-based scholarship or grant aid	41
% UG rec. non-need-based scholarship or grant aid	37
% frosh rec. need-based self-help aid	45
% UG rec. need-based self-help aid	43
% frosh rec. athletic scholarships	4
% UG rec. athletic scholarships	5
% frosh rec. any financial aid	92
% UG rec. any financial aid	92
% UG borrow to pay for school	64
Average cumulative indebtedness	$29,074

DARTMOUTH COLLEGE

6016 McNutt Hall, Hanover, NH 03755 • Admissions: 603-646-2875 • Fax: 603-646-1216

STUDENTS SAY ". . ."

Academics

Dartmouth College "has a reputation of being like summer camp, and it's true: Students take their academic work very seriously, but they're also all extremely happy to be here, and they have a lot of fun, no matter what their idea of fun is." A school that is small "without being suffocating or lacking opportunities, challenging but not too competitive, has good academics and access to professors, and has its own ski hill" obviously has a lot to offer; how else could it entice "artists, athletes, musicians, and future leaders to all gather together in the middle of nowhere?" Students love that Dartmouth is "very undergraduate-focused, unlike the other Ivies that neglect their undergrads to only concentrate on research." They also love the D-Plan, which divides the academic year into four 10-week terms in order to provide maximum flexibility and study abroad opportunities ("Many students use the D-Plan to study abroad up to three times"). On the downside, it "makes being friends with members of other classes difficult," since "D-Plan means consistently being on campus . . . is tricky." Dartmouth professors "are some of the greatest minds in the country, and they're almost all willing to just sit and chat if you feel like it. I've had at least one professor each year who's invited the whole class to her/his house for dinner and discussion (sometimes with famous guests). It's a great way to learn information that is above and beyond what you're learning in the classroom." No wonder "everyone is happy here."

Life

Dartmouth's greatest strength, students tell us, "is its incredible sense of community and tradition," traditions that include "singing the Alma Mater, dancing the Salty Dog Rag, and running 100-plus laps around a 40-foot bonfire." One undergrad notes, "[Students] have a ton of school spirit," and "From the first day on campus, students are learning all about what it means to be a Dartmouth student." Situated in the Upper Connecticut River Valley, Dartmouth has "a great location for skiing and outdoor activities," and it's a place "where the student body is very active, both outdoors (i.e., hiking, biking, rock climbing, ice climbing, and skiing) as well as indoors partying. Whatever you want to do, you can find it here." That is, unless what you want is constant big-city entertainment; hometown Hanover is a "very small town," and "Boston and Montreal, though available, are rarely sought." Students are more likely to flock to the campus' popular Greek scene: "Most people like to go drink at frats on weekends and attend parties. I think like 20 percent of the student population abstains from drinking, but everyone else is pretty into it." Students are also "very involved in on campus organizations and sports teams." As one junior explains, "There's always more to do than can ever be done, and the hardest thing is making time for sleep along with classes, clubs, and friends."

Student Body

The typical Dartmouth student "is hard to define. If I mashed them all up into one person, it'd be a kid from Jersey driving a Lexus with a kayak on the top. His collar popped but his pants torn. In his bag there'd be the works of Marx next to those of Friedman. We're all so different, but at the same time, we're just all here to learn, to love, and to live." Dartmouth "strives to create a world of very different people," and its reputation allows it to cherry-pick top students from all around the globe. The school has a reputation for political conservatism that some argue is overblown: "There are very liberal students at Dartmouth, and there are very conservative student s. . ., but most tend to fall in between." Also, while the school "has a stereotype of being a big party school full of jocks," it's "not really that way" and "That should be more recognized." Across the board students tend to be "well-balanced" and "outgoing," and everyone from the "sweet frat dude to the library dweller all find a place to fit in."

FINANCIAL AID: 603-646-2451 • E-MAIL: ADMISSIONS.OFFICE@DARTMOUTH.EDU • WEBSITE: WWW.DARTMOUTH.EDU

THE PRINCETON REVIEW SAYS

Admissions

Very important factors considered include: Class rank, application essay, academic GPA, recommendation(s), rigor of secondary school record, standardized test scores, character/personal qualities, extracurricular activities. *Important factors considered include:* Talent/ability, volunteer work. *Other factors considered include:* Alumni/ae relation, first generation, geographical residence, interview, racial/ethnic status, SAT; ACT with Writing component and any two SAT II Subject Tests required. TOEFL required of all international applicants. High school diploma or equivalent is not required. *Academic units recommended:* 4 English, 4 mathematics, 34 science, 3 social studies, 3 history.

Financial Aid

Students should submit: FAFSA, CSS/Financial Aid PROFILE, noncustodial PROFILE, business/farm supplement, current W2 or Federal Tax Returns. Regular filing deadline is 2/1. The Princeton Review suggests that all financial aid forms be submitted as soon as possible after January 1. *Need-based scholarships/grants offered:* Federal Pell, SEOG, state scholarships/grants, private scholarships, the school's own gift aid. *Loan aid offered:* FFEL Subsidized Stafford, FFEL Unsubsidized Stafford, FFEL PLUS, Federal Perkins, state loans, college/university loans from institutional funds. Applicants will be notified of awards on or about 4/2. Federal Work-Study Program available. Institutional employment available. Off-campus job opportunities are excellent.

The Inside Word

Like other elite schools, Dartmouth is swamped with more applications from qualified students than it can accommodate. Dartmouth's 2007–2008 admission rate of 13.3 percent was the lowest in the school's history. That wasn't because the applicant pool was less competitive; it's because more kids are applying to Dartmouth every year. Give this your best shot, and don't take it personally if you don't get in; unfortunately, many great candidates don't.

THE SCHOOL SAYS "..."

From The Admissions Office

""Dartmouth's mission is to endow students with the knowledge and wisdom needed to make creative and positive contributions to society. The College brings together a breadth of cultures, traditions, and ideas to create a campus that is alive with ongoing debate and exploration. From student-initiated round-table discussions that attempt to make sense of world events to the late-night exchanges in a dormitory lounge, Dartmouth students take advantage of their opportunities to learn from each other. The unique benefits of sharing in this interchange are accompanied by a great sense of responsibility. Each individual's commitment to the College's 'Principles of Community' ensures the vitality of this learning environment, and Dartmouth's size enhances the quality of the experience for all involved.

"To help all Dartmouth students take full advantage of the 'Dartmouth Experience,' the College has eliminated loans from its financial aid packages. Beginning with the Class of 2012, students from families with incomes under $75,000 will receive free tuition to the College.

"All applicants, including those who apply from foreign countries, are required to take the SAT (or ACT) and any two SAT Subject Tests. All testing must be completed by January of the senior year in high school. If standardized testing is repeated, the Admissions Committee only considers highest scores."

SELECTIVITY

Admissions Rating	98
# of applicants	14,176
% of applicants accepted	15
% of acceptees attending	52
# accepting a place on wait list	797
# of early decision applicants	1,285
% accepted early decision	29

FRESHMAN PROFILE

Range SAT Critical Reading	660–770
Range SAT Math	670–780
Range SAT Writing	660–770
Range ACT Composite	29–34
Minimum paper TOEFL	550
Minimum computer TOEFL	213
Minimum web-based TOEFL	79
% graduated top 10% of class	91
% graduated top 50% of class	100

DEADLINES

Early decision	
Deadline	11/1
Notification	12/15
Regular	
Deadline	1/1
Notification	4/1
Nonfall registration?	no

APPLICANTS ALSO LOOK AT

AND OFTEN PREFER
Harvard College
Stanford University
Yale University
Princeton University

AND SOMETIMES PREFER
Massachusetts Institute of Technology
Williams College
Brown University
Amherst College

AND RARELY PREFER
Cornell University
Middlebury College
Northwestern University
University of Pennsylvania

FINANCIAL FACTS

Financial Aid Rating	92
Annual tuition	$36,915
Room and board	$10,930
Required fees	$213
Books and supplies	$1,412
% frosh rec. need-based scholarship or grant aid	48
% UG rec. need-based scholarship or grant aid	49
% frosh rec. need-based self-help aid	48
% UG rec. need-based self-help aid	48
% frosh rec. any financial aid	48
% UG rec. any financial aid	50
% UG borrow to pay for school	51
Average cumulative indebtedness	$20,926

DAVIDSON COLLEGE

PO BOX 7156, DAVIDSON, NC 28035-7156 • ADMISSIONS: 704-894-2230 • FAX: 704-894-2016

CAMPUS LIFE

Quality of Life Rating	97
Fire Safety Rating	60*
Green Rating	60*
Type of school	private
Affiliation	Presbyterian
Environment	village

STUDENTS

Total undergrad enrollment	1,674
% male/female	50/50
% from out of state	80
% from public high school	51
% live on campus	91
% in (# of) fraternities	44 (8)
% African American	7
% Asian	3
% Caucasian	75
% Hispanic	4
% Native American	1
% international	7
# of countries represented	36

SURVEY SAYS . . .

Small classes
No one cheats
Lab facilities are great
School is well run
Students are friendly
Campus feels safe

ACADEMICS

Academic Rating	97
Calendar	semester
Student/faculty ratio	10:1
Profs interesting rating	98
Profs accessible rating	98
Most common reg class size	10–19 students
Most common lab size	10–19 students

MOST POPULAR MAJORS

English language and literature
biology/biological sciences
history

STUDENTS SAY ". . ."

Academics

Davidson College, which students insist is "the best liberal arts college in the South," is the ideal setting for students who are "not afraid to show their academic passions" and who seek "the incorporation of academics into all parts of life." One undergrad explains, "I feel like I am always learning, even when I am not in the classroom. The atmosphere provided by my fellow classmates provides almost as many new intellectual experiences as my time in class." A school "notorious for grade deflation" (according to one student, "This place is not a joke. And you won't be the smartest kid in your class . . . or any other class"), Davidson is a place where "You have to expect a fair bit of work. Classes are tiny and intense, and with the small size and high level of student participation, it is impossible to hide." The upshot is that "you will learn a lot, not just in terms of subject matter but also about your learning styles and how you learn the best." Davidson professors "are amazing. Not only are they renowned in their fields, but they are always available for extra help or even just to chat"—they are "rare combinations of teachers and researchers." Students tell us that "for such a small school, the amount of undergraduate research going on here is surprising," and that undergrads often contribute to faculty work. Davidson's honor code "is a huge part of life; for example, we have 100 community bikes that anyone can use at any time, and we trust them to not get stolen (and they don't!). Every quiz and test in my French class is take-home, and every exam at Davidson is self-scheduled unless that is logistically impossible."

Life

"Students do spend a lot of time studying at Davidson," claim undergrads, "but that doesn't mean they don't have fun." During the week "We study until our minds bleed," but "We find ways to relieve the pressure over the weekend." For those who drink, that often means "court parties at Patterson Court, home of our fraternity/eating house scene." These events, we're told, involve a lot of alcohol. The administration has sought to curtail drinking by "directing nonalcoholic events to the Student Union." Usually these events "are a viable alternative" to the party scene. Movies, free food, and various types of alcohol-free parties fill the Student Union calendar and are favored by the school's substantial religious population. Davidson basketball is popular; other sports aren't as well supported. Many students recommend frequent trips off campus to "nearby Birkdale for a movie or shopping," to the "small (but by no means boring) towns of Mooresville, Huntersville, and Cornelius," or to "downtown Charlotte for dinner and drinks."

Student Body

There are two noticeable populations at Davidson: "the driven, intelligent, likely wealthy White student who likes to party a lot," and "the driven, intelligent, likely wealthy White student who likes to read the Bible and go to church." One student observes, "To secular folks, this is the most religious place they've ever been, and to religious folks, it's the most secular place they've ever been." Money is rather visible on campus; one student claims, "Students drive much nicer cars than their professors." There are "not many African American students, and hardly any Asians here," and "There is not a lot of diversity in terms of economic status." There are lots of jocks, though, as "probably 25 percent of the student body is made up of Division I- or Division I AA-caliber athletes. They get no breaks in admissions or from professors, by the way, and they don't fit the stereotypes of being elitist or separatist. We all work hard." Regardless of differences in background, however, students assert that the school "is remarkably well integrated—while students certainly stick with their fraternity or sports team, often their best friends are from their freshman hall."

DAVIDSON COLLEGE

FINANCIAL AID: 704-894-2232 • E-MAIL: ADMISSION@DAVIDSON.EDU • WEBSITE: WWW.DAVIDSON.EDU

THE PRINCETON REVIEW SAYS

Admissions

Very important factors considered include: Recommendation(s), rigor of secondary school record, character/personal qualities, volunteer work. *Important factors considered include:* Application essay, extracurricular activities, talent/ability. *Other factors considered include:* Class rank, standardized test scores, racial/ethnic status, work experience. SAT or ACT required; SAT and SAT Subject Tests or ACT recommended; TOEFL required of all international applicants. High school diploma is required and GED is not accepted. *Academic units required:* 4 English, 3 mathematics, 2 science, 2 foreign language, 2 Social Studies and History *Academic units recommended:* 4 mathematics, 4 science, 4 foreign language, 4 social studies and history.

Financial Aid

Students should submit: FAFSA, CSS/Financial Aid PROFILE, noncustodial PROFILE, business/farm supplement, Noncustodial (Divorced/Separated) Parent's Statement; corporate tax return and/or noncustodial parent tax return(if applicable); parent and student tax returns and W-2 forms to the IDOC service. Regular filing deadline is 2/15. The Princeton Review suggests that all financial aid forms be submitted as soon as possible after January 1. *Need-based scholarships/grants offered:* Federal Pell, SEOG, state scholarships/grants, private scholarships, the school's own gift aid. *Loan aid offered:* FFEL Subsidized Stafford, FFEL Unsubsidized Stafford, FFEL PLUS, alternative loans. Applicants will be notified of awards on or about 4/1. Federal Work-Study Program available. Institutional employment available. Off-campus job opportunities are excellent.

The Inside Word

The combination of Davidson's low acceptance rate and high yield really packs a punch. Prospective applicants beware: Securing admission at this prestigious school is no easy feat. Admitted students are typically at the top of their high school classes and have strong standardized test scores. Candidates with leadership experience generally garner the favor of Admissions Officers. The college takes its honor code seriously and, as a result, seeks out students of demonstrated reputable character.

THE SCHOOL SAYS ". . ."

From The Admissions Office

"Davidson College is one of the nation's premier academic institutions, a college of the liberal arts and sciences respected for its intellectual vigor, the high quality of its faculty and students, and the achievements of its alumni. Davidson is distinguished by its strong honor code, close collaboration between professors and students, an environment that encourages both intellectual growth and community service, and a commitment to international education. Davidson places great value on student participation in extracurricular activities, intercollegiate athletics, and intramural sports. The college has a strong regional identity, grounded in traditions of civility and mutual respect, and has historic ties to the Presbyterian Church. The college has a strong commitment to making a Davidson education affordable. Beginning with the 2007-2008 academic year, the college no longer includes student loans in its financial aid packages. Through the Davidson Trust, 100% of demonstrated financial need will be met with a combination of grants and student

"Applicants for the Class of 2013 are required to complete and submit scores from the SAT and/or the ACT. SAT Subject Tests (Mathematics and one of your choice) are recommended. Davidson will utilize the scores that place the student in the greatest possible light."

SELECTIVITY
Admissions Rating	97
# of applicants	3,992
% of applicants accepted	28
% of acceptees attending	41
# of early decision applicants	384
% accepted early decision	41

FRESHMAN PROFILE
Range SAT Critical Reading	630–730
Range SAT Math	640–710
Range ACT Composite	28–32
Minimum paper TOEFL	600
Minimum computer TOEFL	250
% graduated top 10% of class	83
% graduated top 25% of class	98
% graduated top 50% of class	100

DEADLINES
Early decision	
Deadline	11/15
Notification	12/15
Regular	
Deadline	1/2
Notification	4/1
Nonfall registration?	no

APPLICANTS ALSO LOOK AT
AND OFTEN PREFER
Dartmouth College
Duke University
Stanford University
Williams College
AND SOMETIMES PREFER
Washington University in St. Louis
Vanderbilt University
University of Virginia
AND RARELY PREFER
University of Richmond
Wake Forest University

FINANCIAL FACTS
Financial Aid Rating	97
Annual tuition	$33,148
Room and board	$9,471
Required fees	$331
Books and supplies	$1,000
% frosh rec. need-based scholarship or grant aid	30
% UG rec. need-based scholarship or grant aid	32
% frosh rec. non-need-based scholarship or grant aid	12
% UG rec. non-need-based scholarship or grant aid	13
% frosh rec. need-based self-help aid	22
% UG rec. need-based self-help aid	25
% frosh rec. athletic scholarships	9
% UG rec. athletic scholarships	10
% frosh rec. any financial aid	32
% UG rec. any financial aid	34
% UG borrow to pay for school	30
Average cumulative indebtedness	$28,100

DEEP SPRINGS COLLEGE

HC 72 Box 45001, Deep Springs, CA via Dyer, NV 89010-9803 • Admissions: 760-872-2000 • Fax: 760-872-4466

CAMPUS LIFE

Quality of Life Rating	**99**
Fire Safety Rating	**82**
Green Rating	**60***
Type of school	private
Environment	rural

STUDENTS

Total undergrad enrollment	26
% male/female	100/
% from out of state	80
% live on campus	100
# of countries represented	3

SURVEY SAYS . . .

Small classes
No one cheats
Registration is a breeze
Great food on campus
Dorms are like palaces
Low cost of living
Intercollegiate sports are
unpopular or nonexistent
Frats and sororities are unpopular
or nonexistent
Student government is popular
Very little drug use

ACADEMICS

Academic Rating	**99**
Calendar	8
Student/faculty ratio	4:1
Profs interesting rating	93
Profs accessible rating	99
Most common reg class size	fewer than 10 students

MOST POPULAR MAJORS

liberal arts and sciences studies and humanities

STUDENTS SAY " . . . "

Academics

The "three pillars" of a Deep Springs education—"labor, academics, and self-governance"—combine to produce "the most intense experience you will ever have." That's what the 26 men who attend Deep Springs tell us, anyway. They basically run their own school, work the ranch where it is located, and complete a curriculum that "is the epitome of higher education," all of which sounds pretty intense to us too. The program "isn't merely vocational. It's about educating a whole human being, and it makes us more responsible, more sensitive people." Students best suited to this approach are those who "want to take as much control of their education as possible. I enjoy knowing that my actions seriously affect the day-to-day life as well as the future of Deep Springs." Because the school is "very small and governed by the students, the smoothness with which many programs run depends largely on the kind of responsibility students take. Sometimes students do a good job taking care of administrative tasks, sometimes a worse job. It's all part of the educational experience." The students "hire the professors and pretty much run the classes. As a result, when the students are motivated, the classes here are better than they can be anywhere else in the world." While the size of the school inevitably means that "lab and library facilities are not what they might be," students tell us that the quality of the students and professors more than makes up for these kinds of problems.

Life

"Deep Springs is totally unlike other colleges in terms of the everyday life of a student," because "No one drinks, everyone helps run the ranch in some way, and no one can be totally self-absorbed (unless they're out hiking in the desert)." Instead, students immerse themselves in the Deep Springs way. As one student explains, "The Deep Springs program is our whole life. The intellectual questions we're asking and the labor we're doing is all bound up with our identity." Students pass their free time by "having a lot of conversations: about life in general, about personal issues, and about intellectual questions." Occasionally "We have dance parties called 'boojies,'" and "We do some other strange things for fun, like sledding naked down 800-foot-tall sand dunes in neighboring Eureka Valley, for example, or watching every episode of *The Wonder Years*." Undergrads concede that Deep Springs "Life can be intense. Students usually are utterly exhausted. But most of the time we know that something good is coming out of this." That "something good" can take many forms; one student writes, "On Thanksgiving, four of my classmates and I took it upon ourselves to do all the cooking. We smoked and roasted seven turkeys, made several stuffings, and baked dozens of loaves of bread while the rest of our classmates played a game of football on one of the alfalfa fields. Afterward, the whole student body did the dishes while listening to upbeat techno and Led Zeppelin. The next day, over a third of the student body put on Shakespeare's *The Tempest*, moving from a reservoir to a dry wash and down to the center of campus as the play demanded. This sort of thing is typical of Deep Springs life."

Student Body

Given the many demands of a Deep Springs education, it should come as no surprise that "everyone is intelligent, motivated, and responsible" here. Students "must demonstrate depth of thought to be accepted" to the school, and most "are very intellectual and philosophically inclined, although there are some who would rather take a science class any day." As one undergrad puts it, Deep Spring students are "looking for a broader experience than can be found at the usual college. Most students are boys looking to become men. Most students are typical and fit in wonderfully because we're all pretty damn weird."

FINANCIAL AID: 760-872-2000 • E-MAIL: APCOM@DEEPSPRING.EDU • WEBSITE: WWW.DEEPSPRINGS.EDU

THE PRINCETON REVIEW SAYS

Admissions

Very important factors considered include: Application essay, character/personal qualities, interview, level of applicant's interest. *Important factors considered include:* Academic GPA, rigor of secondary school record, extracurricular activities, volunteer work, work experience. *Other factors considered include:* Class rank, recommendation(s), standardized test scores, racial/ethnic status, talent/ability, SAT or ACT required; High school diploma or equivalent is not required.

Financial Aid

The Princeton Review suggests that all financial aid forms be submitted as soon as possible after January 1. Applicants will be notified of awards on or about 4/15.

The Inside Word

Students will be hard pressed to find a school that has a more personal or thorough application process than Deep Springs. Given the intimate and collegial atmosphere fostered at the college, matchmaking is the top priority. Candidates are evaluated by a body composed of students, faculty, and staff members. The application is rather writing intensive, and finalists are expected to spend several days on campus, during which time they will also have a lengthy interview.

THE SCHOOL SAYS "..."

From The Admissions Office

"Founded in 1917, Deep Springs College lies isolated in a high desert valley of eastern California, 30 miles from the nearest town. Its enrollment is limited to 26 students, each of whom receives a full scholarship that covers tuition, room and board and is valued at more than $50,000 per year. Students engage in rigorous academics, govern themselves, and participate in the operation of our cattle and alfalfa ranch. After 2 years, students generally transfer to other schools to complete their studies. Students regularly transfer to Harvard, The University of Chicago, and Brown, but also choose Cornell, Columbia, Stanford, Swarthmore, University of California—Berkeley, and Yale.

"In 2002, Deep Springs students garnered four major national scholarship awards: three Truman Scholarships for public service careers—more than any other school in the country—and one Udall scholarship for careers in environmental studies and ecology.

"As of this book's publication, Deep Springs College did not have information available about their policy regarding the new SAT."

SELECTIVITY
Admissions Rating	99
# of applicants	170
% of applicants accepted	7
% of acceptees attending	92
# accepting a place on wait list	3

FRESHMAN PROFILE
Range SAT Critical Reading	750–800
Range SAT Math	700–800
% graduated top 10% of class	86
% graduated top 25% of class	93
% graduated top 50% of class	100

DEADLINES
Regular	
Deadline	11/15
Notification	4/15
Nonfall registration?	no

FINANCIAL FACTS
Financial Aid Rating	60*
Annual tuition	$0*
Books and supplies	$1,200
% frosh rec. any financial aid	100
% UG rec. any financial aid	100

*All students receive scholarships.

DENISON UNIVERSITY

Box H, Granville, OH 43023 • Admissions: 740-587-6276 • Fax: 740-587-6306

CAMPUS LIFE
Quality of Life Rating	83
Fire Safety Rating	88
Green Rating	87
Type of school	private
Environment	village

STUDENTS
Total undergrad enrollment	2,212
% male/female	43/57
% from out of state	64
% from public high school	70
% live on campus	99
% in (# of) fraternities	19 (8)
% in (# of) sororities	26 (6)
% African American	5
% Asian	3
% Caucasian	83
% Hispanic	2
% international	4
# of countries represented	25

SURVEY SAYS . . .
Large classes
Lab facilities are great
Great computer facilities
Great library
Campus feels safe
Lots of beer drinking

ACADEMICS
Academic Rating	89
Calendar	semester
Student/faculty ratio	10:1
Profs interesting rating	86
Profs accessible rating	89
Most common	
reg class size	10–19 students

MOST POPULAR MAJORS
English language and literature
economics

STUDENTS SAY " . . ."

Academics

Students describe Denison University as "a mecca of top-notch academics" located "in the seclusion of rural Ohio." By necessity Denison University may be "huge on community," but regardless of the impetus, students, faculty, and administrators here "become like a big family where everyone takes care of one another." Students agree that that's a good thing, as this environment provides "academically motivated students a chance to excel in their respective studies through a supportive student population and dedicated faculty, while also providing many social opportunities." Denison is "all about educating the whole student, whether it be through classes, speakers, sports, clubs, or even Greek life." Academically, Denison can be "challenging." "It is possible to spend an entire semester stressed out to the extreme with 20-plus academic credits and no time to do the readings for every class. But it is also very possible to manage your time well and get everything done in a mannerly fashion, without overexerting yourself, but still having a successful and productive semester." Students who find themselves in over their heads can count on "professors who are willing to go the extra mile with their students." Professors "have organized study groups before exams and extend their office hours so that you can meet with them about a paper or project." As one student observes, "It's your own fault if you do poorly, because there are so many ways for you to get help through teachers, study groups, tutoring, etc."

Life

"What is nice about Denison is that most people stay on campus during the weekends, so there is always something to do," students here report. The school and the Student Activities Committee "always sponsor concerts, speakers, and events around campus," and, of course, there is always a party or two available on the weekends. "There is so much to do all week, every week," which "is somewhat necessary, as the town of Granville is quite small and offers few diversions." A party scene "is available if that's what you want," and quite a few students do, telling us that "go-out-and-party nights" are Fridays and Saturdays and "Mondays and Wednesdays also, since most students have few classes on Tuesdays and Thursdays." There's a lot of partying on campus ("Greek life encompasses about 40 percent of the student body") in the student residences. Denison has "a number of sports teams that are nationally ranked," but students are just as likely to follow OSU as Denison. While hometown Granville is "small" and "very quiet," Columbus "is only 30 minutes away which allows [students] to visit other restaurants, bars, concerts, and, of course, big sister OSU." Easton "is just 25 minutes away and has a huge shopping center."

Student Body

While "There are not a lot of atypical students on the extreme ends of 'different'" at Denison, students hasten to point out that "Denison does not solely consist of popped collars and Uggs. Those students just like to make themselves known." True, "Most students here are WASPy" and "generally affluent," and there are "a lot of athletes on campus, and fraternities and sororities are pretty big," but most "Kids are hardworking and usually friendly." Also, Denison is not without its "internationals, artsy types, and [even] the socially awkward." There's "even a small counterculture made up of environmentalists and hippies who live at the Homestead and hang out at Bandersnatch." These people "are the minority, but there's a niche for them." As one student explains, "It's pretty easy to find a core group of friends."

FINANCIAL AID: 740-587-6279 • E-MAIL: ADMISSIONS@DENISON.EDU • WEBSITE: WWW.DENISON.EDU

THE PRINCETON REVIEW SAYS

Admissions

Very important factors considered include: Class rank, application essay, academic GPA, recommendation(s), rigor of secondary school record. *Important factors considered include:* Extracurricular activities, interview, talent/ability. *Other factors considered include:* Character/personal qualities, first generation, geographical residence, level of applicant's interest, racial/ethnic status, religious affiliation/commitment, state residency, volunteer work, work experience. TOEFL required of all international applicants. High school diploma is required and GED is accepted. *Academic units required:* 4 English, 4 mathematics, 4 science, 3 foreign language, 2 social studies, 1 history, 1 academic elective.

Financial Aid

Students should submit: FAFSA. The Princeton Review suggests that all financial aid forms be submitted as soon as possible after January 1. *Need-based scholarships/grants offered:* Federal Pell, SEOG, state scholarships/grants, private scholarships, the school's own gift aid. *Loan aid offered:* Direct Subsidized Stafford, Direct Unsubsidized Stafford, Direct PLUS, Federal Perkins, college/university loans from institutional funds. Applicants will be notified of awards on or about 5/1. Federal Work-Study Program available. Institutional employment available. Off-campus job opportunities are fair.

The Inside Word

Admission to Denison is pretty straightforward. The school "suggests" an interview, meaning you should do one if at all possible. It's a great way to demonstrate your interest in the school, which improves your chances of admission, especially if your grades, test scores, and overall profile put you on the admit/reject borderline.

THE SCHOOL SAYS "..."

From The Admissions Office

"Denison is a college that can point with pride to its success in enrolling and retaining intellectually motivated, diverse, and well-balanced students who are being taught to become effective leaders in the twenty-first century. This year, over 50 percent of our first-year students were in the top 10 percent of their high school graduating class; their average SAT scores have risen to nearly 1,300; 20 percent of the class is multicultural; and 95 percent of our student body is receiving some type of financial assistance. Our First-Year Program focuses on helping students make a successful transition from high school to college, and the small classes and accessibility of faculty assure students the opportunity to interact closely with their professors and fellow students. We care about our students, and the loyalty of our 27,000 alumni proves that the Denison experience is one that lasts for a lifetime.

"Denison operates under a 'test optional' admissions policy.""

SELECTIVITY

Admissions Rating	91
# of applicants	5,196
% of applicants accepted	39
% of acceptees attending	29
# accepting a place on wait list	347
% admitted from wait list	10
# of early decision applicants	153
% accepted early decision	67

FRESHMAN PROFILE

Range SAT Critical Reading	580–690
Range SAT Math	580–670
Range ACT Composite	31–28
Minimum paper TOEFL	550
Minimum computer TOEFL	213
Average HS GPA	3.6
% graduated top 10% of class	53
% graduated top 25% of class	29
% graduated top 50% of class	98

DEADLINES

Early decision	
Deadline	11/1
Regular	
Priority	11/1
Deadline	1/15
Notification	4/1
Nonfall registration?	no

FINANCIAL FACTS

Financial Aid Rating	91
Annual tuition	$34,410
Room and board	$8,830
Required fees	$890
Books and supplies	$1,200
% frosh rec. need-based scholarship or grant aid	46
% UG rec. need-based scholarship or grant aid	42
% frosh rec. non-need-based scholarship or grant aid	41
% UG rec. non-need-based scholarship or grant aid	39
% frosh rec. need-based self-help aid	30
% UG rec. need-based self-help aid	29
% frosh rec. any financial aid	95
% UG rec. any financial aid	95

DePaul University

ONE EAST JACKSON BOULEVARD, CHICAGO, IL 60604-2287 • ADMISSIONS: 312-362-8300 • FAX: 312-362-5749

STUDENTS SAY ". . ."

Academics

True to its "Vincentian ideals" of "community service, social justice, and critical thinking," DePaul University "is all about enriching the student not only academically but also socially, mentally, and physically," and "constantly challenging the student with new ideas, cultures, and thoughts to explore and understand." The school's urban setting plays a huge part in helping the school fulfill its mission by providing a diverse student body and endless service opportunities, as well as the widespread "availability of jobs and internships," which the school exploits through "'Discover Chicago' and 'Experiential Learning' requirements that get [students] involved in the city and with local communities." Standout programs include a strong business program and a top-notch theater conservatory; students tell us that the study abroad program is also excellent. DePaul operates on a quarterly academic calendar, which many enjoy: "We're able to learn about so much more than students at semester schools," an English major asserts. Others students feel that "sometimes it seems as though we do not spend enough time on subjects due to the quarter system." Professors earn solid grades as teachers and mentors; the administration, on the other hand, "is a huge bureaucracy, so it's often difficult dealing with issues [that are] non-classroom related." That being said, "Administrators are, for the most part, friendly, and issues always eventually get taken care of even if they require much more time and energy than they should."

Life

"Life at DePaul is just challenging enough so students are pressured to succeed in life but aren't too stressed out," which leaves them enough time to enjoy the benefits of living in one of America's great cities. It's "nearly impossible to be bored in Chicago," a junior writes, "but it's definitely possible to live up to the broke-college-student standard." "The tourist, theatrical, food, and bar scene[s are] amazing," a sophomore adds. "Getting around is easy thanks to the U-Pass students are provided with each quarter," which allows them "to use the CTA [Chicago Transit Authority] system as much as [they] like." DePaul's Lincoln Park location "is not a town based around the college"; rather, it is a well-heeled Chicago neighborhood with "multimillion-dollar homes, parks, boutiques, and families. The shopping is phenomenal, and the food is just as great. Plus, we're close to lots of other colleges." The Loop campus, home to business students, is "so close [to downtown Chicago] that you can do a variety of things based on your interests every weekend and even go shopping between classes." On campus, "DePaul Theater School performances are great and inexpensive for students," and "Student groups on campus hold fun events every weekend." Many undergrads drink at bars in the city, and "Most big drinkers have a fake ID if they're not 21." For the sober set, "There are always festivals, movies, shopping trips, bike rides, concerts, etc." either on campus or around Chicago.

Student Body

"DePaul is an extremely diverse school" with "people of all shapes, sizes, colors, etc.," students tell us. Classes encompass "a wide variety of religions, ethnicities, and orientations . . . I wouldn't have it any other way," beams a political science major. However, while diverse students interact in a friendly manner "on a daily basis," they largely remain segregated by class, major, background, and interests. Many students distinguish themselves through fashion: "There are a lot of very well-dressed students at DePaul"—"Many have the latest Coach, Ugg, and North Face attire." There are also "a lot of bohemian-style dressers" as well as "artists, bookish types, athletes, etc." Students "tend to be fairly liberal," but there's also an active and visible Conservative Club on campus. Many students are "socially conscious and relish the opportunity to work for causes in which they believe."

Financial Aid: 312-362-8091 • E-mail: admitdpu@depaul.edu • Website: www.depaul.edu

THE PRINCETON REVIEW SAYS

Admissions

Very important factors considered include: Rigor of secondary school record. *Important factors considered include:* Class rank, application essay, academic GPA, recommendation(s), standardized test scores, character/personal qualities, extracurricular activities, level of applicant's interest, talent/ability, volunteer work, work experience. *Other factors considered include:* Alumni/ae relation, first generation, geographical residence, interview, racial/ethnic status, religious affiliation/commitment, state residency, SAT or ACT required; TOEFL required of all international applicants. High school diploma is required and GED is accepted. *Academic units required:* 4 English, 3 mathematics, 3 science, (2 science labs), 2 social studies, 4 academic electives.

Financial Aid

Students should submit: FAFSA. Regular filing deadline is 5/1. The Princeton Review suggests that all financial aid forms be submitted as soon as possible after January 1. *Need-based scholarships/grants offered:* Federal Pell, SEOG, state scholarships/grants, private scholarships, the school's own gift aid, Federal Academic Competitiveness Grant and Federal SMART Grant. *Loan aid offered:* Direct Subsidized Stafford, Direct Unsubsidized Stafford, Direct PLUS, Federal Perkins, Private Loans.. Applicants will be notified of awards on a rolling basis beginning 3/15. Federal Work-Study Program available. Institutional employment available. Off-campus job opportunities are excellent.

The Inside Word

DePaul has earned its reputation as one of the most diverse campuses in the United States. The school courts minority students not only as freshmen but also as transfers. It recognizes that its tuition is beyond the means of many (even with financial aid), so it works with area community colleges to allow students to fulfill requirements at a lower cost before completing their degrees at DePaul.

THE SCHOOL SAYS "..."

From The Admissions Office

"The nation's largest Catholic university, DePaul University is nationally recognized for its innovative academic programs that embrace a comprehensive 'learn by doing' approach. DePaul has two residential campuses and four commuter campuses in the suburbs. The Lincoln Park campus is located in one of Chicago's most exciting neighborhoods, filled with theaters, cafés, clubs, and shops. It is home to DePaul's College of Liberal Arts and Sciences, the School of Education, the Theater School, and the School of Music. New buildings on the 36-acre campus include residence halls, a science building, a student recreational facility, and the student center, which features a cybercafé where students can surf the Web or gather with friends. The Loop campus, located in Chicago's downtown—a world-class center for business, government, law, and culture—is home to DePaul's College of Commerce; College of Law; School of Computer Science, Telecommunications, and Information Systems; School for New Learning; and School of Accountancy and Management Information Systems.

"Applicants for the Fall 2008 freshman class are required to take either the ACT or the SAT. The Writing Test on the ACT and the Writing section on the SAT are not required for admission consideration; therefore, we will also accept results from tests taken prior to March 2005."

SELECTIVITY

Admissions Rating	82
# of applicants	12,450
% of applicants accepted	63
% of acceptees attending	32

FRESHMAN PROFILE

Range SAT Critical Reading	520–630
Range SAT Math	510–620
Range SAT Writing	527.5–622.5
Range ACT Composite	22–27
Minimum paper TOEFL	550
Minimum computer TOEFL	213
Minimum web-based TOEFL	80
Average HS GPA	3.4
% graduated top 10% of class	20
% graduated top 25% of class	48.3
% graduated top 50% of class	82.5

DEADLINES

Early action	
Deadline	11/15
Notification	1/15
Regular	
Priority	2/1
Notification	rolling
Nonfall registration?	yes

FINANCIAL FACTS

Financial Aid Rating	69
Annual tuition	$23,820
Room and board	$9,955
Required fees	$574
Books and supplies	$900
% frosh rec. need-based scholarship or grant aid	45
% UG rec. need-based scholarship or grant aid	45
% frosh rec. non-need-based scholarship or grant aid	27
% UG rec. non-need-based scholarship or grant aid	19
% frosh rec. need-based self-help aid	48
% UG rec. need-based self-help aid	50
% frosh rec. athletic scholarships	2
% UG rec. athletic scholarships	2
% frosh rec. any financial aid	79
% UG rec. any financial aid	68
% UG borrow to pay for school	65
Average cumulative indebtedness	$22,569

DePauw University

101 East Seminary, Greencastle, IN 46135 • Admissions: 765-658-4006 • Fax: 765-658-4007

STUDENTS SAY ". . ."

Academics

Serious-minded students are drawn to DePauw University for its "small classes," "encouraging" professors, and the "individual academic attention" they can expect to receive. Academically, DePauw is "demanding but rewarding," and "requires a lot of outside studying and discipline" in order to keep up. Professors' "expectations are very high," which means "You can't slack off and get good grades." Be prepared to pull your "fair share of all-nighters." Fortunately, DePauw professors are more than just stern taskmasters. Though they pile on the work, they "are always helpful and available" to students in need. When things get overwhelming, "They are very understanding and will cut you a break if you really deserve" it. As a result, students come to know their professors "on a personal level," making DePauw the kind of school where it is "common [for students] to have dinner at a professor's house." Beyond stellar professors, DePauw's other academic draws include "extraordinary" study abroad opportunities and a "wonderful" alumni network great for "connections and networking opportunities." Alums also "keep our endowment pretty high, making it easy for the school to give out merit scholarships," which undergraduates appreciate. Student opinion regarding the administration ranges from ambivalent to slightly negative. One especially thorny issue is class registration; you "rarely . . . get into all the classes you want."

Life

Few schools are as Greek as DePauw, but students are quick to point out that "it is by no means *Animal House*." The Greek system here is more holistic than that. It "promotes not only social activities but also philanthropic events." That's not to say there aren't lots of frat parties here. There are. But "The administration has cracked down big time" on the larger frat parties, and "Now there are just small parties in apartments and dorms." One recently issued rule is that freshmen "will not be allowed on Greek property until after Rush, which is the first week of second semester." In addition to administrative regulation, students exercise their own self-restraint; for the typical undergraduate, "[T]he week is mostly reserved for studying." Beyond the frats and sororities, "There is always a theater production, athletic event, or organization-sponsored event going on," and popular bands occasionally perform on campus. It's a good thing so much is happening at the school because off-campus entertainment options are scarce: "If there is really any fun to be had, it's not in Greencastle." The situation could be greatly improved if there were just a few "more restaurants and stores in the town or a nearby town." As things stand, however, students "have to go to Indianapolis (45 miles) to go shopping, watch a good movie, eat at a good restaurant, etc."

Student Body

The typical DePauw student is "upper-middle class," "a little preppy, a little athletic," and "hardworking"; "parties hard on weekends," and "usually becomes involved with the Greek system." Students describe their peers as "driven students" with "polos and pearls." They "have all had multiple internships, international experience, and [held] some type of leadership position." Though these folks may seem "overcommitted," they "always get their work done." For those who don't fit this mold, don't fret; most students seem to be "accepting of the different types" of people on campus. Diversity on campus is augmented through the school's partnership with the Posse Foundation, which brings in urban (though not necessarily minority) "students from Chicago and NYC every year." These students are described as "leaders on campus" and "take real initiative to hold their communities together."

THE PRINCETON REVIEW SAYS

Admissions

Very important factors considered include: Academic GPA, rigor of secondary school record, standardized test scores. *Important factors considered include:* Class rank, application essay, recommendation(s). *Other factors considered include:* Alumni/ae relation, character/personal qualities, extracurricular activities, first generation, geographical residence, interview, level of applicant's interest, state residency, talent/ability, volunteer work, work experience. SAT or ACT required; ACT with Writing component required. TOEFL required of all international applicants. High school diploma is required and GED is accepted. *Academic units recommended:* 4 English, 4 mathematics, 4 science, (2 science labs), 4 foreign language, 4 social studies.

Financial Aid

Students should submit: FAFSA, institution's own financial aid form. The Princeton Review suggests that all financial aid forms be submitted as soon as possible after January 1. *Need-based scholarships/grants offered:* Federal Pell, SEOG, state scholarships/grants, private scholarships, the school's own gift aid. *Loan aid offered:* FFEL Subsidized Stafford, FFEL Unsubsidized Stafford, FFEL PLUS, Federal Perkins, college/university loans from institutional funds. Applicants will be notified of awards on or about 3/27. Federal Work-Study Program available. Institutional employment available. Off-campus job opportunities are fair.

The Inside Word

Prospective applicants should not be deceived by DePauw's high acceptance rate. The students who are accepted and choose to enroll here have the academic goods to justify their admission. Many of them are accepted by more "competitive" schools and still choose DePauw. DePauw's generous merit scholarships have a lot to do with students' choice to enroll.

THE SCHOOL SAYS ". . ."

From The Admissions Office

"DePauw University is nationally recognized for intellectual and experiential challenge that links liberal arts education with life's work, preparing graduates for uncommon professional success, service to others, and personal fulfillment. DePauw graduates count among their ranks a Nobel Laureate, a vice president and U.S. congressman, Pulitzer Prize and Newbery Award authors, and a number of CEOs and humanitarian leaders. Our students demonstrate a love for learning, a willingness to serve others, the reason and judgment to lead, an interest in engaging worlds and cultures unknown to them, the courage to question their assumptions, and a strong commitment to community. Pre-professional and career exploration are encouraged through winter term, when more than 700 students pursue their own off-campus internships. This represents more students in experiential learning opportunities than at any other liberal arts college in the nation. Other innovative programs include Honor Scholars, Information Technology Associates Program, Management Fellows, Media Fellows, and Science Research Fellows, affording selected students additional seminar and internship opportunities.

"Freshman applicants for Fall 2008 and thereafter are required to submit scores of the Writing section of the SAT or the ACT. Scores from previous SAT or ACT administrations will be considered, but a Writing score is required to complete an application for admission."

SELECTIVITY

Admissions Rating	92
# of applicants	3,624
% of applicants accepted	69
% of acceptees attending	27
# accepting a place on wait list	30
# of early decision applicants	50
% accepted early decision	82

FRESHMAN PROFILE

Range SAT Critical Reading	560–660
Range SAT Math	570–660
Range SAT Writing	550–650
Range ACT Composite	25–29
Minimum paper TOEFL	560
Minimum computer TOEFL	225
Average HS GPA	3.6
% graduated top 10% of class	50
% graduated top 25% of class	83
% graduated top 50% of class	99

DEADLINES

Early decision	
Deadline	11/1
Notification	1/1
Early action	
Deadline	12/1
Notification	2/15
Regular	
Deadline	2/1
Notification	4/1
Nonfall registration?	yes

APPLICANTS ALSO LOOK AT

AND OFTEN PREFER
University of Notre Dame
Vanderbilt University
Indiana University at Bloomington
Northwestern University

AND SOMETIMES PREFER
Washington University in St. Louis
Purdue University—West Lafayette
Denison University
University of Illinois at
Urbana–Champaign
Miami University

AND RARELY PREFER
Hanover College

FINANCIAL FACTS

Financial Aid Rating	98
Annual tuition	$29,300
Room and board	$8,100
Required fees	$400
Books and supplies	$700
% frosh rec. any financial aid	97
% UG rec. any financial aid	96

DICKINSON COLLEGE

PO BOX 1773, CARLISLE, PA 17013-2896 • ADMISSIONS: 717-245-1231 • FAX: 717-245-1442

CAMPUS LIFE
Quality of Life Rating	79
Fire Safety Rating	75
Green Rating	89
Type of school	private
Environment	city

STUDENTS
Total undergrad enrollment	2,349
% male/female	45/55
% from out of state	75
% from public high school	62
% live on campus	92
% in (# of) fraternities	16 (5)
% in (# of) sororities	28 (5)
% African American	4
% Asian	5
% Caucasian	78
% Hispanic	5
% international	6
# of countries represented	46

SURVEY SAYS . . .
Large classes
Great computer facilities
Great library
Lots of beer drinking

ACADEMICS
Academic Rating	89
Calendar	semester
Student/faculty ratio	11:1
Profs interesting rating	86
Profs accessible rating	89
Most common	
reg class size	10–19 students

MOST POPULAR MAJORS
international business/trade/
commerce
political science and government
English language and literature

STUDENTS SAY " . . ."

Academics

Dickinson College is a "quintessential small liberal arts school" in a "small town in central Pennsylvania." The big draw here is an "aggressive" global focus. "Dickinson has completely followed through on all of their promises of a campus that supports international experiences," says a sociology major. Courses "have a strong focus on international issues." Studying abroad "fits seamlessly into the curriculum" and is "a huge deal." "Dickinson has exceptional study abroad programs everywhere in the world." The administration is sometimes "preoccupied with rising in the ranks and improving superficial perceptions" of the school but Dickinson's president is insanely popular. He "has weekly office hours." "From the president down, the faculty and administrators make themselves available." "Any complaint is heard and listened to, not just brushed off." The academic atmosphere here is "difficult but doable." Classes are small. "Students do not often skip, as professors do take note." The "completely accommodating" faculty receives high marks. "They are good teachers, passionate about their subjects, and it is very easy for students to develop strong out-of-the-classroom relationships with their professors," says an international business major. "I can honestly say I've only had one professor who I didn't consider high quality," adds one junior.

Life

"The campus is beautiful," observes a senior at Dickinson. "On a nice day, it can take your breath away." It's also "overloaded with clubs and organizations." During the week, "there is a lot to do if you're willing to do it and a lot of it is college sponsored." There is a "consistently full schedule of lectures." There are plenty of arts-related events. "All the different cultural clubs have a dinner every semester." "Intramural sports are a big deal." "The gym is in constant use." "Greek life is really big at Dickinson" as well. "The social scene revolves around frat parties," and "it is difficult to maintain a social life in this school if you are not involved in some kind of fraternity or sorority." "On the weekends, the majority of people get nice and drunk." "Dickinson did not get the name Drinkinson for nothing." Drugs are not uncommon, either. Students who don't party are here too, "trying desperately to make their own fun." There's also "a lot of drama" on campus. "We like to call it Dickinson High," one student admits. The "dull" surrounding town is "not a social mecca." "I love art museums, live music, and cultural diversity," says a senior. "Carlisle does not have any of that." "There is nothing to do in Carlisle unless you are 21 and can get into the bars, where the most exciting thing to do is drink and maybe dance with a nice townie." "If you don't mind small towns, you'll be fine," advises a junior, "but big city people should look elsewhere for their college experience unless they're tired of the rat race."

Student Body

"The most glaring trait of the student body is that it is mostly white." "There are tons of international students," and the "growing" Posse program brings poor minority kids to campus. Still, as a first-year student relates, "the school is not as diverse as some of us would want it to be." Overall, "there is a lot of homogeneity." Most students here are "socially oriented" and come from somewhere on the east coast or in the mid-atlantic states. "Many students are very rich and have no problem spending copious amounts of money." "The parking lots are filled with Jeep Grand Cherokees, Saabs, and BMWs." Other students receive "sweet financial aid deals," though. Academically, Dickinsonians "range anywhere from overzealous to apathetic" but the vast majority "can usually balance a full academic load with an active and rich social life." "The typical student at Dickinson is very preppy. The girls are gorgeous and the guys look like they are straight out of a J. Crew catalog, and everyone is also really athletic." "Finding the oddballs can be difficult." Cliques are common and "the campus is quite split between Greek life and non-Greek life."

FINANCIAL AID: 717-245-1308 • E-MAIL: ADMIT@DICKINSON.EDU • WEBSITE: WWW.DICKINSON.EDU

THE PRINCETON REVIEW SAYS

Admissions

Very important factors considered include: Academic GPA, rigor of secondary school record, extracurricular activities, talent/ability, volunteer work. *Important factors considered include:* Class rank, recommendation(s), standardized test scores, alumni/ae relation, work experience. *Other factors considered include:* Application essay, character/personal qualities, first generation, geographical residence, interview, level of applicant's interest, racial/ethnic status, state residency, SAT or ACT recommended; TOEFL required of all international applicants. High school diploma is required and GED is accepted. *Academic units required:* 4 English, 3 mathematics, 3 science, (2 science labs), 2 foreign language, 2 social studies, 2 academic electives. *Academic units recommended:* 3 foreign language.

Financial Aid

Students should submit: FAFSA, CSS/Financial Aid PROFILE, state aid form, noncustodial PROFILE, business/farm supplement. Regular filing deadline is 2/1. The Princeton Review suggests that all financial aid forms be submitted as soon as possible after January 1. *Need-based scholarships/grants offered:* Federal Pell, SEOG, state scholarships/grants, private scholarships, the school's own gift aid. *Loan aid offered:* FFEL Subsidized Stafford, FFEL Unsubsidized Stafford, FFEL PLUS, Federal Perkins, college/university loans from institutional funds. Applicants will be notified of awards on or about 3/31. Federal Work-Study Program available. Institutional employment available. Off-campus job opportunities are good.

The Inside Word

Dickinson's admissions process is typical of most small liberal arts colleges. The best candidates for such a place are those with solid grades and broad extracurricular involvement—the stereotypical "well-rounded student." Admissions selectivity is kept in check by a strong group of competitor colleges that fight tooth and nail for their cross-applicants.

THE SCHOOL SAYS "..."

From The Admissions Office

"College is more than a collection of courses. It is about crossing traditional boundaries, about seeing the interrelationships among different subjects, about learning a paradigm for solving problems, about developing critical thinking and communication skills, and about speaking out on issues that matter. Dickinson was intended as an alternative to the 15 colleges that existed in the U.S. at the time of its founding; its aim, then as now, was to provide a "useful" education whereby students would 'learn by doing' through hands-on experience and engagement with the community, the region, the nation, and the world. And this is truer today than ever, with workshop science courses replacing traditional lectures, fieldwork experiences in community studies in which students take oral histories, and 12 study centers abroad in nontourist cities where students, under the guidance of a Dickinson faculty director, experience a true international culture. Almost 55 percent of the student body study abroad and a total of 58 percent study off campus, preparing them to compete and succeed in a complex global world.

"Applicants wishing to be considered for academic scholarships are required to submit scores from either the SAT or ACT, but Dickinson does not require results from either test for admission into the 2008 entering class."

SELECTIVITY

Admissions Rating	93
# of applicants	5,844
% of applicants accepted	42
% of acceptees attending	25
# accepting a place on wait list	456
% admitted from wait list	6
# of early decision applicants	425
% accepted early decision	67

FRESHMAN PROFILE

Range SAT Critical Reading	600–690
Range SAT Math	590–680
Range ACT Composite	27–30
Minimum paper TOEFL	600
Minimum computer TOEFL	250
Minimum web-based TOEFL	100
% graduated top 10% of class	48
% graduated top 25% of class	79
% graduated top 50% of class	95

DEADLINES

Early decision	
Deadline	11/15
Notification	12/15
Early action	
Deadline	12/1
Notification	1/15
Regular	
Deadline	2/1
Notification	3/31
Nonfall registration?	no

APPLICANTS ALSO LOOK AT

AND OFTEN PREFER
Colby College, Hamilton College, Georgetown University

AND SOMETIMES PREFER
Bucknell U, Franklin & Marshall College, Gettysburg College, Lafayette College

AND RARELY PREFER
The George Washington University, Kenyon College, Muhlenberg

FINANCIAL FACTS

Financial Aid Rating	91
Annual tuition	$37,900
Room and board	$9,600
Required fees	$334
Books and supplies	$1,000
% frosh rec. need-based scholarship or grant aid	44
% UG rec. need-based scholarship or grant aid	41
% frosh rec. non-need-based scholarship or grant aid	6
% UG rec. non-need-based scholarship or grant aid	5
% frosh rec. need-based self-help aid	42
% UG rec. need-based self-help aid	39
% frosh rec. any financial aid	48
% UG rec. any financial aid	44
% UG borrow to pay for school	54
Average cumulative indebtedness	$22,853

DREW UNIVERSITY

OFFICE OF COLLEGE ADMISSIONS, MADISON, NJ 07940-1493 • ADMISSIONS: 973-408-3739 • FAX: 973-408-3068

STUDENTS SAY "..."

Academics

For fifteen years, Drew University was practically synonymous with Tom Kean, the popular university president who had previously served as Governor of New Jersey. Kean's prominence brought lots of regional and national attention to this small school, to the great benefit of students and the university alike. His departure was bound to ruffle some feathers, and sure enough there are some here who simply can't abide the school's new direction, which includes plans for expansion (plans that, incidentally, were made during Kean's tenure). Fortunately, Drew seems to have weathered the transition well; the vast majority of students here continue to extol this "small school with a beautiful campus and prime location" near New York City. The school's location allows students to take advantage of "programs such as Wall Street Semester and United Nations Semester, as well as field trips to theaters on Broadway and Art museums." They also tell us that location affords "awesome job opportunities in the surrounding areas." Students praise the curriculum's liberal art focus that ensures "that everyone gets exposed to at least a little bit of every other subject before they leave." Drew's "small class sizes allow for the difficulty of the classes to be manageable" and students say "every professor wants to know your name by the end of the semester." While students acknowledge that "Drew is a school that's in the midst of finding and creating its unique identity," they also don't feel any imperative to rush the process. In fact, they tell us that Drew is "one of the best schools in New Jersey when it comes to education," just as it is.

Life

Drew's small size, coupled with the fact that "there are so many clubs, organizations, and sports teams to join" encourages student participation in extracurricular activities. One student opines: "With a school so small, I doubt that anyone who graduates does not have a leadership position in something." An active performing arts program means that there is "lots of involvement in the arts," among students including theater, musical performances, a capella, and student art exhibits." Drew "is not a party school per se" but "for people who do like to party, it's very easy because the alcohol policy is like the world's most un-enforced thing." More often, when students want a wild night they "simply hop on the train a block away and head for Morristown or New York for an evening or weekend" or "when the weather is conducive" they might "take a trip with a few friends down to the beach." Hometown Madison is "adorable" with "a small-town atmosphere." On the downside, "there isn't much to do in town," but with New York City "right around the corner," that's hardly a make-or-break problem.

Student Body

Drew "caters to a lot of wealthy kids from Dirty Jerz (New Jersey)," students who "live within a few hours of campus and have the opportunity to travel home if they choose to, although it does not at all feel like a 'suitcase school.'" Despite this trend, "There is a very wide variety of students at Drew—all different races, ethnicities, and backgrounds." The student body includes "tons of theatre kids" as well as "your typical jocks." (One student observes that "there is definitely a division between jocks and everyone else at this school—not that our sports teams are even good.") Students tell us that "Drew is a reach school for some and a safety for others, so there are very, very brilliant students here, while others…not so much." Women outnumber men by a healthy 3-to-2 ratio.

FINANCIAL AID: 973-408-3112 • E-MAIL: CADM@DREW.EDU • WEBSITE: WWW.DREW.EDU

THE PRINCETON REVIEW SAYS

Admissions

Very important factors considered include: Academic GPA, rigor of secondary school record, talent/ability. *Important factors considered include:* Application essay, recommendation(s), extracurricular activities, interview, level of applicant's interest. *Other factors considered include:* Class rank, standardized test scores, alumni/ae relation, character/personal qualities, first generation, geographical residence, racial/ethnic status, volunteer work, work experience. ACT with Writing component recommended. TOEFL required of all international applicants. High school diploma or equivalent is not required. *Academic units recommended:* 4 English, 3 mathematics, 2 science, 2 foreign language, 2 social studies, 2 history, 3 academic electives.

Financial Aid

Students should submit: FAFSA, CSS/Financial Aid PROFILE. Regular filing deadline is 2/15. The Princeton Review suggests that all financial aid forms be submitted as soon as possible after January 1. *Need-based scholarships/grants offered:* Federal Pell, SEOG, state scholarships/grants, private scholarships, the school's own gift aid. *Loan aid offered:* FFEL Subsidized Stafford, FFEL Unsubsidized Stafford, FFEL PLUS, Federal Perkins, state loans Applicants will be notified of awards on or about 4/1. Federal Work-Study Program available. Institutional employment available. Off-campus job opportunities are excellent.

The Inside Word

Since 2005, Drew University has given applicants the option of submitting a graded writing sample in place of standardized test scores. If the goal was to attract more applicants, all we can say is: mission accomplished. Drew drew over 4,500 applicants last year, an increase of about 50 percent over applicants during the 2003–04 admissions season. The profile of the average admitted student, oddly, hasn't changed; instead, Drew seems to be attracting more applications from those who see the school as a safety.

THE SCHOOL SAYS " . . ."

From The Admissions Office

"At Drew, great teachers are transforming the undergraduate learning experience. With a commitment to teaching, Drew professors have made educating undergraduates their top priority. With a spirit of innovation, they have brought the most advanced technology and distinctive modes of experiential learning into the Drew classroom. The result is a stimulating and challenging education that connects the traditional liberal arts and sciences to the workplace and to the world.

"Drew University will require applicants for the 2008–2009 academic year to take either the new SAT or the ACT. The Selection Committee will consider the highest Verbal, Math, and Writing scores individually in its evaluation of candidates for admission."

SELECTIVITY

Admissions Rating	**87**
# of applicants	3,816
% of applicants accepted	77
% of acceptees attending	16
# of early decision applicants	36
% accepted early decision	86

FRESHMAN PROFILE

Range SAT Critical Reading	520–650
Range SAT Math	510–630
Range SAT Writing	530–650
Range ACT Composite	20–25
Minimum paper TOEFL	550
Minimum computer TOEFL	213
Average HS GPA	3.35
% graduated top 10% of class	28.1
% graduated top 25% of class	64.3
% graduated top 50% of class	90.3

DEADLINES

Early decision	
Deadline	12/1
Notification	12/24
Regular	
Deadline	2/15
Notification	3/21
Nonfall registration?	yes

FINANCIAL FACTS

Financial Aid Rating	**79**
Annual tuition	$2,850
% UG rec. need-based scholarship or grant aid	49
% UG rec. non-need-based scholarship or grant aid	7
% UG rec. need-based self-help aid	42
% frosh rec. any financial aid	90
% UG rec. any financial aid	82
% UG borrow to pay for school	61.9
Average cumulative indebtedness	$16,777

DREXEL UNIVERSITY

3141 CHESTNUT STREET, PHILADELPHIA, PA 19104 • ADMISSIONS: 215-895-2400 • FAX: 215-895-5939

CAMPUS LIFE
Quality of Life Rating	**65**
Fire Safety Rating	**75**
Green Rating	**98**
Type of school	private
Environment	metropolis

STUDENTS
Total undergrad enrollment	12,722
% male/female	56/44
% from out of state	48
% from public high school	70
% live on campus	25
% in (# of) fraternities	3 (12)
% in (# of) sororities	3 (11)
% African American	8
% Asian	12
% Caucasian	63
% Hispanic	3
% international	7
# of countries represented	104

SURVEY SAYS . . .
Great computer facilities
Career services are great
Diverse student types on campus
Students love Philadelphia, PA
Great off-campus food
Lots of beer drinking
Hard liquor is popular
(Almost) everyone smokes

ACADEMICS
Academic Rating	**73**
Calendar	Quarter for most, Semester for College of Medicine
Student/faculty ratio	9:1
Profs interesting rating	62
Profs accessible rating	62
Most common reg class size	10–19 students

MOST POPULAR MAJORS
information science/studies
mechanical engineering
biology/biological sciences

STUDENTS SAY "..."

Academics

Drexel University "is a lot of work squarely aimed at integration into the professional world," whether that world involves the school's popular majors in engineering, technology, and business, or less-known offerings like the school's programs in the music industry or hospitality management. Drexel has a growing digital media program, making it "one of the only schools in the area with a developed program" in the field. Central to the Drexel experience is the "extremely beneficial" co-op program, which many agree is "the best thing about Drexel." Co-op provides 18 months of professional experience during the 5-year undergraduate program. One student writes, "You will learn as much in the first couple of months of working in the real world as you did in any college. Drexel gives you all of that knowledge before you're even out of school and gives you the preparation necessary to succeed in the real world." The school's location in Philadelphia, "a source of endless fun and opportunity," helps co-op considerably. "Engineering dominates" at Drexel, but the school "has a variety of programs fit for almost anyone," with "a lot of classes run with web-based resources. Lectures are posted online in WebCT, as well as course syllabi and assignments. This makes it easy to access information. Teachers are easy to get in touch with via e-mail and are very accessible to meet with as needed." Administrative tasks are not so convenient; students warn of "lots of red tape," adding that "most issues require visits to at least three different offices, sometimes on opposite ends of campus." Fortunately, the campus isn't that large.

Life

Campus life at Drexel must compete with the temptations offered by Philadelphia, one of the nation's largest cities. Philly provides "so many things to do (if you have the money) that it can be hard to know where to begin." Students tell us that "museums are great. Lots of kids go to concerts, and there are all sorts, all the time. First Fridays in Center City is also popular." The area immediately surrounding the school has plenty of "great bars, food, and dancing." Drexel is close to the UPenn campus, "and students often go into their parties, which are extraordinary." On campus, "There are numerous fraternities and societies you can join." Intercollegiate sports "aren't incredibly popular here," but "The basketball team is really taking off and is always sold out." Drexel's grounds, once an unbroken sea of brick and concrete, have been renovated; today "There are plenty of green grassy areas for students to hang out and relax," as well as "a new beautiful amphitheater and some nice tree-lined walkways with benches and tables."

Student Body

There "are no real typical students at Drexel. [It's] is a pretty diverse school, with students involved in different kinds of activities, dressing differently, and motivated differently." The school "is a melting pot" with "many, many international and minority students." One student notes, "Drexel's common factor seems to be not race or economic background, but a sense of personal drive. Drexel students work hard—it's a requirement to keep afloat—and that self-propulsion seems to be the tie that binds the student body together." If undergrads "seem to fit in well together," that may be because "Students here are very casual and easygoing." Some have quirky senses of humor; take the one who reports that "the students tend to be of the human variety, with genders varying from male to female. Everyone has their clique, and it takes quite a bit of effort to be excluded from them all."

FINANCIAL AID: 215-895-2535 • E-MAIL: ENROLL@DREXEL.EDU • WEBSITE: WWW.DREXEL.EDU

THE PRINCETON REVIEW SAYS

Admissions

Very important factors considered include: Class rank, academic GPA, rigor of secondary school record, standardized test scores. *Important factors considered include:* Application essay, recommendation(s), character/personal qualities. *Other factors considered include:* Alumni/ae relation, extracurricular activities, first generation, interview, level of applicant's interest, talent/ability, volunteer work, work experience. SAT or ACT required; TOEFL required of all international applicants. High school diploma is required and GED is accepted. *Academic units required:* 3 mathematics, 1 science, (1 science labs). *Academic units recommended:* 1 foreign language.

Financial Aid

Students should submit: FAFSA. The Princeton Review suggests that all financial aid forms be submitted as soon as possible after January 1. *Need-based scholarships/grants offered:* Federal Pell, SEOG, state scholarships/grants, private scholarships, the school's own gift aid, United Negro College Fund. *Loan aid offered:* FFEL Subsidized Stafford, FFEL Unsubsidized Stafford, FFEL PLUS, Federal Perkins, Federal Nursing, college/university loans from institutional funds. Applicants will be notified of awards on a rolling basis beginning 3/15. Federal Work-Study Program available.

The Inside Word

Drexel operates on a rolling admissions basis, meaning that admissions decisions are made relatively quickly after all application materials reach the school. Rolling admissions tend to favor those who apply early in the process, when schools are still worried about whether they will be able to fill their incoming classes. Regardless of when you apply, you shouldn't have too much trouble here if your application establishes you as firmly above average.

THE SCHOOL SAYS "..."

From The Admissions Office

"Drexel has gained a reputation for academic excellence since its founding in 1891. In 2006, Drexel became the first top-ranked doctoral university in more than 25 years to open a law school. Its main campus is a 10-minute walk from Center City Philadelphia. Students prepare for successful careers through Drexel's prestigious experiential education program—The Drexel Co-op. Alternating periods of full-time professional employment with periods of classroom study, students can earn an average of $14,000 per 6-month co-op. At any one time, about 2,000 full-time undergraduates are on co-op assignments.

"Drexel integrates science and technology into all 70 undergraduate majors. Students looking for a special challenge can apply to one of 14 accelerated degree programs including the BS/MBA in business; BA/BS/MD in medicine; BA/BS/JD in law; BS/MS or BS/PhD in engineering; BS/MS in information technology; and BS/DPT in physical therapy.

"Pennoni Honors College offers high achievers unique opportunities. Students Tackling Advanced Research (STAR) allows qualified undergraduates to participate in a paid summer research project, and the Center for Civic Engagement matches students with community service opportunities. Students in any major can take dance, music, and theater classes offered through Drexel's performing arts programs.

"Drexel's study abroad program allows students to spend a term or more earning credits while gaining international experience. Adventurous students can also enjoy co-op abroad. Locations include London, Costa Rica, Prague, Rome, and Paris. The Admissions Office invites prospective students to schedule a campus visit for a first-hand look at all Drexel offers.

"Drexel University is currently exploring how to use the new Writing component in admission and placement decisions."

"Students who plan to enter in Fall 2008 will be one of the first classes to take the new SAT for college admissions. Drexel is exploring ways in which the additional Writing component can be used in admissions or placement decisions."

SELECTIVITY
Admissions Rating	87
# of applicants	16,867
% of applicants accepted	72
% of acceptees attending	20

FRESHMAN PROFILE
Range SAT Critical Reading	530–630
Range SAT Math	560–670
Range ACT Composite	23–28
Minimum paper TOEFL	550
Minimum computer TOEFL	213
Average HS GPA	3.47
% graduated top 10% of class	30
% graduated top 25% of class	60
% graduated top 50% of class	86

DEADLINES
Regular	
Deadline	3/1
Nonfall registration?	yes

FINANCIAL FACTS
Financial Aid Rating	62
Annual tuition	$28,500
Room and board	$12,135
Required fees	$1,940
Books and supplies	$1,800
% UG rec. need-based scholarship or grant aid	38
% UG rec. need-based self-help aid	40
% frosh rec. any financial aid	94
% UG rec. any financial aid	89
% UG borrow to pay for school	75
Average cumulative indebtedness	$31,333

DUKE UNIVERSITY

2138 CAMPUS DRIVE, DURHAM, NC 27708 • ADMISSIONS: 919-684-3214 • FAX: 919-681-8941

STUDENTS SAY ". . ."

Academics

Duke University "is the complete package: great academics, fun students, exciting athletics, and school spirit," all enjoyed in "an almost Mediterranean climate." Undergraduates choose Duke because they "are passionate about a wide range of things, including academics, sports, community service, research, and fun," and because the school seems equally committed to accommodating all of those pursuits; as one student puts it, "Duke is for the Ivy League candidate who is a little bit more laid back about school and overachieving (but just a bit) and a lot more into the party scene." Academics "are very difficult in the quantitative majors (engineering, math, statistics, economics, premed)" and "much easier in the non-quantitative majors, but still take a lot of work not to fall behind." In all areas, "the laid-back atmosphere makes competition practically nonexistent. It's the norm to have large study groups, and the review sessions, peer tutoring system, writing center, and academic support center are always helpful when students are struggling with anything from math homework to creating a resume." Professors' "number one priority is teaching undergraduates," a situation made more remarkable by the fact that many are engaged in "groundbreaking" research. Because "the school has a lot of confidence in its students," it offers them "many research opportunities," one of many manifestations of Duke's "commitment to the undergraduate experience. Duke doesn't ignore its undergrads in favor of its graduate programs."

Life

Life at Duke "is very relaxed," with "a great balance between academics and fun. People typically work Monday through Thursday and then go out and enjoy themselves Thursday, Friday, and Saturday." Because "The student union and other organizations provide entertainment all the time, from movies to shows to campus wide parties," there "is always something to do on campus." Indeed, "people usually stay on campus for fun," as hometown Durham "has a few quirky streets and squares with restaurants, shops, clubs, etc., but to really do much you have to go to Raleigh or Chapel Hill," each 20 to 30 minutes away by car. The perception that "Durham is pretty dangerous" further dampens students' enthusiasm for the city. Undergrads' fervor for Blue Devils sports, on the other hand, can be boundless; sports, "especially basketball, are a huge deal here," and undergrads "will paint themselves completely blue and wait in line on the sidewalk in K-ville for three days to jump up and down in Cameron Indoor Stadium." Greek life "essentially runs the party scene, but almost all the parties are open so it definitely isn't hard to get in to a party." A solid contingent abjures the Greek scene; some turn to the "several very active Selective Living groups on campus, which are like a watered-down version of a fraternity or sorority. Several are co-ed and some have special themes like service and foreign language, but many are just social groups to join."

Student Body

The typical Duke student "is someone who cares a lot about their education but at the same time won't sacrifice their social life for it. To go to school here is to find the perfect balance, even if that means some late-night cram sessions or last-minute papers. Everyone's focused on success, but that includes social success as well." They tend to be "perfectionists, very involved in seeking out a 'type A' career (read: investment banking or consulting), and go out two to three times a week and always looks polished, even when wasted." An "overwhelming number" are athletes, "not just varsity athletes...but athletes in high school or generally active people. Duke's athletic pride attracts this kind of person." The student body "is surprisingly ethnically diverse, with a number of students of Asian, African, and Hispanic descent."

DUKE UNIVERSITY

Financial Aid: 919-684-6225 • E-mail: undergrad-admissions@duke.edu • Website: www.duke.edu

THE PRINCETON REVIEW SAYS

Admissions

Very important factors considered include: Application essay, recommendation(s), rigor of secondary school record, standardized test scores, extracurricular activities, talent/ability. *Important factors considered include:* character/personal qualities. *Other factors considered include:* Class rank, academic GPA, alumni/ae relation, geographical residence, interview, racial/ethnic status, state residency, volunteer work, work experience. SAT and SAT Subject Tests or ACT required; High school diploma is required and GED is not accepted. *Academic units recommended:* 4 English, 4 mathematics, 4 science, 4 foreign language, 4 social studies.

Financial Aid

Students should submit: FAFSA, CSS/Financial Aid PROFILE, noncustodial PROFILE, business/farm supplement, parent and student income tax returns. Regular filing deadline is 3/1. The Princeton Review suggests that all financial aid forms be submitted as soon as possible after January 1. *Need-based scholarships/grants offered:* Federal Pell, SEOG, state scholarships/grants, private scholarships, the school's own gift aid, ROTC. *Loan aid offered:* FFEL Subsidized Stafford, FFEL Unsubsidized Stafford, FFEL PLUS, Federal Perkins, college/university loans from institutional funds, private loans. Applicants will be notified of awards on or about 4/1. Federal Work-Study Program available. Institutional employment available. Off-campus job opportunities are good.

The Inside Word

Duke is an extremely selective undergraduate institution, which affords the school the luxury of rejecting many qualified applicants. You'll have to present an exceptional record just to be considered; to make the cut, you'll have to impress the Admissions Office that you can contribute something unique and valuable to the incoming class. Being one of the best basketball players in the nation (male or female) helps a lot, but even athletes have to show academic excellence in order to get in the door here.

THE SCHOOL SAYS "..."

From The Admissions Office

"Duke University offers an interesting mix of tradition and innovation, undergraduate college and major research university, Southern hospitality and international presence, and athletic prowess and academic excellence. Students come to Duke from all over the United States and the world and from a range of racial, ethnic, and socioeconomic backgrounds. They enjoy contact with a world-class faculty through small classes and independent study. More than 40 majors are available in the arts and sciences and engineering; arts and sciences students may also design their own curriculum through Program II. Certificate programs are available in a number of interdisciplinary areas. Special academic opportunities include the Focus Program and seminars for first-year students, study abroad, study at the Duke Marine Laboratory and Duke Primate Center, the Duke in New York and Duke in Los Angeles arts programs, and several international exchange programs. While admission to Duke is highly selective, applications of U.S. citizens and permanent residents are evaluated without regard to financial need and the university pledges to meet 100 percent of the demonstrated need of all admitted U.S. students and permanent residents. A limited amount of financial aid is also available for foreign citizens, and the university will meet the full demonstrated financial need for those admitted students as well.

"Applicants must take either the ACT with the Writing exam, or the three-part SAT plus two SAT Subject Tests (Mathematics Subject Test required for applicants to the Pratt School of Engineering)."

SELECTIVITY
Admissions Rating	99
# of applicants	18,090
% of applicants accepted	22
% of acceptees attending	43
# accepting a place on wait list	1,026
% admitted from wait list	10
# of early decision applicants	1,482
% accepted early decision	32

FRESHMAN PROFILE
Range SAT Critical Reading	690–770
Range SAT Math	690–800
Range ACT Composite	29–34
% graduated top 10% of class	90
% graduated top 25% of class	98
% graduated top 50% of class	100

DEADLINES
Early decision	
Deadline	11/1
Notification	12/15
Regular	
Deadline	1/2
Notification	4/1
Nonfall registration?	no

APPLICANTS ALSO LOOK AT
AND OFTEN PREFER
Harvard College
Stanford University
Yale University
Princeton University
AND SOMETIMES PREFER
Test admin CU
Dartmouth College
Cornell University
Brown University
University of Pennsylvania
AND RARELY PREFER
University of Virginia
Georgetown University
University of North Carolina at Chapel Hill

FINANCIAL FACTS
Financial Aid Rating	94
Annual tuition	$31,420
Room and board	$8,950
Required fees	$1,180
Books and supplies	$970
% frosh rec. need-based scholarship or grant aid	38
% UG rec. need-based scholarship or grant aid	37
% frosh rec. non-need-based scholarship or grant aid	1
% UG rec. non-need-based scholarship or grant aid	1
% frosh rec. need-based self-help aid	35
% UG rec. need-based self-help aid	35
% UG borrow to pay for school	40
Average cumulative indebtedness	$16,502

DUQUESNE UNIVERSITY

600 FORBES AVENUE, PITTSBURGH, PA 15282 • ADMISSIONS: 412-396-2222 • FAX: 412-396-5644

CAMPUS LIFE
Quality of Life Rating	**79**
Fire Safety Rating	**88**
Green Rating	**84**
Type of school	private
Affiliation	Roman Catholic
Environment	metropolis

STUDENTS
Total undergrad enrollment	5,562
% male/female	42/58
% from out of state	18
% live on campus	57
% in (# of) fraternities	8 (10)
% in (# of) sororities	11 (9)
% African American	3
% Asian	2
% Caucasian	81
% Hispanic	1
% international	2
# of countries represented	82

SURVEY SAYS . . .
Large classes
Students love Pittsburgh, PA
Great off-campus food
Lots of beer drinking
(Almost) everyone smokes

ACADEMICS
Academic Rating	**76**
Calendar	semester
Student/faculty ratio	15:1
Profs interesting rating	72
Profs accessible rating	76
Most common reg class size	10–19 students
Most common lab size	20–29 students

MOST POPULAR MAJORS
nursing/registered nurse
(RN, ASN, BSN, MSN)
pharmacy (pharmd [usa], pharmd
or bs/bpharm [canada])
psychology

STUDENTS SAY " . . ."

Academics
Located in a great town for both career networking and college fun, Pittsburgh's Duquesne University offers a prestigious private school education to a "smart, ambitious, and very goal-oriented" student body that "prides itself on its 'Catholic' tradition." DU is perhaps best known for its health sciences programs; students laud the "rigorous pharmacy curriculum," the "wonderful" physical therapy program and "great" nursing, occupational, and athletic training programs, all of which benefit from "great access to all the hospitals in the area." The music program at Duquesne is "amazing," and students say "The employment rate of students that have graduated from the music education program is phenomenal. I'm almost positive every senior that graduated was placed at a job already." Students in many of these areas pursue DUs accelerated bachelor's/graduate degree programs. Regardless of what they study, all DU students must complete a core curriculum that stresses broad general knowledge; students have mixed feelings about the core, warning that these classes are "harder than other courses" and are especially labor intensive. Throughout the school, "Most classes are lecture-driven courses" with relatively large class sizes at the lower levels. The majority of professors are "excellent teachers and very knowledgeable of their respective fields," although, as anywhere, "There are a few awful ones." Nearly all "make themselves available to help you anytime you need. . . . If you are not good at a particular subject, they . . . have tutors available to help you."

Life
Student life at Duquesne "is lots of fun," although students say that has more to do with hometown Pittsburgh than with the DU campus. True, the campus offers numerous diversions, including "movies and crafts and sports and tons of organizations," in addition to weekend frat parties which are quite popular with the Greek crowd and underclassmen. However, most students find city life more tempting, reporting that they "like to go downtown to shop, or to the South Side, or to the Waterfront." Oakland is really close by, with "lots of bars, restaurants," and "other colleges." One student explains, "There's always something going on in Pittsburgh, whether it's free concerts, cultural events, or art exhibits, many of which you are admitted into for free or reduced price with a Duquesne ID." The only downside is the weather: "If you're looking for fun, be prepared to bundle up in the winter and to travel by bus or taxi," one student warns. The "beautiful" DU campus features "lots of fountains and grassy areas and stuff." Location is another plus, as the campus is in the middle of Pittsburgh but still has a very private feel. "We have the opportunities of the city but we are secluded on the bluff."

Student Body
The typical Duquesne undergrad is either "well put together" or "cares too much about the way they look"—it's all a matter of perspective. Since most here are the "dress for success" type, the former viewpoint is more popular than the latter, although the "wearing-sweats-and-being-comfortable crowd" make up "about a third" of the campus, so they're hardly a tiny minority. Because "many students at Duquesne went to high school together," the school tends to be quite clique-y. Undergrads also tend to self-segregate by major. As one music student writes, "The typical music major is completely different from the typical student. The majority of music majors have somewhat eclectic taste in fashion, clothing, hobbies . . . which reflects in our personalities. We also talk about stuff we're doing in class outside of school, which isn't very common among other majors." While most students here are Catholic, "There are also people of different religions," and the school "doesn't impose religion" on anyone.

DUQUESNE UNIVERSITY

FINANCIAL AID: 412-396-6607 • E-MAIL: ADMISSIONS@DUQ.EDU • WEBSITE: WWW.DUQ.EDU

THE PRINCETON REVIEW SAYS

Admissions

Very important factors considered include: Application essay, academic GPA, recommendation(s), rigor of secondary school record, standardized test scores. *Important factors considered include:* Class rank, extracurricular activities, interview, talent/ability, volunteer work. *Other factors considered include:* Alumni/ae relation, first generation, level of applicant's interest, racial/ethnic status, work experience. SAT or ACT required; ACT with Writing component required. High school diploma is required and GED is accepted. *Academic units required:* 4 English, 2 mathematics, 2 science, 2 foreign language, 2 social studies, 4 academic electives.

Financial Aid

Students should submit: FAFSA, institution's own financial aid form Regular filing deadline is 5/1. The Princeton Review suggests that all financial aid forms be submitted as soon as possible after January 1. *Need-based scholarships/grants offered:* Federal Pell, SEOG, state scholarships/grants, private scholarships, the school's own gift aid, United Negro College Fund *Loan aid offered:* FFEL Subsidized Stafford, FFEL Unsubsidized Stafford, FFEL PLUS, Federal Perkins, Federal Nursing, Private Alternative Loans. Applicants will be notified of awards on a rolling basis beginning 3/1. Federal Work-Study Program available. Institutional employment available. Off-campus job opportunities are good.

The Inside Word

Duquesne's overall high admit rate masks the competitiveness of its top programs. Applicants seeking admission to programs in pharmacy, physical therapy, physician's assistant, and forensic science should expect a rigorous review. Others should have little difficulty getting through the door provided they present a respectable complement of transcripts and test scores.

THE SCHOOL SAYS ". . ."

From The Admissions Office

"Duquesne University was founded in 1878 by the Holy Ghost Fathers. Although it is a private, Roman Catholic institution, Duquesne is proud of its ecumenical reputation. The total university enrollment is 10,296. Duquesne University's attractive and secluded campus is set on a 48-acre hilltop ('the bluff') overlooking the large corporate metropolis of Pittsburgh's Golden Triangle. It offers a wide variety of educational opportunities, from the liberal arts to modern professional training. Duquesne is a medium-sized university striving to offer personal attention to its students in addition to the versatility and opportunities of a true university. A deep sense of tradition is combined with innovation and flexibility to make the Duquesne experience both challenging and rewarding. The Palumbo Convocation/Recreation Complex features a 6,300-seat arena, home court to the university's Division I basketball teams; racquetball and handball courts, weight rooms, and saunas. Extracurricular activities are recognized as an essential part of college life, complementing academics in the process of total student development. Students are involved in nearly 100 university-sponsored activities, and Duquesne's location gives students the opportunity to enjoy sports and cultural events both on campus and in the city. There are six residence halls with the capacity to house 3,511 students.

"Although SAT Writing scores will not affect admissions decisions, all freshman applicants are required to take the new SAT (or the ACT with the Writing section). Applicants may choose to submit scores from the old (prior to March 2005) version of the SAT (or ACT) as well, and we will use the student's best scores from either test."

SELECTIVITY

Admissions Rating	84
# of applicants	5,374
% of applicants accepted	74
% of acceptees attending	34
# of early decision applicants	76
% accepted early decision	78

FRESHMAN PROFILE

Range SAT Critical Reading	510–600
Range SAT Math	510–610
Range SAT Writing	510–600
Range ACT Composite	22–26
Average HS GPA	3.65
% graduated top 10% of class	26
% graduated top 25% of class	56
% graduated top 50% of class	88

DEADLINES

Early decision	
Deadline	11/1
Notification	12/15
Early action	
Deadline	12/1
Notification	1/15
Regular	
Priority	11/1
Deadline	7/1
Notification	rolling
Nonfall registration?	yes

FINANCIAL FACTS

Financial Aid Rating	85
Annual tuition	$22,054
Room and board	$8,546
Required fees	$1,896
Books and supplies	$600
% frosh rec. need-based scholarship or grant aid	70
% UG rec. need-based scholarship or grant aid	64
% frosh rec. non-need-based scholarship or grant aid	68
% UG rec. non-need-based scholarship or grant aid	53
% frosh rec. need-based self-help aid	59
% UG rec. need-based self-help aid	56
% frosh rec. athletic scholarships	5
% UG rec. athletic scholarships	5
% frosh rec. any financial aid	93
% UG rec. any financial aid	85
% UG borrow to pay for school	80
Average cumulative indebtedness	$27,080

ECKERD COLLEGE

4200 FIFTY-FOURTH AVENUE SOUTH, ST. PETERSBURG, FL 33711 • ADMISSIONS: 727-864-8331 • FAX: 727-866-2304

STUDENTS SAY ". . ."

Academics

Florida's Eckerd College may be small, but it only seems small "where it matters, like class size[s] and relationships with professors." It also offers many "big-school opportunities that make it seem bigger than it is." Among the school's most distinguished offerings are an "amazing" marine science program—"If it's not your passion," students say, "it will eat you alive"—and a "great international relations program." The latter benefits from a school-wide commitment to undergraduate international travel. One student writes: "International education is great. I spent last January (winter term) in Vietnam, Thailand, Laos, and Cambodia, and next semester I'll be in Sweden on an exchange program." Students tell us that academic programs other than the sciences and international relations "aren't nearly as demanding, and professors don't seem to expect as much out of the students." As one student puts it, "There are two kinds of Eckerd students: Those with easy majors and those [who] watch everyone else party on Tuesdays and skip class to go the beach." Eckerd offers "much flexibility for designing your own concentration or for independent studies" as well as many opportunities "to do research with your professors and advance in ways you couldn't imagine at larger schools." How accessible are professors here? "Pitchers with Professors"—"where students and professors can discuss class lectures or [have] general conversation over a pitcher of beer or a soda"—"is a common occurrence each month."

Life

"It's Florida," explains one student. "Life at school is laid-back." The warm weather "definitely has an effect on the attitude of most people who live on campus." Eckerd's environs include various sports grounds, including beach volleyball courts and a private waterfront where students can take sailing and windsurfing classes. If that's not enough, two gorgeous beaches are less than 10 minutes away, downtown Tampa is only a half-hour away, and Busch Gardens and Disney World are 45 and 90 minutes away, respectively. One student sums up, "The location is amazing. Waking up on the Tampa Bay each morning energizes you." The only drawback is that "Eckerd is somewhat separated from St. Petersburg at large. It's [on] the southern tip of the city and you're really out of luck if you don't have a car or don't know someone who does, since mostly everything worth doing is far away." On campus "The most random of events happen. . . . We've got drum circles on the beach, Saturday Morning Market, Kappa Karnival, Pitchers with Professors, Saturday boat trips to Shell Island, Ybor City, and lots of other things to explore."

Student Body

The Eckerd student body includes "science majors (geeks, if you will)" along with "a small dosage of preppy students," "a lot of surfers, sailors, and tanners," "athletes," "church people," and "trustafarians." Athletes "stick together within their groups," and "The marine science majors sort of are a collective," but students report that "it's easy to make friends and know people in every group." "Overall my friends are a varied crowd," a junior declares. While Eckerd's student body is "mostly White and from a middle- to upper-class background" this "is not a typical college," especially by Florida standards: "Don't expect sorority girls and football players," students warn. It's worth noting that Eckerd "is a very liberal campus, with many Democrats, hippies, marijuana, parties, pets, environmental concern, and a basic openness to new things. If you're close-minded and don't want to see others' views, don't come here."

FINANCIAL AID: 727-864-8334 • E-MAIL: ADMISSIONS@ECKERD.EDU • WEBSITE: WWW.ECKERD.EDU

THE PRINCETON REVIEW SAYS

Admissions

Very important factors considered include: Academic GPA, rigor of secondary school record. *Important factors considered include:* Application essay, recommendation(s), standardized test scores, character/personal qualities, extracurricular activities, interview, talent/ability. *Other factors considered include:* Class rank, alumni/ae relation, first generation, level of applicant's interest, volunteer work, work experience. SAT or ACT required; High school diploma is required and GED is accepted. *Academic units required:* 4 English, 3 mathematics, 3 science, (2 science labs), 2 foreign language, 2 social studies, 1 history, 3 academic electives. *Academic units recommended:* 4 mathematics, 4 science, (3 science labs), 3 foreign language, 2 history, 3 academic electives.

Financial Aid

Students should submit: FAFSA. The Princeton Review suggests that all financial aid forms be submitted as soon as possible after January 1. *Need-based scholarships/grants offered:* Federal Pell, SEOG, state scholarships/grants, private scholarships, the school's own gift aid. *Loan aid offered:* FFEL Subsidized Stafford, FFEL Unsubsidized Stafford, FFEL PLUS, Federal Perkins, college/university loans from institutional funds. Applicants will be notified of awards on a rolling basis beginning 2/20. Federal Work-Study Program available. Institutional employment available. Off-campus job opportunities are excellent.

The Inside Word

Eckerd is looking to upgrade its student body, but competition from other small liberal arts schools is stiff; the school is still a relatively easy admit for B-plus students with decent standardized test scores. The school practices rolling admissions, so apply early to improve your chances—Eckerd can afford to be more selective later in the admissions process, especially with candidates who appear to be headed for its most competitive programs (i.e., marine science and international relations).

THE SCHOOL SAYS "..."

From The Admissions Office

"Eckerd's diverse student body comes from 49 states and 49 countries. In this international setting, the majors of international relations and international business are very popular. Close to 70 percent of our graduates spend at least one term studying abroad. The beautiful waterfront campus is a perfect location for the study of marine science and environmental studies. We characterize Eckerd students as competent givers because of their extensive involvement in the life of the campus and their many volunteer service contributions to the local environment and the St. Petersburg community. The Academy of Senior Professionals draws to campus distinguished persons who have retired from fields our students aspire to enter. Academy members, such as the late novelist James Michener, Nobel Prize–winner Elie Wiesel, and noted Black historian John Hope Franklin, enrich classes and offer valuable counsel for career and life planning.

"Students applying for admission into the Fall 2008 freshman class are allowed to submit old or new SAT or ACT examination results, and Eckerd will use the best scores from either test. The Writing portion will not be considered when determining a student's admission or scholarship."

SELECTIVITY

Admissions Rating	82
# of applicants	3,089
% of applicants accepted	68
% of acceptees attending	26
# accepting a place on wait list	35
% admitted from wait list	100

FRESHMAN PROFILE

Range SAT Critical Reading	510–610
Range SAT Math	500–610
Range SAT Writing	500–600
Range ACT Composite	22–27
Average HS GPA	3.28
% graduated top 10% of class	17
% graduated top 25% of class	45
% graduated top 50% of class	81

DEADLINES

Regular	
Notification	rolling
Nonfall registration?	yes

FINANCIAL FACTS

Financial Aid Rating	80
Annual tuition	$30,304
Room and board	$8,754
Required fees	$286
Books and supplies	$1,000
% frosh rec. any financial aid	96
% UG rec. any financial aid	96
% UG borrow to pay for school	64
Average cumulative	
indebtedness	$24,749

ELON UNIVERSITY

2700 CAMPUS BOX, ELON, NC 27244-2010 • ADMISSIONS: 336-278-3566 • FAX: 336-278-7699

CAMPUS LIFE

Quality of Life Rating	85
Fire Safety Rating	79
Green Rating	94
Type of school	private
Affiliation	United Church of Christ
Environment	town

STUDENTS

Total undergrad enrollment	4,939
% male/female	41/59
% from out of state	72
% from public high school	78
% live on campus	58
% in (# of) fraternities	24 (11)
% in (# of) sororities	42 (12)
% African American	6
% Asian	1
% Caucasian	83
% Hispanic	2
% international	2
# of countries represented	45

SURVEY SAYS . . .
Small classes
Lab facilities are great
Great computer facilities
Great library
Frats and sororities dominate
social scene
Lots of beer drinking

ACADEMICS

Academic Rating	86
Calendar	4/1/4
Student/faculty ratio	14:1
Profs interesting rating	85
Profs accessible rating	89
Most common reg class size	10–19 students
Most common lab size	10–19 students

MOST POPULAR MAJORS
education
business/commerce
communication studies/speech
communication and rhetoric

STUDENTS SAY ". . ."

Academics

Elon University, a "small, preppy, somewhat conservative, highly academic private school" in central North Carolina, is "all about teaching you about your role as a global citizen and enabling you to do experiential learning, not only through discussion-based classes but also through opportunities to study abroad, undergrad research, internships, and involvement in a variety of student organizations." With about 4,950 undergraduates, Elon is "just the right size. It's not too small where everyone knows everyone, but small enough to still get the small-school attributes." At the same time, it's large enough to sustain excellence in a variety of disciplines, including business, communications, a "prestigious but extremely competitive music theater program," an "excellent Teaching Fellows program," and a premed program that's bolstered by an undergraduate cadaver lab—one of only five in the United States. Undergrads tell us that "you can choose how hard you want to work at Elon. One can get away with doing the bare minimum, but those who work hard will get more out of their experience as a whole." It's a plus that "teachers want to see students excel and are, for the most part, very supportive." Study abroad opportunities here are "phenomenal. They are easily arranged and add much to the college experience." One student notes, "I will have studied abroad three times (Peru, Namibia, and Australia) before graduating."

Life

The town of Elon is "a small town that has everything you need: a movie theater, bowling alley, and every food chain, as well as plenty of restaurants and pizza places." If you have no car, though, it can "feel like it's in the middle of nowhere." Access to an automobile opens many options, allowing students to "hit the highway and head to Greensboro, Raleigh, Durham, or Chapel Hill," all reasonably lively places. Even those who are campus bound still have plenty of options. One student explains, "Since Elon is not really a commuter school and there is not a great deal to do in the town itself, getting involved in organizations is really important. Many people commit themselves to a number of the over 150 campus organizations." Undergrads also enjoy a "gorgeous," meticulously maintained campus. "Elon's groundskeeping staff has to be among the best in the nation," offers one student. "If you go outside at 6:30 A.M., there is an army dedicated to lawn care!" Community is strong at this school, with Greek life being "a very big thing at Elon. [Many] of us are or have been in a sorority or fraternity." Another large part of Elon is "Elon Volunteers, the collection of Elon's service programs, organizations, and events." Intercollegiate athletics, in contrast, are neglected, since "Everyone knows our teams are most likely going to get beaten," although a winning men's basketball season has helped disprove that. Socially speaking, Elon has a hopping party scene, but though "most people party on the weekends, the library is packed on Sunday afternoons."

Student Body

"Attending Elon is a lot like attending a country club," students tell us, observing that "your typical Elon girl is clad in Vera Bradley and her Greek letters (don't forget the popped collar underneath [her] letter shirt!), and dresses to the max whether it's an 8:00 A.M. class or it's 2:00 A.M. in the library. For the typical Elon boy, it's a polo and shaggy hair. That says it all." There's more to students on this campus than surface appearances, though; as one explains, "The more time you spend here, the more you get to see how diverse the student population really is. Upon a deeper glance, one will find your atypical groups such as the Army ROTC cadets, the theater people, the musicians, and the socialites. The atypical students fit in pretty well but aren't that well advertised." Also, "There are so many students involved in so many cool things, and they're very passionate about what they're doing. Many people are involved in service work and are specifically passionate about eradicating AIDS."

FINANCIAL AID: 800-334-8448 • E-MAIL: ADMISSIONS@ELON.EDU • WEBSITE: WWW.ELON.EDU

THE PRINCETON REVIEW SAYS

Admissions

Very important factors considered include: Academic GPA, rigor of secondary school record, standardized test scores. *Important factors considered include:* Application essay, recommendation(s), alumni/ae relation, extracurricular activities, talent/ability. *Other factors considered include:* Class rank, character/personal qualities, first generation, geographical residence, level of applicant's interest, racial/ethnic status, state residency, volunteer work, work experience. SAT or ACT required; ACT with Writing component required. TOEFL required of all international applicants. High school diploma is required and GED is accepted. *Academic units required:* 4 English, 3 mathematics, 3 science, (1 science labs), 2 foreign language, 3 social studies (U.S. History). *Academic units recommended:* 4 mathematics, 3 foreign language.

Financial Aid

Students should submit: FAFSA, institution's own financial aid form, CSS/Financial Aid PROFILE. The Princeton Review suggests that all financial aid forms be submitted as soon as possible after January 1. *Need-based scholarships/grants offered:* Federal Pell, SEOG, state scholarships/grants, private scholarships, the school's own gift aid. *Loan aid offered:* FFEL Subsidized Stafford, FFEL Unsubsidized Stafford, FFEL PLUS, Federal Perkins, state loans, Privately funded alternative loans. Applicants will be notified of awards on a rolling basis beginning 3/30. Federal Work-Study Program available. Institutional employment available. Off-campus job opportunities are good.

The Inside Word

Admissions standards at Elon are fairly straightforward—solid grades and strong test scores make for a very competitive candidate. Leadership is a valued attribute and demonstrating an active role in extracurriculars augments one's application. Students who find themselves with an acceptance letter will discover a school with abundant internship and study abroad opportunities.

THE SCHOOL SAYS "..."

From The Admissions Office

"Elon offers the comprehensive resources of a university in a close-knit community atmosphere. The university's 4,939 undergraduates choose from 50 majors in the arts and sciences, business, communications and education. Graduate programs in business administration, law, education and physical therapy are also offered. The National Survey of Student Engagement recognizes Elon as one of the nation's most effective universities in promoting hands-on learning experiences. Academic and co-curricular activities are seamlessly blended, especially in the Elon Experiences: study abroad, internships, service, leadership and undergraduate research. Participation is among the highest in the nation. Seventy-three percent of graduating seniors have studied abroad, 80 percent have internship experiences and 91 percent have volunteered in the community. Elon's 4-1-4 academic calendar allows students to devote January to international study or immerse themselves in innovative on-campus courses. Elon's historic and beautiful 575-acre campus has been recognized as one of the most beautiful in the country. New additions include the $10-million Ernest A. Koury Sr. Business Center, featuring a digital theater and finance trading room, The Oaks, a 500-bed residence complex and The Colonnades Dining Hall, a two-story, 24,000-square-foot dining facility that includes a full-service restaurant, an organic market and deli and a fire stone oven for pizzas and bread. Elon's NCAA Division I Phoenix athletics programs compete in the Southern Conference.

"Freshman applicants for Fall 2009 are required to take the SAT (or the ACT with the writing section). The student?s best critical reading, math and writing scores from either test will be used."

SELECTIVITY
Admissions Rating	92
# of applicants	9,380
% of applicants accepted	41
% of acceptees attending	33
# accepting a place on wait list	1,211
% admitted from wait list	3
# of early decision applicants	452
% accepted early decision	69

FRESHMAN PROFILE
Range SAT Critical Reading	560–650
Range SAT Math	570–660
Range SAT Writing	560–660
Range ACT Composite	24–28
Minimum paper TOEFL	550
Minimum computer TOEFL	213
Minimum web-based TOEFL	79
Average HS GPA	3.95
% graduated top 10% of class	29
% graduated top 25% of class	66
% graduated top 50% of class	93

DEADLINES
Early decision	
Deadline	11/1
Notification	12/1
Early action	
Deadline	11/10
Notification	12/20
Regular	
Priority	11/1
Deadline	1/10
Notification	12/20
Nonfall registration?	no

APPLICANTS ALSO LOOK AT
AND OFTEN PREFER
University of North Carolina at Chapel Hill
AND SOMETIMES PREFER
Wake Forest University

FINANCIAL FACTS
Financial Aid Rating	84
Annual tuition	$21,886
Room and board	$7,296
Required fees	$280
Books and supplies	$900
% frosh rec. need-based scholarship or grant aid	28
% UG rec. need-based scholarship or grant aid	29
% frosh rec. non-need-based scholarship or grant aid	5
% UG rec. non-need-based scholarship or grant aid	3
% frosh rec. need-based self-help aid	25
% UG rec. need-based self-help aid	27
% frosh rec. athletic scholarships	7
% UG rec. athletic scholarships	6
% frosh rec. any financial aid	73
% UG rec. any financial aid	68
% UG borrow to pay for school	41
Average cumulative indebtedness	$21,268

EMERSON COLLEGE

120 BOYLSTON STREET, BOSTON, MA 02116-4624 • ADMISSIONS: 617-824-8600 • FAX: 617-824-8609

STUDENTS SAY ". . ."

Academics

God help the future Wall Streeter who somehow finds themselves a member of the student body at Emerson, a big happy group of "creative people" who come together to share their passions ("whether it be on the stage, the page, the big screen or the small") and learn more about their own mediums of self-expressions via collaboration with diverse individuals. The focus on the more creative side of communication and the arts feeds on itself, providing "a community that (usually) understands what an artist needs to thrive and grow." "People come to Emerson knowing exactly what they want to do, and then do that thing all out for four years," says a sophomore. According to its students, Emerson "brings creativity and ingenuity to the arts and communication unlike any other school in the country," and although those that attend the school are more than aware that most of their fellow students might be "part of the next generation of America's starving artists (unless you're a marketing or CSD major)," the school does a tremendous job of offering each a "specialized career-oriented experience," no matter how non-traditional the career path.

The excellent student-teacher ratio means personal attention that goes beyond just office hours, which translates into a lot of time spent with people that are "practicing professionals in their respective fields." The largest classroom at Emerson can only accommodate about 70 students, so lectures (if a student even has any) "are only about 50 students large," and one must "be prepared to do most of your learning outside of the classroom in projects." Design and technology majors in particular get a good deal of hands-on experience. While there can be "a little too much red tape around some of the administrative aspects of Emerson," one student claims that "there is no other school I have encountered where one would feel more easily acknowledged and listened to by their professors."

Life

The drive to succeed in such competitive industries means "a majority of students are busier than the average professional" and "don't really sleep," which is not surprising, considering all of the rehearsals, film shoots, concerts, and organization meetings seemingly required of Emerson life. The school is located right in the heart of downtown Boston, and many admit that it can be hard to concentrate with Boston Common right across the street and the realization that "you live in a city, not a campus bubble." After sophomore year "most people live off-campus," which is where most parties are also hosted; although there's a fair share of partying for those that are interested, "students are more inclined to have an 80s costume and dance party than a frat bash." For those that resist the lure of the cafés, theaters, bars, and performances, plain old-fashioned silliness in the dorms seems equally as exciting, "like coloring or old video games or children's books—everyone just wants to have fun."

Student Body

Around Boston, "an Emerson student can be spotted from a mile away," not because they all look alike, but because they all look so different (although "if you wanted to peg Emerson students as the artsy young adults with an offbeat fashion forward style and a cigarette in one hand and Starbucks in the other, it wouldn't be horribly inaccurate"). Almost all students find a common thread in a love of the arts, which often results in a unifying ambition amongst "people wanting to 'make it' in their field." One film student remarks that Emerson is filled with what she refers to as "my 'type' of people." This "friendly, eclectic and fun" group of students leans pretty far to the left politically, and there is a large gay community at Emerson. There seems to be one student in every class that "can be pretentious and annoying," but these souls are in the minority. Overall, Emersonians are a "very accepting community" of driven individuals.

FINANCIAL AID: 617-824-8655 • E-MAIL: ADMISSION@EMERSON.EDU • WEBSITE: WWW.EMERSON.EDU

THE PRINCETON REVIEW SAYS

Admissions

Very important factors considered include: Academic GPA, standardized test scores. *Important factors considered include:* Class rank, application essay, recommendation(s), rigor of secondary school record, character/personal qualities, extracurricular activities, talent/ability. *Other factors considered include:* Alumni/ae relation, first generation, geographical residence, racial/ethnic status, volunteer work, work experience. SAT or ACT required; ACT with Writing component required. TOEFL required of all international applicants. High school diploma is required and GED is accepted. *Academic units required:* 4 English, 3 mathematics, 3 science, 3 foreign language, 3 social studies. *Academic units recommended:* 4 English, 3 mathematics, 3 science, 3 foreign language, 3 social studies, 4 academic electives.

Financial Aid

Students should submit: FAFSA, CSS/Financial Aid PROFILE, noncustodial PROFILE, business/farm supplement, tax Returns, non-custodial statement. The Princeton Review suggests that all financial aid forms be submitted as soon as possible after January 1. *Need-based scholarships/grants offered:* Federal Pell, SEOG, state scholarships/grants, private scholarships, the school's own gift aid. *Loan aid offered:* FFEL Subsidized Stafford, FFEL Unsubsidized Stafford, FFEL PLUS, Federal Perkins, state loans Applicants will be notified of awards on or about 4/1. Federal Work-Study Program available. Institutional employment available. Off-campus job opportunities are excellent.

The Inside Word

Expect your living situation to be made easier by recent developments on Emerson's campus. The Max Mutchnick Campus Center, named in recognition of the substantial gift made by the Emerson alumnus and co-creator/executive producer of *Will & Grace*, is an 185,000-square-foot building that features a gym, offices, and residence hall. This facility, combined with the recent acquisition of the Colonial Theatre (which will also feature dorm rooms), means nearly three quarters of the students will be able to live on-campus and indulge in affordable rent.

THE SCHOOL SAYS "..."

From The Admissions Office

"Founded in 1880, Emerson is one of the premier colleges in the United States for communication and the arts. Students may choose from more than two-dozen undergraduate and graduate programs supported by state-of-the-art facilities and a nationally renowned faculty. The campus is home to WERS-FM, the first noncommercial station in Boston; the historic 1,200-seat Cutler Majestic Theatre; and Ploughshares, the award-winning literary journal for new writing.

"Located on Boston Common in the heart of the city's Theatre District, Emerson is walking distance from the Massachusetts State House, Chinatown, and historic Freedom Trail. 1,300 students reside on-campus, some in special learning communities such as the Writers' Block and Digital Culture Floor. There is also a fitness center, athletic field, and new gymnasium and campus center.

"Emerson's 3,000 undergraduates come from across the United States and 50 countries. There are more than 60 student organizations and performance groups, 15 NCAA teams, student publications, and honor societies. The College also sponsors programs in Los Angeles; study abroad in the Netherlands, Taiwan, and Czech Republic; and cross-registration with the six-member Boston ProArts Consortium.

"Emerson has the highest quality visual and media arts equipment, including sound-treated television studios, digital editing labs, audio post-production suites with analog and digital peripherals, and a professional marketing suite/focus group room. There are seven on-campus programs to observe speech and hearing therapy, an integrated digital newsroom for aspiring journalists, and an 11-story performance and production center housing rehearsal space, a theatre design/technology center, makeup lab, and costume shop."

SELECTIVITY

Admissions Rating	92
# of applicants	4,981
% of applicants accepted	45
% of acceptees attending	38
# accepting a place on wait list	281
% admitted from wait list	1

FRESHMAN PROFILE

Range SAT Critical Reading	590–680
Range SAT Math	550–650
Range SAT Writing	580–670
Range ACT Composite	25–29
Minimum paper TOEFL	550
Minimum computer TOEFL	213
Minimum web-based TOEFL	80
Average HS GPA	3.62
% graduated top 10% of class	42.4
% graduated top 25% of class	78.6
% graduated top 50% of class	98.3

DEADLINES

Early action	
Deadline	11/1
Notification	12/15
Regular	
Deadline	1/5
Notification	4/1
Nonfall registration?	yes

APPLICANTS ALSO LOOK AT

AND OFTEN PREFER
New York University

AND SOMETIMES PREFER
University of Southern California
Ithaca College

AND RARELY PREFER
Boston University
Syracuse University

FINANCIAL FACTS

Financial Aid Rating	83
Annual tuition	$28,352
Room and board	$11,832
Required fees	$522
Books and supplies	$720
% frosh rec. need-based scholarship or grant aid	44
% UG rec. need-based scholarship or grant aid	40
% frosh rec. non-need-based scholarship or grant aid	8
% UG rec. non-need-based scholarship or grant aid	6
% frosh rec. need-based self-help aid	51
% UG rec. need-based self-help aid	48
% frosh rec. any financial aid	73.3
% UG rec. any financial aid	64.4

EMORY UNIVERSITY

BOISFEUILLET JONES CENTER, ATLANTA, GA 30322 • ADMISSIONS: 404-727-6036 • FAX: 404-727-4303

STUDENTS SAY " . . ."

Academics

Emory University, "a Northern school in the South," is a "school on the rise." It boasts "amazing academic resources" and tremendous "post-graduation employment opportunities," which makes it a strong choice for students who see their educations more as "a step on the way to a professional career" than the acquisition of knowledge for its own sake. Many career opportunities arrive via the school's "strong ties to the CDC [Centers for Disease Control and Prevention], the Carter Center, and Coca Cola as well as the 700 Fortune 1000 companies with offices in Atlanta." Emory's strong undergraduate business program and "great medical school" are big draws, and research-intensive disciplines benefit from "access to state-of-the-art equipment." While there is a sense that "some professors are here for only research," students generally agree that "professors are top-notch and approachable," noting in particular that "those in smaller departments are great! Those in larger departments have less time for students," and many "are less willing to go out of their way to make sure students understand material and are getting something out of the class." Emory's general education requirements earn some complaints, with students telling us that the requirements are "meant to give students a wide base of knowledge," but often "become more a chore than a learning experience." Even so, students here tell us: "On the whole, you leave classes thinking much more than you did when you entered, and class is almost always worthwhile to attend. Many professors place a great emphasis on theoretical application, making the material come alive."

Life

"Emory is interesting because there is a lack of school spirit," but "There is an abundance of support on campus for different activities. Almost everyone participates in some activity. Many people volunteer in some way or another or are extraordinarily active on campus." Greek life is huge at Emory; while "only one-third of the population" is involved, "It feels much stronger than it actually is in numbers. This is because students in Greek life tend to be community leaders." When it's party time, "People basically act like regular college kids: They drink, go out to bars or clubs, or [attend] Greek functions." Freshmen and sophomores are more likely to hang close to campus, while upperclassmen are more likely to explore Atlanta. Students tell us that "life at Emory is tricky," because "while there are a wealth of dining, culture, and sports opportunities [in Atlanta], they must all be commuted to, which spells one thing: High taxi bills, unless you have a car." Popular destinations include Midtown, Virginia Highlands, Toco Hills, Buckhead, and Decatur.

Student Body

Though many people look at Emory as a predominately Jewish school, (about one-third of Emory undergraduates are Jewish) students point out that Jewish students "are definitely not the only type of student here, and everyone has their own niche. Emory is truly diverse." This diversity includes students from "every" "socioeconomic background" and "all over the world." A sophomore boasts that she has friends "from Chad, Senegal, and South Korea, in addition to friends from all over the country." The affluent are definitely well represented here, "giving everyone a slightly skewed world view that tends to overemphasize materialism," but within that context "Everyone is fairly cordial and approachable, and no one is looking to undercut you when you are competing over grades—in that respect, it is a very collegial environment." Some here detect "a split between the wealthier students and those who aren't."

FINANCIAL AID: 800-727-6039 • E-MAIL: ADMISS@EMORY.EDU • WEBSITE: WWW.EMORY.EDU

THE PRINCETON REVIEW SAYS

Admissions

Very important factors considered include: Application essay, academic GPA, recommendation(s), rigor of secondary school record, standardized test scores, extracurricular activities. *Important factors considered include:* Character/personal qualities, level of applicant's interest, talent/ability. *Other factors considered include:* Class rank, alumni/ae relation, first generation, geographical residence, racial/ethnic status, state residency, volunteer work, work experience. SAT or ACT required; ACT with Writing component required. TOEFL required of all international applicants. High school diploma is required and GED is not accepted. *Academic units required:* 4 English, 3 mathematics, 2 science, (2 science labs), 2 foreign language, 2 social studies, 2 history, 1 visual/performing arts, 2 academic electives. *Academic units recommended:* 4 mathematics, 3 science, 3 foreign language.

Financial Aid

Students should submit: FAFSA, CSS/Financial Aid PROFILE, noncustodial PROFILE if parents are divorced or separated. In addition prior year (2008) US Income tax returns are required from the student the parents and the noncustodial parent if applicable. Priority filing deadline is 3/1. The Princeton Review suggests that all financial aid forms be submitted as soon as possible after January 1. *Need-based scholarships/grants offered:* Federal Pell, SEOG, state scholarships/grants, private scholarships, the school's own gift aid. *Loan aid offered:* FFEL Subsidized Stafford, FFEL Unsubsidized Stafford, FFEL PLUS, Federal Perkins, Federal Nursing, state loans, college/university loans from institutional funds. Applicants will be notified of awards beginning 4/1.

The Inside Word

In 2006, early decision applications to Emory rose nearly 20 percent over the previous year, creating a quandary for aspiring Emory students: Do they join the growing crowd of early applicants and presumably increase the likelihood of admission, or do they take their chances with the regular admission date? Locking into one school early in the process can be a blessing or a curse; what if the aid package (which doesn't arrive until mid-April) isn't sufficient? Here's the good news: Emory financial aid has traditionally met 100 percent of applicants' demonstrated need.

THE SCHOOL SAYS "..."

From The Admissions Office

"As a destination for path-breaking researchers, renowned teachers, superb students, and dedicated staff, Emory University strives to help its community members fulfill their highest aspirations. Our vision is to discover truth, share it, and ignite in others a passion for its pursuit. The newly adopted Emory Strategic Plan provides a map to guide our growth and development over the next decade, focusing on strengthening faculty distinction, preparing engaged scholars, creating community, confronting the human condition and experience, and exploring new frontiers in science and technology. Similarly, our revised Campus Master Plan outlines a bold proposal for reshaping Emory's presence in Atlanta. Critical to that presence are programs in the arts, university-community partnerships, and the global reach of our initiatives through such Emory entities as the Carter Center.

"Emory remains more than the sum of its parts—a strong intellectual community that seeks excellence, not to compete with other institutions, but to contribute to the shaping of a better world.

"All applicants are required to submit scores from the SAT or the ACT. For those students applying for the 2008–2009 school year, Emory will require one of the following: the old SAT (without Writing), the ACT (without Writing), the new SAT (which includes a Writing section), or the ACT with Writing."

SELECTIVITY
Admissions Rating	98
# of applicants	15,366
% of applicants accepted	27
% of acceptees attending	30
# accepting a place on wait list	800
% admitted from wait list	14
# of early decision applicants	1,577
% accepted early decision	31

FRESHMAN PROFILE
Range SAT Critical Reading	640–730
Range SAT Math	660–740
Range SAT Writing	640–730
Range ACT Composite	29–33
Minimum paper TOEFL	600
Minimum computer TOEFL	250
Average HS GPA	3.8
% graduated top 10% of class	88
% graduated top 25% of class	95
% graduated top 50% of class	100

DEADLINES
Early decision	
Deadline	11/1
Notification	12/15
Regular	
Deadline	1/15
Notification	4/1
Nonfall registration?	no

FINANCIAL FACTS
Financial Aid Rating	92
Annual tuition	$35,800
Room and board	$10,572
Required fees	$536
Books and supplies	$1,000
% frosh rec. need-based scholarship or grant aid	34
% UG rec. need-based scholarship or grant aid	36
% frosh rec. non-need-based scholarship or grant aid	14
% UG rec. non-need-based scholarship or grant aid	17
% frosh rec. need-based self-help aid	30
% UG rec. need-based self-help aid	33
% frosh rec. any financial aid	61
% UG rec. any financial aid	60
% UG borrow to pay for school	41
Average cumulative indebtedness	$23,374

65 WEST ELEVENTH STREET, OFFICE OF ADMISSION, NEW YORK, NY 10011 • ADMISSIONS: 212-229-5665 • FAX: 212-229-5166

CAMPUS LIFE

Quality of Life Rating	71
Fire Safety Rating	60*
Green Rating	60*
Type of school	private
Environment	metropolis

STUDENTS

Total undergrad enrollment	1,294
% male/female	31/69
% from out of state	68
% live on campus	27
% African American	4
% Asian	5
% Caucasian	61
% Hispanic	6
% Native American	1
% international	3
# of countries represented	36

SURVEY SAYS . . .

Class discussions encouraged
Athletic facilities need improving
Students aren't religious
Students love New York, NY
Great off-campus food
Intercollegiate sports are unpopular
or nonexistent
Intramural sports are unpopular or
nonexistent
Frats and sororities are unpopular
or nonexistent
(Almost) everyone smokes

ACADEMICS

Academic Rating	86
Calendar	semester
Student/faculty ratio	15:1
Profs interesting rating	81
Profs accessible rating	78
Most common reg class size	10–19 students
Most common lab size	20–29 students

STUDENTS SAY ". . ."

Academics

Eugene Lang College is an "unconventional," highly urban school with few academic requirements where courses have "really long poetic titles" and professors "go by their first names." "Lang is about small classes in a big city," summarizes a writing major. There's a "rich intellectual tradition" here and, no matter what your major, an "interdisciplinary curriculum." "At Eugene Lang, you have the freedom to pursue your artistic or intellectual direction with absolute freedom," says a philosophy major. However, "students who are uncomfortable in a city and who are not excited about learning for learning's sake should not come to this school." Lang's "clueless," "incredibly bureaucratic" administration is hugely unpopular. The "approachable" and monolithically "radical" faculty is a mixed bag. "75 percent of the professors are pure gold, but the 25 percent who are not really are awful." "Lang's greatest strength (other than location) is its seminar style of teaching," explains a first-year student. "I've yet to be in a class with more then 15 people." Students say their class discussions are phenomenal. "The students, however, at times can be somewhat draining." "All the teachers are highly susceptible to being led off on long tangents" and some "are too gentle and not comfortable shutting down wandering or irrelevant conversation." Juniors and seniors can take classes at several schools within the larger university (including Parsons The New School for Design and Mannes College The New School for Music). "So if Lang's ultra-liberal, writing-intensive seminars are too much," notes an urban studies major, "you can always take a break." Internships all over Manhattan are common, too.

Life

There are "great talks given on campus every week by a wide variety of academics on almost every social issue imaginable." Otherwise, "Lang is the anti-college experience." "There is very little community" on this speck of a campus on the northern end of Greenwich Village. "Space and facilities are limited." "There is no safe haven in the form of a communal student space" except for "a courtyard of a million cigarette butts." Certainly, "you aren't going to have the traditional college fun" here. On the other hand, few students anywhere else enjoy this glorious level of independence. "Life at Eugene Lang is integrated completely with living in New York City," and "you have the entire city at your fingertips." When you walk out of class, "you walk out into a city of nine million people." There are dorms here but "most students have apartments," especially after freshman year. For fun, Lang students sometimes "hang around other students' apartments and smoke pot." Many "thoroughly enjoy the club scene." Mostly though, "people band into small groups and then go out adventuring in the city" where "there is always something to do that you've never done, or even heard of, before."

Student Body

"Lang offers the kids with dreadlocks and piercings an alternative place to gather, smoke, and write pretentious essays." It's "overrun with rabid hipsters." "Cool hair" and "avant-garde" attitudes proliferate. So do "tight pants." "Every student at Lang thinks they are an atypical student." "There is a running joke that all Lang students were 'that kid' in high school," says a senior. "Shock is very popular around here," and "everyone fits in as long as they are not too mainstream." "It's the normal ones who have the trouble," suggests a sophomore. "But once they take up smoking and embrace their inner hipster, everything's cool." "There are a lot of queer students, who seem to be comfortable." "We're really not all that ethnically diverse," admits a first-year student. There are "less affluent kids due to great financial aid," and there is a strong contingent of "trust fund babies" and "over-privileged communists from Connecticut." "Most students are wealthy but won't admit it," says a senior. "To be from a rich family and have it be apparent is a cardinal sin." "Most students are extremely liberal and on the same wavelength politically." "Conservative kids are the freaks at our school. Left is in. But having a Republican in class is so exciting," suggest a senior. "We can finally have a debate."

FINANCIAL AID: 212-229-8930 • E-MAIL: LANG@NEWSCHOOL.EDU • WEBSITE: WWW.LANG.EDU

THE PRINCETON REVIEW SAYS

Admissions

Very important factors considered include: Application essay, academic GPA, recommendation(s), rigor of secondary school record. *Important factors considered include:* Standardized test scores, character/personal qualities, interview, level of applicant's interest, volunteer work. *Other factors considered include:* Class rank, alumni/ae relation, extracurricular activities, first generation, geographical residence, work experience. SAT or ACT required; TOEFL required of all international applicants. High school diploma is required and GED is accepted. *Academic units required:* 4 English. *Academic units recommended:* 3 mathematics, 3 science, 2 foreign language, 3 social studies, 2 history.

Financial Aid

Students should submit: FAFSA, state aid form. The Princeton Review suggests that all financial aid forms be submitted as soon as possible after January 1. *Need-based scholarships/grants offered:* Federal Pell, SEOG, state scholarships/grants, private scholarships, the school's own gift aid. *Loan aid offered:* FFEL Subsidized Stafford, FFEL Unsubsidized Stafford, Federal Perkins, college/university loans from institutional funds. Applicants will be notified of awards on a rolling basis beginning 3/1. Federal Work-Study Program available. Institutional employment available.

The Inside Word

The college draws a very self-selected and intellectually curious pool. Those who demonstrate little self-motivation will find themselves denied. It would be a terrible idea to blow off the interview here.

THE SCHOOL SAYS "..."

From The Admissions Office

"Eugene Lang College offers students of diverse backgrounds an innovative and creative approach to a liberal arts education, combining the stimulating classroom activity of a small, intimate college with the rich resources of a dynamic, urban university—The New School. The curriculum at Lang is challenging and flexible. Small classes, limited in size to 18 students, promote energetic and thoughtful discussions, and writing is an essential component of all classes. Students can earn a bachelor's degree in Liberal Arts by designing their own program of study within one of 14 interdisciplinary areas in the arts, social sciences, and humanities. Lang also offers bachelor's degrees in the Arts (pending New York State approval), Culture and Media, Economics, Education Studies, Environmental Studies (pending New York State approval), History (pending New York State approval), Philosophy, and Psychology. Students have the opportunity to pursue a five year BA/BFA or BA/MA with other programs offered at the university. Lang's Greenwich Village location puts many of city's cultural treasures—museums, libraries, music venues, theaters, and more—at your doorstep."

SELECTIVITY

Admissions Rating	85
# of applicants	1,670
% of applicants accepted	63
% of acceptees attending	30
# accepting a place on wait list	39
% admitted from wait list	18

FRESHMAN PROFILE

Range SAT Critical Reading	555–665
Range SAT Math	490–610
Range SAT Writing	560–660
Range ACT Composite	23–28
Minimum paper TOEFL	600
Minimum computer TOEFL	250
Minimum web-based TOEFL	100
Average HS GPA	3.19

DEADLINES

Early decision	
Deadline	11/15
Notification	12/15
Regular	
Deadline	2/1
Notification	rolling
Nonfall registration?	yes

APPLICANTS ALSO LOOK AT

AND OFTEN PREFER
New York University
Bard College
Sarah Lawrence College

AND SOMETIMES PREFER
Hampshire College
Reed College

AND RARELY PREFER
St. John's College (MD)
Bennington College

FINANCIAL FACTS

Financial Aid Rating	75
Annual tuition	$30,660
Room and board	$11,750
Required fees	$650
Books and supplies	$2,050
% frosh rec. need-based scholarship or grant aid	50
% UG rec. need-based scholarship or grant aid	49
% frosh rec. non-need-based scholarship or grant aid	18
% UG rec. non-need-based scholarship or grant aid	16
% frosh rec. need-based self-help aid	51
% UG rec. need-based self-help aid	50
% UG borrow to pay for school	76
Average cumulative indebtedness	$16,414

THE EVERGREEN STATE COLLEGE

2700 EVERGREEN PARKWAY, NORTHWEST, OFFICE OF ADMISSIONS, OLYMPIA, WA 98505 • ADMISSIONS: 360-867-6170 • FAX: 360-867-5114

CAMPUS LIFE
Quality of Life Rating	**75**
Fire Safety Rating	**60***
Green Rating	**98**
Type of school	public
Environment	city

STUDENTS
Total undergrad enrollment	4,282
% male/female	44/56
% from out of state	24
% live on campus	22
% African American	4
% Asian	5
% Caucasian	69
% Hispanic	5
% Native American	4
# of countries represented	11

SURVEY SAYS . . .
Lots of liberal students
Small classes
Students are happy
Frats and sororities are unpopular
or nonexistent

ACADEMICS
Academic Rating	**76**
Calendar	quarter
Student/faculty ratio	23:1
Profs interesting rating	86
Profs accessible rating	74
Most common	
reg class size	20–29 students

STUDENTS SAY ". . ."

Academics

The Evergreen State College "is about being in charge of your own education, and not being force-fed what others think you should know." That's because under TESC's "alternative education format" students enroll each quarter in a single program "with various areas of study emphasized rather than in a group of individual classes. You typically take one program for two quarters with the same students and faculty, exploring complexities of the issue of study and new ideas. Students always have a voice and decide on field trips, readings, and lecture topics." TESC undergrads are also encouraged to design their own independent or group studies, an option one student describes as "very rewarding, since you are given much choice and opportunity to make your mark." Another undergrad observes, "You can do almost anything for credit here if you're willing to wade through the red tape. If you have something unconventional or cross-disciplinary in mind for a career, this is the place to be. I want to design computers and digital aides for people with disabilities. There's really no place to do that undergrad but here, where there's the freedom to mix up the art and the computer stuff." Experiential learning—i.e., "learning through doing"—is well integrated into the TESC curriculum through "the many internships with local organizations" that students undertake. TESC undergrads don't receive grades. Rather, professors write narrative evaluations of each student's work (students' evaluations of their own work also becomes part of their academic records).

Life

"People spend a lot of time on homework" at TESC, although "Most may not say so because we don't really have worksheets, quizzes, or . . . reading (I say this as a transfer from a more traditionally 'prestigious' liberal arts college). The Evergreen life is a full-time experience." In their spare time, students like to "hang at local coffee shops, play Frisbee and soccer on the lawn, watch movies, go see live music, the usual stuff." The options for outdoor activity are myriad, with "rainforests, volcanoes, the ocean, dozens of rivers and lakes as well as two unique major cities (Portland and Seattle) within a 2-hour drive." Hometown Olympia "is a great place to live, with the culture of a town twice its size. There are great little shops downtown, and the city has a quaint atmosphere. Not only that, but the Olympia Transit Center links to nearly every bus you need to get through and out of Olympia. It's not hard to see why Greeners tend to settle here."

Student Body

"The hippie stereotype persists" at the Evergreen State College, but they are by far "fairly normal college students: studying, partying occasionally, and experimenting with different styles and points of view." True, "There seem to be more vegetarian, vegan, and health-conscious students at Evergreen" and the 'normal' TESC student "may be atypical elsewhere; when something offbeat or out of the norm happens, we just shrug our shoulders and say, 'Well, that's Evergreen!'" Still, the population runs the gamut from "neurotically brilliant grandmothers to Army veterans to 16-year-old geniuses to queer forestry students to mildly syndicated cartoonists." TESC also "has its fair share of opportunists. The school's reputation, decidedly unearned, is that of a slacker school. That means that some excellent fakers will come to school and dream of partying. They're not bad people. They just didn't realize what they were getting into. I really don't know what happens to these folks; I hope they quietly disappear and find a path that's better for them."

FINANCIAL AID: 360-867-6205 • E-MAIL: ADMISSIONS@EVERGREEN.EDU • WEBSITE: WWW.EVERGREEN.EDU

THE PRINCETON REVIEW SAYS

Admissions

Very important factors considered include: Application essay, academic GPA, rigor of secondary school record. *Important factors considered include:* Standardized test scores, first generation, level of applicant's interest. *Other factors considered include:* Class rank, recommendation(s), extracurricular activities, interview, volunteer work, work experience. SAT or ACT required; TOEFL required of all international applicants. High school diploma is required and GED is accepted. *Academic units required:* 4 English, 3 mathematics, 2 science, (1 science labs), 2 foreign language, 3 social studies, 1 academic elective, 1 Fine, visual or performing arts elective or other college prep elective from the areas above.

Financial Aid

Students should submit: FAFSA, institution's own financial aid form. The Princeton Review suggests that all financial aid forms be submitted as soon as possible after January 1. *Need-based scholarships/grants offered:* Federal Pell, SEOG, state scholarships/grants, private scholarships, the school's own gift aid. *Loan aid offered:* FFEL Subsidized Stafford, FFEL Unsubsidized Stafford, FFEL PLUS, Federal Perkins, Private Alternative Loans. Applicants will be notified of awards on a rolling basis beginning 4/15. Federal Work-Study Program available. Institutional employment available. Off-campus job opportunities are good.

The Inside Word

Evergreen places a lot of credence in character and personal qualities when making admissions decisions. The school's atypical academic program calls for a curious and independent spirit, and Admissions Officers want to ensure that applicants will have the maturity to direct their own educational development.

THE SCHOOL SAYS "..."

From The Admissions Office

"Evergreen, a public college of arts and sciences, is a national leader in developing full-time interdisciplinary studies programs. Students work closely with faculty (there are no teaching assistants) to study an issue or theme from the perspective of several academic disciplines. They apply what's learned to real world issues, complete projects in groups, and discuss concepts in seminars that typically involve a faculty member and 22 students. The emphasis on seminars, interdisciplinary problem solving, and collaboration means students are well prepared for graduate school and the world of work. Our students tend to be politically active, environmentally savvy, and more concerned about social justice than competition and personal gain.

"All applicants are encouraged to complete a Free Application for Federal Student Aid (FAFSA). Evergreen's priority financial aid deadline is March 15, though applicants may submit the form later and may be awarded aid if funds are still available.

"Freshman applicants for Fall 2008 are required to submit test scores from either the SAT or ACT tests. Scores submitted from the old (prior to March 2005) SAT will be accepted. The student's best composite score will be used in the admission process."

SELECTIVITY

Admissions Rating	72
# of applicants	1,806
% of applicants accepted	97
% of acceptees attending	39

FRESHMAN PROFILE

Range SAT Critical Reading	520–640
Range SAT Math	460–590
Range ACT Composite	21–26
Minimum paper TOEFL	550
Minimum computer TOEFL	213
Minimum web-based TOEFL	79
Average HS GPA	3.06
% graduated top 10% of class	10
% graduated top 25% of class	29
% graduated top 50% of class	64

DEADLINES

Priority	3/1
Notification	rolling
Nonfall registration?	yes

APPLICANTS ALSO LOOK AT
AND OFTEN PREFER
Lewis-Clark State College
Western Washington University
University of Washington
AND RARELY PREFER
Saint Martin's University
Warren Wilson College
Eastern Washington University
Lewis & Clark College
Earlham College
Southern Oregon University
University of Vermont

FINANCIAL FACTS

Financial Aid Rating	72
Annual in-state tuition	$4,797
% frosh rec. need-based scholarship or grant aid	25
% UG rec. need-based scholarship or grant aid	45
% frosh rec. non-need-based scholarship or grant aid	24
% UG rec. non-need-based scholarship or grant aid	10
% frosh rec. need-based self-help aid	30
% UG rec. need-based self-help aid	46
% frosh rec. athletic scholarships	2
% UG rec. athletic scholarships	1
% frosh rec. any financial aid	42
% UG rec. any financial aid	57
% UG borrow to pay for school	61
Average cumulative indebtedness	$16,000

FAIRFIELD UNIVERSITY

1073 NORTH BENSON ROAD, FAIRFIELD, CT 06824 • ADMISSIONS: 203-254-4100 • FAX: 203-254-4199

STUDENTS SAY "..."

Academics

Study amongst the trees of the "breathtaking campus" at Fairfield University, a competitive mid-sized school with a Division I basketball team and Jesuit ideals. A stalwart of the preppy New England college scene, the school has wealth and is definitely "image conscious," but financial aid packages are said to be super for students in need; several of the large scholarships also "entitle you to preferred registration for small classes." Fairfield's extremely rigorous and time-consuming core courses ensure that students receive a well-rounded education, and the small enrollment assures students small class sizes once they move beyond the mandatory curriculum. The school's Connecticut location is just an hour away from New York City, which provides a plethora of work study and internship possibilities for the students. This is especially convenient for students in Fairfield's notably strong nursing and business programs, the latter of which is taught by a faculty mostly comprised of current and ex-professionals.

Though students are generally happy here, thanks to an involved student government and a high quality of life, many wish that there was "more school spirit" amongst the student body. The "Leviathan" administration has not curried much favor with students, with the Registrar, Career Planning, and the Division of Student Affairs receiving singular complaints. Complaints of inefficacy and bureaucracy abound, and the various offices "act in distinct bubbles, with one hand not knowing what the other is doing." Opinions of professors are at the opposite end of the spectrum, as most find almost all their teachers "extremely engaging" and "wonderful people." "They actually read your essays and provide constructive criticism," says a student. "Professors have been amazing, inspiring, accessible, and have defined my time at Fairfield," says another.

Life

Not surprising for a school with an "ideal party location on the beaches of the Long Island Sound, only an hour north of New York City by train," students here like to drink. Although all go to "most of the classes," they know that they "must leave time for going out on Tuesdays, Thursdays and the weekend," making Fairfield "the opposite of a suitcase school." "Weekends are usually for partying, whether it's a townhouse party or a party down at the beach. Once you turn 21 there are some great bars in town too." This isn't to say that hedonism completely rules the school; many students remain very active in student activities and service organizations, and for those who don't want to party, the late night programming "offers tons of activities and trips almost every Thursday, Friday, and Saturday night." The student government organizes many of these events, as well as trips into the city for Broadway performances, comedy shows, and sporting events.

Student Body

Almost everyone hails from the northeast at this "homogenous, preppy school" with "generally very intelligent" students. Pockets run pretty deep amongst students, which leads some of this "Ugg wearing, blond haired, Seven for All Mankind-wearing" crowd to "think they're God's gift to mankind." There are plenty of "more mellow, normal folks" here, and even though "it doesn't take much" to be considered an atypical student, those that are usually "find their own niche and have no problems living their lives the way they wish." With the rising enrollment, the school is attempting to increase this diversity, and there's a "growing Gay and Lesbian population."

FINANCIAL AID: 203-254-4125 • E-MAIL: ADMIS@MAIL.FAIRFIELD.EDU • WEBSITE: WWW.FAIRFIELD.EDU

THE PRINCETON REVIEW SAYS

Admissions

Very important factors considered include: Application essay, academic GPA, recommendation(s), rigor of secondary school record. *Important factors considered include:* Standardized test scores, character/personal qualities, extracurricular activities, first generation, talent/ability, volunteer work, work experience. *Other factors considered include:* Class rank, alumni/ae relation, geographical residence, interview, racial/ethnic status, SAT or ACT required; TOEFL required of all international applicants. High school diploma is required and GED is not accepted. *Academic units required:* 4 English, 3 mathematics, 2 science, (2 science labs), 2 foreign language, 2 social studies, 2 history, 1 academic elective. *Academic units recommended:* 4 English, 4 mathematics, 3 science, (2 science labs), 4 foreign language, 2 social studies, 2 history, 1 academic elective.

Financial Aid

Students should submit: FAFSA, CSS/Financial Aid PROFILE, business/farm supplement. Regular filing deadline is 2/15. The Princeton Review suggests that all financial aid forms be submitted as soon as possible after January 1. *Need-based scholarships/grants offered:* Federal Pell, SEOG, state scholarships/grants, private scholarships, the school's own gift aid, United Negro College Fund. *Loan aid offered:* FFEL Subsidized Stafford, FFEL Unsubsidized Stafford, FFEL PLUS, Federal Perkins, Federal Nursing, Grad Plus, Alternative Loans. Applicants will be notified of awards on or about 4/1. Federal Work-Study Program available. Institutional employment available. Off-campus job opportunities are good.

The Inside Word

Steady increases in the number of admission applications has nicely increased selectivity in recent years. Fairfield's campus and central location, combined with improvements to the library, campus center, classrooms, athletic facilities, and campus residences, make this a campus worth seeing.

THE SCHOOL SAYS "..."

From The Admissions Office

"Fairfield University's primary objectives are to develop the creative intellectual potential of its students and to foster in them ethical values and a sense of social responsibility. Towards this end, the application review process is holistic, including not just a student's academic credentials, but their extracurricular pursuits and outside interests. Our students are challenged to be creative and active members of a community in which diversity is not simply accepted, but encouraged and honored. Students learn in a supportive environment with faculty committed to individual development and personal enrichment. As a key to the lifelong process of learning, Fairfield has developed a core curriculum to introduce all students to the broad range of liberal learning. Students choose from 34 majors and 19 interdisciplinary minors. They also have outstanding internship opportunities in Fairfield County and New York City. Additionally, 35 percent of Fairfield's students take advantage of an extensive study abroad program. Fairfield graduates wishing to continue their education are highly successful in gaining graduate and professional school admission, while others pursue extensive job opportunities throughout the region. Thirty-nine Fairfield students have been tapped as Fulbright scholars since 1993.

"Applicants to Fairfield University for Fall 2008 may submit the results from either the SAT or the ACT. We will consider the student's best scores in the application process. Fairfield does not require any SAT Subject Tests."

SELECTIVITY

Admissions Rating	89
# of applicants	8,557
% of applicants accepted	55
% of acceptees attending	18
# accepting a place on wait list	1,196
% admitted from wait list	8

FRESHMAN PROFILE

Range SAT Critical Reading	530–620
Range SAT Math	550–640
Range ACT Composite	23–28
Minimum paper TOEFL	550
Minimum computer TOEFL	213
Average HS GPA	3.4
% graduated top 10% of class	36
% graduated top 25% of class	76
% graduated top 50% of class	96

DEADLINES

Early action	
Deadline	11/15
Notification	1/1
Regular	
Deadline	1/15
Notification	4/1
Nonfall registration?	no

APPLICANTS ALSO LOOK AT
AND OFTEN PREFER
Georgetown University
Boston College
AND SOMETIMES PREFER
Fordham University
College of the Holy Cross
Villanova University
Providence College

FINANCIAL FACTS

Financial Aid Rating	78
Annual tuition	$33,340
Room and board	$10,430
Required fees	$565
Books and supplies	$900
% frosh rec. need-based scholarship or grant aid	46
% UG rec. need-based scholarship or grant aid	46
% frosh rec. non-need-based scholarship or grant aid	18
% UG rec. non-need-based scholarship or grant aid	20
% frosh rec. need-based self-help aid	45
% UG rec. need-based self-help aid	43
% frosh rec. athletic scholarships	8
% UG rec. athletic scholarships	6
% frosh rec. any financial aid	59
% UG rec. any financial aid	59
% UG borrow to pay for school	60
Average cumulative indebtedness	$31,984

Fisk University

1000 Seventeenth Avenue North, Nashville, TN 37208-3051 • Admissions: 615-329-8665 • Fax: 615-329-8774

CAMPUS LIFE

Quality of Life Rating	**62**
Fire Safety Rating	**60***
Green Rating	**60***
Type of school	private
Environment	metropolis

STUDENTS

Total undergrad enrollment	812
% from out of state	71
% from public high school	85
% live on campus	65
% in (# of) fraternities	15 (4)
% in (# of) sororities	20 (4)
% African American	98
% international	2
# of countries represented	5

SURVEY SAYS . . .

Large classes
Great off-campus food
Low cost of living
Frats and sororities dominate
social scene
Musical organizations are popular
Student government is popular

ACADEMICS

Academic Rating	**76**
Calendar	semester
Student/faculty ratio	12:1
Profs interesting rating	67
Profs accessible rating	65
% profs teaching	
UG courses	100
% classes taught by TAs	0

STUDENTS SAY "..."

Academics

With its rich past and impressive list of alumni, Historically Black College/University Fisk University is "about history and continuing a legacy." But history and legacy alone wouldn't be enough to attract top students to this small Nashville school. To do that, Fisk has to deliver the goods, and it does: Fisk graduates over three-quarters of its enrollees, over 70 percent of whom go on to graduate and professional schools. Indeed, for every student who mentioned Fisk's illustrious history as a reason for choosing the school, at least two cite Fisk's reputation for "graduating African Americans to become wonderful professionals" as a reason to attend. As one student puts it, "Fisk University is all about nurturing young Black people with the goal of preparing them to thrive" in the world while remaining committed to "community involvement." With fewer than 1,000 undergraduates and limited finances, Fisk must focus its efforts on a few key disciplines. Departments that track to health care careers—biology, physics, chemistry, nursing, and psychology—fare well here, as do computer science and business administration. A core curriculum encompassing humanities, mathematics, and science ensures that everyone leaves with a well-rounded education. The school's size results in "wonderful" relationships with professors who "actually care about your matriculation through the school." The faculty "is generally very approachable" and they "take the time to work with you when you request help." Academics are "rigorous," and the mantra on campus is "Success is in the details (by which we mean diversity, excellence, teamwork, accountability, integrity, leadership, service)." Fisk also excels at procuring "internships and study abroad" opportunities.

Life

At a school as small as Fisk, "Campus life can be boring," and many students say they are "sheltered and separated from the real world." For some (especially freshmen, who are not yet fully integrated into campus life and often lack automobiles), free time consists of little more than "going out to the yard to throw the football around or hanging in the lounge playing spades, pool, or watching TV. Just enjoying one another's company is making our own fun." The campus sponsors a number of activities, including "step shows, organizational meetings, choir, sports, clubs, dances, yard gatherings, etc." Social life centers on Fisk's Greek organizations and the Jubilee Singers, the school's world-renowned singing group, famous for its repertoire of slave spirituals. On the weekends, "Students go to clubs or Greek-hosted parties," but are just as likely to head out to Nashville for fun. Nashville is a great music town, and as a tourist destination, boasts many attractions, including great restaurants, amusement parks, and plenty of shopping. Fisk fields 15 NCAA Division III athletic teams, seven for men (basketball, baseball, soccer, tennis, cross-country, track, and golf) and eight for women (basketball, softball, volleyball, cross-country, tennis, track, soccer, and golf).

Student Body

Fisk is a "small school" with a "family environment," even though "The only thing most students share in common is that we are all Black. There are, however, many different types of students," from those who "are first-generation college students to others who are fourth- and fifth-generation Fiskites." Undergraduates come from "various regions of the country" and all across the world, and range in personality types from "the really wild kids who are always partying to the students in really hard majors who no one ever sees to the different cliques of rich girls, international students, etc." With many students hailing from Tennessee and nearby states, "Southern hospitality" and "sociable" natures are the norm among students at Fisk.

FINANCIAL AID: 615-329-8735 • E-MAIL: ADMISSIONS@FISK.EDU • WEBSITE: WWW.FISK.EDU

THE PRINCETON REVIEW SAYS

Admissions

Very important factors considered include: Application essay, character/personal qualities, class rank, recommendation(s), rigor of secondary school record, standardized test scores, talent/ability. *Important factors considered include:* Alumni/ae relation, extracurricular activities, interview. *Other factors considered include:* Volunteer work. SAT or ACT required; TOEFL required of all international applicants. High school diploma is required, and GED is accepted. *Academic units required:* 4 English, 3 math, 2 science (2 science labs), 1 foreign language, 1 history, 4 academic electives. *Academic units recommended:* 4 English, 3 math, 3 science (2 science labs), 2 foreign language, 1 social studies, 1 history, 4 academic electives.

Financial Aid

Students should submit: FAFSA. The Princeton Review suggests that all financial aid forms be submitted as soon as possible after January 1. *Need-based scholarships/grants offered:* Pell Grant, SEOG, state scholarships/grants, private scholarships, the school's own gift aid, United Negro College Fund. *Loan aid offered:* Direct Subsidized Stafford, Direct Unsubsidized Stafford, Direct PLUS, FFEL PLUS, Federal Perkins Loan. Applicants will be notified of awards on a rolling basis beginning or about April 1. Federal Work-Study Program available. Off-campus job opportunities are excellent.

The Inside Word

Intangibles can play a big part in the admissions decision at Fisk, especially for borderline candidates. A marked improvement in high school grades during junior and senior years, a demonstrated high level of determination, and commitment to school, community, and/or church can all help create a successful application.

THE SCHOOL SAYS "..."

From The Admissions Office

"Founded in 1866, the university is coeducational, private, and one of America's premier Historically Black Universities. The first Black college to be granted a chapter of Phi Beta Kappa Honor Society, Fisk serves a national student body, with an enrollment of 900 students. There are residence halls for men and women. The focal point of the 40-acre campus and architectural symbol of the university is Jubilee Hall, the first permanent building for the education of Blacks in the South, and named for the internationally renowned Fisk Jubilee Singers, who continue their tradition of singing the Negro spiritual. From its earliest days, Fisk has played a leadership role in the education of African Americans. Faculty and alumni have been among America's intellectual leaders. Among them include Fisk graduates Nikki Giovanni, poet/writer; John Hope Franklin, historian/scholar; David Lewis, professor/recipient of the prestigious Pulitzer Prize; Hazel O'Leary, U.S. Secretary of Energy; John Lewis, U.S. Representative—Georgia; and W. E. B. DuBois, the great social critic and cofounder of the NAACP. Former Fisk students whose distinguished careers bring color to American culture include Judith Jamison, director of the Alvin Ailey Dance Company, and Johnetta B. Cole, president of Spelman College. In proportion to its size, Fisk continues to contribute more alumni to the ranks of scholars pursuing doctoral degrees than any other institution in the United States.

"Fisk University does review all three aspects of the SAT exam. For regular admission, first-time freshman applicants must have a minimum combined (CR, Math, Writing) SAT score of 1410 or ACT composite of 20. Transfer applicants with at least 30 college credit hours at the time of application are not required to submit SAT scores. Transfer applicants with fewer than 30 college credit hours at the time of application must submit high school transcript and test scores. Submitted scores must meet minimum requirement (1410 SAT, 20 composite ACT). SAT Subject Tests are not required for admission or placement."

SELECTIVITY	
Admissions Rating	83
# of applicants	1,146
% of applicants accepted	66
% of acceptees attending	29

FRESHMAN PROFILE	
Range SAT Critical Reading	395–650
Range SAT Math	365–620
Range ACT Composite	17–29
Minimum Paper TOEFL	500
Minimum Computer Based TOEFL	250
Average HS GPA	3.0
% graduated top 10% of class	35
% graduated top 25% of class	48
% graduated top 50% of class	73

DEADLINES	
Early decision application deadline	12/1
Regular application deadline	3/1
Regular notification	rolling
Nonfall registration?	yes

APPLICANTS ALSO LOOK AT AND SOMETIMES PREFER
Belmont University, Hampton University, Morehouse College, Spelman College

FINANCIAL FACTS	
Financial Aid Rating	72
Annual tuition	$12,480
Room & Board	$6,730
Books and supplies	$1,500
Required fees	$700
% frosh rec. need-based scholarship or grant aid	58
% UG rec. need-based scholarship or grant aid	63
% frosh rec. need-based self-help aid	81
% UG rec. need-based self-help aid	85

FLAGLER COLLEGE

74 KING STREET, PO BOX 1027, ST. AUGUSTINE, FL 32085-1027 • ADMISSIONS: 800-304-4208 • FAX: 904-826-0094

STUDENTS SAY ". . ."

Academics

Undergrads at this small Florida liberal arts college love the "intimate campus experience" and the "personal attention" that the school provides. Professors "all have ample office hours and encourage us to use them. They are also accessible through e-mail and telephone. They genuinely care about their students, and this care even extends to non-academic issues." What's more, "The professors here are very understanding of students' personal lives and know that we have a life outside the classroom." The business and education programs are singled out for particular praise. Reviews of the administration, however, are more mixed. While some students assert that the "Members of the administration are some of the nicest people you will ever meet," others see them as the source of more than a little consternation. First on students' lists of complaints "is a stringent policy on attendance that forces the students to attend every class"; some argue that the policy is "why some students refer to Flagler College as 'Flagler High.'" Regardless of how "tightly wound" the administration may be, "They make things work pretty well"—and for a good value; finance-sensitive students appreciate the fact that "tuition is relatively inexpensive for a private school."

Life

"It's exhilarating to be able to wake up, walk downstairs, and step into an interesting little slice of history every day. Our school was once a very pricey and very elegant hotel. Everywhere you turn something has been hand-carved, gold-leafed, frescoed, marbled—you get the idea. It's just beautiful," enthuses one appreciative sophomore. Indeed, if there's one thing the majority of students appreciate about Flagler, it's the beauty of the school itself and of the "quaint, small tourist town" of St. Augustine in which it is located. Undergrads take advantage of "St. Augustine's awesome restaurants, many of which are located only a block away on St. George Street; many of the restaurants also have Flagler student discounts." In addition, "Surfing and the beach [about five miles away] are very, very popular at the school" when the weather is warm. Because Flagler has a "zero-tolerance [policy] for drugs and alcohol," many students "party with friends who have houses off campus." Some students also make the 45-minute drive to Jacksonville to go dancing. Two things about life at Flagler draw the ire of many respondents to our survey. First, the policy of "no interdormitory visits between males and females" can "drive students insane": "There's nowhere even to watch a movie with someone of the opposite sex." Second, the dining hall food is near-universally despised.

Students

Students agree that one can divide most of the Flagler student body into a few visible groups: The majority of students, respondents write, "are from the middle to upper-middle class, and have a car and a good amount of disposable income." They are "White," possibly "religious," and generally have "conservative views on politics." Then there are the surfers, who "all hang out together" and "often miss class when the waves are good." While the appeal for a Gay-Straight Alliance in fall 2004 (to be recognized as an official organization) was not approved, Club Unity, an organization whose purpose is to promote the unity of all people regardless of sexual orientation was approved by the President in October 2007. As far as ethnic diversity is concerned, "There are not many minorities on campus, but the Admissions Office tries to create a better balance each semester."

FLAGLER COLLEGE

THE PRINCETON REVIEW SAYS

Admissions

Very important factors considered include: Academic GPA, rigor of secondary school record. *Important factors considered include:* Application essay, standardized test scores, alumni/ae relation. *Other factors considered include:* Class rank, recommendation(s), character/personal qualities, extracurricular activities, first generation, interview, level of applicant's interest, talent/ability, volunteer work, work experience. SAT or ACT required; TOEFL required of all international applicants. High school diploma is required and GED is accepted. *Academic units required:* 4 English, 3 mathematics, 3 science, (1 science labs), 3 social studies, 1 history, 3 academic electives. *Academic units recommended:* 4 English, 4 mathematics, 4 science, (2 science labs), 2 foreign language, 4 social studies, 2 history, 1 visual/performing arts, 1 computer science, 3 academic electives.

Financial Aid

Students should submit: FAFSA, institution's own financial aid form, state aid form. Regular filing deadline is 4/1. The Princeton Review suggests that all financial aid forms be submitted as soon as possible after January 1. *Need-based scholarships/grants offered:* Federal Pell, SEOG, state scholarships/grants, private scholarships, the school's own gift aid. *Loan aid offered:* Direct Subsidized Stafford, Direct Unsubsidized Stafford, Direct PLUS, Federal Perkins Applicants will be notified of awards on a rolling basis beginning 4/1. Federal Work-Study Program available. Institutional employment available. Off-campus job opportunities are excellent.

The Inside Word

Admission to Flagler is competitive, as evidenced by the low acceptance rate. Successful applicants must be well rounded, not only excelling in rigorous classes but also demonstrating strong writing skills and a willingness to devote significant time to extracurricular interests. Candidates should note that a few majors, such as education, require specific standardized test minimums. Students with a conservative bent will thrive best at Flagler.

THE SCHOOL SAYS "..."

From The Admissions Office

"Flagler College is an independent, 4-year, coeducational, residential institution located in picturesque St. Augustine. A famous historic tourist center in northeast Florida, it is located to the south of Jacksonville and north of Daytona Beach. Flagler students have ample opportunity to explore the rich cultural heritage and international flavor of St. Augustine, and there's always time for a relaxing day at the beach, about four miles from campus. Flagler is one of the least expensive private colleges in the nation and is recognized in *MoneyGuide, U.S. News & World Report,* and *America's Best 100 Buys* as a top value in education at an affordable cost. The annual cost for tuition, room, and board at Flagler is about the same as state universities. The small student body helps to keep one from becoming 'just a number.' Flagler serves a predominately full-time student body and seeks to enroll students who can benefit from the type of educational experience the college offers. Because of the college's unique mission and distinctive characteristics, some students may benefit more from an educational experience at Flagler than others. The college's admission standards and procedures are designed to select from among the applicants those students most likely to succeed academically, to contribute significantly to the student life program at Flagler, and to become graduates of the college. Flagler College provides an exceptional opportunity for a private education at an extremely affordable cost.

"Freshman applicants for Fall 2008 must take the new SAT (or the ACT with the Writing component). In addition, students may submit scores from the old (before March 2005) SAT (or ACT), and we will use their best scores from either test."

SELECTIVITY
Admissions Rating	88
# of applicants	2,353
% of applicants accepted	40
% of acceptees attending	57
# accepting a place on wait list	104
% admitted from wait list	8
# of early decision applicants	629
% accepted early decision	64

FRESHMAN PROFILE
Range SAT Critical Reading	520–610
Range SAT Math	510–590
Range SAT Writing	500–600
Range ACT Composite	21–25
Minimum paper TOEFL	550
Minimum computer TOEFL	213
Average HS GPA	3.33
% graduated top 10% of class	16
% graduated top 25% of class	48
% graduated top 50% of class	84

DEADLINES
Early decision	
Deadline	12/1
Notification	12/15
Regular	
Priority	1/15
Deadline	3/1
Notification	3/30
Nonfall registration?	yes

APPLICANTS ALSO LOOK AT AND RARELY PREFER
Florida Gulf Coast University
Eckerd College
Florida Southern College
Florida International University
Rollins College
Jacksonville State University

FINANCIAL FACTS
Financial Aid Rating	73
Annual tuition	$13,600
Room and board	$6,900
Books and supplies	$900
% frosh rec. need-based scholarship or grant aid	18
% UG rec. need-based scholarship or grant aid	26
% frosh rec. non-need-based scholarship or grant aid	23
% UG rec. non-need-based scholarship or grant aid	29
% frosh rec. need-based self-help aid	26
% UG rec. need-based self-help aid	35
% frosh rec. athletic scholarships	3
% UG rec. athletic scholarships	5
% frosh rec. any financial aid	76
% UG rec. any financial aid	84
% UG borrow to pay for school	54
Average cumulative indebtedness	$15,186

FLORIDA SOUTHERN COLLEGE

OFFICE OF ADMISSIONS, 111 LAKE HOLLINGSWORTH DRIVE, LAKELAND, FL 33801 • ADMISSIONS: 800-274-4131 • FAX: 863-680-4120

CAMPUS LIFE

Quality of Life Rating	**76**
Fire Safety Rating	**81**
Green Rating	**68**
Type of school	private
Affiliation	Methodist
Environment	city

STUDENTS

Total undergrad enrollment	1,710
% male/female	40/60
% from out of state	25
% from public high school	79
% live on campus	74
% in (# of) fraternities	30 (5)
% in (# of) sororities	35 (6)
% African American	7
% Asian	1
% Caucasian	82
% Hispanic	6
% international	4
# of countries represented	31

SURVEY SAYS . . .

Large classes
Intramural sports are popular
Frats and sororities dominate
social scene

ACADEMICS

Academic Rating	**78**
Calendar	semester
Student/faculty ratio	13:1
Profs interesting rating	76
Profs accessible rating	79
Most common	
reg class size	10–19 students
Most common	
lab size	10–19 students

MOST POPULAR MAJORS

marketing/marketing management
psychology
biological and biomedical sciences

STUDENTS SAY ". . ."

Academics

Florida Southern College offers "a fairly strong liberal arts core," "a total community atmosphere," and a throng of degrees and majors. Standout programs include business, music, and the sciences. There is "an incredible education program," too. "Extremely exciting" study-abroad programs will take you to England, China, Australia, and many other places all across the globe. Classes are "small." FSC's "hands-on" administration "is very open to student ideas and easy to contact." The faculty is "a big mix." "Most of the professors are deeply committed to the students and will go to great lengths to help." "Teachers care when you miss class," says one happy student who appreciates the extra attention. "We don't have teaching assistants so the relationships are directly with the professors." "It is very uncommon" to have professors who don't "know you by name," "even if you only had them one time." Some professors "aren't so good," though. "A lot of professors are the only one teaching a particular subject, especially when you get to the upper-level classes in your major," one student told us. Also, the library here "needs more up-to-date resources," though a new wing will open for Fall 2008.

Life

Florida Southern's lakefront campus is home to the largest single-site collection of Frank Lloyd Wright architecture on earth. As such, it's no wonder that students describe it as "very beautiful." Life here is "interactive" and "comfortable." The Greek system is somewhat big. The Wellness Center, the campus pool, and activities on Lake Hollingsworth are popular hang-out spots for students. There are fairly strict rules regarding when males and females can be "in each others' dorms." Also, FSC is "supposed to be a dry campus" but "everybody drinks, anyway." While it's theoretically possible to "go out every night and party," "It's not your typical *Animal House* scene" here. "It's more laid-back." The surrounding city of Lakeland "isn't too thrilling." A few "hole-in-the-wall bars" are the big draw on "Thursday nights" ("which makes Friday the most interesting class day"). For real off-campus fun, "Students often go to Tampa or Orlando," both just "short" rides away.

Students

"Everyone knows each other and gets along," notes one student. It's "one big community." "You can really be yourself here," says a sophomore, so just "being silly with [your] friends" isn't looked down on. "The majority of the campus is female," and from Florida, though about one-third of the students come from out of state. FSC students are "hardworking" and "energetic." Many are "rich" or, at least, "from a decently well-off family." Many others "act rich." Most students are "very friendly," though you will find a few "snotty" types. One student noted that "nearly the entire population is preppy." There is a smattering of minority students and international students but, by and large, ethnic diversity is minimal. There are many "very religious" people on campus. "A lot of students" are "involved in Christian ministries." Politically, you can find "both conservative and liberal extremes" on campus.

FINANCIAL AID: 800-205-1600 • E-MAIL: FSCADM@FLSOUTHERN.EDU • WEBSITE: WWW.FLSOUTHERN.EDU

THE PRINCETON REVIEW SAYS

Admissions

Very important factors considered include: Academic GPA, rigor of secondary school record. *Important factors considered include:* Application essay, recommendation(s), standardized test scores, character/personal qualities, extracurricular activities, talent/ability. *Other factors considered include:* Class rank, alumni/ae relation, first generation, interview, level of applicant's interest, racial/ethnic status, religious affiliation/commitment, volunteer work, work experience. SAT or ACT required; TOEFL or IELTS required of all international applicants. High school diploma is required and GED is accepted. *Academic units required:* 4 English, 3 mathematics, 2 science, (2 science labs). *Academic units recommended:* 2 foreign language, 3 social studies, 3 history, 2 academic electives.

Financial Aid

Students should submit: FAFSA, institution's own financial aid form. Regular filing deadline is 7/1. The Princeton Review suggests that all financial aid forms be submitted as soon as possible after January 1. *Need-based scholarships/grants offered:* Federal Pell, SEOG, state scholarships/grants, private scholarships, the school's own gift aid. *Loan aid offered:* FFEL Subsidized Stafford, FFEL Unsubsidized Stafford, FFEL PLUS, Federal Perkins Applicants will be notified of awards on a rolling basis beginning 3/1. Federal Work-Study Program available. Institutional employment available. Off-campus job opportunities are good.

The Inside Word

Individual attention is the cornerstone of a Florida Southern education and this sentiment extends to the admissions process. A close-knit community, officers seek out applicants who best embody FSC's spirit and are likely to contribute to the campus' vitality. Focus is therefore paid not only to grades and test scores, but personal attributes and experiences that reveal involvement beyond the classroom. Candidates are encouraged to employ creative measures throughout their application and are welcome to submit additional academic materials and portfolio samples.

THE SCHOOL SAYS "..."

From The Admissions Office

"Florida Southern is friendly and dynamic, offering terrific engaged learning opportunities including student-faculty collaborative research and performance, study abroad, service learning, and internships. The College offers an unusually wide choice of undergraduate majors—46—such as art, business, communication, nursing, psychology, education, music performance, and biology, and a new self-designed major. Pre-professional programs include pre-med, pre-dental and pre-law. FSC is known for great professors and faculty mentors with a student-faculty ratio of 13:1. A new technology plan is being implemented to support dynamic instruction. Students have won national competitions in biology, advertising, and psychology. Thirty percent of graduating seniors have studied abroad, 52 percent have completed formal internships, and 94 percent go on to professional or graduate school or land jobs in their chosen fields. Overlooking beautiful Lake Hollingsworth, Florida Southern is home to the world's largest collection of Frank Lloyd Wright architecture, which provides a stunning setting for living and learning. New campus additions include a Residential Life Center with bedroom views to the lake; the phenomenal Nina B. Hollis Wellness Center and adjacent Lakefront Program with kayaks, canoes, and sailboats; a cyber café serving Starbuck's products in the library; and an upcoming humanities building featuring a modern language lab and film studies center. FSC is ranked #5 by U.S. News & World Report among the best "Comprehensive Colleges in the South."

SELECTIVITY

Admissions Rating	83
# of applicants	2,559
% of applicants accepted	58
% of acceptees attending	29
# of early decision applicants	82
% accepted early decision	74

FRESHMAN PROFILE

Range SAT Critical Reading	480–600
Range SAT Math	470–600
Range SAT Writing	460–570
Range ACT Composite	20–25
Minimum paper TOEFL	550
Minimum computer TOEFL	213
Minimum web-based TOEFL	79/80
Average HS GPA	3.51
% graduated top 10% of class	24
% graduated top 25% of class	49
% graduated top 50% of class	82

DEADLINES

Early decision	
Deadline	12/1
Notification	12/15
Regular	
Deadline	3/1
Notification	rolling
Nonfall registration?	yes

FINANCIAL FACTS

Financial Aid Rating	77
% frosh rec. need-based scholarship or grant aid	35
% UG rec. need-based scholarship or grant aid	38
% frosh rec. non-need-based scholarship or grant aid	59
% UG rec. non-need-based scholarship or grant aid	57
% frosh rec. need-based self-help aid	26
% UG rec. need-based self-help aid	30
% frosh rec. athletic scholarships	13
% UG rec. athletic scholarships	10
% frosh rec. any financial aid	98
% UG rec. any financial aid	96
% UG borrow to pay for school	66
Average cumulative indebtedness	$8,914

FLORIDA STATE UNIVERSITY

2500 UNIVERSITY CENTER, TALLAHASSEE, FL 32306-2400 • ADMISSIONS: 850-644-6200 • FAX: 850-644-0197

CAMPUS LIFE
Quality of Life Rating	85
Fire Safety Rating	83
Green Rating	83
Type of school	public
Environment	city

STUDENTS
Total undergrad enrollment	31,595
% male/female	44/56
% from out of state	11
% live on campus	19
% in (# of) fraternities	13 (28)
% in (# of) sororities	13 (23)
% African American	11
% Asian	3
% Caucasian	73
% Hispanic	11
% Native American	1
# of countries represented	129

SURVEY SAYS . . .
Great library
Athletic facilities are great
Everyone loves the Seminoles
Frats and sororities dominate
social scene
Lots of beer drinking

ACADEMICS
Academic Rating	72
Calendar	semester
Student/faculty ratio	21:1
Profs interesting rating	74
Profs accessible rating	74
% classes taught by TAs	28
Most common	
reg class size	20–29 students

MOST POPULAR MAJORS
finance
criminal justice/safety studies
psychology

STUDENTS SAY ". . ."

Academics
You don't have to sell Florida State University to its prospective students; the school has established a clear and recognizable brand based on a tradition of "accomplishment in academics, athletics, and politics," and these are a source of "an enormous sense of school pride" for FSU's myriad devotees. Those traditions include a beloved football program, of course, but they're much more than that; they envelop a complete undergraduate experience that includes "a wonderful mix of both the academic and social spheres" and "an intimate social community," despite the fact that the "school is so large." Academics here "do an excellent job of preparing students for the real world," with standout programs that include an "amazing" international program that "encourages all majors to study abroad and bring many international students and teachers to campus," a college of business that "graduates some of the best businesspeople in the United States," an "extremely competitive" premed program, a "fantastic" music school, merchandising, education, criminology, and the only exercise science program in the state. Workloads in the research-intensive sciences are heavy; elsewhere, "It's just enough so that you have free time, but if you study and work hard you get a lot out of each class and a good grade." FSU's facilities are a mixed bag. Those that are good are fabulous; they include "one of the best career centers in the country, a state-of-the-art school of medicine, and magnet labs that are supposed to be among the most advanced in the country." However, as one student points out, while FSU's "incredible athletic facilities are great," other facilities "could be better taken care of."

Life
Life at FSU is "very social oriented," with "events always happening" either on campus or off. Weekdays, "Campus is always a-bustlin'," with tons of activities, presentations, organization meetings, and casual get-togethers. On weekends, the options are somewhat more limited; some here describe weekends as "calm, even tranquil, except of course on game weekends," but most report that the weekend is a time to blow off steam. One student explains, "A lot of people at FSU are big partiers. [A lot of students] love to drink and have a good time. [A lot of students] find many excuses to drink: holidays, sporting events, or a day at the pool." The administration has created a coalition to change the drinking culture on- and off-campus.The administration has created a coalition to change the drinking culture on- and off-campus. Home football games are the *ne plus ultra* of campus activity, as football "becomes a religion in the fall." The games attract "most students and many out-of-towners," and pre-game and post-game parties are both de rigueur. "Most students here seem to be very physically active and involved in the outdoor pursuits on our campus, such as hiking, running, fishing, skydiving, rock climbing, etc." Intramural sports "are also extremely popular . . . anyone can play and every sport is offered, from football to dodgeball." Greek life at FSU "is everywhere," as the Greeks "have established themselves within the university community portraying strong leadership, service, and scholarship." From "fraternity parties and tailgating to seminars on how to become an effective leader, Greek life at FSU is very interesting."

Student Body
While the typical FSU student is a "sweatpants-wearing, Starbucks-drinking, Dave Matthews Band listener," undergrads point out that "there are so many students of so many different types here that the 'typical student' is a very poor representation of the school as a whole." While that 'typical student' hails "from a middle- to upper-class family in Florida," for example, many students here receive substantial aid packages, and about one in seven undergrads is from out of state. Students tell us that almost everyone is "highly involved in extracurricular activities," whether it's a "fraternity/sorority, sports, the arts, or one of the many school organizations out there." FSU students also tend to be people who "strive for success, but also know how to enjoy the social experiences college has to offer." "Each and every student has their own place at FSU, and all students share a common identity of garnet and gold."

FLORIDA STATE UNIVERSITY

FINANCIAL AID: 850-644-5871 • E-MAIL: ADMISSIONS@ADMIN.FSU.EDU • WEBSITE: WWW.FSU.EDU

THE PRINCETON REVIEW SAYS

Admissions

Very important factors considered include: Academic GPA, rigor of secondary school record. *Important factors considered include:* Class rank, standardized test scores, state residency, talent/ability. *Other factors considered include:* Application essay, recommendation(s), alumni/ae relation, character/personal qualities, extracurricular activities, first generation, geographical residence, volunteer work, work experience. SAT or ACT required; ACT with Writing component required. High school diploma is required and GED is accepted. *Academic units required:* 4 English, 3 mathematics, 3 science, (2 science labs), 2 foreign language, 1 social studies, 2 history, 3 academic electives. *Academic units recommended:* 4 English, 4 mathematics, 4 science, (2 science labs), 4 foreign language, 1 social studies, 2 history, 3 academic electives.

Financial Aid

Students should submit: FAFSA. The Princeton Review suggests that all financial aid forms be submitted as soon as possible after January 1. *Need-based scholarships/grants offered:* Federal Pell, SEOG, state scholarships/grants, private scholarships, the school's own gift aid. *Loan aid offered:* FFEL Subsidized Stafford, FFEL Unsubsidized Stafford, FFEL PLUS, Federal Perkins Applicants will be notified of awards on a rolling basis beginning 3/15. Federal Work-Study Program available. Institutional employment available. Off-campus job opportunities are excellent.

The Inside Word

With 22,000 applications to process each year, FSU must rely on a formula-driven approach to triage its applicant pool. With the exception of those applying to special programs, only the applications of those on the borderline will receive a truly thorough review. Those hoping to study fine arts, creative arts, or the performing arts at FSU must undergo a more rigorous application process that includes a portfolio/audition.

THE SCHOOL SAYS "..."

From The Admissions Office

"Established in 1851, Florida State University is one of the nation's premier research universities, known for attracting leading scholars from all over the world and providing students with some of the best academic mentors of any university in the U.S. Sixteen colleges and schools offer nearly 200 undergraduate majors, 214 graduate degrees, and professional degrees in law and medicine. Florida State enjoys an excellent reputation for groundbreaking academic achievements, including establishing the first new medical college in the nation in 20 years. Technologically enhanced classrooms and wireless networking allow state-of-the-art teaching techniques in every discipline. Through the University Honors Program, faculty and undergraduate students who share academic interests can work on-on-one to design and conduct original research projects. Our innovative student services include an internationally renowned career center, a comprehensive campus-wide leadership learning program, and a center for community-based learning through service. World-class cultural events, championship athletics, extensive recreation facilities, and a friendly, close-knit university community enrich student life and extend learning well beyond the classroom. Our diverse student body hails from all 50 states and over 130 countries, and our many international programs throughout the world include year-round programs in Florence, Italy; London, England; Panama City, Panama; and Valencia, Spain.

"Students applying to the university are required to submit the Writing section of the new SAT or take the optional Writing test of the ACT. We will continue to use the highest subscores on the ACT and SAT for admission purposes."

SELECTIVITY
Admissions Rating	88
# of applicants	24,343
% of applicants accepted	55
% of acceptees attending	46
# accepting a place on wait list	215

FRESHMAN PROFILE
Range SAT Critical Reading	540–630
Range SAT Math	550–640
Range ACT Composite	23–28
Average HS GPA	3.63
% graduated top 10% of class	33
% graduated top 25% of class	69
% graduated top 50% of class	96

DEADLINES
Regular Deadline	2/14
Nonfall registration?	yes

FINANCIAL FACTS
Financial Aid Rating	88
Annual tuition	$3,471
% frosh rec. need-based scholarship or grant aid	21
% UG rec. need-based scholarship or grant aid	21
% frosh rec. non-need-based scholarship or grant aid	30
% UG rec. non-need-based scholarship or grant aid	24
% frosh rec. need-based self-help aid	21
% UG rec. need-based self-help aid	25
% frosh rec. athletic scholarships	7
% UG rec. athletic scholarships	4
% frosh rec. any financial aid	97
% UG rec. any financial aid	87
% UG borrow to pay for school	32.1
Average cumulative indebtedness	$13,855

FORDHAM UNIVERSITY

441 EAST FORDHAM ROAD, THEBAUD HALL, NEW YORK, NY 10458 • ADMISSIONS: 718-817-4000 • FAX: 718-367-9404

STUDENTS SAY " . . ."

Academics
Like Certs breath mints, Fordham University is two schools in one. First, there's the school's long-established campus in the Rose Hill section of the Bronx, which might best be regarded as Fordham's 'conventional' undergraduate site. Then there's the newer campus at Manhattan's Lincoln Center, which is "very small and geared toward theater and dance students [though the school says the largest number of majors is liberal arts]." Students are adamant that "they are two different schools going in different directions with different student bodies and different academic focuses." The campuses do share a number of common traits, however. Each is a Jesuit school "with really big core requirements" that provide undergrads with "a strong background in a broad area of academics before actually specializing in one area, thereby educating the whole mind." The Jesuit influence is also seen in the way each school "promotes social awareness, caring for others, and expanding one's knowledge of the world and helping find one's contribution to it." Each school, of course, benefits from a city location that provides near limitless opportunities for networking, internships, and enriching extracurricular experiences. Rose Hill's students praise Fordham's College of Business ("the school for business professionals"), its pre-law and premedical programs, and its psychology program; undergrads at Lincoln Center boast of "one of the best Theater Departments in the country" and "a great dance program."

Life
Fordham's Rose Hill Campus "is truly beautiful, and the location is pretty much the best of both worlds—the city as well as plenty of green." Here, "life centers around the weekends. Most people go out to local bars, leaving no one on campus on a Tuesday, Friday, or Saturday night. . . . There are numerous events going on on campus all the time, although many of these events are based in religion or politics." Students are also "very involved . . . in intramural sports teams as well as performing arts groups." There's also the city, of course; you can reach it in 15 minutes by Metro North train, or you can save a few bucks and ride the subway. Expect the trip downtown to take about 30 minutes. Closer by is Arthur Avenue, the Bronx's own (and, many say, much better) version of Manhattan's Little Italy. Life at Lincoln Center is understandably less campus-centric; no campus can compete with all that downtown New York City has to offer. One student explains, "The bar and restaurant scene at Lincoln Center is very popular because of the variety of places to go in Manhattan. Dorm parties are not as usual as I would imagine them to be at other colleges. Students from all . . . of Fordham come to Lincoln Center to set out for their various night activities because of the campus's proximity to everything . . . I try to take advantage of the incredible amount of things to do here that one isn't able to do in most other places, but things are very expensive." Lincoln Center dorms "are like apartments, which I know is a definite attraction for many students."

Student Body
Students on the Rose Hill campus tend to be "from an upper-class home in New Jersey, Connecticut, or Long Island . . . [and] wear sandals and jeans and polos, with some popped collars sprinkled in. . . . Off campus (in the Bronx) they stick out like a sore thumb." Many are business and communications majors who favor conservative politics and a businesslike approach to academics. Students at Lincoln Center are more diverse; one writes, "There is no such thing as a typical student at Lincoln Center. Most students who choose to go here are liberal and artsy (writers, dancers, actors). Students tend to be very creative in their clothing choices." The majority of students here are women, and "Most of the boys are gay."

FINANCIAL AID: 718-817-3800 • E-MAIL: ENROLL@FORDHAM.EDU • WEBSITE: WWW.FORDHAM.EDU

THE PRINCETON REVIEW SAYS

Admissions

Very important factors considered include: Class rank, rigor of secondary school record, standardized test scores. *Important factors considered include:* Application essay, recommendation(s), character/personal qualities, extracurricular activities, talent/ability. *Other factors considered include:* Alumni/ae relation, first generation, geographical residence, racial/ethnic status, volunteer work, work experience. SAT Subject Tests recommended; SAT or ACT required; ACT with Writing component recommended. TOEFL required of all international applicants. High school diploma is required and GED is accepted. *Academic units required:* 4 English, 3 mathematics, 3 science, 2 foreign language, 2 social studies, 2 history, 6 academic electives. *Academic units recommended:* 4 English, 4 mathematics, 4 science, 3 foreign language, 2 social studies, 2 history, 6 academic electives.

Financial Aid

Students should submit: FAFSA, CSS/Financial Aid PROFILE, noncustodial PROFILE, business/farm supplement. Regular filing deadline is 2/1. The Princeton Review suggests that all financial aid forms be submitted as soon as possible after January 1. *Need-based scholarships/grants offered:* Federal Pell, SEOG, state scholarships/grants, private scholarships, the school's own gift aid. *Loan aid offered:* FFEL Subsidized Stafford, FFEL Unsubsidized Stafford, FFEL PLUS, Federal Perkins Applicants will be notified of awards on or about 4/1.

The Inside Word

Applicants to Fordham are required to indicate whether they are applying to Fordham College—Rose Hill, Fordham College—Lincoln Center, or the College of Business Administration. Admissions criteria vary by school, but all are very competitive. Graduation from one of the area's many prestigious Catholic high schools is certainly a plus.

THE SCHOOL SAYS "..."

From The Admissions Office

"Fordham University offers a distinctive, values-centered educational experience that is rooted in the Jesuit tradition of intellectual rigor and personal attention. Located in New York City, Fordham offers to students the unparalleled educational, cultural, and recreational advantages of one of the world's greatest cities. Fordham has two residential campuses in New York—the tree-lined, 85-acre Rose Hill in the Bronx, and the cosmopolitan Lincoln Center campus in the heart of Manhattan's performing arts center. The university's state-of-the-art facilities and buildings include one of the most technologically advanced libraries in the country. Fordham offers a variety of majors, concentrations, and programs that can be combined with an extensive career planning and placement program. More than 2,600 organizations in the New York metropolitan area offer students internships that provide hands-on experience and valuable networking opportunities in fields such as business, communications, medicine, law, and education.

"Applicants are required to take SAT or the ACT with or without the Writing section. SAT IIs are recommended but not required."

SELECTIVITY

Admissions Rating	92
# of applicants	22,035
% of applicants accepted	42.1
% of acceptees attending	19.2
# accepting a place on wait list	1,189
% admitted from wait list	10

FRESHMAN PROFILE

Range SAT Critical Reading	570–670
Range SAT Math	560–660
Range SAT Writing	560–660
Range ACT Composite	25–29
Minimum paper TOEFL	575
Minimum computer TOEFL	231
Average HS GPA	3.7
% graduated top 10% of class	42.5
% graduated top 25% of class	73
% graduated top 50% of class	96

DEADLINES

Early action	
Deadline	11/1
Notification	12/25
Priority	
Deadline	1/15
Notification	4/1
Nonfall registration?	yes

APPLICANTS ALSO LOOK AT

AND OFTEN PREFER
Boston College
New York University
The George Washington University

AND SOMETIMES PREFER
Rutgers University
Georgetown University
Loyola College in Maryland
College of the Holy Cross

AND RARELY PREFER
Hofstra University
Pace University
Marist College

FINANCIAL FACTS

Financial Aid Rating	73
Annual tuition	$30,000
Room and board	$11,780
Required fees	$730
Books and supplies	$800
% frosh rec. need-based scholarship or grant aid	66
% UG rec. need-based scholarship or grant aid	62
% frosh rec. non-need-based scholarship or grant aid	8
% UG rec. non-need-based scholarship or grant aid	5
% frosh rec. need-based self-help aid	51
% UG rec. need-based self-help aid	52
% frosh rec. athletic scholarships	2
% UG rec. athletic scholarships	2
% frosh rec. any financial aid	67
% UG rec. any financial aid	62

FRANKLIN & MARSHALL COLLEGE

PO Box 3003, Lancaster, PA 17604-3003 • Admissions: 717-291-3953 • Fax: 717-291-4381

STUDENTS SAY ". . ."

Academics
Franklin and Marshall is widely regarded as a school that "prepares students well for law school and medical school," along with retaining "a stellar reputation in graduate school admissions departments," but there's more to F&M than a bunch of high-strung future doctors and lawyers. True, the school has earned a reputation as a pre-professional powerhouse through its "intense workload" and "very difficult grading structure," conditions that some see as necessary in order to provide "an environment for intense personal and academic growth, and development of the skills necessary to achieve well-rounded success in life." However, students deem the workload "far too academically demanding for an average liberal arts college." But F&M also boasts "amazing departments in German, economics, history, government…and geology/environmental science," among others. And in all areas—not just in the high-profile sciences and business—the school ensures that "independent research, especially for upperclassmen, is a vital part of the academic experience," and that "there are enough resources that can be accessed to make good grades more easily attainable," the "demanding" workload notwithstanding. Close student-teacher relationships help make the experience; professors here "are by far the greatest thing about this school. If you're interested in doing something, you can always find a professor or other staff member who would love to help you."

Life
"There is a grind at F&M" during the week, "not a bad one, but you have to be ready for it. Everyone takes his role as a student here very seriously: class, library, meetings, more class, more library, extracurriculars, most students follow this itinerary during the week." Weeknight respites come in the form of "concerts, movies, amazing lectures and other things to break up the schedule." For most, weekends "are a good time to relax and drink and forget about all of the work that has been done and still needs to be done in the week to come," so "most students like to go to one or more of the numerous fraternity parties or they may go to a party in someone's room or apartment." And "If you aren't into the drinking scene or the partying scene on campus"—and contrary to the school's reputation, some students here aren't—"you can go to Ben's Underground, which is an alcohol-free, student-run club. Students can go to play pool or see comedians. It's really a nice facility to use and open all week." Also, "Athletics are fairly popular for a division three school, and the orchestra draws as well." Hometown Lancaster offers "a bunch of art galleries, really good cafés, an old opera house that has great plays, and a concert venue that has pretty big name bands play." However, by the time most students are juniors, "Lancaster and the frat scene get old, so older students take to the local bars and sometimes take road trips to…Philadelphia or Washington DC."

Student Body
F&M is "an extremely preppy school and many designers are flashed all around campus. Students are not afraid to show that they have money, but they are never in your face about it." Not everyone here is a slave to fashion. "You have students that do not get all dressed up for class that just wear sweats and sweatshirt," says a student. Along with those students "from boarding schools or expensive private schools," you'll find "a handful of international students, a smaller handful of minority students, and a few 'townies.' Everyone finds a niche, though." The small campus sometimes feels smaller because students can be cliquish; undergrads here "can be broken into many groups: frats, sororities, specific athletic groups, similar interests (arts, music, etc)."

FINANCIAL AID: 717-291-3991 • E-MAIL: ADMISSION@FANDM.EDU • WEBSITE: WWW.FANDM.EDU

THE PRINCETON REVIEW SAYS

Admissions

Very important factors considered include: Class rank, academic GPA, rigor of secondary school record, character/personal qualities. *Important factors considered include:* Application essay, recommendation(s), standardized test scores, extracurricular activities, interview, talent/ability, volunteer work. *Other factors considered include:* Alumni/ae relation, geographical residence, level of applicant's interest, racial/ethnic status, work experience. TOEFL required of all international applicants. High school diploma is required and GED is accepted. *Academic units required:* 4 English, 3 mathematics, 2 science, (2 science labs), 2 foreign language, 1 social studies, 2 history, 1 visual/performing arts. *Academic units recommended:* 4 mathematics, 3 science, (3 science labs), 4 foreign language, 3 social studies, 3 history.

Financial Aid

Students should submit: FAFSA, institution's own financial aid form, CSS/Financial Aid PROFILE, noncustodial PROFILE, business/farm supplement. Regular filing deadline is 3/1. The Princeton Review suggests that all financial aid forms be submitted as soon as possible after January 1. *Need-based scholarships/grants offered:* Federal Pell, SEOG, state scholarships/grants, private scholarships, the school's own gift aid. *Loan aid offered:* FFEL Subsidized Stafford, FFEL Unsubsidized Stafford, FFEL PLUS, Federal Perkins, college/university loans from institutional funds. Applicants will be notified of awards on or about 3/15. Federal Work-Study Program available.

The Inside Word

Applicants who feel that their standardized test scores do not accurately reflect their abilities may opt to omit them from their applications, in which case they must instead include two recent (junior or senior year) graded papers, preferably from a humanities or social science course. Since F&M is a school that requires tons of writing from its students, there could hardly be a better way to demonstrate your qualifications to attend than with the written word. Make sure to let F&M know if the school is your first choice. The school loses lots of applicants to 'prestige schools' and will review your application more favorably if you indicate a commitment to attending.

THE SCHOOL SAYS "..."

From The Admissions Office

"Franklin & Marshall students choose from a variety of fields of study, traditional and interdisciplinary, that typify liberal learning. Professors in all of these fields are committed to a common purpose, which is to teach students to think, speak, and write with clarity and confidence. Whether the course is in theater or in physics, the class will be small, engagement will be high, and discussion will dominate over lecture. Thus, throughout their 4 years, beginning with the First-Year Seminar, students at Franklin & Marshall are repeatedly invited to active participation in intellectual play at high levels. Our graduates consistently testify to the high quality of an F&M education as a mental preparation for life.

"Beginning with the Fall 2007 incoming class, the school offers an SAT option policy to all students."

SELECTIVITY

Admissions Rating	95
# of applicants	5,018
% of applicants accepted	37
% of acceptees attending	30
# accepting a place on wait list	511
% admitted from wait list	10
# of early decision applicants	471
% accepted early decision	68

FRESHMAN PROFILE

Range SAT Critical Reading	600–690
Range SAT Math	610–690
Minimum paper TOEFL	600
Minimum computer TOEFL	250
Average HS GPA	3.57
% graduated top 10% of class	57
% graduated top 25% of class	87
% graduated top 50% of class	99

DEADLINES

Early decision	
Deadline	11/15
Notification	12/15
Regular	
Deadline	2/1
Notification	4/1
Nonfall registration?	yes

APPLICANTS ALSO LOOK AT

AND OFTEN PREFER

Hamilton College
Haverford College
Cornell University
University of Pennsylvania

AND SOMETIMES PREFER

Dickinson College
Lehigh University
Lafayette College
Bucknell University
Colgate University

FINANCIAL FACTS

Financial Aid Rating	81
Annual tuition	$36,430
Room and board	$9,174
Required fees	$50
Books and supplies	$650
% frosh rec. need-based scholarship or grant aid	44
% UG rec. need-based scholarship or grant aid	43
% frosh rec. non-need-based scholarship or grant aid	4
% UG rec. non-need-based scholarship or grant aid	3
% frosh rec. need-based self-help aid	45
% UG rec. need-based self-help aid	41
% frosh rec. any financial aid	69
% UG rec. any financial aid	70
% UG borrow to pay for school	58
Average cumulative indebtedness	$24,752

FRANKLIN W. OLIN COLLEGE OF ENGINEERING

OLIN WAY, NEEDHAM, MA 02492-1200 • ADMISSIONS: 781-292-2222 • FAX: 781-292-2210

CAMPUS LIFE
Quality of Life Rating	97
Fire Safety Rating	98
Green Rating	60*
Type of school private	
Environment	town

STUDENTS
Total undergrad enrollment	296
% male/female	58/42
% from out of state	92
% from public high school	71
% live on campus	98
# of countries represented	8

SURVEY SAYS . . .
No one cheats
Lab facilities are great
Great computer facilities
Students are friendly
Dorms are like palaces
Campus feels safe
Students are happy
Frats and sororities are unpopular
or nonexistent

ACADEMICS
Academic Rating	99
Profs interesting rating	99
Profs accessible rating	98

MOST POPULAR MAJORS
engineering
mechanical engineering
electrical, electronics and communications engineering

STUDENTS SAY ". . ."

Academics

An "innovative," "exceptional" "project-based" curriculum attracts the country's math and science whiz kids to Franklin W. Olin College of Engineering. The school's "small size" and "open atmosphere that's supportive of everyone" are very appealing to the approximately 300 undergraduates on campus. But the piece de resistance—the thing that has students choosing this place over schools like MIT and Cal Tech—has got to be the "free tuition." "Academics-wise, the school kicks people's [butts] right and left. It takes the best and the brightest and breaks them, pushing them when they likely have never had to work hard before. Around here, everyone is smart, and professors assume that, so the classes are taken to that level; there is no such thing as an easy class." One might describe professors here as "grown up Olin kids" insofar as they "are geniuses," but also "young" and just "generally awesome people." "They love teaching," and are "mostly on [a] first-name basis" with undergrads, professors bend over backwards to make themselves accessible, either in person or over e-mail, which means "that they always seem to be available." In terms of how smoothly things run, keep in mind that Olin is "an experiment, so you never really know what's going to happen," which "tends to lead to some chaos." That doesn't mean that the administration isn't trying—it's actually trying all the time. There is a "constant dialogue of feedback between the students, staff, and faculty" and the administration "always has open doors to everyone." "You can sit down and eat lunch [in the dining hall] with the president if you want to." Feedback drives a "continual reassessment" of the institution with the aim of constant "improvement in all departments."

Life

A popular saying used to describe student life at Olin goes like this: "Choose two: work, sleep, fun." The majority of students choose the first and the last because "An Oliner at rest is an unhappy Oliner." The "Entrepreneurial spirit is strong" here, leading many people to choose to spend what little free time they have "working on cool projects" like "hacking the thermostat in their room" and "playing with lasers and circuits." Not everyone engages in genius science "geek" endeavors in their free time. Instead many do plain-Jane, run-of-the-mill, vanilla geek activities like "playing DDR" and "video gaming." Still, normal college student stuff happens here, too. "There are definitely typical college parties with drinking games," and "Clubs and student organizations put on a lot of activities." Plenty of students also get heavily involved "with local service groups (FIRST Robotics and Habitat for Humanity are particularly active)." And as it is at every one of the gazillion colleges in the greater Beantown area, "going into Boston for events" is a popular pastime here too. Concerning the more mundane details of day-to-day life on campus, students are pleased. The dorms are "nice and warm," and "The food is amazing."

Student Body

Picture this: "Engineers with social skills." Yes, they really do exist, and about 300 of them live and learn happily together at this small college on the outskirts of Boston. These folks "are all extremely intelligent and very high-achieving." "There are students here that have held patents since high school, [and others] who have worked for NASA." Perhaps because people like this—people who have "already made incredible, insane contributions to the world"—are not in short supply, "The majority [of students] don't seem to feel like they're especially smart." So there's little threat of being smothered by peers' egos if one enrolls here. "Olin has a very diverse student body with regard to everything except race." "The full-tuition scholarship allows for students from less wealthy backgrounds" to attend, and a "strong group of very religious students" coexists peacefully with a "decent number of people who express alternative sexualities." In sum, a live-and-let-live philosophy is pervasive. "People are allowed to have their own passions and opinions so long as they have passions and opinions."

FRANKLIN W. OLIN COLLEGE OF ENGINEERING

FINANCIAL AID: 781-292-2222 • E-MAIL: INFO@OLIN.EDU • WEBSITE: WWW.OLIN.EDU

THE PRINCETON REVIEW SAYS

Admissions

Very important factors considered include: Rigor of secondary school record, Academic GPA, Application Essay, Recommendation(s), Extracurricular activities, Talent/ability, Character/personal qualities, Level of applicant's interest. *Important factors considered include:* Volunteer work, Class rank, Standardized test scores *Other factors considered include:* Interview, First Generation, Geographical residence, State residency, Racial/ethnic status, Work experience.

Financial Aid

The Princeton Review suggests that all financial aid forms be submitted as soon as possible after January 1.

The Inside Word

Not many colleges can boast that they are filled with students who turned down offers from the likes of MIT, Cal Tech, and Carnegie Mellon, but Olin can. Olin is unique among engineering schools in that the Admissions Office really looks for more than just brains. Things like social skills and eloquence are taken extremely seriously here, so reclusive geniuses seeking 4 years of technical monasticism will be at a disadvantage in the application process.

THE SCHOOL SAYS "..."

From The Admissions Office

"Every admitted student at Olin College receives a $130,000 4-year full-tuition scholarship. The endowment to support these scholarships, as well as the funds to build a brand new state-of-the-art campus, was provided by the F. W. Olin Foundation. This commitment, in excess of $460 million, is among the largest grants in the history of U.S. higher education. It is the intention of the founders that this scholarship will be offered in perpetuity.

"The selection process at Olin College is unique to college admission. Each year a highly self-selecting pool of approximately 800 applications is reviewed on traditional selection criteria. Approximately 180 finalists are invited to one of two Candidates' Weekends in February and March. These candidates are grouped into five-person teams for a weekend of design-and-build exercises, group discussions, and interviews with Olin students, faculty, and alumni. Written evaluations and recommendations for each candidate are prepared by all Olin participants and submitted to the faculty Admission Committee. The committee admits about 100 candidates to yield a freshman class of 75. The result is that the freshman class is ultimately chosen on the strength of personal attributes such as leadership, cooperation, creativity, communication, and their enthusiasm for Olin College.

"A waiting list of approximately 20 is also established. Some wait list candidates who are not offered a spot in the class may defer enrollment for 1 year—with the guarantee of the Olin Scholarship. Wait list students are strongly encouraged do something unusual, exciting, and productive during their sabbatical year.

"Students applying for admission in the Fall of 2007 are required to take the SAT (or the ACT with the writing section). Olin College also requires scores from two SAT Subject Tests: Math (level 1 or 2), and a Science of the student's choice."

SELECTIVITY
Admissions Rating	99
# of applicants	1,054
% of applicants accepted	11
% of acceptees attending	71

FRESHMAN PROFILE
Range SAT Critical Reading	700–790
Range SAT Math	740–800
Range ACT Composite	32–35
% graduated top 10% of class	94
% graduated top 25% of class	100
% graduated top 50% of class	100

DEADLINES
Regular	12/01
Nonfall registration?	No

APPLICANTS ALSO LOOK AT
AND OFTEN PREFER
Harvard College
Cornell College
University of California—Berkeley
Stanford University
Massachusetts Institute of Technology
AND SOMETIMES PREFER
Harvey Mudd College
California Institute of Technology
Carnegie Mellon University
Rensselaer Polytechnic Institute
AND RARELY PREFER
Washington University in St. Louis
Rice University
Worcester Polytechnic Institute
Brown University
Northwestern University

FINANCIAL FACTS
Financial Aid Rating	99
Comprehensive fee	$33,600
Room and board	$11,800
Required fees	$175
Books and supplies	$750
% frosh rec. need-based scholarship or grant aid	12
% UG rec. need-based scholarship or grant aid	12
% frosh rec. non-need-based scholarship or grant aid	10
% UG rec. non-need-based scholarship or grant aid	3
% frosh rec. any financial aid	100
% UG rec. any financial aid	100
% UG borrow to pay for school	2
Average cumulative indebtedness	$4,525

FURMAN UNIVERSITY

3300 POINSETT HIGHWAY, GREENVILLE, SC 29613 • ADMISSIONS: 864-294-2034 • FAX: 864-294-3127

STUDENTS SAY ". . ."

Academics

Furman University, "a small, private, liberal arts school with a gorgeous campus," has "a great reputation, especially in the Southeast." These are just some of the reasons that students choose the school. Undergraduates also love the "great collegiate atmosphere," "generous scholarships, plenty of undergraduate research opportunities, and personal attention from professors," and the "sweet downtown scene" in hometown Greenville. In short, they come because they feel that "Furman offers a great overall experience." Students warn that "Furman is hard. There are no 'gimmes' here. You work for what you get and oftentimes the result shocks freshmen who grew accustomed to cruising in high school." As one student writes, "Furman places a great deal of emphasis on class discussion and active participation. This is often quite fun, but it usually is a pretty effective test of whether you read the deconstruction article last night or whether you truly have the Greek aorist passive down." Students' efforts to keep up are abetted by "small class sizes and good faculty" that provide "the feeling that your professors not only know you as a person, but care about you. Even when classes are kicking your butt, Furman still provides a very enjoyable academic experience, and you're left thinking of the good over the bad."

Life

Furman University "is about students who have truly come to get an education but also find an abundance of other activities that they love." Even walking to class offers a pleasant diversion "because of how picturesque the campus is." For some, "Life at Furman is definitely centered around Furman itself. Students call it 'the bubble.' People are generally very active in at least one activity on campus other than their academic responsibilities." Major events include homecoming which is "one of the most fun weeks all year, with competitions and . . . gathering on the mall Friday night for float building, carnival rides, funnel cakes, and for many students, alcohol intake." Others leave campus fairly frequently to take advantage of downtown Greenville ("one of the coolest places") and the many "outdoor opportunities in the surrounding area." Students occasionally venture further a-field: "We're only 2 hours from Atlanta, Charlotte, and Columbia, so we go to concerts there. We're right in the mountains, so we go hiking and camping, and sometimes we make the 4-hour drive to the beach." Just about everyone enjoys the frequent and popular Greek parties; although "only about one-third of the student body is involved in Greek organizations, at least two-thirds go to the parties and other Greek events." A large jock population drives an active athletic scene; music groups and religious organizations are also "very popular."

Student Body

"Furman kids are often viewed as being rich, White, and preppy (soror-adorable and frat-tastic are two common terms)," and "While the majority may fit into those categories," there are also "plenty that are outside that spectrum." True, the typical student is still "a Southern (probably from Tennessee, Georgia, or South Carolina), Protestant Christian of a conservative denomination, athletic, snappily dressed, and hard-studying, but not possessing deep intellectual interest in more than a couple of subjects," but the university is working hard to overcome its reputation as a "a school only for conservative, rich, White kids" by "opening up its doors to many different types of people. Last year, for example, the student body president was a Muslim of Pakistani descent." Most here "are religious to some degree," and many "can quote any and every line of the Bible, making those who are less religious feel a little out of place." Rich or not, religious or agnostic, Southern or otherwise, "The one unifying factor here is the desire for Furman to retain a spirit of Southern hospitality no matter the diversity of its student body."

FINANCIAL AID: 864-294-2204 • E-MAIL: ADMISSIONS@FURMAN.EDU • WEBSITE: WWW.FURMAN.EDU

THE PRINCETON REVIEW SAYS

Admissions

Very important factors considered include: Rigor of secondary school record. *Important factors considered include:* Class rank, application essay, academic GPA, standardized test scores, character/personal qualities, extracurricular activities. *Other factors considered include:* Recommendation(s), alumni/ae relation, first generation, level of applicant's interest, racial/ethnic status, talent/ability, volunteer work, work experience. SAT or ACT recommended; ACT with Writing component recommended. High school diploma is required and GED is accepted. *Academic units required:* 4 English, 3 mathematics, 2 science, (2 science labs), 2 foreign language, 3 social studies. *Academic units recommended:* 4 English, 4 mathematics, 3 science, (3 science labs), 3 foreign language, 4 social studies.

Financial Aid

Students should submit: FAFSA, institution's own financial aid form, state aid form, South Carolina residents must complete required state forms for South Carolina. Regular filing deadline is 1/15. The Princeton Review suggests that all financial aid forms be submitted as soon as possible after January 1. *Need-based scholarships/grants offered:* Federal Pell, SEOG, state scholarships/grants, private scholarships, the school's own gift aid, Federal SMART and ACG grants. *Loan aid offered:* FFEL Subsidized Stafford, FFEL Unsubsidized Stafford, FFEL PLUS, Federal Perkins, state loans, Donor sponsored loans for study abroad. Applicants will be notified of awards on or about 3/15. Federal Work-Study Program available. Institutional employment available. Off-campus job opportunities are excellent.

The Inside Word

Furman's high acceptance rate is deceptive; the applicant pool here is highly self-selected, meaning that most who apply have pretty strong credentials. The following stats are more telling: The average applicant has completed five AP courses, earned an unweighted high school GPA of 3.68, and scored pretty well on standardized tests. In the absence of similarly strong credentials, you'll need to find some way to sell yourself to the Admissions Committee. A demonstrated ability to contribute to the school community—perhaps through athletics, the arts, or community service—will help.

THE SCHOOL SAYS "..."

From The Admissions Office

"From its position as a nationally ranked independent, coeducational liberal arts college of 2,600 students, Furman takes great pride in its beautiful campus, its gifted student body, its distinguished and active faculty, and the many notable accomplishments of its alumni. Furman emphasizes engaged learning, a hands-on, problem-solving, and collaborative educational philosophy that encourages students to put into practice the theories and methods learned from texts and lectures. Using the latest in wired and wireless technology, students have multiple opportunities to become engaged in their academic pursuits through an array of internships, service-learning programs, faculty/student creative projects and significant undergraduate research. Furman offers an unusual combination of a top-tier liberal arts college, 17 Division I men's and women's athletic teams, and a nationally competitive music program that features 26 performing ensembles. Students are involved in hundreds of organizations and clubs on campus ranging from professional organizations to fraternities and sororities. In sum, Furman is a diverse learning community that celebrates its differences and is committed to the development of the whole student. The Admissions Committee believes that standardized testing has an important place in selective college admissions decision-making, but we believe that students should have choices. Furman applicants can meet our standardized test requirement but submitting scores choosing from one of the following options: SAT I; ACT and optional writing test; two SAT II subject tests—one in English, one in Math; two AP exams, one from English (Language and Composition or Literature and Composition) and one from Math (Calculus AB or BC); two IB exams, one in English Language (A1) and one in Mathematics; or the TOEFL (for international students ONLY)."

SELECTIVITY

Admissions Rating	94
# of applicants	3,879
% of applicants accepted	56
% of acceptees attending	32
# accepting a place on wait list	146
% admitted from wait list	14
# of early decision applicants	634
% accepted early decision	69

FRESHMAN PROFILE

Range SAT Critical Reading	590–690
Range SAT Math	590–690
Range SAT Writing	580–680
Range ACT Composite	25–30
Average HS GPA	3.54
% graduated top 10% of class	63
% graduated top 25% of class	85
% graduated top 50% of class	98

DEADLINES

Early decision	
Deadline	11/15
Notification	12/15
Regular	
Deadline	1/15
Notification	3/15
Nonfall registration?	no

FINANCIAL FACTS

Financial Aid Rating	87
Annual tuition	$31,040
Room and board	$8,064
Required fees	$520
Books and supplies	$850
% frosh rec. need-based scholarship or grant aid	41
% UG rec. need-based scholarship or grant aid	41
% frosh rec. non-need-based scholarship or grant aid	34
% UG rec. non-need-based scholarship or grant aid	36
% frosh rec. need-based self-help aid	23
% UG rec. need-based self-help aid	25
% frosh rec. athletic scholarships	8
% UG rec. athletic scholarships	9
% frosh rec. any financial aid	83
% UG rec. any financial aid	85
% UG borrow to pay for school	42
Average cumulative indebtedness	$24,512

GEORGE MASON UNIVERSITY

4400 UNIVERSITY DRIVE MSN 3A4, FAIRFAX, VA 22030-4444 • ADMISSIONS: 703-993-2400 • FAX: 703-993-2392

STUDENTS SAY "..."

Academics

George Mason University, a school in the Virginia suburbs just outside of DC, has spent the past few years trying to get beyond its reputation as a commuter school, and it looks like it has been doing a good job of it. This innovative spirit and focus on "finding a new way to do what every other older school does" is one of Mason's greatest attributes, and though complaints about construction may pop up from time to time, the school is pushing through "the developmental stage" on its way to becoming a top university. Well-known for having one of the best nursing programs in northern Virginia, as well as a similarly strong school of management and economics department, the location of the school means that "students take their own initiative in finding internships and jobs to better their career prospects."

Students are happy with many of their professors, but quite a few people complain that the number of adjuncts teaching make classes too easy, especially for the required courses. "I feel like I'm taking the same classes I took in high school again, just with more homework," says a freshman. However, "once you get into your major courses the classes as well as professors improve." There are many tutoring service and other programs available for students who need help, and due to the close proximity to the nation's capital, the school has the opportunity "to host a large number of guest speakers/special lectures including politicians, CEOs and other professionals from major defense contractors in the area, and non-governmental representatives." At times "it may seem that the administrators are out of touch with reality," but they "generally receive student input well."

Life

While the school has undertaken massive efforts to drop the commuter label by providing more residence halls and events (on-campus housing availability is now completely caught up to demand), most agree that both the quality and the advertising of the weekend activities could use some work. "There is always something going on every weekend, but it may not be exactly what every student wants to do," says a senior. Many of those who do stay on campus for the weekend think the school should "make a better effort to acknowledge that people actually do live on-campus during the weekends...we are all capable of making our own fun, but when the food hours and locations are so restricted we don't feel like we're even supposed to be there, that's taking it a little bit far." Still, the school is doing its best to amuse its students, and programs like Every Freakin' Friday ensure there's an event, well, every Friday, and over 200 organizations (including a strong Greek presence) keep students occupied. Trips to the city for eating, shopping, and nightlife are frequent, and from November through March, basketball games are also popular. The school is almost legendary for its "serious parking problem," which can be a very real concern for the commuter majority here, and people "party pretty hard to relieve the stress accrued from parking on-campus."

Student Body

There are a "wide variety" of students found at this big school, with commuters and non-commuters representing "a mix of traditional and non traditional students," most of who are "moderately preppy" and come from in-state. There are a fair number of international and Muslim students, and "simply walking through the student center you will hear at least three different languages being spoken." Mason has "very little if any discrimination," and in general most students are very aware of global issues and different cultures. With this physical diversity also comes academic diversity, "where some students like to study a lot and some students like to party a lot."

FINANCIAL AID: 703-993-2353 • E-MAIL: ADMISSIONS@GMU.EDU • WEBSITE: WWW.MASONMETRO.EDU

THE PRINCETON REVIEW SAYS

Admissions

Very important factors considered include: Academic GPA, rigor of secondary school record. *Important factors considered include:* Class rank, application essay, recommendation(s), alumni/ae relation, character/personal qualities, talent/ability. *Other factors considered include:* Standardized test scores, extracurricular activities, first generation, level of applicant's interest, volunteer work, work experience. SAT and SAT Subject Tests or ACT recommended; TOEFL required of all international applicants. High school diploma is required and GED is accepted. *Academic units required:* 4 English, 3 mathematics, 3 science, (3 science labs), 2 foreign language, 3 social studies, 3 academic electives. *Academic units recommended:* 4 English, 4 mathematics, 4 science, (4 science labs), 3 foreign language, 4 social studies, 5 academic electives.

Financial Aid

Students should submit: FAFSA. The Princeton Review suggests that all financial aid forms be submitted as soon as possible after January 1. *Need-based scholarships/grants offered:* Federal Pell, SEOG, state scholarships/grants, private scholarships, the school's own gift aid. *Loan aid offered:* FFEL Subsidized Stafford, FFEL Unsubsidized Stafford, FFEL PLUS, Federal Perkins, Federal Nursing Applicants will be notified of awards on a rolling basis beginning 4/1. Federal Work-Study Program available. Institutional employment available. Off-campus job opportunities are excellent.

The Inside Word

George Mason is a popular destination for college for two key reasons: Its proximity to Washington, DC and the fact that it is not nearly as difficult to gain admission at Mason as it is at University of Virginia or William & Mary, the two flagships of the Virginia state system. The university's quality faculty and impressive facilities make it worth taking a look if low-cost, solid programs in the DC area are high on your list.

THE SCHOOL SAYS "..."

From The Admissions Office

"George Mason University enjoys the best location in the world. Our connections to the DC area result in faculty members who are engaged in the top research in their fields. We have professors who are regular contributors on all of the major news networks, and you can hardly listen to a program on National Public Radio without hearing from one of our scholars. This connectivity extends to our students, who take internships and get jobs at some of the best organizations and companies in the world. We have students at AOL/Time Warner, the National Institutes of Health, the Kennedy Center, the World Bank, the White House, and the National Zoo. We have all the advantages of the excitement of our Nation's Capital combined with the comfort and security of this beautiful suburban campus.

"At Mason, we pride ourselves on being among the most innovative universities in the world. Many of our degree programs are the first of their kind, including the first PhD program in biodefense, the first DC-based undergraduate program in conflict resolution, the first integrated school of information technology and engineering based on computer related programs, and one of the most innovative performing arts management programs in the United States. As a result, George Mason University is at the forefront of the emerging field of biotechnology, is a natural leader in the performing arts, and holds a preeminent position in the fields of economics, electronic journalism, and history, just to name a few. George Mason University will accept the ACT, with or without the written portion, and either the old or new version of the SAT. Scores from the Writing section will not be considered in our admission decisions, as our faculty does not feel the Writing section reflects quality or methodology of our award-winning writing across the curriculum program. Mason has the largest score-optional program in the U.S."

SELECTIVITY

Admissions Rating	83
# of applicants	13,327
% of applicants accepted	56
% of acceptees attending	30
# accepting a place on wait list	318
% admitted from wait list	99

FRESHMAN PROFILE

Range SAT Critical Reading	500–600
Range SAT Math	520–610
Range SAT Writing	500–600
Range ACT Composite	22–27
Minimum paper TOEFL	530
Minimum computer TOEFL	71
Average HS GPA	3.46
% graduated top 10% of class	18
% graduated top 25% of class	54
% graduated top 50% of class	93

DEADLINES

Early action	
Deadline	11/1
Notification	12/15
Regular	
Priority	12/1
Deadline	1/15
Notification	4/1
Nonfall registration?	yes

APPLICANTS ALSO LOOK AT AND SOMETIMES PREFER

George Washington University
University of Virginia
Virginia Polytechnic Institute

FINANCIAL FACTS

Financial Aid Rating	70
Annual in-state tuition	$5,035
Annual out-of-state tuition	$17,923
Room and board	$7,020
Required fees	$1,805
Books and supplies	$850
% frosh rec. need-based scholarship or grant aid	27
% UG rec. need-based scholarship or grant aid	26
% frosh rec. non-need-based scholarship or grant aid	11
% UG rec. non-need-based scholarship or grant aid	6
% frosh rec. need-based self-help aid	25
% UG rec. need-based self-help aid	2
% frosh rec. athletic scholarships	2
% UG rec. athletic scholarships	2
% frosh rec. any financial aid	61
% UG rec. any financial aid	49
% UG borrow to pay for school	49
Average cumulative indebtedness	$16,705

THE GEORGE WASHINGTON UNIVERSITY

2121 I STREET NORTHWEST, SUITE 201, WASHINGTON, DC 20052 • ADMISSIONS: 202-994-6040 • FAX: 202-994-0325

CAMPUS LIFE

Quality of Life Rating	**94**
Fire Safety Rating	**60***
Green Rating	**60***
Type of school	private
Environment	metropolis

STUDENTS

Total undergrad enrollment	10,370
% male/female	45/55
% from out of state	98
% live on campus	64
% in (# of) fraternities	19 (12)
% in (# of) sororities	18 (9)
% African American	6
% Asian	10
% Caucasian	62
% Hispanic	6
% international	4
# of countries represented	101

SURVEY SAYS . . .

Athletic facilities are great
Students love Washington, DC
Great off-campus food
Dorms are like palaces
Campus feels safe
Students are happy
Student publications are popular
Student government is popular
Political activism is popular

ACADEMICS

Academic Rating	**86**
Calendar	semester
Student/faculty ratio	13:1
Profs interesting rating	77
Profs accessible rating	75
% classes taught by TAs	3
Most common reg class size	10–19 students
Most common lab size	20–29 students

STUDENTS SAY ". . ."

Academics

At George Washington University, it's all about "being in the center of the most powerful city in the world and deciding where to make your mark," where students can tap "the nation's capital, whether [for] sports, science and medicine, politics, or psychology." Politics are the primary drawing card; the stellar Elliot School of International Affairs trains tomorrow's diplomats, while solid programs in political science and political communication benefit from heavyweight guest speakers (one student writes, "DeeDee Myers came to my Washington Reporters class, and I got to go interview Bob Siegel of NPR—it's experiences like that that make GW special"), and access to incredible internships; as one student puts it, "GW is government's largest source of slave labor. It isn't uncommon . . . [to] see people from your different classes in the halls of Capital Hill." GW doesn't begin and end with government though; the school also has "a wonderful business program with an abundance of internship opportunities," a "computer security and information assurance" program "that's one of the best in the world and is actually one of only a handful accredited by the National Security Agency," and numerous other strengths. GW's administration seems geared toward training future government workers; students describe it as very "bureaucratic." The school maintains a large adjunct faculty; while some love that the adjuncts "have other projects or jobs on the side that can give students firsthand experience with real issues," others complain that "we lose many great adjunct professors every year" and that the large turnover "would be avoided if we just shelled out a little more money [to take on more full-time faculty]."

Life

"Whether it's going to the Kennedy Center, [to] the 9:30 Club, or [for] a midnight monument tour . . . DC is at the center of a GW student's experience." Undergrads boast that "of all DC universities, GW is the best situated. Where else can you party, get drunk, stumble your way to the steps of the Lincoln [Memorial], and attempt to hurry back to get enough sleep to function at your internship on the Hill?" Being in DC "makes it easy to always have something to do, from the monuments to the museums . . . from just hanging out on campus [to] going to sporting events." Speaking of sports, GW basketball "is huge. However than that, we're not much of a sports school. Students are much more interested in joining the College Democrats or the College Republicans." Many are also interested in partying, but a junior stresses that she'd "never call GW a party school. It's definitely there if you want it, but it's not pressured on you at all. Same thing with frats and sororities: Those who want to be in Greek life can be, and those who don't, don't have to [be] in order to have a fulfilling college experience."

Student Body

GW attracts "a lot of wealthy students" (its tuition is among the nation's highest), but there is also "a sense of diversity on campus." Jewish students make up about one-quarter of the undergraduate population; there are also "a lot of international students," "students from each of the 50 states," and, sprinkled among the wealthy, "plenty of middle-class students." At GW, undergrads say, you'll find "people that have disabilities, and people from every race, religion, sexual orientation, and ideology." (While all ideologies are represented, it should be noted that "most students characterize themselves as Democrats.") Students tell us that GW isn't as much "a melting pot as a tossed salad, where people from different backgrounds, frats, and student org[anizations] all blend together and taste pretty darn good." Undergrads here tend to be "very driven, constantly thinking about what their next internship is going to be, and how they're going to get out into Washington more and things like that."

FINANCIAL AID: 202-994-6620 • E-MAIL: GWADM@GWU.EDU • WEBSITE: WWW.GWU.EDU

THE PRINCETON REVIEW SAYS

Admissions

Very important factors considered include: Academic GPA, rigor of secondary school record. *Important factors considered include:* Class rank, application essay, recommendation(s), standardized test scores, extracurricular activities, interview, talent/ability, volunteer work. *Other factors considered include:* Alumni/ae relation, character/personal qualities, first generation, geographical residence, level of applicant's interest, racial/ethnic status, work experience. SAT or ACT required; High school diploma is required and GED is not accepted. *Academic units required:* 4 English, 2 mathematics, 2 science, (1 science labs), 2 foreign language, 2 social studies. *Academic units recommended:* 4 English, 4 mathematics, 4 science, 4 foreign language, 4 social studies.

Financial Aid

Students should submit: FAFSA, CSS/Financial Aid PROFILE Regular filing deadline is 2/1. The Princeton Review suggests that all financial aid forms be submitted as soon as possible after January 1. *Need-based scholarships/grants offered:* Federal Pell, SEOG, state scholarships/grants, the school's own gift aid. *Loan aid offered:* FFEL Subsidized Stafford, FFEL Unsubsidized Stafford, FFEL PLUS, Federal Perkins Federal Work-Study Program available. Institutional employment available. Off-campus job opportunities are excellent.

The Inside Word

With over 20,000 applications to process annually, GW would be forgiven if it gave student essays only a perfunctory glance. However, the school considers essays carefully; a school Admissions Officer recently told the *Washington Times* that student essays represent "the student's voice in the application," adding that the school's low admit rate means that "everything (in the application) takes on significance."

THE SCHOOL SAYS "..."

From The Admissions Office

"At GW, we welcome students who show a measure of impatience with the limitations of traditional education. At many universities, the edge of campus is the real world, but not at GW, where our campus and Washington, DC are seamless. We look for bold, bright students who are ambitious, energetic, and self-motivated. Here, where we are so close to the centers of thought and action in every field we offer, we easily integrate our outstanding academic tradition and faculty connections with the best internship and job opportunities of Washington, DC. A generous scholarship and financial assistance program attracts top students from all parts of the country and the world.

"Students applying for Fall 2008 may send either an old or revised SAT score. Regardless of the version of the SAT submitted, we will use those scores that best work to the student's advantage. Applicants to the BA/MD, IEMP, and BA/JD programs are required to submit SAT Subject Tests. "

SELECTIVITY
Admissions Rating	96
# of applicants	19,606
% of applicants accepted	37
% of acceptees attending	30
# accepting a place on wait list	702
% admitted from wait list	22

FRESHMAN PROFILE
Range SAT Critical Reading	600–690
Range SAT Math	600–690
Range SAT Writing	600–690
Range ACT Composite	26–29
% graduated top 10% of class	66
% graduated top 25% of class	90
% graduated top 50% of class	100

DEADLINES
Early decision	
Deadline	11/10
Notification	12/15
Regular	
Priority	12/1
Deadline	1/10
Notification	4/1
Nonfall registration?	yes

FINANCIAL FACTS
Financial Aid Rating	88
Annual tuition	$38,500
Room and board	$12,155
Required fees	$30
Books and supplies	$1,000
% frosh rec. need-based scholarship or grant aid	35
% UG rec. need-based scholarship or grant aid	39
% frosh rec. non-need-based scholarship or grant aid	11
% UG rec. non-need-based scholarship or grant aid	11
% frosh rec. need-based self-help aid	31
% UG rec. need-based self-help aid	34
% frosh rec. athletic scholarships	1
% UG rec. athletic scholarships	2
% UG borrow to pay for school	49
Average cumulative indebtedness	$30,817

GEORGETOWN UNIVERSITY

THIRTY-SEVENTH AND P STREETS, NORTHWEST, WASHINGTON, DC 20057 • ADMISSIONS: 202-687-3600 • FAX: 202-687-5084

CAMPUS LIFE
Quality of Life Rating	**84**
Fire Safety Rating	**91**
Green Rating	**95**
Type of school	private
Affiliation	Roman Catholic
Environment	metropolis

STUDENTS
Total undergrad enrollment	6,623
% male/female	45/55
% from out of state	98
% live on campus	71
% African American	7
% Asian	9
% Caucasian	67
% Hispanic	7
% international	5
# of countries represented	138

SURVEY SAYS . . .
Students love Washington, DC
Great off-campus food
Students are happy
Frats and sororities are unpopular
or nonexistent
Political activism is popular
Lots of beer drinking

ACADEMICS
Academic Rating	**92**
Calendar	semester
Student/faculty ratio	11:1
Profs interesting rating	82
Profs accessible rating	80
% classes taught by TAs	8

MOST POPULAR MAJORS
political science and government
international relations and affairs
English language and literature

STUDENTS SAY ". . ."

Academics

This moderately-sized elite academic establishment stays true to its Jesuit foundations by educating its students with the idea of Cura Personalis, or "care for the whole person." The "well-informed" student body perpetuates upon itself, creating an atmosphere full of vibrant intellectual life, but "also balanced with extra-curricular learning and development." "Georgetown is…a place where people work very, very hard without feeling like they are in direct competition," says an international politics major. Located in Washington, D.C., there's a noted School of Foreign Service here, and the access to internships is a huge perk for those in political or government programs. In addition, the proximity to the nation's capital fetches "high-profile guest speakers," with many of the most powerful people in global politics speaking regularly, as well as a large number of adjunct professors who either are currently working in the government as a day job, or have retired from high level positions.

Georgetown has on offer a "great selection of very knowledgeable professors, split with a good proportion of those who are experienced in realms outside of academia (such as former government officials) and career academics," though there are a few superstars who might be "somewhat less than totally collegial." Professors tend to be "fantastic scholars and teachers" and are "generally available to students," as well as often being "interested in getting to know you as a person (if you put forth the effort to talk to them and go to office hours)." Though Georgetown has a policy of grade deflation, meaning "A's are hard to come by," there are "a ton of interesting courses available" and TAs are used only for optional discussion sessions and help with grading. The academics "can be challenging or they can be not so much (not that they are ever really easy, just easier)"; it all depends on the courses you choose and how much you actually do the work. The school administration is well-meaning and "usually willing to talk and compromise with students," but the process of planning activities can be full of headaches and bureaucracy, and the administration itself "sometimes is over-stretched or has trouble transmitting its message." Nevertheless, "a motivated student can get done what he or she wants."

Life

Students are "extremely well aware of the world around them," from government to environment, social to economic, and "Georgetown is the only place where an argument over politics, history, and philosophy is preceded by a keg stand." Hoyas like to have a good time on weekends, and parties at campus and off-campus apartments and townhouses "are generally open to all comers and tend to have a somewhat networking atmosphere; meeting people you don't know is a constant theme." With such a motivated group on such a high-energy campus, "people are always headed somewhere, it seems—to rehearsal, athletic practice, a guest speaker, to the gym." Community service and political activism are particularly popular, as is basketball. Everything near Georgetown is in walking distance, including the world of DC's museums, restaurants, and stores, and "grabbing or ordering late night food is a popular option."

Student Body

There are "a lot of wealthy students on campus," and preppy-casual is the fashion de rigueur; this is "definitely not a 'granola' school," but students from diverse backgrounds are typically welcomed by people wanting to learn about different experiences. Indeed, everyone here is well-traveled and well-educated, and there are "a ton of international students." "You better have at least some interest in politics or you will feel out-of-place," says a student. The school can also be "a bit cliquish, with athletes at the top," but there are "plenty of groups for everybody to fit into and find their niche," and "there is much crossover between groups."

FINANCIAL AID: 202-687-4547 • WEBSITE: WWW.GEORGETOWN.EDU

THE PRINCETON REVIEW SAYS

Admissions

Very important factors considered include: Class rank, application essay, academic GPA, recommendation(s), rigor of secondary school record, standardized test scores, character/personal qualities, talent/ability. *Important factors considered include:* Extracurricular activities, interview, volunteer work. *Other factors considered include:* Alumni/ae relation, geographical residence, racial/ethnic status, state residency, work experience. SAT Subject Tests recommended; SAT or ACT required; High school diploma is required and GED is accepted. *Academic units recommended:* 4 English, 2 mathematics, 1 science, 2 foreign language, 2 social studies, 2 history.

Financial Aid

Students should submit: FAFSA, CSS/Financial Aid PROFILE, noncustodial PROFILE, business/farm supplement, tax returns. Regular filing deadline is 2/1. The Princeton Review suggests that all financial aid forms be submitted as soon as possible after January 1. *Need-based scholarships/grants offered:* Federal Pell, SEOG, state scholarships/grants, private scholarships, the school's own gift aid. *Loan aid offered:* FFEL Subsidized Stafford, FFEL Unsubsidized Stafford, FFEL PLUS, Federal Perkins, Federal Nursing, Alternative loans. Applicants will be notified of awards on or about 4/1. Federal Work-Study Program available. Institutional employment available. Off-campus job opportunities are excellent.

The Inside Word

It was always tough to get admitted to Georgetown, but in the early 1980s Patrick Ewing and the Hoyas created a basketball sensation that catapulted the place into position as one of the most selective universities in the nation. There has been no turning back since. GU gets almost 10 applications for every space in the entering class, and the academic strength of the pool is impressive. Virtually 50 percent of the entire student body took AP courses in high school. Candidates who are wait listed should hold little hope for an offer of admission; over the past several years Georgetown has taken very few off their lists.

THE SCHOOL SAYS "..."

From The Admissions Office

"Georgetown was founded in 1789 by John Carroll, who concurred with his contemporaries Benjamin Franklin and Thomas Jefferson in believing that the success of the young democracy depended upon an educated and virtuous citizenry. Carroll founded the school with the dynamic Jesuit tradition of education, characterized by humanism and committed to the assumption of responsibility and action. Georgetown is a national and international university, enrolling students from all 50 states and over 100 foreign countries. Undergraduate students are enrolled in one of four undergraduate schools: the College of Arts and Sciences, School of Foreign Service, Georgetown School of Business, and Georgetown School of Nursing and Health Studies. All students share a common liberal arts core and have access to the entire university curriculum.

"Applicants who graduate from high school in 2008 have the option of submitting scores from either the new or existing version of the SAT. Only the Verbal and Math portions of the new SAT will be considered. The student's best composite score will be used in the admission process."

SELECTIVITY

Admissions Rating	98
# of applicants	16,163
% of applicants accepted	21
% of acceptees attending	47
# accepting a place on wait list	1,035
% admitted from wait list	4

FRESHMAN PROFILE

Range SAT Critical Reading	650–750
Range SAT Math	650–740
% graduated top 10% of class	90
% graduated top 25% of class	96
% graduated top 50% of class	99

DEADLINES

Early action	
Deadline	11/1
Notification	12/15
Regular	
Deadline	1/10
Notification	4/1
Nonfall registration?	no

FINANCIAL FACTS

Financial Aid Rating	93
Annual tuition	$35,568
Room and board	$12,146
Required fees	$396
Books and supplies	$1,060
% frosh rec. need-based scholarship or grant aid	40
% UG rec. need-based scholarship or grant aid	37
% frosh rec. non-need-based scholarship or grant aid	1
% frosh rec. need-based self-help aid	32
% UG rec. need-based self-help aid	34
% frosh rec. athletic scholarships	3
% UG rec. athletic scholarships	3
% frosh rec. any financial aid	40
% UG rec. any financial aid	39
% UG borrow to pay for school	46
Average cumulative indebtedness	$27,117

GEORGIA INSTITUTE OF TECHNOLOGY

219 UNCLE HEINE WAY, ATLANTA, GA 30332-0320 • ADMISSIONS: 404-894-4154 • FAX: 404-894-9511

STUDENTS SAY ". . ."

Academics

Students coming to Georgia Tech should be prepared to be "challenged in many new ways." Here, "Professors are very demanding. They're the most brilliant people I've ever met," and they "don't spoon-feed you"; if you want to succeed at Tech, students advise that "you have to learn how to suck it up and study." There's one big upside to the rigors of Tech's academics. As one student puts it, after being here, "The rest of the world seems easy." Students interested in hands-on learning appreciate the fact that "a lot of the professors are doing major research, so it's [a] great [school] for research opportunities." "Because the professors are deep in their research," however, they sometimes "don't do that great a job teaching." Luckily, "The professors are required to have office hours," and students suggest taking advantage of them: "Professors are mostly great one-on-one. They really want you to talk to them and for you to learn."

Life

As one undergrad puts it, "Basically people bust their asses during the week, and when the weekends arrive they're prepared to let loose a bit." Options for letting loose include "a 'good enough' NCAA Division I sports program, a good social scene," a welcoming Greek community, "and for everyone else, there's the city of Atlanta right at your doorstep. You're just a short ride away from movies, shopping, the Fox Theatre, the High Museum of Art, Piedmont Park, and one of the best club and bar scenes in the South," centered mainly in the neighborhoods of Buckhead and Midtown. For those without cars in this driving city, transportation comes in the form of "a 'Tech Trolley' that takes a route around midtown, and a 'Stinger Shuttle' that goes to the MARTA [Atlanta's subway] station, giving students access to the airport, downtown (although that is walkable), and Lenox Mall." With "over 300 organizations already on campus," students seeking leadership experience can most likely find it, as too they can find other students with like-minded interests.

Student Body

Students claim that "Tech is broken down into two different types of college students. First you have the 'typical' college students, who take their academics seriously, but who enjoy being social, going out on weekends, and interacting with the rest of the student population. Then there's the group of 'Techies' who are sometimes socially awkward and who like to stay in their rooms a lot and only interact with others like them." The guys here bemoan a "70:30 male/female ratio, but" optimistically declare that "The ratio is getting better." And those who have found their talents to be liabilities in the past will be pleased to learn that at GT, "Unlike at high school, no one looks down upon you if you know the entire periodic table, if you can do differential equations, or you can speak three languages; rather, you are respected."

FINANCIAL AID: 404-894-4160 • E-MAIL: ADMISSION@GATECH.EDU • WEBSITE: WWW.GATECH.EDU

THE PRINCETON REVIEW SAYS

Admissions

Very important factors considered include: Academic GPA. *Important factors considered include:* Application essay, rigor of secondary school record, standardized test scores, extracurricular activities, geographical residence, state residency, talent/ability, volunteer work, work experience. SAT or ACT required; ACT with Writing component required. High school diploma is required and GED is accepted. *Academic units required:* 4 English, 4 mathematics, 3 science, (2 science labs), 2 foreign language, 3 social studies.

Financial Aid

Students should submit: FAFSA. Regular filing deadline is 3/1. The Princeton Review suggests that all financial aid forms be submitted as soon as possible after January 1. *Need-based scholarships/grants offered:* Federal Pell, SEOG, state scholarships/grants, private scholarships, the school's own gift aid, Federal ACG & Federal SMART Grants. *Loan aid offered:* FFEL Subsidized Stafford, FFEL Unsubsidized Stafford, FFEL PLUS, Federal Perkins, college/university loans from institutional funds. Applicants will be notified of awards on or about 4/1. Federal Work-Study Program available. Institutional employment available. Off-campus job opportunities are excellent.

The Inside Word

Students considering Georgia Tech should not be deceived by the relatively high acceptance rate. GT is a demanding school, and its applicant pool is largely self-selecting. While Admissions Counselors have begun to implement a more well-rounded approach to the admissions process, grades and test scores are still where candidates make their mark. Requirements vary depending on the school one applies to at GT—applicants are advised to inquire in advance.

THE SCHOOL SAYS "..."

From The Admissions Office

"Georgia Tech consistently ranks among the nation's top public universities producing leaders in engineering, computing, management, architecture, and the sciences while remaining one of the best college buys in the country. The 330-acre campus of red brick buildings and green rolling hills is nestled in the heart of the fun, dynamic, and progressive city of Atlanta in the shadows of a majestic skyline dominated by the work of Georgia Tech–trained architects and designers. During the past decade, over $400 million invested in campus improvements has yielded new state-of-the-art academic and research buildings, apartment-style housing, phenomenal social and recreational facilities, and the most extensive fiber-optic cable system on any college campus. Georgia Tech's combined commitment to technologically focused, hands-on educational experiences, teamwork, great teaching, innovation, leadership development, and community service make it unique. Great things are happening at Georgia Tech. We hope you will join us, become a part of our community, and help us create the future.

"With a Division I ACC sports program and access to Atlanta's music, theater and other cultural venues, Georgia Tech offers its diverse and passionate student body a unique combination of top academics in a thriving and vibrant setting. We encourage you to come visit campus and see why Georgia Tech continues to attract the nation's most motivated, interesting and creative students."

SELECTIVITY

Admissions Rating	93
# of applicants	9,664
% of applicants accepted	63
% of acceptees attending	43
# accepting a place on wait list	118
% admitted from wait list	3

FRESHMAN PROFILE

Range SAT Critical Reading	590–690
Range SAT Math	650–730
Range SAT Writing	580–670
Range ACT Composite	27–31
Average HS GPA	3.73
% graduated top 10% of class	60
% graduated top 25% of class	87
% graduated top 50% of class	99

DEADLINES

Regular	
Deadline	1/15
Notification	3/15
Nonfall registration?	yes

APPLICANTS ALSO LOOK AT

AND OFTEN PREFER
Duke University
Stanford University
Massachusetts Institute of Technology
University of North Carolina at Chapel Hill
Princeton University

AND SOMETIMES PREFER
Emory University
University of Virginia
Clemson University
University of Florida
University of Georgia

AND RARELY PREFER
Vanderbilt University
Virginia Tech
North Carolina State University

FINANCIAL FACTS

Financial Aid Rating	76
Annual tuition	$2,428
% frosh rec. need-based scholarship or grant aid	18
% UG rec. need-based scholarship or grant aid	15
% frosh rec. non-need-based scholarship or grant aid	22
% UG rec. non-need-based scholarship or grant aid	12
% frosh rec. need-based self-help aid	21
% UG rec. need-based self-help aid	18
% frosh rec. athletic scholarships	3
% UG rec. athletic scholarships	2
% frosh rec. any financial aid	89
% UG rec. any financial aid	83
% UG borrow to pay for school	47
Average cumulative indebtedness	$21,436

GETTYSBURG COLLEGE

ADMISSIONS OFFICE, EISENHOWER HOUSE, GETTYSBURG, PA 17325-1484 • ADMISSIONS: 717-337-6100 • FAX: 717-337-6145

STUDENTS SAY " . . ."

Academics

Gettysburg College is a quintessential small liberal arts college, a place where "You can be challenged academically in an intimate environment of smaller class sizes and a smaller student-to-faculty ratio," enabling "students to develop a close rapport with peers and professors." Students here speak glowingly of the "welcoming community with limitless opportunities" to get involved and "grow in and out of the classroom." Those opportunities include "strong study abroad programs, community service activities, internships, and externships." Academically, "Gettysburg isn't a walk in the park. Your professors have expectations of you whether you are a first-year in a 101 class or a senior looking into a research proposal." Help is available to those in danger of falling behind; one student writes, "The offices are there to help you from Calc-Aid [tutors], biology [reviews], and the Writing Center . . . There is so much available; you just need to go take advantage of it." The school's strongest disciplines include political science, music, biology, environmental studies, and (unsurprisingly) Civil War–era studies. Gettysburg also "has a great management department for a small liberal arts school."

Life

"Greek life is where the majority of social life is centered" at Gettysburg, with nearly half of all male students joining a fraternity, "But that's not to say that there are not options beyond that." True, "Greek life is huge at Gettysburg, and for a male who chooses not to 'go Greek' life can be hard socially." It's not as big a deal for females, because "Gettysburg does not have sorority houses." The Greek scene as a whole is "not exclusive"—everyone "goes to the frats." Moreover, "The college doesn't allow rush to take place until second year, so hopefully students have made friends before making the choice to branch out into other social groups such as the frats." "Most everyone makes a conscious effort to get involved on campus in lots of different activities," so the Greeks, while big, aren't the only game in town. The school "does a lot of extras for the students, such as themed dinners, concerts, and special events," and "The Activity Board also brings bands and movies on weekends so there are other things to do." College sports teams "are very strong, both men's and women's," and "lots of students play intramurals or work out." Hometown Gettysburg, with its battlefield and 'ghost tours,' is great for history buffs and has a lot of "small town charm"; others may prefer to "take day trips" to DC and Baltimore for fun, although each requires a 90-minute drive.

Student Body

Gettysburg students tend to be "smart, outgoing, preppy, and determined," the kind of folks who "work real hard during the week and then have fun on the weekend," but also find time to "volunteer and [get] involved in extracurriculars, clubs, and athletics." Students admit that "there is very little diversity on campus, but the majority of the students come from high schools with the same situation," so many "don't notice the lack of diversity, though this can make you stand out if you're different." Students who don't fit the mold tell us they are comfortable here; one writes, "Gettysburg students tend to come from families who are mid- to upper-class, [and] there is a high percentage of legacy students on campus." Quite frequently students show their wealth "in the form of clothing or cars," but "Money isn't the only thing that matters here." While it may be plentiful, "Even if you don't wear Lily Pulitzer or Burberry you will be just fine as long as flip-flops are your favorite footwear!" Students tend to be politically conservative, although the "The Frisbee team is one niche of politically liberal people" on campus.

GETTYSBURG COLLEGE

FINANCIAL AID: 717-337-6611 • E-MAIL: ADMISS@GETTYSBURG.EDU • WEBSITE: WWW.GETTYSBURG.EDU

THE PRINCETON REVIEW SAYS

Admissions

Very important factors considered include: Class rank, academic GPA, recommendation(s), rigor of secondary school record. *Important factors considered include:* Application essay, standardized test scores, character/personal qualities, extracurricular activities, interview, talent/ability, volunteer work. *Other factors considered include:* Alumni/ae relation, first generation, geographical residence, level of applicant's interest, racial/ethnic status, work experience. SAT or ACT required; TOEFL required of all international applicants. High school diploma is required and GED is accepted. *Academic units required:* 4 English, 3 mathematics, 3 science, (3 science labs), 3 foreign language, 3 social studies, 3 history. *Academic units recommended:* 4 English, 4 mathematics, 4 science, (4 science labs), 4 foreign language, 4 social studies, 4 history.

Financial Aid

Students should submit: FAFSA, CSS/Financial Aid PROFILE, business/farm supplement. Regular filing deadline is 2/15. The Princeton Review suggests that all financial aid forms be submitted as soon as possible after January 1. *Need-based scholarships/grants offered:* Federal Pell, SEOG, state scholarships/grants, private scholarships, the school's own gift aid. *Loan aid offered:* FFEL Subsidized Stafford, FFEL Unsubsidized Stafford, FFEL PLUS, Federal Perkins, college/university loans from institutional funds. Applicants will be notified of awards on or about 3/26. Federal Work-Study Program available. Institutional employment available. Off-campus job opportunities are excellent.

The Inside Word

Expect a thorough and highly personalized review of your application at Gettysburg College. Excellent students with relatively weak standardized test scores, take note: Gettysburg no longer requires test scores as part of its application package. The goal of this new policy is to "enrich the classroom environment by encouraging students with a high secondary school grade point average (GPA) and other creative talents who do not perform well on standardized tests to apply for admission." The effect should be to open Gettysburg's doors to capable students who might otherwise not have been previously admitted.

THE SCHOOL SAYS "..."

From The Admissions Office

"Four major goals of Gettysburg College to best prepare students to enter the twenty-first century, include: first, to accelerate the intellectual development of our first-year students by integrating them more quickly into the intellectual life of the campus; second, to use interdisciplinary courses combining the intellectual approaches of various fields; third, to encourage students to develop an international perspective through course work, study abroad, association with international faculty, and a variety of extracurricular activities; and fourth, to encourage students to develop (1) a capacity for independent study by ensuring that all students work closely with individual faculty members on an extensive project during their undergraduate years and (2) the ability to work with their peers by making the small group a central feature in college life.

"Gettysburg College requires that freshman applicants submit scores from the old or new SAT. Students may also choose to submit scores from the ACT (with or without the Writing component) in lieu of the SAT."

SELECTIVITY
Admissions Rating	95
# of applicants	6,126
% of applicants accepted	36
% of acceptees attending	32
# accepting a place on wait list	805
# of early decision applicants	484
% accepted early decision	65

FRESHMAN PROFILE
Range SAT Critical Reading	610–690
Range SAT Math	610–670
Minimum paper TOEFL	525
Minimum computer TOEFL	200
% graduated top 10% of class	66
% graduated top 25% of class	89
% graduated top 50% of class	100

DEADLINES
Early decision	
Deadline	11/15
Notification	12/15
Regular	
Deadline	2/1
Notification	4/1
Nonfall registration?	yes

FINANCIAL FACTS
Financial Aid Rating	98
Annual tuition	$33,700
Room and board	$8,260
Required fees	$250
Books and supplies	$500
% frosh rec. need-based scholarship or grant aid	52
% UG rec. need-based scholarship or grant aid	54
% frosh rec. non-need-based scholarship or grant aid	31
% UG rec. non-need-based scholarship or grant aid	27
% frosh rec. need-based self-help aid	43
% UG rec. need-based self-help aid	47
% frosh rec. any financial aid	70
% UG rec. any financial aid	70
% UG borrow to pay for school	63
Average cumulative indebtedness	$27,440

GONZAGA UNIVERSITY

502 EAST BOONE AVENUE, SPOKANE, WA 99258 • ADMISSIONS: 509-323-6572 • FAX: 509-323-5780

CAMPUS LIFE
Quality of Life Rating	84
Fire Safety Rating	89
Green Rating	60*
Type of school	private
Affiliation	Roman Catholic
Environment	city

STUDENTS
Total undergrad enrollment	4,318
% male/female	47/53
% from out of state	51
% from public high school	71
% live on campus	56
% African American	1
% Asian	5
% Caucasian	78
% Hispanic	4
% Native American	1
% international	2
# of countries represented	36

SURVEY SAYS . . .
Large classes
Great library
Athletic facilities are great
Students are friendly
Everyone loves the Bulldogs
Intramural sports are popular
Frats and sororities are unpopular
or nonexistent

ACADEMICS
Academic Rating	82
Calendar	semester
Student/faculty ratio	11:1
Profs interesting rating	80
Profs accessible rating	86
Most common reg class size	20–29 students
Most common lab size	10–19 students

MOST POPULAR MAJORS
psychology
political science and government

STUDENTS SAY ". . ."

Academics

Students tell us that Jesuit-run Gonzaga University is "one big family comprised of Catholics and non-Catholics alike" who "all work together in achieving success. We embrace the Jesuit traditions of service, spirituality, social justice, and leadership." The Jesuit influence is indeed pervasive. It can be seen in the effort to "educate the entire person" through a broad liberal arts curriculum. Gonzaga requires four semesters of philosophy and three of religious studies. "They are classes that open your eyes to many harsh realities out in the world and ways that we can contribute with our careers to change these," one undergrad observes. It is also seen in the school's commitment to social service; "Almost everyone here is involved in some kind of community service, whether as a class requirement or just for fun," one student explains, adding "GU also requires a social justice class as part of the core curriculum [in the College of Arts and Sciences]." The school is "big enough to have good programs, small enough that you feel cared about"; academic standouts here include engineering, nursing, and business. The fine arts, on the other hand, "could use some more attention" and "need better facilities." The school also "has great support programs. There are endless offices where people can go to get help that include great counselors' offices and homework help." Those same services are "also very good about really helping you figure out what you really want to do with your life."

Life

Gonzaga students "love to go to basketball games," even though "it takes a lot of time out of your week between waiting in line on Sundays to get tickets and waiting in line on game days to get seats. However, when you are in the stands among all those red Kennel Club t-shirts, it is totally worth it." Beyond the hardwood floor, GU's campus "is extremely active, which results in a lot of fun, active ways to entertain oneself," including "extremely popular" intramural and club sports and extracurricular clubs ("everyone is involved in a few"). While "The majority of people do go out and party on the weekends, and most parties take place at off campus houses in the Logan neighborhood surrounding campus," students may also choose from among "lots of things to do here that don't involve drinking. Every other week, the Gonzaga University Theater Sports (GUTS) club puts on an improv comedy show which is hilarious without fail. There are also outdoor programs and trips, a myriad of clubs, and service-learning opportunities." Students also take "a very active role in the surrounding community (The Logan Neighborhood, the poorest neighborhood in all of Spokane). Gonzaga puts on and sponsors a lot of after-school programs for the kids of the local elementary schools and junior highs." Hometown Spokane "has a lot to offer if you know where to look," including "concert venues, cafes, great food, movie theaters showing both mainstream and independent films, and shopping."

Student Body

"There is not a lot of diversity at GU," where "a majority of students are white, upper-middle class." They "are active and generally good students, but they don't take school too seriously" and "like to go out." While they may not love learning for its own sake, they are "intelligent go-getters" who are "eager to grow and eager to explore the world." Most "are or have been involved in sports, either intramural or varsity level. Also, most students are involved with the communities around them, either through services like 'Campus Kitchen,' which serves food to those in the community, or programs like 'Campus Kids' or 'SMILE,' which bring elementary to middle-school kids on campus as an after-school activity to play with and be mentored by the students on campus." Undergrads tend to be "at least moderately religious."

FINANCIAL AID: 800-793-1716 • E-MAIL: ADMISSIONS@GONZAGA.EDU • WEBSITE: WWW.GONZAGA.EDU

THE PRINCETON REVIEW SAYS

Admissions

Very important factors considered include: Academic GPA, rigor of secondary school record, character/personal qualities, first generation. *Important factors considered include:* Application essay, recommendation(s), standardized test scores, extracurricular activities, talent/ability. *Other factors considered include:* Class rank, alumni/ae relation, interview, level of applicant's interest, racial/ethnic status, volunteer work, work experience. SAT or ACT required; TOEFL required of all international applicants. High school diploma is required and GED is not accepted. *Academic units required:* 4 English, 3 mathematics, 3 science, (3 science labs), 2 foreign language, 2 social studies, 2 history, 2 academic electives. *Academic units recommended:* 4 English, 4 mathematics, 4 science, (4 science labs), 3–4 foreign language, 3 social studies, 3 history, 3 academic electives.

Financial Aid

Students should submit: FAFSA. The Princeton Review suggests that all financial aid forms be submitted by February 1. *Need-based scholarships/grants offered:* Federal Pell, SEOG, state scholarships/grants, private scholarships, the school's own gift aid, United Negro College Fund, Federal Nursing Scholarships. *Loan aid offered:* FFEL Subsidized Stafford, FFEL Unsubsidized Stafford, FFEL PLUS, Federal Perkins, Federal Nursing, state loans, college/university loans from institutional funds. Applicants will be notified of awards on a rolling basis beginning 3/1. Federal Work-Study Program available. Institutional employment available. Off-campus job opportunities are excellent.

The Inside Word

Gonzaga is a great example of how a high profile athletic program can transform a competitive school into a highly competitive one. Over the past decade, Gonzaga's admit rate has decreased substantially while class rank, standardized test scores, and high school GPA have all increased measurably. Perhaps the only substandard students admitted here these days are those who can consistently drain three pointers.

THE SCHOOL SAYS "..."

From The Admissions Office

"Education at Gonzaga is not comparable to an academic 'assembly line'; rather, it is person to person and face to face. This personal quality is also true of our admission and financial aid processes. Therefore, allow us to know you beyond the boundaries of your college application. Visit campus, phone us, e-mail us—let us see the person behind the data. Good luck with your college search and your applications. Go Zags!

"All sections of the new SAT will be accepted, but the new Written portion will not receive universal consideration until further studies are done which examine the success of underrepresented college-bound groups. The Written score will be considered in cases where more information specific to writing ability would be helpful in decision making."

SELECTIVITY
Admissions Rating	89
# of applicants	5,744
% of applicants accepted	69
% of acceptees attending	26
# accepting a place on wait list	200
% admitted from wait list	85

FRESHMAN PROFILE
Range SAT Critical Reading	530–640
Range SAT Math	540–650
Range ACT Composite	24–29
Minimum paper TOEFL	550
Minimum computer TOEFL	213
Average HS GPA	3.69
% graduated top 10% of class	42
% graduated top 25% of class	76
% graduated top 50% of class	96

DEADLINES
Early action	
Deadline	11/15
Notification	1/15
Regular	
Priority	2/1
Deadline	2/1
Notification	3/15
Nonfall registration?	yes

APPLICANTS ALSO LOOK AT
AND OFTEN PREFER
University of Notre Dame
AND SOMETIMES PREFER
Loyola Marymount University
University of Washington
Santa Clara University
AND RARELY PREFER
University of San Francisco
Washington State University

FINANCIAL FACTS
Financial Aid Rating	83
Annual tuition	$26,120
Room and board	$7,520
Required fees	$438
Books and supplies	$900
% frosh rec. need-based scholarship or grant aid	52
% UG rec. need-based scholarship or grant aid	57
% frosh rec. non-need-based scholarship or grant aid	19
% UG rec. non-need-based scholarship or grant aid	21
% frosh rec. need-based self-help aid	35
% UG rec. need-based self-help aid	44
% frosh rec. athletic scholarships	4
% UG rec. athletic scholarships	4
% frosh rec. any financial aid	97
% UG rec. any financial aid	95
% UG borrow to pay for school	68
Average cumulative indebtedness	$23,971

GOUCHER COLLEGE

1021 DULANEY VALLEY ROAD, BALTIMORE, MD 21204-2794 • ADMISSIONS: 410-337-6100 • FAX: 410-337-6354

STUDENTS SAY ". . ."

Academics

Goucher College, a "delightfully odd" school at which "Everybody is quirky in some way," offers a surprising number of first-rate programs for a school of its size. The performing and creative arts are big here, and students tout the dance program as "the best non-conservatory program in the country." Goucher's broad "liberal arts education" ensures that all students get to experience "a little bit of everything" academically. Students praise a "great science/premed program," "good writing and theater programs," and a riding program bolstered by "stables right on campus." Goucher's growing international relations program reflects the school's "education without boundaries" philosophy, and includes an "innovative and exciting" study abroad requirement. Most students love this requirement, citing it as a primary reason for choosing Goucher; a few naysayers complain that the program "can add up financially" (despite the $1,200 voucher students receive to help offset costs) and that "there are not many options." There's no disagreement about Goucher's professors, however, whom students describe as "amazing people and great mentors." They expect a lot from you, "but in the end [you] accomplish more than [you] ever thought possible, and they are willing to help you every step of the way." Goucher also offers "very good academic support services for students with learning disabilities."

Life

"Goucher students spend lots of time in class and studying hard," but when it's time to take a break, there is always something to do on campus. "A lot of students are very involved in stereotypically feminine activities like painting, horseback riding, and dancing," while others participate in "various clubs and organizations" on campus. Students "often travel into downtown Baltimore on the weekends, and like to hang out at the local cafes and farmer's markets, and see shows." Inner Harbor is "also a frequent destination for fun." Goucher runs "a free college shuttle that picks students up and drops them off at other area universities (Johns Hopkins, Loyola, College of Notre Dame, Towson University) as well as at Penn Station," from which students can easily access downtown Washington, DC, and the Inner Harbor. Hometown Towson, a satellite of Baltimore, provides "cute restaurants and stores," but little in the way of collegiate nightlife. On campus, undergrads can choose from "100 student clubs and activities, and "Anyone can start a new club (it is really easy)." Many here feel that "the lack of Greek societies [on campus] limits a lot of social life," which "isn't to say that drinking doesn't go on here. It does, but it happens quietly and [is] low-key in dorms." Dating "is pretty difficult" due to the lopsided male-female ratio. "The few straight boys are usually taken or they are extremely awkward. It's not uncommon to walk into any boys' dorm and find Magic cards and posters of *Lord of the Rings* all over."

Student Body

Goucher has "many of the staple groups, such as jocks," but also "a lot of atypical students" including "pirates [there is a Goucher Pirate Alliance], people who play zombies [regular combatants in Humans vs. Zombies, a game played with Nerf guns]," and "lots of aspiring artists and writers who think they are the cream of the crop." In fact, many here tell us that the atypical student in high school is the typical Goucher undergrad, the kid "who was not very popular in high school but rather the creative type, often existing on the periphery." The "only thing that makes Goucher students similar is their acceptance of other students' weirdness." Students also tend to be "laid-back people who enjoy getting an education rather than competing for one." Undergrads report that "there is a strong Jewish community here, but Christian groups are also present." Although "The student body is very friendly as a whole," conservatives warn that "someone with less-than-liberal views is not exactly welcome [on campus]."

FINANCIAL AID: 410-337-6141 • E-MAIL: ADMISSION@GOUCHER.EDU • WEBSITE: WWW.GOUCHER.EDU

THE PRINCETON REVIEW SAYS

Admissions

Very important factors considered include: Academic GPA, rigor of secondary school record. *Important factors considered include:* Application essay, recommendation(s), talent/ability. *Other factors considered include:* Class rank, standardized test scores, alumni/ae relation, character/personal qualities, extracurricular activities, first generation, interview, level of applicant's interest, racial/ethnic status, volunteer work, work experience. TOEFL required of all international applicants. High school diploma is required and GED is accepted. *Academic units required:* 4 English, 3 mathematics, 2 science, 2 foreign language, 3 social studies, 2 academic electives. *Academic units recommended:* 4 English, 4 mathematics, 3 science, 4 foreign language, 3 social studies, 2 academic electives.

Financial Aid

Students should submit: FAFSA, CSS/Financial Aid PROFILE, noncustodial PROFILE, business/farm supplement. Regular filing deadline is 2/15. The Princeton Review suggests that all financial aid forms be submitted as soon as possible after January 1. *Need-based scholarships/grants offered:* Federal Pell, SEOG, state scholarships/grants, private scholarships, the school's own gift aid. *Loan aid offered:* FFEL Subsidized Stafford, FFEL Unsubsidized Stafford, FFEL PLUS, Federal Perkins, college/university loans from institutional funds. Applicants will be notified of awards on a rolling basis beginning 4/1. Federal Work-Study Program available. Institutional employment available. Off-campus job opportunities are excellent.

The Inside Word

Goucher accepts the ACT with Writing in lieu of the new SAT and SAT Subject Tests; for most students, the ACT is the better option. Goucher's high admit rate masks a self-selecting applicant pool; you cannot gain acceptance here without a solid high school transcript and test scores.

THE SCHOOL SAYS "..."

From The Admissions Office

"Through a broad-based arts and sciences curriculum and a groundbreaking approach to study abroad, Goucher College gives students a sweeping view of the world. Goucher is an independent, coeducational institution dedicated to both the interdisciplinary traditions of the liberal arts and a truly international perspective on education. The first college in the nation to pair required study abroad with a special travel stipend of $1,200 for every undergraduate, Goucher believes in complementing its strong majors and rigorous curriculum with abundant opportunities for hands-on experience. In addition to participating in the college's many study abroad programs (including innovative 3-week intensive courses abroad alongside traditional semester and academic year offerings), many students also complete internships and service-learning projects that further enhance their learning.

"The college's 1,350 undergraduate students live and learn on a tree-lined campus of 287 acres just north of Baltimore, Maryland. Goucher boasts a student/faculty ratio of just 10:1, and professors routinely collaborate with students on major research projects—often for publication, and sometimes as early as students' first or second years. The curriculum emphasizes international and intercultural awareness throughout, and students are encouraged to explore their academic interests from a variety of perspectives beyond their major disciplines.

"A Goucher College education encompasses a multitude of experiences that ultimately converge into one cohesive academic program that can truly change lives. Students grow in dramatic and surprising ways here. They graduate with a strong sense of direction and self-confidence, ready to engage the world—and succeed—as true global citizens.

"Freshman applicants to Goucher College are required to submit scores from either the new SAT or ACT (with the Writing component)."

SELECTIVITY

Admissions Rating	85
# of applicants	3,563
% of applicants accepted	66
% of acceptees attending	17
# accepting a place on wait list	213
% admitted from wait list	23

FRESHMAN PROFILE

Range SAT Critical Reading	540–670
Range SAT Math	510–620
Range SAT Writing	540–650
Minimum paper TOEFL	550
Minimum computer TOEFL	213
Minimum web-based TOEFL	79-80
Average HS GPA	3.2
% graduated top 10% of class	16.94
% graduated top 25% of class	58.06
% graduated top 50% of class	94.35

DEADLINES

Early action	
Deadline	12/1
Notification	2/15
Regular	
Priority	2/1
Deadline	2/1
Notification	4/1
Nonfall registration?	yes

APPLICANTS ALSO LOOK AT

AND OFTEN PREFER
Mount Holyoke College
Boston University
Skidmore College

AND SOMETIMES PREFER
The George Washington University
Loyola College in Maryland
Franklin & Marshall College
American University

FINANCIAL FACTS

Financial Aid Rating	78
Annual tuition	$30,363
Room and board	$9,478
Required fees	$446
Books and supplies	$800
% frosh rec. need-based scholarship or grant aid	53
% UG rec. need-based scholarship or grant aid	52
% frosh rec. non-need-based scholarship or grant aid	7
% UG rec. non-need-based scholarship or grant aid	6
% frosh rec. need-based self-help aid	52
% UG rec. need-based self-help aid	49
% frosh rec. any financial aid	80
% UG rec. any financial aid	85
% UG borrow to pay for school	58
Average cumulative indebtedness	$14,221

GRINNELL COLLEGE

OFFICE OF ADMISSION, 1103 PARK STREET, 2ND FLOOR, GRINNELL, IA 50112-1690 • ADMISSIONS: 641-269-3600 • FAX: 641-269-4800

CAMPUS LIFE

Quality of Life Rating	**79**
Fire Safety Rating	**60***
Green Rating	**60***
Type of school	private
Environment	village

STUDENTS

Total undergrad enrollment	1,623
% male/female	47/53
% from out of state	88
% from public high school	74
% live on campus	86
% African American	5
% Asian	7
% Caucasian	65
% Hispanic	5
% international	11
# of countries represented	51

SURVEY SAYS . . .
Small classes
No one cheats
Frats and sororities are unpopular
or nonexistent
Lots of beer drinking

ACADEMICS

Academic Rating	**96**
Calendar	semester
Student/faculty ratio	9:1
Profs interesting rating	91
Profs accessible rating	94
Most common reg class size	10–19 students
Most common lab size	10–19 students

MOST POPULAR MAJORS
economics
psychology
English language and literature

STUDENTS SAY ". . ."

Academics

"Hard work, critical thinking, and social consciousness" define the Grinnell experience. Students at this "haven of a big-city liberal arts college set in the cornfields" know that "professors expect a lot from us. I had one professor tell our class that professors at Grinnell assign their students graduate-level amounts of work and expect graduate-level results. Professors keep expecting that because Grinnell students deliver it." As a result, "Academics here are hard. We live in a culture of stress and constant studying, but we revel in it. You can't go a single day here without having your mind stimulated, your ideas questioned, and your brain flooded with knowledge." Grinnell imposes "no requirements other than freshman tutorial" on its students, granting under-grads incredible "power in the direction of their education." Thanks to a "huge endowment," students have tremendous latitude in plotting their studies. One undergrad observes, "Money never really seems to be an issue here. If you can dream it, Grinnell can pay for it." The school is "full of resources! Students needing to do research in museums, archives, and libraries for thesis-level research projects can easily get funding from the college. Also, the arts and science facilities are top of the line." For students who may stagger under the weight of academic demands, "Grinnell offers a great deal of academic assistance for those in need. There is a writing lab, a math lab, a reading lab; [and] Grinnell also offers tutors free of charge."

Life

The academic rigors at Grinnell are substantial. You "won't have to worry about surviving the Midwest winter" here, because "Being buried in books and papers and paper revisions and articles and essays and book reviews and to-do lists keeps you surprisingly warm." Even so, students still find time for jam-packed extracurricular schedules; undergrads here "are very well rounded. Forty percent are varsity athletes, and almost all participate in some extracurricular activity." The school "brings in a lot of activities and cultural events," such as "concerts by Grammy Award–winning a cappella groups, ambassadors deliver-ing lectures, movies, concerts, [and] even therapy dogs during mid-semester exams." Best of all, "All events on campus are free." When it comes time to kick back and relax, "The school's fairly loose policy of 'self-governance' means that drinking isn't a huge hassle and can be casual and fun, not covert and antago-nistic with the security guards and college administration." Hometown Grinnell is "isolated," but not without its charms. One student explains, "I love the town of Grinnell and think Midwest-nice is a great asset, but that's my personal taste. I like recognizing the lady who walks her dog by our house every day and the kid who bags our groceries. And I love going to the farmer's market and things like the 4-H tractor show that took place this summer."

Student Body

Grinnell undergrads describe themselves and their classmates as "liberal stu-dents interested in social justice and having a good time." Intellect seems to stand out most; as one student explains, "Most Grinnellians are the kids who were labeled as being a little weird in high school, but then they can come here and find other people just like them." Another adds, "Although the average Grinnell student may be a bit geeky, there is a wide variety of passions that drive each student. When you sit in a class with a diverse group of students who are all passionate about different things, it leads to some of the most inter-esting and intense discussions possible. Because I am surrounded by a group of highly intelligent, motivated, and inquisitive peers, I am constantly chal-lenged to examine topics from different perspectives. This constant thinking outside of the box is a primary aspect of a true liberal arts education."

FINANCIAL AID: 641-269-3250 • E-MAIL: ASKGRIN@GRINNELL.EDU • WEBSITE: WWW.GRINNELL.EDU

THE PRINCETON REVIEW SAYS

Admissions '

Very important factors considered include: Class rank, academic GPA, recommendation(s), rigor of secondary school record, standardized test scores, extracurricular activities, talent/ability. *Important factors considered include:* Application essay, interview, racial/ethnic status. *Other factors considered include:* Alumni/ae relation, character/personal qualities, first generation, geographical residence, state residency, volunteer work, work experience. SAT or ACT required; TOEFL required of all international applicants. High school diploma is required and GED is accepted. *Academic units recommended:* 4 English, 4 mathematics, 4 science, (3 science labs), 4 foreign language, 4 social studies.

Financial Aid

Students should submit: FAFSA, institution's own financial aid form, noncustodial PROFILE. Regular filing deadline is 2/1. The Princeton Review suggests that all financial aid forms be submitted as soon as possible after January 1. *Need-based scholarships/grants offered:* Federal Pell, SEOG, state scholarships/grants, private scholarships, the school's own gift aid. *Loan aid offered:* FFEL Subsidized Stafford, FFEL Unsubsidized Stafford, FFEL PLUS, Federal Perkins, college/university loans from institutional funds. Applicants will be notified of awards on or about 4/1. Federal Work-Study Program available. Institutional employment available. Off-campus job opportunities are excellent.

The Inside Word

Grinnell provides a first-rate academic experience and garners a talented applicant pool. You'll need a rigorous course load and top standardized test scores to be a contender. Matchmaking is also an important element of the admissions process; an interview is highly recommended. Admissions Officers will be glad for the opportunity to relay information about Grinnell, and you're likely to leave with a positive impression.

THE SCHOOL SAYS "..."

From The Admissions Office

"Grinnell College is a place where independence of thought and social conscience are instilled. It is a wide-open space of resources, professors, and students in search of truth, understanding, and shared endeavors. Grinnell is a college with the resources of a school 10 times its size, a faculty that reads like a Who's Who of Teaching, and a learning environment where debate does not end in the classroom and often begins in the Campus Center.

"Grinnellians are committed to learning, respect for themselves and others, contributing to global social good, willing collaboration, and the courage to try. Grinnell College is a place of endless possibilities, a place where there are no limits.

"We require that applicants submit either the new SAT (taken prior to January of their senior year) or ACT scores. If students take both the new SAT and ACT, we will consider the higher of the two scores. Unlike our SAT policy, we do not create a best composite score from multiple sittings of the ACT."

SELECTIVITY

Admissions Rating	95
# of applicants	3,077
% of applicants accepted	50
% of acceptees attending	28
# accepting a place on wait list	279
% admitted from wait list	6
# of early decision applicants	164
% accepted early decision	77

FRESHMAN PROFILE

Range SAT Critical Reading	610–750
Range SAT Math	620–740
Range ACT Composite	29–33
Minimum paper TOEFL	550
Minimum computer TOEFL	220
% graduated top 10% of class	66
% graduated top 25% of class	93
% graduated top 50% of class	99

DEADLINES

Early decision	
Deadline	11/20
Notification	12/20
Regular	
Deadline	1/20
Notification	4/1
Nonfall registration?	no

APPLICANTS ALSO LOOK AT
AND SOMETIMES PREFER
Carleton College
AND RARELY PREFER
Macalester College
Kenyon College

FINANCIAL FACTS

Financial Aid Rating	98
Annual tuition	$29,710
Room and board	$8,030
Required fees	$482
Books and supplies	$750
% frosh rec. need-based scholarship or grant aid	62
% UG rec. need-based scholarship or grant aid	55
% frosh rec. non-need-based scholarship or grant aid	9
% UG rec. non-need-based scholarship or grant aid	6
% frosh rec. need-based self-help aid	52
% UG rec. need-based self-help aid	47
% frosh rec. any financial aid	85
% UG rec. any financial aid	87
% UG borrow to pay for school	58
Average cumulative indebtedness	$18,340

GROVE CITY COLLEGE

100 CAMPUS DRIVE, GROVE CITY, PA 16127-2104 • ADMISSIONS: 724-458-2100 • FAX: 724-458-3395

STUDENTS SAY ". . ."

Academics

A small, private liberal arts school dedicated to "cohesive Christian education through academic rigor and integrity," Grove City College provides its students with "a challenging education in a thoroughly Christian environment." In fact, the word *challenge* is frequently used by respondents; says one, "Students here work their butts off." With a course load that many students describe as "insane," "There is a lot of work to be done and not much time to do it. Most of the work, however, is very beneficial." Students credit the school's "high academic standards" as one of the main reasons GCC enjoys "a fantastic job placement rate and reputation in the professional world." And although the professors assign plenty of homework, they are also "friendly and accessible. Professors give you their home phone numbers so that you can call them if you don't understand something after office hours." What's more, they "are interested mainly in teaching students, not publishing books or conducting research." Finally, undergrads appreciate the fact that professors "are also excellent Christian role models" who give their students a "sound moral foundation." All this is available at bargain-basement prices; the tuition at GCC is "incredibly reasonable," at less than half that of many other private colleges.

Life

At GCC, "people are very focused on God. Many are involved in campus ministry groups, and almost everyone attends church on Sundays." As one might suspect at such a place, the kind of fun most students go in for here is of the "good, clean" variety. Since "off-campus life is virtually nonexistent," students looking for fun "go to on-campus events, like coffeehouses, dances, plays, and movies," or play intramural sports. However, funding for these activities and clubs can be limited, students complain, because the school's low tuition necessitates a tight activities budget. The dorms at GCC are single sex, but "Intervis (Dorm Intervisitation) is pretty popular." Intervisitation rules are pretty strict; in the words of one student, "Members of the opposite sex can only come to our rooms to hang out during allotted hours on weekends, provided the door is propped open and the lights are on." Alcohol is forbidden on campus, and for those students who want to party off campus, "You have to be careful. Grove City is technically a dry town, and there are not many places that sell alcohol." Students caught drinking on campus, "whether they're 18 or 35," face strict penalties; the school administration "doesn't take that stuff lightly." Undergrads advise prospective students that at GCC, "There is pressure to find a mate by your senior year, so the opposite sex is often on one's mind." As one student puts it, the school's mission is "to provide a thorough education in a Christian environment (and hopefully get you married in the process)."

Student Body

Students at GCC are the first to point out that "Our school is pretty homogenous." The typical student is "an intelligent, studious, straight-edge Protestant" who "got straight A's in high school and has been pretty much a model person for most of his or her life." Ethnically and economically, undergrads are mainly "White and from middle- to upper-class families." One undergrad notes, "There are not too many atypical students, and everyone knows who those students are." Such atypical "Grovers" include "liberal students" who "face much opposition to their political views, but don't suffer discrimination," and the "very few minorities" on campus. While some students wish that the school would "reach out to minorities and people of different backgrounds more," others feel that the fact that GCC does "not try to be like other colleges is what makes it so unique."

FINANCIAL AID: 724-458-2163 • E-MAIL: ADMISSIONS@GCC.EDU • WEBSITE: WWW.GCC.EDU/PR

THE PRINCETON REVIEW SAYS

Admissions

Very important factors considered include: Application essay, rigor of secondary school record, standardized test scores, character/personal qualities, extracurricular activities, interview, religious affiliation/commitment. *Important factors considered include:* Recommendation(s), talent/ability. *Other factors considered include:* Class rank, alumni/ae relation, geographical residence, racial/ethnic status, state residency, volunteer work, work experience. SAT or ACT required; TOEFL required of all international applicants. High school diploma is required and GED is accepted. *Academic units recommended:* 4 English, 3 mathematics, 3 science, (2 science labs), 3 foreign language, 2 social studies, 2 history.

Financial Aid

Students should submit: institution's own financial aid form. Regular filing deadline is 4/15. The Princeton Review suggests that all financial aid forms be submitted as soon as possible after January 1. *Need-based scholarships/grants offered:* state scholarships/grants, private scholarships, the school's own gift aid, private, alternative loans. Applicants will be notified of awards on a rolling basis beginning 3/20. Institutional employment available. Off-campus job opportunities are good.

The Inside Word

Admission to Grove City has become very competitive, and any serious contender will need to hit the books. While a rigorous class schedule is a given, Admissions Officers also closely assess character and personal qualities. GCC is steeped in Christian values, and the school seeks students who will be comfortable in such an environment. As such, interviews and recommendations hold significant weight.

THE SCHOOL SAYS "..."

From The Admissions Office

"A good college education doesn't have to cost a fortune. For decades, Grove City College has offered a quality education at costs among the lowest nationally. Since the 1990s, increased national academic acclaim has come to Grove City College. Grove City College is a place where professors teach. You will not see graduate assistants or teacher's aides in the classroom. Our professors are also active in the total life of the campus. More than 100 student organizations on campus afford opportunity for a wide variety of cocurricular activities. Outstanding scholars and leaders in education, science, and international affairs visit the campus each year. The environment at GCC is friendly, secure, and dedicated to high standards. Character-building is emphasized and traditional Christian values are supported.

"There is a fresh spiritual vitality on campus that touches every aspect of your college life. In the classroom we don't shy away from discussing all points of view, however we adhere to Christ's teaching as relevant guidance for living. Come and visit and learn more."

SELECTIVITY

Admissions Rating	93
# of applicants	1,916
% of applicants accepted	55
% of acceptees attending	62
# accepting a place on wait list	236
% admitted from wait list	7
# of early decision applicants	630
% accepted early decision	51

FRESHMAN PROFILE

Range SAT Critical Reading	566–702
Range SAT Math	574–691
Range ACT Composite	25–30
Minimum paper TOEFL	550
Minimum computer TOEFL	213
Average HS GPA	3.71
% graduated top 10% of class	52
% graduated top 25% of class	83
% graduated top 50% of class	97

DEADLINES

Early decision	
Deadline	11/15
Notification	12/15
Regular	
Deadline	2/1
Notification	3/15
Nonfall registration?	yes

APPLICANTS ALSO LOOK AT

AND OFTEN PREFER
Wheaton College (IL)
Hillsdale College
Penn State—University Park

AND RARELY PREFER
Slippery Rock University of Pennsylvania
Thiel College

FINANCIAL FACTS

Financial Aid Rating	64
Annual tuition	$12,074
Room and board	$6,134
Books and supplies	$900
% frosh rec. need-based scholarship or grant aid	41
% UG rec. need-based scholarship or grant aid	33
% frosh rec. non-need-based scholarship or grant aid	7
% UG rec. non-need-based scholarship or grant aid	4
% frosh rec. need-based self-help aid	18
% UG rec. need-based self-help aid	19
% frosh rec. any financial aid	42
% UG rec. any financial aid	35
% UG borrow to pay for school	62
Average cumulative indebtedness	$24,721

GUILFORD COLLEGE

5800 WEST FRIENDLY AVENUE, GREENSBORO, NC 27410 • ADMISSIONS: 336-316-2100 • FAX: 336-316-2954

CAMPUS LIFE
Quality of Life Rating	74
Fire Safety Rating	73
Green Rating	60*
Type of school	private
Affiliation	Quaker
Environment	city

STUDENTS
Total undergrad enrollment	2,688
% male/female	39/61
% from out of state	66
% from public high school	68
% live on campus	74
# of countries represented	17

SURVEY SAYS . . .
Small classes
No one cheats
Students are friendly
Frats and sororities are unpopular
or nonexistent
College radio is popular
Lots of beer drinking
(Almost) everyone smokes

ACADEMICS
Academic Rating	83
Calendar	semester
Student/faculty ratio	16:1
Profs interesting rating	86
Profs accessible rating	81
Most common reg class size	10–19 students
Most common lab size	20–29 students

MOST POPULAR MAJORS
biological and biomedical sciences
psychology
business/commerce

STUDENTS SAY " . . ."

Academics

Guilford College, "promotes academic excellence, social and cultural awareness, critical analysis, and community involvement" while "incorporating Quaker ideals and traditions." Undergrads here warn that this small liberal arts school requires "a lot of work," and that the program "is very reading and writing intensive." As one student explains, "I've had to write papers for every class except chemistry, and in one class I've written around 10 papers." Support for students is strong, both from "incredible" professors who "are where they say they are going to be when they say they are going to be there, which makes it incredibly easy to get help." Guilford also offers "many resources" to help students handle the workload, such as "the Academic Skills Center." The school promotes autonomy, providing undergrads "the ability to design their own programs," without sacrificing "personal and positive relationships with most teachers and many members of the administration. They are always open to hear from students on any issue." Especially strong areas of study at Guilford include the Criminal Justice Program (it "rocks"), as well as "great programs for theater and adult studies."

Life

As at most small, rigorous, liberal arts schools, "Classes take up a good deal of time" at Guilford, and students keep themselves busy during their few off hours with "extracurricular activities, hanging out with friends, and going off campus." One student writes, "Considering the relatively small size of the campus, there is a constant list of social, political, and spiritual activities going on for seemingly every preference or belief one might have." Another student concurs: "Whether for class or socially, the campus is always active." The "great Quaker heritage here makes for an open and personal environment" in which "people leave their doors open all the time." Students are "very social . . . I've never heard of someone just sitting alone in their room if that wasn't what they wanted." Guilford's Quaker heritage also attracts a lot of politically active students, who share an "environmental concern." There are also "lots of sports and club activities." Hometown Greensboro is a small city but big enough to support a decent club scene. Students say Guilford "is unique because it is within a fairly cosmopolitan area yet has many natural alcoves and secrets to explore. The lake, the woods, and the meadows on campus are beautiful and fun treasures for students to enjoy. Guilford is also beautifully landscaped and decorated with student-created art, but it isn't pretentious."

Student Body

"Guilford sometimes seems like it attracts the atypical student. People here aren't afraid to express their personal point of view, either vocally or through their activities or style." The population includes a lot of "liberal, granola people," although some here notice a trend toward greater diversity on campus. Recently the school has increased diversity in "ethnic backgrounds and spiritual, political, and socio-cultural beliefs," and has also added to its continuing education population, meaning students here "range from 17 to 60-plus years old." As one student observes, "Because Guilford College promotes a global view of the world, the diverse student body is simply an extension of this academic principle and is nurtured as such." Some students note that "almost everyone who bridges these gaps bonds over a case or keg."

FINANCIAL AID: 336-316-2354 • E-MAIL: ADMISSION@GUILFORD.EDU • WEBSITE: WWW.GUILFORD.EDU

THE PRINCETON REVIEW SAYS

Admissions

Very important factors considered include: Rigor of secondary school record. *Important factors considered include:* Application essay, academic GPA, standardized test scores, character/personal qualities, extracurricular activities, level of applicant's interest, talent/ability. *Other factors considered include:* Class rank, recommendation(s), alumni/ae relation, first generation, geographical residence, interview, racial/ethnic status, religious affiliation/commitment, state residency, volunteer work, work experience. SAT or ACT recommended; TOEFL required of all international applicants. High school diploma is required and GED is accepted. *Academic units recommended:* 4 English, 3 mathematics, 3 science, 2 foreign language.

Financial Aid

Students should submit: FAFSA. Regular filing deadline is 3/1. The Princeton Review suggests that all financial aid forms be submitted as soon as possible after January 1. *Need-based scholarships/grants offered:* Federal Pell, SEOG, state scholarships/grants, private scholarships, the school's own gift aid. *Loan aid offered:* FFEL Subsidized Stafford, FFEL Unsubsidized Stafford, FFEL PLUS, Federal Perkins, college/university loans from institutional funds. Applicants will be notified of awards on a rolling basis beginning 2/1. Federal Work-Study Program available. Institutional employment available. Off-campus job opportunities are good.

The Inside Word

Guilford has traditionally drawn its students primarily from the Mid-Atlantic and Southern states; the school has recently begun to recruit more aggressively outside these areas, and now employs a full-time regional recruiter based in Boston. Additional recruiting should yield additional applications, increasing competition for classroom seats. The upside in terms of admissions is that this effort to build a more national student body creates opportunities for students from outside the school's traditional target zones. If you're willing to travel a long way to attend Guilford, you may find yourself handsomely rewarded.

THE SCHOOL SAYS " . . ."

From The Admissions Office

"Guilford is proud to be included for the seventeenth consecutive year in Princeton Review's "Best College" edition. Guilford can best be described by its academic rigor, preparation for graduate school and its commitment to service, in a caring, socially aware and supportive community.

"Comments from a small sample of Guilford students do not adequately convey the richness of the campus experience. Guilford is building a community that honors traditional as well as alternative lifestyles and viewpoints. No one lifestyle or thought predominates the campus. Regardless of your background, if you are open-minded and willing to interact with others, the Guilford experience can be transformational. If you enroll at Guilford, there will be others like you.

"There is no stereotypical Guilford student. Our students have many passions including athletics and intramurals, community service, social justice and multiculturalism. However the bond that ties them together is the academic curriculum that prepares them for life and a career."

SELECTIVITY

Admissions Rating	**80**
# of applicants	3,493
% of applicants accepted	58
% of acceptees attending	22
# accepting a place on wait list	172
% admitted from wait list	28

FRESHMAN PROFILE

Range SAT Critical Reading	490–630
Range SAT Math	500–610
Range ACT Composite	21–26
Minimum paper TOEFL	550
Minimum computer TOEFL	213
Average HS GPA	3.12
% graduated top 10% of class	20
% graduated top 25% of class	45
% graduated top 50% of class	83

DEADLINES

Early action	
Deadline	1/15
Notification	2/15
Regular	
Priority	1/15
Deadline	2/15
Notification	rolling
Nonfall registration?	yes

APPLICANTS ALSO LOOK AT
AND OFTEN PREFER
Oberlin College
AND SOMETIMES PREFER
Earlham College
University of North Carolina at Chapel Hill
Goucher College
Elon University

FINANCIAL FACTS

Financial Aid Rating	**90**
Annual tuition	$25,700
Required fees	$330
Books and supplies	$1,050
% frosh rec. need-based scholarship or grant aid	88
% UG rec. need-based scholarship or grant aid	89
% frosh rec. need-based self-help aid	56
% UG rec. need-based self-help aid	58
% frosh rec. any financial aid	92
% UG rec. any financial aid	92
% UG borrow to pay for school	68
Average cumulative indebtedness	$23,180

GUSTAVUS ADOLPHUS COLLEGE

800 WEST COLLEGE AVENUE, SAINT PETER, MN 56082 • ADMISSIONS: 507-933-7676 • FAX: 507-933-7474

STUDENTS SAY ". . ."

Academics

Named for a Swedish king and home to the yearly Nobel Conference, Gustavus Adolphus College gets high marks from students for its "demanding, yet encouraging" professors who are "there to help you learn, not just to give you a grade." As one student explains, "The professors are amazing, they will let you call them at home and work with your schedule for everything, whether you need extra help in a class or just want to talk." Although professors have "high expectations," the "extra guidance" that is offered helps students achieve "far beyond graduation." Expect to be challenged by "classes [that] are rigorous and discussion based." Small class sizes allow for "great interaction with professors" but will leave your "empty chair sticking out like a neon sign" if you are absent. According to one student, the administration is "nothing less than competent, articulate, and perceptive" and "is generally very easy to access." Students feel that they are "the number-one priority in everything" and enjoy a "great sense of community" on campus.

Life

In the words of one student, "Life at Gustavus is fun . . . maybe a little too fun." Although "School comes first," on the weekends students "attend a lot of sporting events, parties, and social events on campus and off." "Shows, concerts, and basketball games" are "especially popular," as are the "free movies on Fridays and Saturdays" and the "on-campus student dance club 'The Dive.'" Most students choose to unwind with "a good amount of partying and drinking." As one student explains, "Gusties drink a lot, and the administration doesn't like that reputation, so they are really cracking down on fun." While alcohol and parties are easy to find on campus, abstaining students "never feel any pressure to do either." Being located in a small town is no problem for students who claim that "there are always things going on at school." Students who get cabin fever can head to nearby Mankato with its "excellent mall and restaurants" for entertainment. Finding company for these activities is never a problem since Gustavus "is a small school" and "You get to know people easily." Although the Minnesotan winter may be long, things heat up in January during "J-term" when a light course load gives students a "chance to take a class outside their major" or just "hang out with friends." When students really want a thrill, they'll "borrow a tray from the cafeteria and sled down the many hills behind the dorms" in a Gustavus tradition called "traying."

Student Body

Students at Gustavus describe themselves as "White, suburban, middle-class" and "often of Swedish Lutheran descent." Although the students who "do not fit into this description" may find themselves sticking out "like sore thumbs" in a "land of Abercrombie," any discrimination "is met with the highest degree of denunciation from the administration/faculty/staff and much of the student body." In the words of one student, "Gustavus is a fairly liberal college" that "prides itself on focusing on nonracial diversity." While "most of the students are White, the mix of personalities and lifestyles is amazing," and the university is working to "recruit students of more diverse backgrounds." Despite any surface differences, "The typical student at Gustavus is very studious and cares very much about getting the most out of their education."

FINANCIAL AID: 507-933-7527 • E-MAIL: ADMISSION@GUSTAVUS.EDU • WEBSITE: WWW.GUSTAVUS.EDU

THE PRINCETON REVIEW SAYS

Admissions

Very important factors considered include: Rigor of secondary school record. *Important factors considered include:* Application essay, academic GPA, recommendation(s), standardized test scores, character/personal qualities. *Other factors considered include:* Class rank, alumni/ae relation, extracurricular activities, first generation, geographical residence, interview, level of applicant's interest, racial/ethnic status, religious affiliation/commitment, state residency, talent/ability, volunteer work, work e SAT or ACT recommended; TOEFL required of all international applicants. High school diploma is required and GED is accepted. *Academic units required:* 4 English, 3 mathematics, 2 science, (2 science labs), 2 foreign language, 2 social studies, 2 history. *Academic units recommended:* 4 mathematics, 3 science, (3 science labs), 2 academic electives.

Financial Aid

Students should submit: FAFSA, institution's own financial aid form, CSS/Financial Aid PROFILECSS. Profile required of all students applying for need-based assistance. Regular filing deadline is 4/15. The Princeton Review suggests that all financial aid forms be submitted as soon as possible after January 1. *Need-based scholarships/grants offered:* Federal Pell, SEOG, state scholarships/grants, private scholarships, the school's own gift aid. *Loan aid offered:* Direct Subsidized Stafford, Direct Unsubsidized Stafford, Direct PLUS, Federal Perkins, state loans, Alternative loans from private lenders. Applicants will be notified of awards on a rolling basis beginning 1/20. Federal Work-Study Program available. Institutional employment available. Off-campus job opportunities are good.

The Inside Word

Gustavus Adolphus considers a variety of factors when making admissions decisions. Students should display motivation for tackling challenging courses and a desire to be active participants in their community. The majority of applicants are from local areas—those who can provide some geographic diversity are welcome. The school has a rolling admissions policy, so interested students should think about sending in their applications early. All available slots are usually filled by early spring.

THE SCHOOL SAYS "..."

From The Admissions Office

"To better serve students and their families, there is no application fee.
"Applications completed by November 1 will be notified of an admission decision by November 20. Applications completed after November 1 will be reviewed on a competitive rolling basis beginning December 20.
"Early financial aid awards will be available to admitted students who submit the CSS/Financial Aid PROFILE prior to February 15. Students who submit the FAFSA will continue to receive a financial aid award in a timely fashion.
"The college is committed to excellence, community, justice, service, and faith. These values are pervasive in the college community and can be seen throughout campus activities and events like the 'Our Story' workshop on African American culture, Nobel Conference, Building Bridges Diversity Conference, MAYDAY! Peace Conference, and NYSP summer sports camp. Campus facilities support student life and development. Recent projects include a 200-bed apartment and suite configuration residence hall (also houses an additional 200-bed youth hostel), cardiovascular exercise area, Nobel Hall of Science equipment additions of a DNA sequencer, mass spectrometer microscope, cell growth culture labs, Old Main classroom renovation, International Center for residential living and international education, and, the Jackson Campus Center, which houses student services such as Diversity Center, Market Place cafeteria and Courtyard Café, Ticket Center, student activities offices and work space, Hillstrom Museum, bookstore, and much more.
"Gustavus Adolphus College requires freshman applicants to submit scores from the old or new SAT. Students may also choose to submit scores from the ACT (with or without the Writing component) in lieu of the SAT."

SELECTIVITY

Admissions Rating	87
# of applicants	2,208
% of applicants accepted	80
% of acceptees attending	39
# accepting a place on wait list	30
% admitted from wait list	57

FRESHMAN PROFILE

Range SAT Math	590–680
Range ACT Composite	24–29
Minimum paper TOEFL	550
Minimum computer TOEFL	213
Minimum web-based TOEFL	80
Average HS GPA	3.64
% graduated top 10% of class	36
% graduated top 25% of class	71
% graduated top 50% of class	95

DEADLINES

Early action	
Deadline	11/1
Notification	11/20
Regular	
Deadline	4/1
Notification	rolling
Nonfall registration?	yes

APPLICANTS ALSO LOOK AT AND OFTEN PREFER

University of Wisconsin—Madison
Carleton College

FINANCIAL FACTS

Financial Aid Rating	86
Annual tuition	$28,125
Room and board	$6,275
Required fees	$140
Books and supplies	$900
% frosh rec. need-based scholarship or grant aid	66
% UG rec. need-based scholarship or grant aid	64
% frosh rec. non-need-based scholarship or grant aid	38
% UG rec. non-need-based scholarship or grant aid	37
% frosh rec. need-based self-help aid	66
% UG rec. need-based self-help aid	64
% frosh rec. any financial aid	94
% UG rec. any financial aid	92
% UG borrow to pay for school	69.8
Average cumulative indebtedness	$24,297

HAMILTON COLLEGE

198 COLLEGE HILL ROAD, CLINTON, NY 13323 • ADMISSIONS: 315-859-4421 • FAX: 315-859-4457

CAMPUS LIFE
Quality of Life Rating	80
Fire Safety Rating	79
Green Rating	95
Type of school	private
Environment	town

STUDENTS
Total undergrad enrollment	1,810
% male/female	48/52
% from out of state	66
% from public high school	60
% live on campus	98
% in (# of) fraternities	29 (7)
% in (# of) sororities	19 (3)
% African American	4
% Asian	7
% Caucasian	69
% Hispanic	5
% Native American	1
% international	5
# of countries represented	42

SURVEY SAYS . . .
Small classes
No one cheats
Lab facilities are great
Great computer facilities
Great library
Lots of beer drinking
Hard liquor is popular

ACADEMICS
Academic Rating	95
Calendar	semester
Student/faculty ratio	10:1
Profs interesting rating	96
Profs accessible rating	97
Most common reg class size	10–19 students
Most common lab size	10–19 students

MOST POPULAR MAJORS
economics
government
mathematics
psychology

STUDENTS SAY ". . ."

Academics

"Cold winters, close friends, and great professors who care" are what make Hamilton "the true liberal arts experience." Indeed, "Its small student population, intelligent and accessible professors, and campus size make Hamilton the ideal small liberal arts college." Students praise the dedication and intellectual caliber of professors, who are more "interested in their students' success" than in "the next research grant." Small class sizes bring personal attention and increased responsibility for one's own learning; one student notes, "It is rarely the case for a professor to lecture for the entire class without engaging the students in the discussion. This way, students interact not only with the professor but [also] with each other, listening to each other and building off other students' ideas." Even "In 'big' lectures (50 students is huge for Hamilton), discussion is strongly encouraged." "Extremely knowledgeable" professors demand a lot of their students, and Hamilton's culture of "grade deflation" means that there are no easy A's at this school; one student observes, "Sometimes you're fighting for a B. The classes are that difficult." "I feel very challenged," says another, adding, "but I am learning so much!" Students who feel too challenged, however, can easily get help; the school offers "free tutoring at the Writing Center and the Quantitative Literacy Center," and the "Career Center is always asking you to come visit, even as a freshman." Those looking for international experience also appreciate the fact that the "school makes it so easy to go abroad."

Life

"Work hard, play hard" is the motto among Hamilton students. "Every weekend, without fail, there is at least one party (often three or four) held in one of the social spaces provided by the campus, generally funded by one of Hamilton's many Greek organizations." Off-campus parties are also popular. To wet your whistle closer to home, the college has its own pub, where professors and students (those over 21, that is) are often seen sharing a pint together. While some students complain that drinking draws too great a focus, there are plenty of options for the straight-edge crowd, including substance-free dorms. Those looking for nonalcoholic fun gather at "Cafe Opus, our own little coffee place, and sit and talk for a while." For the "intellectual population," "all kinds of student-run discussion groups" address "topics ranging from politics to religion to psychology," and "We get great name speakers, ranging from B. B. King to Clinton or Nader." Intrepid Hamiltonians brave upstate New York weather to make the most of their bucolic surroundings: "The glen behind campus is great for running, skiing, or other escapades, and cheering on the perpetually bad football team and the much better soccer and hockey teams is a must." Hometown Clinton's "outdoorsy environment, including extensive acres of hiking/cross-country skiing trails and a ropes course make the college often seem more like camp than school when there is no snow." In the words of one student, "It's small, it's isolated, but Hamilton rock 'n' rolls like nowhere else on earth!"

Student Body

"There is a general impression that many students come from places like Fairfield County [Connecticut]," claims one student, but "While there is certainly a healthy representation, their pink polo shirts and yellow shorts probably just make them more conspicuous. We have students from most states, many countries, and just about every ethnic background. There are all kinds of people here, and they generally associate with everyone else." Another states, "Everyone here is different. That's what makes Hamilton so wonderful." Politically, "The student body seems more moderate than most selective Eastern schools and certainly more tolerant of conservatives than most. Still, many seem nostalgic for Clinton." Whatever their political or social differences, Hamilton students unequivocally characterize themselves as friendly and accepting: "Incredible warmth emanates from all people, regardless of age or status, and despite the snow."

FINANCIAL AID: 800-859-4413 • E-MAIL: ADMISSION@HAMILTON.EDU • WEBSITE: WWW.HAMILTON.EDU

THE PRINCETON REVIEW SAYS

Admissions

Very important factors considered include: Class rank, academic GPA, rigor of secondary school record. *Important factors considered include:* Application essay, recommendation(s), standardized test scores, character/personal qualities, extracurricular activities, interview. *Other factors considered include:* Alumni/ae relation, first generation, geographical residence, level of applicant's interest, racial/ethnic status, talent/ability, volunteer work, work experience. TOEFL required of all international applicants. High school diploma is required and GED is accepted. *Academic units recommended:* 4 English, 3 mathematics, 3 science, 3 foreign language, 3 social studies.

Financial Aid

Students should submit: FAFSA, institution's own financial aid form, CSS/Financial Aid PROFILE, state aid form, noncustodial PROFILE, business/farm supplement. Regular filing deadline is 2/8. The Princeton Review suggests that all financial aid forms be submitted as soon as possible after January 1. *Need-based scholarships/grants offered:* Federal Pell, SEOG, state scholarships/grants, private scholarships, the school's own gift aid. *Loan aid offered:* FFEL Subsidized Stafford, FFEL Unsubsidized Stafford, FFEL PLUS, Federal Perkins Applicants will be notified of awards on or about 4/1. Federal Work-Study Program available. Institutional employment available.

The Inside Word

Similar to many prestigious liberal arts schools, Hamilton takes a well-rounded, personal approach to admissions. Academic achievement and intellectual promise are of first importance, but Admissions Officers also put great weight on leadership and diversity. The college strives to attain a complete, accurate profile of each applicant and relies heavily upon interviews either on or off campus with alumni volunteers. Students who decline to interview put themselves at a competitive disadvantage.

THE SCHOOL SAYS "..."

From The Admissions Office

"As a national leader for teaching students to write effectively, learn from one another, and think for themselves, Hamilton produces graduates who have the knowledge, skills, and confidence to make their own voices heard on issues of importance to them and their communities.

"A key component of the Hamilton experience is the college's open, yet rigorous, liberal arts curriculum. In place of distribution requirements that are common at most colleges, Hamilton gives its students freedom to choose the courses that reflect their unique interests and plans. Faculty advisors assist students in planning a coherent and highly individualized academic program. In fact, close student-faculty relationships at Hamilton are a distinguishing characteristic of the college, but ultimately students at Hamilton take responsibility for their own future. Part of that future includes a lifelong relationship with the college. Hamilton alumni are exceptionally loyal and passionate supporters of their alma mater. That support manifests itself through internships, speaking engagements, job-shadowing opportunities, and financial donations.

"The intellectual maturity that distinguishes a Hamilton education extends to the application process. Students are free to choose which standardized tests to submit, based on a specified set of options, so that those who do not test well on the SAT or ACT may decide to submit the results of their AP or SAT Subject Tests. The approach allows students the freedom to decide how to present themselves best to the Committee on Admission."

SELECTIVITY

Admissions Rating	96
# of applicants	4,962
% of applicants accepted	28
% of acceptees attending	34
# accepting a place on wait list	248
% admitted from wait list	10
# of early decision applicants	640
% accepted early decision	36

FRESHMAN PROFILE

Range SAT Critical Reading	640–740
Range SAT Math	640–720
Minimum paper TOEFL	600
Minimum computer TOEFL	250
% graduated top 10% of class	74
% graduated top 25% of class	90
% graduated top 50% of class	99

DEADLINES

Early decision	
Deadline	11/15
Notification	12/15
Regular	
Deadline	1/1
Notification	4/1
Nonfall registration?	yes

APPLICANTS ALSO LOOK AT

AND OFTEN PREFER
Middlebury College
Williams College
Amherst College

AND SOMETIMES PREFER
Colby College
Colgate University
Bowdoin College

AND RARELY PREFER
Dickinson College
Union College (NY)
Skidmore College

FINANCIAL FACTS

Financial Aid Rating	98
Annual tuition	$36,500
Room and board	$9,350
Required fees	$360
Books and supplies	$1,300
% frosh rec. need-based scholarship or grant aid	43
% UG rec. need-based scholarship or grant aid	47
% frosh rec. non-need-based scholarship or grant aid	3
% UG rec. non-need-based scholarship or grant aid	4
% frosh rec. need-based self-help aid	34
% UG rec. need-based self-help aid	38
% UG borrow to pay for school	48
Average cumulative indebtedness	$16,808

HAMPDEN-SYDNEY COLLEGE

PO Box 667, Hampden-Sydney, VA 23943 • Admissions: 434-223-6120 • Fax: 434-223-6346

CAMPUS LIFE

Quality of Life Rating	**83**
Fire Safety Rating	**76**
Green Rating	**71**
Type of school	private
Affiliation	Presbyterian
Environment	rural

STUDENTS

Total undergrad enrollment	1,122
% male/female	100/
% from out of state	34
% from public high school	59
% live on campus	95
% in (# of) fraternities	34 (11)
% African American	5
% Asian	1
% Caucasian	91
% Hispanic	1
% international	2
# of countries represented	17

SURVEY SAYS . . .

Large classes
No one cheats
Great library
Career services are great
Students are happy
Lots of beer drinking

ACADEMICS

Academic Rating	**85**
Calendar	semester
Student/faculty ratio	10:1
Profs interesting rating	98
Profs accessible rating	99
Most common	
reg class size	10–19 students

MOST POPULAR MAJORS
economics
political science and government
history

STUDENTS SAY "..."

Academics

Highlights at tiny, all-male Hampden-Sydney College in Virginia include "insane" study abroad programs, a "very approachable" administration, and "an alumni network that will take care of you." HSC is mostly known for its hardcore liberal arts focus, though. The demanding core curriculum includes foreign language, literature, science, math, fine arts, and a boatload of Western civilization. Students also must "take two semesters of rhetoric, which consists of an intensive study and application of the principles of good writing." "Academically, this school is an orgy of ideas waiting for the next enthusiastic participant." Professors are "absolutely great" and personal attention is "unrivaled." Courses are "very tough," though. "We don't grade-inflate around here," warns a junior. A strict, student-enforced honor code "is taken extremely seriously" as well. "At Sydney, I can leave my laptop unattended in the library for hours, maybe even days, and nobody will touch it," maintains a history major. "I think that's pretty cool." Students say that HSC is "a place where honor lives and boys enter so that they may leave as gentlemen." The word "brotherhood" is omnipresent. There is much talk of "moral integrity." If all that sounds kind of hokey, then, obviously, HSC isn't for you. "It takes a certain kind of man to come to Hampden-Sydney College, and if you want to be here, then you will love it. If you don't want to be here, you will hate it."

Life

"The school is its own little city" and Hamden-Sydney students spend most of their time on campus. "The dorm rooms are huge" and "laundry is free" but the food is "not very good." Clubs and organizations include "a prestigious debating society." "A majority of the student body is involved in some type of sport." Football weekends are "a great time to be on campus." (Students dress "in formal coat and tie.") "Most students work and study hard from Monday to Thursday." "With no females at school, it is easier to focus during the week," claims one student. "During the week, every night is a guys' night," explains a sophomore. "When we aren't studying, we are playing video games or cards, watching a sporting event, and basically just hanging out." Weekends are usually spent "partying incredibly hard" with "females from Sweet Briar, Longwood, Randolph College, and Hollins." "Frat boys run the social scene" but "the fraternities are very open and almost everyone is welcome at parties." Off campus, Farmville lives up to its name. The rural surrounding area offers "breathtaking scenery" and some of the best hunting and outdoor activity anywhere, though. "Shooting guns," i.e., hunting, is generally popular. "No one looks at you twice for walking through your dorm to the parking lot with your deer rifle over your shoulder."

Student Body

Ethnic diversity is negligible. This is a "very homogeneous" school. The small homosexual population is "tolerated" at best. "Gay students probably won't feel too comfortable," suggests a junior. "They typical Hampden-Sydney student comes from the south, enjoys outdoor activities such as hunting and fishing, and is likely conservative and preppy." He "wears polos and khakis." He "can tie a bowtie" and probably has "a ragged, old baseball cap snugly fit over lip-length curly brown hair." "Our reputation for being made up of white middle- to upper-class conservatives who dress preppy most of the time and in camouflage during the winter is unavoidable," concedes one student. Politically, a kind of conservative snobbery reigns supreme. "Overall, they seem invested in the notion of preserving the ideas of the old South," relates a junior. "By this, I mean social stratification and cultural elitism. They're also geographic elitists and somewhat skeptical of outsiders." "Hampden-Sydney has been educating men since before the United States was founded," rejoins a proud sophomore, "and 35 congressmen, 12 senators, 12 governors, one U.S. president, and countless other prominent Americans later, we feel we're doing a fine job—change and political correctness be damned."

FINANCIAL AID: 804-223-6119 • E-MAIL: ADMISSIONS@HSC.EDU • WEBSITE: WWW.HSC.EDU

THE PRINCETON REVIEW SAYS

Admissions

Very important factors considered include: Recommendation(s), rigor of secondary school record, academic GPA, standardized test scores, character/personal qualities. *Important factors considered include:* Class rank, extracurricular activities. *Other factors considered include:* Application essay, alumni/ae relation, first generation, interview, level of applicant's interest, racial/ethnic status, talent/ability, volunteer work, work experience. SAT or ACT required; ACT with Writing component recommended. TOEFL required of all international applicants. High school diploma is required and GED is accepted. *Academic units required:* 4 English, 3 mathematics, 2 science, (1 science labs), 2 foreign language, 1 social studies, 1 history, 3 academic electives. *Academic units recommended:* 4 mathematics, 3 science, 3 foreign language.

Financial Aid

Students should submit: FAFSA, CSS/Financial Aid PROFILE, state aid form. Regular filing deadline is 5/1. The Princeton Review suggests that all financial aid forms be submitted as soon as possible after January 1. *Need-based scholarships/grants offered:* Federal Pell, SEOG, state scholarships/grants, private scholarships, the school's own gift aid. *Loan aid offered:* FFEL Subsidized Stafford, FFEL Unsubsidized Stafford, FFEL PLUS, Federal Perkins, college/university loans from institutional funds, private loans. Applicants will be notified of awards on a rolling basis beginning 12/15. Federal Work-Study Program available. Institutional employment available. Off-campus job opportunities are fair.

The Inside Word

Hampden-Sydney is one of the last of its kind. Understandably, the applicant pool is heavily self-selected, and a fairly significant percentage of those who are admitted choose to enroll. This enables the Admissions Committee to be more selective, which in turn requires candidates to take the process more seriously than might otherwise be necessary. Students with consistently sound academic records should have little to worry about nonetheless.

THE SCHOOL SAYS "..."

From The Admissions Office

"The spirit of Hampden-Sydney is its sense of community. As one of only 1,026 students, you will be in small classes and find it easy to get extra help or inspiration from professors when you want it. Many of our professors live on campus and enjoy being with students in the snack bar as well as in the classroom. They give you the best, most personal education as possible. A big bonus of small-college life is that everybody is invited to go out for everything, and you can be as much of a leader as you want to be. From athletics to debating to publications to fraternity life, this is part of the process that produces a well-rounded Hampden-Sydney graduate.

"Hampden-Sydney College requires either the SAT or ACT standardized test with essay."

SELECTIVITY

Admissions Rating	79
# of applicants	1,470
% of applicants accepted	67
% of acceptees attending	34
# of early decision applicants	89
% accepted early decision	67

FRESHMAN PROFILE

Range SAT Critical Reading	510–600
Range SAT Math	515–630
Range SAT Writing	480–590
Range ACT Composite	20–26
Minimum paper TOEFL	570
Minimum computer TOEFL	230
Average HS GPA	3.26
% graduated top 10% of class	13
% graduated top 25% of class	38
% graduated top 50% of class	70

DEADLINES

Early decision	
Deadline	11/15
Notification	12/15
Early action	
Deadline	1/15
Notification	2/15
Regular	
Deadline	3/1
Notification	4/15
Nonfall registration?	yes

APPLICANTS ALSO LOOK AT

AND OFTEN PREFER
Virginia Tech
University of Virginia

AND SOMETIMES PREFER
Sewanee—The University of the South

AND RARELY PREFER
Randolph–Macon College

FINANCIAL FACTS

Financial Aid Rating	82
Annual tuition	$28,144
Room and board	$9,148
Required fees	$1,110
Books and supplies	$1,000
% frosh rec. need-based scholarship or grant aid	50
% UG rec. need-based scholarship or grant aid	48
% frosh rec. non-need-based scholarship or grant aid	12
% UG rec. non-need-based scholarship or grant aid	10
% frosh rec. need-based self-help aid	38
% UG rec. need-based self-help aid	38
% frosh rec. any financial aid	99
% UG rec. any financial aid	98
% UG borrow to pay for school	63.8
Average cumulative indebtedness	$16,472

HAMPSHIRE COLLEGE

ADMISSIONS OFFICE, 893 WEST STREET, AMHERST, MA 01002 • ADMISSIONS: 413-559-5471 • FAX: 413-559-5631

CAMPUS LIFE

Quality of Life Rating	84
Fire Safety Rating	60*
Green Rating	79
Type of school	private
Environment	town

STUDENTS

Total undergrad enrollment	1,412
% male/female	43/57
% from out of state	83
% from public high school	49
% live on campus	89
% African American	4
% Asian	4
% Caucasian	72
% Hispanic	5
% Native American	1
% international	3
# of countries represented	27

SURVEY SAYS . . .

Lots of liberal students
Small classes
No one cheats
Great off-campus food
Frats and sororities are unpopular
or nonexistent

ACADEMICS

Academic Rating	88
Calendar	4/1/4
Student/faculty ratio	12:1
Profs interesting rating	86
Profs accessible rating	81
Most common	
reg class size	10–19 students

MOST POPULAR MAJORS

English language and literature
social sciences
cinematography and film/video production

STUDENTS SAY ". . ."

Academics

Hampshire College presents a "do-it-yourself, do-it-as-yourself" approach to education, offering students "a self-designed curriculum" facilitated by "close relationships with professors, small classes, and the great combination of communal living and individualism that a true Hampshire student embodies." Here's how it works: "In class, students learn as a group in discussions or hands-on activities (few lectures, no tests), while outside of class one focuses on independent projects (research, reading, writing, art-making)." The experience culminates in a 'Division III,' an all-consuming year-long senior thesis project "that allows students to become excited and completely invested" while "producing a unique product at the end of the year." Students "receive evaluations instead of grades, which we feel is a much more productive system." The goal is a "hands-on, interdisciplinary education, with the option to incorporate internships and experience abroad," and many here say that's exactly what they accomplish. Undergrads see Hampshire as the "embodiment of academic freedom, personal vision, and self-motivation," a place for students "who can handle the huge responsibility that comes with great opportunities" and "great freedom." Hampshire "is very small," which might limit students' choices; fortunately, "It belongs to the Five College[s] consortium," a group that includes the massive University of Massachusetts—Amherst. With the course offerings of five colleges available to them, Hampshire students can "take any course we could dream of."

Life

Hampshire students enjoy domestic pleasures: At this "very community-based school," undergrads "live together in mods, on-campus, apartment-style housing where they can cook together and share a living space while having their own room." "Potlucks are abundant since most people cook for themselves." Students tell us, "We take our class discussions to our dinner tables. We have a lot of passionate people who infect everybody else with their passion." Hampshire students also enjoy "playing music together" and "chilling out and watching a movie or just having some coffee together." Every weekend students can find plenty of parties, which "generally consist of 50 people or fewer—never the roaring, dangerously wild parties that are often found at other colleges." Overall, undergrads describe it as "a very chill campus. There is no Greek life, and the Frisbee team is the closest thing we have to jocks." The surrounding area provides opportunities "for water sports, biking, hikes," or "bonfires in the woods," and "the nearby towns of Amherst and Northampton aren't too bad," offering "lots of art galleries and live music." Of course, the school's proximity to numerous other colleges provides ample opportunities for those who grow bored with the Hampshire campus.

Student Body

As befits their school's curriculum, "Hampshire students tend to be very self-motivated people who would rather invent their own approach to knowledge than follow a pre-established track." This independent bent means that "we were maybe the 'black sheep' of our high schools, the outcasts, the ones looking for more of a challenge, more say in what they were learning or what they were expected to do with their lives." Students here are "usually good at improvising and, because of the emphasis on class discussion and writing papers, very verbal." They also tend to be "socially conscious, left-wing, and artistic. We are fond of do-it-yourself philosophies, from 'zines to music and film production to designing ecologically sustainable communities. We like a wide variety of music, and like to have parties in cramped mods at which we play this music at high volume. We are comfortable with smoking, drinking, and drug use, in a laissez-faire sort of way. We may be vegetarian, vegan, or meat eaters, but we like to cook, and we love to complain about the dining hall."

FINANCIAL AID: 413-559-5484 • E-MAIL: ADMISSIONS@HAMPSHIRE.EDU • WEBSITE: WWW.HAMPSHIRE.EDU

THE PRINCETON REVIEW SAYS

Admissions

Very important factors considered include: Application essay, character/personal qualities. *Important factors considered include:* Recommendation(s), rigor of secondary school record, extracurricular activities, level of applicant's interest, talent/ability. *Other factors considered include:* Class rank, academic GPA, standardized test scores, alumni/ae relation, interview, racial/ethnic status, volunteer work, work experience. TOEFL required of all international applicants. High school diploma is required and GED is accepted. *Academic units required:* 4 English, 4 mathematics, 4 science, (2 science labs), 3 foreign language, 2 social studies, 2 history.

Financial Aid

Students should submit: FAFSA, CSS/Financial Aid PROFILE, noncustodial PROFILE. The Princeton Review suggests that all financial aid forms be submitted as soon as possible after January 1. *Need-based scholarships/grants offered:* Federal Pell, SEOG, state scholarships/grants, private scholarships, the school's own gift aid. *Loan aid offered:* Direct Subsidized Stafford, Direct Unsubsidized Stafford, FFEL PLUS, Federal Perkins Applicants will be notified of awards on a rolling basis beginning 4/1. Federal Work-Study Program available.

The Inside Word

As some prospective students have probably deduced, Hampshire's admissions policies are the antithesis of formula-based practices. Officers want to know the individual behind the transcript, and so personal characteristics hold substantial weight. Demonstrating discipline and an independent and inquisitive spirit may just carry more weight than a perfect 4.0. Writing is seen as pivotal to a Hampshire education, and applicants must put considerable thought into their personal statements.

THE SCHOOL SAYS " . . ."

From The Admissions Office

"Students tell us they like our application. It is less derivative and more open-ended than most. Rather than assigning an essay topic, we ask to learn more about you as an individual and invite your ideas. Instead of just asking for lists of activities, we ask you how those activities (and academic or other endeavors) have shown some of the traits that lead to success at Hampshire (initiative, independence, persistence, for example). This approach parallels the work you will do at Hampshire, defining the questions you will ask and the courses and experiences that will help you to answer them, and integrating your interests.

"Hampshire College requires freshman applicants to submit scores from the old or new SAT. Students may also choose to submit scores from the ACT (with or without the Writing component) in lieu of the SAT."

SELECTIVITY

Admissions Rating	**89**
# of applicants	2,571
% of applicants accepted	55
% of acceptees attending	28
# accepting a place on wait list	102
% admitted from wait list	23
# of early decision applicants	74
% accepted early decision	72

FRESHMAN PROFILE

Range SAT Critical Reading	610–710
Range SAT Math	540–660
Range SAT Writing	590–700
Range ACT Composite	25–30
Minimum paper TOEFL	577
Minimum computer TOEFL	233
Average HS GPA	3.45
% graduated top 10% of class	28
% graduated top 25% of class	58
% graduated top 50% of class	88

DEADLINES

Early decision	
Deadline	11/15
Notification	12/15
Early action	
Deadline	12/1
Notification	2/1
Regular	
Priority	11/15
Deadline	1/15
Notification	4/1
Nonfall registration?	yes

APPLICANTS ALSO LOOK AT
AND OFTEN PREFER
Bard College
AND SOMETIMES PREFER
Sarah Lawrence College
AND RARELY PREFER
Bennington College

FINANCIAL FACTS

Financial Aid Rating	**91**
Annual tuition	$37,789
Books and supplies	$500
% frosh rec. need-based scholarship or grant aid	57
% UG rec. need-based scholarship or grant aid	55
% frosh rec. non-need-based scholarship or grant aid	38
% UG rec. non-need-based scholarship or grant aid	29
% frosh rec. need-based self-help aid	57
% UG rec. need-based self-help aid	52
% frosh rec. any financial aid	61
% UG rec. any financial aid	71
% UG borrow to pay for school	56
Average cumulative indebtedness	$20,300

HAMPTON UNIVERSITY

OFFICE OF ADMISSIONS, HAMPTON UNIVERSITY, HAMPTON, VA 23668 • ADMISSIONS: 757-727-5328 • FAX: 757-727-5095

CAMPUS LIFE

Quality of Life Rating	63
Fire Safety Rating	60*
Green Rating	60*
Type of school	private
Environment	city

STUDENTS

Total undergrad enrollment	5,056
% male/female	36/64
% from out of state	69
% live on campus	59
% in (# of) fraternities	5 (6)
% in (# of) sororities	4 (3)
% African American	96
% Asian	1
% Caucasian	12
% Hispanic	1
# of countries represented	33

SURVEY SAYS . . .

Large classes
Great library
Campus feels safe
Everyone loves the Pirates
Frats and sororities dominate
social scene
Student government is popular

ACADEMICS

Academic Rating	74
Calendar	semester
Student/faculty ratio	16:1
Profs interesting rating	68
Profs accessible rating	66
Most common reg class size	20–29 students
Most common lab size	10–19 students

MOST POPULAR MAJORS
psychology
business/commerce

STUDENTS SAY " . . ."

Academics

Hampton University, "one of the premier Historically Black Colleges and Universities in the country," is "perfect for students who desire to be around other intelligent and focused Black students who have a future and are making plans to achieve their goals. Our students are making changes in this world and will always continue to." With popular programs in business and management, psychology, pharmacy, nursing, sociology, the hard sciences, and communications, Hampton "is about producing successful, bright, and talented professionals." The school has made a special commitment to journalism and communications, opening a state-of-the-art facility in 2002 that includes a full working studio with editing facilities, a student-run radio station, and five computer labs. Throughout its many departments, Hampton stresses the importance of experiential learning, "presenting a host of opportunities for students to get internships and jobs." One student reports, "I have had three internships and have been on the campus radio station for my entire career at HU." Professors here earn good marks for dedication and teaching skills; the administration, on the other hand, is notorious for 'The Hampton Run-Around,' in which "A student spends their day running around campus trying to get a simple form signed or for a person to help them in whatever way, and in the end find out that the initial person they met with could have dealt with the problem." Most agree the inconvenience is worth it for "the connections and networking" Hampton provides. As one student notes, "Everyone here is important, related to, or knows someone important, and everyone will become successful and important."

Life

"Hampton is not the typical party school," students agree. One student writes, "Life at Hampton is pretty boring compared to where I'm from. There, the parties are wack. But, looking on the bright side, I'm not here to party and have fun; I'm here for school and to get my degree." Undergrads report that "most events take place off campus, so you really have to find your own fun." Fortunately the area provides some diversion, including "malls, fine dining, and parties … Also, Hampton is surrounded by cities that are no more than 15 to 20 minutes away," including Norfolk, Newport News, and Virginia Beach. "Nearby amusement parks are also great attractions for the spring and summer." On campus, "There is a really nice student center that turns into a virtual party every day from noon to 2:00 P.M. The student center is tri-level and has everything from a theater to [a] bowling ally and a fitness center." Hampton's Greek system is very popular; the most popular ones "are highly competitive and selective, and the whole process is crazy and oh-so-hard to get into." Some here complain that restrictive regulations dampen campus life. One student writes, "Rules and regulations prevent us from body painting at sporting events. Students are not allowed to have refrigerators apparently due to outdated wiring in the dorms. . . . Administration, faculty, and staff do not respect students as adults."

Student Body

Hampton "is a Historically Black [College and] University, but the range of Black students here is amazing. There is a niche for everyone, and I mean everyone, and most are universally accepted." Many are "very outgoing and professional," and "are well off and come from a nice home." Some "tend to be very materialistic and . . . care a lot about social matters. They all dress well, spend plenty of money on clothes, and drive very nice cars (even better cars than teachers)," but "There are many different types of students" here, not just the well heeled. Atypical students here "mesh well with the others" because Hampton students are a part of a family. "We are called Hamptonians, symbolizing our unity. Here we have a bond that is very strong—we all fit in—and it is not to be broken."

FINANCIAL AID: 800-624-3341 • E-MAIL: ADMIT@HAMPTONU.EDU • WEBSITE: WWW.HAMPTONU.EDU

THE PRINCETON REVIEW SAYS

Admissions

Very important factors considered include: Application essay, rigor of secondary school record, standardized test scores, character/personal qualities. *Important factors considered include:* Class rank, recommendation(s). *Other factors considered include:* Alumni/ae relation, extracurricular activities, talent/ability, volunteer work, SAT or ACT required; High school diploma is required and GED is accepted. *Academic units required:* 4 English, 3 mathematics, 2 science, (2 science labs), 2 social studies, 6 academic electives. *Academic units recommended:* 2 foreign language.

Financial Aid

Students should submit: FAFSA. The Princeton Review suggests that all financial aid forms be submitted as soon as possible after January 1. *Need-based scholarships/grants offered:* Federal Pell, SEOG, state scholarships/grants, private scholarships, the school's own gift aid, Federal Nursing Scholarships. *Loan aid offered:* Direct Subsidized Stafford, Direct Unsubsidized Stafford, Direct PLUS, FFEL Subsidized Stafford, FFEL Unsubsidized Stafford, FFEL PLUS, Federal Perkins, Alternative Loans. Applicants will be notified of awards on a rolling basis beginning 4/15. Federal Work-Study Program available. Off-campus job opportunities are excellent.

The Inside Word

Hampton University allows for early action admissions, meaning that students can receive an early decision without having to commit to attending the school. Well more than half of HU's applicant pool pursues this option. You would be wise to follow suit; the school is bound to be more lenient early in the process than later, when it has already admitted many qualified students. Don't be fooled by the fact that the number of applicants to HU has dropped in recent years; that is the result of more stringent admission standards, not a drop in the school's cachet.

THE SCHOOL SAYS "..."

From The Admissions Office

"Hampton attempts to provide the environment and structures most conducive to the intellectual, emotional, and aesthetic enlargement of the lives of its members. The university gives priority to effective teaching and scholarly research while placing the student at the center of its planning. Hampton will ask you to look inwardly at your own history and culture and examine your relationship to the aspirations and development of the world.

"As of this book's publication, Hampton University did not have information available about their policy regarding the new SAT."

SELECTIVITY
Admissions Rating	87
# of applicants	7,120
% of applicants accepted	37
% of acceptees attending	43

FRESHMAN PROFILE
Range SAT Critical Reading	481–552
Range SAT Math	464–606
Range ACT Composite	17–26
Average HS GPA	3.2
% graduated top 10% of class	20
% graduated top 25% of class	45
% graduated top 50% of class	90

DEADLINES
Early action	
Deadline	12/1
Notification	12/15
Priority	3/1
Nonfall registration?	yes

FINANCIAL FACTS
Financial Aid Rating	62
Annual tuition	$13,358
Room and board	$6,746
Required fees	$1,460
Books and supplies	$750
% frosh rec. need-based scholarship or grant aid	96
% UG rec. need-based scholarship or grant aid	44
% frosh rec. non-need-based scholarship or grant aid	23
% UG rec. non-need-based scholarship or grant aid	13
% frosh rec. need-based self-help aid	79
% UG rec. need-based self-help aid	44
% frosh rec. any financial aid	44
% UG rec. any financial aid	100
% UG borrow to pay for school	51
Average cumulative indebtedness	$17,125

HANOVER COLLEGE

PO Box 108, Hanover, IN 47243-0108 • Admissions: 812-866-7021 • Fax: 812-866-7098

STUDENTS SAY ". . ."

Academics

"Demanding course work" and a "small-school atmosphere" pervade the "picturesque" Georgian-style campus of Hanover College, an "excellent" bastion of the liberal arts and sciences in southeastern Indiana. Hanover operates on a fairly unique 4-4-1 calendar, in which there are two traditional semesters followed by a spring term during which students concentrate on a single class, participate in an array of off-campus internships, or study abroad. Classes are very small, and there is a strong focus on "teaching students to think and write critically." Students must complete a wide range of distribution requirements and agree that the curriculum is "intense." Sometimes "The workload is barely manageable." While the "amazing" and "very intelligent" professors at Hanover may "require a lot from the students," they are "very attentive." "Personal attention from professors" is commonplace and they "spend a lot of time out of class with the students." "Teachers are tough" but in the end, "You really learn." "The professors here are some of the best teachers, mentors, and friends that one could hope to find anywhere," beams a classical studies major. Over 90 percent of all students receive at least some financial assistance and more than a few say they chose Hanover because they got "a lot of scholarship money." Students say the Career Services staff is "really good," although registration can be "a hassle." While the "distant" administration is almost uniformly unpopular, students are happy with the new president. One student tells us "she is a breath of frsh air and I believe she will make a difference."

Life

"Hanover's campus is one of the most beautiful places I have ever been," swears a junior. "This place is beautiful the whole year round," "even in the soggy dreariness of late March." A "family-like" environment "allows people to really get to know each other and have connections." "Academics are very important" but "There are also many opportunities to get involved in extracurricular activities." Greek life is an exceptionally big deal here ("most students on campus are strongly Greek affiliated") and fraternities and sororities dominate the social scene. During the week, "Most students are doing homework and studying" and "just hang out casually"—except for Wednesday. "Wednesday nights and the weekends are when people party." Students say most people on campus "at least talk about partying a lot" and that "parties are pretty much just at the fraternities." "Though the rules about alcohol are rather strict, they are not necessarily heavily enforced (in the fraternities anyway). It is much harder to drink in residence halls." Some students complain that there is little to do "outside of fraternity parties or bars." To be sure, "the surrounding towns of Hanover and Madison" are "not very exciting" and may be a little "too rural" for some tastes. "This is the worst place a college town could be," laments one junior. Students with cars can avail themselves of more urban pursuits available in nearby "Cincinnati, Louisville, and Indianapolis."

Student Body

There are just over 1,000 students here from over 35 states and 18 countries, though "Most tend to be from Indiana, Kentucky, or Ohio." "The typical student is an upper-middle-class White athlete" and very likely "Christian." A lot of students come from "suburbia," while others come from small Midwestern towns. "There are a few Blacks, a few gays, and a lot of Nepalese and Hawaiian students." "The little ethnic diversity here is from the international students, not diverse Americans," though. "There are not a lot of atypical students" and those that are "tend to stick together." The generally homogenous nature of the student population creates a good deal of cohesion. "We pretty much all get along," reports one first-year student. Students describe themselves as "friendly," "easygoing," and "pretty casual." "There's a little bit of everything as far as goals, interests, and ambitions." There are "quite a few [students who] like to party frequently;" "However, most study and work hard." Over 60 percent of Hanover's newly minted graduates eventually go on to graduate and professional schools.

FINANCIAL AID: 812-866-7030 • E-MAIL: ADMISSION@HANOVER.EDU • WEBSITE: WWW.HANOVER.EDU

THE PRINCETON REVIEW SAYS

Admissions

Very important factors considered include: Class rank, academic GPA, rigor of secondary school record. *Important factors considered include:* Recommendation(s), standardized test scores, talent/ability. *Other factors considered include:* Application essay, alumni/ae relation, character/personal qualities, extracurricular activities, first generation, geographical residence, interview, level of applicant's interest, racial/ethnic status, state residency, volunteer work, work experience. SAT or ACT required; ACT with Writing component required. High school diploma is required and GED is not accepted. *Academic units required:* 4 English, 3 mathematics, 3 science, (2 science labs), 2 foreign language, 2 social studies, 2 history, 2 academic electives. *Academic units recommended:* 4 English, 4 mathematics, 4 science, (3 science labs), 4 foreign language, 3 social studies, 3 history, 3 academic electives.

Financial Aid

Students should submit: FAFSA. The Princeton Review suggests that all financial aid forms be submitted as soon as possible after January 1. *Need-based scholarships/grants offered:* Federal Pell, state scholarships/grants, private scholarships, the school's own gift aid. *Loan aid offered:* FFEL Subsidized Stafford, FFEL Unsubsidized Stafford, FFEL PLUS Applicants will be notified of awards on a rolling basis beginning 3/1. Off-campus job opportunities are fair.

The Inside Word

Admission is competitive, but the applicant pool is not huge, and Hanover accepts a relatively high percentage of its applicants. High school grades (especially during your junior and senior years) and class rank are the most important determining factors for the Admissions Committee. If you are vying for an academic scholarship—and many, many applicants will be—it pays to invest some serious thought and time into Hanover's application process.

THE SCHOOL SAYS "..."

From The Admissions Office

"Since our founding in 1827, we have been committed to providing students with a personal, rigorous, and well-rounded liberal arts education. Part of the college search process is finding that school that proves to be a good match. For those who see the value in an education that demands engagement and who see college as a time for exploration and involvement, they will find that Hanover is all they could hope for and more.

"The admission process serves as an introduction to the personal education that students receive at Hanover College. Every application is considered individually with emphasis being placed on a student's high school curriculum and the student's academic performance in that curriculum. While we realize that not every high school has the same course offerings, we expect students to have selected a college preparatory curriculum as challenging as possible within his or her particular high school or academic setting.

"Hanover College accepts both the SAT and ACT. Students taking the ACT are required to take the optional writing section. For students who have taken one or both of the tests multiple times, we will use the highest sub scores when calculating a student's score on either test for admission and scholarship purposes."

SELECTIVITY
Admissions Rating	89
# of applicants	1,894
% of applicants accepted	66
% of acceptees attending	19

FRESHMAN PROFILE
Range SAT Critical Reading	510–630
Range SAT Math	520–630
Range SAT Writing	490–610
Range ACT Composite	22–28
Average HS GPA	3.72
% graduated top 10% of class	39
% graduated top 25% of class	77
% graduated top 50% of class	96

DEADLINES
Early action	
Deadline	12/1
Notification	12/20
Regular	
Deadline	3/1
Notification	rolling
Nonfall registration?	yes

FINANCIAL FACTS
Financial Aid Rating	60*
Annual tuition	$24,700
Room and board	$7,500
Required fees	$520
Books and supplies	$900
% frosh rec. need-based scholarship or grant aid	71
% UG rec. need-based scholarship or grant aid	66
% frosh rec. non-need-based scholarship or grant aid	16
% UG rec. non-need-based scholarship or grant aid	13
% frosh rec. need-based self-help aid	55
% UG rec. need-based self-help aid	52
% frosh rec. any financial aid	99
% UG rec. any financial aid	98
% UG borrow to pay for school	58
Average cumulative indebtedness	$21,597

HARVARD COLLEGE

BYERLY HALL, EIGHT GARDEN STREET, CAMBRIDGE, MA 02138 • ADMISSIONS: 617-495-1551 • FAX: 617-495-8821

STUDENTS SAY ". . ."

Academics

Those who are lucky enough to attend this legendarily "beautiful, fun, historic and academically alive place" in Cambridge, Massachusetts find a "dynamic universe" that has the ability to both inspire and intimidate, and to open up a portal to an "amazing irresistible hell," plus about a billion opportunities beyond that. Needless to say, it's "very difficult academically," but the school "does a good job of watching over its freshmen through extensive advising programs." Those that are not willing to go after what they want—classes, positions in extracurriculars, jobs, etc—do not gain access to the vast resources of the university. With such a definitive grouping of intelligent people, there does tend to be "latent competition"; nobody is cutthroat in classes, but "people find ways to make everything (especially clubs and even partying) competitive." Still, this is a good thing, and one student claims his experience to be "rewarding beyond anything else I've ever done." "It is impossible to 'get the most out of Harvard' because Harvard offers so much," says another. As at any school, "some professors are better than others," but for the most part, the "the brightest minds in the world" here are "incredible" and "every so often, fantastic," and "the level of achievement is unbelievable." says a student. Harvard employs a lot of Teaching Fellows (TFs) for the larger lecture classes, so "you do have to go to office hours to get to know your big lecture class professors on a personal level," but "this is not a deterrent." The administration can be "waaaaay out of touch with students" and "reticent to change," and there are more than a few claims of bureaucracy, but many agree it has the students' best interests at heart.

Life

Most students have resolved their study habits by the time they get to Harvard, so "studying becomes routine and there is a vibrant social atmosphere on campus, and between students and the local community." In Cambridge and Boston, there's always something to do, whether it's "go see a play, a concert, hit up a party, go to the movies, or dine out." The new pub on campus is an excellent place to hang out and see people, "especially if you want to play a game of pool or have a reasonably priced drink"; drinking also occurs on weekends at parties or at Harvard's Finals clubs, though it is by no means a prevalent part of social life here (partly due to the university's less-than-lax alcohol policies). In addition to school-sponsored events such as panels and film screenings, the number of student organizations is staggering. "Basically, if you want to do it, Harvard either has it or has the money to give to you so you can start it," says a student. "Boredom does not exist here. There are endless opportunities and endless passionate people to do them with." During freshman year, the school organizes a lot of holiday/special event parties for people to get to know one another, and conversations are rarely surface-level and "often incorporate some sort of debate or interesting/important topic."

Student Body

Everyone is here to achieve, and this makes for a very common, if broad mold of a typical student. As one junior computer science major succinctly puts it: "Works really hard. Doesn't sleep. Involved in a million extracurriculars." People here have nothing but the highest opinion of their fellow students, and the when it comes to finding the lowest common denominator, it's that "everyone is great for one reason or another." However, all of these virtuosos are down to earth and there are also a lot of well-rounded kids "who aren't geniuses but are pretty good at most things." Admitting the best of the best makes for quite a diverse campus, and "there is a lot of tolerance and acceptance at Harvard for individuals of all races, religions, socio-economic backgrounds, life styles, etc."

FINANCIAL AID: 617-495-1581 • E-MAIL: COLLEGE@FAS.HARVARD.EDU • WEBSITE: WWW.FAS.HARVARD.EDU

THE PRINCETON REVIEW SAYS

Admissions

Other factors considered include: Application essay, academic GPA, recommendation(s), rigor of secondary school record, standardized test scores, alumni/ae relation, character/personal qualities, extracurricular activities, first generation, geographical residence, interview, racial/ethni SAT Subject Tests required; SAT or ACT required; ACT with Writing component required. High school diploma or equivalent is not required. *Academic units recommended:* 4 English, 4 mathematics, 4 science, 4 foreign language, 3 social studies, 2 history.

Financial Aid

Students should submit: FAFSA, CSS/Financial Aid PROFILE, noncustodial PROFILE, business/farm supplement, tax forms through IDOC. Regular filing deadline is 2/1. The Princeton Review suggests that all financial aid forms be submitted as soon as possible after January 1. *Need-based scholarships/grants offered:* Federal Pell, SEOG, state scholarships/grants, private scholarships, the school's own gift aid. *Loan aid offered:* Direct Subsidized Stafford, Direct Unsubsidized Stafford, Direct PLUS, Federal Perkins, state loans, college/university loans from institutional funds. Applicants will be notified of awards on or about 4/1. Federal Work-Study Program available. Institutional employment available. Off-campus job opportunities are excellent.

The Inside Word

It just doesn't get any tougher than this. Candidates to Harvard face dual obstacles—an awe-inspiring applicant pool and, as a result, admissions standards that defy explanation in quantifiable terms. Harvard denies admission to the vast majority, and virtually all of them are top students. It all boils down to splitting hairs, which is quite hard to explain and even harder for candidates to understand. Rather than being as detailed and direct as possible about the selection process and criteria, Harvard keeps things close to the vest—before, during, and after. They even refuse to admit that being from South Dakota is an advantage. Thus the admissions process does more to intimidate candidates than to empower them. Moving to a common application seemed to be a small step in the right direction, but with the current explosion of early decision applicants and a super-high yield of enrollees, things are not likely to change dramatically.

THE SCHOOL SAYS ". . ."

From The Admissions Office

"The Admissions Committee looks for energy, ambition, and the capacity to make the most of opportunities. Academic ability and preparation are important, and so is intellectual curiosity—but many of the strongest applicants have significant non-academic interests and accomplishments as well. There is no formula for admission, and applicants are considered carefully, with attention to future promise.

"Freshman applicants for Fall 2008 may submit either the old SAT taken before March 2005, or the new SAT. The ACT with Writing component is also accepted. All students must also submit three SAT Subject Tests of their choosing."

SELECTIVITY

Admissions Rating	99
# of applicants	22,955
% of applicants accepted	9
% of acceptees attending	79

FRESHMAN PROFILE

Range SAT Critical Reading	700–800
Range SAT Math	700–790
Range SAT Writing	690–790
Range ACT Composite	31–35
% graduated top 10% of class	95
% graduated top 25% of class	100
% graduated top 50% of class	100

DEADLINES

Regular	
Priority	12/1
Deadline	1/1
Notification	4/1
Nonfall registration?	no

FINANCIAL FACTS

Financial Aid Rating	99
Annual tuition	$32,557
Books and supplies	$1,000
% frosh rec. need-based scholarship or grant aid	55
% UG rec. need-based scholarship or grant aid	51
% frosh rec. need-based self-help aid	39
% UG rec. need-based self-help aid	44
% frosh rec. any financial aid	70
% UG rec. any financial aid	70
% UG borrow to pay for school	46
Average cumulative indebtedness	$9,290

HARVEY MUDD COLLEGE

301 PLATT BOULEVARD, CLAREMONT, CA 91711-5990 • ADMISSIONS: 909-621-8011 • FAX: 909-607-7046

CAMPUS LIFE
Quality of Life Rating	**88**
Fire Safety Rating	**74**
Green Rating	**86**
Type of school	private
Environment	town

STUDENTS
Total undergrad enrollment	735
% male/female	67/33
% from out of state	50
% from public high school	70
% live on campus	99
% African American	1
% Asian	21
% Caucasian	52
% Hispanic	8
% Native American	1
% international	4
# of countries represented	15

SURVEY SAYS . . .
Large classes
No one cheats
Lab facilities are great
Great computer facilities
Students are friendly
*Frats and sororities are unpopular
or nonexistent*

ACADEMICS
Academic Rating	**99**
Calendar	semester
Student/faculty ratio	8:1
Profs interesting rating	98
Profs accessible rating	99
Most common reg class size	fewer than 10 students
Most common lab size	10–19 students

MOST POPULAR MAJORS
engineering
computer and information sciences
mathematics

STUDENTS SAY " . . . "

Academics
Harvey Mudd, the math, science, and engineering centerpiece of the five Claremont Colleges, "is a vortex of challenges and opportunities where you work until you drop, but it doesn't bother you because everyone else is in the same exact situation you are." A curriculum that teaches "way more math and science than you knew existed, then adds one third humanities on top of it" means students here leave with "a broad education" that "prepares undergraduates (and undergraduates only) for both industry and grad school." Opportunities are further enhanced by "limitless undergraduate research opportunities." One engineering major reports that "Mudd is extremely good at offering research experience for undergraduates. Engineering majors participate in 'Clinic' where they collaborate with other Mudders to satisfy the requests of an actual company." Best of all, Mudd somehow manages to accomplish all this without creating the high-stress environment common at other tech schools. Many here attribute this to the honor code, "a very strong driving force" providing students with "many freedoms." For example, students can "work collaboratively on the vast majority of their assignments, where people contribute what they know and the group as a whole can find a solution." Moreover, "take-home closed book tests are the norm. We also have full access via our ID cards to all the academic buildings 24/7. Theft is also essentially a non-issue. It's hard to imagine a better setup." Indeed, a school where undergrads are "given all the freedom and resources to explore all the brilliant, not so brilliant, and downright foolish ideas we conceive" can accurately be described as "pretty much as good as it gets. As long as you are serious about learning math and science, you will be happy here."

Life
Even though "Mudd schedules are extremely busy," most students here "know how to lighten up so we aren't completely crushed." "Sports like Ultimate Frisbee are very popular, and each dorm occasionally hosts study breaks where students can watch a movie or relax from work. Art clubs like the Sewing Club or Crafts Club are available for people who like working on artistic things in groups, and there are many political or environmentally-oriented activist groups." Students report that the incidence of pranking—the perpetration of elaborate yet harmless pranks, such as completely filling a classmate's dorm room with inflated garbage bags—is down from past years, but tell us that Mudd remains "known for pretty good parties" among all the Claremont colleges, in part because of "a loose alcohol policy" on the Mudd campus. Even so, the workload here is simply too great for partying to ever get out of hand. As one undergrad explains, "People are pretty busy, so a lot of socializing is done over homework." Dorm communities are "very strong, so people will generally hang out in their own dorms, although there's always crossover between dorms." Hometown Claremont "can be a little lackluster" and pricey as well, but fortunately greater Los Angeles isn't too far off.

Student Body
Mudd undergrads are "intelligent yet social—at least within their own social groups. There are some who don't get out much or at all, but that's going to happen at a nerd school like Mudd." While students readily concede that "there are some odd students" on campus, depending on the exact nature of their eccentricity, "people either leave them alone or they do well socially." As one student observes, "Swordfights in dorm courtyards are not uncommon, but neither are more typical college parties." Unsurprisingly, students here "are all really into science and technology, but there is quite a bit of variation within that." Though "a bit heavy on the white, upper-class males," there has been "a strong effort to recruit talented underrepresented groups and some success recently in recruiting more women." Most students here are "fairly sleep-deprived."

FINANCIAL AID: 909-621-8055 • E-MAIL: ADMISSION@HMC.EDU • WEBSITE: WWW.HMC.EDU

THE PRINCETON REVIEW SAYS

Admissions

Very important factors considered include: Class rank, application essay, academic GPA, recommendation(s), rigor of secondary school record, standardized test scores, character/personal qualities. *Important factors considered include:* Alumni/ae relation, extracurricular activities, first generation, interview, racial/ethnic status, talent/ability. *Other factors considered include:* geographical residence, volunteer work, work experience. SAT or ACT with Writing component, SAT II Math 2 plus any other subjects required. High school diploma is required and GED is accepted. *Academic units required:* 4 English, 4 mathematics, 3 science, (3 science labs), 1 social studies, 1 history. *Academic units recommended:* 2 foreign language.

Financial Aid

Students should submit: FAFSA, CSS/Financial Aid PROFILE, state aid form, noncustodial PROFILE, business/farm supplement. Regular filing deadline is 2/1. The Princeton Review suggests that all financial aid forms be submitted as soon as possible after January 1. *Need-based scholarships/grants offered:* Federal Pell, SEOG, state scholarships/grants, private scholarships, the school's own gift aid. *Loan aid offered:* FFEL Subsidized Stafford, FFEL Unsubsidized Stafford, FFEL PLUS, Federal Perkins, college/university loans from institutional funds, alternative loans. Applicants will be notified of awards on or about 4/1. Federal Work-Study Program available. Institutional employment available. Off-campus job opportunities are excellent. Eighty-five percent of students receive some form of financial aid.

The Inside Word

There's little mystery to the admissions process at Harvey Mudd College. Like most top tier science, math, and engineering schools, Harvey Mudd considers far more qualified applicants than it can accommodate in its incoming class. Give the application your all and accept the fact that being perfectly qualified to attend this school is no guarantee of admission.

THE SCHOOL SAYS "..."

From The Admissions Office

"HMC is a wonderfully unusual combination of a liberal arts college and research institute. Our students love math and science, want to live and learn deeply in an intimate climate of cooperation and trust, thrive on innovation and discovery, and enjoy rigorous coursework in arts, humanities, and social sciences in addition to a technical curriculum. At least a year of research or our innovative Clinic program is required (or guaranteed, if you prefer). The resources at HMC are astounding, and all are accessible to undergraduates: labs, shops, work areas, and most importantly, faculty. You'll find the professors and student body stimulating and supportive – they'll challenge you inside and outside the classroom, and share your love of learning and collaboration. They'll also share your love of fun and sense of humor (math jokes and all). In addition, we benefit from the unique consortium that is the Claremont Colleges.

While we may not take ourselves too seriously, employers and graduate schools do. We enjoy a powerful reputation for preparing our graduates for all kinds of career paths. A wide range of companies are eager to hire our seniors, and HMC sends the highest proportion of graduates to PhD programs of any undergraduate college in the country."

SELECTIVITY
Admissions Rating	99
# of applicants	2,493
% of applicants accepted	28
% of acceptees attending	31
# accepting a place on wait list	186
% admitted from wait list	1
# of early decision applicants	112
% accepted early decision	40

FRESHMAN PROFILE
Range SAT Critical Reading	690–760
Range SAT Math	740–820
Range SAT Writing	680–760
Average HS GPA	3.8
% graduated top 10% of class	93
% graduated top 25% of class	98.7
% graduated top 50% of class	100

DEADLINES
Early decision	
Deadline	11/15
Notification	12/15
Regular	
Deadline	1/2
Notification	4/1
Nonfall registration?	no

APPLICANTS ALSO LOOK AT
AND OFTEN PREFER
Stanford University
Princeton University
Massachusetts Institute of Technology
AND SOMETIMES PREFER
University of California—Berkeley
California Institute of Technology
Franklin W. Olin College of Engineering
AND RARELY PREFER
University of California—Los Angeles
Rensselaer Polytechnic Institute
University of California—San Diego

FINANCIAL FACTS
Financial Aid Rating	96
Annual tuition	$34,669
Room and board	$11,415
Required fees	$222
Books and supplies	$800
% frosh rec. need-based scholarship or grant aid	59
% UG rec. need-based scholarship or grant aid	52
% frosh rec. non-need-based scholarship or grant aid	29
% UG rec. non-need-based scholarship or grant aid	25
% frosh rec. need-based self-help aid	43
% UG rec. need-based self-help aid	42
% frosh rec. any financial aid	88
% UG rec. any financial aid	83
% UG borrow to pay for school	55.29
Average cumulative indebtedness	$16,078

HAVERFORD COLLEGE

370 WEST LANCASTER AVENUE, HAVERFORD, PA 19041 • ADMISSIONS: 610-896-1350 • FAX: 610-896-1338

STUDENTS SAY ". . ."

Academics

Any fitting description of academic life at Haverford College should start with "two words: honor code!" Here "Students are allowed a great deal of freedom and self-governance," and the "honor code holds the students responsible for their learning, and trusts them to have both concern and respect for their fellow students. That is why our school has both unscheduled and unproctored final exams." As one student puts it, "The success of the institution is dependent upon a body of students who are actively concerned and engaged." Equally concerned and engaged are members of the faculty: "Despite the fact that professors here do incredible research and publish regularly, it is evident that they have come to Haverford to teach. Students are their first priority, and they absolutely make themselves available to discuss anything." In the classroom, professors "are funny and interesting, and lead very good discussions. Class discussions even run overtime every so often, and the students voluntarily stay late to continue the discussions." "If you take one small step toward a Haverford professor," attests one student, "that professor will take a giant leap toward you. Our professors like teaching students and developing personal relationships with us." Like professors here, the administration also draws almost exclusively rave reviews: "Only at a school like Haverford would we have something called 'First Thursdays,' where the entire student community is invited to have an open-forum discussion with the president. Even he makes time for student opinions." Proximity to other great colleges means that Haverford students also have the "opportunity to take classes at Bryn Mawr, Swarthmore, or Penn."

Life

Haverford is "a place where people like to study hard and play hard. During the week students are very hardworking, but on the weekends we like to let our hair down and enjoy ourselves, [by] going into Philly, watching an a cappella group perform, or hanging out with friends. We know how to keep ourselves happy. Since we do not have any Greek life, everyone is part of the social life on campus." Another notes, "The lack of Greek life (which goes against the inclusive nature of Haverford's Quaker roots) on campus is a really strong point." Indeed, "Clubs and organizations are always sponsoring events, like dinners, dances, and parties. The hardest thing to do on weekends is to decide what your plans are for the night." Parties on campus "are open to everyone, and "While many students drink," undergrads say, "it is not necessary to do so to have a good time." If you want to stay in, that's okay, too; Haverford's small size means that "everyone knows everyone else by sophomore year, so it's not like you'll really meet anyone new by going out."

Student Body

Undergrads frequently use the term "closet nerd" to describe their peers. One student defines the term as "someone who is very smart and works very hard but also pursues other interests and has fun." Someone who is "a bit awkward," but "often athletic in some way." Another student sums up Haverfordians in this way: "The typical Haverford student is friendly but not bubbly, self-motivated but not obsessive, smart but not obnoxious, slightly eccentric but not truly weird, nerdy but not socially hopeless. We mill around the edges of the liberal arts stereotypes without quite embodying them." In his or her interactions with others, the Haverfordian is "academically honest and socially respectful, and hopes to make a real difference in the world. There's a variety of personalities, but we're all basically geeks"—"idealist geeks who want to change the world."

FINANCIAL AID: 610-896-1350 • E-MAIL: ADMITME@HAVERFORD.EDU • WEBSITE: WWW.HAVERFORD.EDU

THE PRINCETON REVIEW SAYS

Admissions

Very important factors considered include: Application essay, academic GPA, rigor of secondary school record, standardized test scores, character/personal qualities. *Important factors considered include:* Class rank, recommendation(s), extracurricular activities, talent/ability, volunteer work, work experience. *Other factors considered include:* Alumni/ae relation, first generation, geographical residence, interview, level of applicant's interest, racial/ethnic status, ACT with Writing component required. TOEFL required of all international applicants. High school diploma or equivalent is not required. *Academic units required:* 4 English, 3 mathematics, 1 science, (1 science labs), 3 foreign language, 2 social studies. *Academic units recommended:* 4 mathematics, 2 science.

Financial Aid

Students should submit: FAFSA, CSS/Financial Aid PROFILE, business/farm supplement, CSS College Board Noncustodial Parents' Statement is required-not the Noncustodial supplement. Regular filing deadline is 1/31. The Princeton Review suggests that all financial aid forms be submitted as soon as possible after January 1. *Need-based scholarships/grants offered:* Federal Pell, SEOG, state scholarships/grants, the school's own gift aid. *Loan aid offered:* FFEL Subsidized Stafford, FFEL Unsubsidized Stafford, FFEL PLUS, Federal Perkins Applicants will be notified of awards on or about 4/1. Federal Work-Study Program available. Institutional employment available. Off-campus job opportunities are good.

The Inside Word

Haverford's applicant pool is an impressive and competitive lot. Intellectual curiosity is paramount, and applicants are expected to keep a demanding academic schedule in high school. Additionally, the college places a high value on ethics, as evidenced by its honor code. The Admissions Office seeks students who will reflect and promote Haverford's ideals.

THE SCHOOL SAYS "..."

From The Admissions Office

"Haverford strives to be a college in which integrity, honesty, and concern for others are dominant forces. The college does not have many formal rules; rather, it offers an opportunity for students to govern their affairs and conduct themselves with respect and concern for others. Each student is expected to adhere to the honor code as it is adopted each year by the Students' Association. Haverford's Quaker roots show most clearly in the relationship of faculty and students, in the emphasis on integrity, in the interaction of the individual and the community, and through the college's concern for the uses to which its students put their expanding knowledge. Haverford's 1,100 students represent a wide diversity of interests, backgrounds, and talents. They come from public, parochial, and independent schools across the United States, Puerto Rico, and 28 foreign countries. Students of color are an important part of the Haverford community.

"Haverford College requires that all applicants submit the results of the new three-part SAT exam or the ACT with the optional writing test. Two SAT Subject Tests are required."

SELECTIVITY

Admissions Rating	**98**
# of applicants	3,351
% of applicants accepted	26
% of acceptees attending	36
# accepting a place on wait list	312
% admitted from wait list	17
# of early decision applicants	235
% accepted early decision	42

FRESHMAN PROFILE

Range SAT Critical Reading	640–760
Range SAT Math	650–740
Minimum paper TOEFL	600
Minimum computer TOEFL	250
% graduated top 10% of class	88
% graduated top 25% of class	97
% graduated top 50% of class	100

DEADLINES

Early decision	
Deadline	11/15
Notification	12/15
Regular	
Deadline	1/15
Notification	4/15
Nonfall registration?	no

FINANCIAL FACTS

Financial Aid Rating	**96**
Annual tuition	$33,394
Room and board	$10,390
Required fees	$316
Books and supplies	$1,194
% frosh rec. need-based scholarship or grant aid	39
% UG rec. need-based scholarship or grant aid	40
% frosh rec. need-based self-help aid	37
% UG rec. need-based self-help aid	38
% frosh rec. any financial aid	41
% UG rec. any financial aid	42
% UG borrow to pay for school	39
Average cumulative indebtedness	$15,875

HENDRIX COLLEGE

1600 WASHINGTON AVENUE, CONWAY, AR 72032 • ADMISSIONS: 501-450-1362 • FAX: 501-450-3843

CAMPUS LIFE
Quality of Life Rating	**88**
Fire Safety Rating	**65**
Green Rating	**78**
Type of school	private
Affiliation	Methodist
Environment	town

STUDENTS
Total undergrad enrollment	1,189
% male/female	45/55
% from out of state	46
% from public high school	80
% live on campus	84
% African American	4
% Asian	3
% Caucasian	83
% Hispanic	3
% Native American	1
% international	1
# of countries represented	9

SURVEY SAYS . . .
Athletic facilities are great
Frats and sororities are unpopular
or nonexistent

ACADEMICS
Academic Rating	**87**
Calendar	semester
Student/faculty ratio	11:1
Profs interesting rating	94
Profs accessible rating	95
Most common reg class size	10–19 students
Most common lab size	10–19 students

MOST POPULAR MAJORS
psychology
biology/biological sciences
history

STUDENTS SAY "..."

Academics
Hendrix College in Arkansas is strong in the humanities as well as the hard sciences. "The biggest and nicest buildings on campus are definitely the science buildings," notes one student. "The study abroad program is amazing." Internships and research opportunities are readily available. Scholarships are profuse. Many students receive "phenomenal aid that would be ridiculous to turn down." "Academically, Hendrix is not a walk in the park." "Some mandatory classes are pointless" but "dull or otherwise bad classes seem uncommon." "Class sizes are small, which allows for enriching, intimate discussion." The "courageously friendly" professors are "some of the best and most challenging around." "Ninety percent of the professors are amazingly top notch," estimates an American studies major. "Generally, they all push you to do well." "One of Hendrix's selling points is the personal relationships that students build with their professors," adds a political science major. Be forewarned, "They know when you're missing class or when you're really struggling with the material or when you're not even trying." The administration here is "the same as anywhere you will go." It's "competent and keep the school running smoothly" but sometimes "out of touch with the desires of the students." Decisions "seem uninformed or just plain random" now and then.

Life
"Hendrix is one of those schools where you have to really study and work hard." Nevertheless, social life is very active. "On warm days, the pecan grove in the center of campus is bustling with people just hanging out." "There are always activities going on which students can attend for free." Virtually everyone is "active in at least one organization." Many are "very involved" in theater productions. Ultimate Frisbee is pretty big. A decent percentage of students plays intercollegiate sports but "those who don't couldn't care less." There's no frat or sorority scene and students here say that's "a good thing." "On the weekends there is a pretty strong drinking culture" and there are occasionally "big" campus wide parties and "some awesome theme parties." "The food is very good." However, the residence halls are "a universal source of concern." "Housing is a difficult process here" and the dorms are "cramped." Also, the Internet connection can be "truly abysmal." As for the surrounding town of Conway, "There's not much to do" and "there aren't really any bars except the VFW." As a result, "most people hardly ever leave" the "breathtaking" campus. When they do depart, they usually head "a mere" 30 minutes away to the somewhat urban environs of Little Rock. "Outdoorsy" activities are also available. "There is a lot of nature in the surrounding area but no one seems to want to go there."

Student Body
"Hendrix is a cross between a hippie school and a nerd college." It's mostly "off-the-wall and very creative" "southern kids" "I don't think there really is a typical Hendrix student," a junior tells us. "What unites us is our strong sense of individuality and our unerring desire to learn about each other." "If you are different or have little quirks, you fit right in," guarantees a senior. Most students say "it's easy to float from group to group" but "cliques at Hendrix are very obvious." There are "whiny upper-middleclass trustafarians." There are "socially awkward people." There are "granola kids" and "stoners." "Most students lie somewhere on the spectrum from studious to party animal." Gay students are "very out." "The athletes sequester themselves." "Race-wise, you have your choice of 12 flavors of vanilla." "Despite what the administration wants prospective students to think, there are not a lot of minority students at Hendrix," discloses a freshman. "Minorities seemed to be accepted into the social crowd," though. Politically, the atmosphere is "heavily liberal." "Hendrix is kind of like being in a time warp harkening back to the 60s and 70s." Some students note a "slight dislike of conservatives." "Their political beliefs are given little to no respect by a majority of the student body," says a sophomore. Other students don't see the problem. "I myself am a conservative Republican and I have many friends and have never felt unaccepted," asserts a sophomore. "We just agree to disagree."

FINANCIAL AID: 501-450-1368 • E-MAIL: ADM@HENDRIX.EDU • WEBSITE: WWW.HENDRIX.EDU

THE PRINCETON REVIEW SAYS

Admissions

Very important factors considered include: Application essay, academic GPA, rigor of secondary school record, standardized test scores. *Important factors considered include:* Class rank, recommendation(s), character/personal qualities, extracurricular activities, interview. *Other factors considered include:* Racial/ethnic status, talent/ability, volunteer work, SAT or ACT required; TOEFL required of all international applicants. High school diploma is required and GED is accepted. *Academic units recommended:* 4 English, 3 mathematics, 2 science, 2 foreign language, 3 social studies.

Financial Aid

Students should submit: FAFSA. The Princeton Review suggests that all financial aid forms be submitted as soon as possible after January 1. *Need-based scholarships/grants offered:* Federal Pell, SEOG, state scholarships/grants, private scholarships, the school's own gift aid. *Loan aid offered:* FFEL Subsidized Stafford, FFEL Unsubsidized Stafford, FFEL PLUS, Federal Perkins, Methodist Loan. Applicants will be notified of awards on a rolling basis beginning 2/15. Federal Work-Study Program available. Institutional employment available. Off-campus job opportunities are good.

The Inside Word

Hendrix is something of a sleeper school. The acceptance rate is high but the applicant pool is small and well-qualified. Hendrix is an especially good bet for students with strong grades who lack the test scores usually necessary for admission to colleges on a higher level of selectivity. Also, financial aid is stellar here, so don't let the cost of tuition be a deterrent.

THE SCHOOL SAYS "..."

From The Admissions Office

"Hendrix students are participants, not spectators. They like to be involved, and they like to know that what they do makes a difference. Hendrix students are voting members of almost every campus committee, which gives them an important voice in college governance. They are very hands-on about their education as well. Internships, study abroad, research projects, service projects, expressive arts projects, and leadership development—these are all areas that Hendrix students find attractive. In Fall 2005, Hendrix introduced a new program that guarantees every Hendrix student will have at least three hands-on experiences selected from six categories. The program is called *Your Hendrix Odyssey: Engaging in Active Learning.* Students receive transcript credit for their Odyssey projects. The benefits of this hands-on approach to learning are so obvious that we believe every Hendrix student should have the opportunity to participate. The college is raising money to provide grants and fellowships that will help remove the economic barriers to participation in out-of-class experiences. It is an exciting time to be a Hendrix student! The Hendrix curriculum is demanding, but the environment is one of support and cooperation—not competition. Hendrix students form a close-knit, inclusive community. They build lifetime connections and close friendships, the kind of relationships that grow in a residential college where learning is a 24/7 kind of thing. It doesn't hurt that the campus is beautifully maintained and that Hendrix graduates are admitted to top graduate schools and recruited for good jobs around the world.

"Hendrix College has no preference on which standardized test (SAT/ACT) or version (old/new) is taken, but we strongly encourage all applicants to take one of the tests during their senior year. While the Writing scores will be considered, at this point weight will only be given to the Critical Reading and Math sections of the SAT and the required sections of the ACT."

SELECTIVITY
Admissions Rating	88
# of applicants	1,323
% of applicants accepted	83
% of acceptees attending	34
# accepting a place on wait list	31
% admitted from wait list	39

FRESHMAN PROFILE
Range SAT Critical Reading	570–690
Range SAT Math	550–660
Range ACT Composite	25–31
Minimum paper TOEFL	550
Minimum computer TOEFL	215
Average HS GPA	3.7
% graduated top 10% of class	43
% graduated top 25% of class	75
% graduated top 50% of class	92

DEADLINES
Regular	
Priority	2/1
Deadline	8/1
Notification	rolling
Nonfall registration?	yes

APPLICANTS ALSO LOOK AT
AND OFTEN PREFER
Rhodes College
University of Central Arkansas
University of Arkansas—Fayetteville
AND SOMETIMES PREFER
Millsaps College
Trinity University
University of Arkansas—Little Rock
AND RARELY PREFER
Lambuth University
Monmouth University (NJ)

FINANCIAL FACTS
Financial Aid Rating	86
Annual tuition	$24,198
Room and board	$7,200
Required fees	$300
Books and supplies	$900
% frosh rec. need-based scholarship or grant aid	63
% UG rec. need-based scholarship or grant aid	58
% frosh rec. non-need-based scholarship or grant aid	20
% UG rec. non-need-based scholarship or grant aid	16
% frosh rec. need-based self-help aid	45
% UG rec. need-based self-help aid	46
% frosh rec. any financial aid	100
% UG rec. any financial aid	99
% UG borrow to pay for school	80.61
Average cumulative indebtedness	$17,490

HILLSDALE COLLEGE

33 EAST COLLEGE STREET, HILLSDALE, MI 49242 • ADMISSIONS: 517-607-2327 • FAX: 517-607-2223

CAMPUS LIFE

Quality of Life Rating	81
Fire Safety Rating	86
Green Rating	69
Type of school	private
Environment	village

STUDENTS

Total undergrad enrollment	1,326
% male/female	48/52
% from out of state	59
% from public high school	48
% live on campus	86
% in (# of) fraternities	35 (3)
% in (# of) sororities	45 (3)
% international	2
# of countries represented	13

SURVEY SAYS . . .

Large classes
No one cheats
Students are friendly
Students are very religious
Campus feels safe
Students are happy
Very little drug use

ACADEMICS

Academic Rating	92
Calendar	semester
Student/faculty ratio	10:1
Profs interesting rating	98
Profs accessible rating	95
Most common reg class size	fewer than 10 students
Most common lab size	20–29 students

MOST POPULAR MAJORS

education
biology/biological sciences
business administration and management

STUDENTS SAY ". . ."

Academics

"Tiny" Hillsdale College "provides a classic liberal arts education" "grounded in the great traditions of Western Civilization." Students here spend their time "reading dead guys," grappling with "timeless ideas," and "constantly fighting change." A "strong core curriculum" includes the standard liberal arts and sciences requirements as well as mandatory courses on the Constitution, Western civilization, and the Great Books (stuff like *The Odyssey* and Dante's *Inferno*). "Writing skills are heavily addressed" and "academics are very rigorous." There is "no grade inflation" whatsoever, cautions a Spanish major. "Here, the 'C' reigns." While professors "demand a lot," "lectures are engaging" and most students have nothing but praise for the academic experience. The faculty is reportedly full of "profoundly enlightening" "deep thinkers" who are "always available" outside of class. The administration is "well organized" despite "periodic quirks." The single biggest complaint on this campus involves the "awkward" and "archaic" way in which students sign up for classes. "Hillsdale students are begging for an easier and more efficient registration process." Many rules are severe, too. Management has "no qualms about keeping a close eye on the students." Also, you should be aware that "Hillsdale refuses to accept government money." Every scholarship and financial aid dime is privately funded. Don't worry, though. The average aid package is over $12,000.

Life

Hillsdale's "rural" and "boring" location "almost makes it seem like a secret intellectual getaway," but mostly there's a lot to be desired. Consequently, the "beautiful" campus here "is the hub of social life." Residence halls are "spacious" but there are no co-ed dorms and visitation hours are "strict." During the week, students "don't have copious amounts of free time." "Virtually everyone is studying like mad." Nevertheless, students are "involved in many organizations." "The Greek system is strong." Religious groups are "prominent" as well. Varsity athletics "don't get much support" but "intramural sports are always popular." There are "frequent" concerts and recitals. There's "sledding" and "organized snowball fights." "Everyone loves ideas and good debate" and everything from theology and philosophy to sports and popular culture is fair game. "It is not uncommon to walk to the bathroom, only to get sucked into a three-hour debate on the political ramifications of World War II with someone you have barely ever spoken to," swears a sophomore. "We are not one of those evangelical schools that forbids alcohol," declares a junior. "Kegs and drinking games" are occasionally available. Smaller get-togethers "where people have a few drinks" are more common. For road trips, student often head about 70 miles northeast to the "real college town" of Ann Arbor.

Student Body

"Hillsdale prides itself on being one of the first colleges to openly accept anyone irrespective of nation, color, or sex." All the same, the population here is almost entirely composed of "white, upper-middleclass" students. "There certainly isn't a lot of ethnic diversity." There are "leftish students" and plenty of people who don't go to church. "There's a good libertarian crowd," too. However, Christianity and right-wing politics dominate. "The typical student is religious and conservative," relates a sophomore. "That's the nature of the college." Students describe themselves as "ambitious" and "clean cut." They are "very sweet, very friendly, and good people" who "love learning and willingly participate in intellectual discussions." There's a large contingent of "homeschooled" students and there are definitely "Bible-beating people." You'll find the "little Christian ray of sunshine who studies all the time and goes to bed early." "It's not uncommon to see a long-skirted female posse longing for a beau to court them à la chivalry love," observes a senior. Greeks, athletes, and theater people constitute the other main cliques. "Overall, people get along and mesh well" but "there tends to be a large rift between the group of overly conservative students and the group consisting of the partying athletes and fraternity and sorority members."

FINANCIAL AID: 517-437-7341 • E-MAIL: ADMISSIONS@HILLSDALE.EDU/ADMISSIONS • WEBSITE: WWW.HILLSDALE.EDU

THE PRINCETON REVIEW SAYS

Admissions

Very important factors considered include: Academic GPA, rigor of secondary school record, standardized test scores, character/personal qualities, interview. *Important factors considered include:* Class rank, application essay, recommendation(s), extracurricular activities, level of applicant's interest, volunteer work, work experience. *Other factors considered include:* Alumni/ae relation, talent/ability, SAT or ACT required; ACT with Writing component recommended. TOEFL required of all international applicants. High school diploma is required and GED is accepted. *Academic units recommended:* 4 English, 4 mathematics, 3 science, (1 science labs), 2 foreign language, 1 social studies, 2 history.

Financial Aid

Students should submit: institution's own financial aid form, noncustodial PRO-FILE, business/farm supplement. Regular filing deadline is 3/15. The Princeton Review suggests that all financial aid forms be submitted as soon as possible after January 1. *Need-based scholarships/grants offered:* Private scholarships, the school's own gift aid. *Loan aid offered:* College/university loans from institutional funds. Applicants will be notified of awards on a rolling basis beginning 2/15. Institutional employment available. Off-campus job opportunities are good.

Inside Word

Don't be fooled by Hillsdale's high acceptance rate. Only serious, solid candidates bother applying here and the academic profile of incoming freshmen is tremendous. While you don't have to be politically conservative to get in, a passionate and well-reasoned essay defending traditional values or singing the praises of free-market economics certainly can't hurt you.

THE SCHOOL SAYS "..."

From The Admissions Office

"Personal attention is a hallmark at Hillsdale. Small classes are combined with teaching professors who make their students a priority. The academic environment at Hillsdale will actively engage you as a student. Extracurricular activities abound at Hillsdale with the over 50 clubs and organizations that offer excellent leadership opportunities. From athletics and the fine arts, to Greek life and community volunteer programs, you will find it difficult not to be involved in our thriving campus community. In addition, numerous study abroad programs, a conservation research venture in South Africa, a professional sales internship program with national placements and the Washington-Hillsdale Internship Program (WHIP) are just a few of the unique off-campus opportunities available to you at Hillsdale.

"Our strength as a college is found in our mission and in our curriculum. The core curriculum at Hillsdale contains the essence of the classical liberal arts education. Through it you are introduced to the history, the philosophical and theological ideas, the works of literature, and the scientific discoveries that set Western Civilization apart. As explained in our mission statement, 'The college considers itself a trustee of modern man's intellectual and spiritual inheritance from the Judeo-Christian faith and Greco-Roman culture, a heritage finding its clearest expression in the American experiment of self-government under law.'

"We seek students who are ambitious, intellectually curious and who are ready to become leaders worthy of this heritage in their personal as well as professional lives.

"Applicants for Fall of 2008 can meet admissions requirements by submitting the results of one of three tests: the new SAT, the old SAT (taken prior to March 2005), or the ACT (Writing section optional). We will use the student's best composite/combined score in the evaluation process. The SAT Subject Tests in Literature and U.S. History are recommended."

SELECTIVITY

Admissions Rating	91
# of applicants	1,401
% of applicants accepted	64
% of acceptees attending	42
# accepting a place on wait list	35
% admitted from wait list	14
# of early decision applicants	80
% accepted early decision	85

FRESHMAN PROFILE

Range SAT Critical Reading	640–720
Range SAT Math	570–660
Range SAT Writing	610–690
Range ACT Composite	25–30
Minimum paper TOEFL	570
Minimum computer TOEFL	210
Average HS GPA	3.72
% graduated top 10% of class	47
% graduated top 25% of class	75
% graduated top 50% of class	98

DEADLINES

Early decision	
Deadline	11/15
Notification	12/1
Early action	
Deadline	1/1
Notification	1/20
Regular	
Priority	1/1
Deadline	2/15
Nonfall registration?	yes

APPLICANTS ALSO LOOK AT
AND OFTEN PREFER
University of Dallas

FINANCIAL FACTS

Financial Aid Rating	86
Annual tuition	$18,650
Room and board	$7,340
Required fees	$490
Books and supplies	$850
% frosh rec. need-based scholarship or grant aid	47
% UG rec. need-based scholarship or grant aid	41
% frosh rec. non-need-based scholarship or grant aid	32
% UG rec. non-need-based scholarship or grant aid	26
% frosh rec. need-based self-help aid	47
% UG rec. need-based self-help aid	41
% frosh rec. athletic scholarships	17
% UG rec. athletic scholarships	16
% frosh rec. any financial aid	83
% UG rec. any financial aid	86
% UG borrow to pay for school	62
Average cumulative indebtedness	$14,500

HIRAM COLLEGE

PO Box 67, Hiram, OH 44234 • Admissions: 800-362-5280 • Fax: 330-569-5944

CAMPUS LIFE
Quality of Life Rating	72
Fire Safety Rating	60*
Green Rating	60*
Type of school	private
Affiliation	Disciples of Christ
Environment	rural

STUDENTS
Total undergrad enrollment	1,240
% male/female	44/56
% from out of state	16
% from public high school	86
% live on campus	91
% in (# of) fraternities	NR (3)
% in (# of) sororities	NR (3)
% African American	10
% Asian	1
% Caucasian	68
% Hispanic	2
% international	5
# of countries represented	20

SURVEY SAYS . . .
Small classes
Athletic facilities are great
Students are friendly
Low cost of living
Lots of beer drinking

ACADEMICS
Academic Rating	80
Student/faculty ratio	14:1
Profs interesting rating	84
Profs accessible rating	84

MOST POPULAR MAJORS
biology
management
biomedical humanities

STUDENTS SAY ". . ."

Academics
Students at Hiram don't shy away from discussing what most feel to be the best part of the academic experience at their school: the professors. "They genuinely care about their students—I've even had a home-cooked meal at a professor's house," gushes one. According to another, Hiram is a "loving community where students and faculty are encouraged to talk to each other." With a great student/faculty ratio, the average class size is small, which allows professors to "push you to your full potential while guiding you carefully along the way" and "speak to you as equals." Readily available professors "will stop whatever they're doing to help you out" and students find plenty of opportunities to conduct personalized research projects. Most complaints can be traced back to the administration's recent belt-tightening: "Just because we are a small school does not justify the cutting of our tennis and track teams and other programs," asserts a sophomore. A more upbeat undergrad counters that the school "want[s] to have a personal touch with every student, and may sometimes sacrifice other things for that, but it's mostly a good thing." Most students swear that the school as a whole lives by its motto of "intimate learning and global reach," citing strong science programs, a great study-abroad program, and the opportunity to "grow academically inside the classroom and socially outside of it."

Life
Located in small-town Ohio, Hiram strikes more than a few students as being "in the middle of nowhere." Some, however, cite the "quaint" and remote location as a plus, allowing them to make closer friends. Social life at Hiram largely revolves around "improvised activities" and a typical roster of events includes "intramural sports, playing music, intercollegiate sports, hanging out, watching movies, and going to bars." A student-run coffee shop and a swanky new $12.3 million fitness center are also popular on-campus draws. In addition, "Campus groups do a pretty good job of bringing fun things to campus"; student organizations are also big: "You can get involved in as many things as you want, and most people do." Students are "constantly going from one thing to another—this is a Hiram trademark." As far as off-campus life goes, "Having a car gives one a huge advantage, as there are plenty of cities and towns in reasonable driving distance." It also extends one's culinary options beyond on-campus fare.

Student Body
"There is no "typical" Hiram student," says one junior, speaking for most undergraduates. "This is because of the small student body and the many varieties that make [that] body up. Different types of people interact with each other everyday." Nearly all are "outgoing and love to have fun, but able to balance a social life with all of their academic rigors. All students seem to fit in on campus; there is something for everyone here." The "diverse" student body seems to exist in enviable harmony, with "easygoing" and "open-minded" being common descriptors. Of course, "Like on any campus you have those kids who party a lot and do not care about school," but undergrads are quick to point out that many students at Hiram "study all the time." Regardless of what side of the spectrum they fall on, everyone here is friendly: "Our campus is like a little community, everybody knows everybody and they are always willing to help."

FINANCIAL AID: 330-569-5107 • E-MAIL: ADMISSION@HIRAM.EDU • WEBSITE: WWW.ADMISSION.HIRAM.EDU

THE PRINCETON REVIEW SAYS

Admissions

Very important factors considered include: Academic GPA. *Important factors considered include:* Application essay, rigor of secondary school record, standardized test scores, character/personal qualities, extracurricular activities. *Other factors considered include:* Class rank, recommendation(s), alumni/ae relation, first generation, geographical residence, interview, level of applicant's interest, state residency, talent/ability, volunteer work, work experience. SAT or ACT required; TOEFL required of all international applicants. High school diploma is required and GED is accepted. *Academic units required:* 4 English, 3 mathematics, 3 science, (2 science labs), 2 foreign language, 3 social studies,3 social studies/history, 2 academic electives. *Academic units recommended:* 3 foreign language.

Financial Aid

The Princeton Review suggests that all financial aid forms be submitted as soon as possible after January 1.

The Inside Word

Applicants to Hiram can breathe easy. As the high admission rate indicates, students who enroll in a challenging, college-prep curriculum and produce satisfactory grades should not find it too difficult to gain acceptance. Admission is rolling, and students are admitted on a space-available basis. Therefore, it is in each candidate's best interest to apply early.

THE SCHOOL SAYS "..."

From The Admissions Office

"Hiram College offers distinctive programs that set us apart from other small, private liberal arts colleges. About half of Hiram's students study abroad at some point during their four years. In 2007—2008, a group of 17 students led by two faculty members traveled around the world to study climate change, stopping in nine different locations. Common study abroad destinations include France, China, Mexico, Guatemala, Costa Rica, the Galapagos Islands, and several African countries. Because Hiram students receive credits for the courses taught by Hiram faculty on these trips, studying abroad will not impede progress in their majors or delay graduation.

"Another unique aspect of a Hiram education is our academic calendar, known as the Hiram Plan. Our semesters are divided into 12-week and 3-week periods. Students usually enroll in three courses during each 12-week, and one intensive course during the 3-week. Many students spend the 3-week on study abroad trips or taking unusual courses not typically offered during the 12-week. Our small classes encourage interaction between students and their professors. Students can work with professors on original research projects and often participate in musical groups and intramural sports teams alongside faculty members.

"The Hiram College Tuition Guarantee ensures that the annual cost for tuition will not increase between the first year a student is enrolled and the student's senior year.

"Hiram will accept either the new SAT or the old SAT administered without a writing component. The school will also accept the ACT with or without the writing component."

SELECTIVITY

Admissions Rating	76
# of applicants	1,551
% of applicants accepted	77
% of acceptees attending	28

FRESHMAN PROFILE

Range SAT Critical Reading	480–610
Range SAT Math	470–600
Range ACT Composite	20–25
Minimum paper TOEFL	550
Average HS GPA	3.34
% graduated top 10% of class	20
% graduated top 25% of class	48
% graduated top 50% of class	79

DEADLINES

Regular	
Priority	2/15
Deadline	4/15
Notification	rolling
Nonfall registration?	yes

APPLICANTS ALSO LOOK AT

AND OFTEN PREFER
Denison University
Kenyon College

AND SOMETIMES PREFER
The College of Wooster
John Carroll University

AND RARELY PREFER
The University of Akron
Kent State University—Kent Campus

FINANCIAL FACTS

Financial Aid Rating	60*
Annual tuition	$24,940
Room and board	$8,380
Required fees	$670
Books and supplies	$700

HOBART AND WILLIAM SMITH COLLEGES

629 SOUTH MAIN STREET, GENEVA, NY 14456 • ADMISSIONS: 315-781-3472 • FAX: 315-781-3471

CAMPUS LIFE

Quality of Life Rating	70
Fire Safety Rating	60*
Green Rating	60*
Type of school	private
Environment	village

STUDENTS

Total undergrad enrollment	1,855
% male/female	46/54
% from out of state	55
% from public high school	65
% live on campus	90
% in (# of) fraternities	15 (5)
% African American	4
% Asian	2
% Caucasian	88
% Hispanic	4
% international	2
# of countries represented	18

SURVEY SAYS . . .

Large classes
Career services are great
Students are happy
Lots of beer drinking
Hard liquor is popular

ACADEMICS

Academic Rating	87
Calendar	semester
Student/faculty ratio	11:1
Profs interesting rating	87
Profs accessible rating	90
Most common reg class size	10–19 students

MOST POPULAR MAJORS

English language and literature
economics
history

STUDENTS SAY ". . ."

Academics

"Students come before all else" at tiny upstate Hobart and William Smith, a pair of associated single-sex colleges that share a campus, faculty, and administration, yet remain very distinct in their identities, combining to make the academic and social lives of the students as varied and interesting as possible. While "there aren't always tons of options" for classes, "there are lots of interesting choices offered for such a small school," and this "liberal arts education with a flair" places a strong emphasis on study abroad as a part of a student's education. There is quite a bit of money in the student body, so tuition can be a workout for some (there are many grants offered, though), but even the brokest of students is enthralled with the school, from the "beautiful, green campus" offering "a small slice of New England stuck in upstate New York" to the "unrivalled experience."

The "vibrant" professors have "diverse viewpoints," and though "you have to learn to adapt to different teaching styles," they treat students with complete respect, so that "the academic experience is more in the vein of colleagues." Everyone here is happy with their academic experience, and even though there's an occasional dud, "for every professor that seems mediocre, there's two more who are absolute gems of teaching ability." "I have had professors invite me to office hours, send me internship opportunities, discuss my career goals, and even invite me to their house for dinner," says another. As for higher up, the raves are similar; the administration works very hard to accommodate everyone on campus and "is usually successful at it," partly due to the coordinate system, which allows for separate deans for both William Smith and Hobart, granting "more individual attention to the students." They will "get to know you and will stop on the sidewalk and have a chat whenever they see you." However, students do wish the administration was a little less strict in its policies and enforcement.

Life

Life in general is pretty hectic, but students are "very good at balancing school and socializing"; most kids always stay busy with their school work, but "really let loose on the weekends." Bars, frat parties, and campus parties can all occur in the same night, and the school offers "a very positive program" in Safe Rides, which provides late night van rides. Geneva is a beautiful town, but it's no NYC; the cold winter months can be endless, and the rural location means students "make their own fun here," whether through tray sledding, barbequing, or skinny-dipping, and it "kind of works out better." On nice days, the quad acts as a hub of student life, when students "bring horse shoes, Frisbees, footballs, baseballs, and blankets and just spend the day together." There's also skiing, malls and outlets for shopping, and a wildlife refuge not too far away. Without a nearby big urban center, students are "continuously immersed in campus life and happenings," and most are very happy with the offerings from the school and campus groups. Community service is very popular here, as well.

Student Body

"Preppy white person" seems to encapsulate most everyone's perception of the student body, with "Polo, LL Bean, Lily Pulitzer & Lacoste…everywhere." A lot of students come from affluent backgrounds, but in recent years, thanks to scholarships and opportunity programs, there's a significant number of international students and minority students and "they blend in seamlessly." "Rich kids and alternative types melting all together in a pretty good harmony," sums up a student. People "usually get along with each other regardless of being typical or not," partially due to the rampant involvement in student organizations and groups. With fewer than two thousand people in the student body, there's not much mystery left after a couple of years, when "you can walk to class and recognize at 90% of the people you see," but the general pervading friendliness of the school as a whole means that "there is a happy niche here for everyone."

FINANCIAL AID: 315-781-3315 • E-MAIL: ADMISSIONS@HWS.EDU • WEBSITE: WWW.HWS.EDU

THE PRINCETON REVIEW SAYS

Admissions

Very important factors considered include: Rigor of secondary school record. *Important factors considered include:* Class rank, application essay, academic GPA, recommendation(s), standardized test scores, character/personal qualities, extracurricular activities, volunteer work, work experience. *Other factors considered include:* Alumni/ae relation, first generation, geographical residence, interview, level of applicant's interest, racial/ethnic status, talent/ability, SAT or ACT required; ACT with Writing component required. TOEFL required of all international applicants. High school diploma is required and GED is accepted. *Academic units required:* 4 English, 3 mathematics, 3 science, (2 science labs), 2 foreign language, 2 social studies, 2 history, 2 academic electives. *Academic units recommended:* 3 foreign language, 3 social studies, 4 academic electives.

Financial Aid

Students should submit: FAFSA, CSS/Financial Aid PROFILE, state aid form, noncustodial PROFILE, parent's and student's tax return. Regular filing deadline is 2/1. The Princeton Review suggests that all financial aid forms be submitted as soon as possible after January 1. *Need-based scholarships/grants offered:* Federal Pell, SEOG, state scholarships/grants, private scholarships, the school's own gift aid. *Loan aid offered:* FFEL Subsidized Stafford, FFEL Unsubsidized Stafford, FFEL PLUS, Federal Perkins Applicants will be notified of awards on or about 4/1. Federal Work-Study Program available. Institutional employment available. Off-campus job opportunities are good.

The Inside Word

Applicants to the academic side of Seneca Lake's scenic shore should know that HSW likes to see a student who embraces a challenge. They recommend that hopefuls prepare themselves for a rigorous college curriculum by taking at least two years of a foreign language and a couple of AP courses for good measure. Some good news for people who don't like tests: HSW doesn't require standardized test scores.

THE SCHOOL SAYS ". . ."

From The Admissions Office

"Hobart and William Smith Colleges seek students with a sense of adventure and a commitment to the life of the mind. Inside the classroom, students find the academic climate to be rigorous, with a faculty that is deeply involved in teaching and working with them. Outside, they discover a supportive community that helps to cultivate a balance and hopes to foster an integration among academics, extracurricular activities, and social life. Hobart and William Smith, as coordinate colleges, have an awareness of gender differences and equality and are committed to respect and a celebration of diversity.

"Freshman applicants for Fall 2008 class are required to take either the ACT (old or new, with or without the optional Writing portion) or either version of the SAT. Their highest composite score will be used in admissions decisions. Students are encouraged to submit results of any SAT Subject Test they have taken."

SELECTIVITY

Admissions Rating	88
# of applicants	3,410
% of applicants accepted	65
% of acceptees attending	25
# accepting a place on wait list	194
% admitted from wait list	16

FRESHMAN PROFILE

Range SAT Critical Reading	530–640
Range SAT Math	540–630
Range ACT Composite	24–27
Minimum paper TOEFL	550
Minimum computer TOEFL	220
Average HS GPA	3.22
% graduated top 10% of class	33
% graduated top 25% of class	67
% graduated top 50% of class	95

DEADLINES

Early decision	
Deadline	11/15
Notification	12/15
Regular	
Deadline	2/1
Notification	4/1
Nonfall registration?	no

APPLICANTS ALSO LOOK AT

AND OFTEN PREFER
Connecticut College
Colgate University
Trinity College (CT)

AND SOMETIMES PREFER
Dickinson College
Gettysburg College
Kenyon College

AND RARELY PREFER
Ithaca College
University of Vermont

FINANCIAL FACTS

Financial Aid Rating	91
Annual tuition	$31,850
Room and board	$8,386
Required fees	$887
Books and supplies	$850
% frosh rec. need-based scholarship or grant aid	58
% UG rec. need-based scholarship or grant aid	60
% frosh rec. non-need-based scholarship or grant aid	10
% UG rec. non-need-based scholarship or grant aid	7
% frosh rec. need-based self-help aid	48
% UG rec. need-based self-help aid	53
% frosh rec. any financial aid	74
% UG rec. any financial aid	64
% UG borrow to pay for school	65
Average cumulative indebtedness	$21,545

HOFSTRA UNIVERSITY

ADMISSIONS CENTER, BERNON HALL, HEMPSTEAD, NY 11549 • ADMISSIONS: 516-463-6700 • FAX: 516-463-5100

CAMPUS LIFE
Quality of Life Rating	**62**
Fire Safety Rating	**92**
Green Rating	**83**
Type of school	private
Environment	city

STUDENTS
Total undergrad enrollment	8,298
% male/female	47/53
% from out of state	50
% live on campus	80
% in (# of) fraternities	9 (19)
% in (# of) sororities	9 (15)
% African American	9
% Asian	5
% Caucasian	62
% Hispanic	8
% Native American	1
% international	1
# of countries represented	67

SURVEY SAYS . . .
Large classes
Great computer facilities
Great library
Lots of beer drinking
Hard liquor is popular
(Almost) everyone smokes

ACADEMICS
Academic Rating	**77**
Calendar	4/1/4
Student/faculty ratio	14:1
Profs interesting rating	72
Profs accessible rating	69

MOST POPULAR MAJORS
psychology
accounting
marketing/marketing management

STUDENTS SAY " . . . "

Academics

To experience "Long Island in a nutshell," consider Hofstra University, a school that "is dedicated to preparing its students for successful careers." Nearly one-third of the student body are business majors; Hofstra's "great finance program" benefits from "the number-one college Financial Trading Room in the country," while the marketing program supports the Hofstra American Marketing Cub, "which won 'Business Club of the Year.'" Hofstra is also "a great place for accounting majors." Students tell us that the Communications Department is "amazing," with "a state-of-the art radio station" that "offers a large variety of ways to get involved, whether it's having a show or being behind the scenes." It also plays "a large variety of music," from "rap to rock to Irish." Hofstra's education program is also highly regarded, boasting "one of the best music education programs in the country." In all areas, students laud "real-world experience on real-world equipment" and great opportunities for internships. In fact, "There are more internships available than there are people, so we are always informed of new opportunities in our majors as they emerge. Our location [relative] to the city presents many summer and winter internships in Manhattan, especially for communications and business majors." Hofstra is a big university, meaning students can't wait for someone to tell them what to do; one student writes, "If you want to get something done, you definitely can't wait for it to happen. You have to put yourself out there and meet with teachers and join clubs."

Life

Those who live on or near campus tell us that "there is plenty to do here, but you have to have a car to really do it, [because] walking in the area isn't that safe." There are a "ton of malls, movie theaters, and restaurants right around campus." Hofstra "is known as a bar school," and students have many venues to choose from in Hempstead and "cute little surrounding towns" like Mineola and Garden City. On campus, "Interest in [intercollegiate] athletics has grown dramatically"; even so, "Many students don't advantage of the free or discounted activities offered at the campus." But enthusiasts say this just forces students "to be more creative" when it comes to finding fun. "With Manhattan only 45 minutes away via the Long Island Railroad," lots of "people also go into New York City for fun, whether it is to shop, see shows, or go to nightclubs." Hofstra makes it easy for students to take regular trips into the city, offering a "free bus from campus that takes students to the train station."

Student Body

Long Island is a pretty diverse place, and Hofstra University reflects that diversity reasonably well. One student writes, "My first roommate was a White Orthodox Jew, very serious about school; my second set of roommates were White Greek and Italian Christians, loud partiers who played beer pong every night," and "my third roommate is White, Catholic, and gay," and "is the nicest person I know." Undergrads tell us that "there are two types of students at Hofstra University: The kind that work hard, study and succeed, and the other kind who carelessly roll into class 25 minutes late (if they even go at all) with their Chanel sunglasses and Ugg boots, talking on their cell phones to their friends about their fabulous night out." The latter group is sometimes referred to derisively as "the Long Island kids," and some students describe them as "materialistic" and "apathetic" about school. While there might be lot of "stereotypical Long Island kids" on campus, the school also has "a large minority population," and "It's not hard to find someone here who is interested in the same things you are." Over 50% of the class entering in fall 2007 were from out of state.

HOFSTRA UNIVERSITY

FINANCIAL AID: 516-463-6680 • E-MAIL: ADMITME@HOFSTRA.EDU • WEBSITE: WWW.HOFSTRA.EDU

THE PRINCETON REVIEW SAYS

Admissions

Very important factors considered include: Rigor of secondary school record, Class rank, Academic GPA, Standardized test scores, Application Essay, Recommendation(s) *Important factors considered include:* Interview, Extracurricular activities, Talent/ability, Character/personal qualities. *Other factors considered include:* Alumni/ae relation, Geographical residence, Racial/ethnic status, Volunteer work, Work experience, Level of applicant's interest.

Financial Aid

The Princeton Review suggests that all financial aid forms be submitted as soon as possible after January 1. Federal Work-Study Program available. Institutional employment available. Off-campus job opportunities are excellent.

The Inside Word

This is not your father's Hofstra; the school reports that admission requirements have grown tougher over the years. Average GPAs and standardized test scores of admitted students have gone up, and this has been accompanied by a rise in rejection rates among applicants. Expect an especially thorough review if you indicate communications as your intended field of study.

THE SCHOOL SAYS "..."

From The Admissions Office

"Hofstra is a university on the rise. When you step onto campus you feel the energy and sense the momentum of a university building a national reputation as a center for academic excellence.

"At Hofstra, you'll find an outstanding faculty dedicated to teaching, and small classes, averaging just 22 students. Outside the classroom, you'll find a multitude of study abroad options, a vibrant extracurricular life, and amazing internship opportunities and cultural experiences in nearby New York City.

"The Hofstra campus—so beautiful it is recognized as an arboretum—features new and cutting-edge teaching facilities. At Hofstra, you will share your classrooms and residence halls with students from nearly every U.S. state and 65 countries.

"Hofstra also offers new and unique educational opportunities: During the fall 2008 semester students can participate in Educate '08, a series of programs and events leading up to the third and final presidential debate, which will be held at Hofstra in October 15, 2008. His Holiness the 14th Dalai Lama, the inaugural winner of the Hofstra University's Guru Nanak Interfaith Prize, is expected to visit campus in 2009. In addition, the university plans to establish the nation's newest medical school in partnership with the North Shore-LIJ Health System, subject to preliminary accreditation, and hopes to admit the first medical school class in 2011.

"Students applying for admission may submit either SAT or ACT scores, and an essay is required. The admission team at Hofstra realizes that each applicant is unique and gives each one individual attention."

SELECTIVITY

Admissions Rating	85
# of applicants	18,471
% of applicants accepted	54
% of acceptees attending	17

FRESHMAN PROFILE

Range SAT Critical Reading	540–630
Range SAT Math	550–630
Range ACT Composite	23–26
Average HS GPA	3.4
% graduated top 10% of class	26
% graduated top 25% of class	56
% graduated top 50% of class	85

DEADLINES

Nonfall registration?	Yes

APPLICANTS ALSO LOOK AT
AND OFTEN PREFER

Fordham University, New York University, Syracuse University

AND SOMETIMES PREFER

Northeastern University, Penn State—University Park, Quinnipiac University, State University of New York—Stony Brook

APPLICANTS ALSO LOOK AT AND RARELY PREFER

Albany State University, St. John's University

FINANCIAL FACTS

Financial Aid Rating	65
Annual tuition	$25,700
Room and board	$10,300
Required fees	$1,030
Books and supplies	$1,000
% frosh rec. need-based scholarship or grant aid	53
% UG rec. need-based scholarship or grant aid	49
% frosh rec. non-need-based scholarship or grant aid	6
% UG rec. non-need-based scholarship or grant aid	4
% frosh rec. need-based self-help aid	51
% UG rec. need-based self-help aid	49
% frosh rec. athletic scholarships	1
% UG rec. athletic scholarships	1
% frosh rec. any financial aid	90
% UG rec. any financial aid	84
% UG borrow to pay for school	57

HOLLINS UNIVERSITY

PO Box 9707, Roanoke, VA 24020-1707 • Admissions: 540-362-6401 • Fax: 540-362-6218

CAMPUS LIFE

Quality of Life Rating	**79**
Fire Safety Rating	**71**
Green Rating	**78**
Type of school	private
Environment	city

STUDENTS

Total undergrad enrollment	781
% male/female	/100
% from out of state	48
% from public high school	77
% live on campus	80
% African American	8
% Asian	2
% Caucasian	80
% Hispanic	3
% Native American	1
% international	2
# of countries represented	15

SURVEY SAYS . . .

Small classes
No one cheats
Great library
Frats and sororities are unpopular
or nonexistent

ACADEMICS

Academic Rating	**86**
Calendar	4/1/4
Student/faculty ratio	10:1
Profs interesting rating	93
Profs accessible rating	93
Most common reg class size	10–19 students
Most common lab size	fewer than 10 students

MOST POPULAR MAJORS

English language and literature
psychology

STUDENTS SAY ". . ."

Academics

It's all about educating the next generation of women leaders at Hollins University, a women's liberal arts university in Virginia that seeks to provide its students with an "open-minded, highly educational, and nurturing experience." Hollins students are seeking to be "empowered," and the small class sizes and open-discussion format of many lectures makes the classrooms "an overall better environment" for this growth.

Student here speak fondly of the many Hollins traditions (such as Viking Day and Ring Night) that help them "establish strong bonds," while at the same time expressing satisfaction with the administration's work "towards progressively updating traditions on campus that have been here since the school was established" (described by one junior as "breaking free of their finishing school roots"). The administration gets somewhat poor reviews (especially the bursar's and financial aid offices), though a few students mention both a "lack of effort to see things from a student point of view" and a lack of respect for the well-regarded SGA. Professors here are lauded all around as being "dedicated to women's single-sex education," and willing to "go out of their way to help students as long as the student makes the proper effort," and are often willing to wave intro level courses to let students into upperlevel classes if they are qualified. "When I went abroad I had professors who kept in touch with me on a weekly basis to check up on how I was doing," says a senior. The liberal arts philosophy of the university gives students a wide base of courses to choose from, and "classes are very much geared towards preparing you for graduate school." "Hollins will never give you responsibility and let you flounder with it," says one student, and "there is a huge support system for graduates."

Life

These busy girls are usually wrapped up in one organization or another, either attending an event, or leading one. Students sometimes complain about the lack of guys around, but "in the classroom, that is what we prefer," and there are always weekend visits to other nearby colleges (VA Tech, the all-male Hampden-Sydney) and universities to solve that problem. There is "always something going on on-campus, whether it's live music or a theater department production," and horseback riding is a very popular pastime at Hollins. Apartment parties do occur on weekends, especially in the arts dorm, but students make sure to "get our stuff done, especially when it's crunch time." Roanoke itself is a small suburban town that "offers a ton of cute, indie things to do like a co-op for shopping, antiques galore within a 20 mile radius, and lots of good home-cooked food restaurants," which offers a good alternative to the school's "terrible" food. Students are, for the most part, required to live on campus, which makes it so "you have to create your own fun," through which "you cannot help but meet new people and make close connections."

Student Body

Well, "woman" is a good start, but beyond that, it's a pretty diverse group. You have your "Pearl Girls" and your "tree-hugging hippies" and everyone in between, and no one seems to encounter any problems with being or interacting with whatever passes for atypical here. "It isn't necessary to fit into only one group, though groups can get kind of cliquey after awhile," says a sophomore. Perhaps it's due to their "similar goals," but this motivated bunch (most are "involved in at least one organization") is "politically-minded," "conscientious, excepting of others and the environment" (activism is "booming on campus") and "all interact fairly seamlessly."

FINANCIAL AID: 540-362-6332 • E-MAIL: HUADM@HOLLINS.EDU • WEBSITE: WWW.HOLLINS.EDU

THE PRINCETON REVIEW SAYS

Admissions

Very important factors considered include: Academic GPA, standardized test scores, level of applicant's interest. *Important factors considered include:* Application essay, recommendation(s), talent/ability. *Other factors considered include:* Class rank, rigor of secondary school record, alumni/ae relation, character/personal qualities, extracurricular activities, first generation, interview, racial/ethnic status, volunteer work, work experience. SAT or ACT required; TOEFL required of all international applicants. High school diploma is required and GED is accepted. *Academic units required:* 4 English, 3 mathematics, 3 science, 3 foreign language, 3 social studies.

Financial Aid

Students should submit: FAFSA, state aid form. The Princeton Review suggests that all financial aid forms be submitted as soon as possible after January 1. *Need-based scholarships/grants offered:* Federal Pell, SEOG, state scholarships/grants, private scholarships, the school's own gift aid. *Loan aid offered:* Direct Subsidized Stafford, Direct Unsubsidized Stafford, Direct PLUS, Federal Perkins, college/university loans from institutional funds, PLATO, CitiAssist, SallieMae, Nelnet, Campus Door. Applicants will be notified of awards on a rolling basis beginning 3/1. Federal Work-Study Program available. Institutional employment available. Off-campus job opportunities are good.

The Inside Word

Only candidates who overtly display their lack of compatibility with the Hollins milieu are likely to encounter difficulty in gaining admission. A high level of self-selection and its weak-but-improving freshman profile allow most candidates to relax.

THE SCHOOL SAYS "..."

From The Admissions Office

"Hollins University's slogan, 'Women who are going places start at Hollins,' endures because it captures what this independent liberal arts institution means to its students. Hollins has been a motivating force for women to go places creatively, intellectually, and geographically since it was founded over 160 years ago. As Hollins graduate and Pulitzer Prize–winner Annie Dillard said, Hollins is a place 'where friendships thrive, minds catch fire, careers begin, and hearts open to a world of possibility.' "

"Hollins offers majors in 29 fields. While perhaps best known for its creative writing discipline, the university features strong programs in the visual and performing arts (especially dance) and the social and physical sciences. Hollins also has an innovative general education program called Education Through Skills and Perspectives (ESP). In ESP, students acquire knowledge across the curriculum. One of the most sought-after programs at Hollins is the Batten Leadership Institute, a comprehensive curricular program designed to maximize each student's leadership style and potential and teach her skills she will use both now and in the future. It is the only program of its kind in the nation.

"Hollins was among the first colleges in the nation to offer an international study abroad program. Today, almost half of Hollins' students—many times the national average—study abroad. Internship opportunities are another of Hollins' distinctions. Thanks to an active, dedicated network of alumnae and friends of the university, more than 80 percent of Hollins students put their education to work with a diverse group of organizations.

"Hollins' slogan underscores the most important question each student is asked from the moment she arrives until the day she leaves, and it is asked by her professors, her peers, and especially by herself: 'Where do you want to go?'"

SELECTIVITY

Admissions Rating	83
# of applicants	651
% of applicants accepted	84
% of acceptees attending	35
# accepting a place on wait list	12
% admitted from wait list	50
# of early decision applicants	38
% accepted early decision	76

FRESHMAN PROFILE

Range SAT Critical Reading	500–670
Range SAT Math	470–600
Range SAT Writing	490–620
Range ACT Composite	21–28
Minimum paper TOEFL	550
Minimum computer TOEFL	213
Average HS GPA	3.5
% graduated top 10% of class	28
% graduated top 25% of class	56
% graduated top 50% of class	86

DEADLINES

Early decision	
Deadline	12/1
Notification	12/15
Regular	
Priority	2/1
Notification	rolling
Nonfall registration?	yes

FINANCIAL FACTS

Financial Aid Rating	77
Annual tuition	$25,110
Room and board	$9,140
Required fees	$535
Books and supplies	$1,000
% frosh rec. need-based scholarship or grant aid	67
% UG rec. need-based scholarship or grant aid	80
% frosh rec. non-need-based scholarship or grant aid	33
% UG rec. non-need-based scholarship or grant aid	34
% frosh rec. need-based self-help aid	55
% UG rec. need-based self-help aid	63
% frosh rec. any financial aid	97
% UG rec. any financial aid	93
% UG borrow to pay for school	85
Average cumulative indebtedness	$15,227

HOWARD UNIVERSITY

2400 SIXTH STREET NORTHWEST, WASHINGTON, DC 20059 • ADMISSIONS: 202-806-2700 • FAX: 202-806-4462

CAMPUS LIFE
Quality of Life Rating	**65**
Fire Safety Rating	**97**
Green Rating	**60***
Type of school	private
Environment	metropolis

STUDENTS
Total undergrad enrollment	6,963
% male/female	33/67
% from out of state	77
% from public high school	80
% live on campus	55
% in (# of) fraternities	2 (10)
% in (# of) sororities	1 (8)
% African American	67
% Asian	1
% international	5
# of countries represented	86

SURVEY SAYS . . .
Small classes
Students are happy
Frats and sororities dominate social scene
Musical organizations are popular
Student publications are popular
Student government is popular

ACADEMICS
Academic Rating	**80**
Calendar	semester
Student/faculty ratio	8:1
Profs interesting rating	65
Profs accessible rating	63
Most common reg class size	fewer than 10 students
Most common lab size	10–19 students

MOST POPULAR MAJORS
biology/biological sciences

STUDENTS SAY "..."

Academics

Howard University, which students proclaim "the Mecca of black education," parlays a storied history and an excellent location (ideal for students seeking internships and post-graduation job placements) to "prepare students for the future through academic integrity and social enterprise." Recruiters flock to the Howard campus, in part because "academically, Howard is very strong," in part because "the university has connections all over the country and Howard does a great job of bringing those connections to campus," and in part because of the perception that "organizations are forced to come here to employ their minority quotas." Undergrads here report that "The academic experience largely depends on what you major in. If you're going for African-American studies, business or dentistry you'll get what you've paid for." The presence of a College of Medicine (and its affiliated hospital) bolsters offerings in life sciences and premedical studies as well. Other disciplines can present "a challenging and somewhat unfulfilling college experience," students warn. They also caution that "facilities are outdated and need a major technological and physical update" and that "The administration needs some work. There are great, qualified people in places of high authority. However, the people that you have to go through to get to the people who actually care are usually horrible. They never move with a sense of urgency. If it's not their problem, its not a problem, and they usually talk to you like you are 12."

Life

"We always, always, always have something going on" on the "very active" Howard campus. There are "hundreds of organizations that tailor to any needs you can think of," and students are "very active politically and socially, so there are rallies and there are parties. Each and every extreme is met with its opposite here." There's "always somewhere to go" on campus, "whether it be the Punchout Cafe to hang with your friends, Power Hall to relax, study and work with your friends, to 'the yard' to chill and people watch, [or] to the gym to work out…. If you are isolated on Howard's campus it is because you choose to be." The world awaiting off campus is even more active; as one student explains, "There is so much to do in the Washington, DC area that there is rarely any room for boredom. Georgetown, Chinatown, and Pentagon City are just a few of the places that students go." Adams Morgan is another popular destination. No need to bring a car here; "Everything we would want to go to is Metro accessible so there's no problem moving about DC as if we've lived here our whole lives." Fun is typically confined to weekends, as "Many of us work very hard during the week. Sunday through Thursday, we stay on campus and focus on getting school-work done and attending any organizational meetings/events."

Student Body

The typical Howard student "is African American with a deep desire toward success." Undergrads are "extremely serious about their career goals and their academic achievement" and "very involved in political activism, campus organizations, and community." They also tend to be "very fashion-conscious and dwell a lot on others perceptions of us, although many of us profess to be strong individuals." Although nearly all black, the student population "is extremely diverse. I sit in classes with people from Spain, England, Trinidad and Tobago, South Africa, Nigeria, Alaska, etc." Students "come from all walks of life. You can find people with different religious beliefs, ethnic origins, and sexual preferences. There are students with interests in every field imaginable. Howard represents the black world."

FINANCIAL AID: 202-806-2800 • E-MAIL: ADMISSION@HOWARD.EDU • WEBSITE: WWW.HOWARD.EDU

THE PRINCETON REVIEW SAYS

Admissions

Very important factors considered include: Class rank, rigor of secondary school record, standardized test scores. *Important factors considered include:* Recommendation(s), character/personal qualities. *Other factors considered include:* Application essay, alumni/ae relation, extracurricular activities, talent/ability, volunteer work, work experience. SAT or ACT required; ACT with Writing component required. TOEFL required of all international applicants. High school diploma is required and GED is accepted. *Academic units required:* 4 English, 2 mathematics, 2 science, 2 foreign language, 2 social studies, 2 history. *Academic units recommended:* 4 English, 3 mathematics, 4 science, (2 science labs), 2 foreign language, 2 social studies, 2 history, 4 any other academic courses counted toward graduation.

Financial Aid

Students should submit: FAFSA. Regular filing deadline is 8/15. The Princeton Review suggests that all financial aid forms be submitted as soon as possible after January 1. *Need-based scholarships/grants offered:* Federal Pell, SEOG, state scholarships/grants, private scholarships, the school's own gift aid, Federal Nursing Scholarships. *Loan aid offered:* Direct Subsidized Stafford, Direct Unsubsidized Stafford, Direct PLUS, Federal Perkins, Federal Nursing Applicants will be notified of awards on a rolling basis beginning 4/1. Federal Work-Study Program available. Institutional employment available. Off-campus job opportunities are excellent.

The Inside Word

A large applicant pool and solid yield of acceptees who enroll is a combination that adds up to selectivity at Howard. The school is willing to give applicants a pass on standardized test scores if their high school records indicate seriousness about, and the ability to handle, advanced study.

THE SCHOOL SAYS "..."

From The Admissions Office

"Since its founding, Howard has stood among the few institutions of higher learning where African Americans and other minorities have participated freely in a truly comprehensive university experience. Thus, Howard has assumed a special responsibility to prepare its students to exercise leadership wherever their interest and commitments take them. Howard has issued approximately 99,318 degrees, diplomas, and certificates to men and women in the professions, the arts and sciences, and the humanities. The university has produced and continues to produce a high percentage of the nation's African American professionals in the fields of medicine, dentistry, pharmacy, engineering, nursing, architecture, religion, law, music, social work, education, and business. There are more than 8,906 students from across the nation and approximately 85 countries and territories attending the university. Their varied customs, cultures, ideas, and interests contribute to Howard's international character and vitality. More than 1,598 faculty members represent the largest concentration of African American scholars in any single institution of higher education.

"Beginning with the entering class of Fall 2008 all applicants who have never been to college will be required to submit scores from either the new SAT or the ACT (with the Writing component)."

SELECTIVITY

Admissions Rating	87
# of applicants	7,603
% of applicants accepted	54
% of acceptees attending	36

FRESHMAN PROFILE

Range SAT Critical Reading	460–660
Range SAT Math	440–650
Range SAT Writing	410–650
Range ACT Composite	20–28
Minimum paper TOEFL	550
Minimum computer TOEFL	213
Average HS GPA	3.2
% graduated top 10% of class	23
% graduated top 25% of class	49
% graduated top 50% of class	82

DEADLINES

Early decision	
Deadline	11/1
Notification	12/24
Early action	
Deadline	11/1
Notification	12/24
Regular	
Priority	11/1
Deadline	2/15
Nonfall registration?	yes

APPLICANTS ALSO LOOK AT

AND OFTEN PREFER
Spelman College
Morehouse College
Hampton University

AND SOMETIMES PREFER
The George Washington University

FINANCIAL FACTS

Financial Aid Rating	67
Annual tuition	$13,215
Room and board	$6,976
Required fees	$805
Books and supplies	$1,300
% frosh rec. need-based scholarship or grant aid	35
% UG rec. need-based scholarship or grant aid	35
% frosh rec. non-need-based scholarship or grant aid	63
% UG rec. non-need-based scholarship or grant aid	63
% frosh rec. need-based self-help aid	18
% UG rec. need-based self-help aid	25
% frosh rec. athletic scholarships	40
% UG rec. athletic scholarships	33
% frosh rec. any financial aid	96
% UG rec. any financial aid	96
% UG borrow to pay for school	80
Average cumulative indebtedness	$16,473

ILLINOIS INSTITUTE OF TECHNOLOGY

10 WEST THIRTY-THIRD STREET, CHICAGO, IL 60616 • ADMISSIONS: 312-567-3025 • FAX: 312-567-6939

CAMPUS LIFE
Quality of Life Rating	65
Fire Safety Rating	72
Green Rating	82
Type of school	private
Environment	metropolis

STUDENTS
Total undergrad enrollment	2,479
% male/female	74/26
% from out of state	34
% from public high school	85
% live on campus	53
% in (# of) fraternities	13 (7)
% in (# of) sororities	15 (3)
% African American	4
% Asian	14
% Caucasian	50
% Hispanic	7
% international	16
# of countries represented	106

SURVEY SAYS . . .
Large classes
Great computer facilities
Diverse student types on campus
Students love Chicago, IL
Great off-campus food
Very little drug use

ACADEMICS
Academic Rating	77
Calendar	semester
Student/faculty ratio	8:1
Profs interesting rating	61
Profs accessible rating	61
Most common reg class size	10–19 students
Most common lab size	20–29 students

MOST POPULAR MAJORS
architecture (barch, ba/bs, march, ma/ms, phd)
electrical, electronics and communications engineering

STUDENTS SAY ". . ."

Academics

Illinois Institute of Technology "is all about the demanding work and promised payoffs" students report, warning that "the IIT experience is focused on the career afterwards. There is very little pizzazz about the atmosphere (it was designed by Mies van der Rohe, after all) and virtually no social life, unless you can relate to all of the other geeks who either stare at their computers in their rooms or just sit and chat about academics." Not that you'd have time for much of a social life here anyway, since "Classes are difficult and lots of studying is required. If you got straight A's in high school, expect to work hard to get B's and C's." The various Engineering Departments are, of course, a major strength here; civil engineering "is definitely one of the best departments in the school," while the biomedical, electrical, and mechanical engineering programs also earn students' accolades, with "an emphasis on practicality" across the board. The computer science program "is run like a well-oiled machine." IIT is also renowned for its architecture program, which students tell us is "incredible, and quite influential on the Chicago scene." Students in all disciplines benefit from "a small-school environment" that promotes "personal attention" and allows the professors to "get to know you." "For instance, I can walk into my department chair office or my professor's office whenever and they know me personally." Professors "are really accommodating" and explain the material to you "when you have a problem," although whether you'll understand them is another question entirely. "Professors in certain classes may barely speak English, or may be awesome teachers, it varies greatly,"—and sometimes, they're both.

Life

In the past, IIT has earned a reputation for having a dreary extracurricular life; the situation has improved somewhat, as "The school has put forth a great effort and a vast amount of money to create a school-sponsored program every single weekend. This practice started last year, and the school has kept up with it. Whether it's a movie night, a dance, or a comedy act we have at least one thing every weekend, [and] this has improved IIT." Of course, some students "would rather sit in their room and play computer games than socialize" in their free time, but at least the options are expanding, and more students are taking advantage of them. IIT's frat scene "offers numerous chances for social activities from sports to parties and community service," we're told; for many, joining "makes life a lot more enjoyable." Others leave campus whenever they can spare the time away; IIT is only "five miles south of downtown Chicago," a city that "provides a good playground" with "a lot of things to do." For good cheap eats, "Chinatown is just one stop down" on the El.

Student Body

IIT has "plenty of typical math and science students," meaning "many nerds" and more than a few "students who like their computers more than seems humanly possible and whose only human contact occurs when they make a weekly trip to the cafeteria or their biweekly trip to the shower." There are also "many atypical students, enough so that they can form or join a club or group that fits their own personality," and their numbers appear to be growing as a result of "significant outreach by students groups and more social incoming classes." The international population is substantial, with many students from "India, China, and Korea." While "Not everyone talks to each other," "When they do talk, they learn a lot about [each] other's culture." Undergrads tend to be stressed out, "the kind of people who feel guilty when they have no work to do for a day." A lopsided male/female ratio means there are "barely any women on campus."

FINANCIAL AID: 312-567-7219 • E-MAIL: ADMISSION@IIT.EDU • WEBSITE: WWW.IIT.EDU

THE PRINCETON REVIEW SAYS

Admissions

Very important factors considered include: Academic GPA, rigor of secondary school record. *Important factors considered include:* Class rank, application essay, recommendation(s), standardized test scores. *Other factors considered include:* Alumni/ae relation, character/personal qualities, extracurricular activities, first generation, interview, talent/ability, volunteer work, work experience. TOEFL required of all international applicants. High school diploma is required and GED is accepted. *Academic units required:* 4 English, 4 mathematics, 3 science, (2 science labs), 2 social studies, 2 history. *Academic units recommended:* 4 English, 4 mathematics, 3 science, (2 science labs), 2 foreign language, 2 social studies, 2 history, 1 visual/performing arts, 1 computer science.

Financial Aid

Students should submit: FAFSA. The Princeton Review suggests that all financial aid forms be submitted as soon as possible after January 1. *Need-based scholarships/grants offered:* Federal Pell, SEOG, state scholarships/grants, private scholarships, the school's own gift aid. *Loan aid offered:* FFEL Subsidized Stafford, FFEL Unsubsidized Stafford, FFEL PLUS, Federal Perkins, college/university loans from institutional funds. Applicants will be notified of awards on a rolling basis beginning 3/1. Federal Work-Study Program available. Institutional employment available. Off-campus job opportunities are good.

The Inside Word

Students at IIT say it's "easy to get in, tough to get out," but the term "easy" is relative in this case; easy in comparison to MIT or CalTech, perhaps, but not in comparison to the vast majority of undergraduate institutions. IIT's high acceptance rate is deceptive; few bother to apply here unless they suspect they can handle the demanding curriculum, meaning only the extremely bright and/or extremely ambitious actually do.

THE SCHOOL SAYS " . . ."

From The Admissions Office

"IIT is committed to providing students with the highest-caliber education through dedicated teachers, small class sizes, and undergraduate research opportunities. Classes are taught by senior faculty—not teaching assistants—who bring firsthand research experience into daily class discussion. The university's diverse student population mirrors the global work environment faced by all graduates. IIT promotes a unique interdisciplinary approach to learning. Students experience team-based, creative problem solving through two required Interprofessional Projects (IPROs). Our entrepreneurship program challenges students to develop start-up technology companies. The Leadership Academy teaches leadership skills that advance students in their personal and professional development. IIT's location in one of the nation's great cities affords many opportunities for internships and employment. The new, visually enticing McCormick Tribune Campus Center and ultra-modern State Street Village residence halls provide exciting living and campus opportunities that are sure to create a positive student experience for years to come.

"Students applying for admission into the Fall 2008 entering class are required to submit an SAT or ACT score (old and new test versions accepted). We will use the student's best scores from either test. Subject tests are accepted, but not required."

SELECTIVITY

Admissions Rating	92
# of applicants	4,410
% of applicants accepted	56
% of acceptees attending	21

FRESHMAN PROFILE

Range SAT Critical Reading	543–670
Range SAT Math	620–710
Range SAT Writing	530–640
Range ACT Composite	25–30
Minimum paper TOEFL	550
Minimum computer TOEFL	213
Minimum web-based TOEFL	80
Average HS GPA	3.77
% graduated top 10% of class	43
% graduated top 25% of class	72
% graduated top 50% of class	96

DEADLINES

Regular	
Priority	12/1
Notification	rolling
Nonfall registration?	yes

APPLICANTS ALSO LOOK AT
AND OFTEN PREFER
Washington University in St. Louis
University of Michigan—Ann Arbor
Case Western Reserve University

AND SOMETIMES PREFER
Marquette University
Milwaukee School of Engineering
Iowa State University

AND RARELY PREFER
Purdue University—West Lafayette
University of Minnesota—Twin Cities
Rose-Hulman Institute of Technology

FINANCIAL FACTS

Financial Aid Rating	78
Annual tuition	$24,962
Room and board	$8,618
Required fees	$784
% frosh rec. need-based scholarship or grant aid	70
% UG rec. need-based scholarship or grant aid	60
% frosh rec. non-need-based scholarship or grant aid	17
% UG rec. non-need-based scholarship or grant aid	8
% frosh rec. need-based self-help aid	45
% UG rec. need-based self-help aid	47
% frosh rec. athletic scholarships	3
% UG rec. athletic scholarships	4
% frosh rec. any financial aid	100
% UG rec. any financial aid	99.11
% UG borrow to pay for school	61
Average cumulative indebtedness	$21,326

ILLINOIS WESLEYAN UNIVERSITY

PO Box 2900, Bloomington, IL 61702-2900 • Admissions: 309-556-3031 • Fax: 309-556-3820

CAMPUS LIFE

Quality of Life Rating	**82**
Fire Safety Rating	**81**
Green Rating	**77**
Type of school	private
Environment	city

STUDENTS

Total undergrad enrollment	2,088
% male/female	42/58
% from out of state	13
% from public high school	81
% live on campus	77
% in (# of) fraternities	30 (6)
% in (# of) sororities	26 (5)
% African American	5
% Asian	4
% Caucasian	80
% Hispanic	3
% international	2
# of countries represented	22

SURVEY SAYS . . .

Large classes
Lab facilities are great
Great computer facilities
Great library
Athletic facilities are great

ACADEMICS

Academic Rating	**85**
Calendar	4/4/1
Student/faculty ratio	11:1
Profs interesting rating	79
Profs accessible rating	84
Most common reg class size	10–19 students
Most common lab size	10–19 students

MOST POPULAR MAJORS

biology/biological sciences
psychology
business/commerce

STUDENTS SAY ". . ."

Academics

Illinois Wesleyan University, "a small liberal arts school that will give you lots of personal attention," is "the right size, small enough that you feel comfortable walking around because you always see familiar faces wherever you go, but also big enough where you don't know everybody and you can find your own niche." The school strives to "create a personal educational experience with professors, classmates, and staff"; it's the kind of place where professors "make themselves available to read essay drafts, offer career advice, and write letters of recommendation on top of giving great lectures." IWU excels in such diverse areas as biology (the school "has a great reputation in the sciences"), nursing, English, psychology, theater, and music ("extremely competitive," but much more liberal arts–oriented than "conservatory-like"). "The school encourages exploring multiple interests, and double majors and dual degrees are pursued by many students." One student writes, "Right now, I'm a business major with a philosophy minor, and I'm making up my own minor between the Music and Physics Department in electroacoustic music, and I'm still going to graduate in 4 years." You can really "make your degree yours" here. Students on track for graduate study love "the high acceptance rates into grad school" IWU enjoys in many programs, and everyone appreciates the school's May Term, which "gives you a really great option to take inventive, unique classes or travel abroad."

Life

IWU is located in Bloomington-Normal, which "certainly isn't Chicago" but is still a "great place to live with so much to do." While some kids from the Chicago area complain about the location, telling us that "it's not very exciting," those from elsewhere are more generous in their assessments, observing that "it's better than a suburb. Both Bloomington and Normal have downtown areas with quaint boutiques next to new bars and eateries, and the recent boom in the Latino and East Asian populations have provided excellent cuisine options!" With well over one-quarter of the student body involved in Greek life, "Frats and sororities play a large part in social activities" of the campus. Illinois State University is "just down the street," offering another party alternative "to those who want to escape the IWU bubble." The Student Activities Office "brings awesome entertainment to our campus on the weekends like concerts, movies, [and] comedians," and since they are covered by the student activity fee, there is "no charge to the student," though they are usually "over pretty early." IWU has numerous intercollegiate teams, but "Basketball is the only main sports attraction. Very few students actually attend football games or other sporting events." Wesleyan dormitories "are amazing. The majority of students live on campus all 4 years because of all the great living options."

Student Body

IWU draws heavily from the affluent suburbs of Chicago, attracting a student body that "is White," and "somewhat wealthy" although "There are many who do not fit this mold." Most "have very diverse interests, sometimes even majors that you never thought would be possible: music and science, foreign language and pre-professional science, and so on. Furthermore, they are usually involved in a diverse number of extracurricular activities: sports, clubs, organizations, etc." Students tell us that everyone here is "pretty easy-going, though if one is a bio or chem major, studying is constantly on the mind due to the amount needed to be memorized," though for many, "a long week of paper-writing and test taking is rewarded with a few long nights of debauchery." IWU also has a fair number of international students; one woman writes, "My floor alone has girls from Nigeria, Germany, and Bangladesh and there are other girls of Asian, Indian, and African descent as well."

FINANCIAL AID: 309-556-3096 • E-MAIL: IWUADMIT@TITAN.IWU.EDU • WEBSITE: WWW.IWU.EDU

THE PRINCETON REVIEW SAYS

Admissions

Very important factors considered include: Academic GPA, rigor of secondary school record, interview. *Important factors considered include:* Class rank, application essay, standardized test scores, character/personal qualities, extracurricular activities, talent/ability. *Other factors considered include:* Recommendation(s), alumni/ae relation, first generation, geographical residence, level of applicant's interest, racial/ethnic status, state residency, volunteer work, work experience. SAT or ACT required; TOEFL required of all international applicants. High school diploma is required and GED is accepted. *Academic units recommended:* 4 English, 3 mathematics, 3 science, (2 science labs), 3 foreign language, 2 social studies.

Financial Aid

Students should submit: FAFSA, institution's own financial aid form, CSS/Financial Aid PROFILE. Either our own form or the CSS/PROFILE is accepted. Regular filing deadline is 3/1. The Princeton Review suggests that all financial aid forms be submitted as soon as possible after January 1. *Need-based scholarships/grants offered:* Federal Pell, SEOG, state scholarships/grants, private scholarships, the school's own gift aid. *Loan aid offered:* FFEL Subsidized Stafford, FFEL Unsubsidized Stafford, FFEL PLUS, Federal Perkins, Federal Nursing, college/university loans from institutional funds. Applicants will be notified of awards on a rolling basis beginning 2/15. Federal Work-Study Program available. Institutional employment available. Off-campus job opportunities are good.

The Inside Word

There's no application fee at IWU and the school accepts the Common Application (with the IWU Common Application Supplement, which asks for your intended major and an essay explaining your reasons for wanting to attend IWU), so there are few reasons not to apply to IWU if you're at all interested in the school. Don't expect to breeze through, though; you won't get in here without a solid academic profile or a compelling story.

THE SCHOOL SAYS "..."

From The Admissions Office

"Illinois Wesleyan University attracts a wide variety of students who are interested in pursuing diverse fields such as vocal performance, biology, psychology, German, physics, or business administration. At IWU, students are not forced into either/or choices. Rather, they are encouraged to pursue multiple interests simultaneously—a philosophy that is in keeping with the spirit and value of a liberal arts education. The distinctive 4-4-1 calendar allows students to follow their interests each school year in two semesters followed by an optional month-long class in May. May term opportunities include classes on campus; research collaboration with faculty; travel and study in such places as Australia, China, South Africa, and Europe; as well as local, national, and international internships.

"The IWU mission statement reads in part: 'A liberal education at Illinois Wesleyan fosters creativity, critical thinking, effective communication, strength of character, and a spirit of inquiry; it deepens the specialized knowledge of a discipline with a comprehensive world view. It affords the greatest possibilities for realizing individual potential while preparing students for democratic citizenship and life in a global society. . . . The university, through its policies, programs, and practices, is committed to diversity, social justice, and environmental sustainability. A tightly knit, supportive university community, together with a variety of opportunities for close interaction with excellent faculty, both challenges and supports students in their personal and intellectual development.

"Freshman applicants for Fall 2008 may submit scores from either the old or new SAT exams. For the ACT, students may submit scores with or without the Writing section."

SELECTIVITY

Admissions Rating	89
# of applicants	2,963
% of applicants accepted	57
% of acceptees attending	32
# accepting a place on wait list	63
% admitted from wait list	24

FRESHMAN PROFILE

Range SAT Critical Reading	540–680
Range SAT Math	590–690
Range ACT Composite	26–30
Minimum paper TOEFL	550
Minimum computer TOEFL	213
% graduated top 10% of class	45
% graduated top 25% of class	76
% graduated top 50% of class	98

DEADLINES

Regular	
Priority	11/1
Notification	rolling
Nonfall registration?	yes

APPLICANTS ALSO LOOK AT

AND OFTEN PREFER
University of Notre Dame
Northwestern University

AND SOMETIMES PREFER
Washington University in St. Louis
University of Illinois at Urbana—
Champaign

AND RARELY PREFER
Marquette University
Augustana College (IL)

FINANCIAL FACTS

Financial Aid Rating	84
Annual tuition	$32,260
% frosh rec. need-based scholarship or grant aid	57
% UG rec. need-based scholarship or grant aid	58
% frosh rec. non-need-based scholarship or grant aid	8
% UG rec. non-need-based scholarship or grant aid	8
% frosh rec. need-based self-help aid	46
% UG rec. need-based self-help aid	48
% frosh rec. any financial aid	91
% UG rec. any financial aid	89
% UG borrow to pay for school	64
Average cumulative indebtedness	$24,234

INDIANA UNIVERSITY—BLOOMINGTON

300 North Jordan Avenue, Bloomington, IN 47405-1106 • Admissions: 812-855-0661 • Fax: 812-855-5102

CAMPUS LIFE

Quality of Life Rating	91
Fire Safety Rating	60*
Green Rating	60*
Type of school	public
Environment	town

STUDENTS

Total undergrad enrollment	29,734
% male/female	49/51
% from out of state	33
% live on campus	36
% in (# of) fraternities	16 (NR)
% in (# of) sororities	18 (NR)
% African American	4
% Asian	4
% Caucasian	83
% Hispanic	2
% international	5
# of countries represented	132

SURVEY SAYS . . .
Great computer facilities
Great library
Great off-campus food
Students are happy
Everyone loves the Hoosiers
Student publications are popular
Lots of beer drinking
Hard liquor is popular

ACADEMICS

Academic Rating	78
Calendar	semester
Student/faculty ratio	18:1
Profs interesting rating	77
Profs accessible rating	81

MOST POPULAR MAJORS
business/commerce
education
communication, journalism, and
related programs

STUDENTS SAY ". . ."

Academics
Although many think of Indiana University as "a party school with an active Greek population"—an image students reinforce when they insist that IU is "about going to massive parties...and getting the job done, but not being defined by schoolwork"—the school is "in actuality a Big Ten research university that offers a huge variety of classes and majors (even allowing students to create their own) with a surprisingly diverse student body that allows anybody to fit in regardless of whether they enjoy partying or are interested in the Greek system." Most students appreciate both the academic and social aspects of the school, telling us that IU offers "the best combination of academics and extracurriculars one could ask for in a school." IU's "world renowned" business school is taught by professors who "are at the top of their respective fields of expertise. They have a lot to teach us, and they are almost universally excellent at doing so." An equally acclaimed music school and a language department that "has everything from the romance languages to Urdu, Haitian Creole, and Tibetan" also draw students' attention. On the downside, "There is not a lot of emphasis on real-world experience at IU, so if you want an internship you really have to be self-motivated. IUB is one hour away from a metropolitan area, so, although being in this town has its social benefits, it definitely makes it tougher as you prepare for life after college."

Life
"Every day is a new and exciting experience at Indiana University," where "there is too much going on all of the time." The campus is alive with lectures, art exhibits, theatrical and musical shows, and the school's beloved intercollegiate athletics. "We spend a lot of time thinking about basketball and football, depending obviously on the season," students tell us. You don't have to look hard to find a party here, and "A lot of people tend to get drunk as entertainment," but that's hardly the only option, and many pass four happy years here outside the party scene. Undergrads love hometown Bloomington, "a great city to live in" with "amazing cultural events, such as the Lotus World Music Festival and Chocolate Fest" along with "lots of little stores demonstrating their own niches and a wide range of different authentic-ish ethnic restaurants." Campus-wide traditions such as Little 500, a party "at the end of the year when the whole campus stops what they're doing to attend concerts, parties, and the men's and women's bike races," help cement a strong sense of school spirit.

Student Body
While "most IU students are white and come from a middle-class background," the school's "international and minority student populations are growing, and there are a lot of services available to help minority students feel comfortable on campus." Those who aren't native Hoosiers are most often Chicagoans or East Coasters from New York and New Jersey. The school is big enough to accommodate many personality types: "some Greeks, some who are academically oriented, some who enjoy and actively pursue the arts, and others who enjoy sports such as IU basketball...small cultures exist within the larger IU culture." There are "a lot of students who come to IU with the intention of partying all the time, and rarely studying," but most don't last long; those who "work hard all week and worship the weekends," on the other hand, can and often do thrive here.

INDIANA UNIVERSITY—BLOOMINGTON

FINANCIAL AID: 812-855-0321 • E-MAIL: IUADMIT@INDIANA.EDU • WEBSITE: WWW.IUB.EDU

THE PRINCETON REVIEW SAYS

Admissions

Very important factors considered include: Class rank, academic GPA, rigor of secondary school record. *Important factors considered include:* Standardized test scores. *Other factors considered include:* Application essay, recommendation(s), alumni/ae relation, character/personal qualities, extracurricular activities, first generation, geographical residence, interview, level of applicant's interest, racial/ethnic status, state residency, talent/ability, SAT Subject Tests recommended; SAT or ACT required; ACT with Writing component required. High school diploma is required and GED is accepted. *Academic units required:* 4 English, 3 mathematics, 1 science, (1 science labs), 2 social studies, 4 academic electives. *Academic units recommended:* 4 mathematics, 3 science, 3 foreign language, 3 social studies.

Financial Aid

Students should submit: FAFSA. The Princeton Review suggests that all financial aid forms be submitted as soon as possible after January 1. *Need-based scholarships/grants offered:* Federal Pell, SEOG, state scholarships/grants, private scholarships, the school's own gift aid. *Loan aid offered:* Direct Subsidized Stafford, Direct Unsubsidized Stafford, Direct PLUS, FFEL Subsidized Stafford, FFEL Unsubsidized Stafford, FFEL PLUS, Federal Perkins, Federal Nursing, college/university loans from institutional funds. Applicants will be notified of awards on a rolling basis beginning 4/1. Federal Work-Study Program available. Institutional employment available. Off-campus job opportunities are good.

The Inside Word

Above-average high school performers should meet little resistance from the IU admissions office. Others may be able to improve their chances by attending IU recruiting events (the school visits many locations throughout the state) and visiting the campus. Rolling admissions favor those who apply early in the process. IU's music program is highly competitive; admission hinges upon a successful audition.

THE SCHOOL SAYS ". . ."

From The Admissions Office

"Indiana University—Bloomington, one of America's great teaching and research universities, extends learning and teaching beyond the walls of the traditional classroom. When visiting campus, students and parents typically describe IU as 'what a college should look and feel like.' Students bring their diverse experiences, beliefs, and backgrounds from all 50 states and 132 countries, which adds a richness and diversity to life at IU—a campus often cited as one of the most beautiful in the nation. Indiana University—Bloomington truly offers a quintessential college town, campus, and overall experience. Students enjoy all of the advantages, opportunities, and resources that a larger school can offer, while still receiving personal attention and support. For the third year in a row, *U.S. News & World Report* has recognized IU—Bloomington for the range of programs offered to help freshmen succeed. Because of the variety of outstanding academic and cultural resources, students at IU have the best of both worlds.

"Indiana offers more than 5,000 courses and more than 100 undergraduate programs, of which many are known nationally and internationally. IU—Bloomington is known worldwide for outstanding programs in the arts, sciences, humanities, and social sciences as well as for highly rated Schools of Business, Music, Education, Journalism, Optometry; Public and Environmental Affairs; and Health, Physical Education, and Recreation. Students can customize academic programs with double and individualized majors, internships, and research opportunities, while utilizing state-of-the-art technology. Representatives from more than 1,000 businesses, government agencies, and not-for-profit organizations come to campus each year to recruit IU students.

"IUB requires the new version of the SAT with writing and/or the ACT with writing. The university will use the writing sections to determine possible credit, placement or exemption from writing requirements. We encourage, but do not require, SAT Subject Tests."

SELECTIVITY

Admissions Rating	86
# of applicants	29,059
% of applicants accepted	70
% of acceptees attending	35

FRESHMAN PROFILE

Range SAT Critical Reading	510–620
Range SAT Math	520–640
Range ACT Composite	23–28
Average HS GPA	3.57
% graduated top 10% of class	31
% graduated top 25% of class	68
% graduated top 50% of class	98

DEADLINES

Regular	
Priority	4/1
Nonfall registration?	yes

APPLICANTS ALSO LOOK AT
AND OFTEN PREFER
University of Michigan—Ann Arbor
University of Illinois at Urbana-Champaign

AND SOMETIMES PREFER
Purdue University—West Lafayette
University of Wisconsin—Madison
Miami University

FINANCIAL FACTS

Financial Aid Rating	73
Annual in-state tuition	$5,791
Annual out-of-state tuition	$20,200
Room and board	$6,676
Required fees	$837
Books and supplies	$758
% frosh rec. need-based scholarship or grant aid	33
% UG rec. need-based scholarship or grant aid	28
% frosh rec. non-need-based scholarship or grant aid	5
% UG rec. non-need-based scholarship or grant aid	4
% frosh rec. need-based self-help aid	29
% UG rec. need-based self-help aid	30
% frosh rec. athletic scholarships	1
% UG rec. athletic scholarships	1
% frosh rec. any financial aid	79
% UG rec. any financial aid	71
% UG borrow to pay for school	56
Average cumulative indebtedness	$19,763

INDIANA UNIVERSITY OF PENNSYLVANIA

117 SUTTON HALL, INDIANA, PA 15705 • ADMISSIONS: 724-357-2230 • FAX: 724-357-6281

CAMPUS LIFE

Quality of Life Rating	66
Fire Safety Rating	94
Green Rating	60*
Type of school	public
Environment	village

STUDENTS

Total undergrad enrollment	11,724
% male/female	45/55
% from out of state	4
% from public high school	95
% live on campus	31
% in (# of) fraternities	9 (19)
% in (# of) sororities	9 (14)
% African American	11
% Asian	1
% Caucasian	76
% Hispanic	2
% international	2
# of countries represented	56

SURVEY SAYS . . .

Small classes
Frats and sororities dominate
social scene
Student publications are popular
Lots of beer drinking
Hard liquor is popular
(Almost) everyone smokes

ACADEMICS

Academic Rating	70
Calendar	semester
Student/faculty ratio	16:1
Profs interesting rating	75
Profs accessible rating	76
Most common reg class size	20–29 students
Most common lab size	10–19 students

MOST POPULAR MAJORS
criminology
nursing/registered nurse
(rn, asn, bsn, msn)
management

STUDENTS SAY

Academics

Named not for the state, but for the actual town in which the school is located, Indiana University of Pennsylvania (IUP) is "academically challenging but not impossible if you make an honest effort." Students enjoy "awesome professors" who are "concerned with their welfare and academic growth," and find their teachers "ridiculously easy to get into contact with—no need to make an appointment." Thanks to "strong educators" and "small class sizes" students are "pushed to think critically," and those who want even more of a challenge can take part in "excellent honors classes and programs." In recent years, the administration has gone through several changes, leaving some students feeling that it is "often out of touch with the real world." That said, students enjoy an "equal say in the policies that form the foundation of their education" through the University Senate, and "can always access [the administration] when in need." While some students have experienced "scheduling problems" in certain departments, students feel, overall, that they get more for less at IUP: "Anyone attending can achieve the same education as another student at an Ivy League school" as long as "They are truly interested in learning and willing to put forth the effort."

Life

Indiana, Pennsylvania, is the kind of town John Mellencamp would sing about—small, working-class, but not without its charms or bars. As one student explains, "socializing is a large part of IUP life." Since the school is located "in a backwoods kind of area," most students "go to parties for fun," and most but "not all parties involve a keg." While many students "go to fraternities and house parties and drink" there are options available for students "who want no alcohol/drugs involved in their college life whatsoever." For non-partiers, "Life usually consists of movies and games" and "outdoor activities when the weather is nice." The school also boasts a "good selection of clubs" that provides a quick way "to meet people." While "Going to a grocery store or a mall would be much easier" if you "get a car," most students take advantage of the "free bus system" to get to town. There, students enjoy "a pool hall, two bowling alleys, a local theater that shows current, old, and foreign films," as well as "tons of restaurants and bars" and some "great coffeehouses." If you need a taste of city life, "Pittsburgh is an hour and a half away."

Student Body

According to one student, IUP is "more diverse" than the local "predominantly White area," but "less diverse than U.S. Census percentage numbers." As a "public university" the "student body is very mixed," and students have "the opportunity to interact with more people" than they would at "many other colleges," from the "very conservative" to the "extremely unique." As one student explains, "No matter what your interest is, it wouldn't be too hard to find someone that you can share this interest with." While fraternities and sororities are "popular," there is "a place for everyone" on campus. In other words, "No matter who you are, if you go to this college you are going to have a damn good time." Students view themselves as "down to earth" and adept at "balancing academics" with "social outlets." The dorms help instill "a strong feeling of community" as do the honors courses, which provide "a bonding experience without the drinking" for students.

FINANCIAL AID: 724-357-2218 • E-MAIL: ADMISSIONS-INQUIRY@IUP.EDU • WEBSITE: WWW.IUP.EDU

THE PRINCETON REVIEW SAYS

Admissions

Very important factors considered include: Academic GPA, standardized test scores. *Important factors considered include:* Rigor of secondary school record. *Other factors considered include:* Class rank, application essay, recommendation(s), extracurricular activities, SAT or ACT required; TOEFL required of all international applicants. High school diploma is required and GED is accepted. *Academic units recommended:* 3 English, 3 mathematics, 3 science, 2 foreign language, 3 social studies.

Financial Aid

Students should submit: FAFSA. The Princeton Review suggests that all financial aid forms be submitted as soon as possible after January 1. *Need-based scholarships/grants offered:* Federal Pell, SEOG, state scholarships/grants, private scholarships, the school's own gift aid, United Negro College Fund. *Loan aid offered:* FFEL Subsidized Stafford, FFEL Unsubsidized Stafford, FFEL PLUS, Federal Perkins, Private Alternative Loans. Applicants will be notified of awards on a rolling basis beginning 3/15. Federal Work-Study Program available. Institutional employment available. Off-campus job opportunities are good.

The Inside Word

Indiana University of Pennsylvania offers an academic environment unique among most public universities: undergraduate classes taught solely by professors. Pennsylvania residents will find it especially worthwhile to investigate this school as it offers a solid education at an affordable price to state residents. The admissions process should not give much trouble to students with an above-average secondary school record.

THE SCHOOL SAYS "..."

From The Admissions Office

"At IUP, we look at each applicant as an individual, not as a number. That means we'll review your application materials very carefully. When reviewing applications, the Admissions Committee's primary focus is on the student's high school record and SAT scores. In addition, the committee often reviews the optional personal essay and letters of recommendations submitted by the student to help aid in the decision-making process. We're always happy to speak with prospective students. Call us toll-free at 800-422-6830 or 724-357-2230 or e-mail us at admissions-inquiry@iup.edu.

"Students applying for admission into the Fall 2008 entering class are required to take the new version of the SAT. Students will be allowed to submit scores from the old (prior to March 2005) version of the SAT (or ACT) as well, and we will use the student's best scores from either test."

SELECTIVITY

Admissions Rating	**66**
# of applicants	10,116
% of applicants accepted	59
% of acceptees attending	42

FRESHMAN PROFILE

Range SAT Critical Reading	430–530
Range SAT Math	430–540
Range SAT Writing	420–520
Minimum paper TOEFL	500
Minimum computer TOEFL	173
% graduated top 10% of class	8.6
% graduated top 25% of class	27.8
% graduated top 50% of class	62

DEADLINES

Notification	rolling
Nonfall registration?	yes

APPLICANTS ALSO LOOK AT

AND OFTEN PREFER
Duquesne University
Westminster College
Millersville University of Pennsylvania
Clarion University of PA
Shippensburg University of Pennsylvania
Penn State—University Park

AND SOMETIMES PREFER
University of Delaware
West Virginia University
Kutztown University of Pennsylvania

AND RARELY PREFER
Lock Haven University of Pennsylvania
Ohio University—Athens
Mansfield University

FINANCIAL FACTS

Financial Aid Rating	**71**
Annual in-state tuition	$5,178
Annual out-of-state tuition	$12,944
Room and board	$5,436
Required fees	$1,517
Books and supplies	$1,000
% frosh rec. need-based scholarship or grant aid	47
% UG rec. need-based scholarship or grant aid	46
% frosh rec. non-need-based scholarship or grant aid	22
% UG rec. non-need-based scholarship or grant aid	14
% frosh rec. need-based self-help aid	63
% UG rec. need-based self-help aid	58
% frosh rec. athletic scholarships	3
% UG rec. athletic scholarships	2
% frosh rec. any financial aid	81
% UG rec. any financial aid	81
% UG borrow to pay for school	81
Average cumulative indebtedness	$22,431

IOWA STATE UNIVERSITY

100 ALUMNI HALL, AMES, IA 50011-2011 • ADMISSIONS: 515-294-5836 • FAX: 515-294-2592

CAMPUS LIFE

Quality of Life Rating	**89**
Fire Safety Rating	**72**
Green Rating	**60***
Type of school	public
Environment	town

STUDENTS

Total undergrad enrollment	20,613
% male/female	57/43
% from out of state	21
% from public high school	93
% live on campus	39
% in (# of) fraternities	15 (31)
% in (# of) sororities	16 (19)
% African American	3
% Asian	3
% Caucasian	84
% Hispanic	3
% international	3
# of countries represented	106

SURVEY SAYS . . .

Great computer facilities
Great library
Intramural sports are popular

ACADEMICS

Academic Rating	**72**
Calendar	semester
Student/faculty ratio	16:1
Profs interesting rating	62
Profs accessible rating	68
% classes taught by TAs	14
Most common reg class size	20–29 students
Most common lab size	20–29 students

MOST POPULAR MAJORS

marketing/marketing management
mechanical engineering
management science

STUDENTS SAY ". . ."

Academics

Students tell us the academic experience is "tough but fulfilling" at Iowa State University, where "science, engineering, and technology" are all the rage. "Iowa State is a massive engineering school, and that's probably its biggest asset," explains one first-year student. ISU also boasts "one of the top agricultural universities in the nation," "a great program for landscape architecture," and a notable School of Journalism and Communication. Iowa State is also a "great school for internships," bringing big-time recruiters to career fairs. Students do say that "more classes in liberal arts" would be nice. ISU "should offer more opportunities in the humanities since they are still offered as majors at the university," gripes a junior. Like a lot of schools containing the word *state* in their names, Iowa State is really big. Professors "don't hold your hand," especially in lower-level courses that often enroll upwards of "500 people." ISU's faculty gets mixed reviews: "Sixty percent of the professors are good," estimates one student. "The rest are average." "Professors are usually very dedicated, knowledgeable, and fair," counters another. Overall, students tell us that their professors are "approachable and available for help outside class"—"You just have to ask." However, some are "very typical of the stereotypical state school": These professors are "fantastic researchers, which is why they're hired, but sometimes can't teach for their lives." The administration is seen by some students as a little bureaucratic. Otherwise, "The university seems to be running pretty smoothly."

Life

"It is easy to get involved" at ISU. "Hundreds of clubs and organizations" are "available in everything from medieval recreation, to chemistry club (ice cream and explosions), to service organizations, to major-specific professional organizations." Fraternities and sororities don't overwhelm campus life, but "There are a lot of parties," and "Drinking has to be one of the more popular activities," reports a senior. Students here usually start off the weekend by hitting the bars Thursday nights, although students contend that there are activities on campus for nondrinkers, too. Sports play a dominant role in campus life— "Getting involved in intramurals" is very common, and students are "diehard" fans of their beloved Cyclones. Iowa State's "gorgeous" campus is full of "lots of trees and green space," though "During the winter it's a bit of a bummer to have to walk all over campus." "Most of the buildings are pretty modern"—perhaps too modern. "The campus could use a little more color," as opposed to "all the gray," says one student. The "very quaint" and "safe" surrounding town of Ames is a "typical college town" with "decent amenities and activities." When students need a change of pace, the city of Des Moines is "close enough."

Student Body

Iowa State is home to many students "from different countries and backgrounds"—including a noticeable contingent of students from Asia—who "enrich the environment" and "fit in surprisingly well." And you can find "every type of personality," "from your basic frat boy/sorority girl to goth kids to nerds" to "hick-ish" students who "grew up in very rural communities." Overall, you won't find a great deal of ethnic variation on this campus. "The typical student" here is "White, conservative," and "comes from a middle-class Midwestern family." These "basically good students" describe themselves as "very polite," "pretty well-rounded," and often religious. "There is a great sense of community here." One thing you won't see at ISU is too many highfalutin' snobs: "There are a lot of students who are paying for their education themselves and are very motivated to succeed," observes a first-year student.

FINANCIAL AID: 515-294-2223 • E-MAIL: ADMISSIONS@IASTATE.EDU • WEBSITE: WWW.IASTATE.EDU

THE PRINCETON REVIEW SAYS

Admissions

Very important factors considered include: Class rank, academic GPA, rigor of secondary school record, standardized test scores. *Other factors considered include:* Application essay, recommendation(s), character/personal qualities, extracurricular activities, geographical residence, interview, state residency, talent/ability, volunteer work, work experience. SAT or ACT required; TOEFL required of all international applicants. High school diploma is required and GED is accepted. *Academic units required:* 4 English, 3 mathematics, 3 science, (2 science labs), 2 foreign language, 2 social studies. *Academic units recommended:* 4 English, 4 mathematics, 4 science, (3 science labs), 3 foreign language, 4 social studies.

Financial Aid

Students should submit: FAFSA. The Princeton Review suggests that all financial aid forms be submitted as soon as possible after January 1. *Need-based scholarships/grants offered:* Federal Pell, SEOG, state scholarships/grants, the school's own gift aid. *Loan aid offered:* Direct Subsidized Stafford, Direct Unsubsidized Stafford, Direct PLUS, Federal Perkins, state loans, college/university loans from institutional funds, private alternative loans. Applicants will be notified of awards on a rolling basis beginning 4/1. Federal Work-Study Program available. Institutional employment available. Off-campus job opportunities are excellent.

The Inside Word

As is the case at many public institutions, Iowa State is fairly straightforward about its requirements. It's undeniably a numbers game, so prospective students will want to focus on grades and standardized test scores. Candidates to the College of Arts and Sciences will need an extra year of social science course work and 2 years of a single foreign language to remain competitive. Applicants who do not meet these standards need not panic: They will have an opportunity to gain acceptance after an individual review.

THE SCHOOL SAYS ". . ."

From The Admissions Office

"Iowa State University offers all the advantages of a major university along with the friendliness and warmth of a residential campus. There are more than 100 undergraduate programs of study in the Colleges of Agriculture, Business, Design, Education, Engineering, Family and Consumer Sciences, Liberal Arts and Sciences, and Veterinary Medicine. Our 1,700 faculty members include Rhodes Scholars, Fulbright Scholars, and National Academy of Sciences and National Academy of Engineering members. Recognized for its high quality of life, Iowa State has taken practical steps to make the university a place where students feel like they belong. Iowa State has been recognized for the high quality of campus life and the exemplary out-of-class experiences offered to its students. Along with a strong academic experience, students also have opportunities for further developing their leadership skills and interpersonal relationships through any of the more than 500 student organizations, 60 intramural sports, and a multitude of arts and recreational activities. All residence hall rooms are wired for Internet connections, and all students have the opportunity to create their own World Wide Web pages.

"Iowa State University will accept either the new SAT or the old SAT (administered prior to March 2005 and without a Writing component). The school will also accept the ACT with or without the Writing component."

SELECTIVITY

Admissions Rating	81
# of applicants	11,058
% of applicants accepted	89
% of acceptees attending	44

FRESHMAN PROFILE

Range SAT Critical Reading	510–640
Range SAT Math	530–680
Range ACT Composite	22–27
Minimum paper TOEFL	500
Minimum computer TOEFL	173
Average HS GPA	3.47
% graduated top 10% of class	25.62
% graduated top 25% of class	58.43
% graduated top 50% of class	93.32

DEADLINES

Regular	
Deadline	7/1
Notification	rolling
Nonfall registration?	yes

APPLICANTS ALSO LOOK AT AND OFTEN PREFER

Purdue University—West Lafayette
University of Wisconsin—Madison
University of Illinois at Urbana-Champaign
University of Minnesota—Twin Cities

AND RARELY PREFER

Western Michigan University
Baylor University

FINANCIAL FACTS

Financial Aid Rating	82
Annual in-state tuition	$5,524
Annual out-of-state tuition	$16,514
Room and board	$6,715
Required fees	$836
Books and supplies	$978
% frosh rec. need-based scholarship or grant aid	47
% UG rec. need-based scholarship or grant aid	51
% frosh rec. non-need-based scholarship or grant aid	25
% UG rec. non-need-based scholarship or grant aid	23
% frosh rec. need-based self-help aid	36
% UG rec. need-based self-help aid	43
% frosh rec. athletic scholarships	2
% UG rec. athletic scholarships	2
% frosh rec. any financial aid	87.3
% UG rec. any financial aid	79.7
% UG borrow to pay for school	70.4
Average cumulative indebtedness	$31,501

ITHACA COLLEGE

100 Job Hall, Ithaca, NY 14850-7020 • Admissions: 607-274-3124 • Fax: 607-274-1900

CAMPUS LIFE

Quality of Life Rating	**79**
Fire Safety Rating	**75**
Green Rating	**91**
Type of school	private
Environment	town

STUDENTS

Total undergrad enrollment	6,185
% male/female	45/55
% from out of state	54
% from public high school	75
% live on campus	70
% in (# of) fraternities	1 (4)
% in (# of) sororities	1 (1)
% African American	3
% Asian	4
% Caucasian	80
% Hispanic	4
% international	2
# of countries represented	67

SURVEY SAYS . . .

Great off-campus food
Frats and sororities are unpopular
or nonexistent
Musical organizations are popular
College radio is popular
Theater is popular
Student publications are popular
Lots of beer drinking
Hard liquor is popular

ACADEMICS

Academic Rating	**79**
Calendar	semester
Student/faculty ratio	12:1
Profs interesting rating	81
Profs accessible rating	80
% classes taught by TAs	1
Most common	
reg class size	10–19 students

MOST POPULAR MAJORS
business/commerce

STUDENTS SAY " . . ."

Academics

Ithaca College offers "a wonderful liberal arts experience," and it's "an overall excellent place to study for four years." "A huge variety of majors" includes a "renowned" cinema program and an "amazing" theater program. There are "strong," "in-depth" majors in physical therapy, music education, and communications, too. Courses are discussion-heavy and "reasonably easy to complete if you show up and pay attention." "Some lectures don't even feel like lectures because the professor knows everyone's name," says a physical therapy major. "You don't feel like just a number." In general, the IC faculty is full of "nice, funny, generally laidback people" with "real world experience." "Some can teach and some can't." Some are "so enthusiastic it's almost scary." A few "can be very opinionated." After class, professors are "readily available" and they take time to get to know their students. "You would be hard pressed to find a person who hasn't had dinner at a professor's house," claims a communications major. Don't expect many dinners with the administration, though. Management is reportedly "hard to get hold of." Students also complain about IC's general enormity. "This campus is huge and there is a lot of walking." "Some of the buildings look ugly and dated" as well. Costs are another big gripe. "The school nickels and dimes us quite a bit," vents a music education major.

Life

A great deal of student life at Ithaca occurs on campus. "When it's warm out, there are always students outside playing Frisbee and reading on the grass." "The school and student-run activities provide a plethora of opportunities." "There are music concerts nearly every night." There is a "very popular" radio station. "Many students also like to support" the athletic teams. The party scene is strong. "If you walk around the dorms, you will find at least someone to have drinking competitions with," promises a sophomore. Getting stoned is a popular pastime as well. "There is a huge population of people who enjoy it almost every day." Winters are hardcore up here and "getting off campus can be hard." "It can be very isolating if you can't drive." The surrounding town is "safe" and there are "tons of shops and restaurants," but Ithacans usually "don't venture into the city." When they do, they often go "across town" to Cornell "for the frat parties since Ithaca has no social fraternities." "Girls have no problem getting into the frats" but guys have a harder time. "There is a lot of nature to bask in" as well, at least when the water isn't "frozen over." Ithaca "is nothing if not gorges." For somewhat more cosmopolitan fare, "the mall in Syracuse is a nice escape."

Student Body

It's an odd mix of people. There are "quirky communications students, jockish exercise science majors, and weird thespians." There are "diva-like" music majors. "There are many gays and lesbians." There are "the super studious students and the ones who are more concerned with social life." There are a lot of hippies and "radical students" with "sort of a crazy fashion sense." "Anyone who comes here can basically find their niche," says a first-year student. Politically, the environment is "extremely liberal." "There is a lot of activism." "The environmentalists are everywhere and are annoying at times," says a junior. "Ithaca College endlessly brags about how diverse it is" but students tell us that the minority population is "minimal." There are students here from around the country but "it does seem like everyone is from wealthy suburbs in the Northeast." Some students insist that class issues are nonexistent. "There are a lot of rich people on campus," they say, "but that doesn't mean that they'll rub it in." "I'm here because it was cheaper to attend Ithaca with my financial aid package than either of the state schools I applied to," adds a senior. "That says a lot." However, others see a lot of snobbery. "To survive at Ithaca College, it is best to not openly talk about any socioeconomic disadvantages," asserts a sophomore, "because it makes all the white students feel uncomfortable and they'll alienate you."

FINANCIAL AID: 607-274-3131 • E-MAIL: ADMISSION@ITHACA.EDU • WEBSITE: WWW.ITHACA.EDU

THE PRINCETON REVIEW SAYS

Admissions

Very important factors considered include: Academic GPA, rigor of secondary school record, standardized test scores. *Important factors considered include:* Class rank, application essay, recommendation(s), character/personal qualities, extracurricular activities, talent/ability. *Other factors considered include:* Alumni/ae relation, first generation, level of applicant's interest, volunteer work, work experience. SAT or ACT required; ACT with Writing component required. TOEFL required of all international applicants. High school diploma is required and GED is accepted. *Academic units required:* 4 English, 3 mathematics, 3 science, 2 foreign language, 3 social studies, 1 academic elective.

Financial Aid

Students should submit: FAFSA. The Princeton Review suggests that all financial aid forms be submitted as soon as possible after January 1. *Need-based scholarships/grants offered:* Federal Pell, SEOG, state scholarships/grants, private scholarships, the school's own gift aid. *Loan aid offered:* FFEL Subsidized Stafford, FFEL Unsubsidized Stafford, FFEL PLUS, Federal Perkins, Alternative Loans. Applicants will be notified of awards on a rolling basis beginning 2/15. Federal Work-Study Program available. Institutional employment available. Off-campus job opportunities are good.

The Inside Word

Ithaca has a moderately competitive admissions profile and the annual crop of freshmen typically ranges from solid to spectacular. If you apply, expect thorough consideration of your personal background, talents, and achievements in addition to your academic accomplishments. Programs requiring an audition or portfolio are among the most demanding for admission; the arts have always been particularly strong here.

THE SCHOOL SAYS ". . ."

From The Admissions Office

"Ithaca College was founded in 1892 as a music conservatory, and it continues that commitment to performance and excellence. Its modern, residential 750-acre campus, equipped with state-of-the-art facilities, is home to the Schools of Business, Communications, Health Sciences and Human Performance, Humanities and Sciences, and Music and our new Division of Interdisciplinary and International Studies. With more than 100 majors—from biochemistry to business administration, journalism to jazz, philosophy to physical therapy, and special programs in Washington, DC, Los Angeles, London, and Australia—students enjoy the curricular choices of a large campus in a personalized, smaller school environment. And Ithaca's students benefit from an education that emphasizes active learning, small classes, collaborative student-faculty research, and development of the whole student. Located in central New York's spectacular Finger Lakes region in what many consider the classic college town, the college has 25 highly competitive varsity teams, more than 130 campus clubs, two radio stations and a television station, as well as hundreds of concerts, recitals, and theater performances annually.

"Students applying for admission must have official scores from either the SAT or the ACT with the Writing section sent to Ithaca College by the testing agency. The college will also consider results of SAT Subject Tests, if submitted."

SELECTIVITY

Admissions Rating	83
# of applicants	11,235
% of applicants accepted	74
% of acceptees attending	22

FRESHMAN PROFILE

Range SAT Critical Reading	530–630
Range SAT Math	540–630
Minimum paper TOEFL	550
Minimum computer TOEFL	213
Minimum web-based TOEFL	80
% graduated top 10% of class	29.5
% graduated top 25% of class	65.7
% graduated top 50% of class	93.4

DEADLINES

Regular	
Deadline	2/1
Notification	rolling
Nonfall registration?	yes

APPLICANTS ALSO LOOK AT

AND OFTEN PREFER
New York University
Northeastern University
Boston University
Syracuse University

AND SOMETIMES PREFER
Cornell University
University of Vermont
Penn State—University Park

AND RARELY PREFER
University of New Hampshire
Skidmore College
State University of New York at Geneseo

FINANCIAL FACTS

Financial Aid Rating	82
Annual tuition	$30,606
Room and board	$11,162
Books and supplies	$1,130
% frosh rec. need-based scholarship or grant aid	66
% UG rec. need-based scholarship or grant aid	58
% frosh rec. non-need-based scholarship or grant aid	20
% UG rec. non-need-based scholarship or grant aid	14
% frosh rec. need-based self-help aid	60
% UG rec. need-based self-help aid	57
% frosh rec. any financial aid	90
% UG rec. any financial aid	85

JAMES MADISON UNIVERSITY

SONNER HALL, MSC 0101, HARRISONBURG, VA 22807 • ADMISSIONS: 540-568-5681 • FAX: 540-568-3332

CAMPUS LIFE
Quality of Life Rating	**93**
Fire Safety Rating	**67**
Green Rating	**93**
Type of school	public
Environment	town

STUDENTS
Total undergrad enrollment	16,108
% male/female	40/60
% from out of state	30
% live on campus	36
% in (# of) fraternities	10 (14)
% in (# of) sororities	12 (9)
% African American	4
% Asian	5
% Caucasian	83
% Hispanic	2
% international	1
# of countries represented	64

SURVEY SAYS . . .
Athletic facilities are great
Students are friendly
Great food on campus
Students are happy
Student publications are popular
Lots of beer drinking

ACADEMICS
Academic Rating	**77**
Calendar	semester
Student/faculty ratio	16:1
Profs interesting rating	82
Profs accessible rating	82
% classes taught by TAs	2
Most common reg class size	20–29 students
Most common lab size	20–29 students

MOST POPULAR MAJORS
psychology
finance
health and physical education

STUDENTS SAY ". . ."

Academics
Offering "great facilities and great prospects for the future" through "tons of valuable experiences such as a great study abroad program and internships," Virginia's James Madison University "prepares students for the future" with a mix of broad-ranging general education requirements and career-oriented majors. Students grumble about the "gen eds," which require classes in the arts, humanities, and sciences and consume about one-third of all undergraduate credits. But students also admire the school's commitment to "educating students in all areas, not just a] major concentration" and concede that the classes provide "foundation knowledge every graduating student should have." Standout offerings here include undergraduate business, education, and music programs; the School of Media Arts and Design; and the School of Communications. Students also tell us that "The study abroad program at JMU is fabulous" and that "A large number of students study abroad" thanks to an "absolutely flawless" Office of International Programs. JMU's "very good and unique" Integrated Science and Technology (ISAT) program emphasizes cross-disciplinary problem solving and innovation that are "applicable to the real world." All students here benefit from "great recruitment fairs and internship opportunities," "small classes," professors who "go out of their way to help you understand a concept," and administrators who "strive to meet the demands of students and have undertaken many projects around campus to help with the overwhelming expansion of the student body."

Life
"There's tons to keep people occupied on campus" at JMU, including the campus hangout Taylor Down Under (a place "to catch up with one another, grab a smoothie or some coffee, attend events like open mic night or watch the comedy club, etc."), the Graffton Theater ("which shows two different movies each week" at a $2.50 admission price), "sports, bands, frats, a cappella shows, interest groups, everything that a huge university offers but that here is really accessible to everyone"). In addition, there is "a significant amount happening off campus." "A bus line takes you to all the different apartments day and night" as well as "to the different restaurants, the close Wal-Mart, tanning salons, and local mall." In warm weather, "students flock to the quad to sunbathe, play guitar, and play Frisbee" or "go on day trips to go kayaking, rafting, horseback riding etc. through UREC...or swimming in Blue Hole." Off-campus apartments are home to a robust party scene; reports one undergrad, "For fun, people party. Sunday though Wednesday people are involved in school and their clubs and study. Then Thursday through Saturday it's house parties. The beer is free...just with the understanding that when you get a house and you are 21 you flip the bill once or twice." Hometown Harrisonburg "is a great town" with "lots of excellent restaurants, outdoor opportunities, and a great music scene," but "the Harrisonburg community conflicts with the students due to the weekend partying."

Student Body
The face of JMU may well be the "Ugg-Northface-pearls-sweatpants-wearing sorority girl" (one student observes that "That's difficult to get past with the 60:40 ratio of females to males"), but those who dig deeper discover "different crowds" clustered about campus. "A lot of student at JMU are prep kids from up north, but...there is also a great downtown crowd made up of very creative and artistic people. There is a group for everyone." Undergrads tend to be "involved in multiple organizations and clubs while balancing a substantial course load. We tend to be go-getters, we're very motivated to succeed, and we love any and everything JMU." And while the campus "is not known for being as politically involved as larger institutions, JMU finds its niche in community service. Service organizations are extremely popular at JMU, especially the Alternative Spring Break trips (these are so popular, a raffle system has been implemented to cope with the demand)." The student body is "pretty white," and "Although the Center for Multicultural Student Services has a definite voice on campus, whites seem to significantly outnumber other races. In recent years, an effort seems to have been made to diversify campus."

304 ■ THE BEST 368 COLLEGES

FINANCIAL AID: 540-568-7820 • E-MAIL: GOTOJMU@JMU.EDU • WEBSITE: WWW.JMU.EDU

THE PRINCETON REVIEW SAYS

Admissions

Very important factors considered include: Academic GPA, rigor of secondary school record. *Important factors considered include:* Standardized test scores. *Other factors considered include:* Class rank, application essay, recommendation(s), alumni/ae relation, character/personal qualities, extracurricular activities, geographical residence, state residency, talent/ability, volunteer work, work experience. SAT or ACT required; TOEFL required of all international applicants. High school diploma is required and GED is accepted. *Academic units required:* 4 English, 4 mathematics, 3 science, (3 science labs), 3 social studies. *Academic units recommended:* 4 English, 4 mathematics, 4 science, (4 science labs), 3 foreign language, 4 social studies.

Financial Aid

Students should submit: FAFSA. The Princeton Review suggests that all financial aid forms be submitted as soon as possible after January 1. *Need-based scholarships/grants offered:* Federal Pell, SEOG, state scholarships/grants, private scholarships, the school's own gift aid. *Loan aid offered:* FFEL Subsidized Stafford, FFEL Unsubsidized Stafford, FFEL PLUS, Federal Perkins Applicants will be notified of awards on a rolling basis beginning 4/1. Federal Work-Study Program available. Institutional employment available. Off-campus job opportunities are good.

The Inside Word

Virginia boasts one of the most robust public undergraduate education systems in the nation. James Madison ranks third in most students' preference behind University of Virginia and the College of William and Mary, but third place in that company is far from shabby. The school is large enough to accommodate all those who weren't quite solid enough to gain entry to choices one and two. Virginia students are competitive enough that you still need solidly above-average grades and test scores to sail through JMU's admissions process.

THE SCHOOL SAYS "..."

From The Admissions Office

"James Madison University's philosophy of inclusiveness—known as 'all together one'—means that students become a part of a real community that nurtures its own to learn, grow, and succeed. Our professors, many of whom have a wealth of real-world experience, pride themselves on making teaching their top priority. We take seriously the responsibility to maintain an environment that fosters learning and encourages students to excel in and out of the classroom. Our rich variety of educational, social, and extracurricular activities include more than 100 innovative and traditional undergraduate majors and programs, a well-established study abroad program, a cutting-edge information security program, more than 280 student clubs and organizations, and a 147,000-square-foot, state-of-the-art recreation center. The university's picturesque, self-contained campus is located in the heart of the Shenandoah Valley, a four-season area that's easy to call home. Great food, fun times, exciting intercollegiate athletics, and rigorous academics all combine to create the unique James Madison experience. From the library to the residence halls and from our outstanding honors program to our highly successful career placement program, the university is committed to equipping our students with the tools they need to achieve their dreams.

"The new SAT will be used starting with the freshman applicants for Fall 2008. High school students graduating in 2006 or 2007 will have the option of submitting scores from either the new or old versions of the SAT. The highest composite score will be used in admissions decisions."

SELECTIVITY

Admissions Rating	88
# of applicants	18,352
% of applicants accepted	64
% of acceptees attending	33
# accepting a place on wait list	845
% admitted from wait list	31

FRESHMAN PROFILE

Range SAT Critical Reading	520–610
Range SAT Math	530–620
Range SAT Writing	520–610
Range ACT Composite	22–26
Minimum paper TOEFL	550
Minimum computer TOEFL	213
Minimum web-based TOEFL	80-81
Average HS GPA	3.71
% graduated top 10% of class	29
% graduated top 25% of class	75
% graduated top 50% of class	98

DEADLINES

Early action	
Deadline	11/1
Notification	1/15
Regular	
Priority	11/1
Deadline	1/15
Notification	4/1
Nonfall registration?	no

APPLICANTS ALSO LOOK AT

AND OFTEN PREFER
University of Virginia
College of William and Mary

AND SOMETIMES PREFER
University of Delaware
Virginia Tech
University of Maryland—College Park
George Mason University

FINANCIAL FACTS

Financial Aid Rating	64
Annual in-state tuition	$6,964
% frosh rec. need-based scholarship or grant aid	16
% UG rec. need-based scholarship or grant aid	13
% frosh rec. non-need-based scholarship or grant aid	11
% UG rec. non-need-based scholarship or grant aid	7
% frosh rec. need-based self-help aid	29
% UG rec. need-based self-help aid	22
% frosh rec. athletic scholarships	2
% UG rec. athletic scholarships	2
% frosh rec. any financial aid	54
% UG rec. any financial aid	52
% UG borrow to pay for school	48
Average cumulative indebtedness	$16,546

Johns Hopkins University

3400 North Charles Street/140 Garland, Baltimore, MD 21218 • Admissions: 410-516-8171 • Fax: 410-516-6025

CAMPUS LIFE

Quality of Life Rating	68
Fire Safety Rating	70
Green Rating	60*
Type of school	private
Environment	metropolis

STUDENTS

Total undergrad enrollment	4,578
% male/female	52/48
% from out of state	85
% live on campus	60
% in (# of) fraternities	21 (11)
% in (# of) sororities	22 (7)
% African American	6
% Asian	25
% Caucasian	46
% Hispanic	7
% Native American	1
% international	5
# of countries represented	71

SURVEY SAYS . . .

Lab facilities are great
Great computer facilities
Great library
Athletic facilities are great
Diverse student types on campus
Lots of beer drinking

ACADEMICS

Academic Rating	86
Calendar	4/1/4
Profs interesting rating	61
Profs accessible rating	68
Most common reg class size	10–19 students
Most common lab size	10–19 students

MOST POPULAR MAJORS

biomedical/medical engineering
economics
international relations and affairs

STUDENTS SAY ". . ."

Academics

Johns Hopkins University is a premed powerhouse and one of the nation's great producers of tomorrow's prominent doctors and medical researchers. Boasting one of the "top research [hospitals] in the country," the country's "number-one undergraduate biomedical engineering program," and "the number-one school for public health studies," it's no wonder JHU draws so many aspiring doctors that students sometimes think "Almost everyone is premed." That misconception is one of the reasons JHU's many other strengths are often overlooked. Those strengths are many, including "a fantastic international studies program," a highly respected Writing Seminar that "is paving the way for liberal arts on this science-dominated campus," a School of Engineering that offers students "amazing research experience," and "a wonderful relationship with the Peabody Conservatory for those seriously interested in music." No matter what they study, students at JHU inhabit "an intense academic environment that works hard to make us the best applicants we can be for grad school while teaching us how to be a part of a global community." Research is "a big highlight here"; as one student explains, "JHU was the first research university in the U.S.A.," and you'll find "a lot of [research] opportunities" from freshman year on. What you won't find is a lot of hand-holding, since "Hopkins is an institution where students are given a wide range of freedom with their classes and with their social life, but more importantly, it teaches students to be responsible for their own actions and decisions, both academically and socially."

Life

"Johns Hopkins has a reputation for being a living hell; however, it is actually quite nice," students assure us. One explains, "It is true that we have a very rigorous academic program, but that does not prevent us from having fun and enjoying the many activities and enjoyments that are offered by the school and the neighborhood. The frats and sororities are quite active but not ridiculous; there are many trendy areas in Baltimore with good bars, restaurants, and clubs; and there are many events on campus ranging from a cappella concerts to lectures from prominent political figures to concerts by artists like Guster and Talib Kweli." Hometown Baltimore "gets a bad rep" (if you watch HBO's The Wire, you know what that rep is) "but there is a lot to do in and around campus. There is tons of shopping, and lots of really good restaurants to eat at in the city." There's also "a good band scene, as well as really cheap baseball tickets." All in all, "It's a very fun city." For fun on campus, "Students normally go to frat parties." JHU has some "great Division I sports teams"—men's lacrosse and soccer are always highly ranked—and the student body regularly rallies to their support. The "beautiful" campus is a short walk from the Baltimore Museum of Art, a great place to blow off steam when the pressures of school start to build, and "is free for students."

Student Body

JHU students aren't sure "whether there is such a thing as one typical student here, because there is a strong division between engineering and arts and science students." That said, "Most students work hard and play hard." There are "lots of complaints about the workload, but people are secretly proud of the work they do." Many here "are intensely competitive," which is a "reflection of the pressure they feel on campus," but "It is a myth that Hopkins is filled with cutthroat nerds." Though "it is a stressful atmosphere at times because students want to get ahead, most of the students are very helpful and nice." Demographically speaking, "There are all kinds of people here, which means that everyone can fit in. No matter what kind of person someone may appear to be on the outside, you know that if they're at Hopkins they must be pretty nerdy on the inside, so there's a kind of camaraderie there." Most students "are a little of everything, and it seems like everyone here is exceptional at something."

FINANCIAL AID: 410-516-8028 • E-MAIL: GOTOJHU@JHU.EDU • WEBSITE: WWW.JHU.EDU

THE PRINCETON REVIEW SAYS

Admissions

Very important factors considered include: Academic GPA, recommendation(s), rigor of secondary school record, character/personal qualities. *Important factors considered include:* Class rank, application essay, standardized test scores, extracurricular activities, talent/ability, volunteer work, work experience. *Other factors considered include:* Alumni/ae relation, first generation, geographical residence, interview, racial/ethnic status, state residency, SAT or ACT required; SAT and SAT Subject Tests or ACT recommended; ACT with Writing component required. High school diploma or equivalent is not required. *Academic units recommended:* 4 English, 4 mathematics, 4 science, 4 foreign language, 2 social studies, 2 history, 2 foreign language for engineering majors.

Financial Aid

Students should submit: FAFSA, CSS/Financial Aid PROFILE, noncustodial PROFILE, business/farm supplement, prior and current year federal tax returns. Regular filing deadline is 2/15. The Princeton Review suggests that all financial aid forms be submitted as soon as possible after January 1. *Need-based scholarships/grants offered:* Federal Pell, SEOG, state scholarships/grants, private scholarships, the school's own gift aid. *Loan aid offered:* Direct Subsidized Stafford, Direct Unsubsidized Stafford, FFEL PLUS, Federal Perkins, college/university loans from institutional funds. Applicants will be notified of awards on or about 4/1. Federal Work-Study Program available. Institutional employment available.

The Inside Word

Top schools like Hopkins receive more and more applications every year and, as a result, grow harder and harder to get into. With nearly 14,000 applicants for the class of 2010, Hopkins had to reject numerous applicants who were thoroughly qualified. Give your application everything you've got, and don't take it personally if you don't get a fat envelope in the mail.

THE SCHOOL SAYS "..."

From The Admissions Office

"The Hopkins tradition of preeminent academic excellence naturally attracts the very best students in the nation and from around the world. The Admissions Committee carefully examines each application for evidence of compelling intellectual interest and academic performance as well as strong personal recommendations and meaningful extracurricular contributions. Every applicant who matriculates to Johns Hopkins University was found qualified by the Admissions Committee through a 'whole person' assessment, and every applicant accepted for admission is fully expected to graduate. The Admissions Committee determines whom they believe will take full advantage of the exceptional opportunities offered at Hopkins, contribute the most to the educational process of the institution, and be the most successful in using what they have learned and experienced for the benefit of society.

"Freshman applicants for Fall 2008 may take either the old SAT and three SAT Subject Tests (one must be Writing) or the ACT. Alternatively, students may take either the new SAT or the ACT with Writing component. For those submitting SAT scores, submitting scores from three SAT Subject Tests is recommended."

SELECTIVITY

Admissions Rating	98
# of applicants	14,848
% of applicants accepted	24
% of acceptees attending	33
# accepting a place on wait list	1,319
% admitted from wait list	3
# of early decision applicants	997
% accepted early decision	45

FRESHMAN PROFILE

Range SAT Critical Reading	630–730
Range SAT Math	660–770
Range SAT Writing	630–730
Range ACT Composite	28–33
Average HS GPA	3.7
% graduated top 10% of class	82
% graduated top 25% of class	97
% graduated top 50% of class	100

DEADLINES

Early decision	
Deadline	11/1
Notification	12/15
Regular	
Deadline	1/1
Notification	4/1
Nonfall registration?	no

FINANCIAL FACTS

Financial Aid Rating	93
Annual tuition	$33,000
% frosh rec.	
any financial aid	47
% UG rec. any financial aid	46

JUNIATA COLLEGE

1700 MOORE STREET, HUNTINGDON, PA 16652 • ADMISSIONS: 814-641-3420 • FAX: 814-641-3100

STUDENTS SAY "..."

Academics

Juniata College has catapulted from regional to national status in the past decade on the strength of its great natural science programs, housed in the 88,000-square-foot state-of-the-art Von Liebig Center for Science (VLCS) that opened its doors in 2002. Students tell us that while Juniata "is centered around a very tough but rewarding science program," science is hardly the only game in town. The "business, theatre, and education departments are strong, too." Another student explains, "Other departments are beginning to receive support from trustees and alumni now that VLCS is complete. Several buildings will be undergoing renovations to allow for the expansion of the humanities and social sciences." Business, in particular, seems likely to receive a lot of attention as it is among the school's most popular disciplines. Undergrads tout JC's "great entrepreneurial program...where all students are encouraged to start their own businesses and some are given start-up cash." Education is also popular. Students appreciate that they are "given a practicum their first semester freshman year," meaning that "if they don't like being in the classroom, they can change their major right away." "At most other schools, you have to wait until your junior year to get some classroom experience," says a student. Other perks of a Juniata education include the prominence of the study abroad program and that "students are afforded the option to create their own major (Program of Emphasis), which allows us to explore many possibilities that would otherwise be restricted by a designated major."

Life

Juniata "is located in Huntingdon, PA, which is a tiny town in the middle of nowhere, thirty minutes south of State College," so "needless to say, there is not a lot to do off-campus." Fortunately, "The Juniata Activities Board (JAB) brings numerous acts to campus: comedians, musicians, hypnotists, magicians." The campus also hosts "various weekend parties, but they normally don't happen until Saturday nights because a large population of the student body is active in athletics and they have games either Friday night or Saturday afternoon." Since Juniata "doesn't have any Greek societies," students compensate by being "active in many clubs, including the Agriculture Club, Health Occupations Students of America, Student Government, the Equine Club, and the Student Alumni Association." Otherwise, quiet fun ("video games and movie watching are very popular") dominates. One student explains, "The people who are dissatisfied with Juniata were definitely expecting something else, usually something more along the lines of Penn State."

Student Body

Juniata "is notoriously middle class and Caucasian" with "very few minority students." Diversity arrives in the form of "a vast number of international students, both in semester and year-long exchange programs and as four year degree-seeking students. The international presence at Juniata does a lot for class debate, and often opens the eyes of otherwise typically American students to the perspectives of those from other nations." Undergrads here "work hard for their grades. They want to excel. Basically, they're motivated and determined to succeed in the real world," to the point that they often "choose to do homework and study above most other activities." Ultimately, "A typical student is really studious and really cares about their education. Everyone is able to find their own clique in which they fit into and feel comfortable."

FINANCIAL AID: 814-641-3142 • E-MAIL: INFO@JUNIATA.EDU • WEBSITE: WWW.JUNIATA.EDU

THE PRINCETON REVIEW SAYS

Admissions

Very important factors considered include: Application essay, academic GPA, recommendation(s), rigor of secondary school record, standardized test scores, character/personal qualities. *Important factors considered include:* Extracurricular activities, first generation, interview, talent/ability, volunteer work. *Other factors considered include:* Alumni/ae relation, geographical residence, level of applicant's interest, state residency, SAT or ACT recommended; TOEFL required of all international applicants. High school diploma is required and GED is accepted. *Academic units required:* 4 English, 3 mathematics, 3 science, (2 science labs), 2 foreign language, 1 social studies, 3 history. *Academic units recommended:* 4 English, 4 mathematics, 4 science, 2 foreign language, 1 social studies, 3 history.

Financial Aid

Students should submit: FAFSA. Regular filing deadline is 3/1. The Princeton Review suggests that all financial aid forms be submitted as soon as possible after January 1. *Need-based scholarships/grants offered:* Federal Pell, SEOG, state scholarships/grants, private scholarships, the school's own gift aid. *Loan aid offered:* FFEL Subsidized Stafford, FFEL Unsubsidized Stafford, FFEL PLUS, Federal Perkins, college/university loans from institutional funds. Applicants will be notified of awards on a rolling basis beginning 2/21. Federal Work-Study Program available. Institutional employment available. Off-campus job opportunities are good.

The Inside Word

As at many traditional liberal arts schools, the admissions process at Juniata is a personal one. Applications are scoured for evidence that the student is committed to attending Juniata and to remaining there for the full four years. The school is best known for its premedical programs, meaning that applicants to these programs will have the highest hurdles to clear.

THE SCHOOL SAYS "..."

From The Admissions Office

"Juniata's unique approach to learning has a flexible, student-centered focus. With the help of two advisors, over half of Juniata's students design their own majors (called the "Program of Emphasis" or "POE"). Those who choose a more traditional academic journey still benefit from the assistance of two faculty advisors and interdisciplinary collaboration between multiple academic departments.

"In addition, all students benefit from the recent, significant investments in academic facilities that help students actively learn by doing. For example, the new Halbritter Performing Arts Center houses an innovative theater program where theater professionals work side by side with students; the Sill Business Incubator provides $5,000 in seed capital to students with a desire to start their own business; the LEEDS-certified Shuster Environmental Studies Field Station, located on nearby Raystown Lake, gives unparalleled hands-on study opportunities to students; and the von Liebig Center for Science provides opportunities for student/faculty research surpassing those available at even large universities.

"As the 2003 Middle States Accreditation Team noted, 'Juniata is truly a student-centered college. There is a remarkable cohesiveness in this commitment—faculty, students, trustees, staff, and alumni, each from their own vantage point, describe a community in which the growth of the student is central.' This cohesiveness creates a dynamic learning environment that enables students to think and grow intellectually, to evolve in their academic careers, and to graduate as active, successful participants in the global community.

"Freshman applicants for Fall 2008 may submit either the new SAT (or the ACT with the Writing component) or the old (before March 2005) SAT (or ACT); we will use their best scores from either test. "

SELECTIVITY

Admissions Rating	89
# of applicants	1,958
% of applicants accepted	67
% of acceptees attending	29
# of early decision applicants	33
% accepted early decision	94

FRESHMAN PROFILE

Range SAT Critical Reading	525–630
Range SAT Math	540–630
Minimum paper TOEFL	550
Minimum computer TOEFL	213
Average HS GPA	3.78
% graduated top 10% of class	36
% graduated top 25% of class	77
% graduated top 50% of class	99

DEADLINES

Early decision	
Deadline	12/1
Notification	12/31
Early action	
Deadline	1/1
Notification	1/31
Regular	
Priority	12/1
Deadline	3/15
Notification	2/28
Nonfall registration?	yes

APPLICANTS ALSO LOOK AT
AND OFTEN PREFER
Bucknell University
AND SOMETIMES PREFER
Pennsylvania State University
Gettysburg College
Allegheny College
AND RARELY PREFER
Lebanon Valley College
Elizabethtown College

FINANCIAL FACTS

Financial Aid Rating	80
Annual tuition	$29,610
Room and board	$8,420
Required fees	$670
Books and supplies	$600
% frosh rec. need-based scholarship or grant aid	72
% UG rec. need-based scholarship or grant aid	71
% frosh rec. non-need-based scholarship or grant aid	71
% UG rec. non-need-based scholarship or grant aid	64
% frosh rec. need-based self-help aid	59
% UG rec. need-based self-help aid	62
% frosh rec. any financial aid	99
% UG rec. any financial aid	99
% UG borrow to pay for school	83.75
Average cumulative indebtedness	$21,426

KALAMAZOO COLLEGE

1200 ACADEMY STREET, KALAMAZOO, MI 49006 • ADMISSIONS: 269-337-7166 • FAX: 269-337-7390

CAMPUS LIFE

Quality of Life Rating	**80**
Fire Safety Rating	**60***
Green Rating	**84**
Type of school	private
Environment	city

STUDENTS

Total undergrad enrollment	1,340
% male/female	42/58
% from out of state	31
% from public high school	85
% live on campus	77
% African American	4
% Asian	6
% Caucasian	77
% Hispanic	4
% international	1
# of countries represented	20

SURVEY SAYS . . .

Large classes
No one cheats
Great library
Frats and sororities are unpopular or nonexistent

ACADEMICS

Academic Rating	**91**
Calendar	quarter
Student/faculty ratio	13:1
Profs interesting rating	95
Profs accessible rating	89
Most common reg class size	10–19 students
Most common lab size	10–19 students

MOST POPULAR MAJORS

English
psychology
economics
business

STUDENTS SAY " . . ."

Academics

Kalamazoo College "is all about the K-Plan and giving students the best liberal arts education possible." The K-Plan consists of two mandatory components (a core liberal arts curriculum and a Senior Individualized Project) and two voluntary components (externships/internships and study abroad) that the majority of students pursue. Students say the K-Plan makes Kalamazoo "the epitome of experiential education," starting with the optional Land/Sea first-year orientation experience, a team-building exercise that involves hiking, canoeing, climbing, and rappelling, and continuing with an "off-campus internship sophomore year, study abroad junior year, and a senior project before you graduate!" From beginning to end, it's a "very hands-on education." As at many selective small schools, rigorous academics are delivered by "a faculty who shares in the interests of the student" amid "an awesome collection of competitive but supportive peers." The intensity is ratcheted up somewhat by Kalamazoo's accelerated academic calendar; operating on a quarter system means that "courses last only 10 weeks" and "Everything moves extremely quickly. There's a lot of work involved." In other words, this place "is not a playground." Some feel the workload is a bit too much and feel a reduction would mean "less reading but more thinking," and even those who appreciate the challenge concede that "B's at K are like A's at other schools."

Life

Life at Kalamazoo is, "at the most basic level, heavily focused around academics. Everything else is just gravy." That's not to say that there aren't "a great many opportunities in which to take part," but rather that "before [you do any of that], you have to finish your homework" which is usually substantial. When the books are finally closed, "There are always events going on either here or at Western Michigan University [also in Kalamazoo], and nearly everyone at K is part of some club or organization. Political organizations like Campus Republicans and Campus Democrats are very popular, as is our Gay and Lesbian group, Kaleidoscope." Students say, "Choir and sports like tennis are also popular here. Our Theater Department is small but dedicated." And let's not forget the CGC, "the Childish Games Commission, where students play red rover, dodgeball, zombie tag, and jump in leaf piles. It gives us an excuse to goof around for an hour or two and a break from school work." Many here tell us that "Kalamazoo is a great town to live in. We are lucky to be a part of a real, thriving community, with which we can interact through service-learning, jobs, or even shopping and entertainment. There are theater productions, concerts, and festivals year-round." When students want a more conventional undergrad party scene, they head to the "keggers" happening "any day of the week" over at WMU.

Student Body

Kalamazoo students tend to be extremely bright and a little high strung, to the point that many are at least one standard deviation from the norm. As one undergrad puts it, "My friend has this theory: There is a secret question on the application that no one remembers answering. The question is 'On a scale of 1 to 10, 10 being the oddest, how odd are you?' If you don't score at least a 5, you don't get in." Mostly, "Students here are very smart and nice, but a little on the awkward anti-social side." Other, smaller demographics on campus include "the rich, party types who take blow-off classes and get all C's," the "people who can balance work and play but tend to be the type of people who enjoy a game of 'zombie tag'," the fervent feminists, and "the gay community, [which is] very strong, active, and supportive."

FINANCIAL AID: 269-337-7192 • E-MAIL: ADMISSION@KZOO.EDU • WEBSITE: WWW.KZOO.EDU

THE PRINCETON REVIEW SAYS

Admissions

Very important factors considered include: Academic GPA, rigor of secondary school record, standardized test scores, extracurricular activities, talent/ability. *Important factors considered include:* Class rank, application essay, recommendation(s), character/personal qualities, volunteer work, work experience. *Other factors considered include:* Alumni/ae relation, first generation, geographical residence, interview, level of applicant's interest, racial/ethnic status, state residency, SAT or ACT required; ACT with Writing component required. TOEFL required of all international applicants. High school diploma is required and GED is accepted. *Academic units recommended:* 4 English, 3 mathematics, 3 science, 3 foreign language, 3 social studies.

Financial Aid

Students should submit: FAFSA, institution's own financial aid form. The Princeton Review suggests that all financial aid forms be submitted as soon as possible after January 1. *Need-based scholarships/grants offered:* Federal Pell, SEOG, state scholarships/grants, private scholarships, the school's own gift aid. *Loan aid offered:* Direct Subsidized Stafford, Direct Unsubsidized Stafford, Direct PLUS, Federal Perkins, state loans Applicants will be notified of awards on a rolling basis beginning mid-March. Federal Work-Study Program available. Institutional employment available. Off-campus job opportunities are good.

The Inside Word

Kalamazoo offers early decision and one round of early action, indicating that the school works aggressively to fill its incoming class as early in the admissions process as possible. If you are dead certain you want to attend Kalamazoo, apply early decision. If the school is among your top choices, consider applying early action; your application will probably receive a slightly more generous review than will those that arrive later in the admission process.

THE SCHOOL SAYS ". . ."

From The Admissions Office

"Anyone can pursue any component of the K-Plan at any college, but it is rare to see the purposeful integration and high participation rate found at Kalamazoo. Over the last 50 years, 85 percent of our graduates have formally studied in another country while 80 percent have completed an internship or externship, and 100 percent complete a senior project. Our students often pursue international internships and senior project experiences, in addition to their planned study abroad terms. Also, Kalamazoo is one of the few selective liberal arts colleges to be found in a city—the Kalamazoo metro area has a population of approximately 240,000 with the advantage of being near a university of nearly 30,000 students. It is a diverse and vibrant community with wonderful access to the arts, athletics, service-learning, and community-service opportunities. We are a small and personal college with bigger opportunities.

"Kalamazoo College is one of 40 colleges selected to be in Loren Pope's popular book, *Colleges That Change Lives.* Loren selected Kalamazoo and the other 39 colleges based on reasonable cost, unique programs and curricula, and cocurricular activities that all contribute to dramatically changing the lives of those students who find us.

"An SAT or ACT score is required for admission; SAT Subject Tests are not. Because the writing portions of the SAT and ACT are new and still being evaluated, we have not yet determined what weight writing will hold in our decisions. Students taking only the ACT must take the writing portion."

SELECTIVITY

Admissions Rating	89
# of applicants	2,092
% of applicants accepted	63
% of acceptees attending	28
# accepting a place on wait list	130
% admitted from wait list	22
# of early decision applicants	17
% accepted early decision	100

FRESHMAN PROFILE

Range SAT Critical Reading	580–690
Range SAT Math	570–680
Range ACT Composite	26–30
Minimum paper TOEFL	550
Minimum computer TOEFL	213
Average HS GPA	3.63
% graduated top 10% of class	44
% graduated top 25% of class	75
% graduated top 50% of class	98

DEADLINES

Early decision	
Deadline	11/10
Notification	11/20
Early action	
Deadline	11/20
Notification	12/20
Regular	
Priority	2/1
Deadline	2/1
Notification	4/1
Nonfall registration?	no

APPLICANTS ALSO LOOK AT

AND OFTEN PREFER
University of Michigan—Ann Arbor
Dartmouth College

AND SOMETIMES PREFER
University of Notre Dame
Oberlin College

AND RARELY PREFER
Hope College

FINANCIAL FACTS

Financial Aid Rating	70
Annual tuition	$30,723
% frosh rec. need-based scholarship or grant aid	52
% UG rec. need-based scholarship or grant aid	50
% frosh rec. non-need-based scholarship or grant aid	52
% UG rec. non-need-based scholarship or grant aid	52
% frosh rec. need-based self-help aid	40
% UG rec. need-based self-help aid	45
% frosh rec. any financial aid	98
% UG rec. any financial aid	98
% UG borrow to pay for school	66
Average cumulative indebtedness	$24,655

KANSAS STATE UNIVERSITY

119 ANDERSON HALL, MANHATTAN, KS 66506 • ADMISSIONS: 800-432-8270 OR 785-532-6250 • FAX: 785-532-6393

CAMPUS LIFE
Quality of Life Rating	**95**
Fire Safety Rating	**64**
Green Rating	**60***
Type of school	public
Environment	village

STUDENTS
Total undergrad enrollment	18,235
% male/female	52/48
% from out of state	14
% from public high school	81
% live on campus	37
% in (# of) fraternities	20 (28)
% in (# of) sororities	20 (16)
% African American	3
% Asian	1
% Caucasian	86
% Hispanic	3
% Native American	1
% international	2
# of countries represented	111

SURVEY SAYS . . .
Great library
Students are friendly
Everyone loves the Wildcats
Lots of beer drinking

ACADEMICS
Academic Rating	**74**
Calendar	semester
Student/faculty ratio	20:1
Profs interesting rating	73
Profs accessible rating	76
% classes taught by TAs	17
Most common	
reg class size	10–19 students

MOST POPULAR MAJORS
mechanical engineering

STUDENTS SAY ". . ."

Academics
"Underrated" and tremendously affordable Kansas State University is "a big school with a small school feel." Agriculture will always be prevalent here but there are nine colleges and "over 250 majors and options." Other "marquee programs" include engineering, the hard sciences, and a "grueling" architecture program. The library is "amazing." The faculty is "a mixed bag." "Some instructors you'll love and some you won't be able to stand," says a microbiology major. Intro and general education courses can be on the large side. They're "awkward and usually just rehash information from the textbook." "We struggle with graduate teaching assistants, especially those whose first language is not English," notes a political science major. In upper division courses, "it becomes easier to cultivate a relationship with your professor." Administratively, "the school is a pretty well oiled machine." Management is full of "gifted people who genuinely love K-State" and "students have a large say in everything the university does." Also, the top brass is ultra-accessible for such a large institution. The president frequently rides his bike around campus "in his purple sweat suit." In some areas, though, red tape is unavoidable. "If you change your major here," cautions a junior, "you're pretty much screwed as far as trying to graduate on time."

Life
The residence halls could use some sprucing up and some buildings "are about to crumble" but this "very compact" campus is "easy to navigate" and "beautiful in every season." KSU offers a "laidback atmosphere" and "an extensive variety of clubs." "Movies on the lawn are fun." "Greek life is also huge and is responsible for a multitude of events." Hordes of students are "sports crazy." Intramurals are popular and "cheering on the 'Cats is a must." In the fall, "people are obsessed with K-State football." "During game day weekends, the whole town is dressed in purple." "I do get tired of hearing about the football team 24/7," admits a senior, "but whatever." Beyond campus, Manhattan is a "great college town." It's "just big enough and everything you need for college life is available" including "a decent party scene." House parties and frat parties are common but most students head to Aggieville, the Little Apple's "famous" bar district. K-Staters call it "four square blocks of fun" and "one of the greatest places on earth." Watering holes are "usually full on the weekends" and, "a lot of times, a weeknight at the bars can be even more fun." "Every college student should experience Aggieville," recommends one proud junior.

Student Body
The "hardworking and honest" students at K-State tell us they bask in "country hospitality." "The students are the friendliest in the country," asserts a senior. "You cannot walk through campus without people smiling or acknowledging you"—"not in that creepy, stalker way, but the way that makes you feel warm and fuzzy inside." The "typical Midwestern" population here mostly comes in two varieties. There are the "yokels" and "farm boys from small towns in Kansas." There are also the kids from "suburban white neighborhoods" in Kansas City and Wichita. You'll see "punk rock kids," "cowboys in Wranglers," and "the occasional hippie" but "they form their own weird groups." For the most part, the vibe is "very homogeneous" and "hopelessly vanilla." "The vast majority of the students looks, dresses, and acts the same." Politically, K-State "tends towards conservatism." On the whole, though, these students "generally represent the middle of the road in nearly every American way of thought." As for minority enrollment, it's pretty low and many K-Staters lament "the lack of diversity." On the other hand, what can you do? "I understand why certain ethnicities would not choose a school in the middle of nowhere," admits one student.

FINANCIAL AID: 877-817-2287 OR 785-532-6420 • E-MAIL: K-STATE@K-STATE.EDU • WEBSITE: CONSIDER.K-STATE.EDU

THE PRINCETON REVIEW SAYS

Admissions

Very important factors considered include: Class rank, academic GPA, rigor of secondary school record, standardized test scores. *Other factors considered include:* Recommendation(s), SAT recommended; SAT or ACT recommended; ACT recommended; High school diploma is required and GED is accepted. *Academic units recommended:* 4 English, 3 mathematics, 3 science, 2 social studies, 1 history, 1 computer technology.

Financial Aid

Students should submit: FAFSA. The Princeton Review suggests that all financial aid forms be submitted as soon as possible after January 1. *Need-based scholarships/grants offered:* Federal Pell, SEOG, state scholarships/grants, private scholarships, the school's own gift aid. *Loan aid offered:* Direct Subsidized Stafford, Direct Unsubsidized Stafford, Direct PLUS, FFEL Subsidized Stafford, FFEL Unsubsidized Stafford, FFEL PLUS, Federal Perkins, college/university loans from institutional funds, Alternative Student Loans. Applicants will be notified of awards on a rolling basis beginning 4/1.

The Inside Word

Though K-State is chock full of strong students, admission is very undemanding. The process here is also refreshingly straightforward. Basically, get a 21 on the ACT or graduate in the top third of your high school class, and you're in. If you are a Kansas resident, a third way to get accepted is to complete a college-bound curriculum with a 2.0 GPA. Nonresidents need at least a 2.5.

THE SCHOOL SAYS ". . ."

From The Admissions Office

"Kansas State University offers strong academic programs, a lively intellectual atmosphere, a friendly campus community, and an environment where students achieve: K-State's total of Rhodes, Marshall, Truman, Goldwater, and Udall scholars since 1986 ranks first in the nation among state universities. In the Goldwater competition, only Princeton, Harvard, and Duke have produced more winners. K-State's student government was named best in the nation in 1997 and 1995. The forensics squad finished seventh in the 2005 national tournament. A K-State team finished in the top eight at the national debate tournament in 2003. Research facilities include the Konza Prairie, the world's largest tall grass prairie preserve, and the Macdonald Lab, the only university accelerator devoted primarily to atomic physics. Open House, held each spring, is a great way to explore K-State's more than 250 majors and options and 400 student organizations.

"Kansas State University requires ACT or SAT scores to complete a freshman applicant file. The SAT or ACT Writing score is not considered for admission to the university. Students may submit scores from any or all test dates. The best score from any one test date is used."

SELECTIVITY

Admissions Rating	74
# of applicants	6,658
% of applicants accepted	95
% of acceptees attending	50

FRESHMAN PROFILE

Range ACT Composite	27.5–21
% graduated top 25% of class	62
% graduated top 50% of class	90

DEADLINES

Nonfall registration?	yes

FINANCIAL FACTS

Financial Aid Rating	74
Annual in-state tuition	$5,625
Annual out-of-state tuition	$15,360
Room and board	$6,084
Required fees	$610
Books and supplies	$1,100
% frosh rec. need-based scholarship or grant aid	30
% UG rec. need-based scholarship or grant aid	31
% frosh rec. non-need-based scholarship or grant aid	30
% UG rec. non-need-based scholarship or grant aid	19
% frosh rec. need-based self-help aid	39
% UG rec. need-based self-help aid	44
% frosh rec. athletic scholarships	2
% UG rec. athletic scholarships	2
% UG rec. any financial aid	53
% UG borrow to pay for school	57
Average cumulative indebtedness	$18,900

KENYON COLLEGE

ADMISSIONS OFFICE, RANSOM HALL, GAMBIER, OH 43022-9623 • ADMISSIONS: 740-427-5776 • FAX: 740-427-5770

CAMPUS LIFE
Quality of Life Rating	85
Fire Safety Rating	64
Green Rating	77
Type of school	private
Environment	rural

STUDENTS
Total undergrad enrollment	1,653
% male/female	48/52
% from out of state	80
% from public high school	47
% live on campus	98
% in (# of) fraternities	25 (8)
% in (# of) sororities	10 (4)
% African American	4
% Asian	5
% Caucasian	81
% Hispanic	3
% Native American	1
% international	3
# of countries represented	29

SURVEY SAYS . . .
Large classes
No one cheats
Lab facilities are great
Athletic facilities are great
Students are friendly
Campus feels safe
Students are happy
Lots of beer drinking

ACADEMICS
Academic Rating	93
Calendar	semester
Student/faculty ratio	10:1
Profs interesting rating	99
Profs accessible rating	96
Most common reg class size	20–29 students

MOST POPULAR MAJORS
English language and literature
psychology
political science and government

STUDENTS SAY " . . ."

Academics
At Kenyon College, an "entrancingly pretty" campus and "personal, small, and intimate" classes combine to create "a low-stress setting" for a "liberal arts experience that allows you to make profound changes in your approach to life." Kenyon is primarily "known as a writers' college." It seems fitting, then, that the English Department draws the lion's share of students' praise. The school's rep, however, seems to derive more from the fact that written communication skills are valued and emphasized "in all departments, ranging from history to math," rather than from a course catalogue only filled with fascinating fiction and poetry courses. In terms of academic workload, it "is large but manageable and students in general never seem overly worried about it." They seem to know that they can count on their "brilliant," "incredible" professors who "know their stuff" and "are capable of making it accessible and interesting." Professors give students "as much individual time as [they] need" to digest the material. Administratively the school has experienced "a lot of turn-over in the last year," leading many students to feel that administrators are "still getting their bearings." While they don't "always follow the student body's opinion," they are at least aware of it and "willing to listen" to students' input. Both "Professors and administrators love to take an active experience in the lives of Kenyon students outside of the classroom" by doing things like attending student "art shows, sporting events, [and] musical performances." Such beyond-the-books interaction leads many students to feel that "the school is more of a family than a business."

Life
Student life at Kenyon is a unique riff on the typical college social experience. For example, "There are a lot of parties in apartments and fraternity lodges and lounges." Yet though "Frats throw most of the parties," they are "almost always open to anyone," and Greeks are "incorporated into the same housing as everyone else," so it "doesn't feel exclusive." What's more, "People have academic conversations even while out at parties," which is certainly not the case at your typical college bash. Basically, Kenyon undergrads "know how to let go and have a good time, but there's always a slightly intellectual edge to it." Parties aren't the only social options on campus. Considering its small size, Kenyon may "have too much programming rather than too little." "There are movies shown at the KAC [Kenyon Athletic Center]," and regularly scheduled "concerts, theatrical and dance productions, and lectures." For "casual fun," students "go to Middle Ground Cafe or the Gambier Grill for coffee or food." Also, "People go to the bar on campus if [they're] of legal age." "In nice weather, Kenyon students are very outdoorsy." Students enjoy "[going] out to the nature preserve (the BFEC) and play[ing] Frisbee or go[ing] for walks." Off-campus entertainment options are pretty scarce, as hometown Gambier is "in the middle of nowhere." Luckily, "Columbus is under an hour away," so "When people need to go somewhere a little more exciting, they drive [there]."

Student Body
A stereotypical Kenyonian is "generally very smart but not pretentious." Most students are "rich, White, and Democratic," which might explain why they "spend lots of money trying to look like they don't have that much money." Kenyon students "love to party, and [are] generally involved in music, sports, or theater." On this "liberal," "laid-back" campus, students are "not competitive" and describe each other as "seriously friendly." People here "take academics very seriously, but also enjoy social lives." They also have a "wide variety of interests. It's not unusual to see a neuroscience major paired with a dance minor." As one student sums up, "The 'Kenyon Quirk' is something you hear of often—in that way, everyone is atypical, as it is typical to be different. Hippies, collar-poppers, girlie-girls, goths, nerds, and introverts all find their place at Kenyon."

FINANCIAL AID: 740-427-5430 • E-MAIL: ADMISSIONS@KENYON.EDU • WEBSITE: WWW.KENYON.EDU

THE PRINCETON REVIEW SAYS

Admissions

Very important factors considered include: Application essay, academic GPA, recommendation(s), rigor of secondary school record, character/personal qualities. *Important factors considered include:* Class rank, standardized test scores, extracurricular activities, interview, level of applicant's interest, racial/ethnic status, talent/ability. *Other factors considered include:* Alumni/ae relation, first generation, geographical residence, state residency, volunteer work, work experience. SAT or ACT required; TOEFL required of all international applicants. High school diploma is required and GED is accepted. *Academic units required:* 4 English, 3 mathematics, 3 science, (3 science labs), 3 foreign language, 1 social studies, 2 history, 3 academic electives. *Academic units recommended:* 4 English, 4 mathematics, 4 science, (3 science labs), 4 foreign language, 1 social studies, 3 history, 3 academic electives.

Financial Aid

Students should submit: FAFSA, CSS/Financial Aid PROFILE, noncustodial PROFILE Regular filing deadline is 2/15. The Princeton Review suggests that all financial aid forms be submitted as soon as possible after January 1. *Need-based scholarships/grants offered:* Federal Pell, SEOG, state scholarships/grants, private scholarships, the school's own gift aid. *Loan aid offered:* FFEL Subsidized Stafford, FFEL Unsubsidized Stafford, FFEL PLUS, Federal Perkins, college/university loans from institutional funds. Applicants will be notified of awards on or about 4/1. Federal Work-Study Program available. Institutional employment available. Off-campus job opportunities are fair.

The Inside Word

In terms of admissions selectivity, Kenyon is of the first order of selective, small Midwestern, liberal arts schools. Kenyon shares a lot of application and admit overlap with other schools in this niche, and the choice for many students comes down to "best fit." As Kenyon is a writing-intensive institution, applicants should expect that all written material submitted to the school in the admissions process will be scrutinized. Revise and proofread accordingly.

THE SCHOOL SAYS "..."

From The Admissions Office

"Students and alumni alike think of Kenyon as a place that fosters 'learning in the company of friends.' While faculty expectations are rigorous and the work challenging, the academic atmosphere is cooperative, not competitive. Indications of intellectual curiosity and passion for learning, more than just high grades and test scores, are what we look for in applications. Important as well are demonstrated interests in non-academic pursuits, whether in athletics, the arts, writing, or another passion. Life in this small college community is fueled by the talents and enthusiasm of our students, so the Admission Staff seeks students who have a range of talents and interests.

"The high school transcript, recommendations, the personal statement, and answers on the supplement are of primary importance in reviewing preparedness and fit. Standardized tests (SAT or ACT) are of secondary importance."

SELECTIVITY

Admissions Rating	97
# of applicants	4,626
% of applicants accepted	29
% of acceptees attending	34
# accepting a place on wait list	378
% admitted from wait list	3
# of early decision applicants	359
% accepted early decision	60

FRESHMAN PROFILE

Range SAT Critical Reading	630–730
Range SAT Math	630–690
Range SAT Writing	630–710
Range ACT Composite	28–32
Minimum paper TOEFL	600
Minimum computer TOEFL	250
Average HS GPA	3.86
% graduated top 10% of class	73
% graduated top 25% of class	94
% graduated top 50% of class	99

DEADLINES

Early decision	
Deadline	11/15
Notification	12/15
Regular	
Deadline	1/15
Notification	4/1
Nonfall registration?	no

APPLICANTS ALSO LOOK AT

AND OFTEN PREFER
Carleton University
Middlebury College
Bowdoin College

AND SOMETIMES PREFER
Oberlin College
Grinnell College

AND RARELY PREFER
The College of Wooster

FINANCIAL FACTS

Financial Aid Rating	89
Annual tuition	$39,080
Room and board	$6,590
Required fees	$1,160
Books and supplies	$1,300
% frosh rec. need-based scholarship or grant aid	39
% UG rec. need-based scholarship or grant aid	43
% frosh rec. non-need-based scholarship or grant aid	13
% UG rec. non-need-based scholarship or grant aid	11
% frosh rec. need-based self-help aid	31
% UG rec. need-based self-help aid	38
% frosh rec. any financial aid	54
% UG rec. any financial aid	65
% UG borrow to pay for school	62
Average cumulative indebtedness	$19,489

KNOX COLLEGE

BOX K-148, GALESBURG, IL 61401 • ADMISSIONS: 309-341-7100 • FAX: 309-341-7070

STUDENTS SAY ". . ."

Academics

Knox College, a small liberal arts school with "a very strong creative writing program," offers its students the "freedom to flourish" (it's "the school's tagline, and it's actually very accurate") through the opportunity "to create their paths and discover their goals" and "provides a serious foundation for freethinking individuals." A combination of factors makes this degree of freedom possible: One is a relatively small amount of academic "requirements, both in general and within majors, which means that you can honestly take whatever classes interest you." Another is "the ease . . . you can do independent studies or design your own major or minor with a faculty sponsor. You can personalize your education plan to a great degree at Knox." Strengths include the aforementioned writing program, political science, education, and a premed program that offers early acceptance (no later than sophomore year) to Rush Medical School or George Washington University. All this freedom does have its price: One undergrad warns, "The school allows students to do what they want, but expects rigorous academic performance as well as maturity in return." Academics can be grueling in some students' opinion, because of the school's three-term calendar. One student writes, "Though you're only taking three classes at a time, you still have an amazing workload. Getting A's at Knox is no easy business." Undergrads here appreciate "the wide variety of activities and the opportunities students are given. My freshman year I was able to go to Hawaii with Habitat for Humanity, then Florida the following year. There are many opportunities for research and internships, and since there are fewer students competing for these opportunities than at a big school, the odds are better."

Life

Hometown Galesburg "is small and quaint," with "a few things to do if you're looking for something, like the Rootabaga Jazz Festival in the [winter], Carl Sandburg's home, and the railroad museum." Even so, many feel that "there's nothing to do in Galesburg. The reality of it is that we have a great school in the middle of a cornfield." Fortunately, "There is never a lack of things to do on campus, from clubs and Greek life and sports to Casino Nights and musical and theatrical performances." Student organizations present "a lot of programming to keep students busy: speakers, readings, comedians, trips, bands, etc. These events are publicized everywhere, so you can't miss them." Sporting events "are also fun to attend, especially when Knox is playing its rival, Monmouth." Some diversions are improvised, such as "sledding in the Bowl (the bowl-shaped football field) or hanging at a friend's suite and watching movies." There are also "a lot of parties at Knox. But they are not as one might expect. A lot of people even stay away from the official party places for the evening. Alcohol does factor a lot into campus life here but only if you choose to drink. Like many other schools, it is available if desired but easy enough to sidestep if not."

Student Body

It may seem like "The majority of students are middle-class liberal Whites from Midwestern suburbs" at Knox College, but "The school also draws students from both coasts and around the world. Although classes may be largely homogeneous, they nearly always include some students from other countries or more diverse backgrounds." There is also a diversity of personality types here; one student explains, "a Knox student's hair might be magenta and blue, or it might look like it was styled at a salon. Preppie, hippie, and punk styles all mesh together, and friends mix evenly through all crowds. Being weird doesn't make you an outcast, but neither does being average. At Knox you can find someone totally like you or totally opposite you. All at a school that only has 1,200 students."

FINANCIAL AID: 309-341-7149 • E-MAIL: ADMISSION@KNOX.EDU • WEBSITE: WWW.KNOX.EDU

THE PRINCETON REVIEW SAYS

Admissions

Very important factors considered include: Academic GPA, rigor of secondary school record. *Important factors considered include:* Class rank, application essay. *Other factors considered include:* Standardized test scores, alumni/ae relation, character/personal qualities, extracurricular activities, first generation, interview, level of applicant's interest, racial/ethnic status, talent/ability, volunteer work, TOEFL required of all international applicants. High school diploma is required and GED is accepted. *Academic units recommended:* 4 English, 4 mathematics, 3 science, (2 science labs), 3 foreign language, 2 social studies, 2 history.

Financial Aid

Students should submit: FAFSA, institution's own financial aid form. The Princeton Review suggests that all financial aid forms be submitted as soon as possible after January 1. *Need-based scholarships/grants offered:* Federal Pell, SEOG, state scholarships/grants, private scholarships, the school's own gift aid. *Loan aid offered:* Direct Subsidized Stafford, Direct Unsubsidized Stafford, Direct PLUS, Federal Perkins, college/university loans from institutional funds. Applicants will be notified of awards on a rolling basis beginning 3/15. Federal Work-Study Program available. Institutional employment available. Off-campus job opportunities are good.

The Inside Word

Knox prides itself on maintaining a diverse student body. Its Admissions Office truly focuses on the individual, closely assessing applicants in an attempt to predict how each will contribute to the campus. Prospective students who succeed in intellectually challenging classes in high school will set themselves apart.

THE SCHOOL SAYS "..."

From The Admissions Office

"Knox was founded on the idea that education has the power to confer a kind of freedom—what we've come to call 'freedom to flourish.' On the surface, 'freedom to flourish' is a simple and powerful concept—it is the knowledge and skills one needs to live a rewarding personal, professional, and civic life. But 'freedom to flourish' also has more subtle meaning that touches on how education happens at Knox.

"Most schools ask what you want to study and give you a checklist of courses needed for that degree. Knox asks, 'What do you want to know, and what do you want to do with that knowledge?' Within the context of the goals and milestones of one of our many majors, you and your advisor will develop a personalized educational plan of classes, internships, off-campus study, and independent research projects that meet the agenda you set for yourself. In this sense, a Knox education is an act of imagination, an act of entrepreneurship, an act of freedom.'

"That self-direction doesn't end in advising sessions and course selection. You'll be encouraged to bring your own interests and perspective to every class you take, and you'll be challenged to apply what you learn to the world around you. In the end you will learn how to set goals, how to figure out what you need to know to achieve those goals, and how to identify and collaborate with mentors who can help you along the way. That is 'freedom to flourish.'

"At Knox, you'll never be a number. Knox reviews each application holistically, fully considering a student's academic record, course selection, and performance (grades), as well as essays, recommendations, interviews, and other accomplishments. As a result, the submission of SAT or ACT scores is optional for most applicants."

SELECTIVITY

Admissions Rating	87
# of applicants	2,419
% of applicants accepted	61
% of acceptees attending	21
# accepting a place on wait list	108
% admitted from wait list	58

FRESHMAN PROFILE

Range SAT Critical Reading	610–710
Range SAT Math	580–670
Range SAT Writing	590–690
Minimum paper TOEFL	550
Minimum computer TOEFL	213
Minimum web-based TOEFL	83
% graduated top 10% of class	40
% graduated top 25% of class	75
% graduated top 50% of class	97

DEADLINES

Early action	
Deadline	12/1
Notification	12/31
Regular	
Deadline	2/1
Nonfall registration?	yes

FINANCIAL FACTS

Financial Aid Rating	88
Annual tuition	$30,180
Room and board	$6,726
Required fees	$327
Books and supplies	$900
% frosh rec. need-based scholarship or grant aid	72
% UG rec. need-based scholarship or grant aid	66
% frosh rec. non-need-based scholarship or grant aid	10
% UG rec. non-need-based scholarship or grant aid	8
% frosh rec. need-based self-help aid	62
% UG rec. need-based self-help aid	59
% frosh rec. any financial aid	95
% UG rec. any financial aid	94
% UG borrow to pay for school	70
Average cumulative indebtedness	$21,951

LAFAYETTE COLLEGE

118 MARKLE HALL, EASTON, PA 18042 • ADMISSIONS: 610-330-5100 • FAX: 610-330-5355

CAMPUS LIFE
Quality of Life Rating	**81**
Fire Safety Rating	**60***
Green Rating	**95**
Type of school	private
Affiliation	Presbyterian
Environment	village

STUDENTS
Total undergrad enrollment	2,381
% male/female	52/48
% from out of state	70
% from public high school	68
% live on campus	96
% in (# of) fraternities	26 (7)
% in (# of) sororities	45 (6)
% African American	5
% Asian	3
% Caucasian	80
% Hispanic	5
% international	6
# of countries represented	46

SURVEY SAYS . . .
Lab facilities are great
Great computer facilities
Great library
Athletic facilities are great
Career services are great
Campus feels safe
Lots of beer drinking

ACADEMICS
Academic Rating	**89**
Calendar	semester
Student/faculty ratio	11:1
Profs interesting rating	87
Profs accessible rating	88
Most common reg class size	10–19 students
Most common lab size	10–19 students

STUDENTS SAY " . . ."

Academics

Lafayette College is "a small liberal arts college" that is "especially strong in engineering and physical sciences." There are "very cool" undergraduate research opportunities. Career services "is also phenomenal" and "an excellent alumni network" provides abundant career and internship opportunities. The "efficient, helpful, and very accessible" administration "generally listens to the comments of the students" and does "a great job of keeping the school running smoothly." The biggest academic complaint at Lafayette is that the range of courses offered in a typical semester is too narrow. The classes that are offered tend to be "small" and "difficult." "You must study," reports an economics major. "Not every professor is the greatest." "There is the occasional professor who makes you want to tear your hair out." On the whole, though, Lafayette's professors are "really knowledgeable and really do care about how you do and what you take out of the class." "I feel like I get a lot of individual attention," says a chemical engineering major. "Professors will explain difficult material until you understand," relates a math major, "not just say it once and look at you like you're stupid if you still don't understand." Outside of class, faculty members typically remain "extremely available" and "beg you to talk to them and meet with them."

Life

Lafayette is located on a hill above "terrible and disgusting" Easton, Pennsylvania. The "gorgeous," "scenic" campus is full of "picturesque northeastern college-like buildings." A few dorms "are in desperate need of renovation," though, and the "repetitive" food is "not that great tasting." Socially, Lafayette is reportedly "very homey." "At almost any social gathering, there will be people you know." The "amazing" sports center is "a very popular spot." "Lafayette is a very athletic school and most students participate in either varsity athletics or in a club or intramural sport," explains a sophomore. In the fall, "football games are extremely spirited." The annual contest against hated Lehigh "is attended by basically the whole student body." Beyond sports, many students tell us that "there is always something to do on campus." "Everyone is really involved," they say. There are "a capella concerts, comedians, movies, and club-sponsored activities." A "multitude of speakers" visits campus. There's "a broad range" of religious groups. Lafayette also has a "huge" Greek system. Other students contend that "there should be more to do." "I have not experienced the outpouring of entertainment at the school," grumbles a freshman. Whatever the case, "the party scene is really fun." The frats and various sports teams throw parties "Wednesday through Saturday nights" and many students participate. However, many others don't. "Half the campus considers Lafayette a party school and the other half doesn't know what school the first half is talking about," suggests a junior.

Student Body

Lafayette is a haven for "well-rounded," "preppy," "smart jocks," and "your classic white rich kid" "from New York, New Jersey, or Pennsylvania." "There is certainly a mold," admits a senior. "Everyone is pretty similar." "Collar-popping" suburbanites are everywhere. "Crazy colored hair and facial piercings are not really something you see," observes a first-year student. "You will see a lot of smiling and door-holding," though. Students take pride in the "incredibly friendly" vibe at Lafayette. Many students are "hard-partying" types. There are also "the kids who live in the library 20 hours a day." Most students fall somewhere in the middle. "People like to have a good time but they are also serious about their work and are genuinely interested in their area of study." "Both conservatives and liberals" will find soul mates at Lafayette but many students are "almost completely apathetic" when it comes to politics. Some students "have a snobby attitude," but others either don't flaunt their wealth or don't come from money at all. "We're not all running around with iPhones and Fendi bags," says a sophomore. Ethnic diversity is pretty minimal. "There are a few minority and foreign students but they hang out with each other in their own little cliques."

FINANCIAL AID: 610-330-5055 • E-MAIL: ADMISSIONS@LAFAYETTE.EDU • WEBSITE: WWW.LAFAYETTE.EDU

THE PRINCETON REVIEW SAYS

Admissions

Very important factors considered include: Rigor of secondary school record. *Important factors considered include:* Class rank, application essay, recommendation(s), standardized test scores, alumni/ae relation, character/personal qualities, extracurricular activities, racial/ethnic status, talent/ability, volunteer work. *Other factors considered include:* Geographical residence, interview, work experience. SAT or ACT required; ACT with Writing component required. TOEFL required of all international applicants. High school diploma or equivalent is not required. *Academic units recommended:* 4 English, 3 mathematics, 2 science, (2 science labs), 2 foreign language, 5 academic electives.

Financial Aid

Students should submit: FAFSA, CSS/Financial Aid PROFILE, noncustodial PROFILE, business/farm supplement. Regular filing deadline is 2/1. The Princeton Review suggests that all financial aid forms be submitted as soon as possible after January 1. *Need-based scholarships/grants offered:* Federal Pell, SEOG, state scholarships/grants, private scholarships *Loan aid offered:* FFEL Subsidized Stafford, FFEL Unsubsidized Stafford, FFEL PLUS, Federal Perkins, state loans, college/university loans from institutional funds. HELP loans to parents. Applicants will be notified of awards on or about 4/1. Federal Work-Study Program available. Institutional employment available. Off-campus job opportunities are good.

The Inside Word

Applications are reviewed three to five times and evaluated by as many as nine different committee members. In all cases, students who continually seek challenges and are willing to take risks academically win out over those who play it safe to maintain a high GPA.

THE SCHOOL SAYS "..."

From The Admissions Office

"We choose students individually, one by one, and we hope that the ones we choose will approach their education the same way, as a highly individual enterprise. Our first-year seminars have enrollments limited to 15 or 16 students each in order to introduce the concept of learning not as passive receipt of information but as an active, participatory process. Our low average class size and 11:1 student/teacher ratio reflect that same philosophy. We also devote substantial resources to our Marquis Scholars Program, to one-on-one faculty-student mentoring relationships, and to other programs in engineering within a liberal arts context, giving Lafayette its distinctive character, articulated in our second-year seminars exploring values in science and technology. Lafayette provides an environment in which its students can discover their own personal capacity for learning, personal growth, and leadership.

"Submission of scores from either the SAT Reasoning Test or American College Testing Program (ACT) is required. If taking the ACT, the optional Writing Section is required. SAT Subject Test results are recommended, but not required. Scores must be submitted directly from the testing agency or via your college counselor on an 'official' high school transcript or testing summary sheet."

SELECTIVITY

Admissions Rating	96
# of applicants	5,875
% of applicants accepted	37
% of acceptees attending	29
# accepting a place on wait list	636
% admitted from wait list	9
# of early decision applicants	395
% accepted early decision	68

FRESHMAN PROFILE

Range SAT Critical Reading	580–670
Range SAT Math	620–710
Range SAT Writing	580–670
Range ACT Composite	24–29
Minimum paper TOEFL	550
Average HS GPA	3.78
% graduated top 10% of class	62
% graduated top 25% of class	92
% graduated top 50% of class	100

DEADLINES

Early decision	
Deadline	2/15
Notification	12/1
Regular	
Priority	1/1
Deadline	1/1
Notification	4/1
Nonfall registration?	yes

APPLICANTS ALSO LOOK AT

AND OFTEN PREFER
Johns Hopkins University
Cornell University
Boston College
Tufts University

AND SOMETIMES PREFER
Lehigh University
Bucknell University

AND RARELY PREFER
Franklin & Marshall College
Trinity College (CT)

FINANCIAL FACTS

Financial Aid Rating	96
Annual tuition	$33,634
Room and board	$10,377
Required fees	$177
Books and supplies	$600
% frosh rec. need-based scholarship or grant aid	48
% UG rec. need-based scholarship or grant aid	48
% frosh rec. non-need-based scholarship or grant aid	13
% UG rec. non-need-based scholarship or grant aid	7
% frosh rec. need-based self-help aid	32
% UG rec. need-based self-help aid	38
% UG borrow to pay for school	49
Average cumulative indebtedness	$17,576

LAKE FOREST COLLEGE

555 NORTH SHERIDAN ROAD, LAKE FOREST, IL 60045 • ADMISSIONS: 847-735-5000 • FAX: 847-735-6291

STUDENTS SAY ". . ."

Academics

Students at Lake Forest College rave about "an extraordinary educational environment where students share a close bond with their professors while living and studying in an intimate college community amongst an enriching Chicago background." A broad ranging general education curriculum "emphasizes giving each student an individual and well-rounded education in the liberal arts," one that many pursue in their majors; nearly one-in-10 here majors in English, and departments in psychology, history, the social sciences, and communication are all substantial (as are programs in business and in economics). The curriculum also "emphasizes diversity and global activism a lot, which gives many students a broadened worldview," while the entire Lake Forest experience, academic and extracurricular, "does a good job at incorporating Chicago into the academics and social lives of students." The school differs from similar-sized school in one way; students tell us that "Lake Forest is really what you make it for yourself. The opportunities are there for the taking, but no one is going to hold your hand for four years and tell you what to do." The school is not as well known as it might be if it were located in the Northeast, leading some to describe it as "an undercover gem" and explaining why many regard it as "a safety school for those who can't quite make it into the big-name liberal arts, and a decent compromise for geniuses who could get into Harvard but can't afford the tuition."

Life

The area surrounding Lake Forest College "is an extremely wealthy community, so many of the businesses that are there are too expensive for the average student. There is just one bar, and everything shuts down very early," so "there isn't a lot to do in town" for LFC undergraduates. Students do avail themselves of "the basics: a couple of good restaurants (The Lantern, Burger King, Egg Harbor), a grocery store and pharmacy, and a post office," but "students really have to leave the city to have fun." Vernon Hills, "with a large mall and lots of restaurants, "is about 20 minutes away," but "the best thing to do for fun is go to Chicago! It is only an hour away and only costs $5 for the round trip on the weekends." The train ride delivers "a welcome escape from what can eventually get claustrophobic in Lake Forest College/City. A lot of students seem to get bored of Chicago quickly after they've hit downtown and the museums...as a lifelong Chicagoan I find this silly! There's a reason it's called a 'city of neighborhoods,' and the Loop is probably the least exciting one when it comes to finding your niche." On campus, there's "a lack of activities" outside of movies, athletic events ("athletics are easy to get involved in," though the "Athletic Department could place more of a focus on facilities improvement"), occasional performances, and "a few parties thrown by different student organizations." Saturday is the big on-campus party night, "especially in Gregory and Harlan Hall."

Student Body

The typical Lake Forest student "is an intelligent kid who doesn't want to completely devote his life to studying, likes to party, and usually has quite some money coming in from dad and mom," but even though students have the impression that "most of the students in this school come from wealthy families," this doesn't mean there's some kind of class war going on, as everyone is generally quite friendly, and if they aren't, they are at least civil." Minorities are most often represented among the large population of international students, who "give the campus a more diverse feeling." These students "are a great asset to learn about the world outside of the U.S.! There is a special international residence hall, but all of the international students get along really well with everyone else."

FINANCIAL AID: 847-735-5103 • E-MAIL: ADMISSIONS@LAKEFOREST.EDU • WEBSITE: WWW.LAKEFOREST.EDU

THE PRINCETON REVIEW SAYS

Admissions

Very important factors considered include: Academic GPA, recommendation(s), rigor of secondary school record, interview, leadership experience, commitment to community. *Important factors considered include:* Graded paper, character/personal qualities, extracurricular activities, level of applicant's interest, talent/ability. *Other factors considered include:* First generation, geographical residence, volunteer work, work experience. High school diploma is required and GED is accepted. *Academic units required:* 4 English, 3 mathematics, 3 science, (3 science labs), 2 foreign language, 2 social studies, 2 history, 3 academic electives. *Academic units recommended:* 4 English, 4 mathematics, 4 science, (4 science labs), 4 foreign language, 2 social studies, 2 history, 3 academic electives, 1 Honors or AP courses.

Financial Aid

Students should submit: FAFSA, institution's own financial aid form, Federal Income Tax return. Regular filing deadline is 3/1. The Princeton Review suggests that all financial aid forms be submitted as soon as possible after January 1. *Need-based scholarships/grants offered:* Federal Pell, SEOG, state scholarships/grants, private scholarships, the school's own gift aid. *Loan aid offered:* FFEL Subsidized Stafford, FFEL Unsubsidized Stafford, FFEL PLUS, Federal Perkins, college/university loans from institutional funds, private loans. Applicants will be notified of awards on a rolling basis beginning 3/1. Federal Work-Study Program available. Institutional employment available. Off-campus job opportunities are good.

The Inside Word

Lake Forest is small enough to give each application it receives close and careful consideration. Solid high school performers should have little difficulty gaining admission, but keep in mind that Lake Forest has a prep-school-at-the-college-level feel and likes to assess the whole candidate, not just grades and test scores. In fact, test scores are optional. The school will look closely at the graded essay you submit with your application, so choose carefully.

THE SCHOOL SAYS " . . ."

From The Admissions Office

"Lake Forest College is Chicago's national liberal arts college. Located 30 miles north of downtown Chicago, the College's proximity to the city provides Lake Forest students and faculty with unique academic, cultural, and employment resources. Through partnerships with a variety of cultural, educational, financial, research, and scientific institutions in Chicago and its environs, students are engaged in an active learning process that takes them beyond the traditional boundaries of the classroom, integrating the theoretical and the practical.

"The 1,400 students represent 65 countries and 47 states. Lake Forest College fosters interaction among a diverse community of students and faculty with a significant international and minority population. The faculty are dedicated teachers and accomplished scholars and they do all the teaching; you will not find teaching assistants at Lake Forest.

"With more than 80 student-run organizations and clubs, 17 varsity NCAA Division III teams, and a variety of intramural and club sports, students find many opportunities outside the classroom.

"Lake Forest has a test-optional admission process permitting students to choose whether or not to have their ACT or SAT scores considered for admission. International students and students applying for certain academic scholarships will still be required to submit scores. During the admission process Lake Forest evaluates each student based on qualities that determine success in college: strong academic performance in a challenging high-school curriculum, leadership experience and commitment to community, and extracurricular involvement and individual talent."

SELECTIVITY

Admissions Rating	88
# of applicants	2,203
% of applicants accepted	61
% of acceptees attending	26
# accepting a place on wait list	33
% admitted from wait list	48

FRESHMAN PROFILE

Range SAT Critical Reading	560–660
Range SAT Math	540–660
Range SAT Writing	540–640
Range ACT Composite	24–29
Average HS GPA	3.5
% graduated top 10% of class	35
% graduated top 25% of class	56
% graduated top 50% of class	89

DEADLINES

Early decision	
Deadline	12/1
Notification	12/20
Early action	
Deadline	12/1
Notification	1/20
Regular	
Priority	2/15
Notification	3/20
Nonfall registration?	yes

FINANCIAL FACTS

Financial Aid Rating	99
Annual tuition	$30,600
Room and board	$7,326
Required fees	$364
Books and supplies	$700
% frosh rec. need-based scholarship or grant aid	64
% UG rec. need-based scholarship or grant aid	69
% frosh rec. need-based self-help aid	57
% UG rec. need-based self-help aid	63
% frosh rec. any financial aid	88
% UG rec. any financial aid	91
% UG borrow to pay for school	48
Average cumulative indebtedness	$19,352

LAWRENCE UNIVERSITY

PO BOX 599, APPLETON, WI 54912-0599 • ADMISSIONS: 920-832-6500 • FAX: 920-832-6782

CAMPUS LIFE

Quality of Life Rating	**92**
Fire Safety Rating	**60***
Green Rating	**60***
Type of school	private
Environment	city

STUDENTS

Total undergrad enrollment	1,400
% male/female	46/54
% from out of state	61
% live on campus	89
% in (# of) fraternities	9 (5)
% in (# of) sororities	5 (3)
% African American	2
% Asian	3
% Caucasian	76
% Hispanic	2
% international	7
# of countries represented	49

SURVEY SAYS . . .

Large classes
No one cheats
Students are friendly
Campus feels safe
Low cost of living
Students are happy
Musical organizations are popular

ACADEMICS

Academic Rating	**90**
Calendar	trimester
Student/faculty ratio	9:1
Profs interesting rating	91
Profs accessible rating	99
Most common	
reg class size	10–19 students

MOST POPULAR MAJORS

biology/biological sciences
psychology
music performance

STUDENTS SAY ". . ."

Academics

The Lawrence University experience is defined by "intense academics, extreme involvement in extracurricular activities, and a near-obsession with music." Also by cold weather; located between Oshkosh and Green Bay, LU is a place where "You will freeze your butt off walking to class, have a professor say the most profound thing ever, and then not notice that its twenty below as you walk to the library to study your ass off." A prestigious music conservatory and "great science programs" are the top attractions, but the school also excels in the humanities and social sciences. As one student puts it, "Lawrence doesn't have just one strength, it has many unique and diverse strengths, and I think this quality is reflected in the students." Those students help make LU "an intellectual place, as any good college should be. People are all brilliant in their own ways here, and it's fantastic to find out how." A trimester academic calendar means "classes condense a lot of information (and often a lot of work!) in a shorter period of time" so students "are busy from the first week until the end of the finals week. Stress levels never goes down." Fortunately, the student body "is really friendly" and cooperative, resulting in "an intellectually stimulating—not academically cutthroat—environment that fosters both academic and personal growth." LU is a small school where "Professors are really willing to work one-on-one with students" but "lacks some technologies and resources that larger schools might have."

Life

People at Lawrence "are generally very busy. Even though each student has only three classes (music students have more), the terms are only 10 weeks long and there is a lot to study." When they can get a break, students are "at a group meeting (Habitat for Humanity, Lambda Sigma, Health and Wellness, etc.), at practice (varsity sports and club sports), or spending some time with other people." Social life on campus "is very strong. People with a wide variety of interests come together and form diverse groups of friends. Athletes, artists, musicians, and academics can usually all be found at one party, and on any given weekend there is a party catering to each distinct social group." Undergrads "are big into the arts and nerdy things," and because "lots of students are musical and artistic...there are interesting outlets on campus" for their creativity. Music is the biggest; "There are always different concerts, recitals, and performances to go to. Our symphony is very good and popular guest artists visit and perform." All the action on campus helps compensate for the fact that "Appleton is a very small, boring town" with "basically nothing to do," specifically; "no good concert venues, no strong local music scene, and no independent theater or art galleries."

Student Body

The typical Lawrentian "cannot be better described than as a 'cool nerd.'" They seem to be the types of kids who started realizing that being smart and artsy was cool sometime late in high school, so they have no false delusions about how cool they are. They have strong senses of culture and also have strong senses of satire against conventional norms." They "are interested in learning for the sake of learning, not studying for the sake of receiving the highest grade. Students often study in public areas or in small groups, and always become very involved in the course material. Lawrence is a cooperative, rather than a competitive, learning environment." They are "probably from Wisconsin, the Twin Cities, Colorado or Portland." Some here detect "a bit of a Sharks-and-Jets division between conservatory and college students at times as they compete for the title of Busiest Student," but the competition is generally friendly and benign.

FINANCIAL AID: 920-832-6583 • E-MAIL: EXCEL@LAWRENCE.EDU • WEBSITE: WWW.LAWRENCE.EDU

THE PRINCETON REVIEW SAYS

Admissions

Very important factors considered include: Class rank, academic GPA, rigor of secondary school record. *Important factors considered include:* Application essay, recommendation(s), character/personal qualities, extracurricular activities, talent/ability. *Other factors considered include:* Standardized test scores, alumni/ae relation, first generation, interview, racial/ethnic status, volunteer work, work experience. High school diploma is required and GED is not accepted. *Academic units required:* 4 English. *Academic units recommended:* 3 mathematics, 3 science, 2 foreign language, 2 social studies, 2 history.

Financial Aid

Students should submit: FAFSA, institution's own financial aid form, Copies of 2007 Federal Tax Returns and W-2 forms for parent and student. The Princeton Review suggests that all financial aid forms be submitted as soon as possible after January 1. *Need-based scholarships/grants offered:* Federal Pell, SEOG, state scholarships/grants, private scholarships, the school's own gift aid. *Loan aid offered:* Direct Subsidized Stafford, Direct Unsubsidized Stafford, Direct PLUS, FFEL PLUS, Federal Perkins Applicants will be notified of awards on a rolling basis beginning 3/1. Federal Work-Study Program available. Institutional employment available. Off-campus job opportunities are good.

The Inside Word

Lawrence attracts an accomplished applicant pool, so don't let the high admit rate fool you; you'll need solid high school credentials to get in here. The traditional route is the best way to ensure success: a consistently challenging high school curriculum, good standardized test scores, well considered and constructed application essays, and an impressive on-campus interview. Of these, standardized test scores are least important; Lawrence will even ignore them if you ask that the school do so. Lawrence accepts the Common Application.

THE SCHOOL SAYS "..."

From The Admissions Office

"Lawrence students are characterized by their energy, commitment to community service, respect for each other, and desire to achieve their full potential. Campus activities are abundant, off-campus study programs are popular (more than half of the students take advantage of them), small classes are the norm (65 percent of the classes have 10 or fewer students in them), and, yes, winters can be 'character-building.' But the diversity of interests and experiences, the drive to excel, the wealth of cultural opportunities presented by the Art, Theater, and Music Departments, the quality of research students undertake alongside PhD faculty, and the general friendly attitude of everyone at the university contribute to a uniquely engaging living and learning environment.

"We seek students who are intellectual, imaginative, and innovative: qualities best quantified from a thorough review of each applicant's curriculum, academic performance, essay, activities, and recommendations. Accordingly, Lawrence considers—but does not require—the ACT and the SAT in its review of applications for admission and scholarship."

SELECTIVITY

Admissions Rating	92
# of applicants	2,599
% of applicants accepted	56
% of acceptees attending	25
# accepting a place on wait list	101
% admitted from wait list	35
# of early decision applicants	32
% accepted early decision	78

FRESHMAN PROFILE

Range SAT Critical Reading	610–730
Range SAT Math	590–700
Range SAT Writing	600–700
Range ACT Composite	27–31
Average HS GPA	3.59
% graduated top 10% of class	39
% graduated top 25% of class	71
% graduated top 50% of class	96

DEADLINES

Early decision	
Deadline	11/15
Notification	12/1
Early action	
Deadline	12/1
Notification	1/15
Regular	
Deadline	1/15
Notification	4/1
Nonfall registration?	no

FINANCIAL FACTS

Financial Aid Rating	95
Annual tuition	$29,376
% frosh rec. need-based scholarship or grant aid	59
% UG rec. need-based scholarship or grant aid	59
% frosh rec. need-based self-help aid	59
% UG rec. need-based self-help aid	59
% frosh rec. any financial aid	94
% UG rec. any financial aid	94
% UG borrow to pay for school	74
Average cumulative indebtedness	$25,374

LEHIGH UNIVERSITY

27 MEMORIAL DRIVE WEST, BETHLEHEM, PA 18015 • ADMISSIONS: 610-758-3100 • FAX: 610-758-4361

CAMPUS LIFE
Quality of Life Rating	**71**
Fire Safety Rating	**60***
Green Rating	**84**
Type of school	private
Environment	city

STUDENTS
Total undergrad enrollment	4,732
% male/female	59/41
% from out of state	76
% live on campus	71
% in (# of) fraternities	35 (21)
% in (# of) sororities	38 (8)
% African American	3
% Asian	6
% Caucasian	77
% Hispanic	4
% international	2
# of countries represented	44

SURVEY SAYS . . .
Great library
Students are happy
Frats and sororities dominate social scene
Lots of beer drinking
Hard liquor is popular

ACADEMICS
Academic Rating	**87**
Calendar	semester
Student/faculty ratio	9:1
Profs interesting rating	78
Profs accessible rating	85

MOST POPULAR MAJORS
mechanical engineering
finance
accounting

STUDENTS SAY "..."

Academics

The main thing that students at Lehigh University in Bethelehem, Pennsylvania seem to share is a general love for the school and its entire way of life, as evidenced by the "amazing" alumni base that returns to the school frequently (and provides for good networking). Despite rigorous academics, Lehigh "maintains a substantial social scene," and "work hard, play hard is not just a saying here—it's the lifestyle." Students have "to work for grades, they are not just given out," and outside of the classroom, there's a strong emphasis on experiential learning and real-world applications. The engineering and business programs are particularly strong here, and though tuition is dear, new financial aid policies have been put into place and "the school lives up to its academic reputation…you definitely get your money's worth at the end of the day." The level of instruction here is "top-notch," and "the classes aren't necessarily a drag to go to because the teachers easily manifest how much they want us to learn." "Teaching becomes better" as students begin to take more and more upper level classes; instructors "are always available and want to help you out," and they "really try to have a positive relationship with all of the students," though a few professors seem to be more interested in their research than their teachings. "For my Folktales and Fairytales class, we were invited to the professor's house to tell stories around her fireplace," says a senior. The administration "does not take into account student opinion as well as it could," and many students wish it was more transparent in its reasoning for changes (especially concerning the recent crackdown on partying, the surest way to get a Lehigh student up in arms), but most students are satisfied with the level of accessibility.

Life

Unless you have a car, there really isn't much to in the immediate surrounding area, though the school does provide a shuttle to some common off-campus destinations and the town is home to many festivals throughout the year. On campus, studying takes up most weeknights, and though there are events "here and there," "drinking is king at Lehigh" and "Greek life is everything." "It's party hard, work hard. We have all the Ivy League rejects who are crazy competitive combined with crazy parties. What's better?" asks a sophomore. Though the jury is out as to how crucial drinking is to Lehigh social life, "the school provides a lot of alcohol free activities such as game night, comedians, movie nights, etc.," and there is "plenty of socializing" through sports, student organizations, and plain old hanging out. "Even kids who are obsessed with video games won't just sit and play alone in their rooms. They'll find others with the same interest and do so together," says a student. "There are tons of ways to get involved on campus and have a good time, you just have to get creative," says another.

Student Body

It's a "white and preppy" world at Lehigh, where most students come from the northeast and the typical student's economic background can be described as "appreciates the finer things in life." People here "like to look good" and "tend to dress up for classes very often," and the popped collar has a home at Lehigh. There are still "a few splashes of ethnicity" here, and while there used to be a lot of pressure to fit that specific mold, now "there are a lot of different types of students. It's a friendlier campus." The school has actually seen a rise in enrollment by students from underrepresented backgrounds in recent years, and continues to try and build diversity. Socially, there are three types of students at Lehigh: "those who are Greek, those whose friends are Greek, and those who have no friends." The final group is in the extreme minority, as "it isn't hard to find a friend at Lehigh," and even the atypical students "usually just connect with each other." Ever the balanced bunch, Lehigh students "recognize scholastic the opportunity that Lehigh provides but also thrive on the party scene."

FINANCIAL AID: 610-758-3181 • E-MAIL: ADMISSIONS@LEHIGH.EDU • WEBSITE: WWW.LEHIGH.EDU

THE PRINCETON REVIEW SAYS

Admissions

Very important factors considered include: Recommendation(s), rigor of secondary school record. *Important factors considered include:* Application essay, standardized test scores, character/personal qualities, extracurricular activities, talent/ability, volunteer work. *Other factors considered include:* Class rank, academic GPA, alumni/ae relation, first generation, geographical residence, level of applicant's interest, racial/ethnic status, work experience. SAT or ACT required; ACT with Writing component required. TOEFL required of all international applicants. High school diploma or equivalent is not required. *Academic units required:* 4 English, 3 mathematics, 2 science, (2 science labs), 2 foreign language, 2 social studies, 3 academic electives.

Financial Aid

Students should submit: FAFSA, CSS/Financial Aid PROFILE, noncustodial PROFILE, business/farm supplement. Regular filing deadline is 2/15. The Princeton Review suggests that all financial aid forms be submitted as soon as possible after January 1. *Need-based scholarships/grants offered:* Federal Pell, SEOG, state scholarships/grants, private scholarships, the school's own gift aid, United Negro College Fund. *Loan aid offered:* FFEL Subsidized Stafford, FFEL Unsubsidized Stafford, FFEL PLUS, Federal Perkins, college/university loans from institutional funds, Private Educational Alternative Loans. Applicants will be notified of awards on or about 3/30. Federal Work-Study Program available. Institutional employment available. Off-campus job opportunities are good.

The Inside Word

Lots of work at bolstering Lehigh's public recognition for overall academic quality has paid off—liberal arts candidates will now find the admissions process to be highly selective. Students without solidly impressive academic credentials will have a rough time getting in regardless of their choice of programs, as will unenthusiastic, but academically strong candidates who have clearly chosen Lehigh as a safety.

THE SCHOOL SAYS "..."

From The Admissions Office

"Lehigh University is located 50 miles north of Philadelphia and 75 miles southwest of New York City in Bethlehem, Pennsylvania, where a cultural renaissance has taken place with the opening of more than a dozen ethnic restaurants, the addition of several boutiques and galleries, and Lehigh's Campus Square residential/retail complex. Lehigh combines learning opportunities of a large research university with the personal attention of a small, private college, by offering an education that integrates courses from four colleges and dozens of fields of study. Students customize their experience to their interests by tailoring majors and academic programs from more than 2,000 courses, changing majors, carrying a double major, or taking courses outside their college or major field of study. Lehigh offers unique learning opportunities through interdisciplinary programs such as music and engineering and computer science and business (www.lehigh.edu/distinctive programs). The arts are essential to the learning experience and are integrated throughout the curriculum. Students develop their imagination and creativity while acquiring skills that will complement their professional development. Students have access to world-class faculty who offer their time and personal attention to help students learn and succeed. Students gain hands-on, real-world experience and take part in activities that build confidence and help them develop as leaders. Lehigh's vibrant campus life offers many social and extracurricular activities. Choose from 150 and 40 intramural and club sports, in which over 60 percent of undergraduates participate.

"Lehigh requires students to submit scores from the new SAT with the Writing component. Students may also take the ACT with the Writing portion in lieu of the SAT. SAT Subject Tests are recommended but not required."

SELECTIVITY

Admissions Rating	97
# of applicants	12,155
% of applicants accepted	32
% of acceptees attending	30
# accepting a place on wait list	1,096
% admitted from wait list	7
# of early decision applicants	827
% accepted early decision	58

FRESHMAN PROFILE

Range SAT Critical Reading	600–680
Range SAT Math	640–710
Minimum paper TOEFL	570
Minimum computer TOEFL	230
% graduated top 10% of class	93
% graduated top 25% of class	99
% graduated top 50% of class	100

DEADLINES

Early decision	
Deadline	11/15
Notification	12/15
Regular	
Deadline	1/1
Nonfall registration?	yes

APPLICANTS ALSO LOOK AT

AND OFTEN PREFER
Cornell University
Boston College
University of Pennsylvania

AND SOMETIMES PREFER
Johns Hopkins University
Carnegie Mellon University
Tufts University

AND RARELY PREFER
Lafayette College
Bucknell University
Villanova University
Penn State—University Park

FINANCIAL FACTS

Financial Aid Rating	87
Annual tuition	$37,250
% frosh rec. need-based scholarship or grant aid	40
% UG rec. need-based scholarship or grant aid	43
% frosh rec. non-need-based scholarship or grant aid	5
% UG rec. non-need-based scholarship or grant aid	7
% frosh rec. need-based self-help aid	39
% UG rec. need-based self-help aid	42
% frosh rec. athletic scholarships	1
% frosh rec. any financial aid	65
% UG rec. any financial aid	60
% UG borrow to pay for school	53
Average cumulative indebtedness	$26,768

LEWIS & CLARK COLLEGE

0615 SOUTHWEST PALATINE HILL ROAD, PORTLAND, OR 97219-7899 • ADMISSIONS: 503-768-7040 • FAX: 503-768-7055

STUDENTS SAY "..."

Academics
If you want to learn to think for yourself (and meet other people doing the same), try the beautiful environs of Lewis & Clark College in Portland, a school that "makes a community of its anti-community, and is proud of it." The definitively liberal arts curriculum and "self-directed attitude" toward courses of study cultivate "critical thinking and social awareness," and "even lectures tend to include discussions." The academics here are what you make of them, and the course load "can be incredibly simple or very rigorous/challenging" depending on your choices.

The school has been placing "an increasing level of importance on multiculturalism/ethnicity," which is reflected in its "wonderful study abroad programs," but the administration gets a few complaints from students that "don't think that the administration is totally in sync with what the student body believes or wants." The professors, by and large, "are wonderful"; they are passionate in both their teaching and their desire to shape students into independent thinkers, which "really shows in the critical feedback they give and the lengths they go to be accessible to students." Says one familial freshman: "I feel like each one is an aunt or uncle." Availability is not an issue for any aspect of the faculty or staff, as "personal appointments are very easy to get with practically anyone." Facilities also get top marks for their environmental-friendliness and overall degree of pleasantness, as does the number of grants for students looking to do research (often with professors, for those looking to bulk up their grad school resume). Rising tuition costs (without corresponding financial aid) are a main concern at LC.

Life
Those looking to get away for a few hours take a school-chartered shuttle to downtown Portland where bookstores, markets, and coffeeshops offer some respite. A lot of upperclassmen move off-campus, taking them out of the "the LC Bubble," and these apartments are where most parties occur on weekends, for those that are interested (and many here are not). "No frats means no one is exclusive. Every party is usually open to everyone!" says a student. Pot usage is pretty prevalent at Lewis & Clark, which leads to a lot of "evenings spent high out of your mind while watching YouTube videos." The school provides plenty of sponsored events such as seminars and lectures, though these are usually attended by the underclassmen, and most people take advantage of their location and participate in trips with College Outdoors, such as "hikes on the Oregon coast, kayaking, snowshoeing, or rafting." Between the school and the environment, activities are plentiful, and with such a friendly and "chill" student body, "one cannot get left behind at this school."

Student Body
People here are generous and colorful with their adjectives when describing the gestalt of the student body, ranging from "an eclectic explosion of quirky intelligence, green green green, dreadlocks, vintage stores, hipsters" to "extremely atheist, wannabe hippies, that view clothing as optional and knowledge as power!" Perhaps this says it all—it's a diverse group of individuals at LC (at least as far as personalities go, as the ethnic makeup is quite "vanilla"), with very few students not finding a way to fit in (they "either accept that everyone here is different, or transfer"). There's also a large international and gay/lesbian student quotient. One student sums up the LC population: "As the Cheshire Cat said to Alice, 'We're all mad here.'"

Everyone here is politically active and "open to new experiences and challenging assumptions, with a strong vein of idealism running throughout." Students "constantly engage in academic discussion and debate outside of the classroom," but this is more for rhetoric's sake, as there is an "absence of unhealthily competitive attitudes" at Lewis & Clark.

LEWIS & CLARK COLLEGE

FINANCIAL AID: 503-768-7090 • E-MAIL: ADMISSIONS@LCLARK.EDU • WEBSITE: WWW.LCLARK.EDU

THE PRINCETON REVIEW SAYS

Admissions

Very important factors considered include: Academic GPA, rigor of secondary school record, racial/ethnic status. *Important factors considered include:* Class rank, application essay, recommendation(s), standardized test scores, alumni/ae relation, character/personal qualities, extracurricular activities, first generation, talent/ability, volunteer work. *Other factors considered include:* Geographical residence, interview, level of applicant's interest, state residency, work experience. TOEFL required of all international applicants. High school diploma is required and GED is accepted. *Academic units recommended:* 4 English, 4 mathematics, 3 science, (2 science labs), 3 foreign language, 4 social studies, 1 visual/performing arts.

Financial Aid

Students should submit: FAFSA, CSS/Financial Aid PROFILE. The Princeton Review suggests that all financial aid forms be submitted as soon as possible after January 1. *Need-based scholarships/grants offered:* Federal Pell, SEOG, state scholarships/grants, private scholarships, the school's own gift aid. *Loan aid offered:* Direct Subsidized Stafford, Direct Unsubsidized Stafford, Direct PLUS, FFEL Subsidized Stafford, FFEL Unsubsidized Stafford, FFEL PLUS, Federal Perkins Applicants will be notified of awards on a rolling basis beginning 3/1. Federal Work-Study Program available. Institutional employment available. Off-campus job opportunities are fair.

The Inside Word

Admissions evaluations are thorough, and the Portfolio Path is an intriguing option that guarantees a purely personal evaluation. Few colleges of Lewis & Clark's quality are as accommodating to students.

THE SCHOOL SAYS ". . ."

From The Admissions Office

"The record number of applicants in recent years cited a variety of reasons they were drawn to Lewis & Clark. Many had to do with the multiple environments experienced by our students, including a small arts and sciences college with a 13:1 student/faculty ratio; a location only six miles from downtown Portland (metropolitan population 1.9 million); a setting in the heart of the Pacific Northwest, making more than 80 trips per year possible for our College Outdoors Program; and the rest of the world—almost 60 percent of our graduates included an overseas program in their curriculum. Since 1962, more than 9,337 students and 212 faculty members have participated in 578 programs in 66 countries on 6 continents. Our international curriculum has undergone a total review to better prepare graduates going into the twenty-first century.

"At Lewis & Clark College, SAT Subject Test scores are not required."

SELECTIVITY

Admissions Rating	94
# of applicants	5,351
% of applicants accepted	56
% of acceptees attending	17
# accepting a place on wait list	230
% admitted from wait list	14

FRESHMAN PROFILE

Range SAT Critical Reading	610–700
Range SAT Math	590–680
Range SAT Writing	590–680
Range ACT Composite	26–31
Minimum paper TOEFL	550
Minimum computer TOEFL	213
Average HS GPA	3.69
% graduated top 10% of class	46
% graduated top 25% of class	81
% graduated top 50% of class	98

DEADLINES

Early action	
Deadline	11/1
Notification	1/15
Regular	
Priority	2/1
Deadline	2/1
Notification	4/1
Nonfall registration?	yes

APPLICANTS ALSO LOOK AT
AND OFTEN PREFER
Occidental College
University of California—Santa Cruz
Stanford University
AND SOMETIMES PREFER
University of Puget Sound
Reed College
Colorado College
Willamette University
AND RARELY PREFER
University of Colorado—Boulder
Pitzer College

FINANCIAL FACTS

Financial Aid Rating	86
Annual tuition	$31,840
% frosh rec. need-based scholarship or grant aid	53
% UG rec. need-based scholarship or grant aid	56
% frosh rec. non-need-based scholarship or grant aid	3
% UG rec. non-need-based scholarship or grant aid	2
% frosh rec. need-based self-help aid	36
% UG rec. need-based self-help aid	38
% frosh rec. any financial aid	78
% UG rec. any financial aid	80
% UG borrow to pay for school	58
Average cumulative indebtedness	$20,127

LOUISIANA STATE UNIVERSITY

110 THOMAS BOYD HALL, BATON ROUGE, LA 70803 • ADMISSIONS: 225-578-1175 • FAX: 225-575-4433

STUDENTS SAY ". . ."

Academics

At Louisiana State University's flagship campus, you'll find "outstanding academics combined with a great college life." Some students here opt for only the latter; for many, "LSU is about football and partying." "Those who wish to apply themselves," however, "have ample opportunity and resources," and they can learn almost anything, since "The greatest strength of LSU by far is its diversity. [You] can come to LSU for sports, music. . . science, economics, or nearly any sort of humanities discipline you are interested in." Areas of strength include programs in premedical science, engineering, agriculture, and mass communications. The school is huge, which means that "somewhere within that huge number is someone that you can get along with," but also that it is easy to "get lost in the crowd"; "You are just a number to the administration and a good amount of your professors," especially in intro-level classes. However, "Once you get into classes that are smaller and more geared toward your chosen major, you are able to develop more of a one-on-one relationship with your professors." Fortunately "many administrative tasks" (such as "bills and registration") "can be completed online, and computers are available all over campus for students who don't have personal computers," making the bureaucracy somewhat easier to navigate. The school also offers academic lifelines such as "free tutoring all day long. The tutors are students who have already taken [the] courses."

Life

LSU is a big enough school to offer something for everyone, and undergrads here enjoy countless activities within a variety subcultures. Most divisions, however, dissolve on game day, when tailgating is raised to the level of "an art form." A freshman reports, "On Saturdays during football season everyone is on campus before the game with friends, beer, and barbeque." Fans "come from all over and stay out all day. It's the one day when it doesn't matter who you are, as long as you're wearing purple and gold." Other LSU traditions include Thursday nights at the bars of Tigerland, "a street with three popular college bars right next to each other," and parties wherever and whenever possible. The Greek system here is "highly influential," but, students note, "This isn't the kind of school where a student doesn't have a social life if he/she isn't Greek." For the more aesthetically inclined, "LSU has an amazing art center—The Shaw Center—complete with a theater and fancy sushi bar on the top floor, which looks over the Mississippi River." Undergrads report that "the beauty of our campus is amazing. The 100-plus-year-old oaks and the Italian Renaissance architecture wow any visitor to LSU's campus."

Student Body

The typical student at LSU "studies moderately—enough to get the grade he/she desires in a class"—and "frequently spends time with friends, possibly going to parties or places that serve alcohol." Mixed in is "a good number of atypical students who study more and do not go partying over the weekends. These students find fulfillment in their own interests regardless of what others think." While "conservative frat boys and sorority girls dominate the campus," the school is home to a diverse population including "many from foreign countries and other ethnic group[s]" and "a huge subculture of indie-rock nerds, skateboarders, hippies, and liberals." There are even a few who "don't give a damn about LSU football"—hey, at a school this big, anything's possible. The student body also includes a substantial population of legacies.

FINANCIAL AID: 225-578-3103 • E-MAIL: ADMISSIONS@LSU.EDU • WEBSITE: WWW.LSU.EDU

THE PRINCETON REVIEW SAYS

Admissions

Very important factors considered include: Academic GPA, rigor of secondary school record, standardized test scores. *Important factors considered include:* Class rank, talent/ability. *Other factors considered include:* Application essay, recommendation(s), extracurricular activities, first generation, SAT or ACT required; ACT with Writing component required. TOEFL required of all international applicants. High school diploma is required and GED is accepted. *Academic units required:* 4 English, 3 mathematics, 3 science, 2 foreign language, 1 social studies, 2 history, 3 academic electives, 1 half credit of computer studies.

Financial Aid

Students should submit: FAFSA, institution's own financial aid form. The Princeton Review suggests that all financial aid forms be submitted as soon as possible after January 1. *Need-based scholarships/grants offered:* Federal Pell, SEOG, state scholarships/grants, private scholarships, the school's own gift aid, ACG/SMART. *Loan aid offered:* FFEL Subsidized Stafford, FFEL Unsubsidized Stafford, FFEL PLUS, Federal Perkins, Alternative/Grad Plus. Applicants will be notified of awards on or about 3/1. Federal Work-Study Program available. Institutional employment available. Off-campus job opportunities are excellent.

The Inside Word

Good students and great athletes are welcome at LSU, where the annual avalanche of applications necessitates a formula-driven approach to admissions. Check LSU's website to see which combinations of GPA, class rank, and test scores qualify students for admission.

THE SCHOOL SAYS "..."

From The Admissions Office

"LSU holds a prominent position in U.S. higher education and is committed to meeting the challenge of pursuing intellectual development for its students, expanding the bounds of knowledge through research, and creating economic opportunities for Louisiana. LSU, one of only 25 universities nationwide designated as both a land-grant and sea-grant institution, also holds the Carnegie Foundation's doctoral research, extensive designation.

"LSU's instructional programs include 198 undergraduate and graduate/professional degrees. Outside of the classroom, residential colleges, service-learning opportunites, and over 350 registered student organizations contribute to an exciting and meaningful college experience.

"Louisiana State University offers the Southern hospitality of a small community while providing the benefits of a large, technologically advanced institution.

"Freshman applicants for Fall 2008 are required to submit writing scores by taking the new version of the SAT (or the ACT with the Writing component). LSU will use the best scores from either SAT or ACT, including scores from the old (prior to March 2005) versions of the tests, in making admission decisions."

SELECTIVITY

Admissions Rating	83
# of applicants	11,452
% of applicants accepted	73
% of acceptees attending	55

FRESHMAN PROFILE

Range SAT Critical Reading	520–640
Range SAT Math	550–650
Range SAT Writing	490–620
Range ACT Composite	23–28
Minimum paper TOEFL	550
Minimum computer TOEFL	213
Minimum web-based TOEFL	79
Average HS GPA	3.52
% graduated top 10% of class	27
% graduated top 25% of class	55
% graduated top 50% of class	84

DEADLINES

Regular	
Priority	11/15
Deadline	4/15
Nonfall registration?	yes

FINANCIAL FACTS

Financial Aid Rating	66
Annual in-state tuition	$2,981
Annual out-of-state tuition	$11,281
Room and board	$6,852
Required fees	$1,562
Books and supplies	$1,500
% frosh rec. need-based scholarship or grant aid	33
% UG rec. need-based scholarship or grant aid	29
% frosh rec. non-need-based scholarship or grant aid	2
% UG rec. non-need-based scholarship or grant aid	1
% frosh rec. need-based self-help aid	19
% UG rec. need-based self-help aid	25
% frosh rec. athletic scholarships	2
% UG rec. athletic scholarships	2
% frosh rec. any financial aid	94
% UG rec. any financial aid	79
% UG borrow to pay for school	46
Average cumulative indebtedness	$17,057

LOYOLA COLLEGE IN MARYLAND

4501 NORTH CHARLES STREET, BALTIMORE, MD 21210 • ADMISSIONS: 410-617-5012 • FAX: 410-617-2176

CAMPUS LIFE
Quality of Life Rating	**91**
Fire Safety Rating	**78**
Green Rating	**60***
Type of school	private
Affiliation	Roman Catholic
Environment	village

STUDENTS
Total undergrad enrollment	3,580
% male/female	42/58
% from out of state	82
% from public high school	60
% live on campus	78
% African American	5
% Asian	3
% Caucasian	85
% Hispanic	3
% international	1
# of countries represented	31

SURVEY SAYS . . .
Athletic facilities are great
Dorms are like palaces
Frats and sororities are unpopular
or nonexistent

ACADEMICS
Academic Rating	**84**
Calendar	semester
Student/faculty ratio	12:1
Profs interesting rating	96
Profs accessible rating	93
Most common reg class size	20–29 students
Most common lab size	10–19 students

MOST POPULAR MAJORS
business
communications
biology

STUDENTS SAY ". . ."

Academics

A Jesuit school in suburban Baltimore, Loyola College in Maryland "seeks to develop the whole person—intellectually, emotionally, socially, and spiritually." Jesuit values are stressed through the school's "well-rounded curriculum, encouraging participation in community service, and teaching values in diversity both on and off campus." Across the board, students say the Loyola faculty is comprised of accomplished scholars and talented teachers. A senior shares, "Professors are the best part about Loyola College. They love their subjects and their students, and make class interesting with their enthusiasm." When it comes to academic or personal matters, "the professors at Loyola are so caring it almost seems unnatural. They will go out of their way to make sure you understand material and always have their door open after class discussions." What's more, the academic experience is characterized by small class sizes and ample discussion. A sophomore offers, "I could not be happier with my academic experience at Loyola. Even the biggest classes are small enough to facilitate close interaction with the professors." Outside the classroom, academic opportunities abound, and "professors encourage us to become part of the department through research or work-study programs." Likewise, the "administration cares deeply about fostering growth outside of the classroom." A senior attests, "As a three-year member of the student government association at Loyola College I have always been impressed with the openness of the administration and their willingness to work for the best interests of the students."

Life

Despite the demands of coursework, you'll get the full college experience at Loyola College in Maryland. Outgoing and social, most Loyola undergraduates are "motivated to achieve a balance between academic success and the social benefits of college." In the admiring words of one junior, "The typical student at Loyola is genius at time management. They find a way to get to the gym at least three times a week, go out at least three times week, and pull off above a 3.0 GPA every semester." However, Loyola students never lose track of their educational priorities, telling us, "The social life is very important here, but in all honesty, academics come first." In addition to hitting the off-campus bars, there are many attractions in the surrounding city of Baltimore. A sophomore reports, "For fun, my friends and I go out to eat in Baltimore, head to Towson mall, and go to the movies or concerts. Baltimore has a lot to offer to the college student." There are also plenty of extracurricular activities, clubs, and organizations at school, and "Loyola goes to great lengths to develop a sense of community across the campus." On that note, day-to-day life is easygoing and pleasant on Loyola's pretty campus. Happily, campus housing is top-notch, and "many students live in suites or apartments, and can thus cook their own food in their own kitchens."

Student Body

Loyola tends to admit outgoing and well-rounded students who want to benefit from all the academic, extracurricular, and social aspects of college life. On the whole, students "care deeply about their education and realize that they are here to learn. But they also enjoy themselves and are not too uptight." Considering the fact that Loyola is a private, Jesuit college on the East Coast, it's not surprising that "the average student comes from the greater Philadelphia, New Jersey, and New York area (although that seems to be changing) and ranges in economic background from middle to upper class." You'll find a shared affinity for Ugg boots and The North Face apparel on the Loyola campus and "the majority of students are preppy." Even so, you can't judge a book by its cover. A sophomore tells us, "Everyone seems like they may be a typical 'Loyola Girl' but when you look deeper, you find that these people are unique and diverse." No matter what your background or interests, "there are enough clubs and a wonderful student life on-campus that atypical students find their place and become as much a part of Loyola as typical students."

THE PRINCETON REVIEW SAYS

Admissions

Very important factors considered include: Academic GPA, rigor of secondary school record. *Important factors considered include:* Standardized test scores. *Other factors considered include:* Class rank, application essay, recommendation(s), alumni/ae relation, character/personal qualities, extracurricular activities, racial/ethnic status, talent/ability, volunteer work, work experience. SAT or ACT required; TOEFL required of all international applicants. High school diploma is required and GED is accepted. *Academic units required:* 4 English, 3 mathematics, 3 science, 2 history. *Academic units recommended:* 4 English, 4 mathematics, 4 science, 3 history.

Financial Aid

Students should submit: FAFSA, CSS/Financial Aid PROFILE, noncustodial PROFILE, business/farm supplement. Regular filing deadline is 2/15. The Princeton Review suggests that all financial aid forms be submitted as soon as possible after January 1. *Need-based scholarships/grants offered:* Federal Pell, SEOG, state scholarships/grants, private scholarships, the school's own gift aid. *Loan aid offered:* Direct Subsidized Stafford, Direct Unsubsidized Stafford, FFEL PLUS, Federal Perkins, college/university loans from institutional funds. Applicants will be notified of awards on or about 4/1. Off-campus job opportunities are good.

The Inside Word

Grades are more important than standardized test scores in the admissions process at Loyola. Your junior and senior grades are particularly critical. The content of the courses you've taken weighs fairly heavily, too. Obviously, harder courses look better. If your standardized test scores aren't awful and your high school GPA is the equivalent of a "B+" or better, it is extremely likely that you will get admitted here. If your GPA is more like a "B," your odds are still pretty good. If your academic profile is a little thin, definitely take advantage of the opportunity to interview.

THE SCHOOL SAYS " . . ."

From The Admissions Office

"To make a wise choice about your college plans, you will need to find out more. We extend to you these invitations. Question-and-answer periods with an Admissions Counselor are helpful to prospective students. An appointment should be made in advance. Admissions office hours are 9:00 A.M. to 5:00 P.M., Monday through Friday. College day programs and Saturday information programs are scheduled during the academic year. These programs include a video about Loyola, a general information session, a discussion of various majors, a campus tour, and lunch. Summer information programs can help high school juniors to get a head start on investigating colleges. These programs feature an introductory presentation about the college and a campus tour.

"Loyola College will continue to accept results of both the former SAT and ACT. In addition, Loyola will continue to combine the highest sub scores from multiple test administrations from both the old and new tests (SAT: Reading/Math scores). Loyola will not explicitly require submission of results from the new SAT."

SELECTIVITY
Admissions Rating	89
# of applicants	8,594
% of applicants accepted	60
% of acceptees attending	19

FRESHMAN PROFILE
Range SAT Critical Reading	560–650
Range SAT Math	560–660
Minimum paper TOEFL	550
Minimum computer TOEFL	213
Average HS GPA	3.5
% graduated top 10% of class	37
% graduated top 25% of class	75
% graduated top 50% of class	96

DEADLINES
Regular	
Priority	1/15
Deadline	1/15
Notification	4/1
Nonfall registration?	yes

APPLICANTS ALSO LOOK AT
AND OFTEN PREFER
University of Notre Dame
Georgetown University
Boston College
AND SOMETIMES PREFER
University of Richmond
College of the Holy Cross
Villanova University
AND RARELY PREFER
Fairfield University
Fordham University
Providence College

FINANCIAL FACTS
Financial Aid Rating	96
Annual tuition	$35,140
Room and board	$9,740
Required fees	$1,265
Books and supplies	$1,010
% frosh rec. need-based scholarship or grant aid	37
% UG rec. need-based scholarship or grant aid	36
% frosh rec. non-need-based scholarship or grant aid	19
% UG rec. non-need-based scholarship or grant aid	16
% frosh rec. need-based self-help aid	44
% UG rec. need-based self-help aid	42
% frosh rec. athletic scholarships	3
% UG rec. athletic scholarships	3
% frosh rec. any financial aid	66
% UG rec. any financial aid	71
% UG borrow to pay for school	72
Average cumulative indebtedness	$19,730

LOYOLA MARYMOUNT UNIVERSITY

One LMU Drive, Suite 100, Los Angeles, CA 90045 • Admissions: 310-338-2750 • Fax: 310-338-2797

STUDENTS SAY ". . ."

Academics

You may be technically going to school in the midst of bustling LA, but attending Loyola Marymount University is more like having "a little family on the bluff." Offering a "well-rounded Jesuit education" on an "absolutely beautiful and modern campus" as well as "many activities and service opportunities." Students here are dedicated to becoming aware of "the pertinent social issues of today's world and how they relate to each student's chosen field(s) of study." LMU is often referred to as a "hidden gem," but those that go here wouldn't mind seeing a bit more publicity for their school.

A small enrollment means small class sizes, and students report having no trouble getting into the courses they desire. Professorial quality "varies"; basically, "the professors that teach because they love to teach are amazing. The professors that care more about their research than their students are disappointing." There aren't many gripes about availability, though, as most are "more than willing to assist with any questions or problems." As for the higher ups, there is "some resistance and hiding on the part of the administration when students try to stir things up," but those in charge primarily do a good job, remaining active with student life. Several administrators and deans "show their commitment to the students by serving as Club Moderators" in addition to their day jobs. Many students complain that the cost of attending LMU "is a bit ridiculous," and wish that financial aid and scholarships were more available to them, rather than the money being spent on ever-present construction.

Life

Student claim to "feel very comfortable living on campus and walking around late at night due to the security on campus." As with many things located in LA, "parking is an issue that needs to be improved." The small size of the student body creates a "bubble" effect, giving the school a "high school" flavor, but the city and neighboring schools provide plenty of options to any student that feels as though the LMU walls are closing in on her. A lot of freshmen choose to go home on the weekends, but most upperclassmen hang around and go to the beach, Santa Monica, or shopping malls, all located within 15 minutes of the campus. "People do party and drink, but it is nothing compared to most other colleges," says one junior. Greek life is popular but not central to the party scene here, and most parties occur off-campus. For students wishing to remain close to their dorms, the campus has an excellent sit-down restaurant that provides "almost anything that you can find at a classy off-campus restaurant," and the D-1 sports teams "are entertaining and encourage a great deal of campus spirit."

Student Body

"There is quite a bit of money at LMU," enough that "two students brought 49-inch plasma TVs to their freshman dorm this year." Perhaps they are friends with the "skinny, rich-beyond-belief blonde girls whose version of 'scrubbing it' is wearing their Juicy Couture sweatshirts with their Manolo Blahniks." But "Not everyone is rich. The school isn't overly snobby, and there is a niche for everyone." The "most visible" LMU archetype is "the vaguely wholesome, *Saved By the Bell: The College Years* jocky frat/sorority type," but there are also plenty of "serious student types who are always in the library and no one else ever really gets to know them," as well as "the artsy, theater/coffee-shop types who wear whatever expresses their feelings" as part of the "chill underground." Many in this last group "participate in the film department and the radio station and form their own close community." While "some students here are very LA, others are more focused politically and spiritually and are committed to social justice, service, and participation in student life." At LMU, it may be "easy to feel like you belong" but some say there still "needs to be a stronger sense of the differences in people, races, sexual orientations, and cultures."

LOYOLA MARYMOUNT UNIVERSITY

FINANCIAL AID: 310-338-2753 • E-MAIL: ADMISSIONS@LMU.EDU • WEBSITE: WWW.LMU.EDU

THE PRINCETON REVIEW SAYS

Admissions

Very important factors considered include: Academic GPA, rigor of secondary school record. *Important factors considered include:* Class rank, application essay, standardized test scores, character/personal qualities, talent/ability. *Other factors considered include:* Recommendation(s), alumni/ae relation, extracurricular activities, first generation, geographical residence, interview, volunteer work, work experience. SAT or ACT required; TOEFL required of all international applicants. High school diploma is required and GED is accepted. *Academic units recommended:* 4 English, 3 mathematics, 2 science, (2 science labs), 3 foreign language, 3 social studies, 1 academic elective.

Financial Aid

Students should submit: FAFSA, CSS/Financial Aid PROFILE, business/farm supplement. Regular filing deadline is 4/1. The Princeton Review suggests that all financial aid forms be submitted as soon as possible after January 1. *Need-based scholarships/grants offered:* Federal Pell, SEOG, state scholarships/grants, private scholarships, the school's own gift aid. *Loan aid offered:* FFEL Subsidized Stafford, FFEL Unsubsidized Stafford, FFEL PLUS, Federal Perkins, college/university loans from institutional funds. Applicants will be notified of awards on a rolling basis beginning 3/15. Federal Work-Study Program available. Institutional employment available. Off-campus job opportunities are excellent.

The Inside Word

Loyola Marymount's Admissions Committee is particular about candidate evaluation, but a large applicant pool has more to do with the university's moderate acceptance rate than does academic selectivity. Even so, underachievers will have difficulty getting in.

THE SCHOOL SAYS " . . ."

From The Admissions Office

"Loyola Marymount University is a dynamic, student-centered university. We are medium sized (5,000 undergraduates), and we are the only Jesuit university in the Southwestern United States.

"Our campus is located in Westchester, a friendly, residential neighborhood that is removed from the hustle and bustle of Los Angeles, yet offers easy access to all the richnesss of our most cosmopolitan environment. One mile from the ocean, our students enjoy ocean and mountain vistas as well as the moderate climate and crisp breezes characteristic of a coastal location.

"Loyola Marymount is committed to the ideals of Jesuit and Marymount education. We are a student-centered university, dedicated to the education of the whole person and to the preparation of our students for lives of service to their families, communities, and professions. Breadth and rigor are the hallmarks of the curriculum.

"Taken together, our academic program, our Jesuit and Marymount heritage, and our terrific campus environment afford our students unparalleled opportunity to prepare for life and leadership in the twenty-first century.

"Applicants to the Fall 2008 entering class must submit results from either the SAT or ACT. We expect most students will submit scores from the new version of the SAT (or the ACT with the Writing section). We will use the student's best scores from either test."

SELECTIVITY

Admissions Rating	88
# of applicants	8,533
% of applicants accepted	52
% of acceptees attending	28

FRESHMAN PROFILE

Range SAT Critical Reading	530–630
Range SAT Math	540–640
Minimum paper TOEFL	550
Minimum computer TOEFL	213
Average HS GPA	3.6
% graduated top 10% of class	30
% graduated top 25% of class	66
% graduated top 50% of class	99

DEADLINES

Regular	
Priority	1/15
Notification	rolling
Nonfall registration?	yes

APPLICANTS ALSO LOOK AT
AND OFTEN PREFER
University of Southern California
University of California—Berkeley
University of California—Los Angeles
AND SOMETIMES PREFER
University of California—San Diego
Santa Clara University
University of California—Santa Barbara
AND RARELY PREFER
Pepperdine University
University of San Diego
University of California—Irvine
Chapman University

FINANCIAL FACTS

Financial Aid Rating	77
Annual tuition	$33,901
Room and board	$11,808
Required fees	$636
Books and supplies	$3,465
% frosh rec. need-based scholarship or grant aid	46
% UG rec. need-based scholarship or grant aid	46
% frosh rec. non-need-based scholarship or grant aid	9
% UG rec. non-need-based scholarship or grant aid	5
% frosh rec. need-based self-help aid	39
% UG rec. need-based self-help aid	42
% frosh rec. athletic scholarships	7
% UG rec. athletic scholarships	4
% UG borrow to pay for school	66
Average cumulative indebtedness	$28,548

LOYOLA UNIVERSITY—CHICAGO

820 NORTH MICHIGAN AVENUE, CHICAGO, IL 60611 • ADMISSIONS: 312-915-6500 • FAX: 312-915-7216

CAMPUS LIFE
Quality of Life Rating	77
Fire Safety Rating	78
Green Rating	95
Type of school	private
Affiliation	Roman Catholic/Jesuit
Environment	metropolis

STUDENTS
Total undergrad enrollment	9,365
% male/female	35/65
% from out of state	34
% from public high school	66
% live on campus	39
% in (# of) fraternities	6 (7)
% in (# of) sororities	5 (12)
% African American	5
% Asian	12
% Caucasian	62
% Hispanic	10
% international	1
# of countries represented	79

SURVEY SAYS . . .
Small classes
Lab facilities are great
Students love Chicago, IL
Great off-campus food
Lots of beer drinking
(Almost) everyone smokes

ACADEMICS
Academic Rating	77
Calendar	semester
Student/faculty ratio	14:1
Profs interesting rating	74
Profs accessible rating	76
Most common reg class size	10–19 students
Most common lab size	20–29 students

MOST POPULAR MAJORS
biology/biological sciences
psychology
nursing/registered nurse
(RN, ASN, BSN, MSN)

STUDENTS SAY ". . ."

Academics

Standing tall alongside the shore of Lake Michigan, eight miles north of Chicago, many students are quick to affirm that Loyola's greatest asset is "the school's location." Proud of its "strong Jesuit tradition," Loyola University—Chicago "encourages creative thinking and allows students to explore the complexities of the world in and out of the classroom." The professors here are "very knowledgeable" and distinguished in their respective fields, and are always "willing to help students as much as they can." "Small class sizes" help students "feel comfortable asking questions," and professors' "expertise" and "passion" make it "much easier to learn." Many students, however, express disappointment with the administration citing "red tape" and "layers of bureaucracy," which make many offices "a bit inaccessible." Recently, efforts to "streamline university services" have been made, resulting in the creation of "a central location for the Dean's, Bursar, [and] Cash Office" with "easier accessibility" to students. The President's Office also holds regular town meetings and informal gatherings to encourage an ongoing dialogue between students, staff, and administration, and a service excellence initiative also continues to evaluate and enhance student services. The Office of First-Year Experience, created in Fall 2007, provides services to help freshmen and transfer students transition to Loyola through special seminars, mentoring, and more. While the administration can be "daunting," the "Professors are always in reach, and the academic experience is uplifting." As for the Loyola experience, in the words of one student, "I love this school and I love the city it is located in."

Life

It's all about location, location, location. As one student explains, "I've learned some lessons in the classroom, but more on the streets around campus." Living in Chicago, "Students tend to have plenty of options in terms of what to do for fun." There's an active "local bar scene," as well as "concerts, museums, plays, and almost anything else one can think of doing." Getting around town is really easy: "There is a [CTA] station dedicated to the campus which makes it extremely easy to travel anywhere within the city. Each student is also given a U-pass which provides unlimited rides on any Chicago public transportation." Students who prefer to stay on campus will find "plenty of other activities" to capture their attention, including "intramural sports, clubs, and Division I basketball games." Serious sports fans should be warned, however, as "Sports teams do not rule this school," even though the city itself is pretty well-known for its enthusiasm for athletics. Students don't let life in the big city deter their need for the great outdoors either. They enjoy "being right on Lake Michigan" where there are plenty of "parks close by with good running trails." The school itself is located in one of "the most diverse neighborhoods" in Chicago. There are "African, Thai, Chinese, Italian, and Puerto Rican restaurants next to Mexican grocery stores, Middle Eastern bakeries, and vegetarian stores." The entertainment options are so expansive that, as one student claims, "If you get bored in Chicago, it's your own fault."

Student Body

Loyola has a "very diverse mix of students." While many are "White and from the Chicago suburbs," many others are "of all different races, ethnicities, religions, and sexual orientations." One student was surprised to discover that a "large portion of students aren't Catholic." The university supports diversity through its on-campus "ethnic and cultural groups" so that students "rarely feel alone or ostracized." As one student explains, Loyola is a "good place to be surrounded by such a diverse student body" as "There's definitely room for different people." Students here "take academics seriously" and have a "good work ethic." Most are "politically active," "generally liberal," and "social justice oriented." Others caution that most students are "traditional-age, 4-year students who have been there since they were freshmen, making it hard for new transfer students and commuters to fit in."

FINANCIAL AID: 773-508-3155 • E-MAIL: ADMISSION@LUC.EDU • WEBSITE: WWW.LUC.EDU

THE PRINCETON REVIEW SAYS

Admissions

Very important factors considered include: Academic GPA, rigor of secondary school record, standardized test scores. *Important factors considered include:* Application essay, recommendation(s), character/personal qualities, extracurricular activities, level of applicant's interest, volunteer work. *Other factors considered include:* Class rank, alumni/ae relation, first generation, geographical residence, interview, state residency, talent/ability, work experience. SAT or ACT required; TOEFL required of all international applicants. High school diploma is required and GED is accepted. *Academic units required:* 4 English, 3 mathematics, 3 science, 2 foreign language, 2 social studies, 1 history. *Academic units recommended:* 4 English, 4 mathematics, 3 science, 2 foreign language, 2 social studies, 2 history, 3 academic electives.

Financial Aid

Students should submit: FAFSA. The Princeton Review suggests that all financial aid forms be submitted as soon as possible after January 1. *Need-based scholarships/grants offered:* Federal Pell, SEOG, state scholarships/grants, private scholarships, the school's own gift aid. *Loan aid offered:* FFEL Subsidized Stafford, FFEL Unsubsidized Stafford, FFEL PLUS, Federal Perkins, Federal Nursing Applicants will be notified of awards on a rolling basis beginning 2/15. Federal Work-Study Program available. Institutional employment available. Off-campus job opportunities are good.

The Inside Word

Loyola is fairly conventional when it comes to admissions policies. Successful candidates usually have a combination of strong grades, success in a tough college preparatory curriculum, and solid extracurricular activities. The school adheres to Jesuit teachings, so applicants with significant volunteer work should impress Admissions Officers.

THE SCHOOL SAYS " . . . "

From The Admissions Office

"To accommodate recent record-breaking freshman classes, Loyola University—Chicago continues to open new facilities and renovate existing buildings, including the state-of-the-art Quinlan Life Sciences Education and Research Center, new residence halls at both the Lake Shore and Water Tower Campuses, and the Sullivan Center for Student Services, a new one-stop center that consolidates more than a dozen campus offices. The Information Commons, a high-tech lakefront library featuring large group study spaces, more than 250 computers; wireless Internet connections and a lakefront café. Loyola frequently enhances its undergraduate academic programs and adds new majors in emerging fields. A new core curriculum enhances student credentials, because it emphasizes lifelong skills and values, and it gives students the opportunity to more easily complete a second major or additional minor. Nationally recognized researchers and scholars continue to teach freshman-level as well as advanced courses. These new developments build on Loyola's rich Jesuit tradition, which fosters academic excellence, instills service to others, and educates the whole person.

"Loyola's Lake Shore and Water Tower Campuses enable students to experience both traditional residential campus life and a vibrant urban environment. With more than 150 campus organizations offering numerous activities and events, as well as cultural, recreational, and internship opportunities throughout the world-class city of Chicago, undergraduate student education at Loyola extends well beyond the classroom. For more information about undergraduate academics, housing, student life, financial assistance, and more, please visit: www.luc.edu/undergrad. Pending further examination into the validity of the new Writing portions offered by the SAT and ACT, LUC will not require applicants to submit Writing scores from either test. All applicants are required to submit a writing sample with their application materials."

SELECTIVITY

Admissions Rating	86
# of applicants	17,357
% of applicants accepted	73
% of acceptees attending	16

FRESHMAN PROFILE

Range SAT Critical Reading	540–640
Range SAT Math	520–640
Range SAT Writing	510–628
Range ACT Composite	23–28
Minimum paper TOEFL	550
Minimum computer TOEFL	213
Minimum web-based TOEFL	79
Average HS GPA	3.54
% graduated top 10% of class	33
% graduated top 25% of class	69
% graduated top 50% of class	96

DEADLINES

Regular	
Priority	4/1
Notification	rolling
Nonfall registration?	yes

APPLICANTS ALSO LOOK AT

AND OFTEN PREFER
Marquette University
DePaul University
University of Illinois at Chicago
University of Illinois at Urbana—Champaign

AND SOMETIMES PREFER
Washington University in St. Louis
Michigan State University

AND RARELY PREFER
Illinois State University

FINANCIAL FACTS

Financial Aid Rating	71
Annual tuition	$28,700
Room and board	$10,490
Required fees	$786
Books and supplies	$1,200
% frosh rec. need-based scholarship or grant aid	70
% UG rec. need-based scholarship or grant aid	65
% frosh rec. non-need-based scholarship or grant aid	6
% UG rec. non-need-based scholarship or grant aid	5
% frosh rec. need-based self-help aid	64
% UG rec. need-based self-help aid	62
% frosh rec. athletic scholarships	1
% UG rec. athletic scholarships	1
% frosh rec. any financial aid	93.6
% UG rec. any financial aid	89.4
% UG borrow to pay for school	67.3
Average cumulative indebtedness	$25,470

LOYOLA UNIVERSITY—NEW ORLEANS

6363 St. Charles Avenue, Box 18, New Orleans, LA 70118 • Admissions: 504-865-3240 • Fax: 504-865-3383

STUDENTS SAY ". . ."

Academics

Loyola University—New Orleans provides students with "an excellent Jesuit education," that emphasizes a "commitment to the community" in "an intimate college setting," all capped with life in New Orleans, "a great place to go to school." Small by university standards, Loyola has a wonderful "community feeling." "You feel it when you first walk on campus." Professors "know you by name and it's not uncommon to stop by their office hours just to chat. They truly care about their students and how we are doing academically and otherwise." Among Loyola's top offerings is its music industry studies program, "the second-best in the nation," right up there with Berklee College of Music in Boston (but with much better weather!). The communications program is "great," as is the "awesome" College of Business (nearly one in four students here pursues a business major). Loyola also boasts a "strong program in criminal justice, with great internship opportunities in New Orleans," and an "outstanding" music program that "produces many successful musicians." One music student notes, "The greatest thing about the music school here is you are never second to a graduate student. Undergraduates are the priority." All undergraduates must complete a common curriculum covering English, math, natural science, history, philosophy, and religious studies; the common curriculum consumes most of freshman year. Hurricane Katrina robbed Loyola of much-needed tuition funds; cost-cutting measures to deal with subsequent budget shortfalls "have resulted in entire fields of study being cut from the curriculum." While that's been the source of some "discontent" on campus, many feel that under the circumstances, "The university is doing the very best that it can to function under the same ideals that it represented pre-Katrina."

Life

New Orleans, in case you hadn't heard, was hit by a pretty big hurricane in 2005. The city is still rebuilding and will be for some time; Loyola's campus, fortunately, was spared the substantial damage so much of the city endured. Students are undaunted, reporting that "going to school in New Orleans is so much fun, even after Hurricane Katrina. There's salsa dancing on Friday nights at Cafe Brazil, live music every night of the week at Snug Harbor, D.B.A., Maple Leaf, or the Howlin' Wolf (just to name a few!). There's great food everywhere in the city: Cajun, Creole, or ethnic." Audubon Park is right "up the street," and is "a great place to hang out, feed the ducks, relax, and maybe even do homework." Another distinguishing characteristic of the town is that "drinking is a way of life in New Orleans, and it's a way of life for kids on campus. You only have to be 18 to get into the bars." Most Loyola students get involved in service, and, "Post-Katrina, there's a ridiculous amount of community service that's easily accessible through the university." Loyola's frats provide plenty of on-campus diversion, as do "a wide variety of campus organizations."

Student Body

Loyola undergrads "want a real college life, not just an education. They want to have experiences and take advantage of the city and truly care about impacting their community." All students "go out and do service." "So many people mentor kids at area schools. Social justice is a theme you can't escape at Loyola." Post-Katrina, "People are very keenly aware of what's going on in the world at large," and students report feeling "more camaraderie and oneness since the hurricane." The school is home to "a wide range of different ethnicities, interests, and so forth. People mostly tend to stick to their own circles, even though people are almost always nice to each other." Prominent subpopulations include the many "sorority and frat people," sometimes "annoying," but "nice people in the end," and the "bohemians and free spirits" drawn here by the music school. "They don't really clash with the more preppy students here." It's New Orleans, so it should come as no surprise that "most students like to drink." "So-called 'straight-edge' students are a minority, but exist."

LOYOLA UNIVERSITY—NEW ORLEANS

FINANCIAL AID: 504-865-3231 • E-MAIL: ADMIT@LOYNO.EDU • WEBSITE: WWW.LOYNO.EDU

THE PRINCETON REVIEW SAYS

Admissions

Very important factors considered include: Rigor of secondary school record, standardized test scores. *Important factors considered include:* Academic GPA, character/personal qualities, extracurricular activities, first generation, interview, talent/ability. *Other factors considered include:* Class rank, application essay, recommendation(s), alumni/ae relation, level of applicant's interest, volunteer work, work experience. ACT with Writing component required. TOEFL required of all international applicants. High school diploma is required and GED is accepted. *Academic units required:* 4 English, 2 mathematics, 2 science, 2 social studies. *Academic units recommended:* 4 English, 3 mathematics, 3 science, 3 social studies.

Financial Aid

Students should submit: FAFSA Regular filing deadline is 6/1. The Princeton Review suggests that all financial aid forms be submitted as soon as possible after January 1. *Need-based scholarships/grants offered:* Federal Pell, SEOG, private scholarships, the school's own gift aid. *Loan aid offered:* FFEL Subsidized Stafford, FFEL Unsubsidized Stafford, FFEL PLUS, Federal Perkins Applicants will be notified of awards on a rolling basis beginning 3/1. Federal Work-Study Program available. Institutional employment available. Off-campus job opportunities are excellent.

The Inside Word

Volunteer work and community service will serve your application to any school well, but they're especially helpful at this Jesuit institution. Post-Katrina New Orleans has spooked some prospective applicants, causing Loyola to have to dig deeper into its applicant pool to fill its classes. Leverage others' squeamishness to your benefit.

THE SCHOOL SAYS " . . ."

From The Admissions Office

"Founded by the Jesuits in 1912, Loyola University—New Orleans has had more than 35,000 graduates who have excelled in innumerable professions for more than 80 years. Loyola's rich Jesuit tradition, its commitment to academic excellence, and its ideal size set it apart from other academic institutions. The total enrollment is approximately 5,000 students; 3,000 of whom are undergraduates. Loyola welcomed back 91 percent of its student body after Hurricane Katrina and experienced only minor damage to its campus.

"Loyola has a student/faculty ratio of 11:1. Ninety-one percent of our faculty hold the highest degrees in their fields. Loyola offers more than 60 majors, the largest of which are communications, business, psychology, music, and premed. Our undergraduate students enjoy individual attention in a university that strives to educate the whole person, not only intellectually, but also spiritually, socially, and athletically. Students hail from all 50 states, Puerto Rico, the District of Columbia, and 48 foreign countries.

"Students applying for admission for the Fall of 2008 are required to take the new version of the SAT (or the ACT with the writing section), but students may also submit scores from the old (prior to March 2005) version of the SAT (or ACT). The highest composite scores will be used in admissions decisions."

SELECTIVITY

Admissions Rating	88
# of applicants	2,980
% of applicants accepted	61
% of acceptees attending	27

FRESHMAN PROFILE

Range SAT Critical Reading	550–690
Range SAT Math	530–630
Range ACT Composite	23–28
Minimum paper TOEFL	550
Minimum computer TOEFL	213
Average HS GPA	3.55
% graduated top 10% of class	27.4
% graduated top 25% of class	54.2
% graduated top 50% of class	84.9

DEADLINES

Regular	
Priority	1/15
Notification	rolling
Nonfall registration?	yes

APPLICANTS ALSO LOOK AT
AND OFTEN PREFER
Saint Louis University
Tulane University
Southern Methodist University
Louisiana State University
University of Miami
AND SOMETIMES PREFER
College of Charleston
Fordham University
Xavier University of Louisiana
Loyola University of Chicago
Florida State University
Boston University

FINANCIAL FACTS

Financial Aid Rating	86
Annual tuition	$37,380
Room and board	$9,126
Required fees	$1,086
Books and supplies	$1,000
% frosh rec. need-based scholarship or grant aid	38
% UG rec. need-based scholarship or grant aid	37
% frosh rec. non-need-based scholarship or grant aid	58
% UG rec. non-need-based scholarship or grant aid	47
% frosh rec. need-based self-help aid	46
% UG rec. need-based self-help aid	39
% frosh rec. any financial aid	85
% UG rec. any financial aid	85
% UG borrow to pay for school	62
Average cumulative indebtedness	$21,020

LYNCHBURG COLLEGE

1501 Lakeside Drive, Lynchburg, VA 24501 • Admissions: 434-544-8300 • Fax: 434-544-8653

CAMPUS LIFE

Quality of Life Rating	**85**
Fire Safety Rating	**75**
Green Rating	**73**
Type of school	private
Affiliation	Disciples of Christ
Environment	city

STUDENTS

Total undergrad enrollment	2,113
% male/female	41/59
% from out of state	34
% from public high school	78
% live on campus	80
% in (# of) fraternities	9 (4)
% in (# of) sororities	13 (6)
% African American	7
% Asian	2
% Caucasian	87
% Hispanic	2
% international	1
# of countries represented	27

SURVEY SAYS . . .
No one cheats
Lots of beer drinking

ACADEMICS

Academic Rating	**78**
Calendar	semester
Student/faculty ratio	13:1
Profs interesting rating	83
Profs accessible rating	85
Most common reg class size	10–19 students
Most common lab size	10–19 students

MOST POPULAR MAJORS
business administration and management
education
communication studies

Academics

The "tight-knit" sense of community of Lynchburg College in Lynchburg, Virginia is one of the main draws of this liberal arts school. Offering a "pretty little campus and a (pretty) good academic setting," the school provides its students with a solid liberal arts education that also helps "to prepare them for life."

Being a small school, classes are typically not very big and are normally geared toward discussion, and attendance counts towards grading. The quality of teaching here is "above average," with "some truly magnificent professors, but then some really bad ones too." There "are places where students can go for help if they need it," but this isn't really necessary for the more academic minded/honors students, who say that "academic rigor can be lacking," and "classroom discussions can leave the intellectual somewhat disappointed." However, if students are having trouble, "the students have to make a case for themselves—the school doesn't do it for them without effort from the students (a good thing)." Though a few students claim the school has some money management issues, most find the administration here to be "open and accessible," and they really set the course for the school, which "strives to be one of the best private colleges." Freshman orientation does a fantastic job of helping transition students into their new lives; the study abroad programs do a great job of taking them out of it for a bit if they so choose.

Life

There is "not a whole lot to do in Lynchburg" other than "go to Walmart, the dollar theater, and eat," a state that the school attempts to counteract by sponsoring weekend events such as comedians, speakers, concerts, and hypnotists. Outdoor events such as skiing, biking, and rock climbing add to the already well-stocked list of sporty opportunities. "Fridays and Saturdays are crazy" once students stop studying, and partying takes a prominent place in everyone's "loud social life," though "if you want to find somewhere to just chill, you can find that also." Activities that go about on-campus can be anything "from a night in playing *Scene It!* or *Shout About* in a dorm room with a group of friends to a late night out …perusing the frat houses and townhouses." All housing is on-campus, which has its downsides in the myriad complaints about the lack of selection of food in the dining halls.

Student Body

Students use the age-old descriptors of "white" and "middle-class" to portray the typical Lynchburg student, with most hailing from the mid-atlantic region; there is also a noticeably higher percentage of females enrolled. "Kindness is an epidemic at this college," so it shouldn't be surprising that everyone is friendly, and the few atypical students seem to get along well with everyone, or at least find their own niche. Athletics are popular here, and most students keep active with either a sport (club, intramural, or Division III varsity) and/or Greek life. "Everyone always says hi to each other, it is a very friendly environment overall," says a freshman.

FINANCIAL AID: 434-544-8228 • E-MAIL: ADMISSIONS@LYNCHBURG.EDU • WEBSITE: WWW.LYNCHBURG.EDU

THE PRINCETON REVIEW SAYS

Admissions

Very important factors considered include: Academic GPA, rigor of secondary school record, standardized test scores. *Important factors considered include:* Class rank, interview. *Other factors considered include:* Application essay, recommendation(s), extracurricular activities, level of applicant's interest, talent/ability, volunteer work, TOEFL required of all international applicants. High school diploma is required and GED is accepted. *Academic units required:* 4 English, 3 mathematics, 3 science, (2 science labs), 2 foreign language, 2 social studies, 2 history. *Academic units recommended:* 4 mathematics, 4 science, 3 foreign language, 1 academic elective.

Financial Aid

Students should submit: FAFSA, state aid form. The Princeton Review suggests that all financial aid forms be submitted as soon as possible after January 1. *Need-based scholarships/grants offered:* Federal Pell, SEOG, state scholarships/grants, private scholarships, the school's own gift aid. *Loan aid offered:* FFEL Subsidized Stafford, FFEL Unsubsidized Stafford, FFEL PLUS, Federal Perkins Applicants will be notified of awards on a rolling basis beginning 3/1. Federal Work-Study Program available. Institutional employment available. Off-campus job opportunities are good.

Inside Word

The admissions process at Lynchburg is about as typical as they come. The school expects that you will have completed a college preparatory curriculum in high school with a B average and have scored near the national mean on the SAT and/or ACT. Two somewhat unique attributes of the process is that letters of recommendation are not required and applications are reviewed on a rolling basis. For those who know that Lynchburg is their first choice, the school has an early decision option.

THE SCHOOL SAYS "..."

From The Admissions Office

"Lynchburg College is Virginia's most comprehensive private college, nationally recognized for going above and beyond in its commitment to student success. From the moment that prospective students step onto the spectacular campus, they are aware that LC is a place where they will have opportunities to grow intellectually, morally, and spiritually, and that there are faculty, staff, and peer mentors waiting to support them in their quest to achieve their personal goals.

"The emphasis at Lynchburg College is on the development of the whole person, as evidenced by the low student/faculty ratio and an abundance of student organizations, athletic teams, intramural and club sports, and experiential learning opportunities, including service learning, internships, study abroad, and faculty-student collaborative research.

"Lynchburg College seeks to enroll students who wish to take advantage of all that the school has to offer and who want to be part of a caring community. LC welcomes and encourages interested high school students to visit the campus to see for themselves why the college has received record numbers of applications and multiple national honors in recent years. The Admissions Office sponsors open houses and other events for prospective students throughout the year. For more information visit www.lynchburg.edu.

"We allow students to submit scores from either version of the SAT or the ACT, and will use the student's best score from these tests. In regard to the current SAT, and pending further evaluation of Writing scores, the Critical Reading and Math scores will be the primary SAT scores used for admission decisions."

SELECTIVITY

Admissions Rating	77
# of applicants	4,248
% of applicants accepted	69
% of acceptees attending	20
# of early decision applicants	98
% accepted early decision	76

FRESHMAN PROFILE

Range SAT Critical Reading	460–560
Range SAT Math	460–570
Range SAT Writing	450–550
Range ACT Composite	18–22
Minimum paper TOEFL	525
Minimum computer TOEFL	197
Average HS GPA	3.11
% graduated top 10% of class	13
% graduated top 25% of class	37
% graduated top 50% of class	74

DEADLINES

Early decision	
Deadline	11/15
Notification	12/15
Regular	
Notification	rolling
Nonfall registration?	yes

FINANCIAL FACTS

Financial Aid Rating	84
Annual tuition	$27,160
Books and supplies	$600
% frosh rec. need-based scholarship or grant aid	66
% UG rec. need-based scholarship or grant aid	63
% frosh rec. non-need-based scholarship or grant aid	37
% UG rec. non-need-based scholarship or grant aid	40
% frosh rec. need-based self-help aid	57
% UG rec. need-based self-help aid	58
% frosh rec. any financial aid	93
% UG rec. any financial aid	89
% UG borrow to pay for school	68
Average cumulative indebtedness	$22,825

MACALESTER COLLEGE

1600 GRAND AVENUE, ST. PAUL, MN 55105 • ADMISSIONS: 651-696-6357 • FAX: 651-696-6724

CAMPUS LIFE
Quality of Life Rating	**99**
Fire Safety Rating	**88**
Green Rating	**85**
Type of school	private
Affiliation	Presbyterian
Environment	metropolis

STUDENTS
Total undergrad enrollment	1,912
% male/female	42/58
% from out of state	78
% from public high school	76
% live on campus	67
% African American	5
% Asian	9
% Caucasian	69
% Hispanic	4
% Native American	1
% international	12
# of countries represented	87

SURVEY SAYS . . .
Students love St. Paul, MN
Frats and sororities are unpopular
or nonexistent
Political activism is popular

ACADEMICS
Academic Rating	**94**
Calendar	semester
Student/faculty ratio	10:1
Profs interesting rating	89
Profs accessible rating	89
Most common reg class size	10–19 students
Most common lab size	fewer than 10 students

MOST POPULAR MAJORS
English language and literature
economics
political science and government

STUDENTS SAY ". . ."

Academics

"Globalism, liberalism, social justice and environmentalism rule the day" at Macalester College, a small Minnesota liberal arts school where "Academics are taken very seriously and students are expected to perform." Academic offerings "are top notch" here, "particularly chemistry, economics, and international studies," the last of which benefits from "the new Institute for Global Citizenship, study abroad, and the diversity of international students" which together make Macalester "a very worldly place." Departments of psychology, sociology, and political science also have their champions; students warn that because of Macalester's small size, some other departments "are extremely understaffed, and in combination with small class sizes, that leads to a lot of people being turned away from courses they need." Students report that "in true liberal arts style, every department is somehow interconnected to seemingly opposite departments, numerous interdisciplinary majors exist, and even within individual classes, professors approach teaching their given subject from numerous angles. While this may make choosing a specific major somewhat difficult, it absolutely enriches everyone's thoughts and sparks discussion across campus about a variety of issues." This can lead to "The 'Macalester Dilemma,' the oh-so-common problem of so many interests and so little time. With so many ways to involve oneself, Mac students, with their wide-ranging interests and their desire to explore them, often find themselves overcommitted."

Life

"Everything is pretty low key" on the Macalester campus, where "There are rarely large parties. Instead, people will drink and hang out in the dorms (if underclassmen) or friends' houses (if juniors or seniors)" where they tend to discuss 'big ideas.' In this way, "Life at Mac is an extension of classes. We talk about gender, sexuality, multiculturalism, politics, etc. I always learn something new in a conversation with my friends because Mac students love analyzing things." As one student notes, "A joke here at Mac is how often the phrase 'social construct' and the word 'hegemony' are used, both in classes and even in social settings." Mac life is not all hanging out and deconstructing, however; on the contrary, "There's a really strong campus community. There are always events going on on the weekends, both campus-sponsored dances and parties in dorm rooms, etc." as well as "plays, musicals, and other things on campus." And, "When Mac lets us down, there are two cities (Minneapolis and St. Paul) for us to go play in. Everyone should go to the Gay '90s at least once before they graduate." Other urban options include "football or basketball games...some people go clubbing or out to eat. Lots go to the museums or just out shopping." "Getting around on the bus system is easy, although sometimes slow."

Student Body

Macalester "has a very diverse population as far as ethnicity and origin goes, but as a whole is very politically liberal." The typical student "is either a liberal Democrat and environmentalist who wants to make the world a better place, or an international student (who generally doesn't approve of any U.S. politics) who seeks to work in industry in his home country." Undergrads tend to be "fairly relaxed and easygoing," "intelligent, high-achieving, hard-working, and unpretentious but conscientious and on top of the news." Many describe themselves as "awkward," adding "We are nerds and proud of it." Jocks that are "only interested in playing football and partying" are atypical, "but they seem to have fun among themselves, too."

THE PRINCETON REVIEW SAYS

Admissions

Very important factors considered include: Academic GPA, rigor of secondary school record. *Important factors considered include:* Application essay, recommendation(s), standardized test scores, character/personal qualities, extracurricular activities. *Other factors considered include:* Class rank, alumni/ae relation, first generation, interview, racial/ethnic status, talent/ability, volunteer work, work experience. SAT or ACT required; TOEFL required of all international applicants. High school diploma or equivalent is not required. *Academic units recommended:* 4 English, 3 mathematics, 3 science, (3 science labs), 3 foreign language, 3 social studies.

Financial Aid

Students should submit: FAFSA, CSS/Financial Aid PROFILE, noncustodial PROFILE. Regular filing deadline is 2/8. The Princeton Review suggests that all financial aid forms be submitted as soon as possible after January 1. *Need-based scholarships/grants offered:* Federal Pell, SEOG, state scholarships/grants, private scholarships. *Loan aid offered:* FFEL Subsidized Stafford, FFEL Unsubsidized Stafford, FFEL PLUS, Federal Perkins, state loans Applicants will be notified of awards on or about 4/1. Federal Work-Study Program available. Institutional employment available. Off-campus job opportunities are excellent.

The Inside Word

To say that Macalester's star is on the rise is to put it very mildly. From 2001 to 2007, the number of applicants to the school increased by more than 50 percent. The freshman class has grown slightly in that time but not at anything approaching the growth rate of the applicant pool. Accordingly, it has grown substantially more difficult to gain admission here over a very short period of time. Candidates need to put their best foot forward in their applications; expressing a commitment to attending the school if admitted can only help.

THE SCHOOL SAYS "..."

From The Admissions Office

"Macalester has been preparing students for world citizenship and providing an integrated international education for over six decades. The United Nations flag has flown on campus since 1950 and 16 percent of the students are citizens of another country, with 87 countries represented on campus. Over 60% of Mac students study abroad, going to nearly 50 countries all over the world each year. Graduates enter the work force or graduate school with respected scholarship and real experience in a global community, prepared to succeed in their chosen fields. Mac students thrive in a rigorous academic environment, supported by accomplished faculty who love to teach. Located in a friendly residential neighborhood in the heart of a vibrant metropolitan area, Macalester offers unusually broad, easily accessible internship opportunities to add valuable experience, connections and practice at getting things done, often leading to job opportunities after graduation. Two out of three Mac students complete an internship at a Twin Cities business, law firm, hospital, financial institution, museum, theater, state government, research lab, environmental agency or non-profit group (and more), all within a few miles of campus. Students rave about the food at Mac, which includes vegetarian fare, food for meat lovers, plenty of variety and entrées from around the world. A new athletic and recreation center opened in the fall of 2009, including a large fitness center, indoor track, gymnasium, natatorium, field house, gathering spaces, juice bar, atrium and more. Athletic teams frequently earn the highest cumulative GPA in the nation. Macalester meets the full demonstrated need for every admitted student, providing broad socioeconomic representation in the student body. Last year 65% of students received financial assistance and the average first-year award was $24,314.

SELECTIVITY

Admissions Rating	96
# of applicants	4,967
% of applicants accepted	41
% of acceptees attending	24
# accepting a place on wait list	177
% admitted from wait list	19
# of early decision applicants	250
% accepted early decision	46

FRESHMAN PROFILE

Range SAT Critical Reading	630–730
Range SAT Math	620–710
Range SAT Writing	620–720
Range ACT Composite	28–32
Minimum paper TOEFL	573
Minimum computer TOEFL	230
% graduated top 10% of class	68
% graduated top 25% of class	90
% graduated top 50% of class	100

DEADLINES

Early decision	
Deadline	11/15
Notification	12/15
Regular	
Deadline	1/15
Notification	3/30
Nonfall registration?	no

APPLICANTS ALSO LOOK AT

AND OFTEN PREFER
Brown University
AND SOMETIMES PREFER
Oberlin College
University of Minnesota—Twin Cities
AND RARELY PREFER
Colorado College

FINANCIAL FACTS

Financial Aid Rating	98
Annual tuition	$33,494
Room and board	$8,220
Required fees	$200
Books and supplies	$850
% frosh rec. need-based scholarship or grant aid	45
% UG rec. need-based scholarship or grant aid	67
% frosh rec. non-need-based scholarship or grant aid	1
% UG rec. non-need-based scholarship or grant aid	1
% frosh rec. need-based self-help aid	65
% UG rec. need-based self-help aid	67
% frosh rec. any financial aid	71.5
% UG rec. any financial aid	73
% UG borrow to pay for school	70.1
Average cumulative indebtedness	$18,849

MANHATTANVILLE COLLEGE

2900 PURCHASE STREET, ADMISSIONS OFFICE, PURCHASE, NY 10577 • ADMISSIONS: 914-323-5124 • FAX: 914-694-1732

CAMPUS LIFE

Quality of Life Rating	**94**
Fire Safety Rating	**60***
Green Rating	**88**
Type of school	private
Environment	town

STUDENTS

Total undergrad enrollment	1,752
% male/female	33/67
% from out of state	36
% live on campus	80
% African American	7
% Asian	2
% Caucasian	56
% Hispanic	16
% Native American	1
% international	9
# of countries represented	59

SURVEY SAYS . . .
Small classes
Great library
Diverse student types on campus

ACADEMICS

Academic Rating	**82**
Calendar	semester
Student/faculty ratio	11:1
Profs interesting rating	83
Profs accessible rating	86
Most common reg class size	10–19 students

MOST POPULAR MAJORS
psychology
visual and performing arts
business/commerce

STUDENTS SAY ". . ."

Academics

"Qualified and committed" professors, "very involved" administrators, and an "excellent location" near New York City (one still far enough from its "pollution and distractions") all contribute to the "close and supportive community" that is Manhattanville College. Students here have the "unbelievable" opportunity to "exchange ideas" with professors who have "studied in the best universities in the world. There are so many distinguished professors here, ranging from experts in world religions, to former ambassadors in the UN. Almost all of them are well known in their areas of study." Yet regardless of the faculty's impressive credentials, "Each one of them makes you feel comfortable enough to go and see him or her if you need help, and is more than willing to use his or her own time to help you." Getting such help is made easier by the fact that "one-third of professors live on campus." Mville (as it is affectionately called by its students) places a lot of emphasis on experiential learning, and the school's location is an asset in that regard. Not only is Mville close to the myriad internship opportunities of the megalopolis next door, but "We [also] have tons of corporations literally in our neighborhood, like MasterCard, IBM, MBIA, JPMorgan—[these bring] plenty of internships." In addition to internships, the school reportedly "is very successful in finding students interesting jobs in their fields after they graduate." Students praise a "very helpful" administration, and the president is such a hit with students that one goes so far as to say that he "is probably more popular than the star of the basketball team."

Life

Manhattanville's campus "is a quiet place." Students here "generally focus on their academics first and on partying and having fun second." While "There are parties on campus every 2 weeks or so [at which] alcohol is served," the residential directors and RAs "are so strict, the party scene is not so big." Parties are typically "small get-togethers," and "People are usually nervous that they are going to get caught [if they drink]." Such a tame on-campus party scene means that the drinkers here make it a "very big bar school." They take "the Valiant Express [a campus shuttle] to downtown White Plains," where "dozens of bars" can be found. Students can also find "other stuff to do [in White Plains]," such as visiting its "malls, movie theaters, restaurants, and clubs." The "college bus also takes students [to New York City] every Saturday"; people go there to "see Broadway shows or [attend] professional athletic events." For those students seeking more wholesome fun on campus, There are "lots of interest groups and activities that one can join," and "there is also a game room with different things like billiards and Ping-Pong." Finally, "The students here have a lot of school spirit, so there is always a great turnout for games."

Student Body

"The community at Manhattanville is very diverse," with a community that includes students "from 59 different countries around the world." A typical student might even have "lived in more than three countries." Despite the diversity (or perhaps as a natural consequence of it), sometimes "People tend to hang out with the group they feel most comfortable with (i.e., international students hanging out with fellow international students, sport students with fellow sport students, etc.)." Regardless of any cliques, "All of the students at the school are extremely cordial. Since it is such a small school, you get to know everyone's face." "The typical student works hard about half the time," one claims. "There are atypical students who care a lot about their work and do a lot of studying. Some of them stick out, and others fit in fine."

FINANCIAL AID: 914-323-5357 • E-MAIL: ADMISSIONS@MVILLE.EDU • WEBSITE: WWW.MVILLE.EDU

THE PRINCETON REVIEW SAYS

Admissions

Very important factors considered include: Rigor of secondary school record, standardized test scores. *Important factors considered include:* Application essay, recommendation(s), extracurricular activities, interview. *Other factors considered include:* Alumni/ae relation, character/personal qualities, geographical residence, talent/ability, volunteer work, work experience. SAT or ACT required; TOEFL required of all international applicants. High school diploma is required and GED is accepted. *Academic units required:* 4 English, 3 mathematics, 2 science, 2 social studies, 5 academic electives.

Financial Aid

Students should submit: FAFSA, state aid form. The Princeton Review suggests that all financial aid forms be submitted as soon as possible after January 1. *Need-based scholarships/grants offered:* Federal Pell, SEOG, state scholarships/grants, private scholarships, the school's own gift aid. *Loan aid offered:* FFEL Subsidized Stafford, FFEL Unsubsidized Stafford, FFEL PLUS, Federal Perkins Applicants will be notified of awards on a rolling basis beginning 3/1. Federal Work-Study Program available. Institutional employment available. Off-campus job opportunities are excellent.

The Inside Word

Applicants evincing middle-of-the-road academic achievement will most likely find themselves with an acceptance letter from Manhattanville. The college still seeks to achieve greater gender balance, so male candidates enjoy a slightly higher admission rate than female candidates. In addition to meeting regular admissions requirements, students who wish to pursue a degree in fine arts or performing arts must present a portfolio or audition, respectively.

THE SCHOOL SAYS "..."

From The Admissions Office

"Manhattanville's mission—to educate ethically and socially responsible leaders for the global community—is evident throughout the college, from academics to athletics to social and extracurricular activities. With 1,600 undergraduates from 59 nations and 39 states, our diversity spans geographic, cultural, ethnic, religious, socioeconomic, and academic backgrounds. Students are free to express their views in this tight-knit community, where we value the personal as well as the global. Any six students with similar interest can start a club, and most participate in a variety of campus wide programs. Last year, students engaged in more than 23,380 hours of community service and social justice activity. Study abroad opportunities include not only the most desirable international locations, but also a semester-long immersion for living, studying, and working in New York City. In the true liberal arts tradition, students are encouraged to think for themselves and develop new skills—in music, the studio arts, on stage, in the sciences, or on the playing field. With more than 50 areas of study and a popular self-designed major, there is no limit to our academic scope. Our Westchester County location, just 35 miles north of New York City, gives students an edge for jobs and internships. Over the past few years, Manhattanville has been rated among the '100 Most Wired,' the '100 Most Undeservedly Underappreciated,' the '320 Hottest,' and in *U.S. News & World Report*'s first tier. Last year, the men's and women's ice hockey teams were ranked #1 in the nation for Division III.

"As of this book's publication, Manhattanville College did not have information available about their policy regarding the new SAT."

SELECTIVITY

Admissions Rating	80
# of applicants	3,927
% of applicants accepted	50
% of acceptees attending	27

FRESHMAN PROFILE

Range SAT Critical Reading	500–620
Range SAT Math	500–610
Range ACT Composite	20–25
Minimum paper TOEFL	550
Minimum computer TOEFL	217
% graduated top 10% of class	22
% graduated top 25% of class	47
% graduated top 50% of class	80

DEADLINES

Early decision	
Deadline	12/1
Notification	12/31
Regular	
Priority	3/1
Deadline	3/1
Notification	rolling
Nonfall registration?	yes

APPLICANTS ALSO LOOK AT

AND OFTEN PREFER
New York University
AND SOMETIMES PREFER
Fordham University
AND RARELY PREFER
Pace University—White Plains

FINANCIAL FACTS

Financial Aid Rating	78
Annual tuition	$30,400
Room and board	$13,040
Required fees	$1,220
Books and supplies	$800
% frosh rec. need-based scholarship or grant aid	62
% UG rec. need-based scholarship or grant aid	57
% frosh rec. non-need-based scholarship or grant aid	59
% UG rec. non-need-based scholarship or grant aid	57
% frosh rec. need-based self-help aid	58
% UG rec. need-based self-help aid	54
% frosh rec. any financial aid	75
% UG rec. any financial aid	70
% UG borrow to pay for school	67
Average cumulative indebtedness	$23,253

MARIST COLLEGE

3399 NORTH ROAD, POUGHKEEPSIE, NY 12601-1387 • ADMISSIONS: 845-575-3226 • FAX: 845-575-3215

CAMPUS LIFE

Quality of Life Rating	**75**
Fire Safety Rating	**80**
Green Rating	**81**
Type of school	private
Environment	town

STUDENTS

Total undergrad enrollment	4,769
% male/female	43/57
% from out of state	41
% from public high school	72
% live on campus	72
% in (# of) fraternities	1 (3)
% in (# of) sororities	3 (4)
% African American	3
% Asian	2
% Caucasian	77
% Hispanic	5
# of countries represented	11

SURVEY SAYS . . .

Small classes
Great computer facilities
Great library
Lots of beer drinking
Hard liquor is popular

ACADEMICS

Academic Rating	**78**
Calendar	semester
Student/faculty ratio	15:1
Profs interesting rating	75
Profs accessible rating	76
Most common reg class size	10–19 students
Most common lab size	20–29 students

MOST POPULAR MAJORS

special education and teaching
business administration and management
communication & media studies

STUDENTS SAY "..."

Academics

Marist College, a "midsized institute that proudly offers competitive academics, career placement, and a well-rounded college experience," is "the perfect size." Students tell us that it's "small enough that professors remember your name and address you as a person, not a number, but large enough that you are not constantly seeing the same people every day." Pre-professional and career-track programs are most popular here; students laud the "great communications program" with its "unique digital media major" and "strong internship connections," the "very good education program," the popular business programs, and the "excellent Chemistry Department, where personal attention is unmatched." Students here keep their eyes on the prize: They sing the praises of the Center for Career Services, noting that "Our career services and internship opportunities are amazing. By the end of your senior year you will most likely complete an internship with a big-name company, either in the local area or in New York City, which we are in close proximity to." They also love the Study Abroad Office, which "has connected students with many countries around the world, allowing students to study abroad for a semester, year, or short-term period." Further sweetening the deal are the school's "strong connections to IBM" and "an amazing library that is ranked among the top 20 in the country."

Life

"Classes keep you busy" at Marist College, but not so busy that you can't also enjoy a variety of extracurricular activities. These include "social organizations, religious organizations, academic organizations, to name simply a few" as well as "campus events such as sports, plays, lectures, seminars, and concerts. Marist is not a suitcase campus, as students who live on campus stay on campus over the weekends." The bar scene is big; some here see Marist as "very much a bar school. Kids go out Tuesday, Thursday, Friday, and Saturday. House parties happen, but they aren't as popular as the bars. There's tons of nonalcoholic fun, too." While "The city of Poughkeepsie is generally not safe outside of the venues Marist students flock to," the "diverse" area surrounding Poughkeepsie "allows outdoor experiences like hiking, kayaking, and swimming." Undergrads appreciate the fact that "the Marist campus is beautiful, with the most amazing views ever"—"The Hudson River can be seen from almost every dorm."

Student Body

Marist seems to draw "lots of kids from Long Island, New Jersey, and Connecticut, many of them White, upper-middle-class, immigrant-descended Catholics." (One student adds, "They shop at Abercrombie.") Another undergrad notes, "While walking through campus, one may notice that Marist is filled with very similar people." The student body includes "many athletes [Marist fields 10 men's and 11 women's intercollegiate teams] and preppy students. Many are involved in clubs." Students here "are going to school to gain experience, get their degree, and dive into the competitive workforce. They focus on attaining good grades while also being involved in on-campus activities and having a diverse social life. They are fun-loving people." Undergrads are also "extremely friendly and will go out of their way to hold a door for you." All students "fit in well and get along," we're told.

MARIST COLLEGE

FINANCIAL AID: 845-575-3230 • E-MAIL: ADMISSIONS@MARIST.EDU • WEBSITE: WWW.MARIST.EDU

THE PRINCETON REVIEW SAYS

Admissions

Very important factors considered include: Academic GPA, rigor of secondary school record, standardized test scores. *Important factors considered include:* Class rank, application essay, recommendation(s), character/personal qualities, extracurricular activities, geographical residence, state residency, talent/ability, volunteer work, work experience. *Other factors considered include:* Alumni/ae relation, level of applicant's interest, racial/ethnic status, SAT or ACT required; ACT with Writing component required. TOEFL required of all international applicants. High school diploma is required and GED is accepted. *Academic units required:* 4 English, 3 mathematics, 3 science, (2 science labs), 2 foreign language, 2 social studies, 1 history, 2 academic electives. *Academic units recommended:* 4 mathematics, 4 science, (3 science labs), 3 foreign language.

Financial Aid

Students should submit: FAFSA, institution's own financial aid form. Regular filing deadline is 5/1. The Princeton Review suggests that all financial aid forms be submitted as soon as possible after January 1. *Need-based scholarships/grants offered:* Federal Pell, SEOG, state scholarships/grants, private scholarships, the school's own gift aid. *Loan aid offered:* FFEL Subsidized Stafford, FFEL Unsubsidized Stafford, FFEL PLUS, Federal Perkins, Alternative Loans. Applicants will be notified of awards on a rolling basis beginning 3/15. Federal Work-Study Program available. Institutional employment available. Off-campus job opportunities are excellent.

The Inside Word

Marist attracts some solid students, and viable candidates are usually in the top quarter of their class. Additionally, Admissions Counselors tend to favor applicants who have attained leadership roles and contributed to their communities. State residency is also taken into consideration, as Marist aims to maintain a diverse campus.

THE SCHOOL SAYS "..."

From The Admissions Office

"Marist is a 'hot school' among prospective students. We are seeing a record number of applications each year. But the number of seats available for the freshman class remains the same, about 950. Therefore, becoming an accepted applicant is an increasingly competitive process. Our recommendations: keep your grades up, score well on the SAT, participate in community service both in and out of school, and exercise leadership in the classroom, athletics, extracurricular activities, and your place of worship. We encourage a campus visit. When prospective students see Marist—our beautiful location on a scenic stretch of the Hudson River, the quality of our facilities, the interaction between students and faculty, and the fact that everyone really enjoys their time here—they want to become a part of the Marist College community. We'll help you in the transition from high school to college through an innovative first-year program that provides mentors for every student. You'll also learn how to use technology in whatever field you choose. We emphasize three aspects of a true Marist experience: excellence in education, community, and service to others. At Marist, you'll get a premium education, develop your skills, have fun and make lifelong friends, be given the opportunity to gain valuable experience through our great internship and study abroad programs, and be ahead of the competition for graduate school or work.

"Marist requires the SAT with the Writing component. We recommend all students take the test at least twice and the ACT once. Marist will use the best Verbal, Math, and Writing scores from the SAT or the highest composite ACT score."

SELECTIVITY
Admissions Rating	89
# of applicants	8,328
% of applicants accepted	42
% of acceptees attending	29
# accepting a place on wait list	731
% admitted from wait list	8
# of early decision applicants	102
% accepted early decision	83

FRESHMAN PROFILE
Range SAT Critical Reading	520–620
Range SAT Math	540–630
Range SAT Writing	530–630
Range ACT Composite	22–27
Minimum paper TOEFL	550
Minimum computer TOEFL	213
Minimum web-based TOEFL	79
Average HS GPA	3.3
% graduated top 10% of class	29
% graduated top 25% of class	75
% graduated top 50% of class	94

DEADLINES
Early decision	
Deadline	11/15
Notification	12/15
Early action	
Deadline	12/1
Notification	1/30
Regular	
Deadline	2/15
Notification	3/15
Nonfall registration?	yes

APPLICANTS ALSO LOOK AT AND OFTEN PREFER
Boston College

FINANCIAL FACTS
Financial Aid Rating	66
Annual tuition	$23,560
Room and board	$10,250
Required fees	$480
Books and supplies	$1,230
% frosh rec. need-based scholarship or grant aid	59
% UG rec. need-based scholarship or grant aid	57
% frosh rec. non-need-based scholarship or grant aid	43
% UG rec. non-need-based scholarship or grant aid	33
% frosh rec. need-based self-help aid	47
% UG rec. need-based self-help aid	50
% frosh rec. athletic scholarships	8
% UG rec. athletic scholarships	6
% frosh rec. any financial aid	92
% UG rec. any financial aid	86
% UG borrow to pay for school	68
Average cumulative indebtedness	$28,374

MARLBORO COLLEGE

PO Box A, South Road, Marlboro, VT 05344-0300 • Admissions: 802-258-9236 • Fax: 802-451-7555

CAMPUS LIFE

Quality of Life Rating	**81**
Fire Safety Rating	**66**
Green Rating	**72**
Type of school	private
Environment	rural

STUDENTS

Total undergrad enrollment	324
% male/female	47/53
% from out of state	88
% from public high school	70
% live on campus	80
% Asian	2
% Caucasian	67
% Hispanic	2
% Native American	1
# of countries represented	3

SURVEY SAYS . . .

Class discussions encouraged
No one cheats
Campus feels safe
Frats and sororities are unpopular
or nonexistent
(Almost) everyone smokes

ACADEMICS

Academic Rating	**98**
Calendar	semester
Student/faculty ratio	8:1
Profs interesting rating	97
Profs accessible rating	91
Most common reg class size	fewer than 10 students
Most common lab size	fewer than 10 students

MOST POPULAR MAJORS

English language and literature
social sciences
visual and performing arts

STUDENTS SAY ". . ."

Academics

Marlboro College is all about giving students "the freedom to pursue their own interests and study what they want." Here, undergrads design their own junior and senior curricula, then pursue them in one-on-one tutorials with professors. The process, known here simply as 'The Plan,' culminates in a substantial senior thesis. The goal is to "learn how to think critically and find the resources you need in the course of completing a dissertation-level project," and undergrads here "wouldn't settle for anything less in their academic pursuits." Freshmen and sophomores complete more traditional-style courses, albeit in smaller classrooms and with a greater-than-usual focus on writing and discussion. The size of the school—just over 300 undergraduates attend—is sometimes a hindrance. One student observes that "Since there is generally only one professor per field, it is a bit disappointing to realize that there can only be a limited number of classes offered per semester." "Too often a student will reach the final year when his/her Plan sponsor goes on sabbatical and a replacement is not hired in time or hired at all. This presents a problem: Does the student leave the college until their professor returns? Or does the student switch Plan sponsors, potentially altering the focus of their work so much they dislike what their doing?" Despite these issues, "professors are very receptive and try to accommodate individual interests as best they can." Most here feel these are reasonable costs to bear in order to pursue "independent, difficult, intellectually-stimulating work inside a student-centered and directed curriculum."

Life

Marlboro is "a little school on top of a hill" with Brattleboro, the closest town, "about a half an hour away," so "life is pretty intensely focused on the campus." "While we do make the trip to Brattleboro fairly often, most of our time is spent 'on the hill,'" says one student. Students "study a lot, but there is also a lot of hanging out, mainly in small impromptu ways." They "like to debate about philosophy, politics, and religion" while "smoking a lot of cigarettes and pot." As one student puts it, "Parties are fun because, while we drink and smoke just as much as the next college, we'll also engage in deep intellectual discussions while doing said activities." Otherwise, fun "is found in the 300 acres that surround the college: skiing, hiking, long walks in an apple orchard, broomball (a hippie version of hockey), soccer, etc." Trips to Brattleboro are pleasant because it's "an arts town." Students occasionally travel to Massachusetts college towns Amherst and Northampton for concerts or shopping and "frequently classes take field trips to NYC or Boston." Many get involved in grassroots political organization, both on campus and off.

Students

The typical Marlboro student "wouldn't fit quite right anywhere else: academically driven, maybe a little nerdy, politically vocal, and looking for a laid-back environment. There is no atypical student at Marlboro, because we all would have been atypical someplace else." Personality types run the gamut, including "hippie environmentalists, geeks and gamers, theater kids, artists, and so on and so forth and every combination thereof. We're underrepresented in the jock and beauty queen categories, but that doesn't seem to bother anybody." Everyone here, we're told, "is extremely passionate about their own little academic niche, and furthermore each person is one of the smartest people you will ever meet." The school is home to "a large gay population and a few transgender students," but "there are a lack of minority students, Republicans, and financially lower-class students."

FINANCIAL AID: 800-343-0049 • E-MAIL: ADMISSIONS@MARLBORO.EDU • WEBSITE: WWW.MARLBORO.EDU

THE PRINCETON REVIEW SAYS

Admissions

Very important factors considered include: Application essay, academic GPA, rigor of secondary school record, character/personal qualities. *Important factors considered include:* Extracurricular activities, interview, talent/ability. *Other factors considered include:* Class rank, recommendation(s), standardized test scores, alumni/ae relation, first generation, geographical residence, level of applicant's interest, state residency, volunteer work, work experience. SAT or ACT required; TOEFL required of all international applicants. High school diploma is required and GED is accepted. *Academic units recommended:* 4 English, 3 mathematics, 3 science, (1 science labs), 3 foreign language, 3 social studies, 3 history, 3 academic electives.

Financial Aid

Students should submit: FAFSA. Regular filing deadline is 3/1. The Princeton Review suggests that all financial aid forms be submitted as soon as possible after January 1. *Need-based scholarships/grants offered:* Federal Pell, SEOG, state scholarships/grants, private scholarships, the school's own gift aid. *Loan aid offered:* FFEL Subsidized Stafford, FFEL Unsubsidized Stafford, FFEL PLUS, state loans, college/university loans from institutional funds. Applicants will be notified of awards on a rolling basis beginning 3/15. Federal Work-Study Program available. Institutional employment available. Off-campus job opportunities are fair.

The Inside Word

Don't be misled by Marlboro's high acceptance rate—this is not the type of school that attracts many applications from students unsure of whether they belong at Marlboro. Most applicants are qualified both in terms of academic achievement and sincere intellectual curiosity. The school seeks candidates "with intellectual promise, a high degree of self-motivation, self-discipline, personal stability, social concern, and the ability and desire to contribute to the College community." These are the qualities you should stress on your application.

THE SCHOOL SAYS "..."

From The Admissions Office

"Marlboro College is distinguished by its curriculum, praised in higher education circles as unique; it is known for its self-governing philosophy, in which each student, faculty, and staff has an equal vote on many issues affecting the community; and it is recognized for its 60-year history of offering a rigorous, exciting, self-designed course of study taught in very small classes and individualized study with faculty. Marlboro's size also distinguishes it from most other schools. With 300 students and a student/faculty ratio of 8:1, it is one of the nation's smallest liberal arts colleges. Few other schools offer a program where students have such close interaction with faculty, and where community life is inseparable from academic life. The result, the self-designed, self-directed Plan of Concentration, allows students to develop their own unique academic work by defining a problem, setting clear limits on an area of inquiry, and analyzing, evaluating, and reporting on the outcome of a significant project. A Marlboro education teaches you to think for yourself, articulate your thoughts, express your ideas, believe in yourself, and do it all with the clarity, confidence, and self-reliance necessary for later success, no matter what postgraduate path you take.

"Marlboro College requires all applicants for admission to submit results of either the ACT and ACT Writing Test or SAT Reasoning Test. Students who have previously taken older versions of the ACT or SAT may submit those test results and are not required to retake the 'new' ACT or SAT. We do not require SAT Subject Tests."

SELECTIVITY

Admissions Rating	88
# of applicants	459
% of applicants accepted	68
% of acceptees attending	30
# of early decision applicants	19
% accepted early decision	68

FRESHMAN PROFILE

Range SAT Critical Reading	590–690
Range SAT Math	510–650
Range SAT Writing	640–720
Range ACT Composite	24–32
Minimum paper TOEFL	550
Minimum computer TOEFL	213
Minimum web-based TOEFL	80
Average HS GPA	3.2
% graduated top 10% of class	40
% graduated top 25% of class	60
% graduated top 50% of class	95

DEADLINES

Early decision	
Deadline	12/1
Notification	12/15
Early action	
Deadline	2/1
Notification	2/15
Regular	
Priority	1/15
Deadline	2/15
Notification	rolling
Nonfall registration?	yes

APPLICANTS ALSO LOOK AT
AND OFTEN PREFER
Reed College
AND SOMETIMES PREFER
The Evergreen State College
AND RARELY PREFER
Hampshire College

FINANCIAL FACTS

Financial Aid Rating	89
Annual tuition	$31,140
Room and board	$9,040
Required fees	$1,040
Books and supplies	$1,000
% frosh rec. need-based scholarship or grant aid	70
% UG rec. need-based scholarship or grant aid	74
% frosh rec. non-need-based scholarship or grant aid	49
% UG rec. non-need-based scholarship or grant aid	16
% frosh rec. need-based self-help aid	75
% UG rec. need-based self-help aid	72
% frosh rec. any financial aid	77
% UG rec. any financial aid	84
% UG borrow to pay for school	84
Average cumulative indebtedness	$19,758

MARQUETTE UNIVERSITY

PO Box 1881, Milwaukee, WI 53201-1881 • Admissions: 414-288-7302 • Fax: 414-288-3764

STUDENTS SAY ". . ."

Academics

Marquette University, "a small campus in a big city with a big heart and a comfortable atmosphere," serves up "a great Jesuit education" to those "seeking a happy medium between working hard academically, making great friends while having a good social life, and getting prepared for life after college." Marquette is also a great choice for those "really interested in community service and exploring their Catholic faith. Marquette has a lot of opportunities in these areas." Popular majors include business, nursing, engineering, and education; these programs are so popular, in fact, that "as a junior it is really difficult to transfer into them and still graduate in 4 years." Premedical programs in physical therapy and dentistry are also strong. In most areas, Marquette's faculty is "truly top-notch and cares about both teaching and research. Marquette is highly underrated for what we receive. Most professors personally care about the learning experiences of their students and make every effort to offer help or insight inside and outside of class." That help can be important, since "Classes are challenging." Students also appreciate the school's "state-of-the-art computer facilities" and the "amazing new Raynor Memorial Library." The "very generous financial aid packages" also earn praise. The few students with leftist political leanings warn that "the professors and the students are incredibly conservative, which can be difficult because the university requires a ton of theology and philosophy credits."

Life

"It seems as if much of the student body leads two separate lives" at Marquette. "During the week we are very studious, because this is a very demanding school. But on weekends we know how to have a great time. We work hard, but we play hard, too." For many, "having a good time" involves drinking, either at a campus party or in one of Milwaukee's many bars. Students who don't drink tell us they still find plenty to do. Marquette "has many active organizations, especially the student government and the newspaper. These organizations are very involved in campus life and do well at making their presence known." College athletics are also a big draw; men's basketball is especially popular. Other options include the on-campus Varsity Theater, "which has good two-dollar movies every weekend"; an on-campus art museum; events such as "Late Night Marquette, which includes games and other fun stuff"; and strolling along Lake Michigan. Milwaukee brings a lot to the mix, including "professional sports and lots of concerts," but beware of winters here, which "can get pretty cold," to put it mildly.

Student Body

The majority of Marquette undergrads "are White and come either from rural areas in Wisconsin or from Chicago suburbs." Many come from economically comfortable families and "went to private Catholic high schools. Marquette students could be considered preppy and snobby." Dig below the surface, though, and you'll find "a large range of people, at least from an economic standpoint. There are some very rich kids and at the same time there are those who are less fortunate." The same diversity is absent from the school's racial makeup—there are "very few minority students," which, according to one Latina student, "can make it very difficult to feel a part of campus life." Students tend to be "very conservative," but apparently not dogmatically so, since "Despite the Catholic environment, no one is ashamed of being homosexual. There is even a Gay/Straight Alliance club."

FINANCIAL AID: 414-288-7390 • E-MAIL: ADMISSIONS@MARQUETTE.EDU • WEBSITE: WWW.MARQUETTE.EDU

THE PRINCETON REVIEW SAYS

Admissions

Very important factors considered include: Academic GPA, rigor of secondary school record. *Important factors considered include:* Class rank, application essay, recommendation(s), standardized test scores. *Other factors considered include:* Alumni/ae relation, character/personal qualities, extracurricular activities, first generation, geographical residence, racial/ethnic status, religious affiliation/commitment, state residency, talent/ability, SAT or ACT required; ACT with Writing component recommended. High school diploma is required and GED is accepted. *Academic units required:* 4 English, 2 mathematics, 2 science, (2 science labs), 2 foreign language, 2 social studies, 2 academic electives. *Academic units recommended:* 4 English, 4 mathematics, 3 science, (3 science labs), 2 foreign language, 3 social studies, 5 academic electives.

Financial Aid

Students should submit: FAFSA, MU Admissions Application. The Princeton Review suggests that all financial aid forms be submitted as soon as possible after January 1. *Need-based scholarships/grants offered:* Federal Pell, SEOG, state scholarships/grants, private scholarships, the school's own gift aid. *Loan aid offered:* Direct Subsidized Stafford, Direct Unsubsidized Stafford, Direct PLUS, Federal Perkins, Federal Nursing, state loans, college/university loans from institutional funds, Private educational/alternative loans. Applicants will be notified of awards on a rolling basis beginning 3/20.

The Inside Word

Marquette does not take admissions decisions lightly: Each application is evaluated by at least two committee members. Qualified applicants are academically competitive with their peers and maintain consistent grades. Essays are also highly valued, as Admissions Officers seek students with strong writing skills.

THE SCHOOL SAYS "..."

From The Admissions Office

"Since 1881, Marquette has been noted for its commitment to educational excellence in the 450-year-old Catholic/Jesuit tradition. Marquette embraces the philosophy that true education should be more than an acquisition of knowledge; it should develop your intellect as well as your moral and spiritual character. This all-encompassing education will challenge you to develop the goals and values that will shape the rest of your life. Each of Marquette's 7,500 undergraduates are admitted as freshman to one of six colleges: Arts and Sciences, Business Administration, Communication, Engineering, Health Sciences, or Nursing. Many co-enroll in the School of Education. The faculty within these colleges are prolific writers and researchers, but more importantly, they all teach and advise students.

"Marquette is nestled in the financial center of Milwaukee, the nation's eighteenth-largest city, allowing you to take full advantage of the city's cultural, professional, and governmental opportunities. Marquette's urban experience is unique; an 80-acre campus, an outdoor athletic complex, and an internationally diverse student body (90 percent of which live on or near campus) all make Marquette a close-knit community in which you can learn and live.

"Marquette applicants must submit scores from either the new version of the SAT or the ACT with Writing component. The highest composite score will be used in admissions decisions for students that submit scores from multiple administrations of these tests."

SELECTIVITY

Admissions Rating	84
# of applicants	11,514
% of applicants accepted	70
% of acceptees attending	23
# accepting a place on wait list	448
% admitted from wait list	17

FRESHMAN PROFILE

Range SAT Critical Reading	540–640
Range SAT Math	550–660
Range SAT Writing	530–630
Range ACT Composite	24–29
Minimum paper TOEFL	520
Minimum computer TOEFL	190
% graduated top 10% of class	35
% graduated top 25% of class	67
% graduated top 50% of class	92

DEADLINES

Regular	
Priority	12/1
Deadline	12/1
Notification	1/31
Nonfall registration?	yes

APPLICANTS ALSO LOOK AT
AND OFTEN PREFER
University of Notre Dame
University of Michigan—Ann Arbor
Case Western Reserve University
Boston College
AND SOMETIMES PREFER
Michigan State University
University of Wisconsin—Madison
AND RARELY PREFER
Milwaukee School of Engineering
University of Wisconsin—Milwaukee

FINANCIAL FACTS

Financial Aid Rating	76
Annual tuition	$26,270
Room and board	$8,590
Required fees	$408
Books and supplies	$900
% frosh rec. need-based scholarship or grant aid	54
% UG rec. need-based scholarship or grant aid	52
% frosh rec. non-need-based scholarship or grant aid	6
% UG rec. non-need-based scholarship or grant aid	5
% frosh rec. need-based self-help aid	51
% UG rec. need-based self-help aid	50
% frosh rec. athletic scholarships	1
% UG rec. athletic scholarships	2
% frosh rec. any financial aid	88
% UG rec. any financial aid	85
% UG borrow to pay for school	65
Average cumulative indebtedness	$25,753

MASSACHUSETTS INSTITUTE OF TECHNOLOGY

MIT ADMISSIONS OFFICE, ROOM 3-108, 77 MASSACHUSETTS AVENUE, CAMBRIDGE, MA 02139 • ADMISSIONS: 617-253-4791

CAMPUS LIFE

Quality of Life Rating	87
Fire Safety Rating	75
Green Rating	85
Type of school	private
Environment	city

STUDENTS

Total undergrad enrollment	4,163
% male/female	55/45
% from out of state	90
% from public high school	69
% live on campus	90
% in (# of) fraternities	49 (27)
% in (# of) sororities	26 (5)
% African American	7
% Asian	26
% Caucasian	37
% Hispanic	12
% Native American	1
% international	8
# of countries represented	89

SURVEY SAYS . . .

Registration is a breeze
Lab facilities are great
Great computer facilities
Great library
Athletic facilities are great
Diverse student types on campus
Students love Cambridge, MA

ACADEMICS

Academic Rating	97
Calendar	4/1/4
Student/faculty ratio	6:1
Profs interesting rating	70
Profs accessible rating	76
Most common reg class size	fewer than 10 students
Most common lab size	10–19 students

MOST POPULAR MAJORS
computer science
chemical engineering
mechanical engineering

STUDENTS SAY ". . ."

Academics

Massachusetts Institute of Technology, the East Coast mecca of engineering, science, and mathematics, "is the ultimate place for information overload, endless possibilities, and expanding your horizons." The "amazing collection of creative minds" includes enough Nobel laureates to fill a jury box as well as brilliant students who are given substantial control of their educations; one explains, "The administration's attitude towards students is one of respect. As soon as you come on campus, you are bombarded with choices." Students need to be able to manage a workload that "definitely push[es you] beyond your comfort level." A chemical engineering major elaborates: "MIT is different from many schools in that its goal is not to teach you specific facts in each subject. MIT teaches you how to think. Not about opinions, but about problem solving. Facts and memorization are useless unless you know how to approach a tough problem." Professors here range from "excellent teachers who make lectures fun and exciting" to "dull and soporific" ones, but most "make a serious effort to make the material they teach interesting by throwing in jokes and cool demonstrations." "Access to an amazing number of resources, both academic and recreational," "research opportunities for undergrads with some of the nation's leading professors," and a rock-solid alumni network complete the picture. If you ask "MIT alumni where they went to college, most will immediately stick out their hand and show you their 'brass rat' (the MIT ring, the second most recognized ring in the world)."

Life

At MIT "It may seem . . . like there's no life outside problem sets and studying for exams," but "There's always time for extracurricular activities or just relaxing" for those "with good time-management skills" or the "ability to survive on [a] lack of sleep." Options range from "building rides" (recent projects have included a motorized couch and a human-sized hamster wheel) "to partying at fraternities to enjoying the largest collection of science fiction novels in the U.S. at the MIT Science Fiction Library." Students occasionally find time to "pull a hack," which is an ethical prank "like the life-size Wright brothers' plane that appeared on top of the Great Dome for the one-hundredth anniversary of flight." Undergrads tell us that "MIT has great parties—a lot of Wellesley, Harvard, and BU students come to them," but also that "There are tons of things to do other than party" here. "Movies, shopping, museums, and plays are all possible with our location near Boston. There are great restaurants only [blocks] away from campus, too . . . From what I can tell, MIT students have way more fun on the weekends then their Cambridge counterpart[s at] Harvard."

Student Body

"There actually isn't one typical student at MIT," students here assure us, explaining that "Hobbies range from building robots and hacking to getting wasted and partying every weekend. The one thing students all have in common is that they are insanely smart and love to learn. Pretty much anyone can find the perfect group of friends to hang out with at MIT." While "Most students do have some form of 'nerdiness'" (like telling nerdy jokes, being an avid fan of *Star Wars*, etc.), "Contrary to MIT's stereotype, most MIT students are not geeks who study all the time and have no social skills. The majority of the students here are actually quite 'normal.'" The "stereotypical student [who] looks techy and unkempt . . . only represents about 25 percent of the school." The rest include "multiple-sport standouts, political activists, fraternity and sorority members, hippies, clean-cut business types, LARPers, hackers, musicians, and artisans. There are people who look like they stepped out of an Abercrombie & Fitch catalog and people who dress in all black and carry flashlights and multi-tools. Not everyone relates to everyone else, but most people get along, and it's almost a guarantee that you'll fit in somewhere."

FINANCIAL AID: 617-253-4971 • WEBSITE: WEB.MIT.EDU

THE PRINCETON REVIEW SAYS

Admissions

Very important factors considered include: Character/personal qualities. *Important factors considered include:* Class rank, academic GPA, recommendation(s), rigor of secondary school record, standardized test scores, extracurricular activities, interview, talent/ability. *Other factors considered include:* Application essay, alumni/ae relation, first generation, geographical residence, level of applicant's interest, racial/ethnic status, volunteer work, work experience. ACT with Writing component required. High school diploma or equivalent is not required. *Academic units recommended:* 4 English, 4 mathematics, 4 science, 2 foreign language, 2 social studies.

Financial Aid

Students should submit: FAFSA, CSS/Financial Aid PROFILE, noncustodial PROFILE, business/farm supplement, parent's complete federal income tax returns from prior year and W2s. Regular filing deadline is 2/15. The Princeton Review suggests that all financial aid forms be submitted as soon as possible after January 1. *Need-based scholarships/grants offered:* Federal Pell, SEOG, state scholarships/grants, private scholarships, the school's own gift aid. *Loan aid offered:* Direct Subsidized Stafford, Direct Unsubsidized Stafford, Direct PLUS, Federal Perkins, college/university loans from institutional funds. Applicants will be notified of awards on or about 4/1. Federal Work-Study Program available. Institutional employment available. Off-campus job opportunities are excellent.

The Inside Word

MIT has one of the nation's most competitive admissions processes. The school's applicant pool is so rich it turns away numerous qualified candidates each year. Put your best foot forward and take consolation in the fact that rejection doesn't necessarily mean that you don't belong at MIT, but only that there wasn't enough room for you the year you applied. Your best chance to get an edge: Find ways to stress your creativity, a quality that MIT's admissions director told *USA Today* is lacking in many prospective college students.

THE SCHOOL SAYS " . . ."

From The Admissions Office

"The students who come to the Massachusetts Institute of Technology are some of America's—and the world's—best and most creative. As graduates, they leave here to make real contributions—in science, technology, business, education, politics, architecture, and the arts. From any class, many will go on to do work that is historically significant. These young men and women are leaders, achievers, and producers. Helping such students make the most of their talents and dreams would challenge any educational institution. MIT gives them its best advantages: a world-class faculty, unparalleled facilities, and remarkable opportunities. In turn, these students help to make the institute the vital place it is. They bring fresh viewpoints to faculty research: More than three-quarters participate in the Undergraduate Research Opportunities Program. They play on MIT's 41 intercollegiate teams as well as in its 15 musical ensembles. To their classes and to their out-of-class activities, they bring enthusiasm, energy, and individual style.

"For freshman admission, MIT requires scores from either the SAT or the ACT (with or without the optional Writing test). In addition, we require two SAT Subject Tests: one in Math (Level IC or IIC), one in science (Physics, Chemistry, or Biology)."

SELECTIVITY

Admissions Rating	99
# of applicants	12,445
% of applicants accepted	12
% of acceptees attending	69
# accepting a place on wait list	443
% admitted from wait list	5

FRESHMAN PROFILE

Range SAT Critical Reading	660–760
Range SAT Math	720–800
Range SAT Writing	660–750
Range ACT Composite	31–34
Minimum paper TOEFL	577
Minimum computer TOEFL	233
Minimum web-based TOEFL	90
% graduated top 10% of class	97
% graduated top 25% of class	100
% graduated top 50% of class	100

DEADLINES

Early action	
Deadline	11/1
Notification	12/15
Regular	
Deadline	1/1
Notification	3/20
Nonfall registration?	no

APPLICANTS ALSO LOOK AT

AND OFTEN PREFER
Harvard College

AND SOMETIMES PREFER
Stanford University
Yale University
Princeton University

AND RARELY PREFER
Duke University
Columbia University
Cornell University
California Institute of Technology
University of Pennsylvania

FINANCIAL FACTS

Financial Aid Rating	95
Annual tuition	$34,750
Room and board	$10,400
Required fees	$236
Books and supplies	$1,114
% frosh rec. need-based scholarship or grant aid	63
% UG rec. need-based scholarship or grant aid	60
% frosh rec. need-based self-help aid	51
% UG rec. need-based self-help aid	53
% frosh rec. any financial aid	79
% UG rec. any financial aid	71
% UG borrow to pay for school	41
Average cumulative indebtedness	$15,051

McGill University

845 Sherbrooke Street West, Montreal, QC H3A 2T5, Canada • Admissions: 514-398-3910 • Fax: 514-398-3683

CAMPUS LIFE

Quality of Life Rating	85
Fire Safety Rating	67
Green Rating	85
Type of school	public
Environment	metropolis

STUDENTS

Total undergrad enrollment	22,262
% male/female	40/60
% from out of state	36
% live on campus	11
% in (# of) fraternities	NR (8)
% in (# of) sororities	NR (4)
% international	18
# of countries represented	135

SURVEY SAYS . . .
Great library
Diverse student types on campus
Students love Montreal, QC
Great off-campus food
Lots of beer drinking

ACADEMICS

Academic Rating	77
Calendar	semester
Student/faculty ratio	16:1
Profs interesting rating	64
Profs accessible rating	63
Most common reg class size	10–19 students
Most common lab size	20–29 students

MOST POPULAR MAJORS
political science and government
psychology
business/commerce

STUDENTS SAY ". . ."

Academics

McGill University in Montreal, Quebec enjoys "international name recognition," and it's "unapologetically a top-notch, high-powered research university." Many resources rival the best anywhere in the world. "The libraries are amazing." Other facilities are "rather shabby," though, and "McGill is unique in that the administration tends to go against the students' society (SSMU)." The administration is "extremely tedious" and "difficult to navigate." "The sheer amount of red tape, inefficiency, and incompetence is astounding." Also, while registration is "fantastically easy," some students "would have appreciated better academic guidance." "McGill forces you to take responsibility for yourself," cautions a biology major. "Nobody's going to be coddling you, but "once you figure out how to make the school work for you, things are mostly smooth sailing." " There are more than 300 areas of study, and "there does not seem to be a lot of integration between disciplines." Some classes have "over 500 students." Other classes "are not nearly as large." The faculty is a seriously mixed bag. Some professors are "amazingly passionate, talented, dedicated, and interesting" and they "genuinely care about students." Many others are "very disinterested in teaching" or "barely fluent in English." For many students, the workload is "exhausting." "A 'B+' deserves a pat on the back" here and the struggle for good grades can be "cutthroat." Other students aren't as competitive, though, and McGill offers an "easy life for those who just want to pass." "The academic seriousness of each individual student largely correlates to their chosen major."

Life

McGill has a "gorgeous campus," "located in the heart of one of the world's best cities." Students can participate in hundreds of extracurricular clubs and organizations. Intramural sports are reasonably popular. Intercollegiate sports aren't, though, and "school spirit is pretty low." "It's a DIY social experience but there's something for everyone," says a sophomore. Students say they "know when to buckle down and work hard." When the time is right, many students "drink a lot," "but it's done with the same vigor that students give their school work and extra-curriculars." The drinking age in Quebec is 18 and marijuana is not unheard of, but "the only people who really make a big deal about these things are the American students who come up here and are wowed by it all for their first year. Then they settle down and enjoy things in moderation like everyone else." "Housing is not offered after first year so there is no choice" but to live off campus for most students. Nobody cares, though, because the "relatively cheap," "wildly fun," "quasi-European city" of Montreal is "one of the world's greatest college towns." There are "ethnic quarters with every culture and food imaginable." "Nightlife is incomparable" and "the music scene is really good." "There is never a night when there is nothing to do," says a senior. "This is both a good and bad thing." "Outdoorsy stuff" is also plentiful. "Mount Royal, which is a park just north of campus, has bike and running paths and a beautiful observatory overlooking the city at the top which is great for exercising and exploring when the weather is nice," explains a junior. In the winter months, when the weather is decidedly not so nice, opportunities to hit the slopes are "very close."

Student Body

Students here describe themselves as "very smart." They're also "good looking" and they don't mind telling you so. Beyond those characteristics, the undergraduate population is widely varied. "Diversity is one of McGill's best advantages." It's "a melting pot of eclectic people of different cultures and backgrounds." "This environment doesn't allow for cookie cutters," relates a junior. "There are many niches for students to be able to find a place." The international contingent is huge. "McGill recruits students from all over the world" who "speak several languages and have multiple citizenships" "A lot of people seem to take themselves too seriously and always want to win an argument," says a junior. Others are "really down to earth." There are "plenty of preppy students" and "rich, white kids who grew up in Toronto and attended private high school." Other students are emphatically "middle class." There are "jeans-clad, beer-drinking, indie pop-listening" students. There are "academically devoted students, late-night party fiends, hippies," and "elitist, fashion-victim" "scenesters" "adhering to the latest style." Other students are "crunchy," "cry-baby social activists." Still others are "major stoners." McGill is also home to "one of the larger openly gay communities in Canada." "We're interesting kids," reflects a sophomore.

FINANCIAL AID: 514-398-6013 • E-MAIL: ADMISSIONS@MCGILL.CA • WEBSITE: WWW.MCGILL.CA

THE PRINCETON REVIEW SAYS

Admissions

Very important factors considered include: Academic GPA, rigor of secondary school record, standardized test scores. *Important factors considered include:* Class rank. *Other factors considered include:* Recommendation(s), ACT with Writing component required. TOEFL required of all international applicants. High school diploma is required and GED is not accepted. *Academic units recommended:* 4 English, 4 mathematics, 3 science, (3 science labs), 3 foreign language, 2 social studies, 2 history.

Financial Aid

Students should submit: Institution's own financial aid form, Provincial Government Loan Applications. Regular filing deadline is 6/30. The Princeton Review suggests that all financial aid forms be submitted as soon as possible after January 1. *Need-based scholarships/grants offered:* Private scholarships, the school's own gift aid, Canadian (Federal & Provincial) Student Assistance. *Loan aid offered:* FFEL Subsidized Stafford, FFEL Unsubsidized Stafford, FFEL PLUS, college/university loans from institutional funds. Applicants will be notified of awards on a rolling basis beginning 3/1. Institutional employment available. Off-campus job opportunities are fair.

The Inside Word

McGill is as tough as it comes in Canadian higher education. The university is provincially funded. As there are no geographic quotas, competition from applicants around the world is intense. The admissions process is thorough and demanding, and high SAT and SAT Subject Test scores just don't guarantee admission across the board. While English is the language of instruction, French is the language of Montreal, and those who speak it fare much better in everyday life than those who do not.

THE SCHOOL SAYS "..."

From The Admissions Office

"McGill processes over 30,000 online applications a year. Very few programs are available to non-Quebec students for January admission; consult the website for details.

"Applicants for Fall 2008 may submit results from either version (old/new) of the SAT (plus at least two appropriate SAT Subject Tests). The ACT is accepted in lieu of the SAT and SAT Subject Test combination. Please note that certain programs can require specific SAT Subject Tests."

SELECTIVITY

Admissions Rating	**60***
# of applicants	20,391
% of applicants accepted	54
% of acceptees attending	44
# accepting a place on wait list	300
% admitted from wait list	50

FRESHMAN PROFILE

Range SAT Critical Reading	640–740
Range SAT Math	640–720
Range SAT Writing	650–720
Range ACT Composite	29–31
Minimum paper TOEFL	577
Minimum computer TOEFL	233
Minimum web-based TOEFL	90
Average HS GPA	3.53

DEADLINES

Regular	
Deadline	1/15
Notification	rolling
Nonfall registration?	yes

APPLICANTS ALSO LOOK AT

AND OFTEN PREFER
Queen's University
New York University
Cornell University
University of Toronto
Tufts University
Brown University

AND SOMETIMES PREFER
Harvard College
University of Chicago
University of Michigan—Ann Arbor
Massachusetts Institute of Technology
University of Pennsylvania

FINANCIAL FACTS

Financial Aid Rating	**60***
Annual in-state tuition	$1,768
Annual out-of-state tuition	$5,141
Room and board	$10,300
Required fees	$1,450
Books and supplies	$1,000
% UG rec. need-based scholarship or grant aid	16
% UG rec. non-need-based scholarship or grant aid	10
% UG rec. need-based self-help aid	25
% UG rec. any financial aid	26

MERCER UNIVERSITY—MACON

ADMISSIONS OFFICE, 1400 COLEMAN AVENUE, MACON, GA 31207-0001 • ADMISSIONS: 478-301-2650 • FAX: 478-301-2828

CAMPUS LIFE

Quality of Life Rating	**78**
Fire Safety Rating	**73**
Green Rating	**60***
Type of school	private
Affiliation	Baptist
Environment	city

STUDENTS

Total undergrad enrollment	2,245
% male/female	47/53
% from out of state	23
% live on campus	69
% in (# of) fraternities	24 (10)
% in (# of) sororities	28 (7)
% African American	17
% Asian	7
% Caucasian	65
% Hispanic	3
% international	2
# of countries represented	35

SURVEY SAYS . . .
Small classes
Great computer facilities
Great library
Athletic facilities are great
Frats and sororities dominate
social scene

ACADEMICS

Academic Rating	**83**
Calendar	semester
Student/faculty ratio	13:1
Profs interesting rating	86
Profs accessible rating	85

MOST POPULAR MAJORS
business/commerce
engineering
psychology

STUDENTS SAY " . . . "

Academics

"Good scholarships," "challenging courses," an appealing "professor-to-student ratio, small class sizes," and "a great campus" initially convince many students to attend Mercer University in Macon—but it's the "very good professors who actually care about the students" who keep them here. The "professors are very friendly and love to interact with the students," and what's more, professors "can devote more time and energy to students' education" because they "are not required to do research." And that devotion starts on day one: "Even the introductory courses in the School of Engineering are taught only by professors with PhDs. I've never been taught by a TA." Outside of class, professors are "easily accessible, and they're very likely to actually know who you are." As at any college, there may be "some dud teachers, but overall," most students are very "pleased with the level of instruction here." Students have a lot of praise for the administration, as well: "Our administration is focused on what's best for the students and the university, not on money."

Life

Technically, Mercer is a dry campus with a curfew: Men have to leave the women's dorms by a certain hour. But students stress that in reality, the school "is more of a 'moist' campus," and "The curfew rules [are] not [strictly] enforced." As is the case on many campuses, Greek life provides a lot of the party scene, but "The Greeks on campus are cut from a different cloth from most Greeks on other campuses. At Mercer they are more dedicated to philanthropy and community service than to hazing or binge drinking." Greeks "also have higher GPAs and are more active in campus life." To offer alternatives to frat parties, Mercer "has a group called 'Quadworks' that tries to make sure that students aren't stuck on campus with nothing to do. They host bands and sponsor drive-in movies and other events." Off campus "There are lots of great restaurants," and students "frequent bars and clubs in downtown Macon." "Mercer rents a trolley service Thursday–Saturday nights that runs from campus to downtown where all of the bars and clubs are." This makes socializing a little easier for those without wheels. Some "People jet away to Atlanta" for fun and big-city cultural events on weekends. Intercollegiate athletics are not particularly well-supported at Mercer; one student remarks, "No one goes to sporting events. People will [only] go if there is a free t-shirt or cup" giveaway.

Students

Mercer students describe the majority of their peers as "Georgia residents with Judeo-Christian heritages" who are "conservative, from a wealthy family, [and] generally well bred." As one student puts it, a typical Mercer undergrad "is a Friday/Saturday night partier with a knack for Sunday-morning church-going." The numbers reveal a high percentage of minority students in the student body, especially African Americans, "but ethnic/racial groups tend to remain separated." Students emphasize, however, that this separation is "not because of any explicit racism or intolerance—it's mostly self-imposed and self-perpetuating." "A good number of students" are "involved in religious organizations" and Greek life here, but "Nearly everyone is involved in some club or another; everyone can find some niche to fit into." No matter what their niche, though, Mercer undergraduates remain true to their Southern roots by being "welcoming" as well as "friendly and courteous" to all. Though the student body has been reputed to be politically apathetic, the school's recent confrontation with the Georgia Baptist Convention and the debates it stirred up got some students to thinking that "The campus is becoming a little more politically active."

FINANCIAL AID: 478-301-2670 • E-MAIL: ADMISSIONS@MERCER.EDU • WEBSITE: WWW.MERCER.EDU

THE PRINCETON REVIEW SAYS

Admissions

Very important factors considered include: Academic GPA, rigor of secondary school record, standardized test scores, level of applicant's interest. *Important factors considered include:* Class rank, extracurricular activities, talent/ability, character personal qualities, volunteer work. *Other factors considered include:* Application essay, recommendation(s), interview, alumni/ae relation, work experience. SAT or ACT required. TOEFL required of all international applicants. High school diploma is required and GED is accepted. *Academic units required:* 4 English, 4 mathematics, 3 science, (2 science labs), 2 foreign language, 1 social studies, 2 history.

Financial Aid

Students should submit: FAFSA, Institution's own financial aid form, State aid form. The Princeton Review suggests that all financial aid forms be submitted as soon as possible after January 1. *Need-based scholarships/grants offered:* Federal Pell, SEOG, state scholarships/grants, private scholarships, the school's own gift aid, Federal Nursing Scholarships. *Loan aid offered:* Federal Perkins, Federal Nursing, state loans, college/university loans from institutional funds. Applicants will be notified of awards on a rolling basis beginning 4/01. Federal Work-Study Program available. Institutional employment available. Off-campus job opportunities are good.

The Inside Word

Mercer University's approach to the admissions process is fairly conventional—academics are where applicants distinguish themselves. Candidates with solid test scores and moderately challenging college preparatory curricula should be able to secure admittance. Students with a Christian background who want higher education with a religious foundation will thrive best at Mercer.

THE SCHOOL SAYS "..."

From The Admissions Office

"The mission of the Mercer University Office of Admissions is to attract, admit, and enroll qualified and talented students who will ultimately become happy, successful alumni. We do this by becoming personally involved with each admitted student and family during the admissions process. Mercer Admissions Staff takes time to know each admitted applicant on a personal level and are concerned about the family's questions regarding financial assistance, campus life, and academic affairs. High school and campus visits, regional receptions, and programs are all conducted by Admissions Staff who are knowledgeable about the high schools and 2-year colleges in a particular region. This makes for a truly enjoyable and productive admissions experience for all involved.

"Freshman applicants for Fall 2008 must take the new SAT, which includes a written essay, or the ACT with Writing component."

SELECTIVITY
Admissions Rating	87
# of applicants	4,588
% of applicants accepted	60
% of acceptees attending	21

FRESHMAN PROFILE
Range SAT Critical Reading	530–640
Range SAT Math	540–630
Range ACT Composite	23–28
Minimum paper TOEFL	550
Minimum computer TOEFL	213
Average HS GPA	3.6
% graduated top 10% of class	42
% graduated top 25% of class	71
% graduated top 50% of class	92

DEADLINES
Regular	
Deadline	7/1
Notification	rolling
Nonfall registration?	no

APPLICANTS ALSO LOOK AT
AND OFTEN PREFER
Samford University
Georgia Institute of Technology
Emory University
University of Georgia
AND SOMETIMES PREFER
Stetson University
Vanderbilt University
Furman University
Auburn University
AND RARELY PREFER
Clemson University
Georgia Southern University

FINANCIAL FACTS
Financial Aid Rating	87
Annual tuition	$26,760
Room and board	$8,015
Required fees	$200
Books and supplies	$900
% frosh rec. need-based scholarship or grant aid	71
% UG rec. need-based scholarship or grant aid	65
% frosh rec. non-need-based scholarship or grant aid	24
% UG rec. non-need-based scholarship or grant aid	19
% frosh rec. need-based self-help aid	42
% UG rec. need-based self-help aid	40
% frosh rec. athletic scholarships	7
% UG rec. athletic scholarships	7
% frosh rec. any financial aid	96
% UG rec. any financial aid	96
% UG borrow to pay for school	67
Average cumulative indebtedness	$24,251

MIAMI UNIVERSITY

301 SOUTH CAMPUS AVENUE, OXFORD, OH 45056 • ADMISSIONS: 513-529-2531 • FAX: 513-529-1550

CAMPUS LIFE

Quality of Life Rating	73
Fire Safety Rating	76
Green Rating	60*
Type of school	public
Environment	village

STUDENTS

Total undergrad enrollment	14,555
% male/female	46/54
% from out of state	30
% live on campus	48
% in (# of) fraternities	20 (28)
% in (# of) sororities	25 (20)
% African American	3
% Asian	3
% Caucasian	85
% Hispanic	2
% Native American	1
% international	1
# of countries represented	50

SURVEY SAYS . . .
Great library
Athletic facilities are great
Great food on campus
Frats and sororities dominate social scene
Lots of beer drinking
Hard liquor is popular

ACADEMICS

Academic Rating	76
Calendar	semester
Student/faculty ratio	15:1
Profs interesting rating	75
Profs accessible rating	73
% classes taught by TAs	10

MOST POPULAR MAJORS
zoology/animal biology
finance
marketing/marketing management

STUDENTS SAY ". . ."

Academics

The "beautiful" "wooded campus" of Miami University is just one of the reasons "This is a public school that feels like a private school." Another reason is the school's "commitment to the liberal arts via the Miami Plan." The Miami Plan refers to the university's core curriculum of 48 semester hours. Unlike tiny private schools, however, MU offers students scads of prescribed majors. "Miami is very well organized in getting students into internships and onto management fast-tracks." The vast study abroad opportunities and summer program activities draw widespread student praise too. But some students claim that "professors are hit or miss. Some are amazingly available, very dedicated teachers, and some couldn't care less what happens to their students." As Miami prepares to celebrate its bicentennial in 2009, the school is raising $500 million to hire more professors, create scholarships, build a new business school and student center, and has recently opened a new ice arena, a new engineering school, and new parking garages." Students have reported that the administration at times seems preoccupied, but the current president is very involved with students, even playing in the student broomball intramural league.

Life

Miami University is a "work hard, play hard" school. "During a generally tough week throughout campus, most people are studying, and the library is packed. But at the beginning of any semester, a lot of people go out on a Wednesday or Thursday night." Miami's "small rural classic college town" of Oxford "is very college-oriented. The street is lined with bars and restaurants" where lots of students "drink and party." Since "All of the bars pretty much have dance floors" and "People under 21 can go to bars here," under- and upperclassmen alike may take advantage of the nightlife. Greek life is also "strong here, so there are Greek functions to go to as well." There are also "university concerts, plays, and musicals, which are usually pretty well attended. As for athletics, Miami has lots of fair-weather fans," one student contends. "When we are doing well, everyone is at the game; when we aren't doing so well, lots of people are doing something else." As far as opportunities for entertainment outside of town are concerned, "There isn't any public transportation to leave Oxford," but "If you have a car, you can travel to Cincinnati or other neighboring cities for a night on the town."

Student Body

Old stereotypes die hard. Just ask the undergrads here, and they will tell you that, yes, "Miami is 'J. Crew U.'": "The typical student is White, relatively wealthy, equipped with their parents' credit card, good-looking, and only seen in the hottest fashions." (We're serious about the fashions: "Students dress up for their 8:00 A.M. classes," one student claims.). But students are adamant that there are two "sides of the J. Crew U. stereotype. To be sure, if you look at Miami U. from the Goodyear Blimp, it is J. Crew U. If you looked at Miami U. under a microscope and saw students interacting in everyday situations, you would see another school entirely." One undergrad observes that "Minorities seem to be in short supply." Another calls "this student body composition . . . self-perpetuating."

FINANCIAL AID: 513-529-8734 • E-MAIL: ADMISSION@MUOHIO.EDU • WEBSITE: WWW.MUOHIO.EDU

THE PRINCETON REVIEW SAYS

Admissions

Very important factors considered include: Rigor of secondary school record, Class rank, Academic GPA, Standardized test scores, Application Essay, Recommendation(s), Talent/ability, Character/personal qualities. *Other factors considered include:* First Generation, Alumni/ae relation, Geographical residence, State residency, Volunteer work, Work experience.

Financial Aid

The Princeton Review suggests that all financial aid forms be submitted as soon as possible after January 1. Federal Work-Study Program available. Institutional employment available. Off-campus job opportunities are good.

The Inside Word

Miami's Admissions Officers employ a practice that certainly distinguishes the Miami admissions process from that of other large, public universities. While most peer institutions typically adopt a numbers-driven process, this school is concerned about the total package. Counselors closely examine every facet of each application and consider applicants' achievements in the context of their experiences.

THE SCHOOL SAYS "..."

From The Admissions Office

"At Miami, you'll find a level of involvement—in your classes, in your research, in your extracurricular activities—that you won't find at other schools. What sets Miami apart is the ability to give students a small-college experience within the excitement and opportunities of a large university, all at a public school cost. With more than 100 majors to choose from, and a liberal arts foundation that allows students to explore different areas of interest, finding your true passion – in and out of the classroom - is at the heart of what the MU experience is all about. This deep level of engagement is reflected in the 90 percent freshman to sophomore retention rate and Miami's graduate rate, which is among the top graduation rates for public universities across the country. Miami's reputation for producing outstanding leaders with real-world experience makes us a target school for top national firms and our graduates' acceptance rate into law and medical school are far above the national average. Students also benefit from small class sizes – 90 percent of undergraduate classes have fewer than 50 students – and personal attention from faculty members in the classroom, through research opportunities, and through faculty mentoring programs. Outside of the classroom, students can participate in over 300 student organizations, attend social and cultural events, or get involved with one of the most extensive intramural and club sports program in the country."

SELECTIVITY

Admissions Rating	88
# of applicants	15,925
% of applicants accepted	75
% of acceptees attending	29

FRESHMAN PROFILE

Range SAT Critical Reading	540-640
Range SAT Math	570-660
Range ACT Composite	24-28
Average HS GPA	3.7
% graduated top 10% of class	35
% graduated top 25% of class	72
% graduated top 50% of class	98
Minimum paper TOEFL	533
Minimum computer TOEFL	200
Minimum web-based TOEFL	73

DEADLINES

Regular	01/31
Nonfall registration?	Yes

APPLICANTS ALSO LOOK AT

AND OFTEN PREFER
University of Notre Dame
Vanderbilt University
Northwestern University

AND SOMETIMES PREFER
Washington University in St. Louis
University of Wisconsin—Madison
University of Michigan—Ann Arbor
University of Illinois at Urbana-Champaign
Boston College

AND RARELY PREFER
Purdue University—West Lafayette
Xavier University (OH)
University of Dayton
Denison University

FINANCIAL FACTS

Financial Aid Rating	74
Annual in-state tuition	$8,443
Annual out-of-state tuition	$22,270
Room and board	$8,600
Required fees	$2,111
Books and supplies	$1,140
% frosh rec. need-based scholarship or grant aid	34
% UG rec. need-based scholarship or grant aid	31
% frosh rec. non-need-based scholarship or grant aid	24
% UG rec. non-need-based scholarship or grant aid	17
% frosh rec. need-based self-help aid	32
% UG rec. need-based self-help aid	31
% frosh rec. athletic scholarships	3
% UG rec. athletic scholarships	3
% frosh rec. any financial aid	87
% UG rec. any financial aid	85
% UG borrow to pay for school	52
Average cumulative indebtedness	$26,378

MICHIGAN STATE UNIVERSITY

250 ADMINISTRATION BUILDING, EAST LANSING, MI 48824-1046 • ADMISSIONS: 517-355-8332 • FAX: 517-353-1647

CAMPUS LIFE

Quality of Life Rating	86
Fire Safety Rating	60*
Green Rating	93
Type of school	public
Environment	town

STUDENTS

Total undergrad enrollment	35,772
% male/female	47/53
% from out of state	8
% live on campus	43
% in (# of) fraternities	8 (31)
% in (# of) sororities	7 (19)
% African American	8
% Asian	5
% Caucasian	78
% Hispanic	3
% Native American	1
% international	4
# of countries represented	134

SURVEY SAYS . . .

Great library
Students are friendly
Everyone loves the Spartans
Student publications are popular
Lots of beer drinking

ACADEMICS

Academic Rating	73
Calendar	semester
Student/faculty ratio	17:1
Profs interesting rating	71
Profs accessible rating	74
Most common reg class size	20–29 students
Most common lab size	20–29 students

STUDENTS SAY ". . ."

Academics

Michigan State University's large size is both its greatest asset and its greatest potential downside. The benefits of size include near-unlimited choice: "MSU is extremely varied, and there are opportunities for anyone who wishes to take advantage of them," including "over 200 majors to choose from." Those majors include "good engineering and science programs," an "amazing communications program," "the best political science program in Michigan," "the only agriculture school in the state," and "an absolutely amazing School of Hospitality Business." Economies of scale also allow MSU to offer "great study abroad programs," "a lot of helpful free tutoring in math and other subjects," and "great web programs that make it very easy to download class materials and view assignments. You can also e-mail the whole class questions or just your professor, through our Angel system." As far as possible downsides to the school's size, MSU students find that they have to "fend for [themselves]." One student noted, "Initially I came from a smaller college where there was more guidance and interaction with professors. At MSU, this is just not the case, although MSU's residential colleges do make the university seem smaller for students in related majors." That means potential peril for students who aren't self-motivated. One undergrad explains, "There are two roads you can follow when at MSU. You can study hard and earn a degree in a reputable, challenging setting; or you can soak your brain cells with alcohol instead of academia."

Life

Life on the MSU campus "generally revolves around the weekend and the basketball or football team. You get through the week looking forward to one of the two." Indeed, "Sports are huge here, and nothing beats football Saturdays or basketball nights. Tailgating is a religion." The school has a well-known party scene; one undergrad concedes, "We're known as somewhat of a party school, and MSU lives up to the title. Although during the winter there is less to do around campus, being here in the fall more than makes up for it! If you attend MSU, you're bound to have a great time." Even teetotalers can have fun here, since "Between free on-campus movies and club meetings and concerts, there is never a dull moment on campus." East Lansing has its own allures: a student explains, "Walking downtown on Grand River is awesome when it gets warmer out"; there are "decent stores and restaurants. Also, in the warm weather you are bound to see people sitting out on their porches. Many of them are having parties or just hanging out, and a lot of times they'll invite you to come on up!" Or you can just enjoy the "breathtaking beauty of the campus," with its "old buildings and beautiful trees and plants that make every walk to class a great one."

Student Body

MSU's size ensures that "This is a fairly diverse campus, especially considering that it is located in the northern Midwest." Because "Study abroad is emphasized at MSU," there are "a lot of foreign students, and they seem to fit right into the general population." One undergrad observes, "For the most part, everyone seems to do their own thing, and no one seems to have problems with that." The predominant attitude seems to be "live and let live," as "A lot of people tend to associate mostly with members from the same racial or ethnic background, although that's not always the case." What unites students—besides their love of MSU sports—is that most "are extremely friendly. Random people in classes ask you if you need a ride home, and, even better, random people offer you a seat on the bus. It's comforting to know that these are the people soon entering the workforce and 'the real world.'"

FINANCIAL AID: 517-353-5940 • E-MAIL: ADMIS@MSU.EDU • WEBSITE: WWW.MSU.EDU

THE PRINCETON REVIEW SAYS

Admissions

Very important factors considered include: Academic GPA, rigor of secondary school record, standardized test scores. *Important factors considered include:* Application essay, extracurricular activities, first generation, geographical residence. *Other factors considered include:* Class rank, recommendation(s), alumni/ae relation, character/personal qualities, level of applicant's interest, talent/ability, volunteer work, work experience. SAT or ACT required; Writing component required. High school diploma is required and GED is accepted. *Academic units required:* 4 English, 3 mathematics, 2 science, 2 foreign language, 2 social studies, 1 history. *Academic units recommended:* (2 science labs), 2 foreign language, 2 social studies, 2 history.

Financial Aid

Students should submit: FAFSA. The Princeton Review suggests that all financial aid forms be submitted as soon as possible after January 1. *Need-based scholarships/grants offered:* Federal Pell, SEOG, state scholarships/grants, private scholarships, the school's own gift aid, United Negro College Fund. *Loan aid offered:* FFEL Subsidized Stafford, FFEL Unsubsidized Stafford, FFEL PLUS, Federal Perkins, state loans, college/university loans from institutional funds. Applicants will be notified of awards on a rolling basis beginning 3/15. Federal Work-Study Program available. Institutional employment available. Off-campus job opportunities are excellent.

The Inside Word

Given the extraordinary volume of applications the Admissions Office receives, it's no wonder that Michigan State relies primarily on numbers. Decisions typically come down to grades, class rank, and test scores. Applicants who have proven to be capable students in college prep courses are relatively likely to find themselves the proud addressees of fat admissions envelopes.

THE SCHOOL SAYS "..."

From The Admissions Office

"Although Michigan State University is a graduate and research institution of international stature and acclaim, your undergraduate education is a high priority. More than 2,600 instructional faculty members (90 percent of whom hold a terminal degree) are dedicated to providing academic instruction, guidance, and assistance to our undergraduate students. Our 35,000 undergraduate students are a select group of academically motivated men and women. The diversity of ethnic, racial, religious, and socioeconomic heritage makes the student body a microcosm of the state, national, and international community.

"Students applying for admission to Michigan State University are required to take the new version of the SAT or the ACT exam with the Writing section. The Writing assessment will be considered in the holistic review of the application for admission. SAT Subject Tests are not required."

SELECTIVITY

Admissions Rating	85
# of applicants	24,436
% of applicants accepted	74
% of acceptees attending	42

FRESHMAN PROFILE

Range SAT Critical Reading	480–620
Range SAT Math	520–650
Range SAT Writing	470–600
Range ACT Composite	23–27
Average HS GPA	3.59
% graduated top 10% of class	28.9
% graduated top 25% of class	69.2
% graduated top 50% of class	96.2

DEADLINES

Nonfall registration?	yes

FINANCIAL FACTS

Financial Aid Rating	74
Annual in-state tuition	$8,603
Annual out-of-state tuition	$22,343
Room and board	$6,676
Required fees	$1,240
Books and supplies	$906
% frosh rec. need-based scholarship or grant aid	24
% UG rec. need-based scholarship or grant aid	24
% frosh rec. non-need-based scholarship or grant aid	37
% UG rec. non-need-based scholarship or grant aid	25
% frosh rec. need-based self-help aid	38
% UG rec. need-based self-help aid	37
% frosh rec. athletic scholarships	1
% UG rec. athletic scholarships	2
% frosh rec. any financial aid	44
% UG rec. any financial aid	42
% UG borrow to pay for school	59
Average cumulative indebtedness	$21,175

CAMPUS LIFE

Quality of Life Rating	**83**
Fire Safety Rating	**95**
Green Rating	**76**
Type of school	public
Environment	village

STUDENTS

Total undergrad enrollment	5,722
% male/female	77/23
% from out of state	25
% from public high school	90
% live on campus	45
% in (# of) fraternities	7 (13)
% in (# of) sororities	12 (8)
% African American	2
% Asian	1
% Caucasian	85
% Hispanic	1
% Native American	1
% international	5
# of countries represented	72

SURVEY SAYS . . .

Great computer facilities
Great library
Athletic facilities are great
Career services are great
Campus feels safe
Lots of beer drinking

ACADEMICS

Academic Rating	**74**
Calendar	semester
Student/faculty ratio	11:1
Profs interesting rating	63
Profs accessible rating	74
% classes taught by TAs	3
Most common reg class size	20–29 students
Most common lab size	10–19 students

MOST POPULAR MAJORS

mechanical engineering
civil engineering
business administration and
management

STUDENTS SAY "..."

Academics

Future engineers looking for an affordable education in a "remote, small location near the woods" flock to Michigan Technological University, a school that "is nationally ranked in almost all its engineering programs, both undergraduate and graduate." MTU offers more than just engineering—the "strong" Forest Resource and Environmental Science program "is growing significantly" and the School of Business "is gaining momentum" and "starting to grow and be accepted among the engineers of campus." That being said, most still regard the school primarily as "a winter wonderland for math, science, and computer geeks." The school "offers a real hands-on learning experience, not only in the classroom but in life," all while "dealing with being in the middle of nowhere," which students say "makes you tough." Slackers beware: "Classes are rarely canceled due to inclement weather and with the load of homework that is given, good time management skills are necessary to succeed." Perhaps that's why "there are so many companies at our career fair that it's hard not to get an interview." As one student reports, "Everyone in the industry I have talked to recruits Tech graduates because of their work ethic and personalities. This goes back to working and suffering all the time. They know what we have been through." Small class sizes facilitate one-on-one contact with professors but also "tend to make for a more competitive environment. It can be hard for those who are below the curve and trying to do better."

Life

MTU is located on the Upper Peninsula in Houghton, a town so remote that "no one goes home on weekends because it's so far away." Students see this as a plus that encourages campus unity: "My college experience would have been so much different if I had gone home on the weekends. It's on the weekends that you get to know people and actually have fun or meet with a group to study," one student explains. "Hockey is a big deal here" and the campus really comes together for games, as "it's our only Division I sport." Intramural broomball is another huge activity, "and a majority of people get involved with it because it is such a fun winter sport." Outdoor activities are also popular; one student points out that "Because of its location, Michigan Tech is the only college in the Midwest with its own ski hill right on campus, and many students and faculty utilize this luxury when the winter snows hit," which is early—"the grass is almost always buried in snow," one student warns. While some here "would probably joke and say that drinking is the only thing to do up here, and for those students it's probably true," those who seek alternative entertainment rarely have trouble finding it. Finding the time for it, given the amount of schoolwork, is another matter.

Student Body

The typical student at Tech "is the smart person from those small towns who really loves the small-town atmosphere." A good number "enjoy doing things outdoors and being active," (hunting, fishing, skiing, and snowmobiling are all popular) but "this is a technical school, so there is a fair share of people who enjoy staying inside and playing a lot of video games." With a male to female ratio of nearly 4:1, MTU has lots of undergrads "wishing there were more females on campus," although some report optimistically that "more and more women are coming to Tech as well as other ethnic groups, but it needs to grow more."

MICHIGAN TECHNOLOGICAL UNIVERSITY

Financial Aid: 906-487-2622 • E-mail: mtu4u@mtu.edu • Website: www.mtu.edu

THE PRINCETON REVIEW SAYS

Admissions

Very important factors considered include: Class rank, rigor of secondary school record, standardized test scores. *Important factors considered include:* Academic GPA. *Other factors considered include:* Application essay, recommendation(s), alumni/ae relation, character/personal qualities, extracurricular activities, interview, talent/ability, volunteer work, work experience. SAT or ACT required; TOEFL required of all international applicants. High school diploma is required and GED is accepted. *Academic units required:* 3 English, 3 mathematics, 2 science. *Academic units recommended:* 4 English, 4 mathematics, 3 science, 2 foreign language, 3 social studies, 1 history, 1 visual/performing arts, 1 computer science, 1 academic elective.

Financial Aid

Students should submit: FAFSA. The Princeton Review suggests that all financial aid forms be submitted as soon as possible after January 1. *Need-based scholarships/grants offered:* Federal Pell, SEOG, state scholarships/grants, private scholarships, the school's own gift aid. *Loan aid offered:* Direct Subsidized Stafford, Direct Unsubsidized Stafford, Direct PLUS, Federal Perkins, state loans, college/university loans from institutional funds, External Private Loans. Applicants will be notified of awards on a rolling basis beginning 3/1. Federal Work-Study Program available. Institutional employment available. Off-campus job opportunities are excellent.

The Inside Word

Michigan Tech makes applying as easy as can be. Admissions decisions are based entirely on your completed application form, your transcripts, and your standardized test scores; there are no essays or personal recommendations to make you sweat here. Best of all, you can apply online free of cost. Admissions decisions are made on a rolling basis with priority given to applications arriving early. Plan to submit your application as early as possible.

THE SCHOOL SAYS "..."

From The Admissions Office

"At Michigan Tech, our students create the future. Our unique Enterprise Program lets students work on real industry problems involving homeland security, wireless technology, communication, environmental sustainability, and nanotechnology. Through student groups like Engineers without Borders and the campus-wide Make A Difference Day, our students impact lives in our community and around the world. Students can choose from 120 degree programs in arts and human sciences, business, computing, engineering, environmental studies, sciences, and technology as they begin their careers here. We offer exciting degree programs in growing fields including biomedical engineering, applied ecology and environmental science, and pre-health studies.

"Outside of the classrooms and labs, students enjoy our golf course, ski hill, trails and recreational forest, and friendly, small-town atmosphere in beautiful Upper Michigan. Located on Portage Waterway, the campus is only minutes from Lake Superior.

"We recommend that students applying for admission take the new SAT (or the ACT with the writing section).

"Apply online for free at www.mtu.edu."

SELECTIVITY
Admissions Rating	85
# of applicants	4,148
% of applicants accepted	84
% of acceptees attending	35

FRESHMAN PROFILE
Range SAT Critical Reading	530–650
Range SAT Math	590–690
Range SAT Writing	500–620
Range ACT Composite	23–28
Minimum paper TOEFL	550
Minimum computer TOEFL	213
Minimum web-based TOEFL	79
Average HS GPA	3.52
% graduated top 10% of class	30
% graduated top 25% of class	61
% graduated top 50% of class	87

DEADLINES
Regular	
Priority	1/15
Nonfall registration?	yes

APPLICANTS ALSO LOOK AT
AAND SOMETIMES PREFER
Western Michigan University
Milwaukee School of Engineering
Michigan State University
University of Wisconsin—Madison
Kettering University
University of Michigan—Ann Arbor
University of Minnesota—Twin Cities

AND RARELY PREFER
Grand Valley State University
Northern Michigan University
Lawrence Technological University

FINANCIAL FACTS
Financial Aid Rating	78
Annual tuition	$9,828
% frosh rec. need-based scholarship or grant aid	57
% UG rec. need-based scholarship or grant aid	53
% frosh rec. non-need-based scholarship or grant aid	53
% UG rec. non-need-based scholarship or grant aid	37
% frosh rec. need-based self-help aid	56
% UG rec. need-based self-help aid	56
% frosh rec. athletic scholarships	3
% UG rec. athletic scholarships	4
% frosh rec. any financial aid	94
% UG rec. any financial aid	95
% UG borrow to pay for school	65
Average cumulative indebtedness	$14,223

MIDDLEBURY COLLEGE

THE EMMA WILLARD HOUSE, MIDDLEBURY, VT 05753-6002 • ADMISSIONS: 802-443-3000 • FAX: 802-443-2056

STUDENTS SAY ". . ."

Academics

Home to "smart people who enjoy Aristotelian ethics and quantum physics, but aren't too stuck up to go sledding in front of Mead Chapel at midnight," Middlebury College is a small, exclusive liberal arts school with "excellent foreign language programs" as well as standout offerings in environmental studies, the sciences, theater, and writing. Distribution requirements and other general requirements ensure that a Middlebury education "is all about providing students with a complete college experience including excellent teaching, exposure to many other cultures, endless opportunities for growth and success, and a challenging (yet relaxed) environment." Its "small class size and friendly yet competitive atmosphere make for the perfect college experience," as do "the best facilities of a small liberal arts college in the country. The new library, science center, athletic complex, arts center, and a number of the dining halls and dorms have been built in the past 10 years." Expect to work hard here; "It's tough, but this is a mini-Ivy, so what should one expect? There is plenty of time to socialize, and due to the collaborative atmosphere here, studying and socializing can often come hand in hand. The goal of many students here is not to get high grades" but rather "learning in its purest form, and that is perhaps this college's most brightly shining aspect." The collaborative atmosphere is abetted by the fact that "Admissions doesn't just bring in geniuses, they bring in people who are leaders and community servants. Think of the guy or girl in your high school whom everybody describes as 'so nice' . . . that's your typical Middlebury student."

Life

"This high level of involvement in everything translates into an amazing campus atmosphere" at Middlebury, where "Most people are very involved. There is a club for just about everything you can imagine, and if you can imagine one that hasn't yet been created, you go ahead and create it yourself." With great skiing and outdoor activity close by, "Almost everyone is athletic in some way. This can translate into anything from varsity sports to intramural hockey (an extremely popular winter pastime!). People are enthusiastic about being active and having fun." Because the school "is set in a very small town, there aren't too many (if any) problems with violence, drugs, [or] crime. It's the ideal college town because of its rural setting, in that there are no real distractions other than those that are provided within the college campus." Of course, the small-town setting also means that "the only real off-campus activity is going out to eat at the town's quaint restaurants or going to the one bar in town," but fortunately "When it comes to on-campus activities, Middlebury provides the student population with tons of great events. Everything from classy music concerts to late-night movies and dance parties can be found as a Midd-supported activity. The student activity board does a fabulous job with entertaining the students virtually every day."

Student Body

"The typical [Middlebury] student is athletic, outdoorsy, and very intelligent." The two most prominent demographics are "very preppy students (popped collars)" and "extreme hippies." One undergrad explains: "The typical students are one of two types: either 'Polo, Nantucket red, pearls, and summers on the Cape,' or 'Birks, wool socks, granola, and suspicious smells about them.' A lot of people break these two molds, but they often fall somewhere on the spectrum between them." There's also "a huge international student population, which is awesome," but some international students, "tend to separate out and end up living in language houses." There's also "a really strong theater/artsy community" here. One student notes, "Other than a few groups, everyone mingles pretty well. We're all too damn friendly and cheerful for our own good."

FINANCIAL AID: 802-443-5158 • E-MAIL: ADMISSIONS@MIDDLEBURY.EDU • WEBSITE: WWW.MIDDLEBURY.EDU

THE PRINCETON REVIEW SAYS

Admissions

Very important factors considered include: Class rank, academic GPA, rigor of secondary school record, character/personal qualities, extracurricular activities, talent/ability. *Important factors considered include:* Application essay, recommendation(s), standardized test scores, racial/ethnic status. *Other factors considered include:* Alumni/ae relation, first generation, geographical residence, level of applicant's interest, volunteer work, work experience. SAT and SAT Subject Tests or ACT required; High school diploma or equivalent is not required. *Academic units recommended:* 4 English, 4 mathematics, 3 science, (3 science labs), 4 foreign language, 3 social studies, 2 history, 1 academic elective, 1 Fine Arts, Music, or Drama courses recommended.

Financial Aid

Students should submit: FAFSA, CSS/Financial Aid PROFILE, state aid form, noncustodial PROFILE, business/farm supplement. Regular filing deadline is 1/1. The Princeton Review suggests that all financial aid forms be submitted as soon as possible after January 1. *Need-based scholarships/grants offered:* Federal Pell, SEOG, state scholarships/grants, private scholarships, the school's own gift aid. *Loan aid offered:* Direct Subsidized Stafford, Direct Unsubsidized Stafford, Direct PLUS, Federal Perkins, college/university loans from institutional funds. Applicants will be notified of awards on or about 4/1.

The Inside Word

Middlebury gives you options in standardized testing. The school will accept either the SAT or the ACT or three SAT Subject Tests, (the three must be in different subject areas, however). Middlebury is extremely competitive; improve your chances of admission by crafting a standardized test profile that shows you in the best possible light.

THE SCHOOL SAYS "..."

From The Admissions Office

"The successful Middlebury candidate excels in a variety of areas including academics, athletics, the arts, leadership, and service to others. These strengths and interests permit students to grow beyond their traditional 'comfort zones' and conventional limits. Our classrooms are as varied as the Green Mountains, the Metropolitan Museum of Art, or the great cities of Russia and Japan. Outside the classroom, students informally interact with professors in activities such as intramural basketball games and community service. At Middlebury, students develop critical-thinking skills, enduring bonds of friendship, and the ability to challenge themselves.

"Middlebury offers majors and programs in 45 different fields, with particular strengths in languages, international studies, environmental studies, literature and creative writing, and the sciences. Opportunities for engaging in individual research with faculty abound at Middlebury.

"Applicants must submit standardized test results in at least three different areas of study. This requirement may be met by any one of the following three options: the ACT (optional Writing Test recommended, but not required), the new SAT, or three tests in different subject areas from the SAT Subject Tests, Advanced Placement, or International Baccalaureate exams."

SELECTIVITY

Admissions Rating	99
# of applicants	7,180
% of applicants accepted	21
% of acceptees attending	44
# accepting a place on wait list	603
# of early decision applicants	1,011
% accepted early decision	25

FRESHMAN PROFILE

Range SAT Critical Reading	650–750
Range SAT Math	650–740
Range SAT Writing	650–730
Range ACT Composite	29–33
Average HS GPA	4
% graduated top 10% of class	82
% graduated top 25% of class	97
% graduated top 50% of class	100

DEADLINES

Early decision	
Deadline	11/1
Notification	12/15
Regular	
Deadline	1/1
Notification	4/1
Nonfall registration?	yes

APPLICANTS ALSO LOOK AT

AND OFTEN PREFER
Harvard College
Dartmouth College
Williams College
Amherst College

AND SOMETIMES PREFER
Pomona College
Duke University
Stanford University
Yale University
Brown University

AND RARELY PREFER
Hamilton College
Colby College
Colgate University
Bowdoin College

FINANCIAL FACTS

Financial Aid Rating	93
Comprehensive fee	$46,910
Books and supplies	$750
% frosh rec. need-based scholarship or grant aid	45
% UG rec. need-based scholarship or grant aid	41
% frosh rec. need-based self-help aid	43
% UG rec. need-based self-help aid	38
% UG borrow to pay for school	39.2
Average cumulative indebtedness	$20,808

MILLS COLLEGE

5000 MacArthur Boulevard, Oakland, CA 94613 • Admissions: 510-430-2135 • Fax: 510-430-3314

CAMPUS LIFE

Quality of Life Rating	**74**
Fire Safety Rating	**60***
Green Rating	**92**
Type of school	private
Environment	metropolis

STUDENTS

Total undergrad enrollment	948
% male/female	/100
% from out of state	19
% from public high school	80
% live on campus	56
% African American	10
% Asian	8
% Caucasian	43
% Hispanic	15
% Native American	1
% international	2
# of countries represented	22

SURVEY SAYS . . .
Small classes
No one cheats
Frats and sororities are unpopular
or nonexistent
Political activism is popular

ACADEMICS

Academic Rating	**85**
Calendar	semester
Student/faculty ratio	11:1
Profs interesting rating	89
Profs accessible rating	85
Most common reg class size	10–19 students
Most common lab size	fewer than 10 students

MOST POPULAR MAJORS
English language and literature
psychology
political science and government

STUDENTS SAY " . . . "

Academics

Mills College, a Bay Area all-women's liberal arts school "so small that most freshwomen even know the president of the college personally," is "all about the empowerment of women, innovative thought, independence, and activism." The "creative, unique, leftist women" who attend Mills may sometimes be "skeptical of the world in general" and love the "many opportunities to get involved and make a difference" that their academic community encourages. Of course, Mills also has a "rigorous and challenging" curriculum that consumes substantial proportions of each undergrad's time. The workload is considerable here; fortunately, however, undergrads enjoy "plenty of support and guidance from the faculty to aid in each student's individual success." This help may take the form of "workshops and tutoring if you are struggling." Professors "are nurturing in their teaching methods, and they are [also] experts in their fields. The teachers are here to help the students learn, and, therefore, they take the time to give individualized attention." Students lavish praise on the nursing program, computer sciences and mathematics, the "strong Psychology Department," the "amazing Child Development Department," an English Department that "accommodates and often encourages experimentation," and an ethnic studies program "that will challenge and push you." As is the case at many small schools, course availability is sometimes a problem; one undergrad writes, "Incoming students should simply be aware that many classes are only offered every 2 years (and the very rare ones, every 3), so they need to plan carefully if they are expecting to take some of Mills' more unique classes." All told, however, students tend to agree that "the benefits of attending Mills far outweigh these compromises."

Life

"Mills is not for everyone," students concede, pointing out that "If you're looking for a party school, Mills is not for you." One student puts it more bluntly: "Life at Mills is usually pretty dull. Social activities, whether endorsed by the school or not, are scarce. We generally go to UC—Berkeley if we want to interact with other students, either at a party or just a coffee shop. So many things are closed at Mills on the weekends that it doesn't really provide a great atmosphere for socializing once classes are done for the week." Activities are a little more lively during the week, when undergrads "have social lives, but parties do not consume them. We have many free activities such as dances, movie screenings, guest speakers, art shows, outdoor outings such as water rafting and horseback riding, and many sporting events." Many here relish the fact that "campus life is usually quiet and peaceful," and they praise the beautiful campus, which they liken to "a park in the middle of the city" that provides "lots of quiet space to study." At the same time, the urban setting provides the hustle and bustle missing from campus: "The rest of the Bay Area . . . is a great asset. The opportunities for entertainment in Berkeley, San Francisco, etc. are endless."

Student Body

Mills students "tend to differ from socially imposed expectations about what a young woman ought to be in at least one major way. "A typical student at Mills is usually either gay, transgender, minority, impoverished, vegetarian, or anarchist." The student body is thus, to some degree, "reverse mainstream." With students of color representing one-third of the population, a significant lesbian population, and lots of nontraditional undergrads—that is, "a relatively high percentage of older, resuming, and transferring students"—Mills achieves the diversity that its community members enthusiastically champion. One student notes, "The only thing that is 'typical' about the women at Mills is that all of them are smart, independent-thinking, strong women who want to make their lives the best that they can be."

FINANCIAL AID: 510-430-2000 • E-MAIL: ADMISSION@MILLS.EDU • WEBSITE: WWW.MILLS.EDU

THE PRINCETON REVIEW SAYS

Admissions

Very important factors considered include: Rigor of secondary school record. *Important factors considered include:* Class rank, application essay, academic GPA, recommendation(s), standardized test scores, character/personal qualities, extracurricular activities. *Other factors considered include:* Alumni/ae relation, first generation, interview, level of applicant's interest, talent/ability, volunteer work, work experience. SAT Subject Tests recommended; SAT or ACT required; TOEFL required of all international applicants. High school diploma is required and GED is accepted. *Academic units required:* 4 English, 3 mathematics, 2 science, (2 science labs), 2 foreign language, 2 social studies, 2 history. *Academic units recommended:* 4 English, 4 mathematics, 4 science, 4 foreign language, 4 social studies, 4 history, 2 visual/performing arts, 2 academic electives.

Financial Aid

Students should submit: FAFSA, institution's own financial aid form, state aid form. Regular filing deadline is 2/15. The Princeton Review suggests that all financial aid forms be submitted as soon as possible after January 1. *Need-based scholarships/grants offered:* Federal Pell, SEOG, state scholarships/grants, private scholarships, the school's own gift aid. *Loan aid offered:* FFEL Subsidized Stafford, FFEL Unsubsidized Stafford, FFEL PLUS, Federal Perkins, college/university loans from institutional funds. Applicants will be notified of awards on a rolling basis beginning 3/1. Federal Work-Study Program available. Institutional employment available. Off-campus job opportunities are excellent.

Inside Word

Mills recognizes that no individual factor fully encompasses an applicant. The Admissions Office endeavors to give equal attention and weight to all facets of the application, from the secondary school record and standardized test scores to the extracurricular interests and recommendations. While this means that candidates need to concentrate on a variety of areas, it also ensures they won't be discounted due to any one weakness.

THE SCHOOL SAYS " . . ."

From The Admissions Office

"For more than 150 years, Mills College has shaped women's lives. Offering a progressive liberal arts and sciences curriculum taught by nationally renowned faculty, Mills gives students the personal attention that leads to extraordinary learning. Through intensive, collaborative study in a community of forward-thinking individuals, students gain the ability to make their voices heard, the strength to risk bold visions, an eagerness to experiment, and a desire to change the world.

"Nestled on 135 lush acres in the heart of the San Francisco Bay Area, Mills draws energy from the college's location. Mills students connect with centers of learning, business, and technology; pursue research and internship opportunities; and explore the Bay Area's many sources of cultural, social, and recreational enrichment.

"Ranked sixth among top colleges in the West, Mills offers a renowned education for students who are seeking an intimate, collaborative college experience. You'll learn from distinguished professors who are truly dedicated to teaching. You'll interact with dynamic women of different backgrounds, ethnicities, cultures, ages, and mindsets, making your learning rich and inspiring.

"With more than 40 different majors to choose from—including a self-designed program—you'll have lots of educational options. The classroom debate will be your intellectual catalyst, but you'll find plenty of opportunities to express yourself, both in and out of the classroom.

"First-year applicants should submit either the SAT or the ACT. A student's overall candidacy may be enhanced by the submission of SAT Subject Tests."

SELECTIVITY

Admissions Rating	86
# of applicants	1,098
% of applicants accepted	64
% of acceptees attending	26

FRESHMAN PROFILE

Range SAT Critical Reading	520–640
Range SAT Math	490–610
Range SAT Writing	500–630
Range ACT Composite	19–27
Minimum paper TOEFL	550
Minimum computer TOEFL	213
Average HS GPA	3.61
% graduated top 10% of class	40
% graduated top 25% of class	50
% graduated top 50% of class	97

DEADLINES

Early action	
Deadline	11/15
Notification	12/15
Regular	
Priority	2/1
Deadline	5/1
Notification	rolling
Nonfall registration?	yes

APPLICANTS ALSO LOOK AT

AND OFTEN PREFER
University of California—Berkeley
Mount Holyoke College
Smith College

AND SOMETIMES PREFER
Oberlin College
Occidental College
Scripps College
Wellesley College

AND RARELY PREFER
Pitzer College
University of Southern California

FINANCIAL FACTS

Financial Aid Rating	80
Annual tuition	$34,170
Room and board	$11,270
Required fees	$1,020
Books and supplies	$1,300
% frosh rec. need-based scholarship or grant aid	76
% UG rec. need-based scholarship or grant aid	73
% frosh rec. non-need-based scholarship or grant aid	76
% UG rec. non-need-based scholarship or grant aid	73
% frosh rec. need-based self-help aid	76
% UG rec. need-based self-help aid	73
% frosh rec. any financial aid	98
% UG rec. any financial aid	91
% UG borrow to pay for school	91
Average cumulative indebtedness	$25,163

MILLSAPS COLLEGE

1701 NORTH STATE STREET, JACKSON, MS 39210-0001 • ADMISSIONS: 601-974-1050 • FAX: 601-974-1059

STUDENTS SAY ". . ."

Academics

At last, a college where "The brochures are true! The classes are not too big, the instructors love what they do (and do it well), upperclassmen are helpful, and the out-of-class experience is fun." It's hard to find an undergraduate dissatisfied with the academic experience at this small gem of a school in Jackson. Foremost, there are the professors, who "are simply top of the line. They are intellectually stimulating, approachable, and respectable in their fields." And if there's one thing they're not, it's pushovers; one student says, "Professors here have very high standards as a whole, and grade inflation is quite low. Many teachers have reputations for being hard-core graders." But while grading may be "tough," students also agree that it is "fair." Writing is "stressed" in Millsaps classes, so prospective students should "Be prepared to write all the time, in anything and everything." "You have to write a paper for every class, including math classes." Most in-class time "is composed of classroom discussion." The result of all this class discussion and writing, of course, is that "professors teach you how to think, not what to think."

Life

"A little more than half of the girls at Millsaps are in sororities," and nearly the same percentage of guys are in fraternities. Needless to say, "Greek life is very big at Millsaps, and almost all on-campus entertainment options are centered around places like the frat houses." "During the week, class is the focus," but "We have frat parties on Fridays and Saturdays and occasionally on Thursdays. Anyone can come to these parties," including "guys from other fraternities." "During football and basketball season students and faculty turn out to cheer on our team. This is probably when there is the most unity on campus." Beyond campus, "Our city, Jackson, also introduces [us to] many cultural opportunities, such as musicals (sometimes with sponsored tickets for students), gallery and museum exhibits, and more." Jackson also "has plenty of bars, clubs, both 21-plus and 18-plus, parks, and good bands playing somewhere just about every weekend." Students can also find "good concerts" at the Mississippi State Fairgrounds. The civic-minded will appreciate that "community service is huge" at Millsaps, with numerous "philanthropic activities off campus" sponsored by the Greek and other organizations and even "a Habitat for Humanity chapter" based on the campus. One downside to campus? Due to Millsaps' small size, "People gossip like crazy, so if you hook up with somebody, everybody is going to know."

Student Body

"The typical Millsaps student was that cool nerd in high school." You know, "the A student from high school who was involved in every club offered." In other words, Millsaps students are "friendly and eager to engage in conversation about anything! Economically, many students are middle- to upper-middle-class, but almost everyone is on some type of scholarship. Politically, Millsaps students are on both sides of the spectrum, and most people are aware of politics." Students estimate that the "majority of students are religious or spiritual, and typically Millsaps students are interested in social justice issues and service to the community at large." These "friendly, studious, driven" undergraduates "like to party as hard as they work." But even if you don't fit this mold, don't fret: "We're too small to have outcasts."

FINANCIAL AID: 601-974-1220 • E-MAIL: ADMISSIONS@MILLSAPS.EDU • WEBSITE: WWW.GO.MILLSAPS.EDU

THE PRINCETON REVIEW SAYS

Admissions

Very important factors considered include: Academic GPA, rigor of secondary school record, standardized test scores, character/personal qualities. *Important factors considered include:* Class rank, application essay, recommendation(s), extracurricular activities, interview, talent/ability, volunteer work. *Other factors considered include:* work experience. SAT or ACT required; TOEFL required of all international applicants. High school diploma is required and GED is accepted. *Academic units required:* 4 English, 3 mathematics, 3 science, (1 science labs), 2 social studies, 2 history. *Academic units recommended:* 4 English, 4 mathematics, 4 science, (1 science labs), 2 foreign language, 2 social studies, 2 history, 2 academic electives.

Financial Aid

Students should submit: FAFSA, admissions application for freshmen. The Princeton Review suggests that all financial aid forms be submitted as soon as possible after January 1. *Need-based scholarships/grants offered:* Federal Pell, SEOG, state scholarships/grants, private scholarships, the school's own gift aid. *Loan aid offered:* FFEL Subsidized Stafford, FFEL Unsubsidized Stafford, FFEL PLUS, Federal Perkins, college/university loans from institutional funds. Applicants will be notified of awards on a rolling basis beginning January.

The Inside Word

High school seniors looking for a quality liberal arts college with Southern charm should look no further than Millsaps. While the applicant pool is somewhat self-selecting, the high admit rate is indicative of a relatively painless application process. Candidates with solid transcripts and a variety of extracurriculars should make the cut.

THE SCHOOL SAYS "..."

From The Admissions Office

"Millsaps offers outstanding value in nationally ranked liberal arts education. Your academic journey begins with Introduction to Thinking and Writing, a comprehensive freshman experience that develops reasoning, communication, quantitative thinking, historical consciousness, aesthetic judgment, global, and multicultural awareness, and valuing and decision-making. Throughout your Millsaps years you'll be encouraged to think differently; learn critical, analytical skills; embrace independence of thought; and prepare for study in your chosen major. We offer unique opportunities such as study abroad and in the field at our Yucatán Program; an exploration of your personal and professional future in relation to issues of ethics, values, faith, and the common good through our Faith and Work Initiative; highly respected pre-professional programs in law, medicine, and social work; and a 5-year business track leading to an MBA or master's in accountancy with a liberal arts perspective that is accredited by the Association to Advance Collegiate Schools of Business. Our student body included Mississippi's 2003–2004 Rhodes scholar, and the faculty included the Carnegie Foundation's 2006 and 2007 Mississippi Professor of the Year. Our courses are taught without graduate assistants and our intimate student-faculty-community relationship is a hallmark of a Millsaps education. The emerging cultural climate in Jackson, Mississippi's capital city, provides unique artistic, athletic, and social opportunities in the modern South. We encourage you to look at Millsaps College. You'll appreciate the quality of our educational experience in comparison to the costs you'll discover at other national liberal arts institutions. Millsaps College: where minds matter."

SELECTIVITY

Admissions Rating	87
# of applicants	1,250
% of applicants accepted	77
% of acceptees attending	31

FRESHMAN PROFILE

Range SAT Critical Reading	550–670
Range SAT Math	540–650
Range ACT Composite	23–29
Minimum paper TOEFL	550
Minimum computer TOEFL	220
Minimum web-based TOEFL	80
Average HS GPA	3.5
% graduated top 10% of class	40
% graduated top 25% of class	66
% graduated top 50% of class	89

DEADLINES

Early action	
Deadline	1/8
Notification	rolling
Nonfall registration?	yes

APPLICANTS ALSO LOOK AT

AND OFTEN PREFER
Birmingham-Southern College

AND SOMETIMES PREFER
Rhodes College

AND RARELY PREFER
Samford University
Spring Hill College
Furman University
Texas Christian University

FINANCIAL FACTS

Financial Aid Rating	80
Annual tuition	$23,214
Room and board	$8,800
Required fees	$1,540
Books and supplies	$1,000
% frosh rec. need-based scholarship or grant aid	55
% UG rec. need-based scholarship or grant aid	55
% frosh rec. non-need-based scholarship or grant aid	16
% UG rec. non-need-based scholarship or grant aid	10
% frosh rec. need-based self-help aid	37
% UG rec. need-based self-help aid	42
% frosh rec. any financial aid	97
% UG rec. any financial aid	94
% UG borrow to pay for school	58.8
Average cumulative indebtedness	$21,495

MISSOURI U. OF SCIENCE AND TECHNOLOGY

106 PARKER HALL, ROLLA, MO 65409 • ADMISSIONS: 573-341-4165 • FAX: 573-341-4082

CAMPUS LIFE

Quality of Life Rating	**66**
Fire Safety Rating	**80**
Green Rating	**75**
Type of school	public
Environment	town

STUDENTS

Total undergrad enrollment	4,705
% male/female	78/22
% from out of state	20
% from public high school	85
% live on campus	58
% in (# of) fraternities	25 (20)
% in (# of) sororities	24 (5)
% African American	5
% Asian	2
% Caucasian	84
% Hispanic	2
% Native American	1
% international	3
# of countries represented	46

SURVEY SAYS . . .

Small classes
Great computer facilities
Career services are great
Campus feels safe
Frats and sororities dominate
social scene
Lots of beer drinking
Hard liquor is popular

ACADEMICS

Academic Rating	**77**
Calendar	semester
Student/faculty ratio	15:1
Profs interesting rating	67
Profs accessible rating	74
% classes taught by TAs	12
Most common reg class size	20–29 students
Most common lab size	10–19 students

MOST POPULAR MAJORS

civil engineering
electrical, electronics and communications engineering
mechanical engineering

STUDENTS SAY ". . ."

Academics

Prospective Missouri University of Science and Technology students should prepare for "mental boot camp," because hard work is the norm at this engineering, mathematics, science, and business-intensive school. In return for their efforts, UMR undergrads receive an education from "one of the best engineering schools in the country" at state-school prices. While students note that "some classes can be more difficult than anticipated due to the fact that English is not the professor's native tongue" (an issue being addressed internally by the university), they give Rolla professors high marks overall. That's because professors "do a good job of explaining the subjects to the students. Even though the subjects are almost always technical and difficult, they usually try to make sense [of them] and teach well." The "free tutoring sessions available for a variety of courses where the various instructors of that course and other upper-level students from that major help you understand the material" also help a lot. UMR undergrads appreciate the fact that Rolla excels not only in the expected areas of engineering (such as electrical and mechanical engineering), but also in some less common disciplines. A "very good program in ceramic engineering, which is not present at all in most engineering schools," as well as "one of the nation's very few mining engineering degrees," earns students' praise. Students also love the Career Opportunity Center, which "really goes above and beyond to help students find internships and full-time job opportunities and prepare for interviews."

Life

"Students have to dedicate a good portion of their time to studies" at UMR, largely because of the homework-intensive nature of the school's popular engineering programs. During the week, "The mood is all about school. On the weekend, a lot of people still focus on school, but there are a lot of parties and events, especially at the Greek houses." As far as other on-campus diversions are concerned, "Lots of events are planned, such as film screenings, comedians, Broadway plays, music performances, concerts, trivia, and professional meetings." Clubs and organizations "are very common." "You have to make your own fun," possibly a result of the fact that hometown Rolla "is a small hick town with nothing to do: no big sports teams, no shopping, no entertainment, no nice restaurants. It's not the place to be for a city kid." Outdoor enthusiasts find Rolla more accommodating because it "has excellent outdoor possibilities, everything from hiking to camping and skeet shooting. Lots of open federal lands and national forests" add to the outdoorsy appeal. Students add that "we are a little over an hour from St. Louis, Columbia, and Springfield, so if the night is slow, we always have somewhere to go."

Student Body

About 70 percent of UMR students graduate with engineering degrees. As a result, Rolla is characterized by some as "a school of nerds: run by the nerd and for the nerd. Geeks of all looks, smells, and intelligence thrive here." The most antisocial among them are the "computer nerds who play online games all day and have Halo tournaments in their dorms." Others are more outgoing; one undergrad reports, "There are two types of people at UMR: the social people who go out and have fun and get highly involved on campus and the introverts." But fear not: "There are enough fun, normal people on campus to balance out the weird ones." While Rolla is relatively lacking in racial diversity, the school is "geographically diverse, with students from rural areas, big cities, and foreign countries." Gender is another issue: With an almost 3:1 male/female ratio, "girls are often flocked to and very often get a lot of unwanted attention."

FINANCIAL AID: 800-522-0938 • E-MAIL: ADMISSIONS@UMR.EDU • WEBSITE: WWW.UMR.EDU

THE PRINCETON REVIEW SAYS

Admissions

Very important factors considered include: Class rank, academic GPA, rigor of secondary school record, standardized test scores. *Important factors considered include:* Recommendation(s). *Other factors considered include:* Application essay, character/personal qualities, extracurricular activities, interview, talent/ability, volunteer work, work experience. SAT or ACT required; ACT with Writing component recommended. TOEFL required of all international applicants. High school diploma is required and GED is accepted. *Academic units required:* 4 English, 4 mathematics, 3 science, (1 science labs), 2 foreign language, 3 social studies, 1 visual/performing arts.

Financial Aid

Students should submit: FAFSA. The Princeton Review suggests that all financial aid forms be submitted as soon as possible after January 1. *Need-based scholarships/grants offered:* Federal Pell, SEOG, state scholarships/grants, private scholarships, the school's own gift aid. *Loan aid offered:* FFEL Subsidized Stafford, FFEL Unsubsidized Stafford, FFEL PLUS, Federal Perkins, state loans, college/university loans from institutional funds. Federal Work-Study Program available. Institutional employment available. Off-campus job opportunities are good.

The Inside Word

Comparable to other leading public universities, it's a numbers game at Missouri University of Science and Technology. Applicants who meet class rank and standardized test cut-offs, as well as distribution requirements, will be granted admission. But don't let the straightforward application process fool you—the university draws a competitive, self-selecting pool of applicants. Candidates will find it to their advantage to apply early.

THE SCHOOL SAYS "..."

From The Admissions Office

"Widely recognized as one of our nation's best universities for engineering, sciences, computer science, and technology, the Missouri University of Science and Technology also offers programs in information science, business, and liberal arts. Personal attention, access to leadership opportunities, research projects, and co-ops and internships mean students are well prepared for the future. A 96 percent career placement rate across all majors and a 90-plus percent placement rate to medical, law, and other professional schools tell the tale; UMR offers a terrific undergraduate experience and value for your money.

"The Missouri University of Science and Technology makes individual admission decisions based primarily on each applicant's standardized test scores and class rank or GPA. In the case of borderline admission situations, additional factors may be considered.

"As of this book's publication, the Missouri University of Science and Technology did not have information available about their policy regarding the new SAT."

SELECTIVITY

Admissions Rating	86
# of applicants	2,317
% of applicants accepted	67
% of acceptees attending	63

FRESHMAN PROFILE

Range SAT Critical Reading	590–690
Range SAT Math	525–670
Range ACT Composite	25–30
Minimum paper TOEFL	550
Minimum computer TOEFL	213
Average HS GPA	3.71
% graduated top 10% of class	38
% graduated top 25% of class	69
% graduated top 50% of class	92

DEADLINES

Regular	
Priority	12/1
Deadline	7/1
Notification	rolling
Nonfall registration?	yes

APPLICANTS ALSO LOOK AT
AND OFTEN PREFER

Saint Louis University
Washington University in St. Louis
University of Missouri—Columbia
Truman State University
University of Wisconsin—Madison
University of Illinois at Urbana-Champaign
Massachusetts Institute of Technology

AND SOMETIMES PREFER

Purdue University—West Lafayette
University of Iowa
Iowa State University
Georgia Institute of Technology
Colorado School of Mines

FINANCIAL FACTS

Financial Aid Rating	76
Annual in-state tuition	$7,077
Annual out-of-state tuition	$17,733
Room and board	$6,660
Required fees	$1,095
Books and supplies	$900
% frosh rec. need-based scholarship or grant aid	48
% UG rec. need-based scholarship or grant aid	52
% frosh rec. non-need-based scholarship or grant aid	18
% UG rec. non-need-based scholarship or grant aid	11
% frosh rec. need-based self-help aid	32
% UG rec. need-based self-help aid	37
% frosh rec. athletic scholarships	2
% UG rec. athletic scholarships	2

MONMOUTH UNIVERSITY (NJ)

400 CEDAR AVENUE, WEST LONG BRANCH, NJ 07764-1898 • ADMISSIONS: 732-571-3456 • FAX: 732-263-5166

STUDENTS SAY ". . ."

Academics

Monmouth University is "not a large university, but not a tiny one," the sort of place where you "can hang out with friends one day and meet a whole new crowd the next." It's big enough to qualify as "a diverse school with good academics, recognized extracurriculars, and impressive athletics," yet small enough that "students really get to build great academic relationships with their professors and get the attention and education that they need and deserve." Standout departments include communications, business (where most of the professors "have worked for companies prior to teaching so they have a lot of insight"), education, music, criminal justice, and premedical sciences. In all disciplines students must complete "an internship program—what we call the experiential education requirement—that really sets up students for life after college. Many of the students get hired by the people for whom they intern." If there's a drawback here, it's that the student body carries too much dead weight, too many students who "have no interest" in anything but the nearby beach and thus threaten to transform the school into "a post-high school country club." However, "for a student willing to commit himself, Monmouth is a great school. At the same time, it is easy for a student to get by doing marginal work. Basically you get out of it what you put into it."

Life

Life at Monmouth University "is a totally unique experience for each person. Some people go home every weekend and hate it; others choose to get involved and love it. Personally, I chose the latter choice and couldn't be happier about it." One student reports, "when I'm not endlessly slaving away over my senior thesis, you can find me (or any student my age, really) spending time on the beach, shopping, enjoying my wonderful apartment in Pier Village, or frequenting any one of the local bars." The party scene is not what it once was here; one student reports that "Monmouth somehow still has the reputation as a 'party school,' which was true around ten years ago, but not anymore." Students warn, "The MU police are extremely strict about alcohol consumption. Most parties on campus are busted by RAs or the police." As a result, "off-campus parties are popular. Not a lot of people go home on the weekends, but a good number go to different schools around here." Alternatively, "there is lots of nightlife around the area: Long Branch, Seaside Park, Sayreville, Red Bank, Belmar, etc. Lots of dance clubs allow girls 18 and over in with a small cover charge on select days of the week." Finally, "students often take weekend trips into the city (either New York or Philadelphia) by train or by car" when they want to get off campus.

Students

There's a lot of conspicuous wealth at Monmouth in the form of "various expensive cars in the parking lots" and "designer clothes and bags." "Vera Bradley is almost a necessity—it is even sold in the book store." Students are typically "very trendy," and "extremely image-conscious," and "beautiful and very materialistic." Students "are very in tune with the latest fashion and technology trends." They tend to come from "New Jersey, Pennsylvania, Staten Island, or Long Island, New York. We are all from the suburbs and probably have the same family income." Monmouth's proximity to the beach attracts "many skaters and surfers" as well as "a lot of relaxed people." With three women to every two men, "the male-female ratio totally works out in the guy's favor."

FINANCIAL AID: 732-571-3463 • E-MAIL: ADMISSION@MONMOUTH.EDU • WEBSITE: WWW.MONMOUTH.EDU

THE PRINCETON REVIEW SAYS

Admissions

Very important factors considered include: Academic GPA, rigor of secondary school record, standardized test scores, extracurricular activities, volunteer work, work experience. *Other factors considered include:* Application essay, recommendation(s), alumni/ae relation, SAT or ACT required; ACT with Writing component required. TOEFL required of all international applicants. High school diploma is required and GED is accepted. *Academic units required:* 4 English, 3 mathematics, 2 science, (1 science labs), 2 history, 5 academic electives. *Academic units recommended:* 2 foreign language, 2 social studies.

Financial Aid

Students should submit: FAFSA Regular filing deadline is 6/30. The Princeton Review suggests that all financial aid forms be submitted as soon as possible after January 1. *Need-based scholarships/grants offered:* Federal Pell, SEOG, state scholarships/grants, private scholarships, the school's own gift aid, Federal Nursing Scholarships. *Loan aid offered:* Direct Subsidized Stafford, Direct Unsubsidized Stafford, Direct PLUS, FFEL PLUS, Federal Perkins, state loans, college/university loans from institutional funds, Alternative Loans. Applicants will be notified of awards on a rolling basis beginning 2/1. Off-campus job opportunities are good.

Inside Word

"B" students with slightly above average SAT or ACT scores should find little impediment to gaining admission to Monmouth. The school's national stature is on the rise, resulting in a more competitive applicant base, but Monmouth must still compete with many heavy hitters for top regional students.

THE SCHOOL SAYS "..."

From The Admissions Office

"Monmouth University offers a well-rounded but bold academic environment with plenty of opportunities—personal, professional, and social. Monmouth graduates are poised for success and prepared to assume leadership roles in their chosen professions, because the university invests in students beyond the classroom.

"Monmouth emphasizes hands-on learning, while providing exceptional undergraduate and graduate degree programs. There are programs for medical scholars, honors students, marine scientists, software engineers, teachers, musicians, broadcast producers, and more. Faculty members are lively participants in the education of their students. These teacher/scholars, dedicated to excellence, are often recognized experts in their fields. Students may be in a class with no more than 35 students (half of Monmouth's classes have fewer than 21 students) learning from qualified professors who know each student by name.

"Monmouth recognizes its students are the energy of its campus. The Monmouth community celebrates student life with cultural events, festivals, active student clubs, and organizations that reflect its school spirit. Athletics play a big part in campus life. A well-established member of the NCAA Division I, Monmouth athletics is a rising tide supported by some of the best fans in the Northeast.

"The president of Monmouth University, Paul G. Gaffney II, believes the reputation of the university starts with the achievements and successes of its students. At Monmouth, students find the support and guidance needed to make their mark in the world."

SELECTIVITY

Admissions Rating	78
# of applicants	6,982
% of applicants accepted	57
% of acceptees attending	24

FRESHMAN PROFILE

Range SAT Critical Reading	490–560
Range SAT Math	500–580
Range SAT Writing	480–570
Range ACT Composite	21–24
Minimum paper TOEFL	550
Minimum computer TOEFL	213
Minimum web-based TOEFL	79
Average HS GPA	3.17
% graduated top 10% of class	11
% graduated top 25% of class	39
% graduated top 50% of class	72

DEADLINES

Early action	
Deadline	12/1
Notification	1/15
Regular	
Priority	12/1
Deadline	3/1
Nonfall registration?	yes

FINANCIAL FACTS

Financial Aid Rating	71
Annual tuition	$22,406
Room and board	$8,904
Required fees	$628
Books and supplies	$1,000
% frosh rec. need-based scholarship or grant aid	21
% UG rec. need-based scholarship or grant aid	28
% frosh rec. non-need-based scholarship or grant aid	56
% UG rec. non-need-based scholarship or grant aid	53
% frosh rec. need-based self-help aid	48
% UG rec. need-based self-help aid	49
% frosh rec. athletic scholarships	3
% UG rec. athletic scholarships	3
% frosh rec. any financial aid	65
% UG rec. any financial aid	92
% UG borrow to pay for school	76
Average cumulative indebtedness	$34,484

MONTANA TECH OF THE UNIVERSITY OF MONTANA

1300 WEST PARK STREET, BUTTE, MT 59701 • ADMISSIONS: 406-496-4178 • FAX: 406-496-4710

CAMPUS LIFE
Quality of Life Rating	80
Fire Safety Rating	89
Green Rating	60*
Type of school	public
Environment	town

STUDENTS
Total undergrad enrollment	2,236
% male/female	59/41
% from out of state	12
% live on campus	16
% Asian	1
% Caucasian	83
% Hispanic	2
% Native American	1
% international	4
# of countries represented	18

SURVEY SAYS . . .
Large classes
Great computer facilities
Career services are great
Frats and sororities are unpopular
or nonexistent
Lots of beer drinking

ACADEMICS
Academic Rating	76
Calendar	semester
Student/faculty ratio	16:1
Profs interesting rating	80
Profs accessible rating	82
Most common reg class size	fewer than 10 students
Most common lab size	10–19 students

MOST POPULAR MAJORS
resort management
biology/biological sciences
mass communication/media studies

STUDENTS SAY ". . ."

Academics

A division of the University of Montana public school system, Montana Tech is a "small school with an excellent curriculum in science and engineering, complete with small classes, lots of personal attention, many internship opportunities, nearby recreation, and post-graduate success." The school offers a range of "challenging and rewarding" degree programs in engineering, sciences, and technology, with able professors who "know how to push the students without making them feel inadequate or lost in the material." With an undergraduate enrollment of just 2,000, "it is easy to establish a personal relationship with professors," and "the low student to professor ratio allows students to build first-name basis relationships." In fact, "professors are approachable and encourage students to visit them during office hours to discuss anything they would like to." There is no denying the academic rigor of Montana Tech's undergraduate programs; however, the university offers "a lot of support as far as helping you understand anything you're not getting," and "there are always tutors available" at one of the two campus learning centers. While most students admit that they have little contact with the school's administrative offices, most observe that, "the administration seems to be doing a great job of keeping everything running smoothly." In preparing students for life after college, Montana Tech is peerless, giving students "real-world experience while still in an undergraduate learning environment." What's more, with post-graduation job placement at almost 100 percent, "Montana Tech has one of the highest job placement rates in the nation."

Life

To keep up with Montana Tech's demanding coursework, many undergraduates spend a majority of their time with their noses in books. However, many students also get involved in a few extracurricular activities. For example, a sophomore shares, "I'm in the Society of Petroleum Engineers, Ski/Snowboard Club, and an off-campus Homebrewers' Guild." Set in the small mining town of Butte, Montana, halfway between Glacier National Park and Yellowstone, Tech's campus is surrounded by spectacular natural beauty. As a result, "outdoor recreation is popular," and students can easily engage in a range of activities, including "climbing, skiing, snowshoeing, backpacking, hunting, snowmobiling, hiking, mountain biking, and backcountry skiing." On the weekends, Tech students "can usually be found hanging out with large groups of friends at someone's house, just having a good time." Butte also has a number of popular watering holes, and many Tech students "go out to the local bars on the weekend to watch the different bands that come in to play for the locals." A freshman relates, "A lot of time is spent playing pool, having a few drinks, and just getting to know the other students. It can be at the local bar or at a student's house, but it's always a fun time and nothing too crazy."

Student Body

An open and affable vibe permeates the campus atmosphere at Montana Tech and throughout the campus, "students are friendly and always smile and offer a hello when passing by." Generally, Tech undergraduates are neither cliquish nor judgmental, as "most students at Montana Tech are here to study and focus on getting a career instead of how they dress or who they interact with." A junior concurs, "Everyone gets along well because the real measure of a student is not what he or she looks like, but their ability to make connections and see the whole picture." Currently, the school is majority male, and demographically, "Montanans make up most of Tech." In addition to the local men, you'll find "many small town, Canadian, and Middle Eastern Students at Montana Tech," a majority of whom have come to participate in the school's touted petroleum engineering program. While a common interest in math and science unites the student body, the school tends to attract a lot of different personalities. A freshman enthuses, "Everybody's unique and acts that way. We have everybody from cowboy Joe to dreadlock Steve. And they're friends."

MONTANA TECH OF THE UNIVERSITY OF MONTANA

FINANCIAL AID: 406-496-4212 • E-MAIL: ADMISSIONS@MTECH.EDU • WEBSITE: WWW.MTECH.EDU

THE PRINCETON REVIEW SAYS

Admissions

Other factors considered include: Class rank, academic GPA, standardized test scores, SAT or ACT required; ACT with Writing component required. High school diploma is required and GED is accepted. *Academic units required:* 4 English, 3 mathematics, 2 science, (2 science labs), 3 social studies, 2 combined 2 years of foreign language, visual and performing arts, computer science, or vocational ed. *Academic units recommended:* 4 English, 4 mathematics, 4 science, (2 science labs), 2 foreign language.

Financial Aid

Students should submit: FAFSA, institution's own financial aid form. The Princeton Review suggests that all financial aid forms be submitted as soon as possible after January 1. *Need-based scholarships/grants offered:* Federal Pell, SEOG, state scholarships/grants, private scholarships, the school's own gift aid. *Loan aid offered:* FFEL Subsidized Stafford, FFEL Unsubsidized Stafford, FFEL PLUS, Federal Perkins, college/university loans from institutional funds. Applicants will be notified of awards on a rolling basis beginning 3/15. Federal Work-Study Program available. Institutional employment available. Off-campus job opportunities are good.

The Inside Word

Under-recognized schools like Montana Tech can be a godsend for students who are strong academically but not likely to be offered admission to nationally renowned technical institutes. In fact, because of its small size and relatively remote location, Montana Tech is a good choice for anyone leaning toward a technical career. You'd be hard-pressed to find many other places that are as low-key and personal in this realm of academia.

THE SCHOOL SAYS "..."

From The Admissions Office

"Characterize Montana Tech by listening to what employers say. They tell us Tech graduates stand out with an incredible work ethic and top-notch technical skills. Last year, 130 employers came to our small campus competing for our students and graduates. The beneficiaries: the students! Montana Tech has had a 10-year placement rate of over 95 percent. Learning takes place in a personalized environment, in first-class academic facilities, and in the heart of the Rocky Mountains. Student at Tech work hard and play hard. Outdoor recreation provides a great balance to the rigors of the course work at Montana Tech. It's not a large, multifaceted university with lots of frills, but our students get a terrific education, and in the end, great jobs!

"The new version of the SAT (or the ACT with the Writing section) is recommended for all students applying for admission. Students who do not take the tests with the Writing component may be required to take an additional English Placement test from the college before they enroll."

SELECTIVITY

Admissions Rating	73
# of applicants	508
% of applicants accepted	89
% of acceptees attending	98

FRESHMAN PROFILE

Range SAT Critical Reading	470–590
Range SAT Math	500–600
Range SAT Writing	430–560
Range ACT Composite	19–25
Average HS GPA	3.2
% graduated top 10% of class	17
% graduated top 25% of class	38
% graduated top 50% of class	69

DEADLINES

Regular	
Priority	3/1
Notification	rolling
Nonfall registration?	yes

FINANCIAL FACTS

Financial Aid Rating	66
Annual in-state tuition	$5,644
Annual out-of-state tuition	$15,076
Room and board	$5,860
Books and supplies	$800
% UG rec. need-based scholarship or grant aid	1
% frosh rec. non-need-based scholarship or grant aid	39
% UG rec. non-need-based scholarship or grant aid	20
% frosh rec. need-based self-help aid	78
% UG rec. need-based self-help aid	64
% frosh rec. athletic scholarships	13
% UG rec. athletic scholarships	5
% frosh rec. any financial aid	80
% UG rec. any financial aid	68
% UG borrow to pay for school	85
Average cumulative indebtedness	$20,000

MORAVIAN COLLEGE

1200 MAIN STREET, BETHLEHEM, PA 18018 • ADMISSIONS: 610-861-1320 • FAX: 610-625-7930

CAMPUS LIFE
Quality of Life Rating	83
Fire Safety Rating	82
Green Rating	78
Type of school	private
Affiliation	Moravian
Environment	city

STUDENTS
Total undergrad enrollment	1,784
% male/female	42/58
% from out of state	43
% from public high school	73
% live on campus	71
% in (# of) fraternities	13 (3)
% in (# of) sororities	20 (4)
% African American	2
% Asian	2
% Caucasian	90
% Hispanic	3
% international	1
# of countries represented	15

SURVEY SAYS . . .
Large classes
Great library
Low cost of living
Lots of beer drinking

ACADEMICS
Academic Rating	84
Calendar	semester
Student/faculty ratio	11:1
Profs interesting rating	83
Profs accessible rating	85
Most common reg class size	10–19 students
Most common lab size	10–19 students

MOST POPULAR MAJORS
psychology
sociology
business/commerce

STUDENTS SAY ". . ."

Academics

For those students seeking a place where "everybody knows your name," take a look at Moravian College, a tiny school in eastern Pennsylvania that offers the "liberal arts experience," using a "well-rounded education to mold a well-rounded individual." This "outwardly modest institution" disguises a solid academic environment that is "more geared toward learning rather than just getting good grades on tests," which, combined with the cozy community feel of the surroundings, provides the "perfect peaceful atmosphere for studying and socializing." One student, commenting on the school's relatively low weekend retention rate, describes the school as "Camp Moravian—a lot of people may go home, but those who stay behind have a lot more fun."

For the most part, Moravian's "fairly forgiving" professors "are engaging and provide students with challenging questions concerning the real world." Their availability and willingness to help students understand the material gets praise all around, as does their demeanor; more than one student tells of being invited into a teacher's home for dinner. "Students are able to get the individual attention they need," says one. However, this doesn't mean that there aren't a few points that need to be worked on: "All of my professors are intelligent, but not all of them are meant to be teachers," says one freshman. A few students express some discontent with the administration's level of involvement, but the "college president is a regular fixture on campus" and "can be seen eating in the student café or sitting on a bench outside the academic building." Though most find the registration process "archaic," the academic advising system helps keep students on track in their course selection.

Life

With such a small undergrad enrollment, students get to know each other's business pretty easily and quickly, and most see this as a positive thing, listing "the chance for strong relationships" as one of the school's greatest strengths. Hanging out with friends, video games, and cards seems to be a pretty big part of relaxing at Moravian, and "there are a lot of different groups and clubs on campus that also plan activities for the rest of the student body to be part of." Almost everything necessary to amuse oneself in this "safe and nurturing environment" is "within walking distance," making it easy to go check out the events offered by the school, such as "movies every week and comedians a few times a semester," and Moravian runs Friday mall trips for those needing other supplies. The soccer field and basketball arena are located in the center of the campus "which makes it easy to attend the home games," and the school has such a wonderful music program that "the recitals are worth checking out, even if you're not a music major." A Greek scene is present on campus but not in an overwhelming way, so that "if you are looking for a party, you can find one. If you are not into the party scene, that's fine."

Student Body

"I'm not going to lie, Moravian's a very white school," confesses a student. Most of the students are from "Pennsylvania, New Jersey, or New York" and come from middle to upper-class homes, though "not many people question the economic situations of others." There is, at least, some diversity at Moravian (the "Multicultural Club is one of the best clubs on campus"), and the students that make up this "close knit community" are a "very open group of people" in how they relate to atypical students. Since there is a separate campus devoted to art and music, there tends to be a fair number of "artsy" students on the South campus to balance out the healthy portion of student athletes that populate mainly the North campus.

FINANCIAL AID: 610-861-1330 • E-MAIL: ADMISSIONS@MORAVIAN.EDU • WEBSITE: WWW.MORAVIAN.EDU

THE PRINCETON REVIEW SAYS

Admissions

Very important factors considered include: Class rank, academic GPA, rigor of secondary school record, alumni/ae relation, character/personal qualities. *Important factors considered include:* Application essay, recommendation(s), standardized test scores, extracurricular activities, first generation, level of applicant's interest, racial/ethnic status, talent/ability, volunteer work. *Other factors considered include:* Geographical residence, interview, work experience. SAT or ACT required; ACT with Writing component required. TOEFL required of all international applicants. High school diploma is required and GED is accepted. *Academic units required:* 4 English, 3 mathematics, 3 science, (2 science labs), 2 foreign language, 4 social studies. *Academic units recommended:* 4 mathematics, 3 foreign language.

Financial Aid

Students should submit: FAFSA, CSS/Financial Aid PROFILE, noncustodial PROFILE, business/farm supplement, copies of parent and student W2s and 1040s. Regular filing deadline is 3/15. The Princeton Review suggests that all financial aid forms be submitted as soon as possible after January 1. *Need-based scholarships/grants offered:* Federal Pell, SEOG, state scholarships/grants, the school's own gift aid. *Loan aid offered:* FFEL Subsidized Stafford, FFEL Unsubsidized Stafford, FFEL PLUS, Federal Perkins Applicants will be notified of awards on a rolling basis beginning 4/1.

The Inside Word

Moravian is a small liberal arts school with all the bells and whistles. Applicants will find a pretty straightforward admissions process—solid grades and test scores are required. Counselors will look closely to find the extras—community service, extracurricular activities—that make students stand out from the crowd. Moravian has many programs that should not be overlooked, including music, education, and the sciences.

THE SCHOOL SAYS "..."

From The Admissions Office

"Founded in 1742, Moravian is proud of its history as one of the oldest and most respected liberal arts colleges. Students find a supportive environment for self-discovery and academic achievement that nurtures their capacity for leadership, lifelong learning, and positive societal contributions. Moravian enrolls students from a variety of socioeconomic, religious, racial, and ethnic backgrounds. Providing a highly personalized learning experience, the College offers opportunities for students to direct their education toward individual and professional goals. Students are encouraged to collaborate with faculty on original research, pursue honors projects, independent work, internships, and field study. Moravian recently produced 7 Fulbright scholars, a Goldwater scholar, a Rhodes finalist, a Truman Scholarship finalist, and 3 NCAA postgraduate scholars.

"Facilities range from historic to modern, with a $20 million academic complex featuring current educational technology, at the heart of the Main Street Campus. The College is in the process of building a new residence hall on its historic Hurd Campus. The $25 million project will house approximately 230 students, contain classrooms, and other learning spaces that support the academic and co-curricular mission of the College. The Leadership Center fosters student leadership qualities and skills. Moravian encourages the complete college experience for mind, body, and spirit. Its robust varsity sports program, from football to lacrosse, has produced nationally ranked women's softball and track teams, and All-American student athletes—including several Olympic hopefuls—in many sports. Athletes complete on a state-of-the-art synthetic multi-sport field and the eight-lane Olympic track."

SELECTIVITY

Admissions Rating	79
# of applicants	2,189
% of applicants accepted	64
% of acceptees attending	29
# accepting a place on wait list	122
% admitted from wait list	25
# of early decision applicants	210
% accepted early decision	72

FRESHMAN PROFILE

Range SAT Critical Reading	500–600
Range SAT Math	500–610
Range SAT Writing	490–590
Minimum paper TOEFL	550
Minimum computer TOEFL	213
% graduated top 10% of class	29
% graduated top 25% of class	54
% graduated top 50% of class	87

DEADLINES

Early decision	
Deadline	2/1
Notification	12/15
Regular	
Deadline	3/1
Notification	3/15
Nonfall registration?	yes

APPLICANTS ALSO LOOK AT

AND OFTEN PREFER
Lafayette College
Muhlenberg College
Bucknell University

AND SOMETIMES PREFER
Gettysburg College
Ursinus College
Susquehanna University

AND RARELY PREFER
Fairleigh Dickinson University—College at Florham
Kutztown University of Pennsylvania

FINANCIAL FACTS

Financial Aid Rating	75
Annual tuition	$29,547
Room and board	$8,312
Required fees	$515
Books and supplies	$900
% frosh rec. need-based scholarship or grant aid	75
% UG rec. need-based scholarship or grant aid	74
% frosh rec. non-need-based scholarship or grant aid	6
% UG rec. non-need-based scholarship or grant aid	6
% frosh rec. need-based self-help aid	69
% UG rec. need-based self-help aid	68
% frosh rec. any financial aid	95
% UG rec. any financial aid	94

MOUNT HOLYOKE COLLEGE

OFFICE OF ADMISSIONS, NEWHALL CENTER, SOUTH HADLEY, MA 01075 • ADMISSIONS: 413-538-2023 • FAX: 413-538-2409

CAMPUS LIFE

Quality of Life Rating	**90**
Fire Safety Rating	**80**
Green Rating	**82**
Type of school	private
Environment	village

STUDENTS

Total undergrad enrollment	2,185
% male/female	/100
% from out of state	75
% from public high school	61
% live on campus	93
% African American	5
% Asian	12
% Caucasian	50
% Hispanic	5
% Native American	1
% international	16
# of countries represented	64

SURVEY SAYS . . .
Small classes
Lab facilities are great
Great library
Diverse student types on campus
Campus feels safe
Frats and sororities are unpopular
or nonexistent

ACADEMICS

Academic Rating	**94**
Calendar	semester
Student/faculty ratio	10:1
Profs interesting rating	97
Profs accessible rating	93
Most common reg class size	10–19 students
Most common lab size	10–19 students

MOST POPULAR MAJORS
English language and literature
psychology
political science and government

STUDENTS SAY ". . ."

Academics
Mount Holyoke "is a rigorous all women's college that prepares its students to become the leaders of tomorrow by encouraging them to pursue their passions in a safe, comfortable and yet challenging environment," undergrads at this small, prestigious liberal arts school tell us. Biology, chemistry, the humanities, and international studies are among the strong suits of the school; in nearly all disciplines, professors "are highly respected in their fields, many of them being very prominent figures among their respective academic communities" who are also "very kind, excited to impart their knowledge, and very, very accessible outside of class and willing to spend a lot of time helping individual students." They aren't pushovers, though; "Despite their overall generosity, they hold every student to a very high academic standard (no grade inflation here), and the material covered in each course is always challenging and of high academic caliber." Students may supplement their curricula with classes at other area colleges through the Five College Consortium, but they do say that the consortium is "very underused."

Life
"People are very focused on their academics, sometimes too much so" at Mount Holyoke, and "Much of our time is dedicated to class work." Undergrads typically find time for the "fabulous traditions that help to define" school life, such as "Milk and cookies in the evening (a snack put out by dining services at 9:30 on school nights) and class colors and mascots." Otherwise, "Mount Holyoke life is what you make of it. We are an all women's college, but that doesn't mean you are going off to a convent. It is easy to have a social life through the Five College Consortium, and it is easy to go into Boston or New York." Also, "people are active in clubs and sports, and they hang out in the common areas or on the green with friends," and "there are many on-campus events, such as speakers, movie screenings, etc. to keep anyone busy." The campus itself "is so beautiful…between the foliage, the classic brick buildings and the well kept landscape of the college, I was in love!" Off-campus life offers "movie theaters and restaurants, as well as parties at the other four colleges." Hometown South Hadley "is admittedly not the most happening town ever (to put it mildly)," but Amherst and Northhampton—which are "great for eating, shopping, and anything else imaginable"—"are only a free bus ride away."

Student Body
The Mount Holyoke student body "is extremely diverse, from ethnicity to race to religion to sexual orientation to individual interests. However, the community works as a whole because of the common interest in academics and openness of the students who attend." If there is a "typical" student, it's one who "is female and academically motivated," undergrads tell us. Students are also typically "very aware of world issues, politically active, and open-minded," "very concerned about grades and jobs," and, perhaps, "overly politically correct." Among the subpopulations that stand out, "The most visible opposites are the 'pearls and cardigans,' the 'Carhartts and piercings' types, and the hippies. There are a ton of people, however, who are somewhere in between those."

FINANCIAL AID: 413-538-2291 • E-MAIL: ADMISSION@MTHOLYOKE.EDU • WEBSITE: WWW.MTHOLYOKE.EDU

THE PRINCETON REVIEW SAYS

Admissions

Very important factors considered include: Class rank, application essay, academic GPA, recommendation(s), rigor of secondary school record. *Important factors considered include:* Character/personal qualities, extracurricular activities, first generation, interview, talent/ability, volunteer work, work experience. *Other factors considered include:* Standardized test scores, alumni/ae relation, geographical residence, level of applicant's interest, racial/ethnic status, TOEFL required of all international applicants. High school diploma is required and GED is accepted. *Academic units recommended:* 4 English, 3 mathematics, 3 science, (3 science labs), 3 foreign language, 3 history, 1 academic elective.

Financial Aid

Students should submit: FAFSA, CSS/Financial Aid PROFILE, noncustodial PROFILE, business/farm supplement, Federal Tax Returns. Regular filing deadline is 3/1. The Princeton Review suggests that all financial aid forms be submitted as soon as possible after January 1. *Need-based scholarships/grants offered:* Federal Pell, SEOG, state scholarships/grants, private scholarships, the school's own gift aid. *Loan aid offered:* Direct Subsidized Stafford, Direct Unsubsidized Stafford, Direct PLUS, Federal Perkins, college/university loans from institutional funds. Applicants will be notified of awards on or about 4/1. Federal Work-Study Program available. Institutional employment available. Off-campus job opportunities are fair.

The Inside Word

Mount Holyoke has seen a 25 percent increase in the size of its applicant pool since the beginning of the decade, allowing what was already a selective institution to become a highly selective one. Matchmaking is a significant factor here; strong academic performance, well-written essays, and an understanding of and appreciation for "the Mount Holyoke experience" will usually carry the day.

THE SCHOOL SAYS "..."

From The Admissions Office

"The majority of students who choose Mount Holyoke do so simply because it is an outstanding liberal arts college. After a semester or two, they start to appreciate the fact that Mount Holyoke is a women's college, even though most Mount Holyoke students never thought they'd go to a women's college when they started their college search. Students talk of having 'space' to really figure out who they are. They speak about feeling empowered to excel in traditionally male subjects such as science and technology. They talk about the remarkable array of opportunities—for academic achievement, career exploration, and leadership—and the impressive, creative accomplishments of their peers. If you're looking for a college that will challenge you to be your best, most powerful self and to fulfill potential, Mount Holyoke should be at the top of your list.

"Submission of standardized test scores is optional for most applicants to Mount Holyoke College. However, the TOEFL is required of students for whom English is not their primary language, and the SAT Subject Tests are required for homeschooled students."

SELECTIVITY

Admissions Rating	95
# of applicants	3,194
% of applicants accepted	52
% of acceptees attending	31
# accepting a place on wait list	178
# of early decision applicants	225
% accepted early decision	53

FRESHMAN PROFILE

Range SAT Critical Reading	640–730
Range SAT Math	590–690
Range SAT Writing	630–710
Range ACT Composite	26–30
Minimum paper TOEFL	600
Minimum computer TOEFL	250
Average HS GPA	3.67
% graduated top 10% of class	55
% graduated top 25% of class	86
% graduated top 50% of class	99

DEADLINES

Early decision	
Deadline	11/15
Notification	1/1
Regular	
Deadline	1/15
Notification	4/1
Nonfall registration?	yes

APPLICANTS ALSO LOOK AT

AND OFTEN PREFER
Vassar College
Wellesley College
Barnard College

AND SOMETIMES PREFER
Bryn Mawr College
Smith College

AND RARELY PREFER
Scripps College
University of Massachusetts—Amherst
Boston University

FINANCIAL FACTS

Financial Aid Rating	97
Annual tuition	$37,480
% frosh rec. need-based scholarship or grant aid	60
% UG rec. need-based scholarship or grant aid	63
% frosh rec. non-need-based scholarship or grant aid	55
% UG rec. non-need-based scholarship or grant aid	60
% frosh rec. need-based self-help aid	58
% UG rec. need-based self-help aid	60
% frosh rec. any financial aid	67
% UG rec. any financial aid	69
% UG borrow to pay for school	67
Average cumulative indebtedness	$22,270

MUHLENBERG COLLEGE

2400 WEST CHEW STREET, ALLENTOWN, PA 18104-5596 • ADMISSIONS: 484-664-3200 • FAX: 484-664-3234

CAMPUS LIFE
Quality of Life Rating	**72**
Fire Safety Rating	**89**
Green Rating	**75**
Type of school	private
Affiliation	Lutheran
Environment	city

STUDENTS
Total undergrad enrollment	2,324
% male/female	42/58
% from out of state	70
% from public high school	70
% live on campus	92
% in (# of) fraternities	14 (4)
% in (# of) sororities	17 (4)
% African American	2
% Asian	2
% Caucasian	89
% Hispanic	4
# of countries represented	5

SURVEY SAYS . . .
Small classes
Athletic facilities are great
Students are friendly
Theater is popular
Lots of beer drinking
Hard liquor is popular

ACADEMICS
Academic Rating	**87**
Calendar	semester
Student/faculty ratio	12:1
Profs interesting rating	84
Profs accessible rating	88
Most common reg class size	10–19 students
Most common lab size	10–19 students

MOST POPULAR MAJORS
psychology
drama and dramatics/theatre arts
business/commerce

STUDENTS SAY ". . ."

Academics

Muhlenberg bills itself as "the college that cares," and for many students, it more than lives up to that designation. "The small community and small, personal class sizes" allow "professors [to] become friends, mentors, and role models" to students. "They love what they do, they love students, and they love interacting with the students." In addition, professors are "always very approachable. I've become close with many professors and frequently chat with them outside of class. Professors are often on campus with their families, and some hold parties at their houses at the end of the year." But professors aren't just friendly faces; "They are [also] very knowledgeable in their fields" and "challenge students to achieve more than they thought they were capable of." In addition to excellent professors, the school's size also provides students with numerous "research opportunities." Muhlenberg students "write a lot" because of the individual attention made possible in the "small, discussion-based classes." Among many quality majors, the Premedical, Pre-Law, Education, and Political Science Departments get rave reviews, and students note that "the theater and dance programs are extremely well regarded," as well.

Life

Some students claim that hometown Allentown "is not a vibrant place, and prospective students should be aware of this," while others point to the "two bars, an excellent deli, a famous movie and art theater, as well as restaurants and all the normal everyday places that a student needs" within walking distance of the campus. As far as partying goes, "If you are looking for a school with 15 parties to choose from every night of the week, then stop reading about Muhlenberg right now." The "school does have Greek life, but the administration is cracking down on [fraternities and sororities] more and more," largely through "a very strict alcohol and drug policy." As a result, "People go to house parties [off-campus] or the bars." Besides parties, "There is a pretty decent mall nearby and good restaurants." On campus "There are always school-sponsored events going on: bands, movies, magicians, comedians, the works," although many claim that "students don't generally participate in the on-campus activities." Particularly popular are the school's "community-service programs," which "work very well with Allentown," challenging students to carry the school's reputation for "caring" to their fellow citizens beyond the campus gates. To get away from the Muhlenberg scene altogether for some fresh experiences, "It's not too long a drive to Philadelphia." "Also, there are several other colleges in the area." Students do caution, however, that a "parking problem" makes owning a car on campus a little difficult.

Student Body

Although "'preppy' would be the word to describe most students on this campus, there are others who do not fit this category at all." And many students emphasize that the student body is not cliquey: "Students have groups of friends, but that can be very fluid." Such intermixing is a function of how "amazingly nice" the students here are, regardless of the fact that "most of the students come from fairly wealthy homes." Politically, students have liberal leanings, and students report that most of their classmates seem to "come from the surrounding areas of New Jersey, Pennsylvania, and New York." "Muhlenberg is extremely gay-friendly," but in terms of ethnicity, "There is little diversity," a fact "that the college is interested in changing." On the bright side, "The little bit of ethnic and racial diversity that we have here is celebrated." According to one student, however, regardless of social groups or differences, "The majority of people that I have come into contact with are their own selves, and they pride themselves on that. After all, college is about finding out who you are as a person, not conforming to the majority."

FINANCIAL AID: 484-664-3175 • E-MAIL: ADMISSION@MUHLENBERG.EDU • WEBSITE: WWW.MUHLENBERG.EDU

THE PRINCETON REVIEW SAYS

Admissions

Very important factors considered include: Academic GPA, rigor of secondary school record, character/personal qualities, talent/ability. *Important factors considered include:* Extracurricular activities. *Other factors considered include:* Class rank, application essay, recommendation(s), standardized test scores, alumni/ae relation, first generation, interview, level of applicant's interest, racial/ethnic status, volunteer work, work experience. ACT with Writing component required. TOEFL required of all international applicants. High school diploma is required and GED is accepted. *Academic units required:* 4 English, 3 mathematics, 2 science, (2 science labs), 2 foreign language, 1 social studies, 2 history. *Academic units recommended:* 4 mathematics, 4 science, 3 foreign language, 3 history, 2 academic electives.

Financial Aid

Students should submit: FAFSA, institution's own financial aid form, CSS/Financial Aid PROFILE, noncustodial PROFILE. Regular filing deadline is 2/15. The Princeton Review suggests that all financial aid forms be submitted as soon as possible after January 1. *Need-based scholarships/grants offered:* Federal Pell, SEOG, state scholarships/grants, private scholarships, the school's own gift aid. *Loan aid offered:* FFEL Subsidized Stafford, FFEL Unsubsidized Stafford, FFEL PLUS, Federal Perkins, Private. Applicants will be notified of awards on or about 4/1. Federal Work-Study Program available. Institutional employment available. Off-campus job opportunities are excellent.

The Inside Word

Akin to many liberal arts colleges, Muhlenberg doesn't adhere to a set admissions formula. With application numbers on the rise, however, and the school's selectivity increasing, a strong secondary school transcript is necessary. Standardized tests, on the other hand, are optional at Muhlenberg. Those who don't submit scores can provide a graded paper and sit for an interview instead. Prospective students who have determined Muhlenberg to be their top choice will find it advantageous to apply early decision.

THE SCHOOL SAYS "..."

From The Admissions Office

"Listening to our own students, we've learned that most picked Muhlenberg mainly because it has a long-standing reputation for being academically demanding on one hand but personally supportive on the other. We expect a lot from our students, but we also expect a lot from ourselves in providing the challenge and support they need to stretch, grow, and succeed. It's not unusual for professors to put their home phone numbers on the course syllabus and encourage students to call them at home with questions. Upperclassmen are helpful to underclassmen. 'We really know about collegiality here,' says an alumna who now works at Muhlenberg. 'It's that kind of place.' The supportive atmosphere and strong work ethic produce lots of successes. The premed and pre-law programs are very strong, as are programs in theater arts, English, psychology, the sciences, business, and accounting. 'When I was a student here,' recalls Dr. Walter Loy, now a professor emeritus of physics, 'we were encouraged to live life to its fullest, to do our best, to be honest, to deal openly with others, and to treat everyone as an individual. Those are important things, and they haven't changed at Muhlenberg.'

"Students have the option of submitting SAT or ACT scores (including the Writing sections on each), or submitting a graded paper with teacher's comments and grade on it from junior or senior year and interviewing with a member of the Admissions Staff. Muhlenberg will accept old or new SAT scores and will use the student's best scores from either test."

SELECTIVITY

Admissions Rating	94
# of applicants	4,703
% of applicants accepted	37
% of acceptees attending	31
# accepting a place on wait list	541
% admitted from wait list	8
# of early decision applicants	420
% accepted early decision	67

FRESHMAN PROFILE

Range SAT Critical Reading	550–650
Range SAT Math	560–660
Range SAT Writing	560–660
Range ACT Composite	24–29
Minimum paper TOEFL	550
Minimum computer TOEFL	213
Average HS GPA	3.41
% graduated top 10% of class	47
% graduated top 25% of class	80
% graduated top 50% of class	98

DEADLINES

Early decision	
Deadline	2/1
Notification	12/1
Regular	
Deadline	2/15
Notification	1/5
Nonfall registration?	yes

APPLICANTS ALSO LOOK AT

AND OFTEN PREFER
Lehigh University
Lafayette College

AND SOMETIMES PREFER
University of Delaware
Dickinson College

AND RARELY PREFER
Rutgers University—Rutgers College
Drew University

FINANCIAL FACTS

Financial Aid Rating	93
Annual tuition	$32,850
Room and board	$7,790
Required fees	$240
Books and supplies	$800
% frosh rec. need-based scholarship or grant aid	41
% UG rec. need-based scholarship or grant aid	42
% frosh rec. non-need-based scholarship or grant aid	11
% UG rec. non-need-based scholarship or grant aid	10
% frosh rec. need-based self-help aid	30
% UG rec. need-based self-help aid	31
% frosh rec. any financial aid	73.8
% UG rec. any financial aid	72.1
% UG borrow to pay for school	81
Average cumulative indebtedness	$18,052

Nazareth College

424 East Avenue, Rochester NY 14618 • Admissions: 800-762-3944 or 585-389-2860• Fax: 585-389-2826

STUDENTS SAY ". . ."

Academics

Nazareth College is "a very personalized school" in the suburbs, "about 10 miles from downtown Rochester." "Education is a huge degree program" and there are quite a few physical therapy and nursing majors. Naz is also great for theater and music. "All of their productions are always spectacular," gushes a sophomore. "I constantly feel like I'm watching a Broadway show whenever I go see one." The academic pace is reasonable. "I would say that our academic program is rigorous but not mental-illness inducing," suggests an English literature major. "I count this as a strength." "Most of the professors are a lot of fun, and try to make classes interesting. Plus, they take the time to get to know you personally, which is great." "Professors care about how you are doing," declares a nursing major. "You are not just a number." Course selection is limited but classes are wonderfully small. "The administration loves student feedback" and receives generally glowing reviews. Nazareth's president frequently walks around campus and greets students. "I think Naz is doing a fine job," proffers a sophomore.

Life

Students here enjoy an "absolutely gorgeous" campus. The residence halls "are very comfortable and quite spacious," and they offer free laundry machines. However, the food is another story. "The dining hall is disgusting, dirty, and unsatisfying," gripes a hungry sophomore, though renovations are planned for summer 2008. Socially, there is no Greek system but the student activities council does a fantastic job of having activities planned." Some of these activities are "lame events" but many are widely attended. Intramural and varsity sports are also reasonably big. The surrounding town is a little hamlet right on the Erie Canal "with fun shops and places to eat." "Pittsford, as a town, is very safe and very nice to walk around in," says one student. However, if you attend Nazareth, we recommend that you bring a vehicle with you. "Everyone has a car. It's like a requirement," warns a sophomore. "If you want to find a party, you (usually) can." Older students (and students with respectable fake IDs) often frequent the bars and clubs of downtown Rochester for fun. However, "some weekends are slow" and "Nazareth is definitely not a big party school." Road trips are common. "Nazareth isn't really far from anywhere, which makes other colleges, towns, and locations easy to access." Some students also go home on more than a few weekends.

Student Body

"The typical student at Nazareth is a white girl from suburbia"—usually somewhere around Buffalo, Rochester, or Syracuse. Students at Naz are "concerned about their grades." "The same kids you see drunk on Saturday night at the bars are the kids working hard in the library all Sunday." They are a little on the cliquey side but "very friendly," too. "There are a few jerks but nobody likes them, anyway," says one student. "Students here tend to be very liberal." "There are many preppy and sports-oriented people." "There are a lot of artsy and intellectuals," too. "And there are, of course, your weirdoes, but that's normal." There is apparently a notable contingent of gay males as well, "though more straight men are attending as they realize that they have a big sea to fish in."

FINANCIAL AID: 585-389-2310 • E-MAIL: ADMISSIONS@NAZ.EDU • WEBSITE: WWW.NAZ.EDU

THE PRINCETON REVIEW SAYS

Admissions

Very important factors considered include: Class rank, application essay, academic GPA, recommendation(s), rigor of secondary school record. *Important factors considered include:* Character/personal qualities, extracurricular activities, geographical residence, interview, level of applicant's interest, racial/ethnic status, state residency, talent/ability, volunteer work, work experience. *Other factors considered include:* Standardized test scores, alumni/ae relation, first generation, TOEFL required of all international applicants. High school diploma is required and GED is accepted. *Academic units required:* 4 English, 3 mathematics, 3 science, (2 science labs), 3 foreign language, 3 social studies. *Academic units recommended:* 4 English, 4 mathematics, 4 science, 4 foreign language, 4 social studies.

Financial Aid

Students should submit: FAFSA preferred filing deadline is 2/15. The Princeton Review suggests that all financial aid forms be submitted as soon as possible after January 1. *Need-based scholarships/grants offered:* Federal Pell, SEOG, state scholarships/grants, private scholarships, the school's own gift aid. *Loan aid offered:* FFEL Subsidized Stafford, FFEL Unsubsidized Stafford, FFEL PLUS, Federal Perkins Applicants will be notified of awards on a rolling basis beginning 2/20. Federal Work-Study Program available. Institutional employment available. Off-campus job opportunities are excellent.

The Inside Word

Admissions Officers at Nazareth College are looking for candidates who will enhance the college community as a whole. This means that a special talent in athletics, music, the arts, or leadership areas counts; it can be especially helpful to candidates whose academic records are less than exemplary.

THE SCHOOL SAYS "..."

From The Admissions Office

Growing interest in Nazareth—applications have grown 32 percent in five years—is a result of many factors. New facilities have increased and improved academic, performing arts, residential, and athletic spaces. Major offerings now include music/business, international business, communication and rhetoric, and music theatre. Nazareth has worked diligently to keep tuition at $5,000 less than the New York State average for private colleges. Our track record is strong -- retention and graduation rates exceed national averages; 75 percent of our students participate in a career-related internship with 93 percent of them citing this a very worthwhile experience; and 93 percent of our students are employed or in graduate school within one year of graduation. The College has produced 12 Fulbright scholars and six faculty Fulbrights, in the past decade alone, along with two Thomas R. Pickering Graduate Foreign Affairs Fellowships. The Center for International Education has developed more opportunities for our students to study abroad and for international students to study at Nazareth. With civic engagement and service learning as hallmarks of the Nazareth experience, 91 percent of undergrads participate in community service while at Nazareth. A proactive approach to campus security and state-of-the-art emergency notification system places Nazareth ahead of the curve regarding student safety. Student athletes, veterans of conference and national championships, have one of the highest graduation rates among NCAA Division III institutions. The Nazareth College Arts Center brings an international roster of performing art companies to campus, and provides high-quality facilities for student productions."

SELECTIVITY

Admissions Rating	84
# of applicants	2,076
% of applicants accepted	74
% of acceptees attending	30
# of early decision applicants	33
% accepted early decision	94

FRESHMAN PROFILE

Range SAT Critical Reading	530–630
Range SAT Math	530–630
Range SAT Writing	510–610
Range ACT Composite	23–27
Minimum paper TOEFL	550
Minimum computer TOEFL	213
Average HS GPA	3.31
% graduated top 10% of class	30
% graduated top 25% of class	69

DEADLINES

Early decision	
Deadline	11/15
Notification	12/15
Early action	
Deadline	12/15
Notification	1/15
Regular	
Priority	12/15
Deadline	2/15
Notification	3/1
Nonfall registration?	yes

FINANCIAL FACTS

Financial Aid Rating	74
Annual tuition	$21,900
Room and board	$9,500
Required fees	$980
Books and supplies	$900
% frosh rec. need-based scholarship or grant aid	76
% UG rec. need-based scholarship or grant aid	77
% frosh rec. non-need-based scholarship or grant aid	14
% UG rec. non-need-based scholarship or grant aid	10
% frosh rec. need-based self-help aid	60
% UG rec. need-based self-help aid	65
% UG borrow to pay for school	77
Average cumulative indebtedness	$26,795

NEW COLLEGE OF FLORIDA

5800 BAY SHORE ROAD, SARASOTA, FL 34243-2109 • ADMISSIONS: 941-487-5000 • FAX: 941-487-5010

STUDENTS SAY ". . ."

Academics

New College of Florida, a uniquely small and unconventional public institution, "provides challenging courses for highly self-motivated students who want a large amount of control over their academic choices." It's all about "self-directed learning" here ("the student decides what she is going to learn and how she is going to learn it") that leaves undergrads "free to do what they please—with their bodies, their studies, their behavior—but while also being held to high academic standards." Those who choose carefully wind up with "a rounded education that enables them to critically and pragmatically examine and understand the world in which we live...and weird parties." The academics "are undeniably awesome" at NCF, while the small-school setting and the student body "encourage a love of learning, whether it be academic, political, or hobby-related." It's the sort of school where "It is very popular for groups of students to get together to talk about class readings outside of the classroom, usually at the college coffee shop, as a means of socializing." NCF undergrads receive "narrative evaluations instead of grades. These evaluations give advice and help us to become better students." Many here "love having written evaluations in which our process and progress are documented, not only the final outcome. The evaluations force students to fully participate and the professors to pay close attention." All students must write a senior thesis to graduate; reports one undergrad, "Recently we had a survey...on which one of the sections dealt with the possibility of making the senior thesis optional. There was an overwhelming response that this was unacceptable. I think that says a lot about how proud we are of our academic standards."

Life

Having fun "in a glorified retirement community requires ingenuity of the New College student population," but "thankfully, most grew up in suburban Florida" and so "know how to navigate a hellhole." It helps that this hellhole includes Lido Beach, "where we enjoy unlimited swimming, sunning, and Frisbee playing," and that "downtown Sarasota isn't that bad either," since it's home to a number of "ethnic eateries. Thai food, in particular, seems to have a strange cult following on campus—constant debate as to which restaurant is the best or most authentic a student events that advertise Thai food are bound to pull in dozens of followers." On campus, students enjoy everything "from club meetings to public speakers to 'hip' bands playing shows. There's usually something to do, and usually free food to be found!" There are also "school-wide parties every Friday and Saturday night in a courtyard outside of the dorms. Different students get to decide the theme of each dance party and the music to be played. Most on-campus students never leave campus during the weekend because of these dance parties."

Student Body

New College students share "a few things in common: most...are friendly, passionate about the things they believe in, very hard workers, liberal, and most of all, try to be open to new experiences." They are "largely middle-class, white, and liberal. There are of course exceptions, but the school is rather small and unique, and seems to attract a very particular subset of the general population." One student observes that "With such a small school, our small percentages of minorities reflect a more pronounced race divide.... The socially white-washed campus tends to scare off a lot of 'atypical' prospectives. I've spoken to many personally who decided against the school for fear of becoming 'the token.'" There is "a fairly strong queer community here, and many transgendered people who have decided to make New College their coming out grounds. The student body is generally aware of gender issues and respectful of queer people of all types." There are even "some Republicans on campus. Maybe four. I'm not sure. We're not the type of school that generally attracts heavy right-wingers."

Financial Aid: 941-487-5001 • E-mail: admissions@ncf.edu • Website: www.ncf.edu

THE PRINCETON REVIEW SAYS

Admissions

Very important factors considered include: Application essay, academic GPA, rigor of secondary school record, standardized test scores. *Important factors considered include:* Recommendation(s), character/personal qualities, level of applicant's interest. *Other factors considered include:* Class rank, alumni/ae relation, extracurricular activities, geographical residence, interview, state residency, talent/ability, volunteer work, work experience. SAT or ACT required; TOEFL required of all international applicants. High school diploma is required and GED is accepted. *Academic units required:* 4 English, 3 mathematics, 3 science, (2 science labs), 2 foreign language, 3 social studies, 3 academic electives. *Academic units recommended:* 4 English, 3 mathematics, 3 science, (2 science labs), 2 foreign language, 3 social studies, 5 academic electives.

Financial Aid

Students should submit: FAFSA. The Princeton Review suggests that all financial aid forms be submitted as soon as possible after January 1. *Need-based scholarships/grants offered:* Federal Pell, SEOG, state scholarships/grants, private scholarships, the school's own gift aid, Federal Academic Competitiveness Grant. *Loan aid offered:* FFEL Subsidized Stafford, FFEL Unsubsidized Stafford, FFEL PLUS, Alternative Loans. Applicants will be notified of awards on a rolling basis beginning 10/1. Federal Work-Study Program available. Institutional employment available. Off-campus job opportunities are good.

The Inside Word

New College is not your typical public school. The tiny student body allows admissions officers here to review each application carefully; expect a thorough going over of your essays, recommendations, and extracurricular activities. Iconoclastic students tend to thrive here, and the admissions staff knows that. Don't be afraid to let your freak flag fly; it won't get you in here if your academics aren't top flight, but it certainly won't hurt you either.

THE SCHOOL SAYS "..."

From The Admissions Office

"Inspired individualism, with a dash of quirkiness, best describes New College of Florida and its students. At New College, you participate directly in your education by collaborating with faculty to develop an individualized program of classes, seminars, independent research projects, and off-campus experiences designed to meet your personal academic interests and needs. As a result, you receive the high-quality, personalized education of a top-tier private college yet at the affordable cost of a public university. If you are independent, open-minded, and welcome the challenge of a rigorous academic program matched with a relaxed social environment, then New College may be the perfect fit for you.

"Students applying for Fall 2008 must submit scores from the SAT (or ACT). It is not required that they take the new version of the SAT (or the ACT with the Writing section). We will allow students to submit scores from either version of the SAT (or ACT) and will use the student's best scores from either test."

SELECTIVITY

Admissions Rating	94
# of applicants	1,029
% of applicants accepted	57
% of acceptees attending	34
# accepting a place on wait list	69
% admitted from wait list	14

FRESHMAN PROFILE

Range SAT Critical Reading	650–750
Range SAT Math	580–670
Range SAT Writing	600–690
Range ACT Composite	26–30
Minimum paper TOEFL	560
Minimum computer TOEFL	220
Average HS GPA	3.94
% graduated top 10% of class	53
% graduated top 25% of class	81
% graduated top 50% of class	98

DEADLINES

Regular	
Priority	2/15
Deadline	4/15
Notification	4/25
Nonfall registration?	yes

APPLICANTS ALSO LOOK AT

AND OFTEN PREFER
University of Florida
Florida State University

AND SOMETIMES PREFER
University of Miami
Eckerd College
Hampshire College

AND RARELY PREFER
University of South Florida
Truman State University
St. Mary's College of Maryland

FINANCIAL FACTS

Financial Aid Rating	92
Annual in-state tuition	$3,850
Annual out-of-state tuition	$21,625
Room and board	$7,080
Books and supplies	$800
% frosh rec. need-based scholarship or grant aid	39
% UG rec. need-based scholarship or grant aid	38
% frosh rec. non-need-based scholarship or grant aid	100
% UG rec. non-need-based scholarship or grant aid	77
% frosh rec. need-based self-help aid	31
% UG rec. need-based self-help aid	31
% frosh rec. any financial aid	100
% UG rec. any financial aid	97
% UG borrow to pay for school	35
Average cumulative indebtedness	$11,720

NEW JERSEY INSTITUTE OF TECHNOLOGY

UNIVERSITY HEIGHTS, NEWARK, NJ 07102 • ADMISSIONS: 973-596-3300 • FAX: 973-596-3461

STUDENTS SAY " . . . "

Academics

Mathematics, science, technology, and architecture offerings all shine at New Jersey Institute of Technology, a "leader in the field of technology in the Tri-State Area" whose public school pricing allows students to "graduate without the bank owning our first-borns, which is a definite plus." As is the case at many prestigious tech-oriented schools, "The professors are generally hired for research rather than teaching ability, [so] there are some who cannot teach, and they aren't that great at grading assignments or handing back papers either." The demanding undergraduate curriculum means "You have to be serious about studies if you are choosing NJIT. There is no time for fun and games." Students groan about the demands made on them but also recognize the benefits; "NJIT is an intense academic university that allows students to be prepared for the working world," explains one architect. Another plus of studying at NJIT is "how well the students interact, especially during exam time. Seniors help juniors, who help sophomores, who help freshman. It's helpful when someone who has taken the courses you're taking at the moment can put things into perspective, and give you hints about what may be on the test."

Life

NJIT is "not the best school socially, but few engineering schools are," students here concede. Since "a lot of classes give amazing amounts of homework, it is hard to have a normal social life. Most nights are spent doing homework late, then getting a few hours of fun before passing out." Extracurricular life has improved recently with the addition of new recreation facilities; one student notes, "The game room has been improved, with pool tables, bowling, and arcades, and a much-needed pub on campus." The institute also boasts "a pretty good gym to work out in, and a brand-new soccer field." Undergrads note optimistically that "our team sports are all performing better, and the students are starting to feel a sense of competition building. There are plenty of parties on Thursday nights on campus, organized by frats or clubs." And, of course, "Possibilities are endless because New York City is minutes away" by affordable public transportation, opening the door to "major league sports, world-class museums, and theater." Hometown Newark, although much maligned by students and locals, offers "great food and restaurants less than half a mile away from campus, in the Ironbound section." Students do appreciate how the "small classes and campus make a 'small-town' atmosphere during the semester," even though they also acknowledge the school's urban environs.

Student Body

"There are two types of students at NJIT," writes one undergrad, elaborating: "The first are the ones who are involved with athletics, clubs, organizations, and other things. The others are the antisocial ones. These people stay in their dorms and play computer games all day." How many of each category populate this campus? One student offers some pertinent data: "Class attendance dropped 32 percent the day Halo 2 came out." Like the region surrounding it, "NJIT is a total melting pot; the mix of ethnic backgrounds of students is diverse." While many say the various groups interact well, just as many others describe the student body as "clusters of ethnic groups isolated from each other." Because of curricular demands, "Everyone is pretty smart. But you also have the very smart people." When asked in what ways his school could stand to improve, one succinct information technologist wrote "girls!" reflecting a sentiment running through much of the student body. The male/female ratio is about 4:1.

NEW JERSEY INSTITUTE OF TECHNOLOGY

FINANCIAL AID: 973-596-3480 • E-MAIL: ADMISSIONS@NJIT.EDU • WEBSITE: WWW.NJIT.EDU

THE PRINCETON REVIEW SAYS

Admissions

Very important factors considered include: Class rank, rigor of secondary school record, standardized test scores. *Important factors considered include:* Academic GPA. *Other factors considered include:* Application essay, recommendation(s), alumni/ae relation, character/personal qualities, extracurricular activities, geographical residence, interview, level of applicant's interest, racial/ethnic status, religious affiliation/commitment, state residency, SAT or ACT required; TOEFL required of all international applicants. High school diploma is required and GED is accepted. *Academic units required:* 4 English, 4 mathematics, 2 science, (2 science labs). *Academic units recommended:* 2 foreign language, 1 social studies, 1 history, 2 academic electives.

Financial Aid

Students should submit: FAFSA. Regular filing deadline is 5/15. The Princeton Review suggests that all financial aid forms be submitted as soon as possible after January 1. *Need-based scholarships/grants offered:* Federal Pell, SEOG, state scholarships/grants, private scholarships, the school's own gift aid. *Loan aid offered:* Direct Subsidized Stafford, Direct Unsubsidized Stafford, Direct PLUS, Federal Perkins, state loans, college/university loans from institutional funds. Applicants will be notified of awards on a rolling basis beginning 3/1. Federal Work-Study Program available. Institutional employment available. Off-campus job opportunities are good.

The Inside Word

NJIT is a great choice for students who aspire to technical careers but don't meet the requirements for better-known and more selective universities. To top it off, it's a pretty good buy.

THE SCHOOL SAYS "..."

From The Admissions Office

"Talented high school graduates from across the nation come to NJIT to prepare for leadership roles in architecture, business, engineering, medical, legal, science, and technological fields. Students experience a public research university conducting more than $75 million in research that maintains a small-college atmosphere at a modest cost. Our attractive 45-acre campus is just minutes from New York City and less than an hour from the Jersey shore. Students find an outstanding faculty and a safe, diverse, caring learning and residential community. All dormitory rooms have sprinklers. NJIT's academic environment challenges and prepares students for rewarding careers and full-time advanced study after graduation. The campus is computing-intunsive. For 5 consecutive years, *Yahoo! Internet Life* ranked NJIT among America's 'Most Wired Universities.'

"Students applying for admission to NJIT for Fall 2008 may provide scores from either version of the SAT, or the ACT. Writing sample scores will be collected but will not be used for admission purposes for 2008. SAT Subject Test scores are not required for any major."

SELECTIVITY
Admissions Rating	81
# of applicants	3,027
% of applicants accepted	64
% of acceptees attending	38

FRESHMAN PROFILE
Range SAT Critical Reading	480–580
Range SAT Math	550–650
Range SAT Writing	470–570
Minimum paper TOEFL	550
Minimum computer TOEFL	213
% graduated top 10% of class	28
% graduated top 25% of class	56
% graduated top 50% of class	83

DEADLINES
Regular	
Deadline	4/1
Notification	rolling
Nonfall registration?	yes

APPLICANTS ALSO LOOK AT
AND OFTEN PREFER
Drexel University
Rutgers University—Rutgers College
The College of New Jersey
Rensselaer Polytechnic Institute
AND SOMETIMES PREFER
Virginia Tech
Worcester Polytechnic Institute
Penn State—University Park

FINANCIAL FACTS
Financial Aid Rating	83
Annual in-state tuition	$9,700
Annual out-of-state tuition	$18,432
Room and board	$9,264
Required fees	$1,650
Books and supplies	$1,200
% frosh rec. need-based scholarship or grant aid	51
% UG rec. need-based scholarship or grant aid	42
% frosh rec. non-need-based scholarship or grant aid	25
% UG rec. non-need-based scholarship or grant aid	18
% frosh rec. need-based self-help aid	38
% UG rec. need-based self-help aid	34
% frosh rec. athletic scholarships	3
% UG rec. athletic scholarships	2
% frosh rec. any financial aid	70
% UG rec. any financial aid	70
Average cumulative indebtedness	$16,000

NEW MEXICO INSTITUTE OF MINING & TECHNOLOGY

CAMPUS STATION, 801 LEROY PLACE, SOCORRO, NM 87801 • ADMISSIONS: 505-835-5424 • FAX: 505-835-5989

STUDENTS SAY "..."

Academics

New Mexico Institute of Mining and Technology—"Tech" for short—is not your standard-issue state-run engineering and science degree factory. On the contrary, this small school "is about creating close relationships with actual professors who help students think and grow academically so that they can become life-long learners and influential engineers and scientists." Entering students should expect "an intense, rigorous academic experience" designed "for serious students with a love for all things scientific, electronic, or just plain nerdy." The academic program provides "a hands-on education" through "immense internship and experience opportunities, so no person should excuse themselves from achieving an exceptional education in theory and tangible worldly knowledge" here. Research opportunities also abound, another benefit of the school's size; as one student reports, "Within two weeks of attending NMT I was able to obtain a research position working under a professor doing actual research, not grunt work. NMT is a research facility that just so happens to be a university." The workload is tough, but "there are free tutoring centers for nearly every subject, as well as individualized help upon request. Professors are almost always willing to help individual students and love to see students succeed at this school." With all these assets, how does NMT keep the cost of its education so cheap? Public funding is part of the reason, but perhaps "being located in the middle of nowhere"—where property values are traditionally pretty low—also has something to do with it.

Life

Surviving at Tech "involves a lot of work, and so students are usually very busy." Undergrads typically immerse themselves in their studies; they "think about school and getting smarter. That's all anyone thinks about. When you walk by people in the cafeteria, they're talking about algorithms. That's not a joke. I didn't know there were places or people like this. I thought that people like this were a joke stereotype that you only saw on TV, but they're real." Students do find time for leisure, however. "The more athletic students tend to hike, mountain bike, rock climb, or play rugby," while "The more introverted students tend to play computer games on the campus intranet." Social life here "is not so great. Every weekend, people leave town to go home or they get drunk. There are clubs to join and some things to do, but those activities are limited and often stop around midterms." Hometown Socorro offers "absolutely nothing to do" according to some, although others report that "There are also a few cool hangouts if students really want to get out (Socorro Springs Brewery serves wonderful food)."

Student Body

"At a typical school, you see people listening to music because it's popular, not really because they think it sounds good," one Techie explains. "The clothes they wear, the way they talk, everything is done to try to impress others and try to be as 'cool' as possible. Here however, this is not the concern. No one wears the most expensive 'cool' brand-name clothing, no one listens to the music that's popular. Individuality is absolutely held onto tight here because no one cares what anyone else thinks of them. I know people who only shower three times a week because they think that's all they need. They're wrong, but they don't care whether you think they're wrong or not. They do because they want." Another student adds that "High school 'popular kids' will probably feel very out of place here. On the other hand, gamers, nerds, geeks, and students who just never fit the mold will find a friendly home." The population "has many Caucasian students, but there are also quite a few students from India and Japan, in particular. Males outweigh females heavily. As a male student, the male-to-female ratio feels like 15:1!"

FINANCIAL AID: 505-835-5333 • E-MAIL: ADMISSION@ADMIN.NMT.EDU • WEBSITE: WWW.NMT.EDU

THE PRINCETON REVIEW SAYS

Admissions

Very important factors considered include: Academic GPA, rigor of secondary school record, standardized test scores. *Other factors considered include:* Class rank, extracurricular activities, talent/ability, SAT or ACT required; ACT recommended; TOEFL required of all international applicants. High school diploma is required and GED is accepted. *Academic units required:* 4 English, 3 mathematics, 2 science, (2 science labs), 2 social studies, 1 history, 3 academic electives. *Academic units recommended:* 4 English, 4 mathematics, 4 science, (3 science labs), 2 foreign language, 3 social studies, 1 history.

Financial Aid

Students should submit: FAFSA, institution's own financial aid form. Regular filing deadline is 3/1. The Princeton Review suggests that all financial aid forms be submitted as soon as possible after January 1. *Need-based scholarships/grants offered:* Federal Pell, SEOG, state scholarships/grants, private scholarships, the school's own gift aid. *Loan aid offered:* FFEL Subsidized Stafford, FFEL Unsubsidized Stafford, FFEL PLUS, Federal Perkins, state loans Applicants will be notified of awards on a rolling basis beginning 4/1. Federal Work-Study Program available. Institutional employment available. Off-campus job opportunities are fair.

The Inside Word

Tech sets a minimum requirement of 970 combined SAT score or ACT composite score of 21 for admission, but typically students who thrive here do much better; indeed, the average math score is 610 (average composite ACT is 26, math 26). One student puts it this way: "You have to understand, NMT is a geek school. Even though the admission criteria are not particularly rigorous, you will be expected to focus, work hard, and give it your all. The professors are knowledgeable in their subjects and expect a lot of their students." Those unsure whether they can handle the workload are strongly advised to meet with an admissions counselor before deciding whether to apply and/or attend.

THE SCHOOL SAYS "..."

From The Admissions Office

"More than a century old, New Mexico Tech has research programs at the cutting edge of today's technology. This is exciting for students because many of them get jobs working for professors or for one of our many research divisions, learning skills they will use in graduate schools or high-tech careers. Pulsars, thunderstorms, volcanoes, lightning, quasars, earthquakes, energetic materials, and caves are just a few of the areas we study. We also teach and work in areas of computer and information security, business management, and several fields of engineering. Many of our research divisions are known worldwide in their fields, including Magdalena Ridge Observatory, the Energetic Materials Research and Testing Center, and Langmuir Laboratory for Atmospheric Research. Recent graduates with engineering degrees received starting salaries averaging $51,755, those with computer science degrees averaged $55,583; and those with degrees in both computer science and electrical engineering started at $63,333.

"From Fall 2008 on, students are required to submit scores from either the SAT or ACT. New Mexico Institute of Mining and Technology will continue to use the composite score from the ACT and/or the combined score of the Critical Reading and Math components *only* from the new SAT for both admission decisions and merit scholarships. The newly introduced Writing component will not be used for admission decisions and/or merit scholarships. We will continue to allow students to submit scores from the old (prior to March 2005) version of the SAT (or ACT) as well, and will use the student's best scores from either test. New Mexico Tech does not require the SAT Subject Test for consideration for admission or merit scholarships."

SELECTIVITY

Admissions Rating	88
# of applicants	763
% of applicants accepted	55
% of acceptees attending	59

FRESHMAN PROFILE

Range SAT Critical Reading	530–660
Range SAT Math	560–680
Range ACT Composite	23–29
Minimum paper TOEFL	540
Minimum computer TOEFL	207
Average HS GPA	3.6
% graduated top 10% of class	31
% graduated top 25% of class	63
% graduated top 50% of class	91

DEADLINES

Regular	
Priority	3/1
Deadline	8/1
Notification	rolling
Nonfall registration?	yes

APPLICANTS ALSO LOOK AT

AND OFTEN PREFER
California Institute of Technology
Massachusetts Institute of Technology

AND SOMETIMES PREFER
University of New Mexico
Colorado School of Mines

AND RARELY PREFER
New Mexico State University
Arizona State University at the Tempe campus

FINANCIAL FACTS

Financial Aid Rating	87
Annual in-state tuition	$3,543
Annual out-of-state tuition	$11,199
Room and board	$5,300
Required fees	$562
Books and supplies	$1,000
% frosh rec. need-based scholarship or grant aid	17
% UG rec. need-based scholarship or grant aid	26
% frosh rec. non-need-based scholarship or grant aid	26
% UG rec. non-need-based scholarship or grant aid	26
% frosh rec. need-based self-help aid	20
% UG rec. need-based self-help aid	28
% frosh rec. any financial aid	34
% UG rec. any financial aid	39
% UG borrow to pay for school	36
Average cumulative indebtedness	$7,889

NEW YORK UNIVERSITY

22 WASHINGTON SQUARE NORTH, NEW YORK, NY 10011 • ADMISSIONS: 212-998-4500 • FAX: 212-995-4902

CAMPUS LIFE
Quality of Life Rating	75
Fire Safety Rating	74
Green Rating	96
Type of school	private
Environment	metropolis

STUDENTS
Total undergrad enrollment	21,327
% male/female	38/62
% from out of state	64
% from public high school	71
% live on campus	53
% in (# of) fraternities	1 (15)
% in (# of) sororities	2 (10)
% African American	4
% Asian	19
% Caucasian	50
% Hispanic	8
% international	6
# of countries represented	127

SURVEY SAYS . . .
Great library
Students love New York, NY
Great off-campus food
Hard liquor is popular
(Almost) everyone smokes

ACADEMICS
Academic Rating	83
Calendar	semester
Student/faculty ratio	11:1
Profs interesting rating	65
Profs accessible rating	62
Most common reg class size	10–19 students
Most common lab size	10–19 students

MOST POPULAR MAJORS
liberal arts and sciences/liberal studies
drama and dramatics/theatre arts
finance

STUDENTS SAY " . . ."

Academics

Located in the heart of Manhattan's Greenwich Village, New York University feeds off its great home city. The school's layout reinforces this relationship; academic buildings and dormitories are scattered around Washington Square Park and are virtually indistinguishable from the private residences, hotels, and restaurants that are its neighbors. Asked to identify the school's greatest asset, so many students respond "location, location, location" that one could be forgiven for thinking that NYU is a training school for real-estate agents. Nonetheless, the school's location "attracts superb professors and well-known researchers and lecturers" and "It's pretty much guaranteed that you'll have a couple good connections in your field when you leave NYU." While at school, you'll find opportunities for "amazing internship possibilities and real-life experiences," and you'll learn the "independence, maturity, and time-management skills" that come with living in an "expensive place where space is limited but you have access to the best of everything." Students note that NYU "offers a great program for nearly anything you want to major in," including a world-renowned arts school, and excellent programs in business, the humanities, and education. The school's weak spot, undergrads agree, is the administration, where "too much red tape" creates an experience reminiscent of "a daily trip to the Department of Motor Vehicles." A relatively small price to pay, most here agree, for the "endless cultural, culinary, musical, artistic, and academic opportunities" that NYU offers.

Life

NYU isn't merely located in "the city that never sleeps." It is, in fact, located in one of the city's hottest social and cultural areas, an agora of restaurants, clubs, concert venues, movie theaters, retail shops, and galleries. Village life ain't cheap, however, and students warn that "money is always an issue. Kids are either worried about getting more money out of their parents or managing what money they have. But money seems to be considerably less of an issue when we're all going out on a Friday night. There is any number of ways to entertain yourself—it's New York City!" Inexpensive diversions include many of the city's famous museums, cheap ethnic eats, and the ever-popular pastime of people-watching. There are also "many free/discounted events put on by the university (like concerts, plays, forums, etc)." Don't expect a typical college party scene here, however, as "There are no frat parties at NYU, as Greek life is virtually nonexistent, even frowned upon by many students. Instead, students prefer to go out to bars and clubs on weekends." Dorm and apartment parties also "aren't too abundant, though pre-gaming is very popular." In fact, "NYU doesn't really provide much of an emphasis on campus activities, especially during the weekend. You're basically left to find your own entertainment which, thankfully, is always possible."

Student Body

Students agree that "NYU is just a diverse as the city it is surrounded by," noting that the campus "is a conglomeration of the atypical. If you are looking for a student body wearing J. Crew and discussing the next frat party, this isn't the school for you." Each college has a specific archetype—"The somewhat eccentric theater student in Tisch, the mostly international Stern business students, the Steinhardt musicians reminiscent of the band groups in high school"—but "The vast majority of students are really pretty average, just doing their own thing like everybody else." The community "is known for its acceptance of students of any ethnicity, religion, sexual orientation, gender, or race. We live in New York, so absolutely nothing shocks us, and virtually everything is accepted." The lack of a traditional campus attracts students of an "independent" bent and, on occasion, drives away those who discover they crave a more conventional college experience.

FINANCIAL AID: 212-998-4444 • WEBSITE: WWW.NYU.EDU

THE PRINCETON REVIEW SAYS

Admissions

Very important factors considered include: Application essay, academic GPA, recommendation(s), rigor of secondary school record, extracurricular activities. *Important factors considered include:* Class rank, standardized test scores, character/personal qualities, talent/ability. *Other factors considered include:* Alumni/ae relation, first generation, level of applicant's interest, racial/ethnic status, volunteer work, work experience. SAT Subject Tests required; SAT or ACT required; ACT with Writing component required. TOEFL required of all international applicants. High school diploma is required and GED is accepted. *Academic units required:* 4 English, 3 mathematics, 3 science, (3 science labs), 2 foreign language, 3 history. *Academic units recommended:* 4 mathematics, 4 science labs, 3 foreign language.

Financial Aid

Students should submit: FAFSA, state aid form. Early Decision applicants may submit an institutional form for an estimated award. Regular filing deadline is 2/15. The Princeton Review suggests that all financial aid forms be submitted as soon as possible after January 1. *Need-based scholarships/grants offered:* Federal Pell, SEOG, state scholarships/grants, private scholarships, the school's own gift aid. *Loan aid offered:* FFEL Subsidized Stafford, FFEL Unsubsidized Stafford, FFEL PLUS, Federal Perkins, Federal Nursing Applicants will be notified of awards on a rolling basis beginning 4/1. Federal Work-Study Program available. Institutional employment available. Off-campus job opportunities are excellent.

The Inside Word

Undergraduate applicants may apply only to one of NYU's undergraduate schools and colleges. Students applying to the Silver School of Social Work, Steinhardt School of Culture, Education, and Human Development, the Tisch School of the Arts, or the School of Continuing and Professional Studies must indicate an intended major (those applying to the College of Arts and Sciences or the Stern School of Business may indicate that they are undecided on their majors). This is different from the application process at most schools and obviously requires some forethought. Remember that this is a highly competitive school; if your application does not reflect a serious interest in your intended area of study, your chances of getting in will be diminished.

THE SCHOOL SAYS "..."

From The Admissions Office

"Located in Greenwich Village, New York University (NYU) is unlike any other U.S. institution of higher education in the United States. When you enter NYU, you become part of a close-knit community that combines the nurturing atmosphere of a small- to medium-sized college with the myriad offerings and research opportunities of a global, urban university. The energy and resources of New York City serve as an extension of our campus, providing unique opportunities for research, internships, and job placement. With thousands of undergraduate course offerings and over 160 areas of study from which to choose, you can explore and develop your intellectual and professional passions from your very first semester. Along with this extraordinary range of courses and programs, each of our schools offers a strong liberal arts foundation, introducing you to the traditions of scholarship and inquiry that are the keys to success at NYU and throughout life. NYU's intellectual climate is fostered by a faculty of world-famous scholars, researchers, and artists who teach both undergraduate and graduate courses. In addition, an integral element of the NYU academic experience is our study abroad programs. NYU offers nine study abroad sites—in Berlin, Buenos Aires, Florence, Ghana, London, Madrid, Paris, Prague, and Shanghai, with a future site planned for Tel Aviv, Israel.

"At NYU, you will become part of one of the most dynamic universities in the country, in one of the most exciting cities in the world, making NYU's tradition of innovation, learning, and success a part of your future."

SELECTIVITY

Admissions Rating	96
# of applicants	34,389
% of applicants accepted	37
% of acceptees attending	39
# of early decision applicants	2,990
% accepted early decision	35

FRESHMAN PROFILE

Range SAT Critical Reading	620–710
Range SAT Math	620–720
Range SAT Writing	620–710
Range ACT Composite	28–31
Average HS GPA	3.6
% graduated top 10% of class	66
% graduated top 25% of class	93
% graduated top 50% of class	99

DEADLINES

Early decision	
Deadline	11/1
Notification	12/15
Regular	
Deadline	1/1
Notification	4/1
Nonfall registration?	yes

FINANCIAL FACTS

Financial Aid Rating	75
Annual tuition	$35,230
% frosh rec. need-based scholarship or grant aid	50
% UG rec. need-based scholarship or grant aid	48
% frosh rec. need-based self-help aid	50
% UG rec. need-based self-help aid	47
% frosh rec. any financial aid	60
% UG rec. any financial aid	74
% UG borrow to pay for school	58
Average cumulative indebtedness	$33,637

NORTH CAROLINA STATE UNIVERSITY

Box 7103, Raleigh, NC 27695 • Admissions: 919-515-2434 • Fax: 919-515-5039

CAMPUS LIFE

Quality of Life Rating	76
Fire Safety Rating	84
Green Rating	90
Type of school	public
Environment	metropolis

STUDENTS

Total undergrad enrollment	22,070
% male/female	57/43
% from out of state	7
% from public high school	90
% live on campus	34
% in (# of) fraternities	8 (34)
% in (# of) sororities	10 (15)
% African American	9
% Asian	5
% Caucasian	79
% Hispanic	3
% Native American	1
% international	1
# of countries represented	99

SURVEY SAYS . . .

Lab facilities are great
Great computer facilities
Great library
Everyone loves the Wolfpack
Student publications are popular
Lots of beer drinking

ACADEMICS

Academic Rating	76
Calendar	semester
Student/faculty ratio	16:1
Profs interesting rating	74
Profs accessible rating	74
% classes taught by TAs	9
Most common	
reg class size	20–29 students
Most common	
lab size	10–19 students

MOST POPULAR MAJORS

mechanical engineering
biology/biological sciences
business administration and management

STUDENTS SAY ". . ."

Academics

North Carolina State University provides its student body with a combination of practical experience and theoretical knowledge in a curriculum with a technological bent. It offers strong programs in business, textiles and design, engineering, premedical sciences, and a host of agricultural and wildlife sciences. While some here feel that the school "offers no liberal arts program," others point out that its College of Humanities and Social Science is "underrated" and "becoming just as important as [the] engineering and agriculture" colleges. There is no doubt, however, that the school "emphasiz[es] out-of-classroom experiences." A senior boasts, "All I had to do was ask my professors about opportunities in my field and they heaped internships and research studies so high on me I had to reject six of them." A junior adds, "NCSU really cares about students and provid[es] them with great facilities, community resources, and professors—something you can't really say for many schools of this size." Students report that the faculty are "very knowledgeable." "Many people tell you in high school that professors do not care about you [or] your academic success, but from what I have seen here at NCSU, most professors do care as long as you are willing to put forth the effort to ask," a freshman reports. The administration, on the other hand, "is very difficult to get a hold of, unless it's something they themselves care about." Fortunately, many administrative tasks can be handled easily online.

Life

NC State benefits from a great location; "There is always something fun going on" in hometown Raleigh, with "lots of universities within a 30-mile radius, including Duke, UNC, Peace, Meredith, Shaw, and others. . . . There are many people in their early 20s to meet and hang out with." There are also "lots of golf courses, tennis courts, basketball courts, etc. for sports enthusiasts. You will not get bored in Raleigh, [but] if somehow you do . . . drive to Chapel Hill or Greenville." A slightly longer car trip—approximately 2 hours—puts you on the beach (east) or the mountains (west). ACC athletics dominate the thoughts of many in the area; NCSU's rivalries with nearby UNC and Duke are long-standing and legendary, especially in basketball, where all three schools typically field competitive teams; "Wolfpack pride is definitely evident throughout campus and even many portions of Raleigh." The school is home to "plenty of on-campus clubs and activities that many people participate in during the day. No matter what you are interested in, there is normally a club for it, and NCSU students are very active within their campus organizations and with the community." While "Most people stay focused during the week . . . when the weekend comes they leave that behind for the party scene," which centers on Greek houses and student housing until students hit the age of 21, when "Bars become the hang-out spot." Students point out, however, that "this doesn't mean that there aren't other things to do or that you won't have any friends" if "you aren't into drinking."

Student Body

At a school of 20,000, you'll find a little of everything, and NCSU is no exception to that rule; "athletes, computer geeks, frat dogs, sorority girls, skaters, intellects, grad students, goths, exchange students, etc." are peppered among the more populous "agriculture majors who wear overalls and talk with a thick Southern accent" and "engineering majors who are kind of geeky." In the same vein, NCSU "is a very conservative campus," but it is not without its "politically liberal students" and homosexual and minority advocacy groups. Atypical students "fit in really well in certain degree programs, especially textiles," but the campus isn't strife-free in this regard; one student reports, "There is lots of controversy over a new LGBT Center being built on campus."

FINANCIAL AID: 919-515-2421 • E-MAIL: UNDERGRAD_ADMISSIONS@NCSU.EDU • WEBSITE: WWW.NCSU.EDU

THE PRINCETON REVIEW SAYS

Admissions

Very important factors considered include: Class rank, academic GPA, rigor of secondary school record, standardized test scores. *Other factors considered include:* Application essay, recommendation(s), alumni/ae relation, character/personal qualities, extracurricular activities, first generation, geographical residence, racial/ethnic status, state residency, talent/ability, volunteer work, work experience. SAT or ACT required; ACT with Writing component required. TOEFL required of all international applicants. High school diploma is required and GED is not accepted. *Academic units required:* 4 English, 4 mathematics, 3 science, (1 science labs), 2 foreign language, 1 social studies, 1 history, 1 academic elective. *Academic units recommended:* 4 English, 4 mathematics, 4 science, (2 science labs), 2 foreign language, 1 social studies, 1 history, 4 academic electives.

Financial Aid

Students should submit: FAFSA, institution's own financial aid form. The Princeton Review suggests that all financial aid forms be submitted as soon as possible after January 1. *Need-based scholarships/grants offered:* Federal Pell, SEOG, state scholarships/grants, private scholarships, the school's own gift aid, United Negro College Fund. *Loan aid offered:* FFEL Subsidized Stafford, FFEL Unsubsidized Stafford, FFEL PLUS, Federal Perkins, state loans, college/university loans from institutional funds. Applicants will be notified of awards on a rolling basis beginning 3/1. Federal Work-Study Program available. Institutional employment available. Off-campus job opportunities are excellent.

The Inside Word

Back in the mid 1990s, strong applicants could apply to NCSU as a safety school, but things have really changed in the last decade. Soaring tuition rates at private schools and the school's growing reputation in a wide variety of fields have expanded the applicant pool. Freshman applicants must apply to a specific program, and some are more selective than others. Agricultural programs, the College of Textiles, and the College of Natural Resources are not as selective as programs in engineering, mathematics, the sciences, business, and the humanities and social sciences.

THE SCHOOL SAYS ". . ."

From The Admissions Office

"NC State is arguably the most popular university in the state, with more NC students seeking admission than at any other college or university. Over 12,000 students from across the nation seek one of the 3,600 available freshman spaces. Students choose NC State for its strong and varied academic programs (approximately 90), national reputation for excellence, low cost, location in Raleigh and the Research Triangle Park area, and very friendly atmosphere. Our students like the excitement of a large campus and the many opportunities it offers, such as Cooperative Education, Study Abroad, extensive honors programming, and theme residence halls. Each year, hundreds of NC State graduates are accepted into medical or law schools or other areas of advanced professional study. More corporate and government entities recruit graduates from NC State than from any other university in the United States. In 1999, IBM hired more graduates from NC State than from any other university in the United States.

"Freshman applicants for Fall 2008 must take either the new SAT, which includes a written essay, or the ACT with the Writing component. Students may also submit scores from either the old SAT (taken before March 2005) or the ACT, but the new Writing score is still required."

SELECTIVITY

Admissions Rating	89
# of applicants	16,437
% of applicants accepted	60
% of acceptees attending	49

FRESHMAN PROFILE

Range SAT Critical Reading	520–610
Range SAT Math	550–650
Range SAT Writing	510–610
Range ACT Composite	22–27
Minimum paper TOEFL	550
Minimum computer TOEFL	213
Average HS GPA	4.12
% graduated top 10% of class	34
% graduated top 25% of class	78
% graduated top 50% of class	98

DEADLINES

Early action	
Deadline	11/1
Notification	1/30
Regular	
Priority	11/1
Deadline	2/1
Notification	rolling
Nonfall registration?	yes

APPLICANTS ALSO LOOK AT
AND OFTEN PREFER
University of North Carolina at Chapel Hill

AND SOMETIMES PREFER
Wake Forest University
University of North Carolina—Charlotte

AND RARELY PREFER
University of South Carolina—Columbia
Virginia Tech

FINANCIAL FACTS

Financial Aid Rating	79
Annual in-state tuition	$3,760
Annual out-of-state tuition	$15,958
Room and board	$7,373
Required fees	$1,357
Books and supplies	$930
% frosh rec. need-based scholarship or grant aid	39
% UG rec. need-based scholarship or grant aid	37
% frosh rec. non-need-based scholarship or grant aid	4
% UG rec. non-need-based scholarship or grant aid	3
% frosh rec. need-based self-help aid	28
% UG rec. need-based self-help aid	30
% frosh rec. athletic scholarships	1
% UG rec. athletic scholarships	2
% frosh rec. any financial aid	68
% UG rec. any financial aid	61
% UG borrow to pay for school	50
Average cumulative indebtedness	$14,930

NORTHEASTERN UNIVERSITY

360 HUNTINGTON AVENUE, 150 RICHARDS HALL, BOSTON, MA 02115 • ADMISSIONS: 617-373-2200 • FAX: 617-373-8780

STUDENTS SAY ". . ."

Academics

Northeastern "is all about mixing classroom-based instruction with real-world experience" via a robust, justly renowned co-op program (which places students in real-life major-related internships and jobs for up to 18 months) that provides "meaningful work and life experience" to nearly all undergraduates. While some may quibble that co-op "isn't the best thing for all majors, only those oriented toward business, journalism, communications, engineering, some sciences, and architecture," most here insist that "the co-op program is Northeastern's bragging right" and "without any doubt the school's greatest strength." As one student explains, "Experiences on co-op lead to better discussion and learning in the classroom as professors tackle real-world applications of their subjects with the knowledge that we have been there before, rather than stay in the theoretical realm." As an added bonus, "Northeastern students have some of the strongest post-college resumes in the nation" as a result of their co-op experiences. As you might expect, Northeastern's strengths lie in such solidly pre-professional programs as business, health services, engineering, and computer and information sciences. Students caution that it's the type of school "where you get in what you put out...if you sit around and complain about not getting a good job and not having much help from advisers or professors, it's probably because you didn't try very hard. If you put in the effort, you will find many, many people are willing to do a great deal to help you succeed and doors will fly open to ensure your success, and you'll meet a lot of great people (classmates and faculty) and make a lot of friends along the way."

Life

"There is always something to do, either on campus or around the city" at Northeastern, and understandably so; the school is located in Boston, perhaps the nation's preeminent college town. Boston affords "unlimited amounts of things to do like shopping, walking around, movies, etc." Boston is especially accommodating to those over 21, since "there are plenty of bars to enjoy" all over town. For sports fans, "Fenway Park and the TD Banknorth Garden are a short distance away for athletic games," and "Matthews Arena, home of Husky hockey and the men's basketball team," are nearby. On campus, Greek life "is on the rise," and "Greeks...are extremely involved on campus, planning service events, educational speakers or fun events, such as bringing former Red Sox players or popular comedians to campus." Extracurricular clubs "including but not limited to sports, newspaper, religious groups, social awareness, diversity groups, and more" are widely available to students, and "The campus has much to offer as far as recreation from an ice rink to multiple gym facilities. It also has a large student center, multiple outdoor quads, and dorm activities. There is never a dull moment on campus, there is always something to do."

Student Body

"Because of our highly attractive location, there is no 'typical' Northeastern student," undergrads here insist, informing us that "Students come from the local Boston neighborhoods, ivy towns in Connecticut, countries around the world and cities across the country." The university's "wide range of courses to study" further ensures "a wide range of students" on campus. Finally, the school's large population practically ensures a diverse mix, as evidenced by the "250 or so clubs ranging from anime to the Caribbean Student Organization, from fraternities to a gay/lesbian/transsexual organization. You find virtually every race/gender/religious/political type of people here and they all fit in and generally get along." The enticement of co-op, of course, means that most everyone here is "looking to obtain a solid education and prepare themselves for the working world." You won't find a lot of ivory-tower intellectuals here.

FINANCIAL AID: 617-373-3190 • E-MAIL: ADMISSIONS@NEU.EDU • WEBSITE: WWW.NORTHEASTERN.EDU

THE PRINCETON REVIEW SAYS

Admissions

Very important factors considered include: Academic GPA, rigor of secondary school record. *Important factors considered include:* Class rank, application essay, recommendation(s), standardized test scores, character/personal qualities, extracurricular activities, first generation, talent/ability. *Other factors considered include:* Alumni/ae relation, geographical residence, racial/ethnic status, state residency, volunteer work, work experience. SAT or ACT required; ACT with Writing component required. TOEFL required of all international applicants. High school diploma is required and GED is accepted. *Academic units required:* 4 English, 3 mathematics, 3 science, (2 science labs), 2 foreign language, 2 social studies, 2 history. *Academic units recommended:* 4 mathematics, 4 science, (4 science labs), 4 foreign language.

Financial Aid

Students should submit: FAFSA, CSS/Financial Aid PROFILE. The Princeton Review suggests that all financial aid forms be submitted as soon as possible after January 1. *Need-based scholarships/grants offered:* Federal Pell, SEOG, state scholarships/grants, private scholarships, the school's own gift aid, Federal Nursing Scholarships. *Loan aid offered:* FFEL Subsidized Stafford, FFEL Unsubsidized Stafford, FFEL PLUS, Federal Perkins, Federal Nursing, state loans, MEFA, TERI, Signature, Mass. No Interest Loan (NIL), CitiAssist. Applicants will be notified of awards on a rolling basis beginning 2/15. Federal Work-Study Program available. Institutional employment available. Off-campus job opportunities are excellent.

The Inside Word

With more than 30,000 applicants each year, Northeastern admissions officers must wade through an ocean of applications in order to select the incoming class. The volume requires that much of the early winnowing be strictly numbers-based; the school has too many applicants with decent test scores and high school grades to bother with substandard candidates. Those who make the first cut should receive a more personalized review that includes a close look at essays, extracurriculars, and recommendations. A campus visit couldn't hurt.

THE SCHOOL SAYS "..."

From The Admissions Office

"Northeastern students take charge of their education in a way you'll find nowhere else, because a Northeastern education is like no other. We integrate challenging liberal arts and professional studies with a variety of experiential learning opportunities anchored by the our signature cooperativeeducation program. Northeastern's dynamic of academic excellence and experience means that our students are better prepared to succeed in the lives they choose. On top of that, they experience all of this on a beautifully landscaped, 73-acre campus in the heart of Boston, where culture, commerce, civic pride, and college students from around the globe are all a part of the mix."

SELECTIVITY

Admissions Rating	91
# of applicants	30,349
% of applicants accepted	39
% of acceptees attending	24
# accepting a place on wait list	1,342
% admitted from wait list	27

FRESHMAN PROFILE

Range SAT Critical Reading	570–660
Range SAT Math	600–680
Range ACT Composite	25–29
Minimum paper TOEFL	550
Minimum computer TOEFL	213
% graduated top 10% of class	42
% graduated top 25% of class	77
% graduated top 50% of class	96

DEADLINES

Early action	
Deadline	11/15
Notification	12/31
Regular	
Deadline	1/15
Nonfall registration?	yes

APPLICANTS ALSO LOOK AT

AND OFTEN PREFER
The George Washington University
New York University
Boston College

AND SOMETIMES PREFER
Pennsylvania State University
Binghamton University

AND RARELY PREFER
Drexel University
University of Connecticut
University of New Hampshire

FINANCIAL FACTS

Financial Aid Rating	70
Annual tuition	$31,500
Room and board	$11,420
Required fees	$399
Books and supplies	$900
% frosh rec. need-based scholarship or grant aid	55
% UG rec. need-based scholarship or grant aid	52
% frosh rec. non-need-based scholarship or grant aid	9
% UG rec. non-need-based scholarship or grant aid	5
% frosh rec. need-based self-help aid	47
% UG rec. need-based self-help aid	48
% frosh rec. athletic scholarships	2
% UG rec. athletic scholarships	2
% frosh rec. any financial aid	90
% UG rec. any financial aid	83

NORTHWESTERN UNIVERSITY

PO Box 3060, 1801 Hinman Avenue, Evanston, IL 60208-3060 • Admissions: 847-491-7271

STUDENTS SAY ". . ."

Academics

"The strength of the school is its range," Northwestern students agree, arguing that their school "has everything": "Intelligent but laid-back students," "excel[lence] in so many academic fields," "great extracurriculars and good parties," "strong [Big Ten] sports spirit," and "so many connections and opportunities during and after graduation." Undergrads here brag of "nationally acclaimed programs for almost anything anyone could be interested in, from engineering to theater to journalism to music," and report that "everything is given fairly equal weight. Northwestern students and faculty do not show a considerable bias" towards specific fields. The school accomplishes all this while maintaining a manageable scale. While its relatively small size allows for good student-professor interaction, it has "all the perks" of a big school, including "many opportunities" for research and internships. Be aware, however, that "Northwestern is not an easy school; it takes hard work to be average here." If you "learn from your failures quickly and love to learn for the sake of learning rather than the grade," students say it is quite possible to stay afloat and even to excel. Helping matters are numerous resources established by administrators and professors, including tutoring programs such as Northwestern's Gateway Science Workshop. Those who take advantage of these opportunities find the going much easier than those who don't.

Life

There are two distinct sections of the Northwestern campus. The North Campus is where "You can find a party every night of the week" and "The Greek scene is strong." The South Campus, about a one-mile trek from the action to the north, is "more artsy and has minimal partying on weeknights," but is closer to town so "it is easy" to "buy dinner, see a show at the movies, and go shopping. People who live on North Campus have a harder time getting motivated to go into Evanston and tap into all that is offered." As one South Campus resident puts it, "South Campus is nice and quiet in its own way. I enjoy reading and watching movies here, and the quietude is appreciated when study time rolls around. But for more exciting fun, a trip north is a must." Regardless of where students live, extracurriculars are "incredible here. There is a group for every interest, and they are amazingly well-managed by students alone. This goes hand-in-hand with how passionate students at Northwestern are about what they love." Many students "are involved in plays, a cappella groups, comedy troupes, and other organizations geared toward the performing arts. Activism is also very popular, with many involved in political groups, human rights activism, and volunteering." In addition, Northwestern's membership in the Big Ten means students "attend some of the best sporting events in the country." Chicago, of course, "is a wonderful resource. People go into the city for a wide variety of things—daily excursions, jobs, internships, nights out, parties, etc."

Student Body

The typical Northwestern student "was high school class president with a 4.0, swim team captain, and on the chess team." So it makes sense that everyone here "is an excellent student who works hard" and "has a leadership position in at least two clubs, plus an on-campus job." Students also tell us that "there's [a] great separation between North Campus (think: fraternities, engineering, state school mentality) and South Campus (think: closer to Chicago and its culture, arts and letters, liberal arts school mentality). Students segregate themselves depending on background and interests and it's rare for these two groups to interact beyond a superficial level." The student body here includes sizeable Jewish, Indian, and East Asian populations.

FINANCIAL AID: 847-491-7400 • E-MAIL: UG-ADMISSION@NORTHWESTERN.EDU • WEBSITE: WWW.NORTHWESTERN.EDU

THE PRINCETON REVIEW SAYS

Admissions

Very important factors considered include: Class rank, application essay, academic GPA, rigor of secondary school record, standardized test scores. *Important factors considered include:* Recommendation(s), character/personal qualities, extracurricular activities, talent/ability. *Other factors considered include:* Alumni/ae relation, first generation, interview, level of applicant's interest, racial/ethnic status, volunteer work, work experience. SAT or ACT required; ACT with Writing component required. TOEFL required of all international applicants. High school diploma or equivalent is not required. *Academic units recommended:* 4 English, 3 mathematics, 2 science, (2 science labs), 2 foreign language, 2 social studies, 1 academic elective.

Financial Aid

Students should submit: FAFSA, CSS/Financial Aid PROFILE, noncustodial PROFILE, business/farm supplement, parent and student federal tax returns. Regular filing deadline is 2/15. The Princeton Review suggests that all financial aid forms be submitted as soon as possible after January 1. *Need-based scholarships/grants offered:* Federal Pell, SEOG, state scholarships/grants, private scholarships, the school's own gift aid, United Negro College Fund. *Loan aid offered:* FFEL Subsidized Stafford, FFEL Unsubsidized Stafford, FFEL PLUS, Federal Perkins, college/university loans from institutional funds. Applicants will be notified of awards on or about 4/15. Federal Work-Study Program available. Institutional employment available.

The Inside Word

Northwestern is among the nation's most expensive undergraduate institutions, a fact that dissuades some qualified students from applying. The school is working to attract more low-income applicants by increasing the number of full scholarships available for students whose family income is less than $45,000. Low-income students who score well on the ACT may receive a letter from the school encouraging them to apply; even if you don't receive this letter, you should consider applying if you've got the goods—you may be pleasantly surprised by the offer you receive from the Financial Aid Office.

THE SCHOOL SAYS " . . ."

From The Admissions Office

"Consistent with its dedication to excellence, Northwestern provides both an educational and an extracurricular environment that enables its undergraduate students to become accomplished individuals and informed and responsible citizens. To the students in all its undergraduate schools, Northwestern offers liberal learning and professional education to help them gain the depth of knowledge that will empower them to become leaders in their professions and communities. Furthermore, Northwestern fosters in its students a broad understanding of the world in which we live as well as excellence in the competencies that transcend any particular field of study: writing and oral communication, analytical and creative thinking and expression, quantitative and qualitative methods of thinking.

"Applicants for Fall 2008 are required to take the SAT or the ACT with the Writing section. Northwestern will allow students to submit scores from the old (prior to March 2005) SAT (or ACT) as well, and will use the student's best scores from either test. However, Writing scores will be required."

SELECTIVITY
Admissions Rating	98
# of applicants	21,930
% of applicants accepted	27
% of acceptees attending	34
# accepting a place on wait list	1,274
% admitted from wait list	37
# of early decision applicants	1,296
% accepted early decision	44

FRESHMAN PROFILE
Range SAT Critical Reading	670–750
Range SAT Math	680–770
Range SAT Writing	660–750
Range ACT Composite	30–34
Minimum paper TOEFL	600
Minimum computer TOEFL	250
% graduated top 10% of class	85
% graduated top 25% of class	97
% graduated top 50% of class	99

DEADLINES
Early decision	
Deadline	11/1
Notification	12/15
Regular	
Deadline	1/1
Notification	4/15
Nonfall registration?	yes

APPLICANTS ALSO LOOK AT
AND OFTEN PREFER
Harvard College
Yale University
AND SOMETIMES PREFER
University of Chicago
Stanford University
Princeton University
AND RARELY PREFER
Purdue University—West Lafayette
Marquette University
DePaul University

FINANCIAL FACTS
Financial Aid Rating	94
Annual tuition	$36,756
Room and board	$11,295
Required fees	$414
Books and supplies	$1,626
% frosh rec. need-based scholarship or grant aid	41
% UG rec. need-based scholarship or grant aid	41
% frosh rec. need-based self-help aid	36
% UG rec. need-based self-help aid	38
% frosh rec. athletic scholarships	5
% UG rec. athletic scholarships	5
% frosh rec. any financial aid	60
% UG rec. any financial aid	60
% UG borrow to pay for school	46
Average cumulative indebtedness	$18,393

OBERLIN COLLEGE

101 NORTH PROFESSOR STREET, OBERLIN, OH 44074 • ADMISSIONS: 440-775-8411 • FAX: 440-775-6905

STUDENTS SAY ". . ."

Academics

Oberlin College, a school "for laid-back people who enjoy learning and expanding social norms," "allows each and every student to have the undergrad experience for which he or she is looking, all the while challenging the students to change themselves and the world for the better." Oberlin is a place where students "focus on learning for learning's sake rather than making money in a career." As one student explains, "I didn't plan on becoming a scholar when I entered Oberlin. . . . As fate would have it, I ended up loving my college classes and professors. Now I hope to be a professor of religion." At Oberlin, "Academics are very highly valued, but balanced with a strong interest in the arts and a commitment to society." Wags might suggest that Oberlin puts the "liberal" in "liberal arts"; the school's staunchest supporters agree, stressing the school's emphasis on open-mindedness and the belief that "one person can change the world." Among the school's offerings, "the sciences, English, politics, religion, music, environmental studies, and East Asian studies are particularly noteworthy." The presence of a prestigious music school imbues the entire campus community; one undergrad writes, "Oberlin's greatest strength is the combination of the college and the conservatory. They are not separated, so students mix with each other all the time." Professors here—the "heart and soul of the school"—are dedicated teachers who "treat you more like collaborators and realize that even with their PhDs, they can learn and grow from you, as well as you from them." They are "excellent instructors and fantastic people" who are "focused on learning instead of deadlines." Undergrads also appreciate "a cooperative learning environment" in which "Students bond over studying together for difficult exams."

Life

Life during the week at Oberlin can be "pretty bland," as "Almost everyone has to crack the books and study it up." It's not always bland, though; some here manage to find time for the many "events [going on] each weekend—operas, plays, organ pumps, etc.," or "rally to stage to help the oppressed." Thursday afternoons at Oberlin means "Classical Thursdays," an event during which "You get free beer from the college if you bring a professor to the on-campus pub." Another feature of campus life is "the musical scene, which has its heart in the conservatory. All of the other arts—performing, studio, whatever—are intertwined with the talent in the conservatory." On weekends, "People let loose, rip out the bong (no pun intended), and drink beer. Not everyone does this every weekend. Some don't do it at all," and "There is absolutely no pressure on those who don't." There are also "tons of student-produced social events: parties, fundraisers, concerts, dances, etc.," keeping students "very connected to each other and to what's going on in the community." Hometown Oberlin "is a small town, and about all there is to do there is go out for pizza or Chinese, see a movie for $2 or $3 at the Apollo, or go to the Feve, the bar in town."

Student Body

"If you're a liberal, artsy, indie loner who likes to throw around the phrase 'heteronormative White privilege,'" then Oberlin might be the place for you. "We're like the Island of Misfit Toys, but together we make a great toy chest." "We're all different and unusual, which creates a common bond between students." "Musicians, jocks, science geeks, creative writing majors, straight, bi, questioning, queer, and trans [students]," all have their place here, alongside "straight-edge, international, local, and joker students." Oberlin has a reputation for a left-leaning and active student body; one undergrad observes, "They are less active politically than they would like to think, but still more active than most people elsewhere." Another adds, "Most students are very liberal, but the moderates and (few) Republicans have a fine time of it. Every student has different interests and isn't afraid to talk about them." Some here worry that "Oberlin's student body is becoming more and more mainstream each year."

FINANCIAL AID: 440-775-8142 • E-MAIL: COLLEGE.ADMISSIONS@OBERLIN.EDU • WEBSITE: WWW.OBERLIN.EDU

THE PRINCETON REVIEW SAYS

Admissions

Very important factors considered include: Class rank, academic GPA, rigor of secondary school record, standardized test scores. *Important factors considered include:* Application essay, recommendation(s), character/personal qualities, extracurricular activities, talent/ability. *Other factors considered include:* Alumni/ae relation, first generation, geographical residence, interview, level of applicant's interest, racial/ethnic status, state residency, volunteer work, work experience. SAT or ACT required; ACT with Writing component required. TOEFL required of all international applicants. High school diploma is required and GED is accepted. *Academic units required:* 4 English, 4 mathematics, 3 science, 3 foreign language, 3 social studies.

Financial Aid

Students should submit: FAFSA, institution's own financial aid form, CSS/Financial Aid PROFILE, noncustodial PROFILE, business/farm supplement. Regular filing deadline is 2/15. The Princeton Review suggests that all financial aid forms be submitted as soon as possible after January 1. *Need-based scholarships/grants offered:* Federal Pell, SEOG, state scholarships/grants, private scholarships, the school's own gift aid. *Loan aid offered:* FFEL Subsidized Stafford, FFEL Unsubsidized Stafford, FFEL PLUS, Federal Perkins, college/university loans from institutional funds. Applicants will be notified of awards on or about 4/1.

The Inside Word

Oberlin's music conservatory is one of the most elite programs in the nation; aspiring music students should expect stiff competition for one of the 600 available slots. Other applicants won't have a much easier time of it; Oberlin is a highly selective institution that attracts a highly competitive applicant pool. Your personal statement could be the make-or-break factor here.

THE SCHOOL SAYS ". . ."

From The Admissions Office

"Oberlin College is an independent, coeducational, liberal arts college. It comprises two divisions, the College of Arts and Sciences, with roughly 2,200 students enrolled, and the Conservatory of Music, with about 600 students. Students in both divisions share one campus; they also share residence and dining halls as part of one academic community. Many students take courses in both divisions. Oberlin awards the Bachelor of Arts and the Bachelor of Music degrees; a 5-year program leads to both degrees. Selected master's degrees are offered in the conservatory. Oberlin is located 35 miles southwest of Cleveland. Founded in 1833, Oberlin College is highly selective and dedicated to recruiting students from diverse backgrounds. Oberlin was the first coeducational college in the United States, as well as a historic leader in educating African Americans. Oberlin's 440-acre campus provides outstanding facilities, modern scientific laboratories, a large computing center, a library unexcelled by other college libraries for the depth and range of its resources, and one of the top-five college- or university-based art museums in the country.

"Freshman applicants for Fall 2008 must take the new SAT (which includes a written essay), or the ACT with Writing component."

SELECTIVITY

Admissions Rating	97
# of applicants	7,014
% of applicants accepted	31
% of acceptees attending	34
# accepting a place on wait list	666
% admitted from wait list	3
# of early decision applicants	342
% accepted early decision	60

FRESHMAN PROFILE

Range SAT Critical Reading	640–750
Range SAT Math	610–710
Range SAT Writing	630–730
Range ACT Composite	26–32
Minimum paper TOEFL	600
Minimum computer TOEFL	200
Average HS GPA	3.58
% graduated top 10% of class	68
% graduated top 25% of class	92
% graduated top 50% of class	100

DEADLINES

Early decision	
Deadline	11/15
Notification	12/20
Regular	
Deadline	1/15
Notification	4/1
Nonfall registration?	no

APPLICANTS ALSO LOOK AT

AND OFTEN PREFER
Stanford University
Wesleyan University

AND SOMETIMES PREFER
Macalester College
Carleton College

AND RARELY PREFER
Connecticut College

FINANCIAL FACTS

Financial Aid Rating	94
Annual tuition	$36,064
Room and board	$9,280
Required fees	$218
Books and supplies	$830
% frosh rec. need-based scholarship or grant aid	49
% UG rec. need-based scholarship or grant aid	50
% frosh rec. non-need-based scholarship or grant aid	35
% UG rec. non-need-based scholarship or grant aid	27
% frosh rec. need-based self-help aid	47
% UG rec. need-based self-help aid	48
% frosh rec. any financial aid	61
% UG rec. any financial aid	60
% UG borrow to pay for school	56
Average cumulative indebtedness	$17,485

OCCIDENTAL COLLEGE

1600 CAMPUS ROAD, OFFICE OF ADMISSION, LOS ANGELES, CA 90041 • ADMISSIONS: 800-825-5262 • FAX: 323-341-4875

CAMPUS LIFE

Quality of Life Rating	87
Fire Safety Rating	60*
Green Rating	60*
Type of school	private
Environment	metropolis

STUDENTS

Total undergrad enrollment	1,863
% male/female	44/56
% from out of state	54
% from public high school	60
% live on campus	80
% in (# of) fraternities	6 (4)
% in (# of) sororities	13 (4)
% African American	6
% Asian	13
% Caucasian	58
% Hispanic	15
% Native American	1
% international	2
# of countries represented	22

SURVEY SAYS . . .
Small classes
No one cheats
Students are friendly
Diverse student types on campus
Lots of beer drinking

ACADEMICS

Academic Rating	88
Calendar	semester
Student/faculty ratio	10:1
Profs interesting rating	83
Profs accessible rating	84
Most common reg class size	10–19 students
Most common lab size	10–19 students

MOST POPULAR MAJORS
international relations and affairs
English
economics

STUDENTS SAY ". . ."

Academics

Located in sunny California, Occidental College has a "rising star" quality to it. Often in the "shadows" of other "heavyweight liberal arts colleges on the West Coast," Oxy is "stepping up its game" and this "striving to become something better embodies the ethos of Oxy." The professors at Oxy are "top quality" and "passionate" about what they teach and all seem to "care about their students." They don't exist to "publish or perish"; "They actually are at Oxy to teach—and not to teach so they can research." That said, Oxy is no slacker when it comes to research either. Students say it is "really easy" to get "independent study, internships, and grants" that would "not be offered anywhere else to undergraduates." At Oxy, there are "no slackers" and the "students are really intelligent and motivated." For students who need it, help is never far out of reach due to "incredible" services like the "Center for Academic Excellence, where student teachers are available for writing and study help." In recent years, the administration has undergone "a lot of changes," leaving some students feeling that "it is unable to help students due to overall bureaucracy." However, the restoration of "student government" after being "dissolved for about a year" has helped smooth out relations. One thing students agree on, however, is that "registration is awful."

Life

As one student quips, "Los Angeles, though the air is not spectacular, is a wonderful place to go to college." Students cite "great resources for academic pursuits," a "beach [that] is accessible practically all year," and "myriad events occurring" in the city. Bear in mind, however, that "a car is essential here" and "Everyone who doesn't have a car wishes they did and hangs out with people who do." Students with cars enjoy free parking on campus and the ability to be "in Chinatown, at Dodger Stadium, or in Hollywood" in less than a "15-minute drive." Other popular destinations include "Pasadena or Glendale where students go "to shop, eat, see movies, or just walk around." Neither is there a dearth of entertainment options on campus. Oxy students "have a great student service called Programming Board, which puts on tons of social events for the students which are really popular" including "a movie series every Wednesday, huge themed dances, debates, and poker tournaments." While most students are "fairly social," Oxy is "not what I would call a party school." Most of the parties "are all just off campus," and "Drinks are easy to obtain but also easy to refuse." Oxy's "smart and opinionated" students often forgo the party scene for "lively conversations about politics or topics from class" with their friends.

Student Body

Most students agree that "the one thing most everyone has in common" at Oxy is their "left-leaning political views." Republicans on campus "seem to somewhat not fit in" and "make it very known that they feel oppressed by faculty and other students." Everyone else seems to be treated "equally, regardless of ethnicity, sexual orientation, socioeconomic status, [or] religious affiliation." These self-described "Californian/Seattleite Ugg-wearing hipsters" are "very intellectually bright and interesting." Many are quite idealistic and "genuinely" want to "change the world." Although the students are very driven, "There is very little competition" and "very little cliquing." Most students on campus are "pretty laid-back and know how to have fun, but still work pretty hard."

FINANCIAL AID: 323-259-2548 • E-MAIL: ADMISSION@OXY.EDU • WEBSITE: WWW.OXY.EDU

THE PRINCETON REVIEW SAYS

Admissions

Very important factors considered include: Rigor of secondary school record. *Important factors considered include:* Application essay, academic GPA, recommendation(s), standardized test scores, character/personal qualities, extracurricular activities, volunteer work. *Other factors considered include:* Class rank, alumni/ae relation, first generation, geographical residence, interview, level of applicant's interest, racial/ethnic status, talent/ability, work experience. SAT Subject Tests recommended; SAT or ACT required; ACT with Writing component required. TOEFL required of all international applicants. High school diploma is required and GED is accepted. *Academic units recommended:* 4 English, 4 mathematics, 3 science, (2 science labs), 3 foreign language, 2 social studies, 2 history, 2 academic electives.

Financial Aid

Students should submit: FAFSA, CSS/Financial Aid PROFILE, state aid form, noncustodial PROFILE, business/farm supplement. Regular filing deadline is 2/1. The Princeton Review suggests that all financial aid forms be submitted as soon as possible after January 1. *Need-based scholarships/grants offered:* Federal Pell, SEOG, state scholarships/grants, private scholarships, the school's own gift aid. *Loan aid offered:* FFEL Subsidized Stafford, FFEL Unsubsidized Stafford, FFEL PLUS, Federal Perkins, college/university loans from institutional funds. Applicants will be notified of awards on a rolling basis beginning 3/24. Federal Work-Study Program available. Institutional employment available. Off-campus job opportunities are good.

The Inside Word

The Admissions Team at Occidental is adamant about not adhering to formulas. They rely heavily on essays and recommendations in their mission to create a talented and diverse incoming class. The college attracts some excellent students, so a demanding course load in high school is essential for the most competitive candidates. Successful applicants tend to be creative and academically motivated.

THE SCHOOL SAYS "..."

From The Admissions Office

"Here's what our students tell us:

"Tycho Bergquist '05: 'The professors have all been just amazing. Every person's needs are different, and they're all very willing to coordinate times to meet and discuss how you feel about a class and what you want to get out of it.'

"Molly Franz '05: 'I realize the caliber of discussion that occurs at Oxy is not easily matched. It's very uncommon. I've developed very strong relationships with many professors, and that's something I believe is unique to Oxy.'

"Zach Chinn '05: 'The program has been awesome. Whether you want to go to med school or grad school, it's a great experience. The professors really want you to succeed.'

"Stanley Burgos '06: "I've been working with postdoctoral researchers as an undergraduate. It's very rewarding. Oxy challenges me both inside and outside the classroom."

"Candace Ryan '05: 'Occidental opened my eyes to different beliefs, values, and ideas. The range of ideas and beliefs at Occidental is incredible. Discussions in class are much more interesting, because you consider things you might not have thought about before.'

"Sam Phang '06: 'Oxy's close-knit community and its size make me feel this is a place I can call home.'

"Devin Miller '06: 'Oxy instills curiosity and makes students want to go out and learn a subject on their own. I've gotten a broader sense of self and have been able to fulfill my learning goals.' Occidental requires all applicants (including international students) to take either the SAT or ACT with the new Writing component. SAT subject tests are recommended, but not required."

SELECTIVITY

Admissions Rating	**94**
# of applicants	5,275
% of applicants accepted	44
% of acceptees attending	21
# accepting a place on wait list	234
% admitted from wait list	11
# of early decision applicants	78
% accepted early decision	49

FRESHMAN PROFILE

Range SAT Critical Reading	590–700
Range SAT Math	600–690
Range SAT Writing	585–690
Range ACT Composite	26–30
Minimum paper TOEFL	600
Minimum computer TOEFL	250
% graduated top 10% of class	57
% graduated top 25% of class	89
% graduated top 50% of class	99

DEADLINES

Early decision	
Deadline	11/15
Notification	12/15
Regular	
Deadline	1/10
Notification	4/1
Nonfall registration?	no

APPLICANTS ALSO LOOK AT
AND OFTEN PREFER
Pomona College
University of Southern California
University of California—Berkeley
University of California—Los Angeles
Stanford University

AND SOMETIMES PREFER
Macalester College
Claremont McKenna College

FINANCIAL FACTS

Financial Aid Rating	**96**
Annual tuition	$36,160
Room and board	$10,270
Required fees	$911
Books and supplies	$988
% frosh rec. need-based scholarship or grant aid	50
% UG rec. need-based scholarship or grant aid	50
% frosh rec. non-need-based scholarship or grant aid	36
% UG rec. non-need-based scholarship or grant aid	31
% frosh rec. need-based self-help aid	46
% UG rec. need-based self-help aid	46
% frosh rec. any financial aid	82
% UG rec. any financial aid	77
% UG borrow to pay for school	67
Average cumulative indebtedness	$19,756

OGLETHORPE UNIVERSITY

4484 PEACHTREE ROAD, NORTHEAST, ATLANTA, GA 30319 • ADMISSIONS: 404-364-8307 • FAX: 404-364-8491

CAMPUS LIFE
Quality of Life Rating	87
Fire Safety Rating	60*
Green Rating	73
Type of school	private
Environment	metropolis

STUDENTS
Total undergrad enrollment	943
% male/female	39/61
% from out of state	30
% from public high school	79
% live on campus	61
% in (# of) fraternities	25 (4)
% in (# of) sororities	20 (3)
% African American	23
% Asian	5
% Caucasian	50
% Hispanic	3
% Native American	1
% international	5
# of countries represented	35

SURVEY SAYS . . .
Students are friendly
Diverse student types on campus
Students love Atlanta, GA
Great off-campus food
Lots of beer drinking

ACADEMICS
Academic Rating	85
Calendar	semester
Student/faculty ratio	13:1
Profs interesting rating	96
Profs accessible rating	90
Most common reg class size	10–19 students

MOST POPULAR MAJORS
English language and literature
psychology
business/commerce

STUDENTS SAY ". . ."

Academics

Oglethorpe University in Atlanta concerns itself with creating an environment in which students from varying majors can interact so as to broaden each student's experiences. Oglethorpe's liberal arts curriculum naturally lends itself to students learning to be "analytical and engaging in the classroom," and many report that it is "so much easier to learn and broaden your mind and opinions while being able to discuss and debate different ideas in a classroom of less than twenty students" than in the lecture halls of larger universities. "We also have a rep for being a theater school and we really aren't at all," says a student. Though the "pickings are very slim" as far as class options go, "there are many classes here that you would never find at another school, but they are very interesting and definitely prepare you for the real world."

It can be tough to win students over at such a small school, but the administration here is commended for running the place "professionally," although the financial aid, while "pretty darn fair," is "sloppy," "very slow, and loses stuff all the time." Students also wish for an update of many of the systems, so that registration, transcripts, and bill payment can all be done online. The professors, most of whom are experts in their field, are "overall pretty much the bomb, in a very good way," and it shows in the positive experiences that every single Oglethorpe student takes away from the classroom. "I come away from class much more enriched than when I went in," says a senior. "You get what you pay for," says a student as a testament to his satisfaction.

Life

"We live in the big city of Atlanta, but still manage to have a real small town vibe on campus," says a sophomore. Life is made up of strictly school on weekdays, but when the weekend rolls around, students let loose a bit. Theatre is popular, as well as "jamming with musical instruments." Greek life is very popular here, as are their parties on Greek Row, but Oglethorpe has "a much different take on it" than other schools: "It is more based on social fun and networking rather than bordering on a painfully exclusive club." "It's not uncommon to see a group of brothers sitting outside with their beers arguing the nature of humanity or the current applications of Aristotle." There is "a lot of drinking, but you don't have to drink" to have fun; one student says that merely "sitting out in the grass on the quad and talking with friends is the best." There are also many school-sponsored events (usually at least four or five a week), "so no one has any reason to be bored."

Student Body

Diversity is a huge element at Oglethorpe, where a large minority population and many international students mean that "ethnicity and gender are almost irrelevant." While many students still can still be classified into groups, all "interact with each other easily," and the school as a whole "is such a microcosm that everybody stands out a lot." "Oglethorpe embodies everything from pot-head philosophers, wannabe prep jocks, loud outspoken activists, and just your plain average college nerd," says one student. "It is a small campus so it is impossible to completely avoid someone you do not like, but it is easy enough to just not be around them and hang out with that group," says another. Most people are "refined in either the fine arts or sports or sometimes both," and there's also "a strong minority of LGBT students." The strong theater program does give the school an "artsy" feel, but there's also an athletic and frat/sorority scene.

OGLETHORPE UNIVERSITY

FINANCIAL AID: 404-364-8356 • E-MAIL: ADMISSION@OGLETHORPE.EDU • WEBSITE: WWW.OGLETHORPE.EDU

THE PRINCETON REVIEW SAYS

Admissions

Very important factors considered include: Academic GPA, rigor of secondary school record, standardized test scores. *Important factors considered include:* Class rank, application essay, recommendation(s), extracurricular activities, interview, level of applicant's interest, volunteer work. *Other factors considered include:* Alumni/ae relation, character/personal qualities, first generation, talent/ability, work experience. SAT or ACT required; ACT with Writing component recommended. TOEFL required of all international applicants. High school diploma is required and GED is accepted. *Academic units required:* 4 English, 3 mathematics, 2 science, 3 social studies. *Academic units recommended:* 2 foreign language.

Financial Aid

Students should submit: FAFSA, institution's own financial aid form, state aid form. The Princeton Review suggests that all financial aid forms be submitted as soon as possible after January 1. *Need-based scholarships/grants offered:* Federal Pell, SEOG, state scholarships/grants, private scholarships, the school's own gift aid, United Negro College Fund. *Loan aid offered:* Direct Subsidized Stafford, Direct Unsubsidized Stafford, Direct PLUS, FFEL Subsidized Stafford, FFEL Unsubsidized Stafford, FFEL PLUS, Federal Perkins Applicants will be notified of awards on a rolling basis beginning 4/1. Federal Work-Study Program available. Institutional employment available. Off-campus job opportunities are excellent.

The Inside Word

With rising national interest in the South, it won't be long before the academic strength found at Oglethorpe attracts wider attention and more applicants. At present, it's much easier to gain admission here than at many universities of similar quality. Go to Atlanta for a campus interview—you'll leave impressed.

THE SCHOOL SAYS "..."

From The Admissions Office

"Promising students and outstanding teachers come together at Oglethorpe University in an acclaimed program of liberal arts and sciences. Here you'll find an active intellectual community on a beautiful English Gothic campus just 10 miles from the center of Atlanta, capital of the Southeast, site of the 1996 Summer Olympics, and home to 4 million people. If you want challenging academics, the opportunity to work closely with your professors, and the stimulation of a great metropolitan area, consider Oglethorpe, a national liberal arts college in a world-class city.

"Applicants for Fall 2008 are required to take the new SAT (or the ACT with the Writing section). Students may also submit scores from the old (prior to March 2005) SAT (or ACT), and we will use the student's best scores from either test. It is recommended that students submit scores from two SAT Subject Tests."

SELECTIVITY

Admissions Rating	82
# of applicants	1,155
% of applicants accepted	48
% of acceptees attending	32

FRESHMAN PROFILE

Range SAT Critical Reading	510–640
Range SAT Math	500–610
Range SAT Writing	500–610
Range ACT Composite	21–27
Minimum paper TOEFL	550
Minimum computer TOEFL	200
Average HS GPA	3.43
% graduated top 10% of class	23
% graduated top 25% of class	54
% graduated top 50% of class	84

DEADLINES

Early action	
Deadline	12/5
Notification	12/20
Regular	
Notification	rolling
Nonfall registration?	yes

FINANCIAL FACTS

Financial Aid Rating	79
Annual tuition	$25,380
Room and board	$9,500
Required fees	$100
Books and supplies	$800
% frosh rec. need-based scholarship or grant aid	62
% UG rec. need-based scholarship or grant aid	61
% frosh rec. non-need-based scholarship or grant aid	8
% UG rec. non-need-based scholarship or grant aid	8
% frosh rec. need-based self-help aid	45
% UG rec. need-based self-help aid	49
% frosh rec. any financial aid	95
% UG rec. any financial aid	95
% UG borrow to pay for school	58
Average cumulative indebtedness	$26,299

OHIO NORTHERN UNIVERSITY

525 SOUTH MAIN STREET, ADA, OH 45810 • ADMISSIONS: 419-772-2260 • FAX: 419-772-2313

STUDENTS SAY ". . ."

Academics
Ohio Northern's premier attraction is its Raabe College of Pharmacy; the school, which enrolls about one-third of all undergraduates here, offers a six-year Pharm.D. option as well as dual majors in pharmacy/biology and pharmacy/law. Students in the program warn that "the academics can be tough" but "the hands-on opportunities available to students are great," and the school's "good reputation for applying for jobs" justifies the work required to succeed. Less prestigious but equally popular (and, according to students, nearly as excellent) are the James F. Dicke College of Business Administration and the T.J. Smull College of Engineering, each claiming between 15 and 20 percent of the student body. Across all five schools at this small university, students report that they "get involved in major-related activities as soon as they arrive on campus. This is much harder to do at a larger school. The opportunities here are almost endless." As are the challenges; ONU is one of those schools that's fairly easy to get into but not so easy to survive at, as "The school does a good job of weeding out the social-scene-centered students, and by second year most students are overall very academically motivated."

Life
Ohio Northern is located in the town of Ada (app. pop. 5,600), an hour and a half's drive northwest of Columbus. "There isn't a ton of stuff to do off campus unless you want to drive a half an hour" to Lima, so "You really have to make your own fun" at ONU (for those with cars, Lima and Findlay—also a half hour off—"provide lots of eating and shopping places"). Many choose to get involved with campus activities; they tell us that "Life is usually hectic because of classes and organizations students are involved with," and that "There are over 150 student organizations at Ohio Northern so there always seems to be something going on that you can attend." Others indulge in the party scene, explaining that "Obviously, the social scene is limited in such a small isolated town. The weekend scene is no different than any other college in America, lots of alcohol consumption (but mostly on-campus, since there are only three bars in Ada). Random hooking up is also common among the alcohol-impaired. However, "there is a sizeable population of students that keep their fun clean with cards, board games, movies, etc." Some here even insist that "There is a decent amount of drinking that goes on, but not near as much as at some other schools."

Student Body
ONU students are "usually really dedicated to something and have a strong passion for it. It could be politics, music, sports, religion, or anything." They are typically "involved with some organization. Everyone seems to find something that they are good at or interested in, whether it's a club, sports, or Greek life, or all three." Minority students are in short supply; nearly everyone is "white, middle class, and fairly smart," typically "from a rural or suburban community" where they were "honor or merit roll students." They tend to be "conservative and not very open-minded to different cultures, gender-orientations, etc.… There is a small but growing population of students with different ethnicities, cultures, sexual orientations, and political stances that more or less group together to interact within their own subgroup(s)."

OHIO NORTHERN UNIVERSITY

FINANCIAL AID: 419-772-2272 • E-MAIL: ADMISSIONS-UG@ONU.EDU • WEBSITE: WWW.ONU.EDU

THE PRINCETON REVIEW SAYS

Admissions

Very important factors considered include: Academic GPA, rigor of secondary school record, standardized test scores. *Important factors considered include:* Class rank, extracurricular activities, interview. *Other factors considered include:* Application essay, recommendation(s), alumni/ae relation, character/personal qualities, first generation, level of applicant's interest, talent/ability, volunteer work, SAT or ACT required; TOEFL required of all international applicants. High school diploma is required and GED is accepted. *Academic units required:* 4 English, 2 mathematics, 2 science, (2 science labs), 2 social studies, 2 history, 4 academic electives. *Academic units recommended:* 4 English, 4 mathematics, 3 science, (2 science labs), 2 foreign language, 3 social studies, 2 history, 1 visual/performing arts, 1 computer science, 4 academic electives.

Financial Aid

Students should submit: FAFSA, institution's own financial aid form. Regular filing deadline is 6/1. The Princeton Review suggests that all financial aid forms be submitted as soon as possible after January 1. *Need-based scholarships/grants offered:* Federal Pell, SEOG, state scholarships/grants, private scholarships, the school's own gift aid, External Scholarships. *Loan aid offered:* FFEL Subsidized Stafford, FFEL Unsubsidized Stafford, FFEL PLUS, Federal Perkins, college/university loans from institutional funds, Alternative Loans, Federal Health Professions Loan. Applicants will be notified of awards on a rolling basis beginning 2/15. Federal Work-Study Program available. Institutional employment available. Off-campus job opportunities are good.

The Inside Word

Solid high school grades and above average standardized test scores will pretty much punch your ticket to Ohio Northern. Admissions standards for the pharmacy school are considerably more stringent but could hardly be described as highly competitive. Applicants may qualify for substantial merit-based scholarships based on standardized test scores and high school GPA; see the school's website for details.

THE SCHOOL SAYS "..."

From The Admissions Office

"Ohio Northern's purpose is to help students develop into self-reliant, mature men and women capable of clear and logical thinking and sensitive to the higher values of truth, beauty, and goodness. ONU selects its student body from among those students possessing characteristics congruent with the institution's objectives. Generally, a student must be prepared to use the resources of the institution to achieve personal and educational goals.

"Students applying for admission for Fall 2008 are urged to take the new SAT (or the ACT with the Writing section), but we will allow students to submit scores from the old (prior to March 2005) SAT (or ACT) as well. The student's best composite scores will be used for scholarship purposes."

SELECTIVITY

Admissions Rating	85
# of applicants	3,308
% of applicants accepted	88
% of acceptees attending	25

FRESHMAN PROFILE

Range SAT Critical Reading	510–630
Range SAT Math	550–660
Range SAT Writing	510–630
Range ACT Composite	23–29
Minimum paper TOEFL	480
Minimum computer TOEFL	157
Minimum web-based TOEFL	54
Average HS GPA	3.64
% graduated top 10% of class	38
% graduated top 25% of class	65
% graduated top 50% of class	88

DEADLINES

Regular	
Priority	12/1
Deadline	8/15
Notification	rolling
Nonfall registration?	yes

APPLICANTS ALSO LOOK AT AND SOMETIMES PREFER

University of Toledo
Wittenberg University
Bowling Green State University
Miami University
The Ohio State University—Columbus

FINANCIAL FACTS

Financial Aid Rating	84
Annual tuition	$30,555
Room and board	$7,890
Required fees	$210
Books and supplies	$1,500
% frosh rec. need-based scholarship or grant aid	86
% UG rec. need-based scholarship or grant aid	83
% frosh rec. non-need-based scholarship or grant aid	84
% UG rec. non-need-based scholarship or grant aid	79
% frosh rec. need-based self-help aid	86
% UG rec. need-based self-help aid	83
% UG borrow to pay for school	79
Average cumulative indebtedness	$20,740

THE OHIO STATE UNIVERSITY—COLUMBUS

110 ENARSON HALL, 54 WEST TWELFTH AVENUE, COLUMBUS, OH 43210 • ADMISSIONS: 614-292-3980 • FAX: 614-292-4818

CAMPUS LIFE
Quality of Life Rating	85
Fire Safety Rating	65
Green Rating	60*
Type of school	public
Environment	metropolis

STUDENTS
Total undergrad enrollment	37,088
% male/female	53/47
% from out of state	10
% from public high school	88
% live on campus	24
% in (# of) fraternities	6 (39)
% in (# of) sororities	6 (21)
% African American	7
% Asian	5
% Caucasian	80
% Hispanic	3
% international	2

SURVEY SAYS . . .
Athletic facilities are great
Diverse student types on campus
Great off-campus food
Everyone loves the Buckeyes
Lots of beer drinking

ACADEMICS
Academic Rating	71
Calendar	quarter
Student/faculty ratio	13:1
Profs interesting rating	66
Profs accessible rating	71

MOST POPULAR MAJORS
biology/biological sciences
psychology
political science and government

STUDENTS SAY ". . ."

Academics

The Ohio State University in Columbus is "a great blend of academics, opportunity, and fun." This is one of the largest universities in the country, and as such, you'll find "every resource you could possibly need" and "unlimited" academic opportunities. "Everything from music to biochemical engineering and anything and everything in between" is available. "You name it and we've got it," guarantees an English major. "The size of campus can be in some ways intimidating," though. It's a "cattle call" here. Classes are often enormous, and it can be hard to get the ones you want. Also, while "the administration seems to run the school fairly smoothly," "red tape" is a problem. "If you want to do anything out of the ordinary, such as apply a scholarship to the summer quarter, or take a leave of absence, it is very difficult." "You have to kind of fend for yourself to figure out how the school works." "OSU is not a school which holds your hand though planning and logistical matters," cautions a business major. The general education curriculum is unpopular with many students, but Ohio State is on a quarter system and coursework moves pretty fast. Any class you don't like will be over relatively quickly. Some professors are "incredibly eager to work with students" and are "as interesting and entertaining as they can be when lecturing." "There are a lot of mediocre professors," too. Still other faculty members are "too wrapped up in their research" and "don't pay attention to whether the students are learning or not." Also, just like at any big state school, there are plenty of teaching assistants here and they are "sometimes sub par."

Life

For many students, life at Ohio State comes down to "drinking and sports." The entire campus is fulled up with "a ton of Buckeye spirit." "Attending the varsity sports events is popular." "Everyone is obsessed with Buckeye football." It's a little bit "like a religion" and the team is "idolized." Students also "party a lot in general." "It's hard to tell exactly how many people really are partying," explains a senior. "It just seems like a lot." For many students, "awesome" house parties "are the preferred medium" for social activity, but there is "always a party, always a bar" "Thursday through Saturday." "There are other scenes than just the party scene," of course. The "great" recreation center here is absolutely gargantuan. "There is always an interesting event, conference, or performance," and OSU brings in plenty of "big entertainment acts." There are about 800 student organizations as well. "Greek life here isn't dominant" but it's noticeable and a few thousand students are involved. "It's impossible to not find something that fits you," promises a senior. "You're never bored." Off campus, Columbus boasts a population of over one million souls and "is its own city." Many students "gallery hop in the art district" or regularly take advantage of the area's "great shopping."

Student Body

"It's hard to categorize students here," says a sophomore. The vibe is "middle class" and "very Midwestern," and just about everyone is either "from small Ohio towns" or from "from a suburban-type setting" around Columbus, Toledo, Cincinnati, or Cleveland. Otherwise, "Ohio State is a melting pot," and "it easy to blend into the crowd." "There is no real homogenous, average student." Several ethnic minorities are solidly represented. Many students dress "like they shopped in a department store, albeit a nice department store," observes a senior. "There is a lot of style and fashion walking around campus," too. There are also hordes of students clad in "OSU clothing." A huge contingent of students is "smart, outgoing, athletic, and involved," but "the stereotypical weird kids at other universities have several hundred like-minded classmates at OSU." There are "drunks, nerds, overachievers, underachievers," "artists," outcasts, and hippies. Many students are "working a job or two." "The large community provides diversity," relates a senior. "However, we have our own smaller communities to help campus feel like home."

THE OHIO STATE UNIVERSITY—COLUMBUS

FINANCIAL AID: 614-292-0300 • E-MAIL: ASKABUCKEYE@OSU.EDU (FRESHMEN AND TRANSFER)• WEBSITE: WWW.OSU.EDU

THE PRINCETON REVIEW SAYS

Admissions

Very important factors considered include: Class rank, academic GPA, rigor of secondary school record, standardized test scores. *Important factors considered include:* Application essay, extracurricular activities, first generation, talent/ability, volunteer work, work experience. *Other factors considered include:* Recommendation(s), character/personal qualities, geographical residence, racial/ethnic status, state residency, SAT or ACT required; ACT with Writing component required. TOEFL required of all international applicants. High school diploma is required and GED is accepted. *Academic units required:* 4 English, 3 mathematics, 2 science, (2 science labs), 2 foreign language, 2 social studies, 1 academic elective, 1 visual and performing Arts. *Academic units recommended:* 4 English, 4 mathematics, 4 science, (3 science labs), 3 foreign language, 3 social studies, 1 academic elective, 1 visual and performing arts.

Financial Aid

Students should submit: FAFSA. The Princeton Review suggests that all financial aid forms be submitted as soon as possible after January 1. *Need-based scholarships/grants offered:* Federal Pell, SEOG, state scholarships/grants, private scholarships, the school's own gift aid. *Loan aid offered:* Direct Subsidized Stafford, Direct Unsubsidized Stafford, Direct PLUS, Federal Perkins, Federal Nursing, college/university loans from institutional funds. Applicants will be notified of awards on or about 4/5.

The Inside Word

Although the admissions staff takes extracurricular activities and other personal characteristics into account, the sheer volume of applications usually makes anything more than a cursory look impractical. Mostly, there is a heavy emphasis on numbers—grades, class rank, and test scores. Standards are high, but OSU is certainly worth a shot for the average student. The university's great reputation and affordable cost make it a good choice for anyone looking at large schools.

THE SCHOOL SAYS "..."

From The Admissions Office

"Few universities have changed as much as the Ohio State University has in the last decade. Ohio State has undergone a physical transformation, attracted undergraduates of exceptional scholarly talent, and seen its reputation for academic excellence thrive.

"Despite remarkable rankings in most academic programs, the true strength of Ohio State's academic experience is the dialogue between faculty and students that is rarely found among large, research universities.

"With each incoming class, a new academic standard is set as the quality of its students reaches new heights. One of the nation's richest First-Year Experience programs helps students transition from talented freshmen to distinguished graduates.

"Ohio State is undergoing unprecedented physical change. The Fisher College of Business complex has been joined by a unique World Media and Culture Center, the $30 million Knowlton School of Architecture, two state-of-the-art recreation centers, and even a university-dedicated highway exit. The university's commitment to both tradition and technology make Ohio State an historic and modern atmosphere in which to learn.

"Although Ohio State is a university of change, it still has phenomenal faculty, incredible programs, competitive tuition, supportive environments, and distinctive tradition. Students never lack for something to do or fail to find a unique place. Whether participating in one of 650 student organizations, attending a lecture by a renowned author or politician, or simply sitting on the Oval, students find their niche at Ohio State, and become part of its living history.

"Students applying for admission are required to submit one writing score (SAT or the ACT with Writing) in order for their applications to be considered complete. The Writing score will not be used to determine admissibility for students entering in 2008. It will be used for research purposes only."

SELECTIVITY

Admissions Rating	86
# of applicants	18,286
% of applicants accepted	68
% of acceptees attending	51
# accepting a place on wait list	149
% admitted from wait list	2

FRESHMAN PROFILE

Range SAT Critical Reading	530–640
Range SAT Math	560–670
Range SAT Writing	520–630
Range ACT Composite	24–29
Minimum paper TOEFL	527
Minimum computer TOEFL	197
% graduated top 10% of class	43
% graduated top 25% of class	80
% graduated top 50% of class	98

DEADLINES

Regular	
Deadline	2/1
Notification	rolling
Nonfall registration?	yes

APPLICANTS ALSO LOOK AT AND OFTEN PREFER

Purdue University—West Lafayette
University of Cincinnati
Ohio University—Athens
Bowling Green State University
Case Western Reserve University
Miami University

FINANCIAL FACTS

Financial Aid Rating	72
Annual in-state tuition	$8,676
% frosh rec. need-based scholarship or grant aid	52
% UG rec. need-based scholarship or grant aid	46
% frosh rec. non-need-based scholarship or grant aid	4
% UG rec. non-need-based scholarship or grant aid	2
% frosh rec. need-based self-help aid	46
% UG rec. need-based self-help aid	48
% frosh rec. athletic scholarships	1
% UG rec. athletic scholarships	1
% frosh rec. any financial aid	54
% UG rec. any financial aid	49
% UG borrow to pay for school	58
Average cumulative indebtedness	$17,821

OHIO UNIVERSITY—ATHENS

120 CHUBB HALL, ATHENS, OH 45701 • ADMISSIONS: 740-593-4100 • FAX: 740-593-0560

STUDENTS SAY ". . ."

Academics

OU has a well-deserved reputation for wild parties, but that's hardly all there is to the school; as one student explains, "OU will give you the college experience you want. If you want a good education, it's there for the taking. If you want to mess around, get drunk, high and just party, well, you will definitely be able to get that. If you want a great education while still having a lot of fun, there is no better place than OU." Serious students will find "enclaves of intellectual curiosity" amid the slackers and revelers, especially in the Honors Tutorial College, "the greatest strength of OU." Writes one participant, "Without it, OU would be just another state school with some decent programs." Top programs here include "nationally respected schools in journalism, the arts, and business," and "a good communications program." Across all disciplines students "have a lot of great facilities and resources to use," including professors who "are very intelligent and passionate about what they are teaching. Most are accessible and eager to help, but of course there are the occasional professors here simply treating it as a job and not a passion." OU operates on a quarterly academic calendar, meaning that academic demands can occasionally be "utter hell, as in caught-in-a-bathtub-with-a-bleeding-iguana-and-a-piranha hell." Some feel that "considering we are on quarters, sometimes I don't feel like I retain that much information" from classes. Even so, academics are generally manageable; as one student puts it, "There have been a handful of classes that blew me away (in a good way) and a handful that made me feel like I was in high school, while the rest fall somewhere in between."

Life

Not all OU students party out of bounds, but enough students love to recreate that "On the weekends you could definitely find a party anywhere on campus, and all the bars are packed, especially on game nights." The school throws a number of organized campus-wide parties, including a legendary Halloween festival that involves "the largest block party in the US." "No one misses out on Halloween. Even the graduates come back," one student reports. The OU party scene is large but it's not the only game in town: While "many people in Athens look forward to getting smashed every weekend, an alarmingly large number of students do not. There are a great many critical thinkers and politically active people on campus. Many people just sit around and drink, but others go to Donkey Coffee and Espresso, spend time in the library, and hang out with friends." Hometown Athens is small but has an active music scene; "Rock, punk and folk bands flourish in the many bars and cafes downtown." Also, "The university offers several social activities that do not revolve around drinking—comedy sketches, theater and music."

Student Body

"The typical student at Ohio University is white upper-middle class," "but there are growing African American and Asian American populations" and "Students from lower incomes are increasing because of a new scholarship enacted for students who live in the Appalachians." A panoramic snapshot of the student body would still look pretty homogeneous—with the typical student fitting "the frat boy stereotype"—but if you pull in closer you'll find "numerous groups and individuals to encounter. They may not be the major organizations on campus, but you'll certainly be able to find a place to fit in via talking to people and seeing flyers around campus." Size helps; with more than 16,000 undergrads there are enough folks to support almost any subpopulation, including "a large and active gay population that for the most part is accepted by the students and faculty of the university."

FINANCIAL AID: 740-593-4141 • E-MAIL: ADMISSIONS.FRESHMEN@OHIOU.EDU • WEBSITE: WWW.OHIOU.EDU

THE PRINCETON REVIEW SAYS

Admissions

Very important factors considered include: Academic GPA, rigor of secondary school record. *Important factors considered include:* Class rank, standardized test scores. *Other factors considered include:* Application essay, recommendation(s), alumni/ae relation, character/personal qualities, extracurricular activities, racial/ethnic status, talent/ability, volunteer work, work experience. SAT or ACT required; High school diploma is required and GED is accepted. *Academic units required:* 4 English, 3 mathematics, 3 science, 2 foreign language, 3 social studies, 1 Visual or Performing Arts.

Financial Aid

Students should submit: FAFSA Regular filing deadline is 3/15. The Princeton Review suggests that all financial aid forms be submitted as soon as possible after January 1. *Need-based scholarships/grants offered:* Federal Pell, SEOG, state scholarships/grants, private scholarships, the school's own gift aid. *Loan aid offered:* Direct Subsidized Stafford, Direct Unsubsidized Stafford, Direct PLUS, Federal Perkins, Institutional short term loans are repaid in 30-60 days. Applicants will be notified of awards on or about 4/1.

The Inside Word

It's pretty much a numbers game at OU. Meet the targets on your standardized test scores and high school grades and you're in; fall short and you'll have to compensate elsewhere or make other plans for college. Marginal students may wish to submit a raft of optional materials including essays, a list of extracurricular activities, and descriptions of honors, awards, and achievements. At the very least the extra materials will signal admissions that you're serious about getting in. In a best-case scenario, the supplemental materials will counter poor numbers and cause an admissions officer to give your entire application a thorough review.

THE SCHOOL SAYS "..."

From The Admissions Office

"Pursuing your academic studies at Ohio University means immersing yourself in the quintessential college experience. The tree-lined streets and rolling hills of Athens provide a picture-perfect backdrop for this historic campus beloved for its brick paths and stately Georgian architecture. Live and learn in this classic, residential college town and you join a tight-knit academic community of faculty and student scholars who are welcoming, intellectually challenging, and civic-minded.

"Ohio is highly regarded for the strength of it undergraduate and graduate programs. As the oldest college in Ohio and the entire Northwest Territory, Ohio University offers an irrefutable history of academic excellence and prominence. Our students' success in winning many of the nation's most prestigious and competitive academic awards is at a record high. Our total number of Fulbright winners, for example, currently ranks us first in the state for the fourth straight year and ties us with the likes of Boston College, Princeton, and UCLA. The Honors Tutorial College is the only degree-granting college of its kind in the country and mirrors the same one-on-one tutorial system practiced for centuries Cambridge and Oxford. Close faculty mentoring and personal involvement is a university value that benefits all Ohio students.

"Visit our campus and you'll discover why students' first and lasting impression of Ohio University is 'It's what I always dreamed college would be.'"

SELECTIVITY

Admissions Rating	75
# of applicants	13,020
% of applicants accepted	82
% of acceptees attending	38

FRESHMAN PROFILE

Range SAT Critical Reading	480–600
Range SAT Math	490–600
Range SAT Writing	480–580
Range ACT Composite	21–26
Average HS GPA	3.34
% graduated top 10% of class	15
% graduated top 25% of class	41
% graduated top 50% of class	83

DEADLINES

Regular	
Deadline	2/1
Notification	rolling
Nonfall registration?	yes

FINANCIAL FACTS

Financial Aid Rating	65
Annual in-state tuition	$8,907
Annual out-of-state tuition	$17,871
Room and board	$8,427
Books and supplies	$870
% frosh rec. need-based scholarship or grant aid	24
% UG rec. need-based scholarship or grant aid	22
% frosh rec. non-need-based scholarship or grant aid	31
% UG rec. non-need-based scholarship or grant aid	20
% frosh rec. need-based self-help aid	48
% UG rec. need-based self-help aid	43
% frosh rec. athletic scholarships	2
% UG rec. athletic scholarships	2
% frosh rec. any financial aid	48
% UG rec. any financial aid	45
% UG borrow to pay for school	65
Average cumulative indebtedness	$20,880

OHIO WESLEYAN UNIVERSITY

ADMISSIONS OFFICE, 61 SOUTH SANDUSKY STREET, DELAWARE, OH 43015 • ADMISSIONS: 740-368-3020 • FAX: 740-368-3314

STUDENTS SAY ". . ."

Academics

Students at Ohio Wesleyan University describe it as "a combination of all the things one might look for in a school. It isn't too small, but it isn't too big; it isn't too rural, but it also isn't too urban; it has a big focus on academics, but there is plenty of partying to be done, too. It seems to, and does, have the best of all worlds." An "excellent Science Department" is the star of the show here, with "professors who are amazing, very friendly and approachable, and always willing to help you and share their own knowledge, research, and insights." But the school also boasts a "reputable psychology program," strong Music and Foreign Language Departments, and "a great education program that sets you up for a job after 4 years." OWU undergrads warn that "classes are small, but the workload and intellectual participation required from students are rigorous. Making good grades here is really an achievement, and it won't happen without a lot of work." The environment at the school is "supportive but not coddling; students are expected to manage most of their own affairs. That said, professors and administrators are more than willing to provide whatever help they can." Dedicated professors will even spend free time "advising students on independent studies, even when they have no obligation to do so. They are interested in teaching and talking about what they know."

Life

OWU "is in a very small town, so don't expect packed dance clubs or huge theater productions." There are "two downtown bars that are popular hangout spots, and there are a few pretty good restaurants that are frequented by students," but students claim that this is about it for hometown Delaware. The small-town location makes life here "highly residential, with lots of activities centered [on] campus life." That life can include "a lot of drinking" for some, "But if you're not into it, there are other things you can do," including "different lectures and speakers to go to during the week," "the Strand, which is the university-owned movie theater in town," and "lots of shows, bands, and comedians." Those who find their way into the Small Living Units (SLU), nine "themed houses" based on specific areas of study or extracurricular interests, usually become deeply involved in their residential communities. One such student writes, "We at the House of Peace and Justice focus on promoting social justice activism on campus and educating students about world events." Columbus is less than a half-hour drive from the school, so "If you have a car, there is more to do than if you don't." But even for those who can't get off campus, "There is always some event happening."

Student Body

"The high percentage of international students" is one factor that causes OWU students to describe the school as "very diverse," although they also acknowledge the presence of "your usual preps with popped-up collars." As one student puts it, this "snobby, preppy image" is in fact "a stereotype that belies the camaraderie that really pervades the campus." The school's "Numerous student organizations facilitate cross-cultural discourse. OWU is also very GBLT friendly, with sexual identity courses and discussion forums a regular aspect of OWU's social and cultural scene." One student observes, "It is not unusual to see people walking around with mohawks, or to see people walking around in seersuckers." In other words, "There's a place here for everyone."

FINANCIAL AID: 740-368-3050 • E-MAIL: OWUADMIT@OWU.EDU • WEBSITE: WWW.OWU.EDU

THE PRINCETON REVIEW SAYS

Admissions

Very important factors considered include: Application essay, academic GPA, recommendation(s), rigor of secondary school record, character/personal qualities, interview. *Important factors considered include:* Class rank, standardized test scores, extracurricular activities, talent/ability. *Other factors considered include:* Alumni/ae relation, first generation, geographical residence, level of applicant's interest, racial/ethnic status, volunteer work, work experience. SAT or ACT required; TOEFL required of all international applicants. High school diploma is required and GED is accepted. *Academic units required:* 4 English, 3 mathematics, 3 science, 2 foreign language, 3 social studies. *Academic units recommended:* 4 mathematics, 4 science, 3 foreign language, 4 social studies.

Financial Aid

Students should submit: FAFSA, institution's own financial aid form. Regular filing deadline is 5/1. The Princeton Review suggests that all financial aid forms be submitted as soon as possible after January 1. *Need-based scholarships/grants offered:* Federal Pell, SEOG, state scholarships/grants, private scholarships, the school's own gift aid. *Loan aid offered:* FFEL Subsidized Stafford, FFEL Unsubsidized Stafford, FFEL PLUS, Federal Perkins, college/university loans from institutional funds. Applicants will be notified of awards on a rolling basis beginning 2/15. Federal Work-Study Program available. Institutional employment available. Off-campus job opportunities are excellent.

The Inside Word

Ohio Wesleyan takes a multitude of factors into consideration when examining applicants, and prospective students are expected to put a great deal of thought into every facet of the application. Notably, all candidates are automatically considered for merit-based scholarships.

THE SCHOOL SAYS "..."

From The Admissions Office

"Balance and opportunity describe Ohio Wesleyan. Males make up 48 percent of the student body. There are 35 percent of all students who are members of Greek life. Eight percent of all students are international and 8 percent of them are U.S. minorities. Exceptional teaching and academics are hallmarks of an OWU education, and features such as the Woltemade Center for Economics, Business and Entrepreneurship, and the Arneson Institute for Practical Politics set us apart from other institutions of our kind. OWU houses a newly renovated $34-million science center and newly renovated fine art facilities. Our mission places a premium on community service-learning and interactive learning with more than 85 percent of students participating in community-service activities before graduation. Our annual Sagan National Colloquium is a semester-long program that brings leaders in academics, business, science, and the arts to campus for lectures, panel discussions, readings, exhibits, and performances related to a selected topic of importance to the community and the world. Ohio Wesleyan University is a competitive member of NCAA Division III and the North Coast Athletic Conference, with three National Championships in soccer in the last 6 years.

"Ohio Wesleyan is located in a small-town setting and is near Columbus, the state capital and the sixteenth-largest city in the United States.

"Applicants for Fall 2008 may submit the old SAT (taken before March 2005), the new SAT, or both. Best scores from either test will be considered in the application review. Additionally, students may submit the ACT in lieu of the SAT."

SELECTIVITY

Admissions Rating	86
# of applicants	3,814
% of applicants accepted	66
% of acceptees attending	23
# accepting a place on wait list	12
% admitted from wait list	50
# of early decision applicants	53
% accepted early decision	32

FRESHMAN PROFILE

Range SAT Critical Reading	530–650
Range SAT Math	540–650
Range ACT Composite	24–29
Minimum paper TOEFL	550
Minimum computer TOEFL	213
Average HS GPA	3.27
% graduated top 10% of class	26
% graduated top 25% of class	49
% graduated top 50% of class	79

DEADLINES

Early decision	
Deadline	12/1
Notification	12/15
Early action	
Deadline	12/15
Notification	1/15
Regular	
Priority	3/1
Notification	rolling
Nonfall registration?	yes

APPLICANTS ALSO LOOK AT

AND OFTEN PREFER
Denison University
College of Wooster
Miami University (OH)

AND SOMETIMES PREFER
Rhodes College
Allegheny College

FINANCIAL FACTS

Financial Aid Rating	81
Annual tuition	$31,510
Room and board	$8,030
Required fees	$420
Books and supplies	$2,050
% frosh rec. need-based scholarship or grant aid	60
% UG rec. need-based scholarship or grant aid	56
% frosh rec. non-need-based scholarship or grant aid	11
% UG rec. non-need-based scholarship or grant aid	9
% frosh rec. need-based self-help aid	50
% UG rec. need-based self-help aid	47
% frosh rec. any financial aid	99
% UG rec. any financial aid	98
% UG borrow to pay for school	76
Average cumulative indebtedness	$25,627

PENNSYLVANIA STATE UNIVERSITY—UNIVERSITY PARK

201 SHIELDS BUILDING, BOX 3000, UNIVERSITY PARK, PA 16802-3000 • ADMISSIONS: 814-865-5471 • FAX: 814-863-7590

CAMPUS LIFE

Quality of Life Rating	**84**
Fire Safety Rating	**94**
Green Rating	**97**
Type of school	public
Environment	town

STUDENTS

Total undergrad enrollment	35,876
% male/female	55/45
% from out of state	24
% live on campus	36
% in (# of) fraternities	12 (53)
% in (# of) sororities	11 (34)
% African American	4
% Asian	5
% Caucasian	84
% Hispanic	4
% international	2
# of countries represented	121

SURVEY SAYS . . .

Great library
Athletic facilities are great
Everyone loves the Nittany Lions
Intramural sports are popular
Student publications are popular
Lots of beer drinking
Hard liquor is popular

ACADEMICS

Academic Rating	**74**
Calendar	semester
Student/faculty ratio	17:1
Profs interesting rating	65
Profs accessible rating	65
Most common reg class size	20–29 students
Most common lab size	20–29 students

MOST POPULAR MAJORS

engineering
business administration and
management

STUDENTS SAY ". . ."

Academics

At Penn State "You can do anything you want" academically because with "over 160 majors" to choose from, "There are unlimited opportunities" for every undergraduate. Such vast resources are typical of a sprawling public flagship university, but it's the personal touches that leave students "pretty impressed with how such a large school can run like a small one." For example, "Professors do a lot to facilitate personal interactions." They are "really easy to talk to both in and out of class, and they're always accessible." Unfortunately, it's not always a professor students end up with: "They do use a lot of teaching assistants, which can get frustrating." Still, professors are "thought-provoking" and "You can tell that a lot of them really do want to be teaching." If you can manage to get into it, the Schreyer Honors College's "rigorous" curriculum presents "tremendous opportunities." In addition to more challenging courses, it "offers incredible amounts of money for study abroad, internships, and faculty co-ops," and its students get perks like "priority registration for classes." Administratively, "Penn State is a huge machine . . . run with amazing efficiency." Credit is given to President Graham Spanier, who is praised for not only "holding office hours" and "responding personally to e-mails," but also for being "very involved in student life." Despite having "created Late-Night Penn State and the News Readership Program," he also finds time to be the "advisor to the magician's club" and "play the washboard in a bar downtown." Perhaps the greatest long-term benefit of a Penn State education is "the social networking." With an alumni association of over 159,000 members and growing, opportunities for success through networking are "well in your favor" at Penn State.

Life

At a university this size, "you can do anything and everything" in your free time. There are, however, a couple of common threads. First, "PSU football is a religion." During the fall, "Everyone goes to the football games and tailgates on Saturdays." Second, is the partying. "People party as hard on the weekends as they study during the week." "Popular choices" for freshmen and sophomores are "frat or apartment parties," while "For those over 21, Penn State's College Avenue has a great range of over 20 bars for students to choose from." However, "If someone is not a partier, there are plenty of activities and organizations" he or she can devote her time to. For example, "substance-free activities that occur during the weekends at the Student Union (such as movies, video game tournaments, concerts)" are alternatives for those that decline to imbibe. In terms of extracurriculars, the options are practically endless. According to several students, "with over 700 student clubs and organizations, there's something for everyone" at Penn State, offering "virtually limitless possibilities to carve out your own corner" and "help students get involved, build a resume, and network."

Student Body

"There is a bit of everything" on this huge campus in the center of the Keystone State. That's why some students find it so difficult to describe their peers succinctly. Rather than a "typical" student at Penn State, for some survey respondents it makes more sense to describe the school's "multitude of groups of 'atypical' students: frat boys . . . jocks, internationals, loners, skaters . . . 'jokers, smokers, midnight tokers' . . . city kids, rednecks, country bumpkins, and so on." In this way, "It's like a large high school, where everyone is in their own group." So "if you come to Penn State, don't worry about finding friends because there is someone up here for everyone." Yet even "Though there are a lot of differences, everyone wears blue and white on their sleeve." Ultimately, "All Penn State students . . . love this college."

FINANCIAL AID: 814-865-6301 • E-MAIL: ADMISSIONS@PSU.EDU • WEBSITE: WWW.PSU.EDU

THE PRINCETON REVIEW SAYS
Admissions
Very important factors considered include: Academic GPA, standardized test scores. *Important factors considered include:* Rigor of secondary school record. *Other factors considered include:* Class rank, application essay, recommendation(s), alumni/ae relation, character/personal qualities, extracurricular activities, talent/ability, volunteer work, work experience. SAT or ACT required; ACT with Writing component required. TOEFL required of all international applicants. High school diploma is required and GED is accepted. *Academic units required:* 4 English, 3 mathematics, 3 science, 2 foreign language, 3 social studies.

Financial Aid
Students should submit: FAFSA. The Princeton Review suggests that all financial aid forms be submitted as soon as possible after January 1. *Need-based scholarships/grants offered:* Federal Pell, SEOG, state scholarships/grants, private scholarships, the school's own gift aid. *Loan aid offered:* FFEL Subsidized Stafford, FFEL Unsubsidized Stafford, FFEL PLUS, Federal Perkins, college/university loans from institutional funds, Private Loans. Applicants will be notified of awards on a rolling basis beginning 3/1. Federal Work-Study Program available. Institutional employment available. Off-campus job opportunities are good.

The Inside Word
Penn State evaluates applications on a rolling basis. As it is the first choice of a lot of students, the Admissions Office's recommended filing date for applications is about the same time as many other schools' early application deadlines—keep this in mind to avoid the cut-off date. In terms of what factors weigh heavily in terms of admissions decisions, Penn State is quite open, though high school GPA is paramount to securing your blue and white bid.

THE SCHOOL SAYS "..."
From The Admissions Office
"Unique among large public universities, Penn State combines the over-35,000-student setting of its University Park campus with 20 academically and administratively integrated undergraduate locations—small-college settings ranging in size from 600 to 3,400 students. Each year, more than 60 percent of incoming freshmen begin their studies at these residential and commuter campuses, while nearly 40 percent begin at the University Park campus. The smaller locations focus on the needs of new students by offering the first 2 years of most Penn State baccalaureate degrees in settings that stress close interaction with faculty. Depending on the major selected, students may choose to complete their degree at University Park or one of the smaller locations. Your application to Penn State qualifies you for review for any of our campuses. Your two choices of location are reviewed in the order given. Entrance difficulty is based, in part, on the demand. Due to its popularity, the University Park campus is the most competitive for admission.

"Freshman applicants for Fall 2008 may submit the results from the current version of the SAT, the current ACT, the new version of the SAT, or the results of the new ACT with Writing test. The Writing portions of these tests will not necessarily be factored into admission decisions."

SELECTIVITY
Admissions Rating	91
# of applicants	39,551
% of applicants accepted	51
% of acceptees attending	32
# accepting a place on wait list	1,704
% admitted from wait list	80

FRESHMAN PROFILE
Range SAT Critical Reading	530–630
Range SAT Math	560–670
Minimum paper TOEFL	550
Minimum computer TOEFL	213
Minimum web-based TOEFL	80
Average HS GPA	3.58
% graduated top 10% of class	44.65
% graduated top 25% of class	81.3
% graduated top 50% of class	97.44

DEADLINES
Regular	
Priority	11/30
Notification	rolling
Nonfall registration?	yes

APPLICANTS ALSO LOOK AT
AND OFTEN PREFER
University of Maryland—College Park
University of Michigan—Ann Arbor
Cornell University
Lehigh University
AND SOMETIMES PREFER
University of Virginia
Johns Hopkins University
Harvard College
Emory University

FINANCIAL FACTS
Financial Aid Rating	66
Annual in-state tuition	$12,284
Annual out-of-state tuition	$23,152
Room and board	$7,180
Required fees	$560
Books and supplies	$1,168
% frosh rec. need-based scholarship or grant aid	24
% UG rec. need-based scholarship or grant aid	30
% frosh rec. non-need-based scholarship or grant aid	20
% UG rec. non-need-based scholarship or grant aid	17
% frosh rec. need-based self-help aid	37
% UG rec. need-based self-help aid	42
% frosh rec. athletic scholarships	2
% UG rec. athletic scholarships	2
% frosh rec. any financial aid	75
% UG rec. any financial aid	73
% UG borrow to pay for school	67
Average cumulative indebtedness	$26,300

PEPPERDINE UNIVERSITY

24255 PACIFIC COAST HIGHWAY, MALIBU, CA 90263-4392 • ADMISSIONS: 310-456-4861 • FAX: 310-506-4861

CAMPUS LIFE
Quality of Life Rating	**92**
Fire Safety Rating	**70**
Green Rating	**80**
Type of school	private
Affiliation	Church of Christ
Environment	city

STUDENTS
Total undergrad enrollment	3,381
% male/female	44/56
% from out of state	50
% live on campus	67
% in (# of) fraternities	18 (5)
% in (# of) sororities	33 (7)
% African American	7
% Asian	10
% Caucasian	59
% Hispanic	10
% Native American	1
% international	6

SURVEY SAYS . . .
Lab facilities are great
Great computer facilities
Students are friendly
Dorms are like palaces
Campus feels safe
Students are happy

ACADEMICS
Academic Rating	**88**
Calendar	semester
Student/faculty ratio	13:1
Profs interesting rating	87
Profs accessible rating	88
Most common reg class size	10–19 students
Most common lab size	fewer than 10 students

MOST POPULAR MAJORS
business administration and management
communication/journalism
social sciences

STUDENTS SAY ". . ."

Academics

Pepperdine University, in sunny, "calm" Malibu, California, is a smaller liberal arts school affiliated with the Churches of Christ "where students are given numerous opportunities to mature and develop academically in a spiritually nurturing environment." "Christian values" are unmistakable here. Attendance at chapel is required and the mandatory core curriculum (which includes an optional, highly recommended Great Books sequence) involves religion courses. The faculty is "pretty much all Christian" as well and, while "some of the professors need to be fired," most are "challenging" and "truly passionate." "My professors have all been excellent with the exception of maybe two in all my four years," says a biology major, "and they really look out for their students." The administration is full of "religious zealots" who "tend to shelter students way too much," but staffers all the way up to the top brass are "very easy to communicate with" and the school is "very well managed." "You feel like a student and not a number at Pepperdine," says a journalism major. Study abroad programs in Germany, Hong Kong, France, Argentina, and a host of other places far flung are reportedly "beyond compare." About half the undergrads here go overseas at least once. "Right now, I'm studying abroad in Switzerland and loving every minute of it," declares an advertising major.

Life

The gym is pretty bad and "the food is far too expensive for its quality." However, "the dorms are very nice," and students at Pepperdine enjoy "amazing weather" and a "uniquely breathtaking" campus "with a killer view" of the ocean. During the week, life is "vibrant." "Speakers and musicians come to campus" frequently, and "students are very active with organizations, clubs, and social life in general." "Sororities and fraternities are really big at Pepperdine," and some students "party like rock stars." Be warned, though: Drug and alcohol policies are "zero tolerance." "Rarely do students drink on campus," says a junior. "It's a big risk." There are "curfew rules" and "restrictions for when opposite genders can be in one another's rooms," too. Mostly, students "go off campus if they want to get wild and crazy," and the parties tend to be "fairly exclusive." Many students avoid the party scene altogether. "Instead we go out to dinner, go stargazing, have political discussions, go shopping, or catch the latest movies," explains a proudly sober senior. "Church-related functions" are also popular and the there is "a big emphasis on service." The number of volunteer opportunities is "almost overwhelming." Outdoor activities are outrageously abundant, too. "Running into celebs at local restaurants and businesses is pretty cool" in the glitzy surrounding enclave of Malibu, but otherwise it's "pricey" and "everything closes down at 10:00 P.M." "Even the beauty of the Pacific, sadly, can become old." Santa Monica and Hollywood aren't terribly far but Pepperdine often feels "totally isolated." Having your own car is "almost necessary."

Student Body

"There are many students receiving financial aid" here. "It's mostly white and rich and, if not white, just rich," though. Pepperdine has its "fair share of millionaires' kids and minor celebrities." "Appearances and brand names are important" and the atmosphere is "somewhat superficial." "There are two types at Pepperdine," suggests a sophomore, "the type who has a scholarship or financial aid and is exceedingly intelligent and the type who is pretty stupid but whose parents pay full tuition to the school and give them BMW's and beach houses." Politically, conservatives tend to dominate. Many, many students are "active Christians." Some are "Church of Christ diehards" "who are totally on fire for God." Pepperdine students are also "sun-kissed" and "very beautiful," if they don't mind saying so themselves. They're "social," "excited about life," and "high in character" as well. There are surfers, athletes, frat boys, "Barbie girls," quite a few Texans, and some "eclectic" students but, all in all, it's a "slightly preppy" and "typical Southern Californian" crowd. "Not very many people who attend this school are unique or radical or experimental in any way."

FINANCIAL AID: 310-506-4301 • E-MAIL: ADMISSION-SEAVER@PEPPERDINE.EDU • WEBSITE: WWW.PEPPERDINE.EDU

THE PRINCETON REVIEW SAYS

Admissions

Very important factors considered include: Application essay, academic GPA, recommendation(s), rigor of secondary school record, standardized test scores, character/personal qualities, extracurricular activities, talent/ability. *Important factors considered include:* Religious affiliation/commitment, volunteer work. *Other factors considered include:* Alumni/ae relation, first generation, racial/ethnic status, work experience. SAT or ACT required; ACT with Writing component required. TOEFL required of all international applicants. High school diploma is required and GED is accepted. *Academic units recommended:* 4 English, 4 mathematics, 4 science, (3 science labs), 3 foreign language, 3 social studies, 3 history, 3 academic electives, 1 speech.

Financial Aid

Students should submit: FAFSA, institution's own financial aid form. Regular filing deadline is 2/15. The Princeton Review suggests that all financial aid forms be submitted as soon as possible after January 1. *Need-based scholarships/grants offered:* Federal Pell, SEOG, state scholarships/grants, private scholarships, the school's own gift aid, United Negro College Fund, *Loan aid offered:* FFEL Subsidized Stafford, FFEL Unsubsidized Stafford, FFEL PLUS, Federal Perkins, college/university loans from institutional funds. Applicants will be notified of awards on or about 4/15. Federal Work-Study Program available. Institutional employment available. Off-campus job opportunities are good.

The Inside Word

A stunning physical location enables the Admissions Office to produce beautiful catalogs and viewbooks, which, when combined with the university's reputation for academic quality, help to attract a large applicant pool. In addition to solid grades and test scores, successful applicants typically have well-rounded extracurricular backgrounds. Involvement in school, church, and community is an overused cliché in the world of college admissions, but at Pepperdine it's definitely one of the ingredients in successful applications.

THE SCHOOL SAYS "..."

From The Admissions Office

"As a selective university, Pepperdine seeks students who show promise of academic achievement at the collegiate level. However, we also seek students who are committed to serving the university community, as well as others with whom they come into contact. We look for community-service activities, volunteer efforts, and strong leadership qualities, as well as a demonstrated commitment to academic studies and an interest in the liberal arts.

"Seaver College of Pepperdine University requires freshman applicants to submit scores from either the Scholastic Aptitude Test (SAT Reasoning Test including the Writing portion) or the American College Test (ACT) (including the Writing test). The scores are evaluated in conjunction with the grade point average in specific courses completed."

SELECTIVITY

Admissions Rating	94
# of applicants	6,661
% of applicants accepted	35
% of acceptees attending	33
# accepting a place on wait list	389
% admitted from wait list	3

FRESHMAN PROFILE

Range SAT Critical Reading	560–670
Range SAT Math	570–680
Range SAT Writing	560–670
Range ACT Composite	24–29
Minimum paper TOEFL	550
Minimum computer TOEFL	220
Minimum web-based TOEFL	80
Average HS GPA	3.65
% graduated top 10% of class	46
% graduated top 25% of class	74
% graduated top 50% of class	95

DEADLINES

Regular	
Priority	11/15
Deadline	1/15
Notification	4/1
Nonfall registration?	yes

APPLICANTS ALSO LOOK AT

AND OFTEN PREFER
University of Southern California
University of California—Los Angeles
University of San Diego
University of California—San Diego

AND SOMETIMES PREFER
Vanderbilt University
New York University

AND RARELY PREFER
Occidental College
Biola University

FINANCIAL FACTS

Financial Aid Rating	88
Annual tuition	$36,650
% frosh rec. need-based scholarship or grant aid	32
% UG rec. need-based scholarship or grant aid	32
% frosh rec. non-need-based scholarship or grant aid	7
% UG rec. non-need-based scholarship or grant aid	8
% frosh rec. need-based self-help aid	34
% UG rec. need-based self-help aid	32
% frosh rec. athletic scholarships	6
% UG rec. athletic scholarships	4
% frosh rec. any financial aid	35
% UG rec. any financial aid	34
% UG borrow to pay for school	62
Average cumulative indebtedness	$33,234

PITZER COLLEGE

1050 NORTH MILLS AVENUE, CLAREMONT, CA 91711-6101 • ADMISSIONS: 909-621-8129 • FAX: 909-621-8770

STUDENTS SAY ". . ."

Academics

Though the 60s-style academic buildings on the campus of Pitzer College "are not too visually appealing," "progressive learning" and academic flexibility abound. "People have to take courses within a couple of key areas, but within those areas the specific courses are not dictated," explains a history major. As a result, you can chart your own course "within enough of a structure to ensure that everyone gets a real liberal arts education." Students can also take courses at the "four other amazing colleges" that make up The Claremont Colleges consortium. "It's a great mix of a classic college experience and a small liberal arts oasis." Classes are "discussion-oriented" and "writing-based." Pitzer's professors are "really great at being accessible outside of class whether you want to talk about things related to the class, or anything else under the sun." "They are fascinating, helpful, warm people, who often have a wicked sense of humor," beams an art history major. While it can be difficult to determine "who is actually in charge of what," the "friendly" administration "makes sure the students play a real part" in everything from planning new construction to faculty tenure. Overall, Pitzer students seem extremely happy with their academic experience. "Pitzer is my own little utopia," confides a sociology major. "It just sucks I'm graduating."

Life

"Life at Pitzer College is very on-campus oriented." "Pitzer and the other Claremont Colleges strongly encourage campus life"—everything from guest lectures to deejays. Students "tend to enjoy the outdoors" as well. Biking is big, along with "surf trips" and hiking at Mount Baldy. "Most people are pretty involved, or at least they show up to a lot of stuff," says one student. "I play soccer and participate in the theater," comments another. "I go to Thursday night Groove at the Grove," says another. Other students "just do their own thing," which is cool too, because Pitzer is "the chillest place on Earth." The lifestyle is "Southern Californian." "The sun is always out and people are always on the mounds," deep in discussion. "There is always music and laughter to be found." "If you talk to the right people you can find the marijuana/free love culture, but on average people are pretty normal. On weekends people mostly hang out in small groups and goof around." While there's no Greek system, the social mood is festive. "Weekends start on Thursdays," though parties "mostly occur on the other campuses." Younger carousers "tend to go on the grand expeditions to find the party around the Five C's." "Upperclassmen tend to go off-campus to house parties." Complaints include the hit-or-miss housing situation. New green dorms were completed in fall 2007, but "the old dorms are getting a little funky." The "borderline inedible" campus food needs improvement. And "gossip spreads like wildfire" on this small campus. Getting away to the anonymous confines of nearby Los Angeles is always an option, but the trip "can be quite difficult" without a car.

Student Body

Students are "motivated" yet "very laidback." There is a strong sense of "togetherness and community." "Cliques are not as noticeable as in high school; everyone is simply friends with everyone." "The typical Pitzer student is rarely typical," observes an ironic anthropology major. "Everyone is a bit quirky but it seems like there's a sense of pride that comes with being labeled as a wacky Pitzer student." "We are all oddballs," adds one student. However, "as Pitzer has become increasingly more competitive over the years, the student body has gradually branched out from the 'tree-hugging stoner' prototype to include a wider array of students." "In my freshman class I would say we only have five to 20 true hippies," surveys a first-year student. Politically, while "you can experience a lot of diversity of thought" among the five Claremont Colleges, you'll be experiencing mostly liberalism here. "Pitzer is a haven for those who want to change the world" and students are "passionate about their personal causes." "The few conservatives on campus get a lot of grief, I'm sure," muses one student.

FINANCIAL AID: 909-621-8208 • E-MAIL: ADMISSION@PITZER.EDU • WEBSITE: WWW.PITZER.EDU

THE PRINCETON REVIEW SAYS

Admissions

Very important factors considered include: Class rank, application essay, academic GPA, recommendation(s), rigor of secondary school record, character/personal qualities, extracurricular activities, racial/ethnic status. *Important factors considered include:* First generation, geographical residence, interview, level of applicant's interest, talent/ability, volunteer work. *Other factors considered include:* Standardized test scores, alumni/ae relation, work experience. ACT with Writing component recommended. TOEFL required of all international applicants. High school diploma is required and GED is accepted. *Academic units required:* 4 English, 3 mathematics, 3 science, (3 science labs), 3 foreign language, 3 social studies, 1 history, 1 visual/performing arts.

Financial Aid

Students should submit: FAFSA, CSS/Financial Aid PROFILE, state aid form, noncustodial PROFILE, business/farm supplement. Regular filing deadline is 2/1. The Princeton Review suggests that all financial aid forms be submitted as soon as possible after January 1. *Need-based scholarships/grants offered:* Federal Pell, SEOG, state scholarships/grants, private scholarships, the school's own gift aid, ACG and National SMART. *Loan aid offered:* FFEL Subsidized Stafford, FFEL Unsubsidized Stafford, FFEL PLUS, Federal Perkins, college/university loans from institutional funds. Applicants will be notified of awards on or about 4/1. Federal Work-Study Program available. Institutional employment available. Off-campus job opportunities are fair.

The Inside Word

Pitzer emphasizes admissions essays, and it's no coincidence that unique students find themselves admitted here year after year. Let your thoughts flow freely when you write yours. Show the admissions committee what makes you who you are. Be passionate about whatever you are passionate about. What you have to say about yourself will go much further than numbers in determining your fate. Also worth noting: If you graduate in the top 10 percent of your high school class or have a 3.5 GPA (in your serious classes), you don't have to submit standardized test scores. You still can, but it's not required.

THE SCHOOL SAYS "..."

From The Admissions Office

"Pitzer is about opportunities. It's about possibilities. The students who come here are looking for something different from the usual 'take two courses from column A, two courses from column B, and two courses from column C.' That kind of arbitrary selection doesn't make a satisfying education at Pitzer. So we look for students who want to have an impact on their own education, who want the chief responsibility—with help from their faculty advisors—in designing their own futures.

"Pitzer's admission policy uses a test-optional policy. Students in the top 10 percent of their class or those who have an unweighted academic GPA of 3.5 or higher are not required to submit test scores. Others are allowed to choose from a variety of choices, including standardized tests (i.e., the new SAT and ACT with the Writing component)."

SELECTIVITY

Admissions Rating	90
# of applicants	3,748
% of applicants accepted	26
% of acceptees attending	25
# of early decision applicants	94
% accepted early decision	55

FRESHMAN PROFILE

Range SAT Critical Reading	570–680
Range SAT Math	550–650
Minimum paper TOEFL	520
Minimum web-based TOEFL	70
Average HS GPA	3.72
% graduated top 10% of class	32
% graduated top 25% of class	52
% graduated top 50% of class	100

DEADLINES

Early decision	
Deadline	11/15
Notification	1/1
Regular	
Deadline	1/1
Notification	4/1
Nonfall registration?	no

APPLICANTS ALSO LOOK AT

AND OFTEN PREFER
Pomona College
Occidental College
University of Southern California
University of California—Berkeley
University of California—Los Angeles
Scripps College
Claremont McKenna College

AND SOMETIMES PREFER
New York University
Lewis & Clark College
Colorado College
Whitman College
Boston University

FINANCIAL FACTS

Financial Aid Rating	95
Annual tuition	$32,704
Books and supplies	$900
% frosh rec. need-based scholarship or grant aid	34
% UG rec. need-based scholarship or grant aid	36
% frosh rec. need-based self-help aid	32
% UG rec. need-based self-help aid	34
% frosh rec. any financial aid	41.2
% UG rec. any financial aid	42
% UG borrow to pay for school	43
Average cumulative indebtedness	$24,790

POMONA COLLEGE

333 NORTH COLLEGE WAY, CLAREMONT, CA 91711-6312 • ADMISSIONS: 909-621-8134 • FAX: 909-621-8952

STUDENTS SAY ". . ."

Academics

"No place is perfect, but Pomona comes awfully close," agree students. "We probably are the most spoiled group of kids in the nation," raves one student. "Pomona is like Disneyland." "Luscious comforts and opportunities" abound on campus, as "It's nearly impossible not to be happy." There are "many classes to choose from" with an academic menu that offers a host of typical as well as "unusual programs." Pomona students are able to cross register and utilize the tremendous resources of the four other Claremont Colleges (Claremont McKenna, Harvey Mudd, Pitzer, and Scripps). There are opportunities to do "research that most students don't get the chance to do until graduate school." There's also a "great library" and "a healthy endowment." ("It's freakin' loaded," discloses a history major.) Class sizes are "relatively small," professors "will not let you slip through the cracks" and "love teaching students," and students generally reciprocate. "It's kind of crazy how many people here really love what they study." The big academic complaint is an unwelcome influx of visiting professors. Administratively, "the school is run so well that you do not even think about it." Management is "constantly keeping the students informed and involved." "They pay attention to every detail and make sure everything is perfect."

Life

"Pomona is about getting out of Chinese class and longboarding down College Avenue and smiling because you know you're in an awesome place." The quad is usually full of students playing volleyball, debating, or "pounding away on the keys of their laptops about Voltaire's philosophy." "Everyone here is extremely active," explains an economics major. "Kids don't sit around much." "For a small college, it is shocking how much goes on." With four other colleges within walking distance that share a tight social bond, there are "unlimited opportunities to get involved." Concerts, seminars, and political events are "virtually endless." "Outdoorsy activities are a big part" of Pomona's culture. "Numerous" skiing, hiking, and surfing trips "are pretty much free." Students manage to strike a delicate balance between work and play. "People work their asses off and then party hard," relates one student. "At least that's been my experience." "During the week, just about everyone does schoolwork." On weekends, there are "huge school-sponsored parties" (with "free beer and wine if you're 21"). While drinking is "prevalent" around campus, "no one ever, ever forces you to drink if you don't want to." Substance-free housing is an option, but "people living in other halls tend to disassociate themselves with residents there." "You can be sub-free," advises one student, "just don't live there." Speaking of dorms, we note that "almost all the dorms don't have air conditioning," which can be a problem in perpetually sunny Southern California.

Student Body

Pomona's students are "dedicated to their work but also dedicated to maintaining their sanity." "They work really hard in private, and pretend that they don't in public," observes one student. The political atmosphere is "very, very liberal." "Many of the school's leftist students and teachers are militant and unflinching in their dedication." However, "this doesn't necessarily isolate anyone" and the token conservatives seem pretty happy. "There isn't much of a counterculture," but at the same time, "many different lifestyles are represented." Pomona runs the gamut from "hippie to cool geek to social butterfly." There are "idiosyncratic" students who "don't pay much attention to their looks." There are "pretentious and irritating" intellectuals. "There are the jocks, the activists, the stoners, and the techies." "There are also the party-all-the-time people and the party-never people." Lots of students come from considerable wealth, but others don't. "The advantage is that you're forced to make friends outside of you usual comfort zone. The metal heads can't just hang out with other metal heads." "People here really, honestly think the nerdy things you have done in the past are cool," adds one satisfied student.

FINANCIAL AID: 909-621-8205 • E-MAIL: ADMISSIONS@POMONA.EDU • WEBSITE: WWW.POMONA.EDU

THE PRINCETON REVIEW SAYS

Admissions

Very important factors considered include: Class rank, application essay, academic GPA, recommendation(s), rigor of secondary school record, standardized test scores, character/personal qualities, extracurricular activities, talent/ability. *Important factors considered include:* interview. *Other factors considered include:* Alumni/ae relation, first generation, geographical residence, racial/ethnic status, volunteer work, work experience. SAT and SAT Subject Tests or ACT required; ACT with Writing component recommended. TOEFL required of all international applicants. High school diploma or equivalent is not required. *Academic units required:* 4 English, 3 mathematics, 3 science, (2 science labs), 2 foreign language, 2 social studies, 3 history. *Academic units recommended:* 4 mathematics, 3 science, (3 science labs), 3 foreign language, 2 social studies, 3 history.

Financial Aid

Students should submit: FAFSA, CSS/Financial Aid PROFILE, state aid form, noncustodial PROFILE, business/farm supplement, tax returns for both the student and parents. Regular filing deadline is 2/1. The Princeton Review suggests that all financial aid forms be submitted as soon as possible after January 1. *Need-based scholarships/grants offered:* Federal Pell, SEOG, state scholarships/grants, the school's own gift aid. *Loan aid offered:* FFEL Subsidized Stafford, FFEL Unsubsidized Stafford, FFEL PLUS, Federal Perkins, college/university loans from institutional funds. Applicants will be notified of awards on or about 4/10. Federal Work-Study Program available. Institutional employment available. Off-campus job opportunities are good.

The Inside Word

Even though it is tough to get admitted to Pomona, students will find the Admissions Staff to be accessible and engaging. An applicant pool full of such well-qualified students as those who typically apply, in combination with the college's small size, necessitates that candidates undergo as personal an admissions evaluation as possible. This is how solid matches are made and how Pomona does a commendable job of keeping an edge on the competition.

THE SCHOOL SAYS "..."

From The Admissions Office

"Perhaps the most important thing to know about Pomona College is that we are what we say we are. There is enormous integrity between the statements of mission and philosophy governing the college and the reality that students, faculty, and administrators experience. The balance in the curriculum is unusual. Sciences, social sciences, humanities, and the arts receive equal attention, support, and emphasis. Most importantly, the commitment to undergraduate education is absolute. Teaching awards remain the highest honor the trustees can bestow upon faculty. The typical method of instruction is the seminar and the average class size of 14 offers students the opportunity to become full partners in the learning process. Our location in the Los Angeles basin and in Claremont, with five other colleges, provides a remarkable community.

"Pomona College requires either the new SAT plus two SAT Subject Tests (in different fields) or the ACT. Scores from the old SAT (pre-March 2005) and the ACT are acceptable. For the old SAT, scores must be submitted with the results of three SAT Subject Tests, one of which must be the Writing test."

SELECTIVITY

Admissions Rating	99
# of applicants	5,440
% of applicants accepted	18
% of acceptees attending	39

FRESHMAN PROFILE

Range SAT Critical Reading	690–760
Range SAT Math	680–760
Range SAT Writing	680–760
Range ACT Composite	29–34
Minimum paper TOEFL	600
Minimum computer TOEFL	250
Average HS GPA	3.9
% graduated top 10% of class	87
% graduated top 25% of class	98
% graduated top 50% of class	100

DEADLINES

Early decision	
Deadline	11/15
Notification	12/15
Regular	
Deadline	1/2
Notification	4/10
Nonfall registration?	no

APPLICANTS ALSO LOOK AT
AND OFTEN PREFER
Harvard College
University of California—Berkeley
Stanford University
Yale University
Princeton University
AND SOMETIMES PREFER
Dartmouth College
University of California—Los Angeles
Claremont McKenna College
Wesleyan University
Williams College
AND RARELY PREFER
Pitzer College
University of California—Davis

FINANCIAL FACTS

Financial Aid Rating	99
Annual tuition	$33,635
Room and board	$11,748
Required fees	$297
Books and supplies	$850
% frosh rec. need-based scholarship or grant aid	54
% UG rec. need-based scholarship or grant aid	53
% frosh rec. need-based self-help aid	54
% UG rec. need-based self-help aid	53
% frosh rec. any financial aid	53
% UG rec. any financial aid	50
% UG borrow to pay for school	53
Average cumulative indebtedness	$11,500

PRESCOTT COLLEGE

ADDRESS? • ADMISSIONS: TK • FAX: TK

CAMPUS LIFE
Quality of Life Rating	95
Fire Safety Rating	60*
Green Rating	79
Type of school	private
Environment	town

STUDENTS
Total undergrad enrollment	689
% male/female	50/50
% from out of state	62
% from public high school	78
% live on campus	2
% African American	1
% Asian	1
% Caucasian	89
% Hispanic	6
% Native American	1
% international	1

SURVEY SAYS . . .
No one cheats
Students are friendly
Students are happy
Intercollegiate sports are unpopular
or nonexistent
Frats and sororities are unpopular
or nonexistent
Political activism is popular

ACADEMICS
Academic Rating	87
Calendar	semester
Student/faculty ratio	9:1
Profs interesting rating	98
Profs accessible rating	93
Most common	
reg class size	10–19 students

MOST POPULAR MAJORS
adventure education
human development
cultural & regional studies
arts & letters
environmental studies

STUDENTS SAY ". . ."

Academics

Tiny, innovative Prescott College in the Arizona mountains has "a reputation for being about the environment." The wilderness orientation program features a three-week backcountry excursion, just for instance. Undergrads here pursue "experientially-based," highly "self-directed" curricula on an alternating block and quarterly academic schedule. They receive narrative evaluations of their work instead of actual grades (though letter grades are also available). The "truly interdisciplinary" class offerings, "while somewhat limited, can be amazing." "We don't have lecture classes," explains a senior. "Class sizes are limited to the number of people who can fit in a 15-passenger van, which makes for discussions that include everybody." "My first semester, I was down at a field station in Mexico studying marine biology out on boats and islands every day," reminisces another senior. "Personal attention" is ample and Prescott's professors "are passionate about the topics they teach." The very personable administration is "very flexible and open when it comes to student ideas." The big gripe here involves the limited amount of resources. There is "very little state-of-the-art." Technology, though the design and sustainability aspects of many of the buildings are top of the line. Those who are seeking out the resources, name recognition, and larger-scale community of a large university may "find it very difficult to survive this educational experience." Freshman orientation is a key element of the school: all willing students attend wilderness orientation, spending some twenty days hiking and living in the field. "This is one of the most formative events in Prescott College culture, and cannot be ignored," says a student.

Life

Political activism and community service are widespread but life at Prescott College is mostly idiosyncratic. "People always seem to be involved with a million projects for classes or just for stuff they are interested in and believe in." Students might attend "a lecture about the ecology of peace, or a workshop on digital storytelling, or someone's presentation of the semester they spent hiking around Thailand for their senior project." "Everyone knows everyone" and virtually all students live off-campus. "I live in a yurt," notes a junior. The surrounding town "offers little" except for "a lot of retirees," so students make their own fun. "Adrenaline sports" and outdoor activities are popular. "It is common for students (or classes) to take trips into the wilderness, or to go camping or backpacking." Potluck dinners "are big." Parties are "there if you look for them" and drinking, dancing, bonfires, and "music jams" definitely have their place; however, "not a lot of people get wasted every weekend."

Student Body

"Generally speaking, a 'typical' student is one who prefers a style of life and education that differs with societal norms." "Racial and political diversity are almost nonexistent but just about any other diversity you could think of is represented here." Many students "attended a different college previously or spent some time in the workforce after high school." Prescott reportedly "puts a lot of effort into being queer friendly" as well and "there are many gay and several transgendered students." Students tell us that most everyone is "diligent in their studies" and "truly interested in bettering the community." They are very intellectual students that happen to wear tye dye t-shirts and chaco sandals that also love the environment and put all their energy into saving it!" says a student. "Most people here are intelligent, caring people who shower at least twice a week," declares a senior. "Almost no one is religious in a traditional sense but there is a spiritual element." Politically, students are "extremely leftwing." Conservatives are exotic. "I had one Republican classmate once," says a senior.

FINANCIAL AID: TK • E-MAIL: TK • WEBSITE: TK

THE PRINCETON REVIEW SAYS

Admissions

Very important factors considered include: Application essay, recommendation(s), rigor of secondary school record. *Important factors considered include:* Academic GPA, standardized test scores, character/personal qualities, extracurricular activities, interview, level of applicant's interest, talent/ability. *Other factors considered include:* First generation, volunteer work, work experience. SAT or ACT required; TOEFL required of all international applicants. High school diploma is required and GED is accepted. *Academic units recommended:* 4 English, 3 mathematics, 2 science, 3 foreign language, 1 social studies, 2 history, 1 arts.

Financial Aid

Students should submit: FAFSA. The Princeton Review suggests that all financial aid forms be submitted as soon as possible after January 1. *Need-based scholarships/grants offered:* Federal Pell, SEOG, state scholarships/grants, private scholarships, the school's own gift aid, ACT & SMART. *Loan aid offered:* FFEL Subsidized Stafford, FFEL Unsubsidized Stafford, FFEL PLUS Applicants will be notified of awards on a rolling basis beginning 3/15. Federal Work-Study Program available. Institutional employment available. Off-campus job opportunities are good.

The Inside Word

The acceptance rate at Prescott is high. However, the applicant pool is very self-selecting and Prescott is the kind of place that pays a lot of careful attention to each and every application. Decent grades are important but well-articulated essays are equally vital. Mentioning how dedicated you are to ecological concerns certainly won't hurt your cause. You also want to demonstrate the ability to self-motivate. Students here design their own academic programs and self-direction is nothing less than the bedrock of Prescott's culture. Standardized test score aren't required (though you should definitely send them if you've done well).

THE SCHOOL SAYS "..."

From The Admissions Office

Prescott College highlights the dramatic educational return on investment when experience is at the center of learning. Tucked into a corner of the town in central Arizona of the same name, Prescott College is an evolving experiment in rejecting hierarchical thinking for collaboration and teamwork as the cornerstone of learning. This is an educational institution that puts students at the center in everything it does and is. Optional Grades. Narrative Evaluations. No barriers. Limited bureaucracy. No summa or magna or "best in show" ribbons. Just a peripatetic community of lively intellects and fearless explorers whose connecting threads are a passion for social responsibility and the environment, and a keen sense of adventure.

"At Prescott College, our goal is to fuel your passion and give you a deeper understanding of the world around you through collaborative learning and personal experience. We don't settle for the mundane college experience. Instead, we take learning outside the classroom and into the real world through experiential and field-based learning. From field studies, internships, and independent studies to community service and study abroad opportunities, our students are challenged to think critically, explore the world up close, and form solutions through collaborative efforts.

"If you're looking for a college experience unlike any other—the kind that enables you to take control of your education and truly make a positive impact in your community and in the world—then Prescott College is the ideal college for you..

SELECTIVITY

Admissions Rating	77
# of applicants	252
% of applicants accepted	83
% of acceptees attending	34
# of early decision applicants	27
% accepted early decision	89

FRESHMAN PROFILE

Range SAT Critical Reading	510–660
Range SAT Math	500–610
Range SAT Writing	490–600
Range ACT Composite	21–27
Minimum paper TOEFL	500
Minimum computer TOEFL	173
Minimum web-based TOEFL	61
Average HS GPA	3.09
% graduated top 10% of class	11
% graduated top 25% of class	32
% graduated top 50% of class	57

DEADLINES

Early decision	
Deadline	12/1
Notification	12/15
Priority	3/1
Deadline	8/15
Notification	rolling
Nonfall registration?	yes

APPLICANTS ALSO LOOK AT

AND OFTEN PREFER
Mills College
Earlham College
College of the Atlantic

AND SOMETIMES PREFER
Lewis—Clark State College
Whitman College

AND RARELY PREFER
Hendrix College
Sterling College
Reed College

FINANCIAL FACTS

Financial Aid Rating	77
Annual tuition	$21,492
Required fees	$1,250
% frosh rec. need-based scholarship or grant aid	57
% UG rec. need-based scholarship or grant aid	46
% frosh rec. non-need-based scholarship or grant aid	53
% UG rec. non-need-based scholarship or grant aid	6
% frosh rec. need-based self-help aid	28
% UG rec. need-based self-help aid	74
% frosh rec. any financial aid	75
% UG rec. any financial aid	63
% UG borrow to pay for school	71
Average cumulative indebtedness	$21,723

PRINCETON UNIVERSITY

PO Box 430, Admission Office, Princeton, NJ 08544-0430 • Admissions: 609-258-3060 • Fax: 609-258-6743

STUDENTS SAY ". . ."

Academics

Perhaps you might have heard something about Princeton, a "little suburban oasis in New Jersey" proffering a storied history, a high profile academic curriculum, and stellar financial aid policies, all of which combine to provide "an experience and a network that will transform your life." Or, as one student puts it, "A Princeton education is worth its weight in gold, especially if you didn't have to pay anything." The undergraduate focus (there are no law, med, or business schools here) gives students access to tremendous resources, and everyone enrolled is granted access not just to classes but to a "scholarly community"; in the math department, for instance, tea is open to everyone. "The school has plenty of funding to put toward your research, and it is amazing to work on something that is completely yours," says a senior history major. With one of the nation's largest endowments, the school is happy to share the wealth, as well. "If you have something reasonable you want to do over the summer, for example, you can do it regardless of your financial situation. Princeton has paid for me to study abroad, work abroad, go on a class trip abroad, and compete internationally at a variety of wonderful locales abroad," says a junior. The rigorous admission process brings together some of the top young adults in America to "study seriously, to party seriously, or to pursue a job seriously, or a combination of the three," and the school has "very high expectations…you have to work extremely hard to succeed." Since "Princeton students rarely do things half-way," the learning here is "demanding and competitive, but enlightening." Professors, "even the famous ones," are very down-to-earth and "love talking to students one-on-one about their goals and ideas," but "they have to be sought out; they won't come to you." The administration "is remarkably cooperative," and have done an "excellent job of incorporating student opinions into actual decisions," with, of course, "the notable exception of grade deflation."

Life

People at Princeton really use the 'work hard, play hard' logic. "Academic discipline is on everyone's mind," but on any given day, "there are soo many interesting events being coordinated by students and the university" that everyone here is "always running from one commitment to the next, and studying in between," but students make plenty of time on weekends for fun, "often at the expense of studying or sleeping." Princeton has a relatively small, "gorgeous campus," and "everyone lives on campus and close to one another." The bulk of students don't have class on Fridays, which is good, because there's "never a dull moment," thanks to lectures, concerts, sporting events, performances, and movies. Most people belong to or go out to the eating clubs, which are a unique Princeton institution that acts as a coed frat/dining hall that provide upper-class students with both meals and social events (such as DJ's and theme nights), and offers "great ways to drink and dance in a safe environment, only with other Princeton students." "Princeton is a lifestyle, not a school," says a junior. "The best of everything is here…you're at the center of the world in a very real sense."

Student Body

Everyone at Princeton "has a nerdy streak in them" and there's a fair share of "hyper-ambitious kids who spend all their time studying," but it's a "pretty friendly environment" and people here are "always ready to have fun." These "driven" students are "all over the map in terms of ethnicity, beliefs, passions, and priorities," though students are all very focused on their future careers. "Your average Princetonian wants to run the world, not change it," says a student. While there are still plenty of people fulfilling the "clean-cut, preppy, and well-dressed" stereotype, this is one that Princetonians "are very aware of and hardly take seriously, even when they conform to it"; most "invariably come from different backgrounds and have different pursuits," anyway. There are fringe groups, but "they do not have a large presence." You will still find kids with mohawks here, and "they're often even more treasured by the student community for their exoticness." The small campus means that "everyone is somehow interconnected," but it's also "big enough that you are always meeting new people."

FINANCIAL AID: 609-258-3330 • E-MAIL: UAOFFICE@PRINCETON.EDU • WEBSITE: WWW.PRINCETON.EDU

THE PRINCETON REVIEW SAYS

Admissions

Very important factors considered include: Class rank, application essay, academic GPA, recommendation(s), rigor of secondary school record, standardized test scores, character/personal qualities, extracurricular activities, first generation, talent/ability. *Important factors considered include:* Alumni/ae relation. *Other factors considered include:* Geographical residence, interview, level of applicant's interest, racial/ethnic status, volunteer work, work experience. SAT Subject Tests required; SAT or ACT required; ACT with Writing component recommended. TOEFL required of all international applicants. High school diploma or equivalent is not required. *Academic units recommended:* 4 English, 4 mathematics, 4 science, (2 science labs), 4 foreign language, 2 history.

Financial Aid

Students should submit: FAFSA, institution's own financial aid form, Institutional Noncustodial Parent's Form. The Princeton Review suggests that all financial aid forms be submitted as soon as possible after January 1. *Need-based scholarships/grants offered:* Federal Pell, SEOG, state scholarships/grants, the school's own gift aid. *Loan aid offered:* FFEL Subsidized Stafford, FFEL Unsubsidized Stafford, FFEL PLUS, Federal Perkins, college/university loans from institutional funds. Applicants will be notified of awards on or about 4/1. Federal Work-Study Program available. Institutional employment available. Off-campus job opportunities are good.

The Inside Word

Princeton is much more open about the admissions process than the rest of their Ivy compatriots. The Admissions Staff evaluates candidates' credentials using a 1–5 rating scale, common among highly selective colleges. Princeton's recommendation to interview should be considered a requirement, given the ultracompetitive nature of the applicant pool. In addition, three SAT Subject Tests are required.

THE SCHOOL SAYS "..."

From The Admissions Office

"Methods of instruction [at Princeton] vary widely, but common to all areas is a strong emphasis on individual responsibility and the free interchange of ideas. This is displayed most notably in the wide use of preceptorials and seminars, in the provision of independent study for all upperclass students and qualified underclass students, and in the availability of a series of special programs to meet a range of individual interests. The undergraduate college encourages the student to be an independent seeker of information and to assume responsibility for gaining both knowledge and judgment that will strengthen later contributions to society.

Princeton offers a distinctive financial aid program that provides grants, which do not have to be repaid, rather than loans. Princeton meets the full demonstrated financial need of all students—domestic and international—offered admission. More than half of Princeton's undergraduates receive financial aid.

"All applicants must submit results of either the new or old SAT, as well as SAT Subject Tests in three different subject areas. Students applying for the Class of 2010 and beyond will be required to submit results from the new version of the SAT."

SELECTIVITY

Admissions Rating	99
# of applicants	18,942
% of applicants accepted	10
% of acceptees attending	68
# accepting a place on wait list	483
% admitted from wait list	10

FRESHMAN PROFILE

Range SAT Critical Reading	690–790
Range SAT Math	700–790
Range SAT Writing	690–780
Range ACT Composite	30–34
Minimum paper TOEFL	600
Minimum computer TOEFL	250
Average HS GPA	3.87
% graduated top 10% of class	96
% graduated top 25% of class	99
% graduated top 50% of class	100

DEADLINES

Regular	
Deadline	1/1
Notification	4/1
Nonfall registration?	no

APPLICANTS ALSO LOOK AT

AND SOMETIMES PREFER
Harvard College
Stanford University
Massachusetts Institute of Technology
Yale University

AND RARELY PREFER
Brown University
University of Pennsylvania

FINANCIAL FACTS

Financial Aid Rating	99
Annual tuition	$34,290
Room and board	$11,405
Books and supplies	$1,200
% frosh rec. need-based scholarship or grant aid	55
% UG rec. need-based scholarship or grant aid	52
% frosh rec. need-based self-help aid	55
% UG rec. need-based self-help aid	52
% frosh rec. any financial aid	55
% UG rec. any financial aid	53
% UG borrow to pay for school	22
Average cumulative indebtedness	$5,592

PROVIDENCE COLLEGE

RIVER AVENUE AND EATON STREET, PROVIDENCE, RI 02918 • ADMISSIONS: 401-865-2535 • FAX: 401-865-2826

STUDENTS SAY ". . ."

Academics

Providence College, "a solid, respectable school with a reputation for having fun," appeals both to those who seek an "intense curriculum" ("especially the Development of Western Civilization course" that can be "stressful and time-consuming" though "It offers a great liberal arts background") and to those who simply want "challenging classes" in an atmosphere that balances "academic and personal growth with an incredibly fun social scene." The centerpiece of the PC experience is "the four-semester Civ program, through which the school truly molds the mind with classical training and gives us a basic understanding of how our civilization came to be where it is today." While some students dismiss the sequence as "unnecessary to our success in the future," others appreciate the forced immersion in philosophy, history, art, and theology, noting "I am happy that I am forced to take Civ because I would not have enrolled into any other courses that deal with the topics introduced in Civ." PC academics are "demanding," but "The school has great support systems for academics" "even outside the classroom stuff. The library has lots of different resources and there's always someone around to help." Undergrads also appreciate how "Being in a smaller school, there are more opportunities to excel in one's chosen field, whether it's getting an internship in a biology lab, writing for the newspaper, or starring in a theatrical production."

Life

Social life at Providence College "revolves around the off-campus bars and the off-campus houses. While there are other activities to participate in, the main focus is drinking." One undergrad reports, "Kids work hard from Sunday night to Thursday afternoon; then the weekend starts, and everyone hits the bars." However, it would be remiss to assume students here do nothing but study and drink—on the contrary, there is "a huge focus on extracurriculars," so much so that students always try to "balance and manage" their time between "schoolwork and a social life." Intercollegiate athletics "are extremely popular (all the hockey games are packed) and bring a great atmosphere to the campus," and intramurals "are lots of fun. There's even a noncompetitive division for students who only want to have fun." Community service "is also really popular. Students are always busy donating their time to different groups." Downtown Providence has a lot more to offer than bars; it has "a great music scene, theater, and lots of art venues. The restaurants are good too." Students can access the city easily as "public transportation is free for us. It's only 5 minutes to downtown, and the bus runs right through campus."

Student Body

Though Providence students "are not the most diverse group," "The administration is really emphasizing our need for people who are different" from what some perceive to be the usual "cookie-cutter" student. That said, students report, by and large, that they are "all comfortable with one another and it is easy to fit in," noting a "strong sense of community." The typical student here "is a White, upper-middle class kid who went to a private/Catholic prep school in New England" and "looks as though he stepped of the pages of the Hollister/Abercrombie catalogue." Students who do not fit the mold "seem to form their own peer groups for the most part. Interaction between atypical and typical students is not a problem." One student says that "Everyone is working together to try to come up with ways to make our student population more diverse, both ethnically and economically." Most here are "friendly and hard-working and are very involved in various organizations, from Student Government to intramural sports to the Board of Multicultural Student Affairs . . . we are proud of our school."

FINANCIAL AID: 401-865-2286 • E-MAIL: PCADMISS@PROVIDENCE.EDU • WEBSITE: WWW.PROVIDENCE.EDU

THE PRINCETON REVIEW SAYS
Admissions
Very important factors considered include: Academic GPA, recommendation(s), rigor of secondary school record. *Important factors considered include:* Application essay, character/personal qualities, extracurricular activities. *Other factors considered include:* Class rank, standardized test scores, alumni/ae relation, first generation, geographical residence, level of applicant's interest, racial/ethnic status, talent/ability, volunteer work, work experience. ACT with Writing component required. TOEFL required of all international applicants. High school diploma is required and GED is not accepted. *Academic units required:* 4 English, 4 mathematics, 3 science, (2 science labs), 3 foreign language, 2 social studies, 2 history. *Academic units recommended:* 4 English, 4 mathematics, 4 science, (2 science labs), 3 foreign language, 2 social studies, 2 history.

Financial Aid
Students should submit: FAFSA, CSS/Financial Aid PROFILE, business/farm supplement. Regular filing deadline is 2/1. The Princeton Review suggests that all financial aid forms be submitted as soon as possible after January 1. *Need-based scholarships/grants offered:* Federal Pell, SEOG, state scholarships/grants, private scholarships, the school's own gift aid, Federal Academic Competitive Grant/Smart Grant. *Loan aid offered:* Direct Subsidized Stafford, Direct Unsubsidized Stafford, Direct PLUS, FFEL Subsidized Stafford, FFEL Unsubsidized Stafford, FFEL PLUS, Federal Perkins Applicants will be notified of awards on or about 4/1. Federal Work-Study Program available. Institutional employment available. Off-campus job opportunities are good.

The Inside Word
Few schools can claim a more transparent admissions process than Providence College. The admissions section of the school's website includes a voluminous blog authored by the school's senior Admissions Counselor. Surf on over to http://blogs.targetx.com/providence/ScottSeseske and learn everything you could possibly want to know about the how, what, when, and why of admissions decisions at Providence.

THE SCHOOL SAYS "..."
From The Admissions Office
"Infused with the history, tradition, and learning of a 700-year-old Catholic teaching order, the Dominican Friars, Providence College offers a value-affirming environment where students are enriched through spiritual, social, physical, and cultural growth as well as through intellectual development. Providence College offers over 51 programs of study leading to baccalaureate degrees in business, education, the sciences, arts, and humanities. Our faculty is noted for a strong commitment to teaching. A close student/faculty relationship allows for in-depth classwork, independent research projects, and detailed career exploration. While noted for the physical facilities and academic opportunities associated with larger universities, Providence also fosters personal growth through a small, spirited, family-like atmosphere that encourages involvement in student activities and athletics.

"Submission of standardized test scores is optional for students applying for admission. This policy change allows each student to decide whether they wish to have their standardized test results considered as part of their application for admission. Students who choose not to submit SAT or ACT test scores will not be penalized in the review for admission. Additional details about the test-optional policy can be found on our website at Providence.edu/testoptionalpolicy."

SELECTIVITY
Admissions Rating	93
# of applicants	9,802
% of applicants accepted	41
% of acceptees attending	24
# accepting a place on wait list	879
% admitted from wait list	13

FRESHMAN PROFILE
Range SAT Critical Reading	530–630
Range SAT Math	540–640
Range SAT Writing	540–650
Range ACT Composite	23–28
Minimum paper TOEFL	550
Minimum computer TOEFL	213
Minimum web-based TOEFL	79
Average HS GPA	3.47
% graduated top 10% of class	45
% graduated top 25% of class	83
% graduated top 50% of class	98

DEADLINES
Early action	
Deadline	11/1
Notification	1/1
Regular	
Deadline	1/15
Notification	4/1
Nonfall registration?	yes

APPLICANTS ALSO LOOK AT
AND OFTEN PREFER
University of Notre Dame
University of Richmond
AND SOMETIMES PREFER
Northeastern University
AND RARELY PREFER
Fairfield University

FINANCIAL FACTS
Financial Aid Rating	73
Annual tuition	$28,920
Room and board	$10,335
Required fees	$579
Books and supplies	$800
% frosh rec. need-based scholarship or grant aid	49
% UG rec. need-based scholarship or grant aid	47
% frosh rec. non-need-based scholarship or grant aid	8
% UG rec. non-need-based scholarship or grant aid	8
% frosh rec. need-based self-help aid	54
% UG rec. need-based self-help aid	49
% frosh rec. athletic scholarships	4
% UG rec. athletic scholarships	5
% frosh rec. any financial aid	70
% UG rec. any financial aid	66
% UG borrow to pay for school	72
Average cumulative indebtedness	$35,216

PURDUE UNIVERSITY—WEST LAFAYETTE

1080 SCHLEMAN HALL, WEST LAFAYETTE, IN 47907 • ADMISSIONS: 765-494-1776 • FAX: 765-494-0544

STUDENTS SAY ". . ."

Academics

Purdue University is a large public school in Indiana that has a "hardcore engineering" reputation far and wide. However, there are over 200 majors here and many students insist that Purdue's liberal arts programs are "underrated" and "much bigger than people think." Programs in pharmacy, nursing, business, hotel management, agriculture, and education are also laudable. The "student-oriented" top brass is reportedly "great." The "archaic" registration process is "a hassle for everyone," but "everything is very organized and the people who work in the administration are genuinely there to help the students." While classes do get smaller at the upper levels, Purdue's general education courses are "always packed." The faculty really runs the gamut. "Professors are here to do two things: research and teach, usually in that order," explains a molecular biology major. "As such, they are very intelligent people. Their ability to express their information, however, is a case-by-case situation." There are professors who "only teach classes because they have to" and "there are some teaching assistants who can barely speak English." Other professors "like teaching" and are "willing to help students outside of class." The academic experience at Purdue can also vary wildly from major to major. For engineers, "classes are insanely tough yet satisfying." Getting through the introductory courses is a grueling rite of passage. "While some of the weed-out classes seem difficult and pointless, they really do prepare you for upper level courses," promises a chemical engineering major.

Life

Purdue boasts an "absolutely amazing" freshman orientation program and, with more than 800 clubs and organizations, "there is something for everyone." "Purdue is a party school if you're a partier, a place to succeed for the academically oriented, a Big Ten school for the sports fan, and a place for anyone to completely blend in or stand out," explains a sophomore. Intramural sports are popular. If you enjoy large percussion instruments, Purdue's Big Bass Drum is the planet's largest. The Greek system is also considerable and "fraternity parties are huge." Students who are of age or who have quality fake ID's frequently take advantage of a thriving bar scene. Tradition is also a noticeable part of campus life. Purdue students love being Boilermakers. "During football season, we have the great tradition of Breakfast Club, where people dress in ridiculous costumes and wake up at the crack of dawn because the bars open at 7:00 A.M.," explains a sophomore, "but make sure you get there early, because they start lining up around 6:00." Purdue is located in a "typical college town" "in the middle of cornfields." On campus, "there is a lot of concrete." "You can walk to everything" and "some buildings are wonderful and state of the art." Others could use renovation. Dorm rooms are "a little small." The student recreation facilities are "crowded." "Parking can be a little hectic." Some students also complain that the weather around here is "awful." While the climates in Indianapolis and Chicago aren't any better, both cities are a reasonable drive away.

Student Body

"Many students at Purdue are typical Midwesterners from a suburb of Chicago or Indianapolis." Others are "country kids" from the rural towns that dot Indiana. There are substantially more men here than women, which you will find to be the case at almost any engineering-heavy school. Ethnic diversity is not atrocious. Students note that there are "lots of international students" and they argue that "Purdue is a lot more diverse than it is given credit for." "Students take academics very seriously here." They are "laid back but not lazy." "They're friendly, amiable, and open to many different people and experiences." "The Greeks and non-Greeks mix pretty well." In fact, though there is some tension because "many of the engineering and science students look at anyone else as stupid and destined to work at McDonald's," everyone else gets along for the most part. Politically, "liberalism is very alive," but Purdue is "a more conservative" campus. Mostly, though, it doesn't matter because "no one is really politically motivated."

PURDUE UNIVERSITY—WEST LAFAYETTE

FINANCIAL AID: 765-494-5050 • E-MAIL: ADMISSIONS@PURDUE.EDU • WEBSITE: WWW.PURDUE.EDU

THE PRINCETON REVIEW SAYS

Admissions

Very important factors considered include: Academic GPA, rigor of secondary school record, standardized test scores. *Important factors considered include:* Class rank, geographical residence, racial/ethnic status. *Other factors considered include:* Recommendation(s), alumni/ae relation, extracurricular activities, first generation, volunteer work, work experience. SAT or ACT required; ACT with Writing component required. TOEFL required of all international applicants. High school diploma is required and GED is accepted. *Academic units required:* 4 English, 3 mathematics, 2 science, (2 science labs), 2 foreign language. *Academic units recommended:* 3 science, (3 science labs).

Financial Aid

Students should submit: FAFSA. The Princeton Review suggests that all financial aid forms be submitted as soon as possible after January 1. *Need-based scholarships/grants offered:* Federal Pell, SEOG, state scholarships/grants, private scholarships, the school's own gift aid. *Loan aid offered:* FFEL Subsidized Stafford, FFEL Unsubsidized Stafford, FFEL PLUS, Federal Perkins, college/university loans from institutional funds. Applicants will be notified of awards on or about 4/15. Federal Work-Study Program available. Institutional employment available. Off-campus job opportunities are good.

The Inside Word

The fact that Purdue holds class rank as one of its most important considerations in the admission of candidates is troublesome. There are far too many inconsistencies in ranking policies and class size among the 25,000-plus high schools in the United States to place so much weight on an essentially incomparable number. The university's high admit rate thankfully renders the issue relatively moot.

THE SCHOOL SAYS " . . ."

From The Admissions Office

"Although it is one of America's largest universities, Purdue does not 'feel' big to its students. The campus is very compact when compared to universities with similar enrollment. Purdue is a comprehensive university with an international reputation in a wide range of academic fields. A strong work ethic prevails at Purdue. As a member of the Big Ten, Purdue has a strong and diverse athletic program. Purdue offers over 800 clubs and organizations. The residence halls and Greek community offer many participatory activities for students. Numerous convocations and lectures are presented each year. Purdue is all about people, and allowing students to grow academically as well as socially, preparing them for the real world.

"Applicants seeking admission are required to submit scores from the new Writing component of the SAT (or ACT)."

SELECTIVITY

Admissions Rating	83
# of applicants	25,929
% of applicants accepted	79
% of acceptees attending	34

FRESHMAN PROFILE

Range SAT Critical Reading	490–610
Range SAT Math	530–660
Range ACT Composite	23–28
Minimum paper TOEFL	550
Minimum computer TOEFL	213
Minimum web-based TOEFL	79
Average HS GPA	3.5
% graduated top 10% of class	31
% graduated top 25% of class	63
% graduated top 50% of class	92

DEADLINES

Regular	
Priority	3/1
Notification	rolling
Nonfall registration?	yes

APPLICANTS ALSO LOOK AT AND SOMETIMES PREFER

Valparaiso University
University of Illinois at Urbana-Champaign
Rose-Hulman Institute of Technology
Indiana University—Bloomington

FINANCIAL FACTS

Financial Aid Rating	83
Annual in-state tuition	$7,317
Annual out-of-state tuition	$22,791
Room and board	$7,530
Required fees	$430
Books and supplies	$1,050
% frosh rec. need-based scholarship or grant aid	17
% UG rec. need-based scholarship or grant aid	16
% frosh rec. non-need-based scholarship or grant aid	11
% UG rec. non-need-based scholarship or grant aid	6
% frosh rec. need-based self-help aid	36
% UG rec. need-based self-help aid	37
% frosh rec. athletic scholarships	1
% UG rec. athletic scholarships	1
% frosh rec. any financial aid	72
% UG rec. any financial aid	75
% UG borrow to pay for school	48
Average cumulative indebtedness	$21,266

QUINNIPIAC UNIVERSITY

275 MOUNT CARMEL AVENUE, HAMDEN, CT 06518 • ADMISSIONS: 203-582-8600 • FAX: 203-582-8906

STUDENTS SAY ". . ."

Academics

The physical beauty of Quinnipiac University is a particularly appealing attribute. The "beautiful campus with Sleeping Giant Mountain in the background" boasts many a picturesque vista, both natural and man-made. As far as the latter is concerned, the library "is gorgeous, with huge three-story windows and leather armchairs everywhere!" Quinnipiac's "great" academics manage to draw students away from the windows and into the classrooms. Undergraduate academics at Quinnipiac are divided into five schools (and one new Division of Education), with the School of Health Sciences offering especially outstanding majors. Among these is a 6.5-year physical therapy program that leads to a Doctor of Physical Therapy degree. Students appreciate the fact that "classes here at Quinnipiac are small, with generally less than 30 students," that "not one class in the university is taught by a teacher's assistant" and that professors "have so much experience in the 'real world' with the subject they teach." They warn, however, that "sometimes you can have a little bit of trouble with the adjuncts." Regardless of how good they are as teachers and lecturers, professors "all seem to be willing to help outside of the class time and communicate rapidly through e-mail."

Life

According to students, life at Quinnipiac outside of class follows a regular schedule to it. "Thursday night everyone goes to the clubs in New Haven. Friday night everyone parties on campus. Saturday night most people go to Toad's (a popular New Haven nightclub)." And if you have "no transportation, no problem. Quinnipiac shuttles will take you into New Haven to the clubs." "However, if partying is not your thing, don't worry because Quinnipiac sends out e-mails every week with the [school-sponsored] weekend events. These events include comedians, movies, game room nights, and much more." For outdoorsy types, miles of hiking trails lie right across the street, and "climbing the Sleeping Giant" is a popular pastime here, weather permitting. When it's "nice out," students take full advantage of their gorgeous surroundings: "You will always see kids with their towels lying on the Quad doing work. Others also enjoy playing Frisbee on the beautiful grass." "Support for the athletic teams," however, "is so-so. Men's ice hockey draws the best. Students also support the men's basketball team pretty well."

Student Body

To get a picture of what students here look like, just grab the nearest name-brand clothing catalog: "J. Crew, Ralph Lauren, and the North Face could do a magazine shoot here. [There are lots of] very preppy-looking, clean-cut kids." If their clothes aren't enough to give you a sense of the socioeconomic background from which most QU students come, take a stroll through "the student parking lot, [which] is full of Mercedes, Lexus, BMW, and Acura cars." Intellectually, "Most students don't seem to be their high school class president or their high school overachiever," but respondents emphasize that QU students are "hard workers." Given QU's location, it's not completely shocking to learn that "Many of the students come from surrounding New England states as well as New York and New Jersey." Many respondents lament the female/male ratio (about 3:2), and the fact that there are "very, very, very few minorities"—"but with each entering freshman class the diversity does grow slightly." And regardless of their backgrounds, friendly students make Quinnipiac "a comfortable, enjoyable place to live. The students are understanding of one another."

QUINNIPIAC UNIVERSITY

FINANCIAL AID: 203-582-8750 • E-MAIL: ADMISSIONS@QUINNIPIAC.EDU • WEBSITE: WWW.QUINNIPIAC.EDU

THE PRINCETON REVIEW SAYS

Admissions

Very important factors considered include: Rigor of secondary school record. *Important factors considered include:* Class rank, application essay, academic GPA, standardized test scores. *Other factors considered include:* Recommendation(s), alumni/ae relation, character/personal qualities, extracurricular activities, interview, level of applicant's interest, racial/ethnic status, talent/ability, volunteer work, work experience. SAT or ACT required; TOEFL required of all international applicants. High school diploma is required and GED is accepted. *Academic units required:* 4 English, 3 mathematics, 3 science, (2 science labs), 2 foreign language, 2 social studies, 4 4 years of Science and Math req. in PT,OT, Nursing, and PA. *Academic units recommended:* 4 English, 4 mathematics, 4 science, (3 science labs), 2 foreign language, 3 social studies.

Financial Aid

Students should submit: FAFSA. The Princeton Review suggests that all financial aid forms be submitted as soon as possible after January 1. *Need-based scholarships/grants offered:* Federal Pell, SEOG, state scholarships/grants, private scholarships, the school's own gift aid, Federal Nursing Scholarships. *Loan aid offered:* FFEL Subsidized Stafford, FFEL Unsubsidized Stafford, FFEL PLUS, Federal Perkins, Federal Nursing, state loans Applicants will be notified of awards on a rolling basis beginning 2/15. Federal Work-Study Program available. Institutional employment available. Off-campus job opportunities are excellent.

The Inside Word

Applicants with solid grades and test scores won't have much trouble gaining admission to Quinnipiac as long as they apply early in their senior year. Competition grows fiercer, however, as D-Day approaches. With the recent spike in applications, Admissions Officers have established the wait list in January. Students interested in either physical therapy or physician assistant should be aware that they face more stringent requirements.

THE SCHOOL SAYS "..."

From The Admissions Office

"The appeal of Quinnipiac University continues to grow each year. Our students come from a variety of states and backgrounds. Seventy-five percent of the freshman class is from out of state. Students come from 25 states and 18 countries. Nearly 30 percent of current undergraduates plan to stay at Quinnipiac to complete their graduate degrees. As admission becomes more competitive and our enrollment remains stable, the university continues to focus on its mission: to provide outstanding academic programs in a student-oriented environment on a campus with a strong sense of community. The development of an honors program, a highly regarded emerging leaders student-life program, and a 'writing across the curriculum' initiative in academic affairs, form the foundation for excellence in business, communications, health sciences, education, liberal arts, and law. The university has a fully digital high-definition production studio in the School of Communications; the Terry Goodwin '67 Financial Technology Center which provides a high-tech simulated trading floor in the School of Business; and a critical care lab for our nursing and physician assistant majors. All incoming students purchase a university-recommended laptop with wireless capabilities supported by a campus wide network. More than 70 student organizations, 21 Division I teams, recreation and intramurals, community service, student publications, and a strong student government offer a variety of outside-of-class experiences. There are many clubs that get students involved in campus life. Multicultural awareness is supported through the Black Student Union, Asian/Pacific Islander Association, Latino Cultural Society, and GLASS. An active alumni association reflects the strong connection Quinnipiac has with its graduates, and they give the faculty high marks for career preparation. Students are encouraged to apply early in the fall of their senior year and can access our online application or the Common Application easily from our website. We use the best individual scores on the SAT Reasoning Test (no Subject Tests required), or the ACT composite. We begin notifying students of our decisions in early January."

SELECTIVITY

Admissions Rating	88
# of applicants	12,060
% of applicants accepted	47
% of acceptees attending	24
# accepting a place on wait list	562
% admitted from wait list	10

FRESHMAN PROFILE

Range SAT Critical Reading	540–610
Range SAT Math	560–630
Range ACT Composite	23–27
Minimum paper TOEFL	550
Minimum computer TOEFL	213
Minimum web-based TOEFL	77
Average HS GPA	3.4
% graduated top 10% of class	25
% graduated top 25% of class	66
% graduated top 50% of class	95

DEADLINES

Regular	
Priority	2/1
Notification	rolling
Nonfall registration?	yes

APPLICANTS ALSO LOOK AT

AND OFTEN PREFER
University of Connecticut
Villanova University

AND SOMETIMES PREFER
University of Delaware
Fairfield University

AND RARELY PREFER
Northeastern University
Ithaca College

FINANCIAL FACTS

Financial Aid Rating	68
Annual tuition	$29,700
Room and board	$12,200
Required fees	$1,200
Books and supplies	$800
% frosh rec. need-based scholarship or grant aid	55
% UG rec. need-based scholarship or grant aid	56
% frosh rec. non-need-based scholarship or grant aid	26
% UG rec. non-need-based scholarship or grant aid	21
% frosh rec. need-based self-help aid	46
% UG rec. need-based self-help aid	50
% frosh rec. athletic scholarships	4
% UG rec. athletic scholarships	4
% frosh rec. any financial aid	70
% UG rec. any financial aid	68
% UG borrow to pay for school	71
Average cumulative indebtedness	$35,086

RANDOLPH COLLEGE

2500 RIVERMONT AVENUE, LYNCHBURG, VA 24503-1526 • ADMISSIONS: 434-947-8100 • FAX: 434-947-8996

CAMPUS LIFE

Quality of Life Rating	**88**
Fire Safety Rating	**88**
Green Rating	**72**
Type of school	private
Affiliation	Methodist
Environment	city

STUDENTS

Total undergrad enrollment	618
% male/female	11/89
% from out of state	52
% live on campus	88
% African American	9
% Asian	3
% Caucasian	67
% Hispanic	6
% Native American	1
% international	12
# of countries represented	46

SURVEY SAYS . . .

Small classes
No one cheats
Diverse student types on campus
Campus feels safe
Frats and sororities are unpopular
or nonexistent

ACADEMICS

Academic Rating	**90**
Calendar	semester
Student/faculty ratio	8:1
Profs interesting rating	95
Profs accessible rating	88
Most common reg class size	10–19 students
Most common lab size	fewer than 10 students

MOST POPULAR MAJORS

biology/biological sciences
psychology
political science and government

STUDENTS SAY ". . ."

Academics

Randolph College "is all about traditions: of learning, of excellence, of experiences, and of fun." Learning comes first in the "very academically oriented atmosphere" of this small, recently coed college with a "writing-intensive curriculum." Students here warn that "this school is difficult. It is really worth it, though, when, at the end of the day, you see that you were successful and made the grade. There is no feeling like it! My favorite saying from the professors here is: 'That C would have been an A at any other college.'" To help them handle the workload, students receive "a lot of personal time with teachers, and the teachers are very willing to work with you. They have lots of office hours and will have more if you want them to. There is a lot of class discussion, which I like because the classes are small." Also, while "You have to learn and you feel pressed to excel," "It's not like being pushed out onto a ship deck in a hurricane; they do give a lot of tutoring resources." Randolph's strong areas include a "great dance program," "solid foreign language departments," science programs "that have equipment my dad didn't even get to use until grad school," an "amazing riding program" with "a wonderful riding center," and "a good nursing program." Because the school is located "in the middle of nowhere," students tell us that it's easy to focus on academics and "not get yourself into too much trouble" at Randolph.

Life

Traditions "are what truly make Randolph so unique, and also so much fun to be at." And there are lots of them: There's Ring Week, when "First-years select a junior and spend a week decorating that junior's door and giving them (anonymous) presents; at the end of the week, the first-years present the juniors with their class ring." Then there's Even-Odd rivalry, a competition between classes teamed on the basis of their graduation year. There's also Pumpkin Parade, an October event in which sophomores gift seniors with lighted pumpkins. The traditions are fun, but more importantly, they "further strengthen the family bond" enjoyed by the Randolph community. Otherwise, life on the Randolph campus is "laid-back," with students "very focused on their studies during the week. Friday and Saturday are the nights that most students go out or have parties in their rooms. We seem to watch a lot of movies on campus and off (we have a dollar theater in Lynchburg) and there are a lot of fairly active clubs on campus." Many students "go to Hampden-Sydney College, University of Virginia, or Virginia Tech to party or meet people on weekends."

Student Body

Randolph students "study a lot and do a lot of work for classes. We also are all involved in a zillion different clubs and extracurricular activities at the same time. We're all always very busy, but we make time for hanging out with friends and having fun too." Students tend to be "very strong willed in their opinions and get done what they need to get done." One student elaborates: "The typical student at Randolph is a self-proclaimed hard worker. She is, in some way, a feminist. [Students have] a strong sense of self and are seeking a career in which [they] may exercise [their] talents; [they] feel the world is open to [them], and [they] would like to prove [themselves] in it. [Their] goals are endless, and [their] studies will bring [them] into the realm of accomplishment. Above all, [they are] forward thinkers, asking questions to which there may be no answers, and questioning answers which do not address the questions." While "Most students are Caucasian," Randolph also has "a surprising number of students from abroad—thriving Jamaican and Nepalese communities, as well as students from Saudi Arabia, India, and Argentina."

FINANCIAL AID: 434-947-8128 • E-MAIL: ADMISSIONS@RANDOLPHCOLLEGE.EDU • WEBSITE: WWW.RANDOLPHCOLLEGE.EDU

THE PRINCETON REVIEW SAYS

Admissions

Very important factors considered include: Academic GPA, rigor of secondary school record, character/personal qualities. *Important factors considered include:* Class rank, application essay, recommendation(s), standardized test scores, extracurricular activities, talent/ability. *Other factors considered include:* Alumni/ae relation, first generation, interview, level of applicant's interest, volunteer work, work experience. SAT or ACT required; High school diploma is required and GED is accepted. *Academic units required:* 4 English, 3 mathematics, 2 science, (2 science labs), 3 foreign language, 2 history, 2 academic electives.

Financial Aid

Students should submit: FAFSA, state aid form. The Princeton Review suggests that all financial aid forms be submitted as soon as possible after January 1. *Need-based scholarships/grants offered:* Federal Pell, SEOG, state scholarships/grants, private scholarships, the school's own gift aid. *Loan aid offered:* FFEL Subsidized Stafford, FFEL Unsubsidized Stafford, FFEL PLUS, Federal Perkins, college/university loans from institutional funds, Private. Applicants will be notified of awards on a rolling basis beginning 3/1. Federal Work-Study Program available. Institutional employment available. Off-campus job opportunities are good.

The Inside Word

Finding well-matched students is a top priority at Randolph, and applicants can rest assured that their applications will be given due consideration. While there are no minimum GPA or standardized test score requirements, most candidates have proven successful in the classroom. Character also plays an important role in admissions decisions; officers especially value independent, confident women and men who are proactive about their educations.

THE SCHOOL SAYS "..."

From The Admissions Office

"Randolph College gives a liberal arts education new relevance. The college's global honors emphasis offers the best features of an honors education with a global outlook. All students are encouraged to travel, to take on real problems, to pursue and achieve a goal with personal meaning. Embedded within a student's education are opportunities to study abroad, national and international internships, career guidance, leadership development, and one-on-one faculty advising.

"A graduate of Randolph understands the intellectual foundations of the arts, sciences, and humanities and can pursue an idea with the goal of creating new knowledge. The college's strong emphasis on writing enables students to communicate clearly and persuasively, and our diverse student population and study abroad emphasis enable students to 'see through the eyes of another culture.' The honor system is a vital part of life at Randolph and all students are expected to behave ethically and honorably in all circumstances, to care for others less fortunate, and to act on their behalf.

"If you want to live in a world in which your intelligence, energy, and purpose make a difference, this is the education you need.

"At this time, first-year applicants for Fall 2008 must submit either the SAT or ACT; the Writing component scores for the new SAT and the new ACT are not required. Randolph College will accept the scores from either the new or old versions of both tests."

SELECTIVITY

Admissions Rating	81
# of applicants	1,222
% of applicants accepted	83
% of acceptees attending	17
# of early decision applicants	15
% accepted early decision	73

FRESHMAN PROFILE

Range SAT Critical Reading	510–640
Range SAT Math	500–610
Range ACT Composite	23–27
Average HS GPA	3.2
% graduated top 10% of class	30
% graduated top 25% of class	59
% graduated top 50% of class	86

DEADLINES

Early decision	
Deadline	11/15
Notification	12/15
Regular	
Deadline	3/1
Notification	rolling
Nonfall registration?	yes

FINANCIAL FACTS

Financial Aid Rating	86
Annual tuition	$25,350
Room and board	$9,000
Required fees	$510
Books and supplies	$800
% frosh rec. need-based scholarship or grant aid	66
% UG rec. need-based scholarship or grant aid	65
% frosh rec. non-need-based scholarship or grant aid	10
% UG rec. non-need-based scholarship or grant aid	9
% frosh rec. need-based self-help aid	55
% UG rec. need-based self-help aid	55
% frosh rec. any financial aid	99
% UG rec. any financial aid	96
% UG borrow to pay for school	75
Average cumulative indebtedness	$28,218

RANDOLPH-MACON COLLEGE

PO Box 5005, ASHLAND, VA 23005 • ADMISSIONS: 804-752-7305 • FAX: 804-752-4707

STUDENTS SAY ". . ."

Academics

An "intimate and community-based campus" is what students find at Randolph-Macon College, a Virginia liberal arts school just north of Richmond, Virginia. Students rave that "the professors are the best part of Randolph-Macon"; professors are almost universally praised as "amazing, very social and easy to talk to and approach with problems." Often they won't just wait for you to come to them, but rather "will let you know when you [are] messing up, either by pulling you aside or arranging a meeting." Professors are not just caring people, however; they're also "very intelligent" and "extremely qualified" professionals "who have achieved amazing things during their careers." In at least one student's "opinion, the professors need to be given raises" for the hard work they do. Rather than singling out particular programs as standouts, students praise the overall "great liberal arts education" that RMC offers. Student opinion of the administration is somewhat negative, but many undergraduates are finding hope in the new president, whom R-MC students have dubbed the "Student's President."

Life

"Greek life is key" at R-MC. "When people say there is nothing going on, it is usually because no fraternity is having any parties for the students to go to." Whether at frat parties on campus or at bars in Richmond (which is just 10 miles away), drinking is a popular activity, many students claim. Even if you're not the type of person who likes to drink, "There are plenty of other things to do. There are places around to rent movies, places to go out to eat, or if you want to stay on campus, the school has a college movie channel [on which] they show specific movies each night." "Sporting events" are "also a large part of the social life": "We go to the football games in the fall, and grill out on the lawn in the spring while watching the lacrosse and softball games. Basketball games are always a big deal because we have a really good program here and usually do pretty well in the conference, or in the girls' [case], the nation." Intramural sports "are also very popular on campus," and competition for the "plaques and t-shirts" that are awarded to the best teams in each sport can be fierce. Regardless of the activities they engage in, however, R-MC students "aren't easygoing about academic commitments. They mean a lot to us!" "We are able to go out and party while still accomplishing our work," but "We take academics seriously."

Student Body

At RMC, "The typical student is White, wealthy, has a nice car, is a member of Greek life, dresses like a prep, drinks like a fish, parties like an animal, wears flip-flops all year round, and occasionally goes to the library to study," writes one student. Others claim that typical students are "conservative, Southern, polite, friendly" and "involved in sports." A lot of people seem to be "from Virginia, Maryland, Pennsylvania, New Jersey, or Connecticut" and exude certain "boarding school" manners, even though the majority of students come from public high schools. Many respondents lament the noticeable lack of diversity on campus, but also insist that "minorities do not seem to have a problem fitting in." Finally, at a school this small, "Everyone knows everyone," "so of course, the rumor mill" is a "strong" social force.

FINANCIAL AID: 804-752-7259 • E-MAIL: ADMISSIONS@RMC.EDU • WEBSITE: WWW.RMC.EDU

THE PRINCETON REVIEW SAYS

Admissions

Very important factors considered include: Academic GPA, rigor of secondary school record. *Important factors considered include:* Class rank, application essay, recommendation(s), standardized test scores. *Other factors considered include:* Alumni/ae relation, character/personal qualities, extracurricular activities, first generation, interview, racial/ethnic status, talent/ability, volunteer work, work experience. SAT or ACT required; ACT with Writing component recommended. TOEFL required of all international applicants. High school diploma is required and GED is accepted. *Academic units required:* 4 English, 3 mathematics, 3 science, (2 science labs), 2 foreign language, 1 social studies, 2 history, 1 academic elective. *Academic units recommended:* 4 English, 4 mathematics, 4 science, (4 science labs), 4 foreign language, 4 social studies, 2 history, 2 academic electives.

Financial Aid

Students should submit: FAFSA, state aid form, R-MC Entitlement Eligibility Form(If applicable) College Prepaid Education Program Form. Regular filing deadline is 3/1. The Princeton Review suggests that all financial aid forms be submitted as soon as possible after January 1. *Need-based scholarships/grants offered:* Federal Pell, SEOG, state scholarships/grants, private scholarships, the school's own gift aid. *Loan aid offered:* FFEL Subsidized Stafford, FFEL Unsubsidized Stafford, FFEL PLUS, Federal Perkins, college/university loans from institutional funds. Applicants will be notified of awards on or about 3/15. Federal Work-Study Program available. Institutional employment available. Off-campus job opportunities are excellent.

The Inside Word

Randolph-Macon is a solid liberal arts college, but it must contend with a wealth of Virginia schools for applicants. Students who are academically competitive should easily gain acceptance. Admissions Officers ascribe the most weight to objective data, primarily grades and test scores.

THE SCHOOL SAYS "..."

From The Admissions Office

"Randolph-Macon College, located in historic Ashland, just north of Richmond, is a coeducational, liberal arts and sciences college with a mission fulfilled through a combination of personal interaction and academic rigor. The student/faculty ratio is 11:1 and the average class size is 16 students. Enrollment is kept at approximately 1,150 to maintain this intimate atmosphere. Randolph-Macon College has an outstanding national reputation for its internships, study abroad, and undergraduate research. Founded in 1830, Randolph-Macon College is the oldest United Methodist Church–affiliated college in the nation, is a Phi Beta Kappa college, and is ranked as a Baccalaureate I college by the Carnegie Foundation. It offers the broadest liberal arts core curriculum of any college in Virginia.

"The college prepares students for any future, including success in securing a job or in gaining acceptance to graduate or professional school. The college offers a wide variety of social and recreational opportunities through more than 100 campus organizations. Forty percent of the students participate in one or more community-service activities; 70 percent play intramural sports; 40 percent join a fraternity or sorority; and everyone has a voice in student government. A $9.5 million sports and recreation center is very popular with students, and a new performing arts center offers a wealth of cultural arts programs. In addition, freshmen residence halls were recently renovated. 'Peaks of Excellence' center is now open to assist students with internships, study abroad, and undergraduate research.

"Freshman applicants for Fall 2008 must take the new SAT, which includes a written essay, or the ACT with Writing component."

SELECTIVITY

Admissions Rating	82
# of applicants	3,177
% of applicants accepted	61
% of acceptees attending	20
# accepting a place on wait list	127
% admitted from wait list	25
# of early decision applicants	33
% accepted early decision	73

FRESHMAN PROFILE

Range SAT Critical Reading	490–580
Range SAT Math	500–590
Range SAT Writing	490–580
Minimum paper TOEFL	550
Minimum computer TOEFL	213
Average HS GPA	3.3
% graduated top 10% of class	17
% graduated top 25% of class	46
% graduated top 50% of class	77

DEADLINES

Early decision	
Deadline	11/15
Notification	12/1
Early action	
Deadline	12/1
Notification	1/1
Regular	
Priority	2/1
Deadline	3/1
Notification	4/1
Nonfall registration?	yes

APPLICANTS ALSO LOOK AT
AND OFTEN PREFER
University of Virginia
AND SOMETIMES PREFER
Roanoke College
Virginia Tech
Christopher Newport University
AND RARELY PREFER
Randolph College
Lynchburg College

FINANCIAL FACTS

Financial Aid Rating	80
Annual tuition	$26,195
Room and board	$8,180
Required fees	$635
Books and supplies	$1,000
% frosh rec. need-based scholarship or grant aid	62
% UG rec. need-based scholarship or grant aid	56
% frosh rec. non-need-based scholarship or grant aid	8
% UG rec. non-need-based scholarship or grant aid	8
% frosh rec. need-based self-help aid	53
% UG rec. need-based self-help aid	48
% frosh rec. any financial aid	100
% UG rec. any financial aid	95

REED COLLEGE

3203 SOUTHEAST WOODSTOCK BOULEVARD, PORTLAND, OR 97202-8199 • ADMISSIONS: 503-777-7511 • FAX: 503-777-7553

CAMPUS LIFE

Quality of Life Rating	**93**
Fire Safety Rating	**60***
Green Rating	**79**
Type of school	private
Environment	metropolis

STUDENTS

Total undergrad enrollment	1,426
% male/female	45/55
% from out of state	87
% from public high school	59
% live on campus	59
% African American	2
% Asian	9
% Caucasian	57
% Hispanic	6
% Native American	1
% international	8
# of countries represented	43

SURVEY SAYS . . .

Great computer facilities
Campus feels safe
Frats and sororities are unpopular
or nonexistent

ACADEMICS

Academic Rating	**99**
Calendar	semester
Student/faculty ratio	10:1
Profs interesting rating	99
Profs accessible rating	95
Most common reg class size	10–19 students
Most common lab size	10–19 students

MOST POPULAR MAJORS

English language and literature
biology/biological sciences
psychology

STUDENTS SAY ". . ."

Academics

"Quirky and intellectual," Reed College is an elite liberal arts school where students "can embrace academia without being ridiculed and can love to learn without fear of being ostracized." It's the type of place where students brag about the classics department and proudly report that "Preparation for professional disciplines is somewhat light." With "superior faculty and facilities" that include "an amazing library, lots of computers, a huge amount of free tutoring, [and] a computer help desk where assistance is free," Reed "very much cares what the students think, and is there to serve" students with whatever they might need. Except the work itself, of course; students here "work hard constantly." Most relish the challenge; one undergrad explains, "We take a great deal of pleasure in complaining about the amount of work we have on a daily basis, but never feel as though we are doing something that does not contribute to our ultimate academic project. I had never before understood the intrinsic value of learning. . . . Reed's academic experience is a catalyst for this kind of attitude." Students take a substantial role in running the school, as the administration "keeps a hands-off approach to management of student and faculty affairs, which is well appreciated by both groups. This also allows them to focus on funding the school and maintaining its facilities."

Life

"People spend a lot of time studying, frequently late into the night and on weekends" at Reed. As one undergrad puts it, "Reed allows only three of the following: sleep, a serious relationship, friends, academic success, extracurriculars, a job." Still, once they finish their work, most students find time to "take full advantage of every part of the world outside the library, be it the fantastic Portland restaurants, the huge outdoor sports scene in the Pacific Northwest, or other cultural events around the city, like the art walks that happen twice a month in Portland." On campus, "The Reed social environment is student generated, as all students decide what clubs get funding each semester. I like how this ensures all kinds of opportunities from the outdoors to dance parties to music shows to building crazy 10-foot bikes." Parties and recreational drugs are readily available, but "Overall, people here tend to smaller get-togethers rather than ragers; they tend to prefer doing unique and crazy things rather than the same old beer-drinkin' frat-goin' crapola; and they tend to do cultural activities if those are available to them rather than just go out and get smashed."

Student Body

Reed students "are characterized by a love of learning for its own sake as well as an inability to dance like normal people. Skilled dancers can be integrated into the community with little difficulty, but academic slackers are quickly weeded out." Most "are the kind of 'closet geeks' that you'd never have known about in high school—that is, the ones who looked really cool on the outside but on the inside were all about physics or classics or what-have-you—or 'closet cool kids,' the geeks who were actually really awesome if only you'd bothered to get to know them." There's "one type of student you won't find much of: neo-conservatives. There's a good minority of conservatives on the campus—Libertarians and Republicans who are pissed off by Bush." Mostly "students are left wing in political persuasion and are proud of it."

FINANCIAL AID: 800-547-4750 • E-MAIL: ADMISSION@REED.EDU • WEBSITE: WWW.REED.EDU

THE PRINCETON REVIEW SAYS

Admissions

Very important factors considered include: Application essay, academic GPA, rigor of secondary school record. *Important factors considered include:* Class rank, recommendation(s), standardized test scores, interview, level of applicant's interest. *Other factors considered include:* Alumni/ae relation, character/personal qualities, extracurricular activities, first generation, racial/ethnic status, talent/ability, volunteer work, work experience. SAT Subject Tests recommended; SAT or ACT required; TOEFL required of all international applicants. High school diploma is required and GED is accepted. *Academic units recommended:* 4 English, 4 mathematics, 3 science, 3 foreign language, 1 social studies, 3 history.

Financial Aid

Students should submit: FAFSA, institution's own financial aid form, CSS/Financial Aid PROFILE, noncustodial PROFILE. Regular filing deadline is 1/15. The Princeton Review suggests that all financial aid forms be submitted as soon as possible after January 1. *Need-based scholarships/grants offered:* Federal Pell, SEOG, state scholarships/grants, private scholarships, the school's own gift aid. *Loan aid offered:* FFEL Subsidized Stafford, FFEL Unsubsidized Stafford, FFEL PLUS, Federal Perkins Applicants will be notified of awards on or about 4/1. Federal Work-Study Program available. Institutional employment available.

The Inside Word

The prototypical Reed undergraduate is one who is more concerned with academic pursuits for their own sake than with the potential return on investment of their educations. Think The University of Chicago without the preponderance of math and science majors. You'll need solid credentials and positive indicators of genuine intellectual curiosity to get in the door here—just being smart isn't enough.

THE SCHOOL SAYS "..."

From The Admissions Office

"Reed is animated and energized by its seemingly paradoxical features. Reed has, for example: 1) a traditional, classical, highly structured curriculum—yet, at the same time, a progressive, free-thinking, decidedly unstructured community culture; 2) a powerful emphasis on intellectuality, serious study, and the very highest standards of academic achievement—yet, at the same time, a rich and rewarding program of recreational and extracurricular activity, including a physical education requirement; 3) a refusal to overemphasize grades—yet, third in the nation in the production of future PhDs; 4) a faculty culture absolutely dedicated to superb undergraduate teaching—yet, at the same time, a faculty culture that supports and celebrates high-level research and scholarship at the cutting edge of each academic discipline.

"Reed is not a simple place. It's a complex amalgam of diverse elements. But those elements have been chosen and developed over the years with great care. The result is an intricate—even ornate—but utterly coherent and clearly articulated architecture that has been called by at least one outside observer 'exquisite' and by another 'the most intellectual college in the country.' Reed is not for everyone. But for students who are interested both in exploring great ideas and in developing personal autonomy, it makes very good sense indeed.

"Reed accepts either the ACT or SAT and does not require SAT Subject Tests or the ACT Writing exam. Until we are convinced that the new SAT and ACT Writing exams offer us significant information that we do not already factor into the admission matrix, Reed will not change its approach to standardized tests. Writing sections are recommended, though not required. With the SAT, we will continue to look most closely at the Critical Reading and Math sections and think of test scores on a 1,600-point, as opposed to a 2,400-point scale."

SELECTIVITY
Admissions Rating	97
# of applicants	3,365
% of applicants accepted	34
% of acceptees attending	30
# accepting a place on wait list	43
% admitted from wait list	63
# of early decision applicants	214
% accepted early decision	57

FRESHMAN PROFILE
Range SAT Critical Reading	680–760
Range SAT Math	630–710
Range SAT Writing	650–730
Range ACT Composite	28–32
Minimum paper TOEFL	600
Minimum computer TOEFL	250
Minimum web-based TOEFL	100
Average HS GPA	3.9
% graduated top 10% of class	61
% graduated top 25% of class	92
% graduated top 50% of class	99

DEADLINES
Early decision	
Deadline	11/15
Notification	12/15
Regular	
Deadline	1/15
Notification	4/1
Nonfall registration?	no

APPLICANTS ALSO LOOK AT
AND OFTEN PREFER
University of Chicago
University of California—Berkeley
AND SOMETIMES PREFER
Oberlin College
Carleton College
AND RARELY PREFER
Harvard College
Carleton College
Haverford College
Grinnell College
Stanford University

FINANCIAL FACTS
Financial Aid Rating	95
Annual tuition	$36,190
Room and board	$9,460
Required fees	$230
Books and supplies	$950
% frosh rec. need-based scholarship or grant aid	40
% UG rec. need-based scholarship or grant aid	44
% frosh rec. need-based self-help aid	44
% UG rec. need-based self-help aid	43
% frosh rec. any financial aid	49
% UG rec. any financial aid	50
% UG borrow to pay for school	59
Average cumulative indebtedness	$17,098

RENSSELAER POLYTECHNIC INSTITUTE

110 EIGHTH STREET, TROY, NY 12180-3590 • ADMISSIONS: 518-276-6216 • FAX: 518-276-4072

CAMPUS LIFE

Quality of Life Rating	**68**
Fire Safety Rating	**73**
Green Rating	**88**
Type of school	private
Environment	city

STUDENTS

Total undergrad enrollment	5,119
% male/female	73/27
% from out of state	57
% from public high school	78
% live on campus	53
% in (# of) fraternities	25 (32)
% in (# of) sororities	18 (5)
% African American	4
% Asian	10
% Caucasian	75
% Hispanic	6
% international	2
# of countries represented	62

SURVEY SAYS . . .

Lab facilities are great
Great computer facilities
Great library
Students are happy
Frats and sororities dominate
social scene
Lots of beer drinking

ACADEMICS

Academic Rating	**79**
Calendar	semester
Student/faculty ratio	14:1
Profs interesting rating	61
Profs accessible rating	73
Most common reg class size	20–29 students
Most common lab size	20–29 students

MOST POPULAR MAJORS

computer engineering
electrical, electronics and communications engineering
business/commerce

STUDENTS SAY " . . ."

Academics

Rensselaer Polytechnic Institute, which proud students declare "a small research institute making a large impact on the world," is "essentially a hard-core technical school; heavily oriented towards engineering in the sciences, although it is trying to expand its offerings" in the humanities and arts. The school has already made some headway in that area; as one student points out, "There are a lot of students who are dedicated to their single major in a science or technology field here, which leads to a somewhat narrow-minded type of person...but RPI's saving grace is that it also offers rigorous degrees in architecture and the arts that make this technical institution more like a liberal arts college, as opposed to a strict technical college." Students in all disciplines face "rigorous course loads" that provide "a lesson in perseverance and innovation to overcome future challenges." Most programs incorporate "a hands-on studio-based method" supplemented by "top-of-the-line facilities...and numerous resources for all students to use." RPI's identity as a research center helps here; according to one undergrad, "The greatest resource for students at RPI are the researchers. It's easy to go to any top-ranked school and take hard classes. It's much harder to find as many professors who are on the cutting edge of their disciplines and actively taking undergraduate students into their labs. RPI excels in this, and any RPI student who wants a research position can usually find one." RPI's co-op program and Career Development Center "are also outstanding, leading to a high placement rate in excellent jobs," although of the latter some warn that "many engineering firms are familiar with Rensselaer, but employers in other fields still have yet to learn of the students available."

Life

"The academics are challenging" at RPI, making life "stressful, but in a good way. Time management is a key to success here." A few students have trouble walking away from the books, but most "enjoy relaxing through various clubs and intramural sports" available to all. The Greek scene is popular, but it's not your stereotypical Animal House variety; sure, "There are definitely a bunch of parties every weekend if you're into that," but "they're all pretty much very responsible with sober bartenders and sober drivers." RPI's Greek organizations also "do a lot of community service in the area and philanthropy events on campus." Greek or not, many here agree that "One of the greatest things to do for fun is to head up to the field house on a Friday or Saturday night and watch some Division 1 men's hockey." For those who want something a little more active, "Intramural and inter-fraternity sports are a great way to unwind as well as just hanging out in our student-run union." Hometown Troy "is not the best town to live in, although it has a few cool things to do. But, Albany is only a 20-minute drive away (and the bus is free) and there's always something to do there."

Student Body

"There are a lot of very, very nerdy kids here at RPI, as can be imagined at a school with primarily engineering students," but "There are a large number of 'normal' people as well, and each year, the percent of females in each incoming class increases." While the gender gap may be narrowing, it's still pretty wide, meaning that "there is only one typical student at RPI: a white male. They might be into sports, video games, drinking, Greek life, computers, RPG, or whatever, but they're an overwhelming aspect of campus." The minority population includes "many Asian and Indian students." Nearly everyone "comes from the top of their classes so they are all very intelligent people" who are "driven and hardworking, and think on a global level."

FINANCIAL AID: 518-276-6813 • E-MAIL: ADMISSIONS@RPI.EDU • WEBSITE: WWW.RPI.EDU

THE PRINCETON REVIEW SAYS

Admissions

Very important factors considered include: Class rank, academic GPA, rigor of secondary school record, standardized test scores. *Important factors considered include:* Application essay, recommendation(s), character/personal qualities, extracurricular activities. *Other factors considered include:* Alumni/ae relation, geographical residence, level of applicant's interest, racial/ethnic status, talent/ability, volunteer work, work experience. SAT or ACT required; ACT with Writing component required. TOEFL required of all international applicants. High school diploma is required and GED is accepted. *Academic units required:* 4 English, 4 mathematics, 3 science, 2 social studies. *Academic units recommended:* 4 science, 3 social studies.

Financial Aid

Students should submit: FAFSA, CSS/Financial Aid PROFILE. The Princeton Review suggests that all financial aid forms be submitted as soon as possible after January 1. *Need-based scholarships/grants offered:* Federal Pell, SEOG, state scholarships/grants, private scholarships, the school's own gift aid, Gates Millennium Scholarship, ACG, Smart Grants. *Loan aid offered:* FFEL Subsidized Stafford, FFEL Unsubsidized Stafford, FFEL PLUS, Federal Perkins, state loans, college/university loans from institutional funds. Applicants will be notified of awards on or about 3/25. Federal Work-Study Program available. Institutional employment available. Off-campus job opportunities are good.

The Inside Word

Outstanding test scores and grades are pretty much a must for any applicant hopeful of impressing the RPI Admissions Committee. Underrepresented minorities and women—two demographics the school would like to augment—will get a little more leeway here than others, but in all cases the school is unlikely to admit anyone who lacks the skills and background to survive here. RPI offers many students January admission in order to allow them to pursue productive activities (work, travel, volunteering) in the fall semester following high school graduation.

THE SCHOOL SAYS "..."

From The Admissions Office

"The oldest degree-granting technological research university in North America, Rensselaer was founded in 1824 to instruct students to apply 'science to the common purposes of life.' Rensselaer offers more than 100 programs and 1,000 courses leading to bachelor's, master's, and doctoral degrees. Undergraduates pursue studies in architecture, engineering, humanities and social sciences, management and technology, science, and information technology (IT). A pioneer in interactive learning, Rensselaer provides real-world, hands-on educational opportunities that cut across academic disciplines. Students have ready access to laboratories and attend classes involving lively discussion, problem solving, and faculty mentoring. New programs and facilities are enriching the student experience. The Office of First-Year Experience provides programs for students and their primary support persons that begin even before students arrive on campus. The new $80-million Biotechnology and Interdisciplinary Studies Center offers space for scientific research and discovery, while newly renovated residence halls, wireless computing network, and studio classrooms create a fertile environment for study and learning. The Experimental Media and Performing Arts Center opening in 2008 will encourage students to explore and create at the intersection of engineering and the arts. Rensselaer offers recreational and fitness facilities plus numerous student-run organizations and activities, including fraternities and sororities, a newspaper, a radio station, drama and musical groups, and more than 160 clubs. In addition to intramural sports, NCAA varsity sports include Division I men's and women's ice hockey teams and 21 Division III men's and women's teams in 13 sports. Applicants may submit scores from either SAT (Critical Reading, Math, and Writing) or ACT (which must include optional Writing component). Applicants to the accelerated program must either take the ACT or submit Math and Science scores from SAT Subject Tests."

SELECTIVITY

Admissions Rating	93
# of applicants	10,162
% of applicants accepted	49
% of acceptees attending	26
# accepting a place on wait list	811
% admitted from wait list	6
# of early decision applicants	326
% accepted early decision	57

FRESHMAN PROFILE

Range SAT Critical Reading	600–690
Range SAT Math	650–730
Range SAT Writing	580–670
Range ACT Composite	25–29
Minimum paper TOEFL	570
Minimum computer TOEFL	230
Minimum web-based TOEFL	88
% graduated top 10% of class	64
% graduated top 25% of class	95
% graduated top 50% of class	100

DEADLINES

Early decision	
Deadline	11/1
Notification	12/7
Regular	
Deadline	1/15
Notification	3/14
Nonfall registration?	yes

APPLICANTS ALSO LOOK AT

AND OFTEN PREFER
Cornell University
Massachusetts Institute of Technology

AND SOMETIMES PREFER
Carnegie Mellon University
Boston University

FINANCIAL FACTS

Financial Aid Rating	86
Annual tuition	$36,950
Room and board	$10,730
Required fees	$1,040
Books and supplies	$1,802
% frosh rec. need-based scholarship or grant aid	63
% UG rec. need-based scholarship or grant aid	60
% frosh rec. non-need-based scholarship or grant aid	15
% UG rec. non-need-based scholarship or grant aid	10
% frosh rec. need-based self-help aid	48
% UG rec. need-based self-help aid	48
% frosh rec. athletic scholarships	1
% UG rec. athletic scholarships	1
% frosh rec. any financial aid	99
% UG rec. any financial aid	95
% UG borrow to pay for school	74
Average cumulative indebtedness	$27,125

RHODES COLLEGE

OFFICE OF ADMISSIONS, 2000 NORTH PARKWAY, MEMPHIS, TN 38112 • ADMISSIONS: 901-843-3700 • FAX: 901-843-3631

CAMPUS LIFE

Quality of Life Rating	75
Fire Safety Rating	81
Green Rating	82
Type of school	private
Affiliation	Presbyterian
Environment	metropolis

STUDENTS

Total undergrad enrollment	1,670
% male/female	42/58
% from out of state	73
% from public high school	55
% live on campus	79
% in (# of) fraternities	45 (7)
% in (# of) sororities	51 (6)
% African American	6
% Asian	5
% Caucasian	82
% Hispanic	2
# of countries represented	9

SURVEY SAYS . . .

No one cheats
Great computer facilities
Great library
Students are friendly
Great off-campus food
Frats and sororities dominate
social scene
Lots of beer drinking
Hard liquor is popular

ACADEMICS

Academic Rating	91
Calendar	semester
Student/faculty ratio	11:1
Profs interesting rating	85
Profs accessible rating	85
Most common reg class size	10–19 students
Most common lab size	20–29 students

MOST POPULAR MAJORS

English language and literature
biology/biological sciences
business/commerce

STUDENTS SAY ". . ."

Academics

As "an academically intense liberal arts college with outstanding opportunities for community service and study abroad," Rhodes College lures top area undergrads with "fabulous grad school acceptance ratings, great professor-student interactions and research, and great opportunities in Memphis" of both the career-building and leisure-time variety. Undergrads here praise the "exceptionally high quality of the academics, defined primarily by the small seminar-style classes and the highly approachable and knowledgeable professors," noting that "a distinct majority of professors genuinely love to teach and are just as passionate about their fields and research as they are with the progress [of] their students." As at similar small elite schools, "Academics are tough and the professors demand that you think for yourself. Academic life is characterized by writing papers all the time." Students see the rigors of their curriculum as "preparation and training to effectively translate academic ideas into leadership skills, with the ultimate goal of building stronger, more stable communities."

Life

Rhodes undergrads shoulder a "high commitment to schoolwork" and "often seem overwhelmed by the amount to do," but that doesn't keep them from being able "to balance work and play." "Most are involved either with some sort of on-campus job, internship, student organization or community service effort in the Memphis area." Campus life offers "something to do any night of the week," with "many students very involved in Greek life" and "lots of creative activities provided by the administration." Parties "are the norm on weekends, usually at the frat houses, although recently more parties have been off campus due to an administration crackdown." However, "If you are not into partying, then downtown Memphis is only a few minutes down the road, and there are tons of things to do there. Memphis seems like a little town, but it's really not. If you like music, Memphis is the capital of all music from blues to rock. I came from a city that was about three times larger than Memphis, and I will tell you that Memphis has more unique things…to do than anywhere I have ever been. It really is amazing." While some students worry about crime in Memphis ("It is often in the back of our minds but has never been a problem on campus"), most don't let it deter them from enjoying "one of the most fun cities to live in." As an added bonus, "Rhodes is across the street from the zoo, and Tuesdays are free, so it's a lot of fun to go see the pandas and polar bears."

Student Body

There is "a definite stereotype for the typical Rhodes student, but like all stereotypes, it does not accurately describe and assess the student body as a whole." It "is often tempting to describe the typical Rhodes student as a wealthy, White, Protestant Southerner," but as one student points out, "the fact that I am a liberal Jew from California shows that many students defy the stereotype. There are many atypical students, but students of different races, financial backgrounds, and religions upbringings still manage to interact with each other and with the Memphis community." Even so, a casual observer could be forgiven for drawing overly general conclusions based on the students' appearance, for there is definitely "a Rhodes look" consisting of "pastel polo shirts and pressed khaki pants." Undergrads tend to be "goal-oriented overachievers" who "work extremely hard" to "realize a future at a good law school, med school, or other graduate program." Many students are seen as being "very religious," and while it can be "a bit difficult" to find your "own niche," "You make a lot of good connections and friends here."

FINANCIAL AID: 901-843-3810 • E-MAIL: ADMINFO@RHODES.EDU • WEBSITE: WWW.RHODES.EDU

THE PRINCETON REVIEW SAYS

Admissions

Very important factors considered include: Class rank, academic GPA, secondary school attending, rigor of secondary school record. *Important factors considered include:* Application essay, recommendation(s), standardized test scores, alumni/ae relation, character/personal qualities, racial/ethnic status. *Other factors considered include:* Extracurricular activities, first generation, geographical residence, interview, level of applicant's interest, state residency, talent/ability, volunteer work, work experience. SAT or ACT required; TOEFL required of all non-English speaking international applicants. High school diploma is required and GED is accepted. *Academic units required:* 4 English, 3 mathematics, 2 science, (2 science labs), 2 foreign language, 2 social studies, 3 academic electives. *Academic units recommended:* 4 mathematics.

Financial Aid

Students should submit: FAFSA, CSS/Financial Aid PROFILE, noncustodial PROFILE Regular filing deadline is 3/1. The Princeton Review suggests that all financial aid forms be submitted as soon as possible after January 1. *Need-based scholarships/grants offered:* Federal Pell, SEOG, ACG, SMART, state scholarships/grants, private scholarships, the school's own gift aid. *Loan aid offered:* FFEL Subsidized Stafford, FFEL Unsubsidized Stafford, FFEL PLUS, Federal Perkins Federal Work-Study Program available. Institutional employment available. Off-campus job opportunities are good.

The Inside Word

Rhodes' profile is rising, and as it does, so do both the number of applications it receives and its rejection rate. You can improve your chances of acceptance by showing an active interest in attending—visit the school, meet with an Admissions Counselor, and maintain contact with the Admissions Office to remind administrators that Rhodes is high on your wish list, and hopefully, in return you'll be high on theirs.

THE SCHOOL SAYS "..."

From The Admissions Office

"It's not just one characteristic that makes Rhodes different from other colleges; it's a special blend of features that sets us apart. We are a selective liberal arts college yet without a cutthroat atmosphere; we are a small community yet located in a major city; we are in a metropolitan area yet offer one of the most beautiful and serene campuses in the nation. Our students are serious about learning and yet know how to have fun in an atmosphere of trust and respect brought about by adherence to the honor code. And they know that learning at Rhodes doesn't mean sitting in a lecture hall and memorizing the professor's lecture. It means interaction, discussion, and a process of teacher and student discovering knowledge together. Community service is an integral part of the culture at Rhodes. Our students are keenly aware of their social responsibility, and over 80 percent are involved as volunteers throughout their college years. Rhodes is a place that welcomes new people and new ideas. It's a place of energy and enlightenment, not of apathy and complacency. Everyone who is a part of the Rhodes community is striving to be the best at what she/he does.

"Applicants for Fall 2008 are required to take the SAT or the ACT. The ACT Writing section is optional. Homeschool students must submit two SAT Subject Tests from areas other than English and Mathematics."

SELECTIVITY

Admissions Rating	**94**
# of applicants	3,709
% of applicants accepted	51
% of acceptees attending	24
# accepting a place on wait list	178
% admitted from wait list	25
# of early decision applicants	140
% accepted early decision	48

FRESHMAN PROFILE

Range SAT Critical Reading	590–690
Range SAT Math	590–690
Range ACT Composite	26–30
Minimum paper TOEFL	550
Minimum computer TOEFL	213
Average HS GPA	3.81
% graduated top 10% of class	51
% graduated top 25% of class	83
% graduated top 50% of class	98

DEADLINES

Early decision	
Deadline	11/1
Notification	12/1
Regular	
Priority	1/15
Notification	4/1
Nonfall registration?	yes

APPLICANTS ALSO LOOK AT
AND OFTEN PREFER
Washington University in St. Louis
Washington and Lee University
Davidson College

AND SOMETIMES PREFER
University of Richmond
Sewanee—The University of the South
Vanderbilt University

AND RARELY PREFER
The University of Memphis

FINANCIAL FACTS

Financial Aid Rating	**83**
Annual tuition	$28,232
Room and board	$7,468
Required fees	$310
Books and supplies	$904
% frosh rec. need-based scholarship or grant aid	43
% UG rec. need-based scholarship or grant aid	39
% frosh rec. non-need-based scholarship or grant aid	19
% UG rec. non-need-based scholarship or grant aid	16
% frosh rec. need-based self-help aid	26
% UG rec. need-based self-help aid	25
% frosh rec. any financial aid	80
% UG rec. any financial aid	80
% UG borrow to pay for school	45
Average cumulative indebtedness	$21,035

RICE UNIVERSITY

OFFICE OF ADMISSION MS 17, PO BOX 1892, HOUSTON, TX 77251-1892 • ADMISSIONS: 713-348-7423 • FAX: 713-348-5952

STUDENTS SAY ". . ."

Academics

Students tell us that Rice University provides "an Ivy League education without the Eastern establishment elitism and cutthroat competition." As at the Ivies, there's a lot of high-profile research going on here; unlike at least some of the Ivies, though, "Many of the top researchers at the school teach intro level classes in their fields." Undergrads here benefit from Rice's relatively small size; as one student explains, the school "is small enough that you're always running into someone you know, but big enough that you can easily do awesome research, be a part of a radio station reaching all of Houston, or get involved in the performing arts." Academically, the school "is heavily focused on the sciences and engineering," and although the school has made efforts to bolster its other disciplines, for at least the time being "the humanities and social sciences are perceived as 'easy' majors, and while there are a lot of great resources for these disciplines here, sometimes we who study them feel forgotten in a sea of bioengineers and premeds." Perceptions notwithstanding, academics across the board here are "challenging, but there is an extensive support network and it is not a competitive environment." Indeed, undergrads agree that "Rice University is dedicated to its students, whether in the classroom through providing top-notch professors who are approachable...or just around campus by catering to students' professed real needs and desires" by an administration that is "extremely sensitive to students' needs and concerns."

Life

You can't understand life at Rice without understanding the residential college system, which many, many students say is "hands down the best thing about Rice." Under the system, "You are placed in a dorm and you live there all four years. It's great because it gives you another family and allows you to get to know everyone in your college. Rather than having frats or sororities that you have to be approved of to join, your college immediately accepts you without question." Each college "has developed its own personality, traditions, and completely student-led government.... When asked 'Where are you from?' students almost always reply not with their hometown but with their college affiliation." Students are equally enthusiastic about Rice's "wet campus" policy, under which "You can have alcohol in your room, you can drink it at Pub, and you can drink it at on-campus public parties (for free!)." While this results in "a fairly large drinking culture" on campus, "there are also tons of people who don't ever drink.... There's something for everyone at Rice, and there's very little pressure to enter a sphere of activity that makes you uncomfortable." Hometown Houston "is not the prettiest or most pedestrian-friendly city in America, but it is one of the most vibrant, futuristic places you can live right now, and the opportunities for research within the Houston community are unparalleled." Rice wants students to explore the city; explains one student, "The serveries are closed on Saturday nights, so people have to get off campus.... There are shuttles that take you to the Village, a fun place with shops, restaurants, and bars not to far from campus.... It's a really great excuse to find out what Houston has to offer."

Student Body

"Everyone at Rice is weird with some talent, oddity, or quirk that would otherwise attract attention in the normal world, but is accepted as totally normal here," students inform us. "Through the madness is how people bond." The residential college system also helps, as it "ensures a lot of mixing among different majors, races, interests, and geographic origins. People are similar enough and smart enough and have enough converging interests to make good friends with each other." Elite schools are best positioned to build a diverse student body, and Rice is no exception to the rule; here you'll find "people with extremely diverse beliefs and backgrounds. We are not overly Democrat or Republican, we are not overly religious (though we do have a good number of active organizations, particularly Campus Crusade for Christ and Hillel), and we come from anything ranging from public high schools to boarding schools." However, the school "is not very diverse geographically, as 50 percent come from Texas."

RICE UNIVERSITY

FINANCIAL AID: 713-348-4958 • E-MAIL: ADMISSION@RICE.EDU • WEBSITE: WWW.RICE.EDU

THE PRINCETON REVIEW SAYS

Admissions

Very important factors considered include: Class rank, application essay, academic GPA, recommendation(s), rigor of secondary school record, standardized test scores, character/personal qualities, extracurricular activities, talent/ability. *Other factors considered include:* Alumni/ae relation, first generation, geographical residence, interview, level of applicant's interest, racial/ethnic status, state residency, volunteer work, work experience. SAT Subject Tests required; SAT or ACT required; ACT with Writing component required. TOEFL required of all international applicants. High school diploma or equivalent is not required. *Academic units required:* 4 English, 3 mathematics, 2 science, (2 science labs), 2 foreign language, 2 social studies, 3 academic electives. *Academic units recommended:* 4 English, 4 mathematics, 4 science, (3 science labs), 4 foreign language, 2 social studies, 2 academic electives.

Financial Aid

Students should submit: FAFSA, CSS/Financial Aid PROFILE, noncustodial PROFILE, business/farm supplement, Tax returns and W-2s. The Princeton Review suggests that all financial aid forms be submitted as soon as possible after January 1. *Need-based scholarships/grants offered:* Federal Pell, SEOG, state scholarships/grants, private scholarships, the school's own gift aid. *Loan aid offered:* FFEL Subsidized Stafford, FFEL Unsubsidized Stafford, FFEL PLUS, Federal Perkins, state loans Applicants will be notified of awards on a rolling basis beginning 3/1. Federal Work-Study Program available. Institutional employment available. Off-campus job opportunities are excellent.

The Inside Word

Rice is among the nation's most selective undergraduate institutions. Legacies, athletes, and others thought to bring added value to the campus may receive a few breaks when their applications are assessed; all others need to present a very compelling profile that includes a challenging high school curriculum, solid grades, and superior test scores.

THE SCHOOL SAYS "..."

From The Admissions Office

"We seek students of keen intellect and diverse backgrounds who show potential to succeed at Rice and will also contribute to the educational environment of those around them.

"Student applications are reviewed within the context of the division to which they apply. Admission Committee decisions are based not only on high school grades and test scores but also on such qualities as leadership, participation in extracurricular activities, and personal creativity. Admission is extremely competitive; Rice attempts to seek out and identify those students who have demonstrated exceptional ability and the potential for personal and intellectual growth.

"Our individualized, holistic evaluation process employs many different means to identify these qualities in applicants.

"Required admission testing includes the SAT or ACT with Writing. In addition, Rice requires all freshman applicants to take two SAT Subject Tests. All test scores must be sent to Rice directly from the official testing agency."

SELECTIVITY
Admissions Rating	98
# of applicants	8,776
% of applicants accepted	24
% of acceptees attending	34
# accepting a place on wait list	498
% admitted from wait list	22
# of early decision applicants	596
% accepted early decision	29

FRESHMAN PROFILE
Range SAT Critical Reading	650–760
Range SAT Math	680–780
Range SAT Writing	640–740
Range ACT Composite	30–34
Minimum paper TOEFL	600
Minimum computer TOEFL	250
% graduated top 10% of class	87
% graduated top 25% of class	95
% graduated top 50% of class	99

DEADLINES
Early decision	
Deadline	11/1
Notification	12/15
Early action	
Deadline	12/1
Notification	2/10
Regular	
Deadline	1/10
Notification	4/1
Nonfall registration?	no

APPLICANTS ALSO LOOK AT AND OFTEN PREFER
Harvard College
Stanford University

FINANCIAL FACTS
Financial Aid Rating	95
Annual tuition	$25,606
Room and board	$10,250
Required fees	$500
Books and supplies	$800
% frosh rec. need-based scholarship or grant aid	37
% UG rec. need-based scholarship or grant aid	36
% frosh rec. non-need-based scholarship or grant aid	10
% UG rec. non-need-based scholarship or grant aid	9
% frosh rec. need-based self-help aid	29
% UG rec. need-based self-help aid	34
% frosh rec. athletic scholarships	10
% UG rec. athletic scholarships	9
% frosh rec. any financial aid	65
% UG rec. any financial aid	64
% UG borrow to pay for school	41
Average cumulative indebtedness	$15,876

RIDER UNIVERSITY

2083 LAWRENCEVILLE ROAD, LAWRENCEVILLE, NJ 08648 • ADMISSIONS: 609-896-5042 • FAX: 609-895-6645

STUDENTS SAY ". . ."

Academics

Rider University is a smallish suburban liberal arts school in New Jersey that offers internships galore and a wide variety of majors. Rider's Westminster Choir College (in nearby Princeton) is worth looking into if you can hum a tune exceptionally well, but the biggest draw here is probably the "very good business program." Academically, "the classes aren't too big." "Last semester my biggest class had 17 kids in it," notes a public relations major. Coursework is generally "engaging." A few members of the faculty "should not be teaching," but most professors are "intelligent people with a lot to offer." They're "very interested and involved within their respective fields." "Professors are very easy to contact and are always excited to help answer a question even when you don't have them as a professor anymore," relates an accounting major. "It is easy to build close personal relationships with your professors and that really helps students do well in the classroom." Views of the administration differ pretty radically. Some students call management "very efficient" and "simply wonderful." "Customer service is excellent," they say. Other students say that the staff is "rude and very unhelpful." "It is very hard for me to get a straight answer," gripes an education major.

Life

Rider's main campus is "secluded from town" and full of too many "outdated and jail-like" buildings. Also, some dorms could stand to be "spruced up." The newer residence halls are "great" though, and the gleaming student recreation center is a big hit with many students. There's also a nice on-campus pub. Otherwise, "fun is a touchy topic." Disgruntled students tell us that life at Rider "is not amazingly exciting." It's "a suitcase school," they say, and "a ghost town on the weekends" because so many students "drive home" on Friday night. "Basically there's not a lot to do around here," laments a sophomore. Happier students report an "overwhelming" number of activities and a good amount of free food at weekend events. "One of the biggest perks about staying on the weekend is that you get a really good parking spot," says an optimistic sophomore. Many students who stick around also participate in the Greek system. "A lot of people party," too, but "the alcohol policies are extreme." As a result, there are "numerous parties off campus." Students also frequent "clubs and bars" in the area. While "there's nothing to do anywhere in Lawrenceville without having a car," Rider is situated "directly between" Philadelphia and New York City and those cities are easily accessible.

Student Body

"Mostly, everyone is from New Jersey," but ethnic diversity is pretty laudable at Rider and "students come from many different backgrounds." "It's not too hard to fit in." "There are a lot of students who take their work seriously." "There are the weird people who don't really socialize." There are also "slacker types" with "no sense of the real world" who are "trying to float through college" and "are more concerned with the party scene than academics." There are students "from middleclass homes" and wealthy students "with nice cars." You'll see quite a few women with "skinny jeans, Uggs, and poofy hair." There are "many clone students," too. "Your average student looks like your average kid that you would see in your own town," guesses a junior. "Overall, everyone has a niche" but "you have to join a group to make friends." "There are a lot of cliques," observes a senior. "The athletes stay with the athletes; the Greeks stay with the Greeks; and so on." Many people "stay connected to their high school friends."

FINANCIAL AID: 609-896-5360 • E-MAIL: ADMISSIONS@RIDER.EDU • WEBSITE: WWW.RIDER.EDU

THE PRINCETON REVIEW SAYS

Admissions

Very important factors considered include: Application essay, academic GPA, recommendation(s), rigor of secondary school record, standardized test scores. *Important factors considered include:* Class rank, level of applicant's interest. *Other factors considered include:* Alumni/ae relation, character/personal qualities, extracurricular activities, geographical residence, interview, state residency, talent/ability, volunteer work, work experience. SAT or ACT required; High school diploma is required and GED is accepted. *Academic units required:* 4 English, 3 mathematics (including algebra I, II, and geometry). *Academic units recommended:* 4 mathematics, 4 science, (2 science labs), 2 foreign language, 2 social studies, 2 history.

Financial Aid

Students should submit: FAFSA. The Princeton Review suggests that all financial aid forms be submitted as soon as possible after January 1. *Need-based scholarships/grants offered:* Federal Pell, SEOG, state scholarships/grants, private scholarships, the school's own gift aid. *Loan aid offered:* FFEL Subsidized Stafford, FFEL Unsubsidized Stafford, FFEL PLUS, Federal Perkins, state loans, college/university loans from institutional funds, Alternative loans. Applicants will be notified of awards on a rolling basis beginning 3/15. Federal Work-Study Program available. Student employment available.

The Inside Word

In the admissions world there are two all-important mandates: recruit the college's home state, and recruit *Jersey*! As a school in the Garden State, Rider deserves some special attention for the diverse group of students it brings in each year. Students who wish to attend need to have a solid academic record and good test scores. A few bumps in your academic past, however, shouldn't pose too much of a threat.

THE SCHOOL SAYS "..."

From The Admissions Office

"Rider students are driven by their dreams of a fulfilling career and a desire to have an impact on the world around them. Rider is a place to apply your imagination, talents and aspirations in ways that will make a difference. A Rider education will prepare you as a leader and as a member of a team. When you graduate from Rider, you'll be a different person, confidently ready for your life's challenges and opportunities.

"We invite you to visit and experience Rider firsthand. Open Houses are offered in the fall and late spring, tours are available daily and Information Sessions are offered most weekends. Please see our website (www.rider.edu) for further details.

"Freshmen applicants for Fall 2009 are required to submit the results of either the SAT or ACT exam, the writing component is required for both. The highest scores from either test will be considered for admission."

SELECTIVITY
Admissions Rating	75
# of applicants	6,213
% of applicants accepted	75
% of acceptees attending	21
# accepting a place on wait list	93
% admitted from wait list	12

FRESHMAN PROFILE
Range SAT Critical Reading	470–570
Range SAT Math	480–590
Range SAT Writing	470–570
Range ACT Composite	20–24
Average HS GPA	3.24
% graduated top 10% of class	12
% graduated top 25% of class	38
% graduated top 50% of class	75

DEADLINES
Early decision	
Deadline	11/15
Notification	12/15
Early action	
Deadline	12/15
Notification	1/15
Regular	
Notification	rolling
Nonfall registration?	yes

FINANCIAL FACTS
Financial Aid Rating	71
Annual tuition	$25,650
% frosh rec. need-based scholarship or grant aid	66
% UG rec. need-based scholarship or grant aid	62
% frosh rec. non-need-based scholarship or grant aid	9
% UG rec. non-need-based scholarship or grant aid	8
% frosh rec. need-based self-help aid	51
% UG rec. need-based self-help aid	48
% frosh rec. athletic scholarships	8
% UG rec. athletic scholarships	6
% frosh rec. any financial aid	85
% UG rec. any financial aid	66
% UG borrow to pay for school	76
Average cumulative indebtedness	$32,132

RIPON COLLEGE

300 Seward Street, PO Box 248, Ripon, WI 54971 • Admissions: 920-748-8337 • Fax: 920-748-8335

STUDENTS SAY ". . ."

Academics
"A small liberal arts college that prides itself on promoting close relationships between its students and faculty," Ripon College attracts bright students seeking a "personalized education in a unique learning environment." A "great atmosphere" energizes the "small but friendly campus" of this school; the professors here "get to know you by name as a person, not just as a face in a crowd." Students praise Ripon's "emphasis on written and oral communication" and the liberal arts curriculum that gives students "very personalized opportunities for broad-based learning, both inside and outside of the classroom." As one student puts it, "As clichéd as it sounds, the community is what makes Ripon worthwhile. Going to a professor's house for dinner or having class in the local coffee shop is common. A friend of mine slept through an exam, and her professor noticed her absence. The professor called the Dean of Students, who then called her hall director. Her hall director went to her room to check on her, waking her up in enough time to take the exam, albeit a little late. Stories like that might be unheard of at large universities, but they are really characteristic of Ripon."

Life
At many small rural schools, students complain about the tedium of campus life, but no such complaints are heard at Ripon, where undergrads insist that "there's tons to do for fun." Popular activities include seeing "comedians, movies, or speakers. There are always athletic events, musical concerts, or plays to watch. There are also many intramural sports to participate in. And if you want to get away, there are a campus theater and a bowling alley in town, not to mention the cute downtown [area], which is just a block away." Ripon's robust Greek scene keeps things hopping with "lounge parties and festivals," while other student organizations offer "every type of group you could possibly want to participate in. And if you don't want to join, you can still participate in their events." In addition to clubs, "Collegiate sports are another one of our strengths. Everyone has the opportunity to participate, play, and even be a superstar." Undergrads here really love "the friendliness on campus. Doors are unlocked, and people leave their backpacks in the foyer before going up to eat lunch. The fact that things are not stolen really shows just how much we respect each other."

Student Body
The majority of Ripon undergrads are Wisconsin natives, with many "coming from middle-class families from small rural Wisconsin towns. Most are outgoing and very friendly, and are quick to say hello even if they don't know your name." The school's size fosters this gregarious nature; as one student explains, "You don't go to a small liberal arts school if you don't enjoy participating in class discussions. That's why most students here are outgoing." The size and Midwestern setting can breed homogeneity as well as friendliness: In the past, "The stereotypical Ripon student has been White, likely from a small town or rural area, and conservative." But "The image is changing as each class becomes more diverse. Because of this increasing diversity, I don't think there is really an atypical student at Ripon." What is typical of Ripon students is their energetic involvement in all aspects of school life; students at Ripon are "smart and enjoy school, but also like to have fun. There are many students involved with sports, student organizations, student government, and Greek life. Students on campus are very involved in the activities that they do."

FINANCIAL AID: 920-748-8101 • E-MAIL: ADMINFO@RIPON.EDU • WEBSITE: WWW.RIPON.EDU

THE PRINCETON REVIEW SAYS

Admissions

Very important factors considered include: Rigor of secondary school record, interview. *Important factors considered include:* Class rank, academic GPA, recommendation(s), standardized test scores, character/personal qualities, extracurricular activities. *Other factors considered include:* Application essay, talent/ability, volunteer work, SAT or ACT required; TOEFL required of all international applicants. High school diploma is required and GED is accepted. *Academic units required:* 4 English, 2 mathematics, 2 science, 2 social studies. *Academic units recommended:* 4 mathematics, 4 science, 2 foreign language, 4 social studies.

Financial Aid

Students should submit: FAFSA. The Princeton Review suggests that all financial aid forms be submitted as soon as possible after January 1. *Need-based scholarships/grants offered:* Federal Pell, SEOG, state scholarships/grants, private scholarships, the school's own gift aid. *Loan aid offered:* FFEL Subsidized Stafford, FFEL Unsubsidized Stafford, FFEL PLUS, Federal Perkins Applicants will be notified of awards on a rolling basis beginning 3/1. Federal Work-Study Program available. Institutional employment available. Off-campus job opportunities are good.

The Inside Word

The admissions process at Ripon College reflects the school's familial atmosphere. Matchmaking is a top priority and Admissions Officers are thorough in their assessments. They closely evaluate qualitative components such as interviews and extracurricular activities, searching for eager and committed applicants.

THE SCHOOL SAYS "..."

From The Admissions Office

"Since its founding in 1851, Ripon College has adhered to the philosophy that the liberal arts offer the richest foundation for intellectual, cultural, social, and spiritual growth. Academic strength is a 150-year tradition at Ripon. We attract excellent professors who are dedicated to their disciplines; they in turn attract bright, committed students. Together with the other members of our tightly knit learning community, students at Ripon learn more deeply, live more fully, and achieve more success. Students are surprised to discover that here there are more opportunities—to be involved, to lead, to speak out, to make a difference, to explore new interests—than at a college 10 times our size. Through collaborative learning, group living, teamwork, and networking, students tap into the power of a community where we all work together to ensure success—at Ripon and beyond.

"All of the best residential liberal arts colleges strive to be true learning communities like Ripon. We succeed better than most because our enrollment of about 1,000 students is perfect for fostering connections inside and outside the classroom. Our students flourish in this environment of mutual respect, where shared values are elevated and diverse ideas are valued. If you are seeking academic challenge and want to benefit from an environment of personal attention and support—then you should take a closer look at Ripon.

"Applicants to Ripon College must submit scores from either the ACT (Writing section not required) or the SAT. We will allow students to submit scores from the old (prior to March 2005) version of either test and will use their best scores for admission decisions."

SELECTIVITY

Admissions Rating	79
# of applicants	974
% of applicants accepted	80
% of acceptees attending	34

FRESHMAN PROFILE

Range SAT Critical Reading	440–610
Range SAT Math	480–650
Range ACT Composite	21–27
Minimum paper TOEFL	550
Minimum computer TOEFL	213
Minimum web-based TOEFL	79
Average HS GPA	3.38
% graduated top 10% of class	21
% graduated top 25% of class	51
% graduated top 50% of class	84

DEADLINES

Regular	
Priority	3/15
Notification	rolling
Nonfall registration?	yes

APPLICANTS ALSO LOOK AT

AND OFTEN PREFER
University of Wisconsin—Oshkosh
University of Wisconsin—Madison
St. Norbert College

AND SOMETIMES PREFER
Carroll College (WI)

AND RARELY PREFER
Lawrence University

FINANCIAL FACTS

Financial Aid Rating	87
Annual tuition	$23,970
Room and board	$6,770
Required fees	$275
Books and supplies	$800
% frosh rec. need-based scholarship or grant aid	82
% UG rec. need-based scholarship or grant aid	77
% frosh rec. non-need-based scholarship or grant aid	16
% UG rec. non-need-based scholarship or grant aid	13
% frosh rec. need-based self-help aid	66
% UG rec. need-based self-help aid	77
% frosh rec. any financial aid	100
% UG rec. any financial aid	98
% UG borrow to pay for school	87
Average cumulative indebtedness	$19,929

ROCHESTER INSTITUTE OF TECHNOLOGY

60 LOMB MEMORIAL DRIVE, ROCHESTER, NY 14623-5604 • ADMISSIONS: 585-475-6631 • FAX: 585-475-7424

STUDENTS SAY ". . ."

Academics

Rochester Institute of Technology is a "serious, no-nonsense school" "with amazing facilities" and a "unique" cooperative education program which is "very good" at "preparing you to work in the real world." The "great technical education" is a main draw for students. Other "high-quality programs" include animation, design, and the "renowned" College of Business. The National Technical Institute for the Deaf "makes for a diverse population." "Hard work" and a "fast pace" define academic life. Courses "go by fast" on RIT's "hard-core" 10-week quarter system. "Classes require a lot of outside work," says a junior. One bonus of attending RIT is that "the best employers in the country hold on-campus interviews frequently." Upon graduation, "Job placement is really high" thanks to RIT's co-op program that "is required for many majors and encouraged for all." Co-op students graduate with "hands-on" experience at firms across the country. The "very passionate" professors here "come to teach, not to do research." "Academic support" is ubiquitous. "Even the worst professors I've had in lecture have been helpful after class," says an engineering major. "If you don't do well, it's your own fault." The "visible" administration is "fairly helpful." Some students wish administrators would "listen to their students a little bit more," but "The dean of your college is just an e-mail and appointment away."

Life

"Everything is made of brick" here and the "freezing" winters can be "very hard to walk through every day." "They should put us in a dome," helpfully suggests a first-year student. The weather notwithstanding, "RIT is a place where you come to work hard and make a lot of money when you graduate," explains a senior. The "competitive academic environment" "makes a lot of the students stress out," and students really "have to study." "On weekends, people tend to relax." "If you're looking for a party school," look elsewhere. "Big parties" are sometimes held "off-campus," but "not like the ones that happen at other schools." "Very intense alcohol-free policies" also stifle the party scene, and Greek organizations "are kept on an annoyingly tight leash." "School spirit" is not the highest, but "There are many different types of activities on campus." "Almost anyone who is looking for something to do can find a place to fit in." Engineering clubs "give students hands-on experience and knowledge that they can apply to both their schoolwork and the career world." The campus "is a great venue for influential speakers" and "The College Activities Board does a great job of getting big acts to come perform." There is also "an amazing gym," and "downtown Rochester is close and has a lot" to offer, including "amazing Indian and sushi restaurants."

Student Body

RIT students are "very hardworking" and "career-motivated." "Grades are taken very seriously." Students say "super-smart" engineering majors and "crazy science students" are typical, as are "ragtag art students, preppy business students, jocks, [and] hippies." Many students "like to fool around with computers." Some students assert that "RIT is a nerd haven." Others complain that RIT has a "reputation of being a dork school when it really isn't." "There is a stereotype that students here are unsocial and like to sit in their room playing video games," complains a senior. Without question, there are "kids who don't come out of their rooms," but those that do leave their confines "are awesome." "The variety of programs offered draws a very diverse group of students that can in no way fit under one general description," explains a junior. "The interaction of these extremely different groups of students is part of what makes life on campus so interesting." That said, RIT is "predominantly male" and many would like to see the male/female ratio improved.

ROCHESTER INSTITUTE OF TECHNOLOGY

FINANCIAL AID: 585-475-2186 • E-MAIL: ADMISSIONS@RIT.EDU • WEBSITE: WWW.RIT.EDU

THE PRINCETON REVIEW SAYS

Admissions

Very important factors considered include: Academic GPA, rigor of secondary school record. *Important factors considered include:* Class rank, standardized test scores. *Other factors considered include:* Application essay, recommendation(s), alumni/ae relation, character/personal qualities, extracurricular activities, first generation, geographical residence, interview, level of applicant's interest, racial/ethnic status, talent/ability, volunteer work, SAT or ACT required; High school diploma is required and GED is accepted. *Academic units required:* 4 English, 2 mathematics, 2 science, (1 science labs), 4 social studies, 10 academic electives. *Academic units recommended:* 4 English, 3 mathematics, 3 science, (2 science labs), 3 foreign language, 4 social studies, 5 academic electives.

Financial Aid

Students should submit: FAFSA, state aid form. The Princeton Review suggests that all financial aid forms be submitted as soon as possible after January 1. *Need-based scholarships/grants offered:* Federal Pell, SEOG, state scholarships/grants, private scholarships, the school's own gift aid, NACME. *Loan aid offered:* Direct Subsidized Stafford, Direct Unsubsidized Stafford, Direct PLUS, Federal Perkins, RIT Loan program; Alternative loans. Applicants will be notified of awards on a rolling basis beginning 3/15. Federal Work-Study Program available. Institutional employment available. Off-campus job opportunities are excellent.

The Inside Word

Admission here is nowhere near as cutthroat as it is at other top-tier technical schools on the East Coast. But that doesn't mean admission isn't competitive, since RIT's co-op programs and its tremendous record of job placement with prestigious employers all over the country make it an attractive choice for many academically-talented applicants. The relatively high acceptance rate is somewhat deceiving because the applicant pool is largely self-selecting. The applicant pool is also small enough that RIT can go over your application with the finest-toothed of combs, for better or worse.

THE SCHOOL SAYS ". . ."

From The Admissions Office

"RIT is among the world's leading career-oriented, technological institutions. Ambitious, creative, diverse, and career-oriented students from every state and more than 95 foreign countries find a home in RIT's innovative, vibrant living/learning community. The university's eight colleges offer undergraduate and graduate programs areas such as engineering, computing, information technology, engineering technology, business, hospitality, science, art, design, photography, biomedical sciences, game design and development, and the liberal arts including psychology, advertising and public relations, and public policy Distinctive academic offerings include microelectronic and software engineering, imaging science, film and animation, biotechnology, physician assistant, new media, international business, telecommunications, and the programs in the School for American Crafts. In addition, students may choose from more than seventy different minors to develop personal and professional interests that complement their academic program. As home of the National Technical Institute for the Deaf (NTID), RIT is a leader in providing educational opportunities and access services for deaf and hard-of-hearing students. Experiential learning has been a hallmark of an RIT education since 1912. Every academic program at RIT offers some form of experiential education opportunity which may include cooperative education, internships, study abroad, and undergraduate research. Students work hard, but learning is complemented with plenty of organized and spontaneous events and activities. RIT is a unique blend of rigor and fun, creativity and specialization, intellect and practice that prepares alumni for long-term career success in global society."

SELECTIVITY
Admissions Rating	83
# of applicants	11,012
% of applicants accepted	65
% of acceptees attending	35
# accepting a place on wait list	174
% admitted from wait list	36
# of early decision applicants	1,130
% accepted early decision	69

FRESHMAN PROFILE
Range SAT Critical Reading	530–630
Range SAT Math	560–670
Range ACT Composite	24–29
% graduated top 10% of class	26
% graduated top 25% of class	59
% graduated top 50% of class	88

DEADLINES
Early decision	
Deadline	12/1
Notification	1/15
Regular	
Priority	2/1
Deadline	2/1
Notification	rolling
Nonfall registration?	yes

FINANCIAL FACTS
Financial Aid Rating	90
Annual tuition	$27,624
Room and board	$9,381
Required fees	$411
Books and supplies	$900
% frosh rec. need-based scholarship or grant aid	69
% UG rec. need-based scholarship or grant aid	64
% frosh rec. non-need-based scholarship or grant aid	20
% UG rec. non-need-based scholarship or grant aid	21
% frosh rec. need-based self-help aid	65
% UG rec. need-based self-help aid	60
% frosh rec. any financial aid	88
% UG rec. any financial aid	77
% UG borrow to pay for school	77
Average cumulative indebtedness	$22,000

ROLLINS COLLEGE

CAMPUS BOX 2720, WINTER PARK, FL 32789-4499 • ADMISSIONS: 407-646-2161 • FAX: 407-646-1502

CAMPUS LIFE

Quality of Life Rating	82
Fire Safety Rating	87
Green Rating	72
Type of school	private
Environment	town

STUDENTS

Total undergrad enrollment	1,778
% male/female	42/58
% from out of state	47
% from public high school	53
% live on campus	70
% in (# of) fraternities	25 (5)
% in (# of) sororities	24 (6)
% African American	4
% Asian	4
% Caucasian	72
% Hispanic	10
% international	4
# of countries represented	34

SURVEY SAYS . . .
Small classes
Great computer facilities
Students love Winter Park, FL
Great off-campus food
Frats and sororities dominate
social scene
Lots of beer drinking
Hard liquor is popular

ACADEMICS

Academic Rating	87
Calendar	semester
Student/faculty ratio	10:1
Profs interesting rating	90
Profs accessible rating	88
Most common reg class size	10–19 students

MOST POPULAR MAJORS
international business/trade/commerce
economics
English language and literature

STUDENTS SAY ". . ."

Academics

Students seeking "strong academics in a country-club setting" should consider Rollins College. Undergrads proudly describe it as "one of the best liberal arts schools in the South." Students here form "a community of learners seeking an education experience that advances responsible citizenship in a lively, comfortable, and intimate liberal arts setting." They pursue their goals through a "solid interdisciplinary education" that "draws connections across the curriculum to engage the student in the learning process, putting them in the driver's seat of their education instead of making them passengers." Rollins' "extremely challenging academics" include "a writing-intensive curriculum" that "helps you become a critical thinker and a better writer and communicator." Areas of strength include "an impressive Physics Department, [a] great theater program with professors who are working professionals, [a] strong pre-law program, [and] a good Education Department." In all areas "There are small classes, which gives students the opportunity to build strong relationships with professors and other students in the same field." While the Rollins experience "is whatever a student makes it, because it is a great place to grow academically for those interested in academic experiences or it is a party for those looking for social life," the school "is becoming more serious each year, with better teachers, a wider variety of classes/majors, and better support from the alumni, so the endowment is only getting bigger. Better students are coming to Rollins, making it a better school."

Life

Rollins College is "in a perfect location in Winter Park. We're close to movies, shopping, parks, museums, and nightlife in downtown Orlando. The beach is only 45 minutes away, Disney World and Universal Studios are only 25 minutes away, and there are golf courses all over the place." "Close" is a relative term, of course; the campus is close to all these destinations for students who have cars, but "If you don't have a car, don't plan on going anywhere. Nothing's in walking distance except a couple of great bars that are loaded with Rollins students 24/7." On campus and close by, "There's not much to do other than party. Fraternity and sorority parties are big, and everyone goes. Greek life is huge," with more than one-third of the student body actively involved and many others peripherally involved (attending parties "thrown throughout the year that are open to the whole campus"). Intercollegiate athletics "are not as popular here for some reason. No one knows when games are or who's playing." Students are big fans, however, of Rollins' "absolutely gorgeous campus," which is "located on a lake where students love to sail or wakeboard." Its "structures and landscaping are very pretty and well kept."

Student Body

The typical Rollins student "is blond, very attractive, and wealthy"—and well-dressed. One undergrad elaborates, "The typical female student is one who carries a very expensive purse, wears huge dark sunglasses, has long hair, wears polo shirts, and dresses up to go to afternoon classes but will always be seen in the morning wearing glasses and sweatpants. A typical male student is cocky but, once you get through that, generally sweet. Guys are always sporting collared polo shirts in bright colors and extravagantly colored pants." Undergrads here report that "the student body seems to be changing in makeup in recent years. Still, the majority is wealthy and flaunts it." The growing diversity includes "some kids on scholarship, some smart kids, some minority students, etc." One student observes, "There are enough atypical students that there is some variety and everyone has a place to fit in."

FINANCIAL AID: 407-646-2395 • E-MAIL: ADMISSION@ROLLINS.EDU • WEBSITE: WWW.ROLLINS.EDU

THE PRINCETON REVIEW SAYS

Admissions

Very important factors considered include: Academic GPA, rigor of secondary school record. *Important factors considered include:* Application essay, recommendation(s), standardized test scores, extracurricular activities, talent/ability. *Other factors considered include:* Class rank, alumni/ae relation, character/personal qualities, first generation, interview, level of applicant's interest, volunteer work, work experience. ACT with Writing component recommended. TOEFL required of all international applicants. High school diploma is required and GED is accepted. *Academic units required:* 4 English, 3 mathematics, 2 science, 2 foreign language, 2 social studies, 2 history, 2 academic electives. *Academic units recommended:* 4 English, 4 mathematics, 4 science, 3 foreign language, 3 social studies, 3 history, 3 academic electives.

Financial Aid

Students should submit: FAFSA, institution's own financial aid form. Regular filing deadline is 3/1. The Princeton Review suggests that all financial aid forms be submitted as soon as possible after January 1. *Need-based scholarships/grants offered:* Federal Pell, SEOG, state scholarships/grants, private scholarships, the school's own gift aid. *Loan aid offered:* Direct Subsidized Stafford, Direct Unsubsidized Stafford, Direct PLUS, Federal Perkins, college/university loans from institutional funds. Applicants will be notified of awards on a rolling basis beginning 3/1.

The Inside Word

The personalized nature and nurturing environment that Rollins College fosters even extends to its treatment of prospective students. Each applicant is assigned an Admissions Officer who acts as his or her liaison. The college gives equal weight to most admissions factors and favors well-rounded candidates. Students who have enrolled in challenging courses will also find themselves well positioned for admission. Early decision applicants are given priority in admissions as well as in considerations for merit-based scholarships and need-based financial aid.

THE SCHOOL SAYS "..."

From The Admissions Office

"As you begin the college selection process, remember that you are in control of your destiny. Your academic record—course load, grades earned, test scores—are the most important part of your application credentials. But Rollins also pays close attention to your personal dimension—interests, strengths, values, and potential to contribute to college life. Don't sell yourself short in the application process. Be proud of what you've accomplished and who you are, and be honest when you describe yourself. Finally, the Admission Committee always likes to see candidates who express interest in the college. If we're your first choice, apply early decision. Each year we admit approximately one-third of the entering class through the early decision process. Are you unsure about your choice? If you can, schedule some visits, meet with an Admission Counselor, tour campus, and spend time in a class so you can see for yourself what Rollins and other colleges are all about. Take control of your destiny, and enjoy the process along the way.

"First-year applicants for Fall 2008 may submit either SAT or ACT scores for admission consideration. Candidates are strongly encouraged to complete the new Writing components, but results without Writing will be considered. Each candidate's best score combination will be used in the selection process; we strongly recommend that candidates consider taking both the SAT and the ACT."

SELECTIVITY
Admissions Rating	91
# of applicants	2,900
% of applicants accepted	58
% of acceptees attending	31
# accepting a place on wait list	347
% admitted from wait list	20
# of early decision applicants	278
% accepted early decision	68

FRESHMAN PROFILE
Range SAT Critical Reading	555–640
Range SAT Math	555–640
Range ACT Composite	23–28
Minimum paper TOEFL	550
Minimum computer TOEFL	213
Minimum web-based TOEFL	80
Average HS GPA	3.4
% graduated top 10% of class	45
% graduated top 25% of class	75
% graduated top 50% of class	93

DEADLINES
Early decision	
Deadline	11/15
Notification	12/15
Early action	
Deadline	12/1
Notification	2/1
Regular	
Deadline	2/15
Notification	4/1
Nonfall registration?	yes

APPLICANTS ALSO LOOK AT
AND OFTEN PREFER
University of Richmond
Vanderbilt University
AND SOMETIMES PREFER
Southern Methodist University
University of Miami

FINANCIAL FACTS
Financial Aid Rating	88
Annual tuition	$34,520
% frosh rec. need-based scholarship or grant aid	40
% UG rec. need-based scholarship or grant aid	40
% frosh rec. non-need-based scholarship or grant aid	7
% UG rec. non-need-based scholarship or grant aid	4
% frosh rec. need-based self-help aid	28
% UG rec. need-based self-help aid	34
% frosh rec. athletic scholarships	5
% UG rec. athletic scholarships	5
% frosh rec. any financial aid	70
% UG rec. any financial aid	70
% UG borrow to pay for school	45
Average cumulative indebtedness	$23,298

ROSE-HULMAN INSTITUTE OF TECHNOLOGY

5500 WABASH AVENUE-CM 1, TERRE HAUTE, IN 47803-3999 • ADMISSIONS: 812-877-8213 • FAX: 812-877-8941

CAMPUS LIFE
Quality of Life Rating	**82**
Fire Safety Rating	**93**
Green Rating	**77**
Type of school	private
Environment	town

STUDENTS
Total undergrad enrollment	1,821
% male/female	79/21
% from out of state	58
% from public high school	82.7
% live on campus	60
% in (# of) fraternities	42 (9)
% in (# of) sororities	53 (4)
% African American	2
% Asian	5
% Caucasian	90
% Hispanic	2
% international	2
# of countries represented	20

SURVEY SAYS . . .
Small classes
Lab facilities are great
Great computer facilities
Athletic facilities are great
Career services are great
School is well run
Campus feels safe

ACADEMICS
Academic Rating	**83**
Calendar	quarter
Student/faculty ratio	12:1
Profs interesting rating	84
Profs accessible rating	95
Most common reg class size	20–29 students
Most common lab size	20–29 students

MOST POPULAR MAJORS
mechanical engineering
chemical engineering
biomedical/medical engineering

STUDENTS SAY ". . ."

Academics

"It's all about the family" at the Rose-Hulman Institute of Technology, that rare engineering school "where everyone either knows you or smiles at you anyway" and "The classes are really small, so the professors know you and remember things that you are involved in and ask about them." Tech schools are not typically known for their nurturing environments, but then again most tech schools don't have "faculty who love teaching and staff who are outgoing and friendly." Rose's small size is one of the keys to its success; here "You will never have a class of more than 30 students—even as a freshman in something like Calculus I—so professors always have time to help students who are struggling or who are just really interested in something mentioned in class." Undergrads can also seek help at the Learning Center, "which provides upperclassmen as tutors to help the freshmen and sophomores on homework and such." Students can use the help, since "The typical policy at Rose is to give students 3 hours of homework per credit hour per week. Most students take 18 credit hours per quarter, so this means 54 hours of homework per week, and that does not include lab write-ups, pre-labs, etc. . . . The courses are very difficult and require a lot of work." The reward for this hard work is opportunity, especially for those looking to stay in the Midwest. One senior observes, "There are 31 seniors in my major looking for jobs, and there were over 40 companies on campus looking for seniors in my major at the career fair."

Life

"There are lots of activities provided to the student body" at Rose and "The school works really hard to make campus life as wonderful as possible, with things like free photocopying and printing, free comedians, hypnotists, music performances, 3-D virtual Pac-Man on a random Friday, free movie rentals . . . the list goes on." The Student Activities Board "has bimonthly to monthly activities which students can attend for free! These include recent movies, concerts, motivational speakers, etc. It's very cool." In a way, entertainment has to come to Rose students, because they're usually too busy to go find it on their own. Not that they'd have much success in Terre Haute, where options seem to be somewhat limited: "You can go to one of the two movie theaters (three if you count the really old one) or to one of the 20-plus bars in the area. Most people choose the bars." On campus, "Many social activities revolve around the Greek community." Intramurals are also a big part of life, as "Many students come to Rose first for the academics but still enjoying getting down to the intramural fields for a little stress relief."

Student Body

"Rose-Hulman caters to a somewhat nerdy student," writes one engineer, "but we love it because we are all way past the too-cool-to-care attitude that seems so prominent in high school. Rose students are here to learn and to try new things, and everyone puts a lot of time and effort into their projects, their presentations, their homework, and their studying." White males "probably make up 80 percent of the student body," with students divided among "those who play computers and stay in their rooms and those who do sports and get out." "The great thing is, none of this matters to the student body, as everyone is treated with equal respect." Students at Rose-Hulman seem to agree, adding that "no matter what" type of student you are, "You are definitely going to be doing a lot of homework." Some here do feel that the school "could stand to use more variation in political views. The extreme conservative Republican viewpoint of most of the students gets a little old after 4 years."

ROSE-HULMAN INSTITUTE OF TECHNOLOGY

FINANCIAL AID: 812-877-8259 • E-MAIL: ADMIS.OFC@ROSE-HULMAN.EDU • WEBSITE: WWW.ROSE-HULMAN.EDU

THE PRINCETON REVIEW SAYS

Admissions

Very important factors considered include: Class rank, rigor of secondary school record. *Important factors considered include:* Academic GPA, recommendation(s), standardized test scores, character/personal qualities. *Other factors considered include:* Application essay, alumni/ae relation, extracurricular activities, interview, talent/ability, volunteer work, work experience. SAT or ACT required; TOEFL required of all international applicants. High school diploma is required and GED is not accepted. *Academic units required:* 4 English, 4 mathematics, 2 science, (2 science labs), 2 social studies, 4 academic electives. *Academic units recommended:* 5 mathematics, 3 science.

Financial Aid

Students should submit: FAFSA. The Princeton Review suggests that all financial aid forms be submitted as soon as possible after January 1. *Need-based scholarships/grants offered:* Federal Pell, SEOG, state scholarships/grants, the school's own gift aid. *Loan aid offered:* Direct Subsidized Stafford, Direct Unsubsidized Stafford, Direct PLUS, Federal Perkins Applicants will be notified of awards on or about 3/10. Federal Work-Study Program available. Institutional employment available.

The Inside Word

Embracing the school's engineering roots, Admissions Counselors at Rose-Hulman really rely on numbers and statistics. Class rank and test scores are obvious areas in which applicants may distinguish themselves. Don't be misled by the straightforward process, though; academic standards here are high, and students must prove they are capable of success during what promises to be a rigorous 4 years. Women would do well to apply here, as the college continues to seek out additional female applicants.

THE SCHOOL SAYS "..."

From The Admissions Office

"Rose-Hulman is generally considered one of the premier undergraduate colleges of engineering and science. We are nationally known as an institution that puts teaching above research and graduate programs. At Rose-Hulman, professors (not graduate students) teach the courses and conduct their own labs. Department chairmen teach freshmen. To enhance the teaching at Rose-Hulman, computers have become a prominent addition to not only our labs but also in our classrooms and residence halls. Additionally, all students are now required to purchase laptop computers. Ninety million dollars in new facilities have been added in the last 6 years.

"Students applying for admission into the Fall 2008 class may submit either the SAT or ACT, and the student's best scores from either test will be considered. Both new and old SAT test scores are acceptable. The Writing portion of either test will not be required for admission to the freshman class of 2008."

SELECTIVITY

Admissions Rating	91
# of applicants	3,088
% of applicants accepted	70
% of acceptees attending	22

FRESHMAN PROFILE

Range SAT Critical Reading	560–680
Range SAT Math	630–710
Range SAT Writing	550–650
Range ACT Composite	27–31
Minimum paper TOEFL	580
Minimum computer TOEFL	237
Minimum web-based TOEFL	92
% graduated top 10% of class	59.3
% graduated top 25% of class	91.8
% graduated top 50% of class	99.5

DEADLINES

Regular	
Priority	12/1
Deadline	3/1
Notification	rolling
Nonfall registration?	no

APPLICANTS ALSO LOOK AT AND OFTEN PREFER

Purdue University—West Lafayette
Case Western Reserve University
University of Illinois at Urbana-Champaign

AND SOMETIMES PREFER

Georgia Institute of Technology
Worcester Polytechnic Institute
Rensselaer Polytechnic Institute

AND RARELY PREFER

Kettering University
Rochester Institute of Technology

FINANCIAL FACTS

Financial Aid Rating	60*
Annual tuition	$30,243
Room and board	$8,343
Required fees	$480
Books and supplies	$1,500
% frosh rec. need-based scholarship or grant aid	70
% UG rec. need-based scholarship or grant aid	67
% frosh rec. need-based self-help aid	65
% UG rec. need-based self-help aid	62
% frosh rec. any financial aid	100
% UG rec. any financial aid	99
% UG borrow to pay for school	74
Average cumulative indebtedness	$32,612

RUTGERS, THE STATE UNIVERSITY OF NEW JERSEY—NEW BRUNSWICK

65 DAVIDSON ROAD, PISCATAWAY, NJ 08854-8097 • ADMISSIONS: 732-932-4636 • FAX: 732-445-0237

CAMPUS LIFE

Quality of Life Rating	63
Fire Safety Rating	81
Green Rating	60*
Type of school	public
Environment	town

STUDENTS

Total undergrad enrollment	26,479
% male/female	51/49
% from out of state	7
% live on campus	49
% in (# of) fraternities	NR (29)
% in (# of) sororities	NR (15)
% African American	9
% Asian	24
% Caucasian	52
% Hispanic	8
% international	2
# of countries represented	117

SURVEY SAYS . . .

Great computer facilities
Great library
Athletic facilities are great
Diverse student types on campus
Everyone loves the Scarlet Knights
Student publications are popular
Lots of beer drinking
Hard liquor is popular

ACADEMICS

Academic Rating	71
Calendar	semester
Student/faculty ratio	14:1
Profs interesting rating	61
Profs accessible rating	61
% classes taught by TAs	20

MOST POPULAR MAJORS

engineering
biology/biological sciences

STUDENTS SAY ". . ."

Academics

Rutgers, The State University of New Jersey—New Brunswick, "is the kind of university [at which], if you make the effort to create your niche and find opportunities to succeed, you will have one of the best experiences of your life." With "a great study abroad program, solid academic departments and professors, the vast resources of a large research . . . and lots of scholarship money for honors students," Rutgers "offers boundless opportunity, both educational and professional, but you have to be willing to go out and seek it." Rutgers' immenseness is made more manageable by its subdivision into 13 colleges, "each with its own unique community and environment, all unified under one entity that can afford all the opportunities of a large university." Even so, the university's bureaucracy is legendary; one student writes, "The school seems to take pride in its web of red tape. The famous 'RU Screw' has become so notorious that the university president had to publicly denounce it." It's a good sign that Rutgers "is progressively changing its administrative policies under the administration of its relatively new president. There is a renewed focus on student service, and the changes are evident." As at many state schools, "Good things will not happen at Rutgers by sitting in the corner and waiting for opportunity to knock. It is a big school, so the more you put yourself out and make yourself known, the more likely you'll be able to find help in academics and administration." For self-starters, the rewards can be great; one writes, "I've had the opportunity to [conduct] my own research in the Rutgers facilities." Indeed, "There is a lot of research going on at Rutgers. The topics are numerous, and there are plenty of spots to fill if you look around well enough."

Life

"Weekdays are busy, and you can find places crowded at any time of the day" on the Rutgers campus, as "There's always something going on: concerts, free movies, talks. It's all about diversity and going out to find what you want to do." Student government "is huge, as is Rock the Vote. . . . There's always voter registration drives, and we even have Tent State University in the spring, during which a bunch of political student groups set up tents on the main courtyard and camp out for a week handing out literature, having fun stuff (concerts, etc.), and talking to people about what they do and how they can get involved." For some, "drinking is a big thing." One student writes, "If there was no such thing as getting inebriated, there would be nothing to do here." Many refute that position, noting that "there are other things you can do as well besides. There are lots of places to eat and drink coffee, . . . stuff like Jazz 'n' Java put on by the Douglass Black Students Caucus, . . . or going to a small discussion group with Jhumpa Lahiri, the Pulitzer Prize–winning writer," to name a few. While weekdays are lively, weekends are another story. One student comments, "Life at Rutgers would feel more college-y if people didn't leave on weekends and it [didn't feel] so deserted."

Student Body

Rutgers "is huge, so there is just about every type of person you could think of here." One undergrad observes, "With so many students, it's hard not to find others with whom you fit in. But the drawback to such a large student body is that you need to go out and make friends; you can't expect them to come to you." Another student adds, "To be fair, sometimes it feels a bit like high school (there are 'skaters' and 'preps' and 'thugs' and all that), but once you're an upperclassmen you kind of learn to ignore it."

RUTGERS, THE STATE UNIVERSITY OF NEW JERSEY—NEW BRUNSWICK

FINANCIAL AID: 732-932-7057 • WEBSITE: WWW.RUTGERS.EDU

THE PRINCETON REVIEW SAYS

Admissions

Very important factors considered include: Class rank, academic GPA, rigor of secondary school record, standardized test scores. *Other factors considered include:* Application essay, recommendation(s), extracurricular activities, first generation, geographical residence, interview, racial/ethnic status, state residency, talent/ability, volunteer work, work experience. SAT or ACT required; High school diploma is required and GED is accepted. *Academic units required:* 4 English, 3 mathematics, 2 science, 2 foreign language, 5 academic electives. *Academic units recommended:* 4 mathematics, 2 foreign language.

Financial Aid

Students should submit: FAFSA. The Princeton Review suggests that all financial aid forms be submitted as soon as possible after January 1. *Need-based scholarships/grants offered:* Federal Pell, SEOG, state scholarships/grants, private scholarships, the school's own gift aid, Outside Scholarships. *Loan aid offered:* Direct Subsidized Stafford, Direct Unsubsidized Stafford, Direct PLUS, Federal Perkins, Federal Nursing, state loans, college/university loans from institutional funds. Educational Loans. Applicants will be notified of awards on a rolling basis beginning 2/1.

The Inside Word

With a literal mountain of applications to process each admissions season, Rutgers does not have the luxury of time. The school looks at your grades, the quality of your high school curriculum, your standardized test scores, and your essay to decide whether you can make the grade at Rutgers. Although the school grows more competitive each year, solid students should still find little difficulty getting in.

THE SCHOOL SAYS "..."

From The Admissions Office

"Rutgers, The State University of New Jersey, one of only 62 members of the Association of American Universities, is a research university that attracts students from across the nation and around the world. What does it take to be accepted for admission to Rutgers University? Our primary emphasis is on your past academic performance as indicated by your high school grades (particularly in required academic subjects), your class rank or cumulative average, the strength of your academic program, your standardized test scores on the SAT or ACT, any special talents you may have, and your participation in school and community activities. We seek students with a broad diversity of talents, interests, and backgrounds. Above all else, we're looking for students who will get the most out of a Rutgers education—students with the intellect, initiative, and motivation to make full use of the opportunities we have to offer.

"Fall 2008 first-year applicants should take the SAT Reasoning Test or the ACT (with Writing component) no later than November 2007 in order to meet our December 1 priority application date. SAT scores from the March 2007 test administration and later are acceptable. Test scores are not required for students who graduated high school more than 2 years ago or have completed more than 12 college credits since graduating."

SELECTIVITY

Admissions Rating	87
# of applicants	28,208
% of applicants accepted	56
% of acceptees attending	35

FRESHMAN PROFILE

Range SAT Critical Reading	530–630
Range SAT Math	560–670
% graduated top 10% of class	40
% graduated top 25% of class	81
% graduated top 50% of class	99

DEADLINES

Regular	
Priority	12/1
Notification	3/1
Nonfall registration?	yes

FINANCIAL FACTS

Financial Aid Rating	72
Annual tuition	$8,541
% frosh rec. need-based scholarship or grant aid	31
% UG rec. need-based scholarship or grant aid	32
% frosh rec. non-need-based scholarship or grant aid	30
% UG rec. non-need-based scholarship or grant aid	25
% frosh rec. need-based self-help aid	44
% UG rec. need-based self-help aid	44
% frosh rec. athletic scholarships	1
% UG rec. athletic scholarships	1
% frosh rec. any financial aid	67
% UG rec. any financial aid	69
% UG borrow to pay for school	65
Average cumulative indebtedness	$16,283

SACRED HEART UNIVERSITY

5151 PARK AVENUE, FAIRFIELD, CT 06825 • ADMISSIONS: 203-371-7880 • FAX: 203-365-7607

CAMPUS LIFE
Quality of Life Rating	**79**
Fire Safety Rating	**82**
Green Rating	**70**
Type of school	private
Affiliation	Roman Catholic
Environment	town

STUDENTS
Total undergrad enrollment	4,188
% male/female	39/61
% from out of state	69
% from public high school	70
% live on campus	66
% in (# of) fraternities	5 (3)
% in (# of) sororities	5 (6)
% African American	4
% Asian	2
% Caucasian	85
% Hispanic	6
% international	1
# of countries represented	40

SURVEY SAYS . . .
Large classes
Great computer facilities
Athletic facilities are great
Career services are great
Campus feels safe
Everyone loves the Pioneers

ACADEMICS
Academic Rating	**78**
Calendar	semester
Student/faculty ratio	13:1
Profs interesting rating	79
Profs accessible rating	80
Most common reg class size	10–19 students

MOST POPULAR MAJORS
kinesiology and exercise science
psychology
business/commerce

STUDENTS SAY ". . ."

Academics

Looking for an "excellent education" in Southern New England? Then Sacred Heart University may be the place for you. As one undergrad says, "I feel as though Sacred Heart offers some of the most brilliant professors available in the academic world." High praise, though as another explains, "At SHU, you can really connect with your professors. It is the kind of school where professors know the names of all of their students and remember them after the semester ends." The net result is an academic atmosphere that is "both stimulating and intellectually fulfilling." Learning is enhanced by SHU's "advanced" technology, which means that "the whole campus is wireless and most professors use this to their advantage by putting notes and assignments online, which saves paper and students from arthritis." Some students do complain that some upper-level administrators "seem disconnected." Others note that they would like to see the "registration process improve." But, all in all, if you're willing to suffer a few administrative headaches, you just might discover that "the academic experience is great!"

Life

"If you don't get involved then you don't get the most of the life on campus"— and yes, there's plenty to pick from at SHU. According to one freshman, "There's pretty much a club for anyone, making it easy to become involved. There are also community service projects happening all the time." A classmate adds, "Every day they e-mail us with the 'Events of the Day,' and there's always something going on . . . midnight volleyball, acoustic shows at the Outpost, concerts, sports games, and even Ping-Pong tournaments." Athletics are also a "big part" of student life. "I'm usually at almost every athletic event with my face painted red and a crazy wig on," says an enthusiastic supporter. Though SHU is officially a "dry campus," there are many wet appetites here. "It is a big bar school," explains one student. "There are some parties that go on, but the bars are where people go." To get to the bars in nearby Fairfield or Bridgeport, most students take cabs—"and the cabs are very expensive." There's also "a shuttle that takes everyone to the mall and runs on the hour." Other popular weekend destinations include New Haven, only "20 minutes away," and New York is "an hour" from campus.

Student Body

Your typical SHU student "is either a Yankee or Red Sox fan." In other words, most undergrads hail from the Northeast—"from Massachusetts, New York, and Connecticut," in particular. But if you call some far-off land home, don't worry: "Everyone seems to fit in, even if you're not from these states." A freshman describes her fellow Pioneers as "easily approachable, kind, courteous, respectful, and outgoing." But another first-year says that the four words that best describe your average SHU undergrad are "White, rich, preppy, and Catholic." Look beyond the "average" undergrad and you'll see that "the students at Sacred Heart come in all different shapes and colors, and come from different backgrounds and come from all over the world."

E-MAIL: ENROLL@SACREDHEART.EDU • WEBSITE: WWW.SACREDHEART.EDU

THE PRINCETON REVIEW SAYS

Admissions

Very important factors considered include: Academic GPA, rigor of secondary school record. *Important factors considered include:* Class rank, recommendation(s), standardized test scores, character/personal qualities, extracurricular activities, interview, talent/ability, volunteer work, work experience. *Other factors considered include:* Application essay, alumni/ae relation, first generation, geographical residence, level of applicant's interest, racial/ethnic status, religious affiliation/commitment, state residency, SAT or ACT required; ACT with Writing component required. TOEFL required of all international applicants. High school diploma is required and GED is accepted. *Academic units required:* 4 English, 3 mathematics, 3 science, (1 science labs), 2 foreign language, 3 social studies, 3 history, 3 academic electives. *Academic units recommended:* 4 English, 4 mathematics, 4 science, (2 science labs), 4 foreign language, 4 social studies, 4 history, 4 academic electives.

Financial Aid

Students should submit: FAFSA, CSS/Financial Aid PROFILE, noncustodial PROFILE. The Princeton Review suggests that all financial aid forms be submitted as soon as possible after January 1. *Need-based scholarships/grants offered:* Federal Pell, SEOG, state scholarships/grants, private scholarships, the school's own gift aid, Federal Nursing Scholarships. *Loan aid offered:* FFEL Subsidized Stafford, FFEL Unsubsidized Stafford, FFEL PLUS, Federal Perkins, state loans, Alternative loans. Applicants will be notified of awards on a rolling basis beginning 3/1. Federal Work-Study Program available. Institutional employment available. Off-campus job opportunities are excellent.

The Inside Word

Who's the person behind the application? This is what the Admissions Officers at student-friendly Sacred Heart University want to know. While they place heavy emphasis on traditional academic indicators like high-school curriculum and GPA, they also spend time reading each applicant's admissions essay. If you really want to make an impact, why not head to Sacred Heart for a campus visit? A strong interview can turn many tides to your favor.

THE SCHOOL SAYS "..."

From The Admissions Office

"Sacred Heart University, distinguished by the personal attention it provides its students, is a thriving, dynamic university known for its commitment to academic excellence, cutting-edge technology, and community service. The second-largest Catholic university in New England, Sacred Heart continues to be innovative in its offerings to students; recently launched programs include Connecticut's first doctoral program in physical therapy, an MBA program for liberal arts undergraduates at the newly AACSB-accredited John F. Welch College of Business, and a campus in County Kerry, Ireland. The university's commitment to experiential learning incorporates concrete, real-life study for students in all majors. Drawing on the rich resources in New England and New York City, students are connected with research and internship opportunities ranging from co-ops at international advertising agencies to research with faculty on marine life in the Long Island Sound. These experiential learning opportunities are complemented by a rich student life program offering over 80 student organizations including strong music programs, media clubs, and academic honor societies. To help students transition to college life and navigate the many opportunities available, all freshmen are assigned mentors, who work one-on-one to facilitate students' personal development and enhance the learning process both in and out of the classroom. Students applying to Sacred Heart University benefit from a comprehensive, holistic admissions process which takes into account not only applicants' grade point averages and standardized test scores, but also their overall student profiles including strength of college preparatory curricula, leadership and community service experience, character, and extraordinary talents. Either the SAT or the ACT (with Writing component) is required for admission. For students taking the SAT more than once, the highest Math score and the highest Critical Reading score will be evaluated by the Admissions Committee. No current policy exists for the use of the SAT Writing component."

SELECTIVITY

Admissions Rating	83
# of applicants	7,532
% of applicants accepted	62
% of acceptees attending	21
# of early decision applicants	359
% accepted early decision	47

FRESHMAN PROFILE

Range SAT Critical Reading	490–570
Range SAT Math	500–580
Range ACT Composite	21–25
Minimum paper TOEFL	500
Minimum computer TOEFL	70
Average HS GPA	3.3
% graduated top 10% of class	14
% graduated top 25% of class	45
% graduated top 50% of class	85

DEADLINES

Early decision	
Deadline	11/15
Notification	12/15
Regular	
Priority	2/1
Notification	rolling
Nonfall registration?	yes

APPLICANTS ALSO LOOK AT

AND OFTEN PREFER
University of Connecticut
Villanova University

AND SOMETIMES PREFER
Fordham University
Providence College

AND RARELY PREFER
Hofstra University

FINANCIAL FACTS

Financial Aid Rating	74
Annual tuition	$26,950
Room and board	$10,816
Required fees	$200
Books and supplies	$700
% frosh rec. need-based scholarship or grant aid	66
% UG rec. need-based scholarship or grant aid	64
% frosh rec. non-need-based scholarship or grant aid	21
% UG rec. non-need-based scholarship or grant aid	20
% frosh rec. need-based self-help aid	57
% UG rec. need-based self-help aid	56
% frosh rec. athletic scholarships	5
% UG rec. athletic scholarships	5
% frosh rec. any financial aid	87
% UG rec. any financial aid	91
% UG borrow to pay for school	94
Average cumulative indebtedness	$25,505

SAINT ANSELM COLLEGE

100 SAINT ANSELM DRIVE, MANCHESTER, NH 03102-1310 • ADMISSIONS: 603-641-7500 • FAX: 603-641-7550

CAMPUS LIFE
Quality of Life Rating	86
Fire Safety Rating	60*
Green Rating	60*
Type of school	private
Affiliation	Roman Catholic
Environment	city

STUDENTS
Total undergrad enrollment	1,936
% male/female	43/57
% from out of state	78
% from public high school	45
% live on campus	89
% African American	1
% Asian	1
% Caucasian	77
% Hispanic	1
% Native American	1
# of countries represented	18

SURVEY SAYS . . .
Great library
Students are friendly
Lots of beer drinking

ACADEMICS
Academic Rating	84
Calendar	semester
Student/faculty ratio	12:1
Profs interesting rating	89
Profs accessible rating	86
Most common reg class size	10–19 students
Most common lab size	10–19 students

STUDENTS SAY "..."

Academics

If you long for four years of "Catholic faith and hard classes," consider "wonderful, small" Saint Anselm College in Manchester, New Hampshire. The nursing program is reportedly "awesome" but Saint Anselm is best known for providing "a true liberal arts education." In addition to comprehensive exams in every major, all students must complete three courses each in philosophy and theology, two English courses, two science courses, a year of foreign language, and four common humanities courses. "Some people enjoy the humanities program." Others say "the lectures can be absolute torture." Depending on who you talk to, the administration either "functions smoothly" or is "too Catholic" and "takes its sweet ass time with everything." Students almost universally gush about their "passionate" professors. "I get tons of individual attention," brags a nursing major. "They are always willing to set a time with you outside of class for help." However, "essays are numerous," and "classes are very difficult." "The library is always filled." There is something of a "crusade against grade inflation" on this campus as well. "St. A's is known as St. C's," explains a junior. "Despite how hard you work, you may not see the results you want," warns an English major. Other students tell us that "the work is not excruciatingly hard." "It's definitely not impossible," says a biochemistry major. "I'm no rocket scientist, and I'm taking in at least two A's this semester," agrees a classics major. "St. A's requires you to work very hard, but in a warm, friendly, and respectful atmosphere where there are plenty of opportunities to make your college years fantastic," reflects a business major.

Life

This "absolutely gorgeous" campus boasts "spectacular" food. "Internet technology is a joke" though, and the recreational facilities aren't much. A few students complain that Saint Anselm is "a suitcase school" but others say that "you can be involved in numerous things." "It is a small, tight-knit school, where if you stick around on-campus and get involved you will have the best time ever," declares a senior. "Community service is big." "I've never seen such a giving school," gloats a first-year student. There's Mass every day, and you'll always find a few Benedictine monks around campus. "The monks are awesome," says a junior. "For students who are interested, Saint Anselm is a haven for politics." The "really cool" New Hampshire Institute of Politics provides "a lot of speakers and political candidates," particularly when primary season rolls around. "It's a big deal to go to the hockey games." "Intramural sports are very popular," too. "The pub is a great place on campus for juniors and seniors who are 21 to grab a drink and relax." Various campus policies are "strict" though. First year residence halls are not co-ed and visitation hours for members of the opposite sex are limited. "If you're looking for an intense party scene, Saint Anselm College isn't the place," advises a senior. Nevertheless, "the senior housing always has something going on" and "drinking is very prevalent" on the weekends, "though students must be sneaky." Nearby Boston is "a great option for the weekends" as well.

Student Body

The stereotype at Saint Anselm is definitely a "white, Catholic Red Sox fan." "Most students I've met here have Boston accents, at least half are Irish, and went to a private school," observes a freshman. There's "only a handful of minorities." "The student body is not the most diverse community but most people are very welcoming," adds a senior. "Social groups here tend to be well defined and yet somehow still permeable, or at least, amiable to one another." There are "sheltered, ignorant snobs," but "the majority of students is middle-class and receives some sort of financial aid." Students at Saint A's describe themselves as "smart, hardworking, involved in community service," and "very preppy." "There are a select few who are rebellious, artsy, and try to stand out but they generally get along with the preppy kids." "Most kids are on an athletic team of some type." Many are serious about religion, "but many are not." Politically, opinions "are surprisingly varied for a campus that is pretty conservative."

SAINT ANSELM COLLEGE

FINANCIAL AID: 603-641-7110 • E-MAIL: ADMISSION@ANSELM.EDU • WEBSITE: WWW.ANSELM.EDU

THE PRINCETON REVIEW SAYS

Admissions
Very important factors considered include: Academic GPA, rigor of secondary school record, character/personal qualities. *Important factors considered include:* Class rank, application essay, recommendation(s), standardized test scores, talent/ability. *Other factors considered include:* Alumni/ae relation, extracurricular activities, geographical residence, level of applicant's interest, racial/ethnic status, volunteer work, work experience. SAT or ACT required; TOEFL required of all international applicants. High school diploma is required and GED is accepted. *Academic units required:* 4 English, 3 mathematics, 3 science, (3 science labs), 2 foreign language, 2 social studies, 1 history, 3 academic electives. *Academic units recommended:* 4 mathematics, 4 science, 4 foreign language, 2 history.

Financial Aid
Students should submit: FAFSA, CSS/Financial Aid PROFILE. Regular filing deadline is 3/15. The Princeton Review suggests that all financial aid forms be submitted as soon as possible after January 1. *Need-based scholarships/grants offered:* Federal Pell, SEOG, state scholarships/grants, private scholarships *Loan aid offered:* FFEL Subsidized Stafford, FFEL Unsubsidized Stafford, FFEL PLUS, Federal Perkins, GATE student loans. Applicants will be notified of awards on a rolling basis beginning 3/1. Federal Work-Study Program available. Institutional employment available. Off-campus job opportunities are excellent.

The Inside Word
St. Anselm gets a predominately regional applicant pool, and Massachusetts is one of its biggest suppliers of students. An above-average academic record should be more than adequate to gain admission.

THE SCHOOL SAYS ". . ."

From The Admissions Office
"Why Saint Anselm? The answer lies with our graduates. Not only do our alumni go on to successful careers in medicine, law, human services, and other areas, but they also make connections on campus that last a lifetime. With small classes, professors are accessible and approachable. The Benedictine monks serve not only as founders of the college but as teachers, mentors, and spiritual leaders.

"Saint Anselm is rich in history, but certainly not stuck in a bygone era. In fact, the college has launched a $50-million fund-raising campaign, which will significantly increase funding for financial aid, academic programs, and technology. New initiatives include the New Hampshire Institute of Politics, where the guest list includes every major candidate from the 2000 presidential race, as well as other political movers and shakers. Not a political junkie? No problem. The NHIOP is a diverse undertaking that also involves elements of psychology, history, theology, ethics, and statistics.

"Saint Anselm encourages students to challenge themselves academically and to lead lives that are both creative and generous. On that note, more than 40 percent of our students participate in community service locally and globally. Each year, about 150 students take part in Spring Break Alternative to help those less fortunate across the United States and Latin America. High expectations and lofty goals are hallmarks of a Saint Anselm College education, and each student is encouraged to achieve his/her full potential here. Why Saint Anselm? Accept the challenge and soon you will discover your own answers.

"Freshman applicants for Fall 2008 must take the SAT or the ACT. Students may submit scores from the old or new SAT. The best scores from either test will be used in admissions decisions."

SELECTIVITY
Admissions Rating	84
# of applicants	3,521
% of applicants accepted	69
% of acceptees attending	23
# accepting a place on wait list	368
# of early decision applicants	106
% accepted early decision	77

FRESHMAN PROFILE
Range SAT Critical Reading	510–600
Range SAT Math	510–600
Range SAT Writing	510–610
Range ACT Composite	22–26
Minimum paper TOEFL	550
Minimum computer TOEFL	213
Minimum web-based TOEFL	80
Average HS GPA	3.15
% graduated top 10% of class	21
% graduated top 25% of class	53
% graduated top 50% of class	87

DEADLINES
Early decision	
Deadline	11/15
Notification	12/1
Regular	
Priority	3/1
Notification	rolling
Nonfall registration?	yes

APPLICANTS ALSO LOOK AT
AND OFTEN PREFER
Fairfield University
College of the Holy Cross
AND SOMETIMES PREFER
University of New Hampshire
University of Massachusetts—Amherst
AND RARELY PREFER
Merrimack College

FINANCIAL FACTS
Financial Aid Rating	79
Annual tuition	$26,960
Room and board	$10,200
Required fees	$750
Books and supplies	$750
% frosh rec. need-based scholarship or grant aid	67
% UG rec. need-based scholarship or grant aid	67
% frosh rec. non-need-based scholarship or grant aid	41
% UG rec. non-need-based scholarship or grant aid	39
% frosh rec. need-based self-help aid	60
% UG rec. need-based self-help aid	62
% frosh rec. athletic scholarships	1
% UG rec. athletic scholarships	1
% UG borrow to pay for school	81.69
Average cumulative indebtedness	$33,656

THE BEST 368 COLLEGES ■ 455

SAINT LOUIS UNIVERSITY

221 NORTH GRAND BOULEVARD, SAINT LOUIS, MO 63103 • ADMISSIONS: 314-977-2500 • FAX: 314-977-7136

STUDENTS SAY ". . ."

Academics

"A medium-sized Jesuit school with solid academic programs and a campus that feels close-knit," Saint Louis University is best known for its "great premedical programs," which include "a great direct-entry physical therapy program" and "a well-respected accelerated nursing program" as well as the school's pre-MD tracks. Students also speak highly of SLU's offerings in business and pre-law, as well as its unique programs in aviation and "the one-of-a-kind nutrition program with a culinary emphasis." Since SLU is a Catholic school, nearly all programs here require a solid core curriculum that emphasizes religion and ethics; students praise the way this curriculum "forces you to examine your worldview from the moment you step on campus and helps you discover what your beliefs really are." One student writes, "The Jesuit tradition means that SLU really strives to instill the values of service, leadership, and diversity in the students." Academics, especially in the high-profile departments, can be rigorous. In this regard, SLU is "perfect for high achievers and scholars who strive for the best. The professors are nice and professional but are very stern about assignments being turned in on time." One student says, "When it comes to natural sciences, particularly chemistry, biology, etc., I think SLU can be very hard. I guess it works, though. A nursing degree or physical therapy degree from SLU is very highly respected in the health care profession."

Life

St. Louis is a major city that "offers a lot of things to do off campus, with great attractions such as national sports teams, the zoo, Moolah Temple, malls, and other places downtown." The city also boasts "a very good variety of concerts at many different venues," while the presence of major league sports teams such as the Cardinals, Rams, and Blues helps make up for the fact that "SLU doesn't have genuine sports programs." A student observes, "The great thing about our campus is its location in the heart of downtown St. Louis. It is very easy to get around to the city." For those who prefer to stick closer to campus, "SLU has much to offer for just about every interest. There are so many clubs and organizations to get involved with. Plus, the Busch Student Center provides many opportunities for fun, with dining options, places to study and have meetings, and large auditoriums for special guests and movies." Service is a big part of many students' lives, and "SLU's Jesuit influence encourages the student body to become active in the community. SLU's efforts to encourage community service give many students their first taste of the real world and better prepare them to venture out into it after graduation."

Student Body

Naturally, "a large Catholic population attends Saint Louis University," and "many students here are from the Midwest." The student population includes "a lot of middle- to upper-class kids" who "have been through the Catholic school system their entire lives." There are also "quite a few kids who went to public school and kids who are lower-middle-class," but still the predominant vibe, students say, is "preppy, with pearls, polos, pink, Birkenstocks, etc." No matter what his or her background, though, "The typical SLU student is involved in various organizations and enjoys college life while staying focused and studying hard."

FINANCIAL AID: 314-977-2350 • E-MAIL: ADMITME@SLU.EDU • WEBSITE: WWW.SLU.EDU

THE PRINCETON REVIEW SAYS

Admissions

Very important factors considered include: Academic GPA, standardized test scores. *Important factors considered include:* Application essay, rigor of secondary school record, extracurricular activities. *Other factors considered include:* Recommendation(s), alumni/ae relation, character/personal qualities, first generation, interview, level of applicant's interest, talent/ability, volunteer work, SAT or ACT required; High school diploma is required and GED is accepted. *Academic units required:* 4 English, 4 mathematics, 3 science, 3 foreign language, 3 social studies, 3 academic electives. *Academic units recommended:* 4 English, 4 mathematics, 3 science, 3 foreign language, 3 social studies, 3 academic electives.

Financial Aid

Students should submit: FAFSA. The Princeton Review suggests that all financial aid forms be submitted as soon as possible after January 1. *Need-based scholarships/grants offered:* Federal Pell, SEOG, state scholarships/grants, private scholarships, the school's own gift aid, Federal Nursing Scholarships. *Loan aid offered:* FFEL Subsidized Stafford, FFEL Unsubsidized Stafford, FFEL PLUS, Federal Perkins, Federal Nursing Applicants will be notified of awards on a rolling basis beginning 3/1. Federal Work-Study Program available. Institutional employment available. Off-campus job opportunities are good.

The Inside Word

Saint Louis University has become more competitive in recent years. Admissions officers look for students who display a commitment to both scholarship and Jesuit principles. Applicants must demonstrate success in college preparatory classes and a desire to be active participants in the community.

THE SCHOOL SAYS "..."

From The Admissions Office

"A hot Midwestern university with a growing national and international reputation, Saint Louis University gives students the knowledge, skills, and values to build a successful career and make a difference in the lives of those around them.

"Students live and learn in a safe and attractive campus environment. The beautiful urban, residential campus offers loads of internship, outreach, and recreational opportunities. Ranked as one of the best educational values in the country, the university welcomes students from all 50 states and 80 foreign countries who pursue rigorous majors that invite individualization. Accessible faculty, study abroad opportunities, and many small, interactive classes make SLU a great place to learn.

"A leading Jesuit, Catholic university, SLU's goal is to graduate men and women of competence and conscience—individuals who are not only capable of making wise decisions but who also understand why they made them. Since 1818, Saint Louis University has been dedicated to academic excellence, service to others, and preparing students to be leaders in society. Saint Louis University truly is the place *where knowledge touches lives*.

"For Fall 2008 admission, Saint Louis University will accept either the new SAT or the old SAT (administered prior to March 2005 and without a Writing component). The school will also accept the ACT with or without the Writing component."

SELECTIVITY

Admissions Rating	89
# of applicants	9,169
% of applicants accepted	80
% of acceptees attending	22

FRESHMAN PROFILE

Range SAT Critical Reading	540–650
Range SAT Math	540–670
Range ACT Composite	24–29
Average HS GPA	3.67
% graduated top 10% of class	37
% graduated top 25% of class	68
% graduated top 50% of class	90

DEADLINES

Regular	
Priority	12/1
Deadline	8/1
Notification	rolling
Nonfall registration?	yes

FINANCIAL FACTS

Financial Aid Rating	70
Annual tuition	$28,480
Room and board	$8,550
Required fees	$398
Books and supplies	$1,040
% frosh rec. need-based scholarship or grant aid	58
% UG rec. need-based scholarship or grant aid	54
% frosh rec. non-need-based scholarship or grant aid	7
% UG rec. non-need-based scholarship or grant aid	5
% frosh rec. need-based self-help aid	44
% UG rec. need-based self-help aid	44
% frosh rec. athletic scholarships	3
% UG rec. athletic scholarships	2
% frosh rec. any financial aid	97
% UG rec. any financial aid	87
% UG borrow to pay for school	66
Average cumulative indebtedness	$27,013

SAINT MARY'S COLLEGE OF CALIFORNIA

PO BOX 4800, MORAGA, CA 94575-4800 • ADMISSIONS: 925-631-4224 • FAX: 925-376-7193

CAMPUS LIFE
Quality of Life Rating	71
Fire Safety Rating	86
Green Rating	79
Type of school	private
Affiliation	Roman Catholic
Environment	village

STUDENTS
Total undergrad enrollment	2,504
% male/female	39/61
% from out of state	12
% from public high school	58
% live on campus	58
% African American	6
% Asian	11
% Caucasian	53
% Hispanic	21
% Native American	1
% international	2
# of countries represented	14

SURVEY SAYS . . .
Frats and sororities are unpopular
or nonexistent
Lots of beer drinking
Hard liquor is popular

ACADEMICS
Academic Rating	60*
Calendar	4/1/4
Student/faculty ratio	11:1
Profs interesting rating	82
Profs accessible rating	83
Most common reg class size	20–29 students

MOST POPULAR MAJORS
business administration
communication
psychology

STUDENTS SAY ". . ."
Academics
The "Lasallian tradition" on which Saint Mary's College of California is based "is about quality education, faith, concern for the poor and social justice, respect for all persons, and inclusive community." A junior explains, "It is about learning about all aspects of life, and growth through that learning." SMC students tell us time and again that their school truly embodies these ideals, living up to its motto, "Enter to learn, leave to serve," through its emphasis on "learning and service." The former is embodied by the school's Seminar Program, which focuses on classics of Western literature ("You'll like at least 25 percent of the books," promises one student, adding, "as for the rest, you'll have to accept that you're going to be a little confused"); wide-ranging Area Requirements that ensure "You learn a little bit about everything"; and "seminar-style classes" that "teach critical thinking." Students "enjoy the small class sizes" and appreciate that they "are able to actually go to teachers for help rather than seek the help of some random teacher's aide." Also, "If you're still having trouble in classes, you can seek out the help of a free tutor." Undergrads note that "the facilities could be better, but it is the people, the professors, and the administration that makes academics here so enjoyable."

Life
"Life at Saint Mary's is pretty easygoing." The pace is set by the low (some say "nonexistent") level of activity in hometown Moraga, a "mountain town where everything closes early, even the Jack in the Box." Students report that "due to the small size of the school, there is little to do on campus. This year, though, the main focus is to create more campus activities. The Program Board has organized many events, but most people don't take the time to check them out." The Lasallian tradition means that students are always "putting on community-service events." Intercollegiate sports are also popular, particularly basketball, which "is really big here." Some students "leave campus for the weekend," while those who "stay usually party." One benefit of the school's location is that students are "very close to Berkeley, San Francisco, and the little up-and-coming Walnut Creek." Many students appreciate that SMC is "close enough to San Francisco to have fun, but far enough that you don't have to deal with the issues of city life."

Student Body
SMC offers a "tight-knit community," though as many note, "The typical Saint Mary's student is white and comes from money" and "probably attended a Catholic high school in the Bay Area." However, "There are many other types of people on campus," and one undergrad explains, "The great thing about this school is that everyone is treated the same among teachers and students no matter what their background." Saint Mary's has "a healthy population of international students, many of whom are athletes, and there are a great number of ethnic clubs on campus that host different events throughout the year for anybody to attend." What you won't find here is "many goth types or hippies or anything that's not mainstream. However, that doesn't mean that they wouldn't be accepted into our communities." Some note that "the school is pretty clique-y," though the average student is "athletic and academically oriented," looking to "further themselves."

FINANCIAL AID: 925-631-4370 • E-MAIL: SMCADMIT@STMARYS-CA.EDU • WEBSITE: WWW.STMARYS-CA.EDU

THE PRINCETON REVIEW SAYS

Admissions

Very important factors considered include: Academic GPA, rigor of secondary school record, standardized test scores. *Important factors considered include:* Application essay, recommendation(s), first generation. *Other factors considered include:* Class rank, alumni/ae relation, character/personal qualities, extracurricular activities, geographical residence, interview, level of applicant's interest, racial/ethnic status, religious affiliation/commitment, talent/ability, volunteer work, work experi SAT or ACT required; TOEFL required of all international applicants. High school diploma is required and GED is accepted. *Academic units required:* 4 English, 3 mathematics, 2 science, (1 science labs), 2 foreign language, 1 social studies, 1 history, 2 academic electives. *Academic units recommended:* 4 English, 4 mathematics, 3 science, (1 science labs), 3 foreign language, 1 social studies, 1 history, 2 academic electives.

Financial Aid

Students should submit: FAFSA, state aid form. The Princeton Review suggests that all financial aid forms be submitted as soon as possible after January 1. *Need-based scholarships/grants offered:* Federal Pell, SEOG, state scholarships/grants, private scholarships, the school's own gift aid. *Loan aid offered:* FFEL Subsidized Stafford, FFEL Unsubsidized Stafford, FFEL PLUS, Federal Perkins Applicants will be notified of awards on a rolling basis beginning 3/15. Federal Work-Study Program available. Institutional employment available. Off-campus job opportunities are good.

The Inside Word

The Lasallian tradition that Saint Mary's adheres to is an awareness of social and economic injustice. In line with this, Saint Mary's reserves one quarter of its undergraduate population for students from the lowest economic strata. In spring 2006, the school announced that it would boost its own funding of financial aid by 13.5 percent in order to help such students attend the school. Saint Mary's commitment to serving the underprivileged provides a great opportunity for low-income students with strong academic potential.

THE SCHOOL SAYS " . . . "

From The Admissions Office

"Today, Saint Mary's College continues to offer a value-oriented education by providing a classical liberal arts background second to none. The emphasis is on teaching an individual how to think independently and responsibly, how to analyze information in all situations, and how to make choices based on logical thinking and rational examination. Such a program develops students' ability to ask the right questions and to formulate meaningful answers, not only within their professional careers but also for the rest of their lives. Saint Mary's College is committed to preparing young men and women for the challenge of an ever-changing world, while remaining faithful to an enduring academic and spiritual heritage. We believe the purpose of a college experience is to prepare men and women for an unlimited number of opportunities, and that this is best accomplished by educating the whole person, both intellectually and ethically. We strive to recruit, admit, enroll, and graduate students who are generous, faith-filled, and human, and we believe this is reaffirmed in our community of brothers, in our faculty, and in our personal concern for each student.

"For freshman applicants Fall 2008, we will accept either version of the SAT. The ACT is also accepted. The ACT Writing assessment is optional. The highest critical reading and the highest Math scores attained on the SAT will be used. SAT Subject Tests are not required."

SELECTIVITY

Admissions Rating	60*
# of applicants	3,929
% of applicants accepted	82
% of acceptees attending	19
# accepting a place on wait list	64
% admitted from wait list	83

FRESHMAN PROFILE

Range SAT Critical Reading	480–590
Range SAT Math	480–590
Minimum paper TOEFL	525
Minimum computer TOEFL	197
Minimum web-based TOEFL	71
Average HS GPA	3.33

DEADLINES

Early action	
Deadline	11/15
Notification	12/20
Regular	
Priority	11/15
Deadline	2/1
Notification	3/15
Nonfall registration?	yes

APPLICANTS ALSO LOOK AT

AND OFTEN PREFER
University of Notre Dame
University of California—Berkeley
Stanford University

AND SOMETIMES PREFER
University of California—San Diego
Loyola Marymount University
Santa Clara University

AND RARELY PREFER
University of California—Santa Cruz
University of the Pacific

FINANCIAL FACTS

Financial Aid Rating	72
Annual tuition	$33,100
Room and board	$11,680
Required fees	$150
Books and supplies	$1,206
% frosh rec. need-based scholarship or grant aid	57
% UG rec. need-based scholarship or grant aid	61
% frosh rec. non-need-based scholarship or grant aid	11
% UG rec. non-need-based scholarship or grant aid	9
% frosh rec. need-based self-help aid	52
% UG rec. need-based self-help aid	51
% frosh rec. athletic scholarships	8
% UG rec. athletic scholarships	8
% frosh rec. any financial aid	72
% UG rec. any financial aid	69
% UG borrow to pay for school	51
Average cumulative indebtedness	$26,690

SAINT MICHAEL'S COLLEGE

One Winooski Park, Colchester, VT 05439 • Admissions: 802-654-3000 • Fax: 802-654-2906

Academics

St Michael's College is a Catholic liberal art college that boasts "an absolutely unbeatable location" in the heart of "prime" Vermont ski territory. A reasonably broad set of core course requirements includes two mandatory religion classes. Study abroad is "huge." "Sciences are a very popular." "The education department, in general, is amazing." Coursework at SMC "can be very challenging—by no means is everything a breeze." However, classes tend to be manageably small. "Rarely do you have a class larger than 30 students which gives you a nice, intimate classroom experience." "The administration and professors at the school are all very open and welcoming to every student," promises a junior. "Like any school, there are the good and the bad teachers." For the most part, though, "professors are really passionate and devoted to the subjects that they teach." They are "available outside of class and open to lots of discussion in the classroom, and always are willing to help." The biggest academic gripe here is probably the "insufficient" course selection, since "The size of the college limits the overall variety of courses."

Life

Saint Mike's is lively. "It's my opinion that you cannot be bored on this campus," asserts one student. "The theater kids, the sports kids, the campus ministry kids, the volunteer program kids, the fire and rescue kids—there are groups for everyone." The community service program is "extremely popular." Rallies and demonstrations are common. "Most people are moderately interested in the outdoors" and the Wilderness Program runs student-led trips each weekend." Socially, SMC is "really close knit." "The big family aspect of Saint Mike's makes it easy to meet people and make friends. That boils down to awesome weekends." "Monday through Thursday, people tend to really focus on classes." Thursday marks the beginning of the weekend, which continues until late Saturday night. Mostly, "people get absolutely hammered in their rooms," then amble around campus to "various parties and get-togethers." There's a drug scene, too, if that's your bag. If you choose not to partake in the festivities, it's fine. However, virtually all students "are required to live on campus all four years," and the "overcrowded" dorms are "a mess." Also, the Internet is "slower than death," and Vermont winters are "brutal." On the plus side, if you ski or snowboard, "several great mountains" are nearby. (Smugglers' Notch offers ridiculously cheap season passes through a special offer to Saint Mike's students.) In warmer weather, "many activities—even parties—happen outside in the beautiful Vermont scenery." For a change of pace, students take the free bus to "artsy," "adorable" Burlington, "a hubbub of fun."

Student Body

"We have little to no ethnic or racial diversity at our school," admits a senior. "For what it's worth, however, the minorities here blend in with the rest of the student body." "A typical student is a solid 'B' student in high school who's really involved" and hails from "20 minutes outside Boston," observes one student. There are plenty of "hockey/rugby player types" and many students are "involved in sports." Quite a few students grew up wealthy. "New, expensive cars" dot the campus. "There is an abundance of preppy kids." You'll know them by their "Ugg boots, North Face fleeces, and Vera Bradley bags." "Hippies" are around, but not pervasive. "St Mike's is painted as more of a hippie college than it really is," reports one student. Politically, there are conservatives, but there are a lot more "left-wing liberals who care too much about the environment." Overall, there's an "open, welcoming" vibe. "Everyone is pretty low key about fitting in." "You can see a hippie hugging a preppie or a Yankees fan and Red Sox fan eating lunch together," swears one student. "Everyone gets along here."

FINANCIAL AID: 802-654-3243 • E-MAIL: ADMISSION@SMCVT.EDU • WEBSITE: WWW.SMCVT.EDU

THE PRINCETON REVIEW SAYS

Admissions

Very important factors considered include: Class rank, academic GPA, rigor of secondary school record. *Important factors considered include:* Application essay, recommendation(s), standardized test scores, character/personal qualities, extracurricular activities, talent/ability. *Other factors considered include:* Alumni/ae relation, first generation, geographical residence, level of applicant's interest, racial/ethnic status, state residency, volunteer work, work experience. SAT or ACT required; ACT with Writing component required. TOEFL required of all international applicants. High school diploma is required and GED is accepted. *Academic units required:* 4 English, 3 mathematics, 3 science, (2 science labs), 3 foreign language, 3 social studies. *Academic units recommended:* 4 English, 4 mathematics, 4 science, (3 science labs), 4 foreign language, 4 social studies.

Financial Aid

Students should submit: FAFSA, Signed copies of Parent's 2007 Federal Tax Return, Parent's Federal W-2 forms, Signed copies of Student's 2007 Federal Tax Return, Student's Federal W-2 forms, Dependent 2008-09 Verification Worksheet (Please check the Student Financial Services fo The Princeton Review suggests that all financial aid forms be submitted as soon as possible after January 1. *Need-based scholarships/grants offered:* Federal Pell, SEOG, state scholarships/grants, private scholarships, the school's own gift aid. *Loan aid offered:* Direct Subsidized Stafford, FFEL Subsidized Stafford, FFEL Unsubsidized Stafford, FFEL PLUS, Federal Perkins Applicants will be notified of awards on a rolling basis beginning 1/15. Federal Work-Study Program available. Institutional employment available. Off-campus job opportunities are excellent.

Inside Word

Saint Mike's is a pretty easy admit if you've shown a reasonable level of consistency in solid college prep curriculum. Candidates who goofed around a little too much in high school would be well advised to strongly highlight their extracurricular activities.

THE SCHOOL SAYS "..."

From The Admissions Office

"Saint Michael's is a residential, Catholic, liberal arts college for students who want to make the world a better place.

A Saint Michael's education will prepare you for life, as each of our 30 majors is grounded in our liberal studies core. Our superb faculty are committed first and foremost to teaching, and are known for really caring about their students while simultaneously challenging them to reach higher than they ever thought possible. Because of our holistic approach, Saint Michael's graduates are prepared for their entire careers, not just their first jobs out of college.

"With nearly 100% of students living on campus, our "24/7" learning environment means exceptional teaching goes beyond the classroom and into the living areas which include three new suite-style residences, townhouse apartments and traditional residence halls. The remarkable sense of community encourages students to get involved, take risks and think differently. A unique passion for social justice issues on campus reflects the heritage of the Edmundite priests who founded Saint Michael's in 1904.

"Saint Michael's is situated just outside of Burlington, Vermont's largest city and a true college town. A unique Cultural Pass program allows students to see an array of music, dance, theater and Broadway productions at the Flynn Center downtown. They also take advantage of some of the best skiing in the East through an agreement with Smugglers' Notch ski resort—an all-access season pass is provided to any Saint Michael's student in good academic standing."

SELECTIVITY

Admissions Rating	84
# of applicants	3,504
% of applicants accepted	69
% of acceptees attending	22
# accepting a place on wait list	203
% admitted from wait list	17

FRESHMAN PROFILE

Range SAT Critical Reading	520–620
Range SAT Math	520–610
Range SAT Writing	520–620
Range ACT Composite	22–26
Minimum paper TOEFL	550
Minimum computer TOEFL	213
Minimum web-based TOEFL	79-80
Average HS GPA	3.4
% graduated top 10% of class	23
% graduated top 25% of class	50
% graduated top 50% of class	86

DEADLINES

Early action	
Deadline	11/1
Notification	1/1
Regular	
Priority	11/1
Deadline	2/1
Notification	4/1
Nonfall registration?	yes

APPLICANTS ALSO LOOK AT

AND OFTEN PREFER
College of the Holy Cross
Boston College

AND SOMETIMES PREFER
Fairfield University

FINANCIAL FACTS

Financial Aid Rating	77
Annual tuition	$31,675
Room and board	$7,960
Required fees	$265
Books and supplies	$1,200
% frosh rec. need-based scholarship or grant aid	53
% UG rec. need-based scholarship or grant aid	61
% frosh rec. non-need-based scholarship or grant aid	8
% UG rec. non-need-based scholarship or grant aid	7
% frosh rec. need-based self-help aid	47
% UG rec. need-based self-help aid	55
% frosh rec. athletic scholarships	1
% UG rec. athletic scholarships	1
% frosh rec. any financial aid	90.7
% UG rec. any financial aid	89.8
% UG borrow to pay for school	75
Average cumulative indebtedness	$24,451

SALISBURY UNIVERSITY

ADMISSIONS OFFICE, 1101 CAMDEN AVENUE, SALISBURY, MD 21801 • ADMISSIONS: 410-543-6161 • FAX: 410-546-6016

CAMPUS LIFE

Quality of Life Rating	78
Fire Safety Rating	72
Green Rating	77
Type of school	public
Environment	town

STUDENTS

Total undergrad enrollment	6,726
% male/female	45/55
% from out of state	14
% from public high school	85
% live on campus	40
% in (# of) fraternities	5 (6)
% in (# of) sororities	6 (5)
% African American	11
% Asian	3
% Caucasian	81
% Hispanic	2
% Native American	1
% international	1
# of countries represented	60

SURVEY SAYS . . .

Lab facilities are great
Great computer facilities
Intramural sports are popular
Lots of beer drinking
Hard liquor is popular

ACADEMICS

Academic Rating	73
Calendar	4/1/4
Student/faculty ratio	18:1
Profs interesting rating	72
Profs accessible rating	76
% classes taught by TAs	2
Most common reg class size	20–29 students
Most common lab size	20–29 students

MOST POPULAR MAJORS

elementary education and teaching
business administration and management

STUDENTS SAY ". . ."

Academics

Salisbury University has come a long way since it first opened its doors in 1925. Originally a two-year college, Salisbury gradually grew into a four-year BA-conferring school, then added graduate programs in education, business, and nursing. The pace of ascendance has quickened over the past decade, transforming Salisbury from a local school to a regional favorite to, most recently, a university with some national draw. As one student observes, SU is "rapidly gaining respect and a reputation as a challenging, high-level academic institution." Part of the school's allure has to do with cost; SU is extremely affordable for Maryland residents and not much more expensive for out-of-state students. Scale is another factor at this "laid back, perfectly sized university" small enough to be "your home away from home," but large enough to "offer a top-notch education." Undergraduate business programs are the biggest draw here, attracting nearly 20 percent of all undergrads. Students love that the business curriculum prepares "well-rounded individuals" by "requiring us to have an internship to graduate, which forces one to get some real-world experience." The nursing, education, and communication programs also attract big crowds. In all programs, students enjoy "small class sizes, a compact campus, nice accessible professors, great majors, and fun trips." One student tells us that Salisbury "is about life learning, not just from textbooks and lectures, but from opportunity and diversity." Another adds that the university "is on its way to great things very soon."

Life

Life at SU "depends on what you are looking for. There is a club or organization for everything," and "all kinds of work, volunteer opportunities, and internships available through the school." The Student Office of Activity Programming (SOAP) "brings concerts, comedians, imitations of game shows, and open mic nights to campus and gives us students something fun and constructive to do!" The school's "amazing" Division III sports teams are well supported as well. Even so, many here tell us that life at SU "can get boring a lot of the time though because everything except bars and Taco Bell shuts down early, so many people end up going off-campus or to bars and getting drunk." This does not sit well with the conservative rural locals, and as a result, "We have a bad reputation with the Salisbury community. We are known for being a drinking school." And indeed, "Students do drink here at SU. I mean, we are known to be a party school and it's not a lie. But if you don't do that sort of thing then it's not a big deal. I had a hard time my freshman year first semester because I thought every one on campus went to parties and that's all there was to do. However, I found people who didn't go to parties to be friends with, and I started becoming more active in theatre and the Honors Student Association and I found my niche here at SU." As one student sums up, "Basically anything you want, SU has."

Student Body

SU undergrads are typically "laid back and like to hang out with friends, yet they know how and when to get work done when it needs to be done," although there are some here who "drink too much and complain when they don't get the grades they want even though they've skipped most classes due to hangovers." Most of the latter are presumably gone by sophomore year. There are "a lot of student athletes" here as well as "a D&D crowd who are really nice. They sort of hang out with other Starnet (SciFi club) members." Insofar as diversity, SU apparently has "a department devoted to it."

FINANCIAL AID: 410-543-6165 • E-MAIL: ADMISSIONS@SALISBURY.EDU • WEBSITE: WWW.SALISBURY.EDU

THE PRINCETON REVIEW SAYS

Admissions

Very important factors considered include: Academic GPA, rigor of secondary school record, extracurricular activities, talent/ability. *Important factors considered include:* Class rank, standardized test scores, alumni/ae relation, geographical residence, volunteer work. *Other factors considered include:* Application essay, recommendation(s), character/personal qualities, racial/ethnic status, work experience. TOEFL required of all international applicants. High school diploma is required and GED is accepted. *Academic units required:* 4 English, 3 mathematics, 3 science, (2 science labs), 2 foreign language, 3 social studies. *Academic units recommended:* 4 English, 4 mathematics, 4 science, (3 science labs), 3 foreign language, 3 social studies, 3 academic electives.

Financial Aid

Students should submit: FAFSA Regular filing deadline is 12/31. The Princeton Review suggests that all financial aid forms be submitted as soon as possible after January 1. *Need-based scholarships/grants offered:* Federal Pell, SEOG, state scholarships/grants, private scholarships, the school's own gift aid. *Loan aid offered:* Direct Subsidized Stafford, Direct Unsubsidized Stafford, Direct PLUS, Federal Perkins Applicants will be notified of awards on a rolling basis beginning 3/15. Federal Work-Study Program available. Institutional employment available. Off-campus job opportunities are fair.

The Inside Word

Salisbury has increased its undergraduate population by nearly 20 percent since the start of the decade, which hasn't made admission here any easier. On the contrary, the expansion was a reaction to a growing national profile and corresponding increase in the number of applications. Despite the trend, you can still expect a careful, personalized reading of your application here. It's about a lot more than just the numbers at Salisbury; prepare your application accordingly.

THE SCHOOL SAYS "..."

From The Admissions Office

"Friendly, convenient, safe, and beautiful are just a few of the words used to describe the campus of Salisbury University. The campus is a compact, self-contained community that offers the full range of student services. Beautiful, traditional-style architecture and impeccably landscaped grounds combine to create an atmosphere that inspires learning and fosters student pride. Located just 30 minutes from the beaches of Ocean City, Maryland, SU students enjoy a year-round resort social life as well as an inside track on summer jobs. Situated less than 2 hours from the urban excitement of Baltimore and Washington, DC, greater Salisbury makes up for its lack of size—its population is about 80,000—by being strategically located. Within easy driving distance of a number of other major cities, including New York City, Philadelphia, and Norfolk, Salisbury is the hub of the Delmarva Peninsula, a mostly rural region flavored by the salty air of the Chesapeake Bay and Atlantic Ocean.

"Submission of SAT and/or ACT scores when applying would be optional to freshman applicants who present a weighted high school grade point average (GPA) of 3.5 or higher on a 4.0 scale. Any student applying with less than a 3.5 would still need to submit a standardized test score to supplement the official high school transcript. Additionally, an applicant may wish to submit a standardized test score subsequent to admission for full scholarship consideration as the majority of the University scholarships include test scores as a requirement."

SELECTIVITY

Admissions Rating	86
# of applicants	6,593
% of applicants accepted	56
% of acceptees attending	31

FRESHMAN PROFILE

Range SAT Critical Reading	510–590
Range SAT Math	520–610
Range SAT Writing	520–589
Range ACT Composite	20–24
Minimum paper TOEFL	550
Minimum computer TOEFL	213
Average HS GPA	3.5
% graduated top 10% of class	23.4
% graduated top 25% of class	60.9
% graduated top 50% of class	91.7

DEADLINES

Early action	
Deadline	12/1
Notification	1/15
Regular	
Priority	12/1
Notification	3/15
Nonfall registration?	yes

APPLICANTS ALSO LOOK AT
AND SOMETIMES PREFER

St. Mary's College of Maryland
Towson University
University of Maryland—
Baltimore County

AND RARELY PREFER

University of Maryland—College Park

FINANCIAL FACTS

Financial Aid Rating	70
Annual tuition	$4,814
Books and supplies	$100
% frosh rec. need-based scholarship or grant aid	34
% UG rec. need-based scholarship or grant aid	28
% frosh rec. need-based self-help aid	31
% UG rec. need-based self-help aid	32
% frosh rec. any financial aid	73
% UG rec. any financial aid	67
% UG borrow to pay for school	52
Average cumulative indebtedness	$17,669

SAMFORD UNIVERSITY

800 LAKESHORE DRIVE, BIRMINGHAM, AL 35229 • ADMISSIONS: 205-726-3673 • FAX: 205-726-2171

CAMPUS LIFE

Quality of Life Rating	**92**
Fire Safety Rating	**88**
Green Rating	**74**
Type of school	private
Affiliation	Baptist
Environment	town

STUDENTS

Total undergrad enrollment	2,841
% male/female	36/64
% from out of state	34
% from public high school	55
% live on campus	42
% in (# of) fraternities	28 (7)
% in (# of) sororities	38 (7)
% African American	6
% Asian	1
% Caucasian	90
% Hispanic	1
# of countries represented	20

SURVEY SAYS . . .

Large classes
Athletic facilities are great
Students are friendly
Students love Birmingham, AL
Great off-campus food
Students are happy

ACADEMICS

Academic Rating	**83**
Calendar	4/1/4
Student/faculty ratio	12:1
Profs interesting rating	88
Profs accessible rating	84
Most common reg class size	10–19 students
Most common lab size	10–19 students

MOST POPULAR MAJORS

pharmacy (pharmd [USA], pharmd
or bs/bpharm [Canada])
law (ll.b.,j.d.)
business administration
and management

STUDENTS SAY ". . ."

Academics

Samford University, "a beautiful liberal arts college with amazing Christian values," draws undergrads seeking "a close-knit community in which high value is placed on morality, academic excellence and communication skills." Students tell us that "Samford represents what is great about a Christian university. It provides an environment that is diverse and not typically conservative Christian." A "well-rounded, challenging curriculum" ensures that students transcend indoctrination while still experiencing "some aspect of religious discussion…in classes where you would not usually encounter it." High expectations ensure that they don't coast through to an easy degree. As one student explains, "Samford professors expect a lot from their students, and in return we expect a lot from them. It's been said that academics at Samford are quite a bit harder than most universities, so when someone gets a B people see it as an A, when they get a C it's seen as a B, and so forth." Outstanding disciplines here include English, journalism, nursing, pharmacy, business, music, and theater. But perhaps Samford's most outstanding quality is its "incredibly friendly, welcoming, and genuine atmosphere that makes the transition to college life a pleasant one. The campus is positively breathtaking, the facilities are excellent, class sizes are relatively small, and professors are available and helpful…. There is an overall feeling of contentment on campus."

Life

"There are people who party and those who don't" at Samford; despite the campus' official "dry" status, "There will always be those few people who break the rules," and furthermore, Birmingham offers "some fun nightlife" that can, and occasionally does, involve intoxicants. As a whole, however, "Students generally are not big partiers, but like to have fun. Most weekends are spent hanging out with friends or traveling." "There is a strong Greek presence" on the Samford campus, "and many weekends include Greek parties or fundraisers and activities." Religious groups "are especially popular, and the majority of the student body is involved in at least one college ministry throughout the week." Students enjoy "at least five opportunities a week to worship" and "are very engaged in the community and local churches." These activities include "a strong awareness of global issues: fair trade, Darfur, etc." Samford "is located in a very safe part of Birmingham," providing students a secure enclave from which to launch their explorations of the city. Students tell us the city is "awesome," "with plenty of places to eat, shop, and play. There are several movie theaters and shopping centers within a ten-mile radius, as well as a roller skating rink, plenty of gorgeous parks, and a thriving downtown."

Student Body

"The Samford stereotype is a white, wealthy, southern, Protestant (usually Baptist) female, decked out in country club attire," but "while that accounts for maybe an (admittedly vocal) 20 percent of the school, there is a lot of diversity otherwise, especially outside the Greek system." Students who don't fit the mold "often hang out on the quad and are active in various campus organizations or other activities. There actually are hippies, druggies, minorities, political extremists of all stripes, gay people, and people from all over the world at Samford. Don't be deceived by your first glance." Many here are Christian; quite a few respondents told us that while "a wide variety of people attend" Samford, "a large percent were raised in a very sheltered environment" and the majority are "white, upper class, Southern Christians" "with strong Christian values and beliefs." Students tend to be highly ambitious, with "a generally heavy interest in their future and…a plan for achieving their goals."

FINANCIAL AID: 800-888-7245 • E-MAIL: ADMISS@SAMFORD.EDU • WEBSITE: WWW.SAMFORD.EDU

THE PRINCETON REVIEW SAYS

Admissions

Very important factors considered include: Application essay, academic GPA, recommendation(s), rigor of secondary school record, standardized test scores, character/personal qualities, religious affiliation/commitment. *Important factors considered include:* Class rank, alumni/ae relation, extracurricular activities, interview. *Other factors considered include:* Geographical residence, level of applicant's interest, racial/ethnic status, state residency, talent/ability, volunteer work, work experience. SAT or ACT required; ACT with Writing component recommended. TOEFL required of all international applicants. High school diploma is required and GED is accepted. *Academic units required:* 4 English, 3 mathematics, 3 science, (2 science labs), 2 social studies, 2 history. *Academic units recommended:* 2 foreign language.

Financial Aid

Students should submit: FAFSA. The Princeton Review suggests that all financial aid forms be submitted as soon as possible after January 1. *Need-based scholarships/grants offered:* Federal Pell, SEOG, state scholarships/grants, private scholarships, the school's own gift aid. *Loan aid offered:* FFEL Subsidized Stafford, FFEL Unsubsidized Stafford, FFEL PLUS, Federal Perkins, college/university loans from institutional funds. Applicants will be notified of awards on or about 4/1. Federal Work-Study Program available. Institutional employment available. Off-campus job opportunities are excellent.

The Inside Word

Samford admits applicants on a rolling basis; the first acceptance letters go out as early as October. As is often the case with rolling admissions, those who apply early in the process are most likely to receive a generous review. The school strongly recommends a campus visit, meaning you ought to make one if at all possible. A campus visit is a great way of signaling your desire to attend the school, which in turn improves your chances of being admitted.

THE SCHOOL SAYS "..."

From The Admissions Office

"Students who are drawn to Samford are well-rounded individuals who not only expect to be challenged but are excited by the prospect. It is the critical and creative way you think, it is the articulate way you write and speak, it is the joy of learning that stays with you throughout your life, and it is the clarity of decision making guided by Christian principles."

"As of this book's publication, Samford University did not have information available about their policy regarding the new SAT."

SELECTIVITY

Admissions Rating	84
# of applicants	1,810
% of applicants accepted	92
% of acceptees attending	43

FRESHMAN PROFILE

Range SAT Critical Reading	510–620
Range SAT Math	490–630
Range ACT Composite	22–28
Minimum paper TOEFL	550
Minimum computer TOEFL	213
Average HS GPA	3.61
% graduated top 10% of class	32
% graduated top 25% of class	59
% graduated top 50% of class	86

DEADLINES

Regular	
Priority	3/1
Notification	rolling
Nonfall registration?	yes

APPLICANTS ALSO LOOK AT AND SOMETIMES PREFER

Auburn University
Baylor University
Florida State University
University of Georgia

FINANCIAL FACTS

Financial Aid Rating	74
Annual tuition	$9,300
% frosh rec. need-based scholarship or grant aid	35
% UG rec. need-based scholarship or grant aid	34
% frosh rec. need-based self-help aid	31
% UG rec. need-based self-help aid	34
% frosh rec. athletic scholarships	8
% UG rec. athletic scholarships	7
% frosh rec. any financial aid	39
% UG rec. any financial aid	37
% UG borrow to pay for school	46
Average cumulative indebtedness	$18,501

SANTA CLARA UNIVERSITY

500 El Camino Real, Santa Clara, CA 95053 • Admissions: 408-554-4700 • Fax: 408-554-5255

STUDENTS SAY ". . ."

Academics

Santa Clara University is a small Jesuit institution that "teaches Catholic values and strives for global solidarity" while offering "a great academic program that stresses the development of critical thinking" and real-world application of classroom lessons. Here the Jesuit ideals of broad education and "conscience, compassion, and community" are stressed not only through a thorough core curriculum (which "develops better-rounded students who are more aware of the world around them") but also through "a large emphasis on immersion trips and getting students to volunteer and to go out into the community." Science, business, and engineering are the school's academic fortes, although students identify many other strong points: Art history, English, mathematics, and communications all have their boosters. SCU operates on a quarter system that "is very fast paced." For some it means "constantly worrying about the next midterm, final, or paper that's due," resulting in "chronic stress." Others, however, "love having classes for ten weeks, plus one week of finals," describing it as "a short enough time that you don't get sick of a course" but long enough to "really develop a relationship with your professor." As one student explains, "The engineering program is notoriously difficult and has a reputation for losing eager freshman to easier majors such as communications or sociology. Other programs are extremely challenging" but manageable. In all areas, the school's small size "fosters an excellent community and strong access to and interaction with faculty." An added bonus: "Professional placement in the Bay Area is extraordinary."

Life

"There are two categories of students" at SCU: "the drinkers and the thinkers." In both camps, "most are very academic and stay in and study during the week," but the former are more likely on weekends to "hit the parties or visit San Francisco. Everyone needs a break sometime!" The latter tend to be "very busy pursuing their careers" through internships, workshops, and interest-related clubs. The party scene typically revs up on Wednesdays, Fridays, and Saturdays. "House parties off campus are a really fun way for everyone to interact" and represent the party venue of choice. Partying is hardly the only leisure alternative, however; as one student explains, "What most students do for fun depends on the person. Many find fun in staying in their dorm playing video games with friends, while others enjoy going to the handful of local bars that cater to SCU students. Also, the Activities Planning Board has concerts and comedy shows…that students can attend for ridiculously cheap prices." Many here are athletically inclined; for spectators, "Basketball season is when our student fan group is most active, and a lot of students come out for the men's games. Our volleyball and soccer teams pull a good amount of fans in the fall." Because SCU "is located right next to a Cal Train station; a weekend trip to San Francisco is affordable and fun!" Many take advantage of the opportunity.

Student Body

"The typical student at Santa Clara is probably from an upper-middle class family," making the student body "somewhat homogenous in terms of economic background, but that is expected since it is a private school in California." Writes one student, "My one problem with Santa Clara is that we have a very limited demographic. The people here are the people who can pay to be here. There are different, atypical people here; you just have to look slightly harder to find them." SCU undergrads typically "work hard and are intelligent, but know how to have fun and go out. They have balance in their lives" and are "outgoing and very involved in clubs and organizations." They tend to be "relatively conservative and success-oriented."

THE PRINCETON REVIEW SAYS

Admissions

Very important factors considered include: Application essay, academic GPA, recommendation(s), rigor of secondary school record. *Important factors considered include:* Standardized test scores, extracurricular activities, racial/ethnic status, talent/ability, volunteer work. *Other factors considered include:* Class rank, alumni/ae relation, character/personal qualities, first generation, geographical residence, level of applicant's interest, religious affiliation/commitment, state residency, work experience. SAT or ACT required; High school diploma is required and GED is not accepted. *Academic units required:* 4 English, 3 mathematics, 2 science, 2 foreign language, 3 social studies, 1 academic elective. *Academic units recommended:* 4 English, 4 mathematics, 3 science, 3 foreign language, 3 social studies, 1 visual/performing arts, 1 academic elective.

Financial Aid

Students should submit: FAFSA, CSS/Financial Aid PROFILE The Princeton Review suggests that all financial aid forms be submitted as soon as possible after January 1. *Need-based scholarships/grants offered:* Federal Pell, SEOG, state scholarships/grants, private scholarships, the school's own gift aid. *Loan aid offered:* Direct Subsidized Stafford, Direct Unsubsidized Stafford, Direct PLUS, Federal Perkins, Private alternative loans. Applicants will be notified of awards on or about 4/1. Off-campus job opportunities are good.

The Inside Word

Each year, the Santa Clara admissions office works hard to assemble a diverse incoming class. The result is a student body with large Asian and Hispanic populations; this isn't your typical lily-white private school. One area in which the school falls short is in gender balance; women outnumber men here, and the school "makes a special pitch to men to talk about the benefits of Santa Clara," according to *The Los Angeles Times*. The school won't compromise its standards simply to erase the gender gap, but men enjoy a slight advantage as a result of the school's efforts in this area.

THE SCHOOL SAYS ". . ."

From The Admissions Office

"Santa Clara University, located one hour south of San Francisco, offers its undergraduates an opportunity to be educated within a challenging, dynamic, and caring community. The university blends a sense of tradition and history (as the oldest college in California) with a vision that values innovation and a deep commitment to social justice. Santa Clara's faculty members are talented scholars who are demanding, supportive, and accessible. The students are serious about academics, are ethnically diverse, and enjoy a full range of athletic, social, community-service, religious, and cultural activities—both on campus and through the many options presented by our northern California location. The undergraduate program includes three divisions: the College of Arts and Sciences, the School of Business, and the School of Engineering.

"For Fall 2008, Santa Clara University will accept either the new SAT or the old SAT. The ACT may be taken in lieu of, or in addition to, the SAT. The ACT Writing component is optional. The highest verbal and the highest math scores attained on the SAT will be used."

SELECTIVITY

Admissions Rating	89
# of applicants	9,459
% of applicants accepted	61
% of acceptees attending	21
# accepting a place on wait list	811
% admitted from wait list	21

FRESHMAN PROFILE

Range SAT Critical Reading	540–650
Range SAT Math	570–670
Range ACT Composite	24–29
Average HS GPA	3.5
% graduated top 10% of class	36
% graduated top 25% of class	73
% graduated top 50% of class	94

DEADLINES

Early action	
Deadline	11/1
Notification	12/31
Regular	
Deadline	1/7
Notification	rolling
Nonfall registration?	no

FINANCIAL FACTS

Financial Aid Rating	77
Annual tuition	$33,000
Room and board	$10,644
Books and supplies	$1,386
% frosh rec. need-based scholarship or grant aid	27
% UG rec. need-based scholarship or grant aid	29
% frosh rec. non-need-based scholarship or grant aid	15
% UG rec. non-need-based scholarship or grant aid	10
% frosh rec. need-based self-help aid	20
% UG rec. need-based self-help aid	23
% frosh rec. athletic scholarships	4
% UG rec. athletic scholarships	4
% frosh rec. any financial aid	78
% UG rec. any financial aid	76
% UG borrow to pay for school	46.1
Average cumulative indebtedness	$23,773

SARAH LAWRENCE COLLEGE

ONE MEAD WAY, BRONXVILLE, NY 10708-5999 • ADMISSIONS: 914-395-2510 • FAX: 914-395-2676

STUDENTS SAY ". . ."

Academics
Offering a unique approach to liberal arts education, Sarah Lawrence College is a "serious academic and artistic environment where individual passion fuels learning." Through SLC's distinctive curriculum, students are the architects of their own educational experience and the school "places a great emphasis on personal research and personal responsibility." In their first year, undergrads meet with their advisors every week to discuss their academic plans, and "besides your don (permanent counselor), you have a slew of people who really want you to be the best that you can be." Of particular note, students benefit from "inordinate amounts of individual time with each professor," who are all "enormously educated, good teachers, and passionate about their subjects." Across disciplines, Sarah Lawrence professors "are generally willing to give over copious amounts of time to undergraduate research papers, projects, ideas, and extracurricular discussion." A student shares this noteworthy story: "I am in a lecture about Epic Poetry but I'm not really interested in poetry, so I talked to the professor and he was totally cool with all my papers being about anthropological elements of the text and not poetic one." Among other innovations, SLC's unusual (but, some say, inefficient) course registration system allows students to interview teachers before signing up for classes. Fortunately, "all of the classes here are excellent, so if one doesn't get into a desired class, it isn't the end of the world." Unfortunately, many students feel SLC's administration can be bureaucratic and out-of-step with the school's dominant philosophy and culture. When discussing these shortcomings, however, students acknowledge that the administration faces many challenges in that the school is "expensive to run" and funds are more limited than at larger colleges.

Life
Whether you enjoy attending "study parties" or playing Frisbee in your underwear, "life at Sarah Lawrence is about as quirky as the college itself." Club meetings and school-sponsored activities are lightly attended; however, poetry readings, artistic pursuits, live music shows, and political organizing are widely popular, and "there is a growing athletic community on campus" as well. On campus, there are occasional dance parties, as well as casual get-togethers; however, on the whole, campus life is fairly subdued. A student claims, "The best way to relax is to get together with a few friends, put on some music, and just hang out. Conversations range from deep political or philosophical debates to discussing cartoons." Located in Bronxville, "everybody enjoys the fact that we're a hop, skip and a jump away from wonderful Manhattan," and a majority of students head to the city on the weekend. For those who stay on campus, "weekends include a lot of wandering around, but mostly just sitting and talking in friends dorm rooms about typical stuff, you know, Nietzsche and the importance of green architecture." In addition, students might be found "playing music together, listening to music, throwing dinner parties, drinking beer, playing board games, playing drinking games, talking about music, going to the city, eating a lot of Chinese and Sushi take-out, [or] playing in the snow."

Student Body
With a motto like "we're different, so are you," it's not surprising that "Sarah Lawrence is like Mecca for creative, proactive, outrageous, and independent students who want ultimate freedom in designing their education." Bohemian attire and alternative music are culturally prevalent, and "writers, artists, eccentrics, musicians, academics, activists, and scientists all call Sarah Lawrence home." In fact, many students say that, "the typical Sarah Lawrence student looks like the atypical student at any mainstream university." Students agree that the SLC "environment is very inclusive of all people and walks of life;" however, many complain that the "indie" or bohemian veneer attracts students who are unfriendly, self-absorbed, or who are "so used to being the "different" ones that they can't deal with the fact that they aren't "special" here." While some would like a warmer and friendlier college atmosphere, students reassure us that "there is a wide spectrum of interests and lifestyles so almost everyone can find a crowd of friends that suits them."

FINANCIAL AID: 914-395-2570 • E-MAIL: SLCADMIT@SLC.EDU • WEBSITE: WWW.SARAHLAWRENCE.EDU

THE PRINCETON REVIEW SAYS

Admissions

Very important factors considered include: Application essay, recommendation(s), rigor of secondary school record. *Important factors considered include:* Academic GPA, character/personal qualities, extracurricular activities, talent/ability. *Other factors considered include:* Class rank, alumni/ae relation, first generation, geographical residence, interview, level of applicant's interest, racial/ethnic status, volunteer work, work experience. High school diploma is required and GED is accepted. *Academic units required:* 4 English, 2 mathematics, 2 science, 2 foreign language, 2 history. *Academic units recommended:* 4 mathematics, 4 science, 4 foreign language, 4 history.

Financial Aid

Students should submit: FAFSA, CSS/Financial Aid PROFILE, state aid form, noncustodial PROFILE. Regular filing deadline is 2/1. The Princeton Review suggests that all financial aid forms be submitted as soon as possible after January 1. *Need-based scholarships/grants offered:* Federal Pell, SEOG, state scholarships/grants, private scholarships, the school's own gift aid. *Loan aid offered:* FFEL Subsidized Stafford, FFEL Unsubsidized Stafford, FFEL PLUS, Federal Perkins Applicants will be notified of awards on or about 4/1.

The Inside Word

In addition to three required essay questions, Sarah Lawrence College requests that candidates submit a graded, academic writing sample. Students say you shouldn't underestimate the importance of this unusual requirement, as SLC's curriculum is writing-based and a good sample can make your application stand out. Sarah Lawrence College doesn't believe that standardized test scores accurately reflect a student's ability to succeed in their academic program, and therefore, they do not review ACT or SAT scores.

THE SCHOOL SAYS "..."

From The Admissions Office

"Students who come to Sarah Lawrence are curious about the world, and they have an ardent desire to satisfy that curiosity. Sarah Lawrence offers such students two innovative academic structures: the seminar/conference system and the arts components. Courses in the humanities, social sciences, natural sciences, and mathematics are taught in the seminar/conference style. The seminars enroll an average of 11 students and consist of lecture, discussion, readings, and assigned papers. For each seminar, students also have private tutorials, called conferences, for which they conceive of individualized projects and shape them under the direction of professors. Arts components let students combine history and theory with practice. Painters, printmakers, photographers, sculptors, filmmakers, composers, musicians, choreographers, dancers, actors, and directors work in readily available studios, editing facilities, and darkrooms, guided by accomplished professionals. The secure, wooded campus is 30 minutes from midtown Manhattan, and the diversity of people and ideas at Sarah Lawrence make it an extraordinary educational environment.

"Sarah Lawrence College no longer uses standardized test scores in the admissions process. This decision reflects our conviction that overemphasis on test preparation can distort results and make the application process inordinately stressful, and that academic success is better predicted by the student's course rigor, their grades, recommendations, and writing ability."

SELECTIVITY

Admissions Rating	89
# of applicants	2,801
% of applicants accepted	44
% of acceptees attending	29
# accepting a place on wait list	271
% admitted from wait list	31
# of early decision applicants	164
% accepted early decision	48

FRESHMAN PROFILE

Average HS GPA	3.6
% graduated top 10% of class	37
% graduated top 25% of class	84
% graduated top 50% of class	98

DEADLINES

Early decision	
Deadline	11/15
Notification	12/15
Regular	
Deadline	1/1
Notification	4/1
Nonfall registration?	no

FINANCIAL FACTS

Financial Aid Rating	79
Annual tuition	$39,450
Room and board	$13,104
Required fees	$960
% frosh rec. need-based scholarship or grant aid	44
% UG rec. need-based scholarship or grant aid	48
% frosh rec. non-need-based scholarship or grant aid	1
% UG rec. non-need-based scholarship or grant aid	1
% frosh rec. need-based self-help aid	43
% UG rec. need-based self-help aid	49
% frosh rec. any financial aid	48
% UG rec. any financial aid	54
% UG borrow to pay for school	61
Average cumulative indebtedness	$16,332

SCRIPPS COLLEGE

1030 COLUMBIA AVENUE, MAILBOX #1265, CLAREMONT, CA 91711 • ADMISSIONS: 909-621-8149 • FAX: 909-607-7508

CAMPUS LIFE

Quality of Life Rating	94
Fire Safety Rating	71
Green Rating	77
Type of school	private
Environment	town

STUDENTS

Total undergrad enrollment	888
% male/female	/100
% from out of state	58
% from public high school	63
% live on campus	95
% African American	4
% Asian	13
% Caucasian	51
% Hispanic	8
% Native American	1
% international	1
# of countries represented	10

SURVEY SAYS . . .

Small classes
No one cheats
Great library
Great food on campus
Dorms are like palaces
Frats and sororities are unpopular
or nonexistent

ACADEMICS

Academic Rating	96
Calendar	semester
Student/faculty ratio	11:1
Profs interesting rating	91
Profs accessible rating	90
Most common reg class size	10–19 students
Most common lab size	10–19 students

MOST POPULAR MAJORS

psychology
English language and literature
international relations and affairs

STUDENTS SAY ". . ."

Academics

With more than 800 undergraduates, the all-women's Scripps College "truly provides a small-college experience" with "an atmosphere that is vibrant, challenging, and conducive not only to learning but also to out-of-class academic discussion." Thanks to the school's membership in the Claremont Consortium (composed of Scripps, Harvey Mudd, McKenna, Pitzer, and Pomona), Scripps also offers "the amazing resources of a bigger school, including excellent faculty, tons of course options, and competitive athletics." Scripps specializes in "teaching students to be independent, intelligent, thoughtful women who are interested in improving both themselves and their world." A feminist perspective informs many classes; one student writes, "We're learning about feminism and being detoxed of the common view that it is evil or man-hating, which is truly liberating and fun to experience." Another jokes, "If you don't come out of here a hard-boiled feminist who still enjoys dressing up for tea, we've done something wrong." Central to any Scripps education is the core program, which is "basically a three-semester humanities course. It is excellent, and it makes for a well-rounded student." Students also love "how everyone takes Core I together, because of the community it creates [during the] freshman year." In addition to these opportunities, Scripps also "has a great off-campus study program, and students are encouraged to study in a foreign country."

Life

Attending Scripps "is like being at a resort," students tell us, because "It's always sunny, the food is great," and "The dorms are incredibly spacious and comfortable." In fact, the entire campus is "exquisite. Even if you wake up in a bad mood, once you step outside and see the beauty of the trees and gardens and fountains, everything seems a little better." Life here is relatively quiet during the week, when "Everyone works hard during the day and then studies or does homework at night." For a break, students often drop by "the Motley, the student-run coffeehouses, where there are always a bunch of people studying, chatting, or just enjoying the great drinks and snacks they serve there." On Thursdays and weekends, "There are always campus parties that are fun to drop by." Most of the parties take place on the campuses of the other 4 C's "because they have more lenient drinking policies, and Scripps generally prefers to keep its campus quiet and clean." These parties "are really fun and take place every weekend; some are large, some small. Many of them are themed parties, and people dress up in costumes. People get pretty into it, and that's fun." Students see hometown Claremont as "not all that thrilling, but it's safe and has nice restaurants and a farmer's market every Sunday, so sometimes it's nice to walk into town with friends." Students note that "the Metrolink train system has a stop that is a 10-minute walk from campus. [It] makes several stops in Claremont every day and travels straight into downtown LA."

Student Body

"Scripps has two stereotypes: the blond Barbie princess and the raging feminist," and while students grudgingly admit that "there is some validity" to the stereotypes, "Most of the students are in fact mild-mannered and [have] fairly studious habits." One student writes, "You can find anyone from the most outspoken social activist to the quietest bookworm, from the artsy type to the scientist. All Scripps women are extremely multifaceted, and you cannot possibly put them in one category." Women here tend to be "very hardworking, givers instead of takers, thoughtful, motivated, approachable, and impressive."

FINANCIAL AID: 909-621-8275 • E-MAIL: ADMISSION@SCRIPPSCOLLEGE.EDU • WEBSITE: WWW.SCRIPPSCOLLEGE.EDU

THE PRINCETON REVIEW SAYS

Admissions

Very important factors considered include: Class rank, application essay, academic GPA, recommendation(s), rigor of secondary school record, standardized test scores, alumni/ae relation, character/personal qualities, extracurricular activities, first generation, interview, racial/ethnic status. *Important factors considered include:* Geographical residence, SAT or ACT required; TOEFL required of all international applicants. High school diploma is required and GED is accepted. *Academic units required:* 4 English, 3 mathematics, 3 science, 3 foreign language, 3 social studies. *Academic units recommended:* 4 English.

Financial Aid

Students should submit: FAFSA, CSS/Financial Aid PROFILE, noncustodial PROFILE, business/farm supplement, Verification worksheet, parent and student federal tax returns. The Princeton Review suggests that all financial aid forms be submitted as soon as possible after January 1. *Need-based scholarships/grants offered:* Federal Pell, SEOG, state scholarships/grants, private scholarships, the school's own gift aid, Federal work-study. *Loan aid offered:* FFEL Subsidized Stafford, FFEL Unsubsidized Stafford, FFEL PLUS, Federal Perkins, college/university loans from institutional funds. Applicants will be notified of awards on or about 4/1. Federal Work-Study Program available. Institutional employment available. Off-campus job opportunities are good.

The Inside Word

Applicants to Scripps won't encounter any admissions formulas or standardized test minimums. Admissions Officers aim to establish a diverse and talented freshman class and do so by evaluating a variety of factors. Serious candidates should give equal time to each facet of their application. Strong writing skills and intellectual curiosity are viewed as essential qualities in successful applicants.

THE SCHOOL SAYS ". . ."

From The Admissions Office

"At Scripps, we believe that learning involves much more than amassing information. The truly educated person is one who can think analytically, communicate effectively, and make confident, responsible choices. Scripps classes are small (the average class size is 15) so that they foster an atmosphere where students feel comfortable participating, testing old assumptions, and exploring new ideas. Our curriculum is based on the traditional components of a liberal arts education: a set of general requirements in a wide variety of disciplines including foreign language, natural science, and writing; a multicultural requirement; a major that asks students to study one particular field in depth; and a variety of electives that allows considerable flexibility. What distinguishes Scripps from other liberal arts colleges is an emphasis on interdisciplinary courses.

"First-year applicants for Fall 2008 must submit results of the new SAT or the ACT. SAT Subject Tests are not required."

SELECTIVITY
Admissions Rating	96
# of applicants	1,969
% of applicants accepted	43
% of acceptees attending	27
# accepting a place on wait list	201
% admitted from wait list	1
# of early decision applicants	84
% accepted early decision	60

FRESHMAN PROFILE
Range SAT Critical Reading	650–740
Range SAT Math	630–700
Range SAT Writing	640–720
Range ACT Composite	28–31
Minimum paper TOEFL	600
Minimum computer TOEFL	250
Average HS GPA	4
% graduated top 10% of class	72
% graduated top 25% of class	95
% graduated top 50% of class	100

DEADLINES
Early decision	
Deadline	11/1
Notification	12/15
Regular	
Deadline	1/1
Notification	4/1
Nonfall registration?	yes

APPLICANTS ALSO LOOK AT
AND OFTEN PREFER
Occidental College
University of Southern California
University of California—Berkeley
Wellesley College

AND SOMETIMES PREFER
Pomona College
University of California—Los Angeles
Stanford University

FINANCIAL FACTS
Financial Aid Rating	97
Annual tuition	$35,636
Room and board	$10,800
Required fees	$214
Books and supplies	$800
% frosh rec. need-based scholarship or grant aid	42
% UG rec. need-based scholarship or grant aid	41
% frosh rec. non-need-based scholarship or grant aid	7
% UG rec. non-need-based scholarship or grant aid	5
% frosh rec. need-based self-help aid	33
% UG rec. need-based self-help aid	37
% frosh rec. any financial aid	57
% UG rec. any financial aid	61
% UG borrow to pay for school	42
Average cumulative indebtedness	$11,235

SEATTLE UNIVERSITY

ADMISSIONS OFFICE, 900 BROADWAY, SEATTLE, WA 98122-4340 • ADMISSIONS: 206-296-2000 • FAX: 206-296-5656

CAMPUS LIFE

Quality of Life Rating	**98**
Fire Safety Rating	**60***
Green Rating	**97**
Type of school	private
Affiliation	Roman Catholic/Jesuit
Environment	metropolis

STUDENTS

Total undergrad enrollment	4,253
% male/female	39/61
% from out of state	45
% from public high school	63
% live on campus	39
% African American	5
% Asian	20
% Caucasian	52
% Hispanic	7
% Native American	1
% international	8
# of countries represented	74

SURVEY SAYS . . .
Small classes
Students love Seattle, WA
Great off-campus food
Frats and sororities are unpopular
or nonexistent

ACADEMICS

Academic Rating	**86**
Calendar	quarter
Student/faculty ratio	13:1
Profs interesting rating	90
Profs accessible rating	89
Most common reg class size	10–19 students
Most common lab size	20–29 students

MOST POPULAR MAJORS
nursing/registered nurse
(RN, ASN, BSN, MSN)
finance
marketing/marketing management

STUDENTS SAY ". . ."

Academics

Seattle University is a midsize Jesuit university "dedicated to growth, not only educational but also spiritual, as well as the overall well-being of the person." Issues of "community and social justice in a complex world" permeate the curriculum here, "pushing students to reevaluate their presuppositions about the world in a just and humane manner." For example, "Community-service hours are actually a requirement with specific required freshman-level courses. This is helpful to freshmen, because it gets them to experience at least one aspect of Seattle's community." Academically, SU "is very strong and very challenging" with "time-consuming homework," but "with services like the Writing Center, Math Lab, and professors who check their e-mail even more regularly than the students themselves, it's not hard to find the resources you need to produce quality work." Standout departments include Public Affairs, Criminal Justice, Civil Engineering, Business, English, Psychology, and a nursing program that "rigorously prepares students to be dependable, altruistic nurses who will be leaders in the community." Across disciplines, "small class sizes and personal attention to one's education and career development" as well as "high-quality professors who get to know individual students and focus entirely on each student's learning" define the SU academic experience.

Student Life

Seattle University "is located on one of the liveliest streets in Seattle," and that naturally has a huge impact on students' lives here. After all, "Seattle is one of the best playgrounds a college student could ever ask for," so, "if there's not something going on at the campus, such as an international dinner, formal, game competition between dorms, or BBQ," then "There's always something to do downtown." "Within walking distance of the campus students can find handfuls of amazing restaurants, small venues for concerts, the Seattle Center, movie theaters, and coffee shops. The possibilities are endless." A little farther afield, students can access "professional sports, art, music, beautiful buildings, and a lot of nature. Not too big and definitely not small, Seattle is a very diverse city in many aspects." On campus, "Many of us like to attend school sporting events. There are generally parties afterwards, and also just about every weekend." There are "also lots of clubs and activities on campus," such as "social, political, and cultural clubs that meet once a week on a weeknight and offer activities such as movie nights, casino nights, club nights, guest speakers, camping and snowboarding trips, as well as an annual 'showcase' of sorts including student-organized dinner and entertainment." For a quieter evening, "The residence halls and the student center offer community rooms to watch TV, play video games, or shoot pool."

Students

The typical SU student "would be described in terms of attitude, not any particular look. A typical student is balanced, having a desire to do well in whatever he or she tackles, but especially wherever his or her passion lies. Nearly all students are involved in some organization, club, or volunteer effort in order to make sure that they maintain a connection to the needs of the greater global reality and outside community." The population is "pretty diverse," with "a lot of international students," a "large gay population," and "quite a few nontraditional [over age 25] students" in the mix. Despite the fact that SU is a Jesuit school, "all religions you can think of are present here." Different groups "tend to mesh very well. The diversity is a wonderful tool for shaping us as students." Asians and Latinos account for the lion's share of the racial diversity here.

SEATTLE UNIVERSITY

FINANCIAL AID: 206-296-2000 • E-MAIL: ADMISSIONS@SEATTLEU.EDU • WEBSITE: WWW.SEATTLEU.EDU

THE PRINCETON REVIEW SAYS
Admissions
Very important factors considered include: Rigor of secondary school record, standardized test scores. *Important factors considered include:* Application essay, academic GPA, recommendation(s), character/personal qualities, extracurricular activities, volunteer work. *Other factors considered include:* Class rank, alumni/ae relation, first generation, geographical residence, interview, level of applicant's interest, racial/ethnic status, state residency, talent/ability, work experience. SAT or ACT required; TOEFL required of all international applicants. High school diploma is required and GED is accepted. *Academic units required:* 4 English, 3 mathematics, 2 science, (2 science labs), 2 foreign language, 3 academic electives. *Academic units recommended:* 4 English, 4 mathematics, 3 science, (2 science labs), 2 foreign language, 3 academic electives.

Financial Aid
Students should submit: FAFSA. The Princeton Review suggests that all financial aid forms be submitted as soon as possible after January 1. *Need-based scholarships/grants offered:* Federal Pell, SEOG, state scholarships/grants, private scholarships, the school's own gift aid. *Loan aid offered:* Direct Subsidized Stafford, Direct Unsubsidized Stafford, Direct PLUS, Federal Perkins, Federal Nursing Applicants will be notified of awards on a rolling basis beginning 3/21.

The Inside Word
Seattle University requires all students to declare their intended areas of study on their applications. Candidates should research their prospective major because the academic demands here do vary. Because this is a Jesuit school, Admissions Officers tend to value community service. Those who demonstrate significant commitment to volunteering will find themselves at an advantage, as will those who convey a relatively clear sense of their academic and career goals.

THE SCHOOL SAYS "..."
From The Admissions Office
"Seattle University provides an ideal environment for motivated students interested in self-reliance, awareness of different cultures, social justice, and the fulfillment that comes from making a difference. Our urban setting promotes the development of leadership skills and independence as well as providing a variety of opportunities for students to apply what they learn through internships, clinical experiences, and volunteer work. It is an environment that allows us to 'connect the mind to what matters.'

"Our academic offerings are designed to provide leadership opportunities as well as to develop global awareness and enable graduates to serve society through a demanding liberal arts and sciences foundation. In the Jesuit tradition, we teach our students how to think, not what to think. Professional undergraduate offerings include highly respected schools of business, nursing, and science and engineering, as well as career-oriented liberal arts programs such as creative writing, journalism, communications, and criminal justice.

"While located in the center of the city, Seattle University is a true residential campus, including students from 48 states and territories and 76 different nations. Washington State has designated the campus as an 'official backyard sanctuary' for its striking landscaping and environmentally conscious practices—several buildings enjoy official 'green' designations, and the student-run recycling program continually receives national recognition. Additionally, Seattle University is proud of its distinction as the most ethnically diverse institution in the Northwest—all students are valued and respected for their individual strengths, experiences, and worth."

SELECTIVITY
Admissions Rating	87
# of applicants	4,923
% of applicants accepted	64
% of acceptees attending	25

FRESHMAN PROFILE
Range SAT Critical Reading	520–640
Range SAT Math	530–630
Range SAT Writing	510–620
Range ACT Composite	23–28
Minimum paper TOEFL	520
Minimum computer TOEFL	190
Average HS GPA	3.55
% graduated top 10% of class	32
% graduated top 25% of class	63
% graduated top 50% of class	91

DEADLINES
Early action	
Deadline	11/15
Notification	12/22
Regular	
Priority	2/1
Deadline	2/1
Notification	rolling
Nonfall registration?	yes

APPLICANTS ALSO LOOK AT
AND OFTEN PREFER
University of Washington
Gonzaga University
University of Portland
AND SOMETIMES PREFER
Santa Clara University
Washington State Universiy
AND RARELY PREFER
Pacific Lutheran University
Western Washington University

FINANCIAL FACTS
Financial Aid Rating	73
Annual tuition	$28,260
Room and board	$8,340
Books and supplies	$1,350
% frosh rec. need-based scholarship or grant aid	59
% UG rec. need-based scholarship or grant aid	57
% frosh rec. non-need-based scholarship or grant aid	33
% UG rec. non-need-based scholarship or grant aid	37
% frosh rec. need-based self-help aid	48
% UG rec. need-based self-help aid	53
% frosh rec. athletic scholarships	4
% UG rec. athletic scholarships	3
% frosh rec. any financial aid	88
% UG rec. any financial aid	76
% UG borrow to pay for school	80
Average cumulative indebtedness	$20,067

SETON HALL UNIVERSITY

ENROLLMENT SERVICES, 400 SOUTH ORANGE AVENUE, SOUTH ORANGE, NJ 07079 • ADMISSIONS: 973-761-9332 • FAX: 973-275-2040

CAMPUS LIFE

Quality of Life Rating	**70**
Fire Safety Rating	**84**
Green Rating	**60***
Type of school	private
Environment	city

STUDENTS

Total undergrad enrollment	4,896
% male/female	44/56
% from out of state	26
% live on campus	46
% African American	12
% Asian	6
% Caucasian	52
% Hispanic	11
% international	2
# of countries represented	43

SURVEY SAYS . . .

Small classes
Great computer facilities
Great library
Diverse student types on campus
College radio is popular
Student publications are popular
Lots of beer drinking

ACADEMICS

Academic Rating	**77**
Student/faculty ratio	14:1
Profs interesting rating	76
Profs accessible rating	74

MOST POPULAR MAJORS

Communication Studies/Speech
Nursing/Registered Nurse
Diplomacy Finance

STUDENTS SAY ". . ."

Academics

Named after Saint Elizabeth Ann Seton, Seton Hall is a Catholic university dedicated to "shaping students into servant leaders by enriching the mind, heart, and spirit." Servant leaders are people "who help to change the world" by offering their talents to the improvement of the community, as did the person for whom the university is a namesake. Professors are at the forefront of this intellectual, emotional, and spiritual enrichment, and students say "You won't find better anywhere." "They are always willing to meet with you outside of class and will do anything to help." Professors in the specialty Schools of Diplomacy, Nursing, Education, and Business receive especially high marks. Although students in the honors program "get the best professors" and benefit from "discussion-based classes," all students enjoy "small class sizes" in which "questions are always welcome." Students are much less enthusiastic about the "very conservative" administration, which for many is a "typical bureaucracy that could be improved but could also be much, much worse." Despite the administration's overall conservatism, it has fully embraced certain forms of progress. "One of Seton Hall's greatest strengths is probably its student technology program where every incoming student is issued a laptop that they can use anywhere on campus thanks to wireless Internet."

Life

As one student explains, "Life in general here is what happens at most colleges." "During the week everyone is stressed and a lot of work gets done." On the weekends, students spend their "free time watching movies, attending on-campus events, going to parties, hanging out, and exploring New York." With fewer than half of the students living on campus, Seton Hall is "very much a commuter school." A lot of students come for class and head home afterwards. Even among resident students, "Seton Hall is a suitcase school," which means "a lot of the Jersey kids go home on the weekends." Still, there are "plenty of things to do for those who stay on campus." "The Greek population is relatively small but is highly visible." Students enjoy "a lot of frat parties on the weekends" as well as "drive-in movies" and "dance lessons." Additionally, "extracurricular activities abound" with many students playing "intramural and intercollegiate sports." Even with all these options, students often "hop on the train" and "go into New York City for fun" which can make the campus feel "deserted on the weekends."

Student Body

While the typical student is "probably Catholic" and from "local towns in New Jersey or New York," diversity is "highly valued" on campus, with many students from "different backgrounds, religious beliefs, sexual orientation, everything." Most students manage to "mix in and feel like they're part of the student body." One student warns, however, that there is "very little tolerance for certain groups," especially gay students who are "targets of active discrimination by the university." While many students think the administration "does not handle GLBT issues well," those who are GLBT have "great support from the rest of the SHU community." Students describe themselves as "friendly" and "pretty motivated," conversant in everything from "political and historical issues to fashion." SHU students concentrate on their "work during the week" and "enjoying themselves on the weekend." As one student sums up, "Most students are just average people" with a "broad variance in personalities and interests."

FINANCIAL AID: 973-761-9332 • E-MAIL: THEHALL@SHU.EDU • WEBSITE: WWW.SHU.EDU

THE PRINCETON REVIEW SAYS

Admissions

Very important factors considered include: Rigor of secondary school record, Academic GPA, Standardized test scores, Application Essay,Recommendation(s). *Important factors considered include:* Volunteer work, Work experience. *Other factors considered include:* Class rank, Talent/ability, Character/personal qualities.

Financial Aid

Students should submit: FAFSA *Need-based scholarships/grants offered:* Federal Pell, SEOG, State scholarships/grants, Private scholarships, College/university scholarship or grant aid from institutional fund. *Loan aid offered:* FFEL Subsidized Stafford Loans, FFEL Unsubsidized Stafford Loans, FFEL PLUS loans, Federal Perkins Loans, State Loans.

The Inside Word

Students looking for a good school with solid Catholic roots should consider Seton Hall. Decent grades in college preparatory courses coupled with strong recommendations will net an acceptance for most students. Applicants with above-average marks are often recipients of scholarship money. The university's close proximity to New York allows for myriad educational, internship, and entertainment opportunities.

THE SCHOOL SAYS "..."

From The Admissions Office

"For more than 150 years, Seton Hall University has been a catalyst for leadership, developing the whole student—mind, heart and spirit. As a Catholic university that embraces students of all races and religions, Seton Hall combines the resources of a large university with the personal attention of a small liberal arts college. The University's attractive suburban campus is only 14 miles by train, bus or car to New York City, with the wealth of employment, internship, cultural and entertainment opportunities the city offers. Outstanding faculty, a technologically advanced campus, and a values-centered curriculum challenge Seton Hall students. Students are exposed to a world of ideas from great scholars, opening their minds to the perspectives, history and achievements of many cultures. Our new core curriculum focuses on the need for our students to have common experiences and encourages them to become thinking, caring, communicative and ethically responsible leaders while emphasizing practical proficiencies and intellectual development Our commitment to our students goes beyond textbooks and homework assignments, though. At Seton Hall, developing servant leaders who will make a difference in the world is a priority. That's why all students take classes in ethics and learn in a community informed by Catholic ideals and universal values. While Seton Hall certainly enjoys a big reputation, our campus community is close-knit and inclusive. Students, faculty and staff come from around the world, bringing with them a kaleidoscope of experiences and perspectives to create a diverse yet unified campus environment."

SELECTIVITY

Admissions Rating	81
# of applicants	6,626
% of applicants accepted	72
% of acceptees attending	27

FRESHMAN PROFILE

Range SAT Critical Reading	470–580
Range SAT Math	480–590
Average HS GPA	3.2
% graduated top 10% of class	21
% graduated top 25% of class	49
% graduated top 50% of class	80

DEADLINES

Priority	03/01
Nonfall registration?	Yes

APPLICANTS ALSO LOOK AT

AND OFTEN PREFER
New York University, Penn State—University Park, William Paterson University

AND SOMETIMES PREFER
Fairfield University, Fordham University, Rider University, University of Connecticut

AND RARELY PREFER
Hofstra University, Monmouth University (NJ), Ramapo College of New Jersey, St. Bonaventure University

FINANCIAL FACTS

Financial Aid Rating	74
Annual tuition	$27,680
Room and board	$11,360
Required fees	$2,250.00
Books and supplies	$1,300
% frosh rec. need-based scholarship or grant aid	70
% UG rec. need-based scholarship or grant aid	51
% frosh rec. non-need-based scholarship or grant aid	46
% UG rec. non-need-based scholarship or grant aid	36
% frosh rec. need-based self-help aid	41
% UG rec. need-based self-help aid	43
% frosh rec. athletic scholarships	5
% UG rec. athletic scholarships	4
% frosh rec. any financial aid	79
% UG rec. any financial aid	69
% UG borrow to pay for school	6
Average cumulative indebtedness	$16,566

Sewanee—The University of the South

735 University Avenue, Sewanee, TN 37383-1000 • Admissions: 931-598-1238 • Fax: 931-538-3248

CAMPUS LIFE

Quality of Life Rating	**87**
Fire Safety Rating	**79**
Green Rating	**88**
Type of school	private
Affiliation	Episcopal
Environment	rural

STUDENTS

Total undergrad enrollment	1,455
% male/female	47/53
% from out of state	78
% from public high school	45
% live on campus	93
% in (# of) fraternities	82 (12)
% in (# of) sororities	88 (9)
% African American	4
% Asian	2
% Caucasian	89
% Hispanic	2
% Native American	1
% international	2
# of countries represented	22

SURVEY SAYS . . .

Large classes
No one cheats
Students are friendly
Campus feels safe
Students are happy
Frats and sororities dominate
social scene
Lots of beer drinking
Hard liquor is popular

ACADEMICS

Academic Rating	**92**
Calendar	semester
Student/faculty ratio	11:1
Profs interesting rating	97
Profs accessible rating	96
Most common	
reg class size	10–19 students
Most common	
lab size	10–19 students

MOST POPULAR MAJORS

English language and literature
visual and performing arts
history

STUDENTS SAY ". . ."

Academics

The University of the South is a small, "very demanding" school "in the middle of rural Tennessee." Students describe it as "an oasis of perfection" "dripping with both southern and academic tradition." "Sewanee embodies what a liberal arts education should," beams a history major. Classes are "small" and there's a "well-rounded curriculum." About a third of all your courses here will be general education requirements and you have to pass a comprehensive exam in your major. "The volume of work can make you want to pull your hair out," warns an economics major. "Sewanee does not inflate grades," either. "You must work hard to earn an A." "Occasionally a professor or two takes the absent-minded professor stereotype to a ridiculous level" but "it is hard to find a truly bad teacher among the whole lot." Professors here "care about their students." "Their passion for their fields and students is unparalleled." Profs are also very approachable. "We have incredible access to the faculty," gushes a religion major. "Many professors invite students to their homes for social and educational activities somewhat regularly," adds a music major. Students also love the "extremely reachable" administration. The only complaint we hear about academic life concerns the lack of course availability.

Life

Some dorms at Sewanee "really need some work." "Give me air conditioning," demands a sweaty sophomore. The school is generally "behind technologically" as well. The "secluded" town that surrounds the school is "void of any good restaurants, bars, and general distractions a city provides." The campus is "absolutely gorgeous," though. It's a "serene haven" in "an idyllic setting" atop a mountain. Also, the school owns an "incredible amount of land." "Hiking the beautiful perimeter trail" is a favorite pastime, and students can bike, kayak, and "play in the woods" to their hearts' content. Socially, "Sewanee is unique in its quirks." There's a revered honor code. Faculty members wear academic gowns when they teach, and "most Sewanee students follow the tradition of dressing up for class." You'll see men in bow ties and seersucker suits and women in "pointy heels and pearls." There's also an "ever-present" sense of community. "You can't compartmentalize your life here," and for good or ill, "everyone knows what everyone else did last night." Otherwise, this school is "an uncanny combination of academic suicide and rampant partying." During the week, studying is paramount. "We spend a lot of time in the library," notes a sophomore. However, alcohol policies here are "lenient" and "Sewanee is a pretty big party school." Booze is "by no means forced upon you," but "students here drink often and heavily." The frat scene is absolutely massive. "Almost everyone becomes involved in a fraternity or a sorority." "The administration requires all Greek events to be open to the entire campus," but "there is no other social network except the Greek organizations."

Student Body

Even though the administration here is "pushing the diversity card to the nth degree," Sewanee is "strikingly homogenous." "A lot more students here are liberal than you would guess" and Yankees are "not viewed as aliens," but "Sewanee is a southern and conservative school in every sense of the word." Students are typically "laidback," "rich, conservative, and fun" "children of the Southern aristocracy" who like to "get drunk on the weekends." Some are "heavily spoiled and coddled." Sewanee is affiliated with the Episcopalian church and some students are pious, but on the whole, religion is not a big deal here. "We have lots of cookie-cutter, preppy, extreme social drinkers, but then again you can also find people who wear only organic hemp, sleep outside, and have dreadlocks," explains a junior. "There are a lot of outdoorsy styles mixed in as well." While "social arrangements are very cliquish," students tell us they are "relatively peacefully coexisting." "It really is one of the friendliest communities that I have ever seen," declares a sophomore.

Sewanee—The University of the South

FINANCIAL AID: 931-598-1312 • E-MAIL: COLLEGEADMISSION@SEWANEE.EDU • WEBSITE: WWW.SEWANEE.EDU

THE PRINCETON REVIEW SAYS

Admissions

Very important factors considered include: Academic GPA, recommendation(s), rigor of secondary school record. *Important factors considered include:* Application essay, standardized test scores, character/personal qualities, extracurricular activities, volunteer work, work experience. *Other factors considered include:* Class rank, alumni/ae relation, first generation, geographical residence, interview, level of applicant's interest, racial/ethnic status, talent/ability, SAT or ACT required; ACT with Writing component required. TOEFL required of all international applicants. High school diploma is required and GED is not accepted. *Academic units required:* 4 English, 3 mathematics, 2 science, (2 science labs), 2 foreign language, 1 social studies, 1 history. *Academic units recommended:* 4 English, 4 mathematics, 4 science, (3 science labs), 4 foreign language, 2 social studies, 2 history.

Financial Aid

Students should submit: FAFSA, institution's own financial aid form, Student and/or parent U.S. Income Tax Returns if applicable. The Princeton Review suggests that all financial aid forms be submitted as soon as possible after January 1. *Need-based scholarships/grants offered:* Federal Pell, SEOG, state scholarships/grants, private scholarships, the school's own gift aid. *Loan aid offered:* FFEL Subsidized Stafford, FFEL Unsubsidized Stafford, FFEL PLUS, Federal Perkins, state loans, college/university loans from institutional funds, private alternative loans. Applicants will be notified of awards on or about 4/1. Federal Work-Study Program available. Institutional employment available. Off-campus job opportunities are fair.

The Inside Word

The Admissions Office at Sewanee is very personable and accessible to students. Its staff includes some of the most well-respected admissions professionals in the South, and it shows in the way they work with students. Despite a fairly high acceptance rate, candidates who take the admissions process here lightly may find themselves disappointed. Applicant evaluation is too personal for a lackadaisical approach to succeed.

THE SCHOOL SAYS "..."

From The Admissions Office

"Sewanee is consistently ranked among the top tier of national liberal arts universities. Sewanee is committed to an academic curriculum that focuses on the liberal arts as the most enlightening and valuable form of undergraduate education. Founded by leaders of the Episcopal church in 1857, Sewanee continues to be owned by 28 Episcopal dioceses in 12 states. The university is located on a 10,000-acre campus atop Tennessee's Cumberland Plateau between Chattanooga and Nashville. The university has an impressive record of academic achievement—25 Rhodes scholars and 26 NCAA postgraduate scholarship recipients have graduated from Sewanee.

"Sewanee will require all applicants for Fall 2008 to take the new SAT or the ACT with the Writing test. We will consider previous scores in Math and Critical Reading from previous administrations of the SAT when calculating a student's highest composite score, but students are required to take the new SAT."

SELECTIVITY

Admissions Rating	90
# of applicants	2,424
% of applicants accepted	64
% of acceptees attending	26
# accepting a place on wait list	32
% admitted from wait list	91
# of early decision applicants	221
% accepted early decision	50

FRESHMAN PROFILE

Range SAT Critical Reading	570–680
Range SAT Math	560–650
Range SAT Writing	580–670
Range ACT Composite	25–30
Minimum paper TOEFL	550
Minimum computer TOEFL	220
Average HS GPA	3.5
% graduated top 10% of class	47
% graduated top 25% of class	78
% graduated top 50% of class	94

DEADLINES

Early decision	
Deadline	11/15
Notification	12/15
Regular	
Deadline	2/1
Notification	3/17
Nonfall registration?	no

APPLICANTS ALSO LOOK AT

AND OFTEN PREFER
Washington and Lee University
University of North Carolina at Chapel Hill

AND SOMETIMES PREFER
Vanderbilt University
Wake Forest University
Davidson College

AND RARELY PREFER
Rhodes College
University of Tennessee—Knoxville
University of Georgia

FINANCIAL FACTS

Financial Aid Rating	92
Annual tuition	$30,438
Room and board	$8,780
Required fees	$222
Books and supplies	$800
% frosh rec. need-based scholarship or grant aid	41
% UG rec. need-based scholarship or grant aid	47
% frosh rec. need-based self-help aid	31
% UG rec. need-based self-help aid	34
% frosh rec. any financial aid	93
% UG rec. any financial aid	95
% UG borrow to pay for school	44
Average cumulative indebtedness	$17,958

THE BEST 368 COLLEGES ■ 477

SIENA COLLEGE

515 LOUDON ROAD, LOUDONVILLE, NY 12211 • ADMISSIONS: 518-783-2423 • FAX: 518-783-2436

CAMPUS LIFE
Quality of Life Rating	80
Fire Safety Rating	60*
Green Rating	60*
Type of school	private
Affiliation	Roman Catholic
Environment	town

STUDENTS
Total undergrad enrollment	3,151
% male/female	44/56
% from out of state	13
% live on campus	74
% African American	2
% Asian	4
% Caucasian	84
% Hispanic	4
# of countries represented	6

SURVEY SAYS . . .
Large classes
Great library
Students love Loudonville, NY
*Frats and sororities are unpopular
or nonexistent*
Lots of beer drinking

ACADEMICS
Academic Rating	80
Calendar	semester
Student/faculty ratio	13:1
Profs interesting rating	80
Profs accessible rating	84
Most common reg class size	20–29 students
Most common lab size	10–19 students

MOST POPULAR MAJORS
marketing/marketing management
psychology
accounting

STUDENTS SAY ". . ."

Academics

The Franciscan tradition "is all about community," and, at Siena College, a small school with "a strong Franciscan atmosphere," students benefit from a friendly community in which "there is always someone to lend a helping hand." That someone may be a professor, a tutor, or, on occasion, a Rollerblading friar in robes. No matter whose hand is extended, however, "Every student really has a lot of opportunities to get any amount of personal academic attention or other scholastic opportunities that they want." Biology and other premedical disciplines are highly regarded, and students especially love the Siena College–Albany Medical College Program, a joint acceptance program that focuses on humanities and community service. In addition, the school's many business undergrads feel their program, which is enhanced by a loyal alumni base that helps newly minted grads quickly find jobs, is the school's "greatest strength." Regardless of discipline, Siena "Teachers know who you are and do not just consider you a number, as opposed [how it is at] larger colleges and universities." An honors program offers "even smaller classes, preferential registration, and seminars" to those seeking an extra challenge.

Life

For many students, recreation time at Siena means it's time for a beer or two, and lately that's become a point of contention with the administration. Students tell us that the administration, in its effort to crack down on under-age drinking, has instituted security checkpoints at the townhouses (where upperclassmen live and, in previous years, had hosted parties) and limits on the amount of alcohol allowed in the rooms of students over 21. Security can be aggressive, we're told, to the point that more than one undergraduate told us that students sometimes feel "like prisoners." Though this has driven the drinking crowd off campus to nearby clubs and the bars of Albany, on-campus drinking still occurs, but it's more often of the pre-gaming or small-quiet-party variety. The campus still bustles during the week, however, as "Most people are involved in clubs" and at least "one sport, whether intramural or intercollegiate." Other diversions include a school-sponsored bus that takes students to the Crossgates Mall, which "is pretty large and houses a bunch of amazing stores," and "a whole strip of dining-out places." Still, an English major admits, "If you don't drink, I can see where weekends would be boring, especially in the winter." The school does sponsor activities on campus designed "to draw students away from the drinking scene," but "There is often a stigma about the 'coolness' of these events."

Student Body

There "isn't much diversity" on the Siena campus, where it seems just about everyone "is from an upper-middle-class Catholic family from Long Island" or "upstate New York." There are some who don't fit the mold, but not many; students speculate that they're mostly nontraditional or international students. Minority students tend to "stick together, but all seem well-liked." Many students "are involved either in D1 athletics, intramural teams, or clubs and Student Senate activities"; students in these groups tend to party together on the weekends "and generally create a strong group of friends easily." While there's a solid contingent of folks at Siena who "drink, party, and hardly ever study," there are also students, particularly in the sciences, who work hard but "don't socialize much outside of their departments, due to the nature of their program."

FINANCIAL AID: 518-783-2427 • E-MAIL: ADMIT@SIENA.EDU • WEBSITE: WWW.SIENA.EDU

THE PRINCETON REVIEW SAYS

Admissions

Very important factors considered include: Academic GPA, rigor of secondary school record. *Important factors considered include:* Recommendation(s), standardized test scores. *Other factors considered include:* Class rank, application essay, alumni/ae relation, character/personal qualities, extracurricular activities, first generation, interview, level of applicant's interest, racial/ethnic status, talent/ability, volunteer work, work experience. SAT or ACT required; ACT with Writing component required. TOEFL required of all international applicants. High school diploma is required and GED is accepted. *Academic units required:* 4 English, 3 mathematics, 3 science, (3 science labs), 1 social studies, 2 history. *Academic units recommended:* 4 English, 4 mathematics, 4 science, (4 science labs), 3 foreign language, 1 social studies, 3 history.

Financial Aid

Students should submit: FAFSA, state aid form. The Princeton Review suggests that all financial aid forms be submitted as soon as possible after January 1. *Need-based scholarships/grants offered:* Federal Pell, SEOG, state scholarships/grants, private scholarships, the school's own gift aid, Siena Grants, St. Francis Community Grants. *Loan aid offered:* FFEL Subsidized Stafford, FFEL Unsubsidized Stafford, FFEL PLUS, Federal Perkins Applicants will be notified of awards on or about 4/1.

The Inside Word

Siena's draw is still primarily regional, with the vast majority of students arriving from in state. Standards aren't especially high; the admit rate says as much about the applicant pool as it does about the school's selectivity. Expect to meet higher standards if you indicate an interest in the School of Science, as it is the gateway to the school's desirable premedical programs. The school does applicants a favor here—substandard students stand little chance of surviving the school's science regimen.

THE SCHOOL SAYS "..."

From The Admissions Office

"Siena is a coeducational, independent liberal arts college with a Franciscan tradition. It is a community where the intellectual, personal, and social growth of all students is paramount. Siena's faculty calls forth the best Siena students have to give—and the students do the same for them. Students are competitive, but not at each other's expense. Siena's curriculum includes 23 majors in three schools—liberal arts, science, and business. In addition, there are over a dozen pre-professional and special academic programs. With a student/faculty ratio of 14:1, class size ranges between 15 and 35 students. Siena's 152-acre campus is located in Loudonville, a suburban community within two miles of the New York State seat of government in Albany. With 15 colleges in the area, there is a wide variety of activities on weekends. Regional theater, performances by major concert artists, and professional sports events compete with the activities on the campus. Within 50 miles are the Adirondacks, the Berkshires, and the Catskills, providing outdoor recreation throughout the year. Because the capital region's easy, friendly lifestyle is so appealing, many Siena graduates try to find their first jobs in upstate New York.

"Freshman applicants must submit the SAT or ACT with the Writing component."

SELECTIVITY

Admissions Rating	86
# of applicants	5,792
% of applicants accepted	54
% of acceptees attending	25
# accepting a place on wait list	318
% admitted from wait list	5
# of early decision applicants	130
% accepted early decision	33

FRESHMAN PROFILE

Range SAT Critical Reading	500–590
Range SAT Math	520–620
Range SAT Writing	490–590
Range ACT Composite	20–24
Minimum paper TOEFL	550
Minimum web-based TOEFL	79
Average HS GPA	89.4
% graduated top 10% of class	21
% graduated top 25% of class	57
% graduated top 50% of class	91

DEADLINES

Early decision	
Deadline	12/1
Notification	12/15
Early action	
Deadline	12/1
Notification	1/1
Regular	
Priority	3/1
Deadline	3/1
Notification	3/15
Nonfall registration?	yes

APPLICANTS ALSO LOOK AT
AND OFTEN PREFER
Villanova University

FINANCIAL FACTS

Financial Aid Rating	74
Annual tuition	$22,510
Room and board	$8,875
Required fees	$175
Books and supplies	$930
% frosh rec. need-based scholarship or grant aid	69
% UG rec. need-based scholarship or grant aid	66
% frosh rec. non-need-based scholarship or grant aid	6
% UG rec. non-need-based scholarship or grant aid	4
% frosh rec. need-based self-help aid	57
% UG rec. need-based self-help aid	55
% frosh rec. athletic scholarships	9
% UG rec. athletic scholarships	8
% frosh rec. any financial aid	96.1
% UG rec. any financial aid	95.3
% UG borrow to pay for school	77
Average cumulative indebtedness	$21,800

SIMMONS COLLEGE

300 THE FENWAY, BOSTON, MA 02115 • ADMISSIONS: 617-521-2051 • FAX: 617-521-3190

CAMPUS LIFE
Quality of Life Rating	**87**
Fire Safety Rating	**89**
Green Rating	**90**
Type of school	private
Environment	city

STUDENTS
Total undergrad enrollment	2,069
% male/female	/100
% from out of state	40
% live on campus	56
# of countries represented	45

SURVEY SAYS . . .
Large classes
Great computer facilities
Great library
Students love Boston, MA
Great off-campus food
Frats and sororities are unpopular
or nonexistent

ACADEMICS
Academic Rating	**85**
Calendar	semester
Student/faculty ratio	13:1
Profs interesting rating	83
Profs accessible rating	83
Most common	
reg class size	10–19 students

MOST POPULAR MAJORS
psychology
nursing/registered nurse
(RN, ASN, BSN, MSN)

STUDENTS SAY " . . ."

Academics

Simmons College, an "all-women's college located in the Fenway area of Boston," provides students with "lots of opportunities to work closely with faculty and interact with local Boston communities." The school excels in pre-professional programs in nursing and physical therapy, each of which capitalizes on the school's location to "give students opportunities to do internships/clinical placements at world-renowned hospitals that are only a few blocks away (e.g. Children's Hospital Boston, Brigham and Women's, Mass General)." Students also rave about Simmons' offerings in psychology, biology, pre-dental sciences, economics, and management, and they praise the school's "excellent facilities, including an amazing new library" and the "large career resource department." Small classes here "allow great discussions, because those who want to participate have the opportunity to do so," which can be both a blessing and a curse. As one student points out, "Because Simmons is not the most selective school there are some students who don't study very much." The same students add that "If you work hard, you get out of it what you put in." Another drawback is the study abroad program. One undergrad gripes, "There just aren't enough choices! And if there are, they are all usually around the same time, making it quite difficult to choose."

Life

Life at Simmons College "is more academic in nature: the classes are teaching-based, and life on campus revolves around schoolwork." One student agrees, "Simmons is pretty much where students go to school. We go elsewhere to have fun/party/live." With downtown Boston outside the school's front door, the options are plentiful. There are museums ("great things to do in the area" include "free gallery talks at the Museum of Fine Arts"), "shopping on Newbury Street," and "eating great food on the North End." Public transportation means "getting around is easy and exploring the city is amazing." When students seek a party, they typically "go to other local colleges...like MIT, Harvard, Boston University, and Northeastern." On-campus fun is more subdued. There's "a lot of random friendly girl-time things going on, like decorating our doors for the holidays, making paper chains, or watching television. For entertainment here, you really have to turn to your friends, because almost nothing worth attending happens on campus," a female student notes. Most see this as a boon; writes one student, "What's nice about living at Simmons is that it is a peaceful and nice place to live, but when you want to go to a party, Northeastern and BU are just minutes away. After spending a night there, you realize how thankful you are for clean dorms and the lack of boys."

Student Body

The student body at Simmons is "mostly middle- to upper-class women who hail from all over the United States and many other countries. The school is predominately white, but a range of ethnicities are represented." One student reports that her study group consists of "an orthodox Jew, a Saudi Arabian, an African American, a Cambodian, an Indian, and two Caucasians. The UN could take lessons from us." Politically, "Most students are liberal and involved with their community." Left-leaning politics dominates to the point that "it can be challenging to express conservative viewpoints." Sexual orientation "tends not to be a question, and it is very common for girls to be open about being straight, gay, or bisexual." While "there are a lot of lesbians here," they are "not at all the majority." Simmons hosts a conspicuous butch subculture. As one women explains, "Even though you know going into it that Simmons is an all-women's college, you may be shocked to see some guys walking around attending your classes...until you realize that they are girls! It's great that everyone is cool with everyone else and the people who are narrow-minded stick to themselves."

FINANCIAL AID: 617-521-2001 • E-MAIL: UGADM@SIMMONS.EDU • WEBSITE: WWW.SIMMONS.EDU

THE PRINCETON REVIEW SAYS

Admissions

Very important factors considered include: Academic GPA, rigor of secondary school record. *Important factors considered include:* Class rank, application essay, recommendation(s), standardized test scores. *Other factors considered include:* Extracurricular activities, interview, talent/ability, volunteer work, work experience. SAT or ACT required; TOEFL required of all international applicants. High school diploma or equivalent is not required. *Academic units required:* 4 English, 3 mathematics, 3 science, 3 foreign language, 3 social studies, 3 history. *Academic units recommended:* 4 English, 4 mathematics, 3 science, 4 foreign language, 4 social studies, 3 history.

Financial Aid

Students should submit: FAFSA. Regular filing deadline is 3/1. The Princeton Review suggests that all financial aid forms be submitted as soon as possible after January 1. *Need-based scholarships/grants offered:* Federal Pell, SEOG, state scholarships/grants, private scholarships, the school's own gift aid. *Loan aid offered:* FFEL Subsidized Stafford, FFEL Unsubsidized Stafford, FFEL PLUS, Federal Perkins, state loans, college/university loans from institutional funds. Applicants will be notified of awards on a rolling basis beginning 3/15. Federal Work-Study Program available. Institutional employment available. Off-campus job opportunities are excellent.

The Inside Word

Most of the nation's best all-women's colleges are in the Northeast, including those Seven Sister schools (roughly the female equivalent of the formerly all-male Ivies) that remain single-sex institutions. The competition for students is intense, and although Simmons is a solid school, there are at least a half-dozen competitors more appealing to most candidates. Solid high school performers should have little need to worry here. The school's excellent academics and Boston location make Simmons a worthy option for any woman interested in single-sex education.

THE SCHOOL SAYS " . . ."

From The Admissions Office

"Simmons believes passionately in an 'educational contract' that places students first and helps them build successful careers, lead meaningful lives, and realize a powerful return on their investment. Simmons honors this contract by delivering a quality education and measurable success through singular approach to professional preparation, intellectual exploration, and community orientation.

"Simmons is a 100-year-old university in Boston, with a tradition of providing women with a collaborative environment that stimulates dialogue, enhances listening, catalyzes action, and spurs personal and professional growth.

"Simmons College accepts both the ACT and SAT. Students who enroll in September 2007 and thereafter are required to submit the SAT or the ACT with Writing. Additionally, if English is not your native language a TOEFL is required."

SELECTIVITY
Admissions Rating	84
# of applicants	2,937
% of applicants accepted	57
% of acceptees attending	28
# accepting a place on wait list	22
% admitted from wait list	5

FRESHMAN PROFILE
Range SAT Critical Reading	500–600
Range SAT Math	480–590
Range SAT Writing	510–610
Range ACT Composite	21–26
Minimum paper TOEFL	560
Minimum computer TOEFL	220
Minimum web-based TOEFL	83
Average HS GPA	3.17
% graduated top 10% of class	18
% graduated top 25% of class	58
% graduated top 50% of class	92

DEADLINES
Early action	
Deadline	12/1
Notification	1/20
Regular	
Priority	2/1
Deadline	2/1
Notification	4/15
Nonfall registration?	yes

APPLICANTS ALSO LOOK AT
AND OFTEN PREFER
Northeastern University
Mount Holyoke College
Boston University

AND SOMETIMES PREFER
University of New Hampshire
University of Connecticut

AND RARELY PREFER
Emmanuel College

FINANCIAL FACTS
Financial Aid Rating	65
Annual tuition	$27,468
Room and board	$11,138
Required fees	$834
Books and supplies	$800
% frosh rec. need-based scholarship or grant aid	63
% UG rec. need-based scholarship or grant aid	67
% frosh rec. non-need-based scholarship or grant aid	4
% UG rec. non-need-based scholarship or grant aid	2
% frosh rec. need-based self-help aid	60
% UG rec. need-based self-help aid	65
% frosh rec. any financial aid	72
% UG rec. any financial aid	70
% UG borrow to pay for school	82
Average cumulative indebtedness	$34,940

SIMON'S ROCK COLLEGE OF BARD

84 ALFORD ROAD, GREAT BARRINGTON, MA 01230 • ADMISSIONS: 413-528-7312 • FAX: 413-528-7334

CAMPUS LIFE

Quality of Life Rating	86
Fire Safety Rating	60*
Green Rating	60*
Type of school	private
Environment	village

STUDENTS

Total undergrad enrollment	368
% male/female	43/57
% from out of state	80
% live on campus	85
% African American	7
% Asian	4
% Caucasian	58
% Hispanic	6
% Native American	1
% international	4

SURVEY SAYS . . .
Small classes
Athletic facilities are great
Campus feels safe
Frats and sororities are unpopular
or nonexistent
(Almost) everyone smokes

ACADEMICS

Academic Rating	97
Calendar	semester
Student/faculty ratio	8:1
Profs interesting rating	99
Profs accessible rating	97
Most common	
reg class size	10–19 students
Most common	
lab size	10–19 students

MOST POPULAR MAJORS
creative writing
cell/cellular biology and histology
psychology

STUDENTS SAY ". . ."

Academics

Simon's Rock, "the only college in the country that is specifically designed for students of high school age who are ready for college," offers "brilliant and creative kids a combination of a lot of freedom and a lot of very demanding work so that they can begin college early and move forward with their lives earlier. It's the perfect environment for kids who think outside the box." Students at the Rock are given a challenging curriculum; one student jokingly describes the approach as "do as you please, and also 400 pages of reading." Undergrads report that "the average student spends more than 7 hours on homework a night and writes at least one six- to ten-page paper a week." In return for their hard work, students receive "up-close and personal attention of teachers who care about you and are not afraid to tell you when you've screwed up," and who are also "more than willing to set up tutorials and even arrange courses that match your academic interests, regardless of how off-the-wall they may be." Slightly more than half the students at Simon's Rock stick around for 2 years, long enough to earn an associate's degree, and then transfer to a larger school. Those who remain here enter the Upper College through "a self-selection process that tends to weed out the people who aren't as serious about the work they want to do. While the Lower College students can be, from time to time, indolent pot-smokers, by and large the juniors and seniors are extremely serious students."

Life

Simon's Rock is located "on top of a mountain in the middle-of-nowhere New England," with the closest town "a mile and a half away." Those who make the trek to town are rewarded with "yummy burritos, groceries, thrift-store shopping and a rad toy store." Because of the school's remote locale, "Students have to make their own fun," and they do so in a variety of ways: "Lots of kids meditate. Lots of kids ride bikes, fence, play soccer, go to the rock wall, or otherwise work out." Others "watch lots of movies, hang out with friends, and play intellectual games," and still others "go to one of the many swimming holes around here." Those with cars (or those who have friends with cars) are most likely to be completely satisfied; they point out that "we're only an hour from Northampton, where there's everything from lectures to concerts, and we also get to live in a nice, quiet New England town." They also note that "going to New York City and Boston is a breeze, and that's what most upperclassmen do on the weekends." Those who are campus-bound, however, caution that "if you're not a nature person, you might not be as happy here as [you would be] somewhere more urban."

Student Body

Who attends Simon's Rock? "Those [students] who are frustrated with the social and academic limitations of high school" are the school's target market, and they are mostly the ones who find their way here. One such student explains, "Simon's Rock is an exceptionally self-selecting institution. Most of us are atypical because if we weren't, we would not be at Simon's Rock." Undergrads "are very smart, or at least smart enough to realize the conformity and uselessness of high school" and "are either very studious or very artistic, or caught somewhere in the middle." Some see Simon's Rock as "'nerd camp' all over again. From neon hair to preppy-looking science students, the Simon's Rock type is that there isn't one." Contrary to popular perception, "We're not all communist beat poets majoring in Movement Studies. Yeah, we have lots of vegetarian liberal kids in sandals from Vermont, but they [also] carry 3.3 GPAs and head our Community Counsel and Fencing Club."

FINANCIAL AID: 413-528-7297 • E-MAIL: ADMIT@SIMONS-ROCK.EDU • WEBSITE: WWW.SIMONS-ROCK.EDU

THE PRINCETON REVIEW SAYS

Admissions

Very important factors considered include: Application essay, recommendation(s), rigor of secondary school record, character/personal qualities, interview, talent/ability. *Important factors considered include:* Class rank, academic GPA, level of applicant's interest. *Other factors considered include:* Standardized test scores, alumni/ae relation, extracurricular activities, first generation, racial/ethnic status, volunteer work, work experience. TOEFL required of all international applicants. High school diploma or equivalent is not required. *Academic units recommended:* 2 English, 2 mathematics, 2 science, (1 science labs), 2 foreign language, 2 social studies, 2 history.

Financial Aid

Students should submit: FAFSA, CSS/Financial Aid PROFILE, business/farm supplement, Parent and Student Federal Taxes/ Federal Verification Worksheet. The Princeton Review suggests that all financial aid forms be submitted as soon as possible after January 1. *Need-based scholarships/grants offered:* Federal Pell, SEOG, state scholarships/grants, private scholarships, the school's own gift aid. *Loan aid offered:* FFEL Subsidized Stafford, FFEL Unsubsidized Stafford, FFEL PLUS, Federal Perkins, state loans, Alternative Educational Loans. Applicants will be notified of awards on a rolling basis beginning 4/15. Federal Work-Study Program available. Institutional employment available. Off-campus job opportunities are good.

The Inside Word

The application process at Simon's Rock is highly personalized. The school's unique composition calls for Admissions Officers to thoroughly assess candidates and evaluate whether the college will be a good fit. Prospective students must be extremely motivated and thrive in intellectual environments. They also need to demonstrate a high degree of maturity and an ability to work independently. Officers tend to focus on personal statements, recommendations, and interviews.

THE SCHOOL SAYS "..."

From The Admissions Office

"Simon's Rock is dedicated to one thing: To allow bright, highly motivated students the opportunity to pursue college work leading to the AA and BA degrees at an age earlier than our national norm.

"Simon's Rock College of Bard will accept either the new SAT or the old SAT (administered prior to March 2005 and without a Writing component), as well as the ACT with or without the Writing component."

SELECTIVITY

Admissions Rating	90
# of applicants	204
% of applicants accepted	84
% of acceptees attending	74

FRESHMAN PROFILE

Range SAT Critical Reading	560–690
Range SAT Math	530–680
Range ACT Composite	25–30
Minimum paper TOEFL	550
Minimum computer TOEFL	200
Average HS GPA	3.36
% graduated top 10% of class	60
% graduated top 25% of class	82
% graduated top 50% of class	94

DEADLINES

Regular	
Priority	4/15
Deadline	5/31
Notification	rolling
Nonfall registration?	yes

FINANCIAL FACTS

Financial Aid Rating	88
Annual tuition	$34,804
Room and board	$9,260
Required fees	$530
Books and supplies	$1,000
% frosh rec. need-based scholarship or grant aid	51
% UG rec. need-based scholarship or grant aid	39
% frosh rec. non-need-based scholarship or grant aid	50
% UG rec. non-need-based scholarship or grant aid	33
% frosh rec. need-based self-help aid	47
% UG rec. need-based self-help aid	43
% frosh rec. any financial aid	78
% UG rec. any financial aid	71
% UG borrow to pay for school	70
Average cumulative indebtedness	$15,000

SKIDMORE COLLEGE

815 NORTH BROADWAY, SARATOGA SPRINGS, NY 12866-1632 • ADMISSIONS: 518-580-5570 • FAX: 518-580-5584

STUDENTS SAY ". . ."

Academics

"Creative thought matters" is Skidmore's slogan, and students here echo it frequently enough to convince us that it's more than your standard college hype; nearly one in five undergrads major in the visual or performing arts. Skidmore also boasts "great science programs," a "superb" English Department, and an "excellent" business program. The combined effect produces "a haven for inquisitive, artsy, liberal-minded students looking for a place to get a good education with minimal pretentiousness." Arts students laud the school's "great artistic community, populated by so many musicians, artists, actors, and dancers who are all passionate about what they do. This leads to collaboration in and outside of schoolwork, making it a great place to develop as an artist." Undergrads in more traditional liberal arts and sciences disciplines love the "opportunities for real work"—such as working as a "lab assistant for research projects" or "in local schools"—and "the very enthusiastic professors who are passionate about their work." Those for whom Skidmore is a fit feel it represents the "perfect balance between structure and freedom."

Life

Students tell us that Skidmore's Saratoga Springs location is one of the best things about the school. "The town is great," a senior raves. "The nightlife is fantastic, internships and volunteer opportunities abound, you have access to the Adirondacks and all of the best ski sites, it's a great place for friends and family to visit . . . everyone loves the place. Most students end up spending a summer or two in Saratoga just so they can enjoy everything about it without being distracted by studies." On campus, life is "very relaxed, and there is generally little pressure on students to do anything. However, the campus is a very involved one and there are countless extracurricular clubs and events going on at any point." Many students "get drunk and go to parties on the weekend," often at upperclassmen's houses, but "It is really easy to find other activities to participate in if partying isn't your scene. There are tons of events every night and lots of people who don't make partying their number one choice." These activities include "tons of campus concerts, performances, and shows" produced by the campus' glut of artists and performers.

Student Body

"Artistic/liberal kids" and "business major/athletic kids" form the two most conspicuous and readily identifiable populations on the Skidmore campus; one student explains, "You can usually tell who is who by the way they dress." While those two groups do "make a large part of the student body," undergrads point out that "there are all types of students that are not in those categories, or lie somewhere in between the two." For example, "We have kids who double major in business and art, athletes who are in the orchestra—you can be anyone you want to be and be accepted as an individual and as a part of the Skidmore community." Indeed, "The student body as a whole is extremely open-minded to diversity. There are a number of LGBT students who are strongly supported by the student body." "Although there is not a large amount of ethnic diversity," one student reports, "I have never seen a student of a different ethnicity be discriminated against, or even heard another student make any racist statement[s]." Are Skidmore students entirely free of prejudice? No, not entirely; one student explains, "The only discrimination I have seen here is against Republicans. Skidmore is extremely liberal, and I would say it is pretty hard to fit in here with extremely conservative beliefs."

FINANCIAL AID: 518-580-5750 • E-MAIL: ADMISSIONS@SKIDMORE.EDU • WEBSITE: WWW.SKIDMORE.EDU

THE PRINCETON REVIEW SAYS

Admissions

Very important factors considered include: Rigor of secondary school record. *Important factors considered include:* Class rank, application essay, academic GPA, recommendation(s), character/personal qualities, extracurricular activities, talent/ability, volunteer work, work experience. *Other factors considered include:* Standardized test scores, alumni/ae relation, first generation, geographical residence, interview, racial/ethnic status, SAT Subject Tests recommended; SAT or ACT required; ACT with Writing component required. TOEFL required of all international applicants. High school diploma is required and GED is accepted. *Academic units recommended:* 4 English, 4 mathematics, 4 science, (3 science labs), 4 foreign language, 4 social studies.

Financial Aid

Students should submit: FAFSA, CSS/Financial Aid PROFILE. Regular filing deadline is 1/15. The Princeton Review suggests that all financial aid forms be submitted as soon as possible after January 1. *Need-based scholarships/grants offered:* Federal Pell, SEOG, state scholarships/grants, the school's own gift aid. *Loan aid offered:* FFEL Subsidized Stafford, FFEL Unsubsidized Stafford, FFEL PLUS, Federal Perkins Applicants will be notified of awards on or about 4/1.

The Inside Word

Skidmore remains a fallback option for Northeastern kids who don't get into their top choices. Admits are very bright kids and a successful applicant must present the Admissions Office with a fairly compelling picture. You'll receive friendly, personalized assistance from the Admissions Office here, especially if you communicate a strong desire to attend Skidmore.

THE SCHOOL SAYS "..."

From The Admissions Office

"Launched in 2005, Skidmore's First-Year Experience (FYE) is a year-long academic, co-curricular, and residential initiative that immediately engages each first-year student with a faculty mentor-advisor, with 14 other students in an innovative Scribner Seminar, and with the entire college community through a series of artistic, cultural, and social events. FYE's centerpiece, 50 distinctive seminars—ranging from the human colonization of space to lessons learned from Hurricane Katrina to British national identity—requires each student to participate actively and creatively in his or her own learning. Seminar instructors function as faculty mentor-advisors for their 15 students, and provide curricular and co-curricular perspectives not only on the specific seminar topic but on the liberal arts in general. In most cases, students live in residence halls in close proximity to classmates from their seminar.

"In terms of skills and habits of mind, seminar participants will learn to distinguish among and formulate the types of questions asked by different disciplines; read critically and gather and interpret evidence; consider and address complexities and ambiguities; recognize choices, examine assumptions, and take a skeptical stance; formulate conclusions based upon evidence; and communicate those conclusions orally and in writing. These are the fundamentals for academic excellence.

"The First-Year Experience is just the beginning of the expectation that students will creatively craft an experience leading to intensive work in a major field of study, often via a double major or major and minor, supplemented by a semester abroad, collaborative research with a faculty member, and internships. It is also a singular manifestation of Skidmore's commitment to the belief that 'Creative Thought Matters'—that every life, career, and endeavor is made more profound with creative ability at its core.

"Applicants for Fall 2008 are required to take the SAT or the ACT with the Writing section. We recommend that students provide scores for two SAT Subject Test examinations."

SELECTIVITY

Admissions Rating	94
# of applicants	6,768
% of applicants accepted	37
% of acceptees attending	28
# accepting a place on wait list	522
% admitted from wait list	11
# of early decision applicants	418
% accepted early decision	64

FRESHMAN PROFILE

Range SAT Critical Reading	580–680
Range SAT Math	580–670
Range SAT Writing	590–690
Range ACT Composite	26–30
Minimum paper TOEFL	590
Minimum computer TOEFL	243
Average HS GPA	3.335
% graduated top 10% of class	38.8
% graduated top 25% of class	79.8
% graduated top 50% of class	96.8

DEADLINES

Early decision	
Deadline	11/15
Notification	12/15
Regular	
Deadline	1/15
Notification	4/1
Nonfall registration?	no

APPLICANTS ALSO LOOK AT

AND OFTEN PREFER
Wesleyan University
Colby College

AND SOMETIMES PREFER
New York University
Connecticut College

AND RARELY PREFER
Ithaca College
University of Vermont

FINANCIAL FACTS

Financial Aid Rating	93
Annual tuition	$36,126
Room and board	$9,836
Required fees	$734
Books and supplies	$1,000
% frosh rec. need-based scholarship or grant aid	40
% UG rec. need-based scholarship or grant aid	41
% frosh rec. non-need-based scholarship or grant aid	2
% UG rec. non-need-based scholarship or grant aid	2
% frosh rec. need-based self-help aid	49
% UG rec. need-based self-help aid	50
% frosh rec. any financial aid	49
% UG rec. any financial aid	50
% UG borrow to pay for school	47
Average cumulative indebtedness	$16,078

SMITH COLLEGE

SEVEN COLLEGE LANE, NORTHAMPTON, MA 01063 • ADMISSIONS: 413-585-2500 • FAX: 413-585-2527

STUDENTS SAY ". . ."

Academics

Smith College, one of the nation's most prestigious all-women's undergraduate institutions, empowers "incredible women to discover where there true passions lie while allowing them to develop the confidence and skills needed to really make a difference, while dispelling any self-doubt" about making their way in "a world still dominated by men." Academics are legendarily demanding here. "Life at Smith is dominated by work," notes one student. "If you don't want to study hard and take school seriously, you won't survive here." An open curriculum—no required classes here—motivates students to work hard by allowing them to immerse themselves only in what most intrigues them. As one undergrad explains, "I've never had this much work before, but I've also never been able to choose all my classes. I have a ton of work, but it's all stuff I'm interested in. Plus, Smith professors rarely get busy-work-happy, so it's all relevant work. Smith just expects that all its students can handle an academically rigorous schedule, so they aren't shy about assigning a large volume of work." "Fantastic free tutoring and editing available for every class" also help lighten the load a bit. What makes the Smith experience worth the hard work are the "phenomenal" resources and "tons of opportunities." Chief among Smith's assets is its "friendly and accessible" faculty whose "first priority obviously is teaching." The school also boasts a great Career Development Office and an exceptional alumnae network. "Before the Ivies went co-ed, Smith was the place for women to get educated. Our alumnae connections are insane, and our career development office keeps track of all of them," writes one student. Though small, Smith offers "a great selection of courses," and "If you can't find a class you want on campus, Smith s a part of the Five College Consortium of Amherst, Hampshire, UMass Amherst, and Mount Holyoke, where you can participate in clubs and take classes that you find interesting."

Life

Smith is located in Northampton, "a perfect college town." "The residents love Smithies and vise versa," explains one student. "It doesn't feel like a small town, but it isn't by any means an overwhelming city. The Pleasant Street Theater shows great independent films, and there are plenty of delicious restaurants ranging from fancy cuisines to casual weekend brunches. The music scene in Northampton is also extremely popular. There are about five venues where fantastic musicians often play at." All in all, "It's hard not to immerse yourself in the wide variety of concerts available in Northampton." In the spring and fall, "canoeing and kayaking on Paradise Pond and walking through the surrounding trails" entice many. On campus, "Most people participate in some sort of extracurricular activity, whether they are singing in an a cappella group or part of a play or on a sports team. In terms of weekends, there are at least two parties on most weekends and a number of lectures, performances, movies, and many other activities to attend. Thus, Smith is a place where you do not need to drink to have a good time but that is also available if that's what you want to do. There is something for everyone." Smith parties tend to be more subdued than your average college bash, so those seeking a more conventional college experience trek on over to UMass or Amherst.

Student Body

There is "a wide diversity of types of people at Smith. You'll walk to class and pass by a jock, a cardigan set and pearls-type person, a Dungeon and Dragons addict…there's a niche for everyone. You just have to find it." Smith women are typically "smart, competitive, motivated, and wants to make a difference in her community." Many are "politically liberal, opinionated, pride themselves on being well-informed, and can be overly sensitive and overly politically correct." They also share "a strong acceptance of lesbian/bisexual/same gender loving identities, which usually changes back to 'straight' once people graduate. This is usually referred to as LUGs (Lesbians Until Gradation) or BUGs (Bisexual Until Graduation)."

FINANCIAL AID: 413-585-2530 • E-MAIL: ADMISSION@SMITH.EDU • WEBSITE: WWW.SMITH.EDU

THE PRINCETON REVIEW SAYS

Admissions

Very important factors considered include: Academic GPA, recommendation(s), rigor of secondary school record, character/personal qualities. *Important factors considered include:* Class rank, application essay, standardized test scores, extracurricular activities, interview, talent/ability. *Other factors considered include:* Alumni/ae relation, first generation, racial/ethnic status, volunteer work, work experience. SAT or ACT required; TOEFL required of all international applicants. High school diploma or equivalent is not required. *Academic units recommended:* 4 English, 4 mathematics, 3 science, (3 science labs), 3 foreign language, 2 history.

Financial Aid

Students should submit: FAFSA, CSS/Financial Aid PROFILE, noncustodial PROFILE, business/farm supplement. Regular filing deadline is 2/1. The Princeton Review suggests that all financial aid forms be submitted as soon as possible after January 1. *Need-based scholarships/grants offered:* Federal Pell, SEOG, state scholarships/grants, the school's own gift aid. *Loan aid offered:* Direct Subsidized Stafford, Direct Unsubsidized Stafford, FFEL PLUS, Federal Perkins, state loans, college/university loans from institutional funds. Applicants will be notified of awards on or about 4/1. Federal Work-Study Program available. Institutional employment available. Off-campus job opportunities are excellent.

The Inside Word

Smith's relatively high acceptance rate results from its self-selecting applicant pool, meaning that students with no chance of getting in here simply don't bother applying. The fact that the school has no intention of admitting men tells you all you need to know about its success in attracting accomplished, highly talented women. Put your best foot forward here and hope for the best.

THE SCHOOL SAYS ". . ."

From The Admissions Office

"Smith students choose from 1,000 courses in more than 50 areas of study. There are no specific course requirements outside the major; students meet individually with faculty advisers to plan a balanced curriculum. Smith programs offer unique opportunities, including the chance to study abroad, or at another college in the United States, and a semester in Washington, DC. The Ada Comstock Scholars Program encourages women beyond the traditional age to return to college and complete their undergraduate studies. Smith is located in the scenic Connecticut River valley of western Massachusetts near a number of other outstanding educational institutions. Through the Five College Consortium, Smith, Amherst, Hampshire, and Mount Holyoke colleges and the University of Massachusetts enrich their academic, social, and cultural offerings by means of joint faculty appointments, joint courses, student and faculty exchanges, shared facilities, and other cooperative arrangements. Smith is the only women's college to offer an accredited major in engineering; it's also the only college in the country that offers a guaranteed paid internship program ("Praxis").

"Smith requires either the SAT or the ACT. Scores from older versions of the SAT (pre-March 2005 version) and the ACT are acceptable."

SELECTIVITY

Admissions Rating	95
# of applicants	3,427
% of applicants accepted	53
% of acceptees attending	37
# accepting a place on wait list	286
% admitted from wait list	6
# of early decision applicants	212
% accepted early decision	78

FRESHMAN PROFILE

Range SAT Critical Reading	580–700
Range SAT Math	560–670
Range SAT Writing	640–730
Range ACT Composite	25–29
Minimum paper TOEFL	600
Minimum computer TOEFL	250
Average HS GPA	4
% graduated top 10% of class	61
% graduated top 25% of class	91
% graduated top 50% of class	100

DEADLINES

Early decision	
Deadline	11/15
Notification	12/15
Regular	
Deadline	1/15
Notification	4/1
Nonfall registration?	no

APPLICANTS ALSO LOOK AT

AND OFTEN PREFER
Brown University
AND SOMETIMES PREFER
Wellesley College
AND RARELY PREFER
Mount Holyoke College

FINANCIAL FACTS

Financial Aid Rating	96
Annual tuition	$32,320
Room and board	$10,880
Required fees	$238
Books and supplies	$600
% frosh rec. need-based scholarship or grant aid	59
% UG rec. need-based scholarship or grant aid	59
% frosh rec. need-based self-help aid	58
% UG rec. need-based self-help aid	58
% frosh rec. any financial aid	66
% UG rec. any financial aid	65
% UG borrow to pay for school	71
Average cumulative indebtedness	$19,760

SONOMA STATE UNIVERSITY

1801 EAST COTATI AVENUE, ROHNERT PARK, CA 94928 • ADMISSIONS: 707-664-2778 • FAX: 707-664-2060

STUDENTS SAY ". . ."

Academics

Californians seeking a first-rate public-school education that allows them to "take a step back from the fast pace of the city without taking away the fun and activities" look to Sonoma State University, a rural campus that is "very relaxing and beautiful"—but also close enough to San Francisco and Sacramento to benefit from the activities these cities offer. Standout programs here include the Hutchins School of Liberal Studies, which offers interdisciplinary instruction that fosters "cross-disciplinary development of critical-thinking abilities" (many Hutchins students ultimately pursue teaching degrees); a "wonderful" psychology program; a business program that "is very well put together, with very helpful, good teachers"; and "excellent health care and science majors," including a unique environmental management and design program. Students love the fact that the small size of the school allows for "a very personal connection between the student and the professor." Size constraints conspire to make it "harder to get the classes you need," however, and this causes some frustration. Respondents report that "many students take more than 4 years to graduate" because of these limitations. Great funding for the library, on the other hand, means that "it's the best you'll find anywhere, thanks to a donation from *Peanuts* cartoonist Charles Schulz."

Life

The "laid-back and beautiful campus" of Sonoma State "can be too quiet for some people, but for the general population, it is a place to relax and get some peace in their busy schedules." Students who "want a place where you can hear a pin drop, view the stars, and breathe actual air rather than LA smog" will feel most at home here. The downside of all this tranquility is that accompanying it is sometimes a "lack of school spirit. Back in the 1990s we had a football team. No more, and some of us feel like we're really missing out. These days, if you go to any game on campus you will see fewer than 100 students." Even the "amazing lacrosse team" can't draw much of a crowd here, though the school does offer a variety of concerts, rallys and other events for students' benefit. Hometown Rohnert Park "is about an hour from San Francisco," but there's also much to be said for closer destinations. Sonoma County "is full of beautiful hillsides that make for great hiking. The beach is a 40-minute drive west, and many students venture out that way when weather permits." Campus housing "is great; we live in apartments instead of rooms," and with the school "currently focusing on renovating old buildings as well as adding new facilities (a music center and a recently opened recreation center, for example)," the campus promises to improve even more in coming years.

Student Body

"The typical student at SSU is a young White female," undergrads here report, estimating that "probably two-thirds of the students are women." Many students can be described as you would expect of native Californians: "Very relaxed, mostly liberal, and left-wing." Those outside the majority demographic "can appear socially removed," but "It seems like everyone can find a niche." SSU has "very few minority students, though that percentage has increased slowly over the years" as "The administration has reached out to city kids as well as minority kids, thus integrating more diversity into the university."

FINANCIAL AID: 707-664-2389 • E-MAIL: ADMITME.@SONOMA.EDU • WEBSITE: WWW.SONOMA.EDU

THE PRINCETON REVIEW SAYS

Admissions

Very important factors considered include: Academic GPA, rigor of secondary school record, standardized test scores. *Other factors considered include:* First generation, geographical residence, state residency, SAT or ACT required; TOEFL required of all international applicants. High school diploma is required and GED is accepted. *Academic units required:* 4 English, 3 mathematics, 2 science, (1 science labs), 2 foreign language, 1 history, 3 academic electives, 1 visual/performing arts.

Financial Aid

Students should submit: FAFSA. The Princeton Review suggests that all financial aid forms be submitted as soon as possible after January 1. *Need-based scholarships/grants offered:* Federal Pell, SEOG, state scholarships/grants, private scholarships, the school's own gift aid, ACG, SMART. *Loan aid offered:* Direct Subsidized Stafford, Direct Unsubsidized Stafford, Direct PLUS, Federal Perkins Applicants will be notified of awards on a rolling basis beginning 4/15. Federal Work-Study Program available. Institutional employment available. Off-campus job opportunities are good.

The Inside Word

Sonoma State's admissions philosophy can be summed up in one word: objectivity. Standardized test scores and GPAs are the overriding factors. Assuming they meet the minimum standards, applicants are guaranteed an acceptance letter. Students should take a moment to peruse the requirements as some of the more popular majors stipulate higher grades.

THE SCHOOL SAYS ". . ."

From The Admissions Office

"Sonoma State University occupies 275 acres in the beautiful wine country of Sonoma County, in Northern California. Located at the foot of the Sonoma hills, the campus is an hour's drive north of San Francisco and centrally located between the Pacific Ocean to the west and the wine country to the north and east. SSU is deeply committed to the teaching of the liberal arts and sciences. The campus has earned a national reputation as a leader in integrating the use of technology into its curriculum. Within its 32 academic departments, SSU awards bachelor's degrees in 41 areas of specialization and master's degrees in 14 areas. In addition, the university offers a joint master's degree in mathematics with San Francisco State University. The campus ushered in the twenty-first century with the opening of a new library and technology center, the Jean and Charles Schulz Information Center.

"All freshmen applicants are required to provide SAT or ACT scores. Fall 2008 applicants are encouraged to take the new SAT or the ACT. In addition, students may submit scores from the old (before March 2005) SAT, and we will use their best scores from either test."

SELECTIVITY
Admissions Rating	60*
# of applicants	10,382
% of applicants accepted	73
% of acceptees attending	23

FRESHMAN PROFILE
Range SAT Critical Reading	460–560
Range SAT Math	460–550
Range ACT Composite	19–24
Minimum paper TOEFL	500
Minimum computer TOEFL	173
Average HS GPA	3.23

DEADLINES
Regular	
Priority	11/30
Deadline	1/31
Notification	rolling
Nonfall registration?	yes

FINANCIAL FACTS
Financial Aid Rating	75
Annual out-of-state tuition	$8,136
Room and board	$8,820
Required fees	$3,946
Books and supplies	$1,386
% frosh rec. need-based scholarship or grant aid	18
% UG rec. need-based scholarship or grant aid	24
% frosh rec. non-need-based scholarship or grant aid	15
% UG rec. non-need-based scholarship or grant aid	17
% frosh rec. need-based self-help aid	19
% UG rec. need-based self-help aid	27
% frosh rec. any financial aid	32
% UG rec. any financial aid	42
% UG borrow to pay for school	20
Average cumulative indebtedness	$15,170

SOUTHERN METHODIST UNIVERSITY

PO Box 750181, Dallas, TX 75275-0181 • Admissions: 214-768-0103 • Fax: 214-768-2507

STUDENTS SAY ". . ."

Academics

Southern Methodist University seeks "to challenge and develop students intellectually and socially in order to provide a fulfilling higher education." Others agree that students here are "making valuable connections that can serve [them] well in the working world." They "work hard and play hard" so it's all about finding balance between "making the grades and having fun." Good news for grads: Future opportunities abound as "You won't struggle to find a job because of SMU's outstanding reputation in the Dallas market. Its strong name has also branched out into the greater South. Most of the alums are very successful, and they seek out SMU students." The school works its magic most effectively in such popular disciplines as business, advertising, pre-law, and premedical study; its Meadows School of Performing Arts is home to "an incredible music program" and equally strong programs in dance, theater, arts administration, and advertising. Students are keen to brag that SMU professors "go above and beyond their duties" and are always "looking after your best interests." Combine this with a "great administration" that "really strives to stay in touch with their students and uses their feedback to make beneficial changes." SMU's Dallas address means "there are a lot of ways to get involved in the community or resources for your career path." As one student explains, "My school does a great job at helping students decide what they want out of their future and assisting them on making it possible."

Life

"School is hard," notes one student, "but you make it through somehow" thanks to "parties, movies, clubs, bars, [and a] very Greek" campus. In fact, the typical student is described as "sporting a Greek affiliation" (and they don't mean the nationality). The Greeks serve as the nexus of social life and account for a large "sense of community" among students. In short, writes one Greek student, "We run this place. Everyone who is anyone is in it. Tailgating wouldn't happen without us. Homecoming wouldn't happen without us." Togas aside, SMU's "beautiful" campus garners even more accolades. "It is definitely the prettiest campus in Texas, and one of the greatest in the South," says a student. Beyond campus awaits Dallas, where "There is always a party going on, whether it is downtown or at a local bar. Because of the location (in upscale Highland Park), bars are always new and safe with the best DJs. There are more places to eat near SMU than anywhere I have ever been."

Student Body

First, let's address the stereotypes. The typical SMU student is described largely as "upper-class, White, and wealthy—though looks can be deceiving." That said, many note that SMU could use "more diversity" and "Atypical students can feel left out." Another student claims that the school has "a huge mix of students" though "you have to look hard." One unifying factor? All things "Dixie." "Every student here seems to know the words to Dixie," explains a student. "You'll see Texas flags in all the dorm rooms. But it's more of a statement of the genteel Southern style of living people appreciate. Everyone is Republican . . . and very conservative." Though many agree that a majority of students "come from high-income households," SMU is a "dynamic community" that manages "to offer something for everyone. You just have to find your niche."

FINANCIAL AID: 214-768-2058 • E-MAIL: UGADMISSION@SMU.EDU • WEBSITE: WWW.SMU.EDU/ADMISSION

THE PRINCETON REVIEW SAYS

Admissions

Very important factors considered include: Class rank, application essay, academic GPA, recommendation(s), rigor of secondary school record, standardized test scores. *Important factors considered include:* Character/personal qualities, extracurricular activities, talent/ability, volunteer work, work experience. *Other factors considered include:* Alumni/ae relation, first generation, interview, level of applicant's interest, SAT or ACT required; TOEFL required of all international applicants. High school diploma is required and GED is not accepted. *Academic units required:* 4 English, 3 mathematics, 3 science, (2 science labs), 2 foreign language, 1 social studies, 2 history. *Academic units recommended:* 4 English, 4 mathematics, 4 science, (3 science labs), 3 foreign language, 2 social studies, 3 history.

Financial Aid

Students should submit: FAFSA, CSS/Financial Aid PROFILE, noncustodial PROFILE, business/farm supplement. The Princeton Review suggests that all financial aid forms be submitted as soon as possible after January 1. *Need-based scholarships/grants offered:* Federal Pell, SEOG, state scholarships/grants, private scholarships, the school's own gift aid. *Loan aid offered:* FFEL Subsidized Stafford, FFEL Unsubsidized Stafford, FFEL PLUS, Federal Perkins, state loans, college/university loans from institutional funds. Applicants will be notified of awards on a rolling basis beginning 3/15. Off-campus job opportunities are good.

The Inside Word

With a potent combination of high-caliber academics, Texan weather, and classic architecture, admissions standards at SMU have been steadily rising over the last decade, meaning that securing a seat here is getting more and more competitive. Solid high school grades and a roster of activities will usually do the trick, but keep in mind that performing arts majors must audition. Interestingly, all other applicants, regardless of declared major, are listed as "pre-majors" to the Dedman College of Humanities and Sciences.

THE SCHOOL SAYS "..."

From The Admissions Office

"SMU students balance challenging academic programs with a total campus experience that enables them to choose their own path of achievement. Small classes ensure that students receive personal attention. Classes are taught by professors who are dedicated to teaching undergraduates while producing new knowledge, enriching the classroom. Students also have access to visiting dignitaries ranging from former presidents to Nobel laureates. Reflecting its student-centered focus, SMU is one of the few universities to have a voting student member on its Board of Trustees. Internships, community service, student research opportunities, and study abroad programs abound. SMU also offers a thriving honors program and one of the top merit scholarship programs in the nation. More than 400 arts events each year add a special vitality to campus life, and nearly 200 student organizations provide opportunities for leadership. SMU welcomes a diverse student body from every state and over 90 countries; 72 percent of students receive some form of financial aid. Graduates attend some of the best graduate and professional schools in the nation. They find promising career opportunities through SMU's close ties with Dallas, a center of commerce and culture and gateway to the global community.

"SMU requires either the ACT or SAT. Assessment of written communication skills remains an important component of the SMU application review process. To that end, it is recommended that applicants use every opportunity, including the ACT or SAT, to display their writing skills in the application process."

SELECTIVITY

Admissions Rating	91
# of applicants	8,253
% of applicants accepted	50
% of acceptees attending	32
# accepting a place on wait list	390
% admitted from wait list	32

FRESHMAN PROFILE

Range SAT Critical Reading	560–660
Range SAT Math	570–670
Range SAT Writing	560–650
Range ACT Composite	25–29
Minimum paper TOEFL	550
Minimum computer TOEFL	213
Average HS GPA	3.55
% graduated top 10% of class	40
% graduated top 25% of class	71
% graduated top 50% of class	94

DEADLINES

Early action	
Deadline	11/1
Notification	12/31
Regular	
Priority	1/15
Deadline	3/15
Notification	rolling
Nonfall registration?	yes

APPLICANTS ALSO LOOK AT

AND OFTEN PREFER
Vanderbilt University
University of Southern California

AND SOMETIMES PREFER
Tulane University
University of Miami

FINANCIAL FACTS

Financial Aid Rating	80
Annual tuition	$29,430
Room and board	$11,875
Required fees	$3,740
Books and supplies	$800
% frosh rec. need-based scholarship or grant aid	25
% UG rec. need-based scholarship or grant aid	28
% frosh rec. non-need-based scholarship or grant aid	24
% UG rec. non-need-based scholarship or grant aid	20
% frosh rec. need-based self-help aid	27
% UG rec. need-based self-help aid	30
% frosh rec. athletic scholarships	5
% UG rec. athletic scholarships	5
% frosh rec. any financial aid	82
% UG rec. any financial aid	65
% UG borrow to pay for school	33
Average cumulative indebtedness	$16,756

SOUTHWESTERN UNIVERSITY

ADMISSIONS OFFICE, PO BOX 770, GEORGETOWN, TX 78627-0770 • ADMISSIONS: 512-863-1200 • FAX: 512-863-9601

CAMPUS LIFE

Quality of Life Rating	**83**
Fire Safety Rating	**76**
Green Rating	**74**
Type of school	private
Affiliation	Methodist
Environment	town

STUDENTS

Total undergrad enrollment	1,294
% male/female	40/60
% from out of state	5
% from public high school	82
% live on campus	77
% in (# of) fraternities	29 (4)
% in (# of) sororities	30 (4)
% African American	3
% Asian	5
% Caucasian	77
% Hispanic	14
% Native American	1
# of countries represented	8

SURVEY SAYS . . .
Great computer facilities
Great library
Career services are great
Students are happy
Lots of beer drinking

ACADEMICS

Academic Rating	**87**
Calendar	semester
Student/faculty ratio	10:1
Profs interesting rating	93
Profs accessible rating	92
Most common reg class size	10–19 students
Most common lab size	10–19 students

MOST POPULAR MAJORS
communication studies
political studies
biology
psychology

STUDENTS SAY ". . ."

Academics

"Camouflaged behind a directional name," Southwestern University offers "a lot of personal attention" and seriously good financial aid. However, "Southwestern's greatest asset" is its "enthusiastic" and "delightfully eccentric" faculty. They are "extraordinary teachers" who "really care" and "form close and long lasting friendships" with students. "Professors will meet with you outside of class every day," promises a history major. While course selection is "limited," students also rave about their "really small" classes. The "responsive" administration is "extremely involved," and the career services staff is reportedly "outstanding." Newly-minted SU grads have a great track record at finding real jobs and getting into graduate and professional schools. If you come here, though, be prepared for a "crazy hard" academic experience. Class attendance is required. Homework is ample. While "getting A's is definitely not impossible, it does require work." "There is almost no such thing as a blow-off class," and the broad core curriculum typically culminates in "a sizable research thesis" or a special project. "You learn a whole lot and are insanely prepared for whatever you want to do when you leave," reports a psychology major.

Life

Southwestern's campus is "absolutely beautiful," some "weird and unattractive architecture" notwithstanding. "The dorms don't completely suck." On the other hand, the "mediocre" food "gets old pretty fast." Campus life is largely "self contained," and despite "constant drama," it's "predictable." In a nutshell, "life at Southwestern is a struggle to maintain the fine balance between a very heavy workload and a very fun social life." SU students "spend a near-absurd amount of time studying" every weeknight. On Wednesday nights and on the weekends, though, they find time to "court death with alcohol, cigarettes, and general idiocies." "Greek life really is a large part of Southwestern's campus" and fraternities definitely "drive the social scene." However, "students not involved in Greek life are still welcome at Greek events and go often." There are also various house parties and "big themed parties" in the student apartments. For sober students, "there are tons of plays and concerts all the time," and "the school does a good job of providing some form of entertainment every weekend." Extracurricular activities are also abundant. "It's all a pretty open, nonexclusive atmosphere where pretty much anybody is welcome to participate in the sports, organizations, or whatever," relates a senior. Off campus, the city of Georgetown is "boring" and "the townies don't like the students very much." Luckily, the "much cooler" environs of Austin are just a short drive away.

Student Body

Students come to Southwestern "from any number of small towns" and from "suburbia" but "it seems like everybody is from Texas." It seems like everyone is white, too. "There are definitely not enough minorities here, that's for sure," asserts a senior. "The school is not as racially diverse as the administration likes to pretend." Many females also lament the male "shortage." "It's a guy's paradise," says a freshman. "You will see the most gorgeous girls with the geekiest guys." "There's also a pretty open gay population." Students at SU describe themselves as "highly motivated," "very eclectic," and "quirky." "Unconventional appearances" are common. There aren't too many jocks here. It's mostly a "nerdy, skinny, non-athletic" crowd. "Most of us are the brainy, slightly eccentric kid you sat behind in any AP or IB class you took in high school," admits a sophomore. Most students are Christian, but at the same time, "not very religious." Some students are "ultra conservative." Others are "liberal as hell." Many are "loaded, money-wise." "The typical student is either an extremely conservative trust fund baby, or a lip-service hippie trust fund baby," suggests a junior. However, a very large contingent of students is also here "on scholarship" or thanks to Southwestern's generous financial aid packages.

FINANCIAL AID: 512-863-1259 • E-MAIL: ADMISSION@SOUTHWESTERN.EDU • WEBSITE: WWW.SOUTHWESTERN.EDU

THE PRINCETON REVIEW SAYS

Admissions

Very important factors considered include: Class rank, application essay, academic GPA, recommendation(s), rigor of secondary school record, standardized test scores. *Important factors considered include:* Alumni/ae relation, character/personal qualities, extracurricular activities, first generation, geographical residence, interview, level of applicant's interest, racial/ethnic status, talent/ability, volunteer work, work experience. SAT or ACT required; ACT with Writing component required. TOEFL required of all international applicants. High school diploma is required and GED is accepted. *Academic units required:* 4 English, 4 mathematics, 3 science, (2 science labs), 2 foreign language, 2 social studies, 1 history, 1 academic elective. *Academic units recommended:* 4 English, 4 mathematics, 4 science, (3 science labs), 3 foreign language, 3 social studies, 2 history.

Financial Aid

Students should submit: FAFSA Regular filing deadline is 3/1. The Princeton Review suggests that all financial aid forms be submitted as soon as possible after January 1. *Need-based scholarships/grants offered:* Federal Pell, SEOG, state scholarships/grants, private scholarships, the school's own gift aid. *Loan aid offered:* FFEL Subsidized Stafford, FFEL Unsubsidized Stafford, FFEL PLUS, Federal Perkins, state loans, college/university loans from institutional funds. Applicants will be notified of awards on a rolling basis beginning 3/1. Federal Work-Study Program available. Institutional employment available. Off-campus job opportunities are good.

The Inside Word

Southwestern is one of the best "sleepers" in the nation. Admissions standards are high, but they would be even higher if more people know about this place. Academic excellence abounds, the administration is earnest and helpful, and financial aid packages are frequently tremendous. If you could thrive in a small-town, close-knit environment, Southwestern definitely deserves a look.

THE SCHOOL SAYS "..."

From The Admissions Office

"On the outskirts of Texas's vibrant capital city of Austin is Southwestern University, the state's first institution of higher learning. Southwestern is committed to helping students achieve personal and professional success as well as a passion for lifelong learning. The Paideia Program, funded in 2002 by an $8.5 million grant, is a distinctive new option for select students beginning the sophomore year that provides opportunities to compare, contrast, and integrate knowledge and skills gained in various areas of study. In addition to their regular studies, students work with the same Paideia professor over a 3-year period in seminar groups of ten. They work to discover the powerful connections between Southwestern's rigorous academic experience and the dynamic programs available outside the classroom—through leadership, service, intercultural learning, and collaborative research or creative works. All Southwestern students discover that a premier liberal arts education leads to high acceptance rates into prestigious graduate and professional programs and careers right out of college. Southwestern is today what it has always been: a highly personal liberal arts experience that equips students with the strengths they need to develop fulfilling lives.

"Southwestern University will accept both the old and new SAT score formats. The Writing component of the new SAT will be considered in a comprehensive manner, along with overall academic record, application essay, extracurricular activities, recommendations, and a personal interview."

SELECTIVITY

Admissions Rating	88
# of applicants	1,916
% of applicants accepted	67
% of acceptees attending	29
# accepting a place on wait list	16
% admitted from wait list	44
# of early decision applicants	72
% accepted early decision	88

FRESHMAN PROFILE

Range SAT Critical Reading	560–680
Range SAT Math	570–660
Range ACT Composite	24–29
Minimum paper TOEFL	570
Minimum computer TOEFL	230
% graduated top 10% of class	50
% graduated top 25% of class	81
% graduated top 50% of class	96

DEADLINES

Early decision	
Deadline	11/1
Notification	12/1
Regular	
Priority	2/15
Deadline	2/15
Notification	4/1
Nonfall registration?	yes

APPLICANTS ALSO LOOK AT

AND OFTEN PREFER
Trinity University
Rice University

AND SOMETIMES PREFER
Rhodes College
Tulane University
Vanderbilt University
Texas A&M University—College Station

AND RARELY PREFER
Southern Methodist University
Baylor University

FINANCIAL FACTS

Financial Aid Rating	86
Annual tuition	$27,940
Room and board	$8,870
Books and supplies	$1,000
% frosh rec. need-based scholarship or grant aid	53
% UG rec. need-based scholarship or grant aid	49
% frosh rec. non-need-based scholarship or grant aid	35
% UG rec. non-need-based scholarship or grant aid	30
% frosh rec. need-based self-help aid	44
% UG rec. need-based self-help aid	42
% frosh rec. any financial aid	88
% UG rec. any financial aid	86
% UG borrow to pay for school	57
Average cumulative indebtedness	$24,057

SPELMAN COLLEGE

350 SPELMAN LANE, SOUTHWEST, ATLANTA, GA 30314 • ADMISSIONS: 404-270-5193 • FAX: 404-270-5201

CAMPUS LIFE
Quality of Life Rating	69
Fire Safety Rating	60*
Green Rating	60*
Type of school	private
Environment	metropolis

STUDENTS
Total undergrad enrollment	2,337
% male/female	/100
% from out of state	69
% from public high school	84
% live on campus	48
% in (# of) sororities	NR (4)
% African American	96
% international	2
# of countries represented	18

SURVEY SAYS . . .
Small classes
Lab facilities are great
Campus feels safe
Frats and sororities dominate social scene
Student government is popular
Very little drug use

ACADEMICS
Academic Rating	77
Calendar	semester
Student/faculty ratio	12:1
Profs interesting rating	66
Profs accessible rating	62
Most common reg class size	10–19 students
Most common lab size	20–29 students

MOST POPULAR MAJORS
psychology
political science and government

STUDENTS SAY ". . ."

Academics

In a nutshell, sums up a senior, small Spelman College in Atlanta is "political awareness, intellectual nirvana, and warm sisterhood in a pair of Prada shoes." It's also "the premier college for black women in the United States." The hard sciences are especially notable but "academics are very strong" across the board. Spelman makes you analyze every situation," emphasizes a sociology major. "It makes you think." "Small classes" allow for plenty of "individual attention." Outside of class, professors are "easy to talk to" as well. The women of Spelman are split in their views of the administration. Proponents say that management is "friendly and as available as regular professors, sometimes more so." Critics charge that the staff can be "rude." "At times, school administration takes patience," says a junior, "but I guess you could look at it as another thing Spelman instills in you." Most students tend to agree that "Spelman could stand to improve financial aid." The curriculum here is strongly oriented toward the liberal arts and sciences, and there is something of a "lack of relevant career-based majors." For programs not offered on campus, though, Spelman belongs to the Atlanta University Center, "the largest consortium" of historically black colleges in the nation," and students can take classes and utilize resources at a handful of schools nearby.

Life

"The food is horrible" and parking needs to improve, but overall, students here are very pleased with their "sisterly community." "Spelman College allows for its students to participate in a lot of different things," says a junior. There are "comedy shows, concerts (for all tastes), coronation ball, pageants—everything you can think of." On Market Friday, "there is music and vendors come to sell their merchandise. Students from Morehouse College and Clark Atlanta University come over and occasionally a celebrity walks through." Greek life is noticeable but "Spelman's campus really isn't the place to be for great parties or socializing." In fact, it's "practically a ghost town on the weekends." Older students often go to house parties or frequent Atlanta's nightclubs. "You have the city of Atlanta at your disposal, which never allows for a dull moment." "It is mandatory for first-year students to live on campus," and they can't have cars, "so the shuttle buses wait outside to pick them up and take them to the party," wherever it is. If you have an interest in men, don't worry. "I don't want anyone to be afraid to come to Spelman because it's a women's college and they're afraid they'll never see men," admonishes a senior. "A lot of times I forget that I go to a women's college. The social scene is never lacking. Morehouse—an HBCU and a men's college—is literally right across the street from us, and they take classes with us, join in activities and clubs with us, and throw parties with us." There's also a joint homecoming, which is "ridiculously fun."

Student Body

"Because most of us are women of African descent, people believe that we will all be the same, but at times I believe Spelman is more diverse than many other schools," suggests a sophomore. "We have students of many different ethnic backgrounds (Jamaican, Trinidadian, Nigerian, etc.). Students come from various socioeconomic backgrounds. This is contrary to what many people think about the typical Spelmanite." "The only things that I'd say are common to nearly all Spelman students are that we are (1) black and (2) female," agrees a senior. "Other than that, everyone's different, and I don't mean to make that a cliché. You'd be surprised how much diversity can be found at a historically black college for women." The students here describe themselves as "hardworking, friendly, competitive, and fashionable." They often come "from a middleclass to upper middleclass background." "People think Spelman women have a lot of money and are generally stuck up," observes one senior. Students here are also "politically active." "Our school has historically been involved in a lot of political movements," relates another senior, "and it's a joke around Morehouse and Spelman that every year we have a new issue."

FINANCIAL AID: 404-270-5212 • E-MAIL: ADMISS@SPELMAN.EDU • WEBSITE: WWW.SPELMAN.EDU

THE PRINCETON REVIEW SAYS

Admissions

Very important factors considered include: Application essay, academic GPA, rigor of secondary school record, standardized test scores, character/personal qualities. *Important factors considered include:* Recommendation(s), extracurricular activities. *Other factors considered include:* Class rank, alumni/ae relation, first generation, geographical residence, level of applicant's interest, volunteer work, work experience. SAT or ACT required; TOEFL required of all international applicants. High school diploma is required and GED is accepted. *Academic units required:* 4 English, 3 mathematics, 3 science, (2 science labs), 2 foreign language, 3 social studies, 2 history, 2 academic electives. *Academic units recommended:* 4 English, 4 mathematics, 4 science, (3 science labs), 4 foreign language, 4 social studies, 3 history, 2 academic electives.

Financial Aid

Students should submit: Institution's own financial aid form, CSS/Financial Aid PROFILE The Princeton Review suggests that all financial aid forms be submitted as soon as possible after January 1. *Need-based scholarships/grants offered:* Federal Pell, SEOG, state scholarships/grants, private scholarships, the school's own gift aid, United Negro College Fund. *Loan aid offered:* FFEL Subsidized Stafford, FFEL Unsubsidized Stafford, FFEL PLUS Federal Work-Study Program available. Institutional employment available. Off-campus job opportunities are good.

The Inside Word

No Historically Black College in the country has more competitive admissions process than Spelman. Successful candidates show strong academic records with challenging course loads and solid grades. Applicant evaluation is very personal; it is quite important to show depth of character and social consciousness.

THE SCHOOL SAYS "..."

From The Admissions Office

"As an outstanding Historically Black College for women, Spelman strives for academic excellence in liberal arts education. This predominantly residential private college provides students with an academic climate conducive to the full development of their intellectual and leadership potential. The college is a member of the Atlanta University Center consortium, and Spelman students enjoy the benefits of a small college while having access to the resources of the other three participating institutions. The purpose extends beyond intellectual development and professional career preparation of students. It seeks to develop the total person. The college provides an academic and social environment that strengthens those qualities that enable women to be self-confident as well as culturally and spiritually enriched. This environment attempts to instill in students both an appreciation for the multicultural communities of the world and a sense of responsibility for bringing about positive change in those communities.

"Applicants for Fall 2008 are required to submit standardized test scores from an appropriate venue (i.e. ACT, TOEFL, SAT). The highest composite score will be used in admissions decisions. Writing scores from either the SAT or ACT will not be taken into consideration in the admission process."

SELECTIVITY
Admissions Rating	92
# of applicants	5,656
% of applicants accepted	33
% of acceptees attending	30

FRESHMAN PROFILE
Range SAT Critical Reading	500–580
Range SAT Math	490–570
Range ACT Composite	21–25
Minimum paper TOEFL	500
Minimum computer TOEFL	250
Average HS GPA	3.59
% graduated top 10% of class	40
% graduated top 25% of class	73
% graduated top 50% of class	95

DEADLINES
Early decision	
Deadline	11/1
Notification	12/15
Early action	
Deadline	11/15
Notification	12/31
Regular	
Deadline	2/1
Notification	4/1
Nonfall registration?	no

APPLICANTS ALSO LOOK AT
AND OFTEN PREFER
Georgia Institute of Technology
AND SOMETIMES PREFER
Tuskegee University
Clark Atlanta University
Howard University
Hampton University
Florida A&M University
AND RARELY PREFER
University of Maryland—College Park
Emory University
University of Georgia

FINANCIAL FACTS
Financial Aid Rating	65
Annual tuition	$14,470
Room and board	$8,750
Required fees	$2,535
Books and supplies	$1,150
% frosh rec. need-based scholarship or grant aid	80
% UG rec. need-based scholarship or grant aid	54
% frosh rec. non-need-based scholarship or grant aid	49
% UG rec. non-need-based scholarship or grant aid	21
% frosh rec. need-based self-help aid	11
% UG rec. need-based self-help aid	72
% frosh rec. any financial aid	82
% UG rec. any financial aid	75
% UG borrow to pay for school	75

ST. BONAVENTURE UNIVERSITY

PO BOX D, ST. BONAVENTURE, NY 14778 • ADMISSIONS: 716-375-2400 • FAX: 716-375-4005

CAMPUS LIFE
Quality of Life Rating	73
Fire Safety Rating	60*
Green Rating	60*
Type of school	private
Affiliation	Roman Catholic
Environment	village

STUDENTS
Total undergrad enrollment	2,072
% male/female	51/49
% from out of state	24
% from public high school	70
% live on campus	77
# of countries represented	24

SURVEY SAYS . . .
Large classes
Athletic facilities are great
Students are friendly
Frats and sororities are unpopular
or nonexistent
College radio is popular
Lots of beer drinking
Hard liquor is popular

ACADEMICS
Academic Rating	76
Calendar	semester
Student/faculty ratio	15:1
Profs interesting rating	81
Profs accessible rating	82
Most common reg class size	10–19 students
Most common lab size	10–19 students

MOST POPULAR MAJORS
elementary education and teaching
business/commerce

STUDENTS SAY ". . ."
Academics
St. Bonaventure is "a small-town university with a lot to offer," including a "simply stellar" journalism and mass communications program that features "an amazing faculty" that "wants you to get the best job possible." SBU's business program is also "very strong," and its education department "has a good reputation"; a new science building, scheduled for completion in the fall of 2008, should bolster the university's small but growing biology, chemistry, and computer science departments. Regardless of major, all students must complete a core curriculum offered through SBU's Clare College. While a few here insist that "Clare College is not that bad, and a lot of the classes are interesting," the majority complain that the "required Catholic core curriculum" is "a complete drag and a waste of students' time and effort, in addition to being a GPA reducer." Somewhere in between are those pragmatists who tell us that "Clare College courses are annoying but not over demanding. If you didn't want to learn about Catholic heritage, you shouldn't come to a Catholic school." Amen! While SBU undergrads may not agree on the value of the core curriculum, nearly all concur that professors here "are easy to talk to and are always available after class and outside of class. They make students feel comfortable and want to get to know the students. We are not just numbers." They also agree that their degree provides them access to "great connections with alumni" and that, all things considered, SBU leaves them "as well equipped to take the jobs of their choosing out of college as students at any other college, period."

Life
"When the weekend arrives, the general consensus of the students is one thing: partying. Off campus houses host triple keggers every weekends and the four local bars begin to draw crowds on Wednesday nights." Almost everyone agrees that "Drinking is huge...and so are basketball games"—as one student explains it, "we all love love love basketball games; the entire student population will be at a basketball game on a Saturday night, without fail"—but undergrads add that "there are lots of other things to keep busy" for those outliers to whom neither beer nor hoops appeals. Winter sports such as snowboarding and skiing are quite popular, and students have access to numerous parks and trails for hiking during the warm months. Furthermore, "The radio station and Campus Activities Board work very hard to bring in an up-and-coming band probably once a week." Students add that "The radio station is also great thing to do, it's very easy to get involved in." Finally, the school's many community-spirited undergrads can participate in "the oldest student-run soup kitchen in the country" or "a program called Bona Buddies that matches up students with underprivileged local kids to mentor them."

Student Body
The typical Bona undergrad "is white and Catholic, with a desire to do well and succeed but a stronger desire to have fun while doing so." Most "wear jeans and a North Face jacket or something very similar"; students are "trendy" but casual. A great number "hail from within three hours of the school, mostly in the Rochester and Buffalo area." Western New York is conservative terrain so SBU "has a good number of conservative students." They are typically "involved, whether it be in our soup kitchen or radio station." While the demographic is largely white, "There are more and more minority students every year," and the school offers "a plethora of activities, groups and policies that seem to provide a soaring number of opportunities for minority students."

St. Bonaventure University

Financial Aid: 716-375-2528 • E-mail: admissions@sbu.edu • Website: www.sbu.edu

THE PRINCETON REVIEW SAYS

Admissions

Very important factors considered include: Academic GPA, recommendation(s), rigor of secondary school record, character/personal qualities, interview. *Important factors considered include:* Application essay, standardized test scores, extracurricular activities, level of applicant's interest, talent/ability, volunteer work. *Other factors considered include:* Class rank, alumni/ae relation, first generation, work experience. SAT recommended; SAT or ACT required; ACT recommended; TOEFL required of all international applicants. High school diploma is required and GED is accepted. *Academic units required:* 4 English, 3 mathematics, 3 science, 2 foreign language, 4 social studies. *Academic units recommended:* 4 English, 3 mathematics, 3 science, (3 science labs), 2 foreign language, 4 social studies.

Financial Aid

Students should submit: FAFSA, institution's own financial aid form, state aid form. The Princeton Review suggests that all financial aid forms be submitted as soon as possible after January 1. *Need-based scholarships/grants offered:* Federal Pell, SEOG, state scholarships/grants, private scholarships, the school's own gift aid. *Loan aid offered:* FFEL Subsidized Stafford, FFEL Unsubsidized Stafford, FFEL PLUS, Federal Perkins, college/university loans from institutional funds. Applicants will be notified of awards on a rolling basis beginning 4/1.

The Inside Word

Above average students should meet little resistance from the St. Bonaventure admissions office; nearly nine in ten applicants here are accepted, and the academic profile of the median admitted student is respectable but hardly overwhelming. A personal essay and interview are optional; barring a misstep of catastrophic proportions, they can only improve your chances of getting in.

THE SCHOOL SAYS "..."

From The Admissions Office

"The St. Bonaventure University family has been imparting the Franciscan tradition to men and women of a rich diversity of backgrounds for more than 130 years. This tradition encourages all who become a part of it to face the world confidently, respect the earthly environment, and work for productive change in the world. The charm of our campus and the inspirational beauty of the surrounding hills provide a special place where growth in learning and living is abundantly realized. The Richter Student Fitness Center, scheduled to be completed in 2004, will provide all students with state-of-the-art facilities for athletics and wellness. Academics at St. Bonaventure are challenging. Small classes and personalized attention encourage individual growth and development for students. St. Bonaventure's nationally known Schools of Arts and Sciences, Business Administration, Journalism/Mass Communication, and Education offer majors in 31 disciplines. The School of Graduate Studies also offers several programs leading to the master's degree.

"Applicants for Fall 2008 can submit scores from either the old or new SAT, as well as the ACT. For students who have taken both versions, the best composite score from either the old or new SAT will be used. The Biology Subject Test is required only for students applying to one of our Dual Admission medical programs. "

SELECTIVITY

Admissions Rating	73
# of applicants	1,730
% of applicants accepted	86
% of acceptees attending	32

FRESHMAN PROFILE

Range SAT Critical Reading	480–570
Range SAT Math	470–570
Range ACT Composite	19–23
Minimum paper TOEFL	550
Minimum computer TOEFL	213
Average HS GPA	3.13
% graduated top 10% of class	11
% graduated top 25% of class	31
% graduated top 50% of class	68

DEADLINES

Regular	
Priority	2/1
Deadline	4/15
Notification	rolling
Nonfall registration?	yes

APPLICANTS ALSO LOOK AT

AND OFTEN PREFER
Villanova University
State University of New York at Geneseo
Providence College

AND SOMETIMES PREFER
Le Moyne College
Ithaca College
Niagara University
Siena College
State University of New York—University at Buffalo

AND RARELY PREFER
Syracuse University

FINANCIAL FACTS

Financial Aid Rating	80
Annual tuition	$21,650
Room and board	$7,760
Required fees	$865
Books and supplies	$650
% frosh rec. need-based scholarship or grant aid	73
% UG rec. need-based scholarship or grant aid	71
% frosh rec. non-need-based scholarship or grant aid	13
% UG rec. non-need-based scholarship or grant aid	12
% frosh rec. need-based self-help aid	60
% UG rec. need-based self-help aid	59
% frosh rec. athletic scholarships	3
% UG rec. athletic scholarships	4
% UG borrow to pay for school	72
Average cumulative indebtedness	$16,900

ST. JOHN'S COLLEGE (MD)

PO Box 2800, Annapolis, MD 21404 • Admissions: 1-800-727-9238 • Fax: 410-269-7916

CAMPUS LIFE

Quality of Life Rating	91
Fire Safety Rating	84
Green Rating	78
Type of school	private
Environment	town

STUDENTS

Total undergrad enrollment	481
% male/female	53/47
% from out of state	83
% from public high school	53
% live on campus	73
% African American	1
% Asian	3
% Caucasian	90
% Hispanic	3
# of countries represented	12

SURVEY SAYS . . .

Class discussions encouraged
No one cheats
Frats and sororities are unpopular
or nonexistent
(Almost) everyone smokes

ACADEMICS

Academic Rating	94
Calendar	semester
Student/faculty ratio	87:1
Profs interesting rating	98
Profs accessible rating	97
Most common	
reg class size	10–19 students

MOST POPULAR MAJORS

liberal arts and sciences studies and
humanities

STUDENTS SAY " . . ."

Academics

Tiny St. John's College specializes in the great books. The entire four-year curriculum is an "exhilarating and exhausting" survey of intellectual history, starting with ancient Greece and ending in modern times. Virtually all classes are required. There are no majors. There are no textbooks. And there are no tests, except for "occasional grammar and vocab quizzes" in Ancient Greek and French. Grades are based on papers and class participation. Students here encounter the works of "the greatest minds of Western Civilization" in their original, unadulterated form. While students at others schools may occasionally think outside the box, students at St. John's critically examine "the eternal questions of this world," namely "what it is to be a human." It's "certainly not the best education for everyone (especially students who want to learn certain technical skills)." For these students, though, it is a little slice of heaven. Classes are small— "never larger than 20 students"—and "discussion-based." Professors (called "tutors" here, incidentally) are "deeply intelligent" and "can bounce from Newton to Leibniz to Baudelaire to Bach" with ease. They "do little or no lecturing," favoring instead to "facilitate discussion." Students engage in conversation, "instead of sitting through lectures on other people's interpretations." "There's a wonderful sense of camaraderie that develops in the classroom, as we wrestle with the Great Questions of the ages," enthuses one student.

Life

Despite the "overbearing" workload, "there is an almost snuggly feeling of community here." "The academic atmosphere is immersing and supportive, especially since everyone is in or has had or will have all the same classes." Social life is "alarmingly insular." "We at St. John's are removed from the world to a truly shocking degree," elaborates one student. "The campus feels not like a campus, but a miniature world, which actually is not very much like the real world." Extracurricular activities include "heaps of clubs." "Most everyone attends the Shakespeare plays and classical music concerts." Intramural sports are "incredibly fun" and a big part of Johnnie life. "Skill is optional but enthusiasm is required." "It is a great stress reliever," explains one student. "The books tear your soul apart," but sports here are a way of "pasting it back together." Campus-wide parties on the weekends include "raucous" reality dance parties as well as waltz and swing dancing parties. Drinking is popular. Coffee and cigarettes are big. Johnnies also "sail, watch movies," and play board games. Or they just hang out, "finding adventures where they pop up." Students also talk late into the night "about set theory, socks, art history, Moby Dick, why macaroni is so orange," and pretty much everything except politics. "Johnnies are extraordinarily uninterested in politics." While the food on campus "sucks," students find epicurean delights in "Annapolis, Baltimore, Washington DC, or New York."

Student Body

"St. John's is a unique program, and it takes a unique group of people to keep it going." "The one thing Johnnies have in common is their love of learning and their love for thought," says a junior. "A Johnnie is a bookworm, socially awkward in some fashion, an intense thinker." Eyeglasses are common. "This campus may have the worst collective eyesight in America." "Many students are quite intelligent, and most are highly eccentric." "'Intellectual elitism' can be a problem." "Upperclassmen especially have an esprit de corps and traditionalist spirit that borders on crotchetiness." "Most people here are strange." Many are "brash and freakish." "There is definitely a certain type of person that picks St. John's, but how that quality reveals itself is different for every person," notes one student. "St. John's is entirely made up of atypical students, so none of them fit in, and they don't feel like they need to." Johnnies are "an amazing conglomeration of artists, mathematicians, jocks, role-playing enthusiasts, poets, iconoclasts, activists, and some who are all of these." That said, there's a serious lack of "ethnic diversity." However, intellectual diversity abounds. Students are "willing to assert opinions, and, more importantly, to reconsider them."

FINANCIAL AID: 410-626-2502 • E-MAIL: ADMISSIONS@SJCA.EDU • WEBSITE: WWW.STJOHNSCOLLEGE.EDU

THE PRINCETON REVIEW SAYS

Admissions

Very important factors considered include: Application essay. *Important factors considered include:* Recommendation(s), rigor of secondary school record, character/personal qualities. *Other factors considered include:* Class rank, academic GPA, standardized test scores, alumni/ae relation, extracurricular activities, first generation, interview, racial/ethnic status, talent/ability, TOEFL required of all international applicants. High school diploma is required and GED is accepted. *Academic units required:* 3 mathematics, 2 foreign language. *Academic units recommended:* 4 English, 4 mathematics, 3 science, (3 science labs), 4 foreign language, 2 social studies, 2 history.

Financial Aid

Students should submit: FAFSA, CSS/Financial Aid PROFILE, state aid form, noncustodial PROFILE, business/farm supplement. The Princeton Review suggests that all financial aid forms be submitted as soon as possible after January 1. *Need-based scholarships/grants offered:* Federal Pell, SEOG, state scholarships/grants, the school's own gift aid. *Loan aid offered:* FFEL Subsidized Stafford, FFEL Unsubsidized Stafford, FFEL PLUS, Federal Perkins, college/university loans from institutional funds. Applicants will be notified of awards on a rolling basis beginning 12/1. Off-campus job opportunities are good.

The Inside Word

St. John's has one of the most personal admissions processes in the country. The applicant pool is highly self-selected and extremely bright, so don't be fooled by the high acceptance rate—every student who is offered admission deserves to be here. Candidates who don't give serious thought to the kind of match they make with the college and devote serious energy to their essays are not likely to be successful.

THE SCHOOL SAYS "..."

From The Admissions Office

"The purpose of the admission process is to determine whether an applicant has the necessary preparation and ability to complete the St. John's program satisfactorily. The essays are designed to enable applicants to give a full account of themselves. They can tell the committee much more than statistical records reveal. Previous academic records show whether an applicant has the habits of study necessary at St. John's. Letters of reference, particularly those of teachers, are carefully read for indications that the applicant has the maturity, self-discipline, ability, energy, and initiative to succeed in the St. John's program. St. John's attaches little importance to 'objective' test scores, and no applicant is accepted or rejected because of such scores.

"St. John's College does not require the results of standardized tests, except in the case of international students, homeschooled students, and those who will not receive a high school diploma. Results of the ACT or SAT are sufficient for these students."

SELECTIVITY

Admissions Rating	86
# of applicants	441
% of applicants accepted	81
% of acceptees attending	40

FRESHMAN PROFILE

Range SAT Critical Reading	660–770
Range SAT Math	580–680
Minimum paper TOEFL	600
Minimum computer TOEFL	270
% graduated top 10% of class	32
% graduated top 25% of class	65
% graduated top 50% of class	87

DEADLINES

Regular	Rolling
Priority	3/1
Nonfall registration?	yes

APPLICANTS ALSO LOOK AT

AND OFTEN PREFER
University of Virginia
University of Chicago
Swarthmore College

AND SOMETIMES PREFER
Oberlin College
Reed College
Kenyon College
Smith College

AND RARELY PREFER
Bard College

FINANCIAL FACTS

Financial Aid Rating	92
Annual tuition	$36,346
Room and board	$8,684
Required fees	$250
Books and supplies	$280
% frosh rec. need-based scholarship or grant aid	56
% UG rec. need-based scholarship or grant aid	77
% frosh rec. need-based self-help aid	62
% UG rec. need-based self-help aid	85
% frosh rec. any financial aid	76
% UG rec. any financial aid	52

ST. JOHN'S COLLEGE (NM)

1160 CAMINO CRUZ BLANCA, SANTA FE, NM 87505 • ADMISSIONS: 505-984-6060 • FAX: 505-984-6162

CAMPUS LIFE
Quality of Life Rating	**92**
Fire Safety Rating	**60***
Green Rating	**81**
Type of school	private
Environment	city

STUDENTS
Total undergrad enrollment	436
% male/female	60/40
% from out of state	95
% from public high school	70
% African American	1
% Asian	3
% Caucasian	86
% Hispanic	6
% Native American	1
% international	2
# of countries represented	22

SURVEY SAYS . . .
Class discussions encouraged
Large classes
No one cheats
Registration is a breeze
Students are happy
Intercollegiate sports are unpopular
or nonexistent
Frats and sororities are unpopular
or nonexistent
(Almost) everyone smokes

ACADEMICS
Academic Rating	**98**
Calendar	semester
Student/faculty ratio	8:1
Profs interesting rating	95
Profs accessible rating	98
Most common reg class size	10–19 students

STUDENTS SAY ". . ."

Academics
The "mind-blowing," all-mandatory curriculum at "incredibly small" St. John's College in Santa Fe, New Mexico, includes "copious amounts" of philosophy, literature, language, math, and science. Students "read only primary texts as opposed to textbooks." "There are no majors." There are no lectures. "Every class is a discussion." There are few tests. Grades are based almost exclusively on papers. While students love the academic experience, they caution that it is full of "relentless intellectual duress." "The program is very difficult and you get kicked out if you can't keep up," warns a senior. "You have to be prepared to work hard without being rewarded with simple answers." Professors at St. John's are called tutors "because they are not professing anything." Instead, they guide students through a few thousand years of Western thought, starting with ancient Greece and ending in modern times, and allow you "to form your own opinions." Some faculty members "are terrible" but most are "insightful, brilliant, and dedicated." Virtually all of them are "absurdly accessible" as well. "Students meet with the dean all the time." However, when difficulties arise, the administration sometimes causes "an ordeal far out of proportion to the problem." "Financial aid is scarce," too. Other complaints include the "often less modern" condition of the campus. There are some "shabby" classrooms, and the Internet connection "needs to be upgraded by an order of magnitude."

Life
Campus life at St. John's in Santa Fe is "a strange boot camp" where "the dating scene is a nightmare" and "the food needs improvement." The "life-consuming" curriculum here forces students to put in many hours of difficult reading. "We read the great, earthshaking books all the time, which necessarily takes a toll on our psychology," explains a junior. "You can only have your conception of the world shattered so many times before you feel emotionally drained." "Social life in general tends to be a less formal (frequently rather irreverent) extension of our classroom life," explains a junior. "A typical dining hall conversation might cycle between Star Wars, the Roman Empire, various videogames, Socrates, world religions, and the nature and existence of divine truth." Beyond stimulating banter, "there is no universally popular activity." "There are lectures every Friday night." "Pickup sports are popular." Martial arts are reasonably big, "as is fencing." "Organized trips for skiing, hiking, rafting," and other outdoor activities are common. Many students "tend to drink now and then, some smoke pot with more frequency, or occasionally use other drugs." There's no pressure to participate, though. "There are definitely people, like myself, who don't drink or smoke or do other drugs," asserts a senior. Surrounding Santa Fe boasts "excellent restaurants" and a nice view of the mountains. Otherwise, it's "a town for rich, retired hippies."

Student Body
"This is a school for super geeks." Everyone is a "voracious reader" and "kind of neurotic." "For many students, St. John's is a funny interlude—a bizarre and startlingly wonderful place to reflect on the world around them and think about themselves and how they want to live their own lives." "People here tend to have considered the big questions," suggests a senior. "How can I be a good person? Why does the world work the way it does?" Some students suffer from "academic haughtiness." "Johnnies tend to have an underlying pretension regarding their role in the world as philosophers and avant-garde thinkers and writers." A lot of people smoke cigarettes, too. "If you're not a smoker before you come here, you will be when you leave." "The population is not diverse ethnically but it is tolerant politically, religiously, and socially." There are "churchgoing Christians and radical atheists." "Every St. John's student is atypical in one way or another." "Although they might not fit in elsewhere, they feel quite comfortable at St. John's." "People here go after what they want," agrees a sophomore, "whether it's getting too stoned to think or finding a job as a ranch hand in the middle of nowhere."

St. John's College (NM)

Financial Aid: 505-984-6058 • E-mail: ADMISSIONS@MAIL.SJCSF.EDU • Website: WWW.SJCSF.EDU

THE PRINCETON REVIEW SAYS

Admissions

Very important factors considered include: Application essay. *Important factors considered include:* Recommendation(s), rigor of secondary school record, character/personal qualities, level of applicant's interest. *Other factors considered include:* Class rank, academic GPA, standardized test scores, alumni/ae relation, extracurricular activities, first generation, interview, racial/ethnic status, talent/ability, volunteer work, work experience. TOEFL required of all international applicants. High school diploma is required and GED is accepted. High school diploma or equivalent is not required. *Academic units required:* 3 mathematics, 2 foreign language. *Academic units recommended:* 4 English, 1 mathematics, 3 science, (3 science labs), 4 foreign language, 2 history.

Financial Aid

Students should submit: FAFSA, CSS/Financial Aid PROFILE, noncustodial PROFILE, business/farm supplement. The Princeton Review suggests that all financial aid forms be submitted as soon as possible after January 1. *Need-based scholarships/grants offered:* Federal Pell, SEOG, state scholarships/grants, private scholarships, the school's own gift aid, academic competitiveness grant. *Loan aid offered:* FFEL Subsidized Stafford, FFEL Unsubsidized Stafford, FFEL PLUS, Federal Perkins, college/university loans from institutional funds. Applicants will be notified of awards on a rolling basis beginning 12/10. Federal Work-Study Program available. Institutional employment available. Off-campus job opportunities are excellent.

The Inside Word

Self-selection drives this admissions process—over one-half of the entire applicant pool each year indicates that St. John's is their first choice, and half of those admitted send in tuition deposits. Even so, no one in admissions takes things for granted, and neither should any student considering an application. The admissions process is highly personal on both sides of the coin. Only the intellectually curious and highly motivated need apply.

THE SCHOOL SAYS ". . ."

From The Admissions Office

"St. John's appeals to students who value good books, love to read, and are passionate about discourse and debate. There are no lectures and virtually no tests or electives. Instead, classes of 16–20 students occur around conference tables where professors are as likely to be asked to defend their points of view as are students. Great books provide the direction, context, and stimulus for conversation. The entire student body adheres to the same, all-required arts and science curriculum. Someone once said, 'A classic is a house we still live in,' and at St. John's, students and professors alike approach each reading on the list as if the ideas it holds were being expressed for the first time—questioning the logic behind a geometrical proof, challenging the premise of a scientific development, or dissecting the progression of modern political theory as it unfolds.

"As of this book's publication, St. John's College (NM) did not have information available about their policy regarding the new SAT."

SELECTIVITY	
Admissions Rating	85
# of applicants	344
% of applicants accepted	79
% of acceptees attending	49
# accepting a place on wait list	4
% admitted from wait list	50

FRESHMAN PROFILE	
Range SAT Critical Reading	620–730
Range SAT Math	570–680
Range ACT Composite	25–31
Minimum paper TOEFL	550
Minimum computer TOEFL	213
% graduated top 10% of class	28
% graduated top 25% of class	64
% graduated top 50% of class	81

DEADLINES	
Regular	
Priority	3/1
Nonfall registration?	yes

APPLICANTS ALSO LOOK AT

AND OFTEN PREFER
Stanford University
Deep Springs College

AND SOMETIMES PREFER
University of Chicago
Claremont McKenna College
Rice University
Bard College

AND RARELY PREFER
Oberlin College
Grinnell College
Whitman College

FINANCIAL FACTS	
Financial Aid Rating	93
Annual tuition	$36,346
Books and supplies	$275
% frosh rec. need-based scholarship or grant aid	51
% UG rec. need-based scholarship or grant aid	58
% frosh rec. need-based self-help aid	56
% UG rec. need-based self-help aid	62
% frosh rec. any financial aid	93
% UG rec. any financial aid	94
% UG borrow to pay for school	68
Average cumulative indebtedness	$26,263

ST. JOHN'S UNIVERSITY

8000 UTOPIA PARKWAY, QUEENS, NY 11439 • ADMISSIONS: 718-990-2000 • FAX: 718-990-5728

CAMPUS LIFE

Quality of Life Rating	75
Fire Safety Rating	92
Green Rating	89
Type of school	private
Affiliation	Roman Catholic
Environment	metropolis

STUDENTS

Total undergrad enrollment	12,178
% male/female	45/55
% from out of state	15
% from public high school	64
% live on campus	19
% in (# of) fraternities	3 (22)
% in (# of) sororities	2 (24)
% African American	16
% Asian	16
% Caucasian	38
% Hispanic	14
% international	4
# of countries represented	125

SURVEY SAYS . . .

Large classes
Great computer facilities
Athletic facilities are great
Diverse student types on campus

ACADEMICS

Academic Rating	71
Calendar	semester
Student/faculty ratio	17:1
Profs interesting rating	63
Profs accessible rating	61
Most common reg class size	10-19 students
Most common lab size	10-19 students

MOST POPULAR MAJORS
biology/biological sciences
psychology
pharmacy (pharmd [USA], pharmd
or bs/bpharm [Canada])

STUDENTS SAY ". . ."

Academics

Like its hometown of Queens, NY, St. John's moves inexorably forward without forgetting its history and traditions. The school's administration is committed to constantly "updating the university's facilities." Recent improvements include "a state-of-the-art athletic training facility and revamped cafeterias,"as well as a $20 million upgrade to science facilities. In addition, the school distributes "brand-new laptops to all incoming students" and has "done a tremendous job of implementing technology throughout the campus," which "is completely wireless except for a few athletic fields and parking lots." On the traditions side of the balance, the school recently built "a beautiful brand-new, free-standing church" and maintains "a lot of policies and politics opposed by typical college students . . . [such as] the visitor policies in the dorms." Regarding academics, the university offers some amazing opportunities such as the Institute for Writing Studies and the "Discover the World" study-abroad program. When it comes to classroom experience, "Professors are professors. Like [at] any school, some are better than others." Students report that "the experience you have at St. John's really depends on what you do with it. Don't take a professor just because he/she is easy—chances are that means they suck! If you are self-motivated . . . you will find challenging professors." Big-picture people will see that St. John's offers "a quality private education" and, in many instances, a "generous" financial aid package that translates to an overall "low cost."

Life

Historically, St. John's has been known as "basically a school for commuters." According to many students, it still is. They argue that because "There aren't many on-campus students," "On the weekends this place is a ghost town." Others counter that "Recently there has been an amazing effort" by the school's Residence Life Department "to bring back campus life," an effort which includes posting "weekly calendars informing us about campus events and activities." For those who prefer off-campus activities in their spare time, the school helps to make that possible, too. There are "shuttles that can take us into the city [aka Manhattan, to those outside New York City] and on weekends . . . to the mall." In addition, the "school runs programs to see Broadway shows for free." Even without the school's help, however, New York is at students' fingertips; almost everything the city has to offer "is just a subway ride away." "Clubs, sports events, parties, restaurants"—you name it, NYC's got it, and St. John's students sample it. The faithful will be happy to know that "St. John's makes it easy to incorporate a spiritual life with an academic one." For the altruistic, there are "community-service initiatives galore."

Student Body

Because it is "located in Queens, the most diverse place on Earth," it's no surprise that St. John's itself is "very, very diverse." Though "everyone gets along exceptionally well," getting along well doesn't equal total integration. There are "major ethnic lines" at St. John's, and each "ethnic group tends [to] hang around with itself, a sight typical of New York in general." Yet students' external differences belie intangible similarities. Many students may be the first in their family to attend college, so a strong work ethic is pervasive. Everyone "wants to achieve something greater than their parents." The second major similarity stems from the first: Students here generally have many responsibilities outside of their schoolwork."

FINANCIAL AID: 1-888-9-STJOHNS • E-MAIL: ADMISSIONS@STJOHNS.EDU • WEBSITE: WWW.STJOHNS.EDU

THE PRINCETON REVIEW SAYS

Admissions

Very important factors considered include: Academic GPA, standardized test scores. *Important factors considered include:* Application essay, recommendation(s), rigor of secondary school record, character/personal qualities, volunteer work. *Other factors considered include:* Class rank, alumni/ae relation, extracurricular activities, interview, level of applicant's interest, work experience. SAT or ACT required; ACT with Writing component recommended. TOEFL required of all international applicants. High school diploma is required and GED is accepted. *Academic units required:* 4 English, 3 mathematics, 3 science, (3 science labs), 2 foreign language, 3 social studies, 5 academic electives.

Financial Aid

Students should submit: FAFSA. The Princeton Review suggests that all financial aid forms be submitted as soon as possible after January 1. *Need-based scholarships/grants offered:* Federal Pell, SEOG, state scholarships/grants, private scholarships, the school's own gift aid. *Loan aid offered:* FFEL Subsidized Stafford, FFEL Unsubsidized Stafford, FFEL PLUS, Federal Perkins Applicants will be notified of awards on a rolling basis beginning 3/15. Federal Work-Study Program available. Institutional employment available. Off-campus job opportunities are good.

The Inside Word

The admissions process at St. John's doesn't include many surprises. High school grades and standardized test scores are undoubtedly the most important factors though volunteer work and extracurricular activities are also highly regarded. What is surprising is that this Catholic university doesn't consider religious affiliation at all when making admissions decisions; there are students of every religious stripe here (see the "Student Body" section).

THE SCHOOL SAYS "..."

From The Admissions Office

"Founded by the Vincentian Fathers in 1870, St. John's is a world-class Catholic university that prepares students for leadership in today's global society. St. John's combines a friendly, residential college experience with full access to the resources and opportunities only available in exciting New York City.

Students pursue more than 100 quality programs in the arts, sciences, business, education, pharmacy and allied health. Professors are internationally respected scholars, 90 % of whom hold a Ph.D. or comparable degree. The 17:1 student-faculty ratio ensures personal attention in the classroom.

Representing 45 states and 125 foreign countries, students also benefit from these advantages:

- A dynamic freshman year featuring "Learning Communities" – themed clusters of like-minded students sharing classes, activities and residence hall suites.

- Unequaled opportunities to experience the "Big Apple" through unique core courses like Discover New York.

- Wireless laptop computers for entering students, with access to our award-winning campus network.

- Academic Service-Learning – course-related volunteer activities that give students real-world experience while assisting those in need.

- Unique study abroad programs like Discover the World, allowing students to earn 15 credits while living and learning in three foreign cities in a single semester.

- Vibrant campus activities with 180 student clubs and organizations that keep students engaged around the clock.

St. John's has three residential New York City campuses: a 105-acre flagship campus in Queens, NY; a wooded Staten Island, NY, campus; and an award-winning Manhattan campus. St. John's also has campuses in Oakdale, NY, and Rome, Italy."

SELECTIVITY

Admissions Rating	81
# of applicants	27,754
% of applicants accepted	56
% of acceptees attending	21
# accepting a place on wait list	63

FRESHMAN PROFILE

Range SAT Critical Reading	480–580
Range SAT Math	480–600
Minimum paper TOEFL	500
Minimum computer TOEFL	173
Minimum web-based TOEFL	61
Average HS GPA	3.2
% graduated top 10% of class	22
% graduated top 25% of class	44
% graduated top 50% of class	67

DEADLINES

Notification	rolling
Nonfall registration?	yes

APPLICANTS ALSO LOOK AT

AND OFTEN PREFER
City University of New York—
Baruch College
State University of New York—Stony
Brook University

AND SOMETIMES PREFER
Fordham University
Rutgers University

AND RARELY PREFER
Siena College
St. Bonaventure University

FINANCIAL FACTS

Financial Aid Rating	70
Annual tuition	$26,200
Room and board	$12,070
Required fees	$690
Books and supplies	$1,000
% frosh rec. need-based scholarship or grant aid	74
% UG rec. need-based scholarship or grant aid	69
% frosh rec. non-need-based scholarship or grant aid	75
% UG rec. non-need-based scholarship or grant aid	66
% frosh rec. need-based self-help aid	58
% UG rec. need-based self-help aid	70
% frosh rec. athletic scholarships	2
% UG rec. athletic scholarships	2
% frosh rec. any financial aid	97
% UG rec. any financial aid	98
% UG borrow to pay for school	74
Average cumulative indebtedness	$28,010

ST. LAWRENCE UNIVERSITY

PAYSON HALL, CANTON, NY 13617 • ADMISSIONS: 315-229-5261 • FAX: 315-229-5818

CAMPUS LIFE

Quality of Life Rating	83
Fire Safety Rating	68
Green Rating	87
Type of school	private
Environment	village

STUDENTS

Total undergrad enrollment	2,198
% male/female	46/54
% from out of state	52
% from public high school	70
% live on campus	99
% in (# of) fraternities	3 (1)
% in (# of) sororities	19 (4)
% African American	3
% Asian	2
% Caucasian	71
% Hispanic	3
% Native American	1
% international	5
# of countries represented	42

SURVEY SAYS . . .

Small classes
Great computer facilities
Great library
Athletic facilities are great
Everyone loves the Saints
Lots of beer drinking

ACADEMICS

Academic Rating	88
Calendar	semester
Student/faculty ratio	11:1
Profs interesting rating	92
Profs accessible rating	88
Most common reg class size	10–19 students
Most common lab size	10–19 students

MOST POPULAR MAJORS

psychology
economics
government

STUDENTS SAY ". . ."

Academics

Described by one student as a "hidden jewel tucked away in the tundra of the North Country," St. Lawrence University offers a "unique liberal arts education" to prospective undergraduates. Two things that "really stand out" at this small university are the "study abroad programs and the First-Year Program (FYP)." FYP is one of the oldest living-learning programs in the country and all first-year students are required to participate, which "helps strengthen skills and better prepares students for their next 3 years in college." Moreover, nearly 50 percent of the student body "participates in the study abroad programs offered" at some point during their time here. According to one student, "The professors are the best asset of St. Lawrence . . . they are very knowledgeable, and they love what they teach." Classes emphasize "critical thinking and writing," and "Professors are always there for students." Many students "form long-lasting friendships with their professors." Despite the university's small size there are "many class offerings," and students praise a "wonderful president" who leads a "very accessible" administration.

Life

Students at St. Lawrence "work hard [and] play harder!" Most students "socialize frequently" through a variety of outlets, from "theme parties [and] midnight breakfasts" to hanging out at "local bars." Although the surrounding area is "fairly void of cultural experiences," many students participate in "outdoor trips to the accessible Adirondacks or to cosmopolitan Montreal or Ottawa . . . all of which are between 1 to 2 and a half hours away from campus." The university makes "a lot of the accessories for these [outdoor] activities available for little or no upfront price." In addition, "There is always something happening at the student center for those who might prefer a more low-key night, like free movies." Most students "enjoy attending collegiate athletics, especially hockey" with "more than 60 percent of students involved with some sport." All of this contributes to a "very energetic atmosphere" on campus where there is "always an event to watch or participate in." Some students see the relatively isolated location of St. Lawrence as a blessing because it "forces students to form tighter bonds than at schools in cities where there is easy access to many different activities."

Student Body

The typical student at St. Lawrence is "very preppy" and "comes from the New England area." Here, "The guys are called 'Larrys' and the girls are 'Muffies,'" but "Most personalities do not fit the 'snobby preppy' stereotype." Many students qualify as "outdoorsy" types and there are "quite a few jocks." While students acknowledge a "lack of diversity" on campus, they say this is "slowly improving." Even though there are "not many atypical students"—"students all in black or with several piercings"—those who deviate from the "popped collar" and "Vera Bradley bag" trends "fit in regardless." While one student warns that some St. Lawrence students can be "very cliquey" and "difficult to approach," most students describe themselves as "friendly, enthusiastic, and open-minded." Typical or not, an SLU student is primarily "dedicated to academics and is very involved outside of the classroom." "Be it sports or other clubs, SLU students rarely spend time just sitting in their dorm rooms doing nothing."

FINANCIAL AID: 315-229-5265 • E-MAIL: ADMISSIONS@STLAWU.EDU • WEBSITE: WWW.STLAWU.EDU

THE PRINCETON REVIEW SAYS

Admissions

Very important factors considered include: Application essay, academic GPA, recommendation(s), character/personal qualities. *Important factors considered include:* Class rank, rigor of secondary school record, extracurricular activities, interview, racial/ethnic status. *Other factors considered include:* Standardized test scores, alumni/ae relation, first generation, geographical residence, level of applicant's interest, talent/ability, volunteer work, work experience. TOEFL required of international applicants for whom English is a foreign language. High school diploma is required and GED is accepted. *Academic units recommended:* 4 English, 4 mathematics, 4 science, 4 foreign language, 2 social studies, 2 history.

Financial Aid

Students should submit: FAFSA, PROFILE, business/farm supplement, Income Tax Returns/W-2s. Regular filing deadline is 2/1. The Princeton Review suggests that all financial aid forms be submitted as soon as possible after January 1. *Need-based scholarships/grants offered:* Federal Pell, SEOG, ACG, state scholarships/grants, the school's own gift aid. *Loan aid offered:* FFEL Subsidized Stafford, FFEL Unsubsidized Stafford, FFEL PLUS, Federal Perkins, college/university loans from institutional funds. Applicants will be notified of awards on or about 3/30. Federal Work-Study Program available. Institutional employment available. Off-campus job opportunities are poor.

The Inside Word

Despite facing stiff competition from many regional competitors, St. Lawrence University has managed to increase its application numbers over the past several years. Because it's increasingly selective, candidates must post decent grades in challenging courses if they hope to be accepted. The Admissions Committee appreciates the time each student puts into his or her application and recognizes those efforts by having three different counselors read each one. The school is a great choice for students looking to attend a small college in the Northeast.

THE SCHOOL SAYS ". . ."

From The Admissions Office

"In an ideal location, St. Lawrence is a diverse liberal arts learning community of inspiring faculty and talented students guided by tradition and focused on the future. The students who live and learn at St. Lawrence are interesting and interested; they enroll with myriad accomplishments and talents, as well as desire to explore new challenges. Our faculty has chosen St. Lawrence intentionally because they know that there is institutional commitment to support great teaching. They are dedicated to making each student's experience challenging and rewarding. Our graduates make up one of the strongest networks of support among any alumni body and are ready, willing, and able to connect with students and help them succeed.

"Which students are happiest at St. Lawrence? Students who like to be actively involved. Students who are open-minded and interested in meeting people with backgrounds different from their own. Students who value having a voice in decisions that affect them. Students who appreciate all that is available to them and cannot wait to take advantage of both the curriculum and the co-curricular options. Students who want to enjoy their college experience and are able to find joy in working hard.

"You can learn the facts about us from this guidebook: We have about 2,200 students; we offer more than 30 majors; the average class size is 16 students; a great new science center is open as of 2007; close to 50 percent of our students study abroad; and we have an environmental consciousness that fits our natural setting between the Adirondack Mountains and St. Lawrence River. You must visit, meet students and faculty, and sense the energy on campus to begin to understand just how special St. Lawrence University is.

"Beginning with applications for entry in Fall 2006, the submission of standardized test scores (SAT or ACT) is optional. Students must indicate on the St. Lawrence Common Application supplement which scores, if any, they wish to have considered in the application process. "

SELECTIVITY
Admissions Rating	89
# of applicants	4,645
% of applicants accepted	44
% of acceptees attending	31
# accepting a place on wait list	151
# of early decision applicants	209
% accepted early decision	79

FRESHMAN PROFILE
Range SAT Critical Reading	560–640
Range SAT Math	560–640
Range SAT Writing	560–640
Range ACT Composite	25–29
Minimum paper TOEFL	600
Minimum computer TOEFL	250
Average HS GPA	3.49
% graduated top 10% of class	35
% graduated top 25% of class	74
% graduated top 50% of class	96

DEADLINES
Early decision	
Deadline	11/15
Notification	12/15
Regular	
Deadline	2/1
Notification	3/30
Nonfall registration?	yes

APPLICANTS ALSO LOOK AT
AND OFTEN PREFER
Dartmouth College
Middlebury College
AND SOMETIMES PREFER
Colby College
Colgate University
AND RARELY PREFER
Hobart and William Smith Colleges
Ithaca College

FINANCIAL FACTS
Financial Aid Rating	88
Annual tuition	$33,690
% frosh rec. need-based scholarship or grant aid	61
% UG rec. need-based scholarship or grant aid	63
% frosh rec. non-need-based scholarship or grant aid	11
% UG rec. non-need-based scholarship or grant aid	8
% frosh rec. need-based self-help aid	58
% UG rec. need-based self-help aid	59
% frosh rec. athletic scholarships	1
% UG rec. athletic scholarships	2
% frosh rec. any financial aid	81
% UG rec. any financial aid	82
% UG borrow to pay for school	74
Average cumulative indebtedness	$28,776

ST. MARY'S COLLEGE OF MARYLAND

ADMISSIONS OFFICE, 18952 EAST FISHER ROAD, ST. MARY'S CITY, MD 20686-3001 • ADMISSIONS: 240-895-5000 • FAX: 240-895-5001

CAMPUS LIFE

Quality of Life Rating	93
Fire Safety Rating	79
Green Rating	84
Type of school	public
Environment	rural

STUDENTS

Total undergrad enrollment	1,922
% male/female	43/57
% from out of state	16
% live on campus	84
% African American	8
% Asian	4
% Caucasian	76
% Hispanic	5
% Native American	1
% international	2
# of countries represented	37

SURVEY SAYS . . .

Large classes
Athletic facilities are great
Students are friendly
Campus feels safe
Students are happy
Frats and sororities are unpopular
or nonexistent

ACADEMICS

Academic Rating	87
Calendar	semester
Student/faculty ratio	12:1
Profs interesting rating	96
Profs accessible rating	96
Most common reg class size	10–19 students
Most common lab size	10–19 students

MOST POPULAR MAJORS
economics
English language and literature
biology/biological sciences

STUDENTS SAY " . . ."

Academics

Set on the "beautiful St. Mary's River", St. Mary's College of Maryland is a "humble oasis" that "has all of the intellectual stimulation of a private liberal arts school with none of the academic rivalry." The blissfully content students at SMCM throw around the word "community" like rice at a wedding, and always precede it with some sort of positive lead-in: "small," "open-minded," "social justice minded, environmentally-friendly, hippie-loving, and very diverse and accepting" are just some of the descriptors used. Classes here are "rigorous" and "very engaging, requiring participation and input from all of the students," and the "amazing" professors are lauded for their brilliance, love of the material, and sheer accessibility; students talk of having seen professors "at school events not related to their classes and been invited to class dinners at their houses." Not only does the small size of the school mean that the faculty knows each student's name—"you are NEVER a number"—but "you get to know your professors on a personal level, which is great when it comes time for them to write recommendations for scholarships, graduate school, or future jobs." The administration gets positive reviews with just a few naysayers. The deans are commended for being "everywhere, participating in athletics, music programs, etc." and making it clear " that the students are the first priority," but a few students still say that the administration "can be a little bit withdrawn from the student body." Although there are complaints of too much construction around the campus, most students know that improvements and growth are necessary for the growth of the college, though they do wish to see more immediate changes to the health services, which "need some serious work."

Life

The phrase "summer camp setting" doesn't just refer to the campus' looks; Frisbee golf, sailing, bonfires, sun tanning, and kayaking in the school-provided kayaks are some of the main activities for students taking a break from their studies (which often occur outside). The river seems to be the hub of student life, not only acting as a "tremendous stress reliever"," but a sort of ad hoc campus center. Since the "very outdoorsy" campus is located in a remote location, "most of the fun that happens occurs on campus," and "the cold winter months are often difficult to bear and result in cabin fever." The lack of metropolitan areas (the nearest being Annapolis) means SMCM is "very residential," and "you really develop your own home and nest here with your friends as family." "There is a decent party scene on campus" with "parties on the weekends, studying during the week," but "students are rarely pressured to drink and many don't do it all." The plethora of clubs and other activities mean no one goes home bored. "I couldn't ask for a better college experience," says a junior.

Student Body

The diversity rate here isn't all that high (though it's not expected to be at such a small school), but no one has any real complaints. Most here are very environmentally oriented, "both in terms of their leisure activities and in terms of their political leanings." Some affectionately refer to their "hippie" classmates, but the "very accepting" student body has plenty of "pearl-wearing preps" and jocks in its "big social mosh pit," so "even the non-tree huggers amongst us can find a comfortable niche with little trouble." "It's entirely acceptable to be a bit quirky," says a junior. SMCM "is truly its own place," and this extreme love of the campus and its surroundings creates a sort of communal understanding anyone not contributing to its betterment will find themselves answering to the angry masses. "Word gets around on a small campus, and if you are mean or vandalize or something, people will know and shun you for that bad action."

ST. MARY'S COLLEGE OF MARYLAND

FINANCIAL AID: 240-895-3000 • E-MAIL: ADMISSIONS@SMCM.EDU • WEBSITE: WWW.SMCM.EDU

THE PRINCETON REVIEW SAYS

Admissions

Very important factors considered include: Academic GPA, rigor of secondary school record. *Important factors considered include:* Application essay, recommendation(s), standardized test scores, alumni/ae relation, character/personal qualities, extracurricular activities, first generation, talent/ability, volunteer work. *Other factors considered include:* Class rank, geographical residence, interview, racial/ethnic status, state residency, work experience. SAT or ACT required; High school diploma is required and GED is accepted. *Academic units required:* 4 English, 3 mathematics, 3 science, (2 science labs), 2 foreign language, 2 social studies, 1 history, 3 academic electives. *Academic units recommended:* 4 English, 4 mathematics, 3 science, (2 science labs), 4 foreign language, 2 social studies, 2 history, 3 academic electives.

Financial Aid

Students should submit: FAFSA Regular filing deadline is 3/1. The Princeton Review suggests that all financial aid forms be submitted as soon as possible after January 1. *Need-based scholarships/grants offered:* Federal Pell, SEOG, state scholarships/grants, private scholarships, the school's own gift aid. *Loan aid offered:* FFEL Subsidized Stafford, FFEL Unsubsidized Stafford, FFEL PLUS, Federal Perkins Applicants will be notified of awards on or about 4/1. Federal Work-Study Program available. Institutional employment available. Off-campus job opportunities are good.

The Inside Word

There are few better choices than St. Mary's for better-than-average students who are not likely to get admitted to one of the top 50 or so colleges in the country. It is likely that if funding for public colleges is able to stabilize, or even grow, that this place will soon be joining the ranks of the best. Now is the time to take advantage, before the academic expectations of the Admissions Committee start to soar.

THE SCHOOL SAYS "..."

From The Admissions Office

"St. Mary's College of Maryland occupies a distinctive niche and represents a real value in American higher education. It is a public college, dedicated to the ideal of affordable, accessible education but committed to quality teaching and excellent programs for undergraduate students. The result is that St. Mary's offers the small college experience of the same high caliber usually found at prestigious private colleges, but at public college prices. Designated by the state of Maryland as 'a public honors college,' one of only two public colleges in the nation to hold that distinction, St. Mary's has become increasingly attractive to high school students. Admission is very selective.

"For Fall 2008, applicants must take the new version of the SAT, but students may submit scores from the old (prior to March 2005) SAT, and admissions will use the student's best scores from either test. The ACT with the Writing section is also accepted."

SELECTIVITY

Admissions Rating	**90**
# of applicants	2,351
% of applicants accepted	55
% of acceptees attending	36
# accepting a place on wait list	132
% admitted from wait list	8
# of early decision applicants	307
% accepted early decision	47

FRESHMAN PROFILE

Range SAT Critical Reading	570–670
Range SAT Math	560–660
Range SAT Writing	560–670
Average HS GPA	3.47
% graduated top 10% of class	42
% graduated top 25% of class	76
% graduated top 50% of class	95

DEADLINES

Early decision	
Deadline	12/1
Notification	1/1
Regular	
Deadline	1/15
Notification	4/1
Nonfall registration?	yes

FINANCIAL FACTS

Financial Aid Rating	**85**
Annual in-state tuition	$10,472
Annual out-of-state tuition	$21,322
Room and board	$9,225
Required fees	$2,132
Books and supplies	$1,000
% frosh rec. need-based scholarship or grant aid	18
% UG rec. need-based scholarship or grant aid	19
% frosh rec. non-need-based scholarship or grant aid	18
% UG rec. non-need-based scholarship or grant aid	19
% frosh rec. need-based self-help aid	18
% UG rec. need-based self-help aid	19
% frosh rec. any financial aid	59
% UG rec. any financial aid	61
% UG borrow to pay for school	69
Average cumulative indebtedness	$17,125

ST. OLAF COLLEGE

1520 St. Olaf Avenue, Northfield, MN 55057 • Admissions: 507-646-3025 • Fax: 507-646-3832

STUDENTS SAY ". . ."

Academics

St. Olaf, a small Lutheran liberal arts school located 40 miles south of downtown Minneapolis, provides its "very Scandinavian" student body a "great liberal arts education rich with musical, academic, and social opportunities in a tight-knit, caring community." The school is renowned for its "amazing and extensive" music department (with which "most students are involved somehow"), but that's hardly the school's only asset. On the contrary, St. Olaf offers "excellent vocational training programs in nursing, social work, and education" (supplemented by "great…hands-on learning in addition to classroom learning through internships") as well as "an amazing science and math program (a state-of-the-art new science center will be finished in the next year). One of the best things about this school is the broad range of academics and academic experiences you can have." For most here, those experiences include study abroad; the school's numerous study abroad programs mean that "almost everyone goes abroad for at least a month." Writes one student, "St. Olaf has an amazing study abroad program. I've ridden camels in Egypt, climbed the Great Wall in China, seen the ruins of the Acropolis, and gone drinking in Switzerland all in the same semester!" Many students here complete a five-course sequence called "the Great Conversation Program, which provides a rigorous introduction to college, exploring the many 'Great Books' of western culture. The liberal arts requirements make everyone somewhat knowledgeable on every field."

Life

"There isn't much to do in Northfield," so life at St. Olaf "is very centered on campus." The school and student organizations make sure that "there is always something to do on campus, despite the small size of the student body. Bands are brought in to the student nightclub; there are over 100 concerts a year. The theater and dance programs put on frequent shows, and sports events are happening constantly. Students have the ability to participate in most of these activities, usually without too much prior experience, either." Also, undergraduates are "very focused on clubs and special interest groups. For about 3,000 students there are over 100 clubs on campus, serving everything from religious beliefs to environmental concerns to just having fun." Undergraduates "are very progressive…. Their passion for creating progressive social and political change often springs from their religious convictions." Intramural sports "are huge, so if varsity sports aren't your thing there are outside options," and because students "walk absolutely everywhere…the freshman 15 is more like the freshman five, if that. We're very healthy." When students need some big-city diversion, the Twin Cities are only about 45 minutes away. "Many students go up there to eat, see a play, sporting event, concert, or just to shop on weekends."

Student Body

"The stereotype that St. Olaf is completely made up of blond-haired, blue-eyed, Scandinavian Lutherans is not true," students insist, although they quickly admit that "We do have a large number of them!" As one student explains, "We joke about how it seems like every girl is 5'4", blonde, and fair skinned, but that isn't totally true. St. Olaf is a Norwegian school, and many students have a Scandinavian background. However, there is a place for more diverse students. It seems like the typical St. Olaf student's mindset is open enough to embrace different religions, races, ideas, and beliefs." The true common ground here is that most St. Olaf undergraduates are "highly motivated toward success, whether academic or vocational," and are "also likely…type A personalities" who are "involved in many extracurricular events yet maintain good grades under a full academic load." While "the majority is Lutheran," students are "not particularly conservative or evangelical. They are more liberal politically and ideologically."

ST. OLAF COLLEGE

FINANCIAL AID: 507-646-3019 • E-MAIL: ADMISSIONS@STOLAF.EDU • WEBSITE: WWW.STOLAF.EDU

THE PRINCETON REVIEW SAYS

Admissions

Very important factors considered include: Application essay, academic GPA, rigor of secondary school record. *Important factors considered include:* Recommendation(s), standardized test scores, character/personal qualities, extracurricular activities, talent/ability. *Other factors considered include:* Class rank, alumni/ae relation, first generation, geographical residence, interview, level of applicant's interest, racial/ethnic status, religious affiliation/commitment, state residency, volunteer work, work experience. SAT or ACT required; TOEFL required of all international applicants. High school diploma is required and GED is accepted. *Academic units required:* 4 English, 2 mathematics, 2 science, (1 science labs), 2 foreign language, 1 social studies, 1 history, 2 academic electives. *Academic units recommended:* 4 English, 4 mathematics, 4 science, (2 science labs), 4 foreign language, 2 social studies, 2 history, 4 academic electives.

Financial Aid

Students should submit: FAFSA, CSS/Financial Aid PROFILE, noncustodial PROFILE, business/farm supplement. Regular filing deadline is 4/15. The Princeton Review suggests that all financial aid forms be submitted as soon as possible after January 1. *Need-based scholarships/grants offered:* Federal Pell, SEOG, state scholarships/grants, private scholarships, the school's own gift aid. *Loan aid offered:* FFEL Subsidized Stafford, FFEL Unsubsidized Stafford, FFEL PLUS, Federal Perkins, Federal Nursing, state loans, college/university loans from institutional funds. Applicants will be notified of awards on a rolling basis beginning 3/1. Federal Work-Study Program available. Off-campus job opportunities are fair.

The Inside Word

St. Olaf's national reputation is sharply on the rise, a fact evidenced by a 50 percent increase in the number of applications since 2001. This elevated prominence means St. Olaf must compete for candidates with more prestigious schools; hence, the acceptance rate hasn't dropped as dramatically as one might expect, as these days the school loses more of its admits to the Harvards and Northwesterns of the world than it did in the past. The artificially high acceptance rate masks a highly selective, highly competitive admissions process. Bring your A game.

THE SCHOOL SAYS "..."

From The Admissions Office

"With 3,000 students, St. Olaf College, a residential campus in Northfield, Minnesota, combines a leading liberal arts experience with the dynamic energy of a small university. Forty-four academic majors, 27 intercollegiate sports, a world-renowned music program, and a nationally recognized commitment to international study help this college of the Lutheran church fulfill its mission to develop mind, body, and spirit. St. Olaf leads the nation in the number of baccalaureate graduates who have earned a PhD in mathematics, and is second in theology/religion. Its rigorous academic program has produced three Rhodes scholars and over 50 Fulbright scholars in the past decade.

"As of this book's publication, St. Olaf College did not have information available about their policy regarding the new SAT."

SELECTIVITY

Admissions Rating	93
# of applicants	4,058
% of applicants accepted	54
% of acceptees attending	34
# accepting a place on wait list	352
% admitted from wait list	4
# of early decision applicants	138
% accepted early decision	86

FRESHMAN PROFILE

Range SAT Critical Reading	600–720
Range SAT Math	600–700
Range ACT Composite	26–31
Minimum paper TOEFL	550
Minimum computer TOEFL	213
Average HS GPA	3.65
% graduated top 10% of class	54.1
% graduated top 25% of class	82.3
% graduated top 50% of class	98.8

DEADLINES

Early decision	
Deadline	11/1
Notification	12/15
Early action	
Deadline	12/1
Notification	2/15
Regular	
Priority	1/15
Nonfall registration?	no

APPLICANTS ALSO LOOK AT AND SOMETIMES PREFER

Gustavus Adolphus College
University of Wisconsin—Madison
Carleton College
University of Minnesota—Twin Cities
University of St. Thomas

FINANCIAL FACTS

Financial Aid Rating	96
Annual tuition	$30,600
Room and board	$7,900
Books and supplies	$900
% frosh rec. need-based scholarship or grant aid	62
% UG rec. need-based scholarship or grant aid	65
% frosh rec. non-need-based scholarship or grant aid	31
% UG rec. non-need-based scholarship or grant aid	29
% frosh rec. need-based self-help aid	62
% UG rec. need-based self-help aid	65
% frosh rec. any financial aid	82
% UG rec. any financial aid	83
% UG borrow to pay for school	64
Average cumulative indebtedness	$25,501

STANFORD UNIVERSITY

UNDERGRADUATE ADMISSION, OLD STUDENT UNION 232, STANFORD, CA 94305-3005 • ADMISSIONS: 650-723-2091 • FAX: 650-723-6050

CAMPUS LIFE

Quality of Life Rating	98
Fire Safety Rating	83
Green Rating	92
Type of school	private
Environment	city

STUDENTS

Total undergrad enrollment	6,520
% male/female	52/48
% from out of state	54
% from public high school	60
% live on campus	88
% in (# of) fraternities	NR (17)
% in (# of) sororities	NR (12)
% African American	9
% Asian	24
% Caucasian	41
% Hispanic	12
% Native American	2
% international	6
# of countries represented	68

SURVEY SAYS . . .

School is well run
Students are friendly
Campus feels safe
Students are happy
Lots of beer drinking

ACADEMICS

Academic Rating	99
Calendar	quarter
Student/faculty ratio	6:1
Profs interesting rating	95
Profs accessible rating	86
% classes taught by TAs	5
Most common reg class size	10–19 students
Most common lab size	10–19 students

MOST POPULAR MAJORS

biology/biological sciences
economics
political science and government

STUDENTS SAY " . . ."

Academics

Students insist that Stanford is "the most amazing school in the country, with a great mix of academics, athletics, and weather," and it's hard to argue with them. The school really does offer it all to the laid-back-but-ambitious crowd lucky enough to receive an invite to attend; as one student puts it, "Stanford essentially disproves the theorem that if it sounds too good to be true, it probably is." Undergrads here "can and are able to do so much." Take, for example, the anthropology major who reported "great opportunities such as researching over the summer in the Peruvian Amazon and working with the Center for Ecotourism and Sustainable Development to create a network of indigenous leaders interested in ecotourism." Or the myriad super-curious here who extol "the many interdisciplinary majors: human biology; history, literature, and the arts; materials science and engineering; symbolic systems; science technology and society; public policy; modern thought and literature; urban studies.... It's amazing how many different fields you can combine." And perhaps best of all, "There is not any counter productive cut-throat competition. Staff and students are all very supportive of each other, and it's really an environment where you can explore and succeed."

Life

"Everyone studies all the time, and a lot of people work and are involved with extracurriculars" at Stanford. They also "work out and volunteer. Basically, people try to be perfect." The school "offers so many extracurriculars that it's impossible for students to not be involved and feel welcome," helping to "offset academic stresses" that can be considerable, especially for engineers and premeds. Indeed, "It would be easy to be at Stanford, not take classes and still be busy. There is always something going on: theater performances, a cappella concerts, small-scale concerts every Thursday, major concerts at least once a year, row house parties every weekend…. It's possible to go out Wednesday through Saturday night." Day to day life here "revolves around the amazing sense of dorm community and the great athletic teams." Stanford prides itself on its robust intercollegiate athletic programs, and "Everyone at Stanford lives and breathes Cardinal red." Residential choices "vary. You can live in a great Row House with a huge room and a private chef, or a one-room double in a dorm with awful food. There are a lot of options: dorms, houses, co-ops, apartments, and suites." Students generally avoid Palo Alto ("It's soooo expensive!"), but do find the cash to visit equally pricey San Francisco when their schedules permit.

Student Body

Stanford undergrads describe each other in terms so rapturous it makes one wonder whether there isn't something a little funny about the campus water supply. These "ambitions, driven, and incredibly intelligent" people include every form of high achiever; writes one, "I have been fortunate enough to meet a professional cartoonist, several Olympic athletes, an international math Olympiad participant, a professional rapper, a concert violinist, an equestrian champion, a national rugby champion, and so many other talented people just in my 89-person dorm. There are people who have run with the bulls in Pamplona, ski race every weekend, have written published books, and that ever-elusive person who actually won the national science fair in eighth grade." The vibe is "definitely chill…. There isn't any of the East Coast snobbery/aristocracy here that I picture at the Ivies." Is there anything negative one can say about these people? "There are barely any fat people," one student offers. Ah ha, but there are some. That will likely have to do.

STANFORD UNIVERSITY

FINANCIAL AID: 650-723-3058 • E-MAIL: ADMISSION@STANFORD.EDU • WEBSITE: WWW.STANFORD.EDU

THE PRINCETON REVIEW SAYS

Admissions

Very important factors considered include: Class rank, application essay, academic GPA, recommendation(s), rigor of secondary school record, standardized test scores, character/personal qualities, extracurricular activities, talent/ability. *Other factors considered include:* Alumni/ae relation, first generation, geographical residence, racial/ethnic status, volunteer work, work experience. SAT or ACT required; ACT with Writing component required. High school diploma is required and GED is accepted. *Academic units recommended:* 4 English, 4 mathematics, 3 science, (3 science labs), 3 foreign language, 2 social studies, 1 history.

Financial Aid

Students should submit: FAFSA, CSS/Financial Aid PROFILE. The Princeton Review suggests that all financial aid forms be submitted as soon as possible after January 1. *Need-based scholarships/grants offered:* Federal Pell, SEOG, state scholarships/grants, private scholarships, the school's own gift aid. *Loan aid offered:* FFEL Subsidized Stafford, FFEL Unsubsidized Stafford, FFEL PLUS, Federal Perkins, GATE Loans, SNAP Loans. Applicants will be notified of awards on a rolling basis beginning 4/3. Federal Work-Study Program available. Institutional employment available. Off-campus job opportunities are excellent.

The Inside Word

Stanford admissions is justly praised for its compassionate approach toward applicants, not only those it accepts but those many, many highly qualified candidates whom it must reject. The admissions staff here may be the nation's best at saying "no" without breaking hearts. Applicants should remember that the vast majority of their competition is qualified to attend this school, yet only 11 percent of them will receive the thick envelope. Good luck!

THE SCHOOL SAYS " . . ."

From The Admissions Office

"Stanford looks for distinctive students who exhibit energy, personality, a sense of intellectual vitality and extraordinary impact outside the classroom. While there is no minimum grade point average, class rank, or test score one needs to be admitted to Stanford, the vast majority of successful applicants will be among the strongest students (academically) in their secondary schools. The most compelling applicants for admission will be those who have thus far achieved state, regional, national, and international recognition in their academic and extracurricular areas of interest.

"Stanford currently accepts the Common Application as its exclusive application for admission. In addition to the on-line version of the Common Application, all applicants must submit an on-line Stanford-specific supplement to be considered for admission. The on-line supplement allows candidates to: detail information about an experience they find intellectually engaging; write a note to their freshman year roommate sharing a personal experience they have had; and explain why they feel Stanford is a good fit for them.

"While the SAT or ACT is required for admission, SAT subject tests are not required (and only recommended). AP scores are also not required but may be influential in admission decisions and can be used for placement/credit purposes if an applicant decides to enroll."

SELECTIVITY

Admissions Rating	99
# of applicants	23,958
% of applicants accepted	10
% of acceptees attending	70
# accepting a place on wait list	967

FRESHMAN PROFILE

Range SAT Critical Reading	660–760
Range SAT Math	680–790
Range SAT Writing	660–760
Range ACT Composite	29–33
% graduated top 10% of class	91
% graduated top 25% of class	98
% graduated top 50% of class	100

DEADLINES

Early action	
Deadline	11/1
Notification	12/15
Regular	
Deadline	1/1
Notification	4/1
Nonfall registration?	no

APPLICANTS ALSO LOOK AT AND OFTEN PREFER

Harvard College
Massachusetts Institute of Technology
Yale University

AND SOMETIMES PREFER

California Institute of Technology
Princeton University

FINANCIAL FACTS

Financial Aid Rating	99
Annual tuition	$34,800
Room and board	$10,808
Books and supplies	$1,335
% frosh rec. need-based scholarship or grant aid	45
% UG rec. need-based scholarship or grant aid	44
% frosh rec. non-need-based scholarship or grant aid	2
% UG rec. non-need-based scholarship or grant aid	2
% frosh rec. need-based self-help aid	29
% UG rec. need-based self-help aid	30
% frosh rec. athletic scholarships	7
% UG rec. athletic scholarships	7
% UG rec. any financial aid	78
% UG borrow to pay for school	44
Average cumulative indebtedness	$16,728

STATE UNIVERSITY OF NEW YORK AT BINGHAMTON

PO Box 6000, Binghamton, NY 13902-6001 • Admissions: 607-777-2171 • Fax: 607-777-4445

STUDENTS SAY ". . ."

Academics

With fewer than 12,000 undergraduates, Binghamton University is "a decent sized school that doesn't feel that big." It's thanks to this that "you get to know people easily" here. Yet the school is also large enough to accommodate "a great education in a variety of fields, ranging from the liberal arts to engineering to business to education to nursing." Students report that "the school does the best it can to prepare its students at an Ivy level. It knows that it does not have the name recognition of others but teaches its students the values of hard work so that they can compete with Ivy students for jobs. Students aim for these jobs and are often successful getting them." Professional programs, which are among the most popular here, are "amazing" and "the connection with alumni is great," not to mention "the career development center is awesome," all huge pluses when it comes time for the job search. And the school accomplishes all this at a very reasonable cost. "Everyone here says value is a huge strength for this school," one student explains. Like most state schools, BU has some problems at the administrative level. Administrators "can sometimes be frustrating to deal with. It seems like if you have a problem you end up getting sent to another office. Once you get to that office you're then directed to yet another office, as though the administration really doesn't know the system…. It can be a wild goose chase." Students also warn that "academic advising is atrocious and unhelpful." When it comes to managing its own bureaucracy, some here feel that "the school is too large for itself to handle."

Life

Students tell us that "campus life is really great" at Binghamton, offering "tons of activities to participate in, including club or intramural sports, student government, fraternities/sororities (both social and professional), student groups, and more." Dorms are "convenient" and "clean" (although "living off-campus is less expensive"), and undergrads are kept busy "trying to balance classes, school work, jobs, volunteer work and sports…. There's never enough time for everything you want to do." Some complain that "The weekends can get pretty dull on campus," which is why they opt for beer-soaked fraternity parties or "the bars downtown that don't check ID." According to the drinking crowd, "The weeks can be stressful with a lot of classes, papers and tests, so students tend to unwind on the weekends. Because there is no major city nearby besides Ithaca—which is an hour away—students are forced to drink in their dorms and then head downtown to one of the many frats. Once the frats run out of alcohol, people generally walk about 10 minutes to the bars." However, the drinking scene is by no means the only weekend alternative. As one student explains, "For people not interested in that, there is Late Night Binghamton," which "shows movies, has hypnotists, magicians, or comedians come, has crafts to do, and it's all free."

Student Body

The typical BU undergrad "is someone who was smart in high school"—they had to be to get in here—but were "well-rounded enough so as to not be only invested in academics. In general, although people are relatively smart, they have other things on their mind than pure academics." The campus is "very ethnically diverse," with "a lot of Jewish students and a lot of Asians" factoring into the mix. Geographically, Long Island and New York City are extremely well represented, "but there are many others from around the country and the world." Class background and local weather conspire to make "The North Face" a conspicuous brand on campus.

STATE UNIVERSITY OF NEW YORK AT BINGHAMTON

FINANCIAL AID: 607-777-2428 • E-MAIL: ADMIT@BINGHAMTON.EDU • WEBSITE: WWW.BINGHAMTON.EDU

THE PRINCETON REVIEW SAYS

Admissions

Very important factors considered include: Academic GPA, rigor of secondary school record, standardized test scores. *Important factors considered include:* Class rank, application essay, recommendation(s), extracurricular activities, first generation, volunteer work. *Other factors considered include:* Alumni/ae relation, character/personal qualities, geographical residence, level of applicant's interest, racial/ethnic status, state residency, talent/ability, work experience. SAT or ACT required; ACT with Writing component required. TOEFL required of all international applicants. High school diploma is required and GED is accepted. *Academic units required:* 4 English, 3 mathematics, 2 science, 3 foreign language, 2 social studies. *Academic units recommended:* 4 mathematics, 4 science, 3 foreign language, 3 history.

Financial Aid

Students should submit: FAFSA, state aid form. The Princeton Review suggests that all financial aid forms be submitted as soon as possible after January 1. *Need-based scholarships/grants offered:* Federal Pell, SEOG, state scholarships/grants, private scholarships, the school's own gift aid. *Loan aid offered:* Direct Subsidized Stafford, Direct Unsubsidized Stafford, Direct PLUS, Federal Perkins, Federal Nursing, college/university loans from institutional funds. Applicants will be notified of awards on a rolling basis beginning 3/17. Federal Work-Study Program available. Institutional employment available. Off-campus job opportunities are excellent.

The Inside Word

Binghamton receives nearly 11 applications for every slot in its freshman class. That's bad news for marginal candidates, who should probably start looking elsewhere in the SUNY system if they have their hearts set on attending one. With competition this stiff, you'll need solid test scores and high school grades just to get past the first winnowing stage.

THE SCHOOL SAYS "..."

From The Admissions Office

"SUNY Binghamton has established itself as the premier public university in the Northeast, because of our outstanding undergraduate programs, vibrant campus culture, and committed faculty. Students are academically motivated, but there is a great deal of mutual help as they compete against the standard of a class rather than each other. Faculty and students work side by side in research labs or on artistic pursuits. Achievement, exploration, and leadership are hallmarks of a Binghamton education. Add to that a campus wide commitment to internationalization that includes a robust study abroad program, cultural offerings, languages and international studies, and you have a place where graduates leave prepared for success.

"Students applying for freshman admission for Fall 2008 are required to take the new version of the SAT (or the ACT with the Writing section). SAT Subject Test scores are not required for admission."

SELECTIVITY

Admissions Rating	94
# of applicants	25,242
% of applicants accepted	39
% of acceptees attending	24
# accepting a place on wait list	664
% admitted from wait list	15

FRESHMAN PROFILE

Range SAT Critical Reading	570–660
Range SAT Math	610–690
Range ACT Composite	25–29
Minimum paper TOEFL	550
Minimum computer TOEFL	213
Minimum web-based TOEFL	80
Average HS GPA	3.7
% graduated top 10% of class	49
% graduated top 25% of class	85
% graduated top 50% of class	99

DEADLINES

Early action	
Deadline	11/15
Notification	1/1
Regular	
Priority	12/1
Notification	4/1
Nonfall registration?	yes

APPLICANTS ALSO LOOK AT
AND OFTEN PREFER
Cornell University
University of Pennsylvania
AND SOMETIMES PREFER
New York University
Boston University

FINANCIAL FACTS

Financial Aid Rating	87
Annual in-state tuition	$4,350
Annual out-of-state tuition	$10,610
Room and board	$9,188
Required fees	$1,662
Books and supplies	$800
% frosh rec. need-based scholarship or grant aid	35
% UG rec. need-based scholarship or grant aid	39
% frosh rec. non-need-based scholarship or grant aid	13
% UG rec. non-need-based scholarship or grant aid	10
% frosh rec. need-based self-help aid	40
% UG rec. need-based self-help aid	42
% frosh rec. athletic scholarships	4
% UG rec. athletic scholarships	2
% frosh rec. any financial aid	78
% UG rec. any financial aid	68
% UG borrow to pay for school	56
Average cumulative indebtedness	$14,530

STATE UNIVERSITY OF NEW YORK AT GENESEO

ONE COLLEGE CIRCLE, GENESEO, NY 14454-1401 • ADMISSIONS: 585-245-5571 • FAX: 585-245-5550

CAMPUS LIFE

Quality of Life Rating	**81**
Fire Safety Rating	**84**
Green Rating	**77**
Type of school	public
Environment	village

STUDENTS

Total undergrad enrollment	5,376
% male/female	42/58
% from out of state	1
% from public high school	81
% live on campus	56
% in (# of) fraternities	9 (9)
% in (# of) sororities	11 (11)
% African American	2
% Asian	6
% Caucasian	73
% Hispanic	3
% international	2
# of countries represented	30

SURVEY SAYS . . .

Lab facilities are great
Great computer facilities
Students are friendly
Campus feels safe
Low cost of living
Students are happy
Lots of beer drinking
Hard liquor is popular

ACADEMICS

Academic Rating	**80**
Calendar	semester
Student/faculty ratio	19:1
Profs interesting rating	73
Profs accessible rating	79
Most common reg class size	10–19 students

MOST POPULAR MAJORS
elementary education and teaching
biology/biological sciences
business/commerce

STUDENTS SAY ". . ."

Academics

State University of New York—Geneseo, the school that considers itself the Honors College of the SUNY system, offers "challenging academics in a very home-like atmosphere" where "you don't get lost in the crowd like bigger schools." As one student puts it, "Geneseo is all about the classic college experience: a small town, rigorous academics, and having fun at the same time." One in five students pursues a teaching degree here, leading some to conclude that "Geneseo focuses mainly on training future teachers, but for the rest of us, they are preparing us for our next step into employment or further education." Nearly as many study business and marketing; the "best academic departments are by far the natural sciences," however, where "the students are the brightest, the courses are the toughest, and the professors really know their stuff." Geneseo also provides "great pre-professional (medical, dental, pharmacological) preparation in sciences." Students here enjoy a small-school experience that includes "superior academics, small, intimate classes, and professors who truly care about students and will offer them every opportunity to succeed" as well as "many study abroad options (students are encouraged to explore the world)." They also point out that "Leadership and research are also a great focus at SUNY Geneseo. If a student wants to do individual research, professors are more than willing to help students organize projects and carry them out." For these and other reasons, students describe Geneseo as a school "for the academically inclined non-rich citizen. It's the Harvard of the SUNY system."

Life

"The great thing about Geneseo is that there's always a party to go to if you want, but there's no pressure to go," and "It's perfectly acceptable to stay home and watch movies with friends on the weekends or even study on Saturday nights." Indeed, students tell us that "There is so much more to do than just party. The college always has amazing activities going on in the union. Every weekend there are crafts and games, and sometimes they bring in comedians or performers…. At the Halloween Monster Mash Bash, there is a costume ball and activities as well as a raffle for really great prizes. There are far too many activities to list here!" Intercollegiate hockey games "are a big hit, and lots of students go to them on weekends." There are "also many different organizations you can get involved in, including several volunteer organizations, intramural sports, and different hobbies." Despite all the alternatives, some students tell us that because "the student body isn't all that creative with what they come up with to do on the weekends… most weekends most students just end up drinking themselves stupid." The town of Geneseo is little help; "There is nothing to do in town, and the closest city is a 45-minute drive away (Rochester, NY)."

Student Body

"The typical student here at SUNY Geneseo is much like that of the ordinary New York State public high school," except that "Most of the school is white (the college is making efforts to diversify). Despite the majority being white, there is still a wide diversity of student types, be it that they are from different backgrounds, economic classes, or simply around the nation." Undergrads "spend most of their time studying in Milne Library, and those who choose not to study usually don't make it to graduation." There are "a few minority and gay/lesbian/bisexual students" here, "but they really are the minority and often have difficulty adjusting. Many students feel like outsiders and transfer before graduating." Students tell us that "The two largest minorities are Asian and African American…the different ethnic groups tend to clump together."

FINANCIAL AID: 716-245-5731 • E-MAIL: ADMISSIONS@GENESEO.EDU • WEBSITE: WWW.GENESEO.EDU

THE PRINCETON REVIEW SAYS

Admissions

Very important factors considered include: Rigor of secondary school record, standardized test scores. *Important factors considered include:* Application essay, academic GPA, recommendation(s), extracurricular activities, racial/ethnic status, talent/ability. *Other factors considered include:* Class rank, first generation, level of applicant's interest, volunteer work, work experience. SAT or ACT required; TOEFL required of all international applicants. High school diploma is required and GED is accepted. *Academic units recommended:* 4 English, 4 mathematics, 4 science, 4 foreign language, 4 social studies.

Financial Aid

Students should submit: FAFSA, state aid form. Regular filing deadline is 2/15. The Princeton Review suggests that all financial aid forms be submitted as soon as possible after January 1. *Need-based scholarships/grants offered:* Federal Pell, SEOG, state scholarships/grants, private scholarships, the school's own gift aid. *Loan aid offered:* FFEL Subsidized Stafford, FFEL Unsubsidized Stafford, FFEL PLUS, Federal Perkins, state loans, alternative loans. Applicants will be notified of awards on a rolling basis beginning 3/15. Federal Work-Study Program available. Institutional employment available. Off-campus job opportunities are poor.

The Inside Word

Geneseo is the most selective of SUNY's 13 undergraduate colleges and more selective than three of SUNY's university centers. No formulaic approach is used here. Expect a thorough review of your academic accomplishments (over half the student body graduated in the top 10 percent of their class) and your extracurricular/personal side. Admissions standards are tempered only by a somewhat low yield of admits who enroll. The school competes for students with some big-time schools, meaning it must admit many more students than it expects will attend.

THE SCHOOL SAYS "..."

From The Admissions Office

"Geneseo has carved a distinctive niche among the nation's premier public liberal arts colleges. The college now competes for students with some of the nation's most selective private colleges, including Colgate, Vassar, Hamilton, and Boston College. Founded in 1871, the college occupies a 220-acre hillside campus in the historic Village of Geneseo, overlooking the scenic Genesee Valley. As a residential campus—with nearly two-thirds of the students living in college residence halls—it provides a rich and varied program of social, cultural, recreational, and scholarly activities. Geneseo is noted for its distinctive core curriculum and the extraordinary opportunities it offers undergraduates to pursue independent study and research with faculty who value close working relationships with talented students. Equally impressive is the remarkable success of its graduates, nearly one-third of whom study at leading graduate and professional schools immediately following graduation.

"For Fall 2008, SUNY Geneseo will use either SAT or ACT test results in the admission selection process. The SAT Writing test result will not be used. SAT Subject Test results are not required but will be considered if the applicant submits the test results."

SELECTIVITY

Admissions Rating	94
# of applicants	10,274
% of applicants accepted	36
% of acceptees attending	28
# accepting a place on wait list	320
# of early decision applicants	323
% accepted early decision	42

FRESHMAN PROFILE

Range SAT Critical Reading	600–690
Range SAT Math	620–690
Range ACT Composite	28–30
Minimum paper TOEFL	525
Minimum computer TOEFL	197
Average HS GPA	3.8
% graduated top 10% of class	57
% graduated top 25% of class	88
% graduated top 50% of class	99

DEADLINES

Early decision	
Deadline	11/15
Notification	12/15
Regular	
Deadline	1/1
Notification	3/1
Nonfall registration?	yes

APPLICANTS ALSO LOOK AT

AND OFTEN PREFER
Hamilton College
Cornell University
Colgate University

AND SOMETIMES PREFER
Vassar College
Skidmore College

AND RARELY PREFER
Nazareth College of Rochester
State University of New York—Stony Brook University

FINANCIAL FACTS

Financial Aid Rating	89
Annual in-state tuition	$4,350
Annual out-of-state tuition	$10,610
Room and board	$8,550
Required fees	$1,266
Books and supplies	$800
% frosh rec. need-based scholarship or grant aid	25
% UG rec. need-based scholarship or grant aid	43
% frosh rec. non-need-based scholarship or grant aid	27
% UG rec. non-need-based scholarship or grant aid	8
% frosh rec. need-based self-help aid	20
% UG rec. need-based self-help aid	37
% frosh rec. any financial aid	68
% UG rec. any financial aid	75
% UG borrow to pay for school	65
Average cumulative indebtedness	$18,300

STATE UNIVERSITY OF NEW YORK—PURCHASE COLLEGE

ADMISSIONS OFFICE, 735 ANDERSON HILL ROAD, PURCHASE, NY 10577 • ADMISSIONS: 914-251-6300 • FAX: 914-251-6314

STUDENTS SAY ". . ."

Academics

Purchase College is the SUNY system's answer to the region's many high-priced conservatories and arts schools set within a public liberal arts and sciences college. While it may not have the cache of Julliard or Rhode Island School of Design, students here don't feel they're getting shorted. On the contrary, they laud the teachers with professional experience (the school's proximity to New York City helps here) who "are caring, inspirational, and focused." They also appreciate the fact that access to Purchase's School of Liberal Arts and Sciences provides "a diverse curriculum" with a greater liberal arts focus than you'll find at most arts schools. Of course, they also love how they're "paying state tuition for a school full of ex-Ivy League teachers who were all too eccentric for Ivy schools, so now they teach at Purchase!" The school's more conventional liberal arts and science offerings notwithstanding, Purchase is primarily "an artistic community." Peer "work in the dance, music, photography, film, art, and acting conservator[ies] is amazing, and it is wonderful to be able to experience the work of these students." Classes tend to be small "with a heavy emphasis on writing skills." Students "are usually well-read and prepared for discussion," and, because "Class sizes are not too large," they "are able to contribute to both the structure of the class and the content." Outside the creative arts, Purchase excels in psychology, journalism, premed, biology, and creative writing.

Life

"Campus activities are amazing" at Purchase, a result of the art school/proximity-to-New York combo, which helps bring "nationally recognized figures in the arts to speak on a regular basis, including Art Speigelman and Tony Kushner. There are also free shows several days a week performed by excellent indie bands like My Brightest Diamond and Gregory and the Hawk" as well as numerous events featuring student performances, such as "Fall Ball, a major campus event [that] features a drag show performed by students. Given that many people who dance or sing are in one of the conservatories, it's very entertaining." And then there's New York City, "just a 40-minute train ride away" and "the most popular destination for entertainment." When students "plan on doing something special, [they] plan on going there for the weekend." Purchase has the requisite college parties, but "Excessive drinking is probably far less common at Purchase than at a more frat-oriented school." Students tend to keep very busy with schoolwork, especially those in the conservatories, who "spend a great deal of time practicing and studying."

Student Body

At Purchase, "many students who would be stereotyped as 'freaks' are not that freaky." This group includes "the 'artsy' type" who has "green hair" and "piercings" and is "blatantly alternative to pop culture." Such students "comprise a good half of the student population," and, as a result, "they make everyone else considered 'normal' look weird." That being said, the student body here is "extremely diverse." There's "an outspoken gay community and a ton of different ethnicities." Because of the school's "urban feel, racism is virtually obsolete, and there is no hostility towards those of different sexual orientations." "Most everyone finds [his or her] niche at Purchase." In all areas, students "like to dive deep into their interests . . . Purchase is where the dancers, musicians, actors, visual artists, liberal arts and science majors, etc. are all interacting with one another to create a really interesting group of students."

STATE UNIVERSITY OF NEW YORK—PURCHASE COLLEGE

FINANCIAL AID: 914-251-6350 • E-MAIL: ADMISSIONS@PURCHASE.EDU • WEBSITE: WWW.PURCHASE.EDU

THE PRINCETON REVIEW SAYS

Admissions

Very important factors considered include: Application essay, academic GPA, talent/ability. *Important factors considered include:* Standardized test scores. *Other factors considered include:* Recommendation(s), rigor of secondary school record, character/personal qualities, extracurricular activities, interview, SAT recommended; SAT or ACT required; TOEFL required of all international applicants. High school diploma is required and GED is accepted.

Financial Aid

Students should submit: FAFSA, state aid form. The Princeton Review suggests that all financial aid forms be submitted as soon as possible after January 1. *Need-based scholarships/grants offered:* Federal Pell, SEOG, state scholarships/grants, private scholarships, the school's own gift aid. *Loan aid offered:* FFEL Subsidized Stafford, FFEL Unsubsidized Stafford, FFEL PLUS, Federal Perkins Applicants will be notified of awards on a rolling basis beginning 3/1. Federal Work-Study Program available. Institutional employment available. Off-campus job opportunities are excellent.

The Inside Word

About one-third of Purchase College undergraduates enroll in the School of the Arts. All must undergo some type of audition or portfolio review to gain admission; this is the most important piece of the application. Traditional application components—such as high school transcript, test scores, and personal essay—are also considered, but do not figure as prominently. Applicants to the School of Liberal Arts and Sciences undergo a more conventional application review.

THE SCHOOL SAYS "..."

From The Admissions Office

"At Purchase College, you're encouraged to 'Think Wide Open.' The campus combines the energy and excitement of professional training in the performing and the visual arts with the intellectual traditions and spirit of discovery of the humanities and sciences. A Purchase College education emphasizes creativity, individual accomplishment, openness, and exploration. It culminates in a senior research or creative project that may focus on civic engagement or interdisciplinary work to become an excellent springboard to a career or to graduate or professional school. The Conservatories of Art and Design, Dance, Music, and Theatre Arts and Film that make up the School of the Arts deliver a cohort-based education with apprenticeships and other professional opportunities in nearby New York City.

"You'll find a unique and engaging atmosphere at Purchase, whether you are a student in the arts, humanities, natural sciences, or social sciences. You choose among a wide variety of programs, including arts management, journalism, creative writing, environmental science, new media, dramatic writing, premed, pre-law, and education. You'll attend performances by your friends, see world-renowned artists on stage at the Performing Arts Center, and experience the artworks on display in the Neuberger Museum of Art (one of the largest campus art museums in the country)—all without leaving campus. The new student services building, along with an enhanced student services website, is making Purchase a lot more user-friendly for its students.

"Admissions requirements vary with each program in the college and can include auditions, portfolio reviews, essays, writing samples, and interviews.

"In addition to individual program requirements, Purchase College requires SAT or ACT scores to complete your application. You can apply on line through the college website at www.purchase.edu/admissions."

SELECTIVITY

Admissions Rating	**84**
# of applicants	7,388
% of applicants accepted	30
% of acceptees attending	31
# of early decision applicants	11
% accepted early decision	73

FRESHMAN PROFILE

Range SAT Critical Reading	510–620
Range SAT Math	480–590
Minimum paper TOEFL	550
Minimum computer TOEFL	213
Average HS GPA	3.04
% graduated top 10% of class	10
% graduated top 25% of class	32
% graduated top 50% of class	72

DEADLINES

Early decision	
Deadline	11/1
Notification	12/5
Regular	
Priority	3/1
Deadline	7/15
Notification	5/1
Nonfall registration?	yes

APPLICANTS ALSO LOOK AT

AND OFTEN PREFER
New York University
The Juilliard School

AND SOMETIMES PREFER
Brandeis University
Carnegie Mellon University
State University of New York—Stony
Brook University

AND RARELY PREFER
Hofstra University
Emerson College

FINANCIAL FACTS

Financial Aid Rating	**67**
Annual in-state tuition	$4,350
Annual out-of-state tuition	$10,610
Room and board	$9,028
Required fees	$1,359
Books and supplies	$1,500
% frosh rec. any financial aid	78
% UG rec. any financial aid	77
% UG borrow to pay for school	78
Average cumulative	
indebtedness	$20,222

CAMPUS LIFE

Quality of Life Rating	**62**
Fire Safety Rating	**60***
Green Rating	**84**
Type of school	public
Environment	town

STUDENTS

Total undergrad enrollment	15,222
% male/female	50/50
% from out of state	5
% from public high school	90
% live on campus	52
% in (# of) fraternities	1 (17)
% in (# of) sororities	1 (17)
% African American	9
% Asian	22
% Caucasian	35
% Hispanic	8
% international	6
# of countries represented	86

SURVEY SAYS . . .

Class discussions are rare
Great computer facilities
Great library
Diverse student types on campus
Lots of beer drinking
(Almost) everyone smokes

ACADEMICS

Academic Rating	**70**
Calendar	semester
Student/faculty ratio	18:1
Profs interesting rating	62
Profs accessible rating	61

MOST POPULAR MAJORS

psychology
biology/biological sciences
health professions and related
clinical sciences

STUDENTS SAY ". . ."

Academics

Stony Brook University "is a great place for ambitious, focused students who actually want to learn something" at a "great research university in which classes are challenging and interesting." Nearly half the undergraduates here pursue traditionally punishing majors such as biology, computer science ("one of the best undergraduate computer science programs," according to at least one student), and engineering. The school also boasts "a strong marine biology program," a popular undergraduate business program, and a solid selection of liberal arts majors. Students in the science and tech majors describe the school as "challenging but worth it," noting that "the sciences here are amazing. Now that I'm interviewing for medical schools, I'm seeing just how highly they think of Stony Brook's undergraduate science programs!" Professors are accomplished and, while "They can be boring, they know what they're teaching like the back of their hand. They will be very helpful in office hours, as long as you ask questions that show them you're trying." As at similar schools, "The only thing you have to watch out for, occasionally, is getting a professor who does not speak English well; that can cause some problems!" Students have "plenty of research opportunities" here, which is another plus. Stony Brook's administration "may consist of nice people, but it's pretty poorly organized. When there is some sort of paperwork involved, nothing ever goes right the first time around. Also, nothing is convenient, and you'll usually have to go in circles to get something done." Most students find the difficulties worth enduring and focus instead on how the school delivers "a great education for a reasonable price."

Life

"Life at Stony Brook depends on whom you surround yourself with," students tell us. While "a lot of students complain that there's nothing to do on campus," others counter that "the problem is that students aren't willing to put in the effort to find those activities." One undergrad explains, "There are many activities in campus life. However, you won't be aware of them at all if you don't . . . look them up. There are a lot of places where you can go play sports, and most dorms have places to play pool, Ping-Pong, or just watch TV." The school is home to "lots of student clubs with something for everyone" and Division I intercollegiate athletic teams, but "No one goes to athletic games. It's really depressing as a pep band member to play to a dead crowd." Hometown Stony Brook "is basically suburban. It is not the best college town. There are a few clubs and bars in the area that some students go to on Thursday nights. However, you have to have a car to get there. . . . If I want to have fun, I generally have to go into the city [NYC]. The city is about 2 hours away by train."

Student Body

The typical student at Stony Brook University "is a middle-class Long Island or Queens kid of Jewish, East Asian, or Indian background." Minority populations are large across a broad demographic range; the school is home to many who are "either Asian, African American, or Hispanic and very, very liberal." Subpopulations "tends to stick to themselves. . . . The atypical students are probably quite miserable at Stony Brook. There is definitely a very Long Island high school–like atmosphere," in part because of the large commuter population and in part because the student body is so large. One student writes, "All students fit in, but the student body is often impersonal, and it is very difficult to develop lasting friendships and relationships as a result."

FINANCIAL AID: 631-632-6840 • E-MAIL: ENROLL@STONYBROOK.EDU • WEBSITE: WWW.STONYBROOK.EDU

THE PRINCETON REVIEW SAYS

Admissions

Very important factors considered include: Rigor of secondary school record, academic GPA, atandardized test scores. *Important factors considered include:* Class rank, application essay, recommendation(s). *Other factors considered include:* Interview, Extracurricular activities, Talent/ability, Character/personal qualities, Alumni/ae relation, State residency, Volunteer work, Work experience, Level of applicant's interest. TOEFL required of all international applicants.

Financial Aid

The Princeton Review suggests that all financial aid forms be submitted as soon as possible after January 1. Off-campus job opportunities are excellent.

The Inside Word

Liberal arts and social science candidates with above-average grades and test scores should encounter little difficulty gaining entry to SUNY Stony Brook. Students in technical fields (engineering, applied mathematics, computer science), in business, and in music must clear some higher hurdles. You can indicate "undecided" for your major on your application, but know that this does not guarantee you entry into these more competitive majors; you'll still have to meet the admissions requirements when you finally declare a major.

THE SCHOOL SAYS "..."

From The Admissions Office

"Stony Brook is ranked among the top 2 percent of universities worldwide by the *London Times Higher Education Supplement* and is a flagship campus of the State University of New York. *U.S. News & World Report* has ranked Stony Brook among the top 100 best national universities. The Wall Street Journal has ranked us eighth in the nation among public institutions placing students in elite graduate schools in medicine, law, and business. Our graduates include Carolyn Porco, the leader of the Imaging Team for the Cassini mission to Saturn; John Hennessy, the president of Stanford University; and Scott Higham, a Pulitzer Prize-winning investigative journalist for the Washington Post who has come to speak to students at our new School of Journalism.

"Situated on 1,100 wooded acres on the North Shore of Long Island, Stony Brook offers more than 150 majors, minors, and combined-degree programs for undergraduates, including our Fast Track MBA program, a thriving research environment, and a dynamic first-year experience in one of six small undergraduate communities. Stony Brook Southampton is our new residential campus focused on sustainability. Faculty include four members of our School of Marine and Atmospheric Sciences who are recent co-winners of the 2007 Nobel Peace Prize.

"Students enjoy comfortable campus housing, outstanding recreational facilities that include a new stadium, modern student activities center, and indoor sports complex. In addition, the Staller Center for the Arts offers spectacular theatrical and musical performances throughout the year.

"We invite students who possess both intellectual curiosity and academic ability to explore the countless exciting opportunities available at Stony Brook. Freshmen applying for admission to the university for Fall 2008 are required to take the SAT (or the ACT with the Writing section). SAT Subject Test scores are recommended, but not required."

SELECTIVITY

Admissions Rating	60*
# of applicants	24,060
% of applicants accepted	43
% of acceptees attending	27

FRESHMAN PROFILE

Range SAT Critical Reading	520–620
Range SAT Math	560–660
Minimum paper TOEFL	550
Minimum computer TOEFL	213
Minimum web-based TOEFL	80

DEADLINES

Regular	12/01
Nonfall registration?	Yes

APPLICANTS ALSO LOOK AT
AND OFTEN PREFER
New York University
State University of New York at Albany
State University of New York at Binghamton

AND SOMETIMES PREFER
Rutgers, The State University of New Jersey—New Brunswick
University of Connecticut
Penn State—University Park
State University of New York at Geneseo

AND RARELY PREFER
Hofstra University
Pace University
Adelphi University

FINANCIAL FACTS

Financial Aid Rating	65
Annual in-state tuition	$4,350
Annual out-of-state tuition	$10,610
Room and board	$9,170
Required fees	$1,480
Books and supplies	$900
% frosh rec. need-based scholarship or grant aid	51
% UG rec. need-based scholarship or grant aid	51
% frosh rec. non-need-based scholarship or grant aid	5
% UG rec. non-need-based scholarship or grant aid	5
% frosh rec. need-based self-help aid	37
% UG rec. need-based self-help aid	40
% frosh rec. athletic scholarships	2
% UG rec. athletic scholarships	1
% frosh rec. any financial aid	74
% UG rec. any financial aid	67
% UG borrow to pay for school	71
Average cumulative indebtedness	$15,076

STATE UNIVERSITY OF NEW YORK—UNIVERSITY AT ALBANY

OFFICE OF UNDERGRAD ADMISSIONS, 1400 WASHINGTON AVE., ALBANY, NY 12222 • ADMISSIONS: 518-442-5435 • FAX: 518-442-5383

CAMPUS LIFE

Quality of Life Rating	61
Fire Safety Rating	60*
Green Rating	88
Type of school	public
Environment	city

STUDENTS

Total undergrad enrollment	12,449
% male/female	51/49
% from out of state	5
% live on campus	57
% in (# of) fraternities	4 (11)
% in (# of) sororities	5 (18)
% African American	9
% Asian	6
% Caucasian	58
% Hispanic	7
% international	2
# of countries represented	91

SURVEY SAYS . . .
Great library
Diverse student types on campus
Lots of beer drinking
Hard liquor is popular
(Almost) everyone smokes

ACADEMICS

Academic Rating	63
Calendar	semester
Student/faculty ratio	19:1
Profs interesting rating	61
Profs accessible rating	61
% classes taught by TAs	7
Most common reg class size	20–29 students
Most common lab size	10–19 students

MOST POPULAR MAJORS
English language and literature
psychology
business/commerce

STUDENTS SAY " . . ."

Academics
Is SUNY Albany (UAlbany to those in the know) the perfect-sized school? Many here think so. Students describe it as "a big school numbers-wise that feels small." Notes one student, "It has a very broad range of quality academic programs, which is very important for an undecided senior in high school." Another adds, "If you know what you want and are motivated, the sky is the limit." The school exploits its location in the state capital to bolster programs in political science, criminal justice, and business, and it "offers internship opportunities to college students that very few schools can." Other standout departments include psychology, Japanese studies, mathematics, and many of the hard sciences. Professors here vary widely in quality, but a surprising number "are receptive, active, and engaging"—in other words, "a lot more accessible than I would have thought for a school this big." Teachers are especially willing to "go out of their way to help students who are interested in learning, come to class regularly, and care about their academic work." The administration, as at most state-run schools, "is basically an over-bloated bureaucracy. Students are sent from department to department in each of their endeavors. It is advisable to avoid [the] administration if at all possible."

Life
There are three distinct social orbits on the Albany campus. Some students take the initiative "by joining one of the many clubs or groups or getting involved with the student government." Others "party for a good time," telling us that "any night of the week you can find people to go out to the bars and clubs with you" and that "the average night ends between 2:30–4:00 A.M." Both of these groups are likely to tell you that "there is a lot to do in Albany and the surrounding area," including "a great arts district, tons of awesome restaurants, museums, [and] a state park." A third, sizable group primarily complains about the cold weather, and asserts that "there's nothing to do in Albany." The school works to excite these students with "fun programs and entertainers who come to the campus. We have had a series of comedians, rappers/singers, guests from MTV and VH1, authors, political figures, musical performances, sporting events, spirit events, and many other things around campus." School spirit is on the rise among all groups, we're told. The reason? "This year our basketball team began winning, and everyone came out of the woodwork to support them—it was really a great thing to see."

Student Body
Undergrads here believe that the student body is very diverse in terms of ethnicity and also in terms of personality type; one student observes, "You have your motivated students [who] get good grades, are involved, and get amazing jobs in NYC after college. Then you have your unmotivated kids [who] complain, don't go to class, and blame a bad grade on the professor (when really it is because they crammed the night before and didn't go to class)." Geographically, the school is less diverse. Nearly everyone is a New York State resident, with many coming from "downstate New York"—Long Island, New York City, and Westchester County. There's a fair amount of upstate kids as well, and "a lot of people have certain stereotypes in their heads when they first come to Albany. The Long Islander has his idea about the upstater and vice versa. After a few weeks, though, people see that these aren't always true. I think people from anywhere get along pretty well." The international students, who form a small but noticeable contingent, "tend to keep to themselves," perhaps "due to a culture or language barrier." About one-quarter of the campus population is Jewish.

STATE UNIVERSITY OF NEW YORK—UNIVERSITY AT ALBANY

FINANCIAL AID: 518-442-5757 • E-MAIL: UGADMISSIONS@ALBANY.EDU • WEBSITE: WWW.ALBANY.EDU

THE PRINCETON REVIEW SAYS

Admissions

Very important factors considered include: Class rank, academic GPA, recommendation(s), rigor of secondary school record, standardized test scores, character/personal qualities. *Important factors considered include:* Application essay. *Other factors considered include:* Alumni/ae relation, extracurricular activities, first generation, geographical residence, talent/ability, volunteer work, work experience. SAT or ACT required; ACT with Writing component required. TOEFL required of all international applicants. High school diploma is required and GED is accepted. *Academic units required:* 4 English, 2 mathematics, 2 science, (2 science labs), 1 foreign language, 3 social studies, 2 history, 4 academic electives. *Academic units recommended:* 4 mathematics, 3 science, (3 science labs), 3 foreign language.

Financial Aid

Students should submit: FAFSA, NY State residents should apply for TAP on-line at www.tapweb.org. The Princeton Review suggests that all financial aid forms be submitted as soon as possible after January 1. *Need-based scholarships/grants offered:* Federal Pell, SEOG, state scholarships/grants. *Loan aid offered:* FFEL Subsidized Stafford, FFEL Unsubsidized Stafford, FFEL PLUS, Federal Perkins Applicants will be notified of awards on a rolling basis beginning 3/15. Federal Work-Study Program available. Institutional employment available. Off-campus job opportunities are excellent.

The Inside Word

In November 2006, *The Wall Street Journal* noted a growing trend among students who, in the past, had limited their postsecondary options to high-end private schools: More such students, the paper reported, have broadened their vision to include prestigious state schools such as SUNY Albany. The driving force, unsurprisingly, is economic. In the event of an unlikely decline in the cost of private education, expect admissions at schools like UAlbany to grow more competitive in coming years.

THE SCHOOL SAYS "..."

From The Admissions Office

"Increasing numbers of well-prepared students are discovering the benefits of study in UAlbany's nationally ranked programs and are taking advantage of outstanding internship and employment opportunities in Upstate New York's 'Tech Valley.' The already strong undergraduate program is being further enhanced by the recently established Honors College, a university-wide program for ambitious students. Building upon the long-standing success of the University Scholars Program, the Honors College offers enhanced honors courses and co-curricular options including honors housing.

"Ten schools and colleges, including the nation's first College of Nanoscale Science and Engineering, offer bachelor's, master's, and doctoral programs to more than 12,000 undergraduates and 5,000 graduate students. An award-winning advisement program helps students take advantage of all these options by customizing the undergraduate experiences. More than two-thirds of Albany graduates go on for advanced degrees, and acceptance to law and medical school is above the national average.

"Student life on campus includes 200 clubs, honor societies, and other groups, and 19 Division I varsity teams. With 19 other colleges in the region, Albany is a great college town, adjacent to the spectacular natural and recreational centers of New York and New England.

"Freshmen are awarded over $800,000 in merit scholarships each year and nearly three-quarters of our students receive financial aid. Plus, *Kiplinger's Personal Finance* ranks us in the nation's 'Top 50 for Excellence and Affordability.' All applicants must submit either the new SAT or the ACT with Writing component."

SELECTIVITY

Admissions Rating	83
# of applicants	20,249
% of applicants accepted	52
% of acceptees attending	24

FRESHMAN PROFILE

Range SAT Critical Reading	520–600
Range SAT Math	540–620
Range ACT Composite	23–26
Minimum paper TOEFL	550
Minimum computer TOEFL	213
Average HS GPA	3.4
% graduated top 10% of class	15
% graduated top 25% of class	49
% graduated top 50% of class	90

DEADLINES

Early action	
Deadline	11/15
Notification	1/1
Regular	
Priority	1/15
Deadline	3/1
Notification	rolling
Nonfall registration?	yes

FINANCIAL FACTS

Financial Aid Rating	74
Annual in-state tuition	$4,350
Annual out-of-state tuition	$10,610
Room and board	$9,032
Required fees	$1,668
Books and supplies	$1,000
% frosh rec. need-based scholarship or grant aid	50
% UG rec. need-based scholarship or grant aid	49
% frosh rec. non-need-based scholarship or grant aid	2
% UG rec. non-need-based scholarship or grant aid	2
% frosh rec. need-based self-help aid	48
% UG rec. need-based self-help aid	46
% frosh rec. athletic scholarships	1
% UG rec. athletic scholarships	1
% frosh rec. any financial aid	61
% UG rec. any financial aid	60
% UG borrow to pay for school	85
Average cumulative indebtedness	$13,842

THE BEST 368 COLLEGES ■ 521

STATE UNIVERSITY OF NEW YORK—UNIVERSITY AT BUFFALO

15 CAPEN HALL, BUFFALO, NY 14260-1660 • ADMISSIONS: 716-645-6900 • FAX: 716-645-6411

CAMPUS LIFE

Quality of Life Rating	74
Fire Safety Rating	60*
Green Rating	60*
Type of school	public
Environment	metropolis

STUDENTS

Total undergrad enrollment	18,779
% male/female	54/46
% from out of state	4
% live on campus	40
% in (# of) fraternities	2 (19)
% in (# of) sororities	4 (14)
% African American	7
% Asian	9
% Caucasian	60
% Hispanic	4
% international	10
# of countries represented	113

SURVEY SAYS . . .
Great library
Diverse student types on campus
Student publications are popular
Lots of beer drinking
Hard liquor is popular

ACADEMICS

Academic Rating	71
Calendar	semester
Student/faculty ratio	16:1
Profs interesting rating	62
Profs accessible rating	67
% classes taught by TAs	12
Most common	
reg class size	20–29 students
Most common	
lab size	20–29 students

MOST POPULAR MAJORS
engineering
psychology
business/commerce

STUDENTS SAY ". . ."

Academics

Offering "more academic programs per dollar than any other university in the state," SUNY Buffalo (UB for short) "is about choices. You can choose many different . . . combinations of academics and social activities with the support in place." Students brag that UB's "Programs are all of the highest quality, translating [into] a best-value education for students." The School of Engineering and Applied Science in particular "is well respected" and "works with corporate partners in a variety of ways that range from joint-research ventures to continuing education to co-op work arrangements for our students." Other stand-out offerings include: pharmacy, physical therapy, a popular business and management school "that is ranked highly," "a solid undergrad and grad architecture program," and "one of the top nursing programs in the state." Of course, a school with this much to offer is bound to be large, making it "easy not to attend class and fall through the cracks, so one must be self-motivated to do well." Administrative tasks are occasionally Kafkaesque, with "a lot of red tape to go through to get anything done. I feel like a pebble being kicked around when trying to get support or services," notes one student. Many students point out that support services and contact with professors improves during junior and senior years when students are pursuing their majors and forging stronger relationships within their departments.

Life

UB is divided into two campuses. Traditionally, South Campus in Northeast Buffalo has been where "the parties are," though students say, "It's much less safe than North Campus," which is located in the suburban enclave of Amherst. The recent closing of several bars near South Campus has made it less of a party destination than it was in years past; these days many students report going to downtown Buffalo "to go clubbing." Students living on North Campus describe it as "its own little city. We have food services, our own bus system, a highway, even our own zip codes. If you know how to play, North Campus is just as much fun as Main Street [which runs by South Campus]; you just need to know where to go." The North Campus, which features "a lake and a nice bike path for when you want to escape from the hectic [atmosphere]" of academic life, is the more populous of the two; the inter-campus bus system is "convenient," although a car is preferred. Students tell us that "between all of the clubs and organizations, the Office of Student Life, athletics, and the Student Association, there is always something to do" on campus. The school's Division I sports teams "are a big hit around here. Even if we are the worst in the division, we still cheer hard and go crazy for our guys and girls." Those who explore Buffalo extol its "amazing art and music scene."

Student Body

Because of UB's size, "You can find just about every kind of person there is here. Everyone has a place in this large and diverse student population." As one student notes, "Although the typical student is of traditional college age, there really isn't a 'typical' student—the student body is very diverse in terms of religion, ethnicity, nationality, age, gender, and orientation. 'Atypical' students fit in well because of the diversity of the student population." Another student adds, "There are a lot of foreign and minority students, to the point that the actual 'majority' is the minority here at UB." Geographically, UB draws "from urban areas, rural areas, NYC, Long Island, and most every country in the world." As a state school, "A lot of the students are from New York State, but with differing areas of the state, there are many different types of students."

STATE UNIVERSITY OF NEW YORK—UNIVERSITY AT BUFFALO

FINANCIAL AID: 866-838-7257 • E-MAIL: UB-ADMISSIONS@BUFFALO.EDU • WEBSITE: WWW.BUFFALO.EDU

THE PRINCETON REVIEW SAYS

Admissions

Very important factors considered include: Class rank, rigor of secondary school record, standardized test scores. *Other factors considered include:* Application essay, recommendation(s), character/personal qualities, extracurricular activities, geographical residence, racial/ethnic/economic status, talent/ability, volunteer work, work experience. SAT or ACT required; ACT with Writing component required. TOEFL required of all international applicants. High school diploma is required and GED is accepted. *Academic units recommended:* 4 English, 3 mathematics, 3 science, 3 foreign language, 4 social studies.

Financial Aid

Students should submit: FAFSA. The Princeton Review suggests that all financial aid forms be submitted as soon as possible after January 1. *Need-based scholarships/grants offered:* Federal Pell, SEOG, state scholarships/grants, private scholarships, the school's own gift aid, Federal Nursing Scholarships. *Loan aid offered:* Direct Subsidized Stafford, Direct Unsubsidized Stafford, Direct PLUS, Federal Perkins, Federal Nursing, college/university loans from institutional funds. Applicants will be notified of awards on a rolling basis beginning 2/1.

The Inside Word

As students point out, UB "is famous for its architecture, nursing, and pharmacy school[s]"; as such, it makes sense that "those majors are a harder to get into." In fact, admissions standards at UB have grown more demanding across all programs in recent years. Despite the school's large applicant pool, it takes a close look at applications, searching for evidence of special talents and experiences that will enrich campus life.

THE SCHOOL SAYS "..."

From The Admissions Office

"The University at Buffalo (UB) is among the nation's finest public research universities—a learning community where you'll work side by side with world-renowned faculty, including Nobel, Pulitzer, National Medal of Science, and other award winners. As the largest, most comprehensive university center in the State University of New York (SUNY) system, UB offers more undergraduate majors than any public university in New York or New England. Through innovative resources like our Undergraduate Research and Creative Activities, Discovery Seminars, and Undergraduate Academics, you'll be free to chart an academic course that meets your individual goals. At UB you can even design your own major. Our unique University Honors College and University Scholars Program scholarship programs offer an enhanced academic experience, including opportunities for independent study, advanced research, and specialized advisement. The university is committed to providing the latest information technology—and is widely considered to be one of the most wired (and wireless) universities in the country. UB also places a high priority on offering an exciting campus environment. With nonstop festivals, Division I sporting events, concerts, and visiting lecturers, you'll have plenty to do outside of the classroom. We encourage you and your family to visit campus to see UB up close and in person. Our Visit UB campus tours and presentations are offered year-round.

"Freshman applicants for Fall 2008 must take the new SAT (or the ACT with Writing component)."

SELECTIVITY

Admissions Rating	85
# of applicants	19,831
% of applicants accepted	52
% of acceptees attending	32
# accepting a place on wait list	344
% admitted from wait list	80
# of early decision applicants	512
% accepted early decision	69

FRESHMAN PROFILE

Range SAT Critical Reading	500–610
Range SAT Math	540–650
Range ACT Composite	23–27
Minimum paper TOEFL	550
Minimum computer TOEFL	213
Average HS GPA	3.2
% graduated top 10% of class	24
% graduated top 25% of class	62
% graduated top 50% of class	93

DEADLINES

Early decision	
Deadline	11/1
Notification	12/15
Regular	
Priority	11/1
Notification	rolling
Nonfall registration?	yes

FINANCIAL FACTS

Financial Aid Rating	81
Annual in-state tuition	$4,350
Annual out-of-state tuition	$10,610
Room and board	$9,132
Required fees	$1,867
Books and supplies	$947
% frosh rec. need-based scholarship or grant aid	35
% UG rec. need-based scholarship or grant aid	33
% frosh rec. non-need-based scholarship or grant aid	21
% UG rec. non-need-based scholarship or grant aid	11
% frosh rec. need-based self-help aid	52
% UG rec. need-based self-help aid	50
% frosh rec. athletic scholarships	1
% UG rec. athletic scholarships	1
% frosh rec. any financial aid	67
% UG rec. any financial aid	75
% UG borrow to pay for school	69
Average cumulative indebtedness	$17,657

STEPHENS COLLEGE

1200 EAST BROADWAY, BOX 2121, COLUMBIA, MO 65215 • ADMISSIONS: 800-876-7207 • FAX: 573-876-7237

CAMPUS LIFE
Quality of Life Rating	**96**
Fire Safety Rating	**74**
Green Rating	**65**
Type of school	private
Environment	city

STUDENTS
Total undergrad enrollment	861
% male/female	3/97
% from out of state	50
% from public high school	76
% live on campus	72
% in (# of) sororities	7 (2)
% African American	10
% Asian	2
% Caucasian	82
% Hispanic	3
% Native American	1
# of countries represented	1

SURVEY SAYS . . .
Small classes
Students are friendly
Great off-campus food
Intramural sports are unpopular or nonexistent
Theater is popular

ACADEMICS
Academic Rating	**89**
Calendar	semester
Student/faculty ratio	12:1
Profs interesting rating	93
Profs accessible rating	94
Most common reg class size	10–19 students
Most common lab size	10–19 students

MOST POPULAR MAJORS
drama and dramatics/theatre arts
fashion/apparel design
apparel and textile marketing management

STUDENTS SAY ". . ."

Academics

A small women's college located in the lively college town of Columbia, Missouri, Stephens College is characterized by its intensive liberal arts programs and supportive learning environment. A junior enthuses, "Academics at Stephens are great. Teachers are always available outside of class and the classes are usually challenging and interesting enough to keep students motivated to work hard!" Professors are "completely willing to help in any way, but they also expect a lot from their students," adds a senior. Stephens offers more than 50 majors, of which performing and applied arts (such as theater and fashion design) are among the most popular. Students sing the praises of their major programs, many noting Stephens's strong commitment to hands-on education, alumni networking, and leadership opportunities. A sophomore attests, "Stephens has one of the best fashion design schools in the country. The teachers are highly knowledgeable, and the alumnae network is extensive." Similarly, "The theater program here is unlike any other because we have great alumnae connections and everything we do is hands-on. The students even run their own theater (Warehouse) right next to the Stephens Theater." Students also tell us that "all of the administration is very approachable," often noting in particular the efforts of friendly President Libby.

Life

Ask almost any Stephens undergrad and she will tell you that "the greatest strength of Stephens College is its close community." Stephens women go out of their way to support campus activities and events; for example, "The theater productions and dance productions are wildly popular. They are always on the verge of being sold out." Off campus, Columbia, Missouri (also home to the University of Missouri), is a boisterous college town, boasting "lots of little shops and restaurants, and, of course, tons of bars." Come the weekend, many Stephens women make a beeline for the coed parties at Mizzou. Others "enjoy shopping in the District downtown, hanging out at the Artisan (a coffee shop with live music), and going to concerts at the Blue Note." Many students mention that the campus facilities need a face-lift; even so, they agree that residential life is particularly agreeable at Stephens, in large part because the school offers almost every student a spacious, private dorm room. A junior jokes, "I expect my first studio apartment in New York will be about half the size of my current dorm room." Pet-lovers take note: "Another perk about Stephens is that students are allowed to bring pets! The 'pet floor' program has been very successful. Girls really enjoy having their cat or dog with them at college."

Student Body

Stephens College tends to attract "hardworking, dedicated, and ambitious" young women, most of whom hail from middle-class families in the Midwest. A freshman tells us, "Typically, the students here are average Midwestern girls, and at times there are girls from the coasts who mix things up a bit." "We are not incredibly diverse," adds one junior, "but there are some minorities here on campus." There is a general homogeneity of interests among the students as well, with many gravitating toward similar majors and extracurricular activities. A freshman reports, "There are a lot of theater/dance/fashion majors," so students in other majors can feel like "a bit of a minority. You usually spend time with those in your major since you are in so many classes with them." Stephens undergrads assure us, however, that every student, no matter what her background, fits in on this friendly campus. As one junior attests, "The Stephens community is incredibly accepting and friendly, making it very easy for any student, typical or atypical, to fit in well."

FINANCIAL AID: 573-876-7106 • E-MAIL: APPLY@WC.STEPHENS.EDU • WEBSITE: WWW.STEPHENS.EDU

THE PRINCETON REVIEW SAYS

Admissions

Very important factors considered include: Application essay, rigor of secondary school record, standardized test scores. *Important factors considered include:* Academic GPA, recommendation(s), extracurricular activities. *Other factors considered include:* Class rank, character/personal qualities, interview, level of applicant's interest, talent/ability, volunteer work, work experience. SAT or ACT required; TOEFL required of all international applicants. High school diploma is required and GED is accepted. *Academic units required:* 4 English, 3 mathematics, 2 science, 2 foreign language, 1 social studies. *Academic units recommended:* (2 science labs).

Financial Aid

Students should submit: FAFSA. The Princeton Review suggests that all financial aid forms be submitted as soon as possible after January 1. *Need-based scholarships/grants offered:* Federal Pell, SEOG, state scholarships/grants, private scholarships, the school's own gift aid, Federal ACG Federal SMART Grant. *Loan aid offered:* FFEL Subsidized Stafford, FFEL Unsubsidized Stafford, FFEL PLUS, Federal Perkins Applicants will be notified of awards on a rolling basis beginning 3/1. Federal Work-Study Program available. Institutional employment available. Off-campus job opportunities are good.

The Inside Word

Stephens offers its students a great deal of personal attention—and this extends to its applicants, as well. Character holds significant weight at this college, so expect essays and recommendations to be thoroughly assessed. Weaker candidates who are deemed to have academic promise will most likely find themselves admitted under probationary guidelines. Stephens's impressive yield rate attests to its appeal to prospective students.

THE SCHOOL SAYS "..."

From The Admissions Office

"Historically committed to meeting the changing needs of women, Stephens College engages students in an innovative educational experience that focuses on pre-professional fields and the performing arts and is grounded in the liberal arts. Graduates of Stephens are career-ready women of distinction who are connected through a supportive network of alumnae across the world, confident in themselves, and inspired by our tradition of the 10 ideals as core values that enrich women's lives.

"The women's college setting offers to its students stimulating classroom discussion and close interaction with professors and peers. Bridging theory and application, students engage in hands-on learning opportunities (education majors in our on-campus children's laboratory school and theater in Iowa, for example) as well as internship experiences in their first year of study. The Stephens campus is within walking distance of a thriving downtown, shared by more than 26,000 students at area colleges and universities."

As of this book's publication, Stephens College did not have information available about their policy regarding the new SAT.

SELECTIVITY

Admissions Rating	79
# of applicants	735
% of applicants accepted	71
% of acceptees attending	43

FRESHMAN PROFILE

Range SAT Critical Reading	540–610
Range SAT Math	480–580
Range ACT Composite	21–26
Minimum paper TOEFL	550
Minimum computer TOEFL	213
Average HS GPA	3.3
% graduated top 10% of class	17
% graduated top 25% of class	42
% graduated top 50% of class	72

DEADLINES

Regular	
Priority	4/1
Notification	rolling
Nonfall registration?	yes

APPLICANTS ALSO LOOK AT

AND OFTEN PREFER
University of Missouri—Columbia
State University of New York—Fashion Institute of Technology

AND SOMETIMES PREFER
William Woods University

AND RARELY PREFER
Butler University

FINANCIAL FACTS

Financial Aid Rating	71
Annual tuition	$23,000
Room and board	$8,730
Books and supplies	$1,000
% frosh rec. need-based scholarship or grant aid	58
% UG rec. need-based scholarship or grant aid	65
% frosh rec. non-need-based scholarship or grant aid	64
% UG rec. non-need-based scholarship or grant aid	73
% frosh rec. need-based self-help aid	55
% UG rec. need-based self-help aid	63
% frosh rec. athletic scholarships	1
% UG rec. athletic scholarships	1
% frosh rec. any financial aid	93
% UG rec. any financial aid	97
% UG borrow to pay for school	75
Average cumulative indebtedness	$21,177

STEVENS INSTITUTE OF TECHNOLOGY

CASTLE POINT ON HUDSON, HOBOKEN, NJ 07030 • ADMISSIONS: 201-216-5194 • FAX: 201-216-8348

STUDENTS SAY ". . ."

Academics

Students at the Stevens Institute of Technology tell us time and again that "Stevens' reputation amongst some of the world's best employers is outstanding." This leads to a "high job placement [rate] and great starting salaries," which, for many, are the primary charms of this small Hoboken school. Engineering disciplines claim about two-thirds of all Stevens undergraduates, and "a huge number participate in the co-op program," which "allows students a break from the theoretical nonsense while putting it to use." In this program, "students spend 5 years getting their undergraduate degree [while] work[ing] three semesters at a company getting experience and pay." That's three semesters of work on top of a 156-credit program that awards a "Bachelor's of Engineering, not [a] Bachelor's of Science in engineering. (We are one of [fewer] than half a dozen schools in the country to offer [it].)" It's a calendar that is not for the faint of heart, since it means a freshman "can have eight classes in [his or her] first semester." Stevens also delivers in mathematics and the sciences; students in the latter area brag that Stevens "always gets a high percent[age] of students accepted . . . to medical school." As at most tech and science schools, students here complain that, while "The professors are very intelligent," "Sometimes we get professors who are unable to communicate the material." This is often attributed to professors whose first language is not English; some say it's "50/50" whether you'll be able to understand your professor. Even so, most agree that "the juice is worth the squeeze . . . you'll get a good job" if you graduate.

Life

Stevens is situated in the town of Hoboken, NJ, which is "located right on the doorstep of New York City." Hoboken boosters believe that "there is simply no better spot in the world to have a college." In truth, this small town close to the capital of the world pleases multiple tastes: "Those that don't enjoy the city are quite content in Hoboken, [and] the more city-slicker-type students feel very at home with the Manhattan skyline as a backdrop." Because the train to New York City is only "a 7-minute walk from campus," it's easy for students to touch as well as look. Despite its great location, Stevens' "highly demanding" academics play the largest role in student life, which is driven by the ebb and flow—usually the latter—of course work. Nevertheless, "Students are very involved [on] campus. Whether it [is] a sports team or Greek life, the vast majority of students do at least one extracurricular activity." Stevens boasts "a very good Division III athletic program," and its teams "have been getting larger fan turnouts" in recent years. Students tell us that there's also "no lack of parties and alcohol [at] this school. You can count on a party every Thursday." A 3:1 male/female ratio drives some male students off campus in search of companionship.

Student Body

Like most tech schools, Stevens "is a nerd school, no doubt about it." It's home to many students who are "very smart but lacking social skills," preferring to "play World of Warcraft in their rooms or watch anime on a Friday night." Students point out that you'll also find "musicians, theater junkies, sports fanatics, and bookworms" on campus. And "just about everybody here has a secret hobby or talent you would have never thought of." In addition, Stevens also has a substantial number of international students—and "lots of minorities" who boost the diversity factor. On the downside, students tend to be very cliquish and "don't associate with each other outside of class" unless they are part of "the group."

STEVENS INSTITUTE OF TECHNOLOGY

FINANCIAL AID: 201-216-5194 • E-MAIL: ADMISSIONS@STEVENS.EDU • WEBSITE: WWW.STEVENS.EDU

THE PRINCETON REVIEW SAYS

Admissions

Very important factors considered include: Application essay, academic GPA, recommendation(s), rigor of secondary school record, standardized test scores, character/personal qualities, extracurricular activities, interview, volunteer work, work experience. *Important factors considered include:* Class rank, talent/ability. *Other factors considered include:* Alumni/ae relation, SAT or ACT required; TOEFL required of all international applicants. High school diploma is required and GED is not accepted. *Academic units required:* 4 English, 4 mathematics, 3 science, (3 science labs). *Academic units recommended:* 4 science, (4 science labs), 2 foreign language, 2 social studies, 2 history, 4 academic electives.

Financial Aid

Students should submit: FAFSA. The Princeton Review suggests that all financial aid forms be submitted as soon as possible after January 1. *Need-based scholarships/grants offered:* Federal Pell, SEOG, state scholarships/grants, private scholarships, the school's own gift aid. *Loan aid offered:* Direct Subsidized Stafford, Direct Unsubsidized Stafford, Direct PLUS, FFEL Subsidized Stafford, Federal Perkins, state loans, Signature Loans, TERI Loans, NJ CLASS, CitiAssist. Applicants will be notified of awards on a rolling basis beginning 3/30. Federal Work-Study Program available. Off-campus job opportunities are excellent.

The Inside Word

Stevens is among the most desirable "second tier" engineering/science/math schools; its location and cachet with employers guarantee that. It's a good choice for those who can't get through the door at MIT or Caltech but who are nonetheless extremely smart and unafraid of hard work. Such students will find the Stevens Admissions Office quite sympathetic to their applications.

THE SCHOOL SAYS "..."

From The Admissions Office

"Founded in 1870 as the first American college to devote itself exclusively to engineering education based on scientific principles, Stevens Institute of Technology is a prestigious independent university for study and research. In 2004, Stevens was ranked by the Princeton Review as one of the nation's 'Most Entrepreneurial Campuses' for having tailored their undergraduate business and technology curricula to encourage young entrepreneurs, providing them with the training and guidance they need to start their own businesses. In 2006, Stevens was ranked among the nation's top-20 'Most Wired Campuses' by *PC* Magazine and the Princeton Review. In 2007 Stevens' office of Career Development was ranked among the nation's top 20 (#16) by The Princeton Review.

"At the undergraduate level, Stevens' broad-based education leads to prestigious degrees in business, science, computer science, engineering, or humanities. Research activities are vital to the university's educational mission, thus Stevens attracts world-renowned faculty to complement its exceptional on-campus facilities. In addition, Stevens maintains an honor system that has been in existence since 1908. Stevens' more than 2,000 undergraduates come from more than 42 states and 65 countries, creating a diverse, dynamic environment. Stevens also boasts an outstanding campus life—students will find more than 150 student organizations and 25 NCAA Division III athletics teams.

"Stevens requires the SAT or ACT for all applicants. We recommend that all students take SAT Subject Tests to show their strength in English, math, and a science of their choice. Accelerated premed and pre-dentistry applicants must take the SAT as well as two SAT Subject Tests in Math (Level I or II), and Biology or Chemistry. Accelerated law applicants must take two SAT Subject Tests of their choice."

SELECTIVITY

Admissions Rating	93
# of applicants	3,058
% of applicants accepted	49
% of acceptees attending	38
# accepting a place on wait list	328
% admitted from wait list	17
# of early decision applicants	277
% accepted early decision	79

FRESHMAN PROFILE

Range SAT Critical Reading	550–650
Range SAT Math	620–710
Minimum paper TOEFL	550
Minimum computer TOEFL	213
Average HS GPA	3.7
% graduated top 10% of class	49
% graduated top 25% of class	86
% graduated top 50% of class	97

DEADLINES

Early decision I	
Deadline	11/15
Notification	12/15
Early decision II	
Deadline	1/15
Notification	2/15
Regular	
Priority	11/15
Deadline	2/1
Notification	4/1
Nonfall registration?	no

APPLICANTS ALSO LOOK AT

AND OFTEN PREFER
Cornell University
Massachusetts Institute of Technology

AND SOMETIMES PREFER
Johns Hopkins University
New York University

AND RARELY PREFER
Rutgers, The State University of New Jersey—New Brunswick

FINANCIAL FACTS

Financial Aid Rating	71
Annual tuition	$34,900
Room and board	$11,000
Required fees	$1,800
Books and supplies	$900
% frosh rec. need-based scholarship or grant aid	58
% UG rec. need-based scholarship or grant aid	54
% frosh rec. non-need-based scholarship or grant aid	59
% UG rec. non-need-based scholarship or grant aid	50
% frosh rec. need-based self-help aid	57
% UG rec. need-based self-help aid	56
% frosh rec. any financial aid	83
% UG rec. any financial aid	76
% UG borrow to pay for school	68
Average cumulative indebtedness	$14,700

SUFFOLK UNIVERSITY

Eight Ashburton Place, Boston, MA 02108 • Admissions: 617-573-8460 • Fax: 617-742-4291

CAMPUS LIFE
Quality of Life Rating	**79**
Fire Safety Rating	**99**
Green Rating	**91**
Type of school	private
Environment	metropolis

STUDENTS
Total undergrad enrollment	5,289
% male/female	44/56
% from out of state	27
% from public high school	67
% live on campus	16
% in (# of) fraternities	NR (1)
% in (# of) sororities	NR (1)
% African American	3
% Asian	6
% Caucasian	62
% Hispanic	5
% international	9
# of countries represented	94

SURVEY SAYS . . .
Large classes
Great library
Diverse student types on campus
Students love Boston, MA
Great off-campus food
(Almost) everyone smokes

ACADEMICS
Academic Rating	**73**
Calendar	semester
Student/faculty ratio	12:1
Profs interesting rating	73
Profs accessible rating	72
% classes taught by TAs	1
Most common	
reg class size	20–29 students
Most common	
lab size	10–19 students

MOST POPULAR MAJORS
sociology
interior design
business/corporate communications

STUDENTS SAY ". . ."
Academics
"A small classroom university in the heart of a big city," Boston's Suffolk University "is small enough that you actually recognize students from their pictures in the admissions booklets [and] big enough to attract national speakers like George Bush Sr." It's also a school with a huge international component, thanks to its campuses in Madrid, Spain, and Dakar, Senegal and "a unique partnership with Charles University in Prague," all of which "provide students an easy opportunity to study abroad without the usual hassle of all the paperwork." Academic life on the home campus "includes "down-to-earth professors" who "are always available outside of class and are very helpful" and the Balloti Learning Center, which "offers extra help to students who want or need it." Make no mistake: Academics are "incredibly student oriented" here—"The student and [his or her] concerns come first." Top programs include psychology, government, history, and sociology, which "offers concentrations in criminology and justice or health and human services as opposed to just a general major."

Life
Suffolk lacks a traditional sprawling suburban campus. Simply put, Suffolk students know they ain't in Kansas any more! The university consists of a collection of buildings located in swanky Beacon Hill, literally steps from Boston Common and the Public Gardens. So, if you're a city lover you my have just found heaven! Suffolk students are quick to point out that their urban existence can make some feel "disconnected" compounded by the fact that many students choose to live off campus. One commuter writes, "It's sometimes difficult for me to join in some of the activities that they have going on at the school." Even so, many here are satisfied with the status quo; they'll skip the conventional campus activities and the rah-rah campus unity, preferring to spend their free time enjoying the city of Boston. "Most people have lots of friends [at] other schools" and the prevalence of fun activities in Boston such as "movies at the Museum of Fine Arts" and "local concerts." Undergrads agree that "drinking is definitely a huge part of Suffolk," and "Being 21 in Boston or having a good fake ID makes it a much better time. What you lose in the lack of campus, you gain with the city."

Student Body
Suffolk's overseas ties draw a large international population to the Boston campus, to the point that "in some classes, almost half of the students are foreign-born. Interacting with students from different backgrounds or cultures isn't an option—it's a daily occurrence. In my international business classes it leads to fascinating discussions because, rather than read about business in different cultures, we have firsthand experiences." Most of the American student body comes from Boston and the surrounding area; while "The majority [are] pretty run-of-the mill products of Massachusetts suburbia, the minority is pretty eclectic." This minority includes "art-school hipsters" and a "relatively large gay community." Each group also features a lot of "rich and preppy" students who use "Boston as their playground." Students report that there "isn't a real strong sense of community, unless you live in the dorms" (about one in five does).

Suffolk University

Financial Aid: 617-573-8470 • E-mail: admission@suffolk.edu • Website: www.suffolk.edu

THE PRINCETON REVIEW SAYS

Admissions

Very important factors considered include: Rigor of secondary school record. *Important factors considered include:* Class rank, application essay, academic GPA, standardized test scores. *Other factors considered include:* Recommendation(s), alumni/ae relation, character/personal qualities, extracurricular activities, first generation, geographical residence, interview, level of applicant's interest, talent/ability, volunteer work, work experience. SAT or ACT required; TOEFL required of all international applicants. High school diploma is required and GED is accepted. *Academic units required:* 4 English, 3 mathematics, 2 science, (1 science labs), 2 foreign language, 1 history, 4 academic electives. *Academic units recommended:* 4 mathematics, 3 science, (1 science labs), 3 foreign language, 1 social studies, 1 history, 4 academic electives.

Financial Aid

Students should submit: FAFSA, institution's own financial aid form. Regular filing deadline is 3/1. The Princeton Review suggests that all financial aid forms be submitted as soon as possible after January 1. *Need-based scholarships/grants offered:* Federal Pell, SEOG, state scholarships/grants, private scholarships, the school's own gift aid. *Loan aid offered:* Direct Subsidized Stafford, Direct Unsubsidized Stafford, Direct PLUS, Federal Perkins Applicants will be notified of awards on a rolling basis beginning 2/5. Federal Work-Study Program available. Institutional employment available. Off-campus job opportunities are excellent.

The Inside Word

Suffolk is unapologetic about its mission to provide access and opportunity to college bound students. That said, test scores and high school GPA requirements are average. Applicants who are borderline based on straight numbers should make their case to the Admissions Office directly.

THE SCHOOL SAYS " . . ."

From The Admissions Office

"Ask any student, and they'll tell you: The best thing about Suffolk is the professors. They go the extra mile to help students to succeed. Suffolk faculty members are noted scholars and experienced professionals, but first and foremost, they are teachers and mentors. Suffolk's faculty is of the highest caliber. Ninety-four percent of the faculty hold PhDs. Suffolk maintains a 13:1 student/faculty ratio with an average class size of 19.

"The university was selected by *U.S. News'* 2007 edition as one of 'America's Best Colleges.' Career preparation is a high priority at Suffolk. Many students work during the school year in paid internships, co-op jobs, or work-study positions. Suffolk has an excellent job placement record. More than 94 percent of recent graduates are either employed or enrolled in graduate school at the time of graduation.

"The university's academic programs emphasize quality teaching, small class size, real-world career applications, and an international experience. There are more than 50 study abroad sites available to students. The undergraduate academic program offers more than 70 majors and 1,000 courses.

"We require applicants to submit the SAT with the essay score or the ACT taken with the Writing component. Standardized tests are used for both placement and assessment. International students may submit any of the following tests for admission: the TOEFL or ELPT, IELTS, CPE, CAE, and FCE. The role of standardized testing is still a secondary role when considering admission to the university. The candidate's grades and the overall strength of curriculum are primary factors in the admission decision."

SELECTIVITY

Admissions Rating	72
# of applicants	8,044
% of applicants accepted	80
% of acceptees attending	21
# accepting a place on wait list	391
% admitted from wait list	25

FRESHMAN PROFILE

Range SAT Critical Reading	460–560
Range SAT Math	450–570
Range SAT Writing	460–560
Range ACT Composite	20–24
Minimum paper TOEFL	525
Minimum computer TOEFL	197
Average HS GPA	2.95
% graduated top 10% of class	9
% graduated top 25% of class	31
% graduated top 50% of class	68

DEADLINES

Early action	
Deadline	11/20
Notification	12/20
Regular	
Deadline	3/1
Notification	modified
Nonfall registration?	yes

FINANCIAL FACTS

Financial Aid Rating	68
Annual tuition	$25,850
% frosh rec. need-based scholarship or grant aid	64
% UG rec. need-based scholarship or grant aid	68
% frosh rec. non-need-based scholarship or grant aid	17
% UG rec. non-need-based scholarship or grant aid	16
% frosh rec. need-based self-help aid	72
% UG rec. need-based self-help aid	77
% frosh rec. any financial aid	63
% UG rec. any financial aid	62

SUSQUEHANNA UNIVERSITY

514 UNIVERSITY AVENUE, SELINSGROVE, PA 17870 • ADMISSIONS: 570-372-4260 • FAX: 570-372-2722

CAMPUS LIFE

Quality of Life Rating	**81**
Fire Safety Rating	**84**
Green Rating	**79**
Type of school	private
Affiliation	Lutheran
Environment	town

STUDENTS

Total undergrad enrollment	1,976
% male/female	46/54
% from out of state	43
% from public high school	85
% live on campus	77
% in (# of) fraternities	20 (4)
% in (# of) sororities	25 (5)
% African American	3
% Asian	2
% Caucasian	91
% Hispanic	2
% international	1
# of countries represented	8

SURVEY SAYS . . .

Large classes
Great computer facilities
Athletic facilities are great
Lots of beer drinking

ACADEMICS

Academic Rating	**81**
Calendar	semester
Student/faculty ratio	14:1
Profs interesting rating	81
Profs accessible rating	87
Most common reg class size	10–19 students
Most common lab size	10–19 students

STUDENTS SAY ". . ."

Academics

Students tell us that Susquehanna University's small size makes it "the perfect university to give students the opportunity to excel in all aspects of school—academics, research, athletics, clubs, and many other activities." Located in rural central Pennsylvania, SU is regarded by students as "an oasis of quirky in the middle of nowhere." This quirkiness emanates from the school's strong programs in the fine arts (including a "big music program," solid departments in creative writing and graphic design, and an active theatre program). Less quirky and more populous is the school's popular School of Business—one in four students here pursues a business major. Students note that "This is a liberal arts university requiring you to take classes from many areas," meaning that all here receive a well-rounded education. They also point out that "It is understandable that you aren't going to be the best at all of those areas. The professors know this as well and are there to help." Indeed, what students love most about SU is the sense that "It is all about the student here. There are no graduate students teaching the undergraduates, the advisers want to make sure how you are doing, and the relationships formed with professors are priceless."

Life

SU's hometown of Selinsgrove "doesn't have the most exciting night life," but that "doesn't really matter" because students "don't have much money to spend on nightlife anyway" and "there's a ton of free stuff to do on campus." Popular campus options include TRAX, "a place were students can go and dance and have a few drinks if they are 21," and Charlie's Coffeehouse, a venue "that provides entertainment like live bands, movies, or games on Friday and Saturday nights." Students are also kept busy with the "abundance of student organizations and campus activities. Not only does it seem like students at Susquehanna are eager to get involved in probably more things than they realistically have time for, but the staff in our student life and campus activities office are amazing." As one student explains, "SU tries to provide as many options as it can because there is literally nothing to do around Selinsgrove." Well, maybe not exactly nothing. Some here concede that the town provides "close proximity to restaurants and stores" and a "decent-sized mall just a couple miles away, as well as everything else from Wall-Mart to every type of fast food restaurant you could think of, all within five miles of school." When small town life gets to be too much, students take advantage of "one-day bus trips to big cities like New York."

Student Body

While there is "a broad mix of students in the sense that there are those that relish in the fine arts, others that are greatly involved in the sciences, and others that enjoy the analytical business aspect of Susquehanna," SU undergrads concede that the typical student is "white and moderately well-off financially" and that "atypical students fit in because they hang out with other atypical students." Overall, students here are "somewhat preppy, but with their own style" and "are hard-working" individuals "who are involved in a ton of activities and sports, but still go out on the weekends."

FINANCIAL AID: 570-372-4450 • E-MAIL: SUADMISS@SUSQU.EDU • WEBSITE: WWW.SUSQU.EDU

THE PRINCETON REVIEW SAYS

Admissions

Very important factors considered include: Academic GPA, rigor of secondary school record. *Important factors considered include:* Class rank, application essay, recommendation(s), standardized test scores, alumni/ae relation, character/personal qualities, extracurricular activities, interview, level of applicant's interest, racial/ethnic status, talent/ability, volunteer work, work. *Other factors considered include:* First generation, geographical residence, religious affiliation/commitment, state residency, TOEFL required of all international applicants. High school diploma is required and GED is accepted. *Academic units required:* 4 English, 3 mathematics, 3 science, (2 science labs), 2 foreign language, 1 social studies, 1 history, 2 academic electives. *Academic units recommended:* 4 English, 4 mathematics, 4 science, (3 science labs), 3 foreign language, 3 social studies, 1 history, 3 academic electives.

Financial Aid

Students should submit: FAFSA, CSS/Financial Aid PROFILE, business/farm supplement. , Prior year Federal tax return. Regular filing deadline is 5/1. The Princeton Review suggests that all financial aid forms be submitted as soon as possible after January 1. *Need-based scholarships/grants offered:* Federal Pell, SEOG, state scholarships/grants, private scholarships, the school's own gift aid. *Loan aid offered:* FFEL Subsidized Stafford, FFEL Unsubsidized Stafford, FFEL PLUS, Federal Perkins, college/university loans from institutional funds. Applicants will be notified of awards on a rolling basis beginning 2/15. Federal Work-Study Program available. Institutional employment available. Off-campus job opportunities are good.

The Inside Word

Susquehanna competes with a number of similar area schools for its student body, and as a result cannot afford to be as selective as it might like, thus creating an opportunity for high school underachievers to attend a challenging and prestigious school. Further improving the odds, Susquehanna does not require standardized test scores of applicants. Those who choose not to submit SAT/ACT scores must instead submit two graded writing samples.

THE SCHOOL SAYS "..."

From The Admissions Office

"Students tell us they are getting a first-rate education and making the connections that will help them be competitive upon graduation. Our size makes it easy for students to customize their 4 years here with self-designed majors, internships, volunteer service, research, leadership opportunities, and rewarding off-campus experiences. Many academic programs are interdisciplinary, meaning that you learn to make connections between different fields of knowledge, which will help make you an educated citizen of the world. A high percentage of students do internships at such sites as Morgan Stanley, Cable News Network, Estee Lauder, and Bristol-Myers Squibb. More than 90 percent of our graduates go on for advanced degrees or get jobs in their chosen field within six months of graduation. There are also more than 100 student organizations on campus, which provide lots of opportunity for leadership and involvement in campus life. The campus is known for its beauty and is a few blocks from downtown Selinsgrove and about a mile from shopping and movie theaters at the Susquehanna Valley Mall.

"Susquehanna will consider a student's top standardized test score (SAT or ACT) when evaluating their application. Students are also encouraged to consider SU's alternative to standardized tests, the Write Option. Under the Write Option, a student may submit two graded writing samples instead of SAT or ACT scores."

SELECTIVITY

Admissions Rating	79
# of applicants	2,373
% of applicants accepted	86
% of acceptees attending	29
# accepting a place on wait list	68
% admitted from wait list	21
# of early decision applicants	212
% accepted early decision	62

FRESHMAN PROFILE

Range SAT Critical Reading	520–610
Range SAT Math	530–610
Range SAT Writing	510–610
Range ACT Composite	22–27
Minimum paper TOEFL	550
Minimum computer TOEFL	213
% graduated top 10% of class	34.3
% graduated top 25% of class	60.5
% graduated top 50% of class	90.5

DEADLINES

Early decision	
Deadline	11/15
Notification	12/1
Regular	
Priority	3/1
Deadline	8/1
Notification	rolling
Nonfall registration?	yes

APPLICANTS ALSO LOOK AT

AND OFTEN PREFER
Lafayette College
Franklin & Marshall College
Bucknell University
Villanova University

AND SOMETIMES PREFER
Dickinson State University
Gettysburg College
Muhlenberg College

AND RARELY PREFER
Lebanon Valley College
Lycoming College

FINANCIAL FACTS

Financial Aid Rating	83
Annual tuition	$31,080
Books and supplies	$750
% frosh rec. need-based scholarship or grant aid	58
% UG rec. need-based scholarship or grant aid	57
% frosh rec. non-need-based scholarship or grant aid	9
% UG rec. non-need-based scholarship or grant aid	7
% frosh rec. need-based self-help aid	53
% UG rec. need-based self-help aid	54
% frosh rec. any financial aid	92
% UG rec. any financial aid	92
% UG borrow to pay for school	82
Average cumulative indebtedness	$16,863

SWARTHMORE COLLEGE

500 COLLEGE AVENUE, SWARTHMORE, PA 19081 • ADMISSIONS: 610-328-8300 • FAX: 610-328-8580

STUDENTS SAY ". . ."

Academics

Swarthmore College, a school that is "as intense and stimulating as it claims to be," suits students who prefer "an emphasis on learning because it's fun and interesting rather than learning to get a job." One undergrad writes, "A lot of what unifies its student body is the fact that, whether we're pursuing a degree in engineering or we're planning on writing the next Great American Novel, we're all passionate and devoted to something." Swatties love that "Swarthmore is amazingly flexible. The requirements are very limited, allowing you to explore whatever you are interested in and change your mind millions of times about your major and career path. If they don't offer a major you want, you can design your own with ease." Professors also earn raves: They're "genuinely interested in giving the students the best academic experience possible" and "challenge students to become knowledgeable in so many areas yet force them to create their own thoughts." Best of all, they come to Swarthmore to teach undergraduates, meaning that "here you can interact with A-list professors straight out of high school. At other universities I'd be lucky to interact one-on-one with professors of similar stature in my third year of graduate school." Students also think you should know that "the school has a lot of money and is very generous with spending it on undergrads, as there isn't anyone else to spend it on."

Life

"There is a misconception that Swarthmore students do nothing but study," students tell us. "While we certainly do a lot of it, we still find many ways to have fun." Though there "isn't a lot to do right in the area surrounding Swarthmore," "With a train station on campus, Philly is very accessible." Most students, however, find no need to leave campus on a regular basis: "The campus provides for us all that we need, and we rarely make it out to Philly," one content freshman writes. On-campus activities "are varied, and there is almost always something to do on the weekend. There are student musical performances, drama performances, movies, speakers, and comedy shows," as well as "several parties every weekend, with and without alcohol, and a lot of pre-partying with friends." For many, things that are the most fun are "the low-key events, just hanging out with friends, talking about classes, or playing in the snow." One student sums up, "While it is tough to generalize on the life of a Swarthmore student, one word definitely applies to us all: busy. All of us are either working on extracurriculars, studying, or fighting sleep to do more work."

Student Body

Students are "not sure if there is a typical Swattie," but suspect that "the defining feature among us is that each person is brilliant at something. Maybe dance, maybe quantum physics, maybe philosophy; each person here has at least one thing that [he or she does] extraordinarily well." There's also "a little bit of a nerd in every one of us—much more in some than in others. The people are all truly genuine, though, and everyone tends to get along well. We're all a little idiosyncratic: When anything that you might call eccentric, or maybe even a little weird at Swat occurs, the typical reaction is, 'That is so Swarthmore!'" A Swattie "tends to have a tremendously hectic life because he or she joins organizations for which he or she holds a passion, and then has 28 hours of work to accomplish in a 24-hour day." Swatties also tend to be "politically left-wing. One says, "If you are not left-wing it is more difficult, but still possible, to fit in—you just have to expect a lot of debate about your political . . . views."

FINANCIAL AID: 610-328-8358 • E-MAIL: ADMISSIONS@SWARTHMORE.EDU • WEBSITE: WWW.SWARTHMORE.EDU

THE PRINCETON REVIEW SAYS

Admissions

Very important factors considered include: Rigor of secondary school record, academic GPA, character/personality qualities, application essay, class rank, recommendations. *Important factors considered include:* Standardized test scores, extracurricular activities. *Other factors considered include:* Alumni/ae relation, first generation, geographical diversity, interview, level of applicant's interest, racial/ethnic identity, talent/ability, volunteer work, work experience. Applicants are required to submit scores for any one of the three following testing scenarios: 1) SAT and any two SAT Subject tests; 2) the ACT with Writing; or 3) SAT and ACT (with or without writing). Prospective engineers are encouraged to take the Mathematics Level 2 Subject Test, regardless of whether they opt for the SAT or ACT. High school diploma or equivalent is not required.

Financial Aid

Students should submit: FAFSA, institution's own financial aid form, CSS/Financial Aid PROFILE, state aid form, noncustodial PROFILE, business/farm supplement. , Federal Tax Return, W2 Statements, Year-end paycheck stub. Regular filing deadline is 2/15. The Princeton Review suggests that all financial aid forms be submitted as soon as possible after January 1. *Need-based scholarships/grants offered:* Federal Pell, SEOG, state scholarships/grants, private scholarships, the school's own gift aid. *Loan aid offered:* Beginning with the 2008-09 academic year all Swarthmore financial aid awards will be loan free. Applicants will be notified of awards on or about 4/1. Federal Work-Study Program available. Institutional employment available. Off-campus job opportunities are good.

The Inside Word

Competition for admission to Swarthmore remains fierce, as the school consistently receives applications from top students across the country. With numerous qualified candidates, prospective students can be assured that every aspect of their applications will be thoroughly evaluated. While there might not be a typical admit, successful applicants have all proven themselves intellectually curious, highly motivated, and creative-minded.

THE SCHOOL SAYS "..."

From The Admissions Office

"Swarthmore College, a highly selective college of liberal arts and engineering, celebrates the life of the mind. Since its founding in 1864, Swarthmore has given students of uncommon intellectual ability the knowledge, insight, skills, and experience to become leaders for the common good. The College is private, yet open to all regardless of financial need; American, yet decidedly global in outlook and diversity, drawing students from around the world and all 50 states. So much of what Swarthmore stands for, from its commitment to curricular breadth and rigor to its demonstrated interest in facilitating discovery and fostering ethical intelligence among exceptional young people, lies in the quality and passion of its faculty. A student/faculty ratio of 8:1 ensures that students have close, meaningful engagement with their professors, preparing them to translate the skills and understanding gained at Swarthmore into the mark they want to make on the world. The College's Honors program features small groups of dedicated and accomplished students working closely with faculty; an emphasis on independent learning; students entering into a dialogue with peers, teachers, and examiners; a demanding program of study in major and minor fields; and an examination at the end of two years' study by outside scholars. Located 11 miles southwest of Philadelphia, Swarthmore's idyllic, 357-acre campus is a designated arboretum, complete with rolling lawns, creek, wooded hills, and hiking trails."

SELECTIVITY

Admissions Rating	99
# of applicants	5,242
% of applicants accepted	18
% of acceptees attending	39
# of early decision applicants	424
% accepted early decision	36

FRESHMAN PROFILE

Range SAT Critical Reading	680–780
Range SAT Math	680–760
Range SAT Writing	680–760
Range ACT Composite	27–33
% graduated top 10% of class	90.5
% graduated top 25% of class	96.3
% graduated top 50% of class	100

DEADLINES

Early decision	
Deadline	11/15
Notification	12/15
Regular	
Deadline	1/2
Notification	4/1
Nonfall registration?	no

FINANCIAL FACTS

Financial Aid Rating	98
Annual tuition	$34,564
Room and board	$10,816
Required fees	$320
Books and supplies	$1,080
% frosh rec. need-based scholarship or grant aid	48
% UG rec. need-based scholarship or grant aid	48
% frosh rec. need-based self-help aid	46
% UG rec. need-based self-help aid	47
% frosh rec. any financial aid	48
% UG rec. any financial aid	50
% UG borrow to pay for school	30

SWEET BRIAR COLLEGE

PO Box B, Sweet Briar, VA 24595 • Admissions: 434-381-6142 • Fax: 434-381-6152

STUDENTS SAY " . . ."

Academics

"A traditional all-girl's school providing exceptional educational opportunities on one of the most beautiful campuses in the nation," Sweet Briar is a tiny liberal arts college that "allows women to do it all; it provides a rigorous academic program as well as a flourishing co-curricular life" that includes "activities and leadership opportunities." A "prestigious riding program" attracts many who want to make equestrian pursuits a part of their academic experience. The small campus is another enticing feature, making it possible "to become involved in any and all aspects of campus life, whether it be academic, social, physical, or extracurricular," while also facilitating "the support of the professors." The faculty here "may not live up to the publishing powerhouses," explains one student, "but they are some of the best teachers with whom I have ever interacted. The small size of the school lends to a very close-knit community, even with the professors, deans, and president." Sweet Briar is strong in education, with a Masters of Arts in Teaching (MAT) program enhanced by "an on-campus kindergarten and preschool, so students interested in being teachers can get teaching experience their first year." The small-school setting is not without its drawbacks; there are problems with course availability ("The courses I would like to enroll in are not offered," writes one student), and limited funding means that the school still needs to "bring many of the buildings up to date and work on getting the campus completely wireless." Students say those problems are worth enduring for the personal attention they receive; "From the administration to the professors, these professionals devote countless hours to being accessible to students and allowing the school to run as an institution for its pupils."

Life

Life at Sweet Briar "is firmly established in traditions. This is one of the most attractive features of the college: The many traditions that build a strong sense of community, whether it be convocation, lantern bearing, step singing, or the many tap clubs active on campus." Socially, the campus "is fairly quiet most of the time. There are a couple of parties a week, but most of the partying (especially on the weekend) is done off campus" at schools like UVA and Hampden-Sydney. Students say "This is not a bad thing," as it allows them to "have our fun and not deal with the mess." The surrounding area is also quiet, as the school "is in a very rural area." Students stay busy during the week; "A lot of girls over-commit themselves to clubs and sports." The school's legendarily beautiful campus continues to live up to its reputation; one student writes, "This is my fourth year at Sweet Briar, and the campus still takes my breath away every morning when I wake up. It's exquisite."

Student Body

Writes one eloquent Sweet Briar student: "Many people stereotype the students at Sweet Briar College. Being a women's college in Southern Virginia allows some to believe us all to be Southern belles interested solely in getting an MRS. We're portrayed as those girls in pink with pearls and ribbons. This, however, could not be further from the truth." While there are some on campus who might fit that stereotype, they are "strongly overpowered" by those who don't. Besides being different from the assumed stereotype, students are also varied among themselves. One students says, "My friends and I, a group of our class leaders, are a random and eclectic group. Our one common trait is that each of us has a little bit of strangeness that we love about ourselves." Another student agrees, "In reality, we are diverse. Many of us do not wear pearls and not all of us ride horses, but we all share an enthusiasm for our academics." The college works to bring many different types of people together, "and each person is respected for her own unique characteristics."

FINANCIAL AID: 434-381-6156 • E-MAIL: ADMISSIONS@SBC.EDU • WEBSITE: WWW.SBC.EDU

THE PRINCETON REVIEW SAYS

Admissions

Very important factors considered include: Academic GPA, rigor of secondary school record. *Important factors considered include:* Class rank, application essay, recommendation(s), standardized test scores, interview. *Other factors considered include:* Alumni/ae relation, character/personal qualities, extracurricular activities, first generation, talent/ability, volunteer work, work experience. SAT or ACT required. TOEFL required of all international applicants. High school diploma is required and GED is accepted. *Academic units required:* 4 English, 3 mathematics, 3 science, (2 science labs), 2 foreign language, 3 social studies. *Academic units recommended:* 4 English, 4 mathematics, 4 science, (3 science labs), 4 foreign language, 4 social studies.

Financial Aid

Students should submit: FAFSA, state aid form. Regular filing deadline is 3/1. The Princeton Review suggests that all financial aid forms be submitted as soon as possible after January 1. *Need-based scholarships/grants offered:* Federal Pell, SEOG, state scholarships/grants, private scholarships, the school's own gift aid. *Loan aid offered:* Direct Subsidized Stafford, Direct Unsubsidized Stafford, Direct PLUS, Federal Perkins, college/university loans from institutional funds. Applicants will be notified of awards on a rolling basis beginning 3/1. Federal Work-Study Program available. Institutional employment available. Off-campus job opportunities are fair.

The Inside Word

A tiny applicant pool allows Sweet Briar to consider each application closely. The school looks not only for evidence of academic achievement and ability but also for "fit" with the school. How well will you fit into/fill out the Sweet Briar community? How well can the school deliver quality academics in your areas of interest? (A school this small can't provide in-depth instruction in every discipline, after all.) These are the questions that will determine your admissions status as Sweet Briar, especially if your test scores and/or high school grades are borderline.

THE SCHOOL SAYS "..."

From The Admissions Office

"The woman who applies to Sweet Briar is mature and far-sighted enough to know what she wants from her college experience. She is intellectually adventuresome, more willing to explore new fields, and more open to challenging her boundaries. Sweet Briar attracts the ambitious, confident woman who enjoys being immersed not only in a first-rate academic program, but in a variety of meaningful activities outside the classroom. Our students take charge and revel in their accomplishments. This attitude follows graduates, enabling them to compete confidently in the corporate world and in graduate school.

"The faculty and staff do not simply give students individual attention; rather they pay attention to individuals. As an institution, we commit to every student and our mission is to provide a learning community that prepares her to be successful in whatever she chooses to do after college."

SELECTIVITY

Admissions Rating	82
# of applicants	585
% of applicants accepted	80
% of acceptees attending	40
# of early decision applicants	63
% accepted early decision	92

FRESHMAN PROFILE

Range SAT Critical Reading	510–640
Range SAT Math	470–595
Range SAT Writing	500–600
Range ACT Composite	21–26
Minimum paper TOEFL	550
Minimum computer TOEFL	213
Average HS GPA	3.4
% graduated top 10% of class	24
% graduated top 25% of class	55
% graduated top 50% of class	88

DEADLINES

Early decision	
Deadline	12/1
Notification	12/15
Regular	
Deadline	2/1
Notification	3/15
Nonfall registration?	yes

APPLICANTS ALSO LOOK AT

AND OFTEN PREFER
College of William and Mary
Mount Holyoke College

AND SOMETIMES PREFER
University of Virginia
Agnes Scott College

AND RARELY PREFER
Randolph College
Hollins University

FINANCIAL FACTS

Financial Aid Rating	90
Annual tuition	$24,740
Room and board	$10,040
Required fees	$275
Books and supplies	$600
% frosh rec. need-based scholarship or grant aid	53
% UG rec. need-based scholarship or grant aid	42
% frosh rec. non-need-based scholarship or grant aid	40
% UG rec. non-need-based scholarship or grant aid	49
% frosh rec. need-based self-help aid	49
% UG rec. need-based self-help aid	39
% frosh rec. any financial aid	93
% UG rec. any financial aid	91
% UG borrow to pay for school	54
Average cumulative indebtedness	$5,496

SYRACUSE UNIVERSITY

100 CROSS-HINDS HALL, 900 SOUTH CROUSE AVE., SYRACUSE, NY 13244 • ADMISSIONS: 315-443-3611 • FAX: 315-443-4226

CAMPUS LIFE

Quality of Life Rating	**63**
Fire Safety Rating	**60***
Green Rating	**89**
Type of school	private
Environment	metropolis

STUDENTS

Total undergrad enrollment	11,794
% male/female	45/55
% from out of state	56
% from public high school	75
% live on campus	75
% in (# of) fraternities	18 (27)
% in (# of) sororities	21 (18)
% African American	7
% Asian	9
% Caucasian	64
% Hispanic	6
% Native American	1
% international	4
# of countries represented	115

SURVEY SAYS . . .

Great library
Everyone loves the Orange
Frats and sororities dominate
social scene
Student publications are popular
Lots of beer drinking
Hard liquor is popular

ACADEMICS

Academic Rating	**82**
Calendar	semester
Student/faculty ratio	15:1
Profs interesting rating	70
Profs accessible rating	73
% classes taught by TAs	6
Most common reg class size	10–19 students
Most common lab size	20–29 students

MOST POPULAR MAJORS

commercial and advertising art
radio, television, and digital
communication
business administration and
management

STUDENTS SAY " . . ."

Academics

Syracuse University "is very strong academically" and boasts "some of the nation's top programs" in a broad range of disciplines. Students are especially bullish on the "prestigious" S. I. Newhouse School of Public Communications, which "has some amazing professors who have worked out in the field and are eager to share all of their experiences with their students," as well as the School of Architecture, "an energetic, sleepless journey of collaboration and individuality in an amazingly cool atmosphere." SU's programs in advertising, art, business, music, political science, engineering, and the life sciences also earn plaudits from undergraduates. Best of all, students say, SU delivers the benefits of "both large schools and small schools," which means it can offer the ability "to concentrate in an area while also taking a variety of other classes that do not have to be within your major or college," as well as plenty of research faculty who put "SU at the front of [the] material" and "professors who are always available to meet during office hours [or] by appointment." One undergrad sums it up: "SU is big enough to have a wealth of resources but small enough so that you always fit in." Another adds, "SU is about academics and preparing us as best as possible for our future careers, along with a little bit of men's basketball."

Life

Students tell us that "the social life at Syracuse is the epitome of the great American college experience. Local bars, frats, and house parties are all popular. Partying takes place from Thursday through Sunday, and close friendships are easily cultivated during the recovery period in between." However, it's important to note that "the school is great about providing other activities" as well. "You don't need to drink to find something fun to do at night or on weekends." "People climb trees on the quad, go rock climbing on the weekends, [and] take ballet classes. We're notorious for our frat parties, but, at the same time, the library is packed every Saturday night." "The student union also provides free movies on weekends, and there are loads of speakers, concerts, and cultural events throughout the week." Of course, SU sports "are huge"—"Syracuse Basketball is going to win the national championship!" Students are mixed on the city of Syracuse. Some tell us "It's pretty much dead" and "The weather sucks," while others aver that "upstate New York is a great location with lots of outdoor activities, unless you hate sub-Arctic climates."

Student Body

While SU undergrads report that a typical peer would be "fashionable," "wealthy," and "trend-driven," they also point out that "there are also tons of students who don't fit that description." Indeed there are upstate, out-of-state, and international students in addition to an abundance from Long Island and New Jersey. While the student body includes "a large frat/sorority presence," there's also a fair share of "neo-hippies." Although SU's student population appears homogenous to some, other students say "[This] seems to be proven wrong on many occasions. For example, the guy living next to me is from St. Thomas. I have friends from all over the world. . . . All religions, sexual orientations, and ethnic groups are strongly represented."

FINANCIAL AID: 315-443-1513 • E-MAIL: ORANGE@SYR.EDU • WEBSITE: WWW.SYRACUSE.EDU

THE PRINCETON REVIEW SAYS

Admissions

Very important factors include: Rigor of secondary school record, academic GPA, class rank, standardized test scores, application essay, recommendation(s), character/personal qualities, level of applicant's interest. *Important factors considered include:* Interview, extracurricular activities, talent/ability, volunteer work, work experience. *Other factors considered include:* First generation, alumni/ae relation, racial/ethnic status. SAT or ACT required; TOEFL required of all international applicants. High school diploma is required and GED is accepted. *Academic units required:* 4 English, 4 mathematics, 4 science (4 science labs), 3 foreign language, 4 social studies.

Financial Aid

Students should submit: FAFSA, CSS/Financial Aid PROFILE, business/farm supplement. Regular filing deadline is 2/1. The Princeton Review suggests that all financial aid forms be submitted as soon as possible after January 1. *Need-based scholarships/grants offered:* Federal Pell, SEOG, state scholarships/grants, private scholarships, the school's own gift aid. *Loan aid offered:* FFEL Subsidized Stafford, FFEL Unsubsidized Stafford, FFEL PLUS, Federal Perkins Applicants will be notified of awards on or about 4/1. Federal Work-Study Program available. Institutional employment available. Off-campus job opportunities are good.

The Inside Word

Syracuse University is divided into nine colleges, and applicants apply to the college in which they are interested. Some colleges make specific requirements of applicants (for example: a portfolio, an audition, or specific high school course work) in addition to SU's general admissions requirements. Applicants are allowed to indicate a second and third choice—you may still gain admission even if you don't get into your first-choice program.

THE SCHOOL SAYS "..."

From The Admissions Office

"Syracuse University provides a dynamic learning environment with a focus on scholarship in action, in which excellence is connected to ideas, problems, and professions in the world. Students at SU focus on interactive, collaborative, and interdisciplinary learning while choosing their course of study from more than 200 options. About half of undergraduates study abroad. SU operates centers in Beijing, Florence, Hong Kong, London, Madrid, Santiago, and Strasbourg. New facilities continue to expand scholarship in action opportunities for students. The Newhouse 3 building houses various facilities for public communications students, including research centers, a high-tech convergence lab, and meeting rooms for student activities. A $107 million Life Sciences Complex will promote interdisciplinary research and education, signaling a new era in scientific research.

"A distinction of the SU education is the breadth of opportunity combined with individualized attention. Average class size is 24 students. Only 3 percent of all classes have more than 100 students. Faculty members are experts in their field, who are dedicated to teaching while conducting research, writing, and experiments they can share with students to aid in the learning process.

"Outside of the classroom, students are encouraged to immerse themselves in organizations and take advantage of the opportunities available in the city of Syracuse. The University community collaborates with city residents, organizations, and businesses in such areas as the arts, entrepreneurship and economic development, and scientific research. The Connective Corridor, a three-mile pedestrian pathway and shuttle bus circuit, links SU and downtown Syracuse's arts institutions, entertainment venues, and public spaces."

SELECTIVITY

Admissions Rating	92
# of applicants	21,219
% of applicants accepted	51
% of acceptees attending	29
# accepting a place on wait list	1,761
% admitted from wait list	11
# of early decision applicants	757
% accepted early decision	80

FRESHMAN PROFILE

Range SAT Critical Reading	540–650
Range SAT Math	570–680
Range ACT Composite	24–29
Minimum paper TOEFL	560
Minimum computer TOEFL	213
Minimum web-based TOEFL	80
Average HS GPA	3.6
% graduated top 10% of class	42
% graduated top 25% of class	70
% graduated top 50% of class	94

DEADLINES

Early decision	
Deadline	11/15
Notification	12/15
Regular	
Deadline	1/1
Notification	3/15
Nonfall registration?	yes

APPLICANTS ALSO LOOK AT AND SOMETIMES PREFER

University of Maryland—College Park
New York University
Cornell University
Boston University
Penn State—University Park

FINANCIAL FACTS

Financial Aid Rating	87
Annual tuition	$30,470
Room and board	$10,940
Required fees	$1,216
Books and supplies	$1,230
% frosh rec. need-based scholarship or grant aid	54
% UG rec. need-based scholarship or grant aid	53
% frosh rec. non-need-based scholarship or grant aid	3
% UG rec. non-need-based scholarship or grant aid	2
% frosh rec. need-based self-help aid	53
% UG rec. need-based self-help aid	51
% frosh rec. athletic scholarships	3
% UG rec. athletic scholarships	3
% frosh rec. any financial aid	79
% UG rec. any financial aid	78
% UG borrow to pay for school	63
Average cumulative indebtedness	$27,152

TEMPLE UNIVERSITY

1801 NORTH BROAD STREET, PHILADELPHIA, PA 19122-6096 • ADMISSIONS: 215-204-7200 • FAX: 215-204-5694

CAMPUS LIFE

Quality of Life Rating	**74**
Fire Safety Rating	**85**
Green Rating	**75**
Type of school	public
Environment	metropolis

STUDENTS

Total undergrad enrollment	24,861
% male/female	45/55
% from out of state	22
% from public high school	76.5
% live on campus	20
% in (# of) fraternities	1 (14)
% in (# of) sororities	1 (9)
% African American	17
% Asian	10
% Caucasian	58
% Hispanic	3
% international	3
# of countries represented	133

SURVEY SAYS . . .

Great computer facilities
Great library
Athletic facilities are great
Diverse student types on campus
Great off-campus food
Campus feels safe
Lots of beer drinking
(Almost) everyone smokes

ACADEMICS

Academic Rating	**76**
Calendar	semester
Student/faculty ratio	17:1
Profs interesting rating	67
Profs accessible rating	71
Most common reg class size	10–19 students
Most common lab size	20–29 students

MOST POPULAR MAJORS

psychology
elementary education and teaching
marketing/marketing management

STUDENTS SAY " . . ."

Academics

Students find "very broad choices in classes and majors" within Temple's 12 schools offering undergraduate academic programs. They also find various levels of classroom intimacy, as "class sizes range from about five students up to 200 depending on level and honors." These broad options are a consequence of the school's large enrollment. Another consequence is the fact that "most professors here have a huge number of students to take care of," which means "A student can get lost easily in the numbers." Due to that reality, students who take the initiative are the ones who do best here: "Temple is a great example of a university where you get out what you put in. If you work hard then you will be recognized and succeed." This is not to say that professors are deaf to their students' needs. On the contrary, "Professors are very accessible and genuinely want to help you learn, but you will be working for that A; don't expect it to be handed to you." The academic environment "is intellectually challenging. Due to the diverse nature of both the faculty and student body, professors usually challenge us to assimilate disparate cultural views and to affirm or change our own views of other cultures."

Administratively, "Every Temple student, at one time, has gotten the 'Temple run-around.' In other words, because the school is so big, sometimes finding the exact person you need to talk to is impossible due to limited office hours and [the fact] that the Temple staff has very limited knowledge of other Temple services." Students appreciate the fact that "the technology is outstanding" at Temple, but complain that the school "needs to build more on-campus housing for students." "After sophomore year you are no longer able to live in dorms," and "The surrounding area is not known for having abundant off-campus housing options."

Life

As you consider Temple, keep in mind its hometown: "This is Philly. There are always things to do. There are plenty of museums and historical tours, there are many places to shop, and the food is so diverse and tasty—there is always something new to try." What's more, "There are subway stops at each end of the campus, so it's a breeze to get to Center City." But you don't have to travel far to socialize: "There are a few college bars just steps away from campus which have gotten extremely popular recently." You don't even have to leave campus if you don't want to. "We go to the bars here (there are two on campus); the SAC has food and the new Student Center has everything you could want," writes one satisfied student. "Frats and sororities are pretty unpopular on the whole," however, so "Temple isn't a bona fide party school."

Student Body

The "student body is so diverse," it often feels to students as if "There is a little of everything at Temple University": "From goth to preppy, from European to Asian, from straight male to transsexual, Temple has it all." "Students come from so many diverse backgrounds; no common denominator among them can really be found." This diversity might be "the reason why all students feel welcome here." It also "makes it a great place to learn and live. It's a full cultural experience." If you absolutely had to describe a typical student, you might say that "most students here care about their grades, and you will find lots of people in the library studying at early hours in the morning at finals time."

TEMPLE UNIVERSITY

FINANCIAL AID: 215-204-2244 • E-MAIL: TUADM@TEMPLE.EDU • WEBSITE: WWW.TEMPLE.EDU

THE PRINCETON REVIEW SAYS

Admissions

Very important factors considered include: Academic GPA, rigor of secondary school record. *Important factors considered include:* Class rank, standardized test scores. *Other factors considered include:* Application essay, recommendation(s), alumni/ae relation, character/personal qualities, extracurricular activities, talent/ability, volunteer work, work experience. SAT or ACT required; ACT with Writing component required. TOEFL required of all international applicants. High school diploma is required and GED is accepted. *Academic units required:* 4 English, 3 mathematics, 2 science, (1 science labs), 2 foreign language, 2 social studies, 1 history, 1 academic elective. *Academic units recommended:* 4 English, 4 mathematics, 3 science, (2 science labs), 2 foreign language, 2 social studies, 2 history, 3 academic electives.

Financial Aid

Students should submit: FAFSA. The Princeton Review suggests that all financial aid forms be submitted as soon as possible after January 1. *Need-based scholarships/grants offered:* Federal Pell, SEOG, state scholarships/grants, private scholarships, the school's own gift aid, Federal Nursing Scholarships. *Loan aid offered:* FFEL Subsidized Stafford, FFEL Unsubsidized Stafford, FFEL PLUS, Federal Perkins, Federal Nursing, state loans, college/university loans from institutional funds. Applicants will be notified of awards on a rolling basis beginning 2/15. Federal Work-Study Program available. Institutional employment available. Off-campus job opportunities are excellent.

The Inside Word

Temple's distinguished reputation and urban environment make the university a good choice for many students, especially Pennsylvania residents. Admissions Officers are fairly objective about their approach to application assessment: They tend to focus principally on GPA, class rank, and test scores. There are no minimum requirements, though, so students who show potential in more subjective arenas should make sure they convey their accomplishments in their applications.

THE SCHOOL SAYS "..."

From The Admissions Office

"Temple combines the academic resources and intellectual stimulation of a large research university with the intimacy of a small college. The university experienced record growth in attracting new students from all 50 states and over 125 countries: up 60 percent in 3 years. Students choose from 125 undergraduate majors. Special academic programs include honors, learning communities for first-year undergraduates, co-op education, and study abroad. Temple has seven regional campuses, including Main Campus and the Health Sciences Center in historic Philadelphia, suburban Temple University, Ambler, and overseas campuses in Tokyo and Rome. Main Campus is home to the Tuttleman Learning Center, with 1,000 computer stations linked to Paley Library. Our TECH Center has over 600 computer workstations, 100 laptops, and a Starbucks. The Liacouras Center is a state-of-the-art entertainment, recreation, and sports complex that hosts concerts, plays, trade shows, and college and professional athletics. It also includes the Independence Blue Cross Student Recreation Center, a major fitness facility for students now and in the future. Students can also take advantage of our Student Fieldhouse. The university has constructed two new dorms, built to meet an unprecedented demand for main campus housing.

"Applicants for Fall 2009 are required to take the new version of the SAT (or the ACT with Writing) and will be considered using the 2400 scale. The best Critical Reading, Math and Writing scores from either test will be considered."

SELECTIVITY

Admissions Rating	83
# of applicants	16,659
% of applicants accepted	63
% of acceptees attending	39
# accepting a place on wait list	250
% admitted from wait list	4

FRESHMAN PROFILE

Range SAT Critical Reading	490–590
Range SAT Math	490–590
Range ACT Composite	20–25
Minimum paper TOEFL	550
Minimum computer TOEFL	213
Minimum web-based TOEFL	79
Average HS GPA	3.35
% graduated top 10% of class	19
% graduated top 25% of class	52
% graduated top 50% of class	89

DEADLINES

Regular	
Deadline	3/1
Notification	rolling
Nonfall registration?	yes

APPLICANTS ALSO LOOK AT
AND OFTEN PREFER

Rutgers, The State University of New Jersey—Newark Campus
University of Maryland—College Park
West Chester University of Pennsylvania

AND SOMETIMES PREFER

LaSalle University
Rutgers University—Camden College of Arts & Sciences

AND RARELY PREFER

Widener University
The University of Scranton
Bloomsburg University of Pennsylvania

FINANCIAL FACTS

Financial Aid Rating	79
Annual in-state tuition	$10,252
Annual out-of-state tuition	$18,770
Room and board	$8,518
Required fees	$550
Books and supplies	$1,000
% frosh rec. need-based scholarship or grant aid	68
% UG rec. need-based scholarship or grant aid	63
% frosh rec. non-need-based scholarship or grant aid	41
% UG rec. non-need-based scholarship or grant aid	32
% frosh rec. need-based self-help aid	58
% UG rec. need-based self-help aid	54
% frosh rec. athletic scholarships	1
% UG rec. athletic scholarships	1
% frosh rec. any financial aid	86
% UG rec. any financial aid	89
% UG borrow to pay for school	75
Average cumulative indebtedness	$29,046

TEXAS A&M UNIVERSITY—COLLEGE STATION

ADMISSIONS COUNSELING, COLLEGE STATION, TX 77843-1265 • ADMISSIONS: 979-845-3741 • FAX: 979-847-8737

CAMPUS LIFE
Quality of Life Rating	92
Fire Safety Rating	60*
Green Rating	86
Type of school	public
Environment	city

STUDENTS
Total undergrad enrollment	37,357
% male/female	52/48
% from out of state	4
% live on campus	25
% in (# of) fraternities	6 (33)
% in (# of) sororities	12 (23)
% African American	3
% Asian	4
% Caucasian	78
% Hispanic	12
% Native American	1
% international	1
# of countries represented	125

SURVEY SAYS . . .
Great computer facilities
Great library
Athletic facilities are great
Students are friendly
Everyone loves the Aggies
Student publications are popular

ACADEMICS
Academic Rating	72
Calendar	semester
Student/faculty ratio	19:1
Profs interesting rating	71
Profs accessible rating	78
% classes taught by TAs	25
Most common reg class size	20–29 students
Most common lab size	10–19 students

MOST POPULAR MAJORS
biological and physical sciences
multi-/interdisciplinary studies
operations management and supervision

STUDENTS SAY ". . ."

Academics
"The excellence of a great research university filled with many traditions and the warm hospitality of a safe, small town" are the hallmarks of a Texas A&M education. United by the school's hallowed traditions, undergrads at this agriculture and engineering powerhouse "are the most fiercely loyal people to the school and other Aggies," and they can't stop bragging about how great their academic and extracurricular lives are. One student writes, "During the college search, I always heard about colleges looking for 'the well-rounded student.' Texas A&M's strength is being a 'well-rounded university,'" particularly for those interested in veterinary science, agricultural science, construction and engineering, business, and life sciences. Most departments hold students to "very high standards"; as one student puts it, "At Texas A&M University, students generally get what they give. An A is well earned, an F is deserved." Another adds, "Classes are extremely hard, but the Aggie ring is worth more this way." That ring provides access to "the Aggie network," alumni of A&M who "help make a lot of things possible," especially "finding a job. I've heard stories of some people getting hired at the sight of their Aggie ring." With A&M "taking many steps, especially in the past few years, to really make A&M an even stronger university and research institution"—including "hiring a lot of new faculty," and "construction of new facilities on campus"—there are now more reasons than ever to love being an Aggie. How great is it? Ultimately you have to find out for yourself, because "From the outside looking in, you can't understand it, and from the inside looking out, you can't explain it!"

Life
A&M "is rich in tradition such as the Twelfth Man, Muster, Silvertaps, Reveille, 'Howdy,' the Corps of Cadets, Elephant Walk, and Maroon Out, just to name a few." If you're already familiar with these terms, you probably know how deeply they permeate campus life. Others should check out the school's website to learn more about them; how you feel about the traditions will strongly impact how much you enjoy life at A&M. Aggies tend to be enthusiastic about sports, both attending games and participating in club, intramural, and pickup games. Although social activities are bound to be extremely diverse at a campus this large, many students here tell us that Northgate, a "row of bars and restaurants off the north side of campus," is the place to go; live music ("Texas country music is real big at A&M"), drinks, and dancing are all on the menu. Hometown College Station "is a small city, so there aren't many activities available off-campus, but the city is at the crossroads to the three major areas in Texas: Houston, Dallas–Fort Worth, and the Austin–San Antonio area. Weekend trips to these areas are fairly common."

Student Body
While "It is true that there is a very large Caucasian population at TAMU," there are also "large numbers of Middle Eastern, Asian, and Hispanic students" as well, providing a good deal of diversity on campus. It's Texas, and it's not Austin, so it should come as no surprise that A&M students tend to be politically conservative. Some point out that "conservative students are probably the most vocal, making it appear our school is more conservative [than it is]. From my experience, most students place themselves in the middle of left and right, making informed decisions when it comes to politics." Many here "are involved in student organizations and have a good social life as well." About 5 percent of the student body participates in the Corps of Cadets, "a senior military academy within the university." One cadet tells us that he and his peers "are the most visible people on campus and live with a structured military lifestyle."

FINANCIAL AID: 979-845-3236 • E-MAIL: ADMISSIONS@TAMU.EDU • WEBSITE: WWW.TAMU.EDU

THE PRINCETON REVIEW SAYS

Admissions

Very important factors considered include: Class rank, academic GPA, rigor of secondary school record, standardized test scores, extracurricular activities, talent/ability. *Important factors considered include:* Application essay, first generation, geographical residence, state residency, volunteer work, work experience. *Other factors considered include:* Recommendation(s), character/personal qualities, SAT or ACT required; ACT with Writing component required. TOEFL required of all international applicants. High school diploma is required and GED is accepted. *Academic units required:* 4 English, 3 mathematics, 3 science, (2 science labs), 2 foreign language, 2 social studies, 1 history. *Academic units recommended:* 4 English, 3 mathematics, 3 science, (2 science labs), 2 foreign language, 2 social studies, 1 history, 1 computer course.

Financial Aid

Students should submit: FAFSA, institution's own financial aid form, Financial Aid Transcripts (for transfer students). The Princeton Review suggests that all financial aid forms be submitted as soon as possible after January 1. *Need-based scholarships/grants offered:* Federal Pell, SEOG, state scholarships/grants, private scholarships, the school's own gift aid. *Loan aid offered:* FFEL Subsidized Stafford, FFEL Unsubsidized Stafford, FFEL PLUS, Federal Perkins, state loans, college/university loans from institutional funds. Applicants will be notified of awards on a rolling basis beginning 4/1. Federal Work-Study Program available. Institutional employment available. Off-campus job opportunities are excellent.

The Inside Word

Texas A&M uses some cut-and-dried admissions criteria: Students graduating in the top 10 percent of a recognized public or private high school in the state of Texas are automatically in; all they have to do is get their applications in on time. Applicants in the top quarter of their graduating class who have a combined SAT Math/Critical Reading score of 1300 (minimum score of 600 in each component) are also automatically in, as are such students who earn a composite ACT score of 30 (minimum 27 on the Math and English sections). All other applications are deemed "Review Admits" to be sorted through by the Admissions Committee.

THE SCHOOL SAYS " . . . "

From The Admissions Office

"Established in 1876 as the first public college in the state, Texas A&M University has become a world leader in teaching, research, and public service. Located in College Station in the heart of Texas, it is centrally situated among three of the country's 10 largest cities: Dallas, Houston, and San Antonio. Texas A&M is ranked nationally in these four areas: enrollment (seventh in enrollment, 45,380 for Fall 2006); enrollment of top students (sixteenth in number of new National Merit Scholars for Fall 2005); value of research (sixteenth with $457 million in 2004); and endowment ($5.1 billion as of 2006).

"Freshman applicants for Fall 2008 are required to take the new SAT or the ACT. We will not accept scores from the old SAT. We will use the applicant's best single testing date score in decision-making."

SELECTIVITY
Admissions Rating	83
# of applicants	18,817
% of applicants accepted	76
% of acceptees attending	56

FRESHMAN PROFILE
Range SAT Critical Reading	520–630
Range SAT Math	560–670
Range SAT Writing	500–610
Range ACT Composite	23–28
Minimum paper TOEFL	550
% graduated top 10% of class	45
% graduated top 25% of class	76
% graduated top 50% of class	89

DEADLINES
Regular	
Deadline	2/1
Notification	rolling
Nonfall registration?	yes

APPLICANTS ALSO LOOK AT
AND OFTEN PREFER
Rice University
AND SOMETIMES PREFER
Louisiana State University
Baylor University
Texas Tech University
The University of Texas at Austin
AND RARELY PREFER
Southern Methodist University
Stephen F. Austin State University

FINANCIAL FACTS
Financial Aid Rating	82
Annual in-state tuition	$4,680
Annual out-of-state tuition	$13,020
Room and board	$6,480
Required fees	$2,655
Books and supplies	$1,156
% frosh rec. need-based scholarship or grant aid	34
% UG rec. need-based scholarship or grant aid	29
% frosh rec. non-need-based scholarship or grant aid	5
% UG rec. non-need-based scholarship or grant aid	2
% frosh rec. need-based self-help aid	20
% UG rec. need-based self-help aid	23
% frosh rec. athletic scholarships	1
% UG rec. athletic scholarships	1
% frosh rec. any financial aid	68.1
% UG rec. any financial aid	61.3
% UG borrow to pay for school	54
Average cumulative indebtedness	$19,940

TEXAS CHRISTIAN UNIVERSITY

OFFICE OF ADMISSIONS, TCU BOX 297013, FORT WORTH, TX 76129 • ADMISSIONS: 817-257-7490 • FAX: 817-257-7268

CAMPUS LIFE

Quality of Life Rating	**86**
Fire Safety Rating	**91**
Green Rating	**78**
Type of school	private
Affiliation	Disciples of Christ
Environment	metropolis

STUDENTS

Total undergrad enrollment	7,264
% male/female	41/59
% from out of state	20
% from public high school	73
% live on campus	46
% in (# of) fraternities	37 (13)
% in (# of) sororities	39 (16)
% African American	5
% Asian	3
% Caucasian	76
% Hispanic	8
% international	5
# of countries represented	79

SURVEY SAYS . . .

Small classes
Athletic facilities are great
Students love Fort Worth, TX
Frats and sororities dominate
social scene
Lots of beer drinking

ACADEMICS

Academic Rating	**79**
Calendar	semester
Student/faculty ratio	14:1
Profs interesting rating	84
Profs accessible rating	84
% classes taught by TAs	2
Most common reg class size	10–19 students
Most common lab size	20–29 students

MOST POPULAR MAJORS

biology/biological sciences
business administration and
management

STUDENTS SAY ". . ."

Academics

Texas Christian University is a small private university affiliated with the Disciples of Christ Church. TCU is "highly respected in Texas," which creates "strong" opportunities for "postgrad jobs or further education." This suits the "career-oriented student body" as does "the location in a large city with lots of future job connections and opportunities." Many TCU students pursue business-related majors through the "top-ranked" Neeley School of Business. TCU's advertising program is "one of the best in the nation," and the university also boasts a "great School of Education," an "excellent premedical program," and a "great social work program." In fact, "The school has many different highly ranked programs, which is appealing to students who can't decide on a major." Students appreciate TCU's commitment to developing "ethical leaders" and love the fact that TCU "has a small-campus feel, but offers all the opportunities . . . you would expect to find on a large campus." Since "The vast majority of all departments give the students at least two semesters of working or internship opportunities," almost all TCU students graduate with real-world experience. TCU's professors "know your name" and "care about you as an individual." They "are more than willing to meet with you outside of class" as long as you show "a substantial amount of effort in class."

Life

According to one student, "The two most popular things at TCU are the Greek life and the football team (when they are winning)." Many students survive happily outside the Greek system, but the divide between Greeks and independents is clearly visible. As one student explains, "Greek life is huge," and if you're not in a Greek organization, "Most all of your friends are other non-Greek people as well." For this reason, campus life can be "very clique-oriented" and can lead to a feeling of "two social classes, which really prevents any real student unity." Fortunately, TCU offers "a very wide variety of activities" outside of Greek life. Many students "are into student government and the campus newspaper (*The Skiff*)," and "There are always events taking place, from theater to music to sports." Since the school is located in a major metropolitan area, "Much of the activity takes place off campus." Students enjoy a "big outpouring of support from the community," and Fort Worth and Dallas offer an "abundance of things to do and places to go," including "great bars, clubs, restaurants, and theaters."

Student Body

The typical TCU student is "frat-tastic: girls wear a polo shirt, designer jeans, and the latest trendy handbag. The guys are similar, minus the handbag." Most tend to be "White, upper-middle-class, and good-looking" and "usually from the South." Not everyone fits this mold, though. Students point out that "with such a big Greek concentration here, it seems that everyone is rich, shallow, and snobby, but that just tends to be the people you notice." TCU "emphasizes diversity," and all students "manage to find an organization or a group to fit into." Fitting in, however, is relative: "If you're not Greek at TCU, you're nothing, in many people's opinions." Moreover, students from a "lower-income family" may find that they "fit in all right, but aren't accepted into the 'highest' social circles because they can't afford the parties." Overall, TCU students describe themselves as "friendly, easygoing," with a "fun-loving character," and "very fashionable."

FINANCIAL AID: 817-257-7858 • E-MAIL: FROGMAIL@TCU.EDU • WEBSITE: WWW.TCU.EDU

THE PRINCETON REVIEW SAYS

Admissions

Very important factors considered include: Class rank, application essay, academic GPA, recommendation(s), rigor of secondary school record, standardized test scores, character/personal qualities. *Important factors considered include:* Extracurricular activities, geographical residence, level of applicant's interest, racial/ethnic status, religious affiliation/commitment, talent/ability, volunteer work, work experience. *Other factors considered include:* Alumni/ae relation, first generation, interview, SAT or ACT required; ACT with Writing component recommended. TOEFL required of all international applicants. High school diploma is required and GED is not accepted. *Academic units required:* 4 English, 3 mathematics, 3 science, 2 foreign language, 3 social studies, 2 academic electives. *Academic units recommended:* 4 English, 4 mathematics, 4 science, 4 foreign language, 4 social studies, 4 academic electives.

Financial Aid

Students should submit: FAFSA. Regular filing deadline is 5/1. The Princeton Review suggests that all financial aid forms be submitted as soon as possible after January 1. *Need-based scholarships/grants offered:* Federal Pell, SEOG, state scholarships/grants, private scholarships, the school's own gift aid. *Loan aid offered:* FFEL Subsidized Stafford, FFEL Unsubsidized Stafford, FFEL PLUS, Federal Perkins, Federal Nursing, state loans Applicants will be notified of awards on a rolling basis beginning 3/15. Federal Work-Study Program available. Institutional employment available. Off-campus job opportunities are good.

The Inside Word

Admissions Counselors at TCU make sure they consider a variety of factors before making admit decisions—students are rarely discounted because they are weak in one particular category. That said, most acceptance letters go to well-rounded applicants. As most TCU students are Texas residents, those applying from out of state are at a slight advantage in the admissions process.

THE SCHOOL SAYS "..."

From The Admissions Office

"TCU is a major teaching and research university with the feel of a small college. The TCU academic experience includes small classes with top faculty; cutting-edge technology; a liberal arts and sciences core curriculum; and real-life application though faculty-directed research, group projects, and internships. While TCU faculty members are recognized for research, their main focus is on teaching and mentoring students. The friendly campus community welcomes new students at Frog Camp before classes begin, where students find three days of fun meeting new friends, learning campus traditions, and serving the community. Campus life includes 200 clubs and organizations, a spirited NCAA Division I athletics program, and numerous productions from professional schools of the arts. More than half of the students participate in a wide array of intramural sports, and about 35 percent are involved in Greek organizations, including ones emphasizing ethnic diversity as well as the Christian faith. The historic relationship to the Christian Church (Disciples of Christ) means that instead of teaching a particular viewpoint, TCU encourages students to consider and follow their own beliefs. The university's mission—to educate individuals to think and act as ethical leaders and responsible citizens in a global community—influences everything from course work to study abroad to the way Horned Frogs act and interact. From National Merit Scholars to those just now realizing their academic potential, TCU attracts and serves students who are learning to change the world.

"TCU will accept either the SAT or the ACT (with or without the Writing component) in admission and scholarship processes. The Writing sections will be considered alongside the TCU application essay."

SELECTIVITY

Admissions Rating	**86**
# of applicants	11,888
% of applicants accepted	49
% of acceptees attending	28
# accepting a place on wait list	547
% admitted from wait list	38

FRESHMAN PROFILE

Range SAT Critical Reading	530–620
Range SAT Math	530–640
Range SAT Writing	530–620
Range ACT Composite	23–28
Minimum paper TOEFL	550
Minimum computer TOEFL	213
Minimum web-based TOEFL	80
% graduated top 10% of class	30
% graduated top 25% of class	64
% graduated top 50% of class	93

DEADLINES

Early action	
Deadline	11/15
Notification	1/1
Regular	
Priority	11/15
Deadline	2/15
Notification	4/1
Nonfall registration?	yes

FINANCIAL FACTS

Financial Aid Rating	**78**
Annual tuition	$26,900
% frosh rec. need-based scholarship or grant aid	32
% UG rec. need-based scholarship or grant aid	33
% frosh rec. non-need-based scholarship or grant aid	21
% UG rec. non-need-based scholarship or grant aid	19
% frosh rec. need-based self-help aid	31
% UG rec. need-based self-help aid	35
% frosh rec. athletic scholarships	4
% UG rec. athletic scholarships	4
% frosh rec. any financial aid	73
% UG rec. any financial aid	72
% UG borrow to pay for school	50
Average cumulative indebtedness	$23,651

THOMAS AQUINAS COLLEGE

10000 NORTH OJAI ROAD, SANTA PAULA, CA 93060 • ADMISSION: 800-634-9797 • FAX: 805-525-9342

CAMPUS LIFE
Quality of Life Rating	94
Fire Safety Rating	88
Green Rating	61
Type of school	private
Affiliation	Roman Catholic
Environment	rural

STUDENTS
Total undergrad enrollment	360
% male/female	51/49
% from out of state	55
% from public high school	16
% live on campus	99
% Asian	3
% Caucasian	79
% Hispanic	6
% international	6
# of countries represented	9

SURVEY SAYS . . .
Class discussions encouraged
No one cheats
Students are very religious
Low cost of living
Intercollegiate sports are unpopular
or nonexistent
Frats and sororities are unpopular
or nonexistent
Very little drug use

ACADEMICS
Academic Rating	95
Calendar	semester
Student/faculty ratio	11:1
Profs interesting rating	98
Profs accessible rating	96
Most common reg class size	10–19 students

MOST POPULAR MAJORS
business administration and
management
communication studies/speech
communication and rhetoric
English/language arts teacher
education

STUDENTS SAY ". . ."

Academics

Thomas Aquinas College is a "Great Books" school, a place where students all follow an identical curriculum that requires "reading the original works of some of the greatest thinkers in history" including, of course, Thomas Aquinas. The goal here is "to discover the truth by studying the greatest minds of Western thought," and students agree that this approach "far outstrips most others because eternal Truth is the end goal, not just some credentials for a job later. Not accidentally, this does actually produce more capable, honest, and self-giving individuals." Undergrad here appreciate "the integration of the curriculum" and are "amazed at the way it all fits together.... That it is one integrated program followed by all greatly contributes to the unity" of the TAC community. Of course, any program, no matter how well designed, is only as good as those who execute it; fortunately, at TAC "the academic experience is amazing.... This journey, when it is not self-inspiring, receives infallible impetus from all the professors at the school, who are inspiring models of inquiry, wonder, and disciplined understanding." Teachers, called tutors here, "are incredibly well-rounded people." As one student sums up the TAC approach, the program is all about "teaching students that reason can help them enlighten and hone their faith, and that they don't have to be afraid to encounter the big philosophical questions as a Catholic, because their worldview is well thought-out enough to take on even the biggest challengers."

Life

Life at TAC "centers around the curriculum.... Consequently, we are always talking about the ideas in those books, and even more everyday conversations are influenced by what we read. Some of the more weighty discussions are, for example: Is Newtonian physics legitimate in the light of Aristotelian physics and metaphysics? Does Kant really prove that you can't prove that God exists? Is a line made up of points? Does God predestine people to Hell? What is the order of charity? What is law? And there are many others." Though "this may not sound like fun" to some, students agree that "when conversations like these are placed in the context of a wonderful social and spiritual life and a myriad of activities, whether sports or the performing arts or volunteer work in the local community, the potential for true growth and true betterment of self and others is huge, and this is what we actually experience." It's thanks to this perspective that many here thrive "in an atmosphere of selflessness and progress in grace and understanding." Some here bristle at the administration's "strongly enforced" rules, and others find it "annoying that we're so far from town," but most accept these strictures as an acceptable cost of a TAC education.

Student Body

The typical student at Thomas Aquinas College, according to one among their ranks, "is a devout Catholic, solidly Aristotelian in philosophy and Thomistic in theology, perhaps even to the point of automatically assuming everything they say (except when Aristotle contradicts Thomas Aquinas!).... A large number could be said, perhaps, to have their views shaped primarily by the Republican platform." He or she "studies a lot, because if you want to stay you've got to study hard since we take at least 18 credits per semester and you can't drop any classes." In addition, "The typical student also believes in what he/she is doing, because if you don't, why do all that work?" Home schoolers are well represented here. Students tell us that those uncomfortable with the restrictive rules and "with the extreme geographical isolation...end up withdrawing from the program."

FINANCIAL AID: 800-634-9797 • E-MAIL: ADMISSIONS@THOMASAQUINAS.EDU • WEBSITE: WWW.THOMASAQUINAS.EDU

THE PRINCETON REVIEW SAYS

Admissions

Very important factors considered include: Application essay, recommendation(s), rigor of secondary school record, standardized test scores, character/personal qualities, level of applicant's interest. *Important factors considered include:* Academic GPA, religious affiliation/commitment. *Other factors considered include:* Class rank, extracurricular activities, interview, talent/ability, volunteer work, work experience. SAT or ACT required; TOEFL required of all international applicants. High school diploma is required and GED is accepted. *Academic units required:* 4 English, 3 mathematics, 2 foreign language, 2 history. *Academic units recommended:* 4 mathematics, 3 science, (2 science labs), 2 history, 3 academic electives.

Financial Aid

Students should submit: FAFSA, institution's own financial aid form, state aid form, Tax return, Noncustodial Parent Statement. Regular filing deadline is 3/2. The Princeton Review suggests that all financial aid forms be submitted as soon as possible after January 1. *Need-based scholarships/grants offered:* Federal Pell, state scholarships/grants, private scholarships, the school's own gift aid. *Loan aid offered:* FFEL Subsidized Stafford, FFEL Unsubsidized Stafford, FFEL PLUS, college/university loans from institutional funds, Canadian student Loans. Applicants will be notified of awards on a rolling basis beginning 1/1. Off-campus job opportunities are fair.

The Inside Word

Thomas Aquinas admits applicants on a rolling basis and reports that "in recent years the freshman class has filled relatively quickly." Apply early to improve your chances. Because the school's unique curriculum, candidates must demonstrate a penchant for scholarship and a love of learning for its own sake. You'll get a chance to demonstrate both in your four admission essays (successful candidates' essays typically run 7 to 10 pages in length, according to the school).

THE SCHOOL SAYS ". . ."

From The Admissions Office

"Thomas Aquinas College holds with confidence that the human mind is capable of knowing the truth about reality. The college further holds that living according to the truth is necessary for human happiness, and that truth is best comprehended through the harmonious work of faith and reason. The intellectual virtues are understood to be essential, and the college considers the cultivation of those virtues the primary work of Catholic liberal education.

"The academic program designed to achieve this goal is comprehensive and unified—and it includes no textbooks or lecture classes. In every course—from philosophy, theology, mathematics, and science to language, music, literature and history—students actually read the greatest written works in those disciplines, both ancient and modern: Homer, Plato, Aristotle, Augustine, Aquinas, Newton, Maxwell, Einstein, the Founding Fathers of the American republic, Shakespeare and T. S. Eliot, to name a few. Instead of attending lecture classes, students gather in small tutorials, seminars, and laboratories for Socratic-style discussions.

"One mark of the program's success is the variety of professions and careers that graduates enter. Nearly half attend graduate and professional schools in a wide array of disciplines; among them, philosophy, theology, law, and the sciences are most often chosen.

"SAT or ACT (Writing component encouraged) scores are required, and the essays written for these tests are reviewed by the Admission Committee. However, scores in Critical Reading and Math (SAT) and English and Mathematics (ACT) are more central in the consideration of a student's application."

SELECTIVITY

Admissions Rating	91
# of applicants	222
% of applicants accepted	60
% of acceptees attending	76
# accepting a place on wait list	77
% admitted from wait list	35

FRESHMAN PROFILE

Range SAT Critical Reading	600–740
Range SAT Math	570–660
Range ACT Composite	25–29
Minimum paper TOEFL	570
Minimum computer TOEFL	230
Average HS GPA	3.57
% graduated top 10% of class	75
% graduated top 25% of class	75
% graduated top 50% of class	100

DEADLINES

Regular	
Notification	rolling
Nonfall registration?	no

APPLICANTS ALSO LOOK AT AND SOMETIMES PREFER

Thomas More College of Liberal Arts
University of Dallas
Franciscan University of Steubenville
University of Notre Dame
The Catholic University of America
Benedictine College
Christendom College

FINANCIAL FACTS

Financial Aid Rating	99
Annual tuition	$21,400
Room and board	$6,950
Books and supplies	$450
% frosh rec. need-based scholarship or grant aid	60
% UG rec. need-based scholarship or grant aid	60
% frosh rec. non-need-based scholarship or grant aid	1
% UG rec. non-need-based scholarship or grant aid	1
% frosh rec. need-based self-help aid	69
% UG rec. need-based self-help aid	67
% frosh rec. any financial aid	69
% UG rec. any financial aid	68
% UG borrow to pay for school	62
Average cumulative indebtedness	$14,000

TRANSYLVANIA UNIVERSITY

300 NORTH BROADWAY, LEXINGTON, KY 40508-1797 • ADMISSIONS: 859-233-8242 • FAX: 859-233-8797

STUDENTS SAY "..."

Academics

Transylvania University "in the middle of" Lexington, Kentucky is a small and "very challenging" bastion of the liberal arts and sciences with a "strong premed program," "a remarkable pre-law program," and a broad core curriculum. "You take a variety of courses even though you might not be interested in them," and "writing is an integral part of the academic experience." "Even business, science, and math students must take writing-intensive classes." "The academic standards here are high." Dedication is "required if you want to excel," and studying is definitely a must. "Basically, I spend a lot of time in the library," reports a biochemistry major. "This school is very time-consuming." Classes are very small, though, "which makes it very easy to work with the professors and develop a relationship with them." The "quirky" faculty is "by far the best aspect of the school." They "are really concerned about helping you learn" and are "great to just sit down and talk with during their office hours." The conservative administration "tends to micromanage" but it's accessible as well. "If you have a complaint, going straight to the top will probably get you somewhere." Still, "they can make you jump through way too many hoops," and getting the classes you want can be a major hassle. "We are still in the middle ages when it comes to registration," gripes a French major.

Life

The campus here is "wonderfully historic" and "beautiful," but "some of the buildings are getting a little run down." "Food services are usually hit or miss." "The Internet is really, really bad. A lot of people complain about the speed and the restrictions on file sharing." "The dorms are popular," and most everyone lives on-campus. "Once you're inside the Transy bubble, it's very hard to get out." "Students are often completely absorbed by this community." "The small college atmosphere allows students to participate in many arenas," relates a sophomore. "At many schools, a math major would never be able to sing in the choir, work on the school newspaper, and be a resident assistant." However, the most prominent aspect of Transylvania's social life is the "overwhelming" Greek system. "Everything that happens on campus has some sort of affiliation with sororities or fraternities." "New students almost feel pressured into joining," and if you don't pledge, "it's generally up to you to make your own fun." "Not every student can handle going to school in this environment," cautions a junior. "Others absolutely flourish in it." "Loud" parties are popular, and a strong contingent of students gets "rowdy" and "really intoxicated" on the weekends. "Alcohol laws are lenient." "We are a wet campus," explains a senior, "so, if you are 21, it is legal to have a small amount of alcohol in your room." "People respect you if you say you don't drink but, at the same time, you feel left out if you don't." The "medium-sized city" of Lexington also offers a decent number of options. The downtown area is within "walking distance." The proximity of the University of Kentucky is another plus. "We have access to their library and social scene," notes a sophomore.

Student Body

"Upper middle class white suburbanites" constitute the vast majority. "There are a few odd students who just don't fit in" but "most students have similar backgrounds and get along with each other rather well." "You have your occasional jock and the occasional guy who looks like he just walked out of the country club." However, the typical student here is reportedly "a nerd deep down and was probably called that in high school." Virtually everyone takes academics pretty seriously. Politically, "there is quite a divide between those who are conservative and those who are liberal." Transylvania students also divide themselves by their frats and sororities. Students "have a very strong tendency to associate mostly with members of their Greek chapters." There's still quite a bit of intermingling, though. "It's just too small to be exclusive."

FINANCIAL AID: 859-233-8239 • E-MAIL: ADMISSIONS@TRANSY.EDU • WEBSITE: WWW.TRANSY.EDU

THE PRINCETON REVIEW SAYS

Admissions

Very important factors considered include: Academic GPA, rigor of secondary school record, standardized test scores. *Important factors considered include:* Application essay, recommendation(s), extracurricular activities. *Other factors considered include:* Class rank, alumni/ae relation, character/personal qualities, first generation, geographical residence, interview, talent/ability, volunteer work, work experience. SAT or ACT required; TOEFL required of all international applicants. High school diploma is required and GED is accepted. *Academic units required:* 4 English, 3 mathematics, 3 science, 2 social studies. *Academic units recommended:* 4 English, 4 mathematics, 4 science, (2 science labs), 2 foreign language, 2 social studies, 1 history, 1 academic elective.

Financial Aid

Students should submit: FAFSA. The Princeton Review suggests that all financial aid forms be submitted as soon as possible after January 1. *Need-based scholarships/grants offered:* Federal Pell, SEOG, state scholarships/grants, private scholarships, the school's own gift aid. *Loan aid offered:* Direct Subsidized Stafford, Direct Unsubsidized Stafford, Direct PLUS, FFEL Subsidized Stafford, FFEL Unsubsidized Stafford, FFEL PLUS, Federal Perkins, college/university loans from institutional funds. Applicants will be notified of awards on a rolling basis beginning 3/15. Federal Work-Study Program available. Institutional employment available. Off-campus job opportunities are excellent.

Inside Word

Applicants who become successful students at TU have the wherewithal to rise to challenging academic demands and the discipline to do so in an ethical fashion. If you're looking for a place to disappear into an ocean of faces, try the University of Kentucky down the road.

THE SCHOOL SAYS "..."

From The Admissions Office

"Bright, highly motivated students choose Transylvania for our personal approach to learning and our record of success in preparing them for rewarding careers and fulfilling lives. They attend small classes (many have fewer than 10 students) with highly qualified professors (no teaching assistants) and tackle faculty-directed student research projects in intriguing subjects like neurotransmitters and receptors, computer animation, and local Hispanic culture. Transylvania graduates have won prestigious scholarships and distinguished themselves at highly selective graduate and professional schools.

"Transylvania students consider the world their classroom. They enjoy May term travel courses studying the ancient polis in Greece, language and culture in France, and tropical ecology in Hawaii. Study abroad takes them to Germany, England, Japan, Mexico, and other destinations for a summer, a semester, or a year.

"You'll find Transylvania, a small college, nestled in a big city. Transylvania students soak up the advantages of Lexington, Kentucky, with its population of 270,000, numerous internships and job opportunities, and lots of entertainment. On campus, we have more than 50 co-curricular activities, and 18 varsity teams competing in NCAA Division III.

"While Transylvania is the nation's sixteenth-oldest college and proud of its rich history, its commitments to the exploration of a variety of disciplines, to intellectual inquiry, and to critical thinking have never been more relevant than in today's rapidly changing twenty-first-century world.

"Applicants for Fall 2009 are not required to submit Writing scores from the ACT or the SAT."

SELECTIVITY

Admissions Rating	86
# of applicants	1,420
% of applicants accepted	79
% of acceptees attending	31

FRESHMAN PROFILE

Range SAT Critical Reading	530–640
Range SAT Math	530–650
Range ACT Composite	23–29
Minimum paper TOEFL	550
Minimum computer TOEFL	213
Average HS GPA	3.66
% graduated top 10% of class	47
% graduated top 25% of class	76
% graduated top 50% of class	94

DEADLINES

Early action	
Deadline	12/1
Notification	1/15
Regular	
Priority	12/1
Deadline	2/1
Notification	3/1
Nonfall registration?	yes

APPLICANTS ALSO LOOK AT

AND OFTEN PREFER
Vanderbilt University
Miami University

AND SOMETIMES PREFER
University of Kentucky
Centre College

FINANCIAL FACTS

Financial Aid Rating	82
Annual tuition	$22,840
Room and board	$7,450
Required fees	$970
Books and supplies	$1,000
% frosh rec. need-based scholarship or grant aid	69
% UG rec. need-based scholarship or grant aid	63
% frosh rec. non-need-based scholarship or grant aid	30
% UG rec. non-need-based scholarship or grant aid	35
% frosh rec. need-based self-help aid	52
% UG rec. need-based self-help aid	50
% frosh rec. any financial aid	99
% UG rec. any financial aid	98
% UG borrow to pay for school	62
Average cumulative indebtedness	$17,561

TRINITY COLLEGE (CT)

300 SUMMIT STREET, HARTFORD, CT 06016 • ADMISSIONS: 860-297-2180 • FAX: 860-297-2287

STUDENTS SAY " . . ."

Academics

Connecticut's Trinity College "offers a rare combination of high academic standards, a balanced political climate, intense athletic competitiveness/participation, awesome financial aid" and, last but not least, "a huge party scene," prompting some students to opine that "Trinity offers the most even balance of academics (amazing professors, room to find your niche) and social life" among U.S. colleges. Here, "Monday through Thursday everyone goes to class, studies, and gets their work done," but, "Come the weekend, people let loose and party just as hard as they study." Weekdays offer "a great learning experience that provides ample opportunities," thanks in part to the school's small size (which means undergraduates have opportunities for research), a faculty staffed by "brilliant and caring" professors who "prioritize teaching above publishing," and a library that is "nothing less than phenomenal." Students also appreciate Trinity's urban setting, noting that "the city of Hartford [is used] as a valuable learning tool" and pointing out that, unlike "the majority of top liberal arts schools . . . [where] internship opportunities are limited, Trinity offered me the opportunity [for] many hands-on experiences." This may be particularly true if your field of interest is politics (Trinity's "location in a capital city means lots of opportunities for political internships," explains one student). Other standout departments include English (both literature and creative writing), Engineering, Theater, French, and the interdisciplinary program in human rights.

Life

For many Trinity undergrads, "The fraternities dominate the weekend social scene," and because these groups can be "fairly elitist" when it comes to allowing people into their late-night soirees, "Sometimes it's hard to find something to do." Other students take a broader view of campus life. Such students tell us that new groups are "gaining social power," among them "The Fred (named after late professor Fred Pfiel)," which hosts "open mic evenings, nonalcoholic competitions, [and] theme nights," among other events. They also call out Trinity's Cinestudio, "one of the best on-campus student-run movie theaters in the country." While campus theater, orchestra, a cappella, and chamber groups have limited participation, their performances are often well attended by the student body. Students note that "everything is available on campus so there is minimal effort to find things off campus." Those who have cars "often travel to nicer parts of Hartford or other Connecticut towns." One student observes, "Hartford, Connecticut is not as bad as people make it out to be. It has a lot to offer as long as you are willing to leave campus. There are some great restaurants and lots of shows to go to. Don't let yourself get stuck on campus every weekend."

Student Body

"Despite admissions' efforts, Trinity is still characterized by the New England boarding-school grad in polos and pink pants," undergrads here tell us, although some assert that "what many see as the typical student is actually a minority." Still, "The picture that immediately comes to mind is a blond, blue-eyed girl buying Coach . . . with daddy's money." Adding some diversity is "a growing population of 'Wesleyan-types,' who probably got rejected from our fellow Connecticut school. There's [been] an influx of intelligent, down-to-earth people at Trinity who are passionate about a lot more than getting wasted Thursday through Sunday." Students tend to be "over-wired" when not in class, attached to a "cell phone, IM, computer, [or] iPod, and therefore socially awkward or impolite. . . . In class, they are overachievers, very articulate and competitive. Most spend an impressive amount of time studying."

FINANCIAL AID: 860-297-2046 • E-MAIL: ADMISSIONS.OFFICE@TRINCOLL.EDU • WEBSITE: WWW.TRINCOLL.EDU

THE PRINCETON REVIEW SAYS

Admissions

Very important factors considered include: Rigor of secondary school record. *Important factors considered include:* Class rank, application essay, academic GPA, recommendation(s), standardized test scores, character/personal qualities, extracurricular activities, interview, racial/ethnic status, talent/ability. *Other factors considered include:* Alumni/ae relation, first generation, geographical residence, level of applicant's interest, volunteer work, work experience. SAT or ACT required; ACT with Writing component recommended. High school diploma is required and GED is accepted. *Academic units required:* 4 English, 3 mathematics, 2 science, (2 science labs), 3 foreign language, 2 history.

Financial Aid

Students should submit: FAFSA, CSS/Financial Aid PROFILE, noncustodial PROFILE, business/farm supplement, Federal Income tax returns. Regular filing deadline is 3/1. The Princeton Review suggests that all financial aid forms be submitted as soon as possible after January 1. *Need-based scholarships/grants offered:* Federal Pell, SEOG, state scholarships/grants, private scholarships, the school's own gift aid. *Loan aid offered:* Direct Subsidized Stafford, Direct Unsubsidized Stafford, Direct PLUS, FFEL Subsidized Stafford, FFEL Unsubsidized Stafford, FFEL PLUS, Federal Perkins, college/university loans from institutional funds. Applicants will be notified of awards on or about 4/1. Federal Work-Study Program available. Institutional employment available. Off-campus job opportunities are good.

The Inside Word

Students describe Trinity as "the home of Yale rejects," an appraisal that accurately characterizes the school's rep as an Ivy safety (if not the actual makeup of the student body). The school's high price tag ensures that a large percentage of the student body is made up of wealthy prepsters, but the school does offer generous financial aid packages to top candidates who can't afford the hefty price of attending. The school would love to broaden its student demographic, so competitive minority students should receive a very receptive welcome here.

THE SCHOOL SAYS "..."

From The Admissions Office

"An array of distinctive curricular options—including an interdisciplinary neuroscience major and a professionally accredited engineering degree program, a unique Human Rights Program, a Health Fellows Program, and interdisciplinary programs such as the Cities Program, Interdisciplinary Science Program, and InterArts—is one reason record numbers of students are applying to Trinity. In fact, applications are up 80 percent over the past 5 years. In addition, the college has been recognized for its commitment to diversity; students of color have represented approximately 20 percent of the freshman class for the past 4 years, setting Trinity apart from many of its peers. Trinity's capital city location offers students unparalleled 'real-world' learning experiences to complement classroom learning. Students take advantage of extensive opportunities for internships for academic credit and community service, and these opportunities extend to Trinity's global learning sites in cities around the world. Trinity's faculty is a devoted and accomplished group of exceptional teacher-scholars; our 100-acre campus is beautiful; Hartford is an educational asset that differentiates Trinity from other liberal arts colleges; our global connections and foreign study opportunities prepare students to be good citizens of the world; and our graduates go on to excel in virtually every field. We invite you to learn more about why Trinity might be the best choice for you.

"Students applying for admission for the entering class of Fall 2008 may submit the following testing options: SAT, ACT with Writing."

SELECTIVITY

Admissions Rating	**95**
# of applicants	5,950
% of applicants accepted	34
% of acceptees attending	28
# accepting a place on wait list	460
% admitted from wait list	37
# of early decision applicants	412
% accepted early decision	69

FRESHMAN PROFILE

Range SAT Critical Reading	600–690
Range SAT Math	610–690
Range SAT Writing	608–700
Range ACT Composite	26–29
% graduated top 10% of class	61
% graduated top 25% of class	88
% graduated top 50% of class	96

DEADLINES

Early decision	
Deadline	11/15
Notification	12/15
Regular	
Deadline	1/1
Notification	4/1
Nonfall registration?	no

APPLICANTS ALSO LOOK AT

AND OFTEN PREFER
Harvard College
Yale University
Tufts University
University of Pennsylvania
Amherst College

AND SOMETIMES PREFER
Wesleyan University
Middlebury College

AND RARELY PREFER
Connecticut College
Colgate University
Boston University

FINANCIAL FACTS

Financial Aid Rating	**98**
Annual tuition	$35,110
Room and board	$9,420
Required fees	$1,760
Books and supplies	$900
% frosh rec. need-based scholarship or grant aid	35
% UG rec. need-based scholarship or grant aid	36
% frosh rec. non-need-based scholarship or grant aid	11
% UG rec. non-need-based scholarship or grant aid	9
% frosh rec. need-based self-help aid	28
% UG rec. need-based self-help aid	31
% frosh rec. any financial aid	39
% UG rec. any financial aid	40
% UG borrow to pay for school	43
Average cumulative indebtedness	$19,835

TRINITY UNIVERSITY (TX)

One Trinity Place, San Antonio, TX 78212 • Admissions: 210-999-7207 • Fax: 210-999-8164

STUDENTS SAY ". . ."
Academics

Trinity University is a small private school that, despite its size, offers "a diversity of good programs." The school is "known for its good science and premed programs, but has decent arts programs, too." And students point out that "Not many other schools this size have their own radio station and television station with a full communications department." Throw in "a really good program in education" ("you can graduate with a Masters in five years, and teachers graduated from Trinity are well-known" in the area), a "really great business program," and "a great study abroad program" and you understand why students say "It's rare to have such a well-rounded school of this size." On top of its academic variety Trinity adds "a diverse population, small classes, and a very active social scene; in other words—there's something for everyone!" Students don't forfeit the benefits of a small school here, though. On the contrary, they enjoy "the ability to really get to know our professors and the administration and to work up to leadership positions and opportunities…. No one holds your hand here, yet everyone really has the drive to do well. There are very few people who just show up to class and then peace out when it's over. Everyone interacts and really makes an effort to engage in class time." The school's location in the nation's seventh-largest city also means that there are "great opportunities" for graduates.

Life

Trinity students form "a pretty small, close-knit community, so students spend a lot of time with each other. People study here a lot, but people also go out a lot and know how to have a good time." Campus fun includes "parties, club sports, various organizations to join, good school sport teams (especially soccer), intramural sports, and all sorts of events going on like dances, concerts, and other things." Big-city life dampens the enthusiasm of some for campus events. As one student explains, "Trinity has many on-campus activities such as Trinity Idol, the Tigers Den, and the Roast, but San Antonio is a city full of cultural and unique restaurants and activities. We go to the zoo, the many restaurants, downtown, the many parks, and venues to hear music." One student sizes up the situation this way: "San Antonio has everything you could want in terms of food, clubs, and shopping. First Fridays is the best part of San Antonio. Once a month they have a sort of festival with plenty of art and crafts for sale." Trinity's dormitories earn good marks as they "are pretty big and we have walk-in closets, and the bathrooms are big as well," although some complain that "all of them are the same" and that "there are no single rooms…. It gets tiring sharing a small room with another person for three years (there's a three-year residency requirement)."

Student Body

Trinity undergrads are "smart," "friendly," and "very dedicated to doing well in school" while also maintaining a healthy social life. As one undergrad puts it, "For the most part, students at Trinity have managed to find that delicate balance between an academic and social life (often through trial and error)." Most here "come from well-to-do families," are "talented in unique ways," and "worked hard in high school." While "the majority is Caucasian," "there are tons of international students who enhance the university" by broadening the perspectives represented in Trinity classrooms.

FINANCIAL AID: 210-999-8315 • E-MAIL: ADMISSIONS@TRINITY.EDU • WEBSITE: WWW.TRINITY.EDU

THE PRINCETON REVIEW SAYS

Admissions

Very important factors considered include: Class rank, academic GPA, rigor of secondary school record. *Important factors considered include:* Application essay, recommendation(s), standardized test scores, character/personal qualities, extracurricular activities, interview, talent/ability. *Other factors considered include:* Alumni/ae relation, first generation, geographical residence, level of applicant's interest, volunteer work, work experience. SAT or ACT required; High school diploma is required and GED is accepted. *Academic units required:* 4 English, 3 mathematics, 3 science, (2 science labs), 2 foreign language, 3 social studies. *Academic units recommended:* 4 English, 3 mathematics, 3 science, (2 science labs), 3 foreign language, 3 social studies, 3 academic electives.

Financial Aid

Students should submit: FAFSA preferred filing deadline is 2/15. The Princeton Review suggests that all financial aid forms be submitted as soon as possible after January 1. *Need-based scholarships/grants offered:* Federal Pell, SEOG, state scholarships/grants, private scholarships, the school's own gift aid. *Loan aid offered:* FFEL Subsidized Stafford, FFEL Unsubsidized Stafford, FFEL PLUS, Federal Perkins, state loans, college/university loans from institutional funds. Applicants will be notified of awards by 4/1. Federal Work-Study Program available. Institutional employment available. Off-campus job opportunities are good.

The Inside Word

Trinity accepts the Common Application but requires a supplemental application that includes a personal statement ("Why I want to attend Trinity") and either one long essay or three short essays. The message is clear: If you want to attend Trinity, you'd better be able to write. Spend some time on these essays, particularly if you think you're right on the cut line. A well-written essay could well tip the balance in your favor.

THE SCHOOL SAYS "..."

From The Admissions Office

"Three qualities separate Trinity University from other selective, academically challenging institutions around the country. First, Trinity is unusual in the quality and quantity of resources devoted almost exclusively to its undergraduate students. Those resources give rise to a second distinctive aspect of Trinity—its emphasis on undergraduate research. Our students prefer being involved over observing. With superior laboratory facilities and strong, dedicated faculty, our undergraduates fill many of the roles formerly reserved for graduate students, and our professors often go to their undergraduates for help with their research. Other hands on learning experiences including internships, study-abroad, and service projects are also available to students. Finally, Trinity stands apart for the attitude of its students. In an atmosphere of academic camaraderie and fellowship, our students work together to stretch their minds and broaden their horizons. For quality of resources, for dedication to undergraduate research, and for the disposition of its student body, Trinity University holds a unique position in American higher education.

"Students applying for admission must submit either the ACT or the SAT I. The highest composite test scores from one or multiple dates are evaluated. The SAT Writing section and ACT Writing component are not required."

SELECTIVITY

Admissions Rating	93
# of applicants	4,511
% of applicants accepted	52
% of acceptees attending	27
# of early decision applicants	45
% accepted early decision	64

FRESHMAN PROFILE

Range SAT Critical Reading	600–690
Range SAT Math	610–690
Range ACT Composite	27–31
Average HS GPA	3.53
% graduated top 10% of class	53
% graduated top 25% of class	85
% graduated top 50% of class	100

DEADLINES

Early decision	
Deadline	11/1
Notification	12/1
Early action	
Deadline	12/1
Notification	2/1
Regular	
Deadline	2/1
Notification	4/1
Nonfall registration?	no

FINANCIAL FACTS

Financial Aid Rating	86
Annual tuition	$26,664
Room and board	$8,822
Required fees	$1,035
Books and supplies	$950
% frosh rec. need-based scholarship or grant aid	41
% UG rec. need-based scholarship or grant aid	37
% frosh rec. non-need-based scholarship or grant aid	8
% UG rec. non-need-based scholarship or grant aid	7
% frosh rec. need-based self-help aid	32
% UG rec. need-based self-help aid	30
% frosh rec. any financial aid	86
% UG rec. any financial aid	85

TRUMAN STATE UNIVERSITY

McClain Hall 205, 100 East Normal, Kirksville, MO 63501 • Admissions: 660-785-4114 • Fax: 660-785-7456

CAMPUS LIFE

Quality of Life Rating	83
Fire Safety Rating	77
Green Rating	79
Type of school	public
Environment	village

STUDENTS

Total undergrad enrollment	5,496
% male/female	43/57
% from out of state	24
% from public high school	75
% live on campus	51
% in (# of) fraternities	22 (14)
% in (# of) sororities	18 (6)
% African American	3
% Asian	2
% Caucasian	63
% Hispanic	2
% Native American	1
% international	3
# of countries represented	40

SURVEY SAYS . . .

Small classes
Lab facilities are great
Great computer facilities
Great library
Career services are great
Students are friendly
Campus feels safe
Low cost of living
Students are happy

ACADEMICS

Academic Rating	80
Calendar	semester
Student/faculty ratio	16:1
Profs interesting rating	80
Profs accessible rating	89
% classes taught by TAs	2
Most common reg class size	20–29 students
Most common lab size	10–19 students

MOST POPULAR MAJORS

business administration and management
biology/biological sciences
English language and literature

STUDENTS SAY ". . ."

Academics

Students who attend Truman State University are convinced that "Truman is one of the best public schools in Missouri, demanding high-level thinking" from undergrads. Students praise Truman's "very strong academic program" with a mandatory liberal arts sequence that "gives students the opportunity to take classes that we would otherwise be unable to take. I can take science, art, history, or several foreign languages. It is wonderful to not be confined to one area." While "Some students see taking a lot of classes that are not directly related to one's major program as a bad thing," the majority recognize that it "helps to diversify our knowledge and to make us more well-rounded individuals. Furthermore, sometimes these classes lead you to realize you are more interested in certain areas than you originally thought." Add "helpful teachers and great study abroad and leadership opportunities" to the mix, and you can see how "Truman gives students the complete education that will make them competitive in the job market and graduate school [admissions]." Students tell us that Truman excels in education ("the best teacher preparation program in the state, if not the region," brags one student), biology, and equine science, among other areas. In all disciplines, "Professors do as much as they can to make themselves accessible, and are always open to an office visit or an e-mail from students if they have a question," and, perhaps best of all, "Truman is a great deal financially."

Life

Truman's small hometown of Kirksville "is not exactly the cultural hub of the Midwest," but the school works hard "to keep students from being bored. The Student Activities Board brings in comedians and bands, and other organizations host events for students like mixers, trivia nights, movie nights, and a cappella concerts." One undergrad explains, "Even though Truman is in a small town, there is plenty to do. The difference is that you don't look so much for something to do, as for someone to do something with. Exploring and wandering around town and the surrounding areas are pretty common activities, as are road trips, and small get-togethers any night of the week." And, "Like most colleges, we party," although "In most cases partying is not excessive and doesn't interfere with schoolwork." Truman students enjoy "a solid Greek presence that doesn't dominate campus life. In other words, your social life will not be over if you don't join a fraternity or sorority." This is true in part because "There are tons of organizations at Truman, and if the one you want doesn't exist, all you need is about six students and a constitution to start your own." For road trips, "Columbia is also a quick hour and a half south for [students seeking] more variety than a small town like Kirksville can offer."

Student Body

The "studious" undergrads of Truman include "a lot of overachievers who excel in and out of the classroom." Truman students "are here to learn. Sure, students go to parties, but Truman is not what I'd call a 'party school.' Many people choose alternative ways of having fun." Most here are "Midwesterners, White, and from middle-class or upper-middle-class families." One student confides, "The rumor is that a third of Truman's campus is from St. Louis, White, and Catholic. Fortunately, religiosity isn't so much an 'in-your-face' issue. Students on the whole get along very well across racial, gender, ethnic, age, and major/minor interests." Another undergrad adds, "We joke about the lack of diversity on our campus, but diversity does exist, and everyone seems to get along really well. Furthermore, everyone seems more than willing to open up to other cultures and religions and to learn more about them." A "surprisingly large number of international students" help bump non-White demographics upward.

FINANCIAL AID: 660-785-4130 • E-MAIL: ADMISSIONS@TRUMAN.EDU • WEBSITE: WWW.TRUMAN.EDU

THE PRINCETON REVIEW SAYS

Admissions

Very important factors considered include: Class rank, academic GPA, rigor of secondary school record, standardized test scores. *Important factors considered include:* Application essay. *Other factors considered include:* Alumni/ae relation, character/personal qualities, extracurricular activities, first generation, geographical residence, level of applicant's interest, racial/ethnic status, state residency, talent/ability, volunteer work, work experience. SAT or ACT required; TOEFL required of all international applicants. High school diploma is required and GED is accepted. *Academic units required:* 4 English, 3 mathematics, 3 science, (2 science labs), 2 foreign language, 3 social studies, 1 visual/performing arts. *Academic units recommended:* 4 mathematics.

Financial Aid

Students should submit: FAFSA, institution's own financial aid form. The Princeton Review suggests that all financial aid forms be submitted as soon as possible after January 1. *Need-based scholarships/grants offered:* Federal Pell, SEOG, state scholarships/grants, private scholarships, the school's own gift aid, Federal ACG and SMART. *Loan aid offered:* FFEL Subsidized Stafford, FFEL Unsubsidized Stafford, FFEL PLUS, Federal Perkins, Federal Nursing, state loans, college/university loans from institutional funds, and Alternative Loans. Applicants will be notified of awards on a rolling basis beginning 4/1. Federal Work-Study Program available. Institutional employment available. Off-campus job opportunities are good.

The Inside Word

Students looking to take advantage of Truman State's educational opportunities and low price tag had better hit the books. As the school's profile continues to rise, competition for admission increases. Applicants with high class rank and strong test scores will be given the most consideration. Candidates will find it to their benefit to apply early, as the decision is nonbinding.

THE SCHOOL SAYS "..."

From The Admissions Office

"Truman's talented student body enjoys small classes where undergraduate research and personal interaction with professors are the norm. Truman's commitment to providing an exemplary liberal arts and sciences education with over 200 student organizations and outstanding internship and study abroad opportunities allows students to compete in top graduate schools and the job market.

"Truman offers a variety of competitive scholarships and there is no seperate scholarship application. Students wishing to be considered for all scholarship programs are strongly encouraged to apply for admission by December 15th.

"Students applying for admission to Truman State University can submit scores from both versions of the SAT, as well as the ACT. The best scores from either test will be considered. The Writing section is not currently required for admission to Truman."

SELECTIVITY

Admissions Rating	89
# of applicants	4,076
% of applicants accepted	81
% of acceptees attending	43

FRESHMAN PROFILE

Range SAT Critical Reading	570–690
Range SAT Math	560–670
Range ACT Composite	25–30
Minimum paper TOEFL	550
Minimum computer TOEFL	213
Minimum web-based TOEFL	79
Average HS GPA	3.75
% graduated top 10% of class	48
% graduated top 25% of class	80
% graduated top 50% of class	98

DEADLINES

Regular	
Priority	12/15
Deadline	3/1
Nonfall registration?	yes

APPLICANTS ALSO LOOK AT

AND OFTEN PREFER
Saint Louis University
Washington University in St. Louis
University of Missouri—Columbia

AND SOMETIMES PREFER
Missouri State University
University of Illinois at Urbana-Champaign

AND RARELY PREFER
University of Iowa
Illinois Wesleyan University
Illinois State University

FINANCIAL FACTS

Financial Aid Rating	89
Annual tuition	$6,458
Books and supplies	$1,000
% frosh rec. need-based scholarship or grant aid	21
% UG rec. need-based scholarship or grant aid	18
% frosh rec. non-need-based scholarship or grant aid	91
% UG rec. non-need-based scholarship or grant aid	76
% frosh rec. need-based self-help aid	35
% UG rec. need-based self-help aid	35
% frosh rec. athletic scholarships	6
% UG rec. athletic scholarships	6
% frosh rec. any financial aid	96
% UG rec. any financial aid	95
% UG borrow to pay for school	41
Average cumulative indebtedness	$17,091

TUFTS UNIVERSITY

BENDETSON HALL, MEDFORD, MA 02155 • ADMISSIONS: 617-627-3170 • FAX: 617-627-3860

CAMPUS LIFE

Quality of Life Rating	**85**
Fire Safety Rating	**96**
Green Rating	**94**
Type of school	private
Environment	town

STUDENTS

Total undergrad enrollment	5,015
% male/female	49/51
% from out of state	75
% from public high school	62
% live on campus	75
% in (# of) fraternities	10 (11)
% in (# of) sororities	4 (3)
% African American	7
% Asian	12
% Caucasian	57
% Hispanic	6
% international	6
# of countries represented	93

SURVEY SAYS . . .

Great computer facilities
Great library
Great off-campus food
Campus feels safe
Students are happy
Student publications are popular
Lots of beer drinking

ACADEMICS

Academic Rating	**91**
Calendar	semester
Student/faculty ratio	7:1
Profs interesting rating	83
Profs accessible rating	80
% classes taught by TAs	1
Most common reg class size	10–19 students
Most common lab size	10–19 students

MOST POPULAR MAJORS

English language and literature
economics
international relations and affairs

STUDENTS SAY ". . ."

Academics

Tufts University boasts a "small-campus feel," a "globally recognized" reputation, and "engaging," "personable" faculty. Professors here "know what they are talking about" and "seem to go out of their way to make themselves accessible." These very same professors, however, "flood" students "with tons of work." Lower-level classes can be huge on occasion, but upper-level classes are "small and well-focused." The "transparent" administration tends "to grapple with technology and change" but it is "incredibly helpful" and very well liked, despite "militant political correctness." "President Bacow will generally respond to any e-mail sent to him by a student within about 20 minutes." Academically, while you can choose from a massive number of stellar majors in the liberal arts and engineering, Tufts is probably best known for its "very strong" science programs (especially premed) and its prestigious international relations programs. "Tufts is internationalism," declares one student. "From the Music Department's ethnomusicology [major] to Political Science and International Relations, every facet of Tufts, both in and out of the classroom, revolves around thinking globally." Studying abroad "is highly encouraged"; about 40 percent of students take advantage of awesome study abroad programs in a host of exotic locales including an "amazing" summer program in the Alps.

Life

At Tufts, the campus is "gorgeous," "The food is incredible," and course work is time-consuming, so it's no surprise that social life is basically centered on campus. Students here "know each other." "It's a nice feeling," an undergrad ventures, but "If you want to be anonymous, Tufts is not for you." The "fabulous extracurricular opportunities" include "a daily paper, a dozen student magazines," and "countless service and activism organizations." In addition, a vast array of large-scale, free campus events helps to keep students entertained. While "Drinking is very popular on the weekends," undergrads report that "there is not always a party guaranteed on a Friday or Saturday night, which is unthinkable at bigger schools." When there is one, it can seem as if "The campus police break everything up." This may be why "As you get older and you meet more people, you begin to go to more parties and social events off of campus," a more seasoned student tells us. Many feel that the surrounding town of Medford leaves a lot to be desired, but fortunately, "You have the greatest college city in the nation a subway ride away" if "you get tired [of] the Tufts scene." It should be noted, however, that public transportation into Boston takes "like an hour (counting waiting)." "We're not in Boston," cautions one student. "Don't let the admissions folks fool you."

Students

Some students tell us that Tuft's reputation as a haven for the "Ivy League reject" is accurate. Others vehemently disagree. "The Tufts Ivy complex is over," argues one student. "Anyone here could get into Cornell!" Students describe themselves as "genuinely nice," "painfully liberal," and "very goal-oriented." They are "laid-back" and only "competitive with themselves." One undergrad asserts, "The typical student here is very intelligent and ambitious, but they don't want you to think that." Another adds, "They get their work done so they can have fun too." Ethnic diversity is notable; traditionally underrepresented minorities on campus have a strong presence. However, "People tend to separate into their little cliques after first semester and rarely interact with other people." "Almost all Tufts students are rich" as well. "The frustrating thing is not the lack of ethnic diversity, but the lack of socioeconomic diversity," an English major writes. This student body features "a lot of smart kids in Lacoste polos who are looking to save the world" (or, at least, "convince others they are looking to save to world") and a lot of "preppy," "Louis V. bag," "North Face fleece," "big sunglasses," "rich kids." There are also "the stoners, the die-hard partiers, the activists, the coffeehouse philosophers," and a slew of "obscenely wealthy international kids."

FINANCIAL AID: 617-627-2000 • E-MAIL: ADMISSIONS.INQUIRY@ASE.TUFTS.EDU • WEBSITE: WWW.TUFTS.EDU

THE PRINCETON REVIEW SAYS

Admissions

Very important factors considered include: Application essay, academic GPA, rigor of secondary school record, character/personal qualities. *Important factors considered include:* Class rank, recommendation(s), standardized test scores, extracurricular activities, talent/ability, volunteer work, work experience. *Other factors considered include:* Alumni/ae relation, first generation, geographical residence, interview, racial/ethnic status, SAT and SAT Subject Tests or ACT required; ACT with Writing component required. TOEFL required of international applicant s if appropriate. High school diploma is required and GED is accepted. *Academic units recommended:* 4 English, 3 mathematics, 2 science, 3 foreign language, 2 history.

Financial Aid

Students should submit: FAFSA, CSS/Financial Aid PROFILE, noncustodial PROFILE, business/farm supplement, Parent and Student Federal Income Tax Returns. Regular filing deadline is 2/15. The Princeton Review suggests that all financial aid forms be submitted as soon as possible after January 1. *Need-based scholarships/grants offered:* Federal Pell, SEOG, state scholarships/grants, private scholarships, the school's own gift aid. *Loan aid offered:* FFEL Subsidized Stafford, FFEL Unsubsidized Stafford, FFEL PLUS, Federal Perkins, state loans, college/university loans from institutional funds. Applicants will be notified of awards on or about 4/1. Federal Work-Study Program available. Institutional employment available. Off-campus job opportunities are good.

The Inside Word

The admissions process is rigorous. With an acceptance rate hovering not much over 25 percent and average SAT section scores in the low 700s, you'll need to demonstrate fairly extraordinary academic accomplishments and submit a thorough and well-prepared application in order to get admitted to Tufts. On the bright side, Tufts is still a little bit of a safety school for aspiring Ivy Leaguers. Since many applicants who also get into an Ivy League school will pass on Tufts, it has spots for "mere mortals" at the end of the day.

THE SCHOOL SAYS "..."

From The Admissions Office

"Tufts University, on the boundary between Medford and Somerville, sits on a hill overlooking Boston, five miles northwest of the city. The campus is a tranquil New England setting within easy access by subway and bus to the cultural, social, and entertainment resources of Boston and Somerville. Since its founding in 1852 by members of the Universalist church, Tufts has grown from a small liberal arts college into a nonsectarian university of over 8,000 students with undergraduate programs in Arts & Sciences and Engineering. By 1900 the college had added a medical school, a dental school, and graduate studies. The university now also includes the Fletcher School of Law and Diplomacy, the Graduate School of Arts and Sciences, the Cummings School of Veterinary Medicine, the Friedman School of Nutrition Science and Policy, the Sackler School of Graduate Biomedical Sciences, and the Gordon Institute of Engineering Management.

"Applicants for Fall 2009 are required to submit scores (including the Writing assessment) from either the SAT or ACT. If an applicant submits the SAT, SAT Subject Tests are also required (candidates for the School of Engineering are encouraged to submit Math and either Chemistry or Physics)."

SELECTIVITY
Admissions Rating	97
# of applicants	15,380
% of applicants accepted	28
% of acceptees attending	32
# of early decision applicants	1,321
% accepted early decision	32

FRESHMAN PROFILE
Range SAT Critical Reading	670–750
Range SAT Math	670–740
Range SAT Writing	670–740
Range ACT Composite	30–32
Minimum paper TOEFL	300
Minimum computer TOEFL	100
% graduated top 10% of class	80
% graduated top 25% of class	96
% graduated top 50% of class	99

DEADLINES
Early decision	
Deadline	11/1
Notification	12/15
Regular	
Deadline	1/1
Notification	4/1
Nonfall registration?	no

FINANCIAL FACTS
Financial Aid Rating	94
Annual tuition	$38,840
% frosh rec. need-based scholarship or grant aid	38
% UG rec. need-based scholarship or grant aid	35
% frosh rec. non-need-based scholarship or grant aid	1
% UG rec. non-need-based scholarship or grant aid	1
% frosh rec. need-based self-help aid	38
% UG rec. need-based self-help aid	35
% frosh rec. any financial aid	42
% UG rec. any financial aid	38
% UG borrow to pay for school	42
Average cumulative indebtedness	$14,200

TULANE UNIVERSITY

6823 St. Charles Avenue, New Orleans, LA 70118 • Admissions: 504-865-5731 • Fax: 504-862-8715

STUDENTS SAY ". . ."

Academics

In 2005, Hurricane Katrina sent Tulane students on a forced semester in exile. For most schools, this move would have been a death sentence. Tulane, however, is not most schools; it is uniquely Tulane, "the ultimate work-hard, play-hard school" whose strong academics and laid-back approach make it the place where all the "cool smart kids" go, a place that inspires the type of student devotion rarely found at schools that lack powerhouse sports programs. Student after student praises the school's recovery efforts, observing that "Tulane's administration brought us through Katrina and is helping New Orleans through this time as well," and that "in post-Katrina New Orleans, the professors who have returned are the ones who really want to be here and really have a desire to help students learn." Katrina has actually strengthened students' allegiance to the school; as one put it, "This is the most amazing, out-of-this-world place to be—a college experience that no other school could top. And we know it because we experienced other schools during [the] Hurricane Katrina [hiatus]." The Tulane academic experience is distinguished by small classes, mostly "10 to 20 students," "one of the best study abroad programs in the country," and, of course, New Orleans, the "best city in the country," which allows Tulane to offer "a one-of-a-kind out-of-classroom experience." Standout programs include premed, business, economics, architecture, and exercise and sports science.

Life

Tulane students love New Orleans—and love to explore it—a city full of "art galleries and museums," "amazing" shopping on Magazine Street, "family-owned restaurants in the uptown area," "touristy" places in the French Quarter, and "a lot [of] different bars near campus." The city also boasts Audubon Park, "a really fun place to get exercise or spend some time," and, of course, an "unparalleled music scene." None of this, however, stops "about 30 percent of the campus" from getting involved in Greek life, or "most students" from getting involved "in at least two student organizations." In addition, "community service [and] volunteer work," always "very popular at Tulane," have become "especially popular post-Katrina." Those concerned about safety—New Orleans has traditionally had one of the higher crime rates in the nation—should note that "Tulane is located in a major city, but not in downtown New Orleans." By all accounts, campus security does "an excellent job of making sure campus is secure, and students have the opportunity to be escorted anywhere." As an added bonus, "The weather is nice—you can wear flip flops year round."

Student Body

The typical Tulane student "is serious about academics, but isn't holed up in the library all the time." Similar to students at other big-city schools, Tulane undergrads tend to be "self-reliant, motivated, [and] forward looking." They point out that the school is "one of the most geographically diverse schools in the country," observing that "75 percent of the students come from more than 500 miles away. . . . In my eight-person suite there are two girls from Boston, one from New York, one from Texas, one from Baton Rouge, one from Florida, and I'm from Chicago. It's great!" Diversity is further represented in the "tons of very large, very active, very vocal groups on campus for every minority, including ethnicities, political beliefs, religious beliefs, and sexual orientation[s]. Everyone here manages to find [his or her] own little niche." A strong Jewish Studies program helps Tulane draw one of the largest Jewish student populations in the South; about 25 percent of the student body is Jewish.

FINANCIAL AID: 504-865-5723 • E-MAIL: UNDERGRAD.ADMISSION@TULANE.EDU • WEBSITE: WWW.TULANE.EDU

THE PRINCETON REVIEW SAYS

Admissions

Very important factors considered include: Class rank, academic GPA, rigor of secondary school record, standardized test scores. *Important factors considered include:* Application essay, recommendation(s), character/personal qualities. *Other factors considered include:* Alumni/ae relation, extracurricular activities, first generation, interview, talent/ability, volunteer work, work experience. SAT or ACT required; ACT with Writing component required. TOEFL required of all international applicants. High school diploma is required and GED is accepted. *Academic units recommended:* 4 English, 4 mathematics, 4 science, (4 science labs), 3 foreign language, 3 social studies, 3 academic electives.

Financial Aid

Students should submit: FAFSA, CSS/Financial Aid PROFILE, noncustodial PROFILE, business/farm supplement. Regular filing deadline is 2/1. The Princeton Review suggests that all financial aid forms be submitted as soon as possible after January 1. *Need-based scholarships/grants offered:* Federal Pell, SEOG, state scholarships/grants, private scholarships, the school's own gift aid, Academic Competitiveness Grant, SMART Grant. *Loan aid offered:* FFEL Subsidized Stafford, FFEL Unsubsidized Stafford, FFEL PLUS, Federal Perkins Applicants will be notified of awards on a rolling basis beginning 2/1. Federal Work-Study Program available. Institutional employment available. Off-campus job opportunities are good.

The Inside Word

If you thought Hurricane Katrina would dampen students' enthusiasm for Tulane, think again; the school received nearly 21,000 applications for the class of 2010—a school record. Competition will be further stiffened by the university's decision to reduce future incoming classes by 10 percent. Part of the university's restructuring involves the elimination of some academic programs—before you apply you should check to make sure that your areas of interest are still being served.

THE SCHOOL SAYS ". . ."

From The Admissions Office

"With 6,000 full-time undergraduate students in five schools, Tulane University offers the personal attention and teaching excellence traditionally associated with small colleges together with the facilities and interdisciplinary resources found only at major research universities. Following Hurricane Katrina, the university underwent a spectacular renewal: renovating facilities and restructuring academic programs. The opportunities for students to be involved in the rebirth of New Orleans offer an experience unavailable at any other place, at any other time.

"Tulane is committed to undergraduate education. Senior faculty members teach most introductory and lower-level courses, and 74 percent of the classes have 25 or fewer students. The close student-teacher relationship pays off. Tulane graduates are among the most likely to be selected for several prestigious fellowships that support graduate study abroad. Founded in 1834 and reorganized as Tulane University in 1884, Tulane is one of the major private research universities in the South.

"The Tulane campus offers a traditional collegiate setting in an attractive residential neighborhood, which is now thriving after Hurricane Katrina."

SELECTIVITY	
Admissions Rating	94
# of applicants	16,967
% of applicants accepted	44
% of acceptees attending	18
# accepting a place on wait list	264
% admitted from wait list	8
# of early decision applicants	175
% accepted early decision	32

FRESHMAN PROFILE	
Range SAT Critical Reading	600–690
Range SAT Math	590–680
Range SAT Writing	600–690
Range ACT Composite	27–31
Minimum paper TOEFL	550
Minimum computer TOEFL	213
Average HS GPA	3.39
% graduated top 10% of class	50
% graduated top 25% of class	80
% graduated top 50% of class	96

DEADLINES	
Early decision	
Deadline	11/1
Notification	12/15
Early action	
Deadline	11/1
Notification	12/15
Regular	
Deadline	1/15
Notification	4/1
Nonfall registration?	yes

APPLICANTS ALSO LOOK AT
AND OFTEN PREFER
Vanderbilt U, Duke U, Emory U
AND SOMETIMES PREFER
Washington U in St. Louis, The University of Texas at Austin, Florida State U
AND RARELY PREFER
University of Richmond, Southern Methodist U

FINANCIAL FACTS	
Financial Aid Rating	89
Annual Tuition	$35,500
Room & board	$8,940
Books and supplies	$900
Required fees	$3,100
% frosh rec. need-based scholarship or grant aid	34
% UG rec. need-based scholarship or grant aid	34
% frosh rec. non-need-based scholarship or grant aid	14
% UG rec. non-need-based scholarship or grant aid	11
% frosh rec. need-based self-help aid	18
% UG rec. need-based self-help aid	20
% frosh rec. athletic scholarships	1
% UG rec. athletic scholarships	2
% UG borrow to pay for school	44
Average cumulative indebtedness	$22,378

TUSKEGEE UNIVERSITY

OLD ADMINISTRATION BUILDING, SUITE 101, TUSKEGEE, AL 36088 • ADMISSIONS: 334-727-8500 OR 800-622-65311 • FAX: 334-727-4402

STUDENTS SAY ". . ."

Academics

A sense of history pervades Tuskegee's "beautiful" campus in eastern Alabama, and that's fitting; "Tuskegee is the only HBCU [Historically Black College or University] named by Congress as a National Historic Site." Undergrads here generally sense there is something about "the legacy and good name of Tuskegee University that can propel a student forward." That good name derives mainly from people knowing that if you are a student at Tuskegee, "No one is doing the work for you." Academics are "challenging" here, with "excellent engineering and vet programs," setting especially high standards. Given these demands, students appreciate that "class sizes are small, only slightly larger than the average high school class at times," so it is easy to get to know one's professors. Speaking of professors, they "are not only good teachers, they are also very good mentors." They "want you to succeed" and they prove their dedication by making themselves "available whenever we need them, even if it is 10:00 in the evening." The administration is an entirely different story. Let's just say that "if you can learn to deal with the administrative staff at this school, you will be able to handle anyone in the real world with class and grace." The biggest gripe from the students is that "registration is a hassle. It just doesn't run smoothly at all."

Life

About halfway between Montgomery and Auburn, off I-85, lies the sleepy little town of Tuskegee. "It's a great study environment" because "there are very few distractions." Many students believe "The closest place to go for fun is at least 20 minutes away, and a car is needed. It's in another city and no campus transportation is given." That other city is Auburn, where "You can always mingle with the Auburn University students," go "bowling, or do a little shopping." For those heading in the other direction, there actually is a school shuttle that goes to "Wal-Mart in Montgomery and a small mall." If they stay in Tuskegee, "To have fun, students typically go to local clubs, frat or sorority parties, or have house parties." In addition, "Music is played on the Yard sometimes and SGA arranges all sorts of student activities, such as fashion shows, basketball tournaments, concerts, and game nights." Film buffs appreciate that "a lot of school clubs have movie nights and show really great movies. Even some dorms have movie nights." There are also activities for more wholesome types. For example, "If you like to go to church, they have a lot of church functions." Even with the all these options, some Tuskegee students still say, "Life is boring except for football games." To put it mildly, the "football team is overwhelmingly supported here."

Student Body

"As an HBCU, Tuskegee's student population is composed almost completely of African Americans, though students come from all over, even as far away as Alaska and California." Some report that "the typical student is someone who has a good work ethic and cares a lot about getting the most [he or she] can out [of his or her] school experience"; others note that undergrads prefer "to hurry up and get their degree and live their life and have all the fun they can have." They are "outgoing, smart, and easy to get along with." They also "are very laid-back and rarely cause trouble, unless it's a special occasion (Halloween, Thanksgiving, homecoming, etc.)." Some undergrads offer that "the only atypical students that attend would be Caucasian students who are enrolled in the veterinary school. They have voiced that they come to school just for an education and not to have fun, so they stick together and go to class."

TUSKEGEE UNIVERSITY

FINANCIAL AID: 334-727-8210 OR 800-416-2831 • E-MAIL: ADMI@TUSKEGEE.EDU • WEBSITE: WWW.TUSKEGEE.EDU

THE PRINCETON REVIEW SAYS

Admissions

Very important factors considered include: Class rank, academic GPA, recommendation(s), rigor of secondary school record, standardized test scores, talent/ability. *Important factors considered include:* Alumni/ae relation, character/personal qualities. *Other factors considered include:* Application essay, extracurricular activities, first generation, geographical residence, interview, state residency, volunteer work, work experience. SAT or ACT required; High school diploma is required and GED is accepted. *Academic units required:* 4 English, 3 mathematics, 2 science, 3 social studies, 4 academic electives.

Financial Aid

Students should submit: FAFSA, institution's own financial aid form, CSS/Financial Aid PROFILE. The Princeton Review suggests that all financial aid forms be submitted as soon as possible after January 1. *Need-based scholarships/grants offered:* Federal Pell, SEOG, state scholarships/grants, private scholarships, the school's own gift aid, United Negro College Fund, Federal Nursing Scholarships. *Loan aid offered:* Direct Subsidized Stafford, Direct Unsubsidized Stafford, Direct PLUS, FFEL Subsidized Stafford, FFEL Unsubsidized Stafford, FFEL PLUS, Federal Perkins, Federal Nursing, state loans, college/university loans from institutional funds. Off-campus job opportunities are good.

The Inside Word

Tuskegee presents its students with a myriad of opportunities for discovery and research. Therefore, Admissions Counselors seek applicants who have proven themselves successful in the classroom and are eager to tackle further academic challenges. To gain that coveted acceptance letter, candidates will need a minimum GPA of 3.0 and composite ACT score of 21. Requirements for both the nursing and engineering programs differ slightly from the requirements for other majors. Prospective students interested in either field should investigate the specific criteria.

THE SCHOOL SAYS "..."

From The Admissions Office

"Tuskegee University, located in central Alabama, was founded in 1881 under the dynamic and creative leadership of Booker T. Washington. As a state-related, independent institution, Tuskegee offers undergraduate and graduate programs in five major areas: The College of Agriculture, Environmental, and Natural Sciences; the College of Engineering, Architecture, and Physical Sciences; the College of Business and Information Sciences; the College of Liberal Arts and Education; and the College of Veterinary Medicine, Nursing, and Allied Health. Substantial research and service programs make Tuskegee University an effective comprehensive institution, geared towards preparing tomorrow's leaders today.

"First-year applicants must take the SAT or ACT; the SAT is preferred. International Applicants must complete the TOEFL. Nursing applicants must complete the National League of Nursing exam."

SELECTIVITY

Admissions Rating	80
# of applicants	3,092
% of applicants accepted	58
% of acceptees attending	44

FRESHMAN PROFILE

Range SAT Critical Reading	390–500
Range SAT Math	380–490
Range ACT Composite	17–21
Average HS GPA	3
% graduated top 10% of class	20
% graduated top 25% of class	59
% graduated top 50% of class	100

DEADLINES

Regular	
Priority	5/15
Deadline	7/15
Notification	rolling
Nonfall registration?	yes

FINANCIAL FACTS

Financial Aid Rating	84
Annual tuition	$14,740
Room and board	$7,130
Required fees	$710
Books and supplies	$949
% frosh rec. need-based scholarship or grant aid	66
% UG rec. need-based scholarship or grant aid	66
% frosh rec. non-need-based scholarship or grant aid	44
% UG rec. non-need-based scholarship or grant aid	22
% frosh rec. need-based self-help aid	51
% UG rec. need-based self-help aid	49
% frosh rec. athletic scholarships	7
% UG rec. athletic scholarships	5
% frosh rec. any financial aid	80
% UG rec. any financial aid	92
% UG borrow to pay for school	91
Average cumulative indebtedness	$20,000

UNION COLLEGE (NY)

GRANT HALL, SCHENECTADY, NY 12308 • ADMISSIONS: 518-388-6112 • FAX: 518-388-6986

CAMPUS LIFE

Quality of Life Rating	**63**
Fire Safety Rating	**83**
Green Rating	**85**
Type of school	private
Environment	town

STUDENTS

Total undergrad enrollment	2,134
% male/female	52/48
% from out of state	60
% from public high school	69
% live on campus	89
% in (# of) fraternities	30 (7)
% in (# of) sororities	32 (3)
% African American	3
% Asian	6
% Caucasian	84
% Hispanic	4
% international	2
# of countries represented	26

SURVEY SAYS . . .

Large classes
Great library
Athletic facilities are great
Frats and sororities dominate
social scene
Lots of beer drinking
Hard liquor is popular

ACADEMICS

Academic Rating	**88**
Calendar	trimester
Student/faculty ratio	10:1
Profs interesting rating	85
Profs accessible rating	86
Most common reg class size	10–19 students
Most common lab size	10–19 students

MOST POPULAR MAJORS

psychology
economics
political science and government

STUDENTS SAY ". . ."

Academics

Immersing a bunch of engineers and premeds in an accelerated trimester calendar should be a formula for a high-stress campus, but somehow Union College manages to keep the situation under control. A highly capable student body helps, as does, perhaps, the availability of quality liberal arts classes to intersperse among the science- and math-heavy classes; as one student puts it, "There aren't too many schools that do a good job combining engineering with liberal arts, [but it's] important if you actually want to communicate with people." In fact, many students here believe Union is actually an "excellent liberal arts school with a solid footing in the hard sciences—I wasn't sure exactly what I wanted to do with my life after graduation, [and] Union gave me a myriad of options." Those options include not only "great Science and Engineering Department[s]" but also strong programs in economics, political science, and psychology, all taught by top-notch professors. An economics major writes, "I was really amazed and pleasantly surprised when I saw the caliber of the professors here. They are all interested in their particular field of research, and their enthusiasm in the classroom rubs off on the students and makes for interesting and fun-filled learning exercises." Students even love the trimester system, which "allows a normal course load of only three classes a term." Some feel this allows for "lots of free time." Others caution, "The amount of work is increased, and in addition we must complete courses in only 10 weeks as opposed to the normal 12 to 14. By nature, Union is an accelerated school."

Life

For as long as anyone can remember, the Greeks have dominated the social scene at Union College, and while the frats are still "a big scene on the weekends (30–40 percent of campus is involved in Greek life)," the school is increasing attempts to provide more alternatives. The 2004 creation of seven Minerva Houses—each incoming student is assigned to one—represents the most significant effort; the houses are intended "to provide a nonexclusive (i.e., [non-] Greek) space for students to live and work." It's too early to deem this experiment a success or failure, although almost everyone here has an opinion one way or another. Some report that the Minervas are "a great idea" that are "slowly gaining popularity and momentum," while others see them as "creat[ing] tension over the distribution of funds" or, worse yet, "rapidly becoming small [frat-like] cliques themselves. For example, almost the entire Ultimate Frisbee team lives in Orange House." There's no disagreement over the city of Schenectady; everyone agrees it is less than ideal, and worse, there is "nothing to do." General consensus is that fun means "staying on campus and drinking" or "maybe an excursion to Albany (20 minutes away) for a concert." Campus perks up whenever the hockey team plays, as "Hockey games are huge events here"; football also draws a crowd. While students concede that drinking is big at Union, they also report that "there are other options for students. Every weekend at least one Minerva has to hold an event, [and] there are speakers, lecturers, movies, [and] performances. We always have a lot going on!"

Student Body

While "You can find a variety of people at Union," students say there is definitely "a typical Union student," who can be described as "preppy, Northeastern, [and] middle- to upper-class." By all accounts, you'll find "a lot of athletes, a lot of frat boys," and a lot of students who "wear Polo and Abercrombie" here. Atypical students are those who "find their place on campus in the Minerva House activities and clubs such as Women's Union, Black Student Union, performing arts groups, the college's radio station—WRUC, Ultimate Frisbee, and others." The "terribly cliquish nature of the social scene makes it difficult to provide a decent analysis of individual students."

UNION COLLEGE (NY)

FINANCIAL AID: 518-388-6123 • E-MAIL: ADMISSIONS@UNION.EDU • WEBSITE: WWW.UNION.EDU

THE PRINCETON REVIEW SAYS

Admissions

Very important factors considered include: Academic GPA, rigor of secondary school record. *Important factors considered include:* Class rank, recommendation(s), character/personal qualities, extracurricular activities, talent/ability. *Other factors considered include:* Application essay, standardized test scores, alumni/ae relation, first generation, geographical residence, interview, level of applicant's interest, racial/ethnic status, state residency, volunteer work, work experience. TOEFL required of all international applicants. High school diploma is required and GED is not accepted. *Academic units required:* 4 English, 3 mathematics, 2 science, (2 science labs), 2 foreign language, 1 social studies, 1 history. *Academic units recommended:* 4 English, 4 mathematics, 4 science, (4 science labs), 4 foreign language, 2 social studies, 2 history.

Financial Aid

Students should submit: FAFSA, CSS/Financial Aid PROFILE, state aid form, business/farm supplement, Noncustodial (Divorced/Separated) Parent's Statement. Regular filing deadline is 2/1. The Princeton Review suggests that all financial aid forms be submitted as soon as possible after January 1. *Need-based scholarships/grants offered:* Federal Pell, SEOG, state scholarships/grants, private scholarships, the school's own gift aid. *Loan aid offered:* FFEL Subsidized Stafford, FFEL Unsubsidized Stafford, FFEL PLUS, Federal Perkins, college/university loans from institutional funds. Applicants will be notified of awards on or about 4/1. Federal Work-Study Program available. Institutional employment available. Off-campus job opportunities are good.

The Inside Word

Hoping to produce world-historical progeny some day? Attending Union College may improve your odds; the school is alma mater to Franklin D. Roosevelt's father and Winston Churchill's grandfather. Craft your application package carefully here. Since Union does not require standardized test scores, there is no need to submit these scores unless they strengthen your application.

THE SCHOOL SAYS " . . ."

From The Admissions Office

"'Breadth' and 'flexibility' characterize the Union academic program. Whether the subject is the poetry of ancient Greece or the possibilities of developing fields such as nanotechnology, Union students can choose from among nearly 1,000 courses—a range that is unusual among America's highly selective colleges. Students can major in a single field, combine work in two or more departments, or even create their own organizing-theme major. Undergraduate research is strongly encouraged, and more than half of Union's students take advantage of the college's extensive international study program.

"Admission to Union is merit based and driven by years of academic success. Union seeks students with excellent academic credentials. Those credentials are primarily transcripts. Submission of SAT and ACT scores are optional except for the law and medicine programs. Please check Union.edu/Admissions for details."

SELECTIVITY

Admissions Rating	95
# of applicants	4,837
% of applicants accepted	43
% of acceptees attending	27
# accepting a place on wait list	183
% admitted from wait list	23
# of early decision applicants	259
% accepted early decision	83

FRESHMAN PROFILE

Range SAT Critical Reading	560–660
Range SAT Math	590–680
Range SAT Writing	570–670
Range ACT Composite	25–29
Minimum paper TOEFL	600
Minimum computer TOEFL	250
Minimum web-based TOEFL	90
Average HS GPA	3.5
% graduated top 10% of class	64
% graduated top 25% of class	87
% graduated top 50% of class	97

DEADLINES

Early decision	
Deadline	11/15
Notification	12/15
Regular	
Deadline	1/15
Notification	4/1
Nonfall registration?	no

APPLICANTS ALSO LOOK AT

AND OFTEN PREFER
Lehigh University
Colby College
Colgate University

AND SOMETIMES PREFER
Hamilton College
Lafayette College
Skidmore College

AND RARELY PREFER
Boston University
University of Rochester
Syracuse University

FINANCIAL FACTS

Financial Aid Rating	60*
Comprehensive fee	$46,245
Books and supplies	$450
% frosh rec. need-based scholarship or grant aid	35
% UG rec. need-based scholarship or grant aid	48
% frosh rec. non-need-based scholarship or grant aid	1
% UG rec. non-need-based scholarship or grant aid	2
% frosh rec. need-based self-help aid	35
% UG rec. need-based self-help aid	42
% frosh rec. any financial aid	67
% UG rec. any financial aid	65
% UG borrow to pay for school	54
Average cumulative indebtedness	$24,100

UNITED STATES AIR FORCE ACADEMY

2304 CADET DRIVE, SUITE 2500, USAF ACADEMY, CO 80840-5025 • ADMISSIONS: 719-333-2520 • FAX: 719-333-3012

STUDENTS SAY ". . ."

Academics

If the prospect of "seemingly impossible academic demands" piled atop "mentally and physically demanding experiences, such as military free-fall parachute training, combat survival, and evasion training" appeals to you, you may well be United States Air Force Academy material. The academy "challenges every student on every level" in its pursuit of "building officers who want to serve in the United States Air Force." Students warn that "this is not school, it is work. The training is intense and sometimes demands more hours than there are in a day." The payoff, of course, is a commission as an Air Force officer at graduation, accompanied by a really cool skill set. As one student puts it, "The experiences gained at USAFA cannot be found at any other school—skydiving, internships at national labs, flying programs, emphasis on leadership and character development, etc." Another adds, "This school's academic programs are one of a kind. I was given the opportunity to manage a $150,000 program that involves directing 16 other seniors toward a final event at the end of the year where we will launch a rocket to space off the coast of California." Students tell us that academy professors "are very tough on us, and the curriculum itself is hard, but professors understand that as cadets we are required to do more than just study for quizzes and write papers. Therefore, most of our instructors are very understanding, and they try to make this place run as smoothly as possible. There are always exceptions, but that is all they are: Exceptions to the rule!"

Life

"Life is incredibly busy" at the Air Force Academy. "If it isn't schoolwork, then you are working out or working on military duties. There is free time, but it is limited and often best used doing schoolwork." It's often not possible for students to leave campus to have fun; one student explains, "As a freshman, you have a certain number of passes to go out. Plus, it's possible to be restricted. If you are on probation (for failing academics, athletics, conduct, or honor), you cannot leave [without permission]." Those who can't get passes "are forced to come up with other ways to have fun. Others really love to sleep, and then there are those who are obsessed with the weight room and the athletic facilities." Life becomes a little easier as you rise through the ranks. Upperclassmen look forward to "getting out into the town to see a movie or go to dinner. Of course, skiing and snowboarding are popular too." Students should note that underage "Drinking on campus is unheard of these days; it's illegal and tightly enforced. Drinking off campus is the norm."

Student Body

Air Force cadets tend to be "self-motivated, highly ambitious achievers"; "type-A personalities who don't go looking for extra work but make sure that any job assigned to them is done well." Students observe that "cadets are fairly similar; we have a small student body, and service academies generally attract people with the same kind of views." They tend to be "from conservative backgrounds." Exchange cadets and midshipmen from other academies and international students add some diversity, bringing "representatives of 40 different countries and nearly all ethnic and racial backgrounds to campus." Common personality types range from "type-A athlete" to the "type-A nerd" to "everyone else, who tries to balance academics, athletics, and military training without getting overburdened." Many students claim that your average cadet "is a bit cynical," but "The guy who's yelling at you on Monday is the guy loaning you his car on Saturday." The low number of females makes for a very interesting social environment, and the military aspect also limits how "atypical" anyone can actually be here.

E-MAIL: RR_WEBMAIL@USAFA.AF.MIL • WEBSITE: WWW.USAFA.AF.MIL

THE PRINCETON REVIEW SAYS

Admissions

Very important factors considered include: Rigor of secondary school record, standardized test scores, character/personal qualities, interview. *Important factors considered include:* Class rank, application essay, academic GPA, extracurricular activities, talent/ability, volunteer work, work experience. *Other factors considered include:* Recommendation(s), alumni/ae relation, SAT or ACT required; ACT with Writing component required. High school diploma is required and GED is accepted. *Academic units recommended:* 4 English, 4 mathematics, 4 science, (4 science labs), 2 foreign language, 3 social studies, 3 history, 1 academic elective.

Financial Aid

The Princeton Review suggests that all financial aid forms be submitted as soon as possible after January 1.

The Inside Word

The Air Force Academy promises a demanding 4 years, and the fainthearted need not apply. Due to the arduous nature of the school, it's no wonder that applicants face stringent requirements right at the outset. Aside from an excellent academic record, successful candidates need to be physically fit. They also must win a nomination from their congressperson. Honor is a valued quality at the academy, and Admissions Officers will only accept those with the strength of character and determination necessary to succeed at one of the country's most elite institutions.

THE SCHOOL SAYS ". . ."

From The Admissions Office

"Applicants for Fall 2008 are required to take the new SAT (or the ACT with the Writing section), but students may submit scores from the old SAT or ACT as well, and will use the student's best scores from either test."

SELECTIVITY

Admissions Rating	**96**
# of applicants	9,162
% of applicants accepted	17
% of acceptees attending	80

FRESHMAN PROFILE

Range SAT Critical Reading	570–650
Range SAT Math	600–690
Range SAT Writing	550–650
Range ACT Composite	27–31
Average HS GPA	3.85
% graduated top 10% of class	51
% graduated top 25% of class	83
% graduated top 50% of class	99

DEADLINES

Regular	
Deadline	1/31
Notification	rolling
Nonfall registration?	no

**APPLICANTS ALSO LOOK AT
AND SOMETIMES PREFER**

United States Naval Academy
United States Coast Guard Academy
United States Merchant Marine Academy
United States Military Academy

FINANCIAL FACTS

Financial Aid Rating	60*
Annual in-state tuition	$0*
Annual out-of-state tuition	$0*

*Tuition covered by full scholarship.

United States Coast Guard Academy

31 Mohegan Avenue, New London, CT 06320-8103 • Admissions: 800-883-8724 • Fax: 860-701-6700

STUDENTS SAY ". . ."

Academics

If you're ready to "deal with military rules and discipline along with a rigorous engineering education" so that "in four years you get the job you've always wanted" (provided that job involves military, maritime, or multi-mission humanitarian service), the United States Coast Guard Academy may be the place for you. "Rigorous academics and military training" prepare cadets "for success as junior officers in the [Coast Guard] as ship drivers, pilots, and marine safety officers." The workload is considerable. Students must take a minimum of 19 credits per semester while also handling military training and athletics. Cadets note that this regimen "builds character through intense physical and mental training," although some opine that "It's like a cup of boiling hot chocolate: It smells good, you know it tastes good, but you have wait a long time to let it cool down in order to enjoy it fully." Others simply say that the demands make USCGA "a great place to be from but not always the greatest place to be." The school offers eight majors, most heavily in Science, Technology, Engineering, and Math, including operations research, management, and government. In all disciplines, "The academic program is extremely difficult, but most instructors are willing to work with you one-on-one if necessary."

Life

Life at USCGA, unsurprisingly, is highly regimented. One student sums it up: "We have to wake up at 0600 every day whether we have class or not. We have to have our doors open whether we're in our rooms or not from 0600 to 1600. They tell us exactly what we can and can't do, and what we can wear and what we can't. We have military training period from 0700 to 0800 and class from 0800 to1600. We all eat lunch together at the same time in a family-style fashion. Sports period is from 1600 to 1800. Military training period from 1900 to 2000. Study hour from 2000 to 2200. We all have to stand duty and play sports and get a certain number of community service hours. We can't drink on base, and we can't leave during the week. We have to make our own fun, which involves some creativity sometimes (and demerits), but our fun wouldn't appeal to most college students because it's silly and doesn't involve alcohol." Cadets warn that "The school can be very rigid with the rules. It hurts to see one of your friends get kicked out after having made a stupid decision, as almost all college students do," but they recognize that "that goes with the territory of being a military institution." Students "can only leave campus on the weekends." When they do "there is a bus system that takes cadets to familiar places in the New London area" as well as "a nearby Amtrak station that takes cadets to New York City or Boston when cadets are allowed to leave the Academy for an extended period of time (rare), usually holiday weekends."

Student Body

Service academies tend to attract students from particular demographics, and the USCGA is no exception. Most here are "fairly conservative," "extremely athletic," "very smart," and "were leaders of their schools while in high school." They tend to be "type A personalities" who are "very disciplined or looking for discipline" in their lives. Students tell us that "Although there are exceptions, almost everyone here is very selfless, willing to take one for the team, or sacrifice to help out a buddy. As the saying goes, 'Ship, shipmates, self.' Along those same lines, everyone is held to a high standard by both comrades and superiors. Both have a low tolerance for slacking."

E-MAIL: ADMISSIONS@USCGA.EDU • WEBSITE: WWW.USCGA.EDU

THE PRINCETON REVIEW SAYS

Admissions

Very important factors considered include: Class rank, academic GPA, rigor of secondary school record, standardized test scores, character/personal qualities, extracurricular activities. *Important factors considered include:* Application essay, recommendation(s), talent/ability. *Other factors considered include:* Alumni/ae relation, interview, level of applicant's interest, volunteer work, work experience. SAT or ACT required; ACT with Writing component required. High school diploma is required and GED is accepted. *Academic units required:* 4 English, 4 mathematics, 3 science, (3 science labs).

Financial Aid

The Princeton Review suggests that all financial aid forms be submitted as soon as possible after January 1.

The Inside Word

Though USCGA has a low level of public recognition, gaining admission is still a steep uphill climb. Candidates must go through the rigorous multi-step admissions process as do their other service-academy peers (although no congressional nomination is required) and will encounter a serious roadblock if they fall short on any step. Those who pass muster join a proud, if somewhat under-recognized, student body, virtually equal in accomplishment to those at other service academies.

THE SCHOOL SAYS " . . ."

From The Admissions Office

"Founded in 1876, the United States Coast Guard Academy enjoys a proud tradition of graduating leaders of character. The academy experience melds academic rigor, leadership development, and athletic participation to prepare you to graduate as a commissioned officer. Character development of cadets is founded on the core values of honor, respect, and devotion to duty. You build friendships that last a lifetime, study with inspiring professors in small classes, and train during the summer aboard America's tall ship *Eagle*, as well as the service's ships and aircraft. Top performers spend their senior summer traveling on exciting internships around the nation and overseas. Graduates serve for 5 years and have unmatched opportunities to attend flight school and graduate school, all funded by the Coast Guard.

"Appointments to the Academy are based on a selective admissions process; Congressional nominations are not required. Your leadership potential and desire to serve your country are what counts. Our student body reflects the best America has to offer—with all its potential and diversity!

"Applicants for Fall 2008 are required to take the new SAT (or the ACT with the Writing section), but students may submit scores from the old SAT or ACT as well, and will use the student's best scores from either test."

SELECTIVITY
Admissions Rating	96
# of applicants	1,633
% of applicants accepted	24
% of acceptees attending	70

FRESHMAN PROFILE
Range SAT Critical Reading	570–670
Range SAT Math	610–680
Range ACT Composite	25–29
Average HS GPA	3.76
% graduated top 10% of class	50
% graduated top 25% of class	90
% graduated top 50% of class	99

DEADLINES
Early action	
Deadline	11/1
Notification	12/15
Regular	
Priority	12/15
Deadline	3/1
Notification	rolling
Nonfall registration?	no

FINANCIAL FACTS
Financial Aid Rating	60*
Annual in-state tuition	$0*
Annual out-of-state tuition	$0*

*Tuition covered by full scholarship.

UNITED STATES MERCHANT MARINE ACADEMY

OFFICE OF ADMISSIONS, KINGS POINT, NY 11024-1699 • ADMISSIONS: 516-773-5391 • FAX: 516-773-5390

CAMPUS LIFE

Quality of Life Rating	63
Fire Safety Rating	60*
Green Rating	60*
Type of school	public
Environment	village

STUDENTS

Total undergrad enrollment	995
% male/female	88/12
% from out of state	87
% from public high school	71
% live on campus	100
% international	2
# of countries represented	5

SURVEY SAYS . . .

Small classes
Career services are great
Lousy food on campus
Low cost of living
Frats and sororities are unpopular
or nonexistent
Political activism is unpopular or
nonexistent
Very little drug use

ACADEMICS

Academic Rating	74
Calendar	trimester
Student/faculty ratio	11:1
Profs interesting rating	61
Profs accessible rating	69
Most common	
reg class size	10–19 students
Most common	
lab size	10–19 students

MOST POPULAR MAJORS

engineering
naval architecture and
marine engineering
transportation and materials moving

STUDENTS SAY ". . ."

Academics

"Producing the highest caliber of professional mariners in terms of character and ability" is what it's all about at the federally funded United States Merchant Marine Academy. The USMMA is not a carefree experience; the workload is intense ("17 to 25 hours per week in class," students estimate), because a year spent at sea means students "have to fit four years of college into the three years we are physically on campus." This time spent at sea, however, is "what sets Kings Point [USMMA] apart. Sea year teaches midshipmen how to study independently and work in an adult environment, and it gives us a global perspective." One midshipman notes, "The training that the students get while out at sea is second to none in learning about engineering, navigation, and business." Another thing that makes the hard work worthwhile is the prospect of "incredible options when you graduate." One student explains, "We can become officers in any branch of the military, including the NOAA [National Oceanic and Atmospheric Administration] and Coast Guard. We can sail merchant ships or go into shore-side engineering and management careers. We can go to grad school with a stipend from the government. And the alumni network is unbelievable. Aside from all of that, we graduate having worked in our chosen field and sailed in almost every sea on Earth," and visited "maybe a dozen different countries." Graduates of USMMA walk away with "one of the top maritime educations that can be found in the world."

Life

Life at USMMA is rugged and highly regimented. It's especially difficult for first-year students (called "plebes"), who "are on lockdown most of the time" and "who clean everything. Rather than having a janitor service for the barracks, the plebes clean, and if cleaning isn't done well, we get in trouble with the upperclassmen." While many underclassmen jokingly compare the plebe experience to being "in jail," they also praise the way the experience of being a plebe molds character; as one student states, "Plebes have horrible lives to begin with. However, the structure and environment develop great leaders and provide a solid foundation for success." All students participate in a daily regimen of reveille, morning inspection, colors, classes, muster, more classes, and drills. Upperclassmen, on the other hand, enjoy "more liberty and spend a lot of time off campus, either in Great Neck (the town nearest us) or in New York City." USMMA midshipmen appreciate "the many opportunities for student leadership; every student is required to be a team leader for a room of plebes [during] sophomore year, every junior is required to hold a petty officer position to a student senior officer for at least a trimester, and every senior holds an officer position for at least half of senior year." Students also praise the way academy life presents "various ways to challenge oneself physically, mentally, and emotionally" and to expand one's horizons. One student sums up, "It's a full schedule, but it's fulfilling. I have personally been to Japan, China, Germany, England, New Zealand, Antarctica, Belgium, and up and down the East and West Coasts of the United States."

Students

The stereotypical USMMA student "is a conservative White male, often—but not always—from a military background." Women and students of color are in the minority at USMMA. Regardless of race or sex, however, all students "share a common love for the United States and a desire to serve it admirably." Beyond love for their country, what ties students together is the shared experience: "At USMMA there is a bond that is formed during Indoc [the 2-week indoctrination program], and there is a sense of pride in being a Kings Pointer." Because of "the close bonds developed, race and geographical origin are nonissues among the student body." Or, as another student puts it, "Shared pain makes most people fit in just fine."

UNITED STATES MERCHANT MARINE ACADEMY

FINANCIAL AID: 516-773-5295 • E-MAIL: ADMISSIONS@USMMA.EDU • WEBSITE: WWW.USMMA.EDU

THE PRINCETON REVIEW SAYS

Admissions

Very important factors considered include: Rigor of secondary school record, standardized test scores, character/personal qualities. *Important factors considered include:* Class rank, application essay, academic GPA, recommendation(s), extracurricular activities, geographical residence, talent/ability. *Other factors considered include:* interview, level of applicant's interest, racial/ethnic status, state residency, volunteer work, work experience. SAT or ACT required; TOEFL required of all international applicants. High school diploma is required and GED is accepted. *Academic units required:* 4 English, 3 mathematics, 3 science, (1 science labs), 8 academic electives. *Academic units recommended:* 4 English, 4 mathematics, 4 science, (2 science labs), 2 foreign language, 4 social studies.

Financial Aid

Students should submit: FAFSA, institution's own financial aid form. Regular filing deadline is 5/1. The Princeton Review suggests that all financial aid forms be submitted as soon as possible after January 1. *Need-based scholarships/grants offered:* Federal Pell, private scholarships, Federal SMART Grants & Federal Academic Competitiveness Grants. *Loan aid offered:* FFEL Subsidized Stafford, FFEL Unsubsidized Stafford, FFEL PLUS Applicants will be notified of awards on a rolling basis beginning 1/31. Off-campus job opportunities are poor.

The Inside Word

Prospective midshipmen face demanding admission requirements. The USMMA assesses scholastic achievement, strength of character, and stamina (applicants must meet specific physical standards). Candidates must also be nominated by a proper nominating authority, typically a state representative or senator.

THE SCHOOL SAYS ". . ."

From The Admissions Office

"What makes the U.S. Merchant Marine Academy different from the other federal service academies? The difference can be summarized in two phrases that appear in our publications. The first: 'The World Is Your Campus.' You will spend a year at sea—a third of your sophomore year and two-thirds of your junior year—teamed with a classmate aboard a U.S. merchant ship. You will visit an average of 18 foreign nations while you work and learn in a mariner's true environment. You will graduate with seafaring experience and as a citizen of the world. The second phrase is 'Options and Opportunities.' Unlike students at the other federal academies, who are required to enter the service connected to their academy, you have the option of working in the seagoing merchant marine and transportation industry or applying for active duty in the Navy, Coast Guard, Marine Corps, Air Force, or Army. Nearly 25 percent of our most recent graduating class entered various branches of the armed forces with an officer rank. As a graduate of the U.S. Merchant Marine Academy, you will receive a Bachelor of Science degree, a government-issued merchant marine officer's license, and a Naval Reserve commission (unless you have been accepted for active military duty). No other service academy offers so attractive a package.

"Freshman applicants for the academic year starting in July 2008 must take the new SAT or the ACT with the Writing component. Students may still submit scores from older SAT or ACT tests that did not include a writing/essay component. For homeschooled students, we recommend they also submit scores from SAT Subject Tests in Chemistry and/or Physics."

SELECTIVITY

Admissions Rating	93
# of applicants	1,754
% of applicants accepted	26
% of acceptees attending	60

FRESHMAN PROFILE

Range SAT Critical Reading	540–633
Range SAT Math	588–669
Range ACT Composite	26–29
Minimum paper TOEFL	533
Minimum computer TOEFL	200
Minimum web-based TOEFL	73
Average HS GPA	3.6
% graduated top 10% of class	21
% graduated top 25% of class	53
% graduated top 50% of class	89

DEADLINES

Early decision	
Deadline	11/1
Notification	12/31
Regular	
Deadline	3/1
Notification	rolling
Nonfall registration?	no

APPLICANTS ALSO LOOK AT

AND OFTEN PREFER
United States Naval Academy

AND SOMETIMES PREFER
United States Air Force Academy
United States Coast Guard Academy
United States Military Academy

AND RARELY PREFER
Massachusetts Maritime Academy
State University of New York—Maritime College
Maine Maritime Academy

FINANCIAL FACTS

Financial Aid Rating	97
Required fees	$2,843
% frosh rec. need-based scholarship or grant aid	15
% UG rec. need-based scholarship or grant aid	5
% frosh rec. non-need-based scholarship or grant aid	27
% UG rec. non-need-based scholarship or grant aid	13
% frosh rec. need-based self-help aid	15
% UG rec. need-based self-help aid	8
% UG borrow to pay for school	18
Average cumulative indebtedness	$10,497

UNITED STATES MILITARY ACADEMY

600 THAYER ROAD, WEST POINT, NY 10996-1797 • ADMISSIONS: 845-938-4041 • FAX: 845-938-3021

STUDENTS SAY " . . ."

Academics

A United States Military Academy education "is not easy and not always fun, but it is a great experience to be proud of," and one that is designed "to educate tomorrow's world leaders." Don't come to West Point expecting the typical college experience. As one student explains, "The military atmosphere makes everything different. Teachers are usually commissioned Army officers and strict discipline is maintained within the classroom at all times. Disciplinary actions ensure that students turn in assignments on time, arrive to class on time, and do not miss class." Also, USMA uses "the Thayer method" of education, under which "Cadets are required to teach themselves the material before coming to class and then spend class time clarifying what was self-taught the night before." Though some find the system "unrealistic," most agree that "it is not really enjoyable to endure, but it does help foster individual academic responsibility." It also contributes to the sense that USMA "give you 28 hours of things to do in a 24-hour day." Expect to be "busy," but know that "every teacher makes an explicit point of stating that any help that a cadet needs will be given. If you want to do well here and are willing to work for it, the path is available for you to do so." Take heart; though the program "is as grueling as can be for the first 2 years," you'll find that in the final 2 years "You have a lot more time to do what you want to do."

Life

"Life at West Point is very regimented" and "Just about every hour of every day is busy." As one student puts it, "West Point tries to make sure that we have little free time and are always doing something (physical, academic, or military)." Another adds that there is "not much room for fun." "Physical fitness is a big part of every student's life," as "West Point has corps-wide physical testing events. From the APFT (Army Physical Fitness Test) to the infamous and dreaded IOCT (Indoor Obstacle Course Test), this place will make you stay in shape or get rid of you." In order to leave campus overnight, students need a pass. "During the first year, you are only guaranteed one pass to leave a semester, but everyone is allowed to go on trip sections, plebes included. Plebes are also allowed to go to the mall, visit sponsors' houses, play sports, and go to their own club to hang out—all without having to take pass." Also, "Passes are awarded for grades, physical fitness, attitude, special activities, etc." So as long as you are a "good person" and "take care of your business," the school is "more than happy to reward you and let you get off post for the weekend." Cadets love to "go to New York City on the weekend." Fitness doesn't end with the school day as many "enjoy the thrill of the outdoors and taking things to the extreme."

Student Body

Being a military school, it should come as no surprise that things as USMA are "uniform." "Most students are the same," notes a senior. They're "intelligent, athletic, honest, and committed to serving in the Army." And while it is a coed institution, expect a greater number of "male students." Gender aside, students are "very alike as far as life goals and ambitions . . . all are very intellectual and bring their own views to the school." There are "a lot of type-A personalities" here, all "prepared to do anything and everything to be the best." However, some find that the school "still has a long way to go" in terms of "ethnic diversity." But being part of "The Long Gray Line" comes with a "unifying, competitive spirit" that "levels the playing field" for these "soldiers and students."

FINANCIAL AID: 845-938-3516 • E-MAIL: ADMISSIONS@USMA.EDU • WEBSITE: WWW.USMA.EDU

THE PRINCETON REVIEW SAYS

Admissions

Very important factors considered include: Academic GPA, application essay, character/personal qualities, class rank, extracurricular activities, recommendation(s), rigor of secondary school record, standardized test scores, talent/ability. *Important factors considered include:* Geographical residence, interview, level of applicant's interest, racial/ethnic status, volunteer work. *Other factors considered include:* Alumni/ae relation, state residency, work experience. SAT or ACT required. High school diploma is required, and GED is accepted. *Academic units recommended:* 4 English, 4 math, 4 science (2 science labs), 2 foreign language, 3 social studies, 1 history, 3 academic electives.

Financial Aid

The Princeton Review suggests that all financial aid forms be submitted as soon as possible after January 1. *Need-based scholarships/grants offered:* All cadets are on active duty as members of the United States Army and receive an annual salary of approximately $10,148. Room and board, medical and dental care is provided by the U.S. Army. A one-time deposit of $2,900 is required upon admission.

The Inside Word

America's military academies experienced an increase in applicants after 9/11. They've been experiencing a similar drop in applications as the Iraq War continues, although it should be noted that the academies believe factors other than the war explain the drop. Regardless, fewer applicants means less competition, but it's still plenty tough to get into West Point. You have to begin the process in your junior year in order to get the requisite nomination. You'll need to excel in school to have a prayer; you'll also need to get into great physical condition to survive the vetting process.

THE SCHOOL SAYS "..."

From The Admissions Office

"As a young man or woman considering your options for obtaining a quality college education, you may wonder what unique aspects the United States Military Academy has to offer. West Point offers one of the most highly respected, quality education programs in the nation. A West Point cadetship includes a fully funded 4-year college education. Tuition, room, board, medical, and dental care are provided by the U.S. Army. As members of the armed forces, cadets also receive an annual salary of more than $8,880. This pay covers the cost of uniforms, books, a personal computer, and living incidentals. By law, graduates of West Point are appointed on active duty as commissioned officers.

"Since its founding nearly two centuries ago, the Military Academy has accomplished its mission by developing cadets in four critical areas: intellectual, physical, military, and moral-ethical—a 4-year process called the 'West Point Experience.' Specific developmental goals are addressed through several fully coordinated and integrated programs.

"A challenging academic program that consists of a core of 31 courses provides a balanced education in the arts and sciences. This core curriculum establishes the foundation for elective courses that permit cadets to explore in greater depth a field of study or an optional major. All cadets receive a Bachelor of Science degree, which is designed specifically to meet the intellectual requirements of a commissioned officer in today's army.

"The physical program at West Point includes both physical education classes and competitive athletics. Every cadet participates in an intercollegiate, club, or intramural-level sport each semester. This rigorous physical program contributes to the mental and physical fitness that is required for service as an officer in the army.

"Applicants are required to take the new SAT (or the ACT with the Writing component). Students may also submit scores from the old SAT or ACT, and their best scores will be used regardless of test date."

SELECTIVITY
Admissions Rating	96
# of applicants	10,778
% of applicants accepted	14
% of acceptees attending	77

FRESHMAN PROFILE
Range SAT Critical Reading	570–670
Range SAT Math	600–690
Range ACT Composite	21–36
Average HS GPA	3.75
% graduated top 10% of class	48
% graduated top 25% of class	77
% graduated top 50% of class	94

DEADLINES
Regular application deadline	2/28
Regular notification	rolling
Nonfall registration?	no

APPLICANTS ALSO LOOK AT AND OFTEN PREFER
United States Air Force Academy, United States Naval Academy

FINANCIAL FACTS
Financial Aid Rating	60*
Annual in-state tuition	$0*
Annual out-of-state tuition	$0*

*Tuition covered by full scholarship.

UNITED STATES NAVAL ACADEMY

117 DECATUR ROAD, ANNAPOLIS, MD 21402 • ADMISSIONS: 410-293-4361 • FAX: 410-295-1815

CAMPUS LIFE
Quality of Life Rating	84
Fire Safety Rating	60*
Green Rating	60*
Type of school	public
Environment	town

STUDENTS
Total undergrad enrollment	4,443
% male/female	79/21
% from out of state	95
% from public high school	60
% live on campus	100
% African American	4
% Asian	3
% Caucasian	76
% Hispanic	10
% Native American	1
% international	1
# of countries represented	24

SURVEY SAYS . . .
Lab facilities are great
Great computer facilities
Great library
Career services are great
Campus feels safe
Everyone loves the Navy
Frats and sororities are unpopular
or nonexistent
Very little drug use

ACADEMICS
Academic Rating	91
Calendar	semester
Student/faculty ratio	8:1
Profs interesting rating	81
Profs accessible rating	99
Most common reg class size	10–19 students

MOST POPULAR MAJORS
systems engineering
economics
political science and government

STUDENTS SAY ". . ."

Academics
The United States Naval Academy is "a rugged, in-your-face" "leadership laboratory" that "teaches you to think critically and develops your skills as a future combat leader." You'll find "the highest ideals of duty, honor, and loyalty" here. You'll find "unreal" facilities, too. Few colleges can boast a sub-critical nuclear reactor, just for example. All midshipmen get "a full-ride scholarship" that includes tuition, room and board, medical care, and a stipend. And you'll "have a guaranteed job when you graduate" as a Navy or Marine Corps officer. "Classes are extremely small." Academics "pile on fast." Regardless of major, you'll take a ton of core courses in the humanities, the hard sciences, engineering, and naval science and weapons systems. Though the experience is "grueling," the professors at the Academy are "some of the most caring and well educated people in the world." They "are always accessible outside of class," and "they do whatever it takes for the students to understand the material." To put it mildly, the top brass "practices tough love." "Think of Stalin and Hitler having a child, and then that child running your school." On one hand, "the administration has obligations to the military and the United States government" to train future officers. On the other hand, "there are too many stupid policies." While the atmosphere "tends to brew cynicism," major reform is unlikely. "The administration is what it is," muses a chemistry major. "Deal with it."

Life
Ultimately, the Naval Academy "gives you a great education, a job, and financial security, but at the cost of your freedom for four years." "To quote a popular slogan: 'We're here to defend liberty, not enjoy it,'" quips one midshipman. During the summer before classes start, first-year students get indoctrinated with "yelling, physical training," and basic seamanship. The entire first year is a "stressful" "crucible-type experience," and it's "no fun." Older students have it only slightly better. Life is "extremely micromanaged." "Midshipmen are never allowed outside the walls during the week." "Each day begins for every student at 6:30 A.M. and ends well past 11:00 at night." "You have to wear a uniform almost all the time." There are "mandatory meals, formations," and sports and study periods. "Most people work out, watch movies, and play various videogames." "On weekends, you may or may not be allowed to leave for a night or two, depending on which class year you are." Older midshipmen often spend that time soaking up "the great bar scene" in Annapolis. "Catching up on sleep" is also popular. Graduates usually leave here with "at least some degree of spite." "The food will always suck." Nevertheless, a "strong camaraderie" is pervasive. "Even though people complain, there is no place we'd rather be," declares a junior. "Nobody here was drafted."

Student Body
The overwhelmingly male population here represents "every state and a lot of foreign countries." "Everyone is 100 percent equal regardless of gender, race, or religion." "The only intolerance is that open homosexuals are not allowed in the military under federal law." Politically, there's "a fair share of liberals" but the majority is "conservative-minded." "You can usually point out a midshipman in a crowd." Students "are pretty much the same person" because they are "made to conform." "We try to kick out the 'individuals' early on," dryly notes a junior. Many midshipmen were "the best from where they came from." "The school is full of enormous egos." "Fiercely competitive," "type A" personalities proliferate. "Almost everyone was a sports star in high school," and "everyone is in great physical condition." At the same time, "there are many students who play a lot of videogames and are socially awkward." Deep down, "everyone here is a dork or a geek, even the most macho of athletic commandos. They're "resilient," "hardworking," "intellectual," and "pretty straightedge." They have "a good sense of humor and a level head." The average midshipman is also "a little jaded," and, on some days, "a zombie that just tries to make it to the meals."

THE PRINCETON REVIEW SAYS

Admissions

Very important factors considered include: Class rank, application essay, academic GPA, recommendation(s), rigor of secondary school record, standardized test scores, character/personal qualities, extracurricular activities, interview, level of applicant's interest. *Important factors considered include:* Talent/ability. *Other factors considered include:* Alumni/ae relation, first generation, geographical residence, racial/ethnic status, volunteer work, work experience. SAT or ACT required; TOEFL required of all international applicants. High school diploma or equivalent is not required. *Academic units recommended:* 4 English, 4 mathematics, 2 science, (1 science labs), 2 foreign language, 2 history, 1 Introductory computer and typing courses.

Financial Aid

The Princeton Review suggests that all financial aid forms be submitted as soon as possible after January 1.

The Inside Word

It doesn't take a genius to recognize that getting admitted to the USNA requires true strength of character; simply completing the arduous admissions process is an accomplishment worthy of remembrance. Those who have successful candidacies are strong, motivated students, and leaders in both school and community. Perseverance is an important character trait for anyone considering the life of a midshipman—the application process is only the beginning of a truly challenging and demanding experience.

THE SCHOOL SAYS "..."

From The Admissions Office

"The Naval Academy offers you a unique opportunity to associate with a broad cross-section of the country's finest young men and women. You will have the opportunity to pursue a 4-year program that develops you mentally, morally, and physically as no civilian college can. As you might expect, this program is demanding, but the opportunities are limitless and more than worth the effort. To receive an appointment to the academy, you need 4 years of high school preparation to develop the strong academic, athletic, and extracurricular background required to compete successfully for admission. You should begin preparing in your freshman year and apply for admission at the end of your junior year. Selection for appointment to the academy comes as a result of a complete evaluation of your admissions package and completion of the nomination process. Complete admissions guidance may be found at www.usna.edu.

"SAT results from tests prior to March 2005 and ACT results from tests prior to February 2005 will be used by the Naval Academy, and no conversion of scores is necessary due to compatibility of old and new scoring systems."

SELECTIVITY

Admissions Rating	96
# of applicants	12,003
% of applicants accepted	12
% of acceptees attending	85
# accepting a place on wait list	70
% admitted from wait list	21

FRESHMAN PROFILE

Range SAT Critical Reading	560–660
Range SAT Math	600–690
Minimum paper TOEFL	200
% graduated top 10% of class	56
% graduated top 25% of class	81
% graduated top 50% of class	96

DEADLINES

Regular	
Deadline	1/31
Notification	rolling
Nonfall registration?	no

APPLICANTS ALSO LOOK AT

AND OFTEN PREFER
University of Virginia
Harvard College
Duke University
United States Air Force Academy

AND SOMETIMES PREFER
Georgia Institute of Technology
Massachusetts Institute of Technology
United States Military Academy
Penn State—University Park

AND RARELY PREFER
Purdue University—West Lafayette
St. John's College (MD)
Boston University

FINANCIAL FACTS

Financial Aid Rating	60*
Annual in-state tuition	$0*
Annual out-of-state tuition	$0*
Books and supplies	$1,000

*Tuition covered by full scholarship.

THE UNIVERSITY OF ALABAMA AT BIRMINHAM

ADDRESS? • ADMISSIONS: TK • FAX: TK

STUDENTS SAY ". . ."

Academics

University of Alabama at Birmingham is a refreshingly friendly public college, boasting a strong reputation in pre-health and science, plenty of personalized attention for undergraduate students, and a "faculty that really cares and want you to do your best." "Integrating culture, education, and 'real world' experience into a college degree," the school encourages students to pursue research, internships, or other opportunities by "working in the field they aspire to have a career in, whether it be art history, biomedical engineering, or medicine." A senior enthuses, "No matter what you want to do, the faculty and administration will see to it that you get the experience you want and need. Nothing is too big or off-limits; you can do it all here." Like faculty, UAB's "administration is very helpful and seems very focused on student satisfaction, personally and academically." A sophomore boasts, "I've eaten dinner with the family of several of my professors and the dean as well. Need I say more?"

Life

"Traditionally a commuter school," UAB has recently stepped up efforts to create a more dynamic campus atmosphere, with good results. A junior enthuses, "From the free movie showings, campus dining, volunteer activities, and cultural events, I find myself enjoying my college life." Other popular extracurricular pursuits include intramural sports, campus ministry, research, honors activities, campus jobs, and fraternities and sororities. In addition, UAB is an NCAA Division I school, so many students "love going to sporting events, such as the basketball and football games." Striking a balance between study and relaxation, UAB students "have far too much coursework to have major parties midweek; but on the weekends, no one is in the library, unless its finals week." But when you're ready to go out, "UAB is located close to downtown Birmingham and is right next to Five Points South and the Lakeview District, so nightlife is pretty easy to come across."

Student Body

With diverse academic and extracurricular opportunities, UAB is a school that "fits most every type of person." As a result, the student body is "truly a great American melting pot of different cultures, religions, and races." "Students work together for the common goal of getting an education, and understanding and appreciating the diversity of others," one student says. As the school's reputation grows in fields other than medicine and science, the campus demographics have also been changing. A senior elaborates, "UAB was once a commuter college with a med school but has since become a very undergraduate and non-medicine student-friendly campus. Most students will be entering into some sort of health related profession, but a great number of students are theatre, art, history, and psychology majors." No matter what your interests, "everyone tends to get along with each other, since there is always something to talk about—be it UAB sports or some of the current events on campus."

FINANCIAL AID: TK • E-MAIL: TK • WEBSITE: TK

THE PRINCETON REVIEW SAYS

Admissions

Very important factors considered include: Academic GPA, rigor of secondary school record, standardized test scores, SAT or ACT required; TOEFL required of all international applicants. High school diploma is required and GED is accepted. *Academic units required:* 4 English, 3 mathematics, 3 science, (2 science labs), 1 foreign language, 3 social studies, 3 academic electives.

Financial Aid

Students should submit: FAFSA, institution's own financial aid form. The Princeton Review suggests that all financial aid forms be submitted as soon as possible after January 1. *Need-based scholarships/grants offered:* Federal Pell, SEOG, state scholarships/grants, private scholarships, the school's own gift aid, United Negro College Fund. *Loan aid offered:* Direct Subsidized Stafford, Direct Unsubsidized Stafford, Direct PLUS, Federal Perkins, state loans, college/university loans from institutional funds. Applicants will be notified of awards on a rolling basis beginning 4/1. Federal Work-Study Program available. Institutional employment available. Off-campus job opportunities are excellent.

The Inside Word

It's not very hard to get admitted to UAB and the process is refreshingly uncomplicated. Basically, you need to get either a 20 on the ACT or a combined score of 950 on the critical reading and math sections of the SAT. To complement this, a high school GPA of at least 2.25 is also required.

SELECTIVITY

Admissions Rating	78
# of applicants	4,398
% of applicants accepted	77
% of acceptees attending	42

FRESHMAN PROFILE

Range ACT Composite	21–27
Minimum paper TOEFL	500
Minimum computer TOEFL	173
Minimum web-based TOEFL	61
Average HS GPA	3.43
% graduated top 10% of class	30.1
% graduated top 25% of class	55.9
% graduated top 50% of class	81.6

DEADLINES

Regular	
Deadline	3/1
Nonfall registration?	yes

FINANCIAL FACTS

Financial Aid Rating	69
Annual in-state tuition	$3,384
Annual out-of-state tuition	$8,472
Room and board	$7,950
Required fees	$824
Books and supplies	$900
% frosh rec. need-based scholarship or grant aid	25
% UG rec. need-based scholarship or grant aid	29
% frosh rec. non-need-based scholarship or grant aid	25
% UG rec. non-need-based scholarship or grant aid	16
% frosh rec. need-based self-help aid	40
% UG rec. need-based self-help aid	47
% frosh rec. athletic scholarships	3
% UG rec. athletic scholarships	3
% UG borrow to pay for school	41
Average cumulative indebtedness	$18,764

THE UNIVERSITY OF ALABAMA AT TUSCALOOSA

Box 870132, Tuscaloosa, AL 35487-0132 • Admissions: 205-348-5666 • Fax: 205-348-9046

CAMPUS LIFE

Quality of Life Rating	86
Fire Safety Rating	75
Green Rating	60*
Type of school	public
Environment	city

STUDENTS

Total undergrad enrollment	20,910
% male/female	47/53
% from out of state	23
% from public high school	90
% live on campus	29
% in (# of) fraternities	12 (21)
% in (# of) sororities	15 (31)
% African American	11
% Asian	1
% Caucasian	85
% Hispanic	2
% Native American	1
% international	1
# of countries represented	71

SURVEY SAYS . . .
Great library
Athletic facilities are great
Everyone loves the Crimson Tide
Frats and sororities dominate
social scene
Lots of beer drinking

ACADEMICS

Academic Rating	76
Calendar	semester
Student/faculty ratio	19:1
Profs interesting rating	80
Profs accessible rating	80
% classes taught by TAs	11
Most common	
reg class size	10–19 students
Most common	
lab size	20–29 students

MOST POPULAR MAJORS
nursing/registered nurse
(RN, ASN, BSN, MSN)
public relations/image management
finance

STUDENTS SAY ". . ."

Academics

"Tradition and excellence" go hand in hand at the University of Alabama's flagship Tuscaloosa campus. Combining an atmosphere of "Southern charm with a modern and certainly enriching education," 'Bama offers the best of all worlds to students seeking a "student-centered research university with a rich tradition of academic, athletic, and community excellence where any student can find peers with common interests, enhance his or her knowledge base, and forge friendships that will last a lifetime." Students agree that UA is "a first-rate public university," and that "with 18,000 students and tons of majors and student organizations, this place can be about whatever you want it to be." Standout programs include business, accounting, dance, nutrition and dietetics, social work, communication and information science, and nursing. Honors students praise the administration for offering "strong support" and "incredible research opportunities" to program participants. In many areas, professors are "top researchers or writers in their fields" who "go out of their way to help you with whatever you need." UA also offers "a wide range [of] opportunities for hands-on experience. The colleges work with students to place them in internships that will allow them to grow and learn about their field, and also make contacts for future employment."

Life

Greek life and Crimson Tide football are the twin pillars of UA life. Undergrads report that "UA has a really strong Greek system, so the sororities and fraternities are very present around campus, and they're pretty impressive." The Greeks may be impressive, but they are not monolithic; as one undergrad points out, "The Greeks do pretty much decide the SGA [student government] and homecoming, but they don't control all the clubs or honor societies." Football is the more universal force; it "encompasses the entire campus. Life during football season revolves around football. The vast majority of the students support and enjoy it." The social life of the campus cycles around the season; "During football season, weekends consist of band parties on Fridays, games on Saturdays followed by parties, and recovering on Sundays." Beyond frats and pigskins, "Life on campus is up to the particular students. If they want to fit in, they party with the party kids. If they are not typical party people, they can find others to spend time with doing whatever they feel is fun." With such a large student body, clubs abound: "There is interest in every possible subject under the sun; chances are that no matter what interest a student holds, there are at least half a dozen other students on campus with the same interest."

Student Body

Most UA students are "easygoing, with plenty of Southern hospitality," and have a "very balanced approach between study and social life." While some students feel that "student culture here puts a great deal of pressure on students to fit into the mold that has dominated this campus for so long," and others claim that the campus is "not as integrated as it could be," still others praise the university for embracing diversity among the student body. As one student states, it's true that "[many] students at the University of Alabama are White, middle- to upper-class kids from the South. They tend to come from traditional families, and a lot are religious. [But] the university is increasing diversity." Undergrads report that "minority groups tend to find a great deal of support and develop much pride here, and they experience very little criticism." The student body is also "far more ideologically diverse than most people would like to think; there is a myth that the university is overrun with [those on the] far right, but this is simply not true; there is a wide representation of political views among the student body."

THE UNIVERSITY OF ALABAMA AT TUSCALOOSA

FINANCIAL AID: 205-348-6756 • E-MAIL: ADMISSIONS@UA.EDU • WEBSITE: WWW.UA.EDU

THE PRINCETON REVIEW SAYS

Admissions

Very important factors considered include: Academic GPA, rigor of secondary school record, standardized test scores. *Important factors considered include:* Class rank. *Other factors considered include:* Application essay, recommendation(s), alumni/ae relation, character/personal qualities, extracurricular activities, first generation, interview, talent/ability, volunteer work, work experience. SAT or ACT required; TOEFL required of all international applicants. High school diploma is required and GED is accepted. *Academic units required:* 4 English, 3 mathematics, 3 science, (2 science labs), 1 foreign language, 3 social studies, 1 history, 5 academic electives. *Academic units recommended:* 4 English, 3 mathematics, 3 science, (2 science labs), 1 foreign language, 3 social studies, 1 history, 1 visual/performing arts, 1 computer science, 3 academic electives.

Financial Aid

Students should submit: FAFSA. The Princeton Review suggests that all financial aid forms be submitted as soon as possible after January 1. *Need-based scholarships/grants offered:* Federal Pell, SEOG, state scholarships/grants, private scholarships, the school's own gift aid, Federal Nursing Scholarships. *Loan aid offered:* Direct Subsidized Stafford, Direct Unsubsidized Stafford, Direct PLUS, Federal Perkins, college/university loans from institutional funds. , Alternate (Private) Student Loans. Applicants will be notified of awards on a rolling basis beginning 4/1. Federal Work-Study Program available. Institutional employment available. Off-campus job opportunities are good.

The Inside Word

The University of Alabama at Tuscaloosa relies heavily on objective data in the application process. Admission is not highly competitive, and applicants with satisfactory grades and modest test scores are likely to be accepted.

THE SCHOOL SAYS ". . ."

From The Admissions Office

"Since its founding in 1831 as the first public university in the state, the University of Alabama has been committed to providing the best, most complete education possible for its students. Our commitment to that goal means that as times change, we sharpen our focus and methods to keep our graduates competitive in their fields. By offering outstanding teaching in a solid core curriculum enhanced by multimedia classrooms and campus-wide computer labs, the University of Alabama keeps its focus on the future while maintaining a traditional college atmosphere. Extensive international study opportunities, internship programs, and cooperative education placements help our students prepare for successful futures. Consisting of 11 colleges and schools offering 220 degrees in more than 100 fields of study, the university gives its students a wide range of choices and offers courses of study at the bachelor's, master's, specialist, and doctoral levels. The university emphasizes quality and breadth of academic opportunities and challenging programs for well-prepared students through its Honors College, including the University Honors Program, International Honors Program, and Computer-Based Honors Programs and Blount Undergraduate Initiative (liberal arts program). Twenty-four percent of undergraduates are from out of state, providing an enriching social and cultural environment.

"Applicants for the 2008 freshmen class may submit either the new SAT or the old SAT (administered before March 2005). For those students electing to take the ACT test, the Writing component is not required for admission to the University of Alabama."

SELECTIVITY

Admissions Rating	86
# of applicants	14,313
% of applicants accepted	64
% of acceptees attending	50

FRESHMAN PROFILE

Range SAT Critical Reading	490–610
Range SAT Math	500–620
Range ACT Composite	21–27
Minimum paper TOEFL	500
Minimum computer TOEFL	173
Average HS GPA	3.4
% graduated top 10% of class	37.8
% graduated top 25% of class	57.4
% graduated top 50% of class	81.7

DEADLINES

Regular	
Priority	2/1
Notification	rolling
Nonfall registration?	yes

APPLICANTS ALSO LOOK AT
AND OFTEN PREFER
University of Tennessee—Knoxville
Vanderbilt University
Duke University
Florida State University
University of Georgia

AND SOMETIMES PREFER
Samford University
Tulane University
Auburn University
Louisiana State University

FINANCIAL FACTS

Financial Aid Rating	74
Annual in-state tuition	$5,700
% frosh rec. need-based scholarship or grant aid	14
% UG rec. need-based scholarship or grant aid	18
% frosh rec. non-need-based scholarship or grant aid	13
% UG rec. non-need-based scholarship or grant aid	11
% frosh rec. need-based self-help aid	28
% UG rec. need-based self-help aid	32
% frosh rec. athletic scholarships	2
% UG rec. athletic scholarships	2
% frosh rec. any financial aid	68
% UG rec. any financial aid	74
% UG borrow to pay for school	48
Average cumulative indebtedness	$17,146

UNIVERSITY OF ARIZONA

PO Box 210040, Tucson, AZ 85721-0040 • Admissions: 520-621-3237 • Fax: 520-621-9799

STUDENTS SAY ". . ."

Academics

The weather's warm and the learning is there for the taking at the University of Arizona—come on in. Giving its students the "absolute full package," the U of A provides a quality, affordable education, with "great school spirit and an all-around positive college environment." Though students don't shy away from the fact that the school's fun-loving environment might move their studies to the backseat on the weekends, most still hit the books plenty during the week, and "there are plenty of opportunities to work hard and succeed, academically and otherwise, if you seek them out." "You have to be willing to put time and effort into it," says a sophomore business major. The large university also "has some outstanding programs" for undergraduate research experience, including BRAVO, a program that provides funding for students who want to do scientific research abroad.

Though lectures (especially in the lower levels) can be large, the "amazing" professors make sure they are accessible to students and conduct their classes in a way that "provides real-life scenarios instead of the textbook jargon." Also, all large general education classes have weekly breakout sessions limited to 30 students each. There "is always a bad apple," of course, but on the whole, students are thrilled with their instructors. "You might not know it just from meeting them, but some of our professors are absolute legends in their field," says a junior. Academic advising is also a strong suit of the U of A, as are the science programs, and there are many sections of general education classes offered, making scheduling "very flexible, and allowing classes at the times you want." The administration, "although it is a bureaucracy," still manages to function well, and one can even send an e-mail to the president and receive a real answer in return.

Life

People here enjoy an active social life on top of their studies, and "everyone drinks socially and goes wild on the weekends, but buckles down again come Monday." The "Greek community rules the school," if not in membership numbers than in influence over weekend plans. Popular options include "house parties, frat parties, and definitely 4th Ave. for the bar scene." Everyone on campus gets into Pac-10 sporting events; one student claims to "have lined up four hours before a men's basketball game to get good seats in the student section (this is a common occurrence)." People here are very political active, and clubs like the Young Democrats and the Young Republicans attract large numbers. "There is always something to do both on campus and off," and Tucson is great for the lover of outdoors, as there are "numerous hiking and biking trails that go through the Sonoran Desert," as well as rock climbing and golf. "Life at the University of Arizona is mostly busy, but busy in a good way," says a student.

Student Body

A giant unifying factor on campus is that "everyone shares a love for this school." Combine that with the large size of the student body, and you'll find that each of the groups on campus "interacts very well and in a dignified manner." It's "a good looking campus," and people "generally care about what they look like and are wearing." The number of activities available to each student means that "no one is an outcast," and "finding a group of friends that is right for you is easy." "If you want to fit in, you find a group of people like yourself. We have the atypical groups, but not the atypical person" says a freshman. Most here hail from Tucson, Phoenix, or California, and are pretty laid back, "to go along with the relaxed Tucson atmosphere at the U of A."

FINANCIAL AID: 520-621-1858 • E-MAIL: APPINFO@ARIZONA.EDU • WEBSITE: WWW.ARIZONA.EDU

THE PRINCETON REVIEW SAYS

Admissions

Very important factors considered include: Academic GPA, rigor of secondary school record, class rank, application essay. *Important factors considered include:* Standardized test scores, character/personal qualities, extracurricular activities, first generation, geographical residence, state residency, talent/ability, volunteer work. SAT or ACT required; High school diploma is required and GED is accepted. *Academic units required:* 4 English, 3 mathematics, 3 science, (3 science labs), 2 foreign language, 1 social studies, 1 history, 1 fine art.

Financial Aid

The Princeton Review suggests that all financial aid forms be submitted as soon as possible after January 1. *Need-based scholarships/grants offered:* Federal Pell, SEOG, state scholarships/grants, private scholarships, the school's own gift aid, federal nursing scholarships, and for state residents, Arizona Assurance. *Loan aid offered:* FFEL Subsidized Stafford, FFEL Unsubsidized Stafford, FFEL PLUS, Federal Perkins, Federal Nursing, college/university loans from institutional funds. Federal Work-Study Program available. Institutional employment available. Off-campus job opportunities are good.

The Inside Word

The sun never sets for an Arizona resident—particularly if they're applying to the University of Arizona and have a solid academic record. The university currently offers "assured admission" for freshmen applicants. This essentially guarantees all applicants immediate admission provided they have fulfilled the following requirements, as detailed on the school's website: They must be "an Arizona resident, attend a regionally accredited high school, rank in the top 25 percent of their class, and have no course work deficiencies as prescribed by the Arizona Board of Regents."

THE SCHOOL SAYS "..."

From The Admissions Office

"Surrounded by mountains and the dramatic beauty of the Sonoran Desert, the University of Arizona offers a top-drawer education in a resort-like setting. Some of the nation's highest-ranked departments make their homes at this oasis of learning in the desert. In addition to producing cloudless sunshine 350 days per year, the clear Arizona skies provide an ideal setting for one of the country's best astronomy programs. Other nationally rated programs include nursing, sociology, management information systems, anthropology, creative writing, and computer and aerospace engineering. The university balances a strong research component with an emphasis on teaching—faculty rolls include Nobel and Pulitzer Prize winners. Famous Chinese astrophysicist and political dissident Fang Lizhi continues his landmark studies here; he now teaches physics to undergraduates. A wealth of academic choices—the university offers 114 majors, with myriad academic concentration options within those majors—is supplemented by an active, progressive campus atmosphere; conference-winning and national title-winning basketball, baseball, swimming, softball, and football teams; and countless recreational opportunities."

SELECTIVITY

Admissions Rating	75
# of applicants	25,449
% of applicants accepted	77
% of acceptees attending	43

FRESHMAN PROFILE

Range SAT Critical Reading	480–600
Range SAT Math	490–620
Range ACT Composite	21–26
Average HS GPA	3.39
% graduated top 10% of class	35
% graduated top 25% of class	65
% graduated top 50% of class	90

DEADLINES

Regular	
Deadline	5/1
Notification	rolling
Nonfall registration?	yes

APPLICANTS ALSO LOOK AT

AND OFTEN PREFER
University of Washington
University of California—Irvine

AND SOMETIMES PREFER
University of Colorado—Boulder
University of Wisconsin—Madison
Ohio University—Athens
University of California—Los Angeles
University of California—Santa Barbara

AND RARELY PREFER
Northern Arizona University
Baylor University
Arizona State University at the Tempe campus

FINANCIAL FACTS

Financial Aid Rating	66
Annual in-state tuition	$5,274
Annual out-of-state tuition	$18,408
Room and board	$7,812
Required fees	$257
Books and supplies	$1,000
% frosh rec. need-based scholarship or grant aid	33
% UG rec. need-based scholarship or grant aid	34
% frosh rec. non-need-based scholarship or grant aid	36
% UG rec. non-need-based scholarship or grant aid	22
% frosh rec. need-based self-help aid	17
% UG rec. need-based self-help aid	25
% UG borrow to pay for school	45
Average cumulative indebtedness	$18,241

UNIVERSITY OF ARKANSAS—FAYETTEVILLE

232 SILAS HUNT HALL, FAYETTEVILLE, AR 72701 • ADMISSIONS: 479-575-5346 • FAX: 479-575-7515

CAMPUS LIFE

Quality of Life Rating	84
Fire Safety Rating	60*
Green Rating	97
Type of school	public
Environment	town

STUDENTS

Total undergrad enrollment	14,442
% male/female	51/49
% from out of state	24
% from public high school	95
% live on campus	29
% in (# of) fraternities	16 (15)
% in (# of) sororities	19 (11)
% African American	5
% Asian	3
% Caucasian	83
% Hispanic	3
% Native American	2
% international	2
# of countries represented	103

SURVEY SAYS . . .

Great library
Athletic facilities are great
Students love Fayetteville, AR
Everyone loves the Razorbacks
Frats and sororities dominate
social scene
Lots of beer drinking

ACADEMICS

Academic Rating	72
Calendar	semester
Student/faculty ratio	17:1
Profs interesting rating	71
Profs accessible rating	72
% classes taught by TAs	27
Most common reg class size	20–29 students
Most common lab size	20–29 students

MOST POPULAR MAJORS

elementary education and teaching
finance
marketing/marketing management

STUDENTS SAY ". . ."

Academics

"Football, beer, business, Greek life, research and development, and all things Southern are the way of life" at the University of Arkansas—Fayetteville, a school that, "like most universities, is exactly what each student makes it out to be. It can be an academic haven or a party paradise. Whichever route a student chooses, Fayetteville and the university offer plenty of tools to ensure success." For those pursuing academics, there are the "many science departments that have top-notch research going on" as well as the popular and well-funded Sam Walton College of Business. U of A also boasts "a well-known engineering program," "an excellent Bachelor of Science in Nursing program," a "great creative writing program," and an honors program "that is keen on postgraduate activities and works hard to help students put forth strong applications for graduate school and postgraduate fellowships." No matter what you study here, prepare for an administration that "is a giant, cumbersome bureaucracy. It is impossible to deal with anyone directly about problems related to course credit, tuition, scholarships, etc." On the plus side, "There are tons of scholarships for study abroad and grad school."

Life

"There are a lot of activities on the U of A campus," with "over 250 student organizations and sports clubs providing something for almost everyone. And it is really easy to get involved." The campus also offers "a lot of social opportunities," including "free entertainment several times per month, such as live bands, free food, etc. There's Friday Night Live almost every Friday night, and many students participate in that. The residence halls also host parties for Halloween, Mardi Gras, and other events." During the fall, "Razorback football games dominate." "Not only are students hyped up for football games but the entire town revolves around the university, so it becomes citywide excitement! Parties are everywhere!" Hometown Fayetteville "is a great town to find things to do" and "is the kind of town where you can walk everywhere, so there's really no need for a car. Dickson Street is adjacent to campus and is full of bars, restaurants that serve many different types of food, live music every night, etc. On the weekends it borders on insanity! There is also an arts center, lots of great coffee shops, eclectic stores, and a nice downtown square within a quarter mile of Dickson Street." As if all that weren't enough, "Outdoor activities abound here in northwestern Arkansas; we're in the Boston Mountains, the most rugged part of the Ozark Highlands, and you can go rock climbing, mountain biking, whitewater kayaking, canoeing, fishing, and hunting in the 2-plus- million-acre Ozark National Forest, which is close by." "The weather in northern Arkansas is warm year-round" so "Even winter is quite mild" here.

Student Body

"Most of the kids at U of A are just good, down-home Southerners." Many "take 12 to 15 hours a semester, work part-time, and still manage to have active social lives." Students say they "want to have their weekends free to relax, not work on schoolwork. We work hard, but we want to have fun too." U of A undergrads "are generally pretty friendly. When you walk around campus people might say hi to you even if they don't know you." There is some diversity here, due in part to the international students: "You can hear several different languages just by walking in the student union," undergrads tell us. "Everyone here loves the Razorbacks," and that love unites the student body. The "huge division between Greeks and non-Greeks" occasionally tests that unity.

FINANCIAL AID: 479-575-3806 • E-MAIL: UOFA@UARK.EDU • WEBSITE: WWW.UARK.EDU/ADMISSIONS

THE PRINCETON REVIEW SAYS

Admissions

Very important factors considered include: Class rank, academic GPA, rigor of secondary school record, standardized test scores. *Other factors considered include:* Recommendation(s), alumni/ae relation, character/personal qualities, extracurricular activities, first generation, geographical residence, racial/ethnic status, state residency, talent/ability, volunteer work, work experience. SAT or ACT required; TOEFL required of all international applicants. High school diploma is required and GED is accepted. *Academic units required:* 4 English, 4 mathematics, 3 science, (2 science labs), 3 social studies, 2 academic electives. *Academic units recommended:* 2 foreign language.

Financial Aid

Students should submit: FAFSA. The Princeton Review suggests that all financial aid forms be submitted as soon as possible after January 1. *Need-based scholarships/grants offered:* Federal Pell, SEOG, state scholarships/grants, private scholarships, the school's own gift aid. *Loan aid offered:* FFEL Subsidized Stafford, FFEL Unsubsidized Stafford, FFEL PLUS, Federal Perkins, state loans, college/university loans from institutional funds, Alternative Loans. Applicants will be notified of awards on a rolling basis beginning 4/1.

The Inside Word

The admissions policy at the University of Arkansas—Fayetteville is straightforward. Applicants are guaranteed entrance as long as they meet published GPA requirements and standardized test minimums. Students who do not meet these requirements should not panic. They may still be admitted after an individualized review. As is the case with most rolling admissions policies, candidates will find it in their best interest to apply early. Those who do will have priority for both housing and orientation.

THE SCHOOL SAYS "..."

From The Admissions Office

"The University of Arkansas aims to become one of the top 50 public research universities, fueled by a historic $300 million gift received entirely in cash in March 2003 from the Walton Family Charitable Support Foundation. The largest gift ever to a public university, it established and endowed an undergraduate honors college and provides financial support to nearly 2,000 students. In 2004, the U of A provided more than $250,000 to support undergraduate research and more than $350,000 for study abroad. In 2005, the U of A completed a successful $1 billion campaign.

"The U of A's growing academic stature is exemplified by student accomplishment. Since 1990 U of A undergraduates have won 30 Goldwater Scholarships; 12 have been recognized by the *USA Today* All-USA College Academic Team; 16 have received National Science Foundations graduate fellowships; 10 have received Fulbright scholarships; 11 have received British Marshall scholarships; six have received Truman scholarships; five have received Udall scholarships; three have received Madison scholarships; three have received Tylenol scholarships; and one has received a Rhodes scholarship. All students who attend the U of A benefit from a range of choice in 208 academic programs; and yet, as research universities go, U of A is on the small side. The student/faculty ratio is 17:1, which allows students to receive individual attention from faculty. The university is located in Fayetteville, a small city on the beautiful Ozark Plateau. It's friendly, safe, diverse, and offers awesome recreational opportunities, a robust economy, vibrant cultural life, and a moderate climate. In 2004, a Washington, DC, nonprofit group named it one of the most livable communities in the United States.

"The University of Arkansas—Fayetteville will accept either the new SAT or the old SAT (administered prior to March 2005 and without a Writing component), as well as the ACT with or without the Writing component."

SELECTIVITY

Admissions Rating	87
# of applicants	10,132
% of applicants accepted	62
% of acceptees attending	46

FRESHMAN PROFILE

Range SAT Critical Reading	510–630
Range SAT Math	520–650
Range ACT Composite	23–29
Minimum paper TOEFL	550
Minimum computer TOEFL	213
Average HS GPA	3.59
% graduated top 10% of class	31.7
% graduated top 25% of class	62
% graduated top 50% of class	89.1

DEADLINES

Early action	
Deadline	11/15
Notification	12/15
Regular	
Priority	11/15
Deadline	8/15
Notification	rolling
Nonfall registration?	yes

FINANCIAL FACTS

Financial Aid Rating	75
Annual in-state tuition	$4,772
Annual out-of-state tuition	$13,226
Room and board	$7,017
Required fees	$1,266
Books and supplies	$966
% frosh rec. need-based scholarship or grant aid	22
% UG rec. need-based scholarship or grant aid	23
% frosh rec. non-need-based scholarship or grant aid	19
% UG rec. non-need-based scholarship or grant aid	13
% frosh rec. need-based self-help aid	25
% UG rec. need-based self-help aid	29
% frosh rec. athletic scholarships	4
% UG rec. athletic scholarships	4
% frosh rec. any financial aid	71
% UG rec. any financial aid	67
% UG borrow to pay for school	45.5
Average cumulative indebtedness	$18,172

UNIVERSITY OF CALIFORNIA—BERKELEY

110 SPROUL HALL #5800, BERKELEY, CA 94720-5800 • ADMISSIONS: 510-642-3175 • FAX: 510-642-7333

STUDENTS SAY " . . ."

Academics

"Tough and competitive" University of California—Berkeley "is the epitome of cultural, political, and intellectual diversity," both in its diverse student body (both in background and interests) and its substantial academic offerings. With "many departments ranked in the top five in their field," UCB has the "stunning ability to accommodate nearly every interest and demand of students." One student explains, "The freedom is incredible; there are a great array of majors and minors that all boast excellence in their departments. I feel like no matter what I choose to do at Cal, I will get the best of everything." It won't be handed to you, however; "UCB is a buffet. The opportunities are plentiful and the education is great, but you have to serve yourself." The many standout departments (featuring "many professors who are Nobel laureates and award winners") include the "top-tier science departments," the "very strong business and engineering departments," "the main humanities (history, English, political science)," mathematics, computer science, and music. No matter what you study here, there's a good chance your professors will "have done great things in their fields." "My organic chemistry professor helped name molecules at an international convention," says one student. "My other organic chemistry professor just won an award for finding a drug to help with cancer research. These are real people with amazing lives and I get to learn the tricks of the trade from them." Ambitious students can get in on the groundbreaking work, as the school "provides optimal research experience for students unlike any other university and constantly seeks students that can bring fresh ideas and new perspectives to the table."

Life

For many, "Life is mostly centered around academic-related activities, if not classes and studying, then internships or jobs, or something of that sort." More than a few, in fact, live in a near-perpetual state of academic immersion; they "get too sucked in to their work" and "don't take full advantage of their surroundings," but "if you can get your head out of the books for long enough, there's always a movie to catch, or a good game of Frisbee going on, or a party in one of the co-ops or fraternities." The city of Berkeley is "amazing." "There are so many great restaurants and bookstores and interesting people and just so much stuff to experience and to explore." Better still, San Francisco is "a 30-minute BART ride away," and is "always exciting" with tons of "shopping, eating, concerts, theater, and all the culture of the big city." Around campus, "Many students participate in sports or clubs for fun. Football games are probably the main reason students have school spirit, and they bring the students together for memorable experiences." The university community provides "a lot of opportunities for everyone: clubs, sports, jobs, internships, sororities, fraternities, dance, art, journalism, etc. There are so many opportunities to meet people and have fun inside the Berkeley campus and out of it," as well as an "endless numbers of events going on any given day. Art shows, benefits, plays, operas, live bands (local and touring), there are volunteer events and free classes. There is not enough time to do everything."

Student Body

"The only real common factor among most Berkeley students is that they are studious and/or hard workers," as undergrads here "come from all different socioeconomic and cultural backgrounds....It is such a big school that you are always likely to be able to find someone else like you." The mix includes "a lot of emo grad students, Asian premeds, a handful of jocks, and frat scenesters," "nerds who never leave the library, environmental activists, ground-breaking scientists, party animals," and "New Age hippies," among many others. In short, "Everyone here is unique, from the run-of-the-mill preppy kids to the neo-hippie and goth crowd, to the guy wearing a kilt in your 8 A.M. Japanese class." Asian students "make up a plurality of the student body, and there are loads of Asian cultural groups on campus. Other ethnic groups—such as African Americans and Hispanics—can be seen on campus" but are not as well represented. The Berkeley area "is quite liberal," and many students here fit in well with the surrounding community.

UNIVERSITY OF CALIFORNIA—BERKELEY

FINANCIAL AID: 510-642-6442 • E-MAIL: OUARS@UCLINK.BERKELEY.EDU • WEBSITE: WWW.BERKELEY.EDU

THE PRINCETON REVIEW SAYS

Admissions

Very important factors considered include: Application essay, academic GPA, rigor of secondary school record, state residency. *Important factors considered include:* Standardized test scores, character/personal qualities, extracurricular activities, talent/ability, volunteer work, work experience. *Other factors considered include:* First generation, geographical residence, SAT and SAT Subject Tests or ACT required; ACT with Writing component required. High school diploma is required and GED is accepted. *Academic units required:* 4 English, 3 mathematics, 2 science, (2 science labs), 2 foreign language, 2 history, 1 academic elective, 1 visual or performing arts; note, history can be social science. *Academic units recommended:* 4 English, 4 mathematics, 3 science, (3 science labs), 3 foreign language, 2 history, 1 academic elective, 1 visual or performing Arts; note, history can be social science.

Financial Aid

Students should submit: FAFSA, state aid form. Regular filing deadline is 3/2. The Princeton Review suggests that all financial aid forms be submitted as soon as possible after January 1. *Need-based scholarships/grants offered:* Federal Pell, SEOG, state scholarships/grants, private scholarships, the school's own gift aid. *Loan aid offered:* Direct Subsidized Stafford, Direct Unsubsidized Stafford, Direct PLUS, Federal Perkins, college/university loans from institutional funds. Applicants will be notified of awards on or about 4/15. Federal Work-Study Program available. Institutional employment available. Off-campus job opportunities are excellent.

The Inside Word

The entire UC system is competitive, and Berkeley is the most competitive of the UC campuses. In-state applicants need to be exceptional; out-of-state applicants must be exceptionally exceptional. The 24 percent acceptance rate tells you that a lot of highly qualified applicants receive a very disappointing letter in late March.

THE SCHOOL SAYS " . . . "

From The Admissions Office

"One of the top public universities in the nation and the world, the University of California—Berkeley offers a vast range of courses and a full menu of extracurricular activities. Berkeley's academic programs are internationally recognized for their excellence. Undergraduates can choose one of 100 majors. Thirty-five departments are top ranked, more than any other college or university in the country. Access to one of the foremost university libraries enriches studies. There are 23 specialized libraries on campus and distinguished museums of anthropology, paleontology, and science.

"All applicants must take the ACT Assessment plus the new ACT Writing Test or the new SAT Reasoning Test. In addition, all applicants must take two SAT Subject Tests in two different subject areas. If a Math SAT Subject Test is chosen by the applicant, he/she must take the Math Level II exam (Math 1 is not acceptable)."

SELECTIVITY

Admissions Rating	97
# of applicants	43,983
% of applicants accepted	23
% of acceptees attending	41

FRESHMAN PROFILE

Range SAT Critical Reading	590–710
Range SAT Math	620–750
Range SAT Writing	590–710
% graduated top 10% of class	98
% graduated top 25% of class	100
% graduated top 50% of class	100

DEADLINES

Regular Deadline	11/30
Nonfall registration?	yes

FINANCIAL FACTS

Financial Aid Rating	85
Annual tuition	$8,932
% frosh rec. need-based scholarship or grant aid	44
% UG rec. need-based scholarship or grant aid	45
% frosh rec. non-need-based scholarship or grant aid	1
% UG rec. non-need-based scholarship or grant aid	1
% frosh rec. need-based self-help aid	40
% UG rec. need-based self-help aid	39
% frosh rec. athletic scholarships	2
% UG rec. athletic scholarships	2
% UG borrow to pay for school	47
Average cumulative indebtedness	$13,171

UNIVERSITY OF CALIFORNIA—DAVIS

178 MRAK HALL, DAVIS, CA 95616 • ADMISSIONS: 530-752-2971 • FAX: 530-752-1280

CAMPUS LIFE
Quality of Life Rating	89
Fire Safety Rating	83
Green Rating	96
Type of school	public
Environment	town

STUDENTS
Total undergrad enrollment	23,373
% male/female	44/56
% from out of state	3
% from public high school	84
% live on campus	25
% in (# of) fraternities	9 (28)
% in (# of) sororities	8 (21)
% African American	3
% Asian	41
% Caucasian	35
% Hispanic	12
% Native American	1
% international	2
# of countries represented	113

SURVEY SAYS . . .
Great library
Athletic facilities are great
Student publications are popular

ACADEMICS
Academic Rating	77
Calendar	quarter
Student/faculty ratio	19:1
Profs interesting rating	72
Profs accessible rating	73
Most common reg class size	20–29 students
Most common lab size	20–29 students

MOST POPULAR MAJORS
biology/biological sciences
psychology
economics

STUDENTS SAY ". . ."

Academics

"UC Davis is a huge research university with the atmosphere of an intimate community." The campus known for its cows, and the agricultural and food sciences programs are indeed excellent. There are more than 100 majors. Research opportunities for undergraduates are abundant. Study abroad and internship programs are "fantastic." "Registration is very nerve racking," but on the whole, management is "invisible." "Things seem to work magically around here." "The administration is like Atlantis," offers a linguistics major. "It's rumored to exist, but you've never actually seen it." "As for your academic experience, 90 percent of it is dependent upon who your professor is, and 100 percent is dependent upon your personal interest," explains an international relations major. "I know that adds up to 190 percent. You can blame my statistics professor." UCD's quarter system affords "no time to fool around." "It is not really a school for a slacker." "Although the pace is fast, it's very doable," asserts a communication major. Classes can be quite large here, and the classrooms themselves "could do with some better desks." Some members of the "world class faculty" are "very enthusiastic" and "really profound." "I have consistently found my professors to be wonderful teachers who care deeply about their students," boasts a biology major. "Professors vary a lot depending on subject." As a rule, "upper division professors are generally far better than lower division ones."

Life

UC Davis is located in a "cozy," "rural," and "relaxed" college town in northern California not too far from Sacramento. Most students report a pretty high level of satisfaction with the atmosphere, though a few tell us that Davis "is boring, ugly, and smells." "Downtown Davis is a great place that is located within walking distance of the dorms and most off-campus housing," says a sophomore. It's "filled with interesting non-chain stores" and "great places to eat all types of food." "There are bicycles everywhere." And "if Davis isn't your thing, you can always go to Sacramento or San Francisco." "Tahoe is about two hours away, so it's pretty easy to go snowboarding or skiing," too. On the "sprawling" campus "the food is repetitive," but Davis has "excellent" recreational facilities and "a wide variety of activities, clubs, and groups to get involved in." "The sense of community is pretty good." "Greek life is big" and "keggers at frats" are definitely available. "There is a demographic that enjoys going to parties at the fraternities, but other people who do not enjoy that can easily stay out of it." "Davis is not mainly about parties," though. Mostly, "Davis is a place where you can really sit down and study," and "the best part is just finding a good group of people." "There is a niche for everyone."

Student Body

"Students here are the hardworking, studious, responsible kids," says a sophomore. "The student body is mostly made up of white and Asian students," but "Davis is a melting pot." "Many different cultures, ethnicities, and religions present," and "everybody is really accepting." Students here describe themselves as "goal-orientated," "down to earth, well rounded, balanced, amiable, and intelligent." "Some seem shy and timid." "There are some atypical students who care more about their looks and having fun than just studying but I feel like they are a minority," says a sophomore. There are "the uber-serious premed students who spend all of their waking time in class or in the library having an aneurism." There's "the sorority girl; the band geek, the jock; the crazy, outspoken chick," and "a lot of hippies," too. A pretty high percentage of these students is "really concerned about environmental issues" and many UCD students "take an active stand" on politics.

FINANCIAL AID: 530-752-2390 • E-MAIL: FRESHMANADMISSIONS@UCDAVIS.EDU • WEBSITE: WWW.UCDAVIS.EDU

THE PRINCETON REVIEW SAYS

Admissions

Very important factors considered include: Academic GPA, rigor of secondary school record, standardized test scores. *Important factors considered include:* Application essay, character/personal qualities, extracurricular activities, first generation, talent/ability. *Other factors considered include:* State residency, volunteer work, work experience. SAT Subject Tests required; SAT or ACT required; ACT with Writing component required. TOEFL required of all international applicants. High school diploma is required and GED is accepted. *Academic units required:* 4 English, 3 mathematics, 2 science, (2 science labs), 2 foreign language, 2 social studies, 1 academic elective, 1 visual and performing arts. *Academic units recommended:* 4 English, 4 mathematics, 3 science, (3 science labs), 3 foreign language, 2 social studies, 1 academic elective, 1 visual and performing arts.

Financial Aid

Students should submit: FAFSA, state aid form. The Princeton Review suggests that all financial aid forms be submitted as soon as possible after January 1. *Need-based scholarships/grants offered:* Federal Pell, SEOG, state scholarships/grants, private scholarships, the school's own gift aid. *Loan aid offered:* Direct Subsidized Stafford, Direct Unsubsidized Stafford, Direct PLUS, Federal Perkins, college/university loans from institutional funds. Applicants will be notified of awards on a rolling basis beginning 3/15.

The Inside Word

Admission to UC Davis is considerably easier than, say, admission to Berkeley. Nevertheless, every school in the UC system is world class, and the UC system in general is geared toward the best and brightest of California's high school students.

THE SCHOOL SAYS "..."

From The Admissions Office

"UC—Davis is characterized by a distinguished faculty of scholars, scientists, and artists, a treasured sense of community, and dedication to innovative teaching, research, and public service. Students follow a philosophy of learning, discovery, and engagement. Their involvement in academic, leadership and honors programs, as well as internships, education abroad, and research, typify the undergraduate experience. Students can earn degrees in more than 100 majors, interact with the university's professional schools through select minor programs, and receive pregraduate advising in nearly any field imaginable.

"The friendly, supportive nature of the campus and Davis community also defines the undergraduate experience. UC—Davis offers its active student body more than 450 student organizations, NCAA Division I athletics, and stunning cultural, academic, and recreational facilities such as the Mondavi Center for the Performing Arts, the Genome Center, and the Activities and Recreation Center.

"UC—Davis also provides many resources to help undergraduates build social and career networks before they graduate, so they're well connected by the time they don their cap and gown. Within one year following graduation, 95 percent of June 2003 baccalaureate degree recipients were working full time or were studying for or had completed a postgraduate degree.

"Freshman applicants are required to take the ACT with the Writing component or the SAT, as well as two SAT Subject Tests in two different subject areas."

SELECTIVITY

Admissions Rating	94
# of applicants	35,148
% of applicants accepted	59
% of acceptees attending	24

FRESHMAN PROFILE

Range SAT Critical Reading	490–630
Range SAT Math	540–660
Range SAT Writing	500–630
Range ACT Composite	20–27
Minimum paper TOEFL	550
Minimum computer TOEFL	213
Minimum web-based TOEFL	60
Average HS GPA	3.74
% graduated top 10% of class	95
% graduated top 25% of class	100
% graduated top 50% of class	100

DEADLINES

Regular	
Deadline	11/30
Notification	3/15
Nonfall registration?	no

APPLICANTS ALSO LOOK AT

AND OFTEN PREFER
University of California—Berkeley
University of California—San Diego
University of California—Los Angeles

AND SOMETIMES PREFER
California Polytechnic State University—San Luis Obispo
University of California—Santa Barbara

AND RARELY PREFER
University of California—Riverside

FINANCIAL FACTS

Financial Aid Rating	73
Annual out-of-state tuition	$19,620
Room and board	$11,533
Required fees	$8,124
Books and supplies	$1,508
% frosh rec. need-based scholarship or grant aid	47
% UG rec. need-based scholarship or grant aid	46
% frosh rec. non-need-based scholarship or grant aid	1
% UG rec. non-need-based scholarship or grant aid	1
% frosh rec. need-based self-help aid	34
% UG rec. need-based self-help aid	36
% frosh rec. athletic scholarships	1
% UG rec. athletic scholarships	1
% frosh rec. any financial aid	46
% UG rec. any financial aid	59
% UG borrow to pay for school	46
Average cumulative indebtedness	$13,835

UNIVERSITY OF CALIFORNIA—LOS ANGELES

405 HILGARD AVENUE, BOX 951436, LOS ANGELES, CA 90095-1436 • ADMISSIONS: 310-825-3101 • FAX: 310-206-1206

CAMPUS LIFE

Quality of Life Rating	**95**
Fire Safety Rating	**86**
Green Rating	**87**
Type of school	public
Environment	metropolis

STUDENTS

Total undergrad enrollment	25,928
% male/female	45/55
% from out of state	4
% from public high school	78
% live on campus	36
% in (# of) fraternities	13 (36)
% in (# of) sororities	13 (28)
% African American	3
% Asian	38
% Caucasian	34
% Hispanic	15
% international	4
# of countries represented	132

SURVEY SAYS . . .

Great library
Athletic facilities are great
Students love Los Angeles, CA
Great off-campus food
Everyone loves the Bruins
Student publications are popular

ACADEMICS

Academic Rating	**80**
Calendar	quarter
Student/faculty ratio	16:1
Profs interesting rating	65
Profs accessible rating	63
Most common	
reg class size	10–19 students
Most common	
lab size	20–29 students

MOST POPULAR MAJORS

political science and government
biology/biological sciences
psychology

STUDENTS SAY ". . ."

Academics

It's all about diversity in activities, academics, athletics, race, religion, and sexuality at UCLA; or, as one student puts it, "academically competitive, athletically dominated, and overcrowded." One of the most vaunted schools in the UC system, Bruins take advantage of the school's location and opportunities in order to "learn as much as you want in whatever field you desire, while being engaged in non-academic endeavors that are equally as stimulating and interesting." Students here "have a lot of things going on that are not always academic or on-campus," and "their outside experiences and passions are reflected in their contributions in class and on campus."

Being a large university can be a double-edged sword, and while those enrolled here are thrilled to be able to "take classes in practically any subject you can imagine," many do wish class sizes were smaller, and "it's very difficult to get classes, especially in competitive majors." "In Chinese, most classes get filled very quickly because econ, business, and everyone else wants to learn Chinese right now," says a junior. Though there are a few complaints of disinterested professors at lower levels, once students reach upper-division courses, "the professors are extremely knowledgeable and often have written the book, literally, on the topic they are teaching." With such a wide selection of courses and departments, reviews range from "not always the greatest teachers" to "very smart and make themselves very available." The curve can be tough, and students begin to think of their learning as "studying longer and getting better scores than the person next to you in order to place higher on the curve." As far as step-by-step guidance goes, you "do have to be self-driven at UCLA," but "if you're determined enough you will be able to accomplish whatever you need (within reason, of course)." "It's all on you to get your stuff done," says a sophomore biology major.

Life

While at times, the school can seem large, "there are always programs going on in the buildings to help you meet new people," and most people use some form of club, organization, or sorority/fraternity to narrow down their circles. Since most of the apartments are within walking distance of the dorms, which are all grouped together, "there's a sense of community. You don't lose track of your friends in the crowd." Students here are "really concerned about academics and getting into graduate/professional schools," but on weekends, many still go to parties at the frats or off-campus apartments. "There seem to be times when no one does work, at other times everyone is busy and stays up studying for days at a time," says a student. Westwood offers everything a college student could want, from shopping, movie premieres, going to the beach, or attending the "great concerts in the area, most of which are very well priced." Naturally, sporting events are "a huge part" of the school, and all "take great pride in being part of such great tradition."

Student Body

UCLA's a tough school to get into, and everyone here "was accepted for a reason," so most students are "well-rounded" and "extremely driven," whether it be academically, athletically, or dramatically. That being said, they also chose to go to school in one of the liveliest cities in the US, so the typical student "regards academic success highly but does not make studying the central focus of their lives," and there's a "balance of work and play." There's a "very strong Asian presence," and most people are involved in extracurricular activities, but beyond that, it's difficult to find any other common characteristics of a UCLA student, other than that they "study hard and hate USC." "Everyone, and I mean everyone, belongs here," says a sophomore, referring to the extraordinarily broad student spectrum. "It doesn't matter; there will be a group of people who are EXACTLY like you, and they will probably have formed a club for it already."

FINANCIAL AID: 310-206-0400 • E-MAIL: UGADM@SAONET.UCLA.EDU • WEBSITE: WWW.UCLA.EDU

THE PRINCETON REVIEW SAYS

Admissions

Very important factors considered include: Application essay, academic GPA, rigor of secondary school record, standardized test scores. *Important factors considered include:* Character/personal qualities, extracurricular activities, talent/ability, volunteer work, work experience. *Other factors considered include:* First generation, geographical residence, SAT Subject Tests required; SAT or ACT required; ACT with Writing component required. TOEFL required of all international applicants. High school diploma is required and GED is accepted. *Academic units required:* 4 English, 3 mathematics, 2 science, (2 science labs), 2 foreign language, 2 history, 1 academic elective, 1 Visual and Performing Arts *Academic units recommended:* 4 English, 4 mathematics, 3 science, (3 science labs), 3 foreign language, 2 history, 1 academic elective, 1 visual and performing arts.

Financial Aid

Students should submit: FAFSA. The Princeton Review suggests that all financial aid forms be submitted as soon as possible after January 1. *Need-based scholarships/grants offered:* Federal Pell, SEOG, state scholarships/grants, private scholarships, the school's own gift aid, United Negro College Fund, Federal Nursing Scholarships, National Merit. *Loan aid offered:* FFEL Subsidized Stafford, FFEL Unsubsidized Stafford, FFEL PLUS, Federal Perkins, Federal Nursing, state loans, college/university loans from institutional funds. Applicants will be notified of awards on a rolling basis beginning 3/15. Federal Work-Study Program available. Institutional employment available. Off-campus job opportunities are good.

The Inside Word

A powerhouse within the California system, UCLA has its applicants face a stringent and comprehensive assessment. Each application is evaluated within the context of three categories: academics, personal achievement, and life challenges, and each is reviewed by multiple Admissions Officers. Academic success is a must for any serious contender and enrollment in honors and Advanced Placement courses is highly recommended. Additionally, officers pay close attention to level of commitment in regards to extracurricular activities.

THE SCHOOL SAYS ". . ."

From The Admissions Office

"Undergraduates arrive at UCLA from throughout California and around the world with exceptional levels of academic preparation. They are attracted by our acclaimed degree programs, distinguished faculty, and the beauty of a park-like campus set amid the dynamism of the nation's second-largest city. UCLA's highly ranked undergraduate programs incorporate cutting-edge technology and teaching techniques that hone the critical-thinking skills and the global perspectives necessary for success in our rapidly changing world. The diversity of these programs draws strength from a student body that mirrors the cultural and ethnic vibrancy of Los Angeles. Generally ranked among the nation's top half-dozen universities, UCLA is at once distinguished and dynamic, academically rigorous and responsive.

"All applicants must take the ACT plus Writing or the SAT Reasoning Test. In addition, all applicants must take two SAT Subject Tests in two different subject areas. (If a Math SAT Subject Test is chosen by the applicant, he/she must take the Math Level II exam.)"

SELECTIVITY
Admissions Rating	98
# of applicants	50,755
% of applicants accepted	24
% of acceptees attending	38

FRESHMAN PROFILE
Range SAT Critical Reading	660–720
Range SAT Math	700–760
Range SAT Writing	670–720
Range ACT Composite	28–31
Minimum paper TOEFL	550
Minimum computer TOEFL	220
Average HS GPA	4.17
% graduated top 10% of class	97
% graduated top 25% of class	100
% graduated top 50% of class	100

DEADLINES
Regular Deadline	11/30
Notification	rolling
Nonfall registration?	no

FINANCIAL FACTS
Financial Aid Rating	81
Annual out-of-state tuition	$19,068
Room and board	$12,420
Required fees	$7,590
Books and supplies	$1,515
% frosh rec. need-based scholarship or grant aid	45
% UG rec. need-based scholarship or grant aid	47
% frosh rec. non-need-based scholarship or grant aid	1
% UG rec. non-need-based scholarship or grant aid	1
% frosh rec. need-based self-help aid	34
% UG rec. need-based self-help aid	37
% frosh rec. athletic scholarships	2
% UG rec. athletic scholarships	2
% frosh rec. any financial aid	47
% UG rec. any financial aid	46
% UG borrow to pay for school	46
Average cumulative indebtedness	$15,996

UNIVERSITY OF CALIFORNIA—RIVERSIDE

1138 HINDERAKER HALL, RIVERSIDE, CA 92521 • ADMISSIONS: 951-827-3411 • FAX: 951-827-6344

CAMPUS LIFE
Quality of Life Rating	**62**
Fire Safety Rating	**87**
Green Rating	**96**
Type of school	public
Environment	city

STUDENTS
Total undergrad enrollment	14,973
% male/female	48/52
% from out of state	1
% from public high school	88
% live on campus	35
% in (# of) fraternities	7 (20)
% in (# of) sororities	7 (20)
% African American	7
% Asian	42
% Caucasian	18
% Hispanic	26
% international	2
# of countries represented	66

SURVEY SAYS . . .
Great library
Athletic facilities are great
Diverse student types on campus
Frats and sororities dominate
social scene
(Almost) everyone smokes

ACADEMICS
Academic Rating	**73**
Calendar	quarter
Student/faculty ratio	18:1
Profs interesting rating	62
Profs accessible rating	65
Most common reg class size	20–29 students
Most common lab size	20–29 students

MOST POPULAR MAJORS
biology/biological sciences
psychology
business administration and
management

STUDENTS SAY ". . ."

Academics
Unlike many of its larger UC peers, "UC—Riverside has all the advantages of being a smaller campus: Classes are smaller, and professors are friendly and helpful." Small classes give students the opportunity to get acquainted with their professors and other faculty members, and the school places great emphasis on attending office hours." The premedical sciences are a particular strength at UCR; other popular majors include biology/biological sciences, business administration, and psychology. (Riverside is "one of only two UCs [Berkeley is the other] with an undergrad business administration program"). Across departments, "The professors are very knowledgeable in their fields and expect students to be equally knowledgeable." In addition to assigning rigorous course work, "The faculty also encourages internships and research. Many students also take up a minor or second major." Aside from internships, undergrads here benefit from "the great variety of opportunities, which include education abroad programs, interuniversity programs, postgrad programs, and two great libraries."

Life
Life at Riverside can be "very calm, and the school's atmosphere in general is very quiet." One contributor to this sense of calm is the fact that many students commute to school. "We are not a huge party school," students admit, but "There is always a party to go to if that's what you're into." Although the city of Riverside has "very little to offer in the way of entertainment," students compensate by joining various clubs and student organizations, including sororities and fraternities, which have a noticeable presence on campus. The school also offers "countless events, including free movie screenings, concerts, academic discussion forums, plays, and trips." Popular campus hangouts include "a great rec center," "the student commons," and "a campus movie theater, where some of our classes are held." Students seem to agree, however, that "intercollegiate sports need more student support." Those with cars leave campus relatively frequently on the weekends, finding plenty to do outside of town; one student explains, "Within an hour's drive you can ski in the mountains, go sunbathing at the beach, visit a major theme park, or even hang out in Hollywood for a day."

Student Body
UCR is "one of the most diverse campuses in the UC system"; one thing that makes the school unique is its particularly "large population of Asian students," who constitute a plurality of the student body. As a result of the diversity on campus, the school "has very few 'typical' students." One respondent writes, "I believe that anyone could find a group of friends here because there are so many different types of people going to this school." Students praise the school's "clubs and organizations" for "uniting differences and providing forums for the expression and understanding of these differences." As a result of this unity, "UCR is a very sociable campus, and it seems like everyone, no matter [what] gender, ethnicity, or sexual orientation, is accepted and feels welcomed."

FINANCIAL AID: 951-827-3878 • E-MAIL: UGADMISS@UCR.EDU • WEBSITE: WWW.UCR.EDU

THE PRINCETON REVIEW SAYS

Admissions

Very important factors considered include: Academic GPA, rigor of secondary school record, standardized test scores, state residency, application essay, first generation, talent/ability. *Other factors considered include:* Talent/ability, SAT Subject Tests required; SAT or ACT required; ACT with Writing component required. TOEFL required of all international applicants. High school diploma is required and GED is accepted. *Academic units required:* 4 English, 3 mathematics, 2 science, (2 science labs), 2 foreign language, 2 history, 1 academic elective, 1 Visual/Performing Arts. *Academic units recommended:* 4 mathematics, 3 science, (3 science labs), 3 foreign language.

Financial Aid

Students should submit: FAFSA Regular filing deadline is 3/2. The Princeton Review suggests that all financial aid forms be submitted as soon as possible after January 1. *Need-based scholarships/grants offered:* Federal Pell, SEOG, state scholarships/grants, private scholarships, the school's own gift aid. *Loan aid offered:* Direct Subsidized Stafford, Direct Unsubsidized Stafford, Direct PLUS, Federal Perkins, college/university loans from institutional funds. Applicants will be notified of awards on a rolling basis beginning 3/1. Federal Work-Study Program available. Institutional employment available. Off-campus job opportunities are excellent.

The Inside Word

Formulas are the foundation of the UC—Riverside admission process. Applicants who meet GPA and standardized test minimums should have no problems gaining acceptance. There is a priority filling period so students should apply as early as possible.

THE SCHOOL SAYS "..."

From The Admissions Office

"The University of California—Riverside offers the quality, rigor, and facilities of a major research institution, while assuring its undergraduates personal attention and a sense of community. Academic programs, teaching, advising, and student services all reflect the supportive attitude that characterizes the campus. Among the exceptional opportunities are the UC—Riverside/UCLA Thomas Haider Program in Biomedical Sciences, which provides an exclusive path to UCLA's Geffen School of Medicine; the University Honors Program; an extensive undergraduate research program; UC's only undergraduate degree program in business administration in Southern California; and UC's only bachelor's degree in creative writing. More than 250 student clubs and organizations and a variety of athletic and arts events give students a myriad of ways to get involved and have fun.

"All applicants must take the ACT Assessment plus Writing Test or the SAT Reasoning Test. In addition, all applicants must take two SAT Subject Tests in two different subject areas. If students choose the Math SAT Subject Test, they must take the Math Level II exam."

SELECTIVITY

Admissions Rating	91
# of applicants	20,126
% of applicants accepted	82
% of acceptees attending	22

FRESHMAN PROFILE

Range SAT Critical Reading	450–560
Range SAT Math	470–610
Range SAT Writing	450–560
Range ACT Composite	18–23
Minimum paper TOEFL	550
Minimum computer TOEFL	213
Average HS GPA	3.4
% graduated top 10% of class	94
% graduated top 25% of class	100
% graduated top 50% of class	100

DEADLINES

Regular	
Deadline	11/30
Notification	rolling
Nonfall registration?	no

APPLICANTS ALSO LOOK AT

AND OFTEN PREFER
University of California—Berkeley
University of California—San Diego
University of California—Los Angeles

AND SOMETIMES PREFER
University of California—Irvine
University of California—Santa Barbara
University of California—Davis

AND RARELY PREFER
University of California—Merced
University of California—Santa Cruz

FINANCIAL FACTS

Financial Aid Rating	79
Annual out-of-state tuition	$19,620
Room and board	$10,800
Required fees	$7,355
Books and supplies	$1,700
% frosh rec. need-based scholarship or grant aid	57
% UG rec. need-based scholarship or grant aid	57
% frosh rec. non-need-based scholarship or grant aid	1
% UG rec. non-need-based scholarship or grant aid	1
% frosh rec. need-based self-help aid	52
% UG rec. need-based self-help aid	47
% frosh rec. athletic scholarships	1
% UG rec. athletic scholarships	1
% frosh rec. any financial aid	80
% UG rec. any financial aid	75
% UG borrow to pay for school	64
Average cumulative indebtedness	$14,992

UNIVERSITY OF CALIFORNIA—SAN DIEGO

9500 GILMAN DRIVE, 0021, LA JOLLA, CA 92093-0021 • ADMISSIONS: 858-534-4831 • FAX: 858-534-5723

CAMPUS LIFE
Quality of Life Rating	71
Fire Safety Rating	60*
Green Rating	60*
Type of school	public
Environment	metropolis

STUDENTS
Total undergrad enrollment	20,679
% male/female	48/52
% from out of state	3
% live on campus	33
% in (# of) fraternities	10 (19)
% in (# of) sororities	10 (14)
% African American	1
% Asian	43
% Caucasian	32
% Hispanic	12
% international	3
# of countries represented	70

SURVEY SAYS . . .
Registration is a breeze
Great computer facilities
Great library
Athletic facilities are great
Great off-campus food
Campus feels safe
Student publications are popular

ACADEMICS
Academic Rating	79
Calendar	quarter
Student/faculty ratio	19:1
Profs interesting rating	62
Profs accessible rating	63
% classes taught by TAs	10
Most common reg class size	10–19 students
Most common lab size	30-39 students

MOST POPULAR MAJORS
microbiology
economics
political science and government

STUDENTS SAY ". . ."

Academics

The University of California—San Diego is "a great research facility" that "is all about science," a place where premedical students benefit from "outstanding biological sciences and chemistry programs," and earth sciences and environmental systems programs capitalize on affiliation with the Scripps Institute of Oceanography. The school's hard-science focus means that "for the vast majority of UCSD students, school is all about studying." A quarterly academic calendar ratchets up the academic pressure and leaves precious little time to goof off. While some here report that the "Dedicated faculty are always accessible and willing to help and guide you," many caution that "in many of the hard sciences, there's a massive concentration on research. It really does take preference over the quality of teaching in many courses. Lots of professors would rather spend their entire lives in their labs and never have to speak to a single student. That needs to change." Students outside the hard sciences occasionally feel neglected. "I sometimes feel as if there aren't as many resources for us," writes one social science major. "I've been able to do research, but students who are in the sciences seem to be offered a lot more resources [such as] grad school info sessions and extracurricular opportunities." On the plus side, San Diego is home to many businesses that dovetail with UCSD's specializations, so there are "many opportunities for internships here. They prepare you well for work experience in your major." UCSD's six-college system is also seen as an asset, "allowing students the advantages of a large research university and the feel of a small university within their [individual] colleges."

Life

"You'll read articles saying that UCSD students are generally unhappy and don't get out and do as much stuff as folks at other campuses, and there's a deal of truth to that," students tell us, adding that "it's mostly the individual fault of each person. There's lots to do, but no one will push you out the door." While "UCSD is in one of the best locations for off-campus fun, many people spend hours upon hours studying. The classwork is hard, and focus is necessary to succeed." But the opportunities are not lacking. True, UCSD lacks a Greek Row, and strict enforcement of residential regulations makes on-campus partying difficult. The absence of a football team and "the lackluster nature of our other teams" means that "UCSD students are generally uninterested in UCSD sports" and have "very little school spirit." Still, some students adamantly oppose the stereotype that the school is "socially dead." One student writes, "The best part of UCSD is that if you want to study, you can study; if you want to party, you can do that too, but the two never impinge on one another." To find a party, "All it takes is asking around or even going online." Hometown La Jolla may be a "swanky area," but it is "not friendly to students." Still, students recognize that there are "so many recreational activities in San Diego, and lots of students love the beach." One undergrad sums up, "Life here is pretty decent, as long as you're willing to leave campus on the weekends for fun. I love to go to the beach and surf, snorkel, kayak . . . anything that gets me outside. And this [retreat from campus] is necessary; on the weekends, the campus dies."

Student Body

The stereotypical UCSD student "is a science nerd with the big backpack and glasses, who's just not into the social scene." He or she is the type of kid "you'd find at the campus shuttle stop at nine o'clock on a Saturday night, reading his textbook with a flashlight." Such students "don't have enough fun," we're told, and "are very focused on grades." But not all the students are like this—it's just that the students who defy the stereotype are likely, according to one respondent, to be "non-science majors." "The school is really diverse," contends one student; in particular, there is a large contingent of Asian students. According to at least one respondent, the homosexual community is welcomed: "We have about 10 different queer clubs on campus."

UNIVERSITY OF CALIFORNIA—SAN DIEGO

FINANCIAL AID: 858-534-4480 • E-MAIL: ADMISSIONSINFO@UCSD.EDU • WEBSITE: WWW.UCSD.EDU

THE PRINCETON REVIEW SAYS

Admissions

Very important factors considered include: Application essay, academic GPA, rigor of secondary school record, standardized test scores, character/personal qualities, state residency, talent/ability, volunteer work. *Important factors considered include:* extracurricular activities. *Other factors considered include:* Work experience. SAT or ACT required; SAT and SAT Subject Tests or ACT required; ACT with Writing component required. TOEFL required of all international applicants. High school diploma is required and GED is accepted. *Academic units required:* 4 English, 3 mathematics, (2 science labs), 2 foreign language, 2 history, 1 academic elective, 1 visual and performing arts. *Academic units recommended:* 4 English, 4 mathematics, (3 science labs), 3 foreign language, 2 history, 1 academic elective, 1 visual and performing arts.

Financial Aid

Students should submit: FAFSA, state aid form. Regular filing deadline is 6/1. The Princeton Review suggests that all financial aid forms be submitted as soon as possible after January 1. *Need-based scholarships/grants offered:* Federal Pell, SEOG, state scholarships/grants, private scholarships, the school's own gift aid. *Loan aid offered:* FFEL Subsidized Stafford, FFEL Unsubsidized Stafford, FFEL PLUS, Federal Perkins, college/university loans from institutional funds, Alternative Loans. Applicants will be notified of awards on a rolling basis beginning 3/15.

The Inside Word

While not as lauded as Berkeley or UCLA, UCSD is quickly earning its place as one of the gems of the UC system. It continues to distinguish itself in a number of ways, including its individualized approach to admissions. Although Admissions Officers do implement a formula, they factor in extracurricular pursuits and personal experiences. Applicants will need to be strong in all areas if they hope to attend UCSD.

THE SCHOOL SAYS "..."

From The Admissions Office

"UCSD is recognized for the exceptional quality of its academic programs: a recent Johns Hopkins study rated UCSD faculty first nationally among public institutions in science; *U.S. News & World Report* rates UCSD seventh in the nation among state-supported colleges and universities; Kiplinger's '100 Best Values in Public Colleges' ranks UCSD tenth in the nation. UCSD ranks fifth in the nation and first in the University of California system for the amount of federal research dollars spent on research and development; and the university ranks tenth in the nation in the excellence of its graduate programs and the quality of its faculty, according to the most recent National Research Council college rankings.

"All applicants must take the ACT Assessment plus the new ACT Writing Test or the new SAT Reasoning Test. In addition, all applicants must take two SAT Subject Tests in two different subject areas. (If a Math SAT Subject Test is chosen by the applicant, he/she must take the Math Level II exam.)"

SELECTIVITY

Admissions Rating	96
# of applicants	43,586
% of applicants accepted	49
% of acceptees attending	21

FRESHMAN PROFILE

Range SAT Critical Reading	540–660
Range SAT Math	600–700
Range ACT Composite	23–29
Minimum paper TOEFL	550
Average HS GPA	3.9
% graduated top 10% of class	99
% graduated top 25% of class	100
% graduated top 50% of class	100

DEADLINES

Regular	
Deadline	11/30
Notification	rolling
Nonfall registration?	yes

APPLICANTS ALSO LOOK AT

AND OFTEN PREFER
University of California—Berkeley
University of California—Los Angeles

AND SOMETIMES PREFER
Stanford University
California Polytechnic State University—
San Luis Obispo
University of California—Davis

AND RARELY PREFER
San Diego State University

FINANCIAL FACTS

Financial Aid Rating	75
Annual out-of-state tuition	$19,068
Room and board	$10,237
Required fees	$7,456
Books and supplies	$1,487
% frosh rec. need-based scholarship or grant aid	45
% UG rec. need-based scholarship or grant aid	46
% frosh rec. non-need-based scholarship or grant aid	1
% frosh rec. need-based self-help aid	41
% UG rec. need-based self-help aid	41
% frosh rec. any financial aid	87
% UG rec. any financial aid	84
% UG borrow to pay for school	46
Average cumulative indebtedness	$15,170

UNIVERSITY OF CALIFORNIA—SANTA BARBARA

OFFICE OF ADMISSIONS, 1210 CHEADLE HALL, SANTA BARBARA, CA 93106-2014 • ADMISSIONS: 805-893-2881 • FAX: 805-893-2676

CAMPUS LIFE

Quality of Life Rating	90
Fire Safety Rating	88
Green Rating	94
Type of school	public
Environment	city

STUDENTS

Total undergrad enrollment	18,412
% male/female	45/55
% from out of state	4
% live on campus	31
% in (# of) fraternities	4 (17)
% in (# of) sororities	7 (18)
% African American	3
% Asian	16
% Caucasian	53
% Hispanic	19
% Native American	1
% international	1
# of countries represented	72

SURVEY SAYS . . .
Great library
Athletic facilities are great
Students are friendly
Students love Santa Barbara, CA
Student publications are popular
Lots of beer drinking
Hard liquor is popular

ACADEMICS

Academic Rating	81
Calendar	quarter
Student/faculty ratio	17:1
Profs interesting rating	75
Profs accessible rating	78
Most common reg class size	fewer than 10 students
Most common lab size	20–29 students

MOST POPULAR MAJORS
biology/biological sciences
psychology
economics

STUDENTS SAY ". . ."

Academics

"Don't believe all the hype," students at the University of California—Santa Barbara say, meaning the hype about UCSB being nothing but a hard-core party school. Undergrads want you to know that "UCSB is a serious academic institution" with "outstanding academics" and "opportunities to participate in high-level scientific research," though it "also happens to be the most beautiful place in the world in which to be stressed out." Five Nobel laureates (including three in physics) pepper the faculty, and, "Because this school is [mainly] undergraduates, real professors teach you. . . . My ECON 1 professor was President Reagan's national economic adviser and created Reaganonomics. That is pretty cool." UCSB is most highly regarded in the sciences. The university's Marine Science Institute facilities provide "invaluable fieldwork and lab experience with top-notch biologists," and the school's multiple nanotechnology centers are "revolutionary." Programs in physics and material sciences are also highly regarded. Intro-level lectures can be "gargantuan," but students point out that though "It is easy to complain that the lectures are huge and that it is hard to get into classes," the experience here "all depends on the amount of effort you put in. There is always help if you choose to seek it." One undergrad agrees, "There are hundreds of academically challenging classes and amazingly talented teachers at UCSB, but it is up to the students to go out and make the most of their academic experience. Nothing is handed to us." UCSB has done a good job of moving administrative tasks online: "Grades, registration, communication, transcripts . . . it's all done on the computer. Financial aid is automatically deposited into my account. There really isn't a need to stand in line for services because you don't need to, but if you do they're generally helpful."

Life

"Life here is very chill. I mean that in the best way," a UCSB student reports, adding, "People aren't freaking out about classes or stressing out. People just do their work and then go hang out at the beach" or "in IV (Isla Vista, the local, mostly student community)." A sophomore brags that "everything I need is on campus or nearby in Isla Vista. I hardly ever need to go off campus or drive anywhere." The beach is a constant temptation; as one student points out, "UCSB is on the beach . . . literally. As I'm writing this survey, I'm looking out my dorm window and seeing the ocean, just feet from my building." Surfing, swimming, and sunbathing are all big, as are "hiking up to the waterfalls, rock climbing, spearfishing, kayaking, scuba diving, [and] beach volleyball." Most parties take place in Isla Vista, where "17,000 19-to-21-year-olds are all jam-packed into this six-tenths-of-a-square-mile community, so you can imagine how the parties are. . . . Every night is wild, but, obviously, Friday and Saturday nights are the craziest." For some, Isla Vista "can get boring, because it's the same party every weekend," but for others, it never grows old. Downtown Santa Barbara "is beautiful and perfect for nights out, movies, or an outing."

Student Body

The "stereotype of 'beautiful beach kids' does exist," writes one student, who notes that "I have heard the joke that UCSB is the only UC that requires a head shot in the application. However, there are all types of students that attend the school, and anyone can and does find their niche." Undergrads here are generally "more laid-back and less stressed out about school" than most college kids and "take school seriously, but also know how to enjoy their youth." They are typically "very athletic and in shape. They love the outdoors." Oddly, students perceive their campus as "pretty White" even though Chicano, Latino, and Asian populations are relatively high; their perception suggests a campus on which students of different backgrounds don't often intermix.

UNIVERSITY OF CALIFORNIA—SANTA BARBARA

FINANCIAL AID: 805-893-2432 • E-MAIL: ADMISSIONS@SA.UCSB.EDU • WEBSITE: WWW.UCSB.EDU

THE PRINCETON REVIEW SAYS

Admissions

Very important factors considered include: Application essay, academic GPA, rigor of secondary school record, standardized test scores. *Other factors considered include:* Character/personal qualities, extracurricular activities, first generation, level of applicant's interest, state residency, talent/ability, volunteer work, work experience. SAT or ACT required; two SAT Subject Tests required; ACT with Writing component. High school diploma is required and GED is accepted. *Academic units required:* 4 English, 3 mathematics, (2 science labs), 2 foreign language, 2 history, 1 visual/performing arts, 1 academic elective. *Academic units recommended:* 4 mathematics, (3 science labs), 3 foreign language.

Financial Aid

Students should submit: FAFSA. Regular filing deadline is 5/31. The Princeton Review suggests that all financial aid forms be submitted as soon as possible after January 1. *Need-based scholarships/grants offered:* Federal Pell, SEOG, state scholarships/grants, private scholarships, the school's own gift aid, Work Study is also available as need-based aid. *Loan aid offered:* Direct Subsidized Stafford, Direct Unsubsidized Stafford, Direct PLUS, Federal Perkins Applicants will be notified of awards on a rolling basis beginning 3/15. Federal Work-Study Program available. Institutional employment available. Off-campus job opportunities are good.

The Inside Word

UCSB received over 40,000 freshman applications for the 2006–2007 year, an increase of about 10 percent over the previous year. With that sort of volume, you can't expect personalized treatment from the Admissions Office; admissions decisions are based on the numbers, plus a quick look at extracurriculars, awards, and honors.

THE SCHOOL SAYS "..."

From The Admissions Office

"The University of California—Santa Barbara is a major research institution offering undergraduate and graduate education in the arts, humanities, sciences and technology, and social sciences. Large enough to have excellent facilities for study, research, and other creative activities, the campus is also small enough to foster close relationships among faculty and students. The faculty numbers more than 900. A member of the most distinguished system of public higher education in the nation, UC—Santa Barbara is committed equally to excellence in scholarship and instruction. Through the general education program, students acquire good grounding in the skills, perceptions, and methods of a variety of disciplines. In addition, because they study with a research faculty, they not only acquire basic skills and broad knowledge but also are exposed to the imagination, inventiveness, and intense concentration that scholars bring to their work. UCSB is one of 62 members of the prestigous Association of American Universities.

"All applicants must take the ACT Assessment plus the new ACT Writing Test or the SAT Reasoning Test. In addition, all applicants must take two SAT Subject Tests in two different subject areas. (If a Math SAT Subject Test is chosen by the applicant, he/she must take the Math Level II exam.)"

SELECTIVITY

Admissions Rating	95
# of applicants	40,933
% of applicants accepted	54
% of acceptees attending	19

FRESHMAN PROFILE

Range SAT Critical Reading	530–650
Range SAT Math	540–660
Range SAT Writing	530–650
Range ACT Composite	23–29
Average HS GPA	3.76
% graduated top 10% of class	96
% graduated top 25% of class	98
% graduated top 50% of class	100

DEADLINES

Regular	
Deadline	11/30
Notification	3/1
Nonfall registration?	yes

FINANCIAL FACTS

Financial Aid Rating	78
Annual tuition	$7,896
% frosh rec. need-based scholarship or grant aid	40
% UG rec. need-based scholarship or grant aid	38
% frosh rec. non-need-based scholarship or grant aid	1
% frosh rec. need-based self-help aid	33
% UG rec. need-based self-help aid	34
% UG rec. athletic scholarships	1
% frosh rec. any financial aid	46
% UG rec. any financial aid	44
% UG borrow to pay for school	48
Average cumulative indebtedness	$15,808

UNIVERSITY OF CALIFORNIA—SANTA CRUZ

ADMISSIONS, COOK HOUSE, 1156 HIGH STREET, SANTA CRUZ, CA 95064 • ADMISSIONS: 831-459-4008 • FAX: 831-459-4452

CAMPUS LIFE

Quality of Life Rating	89
Fire Safety Rating	60*
Green Rating	60*
Type of school	public
Environment	city

STUDENTS

Total undergrad enrollment	14,381
% male/female	46/54
% from out of state	3
% from public high school	85
% live on campus	47
% in (# of) fraternities	1 (7)
% in (# of) sororities	1 (13)
% African American	3
% Asian	21
% Caucasian	51
% Hispanic	16
% Native American	1
% international	1
# of countries represented	78

SURVEY SAYS . . .

Great computer facilities
Great library
Students are friendly
Students are happy
Political activism is popular

ACADEMICS

Academic Rating	78
Calendar	quarter
Student/faculty ratio	19:1
Profs interesting rating	74
Profs accessible rating	77
Most common reg class size	20–29 students
Most common lab size	10–19 students

MOST POPULAR MAJORS

English language and literature/
letters
art/art studies
business/commerce

STUDENTS SAY ". . ."

Academics

The University of California—Santa Cruz offers one of the nation's best combinations of "research and education in a comfortable environment" and is, by all accounts "a great place to live and study!" Students attribute their enthusiasm to an "incredibly beautiful" campus, "intelligent, eloquent, and easily accessible professors," academics that are "impressive and challenging," and people who are "happy, open-minded, and a little bit crazy." This school is best suited to those who can motivate themselves in a "chill" environment, the sort of student whose motto might be "There's no point in learning if you're too stressed to enjoy it." The sciences are "world class" at UCSC. The Biology Department is "heading the Human Genome Project," and the Astrophysics Department is "ranked third in the country." The school also boasts "one of the finest engineering programs in the UCs," as well as "a great marine biology program." While the "Professors all do research," what sets them apart from those at the typical research-driven university is that "they really care about teaching" and are "very accessible." As one student sums up, "There are a lot of opportunities offered at UCSC in terms of internships, research opportunities, job opportunities, and networking because of the . . . faculty. It's the people who make this place valuable."

Life

Students say, "There really is a ton to do" in the area surrounding UCSC, "especially if you like being outdoors." Thanks to the sprawling, lush campus, students don't even have to leave school grounds to "explore caves, climb a huge tree in the forest, or walk or bike or jog." With their campus located "right on the coast" students "love to go to the beach for fun" and "A lot of students also take up surfing." The party scene on and off campus consists of "mostly decentralized, smaller parties, due to the near-absence of fraternities and sororities." It also includes "a lot of drug use" that is limited to "specific locations" and "easy to avoid" for abstaining students. Since Santa Cruz is a "small city," students "have to be inventive" when it comes to finding entertainment. Many students cite a "fun nightlife" with a "number of clubs and bars that cater mostly to the younger crowd." There are also "lots of galleries" in Santa Cruz for students who are into art. Ambitious students "may head to San Jose or San Francisco on the weekend for a more rowdy bar or club scene." Both cities are "readily accessible via public transportation."

Student Body

True to UCSC's reputation, there is certainly a "plethora" of "hippie types who climb trees and walk around barefoot" on campus, but they don't crowd out "the intensely athletic students, intellectuals, computer geeks, surfers, punks, preps" and more. As one student explains, "Every kind of person attends UCSC, but I believe we're all united [in] our desire to chill out and have a good time with each other." Being different is "truly embraced and encouraged" here. Politically, students tend to be "very liberal" and sometimes "not willing to hear other opinions." Some students are more committed to their beliefs than others, and there's "plenty of half-hearted activism" on campus. Politics aside, UCSC students are generally "very sociable and considerate." Meat eaters should take note that there is "a relatively large vegetarian/vegan population" on campus.

UNIVERSITY OF CALIFORNIA—SANTA CRUZ

FINANCIAL AID: 831-459-2963 • E-MAIL: ADMISSIONS@UCSC.EDU • WEBSITE: WWW.ADMISSIONS.UCSC.EDU

THE PRINCETON REVIEW SAYS

Admissions

Very important factors considered include: Application essay, academic GPA, rigor of secondary school record, standardized test scores, state residency. *Important factors considered include:* Class rank, character/personal qualities, extracurricular activities, first generation, geographical residence, talent/ability. *Other factors considered include:* volunteer work, work experience. SAT Subject Tests required; SAT or ACT required; ACT with Writing component required. TOEFL required of all international applicants. High school diploma is required and GED is accepted. *Academic units required:* 4 English, 3 mathematics, 2 science, (2 science labs), 2 foreign language, 1 social studies, 1 history, 1 visual/performing arts, 1 academic elective. *Academic units recommended:* 4 English, 4 mathematics, 3 science, (3 science labs), 3 foreign language, 1 social studies, 1 history, 1 visual/performing arts, 1 academic elective.

Financial Aid

Students should submit: FAFSA. Regular filing deadline is 6/1. The Princeton Review suggests that all financial aid forms be submitted as soon as possible after January 1. *Need-based scholarships/grants offered:* Federal Pell, SEOG, state scholarships/grants, private scholarships, the school's own gift aid. *Loan aid offered:* Direct Subsidized Stafford, Direct Unsubsidized Stafford, Direct PLUS, Federal Perkins Applicants will be notified of awards on a rolling basis beginning 4/1. Federal Work-Study Program available. Off-campus job opportunities are excellent.

The Inside Word

UC—Santa Cruz's admissions process can be summed in one word—formula. If prospective students meet the requirements, only then will they be eligible to receive an acceptance letter. Weaker candidates will be reassured to learn that officers award points for a variety of special circumstances, including improvement in academic performance, geographic location, and achievement in special projects. UCSC's acceptance rate belies the high caliber of applicants it regularly receives.

THE SCHOOL SAYS ". . ."

From The Admissions Office

"Since its founding in 1965, UC—Santa Cruz has earned a national reputation as a campus devoted to excellence in undergraduate teaching, graduate study and research, and professional education. Its academic plan and physical design combine the advantages of a small-college setting with the intensive research and academic strengths traditional to the University of California. At UC—Santa Cruz, undergraduate courses are taught by the same faculty who conduct cutting-edge research. In a national survey of more than 60 elite research universities by the Association of American Universities, UC—Santa Cruz ranked fifteenth for students in all disciplines whose bachelor's degrees led to doctorates. The campus is growing selectively and is investing half a billion dollars in new and improved infrastructure.

"All applicants must take the ACT Assessment plus the new ACT Writing Test or the new SAT Reasoning Test. In addition, all applicants must take two SAT Subject Tests in two different subject areas. (If a Math SAT Subject Test is chosen by the applicant, he/she must take the Math Level II exam.)"

SELECTIVITY

Admissions Rating	93
# of applicants	24,453
% of applicants accepted	82
% of acceptees attending	19

FRESHMAN PROFILE

Range SAT Critical Reading	500–620
Range SAT Math	520–630
Range SAT Writing	500–620
Range ACT Composite	21–29
Minimum paper TOEFL	550
Minimum computer TOEFL	220
Minimum web-based TOEFL	83
Average HS GPA	3.5
% graduated top 10% of class	96
% graduated top 25% of class	100
% graduated top 50% of class	100

DEADLINES

Regular	
Deadline	11/30
Notification	rolling
Nonfall registration?	yes

APPLICANTS ALSO LOOK AT

AND OFTEN PREFER
University of California—Berkeley
University of California—Los Angeles
Stanford University

AND SOMETIMES PREFER
University of California—San Diego
University of California—Santa Barbara
University of California—Davis

AND RARELY PREFER
University of California—Riverside
San Jose State University
San Francisco State University

FINANCIAL FACTS

Financial Aid Rating	81
Annual out-of-state tuition	$20,610
Room and board	$12,831
Required fees	$9,534
Books and supplies	$1,356
% frosh rec. need-based scholarship or grant aid	40
% UG rec. need-based scholarship or grant aid	40
% UG rec. non-need-based scholarship or grant aid	1
% frosh rec. need-based self-help aid	40
% UG rec. need-based self-help aid	40

UNIVERSITY OF CENTRAL FLORIDA

PO Box 160111, Orlando, FL 32816-0111 • Admissions: 407-823-3000 • Fax: 407-823-5625

CAMPUS LIFE
Quality of Life Rating	90
Fire Safety Rating	84
Green Rating	60*
Type of school	public
Environment	city

STUDENTS
Total undergrad enrollment	41,051
% male/female	46/54
% from out of state	5
% live on campus	21
% in (# of) fraternities	11 (24)
% in (# of) sororities	9 (17)
% African American	9
% Asian	5
% Caucasian	68
% Hispanic	13
% international	1
# of countries represented	141

SURVEY SAYS . . .
Great computer facilities
Great library
Athletic facilities are great
Great off-campus food

ACADEMICS
Academic Rating	73
Calendar	semester
Student/faculty ratio	29:1
Profs interesting rating	69
Profs accessible rating	71
% classes taught by TAs	6
Most common reg class size	20–29 students
Most common lab size	20–29 students

MOST POPULAR MAJORS
marketing/marketing management
psychology
health services/allied health/health
sciences

Academics

The University of Central Florida is "a growing school with a solid academic image." "Its reputation needs to catch up with how it actually is," urges a junior. The engineering and science programs are renowned and students laud the hospitality, management, and business programs. UCF undergrads also benefit from "awesome technology" all over campus. The Internet is everywhere. Much like the surrounding city of Orlando, UCF has experienced explosive growth in recent decades. Today, UCF is really quite gargantuan. "It's one of the largest schools in the nation." "The massive size of UCF can be intimidating for students who need a personal approach to higher education." "It is easy to feel a bit lost," admits a freshman. Classes are large and most note that professors can be "hit or miss." "Some professors are amazing" and "willing to go out of their way to make sure you understand the lectures." Others "just stand in front of the class and read off PowerPoint slides." The foreign professors, while "highly-specialized," can "be hard to understand." On the bright side, upper-level courses are "fun and taught by professors who are good and know what they're doing." "The administration seems to genuinely care but, because there are so many students, it is hard for them to really do anything about your concerns." Registration is pretty awful. "When you get to the end of your degree, you better plan out your schedule carefully because there are a lot of important classes that are only offered every three semesters," advises one student. In terms of initials, students used to say that "UCF" stood for "U Can't Finish." Now, it stands for "Under Construction Forever," but most don't mind "because the newer facilities are beautiful!"

Life

UCF boasts a "very scenic," "comfortable" campus. "Everything is relatively close together," which is great when it comes to getting to your next class, but not so much when parking your car. "No matter how many garages UCF builds, somehow parking still sucks." Socially, if you're bored here, you just aren't trying very hard. "The campus organizes a wide variety of social events." "We have a ridiculous number of clubs and organizations," boasts a sophomore. "There are about a million events going on at any given time." There is almost every imaginable intramural sport. There is "a huge three-story gym" that features "every kind of workout machine." "Football game days are amazing" as students root for the perennially "up-and-coming" team. Fraternities and sororities are here too, but they "constitute a minority of the culture." UCF's location is a big hit with students. Hot, sunny Orlando is "a large, thriving city" but the area around UCF has "the feel of a college town." "If you live in the dorms your first year, you will definitely get the typical college experience." The "many bars with dance floors around campus" are "a breeding ground for drunken debauchery" and "underage drinking." They "get packed every night." "Downtown Orlando is a different story, which "provides a nice refuge for upperclassmen trying to break away."

Student Body

"The only real thing that many students share in common is sandals," observes a business major. "At a given time, 75 percent of the campus is probably wearing sandals." "The typical student also applied to the University of Florida but didn't get in," claims a UCF Spanish major, "and also to South Florida, but had a grain of sense and avoided Tampa like the plague." UCF students hail overwhelmingly from in-state, too. And "the girls are insanely pretty." Otherwise, "it is difficult to generalize" about some 40,000 undergrads. "There is no possible way to describe a typical student." Students tend to have "their own set of friends, activities, and experiences at UCF." There are vast differences among students in the different schools (business, health and public affairs, communication, hospitality, engineering, etc.) and also within the schools themselves. "This is a melting pot of culture," says one student. "Walking around campus you see a little bit of every culture, every race, and every ethnicity." "There are strong subcultures for the minorities" and ages about with students "right out of high school" and those "older in years [who] are looking to further their careers."

FINANCIAL AID: 407-823-2827 • E-MAIL: ADMISSION@MAIL.UCF.EDU • WEBSITE: WWW.UCF.EDU

THE PRINCETON REVIEW SAYS

Admissions

Very important factors considered include: Academic GPA, rigor of secondary school record, standardized test scores. *Important factors considered include:* Application essay. *Other factors considered include:* Class rank, recommendation(s), alumni/ae relation, character/personal qualities, extracurricular activities, first generation, geographical residence, interview, level of applicant's interest, state residency, talent/ability, volunteer work, work experien SAT or ACT required; ACT with Writing component required. High school diploma is required and GED is accepted. *Academic units required:* 4 English, 3 mathematics, 3 science, (2 science labs), 2 foreign language, 3 social studies, 3 academic electives.

Financial Aid

Students should submit: FAFSA. Regular filing deadline is 6/30. The Princeton Review suggests that all financial aid forms be submitted as soon as possible after January 1. *Need-based scholarships/grants offered:* Federal Pell, SEOG, state scholarships/grants, private scholarships, the school's own gift aid, University scholarships and grants. *Loan aid offered:* FFEL Subsidized Stafford, FFEL Unsubsidized Stafford, FFEL PLUS, Federal Perkins Applicants will be notified of awards on a rolling basis beginning 3/15.

Inside Word

As is the case at many state schools, it's all a numbers game here; students aren't required to interview or submit essays. It's also worth noting that when calculating your GPA, which is a very important criterion for admission, the Admissions Committee weights honors, AP, dual enrollment, and International Baccalaureate academic classes more heavily than regular classes.

THE SCHOOL SAYS "..."

From The Admissions Office

"The University of Central Florida offers competitive advantages to its student body. We're committed to teaching, providing advisement, and academic support services for all students. Our undergraduates have access to state-of-the-art wireless buildings, high-tech classrooms, research labs, web-based classes, and an undergraduate research and mentoring program.

"Our Career Services professionals help students gain practical experiences at NASA, schools, hospitals, high-tech companies, local municipalities, and the entertainment industry. With an international focus to our curricula and research programs, we enroll international students from 126 nations. Our study abroad programs and other study and research opportunities include agreements with 98 institutions and 36 countries.

"UCF's 1,415-acre campus provides a safe and serene setting for learning, with natural lakes and woodlands. The bustle of Orlando lies a short distance away: the pro sport teams, the Kennedy Space Center, film studios, Walt Disney World, Universal Orlando, Sea World, and sandy beaches are all nearby.

"Applicants for Summer 2008 and beyond are required to take the new version of the SAT (or the ACT with the writing section), but we will allow students to submit scores from the old SAT or ACT as well, and will use the student's best scores from either test."

SELECTIVITY

Admissions Rating	89
# of applicants	26,312
% of applicants accepted	50
% of acceptees attending	50
# accepting a place on wait list	498
% admitted from wait list	9

FRESHMAN PROFILE

Range SAT Critical Reading	530–620
Range SAT Math	540–640
Range SAT Writing	510–600
Range ACT Composite	23–27
Average HS GPA	3.63
% graduated top 10% of class	35
% graduated top 25% of class	77
% graduated top 50% of class	93

DEADLINES

Regular	
Priority	1/1
Deadline	5/1
Notification	rolling
Nonfall registration?	yes

FINANCIAL FACTS

Financial Aid Rating	70
Annual in-state tuition	$3,620
Annual out-of-state tuition	$17,821
Room and board	$8,164
Books and supplies	$924
% frosh rec. need-based scholarship or grant aid	24
% UG rec. need-based scholarship or grant aid	30
% frosh rec. non-need-based scholarship or grant aid	48
% UG rec. non-need-based scholarship or grant aid	33
% frosh rec. need-based self-help aid	15
% UG rec. need-based self-help aid	23
% frosh rec. athletic scholarships	1
% UG rec. athletic scholarships	1
% frosh rec. any financial aid	93
% UG rec. any financial aid	80
% UG borrow to pay for school	43.7
Average cumulative indebtedness	$13,373

THE UNIVERSITY OF CHICAGO

1101 EAST FIFTY-EIGHTH STREET, ROSENWALD HALL, SUITE 105, CHICAGO, IL 60637 • ADMISSIONS: 773-702-8650 • FAX: 773-702-4199

STUDENTS SAY ". . ."

Academics

"Dedication to enriching the 'life of the mind' is palpable" at the "incomparable" The University of Chicago. It is home to "the best Economics Department in the country" and one of the best (and most monstrously ugly) main libraries on earth. Chicago students believe that "no university offers a better academic experience," and there is "an unexpectedly vibrant school spirit that comes not from athletics, but [a] shared academic involvement." Undergraduates must complete an intense, "interdisciplinary" core curriculum that "teaches them how to think about literature and philosophy and science." The Core is "rigorous" and "You will spend about a third of your time here on it. But it's [also] fantastic, and you come out an incredibly well-rounded thinker with opinions on a wide variety of subjects." Naturally, "Courses are tough." "Once you're out of the fire," though, "You realize how much more enriched you've become intellectually, with respect [as] to how to learn and . . . knowledge itself." Professors at Chicago "are the best in the world" and are "real celebrities in their fields of study," but they "make every effort to help every student who asks." Still, "there are duds." "Not everyone with the intelligence to do amazing research is capable of teaching." The "incredibly supportive" administration "takes pains to engage the entire campus in a sort of collective, community-wide conversation. . . . They bring in all sorts of speakers, allow student groups almost absolute freedom, and are very supportive of student initiatives."

Life

The quarter system "makes for a particularly fast-paced" schedule. "We wear t-shirts that say U of C: Where fun comes to die, and we're proud of it," explains a first-year student. "Don't come here if you don't plan to work very hard," an economics major warns. "We spend a large chunk of our time studying and should be studying much of the time that we are not." However, according to one student, "As much as a lot of people complain about the extremely rigorous academics at this school, we all secretly love it or we wouldn't be here." And "contrary to popular belief," students "certainly do know how to have fun." There are "concerts, plays, movies," and "tons of truly brilliant events on campus." Students also spend a lot of time "just talking" with "fascinating" classmates "who can hold their own on any topic under the sun." "The frat party scene is not much at all compared to other schools, but it's still there. Room parties with extended friends and random people from the building are usually more popular." While "scorn for the lovely neighborhood" surrounding the campus is "exceedingly common," downtown Chicago is "very accessible." The city "is a huge asset and resource," "whether it's for an internship," "a night out," or "just a day away from campus."

Student Body

Students at Chicago are "intense," "opinionated," "engaged with the world around them," and "somewhat zany." "Most everyone has a quirk," a senior reports, "like the center on the football team who's really into Dungeons & Dragons." Without question, "the popular stereotype" of the Chicago student is "a nerdy, socially awkward person." Living up to the hype are an abundance of students "religiously dedicated to academic performance" and "a bunch of strange people," "usually clutching some fantastic book." However, "There aren't as many extremely strange and nerdy students as there have been in the past." "A portion of the student body at the U of C [are] actually talented, cool, and (gasp!) attractive." "There are loads of people that are fascinating," a sophomore writes. There are "artists, communists, fashionistas, activists," and even "some who aren't posing at all." "Everyone who is at The University of Chicago considers themselves at the best possible university," concludes one student. "It's a self-selecting group," and most people are "happy to be here." Chicago students "look down on other schools, particularly the Ivies."

FINANCIAL AID: 773-702-8666 • WEBSITE: WWW.UCHICAGO.EDU

THE PRINCETON REVIEW SAYS

Admissions

Very important factors considered include: Application essay, recommendation(s), rigor of secondary school record, character/personal qualities, talent/ability. *Important factors considered include:* Class rank, academic GPA, extracurricular activities, volunteer work. *Other factors considered include:* Standardized test scores, alumni/ae relation, first generation, interview, level of applicant's interest, racial/ethnic status, work experience. SAT or ACT required; High school diploma or equivalent is not required. *Academic units recommended:* 4 English, 4 mathematics, 4 science, 3 foreign language, 2 social studies, 2 history.

Financial Aid

Students should submit: FAFSA, institution's own financial aid form, CSS/Financial Aid PROFILE, noncustodial PROFILE, business/farm supplement. Regular filing deadline is 2/1. The Princeton Review suggests that all financial aid forms be submitted as soon as possible after January 1. *Need-based scholarships/grants offered:* Federal Pell, SEOG, state scholarships/grants, private scholarships, the school's own gift aid. *Loan aid offered:* FFEL Subsidized Stafford, FFEL Unsubsidized Stafford, FFEL PLUS, Federal Perkins Applicants will be notified of awards on or about 4/15.

The Inside Word

The University of Chicago this year will leave the beloved "Uncommon Application" and begin to accept the Common Application. Essay topics will continue to be of the thought provoking "Uncommon" type, keeping the spirit of fun and inquiry in the application's supplement. People here dwell on deep thoughts and big ideas. In your application you'll need to demonstrate outstanding grades in the tough courses; really high standardized test scores; and, most of all, that you will fit in with a bunch of thinkers. Think really hard before you write your three essays and try to say really intelligent things during your interview. Under no circumstances whatsoever should you even consider missing the interview.

THE SCHOOL SAYS "..."

From The Admissions Office

"The University of Chicago is a place where talented young people—writers, politicians, activists, artists, mathematicians, and scientists—come to learn in a setting that rewards interesting thought and prizes initiative and creativity. Chicago is also a place where collegiate life is urban, yet friendly and open, and free of empty traditionalism and snobbishness. Chicago is the right choice for students who know that they would thrive in an intimate classroom setting. Classes at Chicago are small, emphasizing discussion with faculty members whose research is always testing the limits of their chosen fields. Students at U of Chicago take chances—delighting professors when they pursue a topic on their own for the fun of it, or display an articulate voice in papers and in discussion. Their good times include the normal collegiate good times—a highly successful Division III sports program, small but active Greek life, 35 student theatrical productions a year, a rich musical life—and the extraordinary opportunities a major city offers our students, who enjoy the politics, music, theater, commerce, architecture, neighborhood life of Chicago.

"Applicants are asked to submit either the SAT or the ACT. Chicago does not require the SAT Subject Tests. The ACT may be taken without the optional Writing section."

SELECTIVITY
Admissions Rating	98
# of applicants	10,362
% of applicants accepted	35
% of acceptees attending	36
# accepting a place on wait list	1,031

FRESHMAN PROFILE
Range SAT Critical Reading	670–770
Range SAT Math	660–760
Range ACT Composite	28–33
% graduated top 10% of class	83
% graduated top 25% of class	98
% graduated top 50% of class	100

DEADLINES
Early action	
Deadline	11/1
Notification	12/15
Regular	
Priority	11/1
Deadline	1/2
Notification	4/1
Nonfall registration?	no

FINANCIAL FACTS
Financial Aid Rating	94
Annual tuition	$35,169
Room and board	$11,139
Required fees	$699
Books and supplies	$1,050
% frosh rec. need-based scholarship or grant aid	47
% UG rec. need-based scholarship or grant aid	43
% frosh rec. need-based self-help aid	39
% UG rec. need-based self-help aid	38
% frosh rec. any financial aid	47.6
% UG rec. any financial aid	45.3
% UG borrow to pay for school	54.49
Average cumulative indebtedness	$25,971

UNIVERSITY OF CINCINNATI

OFFICE OF ADMISSIONS, PO BOX 210091, CINCINNATI, OH 45221-0091 • ADMISSIONS: 513-556-1100 • FAX: 513-556-1105

CAMPUS LIFE

Quality of Life Rating	**71**
Fire Safety Rating	**80**
Green Rating	**87**
Type of school	public
Environment	metropolis

STUDENTS

Total undergrad enrollment	19,796
% male/female	49/51
% from out of state	10
% live on campus	21
% in (# of) fraternities	NR (23)
% in (# of) sororities	NR (10)
% African American	11
% Asian	3
% Caucasian	77
% Hispanic	2
% international	1
# of countries represented	115

SURVEY SAYS . . .

Great computer facilities
Great library
Athletic facilities are great
Diverse student types on campus
Lots of beer drinking

ACADEMICS

Academic Rating	**72**
Calendar	quarter
Student/faculty ratio	14:1
Profs interesting rating	65
Profs accessible rating	65
Most common reg class size	10–19 students

MOST POPULAR MAJORS
psychology
marketing/marketing management
communication studies

STUDENTS SAY ". . ."

Academics

The University of Cincinnati is "an urban university" "in the midst of a renaissance." The expansive campus includes 12 separate colleges, each of which is like a "different world." Even "each major within the individual colleges provides and entirely different experience than the next." The "great" engineering programs afford opportunities for "lots of cutting edge research." The "renowned" Conservatory of Music offers "intense practical experience in the arts." There's "a real sense of ambition and drive" within the "stellar" College of Design, Architecture, Art, and Planning. Also, internships and co-op programs are "huge." As a result, many students "have extensive experience in their field before obtaining a degree." UC's professors run the gamut from "very helpful" to "total crap." Profs are often overly concerned with research and "not as accessible to students as they should be." "Seventy percent of my professors could be classified as very good, with 20 percent being classified as excellent, and the other 10 percent being less than very good," assesses a senior. "Overall, my academic experience at UC has been more defined by my own initiative to seek good faculty and good outside programs (internships, study abroad, etc.)." "The administration is famous for lack of intra-office coordination; they have great intentions, but students are always talking about getting 'the UC run-around.'" Nevertheless, "there are vast opportunities available to students if they are just willing to put in some effort."

Life

Many students praise the "modern and nice" campus as "an urban oasis of amazing architecture" with amenities galore. The campus itself is "usually pretty safe." However, the "shady" surrounding neighborhood "can be extraordinarily hostile." There's "way too much crime." While there's been "a rebirth of on-campus interest and activity" in recent years, UC largely remains "a big commuter school with little cohesive force." A lot of students are from Cincinnati and often spend weekends "at home rather than around campus." Football and basketball games are the biggest extracurricular draws but, otherwise, "people don't have a lot of enthusiasm for campus events." The frat scene is noticeable but not huge. On the weekends, "drinking is inevitable." "For fun we party at houses and in bars," explains one student. Downtown bars are popular destinations." "The urban setting adds excitement to the atmosphere." The Cincinnati area also "has a huge variety of excellent employers and offers an excellent environment for raising a family." It's "a great city for art museums and restaurants," too.

Student Body

Most students here "probably did a little bit above average in high school." Beyond that, few characteristics unite these undergrads. Without question, the University of Cincinnati "does not lack diversity." There are "lots of minority students, particularly Asian- and African-American students." "UC attracts many older students" as well. "Different money backgrounds" proliferate. The campus is "a vibrant quilt of culture" that feels "very realistic." "It really could be considered the melting pot college of the Midwest." Students tend to be really cliquish, though, and disparate little groups "keep to themselves." "Some people are really into partying." Others are very serious about academics. "Everyone has their own group of friends," observes a psychology major. "Ethnic groups stick together and rarely interact outside of their own group." "Engineers hang out with other engineers." The "suburbanite commuter students" stick together. So, too, do the "artsy, hardworking types," "frat boy jock" types, and the "fashionable, mature" architecture students.

FINANCIAL AID: 513-556-1000 • E-MAIL: TRANSFER@UC.EDU • WEBSITE: WWW.ADMISSIONS.UC.EDU

THE PRINCETON REVIEW SAYS

Admissions

Very important factors considered include: Class rank, academic GPA, recommendation(s), rigor of secondary school record. *Other factors considered include:* Application essay, extracurricular activities, SAT or ACT required; ACT with Writing component required. TOEFL required of all international applicants. High school diploma is required and GED is accepted. *Academic units required:* 4 English, 3 mathematics, 2 science, 2 foreign language, 2 social studies, 2 academic electives. *Academic units recommended:* 4 mathematics, 3 science, 1 history.

Financial Aid

Students should submit: FAFSA. The Princeton Review suggests that all financial aid forms be submitted as soon as possible after January 1. *Need-based scholarships/grants offered:* Federal Pell, SEOG, state scholarships/grants, private scholarships, the school's own gift aid, United Negro College Fund, Federal Nursing Scholarships, ACG, SMART. *Loan aid offered:* Direct Subsidized Stafford, Direct Unsubsidized Stafford, Direct PLUS, FFEL Subsidized Stafford, FFEL Unsubsidized Stafford, FFEL PLUS, Federal Perkins, Federal Nursing, state loans, college/university loans from institutional funds. Applicants will be notified of awards on a rolling basis beginning 3/10. Federal Work-Study Program available. Institutional employment available. Off-campus job opportunities are excellent.

The Inside Word

One the University of Cincinnati's greatest strengths is that it boasts several smaller and completely unique colleges within a single large university setting. Each school maintains some autonomy, and this extends to admissions policies. Requirements vary among programs and candidates will need to do their research before completing their applications. Competitive programs tend to fill up rather quickly, so interested students should submit their materials as early as possible.

THE SCHOOL SAYS "..."

From The Admissions Office

"Remarkable architecture, park-like open spaces, engaging student tour guides, and a welcoming Admissions Staff make the University of Cincinnati a must-visit destination. UC campus has been transformed over the past 10 years and is drawing national and international attention for blending student life, learning, research, and recreation in a unique urban environment.

"Freshman application materials include high school transcripts, test scores, a personal statement, and a list of co-curricular activities. Some academic programs require additional materials.

"Sign up for a visit, become a Bearcat VIP, and apply online at Admissions.uc.edu. Information about all UC majors is linked from the website. We also have Tuesday-night online chat sessions for students and parents. Nothing beats a visit, however, for assessing how well you'll fit in here.

"Either the SAT or ACT is required for students applying to bachelor's degree programs; the ACT Writing component is required. SAT Subject Tests are not required."

SELECTIVITY

Admissions Rating	79
# of applicants	11,876
% of applicants accepted	75
% of acceptees attending	40

FRESHMAN PROFILE

Range SAT Critical Reading	490–610
Range SAT Math	500–630
Range SAT Writing	470–590
Range ACT Composite	21–27
Minimum paper TOEFL	515
Average HS GPA	3.375
% graduated top 10% of class	20
% graduated top 25% of class	46
% graduated top 50% of class	77

DEADLINES

Regular	
Priority	1/15
Deadline	9/1
Notification	rolling
Nonfall registration?	yes

FINANCIAL FACTS

Financial Aid Rating	67
Annual in-state tuition	$7,896
Annual out-of-state tuition	$22,419
Room and board	$8,799
Required fees	$1,503
Books and supplies	$1,225
% frosh rec. need-based scholarship or grant aid	24
% UG rec. need-based scholarship or grant aid	24
% frosh rec. non-need-based scholarship or grant aid	28
% UG rec. non-need-based scholarship or grant aid	19
% frosh rec. need-based self-help aid	23
% UG rec. need-based self-help aid	19
% frosh rec. athletic scholarships	1
% UG rec. athletic scholarships	1
% frosh rec. any financial aid	80
% UG rec. any financial aid	73
% UG borrow to pay for school	65
Average cumulative indebtedness	$21,302

UNIVERSITY OF COLORADO—BOULDER

552 UCB, BOULDER, CO 80309-0552 • ADMISSIONS: 303-492-6301 • FAX: 303-492-7115

CAMPUS LIFE
Quality of Life Rating	**83**
Fire Safety Rating	**86**
Green Rating	**88**
Type of school	public
Environment	city

STUDENTS
Total undergrad enrollment	25,521
% male/female	53/47
% from out of state	31
% live on campus	25
% in (# of) fraternities	8 (19)
% in (# of) sororities	10 (17)
% African American	2
% Asian	6
% Caucasian	78
% Hispanic	6
% Native American	1
% international	1
# of countries represented	115

SURVEY SAYS . . .
Great computer facilities
Great library
Athletic facilities are great
Students love Boulder, CO
Great off-campus food
Students are happy
Everyone loves the The Colorado
Buffaloes
Lots of beer drinking
Hard liquor is popular

ACADEMICS
Academic Rating	**72**
Calendar	semester
Student/faculty ratio	16:1
Profs interesting rating	70
Profs accessible rating	71
% classes taught by TAs	10
Most common reg class size	10–19 students
Most common lab size	20–29 students

MOST POPULAR MAJORS
English language and literature
physiology
psychology

STUDENTS SAY ". . ."

Academics

The University of Colorado—Boulder serves everyone from the most committed undergraduates to those who live by the motto "Skis and C's get degrees." The differences among students are many at this large research institution, but everyone agrees on one thing: The place is drop-dead gorgeous. Even those who tout at length the "opportunities to take classes and participate in graduate courses as an undergraduate, often in renowned academic departments" and the "chances for students to get published, receive grants, and develop relationships with prestigious faculty" can't help appreciating the fact that "the skiing and snowboarding are the best here." As one student puts it, CU provides students with plenty of resources "to pursue what they want (whether that be skiing, music, partying, or just about any outdoor activity imaginable) while also receiving a first-class education." CU is also "a top engineering school" that has "great programs in the sciences and a strong commitment to scientific advancement"; the architecture, journalism and mass communications, and aerospace programs are also held in high esteem by students. Since the school is large there are many available academic choices; some here complain, however, that the school's "core curriculum is overwhelming. It's very hard to take classes that you want outside of your major because the requirements are too specific and too many. This contributes in a major way to the fact that it is not uncommon at all for students to graduate in more than 4 years."

Life

CU has endured its fair share of negative publicity in recent years. A football recruiting scandal and a radical professor who exercised his right to free speech to outrageous effect generated headlines, and the alcohol-related death of an underclassman added a tragic exclamation point. Students tell us that "Boulder needs to find a way to get itself out of the spotlight, because despite how wonderful it is, the media find a way of highlighting its problems, and that seems to be all that anyone knows about us, especially outside of Colorado." There is, of course, so much more to life at CU; sure, "There are parties going on all the time where people can drink, but that is not all that CU has to offer. There are [also] hundreds of clubs that students participate in, along with a lot of fun intramural sports." Intercollegiate football remains huge, the scandal notwithstanding. The Greek scene, though, has taken a bigger hit; these days "'The Hill (the campus' largest social scene) is heavily guarded by police, and the Greek system is under constant scrutiny." As a result, "House and dorm parties are becoming very popular." The best options for fun, though, are off campus, where "You can head up to the mountains to ski or snowboard, catch a concert at one of the many local music venues (from small clubs to Red Rocks), go to Denver (for free with your student pass), go camping, hang out on Pearl Street, or just sit at one of the many coffee shops in the city of Boulder."

Student Body

There is a sense that "Most students are from upper-middle-class to upper-class families and are supported heavily by their parents," at CU, although with a student population of more than 25,000 "there are also plenty of students who are not from wealthy families." While "There is not much ethnic diversity" here, there are all types of people, from "liberals, conservatives, vegetarians, self-proclaimed nerds and computer geeks, hippies, jocks, savvy business students, poets, writers, [and] artists" to "scientists, partiers, and introverts. There is a group here for anyone." While not all students are "focused academically," those who are find many who share their interests. An interesting bit of trivia: "Almost everybody has an iPod," several students observe.

FINANCIAL AID: 303-492-5091 • E-MAIL: APPLY@COLORADO.EDU • WEBSITE: WWW.COLORADO.EDU

THE PRINCETON REVIEW SAYS

Admissions

Very important factors considered include: Class rank, academic GPA, rigor of secondary school record, standardized test scores. *Important factors considered include:* Application essay, recommendation(s), character/personal qualities, first generation, state residency. *Other factors considered include:* Alumni/ae relation, extracurricular activities, geographical residence, level of applicant's interest, talent/ability, volunteer work, work experience. SAT or ACT required; TOEFL required of all international applicants. High school diploma is required and GED is accepted. *Academic units required:* 4 English, 3 mathematics, 3 science, (2 science labs), 3 foreign language, 3 social studies, 1 history, 1 geography.

Financial Aid

Students should submit: FAFSA, Tax return required. The Princeton Review suggests that all financial aid forms be submitted as soon as possible after January 1. *Need-based scholarships/grants offered:* Federal Pell, SEOG, state scholarships/grants, private scholarships, the school's own gift aid. *Loan aid offered:* Direct Subsidized Stafford, Direct Unsubsidized Stafford, Direct PLUS, Federal Perkins, college/university loans from institutional funds, Private lenders. Applicants will be notified of awards on a rolling basis beginning 2/1. Federal Work-Study Program available. Institutional employment available. Off-campus job opportunities are excellent.

The Inside Word

Applicants who meet specific standardized test and GPA requirements are guaranteed acceptance to University of Colorado—Boulder. CU makes provisions, however, for candidates who don't meet those requirements but demonstrate academic potential. With nearly a third of the student body from out of state, CU boasts far more geographic diversity than most state schools.

THE SCHOOL SAYS ". . ."

From The Admissions Office

""The University of Colorado at Boulder is a place of beauty and academic prominence at the foot of the Rocky Mountains. A sense of vitality and curiosity fills the campus, and yet it's comfortable and relaxed. It's a place you can be yourself and let your imagination soar.

"We have programs for you if you seek leadership training, research experience, academic honors, international experience (one in four graduates has studied abroad), community involvement, and more. There are a number of enrichment programs that give exceptionally talented and intellectually committed students the opportunity to expand their education outside the classroom, build a sense of community, and help prepare for post-graduate opportunities. Residential Academic Programs (RAPs) and Living and Learning Communities (LLCs) in several residence halls provide undergraduates with shared learning and living experiences.

"Getting involved is easy at CU-Boulder. If you are interested in student government, clubs, athletics, recreation, Greek life, volunteer work, theater, dance, film, exhibits, planetarium shows, or concerts, you will find them here.

"To find out if CU—Boulder is the place for you, we encourage you to visit. Contact the Office of Admissions, or take a virtual tour at www.colorado.edu/prospective.

"The University of Colorado at Boulder requires either SAT or ACT scores for admissions; the Writing tests are currently not used in making decisions. SAT Subject Test scores are not required."

SELECTIVITY

Admissions Rating	82
# of applicants	19,857
% of applicants accepted	82
% of acceptees attending	35
# accepting a place on wait list	471
% admitted from wait list	64

FRESHMAN PROFILE

Range SAT Critical Reading	520–630
Range SAT Math	540–650
Range SAT Total	1080–1260
Range ACT Composite	23–28
Minimum paper TOEFL	500
Minimum computer TOEFL	173
Minimum web-based TOEFL	61
Average HS GPA	3.56
% graduated top 10% of class	25
% graduated top 25% of class	58
% graduated top 50% of class	92

DEADLINES

Regular	
Deadline	1/15
Notification	rolling
Nonfall registration?	yes

APPLICANTS ALSO LOOK AT
AND OFTEN PREFER
Arizona State University at the Tempe campus
University of California—Santa Cruz
Stanford University
AND SOMETIMES PREFER
University of Wisconsin—Madison
University of Miami
San Diego State University
AND RARELY PREFER
University of Utah
University of Wyoming

FINANCIAL FACTS

Financial Aid Rating	86
Annual in-state tuition	$5,418
Annual out-of-state tuition	$21,900
Room and board	$9,088
Required fees	$1,217
Books and supplies	$1,698
% frosh rec. need-based scholarship or grant aid	36
% UG rec. need-based scholarship or grant aid	31
% frosh rec. non-need-based scholarship or grant aid	2
% UG rec. non-need-based scholarship or grant aid	1
% frosh rec. need-based self-help aid	38
% UG rec. need-based self-help aid	31
% frosh rec. athletic scholarships	1
% UG rec. athletic scholarships	1
% frosh rec. any financial aid	81
% UG rec. any financial aid	79
% UG borrow to pay for school	41
Average cumulative indebtedness	$18,037

UNIVERSITY OF CONNECTICUT

2131 HILLSIDE ROAD, UNIT 3088, STORRS, CT 06268-3088 • ADMISSIONS: 860-486-3137 • FAX: 860-486-1476

CAMPUS LIFE
Quality of Life Rating	**74**
Fire Safety Rating	**86**
Green Rating	**88**
Type of school	public
Environment	town

STUDENTS
Total undergrad enrollment	16,036
% male/female	49/51
% from out of state	23
% live on campus	68
% in (# of) fraternities	8 (14)
% in (# of) sororities	8 (12)
% African American	5
% Asian	7
% Caucasian	67
% Hispanic	5
% international	1
# of countries represented	109

SURVEY SAYS . . .
Great library
Campus feels safe
Everyone loves the Huskies
Intramural sports are popular
Student publications are popular
Lots of beer drinking
Hard liquor is popular

ACADEMICS
Academic Rating	**74**
Calendar	semester
Student/faculty ratio	17:1
Profs interesting rating	65
Profs accessible rating	71
% classes taught by TAs	23
Most common reg class size	10–19 students
Most common lab size	10–19 students

MOST POPULAR MAJORS
business
political science
psychology, general

STUDENTS SAY ". . ."

Academics

The hardy students of University of Connecticut recognize that a UConn education "is based on a solid foundation of research and academics" and a pedagogical approach that "promotes learning in and out of the classroom," although that's not to say that there's not a contingency that are "all about partying, having a good time, and doing the least amount of studying possible." UConn is large enough to offer "a wide range of great majors," including programs at the "fantastic School of Business," the "well-known Neag School of Education," and "a solid engineering school with a unique biomedical engineering major." In most areas, UConn "networks to provide students [with] millions of opportunities for students to expand in academics, self, and even careers," including "great internships." The school "does a great job of publicizing these opportunities, as well. We are a big icon of the state, and we keep our prestige." Thanks to the "UConn 2000" and "UConn Twenty-first Century" initiatives, the campus "is improving drastically with a $2.8-billion construction program designated to refurbishing (and adding onto) nearly every building on campus." As is the case at many large state schools, "The success of a UConn student's education is really a matter of personal responsibility. Introductory classes tend to be large and very impersonal, so it is up to the individual to do well." Bureaucratic tasks such as registration "can be a real pain," and "the class enrollment process is very confusing and difficult to use," but overall, students speak warmly of their interactions with administrators. "While usually you have to go through a middleman to get to the administration, it is possible to voice your concerns," sums up a satisfied student.

Life

UConn is located in Storrs, which "is pretty much in the middle of nowhere." It seems especially so to students without cars, of whom there are quite a few (those with wheels can take advantage of Hartford and, occasionally, Boston). Some students feel this predicament "forces us to go out and party simply because there is nothing better to do." Others point out that "people go out a lot, yeah, and there's often alcohol involved, but there are many interesting and fun things to do here for those who don't like that kind of stuff. For instance, there are UConn Late Nights in Student Union at which students can just hang out, meet new people, play games, and have fun. There are also interesting lectures given by guest speakers at the Dodd Research Center, and movie nights and concerts. Since I've been here I've seen Dave Chappelle, Kanye West, NAS, Busta Rhymes, Lewis Black, and more perform." Those eager to join clubs and organizations will also find many to accommodate them here. And then there are the intercollegiate sports. "Basketball and football games are always a blast!" undergraduates assure us (the men's and women's hoops squads are both perennial national contenders).

Student Body

Students report that the typical UConn undergraduate "is a Connecticut resident"—but after that, "it is so hard to generalize a student population of nearly 15,000." Sure, "A lot of students are very similar in appearance" because "They are from in-state, and a lot of the same trends are prevalent. But there are plenty of students who do not follow this stereotype, and everyone fits in fine." Many feel that UConn is "a fantastic representation of the Northeast in all respects," especially the "actively involved, down-to-earth, [and] pretty friendly" student body. The party animal is a vanishing breed here (though the speed at which he or she is vanishing is open to debate); one student explains, "UConn has had its reputation as a drinking school for many years. And every year, the number of students who come here specifically to party and drink declines."

FINANCIAL AID: 860-486-2819 • E-MAIL: BEAHUSKY@UCONN.EDU • WEBSITE: WWW.UCONN.EDU

THE PRINCETON REVIEW SAYS

Admissions

Very important factors considered include: Class rank, academic GPA, rigor of secondary school record, standardized test scores, talent/ability. *Important factors considered include:* Application essay, recommendation(s), character/personal qualities, extracurricular activities, first generation, racial/ethnic status, volunteer work. *Other factors considered include:* Alumni/ae relation, geographical residence, level of applicant's interest, state residency, work experience. SAT or ACT required; ACT with Writing component required. High school diploma is required and GED is accepted. *Academic units required:* 4 English, 3 mathematics, 2 science, (2 science labs), 2 foreign language, 2 social studies, 3 academic electives. *Academic units recommended:* 3 foreign language.

Financial Aid

Students should submit: FAFSA. The Princeton Review suggests that all financial aid forms be submitted as soon as possible after January 1. *Need-based scholarships/grants offered:* Federal Pell, SEOG, ACG, SMART grants, TEACH grants, state scholarships/grants, private scholarships, the school's own gift aid. *Loan aid offered:* FFEL Subsidized Stafford, FFEL Unsubsidized Stafford, FFEL PLUS, Federal Perkins Applicants will be notified of awards on a rolling basis beginning 3/1. Off-campus job opportunities are good.

The Inside Word

Similar to most large, public institutions, UConn focuses primarily on quantifiable data such as grades, class rank, and test scores when making admit decisions. Connecticut residents who demonstrate significant academic achievement stand a good chance of being admitted, though the acceptance rate has decreased significantly over the past few years. Candidates are advised to apply early as the school has a rolling admissions policy and applications are considered on a space-available basis.

THE SCHOOL SAYS "..."

From The Admissions Office

"Thanks to a $2.8-billion construction program that is impacting every area of university life, the University of Connecticut provides students a high-quality and personalized education on one of the most attractive and technologically advanced college campuses in the United States. Applications are soaring nationally as an increasing number of high-achieving students from diverse backgrounds are making UConn their school of choice. From award-winning actors to governmental leaders, students enjoy an assortment of fascinating speakers each year, while performances by premier dance, jazz, and rock musicians enliven student life. Our beautiful New England campus is convenient and safe, and most students walk to class or ride university shuttle buses. State-of-the-art residential facilities include interest-based learning communities and honors housing as well as on-campus suite-style and apartment living. Championship Division I athletics have created fervor known as Huskymania among UConn students.

"Freshman applicants seeking admittance for Fall 2008 are required to submit official score reports from the new SAT or ACT with Writing component."

SELECTIVITY

Admissions Rating	89
# of applicants	21,105
% of applicants accepted	49
% of acceptees attending	30
# accepting a place on wait list	1,373
% admitted from wait list	27

FRESHMAN PROFILE

Range SAT Critical Reading	530–630
Range SAT Math	560–660
Range SAT Writing	540–640
Range ACT Composite	23–28
% graduated top 10% of class	40
% graduated top 25% of class	81
% graduated top 50% of class	98

DEADLINES

Early action	
Deadline	12/1
Notification	2/1
Regular	
Deadline	2/1
Notification	rolling
Nonfall registration?	yes

FINANCIAL FACTS

Financial Aid Rating	73
Annual in-state tuition	$7,200
Annual out-of-state tuition	$21,912
Room and board	$9,300
Required fees	$2,138
Books and supplies	$800
% frosh rec. need-based scholarship or grant aid	41
% UG rec. need-based scholarship or grant aid	36
% frosh rec. non-need-based scholarship or grant aid	32
% UG rec. non-need-based scholarship or grant aid	22
% frosh rec. need-based self-help aid	37
% UG rec. need-based self-help aid	38
% frosh rec. athletic scholarships	3
% UG rec. athletic scholarships	2
% frosh rec. any financial aid	50
% UG rec. any financial aid	48
% UG borrow to pay for school	61
Average cumulative indebtedness	$20,658

UNIVERSITY OF DALLAS

1845 EAST NORTHGATE DRIVE, IRVING, TX 75062 • ADMISSIONS: 972-721-5266 • FAX: 972-721-5017

STUDENTS SAY ". . ."

Academics

For many of the students at this small Catholic school in the Dallas suburbs, the University of Dallas is all about the core curriculum, an integrated survey of Western civilization's great texts and ideas. The Core gobbles up nearly half the credits required to graduate—but few complain about this. On the contrary, most students choose UD precisely because of its reverence for the classics. One observes, "Where else can you find students discussing casually over lunch, as if were the most normal thing in the world, Plato's *Republic*, the concept of divine love in Dante's *Commedia*, or the effects of the French Revolution on modern society?" The other cornerstone of a UD education is the sophomore-year Rome program, through which "about 85 percent of all students" enjoy "an altogether amazing experience" at UD's private campus just outside the city of Rome, Italy. The semester abroad "includes a 5-day guided tour of Italy's famous cities, an 8-day excursion through Greece, and then a 10-day period during which students are allowed [to go] wherever they want. Everyone says that they come back as a family and continue to miss being there for the rest of their lives." One senior gushes, "The Rome semester was probably the single best experience of my life." Both in Rome and stateside, UD classes are "small and very discussion oriented," and professors are "brilliant and concerned with their students—not just helping them do well in the class, but [also] helping them become better people." Students praise UD's humanities offerings, but some feel that "science majors are often put on the back burner."

Life

"I thought it was just a marketing technique when the school kept talking about how important the community is," writes one UD undergrad, "but I've come to know that it is all true." Students unite for "school-sponsored events every week with music or karaoke," "movie nights and cooking nights in the dorms," "weekend parties at the apartments across the street (which are usually pretty controlled; people drink, but there is rarely any binge drinking or drug use)," "Thank God It's Thursday, which celebrates the start of the weekend in the Rathskellar, the on-campus bar," and other special events. An event called Charity Week "is one of the highest points of the year. It helps get the freshmen involved with the campus while reuniting the junior class after being split in two their sophomore year for the Rome semester. It raises money for various organizations and is a week of fun and relaxation." Among the athletic teams, rugby and women's soccer both "draw a large crowd." Students agree that their campus "is not very pretty" and note that "you don't go to UD for the architecture," but also observe that "in the spring, when the trees blossom, it is very beautiful." Because "The campus is really rather isolated" in the suburbs, "You need access to a car in order to survive at UD. There are lots of places to go in Dallas and Fort Worth; you just need a way to get to them."

Student Body

UD's core curriculum attracts serious-minded students who "really think about things. The Core exposes us to philosophy and literature and history, and when you go through that, you can't help but find life more interesting." Many bring a conservative Catholic perspective to their studies, but "a lot of non-Catholics still enjoy this school a great deal." Some are quite religious, others less so; one student writes, "A very small group of students are sometimes so engaged in their religion they wear it like a shiny badge of righteousness, so you might think the school is full of these people, but it is not." For many, coming to UD becomes a family affair; one undergrad explains, "The first person in the family goes to UD, and gets everyone else hooked as well, so all of their younger siblings end up going to UD; several professors know or teach entire families over the years."

FINANCIAL AID: 972-721-5266 • E-MAIL: UGADMIS@UDALLAS.EDU • WEBSITE: WWW.UDALLAS.EDU

THE PRINCETON REVIEW SAYS

Admissions

Very important factors considered include: Application essay, academic GPA, recommendation(s), rigor of secondary school record, standardized test scores, character/personal qualities. *Important factors considered include:* Class rank, talent/ability. *Other factors considered include:* Alumni/ae relation, extracurricular activities, first generation, interview, level of applicant's interest, volunteer work, work experience. SAT or ACT required; ACT with Writing component required. TOEFL required of all international applicants. High school diploma is required and GED is accepted. *Academic units required:* 4 English, 3 mathematics, 3 science, 2 foreign language, 3 social studies, 3 history, 2 visual/performing arts, 4 academic electives. *Academic units recommended:* 4 English, 4 mathematics, 3 science, 3 foreign language, 4 social studies, 4 history, 2 visual/performing arts, 4 academic electives.

Financial Aid

Students should submit: FAFSA. The Princeton Review suggests that all financial aid forms be submitted as soon as possible after January 1. *Need-based scholarships/grants offered:* Federal Pell, SEOG, state scholarships/grants, private scholarships, the school's own gift aid. *Loan aid offered:* FFEL Subsidized Stafford, FFEL Unsubsidized Stafford, FFEL PLUS, Federal Perkins, state loans Applicants will be notified of awards on a rolling basis beginning 3/15. Federal Work-Study Program available. Institutional employment available. Off-campus job opportunities are fair.

The Inside Word

The University of Dallas is a school deeply rooted in Catholic principles. Its unique academic program couples a classic liberal arts education with the pursuit of moral and intellectual virtues. The Admissions Team gives each applicant careful consideration, endeavoring to find candidates likely to benefit from and contribute to the school environment. Scholarship is especially valued, as students at UD are expected to be immersed in their studies and always ready to engage in a philosophical debate.

THE SCHOOL SAYS "..."

From The Admissions Office

"Quite unabashedly, the curriculum at the University of Dallas is based on the supposition that truth and virtue exist and are the proper objects of search in an education. The curriculum further supposes that this search is best pursued through an acquisition of philosophical and theological principles on the part of a student and has for its analogical field a vast body of great literature—perhaps more extensive than is likely to be encountered elsewhere—supplemented by a survey of the sweep of history and an introduction to the political and economic principles of society. An understanding of these subjects, along with an introduction to the quantitative and scientific worldview and a mastery of a language, is expected to form a comprehensive and coherent experience, which, in effect, governs the intellect of a student in a manner that develops independence of thought in its most effective mode.

"Students applying for admission for Fall 2008 are required to take the SAT Reasoning Test or the ACT with Writing Assessment."

SELECTIVITY

Admissions Rating	86
# of applicants	1,161
% of applicants accepted	75
% of acceptees attending	42

FRESHMAN PROFILE

Range SAT Critical Reading	550–680
Range SAT Math	520–650
Range SAT Writing	530–660
Range ACT Composite	24–29
Minimum paper TOEFL	550
Minimum computer TOEFL	213
Minimum web-based TOEFL	79
Average HS GPA	3.6
% graduated top 10% of class	33
% graduated top 25% of class	61
% graduated top 50% of class	88

DEADLINES

Early action	
Deadline	12/1
Notification	1/15
Regular	
Priority	1/15
Deadline	8/1
Notification	rolling
Nonfall registration?	yes

APPLICANTS ALSO LOOK AT

AND OFTEN PREFER
University of Notre Dame
Southern Methodist University

AND SOMETIMES PREFER
Trinity University
Austin College
Texas Christian University

AND RARELY PREFER
Saint Louis University
Spring Hill College
Loyola University—New Orleans
Texas A&M University—College Station
The University of Texas at Austin

FINANCIAL FACTS

Financial Aid Rating	85
Annual tuition	$23,250
Room and board	$7,885
Required fees	$1,520
Books and supplies	$1,700
% frosh rec. need-based scholarship or grant aid	63
% UG rec. need-based scholarship or grant aid	61
% frosh rec. non-need-based scholarship or grant aid	6
% UG rec. non-need-based scholarship or grant aid	4
% frosh rec. need-based self-help aid	50
% UG rec. need-based self-help aid	49
% frosh rec. any financial aid	97
% UG rec. any financial aid	94
% UG borrow to pay for school	70
Average cumulative indebtedness	$21,772

UNIVERSITY OF DAYTON

300 COLLEGE PARK, DAYTON, OH 45469-1300 • ADMISSIONS: 937-229-4411 • FAX: 937-229-4729

STUDENTS SAY ". . ."

Academics

"Academically challenging yet unpretentious, casual yet fun as hell," the University of Dayton is a midsize Catholic school that "is all about community: community when we study, community when we party, community when we are doing service, community when we pray. There are so many opportunities to build community and be accepted in the community here." Both academics and service "are taken very seriously" at UD. One undergrad notes, "You earn what you deserve. As long as you work hard, and your teachers can see that, you won't have a problem." Top programs include "a great premed program," "a wonderful Engineering Department," "an amazing teacher education program," and an "awesome business school" that includes the Davis Center for Portfolio Management, a "student-run fund that invests more than $3 million of the university's endowment." The number of options is unusual for an institution with such a small-school feel; students describe UD as "small enough that you get to know people very well, and you are always seeing someone you know, yet big enough that there are always new people to meet."

Life

"Community is probably the first word that comes to the majority of the student body's minds," agree most of the students we surveyed at UD. While it may "sound really cheesy," undergrads insist that "everyone is family here" and that "you are welcome from the very moment you step onto campus." Nowhere is this more apparent than in the student neighborhood, in which "Porch sitting is a must on sunny days." One student explains, "Porches are symbolic of UD. Everyone sits out on their porch. It's one huge neighborhood where everyone is welcome to party or to chill. And when we party, everyone leaves their door wide open for anyone to come." Campus organizations at UD "sponsor great weekend events," such as "trips to Chicago and Cincinnati, free movies, cookouts, arts and crafts, flag football games, cornhole (a horseshoe-like game played with cloth bags filled with corn) tournaments, comedy tours, karaoke, and retreats." And let's not forget Dayton basketball, "the gem of the community." True to its Marianist tradition, UD also has "the largest campus ministry in the country. We help both the local and global community with things ranging from one-time service days to immersion trips and even an entire year of service." Beyond campus, things get a little less idyllic. "Dayton as a city needs to improve," students say, noting the fact that "UD is neighboring a poverty-stricken area."

Student Body

The typical UD student is "semireligious, overly friendly, welcoming, and accepting of the few diverse students who are here." He or she also "loves UD basketball, community service, beer, and most of all, holding the door for the person behind them." That final attribute is "all part of the Marianist tradition. Complete strangers help each other all the time, and everyone says hi to one another." The UD "look" is casual, as "the average UD student can be found wearing jeans, a UD hoodie, and flip-flops or Birkenstock clogs. Most students are laid-back, down-to-earth, and fun, yet they know how to get down to business and study." Because of the school's Catholic focus, "The majority of students are Catholic, and some students who are not Catholic feel that the university incorporates too much religion in service-type activities. They fit in among the students but may feel left out when it comes to service and retreat activities because there is a heavy Catholic emphasis."

FINANCIAL AID: 937-229-4311 • E-MAIL: ADMISSION@UDAYTON.EDU • WEBSITE: WWW.UDAYTON.EDU

THE PRINCETON REVIEW SAYS

Admissions

Very important factors considered include: Academic GPA. *Important factors considered include:* Class rank, rigor of secondary school record, standardized test scores, talent/ability. *Other factors considered include:* Application essay, recommendation(s), alumni/ae relation, character/personal qualities, extracurricular activities, first generation, interview, racial/ethnic status, volunteer work, work experience. SAT or ACT required; TOEFL required of all international applicants. High school diploma is required and GED is accepted. *Academic units required:* 2 units of foreign language are required for admission to the College of Arts and Sciences. *Academic units recommended:* 4 English, 3 mathematics, 2 science, (1 science labs), 3 social studies, 4 academic electives.

Financial Aid

Students should submit: FAFSA. The Princeton Review suggests that all financial aid forms be submitted as soon as possible after January 1. *Need-based scholarships/grants offered:* Federal Pell, SEOG, state scholarships/grants, private scholarships, the school's own gift aid, ACG, SMART. *Loan aid offered:* FFEL Subsidized Stafford, FFEL Unsubsidized Stafford, FFEL PLUS, Federal Perkins, GATE. Applicants will be notified of awards on a rolling basis beginning 2/20. Federal Work-Study Program available. Institutional employment available. Off-campus job opportunities are good.

The Inside Word

University of Dayton is an excellent option for students who want to attend a Catholic university but don't meet the stringent criteria of a Georgetown or Notre Dame. UD gives equal weight to all academic factors—e.g., class rank, GPA—on the application. Candidates who demonstrate a modicum of success in the classroom and intellectual promise will most likely be accepted.

THE SCHOOL SAYS "..."

From The Admissions Office

"The University of Dayton is a Catholic leader in higher education. We offer the resources and diversity of a comprehensive university and the attention and accessibility of a small college.

"More than 70 challenging academic programs are offered in the College of Arts and Sciences and the Schools of Business Administration, Education and Allied Professions, Engineering, and Law. Classes are small—27 students on average. Our more than 800 full-time and part-time faculty are committed to teaching undergraduate students and involving them in their research projects.

"The University of Dayton Research Institute ranks second in the nation in the amount of materials research performed annually. Technology-enhanced learning and the student computer initiative ensure students gain expertise in the tools that will prepare them for the future. All university-owned housing is fully wired for direct high-speed Internet access, and a wireless network covers several academic buildings, the student union, library, outdoor plazas, and residential buildings.

"Recent campus construction provides a modern home for the university's cutting-edge academic programs. New facilities include ArtStreet, Marianist Hall, and the Science Center. Open in January 2006, a new fitness and recreation complex, the RecPlex, provides 130,000 square feet of space for classrooms, courts, a natatorium, offices, and other recreational facilities.

"A strong sense of community is a hallmark feature of the university; a dual emphasis on leadership and service contributes to students' participation in more than 170 clubs and organizations. Division I intercollegiate athletics, and club and intramural sports, are also popular.

"Students applying for Fall 2008 admission may provide scores from either version of the SAT, or the ACT. Scores from the new Writing component will be collected but will not be used for admission purposes for 2008. The highest composite scores from either test will be used in admissions decisions."

SELECTIVITY

Admissions Rating	81
# of applicants	8,742
% of applicants accepted	82
% of acceptees attending	25

FRESHMAN PROFILE

Range SAT Critical Reading	520–620
Range SAT Math	530–640
Range ACT Composite	23–28
Minimum paper TOEFL	523
Minimum computer TOEFL	193
Minimum web-based TOEFL	70
Average HS GPA	3.46
% graduated top 10% of class	23
% graduated top 25% of class	49
% graduated top 50% of class	81

DEADLINES

Regular	
Priority	12/15
Notification	rolling
Nonfall registration?	yes

APPLICANTS ALSO LOOK AT
AND OFTEN PREFER
University of Notre Dame
AND SOMETIMES PREFER
Saint Louis University
Marquette University
Miami University
John Carroll University
The Ohio State University—Columbus
AND RARELY PREFER
Purdue University—West Lafayette
Xavier University (OH)
University of Cincinnati
Ohio University—Athens

FINANCIAL FACTS

Financial Aid Rating	88
Annual tuition	$24,880
% frosh rec. need-based scholarship or grant aid	54
% UG rec. need-based scholarship or grant aid	54
% frosh rec. non-need-based scholarship or grant aid	43
% UG rec. non-need-based scholarship or grant aid	51
% frosh rec. need-based self-help aid	49
% UG rec. need-based self-help aid	50
% frosh rec. athletic scholarships	1
% UG rec. athletic scholarships	1
% UG borrow to pay for school	59
Average cumulative indebtedness	$20,438

UNIVERSITY OF DELAWARE

ADMISSIONS OFFICE, 116 HULLIHEN HALL, NEWARK, DE 19716-6210 • ADMISSIONS: 302-831-8123 • FAX: 302-831-6905

CAMPUS LIFE

Quality of Life Rating	75
Fire Safety Rating	93
Green Rating	81
Type of school	public
Environment	town

STUDENTS

Total undergrad enrollment	15,211
% male/female	42/58
% from out of state	60
% from public high school	80
% live on campus	47
% in (# of) fraternities	12 (15)
% in (# of) sororities	12 (15)
% African American	5
% Asian	4
% Caucasian	83
% Hispanic	4
% international	1
# of countries represented	100

SURVEY SAYS . . .
Great computer facilities
Great library
Great off-campus food
Students are happy
Lots of beer drinking
Hard liquor is popular

ACADEMICS

Academic Rating	79
Calendar	4/1/4
Student/faculty ratio	12:1
Profs interesting rating	73
Profs accessible rating	77
% classes taught by TAs	5
Most common reg class size	10–19 students
Most common lab size	10–19 students

MOST POPULAR MAJORS
elementary education and teaching
biology/biological sciences
psychology

STUDENTS SAY ". . ."

Academics
The University of Delaware is in the midst of major institutional changes: A new president took the reins in July 2007, and a new class registration system was implemented in 2006. Regarding the former, students are delighted. Because the new president is the former Dean of the Wharton School of Business, undergraduates are hopeful that he will "do wonders for our prestige." Regarding the latter, they couldn't be more displeased. "Registration is a nightmare," making it "near impossible to get the exact schedule you want." Between those two extremes, respondents to our survey describe a middle-of-the-road academic experience. Take professors, for example. Some "are experts in their fields and are excellent at teaching," while others "are purely there for research," or "have no clue how to teach a class." While most may be "genuinely interested in meeting with students and talking about the class material," "They won't hunt you down" to make sure you're getting it. In other words, there is a willingness to help "as long as the student takes the initiative." The same can be said of the administration. Students generally consider it to be of "average quality." It "can be a pain with some administrative tasks (financial aid, anything that involves going to student services), but it's probably par for the course." In a departure from their typically balanced assessments of UD, undergrads maintain an exceptionally positive view of their school's "absolutely beautiful" campus and its "phenomenal" study abroad program.

Life
Student life at UD is characterized by the timeless effort "to balance partying and studying." During the week, which runs from Sunday through Wednesday, "Life usually remains centered around studies." "You will find the libraries [and] computer labs filled," and "Quiet hours are enforced." For many, working out is part of their weekday work regimen: "A lot of people enjoy going to the gym." Come Thursday, however, "Those with good schedules start going out." "Parties are what everyone looks for," especially house parties, and they are reportedly in abundant supply. Those who aren't into drinking but want to stay on campus can take advantage of "a movie theater right on campus that show[s] fairly current movies for only $3." The SCPAB (Student-Centered Programming Advisory Board) also "books some pretty good musicians and comedians." Many students "hang out on Main Street," which "intersects campus" and includes "endless restaurants, the bookstores, a bowling alley, and a movie theater." Because "the campus is close to Baltimore, DC, and Philly, road trips to museums and other universities [are] always possible."

Student Body
Budding psychologists take note: Undergrads here report a collective "tunnel vision," and it's focused on "success." According to a junior, "Most of us come from upper-middle-class homes and won't be satisfied with anything less than what we already have." As a means to an end, "Academics are important." But only so much—course work "won't stop anyone from going out," an international relations major reports. Geographically, students mainly hail "from the New Jersey, Delaware, Maryland, and Pennsylvania region." Sartorially, "People care what they look like" and those "who have money flaunt it by what they wear." Temperamentally, people are "relaxed, friendly, and generally very approachable." There are very few categories UD students can be sorted into, but an in-state/out-of-state divide exists. Students "from Delaware are not considered as smart as those not from Delaware because it is easier for them to get in," and there is also a widespread perception that those from in-state "are not as well off financially."

UNIVERSITY OF DELAWARE

FINANCIAL AID: 302-831-8761 • E-MAIL: ADMISSIONS@UDEL.EDU • WEBSITE: WWW.UDEL.EDU

THE PRINCETON REVIEW SAYS

Admissions

Very important factors considered include: Academic GPA, rigor of secondary school record, state residency. *Important factors considered include:* Application essay, recommendation(s), standardized test scores, character/personal qualities, extracurricular activities, talent/ability, volunteer work, work experience. *Other factors considered include:* Class rank, alumni/ae relation, first generation, geographical residence, interview, level of applicant's interest, racial/ethnic status, SAT Subject Tests recommended; SAT or ACT required; ACT with Writing component required. TOEFL required of all international applicants. High school diploma is required and GED is accepted. *Academic units required:* 4 English, 3 mathematics, 3 science, (2 science labs), 2 foreign language, 2 social studies, 2 history, 2 academic electives. *Academic units recommended:* 4 English, 4 mathematics, 4 science, (3 science labs), 4 foreign language, 2 social studies, 2 history, 2 academic electives.

Financial Aid

Students should submit: FAFSA. Regular filing deadline is 3/15. The Princeton Review suggests that all financial aid forms be submitted as soon as possible after January 1. *Need-based scholarships/grants offered:* Federal Pell, SEOG, state scholarships/grants, private scholarships, the school's own gift aid. *Loan aid offered:* Direct Subsidized Stafford, Direct Unsubsidized Stafford, Direct PLUS, Federal Perkins, Federal Nursing Applicants will be notified of awards on a rolling basis beginning 3/15. Federal Work-Study Program available. Institutional employment available.

Inside Word

It's rare that a flagship state university enrolls more students from out of state than in state, but the University of Delaware does. It is situated near many more-populous states on the East Coast which makes it a viable and desirable alternative for those states' residents. The school is sensitive to this fact, and in-state students will find admission to UD significantly easier than out-of-state students will.

THE SCHOOL SAYS "..."

From The Admissions Office

"The University of Delaware is a major national research university with a long-standing commitment to teaching and serving undergraduates. It is one of only a few universities in the country designated as a land-grant, sea-grant, urban-grant, and space-grant institution. The academic strength of this university is found in its highly selective honors program, nationally recognized Undergraduate Research Program, study abroad opportunities on all seven continents, and its successful alumni, including three Rhodes Scholars since 1998. The University of Delaware offers the wide range of majors and course offerings expected of a university but in spirit remains a small place where you can interact with your professors and feel at home. The beautiful green campus is ideally located at the very center of the East Coast 'megacity' that stretches from New York City to Washington, DC. All of these elements, combined with an endowment approaching $1 billion and a spirited Division I athletics program, make the University of Delaware a tremendous value.

"Freshman applicants for Fall 2008 are required to take the SAT Reasoning Test (or the ACT with the Writing section). If a student takes the new SAT more than once, the best individual scores from each test taken will be combined. Two SAT Subject Tests are recommended for applicants to the University Honors Program."

SELECTIVITY
Admissions Rating	93
# of applicants	21,930
% of applicants accepted	47
% of acceptees attending	31
# accepting a place on wait list	1,237
% admitted from wait list	48

FRESHMAN PROFILE
Range SAT Critical Reading	540–640
Range SAT Math	560–660
Range SAT Writing	540–650
Range ACT Composite	23–28
Minimum paper TOEFL	550
Minimum computer TOEFL	213
Average HS GPA	3.6
% graduated top 10% of class	39
% graduated top 25% of class	80
% graduated top 50% of class	98

DEADLINES
Regular	
Priority	12/1
Deadline	1/15
Notification	3/15
Nonfall registration?	yes

FINANCIAL FACTS
Financial Aid Rating	80
Annual in-state tuition	$7,340
Annual out-of-state tuition	$18,590
Room and board	$7,948
Required fees	$810
Books and supplies	$800
% frosh rec. need-based scholarship or grant aid	26
% UG rec. need-based scholarship or grant aid	24
% frosh rec. non-need-based scholarship or grant aid	20
% UG rec. non-need-based scholarship or grant aid	11
% frosh rec. need-based self-help aid	29
% UG rec. need-based self-help aid	28
% frosh rec. athletic scholarships	3
% UG rec. athletic scholarships	3
% UG borrow to pay for school	44
Average cumulative indebtedness	$17,200

University of Denver

University Hall, Room 110, 2197 South University Boulevard, Denver, CO 80208 • Admissions: 303-871-2036 • Fax: 303-871-3301

CAMPUS LIFE

Quality of Life Rating	**82**
Fire Safety Rating	**82**
Green Rating	**60***
Type of school	private
Environment	metropolis

STUDENTS

Total undergrad enrollment	5,260
% male/female	45/55
% from out of state	44
% live on campus	41
% in (# of) fraternities	20 (10)
% in (# of) sororities	11 (6)
% African American	3
% Asian	5
% Caucasian	75
% Hispanic	7
% Native American	1
% international	4
# of countries represented	77

SURVEY SAYS . . .
Small classes
Great computer facilities
Athletic facilities are great
Students love Denver, CO
Great off-campus food
Everyone loves the Pioneers
Lots of beer drinking

ACADEMICS

Academic Rating	**83**
Calendar	quarter
Student/faculty ratio	10:1
Profs interesting rating	83
Profs accessible rating	82
Most common reg class size	10–19 students
Most common lab size	10–19 students

MOST POPULAR MAJORS
psychology
business, management, marketing,
and related support services
business/commerce

STUDENTS SAY ". . ."

Academics

A little under half of the University of Denver's (DU) undergraduates pursue degrees in business. This pre-MBA focus contributes substantially to the university's overall character. Students are, for the most part, diligent workers focused on obtaining a successful career. That's not to suggest that students pursuing majors other than business receive the short shrift at DU. The university also excels in pre-law studies, music, and communications. In fact, students brag that "there is ample funding for all the departments at DU, and therefore undergrads have incredible opportunities to pursue serious academic projects. A dedicated student can get an education equal to that of a student at any top university." While there's a wide range of opinions regarding the workload—some students describe it as "intense," others find it "super easy"—most agree that "the fact that the school is small benefits everyone. Teachers and students form relationships and work together when in the classroom. Teachers also meet students at The Pub (the on-campus restaurant) for study sessions." Students tell us DU "makes it easy and affordable for anyone to study abroad."

Life

The University of Denver offers "tons of different organizations to participate in. DU Programs Board, the Greek system, DU Alpine Club, and Student Government are just a few of the on-campus activities offered." Unfortunately, most of these activities do not inspire the majority of undergraduates. "In the winter, the campus empties out on the weekends as students head to the mountains to ski and [snow]board," undergrads report. Students also frequent the "nearby Cherry Creek district for dinner and a movie." Because "The campus is officially dry," a good amount of drinking occurs off campus, frequently at the "great neighborhood bars located one to three blocks from campus." Students always return to campus for sporting events, however, especially for games featuring "the great hockey team," which won the NCAA championship in 2004 and 2005. Students also love to take advantage of the Ritchie Center, "a great sports facility [for working out] that is gorgeous and free to students." As one undergraduate puts it, "With a stunning campus and 300 days of sunshine in Denver, you can't go wrong!"

Student Body

Students say DU is the "perfect size to meet new people all the time, but [also] to run into people you know every time you walk across campus." At a school where "Everyone is friendly" and "smile[s] at each other walking to class," undergrads feel this is a boon to their overall experience. While students report a noticeable contingent of undergrads "from affluent backgrounds [who are] trendy and party a lot," they also tell us there are "many students [who] are more interested in academics [and] other areas of student life. These students are also quite easy to find, and fit in just as well." Intellectual interests at DU tend to be "very career- and goal-oriented." One student wryly notes that DU is not the place to find students who "go to coffee shops to discuss Kafka or talk politics in the dining hall." The university does, however, have a considerable jock population. Students "enjoy being outdoors (anything from a snowball fight to a marathon run to speed skiing)" and "like to work out [and] participate in athletics."

FINANCIAL AID: 303-871-4020 • E-MAIL: ADMISSION@DU.EDU • WEBSITE: WWW.DU.EDU/ADMISSION

THE PRINCETON REVIEW SAYS

Admissions

Very important factors considered include: Academic GPA, rigor of secondary school record, standardized test scores, character/personal qualities. *Important factors considered include:* Application essay, recommendation(s), extracurricular activities, interview, talent/ability, volunteer work, work experience. SAT or ACT required; TOEFL required of all international applicants. High school diploma is required and GED is accepted. *Academic units recommended:* 4 English, 4 mathematics, 3 science, (2 science labs), 3 foreign language, 2 social studies, 2 history.

Financial Aid

Students should submit: FAFSA and CSS profile. Regular filing deadline is 3/1. The Princeton Review suggests that all financial aid forms be submitted as soon as possible after January 1. *Need-based scholarships/grants offered:* Federal Pell, SEOG, state scholarships/grants, private scholarships, the school's own gift aid. *Loan aid offered:* Direct Subsidized Stafford, Direct Unsubsidized Stafford, Direct PLUS, FFEL Subsidized Stafford, FFEL Unsubsidized Stafford, FFEL PLUS, Federal Perkins, college/university loans from institutional funds. Applicants will be notified of awards on or about 3/25. Federal Work-Study Program available. Institutional employment available. Off-campus job opportunities are excellent.

The Inside Word

Any good student will find getting admitted to Denver to be a fairly straightforward process.

THE SCHOOL SAYS "..."

From The Admissions Office

"Founded in 1864, the University of Denver offers an educational experience characterized by adventurous learning and innovative mentoring from a caring faculty. Our undergraduate students come from all across the United States and from more than 80 countries to study in an environment that nurtures potential and passion. The Hyde Interview, which is strongly encouraged, provides all applicants the opportunity to give a voice to their application while assisting DU with admission decisions.

"DU is continually developing educational initiatives that help students prepare for an ever-changing world. Among our offerings: residence-based learning communities that provide extracurricular and co-curricular programming in particular areas; a grant program for students that funds everything from research to creative endeavors; and hundreds of internship opportunities that put students in laboratories, corporate offices, government agencies, and cultural settings. In addition, one of the signature offerings is the Cherrington Global Scholars program which allows students to study abroad at the same cost of a term at DU. More than 70 percent of DU students study abroad at some point in their years in school—which ranks DU second nationally among doctoral and research institutions for percentage of students participating.

"DU's 125-acre campus, located in a quiet residential neighborhood, is eight miles from downtown Denver and a half-hour's drive from the Rocky Mountain foothills. DU students enjoy an active lifestyle with plenty of opportunities to enjoy recreation in the Rockies, cheer on one of the city's many professional sports teams, or explore the city's lively arts and entertainment scene. Many DU students partake in these activities by using the new light rail system, an above-ground train that is free to all DU students. There is a station conveniently located on our campus and provides students a great mode of transportation for a variety of purposes such as entertainment, internships, and jobs in the Denver area.

"Applicants may submit either version of the ACT or SAT."

SELECTIVITY

Admissions Rating	89
# of applicants	5,072
% of applicants accepted	74
% of acceptees attending	30
# accepting a place on wait list	279
% admitted from wait list	33

FRESHMAN PROFILE

Range SAT Critical Reading	530–640
Range SAT Math	540–640
Range ACT Composite	23–28
Minimum paper TOEFL	525
Minimum computer TOEFL	193
Average HS GPA	3.59
% graduated top 10% of class	35
% graduated top 25% of class	66
% graduated top 50% of class	95

DEADLINES

Early action	
Deadline	11/1
Notification	1/15
Regular	
Deadline	1/15
Notification	3/15
Nonfall registration?	yes

APPLICANTS ALSO LOOK AT
AND OFTEN PREFER

University of Colorado—Boulder
Colorado College
Colorado State University

AND SOMETIMES PREFER

University of Puget Sound
University of Vermont
Boston University

FINANCIAL FACTS

Financial Aid Rating	72
Annual tuition	$21,984
% frosh rec. need-based scholarship or grant aid	39
% UG rec. need-based scholarship or grant aid	39
% frosh rec. non-need-based scholarship or grant aid	6
% UG rec. non-need-based scholarship or grant aid	5
% frosh rec. need-based self-help aid	34
% UG rec. need-based self-help aid	35
% frosh rec. athletic scholarships	3
% UG rec. athletic scholarships	4
% frosh rec. any financial aid	83
% UG rec. any financial aid	76
% UG borrow to pay for school	45
Average cumulative indebtedness	$25,375

UNIVERSITY OF FLORIDA

201 CRISER HALL, BOX 114000, GAINESVILLE, FL 32611-4000 • ADMISSIONS: 352-392-1365 • FAX: 352-392-3987

STUDENTS SAY ". . ."

Academics

"It is often joked that we only pay tuition so we can have a football team," one University of Florida student writes, but in fact UF provides "a quality education from the state's oldest and most prestigious university" as well as top-flight football to its undergraduates. "The University of Florida is about finding out if you have what it takes to distinguish yourself from 35,000 other intelligent, talented people. It's a reality check." It also provides "tremendous" "networking opportunities." A robust alumni network over 300,000 strong adds to the possibilities, and some undergrads to assert that, in addition to providing a top-notch education, UF delivers "a career in the future." Stand-out programs include engineering, premed, and journalism. While the school "has its share of boring, unapproachable professors," the "vast majority" are "available to help students throughout the week." In fact, both professors and teaching assistants "are easy to access," as they have "set office hours" that are "made very apparent to students." UF's administration "is not too bad, although there is so much red tape to get through that getting anything accomplished is likely to take half the semester." Students appreciate that most administrative tasks can be accomplished "over the computer."

Life

"You can tell that students at UF like to have fun," undergrads here agree, and fortunately for them the opportunities are ample. There is "a lot of stuff to do on campus," and if partying is your thing, there are "37 fraternity/sorority houses" and "an ample number of clubs to check out" in downtown Gainesville. The Student Union also hosts "a bunch of different activities" and "shows recent movies in [its] theater, long before they come out on DVD." Then, of course, there's Gator athletics. "Almost everybody here is crazy about our sports teams, and team spirit is really high," students tell us. One writes, "Sports, both intramural and intercollegiate, are very important. This is one of the main reasons people are drawn to UF." Greater Gainesville "offers enough things to do" that "not being Greek does not hamper one's social life." Indeed, Gainesville "is a true college town—everything is catered to the UF student." For outdoor enthusiasts, "There is a recreational lake that is university-owned, [and] students can go swim, boat, fish, or BBQ [for free]." UF is also located "within 2 hours" of the beach and "under 2 hours" from "theme parks in Orlando." Students here are "always willing to drive the distance" to "away football games within the SEC (Southeastern Conference)."

Student Body

The UF student body conjures to mind the "Greek macho man" and the "Barbie blonde" for many, but with undergrad enrollment around 35,000, "it's hard to define the typical student" here. While the "large, sprawling campus" is home to "more students than can be observed," even a perfunctory glance reveals "all kinds—jocks, Greeks, religious, political, nonreligious, out-of-staters, international people, intense athletes, and everything in between." Some here tell us that "the typical student falls into one of two categories. Either the student is a know-it-all who graduated with an IB diploma and had a 4.0, or [he or she] is a slacker who somehow got into UF and now doesn't take anything seriously except partying." Because of UF's size, "There's a place for everyone to fit in, whether your thing is knitting, rugby, or video games."

FINANCIAL AID: 352-392-1275 • WEBSITE: WWW.UFL.EDU

THE PRINCETON REVIEW SAYS

Admissions

Very important factors considered include: Academic GPA, rigor of secondary school record. *Important factors considered include:* Application essay, character/personal qualities, extracurricular activities, first generation, talent/ability. *Other factors considered include:* Class rank, standardized test scores, alumni/ae relation, geographical residence, level of applicant's interest, state residency, volunteer work, work experience. SAT or ACT required; ACT with Writing component required. High school diploma is required and GED is accepted. *Academic units required:* 4 English, 3 mathematics, 3 science, (2 science labs), 2 foreign language, 3 social studies, 3 academic electives.

Financial Aid

Students should submit: FAFSA. The Princeton Review suggests that all financial aid forms be submitted as soon as possible after January 1. *Need-based scholarships/grants offered:* Federal Pell, SEOG, state scholarships/grants, private scholarships, the school's own gift aid. State, Academic, Creative arts/performance, Special achievements/activities, Special characteristics, Athletic and ROTC. *Loan aid offered:* Direct Subsidized Stafford, Direct Unsubsidized Stafford, Direct PLUS, Federal Perkins, college/university loans from institutional funds. Applicants will be notified of awards on a rolling basis beginning 4/1. Federal Work-Study Program available. Institutional employment available. Off-campus job opportunities are fair.

The Inside Word

Students from low-income families take note: The University of Florida, in an effort to increase enrollment of minority and economically disadvantaged students, has introduced the Florida Opportunity Scholars program, which fully covers 4 years of educational costs for qualifying students (annual family income must not exceed $40,000). If you fit the bill, you should apply; you may be rewarded with a free education at a prestigious school.

THE SCHOOL SAYS "..."

From The Admissions Office

"University of Florida students come from more than 100 countries, all 50 states, and every one of the 67 counties in Florida. Nineteen percent of the student body is comprised of graduate students. Approximately 3,000 African American students, 4,000 Hispanic students, and 2,300 Asian American students attend UF. Ninety percent of the entering freshmen rank above the national mean of scores on standard entrance exams. UF consistently ranks near the top among public universities in the number of new National Merit and Achievement scholars in attendance.

"Students must submit the SAT or ACT. Students who submit the ACT must include the writing component. Sub scores on the SAT will be mixed/matched with other SAT sub scores to achieve the highest score."

SELECTIVITY

Admissions Rating	60*
# of applicants	24,126
% of applicants accepted	42
% of acceptees attending	63

FRESHMAN PROFILE

Range SAT Critical Reading	560–670
Range SAT Math	580–690
Range ACT Composite	25–29

DEADLINES

Regular	
Deadline	11/1
Nonfall registration?	yes

FINANCIAL FACTS

Financial Aid Rating	80
Annual in-state tuition	$3,257
Annual out-of-state tuition	$17,841
Room and board	$7,020
Books and supplies	$940
% frosh rec. need-based scholarship or grant aid	23
% UG rec. need-based scholarship or grant aid	23
% frosh rec. non-need-based scholarship or grant aid	37
% UG rec. non-need-based scholarship or grant aid	28
% frosh rec. need-based self-help aid	14
% UG rec. need-based self-help aid	20
% frosh rec. athletic scholarships	1
% UG rec. athletic scholarships	1
% frosh rec. any financial aid	98
% UG rec. any financial aid	92
% UG borrow to pay for school	44
Average cumulative indebtedness	$15,045

UNIVERSITY OF GEORGIA

TERRELL HALL, ATHENS, GA 30602 • ADMISSIONS: 706-542-8776 • FAX: 706-542-1466

CAMPUS LIFE

Quality of Life Rating	**85**
Fire Safety Rating	**82**
Green Rating	**89**
Type of school	public
Environment	city

STUDENTS

Total undergrad enrollment	24,971
% male/female	43/57
% from out of state	11
% from public high school	81
% live on campus	27
% in (# of) fraternities	20 (34)
% in (# of) sororities	25 (24)
% African American	6
% Asian	6
% Caucasian	83
% Hispanic	2
% international	1
# of countries represented	109

SURVEY SAYS . . .

Great computer facilities
Athletic facilities are great
Students love Athens, GA
Great off-campus food
Everyone loves the Bulldogs
Student publications are popular
Lots of beer drinking
Hard liquor is popular

ACADEMICS

Academic Rating	**73**
Calendar	semester
Student/faculty ratio	18:1
Profs interesting rating	74
Profs accessible rating	65
% classes taught by TAs	29
Most common	
reg class size	20–29 students

MOST POPULAR MAJORS

biology/biological sciences
psychology
art/art studies

STUDENTS SAY ". . ."

Academics

How enthusiastic are UGA students about their school? One typical undergrad assures us that "UGA is the type of school you see in the movies. The sun is always shining and everyone is always having a great time." It's not all about fun and sun at this top-caliber state university, however; on the contrary, UGA is "dedicated to research and the advancement of education" in order to create "a place where a student interested in any field can fit in and thrive." Business, journalism pharmacy, veterinary science, political science, premedical sciences, psychology, you name it, UGA has it and likely does a pretty good job teaching it. Students in many disciplines benefit from "a ton of emphasis placed on internships" as well as an alumni network that is "pretty well connected and willing to help people just starting out." And while navigating the school's academic rigors can be a tough go at first, students assure us that "When you finally declare a major and get into your particular college, that is when you form the bonds with your professors and fellow students." Those hoping to party more than study can rest assured that "UGA can be as easy or as hard as you want to make it." Those hoping to game the system swear by The Key, "an essential tool for class registration." controlled by the SGA. "It is a list of professors and the percentage of grades (A, B, C, etc.) each gives. I know many students who pick teachers by the key."

Life

UGA is "so big that there is never nothing to do," undergrads tell us, adding that "Nothing compares to Georgia football, downtown Athens, the sorority and fraternity scene, the campus, and the staff. Georgia has it all." "For fun, most people head downtown" to explore Athens, "a great college town filled with little hole-in-the-wall shops and restaurants as well as every kind of bar imaginable. Saturdays in Athens are like no other place on Earth. It's incredible how much this town loves their Dawgs," especially during football season. "Football is like a religion here," students insist, noting that "tailgating is insane, but classy." (Do students hold their pinkies out while downing their beers? Sadly, our respondent failed to elaborate.) There "is a lot of partying" here, "but most students know how to balance play with education and maintain good grades." Undergrads also point out that "There's a lot to do outdoors around here, like kayaking or hiking."

Student Body

Despite the fact that "UGA is stereotyped as being a bunch of white, suburban, middle-class kids," most of whom "are strongly affiliated with Greek life," "dress the same, and are clones," the truth is that "with the huge student body comes a wide range of individuals who come from all different walks of life. If somebody can't find somewhere where they fit in at UGA, they would have a hard time doing so anywhere." Students report that "the black population is growing" and that "people come from many parts of Georgia," not predominantly from the Atlanta area (again, despite the stereotype). It is probably true, however, that "the typical student at UGA is very into sports and has a lot of school spirit. They also like to party and get trashed. However, there are a lot of students who couldn't care less about the football and don't drink. I have to say that all the students get along quite well." Students detect a difference among denizens of the North Campus (trendy) and South Campus (ag students, math and science kids, "usually white, from rural Georgia... in Carhartts, boots, t-shirts, tennis shoes and jeans"). The newly added East Campus is home to arts students.

FINANCIAL AID: 706-542-6147 • E-MAIL: UNDERGRAD@ADMISSIONS.UGA.EDU • WEBSITE: WWW.UGA.EDU

THE PRINCETON REVIEW SAYS

Admissions

Very important factors considered include: Academic GPA, rigor of secondary school record. *Important factors considered include:* Standardized test scores. *Other factors considered include:* Application essay, recommendation(s), character/personal qualities, extracurricular activities, talent/ability, volunteer work, work experience. SAT or ACT required; ACT with Writing component required. TOEFL required of all international applicants. High school diploma is required and GED is accepted. *Academic units required:* 4 English, 4 mathematics, 3 science, (2 science labs), 2 foreign language, 3 social studies. *Academic units recommended:* 4 English, 4 mathematics, 3 science, (2 science labs), 3 foreign language, 1 social studies, 2 history, 1 academic elective.

Financial Aid

Students should submit: FAFSA. The Princeton Review suggests that all financial aid forms be submitted as soon as possible after January 1. *Need-based scholarships/grants offered:* Federal Pell, SEOG, state scholarships/grants, private scholarships, the school's own gift aid. *Loan aid offered:* Direct Subsidized Stafford, Direct Unsubsidized Stafford, Direct PLUS, Federal Perkins, state loans, college/university loans from institutional funds. Applicants will be notified of awards on a rolling basis beginning 5/15.

The Inside Word

A school as large as UGA must by necessity start winnowing applicants by the numbers; fail to meet certain baseline curricular, GPA, and standardized test score floors and only exceptional talent elsewhere (a gift for the arts or, better still, throwing a football) will get you past the first cut. Many students here are Georgia residents reaping the benefits of the state's HOPE scholarship program, which pays tuition and most school-related fees for state residents who earn at least a 3.0 GPA in high school, so long as they maintain at least a 3.0 in college.

THE SCHOOL SAYS "..."

From The Admissions Office

"The University of Georgia offers students the advantages and resources of a top public research university, including a wide range of majors and exceptional academic facilities such as the 200,000-square-foot Student Learning Center. At the same time, UGA provides opportunities more common to smaller, private schools, such as first-year seminars led by distinguished faculty and learning communities that connect students with similar academic interests. The university is committed to challenging its academically superior students in the classroom and beyond, with increased emphasis on undergraduate research, service-learning, and study abroad. UGA students taking advantage of such offerings find themselves well positioned to compete with the best undergraduates in the country, as evidenced by their recent string of successes in winning Rhodes, Marshall, Truman, and other major scholarships.

"The UGA campus, considered one of the most beautiful in the nation, adjoins vibrant downtown Athens. Renowned for its local music scene, Athens is also a center for the performing and visual arts, thanks in part to UGA's popular Hodgson School of Music and Lamar Dodd School of Art. Sports—from football to gymnastics—are also a major attraction, with UGA teams perennially ranked among the best in the country.

"To experience the excitement of UGA, most prospective students visit campus, a 90-minute drive northeast of the Atlanta airport. See the Admissions website (www.admissions.uga.edu) to sign up for a tour with the Visitors Center, view the weekday schedule of admissions information sessions, and find application details."

"Applicants for first-year admission will be required to submit either the SAT or ACT. Students submitting only the ACT must also submit the optional ACT Writing Test."

SELECTIVITY

Admissions Rating	92
# of applicants	17,022
% of applicants accepted	55
% of acceptees attending	51
# accepting a place on wait list	342
% admitted from wait list	51

FRESHMAN PROFILE

Range SAT Critical Reading	560–660
Range SAT Math	570–650
Range SAT Writing	560–640
Range ACT Composite	25–29
Minimum paper TOEFL	550
Minimum computer TOEFL	213
Average HS GPA	3.79
% graduated top 10% of class	53
% graduated top 25% of class	87
% graduated top 50% of class	99

DEADLINES

Early action	
Deadline	10/15
Notification	12/15
Regular	
Priority	10/15
Deadline	1/15
Notification	rolling
Nonfall registration?	yes

APPLICANTS ALSO LOOK AT

AND OFTEN PREFER
Georgia Institute of Technology
AND SOMETIMES PREFER
Emory University
University of North Carolina at Chapel Hill
AND RARELY PREFER
University of South Carolina—Columbia
Clemson University

FINANCIAL FACTS

Financial Aid Rating	79
Annual tuition	$5,264
% frosh rec. need-based scholarship or grant aid	30
% UG rec. need-based scholarship or grant aid	23
% frosh rec. non-need-based scholarship or grant aid	8
% UG rec. non-need-based scholarship or grant aid	5
% frosh rec. need-based self-help aid	15
% UG rec. need-based self-help aid	17
% frosh rec. athletic scholarships	2
% UG rec. athletic scholarships	2
% frosh rec. any financial aid	31
% UG rec. any financial aid	27
% UG borrow to pay for school	39
Average cumulative indebtedness	$14,420

UNIVERSITY OF IDAHO

IDAHO ADMISSIONS OFFICE, PO BOX 444264, MOSCOW, ID 83844-4264 • ADMISSIONS: 208-885-6326 • FAX: 208-885-9119

STUDENTS SAY "..."

Academics

A little college in the "middle of nowhere," the University of Idaho isn't your average public university. While huge lectures and inaccessible administrators beleaguer other state schools, the affordable price tag at Idaho comes with a friendly and intimate academic environment. Indeed, the school's major strength is that it offers "a wide range of classes while still remaining personal enough for one-on-one learning." At Idaho, "The teachers prefer [that] you call them by first name," and "Professors are always willing to help if you show an interest in your work." As one student explains, "University of Idaho has top-ranked professors in the nation in their field. I believe they chose to teach here . . . because of [the] community, students, and friendly atmosphere." Despite their generally glowing reviews, Idaho students note that "some of our departments are short on funds," which "puts pressure on department heads to meet educational goals of students with fewer instructors than are necessary." Most students feel that "administrators are trying their best to provide quality education while trying to recuperate from past debts." Some students would also prefer to see a little more academic rigor infused into the programs. As one student explains, "The classes I've taken were challenging but not too ridiculously demanding in terms of busy work."

Life

Located in the teensy town of Moscow, "Drinking and studying are the main activities" at the University of Idaho. For the diligent, "The small-town atmosphere provides a great student environment." Many other students, however, "are highly involved in Greek life and other activities on campus," producing a lively campus atmosphere and a thriving party scene. While Moscow may be "a small town with little going on," students agree that "for its size, the party scene is awesome." For students who are not into the Greek scene, the beautiful campus and close-knit community foster a number of other recreational opportunities, including several highly active community-service organizations. As one student affirms, "University of Idaho is known as a party school and we can live up to that, but we study, attend cultural events, and are active in our communities, in addition to our beer drinking." Students say that the university "always provides things to do from . . . sporting events and theater shows" to "intramural sports, rock climbing, and . . . movies at the Student Union Building." Located in beautiful rural Idaho, many students say that "most of the fun in Moscow consists of outdoor recreation."

Student Body

Idaho draws the majority of its students from the surrounding areas, attracting, "chill North Idahoans" with a mix of "other spices." Given this breakdown, it's no surprise that at University of Idaho, "most are White, as is our state as a whole." A freshman details, "Typical students at Idaho are from middle-class/upper-middle-class, White homes." Another student adds, "I think there is a lot of diversity as far as types of people, but there could be more ethnic diversity." While there are few minorities, you'll find every personality type "from cowboys to cosmopolitan city residents" on campus. Generally speaking, "Most of the campus is very social" and students describe their classmates as "outgoing" and "friendly."

UNIVERSITY OF IDAHO

FINANCIAL AID: 208-885-6312 • E-MAIL: ADMAPPL@UIDAHO.EDU • WEBSITE: WWW.UIDAHO.EDU

THE PRINCETON REVIEW SAYS

Admissions

Very important factors considered include: Academic GPA, standardized test scores. *Other factors considered include:* Recommendation(s), SAT or ACT required; TOEFL required of all international applicants. High school diploma is required and GED is accepted. *Academic credits required:* 3 English, 6 mathematics, 6 science, (2 science labs), 2 humanities/foreign language, 5 social studies, 3 academic electives.

Financial Aid

Students should submit: FAFSA. The Princeton Review suggests that all financial aid forms be submitted as soon as possible after January 1. *Need-based scholarships/grants offered:* Federal Pell, SEOG, ACG, SMART grants, TEACH grants, state scholarships/grants, university scholarships, the school's own gift aid. *Loan aid offered:* Direct Subsidized Stafford, Direct Unsubsidized Stafford, Direct Parent PLUS, Direct Graduate PLUS, Federal Perkins, college/university loans from institutional funds. Applicants will be notified of awards on a rolling basis beginning 3/30. Federal and State Work-Study Program available. Institutional employment available. Off-campus job opportunities are good.

The Inside Word

The University of Idaho's straightforward approach to admissions is a welcome change for students completing more involved applications. In a way that's typical of large, public universities, Admissions Officers arrive at decisions based upon high school GPA and test scores. Most applicants are admitted and welcome the opportunity to attend a strong school at an affordable price.

THE SCHOOL SAYS "..."

From The Admissions Office

"The University of Idaho, in the rolling Palouse hills of northern Idaho, is one of the leading public universities in the Northwest. Idaho attracts nearly 12,000 students and has become known for its academic excellence, exceptional student living and learning environment, outstanding creative and research opportunities, and proven track record of high-achieving graduates. It continues to educate students in fields important to the mountain West and beyond, such as agriculture, water resources, environmental science and Native American studies. Idaho also offers highly-regarded programs in engineering, business, natural resources, architecture, biotechnology, teaching and foreign languages, among others. Through insight and innovation, and a legacy of leadership, the University of Idaho enriches the lives of people throughout the region and the world.

"Students applying for admission into the Fall 2008 entering class are required to take either the SAT or the ACT. Both the new and the old test scores will be accepted. The Writing Test is not required from the ACT. SAT Subject Test scores are not used for admission purposes."

SELECTIVITY
Admissions Rating	78
# of applicants	4,577
% of applicants accepted	77
% of acceptees attending	47

FRESHMAN PROFILE
Range SAT Critical Reading	480–600
Range SAT Math	480–600
Range SAT Writing	450–570
Range ACT Composite	20–25
Minimum paper TOEFL	525
Minimum computer TOEFL	193
Minimum web-based TOEFL	70
Average HS GPA	3.39
% graduated top 10% of class	18
% graduated top 25% of class	42
% graduated top 50% of class	74

DEADLINES
Regular	
Priority	2/15
Deadline	8/1
Nonfall registration?	yes

APPLICANTS ALSO LOOK AT AND SOMETIMES PREFER
Utah State University
Boise State University
AND RARELY PREFER
Idaho State University

FINANCIAL FACTS
Financial Aid Rating	76
Annual out-of-state tuition	$10,080
Room and board	$6,424
Required fees	$4,410
Books and supplies	$1,430
% frosh rec. need-based scholarship or grant aid	34
% UG rec. need-based scholarship or grant aid	37
% frosh rec. non-need-based scholarship or grant aid	44
% UG rec. non-need-based scholarship or grant aid	39
% frosh rec. need-based self-help aid	44
% UG rec. need-based self-help aid	50
% frosh rec. athletic scholarships	3
% UG rec. athletic scholarships	3
% frosh rec. any financial aid	56.3
% UG rec. any financial aid	57.6
% UG borrow to pay for school	66
Average cumulative indebtedness	$21,609

UNIVERSITY OF ILLINOIS AT URBANA-CHAMPAIGN

901 WEST ILLINOIS STREET, URBANA, IL 61801 • ADMISSIONS: 217-333-0302 • FAX: 217-333-9758

CAMPUS LIFE
Quality of Life Rating	79
Fire Safety Rating	63
Green Rating	92
Type of school	public
Environment	city

STUDENTS
Total undergrad enrollment	30,395
% male/female	53/47
% from out of state	7
% from public high school	75
% live on campus	50
% in (# of) fraternities	22 (60)
% in (# of) sororities	23 (36)
% African American	7
% Asian	13
% Caucasian	66
% Hispanic	7
% international	5
# of countries represented	123

SURVEY SAYS . . .
Great computer facilities
Great library
Athletic facilities are great
Everyone loves the Fighting Illini
Frats and sororities dominate social scene
Student publications are popular
Lots of beer drinking
Hard liquor is popular

ACADEMICS
Academic Rating	74
Calendar	semester
Student/faculty ratio	17:1
Profs interesting rating	66
Profs accessible rating	68
% classes taught by TAs	26
Most common reg class size	20–29 students
Most common lab size	20–29 students

MOST POPULAR MAJORS
cell/cellular and molecular biology
psychology
political science and government

STUDENTS SAY "..."

Academics

The epically large flagship campus of the University of Illinois "is very challenging and gives you freedom to do anything." Students here enjoy "all the benefits of a great public university." There are over 150 undergraduate programs. The colleges of engineering and business are of the "most prestigious and hardest to get into," but there are dozens of other "very strong and reputable" departments as well. "The research resources are amazing," raves a Russian literature major. "The library has almost any resource an undergraduate or even an advanced researcher would ever need." However, the drawbacks that come with such an expansive campus are present as well. Lower-level class sizes "are horrendously large." "My largest class had 800 students," notes a biochemistry major. "The massive bureaucracy" is a constant source of irritation. "Simple things like adding or dropping a class a few weeks into a semester can require five or six trips to different buildings to talk to different people, each time requiring you to explain your situation." "Professors are more impersonal to freshmen, but seem to warm up to upperclassmen," explains one student. "There are some professors that should not be teaching anywhere," though. "A lot of times, it's a toss up with bad/good professors," counsels a geology major. "You can learn a lot and have a great teacher, but you need to ask around and find out who that good teacher is." "There are professors and classes that you come across that certainly leave something to be desired," agrees a women's studies major. "But overall, I am very pleased with my academic experience at UIUC and have met some astoundingly intelligent, influential professors."

Life

At the University of Illinois, there is "never a dull moment, despite the surrounding cornfields." Over a thousand clubs and organizations provide students with a wide array of options. "Anything that you are interested in you can do," gloats an engineering major. "It's a huge campus but it's not too spread out," says a Spanish major. "You can get around anywhere by bike or bus and you don't need a car." "The campus is very Greek-oriented," and the students who pledge the myriad frats and sororities "love the Greek life." Some students notice serious animosity between the independent students and students involved in the frat scene. "It seems at times to take over our campus," says one irate independent. Other students just don't see the problem. "I think plenty of non-Greeks associate with Greeks," asserts a finance major. "Drinking is a big thing at U of I." Apartment parties and frat parties rage on the weekends. There is an "outstanding bar culture," too. "If you're 19, or if you can get an ID so you can be 19, it's very popular to frequent the bars even during the week." "If you don't want to party all the time, there are plenty of other options." "Intramural sports and playing sports on the quad and in Frat Park are popular." The campus is "alive with the Big Ten spirit" and students are very supportive of their beloved Illini. "Awesome concerts" proliferate and "there is a really good artsy theater which runs foreign and indie films."

Student Body

The U of I has a decidedly Midwestern feel and "Midwestern hospitality" is abundant. "Kids from out-of-state and small-town farm students" definitely have a presence but, sometimes, it seems like "practically everyone is from the northwest suburbs of Chicago." There's a lot of ethnic diversity "visible on campus." There are many Asian and Asian-American students. On the whole, the majority of students are "very smart kids who like to party." "The typical student is involved and really good at balancing schoolwork, clubs and organizations, and their social life." "They really study fairly hard, and when you ask, it turns out that they're majoring in something like rocket science." Ultimately, there's something for everyone here with students who think about "nothing but drinking" to those who "never miss a class" and are "in the library every night." "There is a niche for everyone."

FINANCIAL AID: 217-333-0100 • E-MAIL: ADMISSIONS@OAR.UIUC.EDU • WEBSITE: WWW.UIUC.EDU

THE PRINCETON REVIEW SAYS

Admissions

Very important factors considered include: Class rank, application essay, academic GPA, rigor of secondary school record, standardized test scores. *Important factors considered include:* Character/personal qualities, extracurricular activities, first generation, talent/ability, volunteer work, work experience. *Other factors considered include:* Geographical residence, racial/ethnic status, state residency, SAT or ACT required; ACT with Writing component required. TOEFL required of all international applicants. High school diploma is required and GED is accepted. *Academic units required:* 4 English, 3 mathematics, 2 science, (2 science labs), 2 foreign language, 2 social studies, 2 academic electives.

Financial Aid

Students should submit: FAFSA. The Princeton Review suggests that all financial aid forms be submitted as soon as possible after January 1. *Need-based scholarships/grants offered:* Federal Pell, SEOG, state scholarships/grants, private scholarships, the school's own gift aid, United Negro College Fund. *Loan aid offered:* Direct Subsidized Stafford, Direct Unsubsidized Stafford, Direct PLUS, Federal Perkins, college/university loans from institutional funds. Federal Work-Study Program available. Institutional employment available. Off-campus job opportunities are excellent.

The Inside Word

Few candidates are deceived by Illinois's relatively high acceptance rate; the university has a well-deserved reputation for expecting applicants to be strong students, and those who aren't usually don't bother to apply. Despite a jumbo applicant pool, the Admissions Office reports that every candidate is individually reviewed, which deserves mention as rare in universities of this size.

THE SCHOOL SAYS " . . ."

From The Admissions Office

"The campus has been aptly described as a collection of neighborhoods constituting a diverse and vibrant city. The neighborhoods are of many types: students and faculty within a department; people sharing a room or house; the members of a professional organization, a service club, or an intramural team; or simply people who, starting out as strangers sharing a class or a study lounge or a fondness for a weekly film series, have become friends. And the city of this description is the university itself—a rich cosmopolitan environment constructed by students and faculty to meet their educational and personal goals. The quality of intellectual life parallels that of other great universities, and many faculty and students who have their choice of top institutions select Illinois over its peers. While such choices are based often on the quality of individual programs of study, another crucial factor is the 'tone' of the campus life that is linked with the virtues of Midwestern culture. There is an informality and a near-absence of pretension, which, coupled with a tradition of commitment to excellence, creates an atmosphere that is unique among the finest institutions.

"Applicants for Fall 2008 are recommended to take the new SAT or the ACT with the Writing section, but we will allow students to submit scores from the old version (prior to March 2005) of the SAT or ACT. Though strongly recommended, the Writing section of the ACT is not required."

SELECTIVITY

Admissions Rating	89
# of applicants	21,645
% of applicants accepted	71
% of acceptees attending	45
# accepting a place on wait list	633
% admitted from wait list	96

FRESHMAN PROFILE

Range SAT Critical Reading	540–670
Range SAT Math	630–740
Range ACT Composite	26–31
Minimum paper TOEFL	550
Minimum computer TOEFL	213
Minimum web-based TOEFL	79
% graduated top 10% of class	55
% graduated top 25% of class	89
% graduated top 50% of class	99

DEADLINES

Early action	
Deadline	11/10
Notification	12/14
Regular	
Priority	11/10
Deadline	1/2
Notification	12/14
Nonfall registration?	no

APPLICANTS ALSO LOOK AT
AND OFTEN PREFER
University of Michigan—Ann Arbor
Northwestern University
AND SOMETIMES PREFER
Washington University in St. Louis
University of Iowa
University of Wisconsin—Madison
AND RARELY PREFER
Purdue University—West Lafayette
Illinois State University

FINANCIAL FACTS

Financial Aid Rating	80
Annual in-state tuition	$8,502
Annual out-of-state tuition	$21,895
Room and board	$8,196
Required fees	$2,001
Books and supplies	$1,200
% frosh rec. need-based scholarship or grant aid	36
% UG rec. need-based scholarship or grant aid	39
% frosh rec. non-need-based scholarship or grant aid	13
% UG rec. non-need-based scholarship or grant aid	12
% frosh rec. need-based self-help aid	34
% UG rec. need-based self-help aid	36
% frosh rec. athletic scholarships	1
% UG rec. athletic scholarships	1
% frosh rec. any financial aid	69
% UG rec. any financial aid	72
% UG borrow to pay for school	51
Average cumulative indebtedness	$17,057

UNIVERSITY OF IOWA

107 Calvin Hall, Iowa City, IA 52242 • Admissions: 319-335-3847 • Fax: 319-333-1535

CAMPUS LIFE

Quality of Life Rating	**88**
Fire Safety Rating	**83**
Green Rating	**75**
Type of school	public
Environment	city

STUDENTS

Total undergrad enrollment	20,207
% male/female	48/52
% from out of state	34
% from public high school	90
% live on campus	30
% in (# of) fraternities	7 (18)
% in (# of) sororities	12 (17)
% African American	2
% Asian	3
% Caucasian	79
% Hispanic	2
% international	1
# of countries represented	110

SURVEY SAYS . . .

Great computer facilities
Students love Iowa City, IA
Great off-campus food
Everyone loves the Hawkeyes
Lots of beer drinking
Hard liquor is popular

ACADEMICS

Academic Rating	**74**
Calendar	semester
Student/faculty ratio	15:1
Profs interesting rating	63
Profs accessible rating	70
Most common reg class size	10–19 students
Most common lab size	20–29 students

MOST POPULAR MAJORS

communication studies/speech communication and rhetoric
psychology
business/commerce

STUDENTS SAY "..."

Academics

"Strong academics in a variety of fields," including "excellent research programs in numerous disciplines for those who desire a more research-oriented curriculum," are the foundation of University of Iowa's success—but they're not the entire picture. There's also the "high-tech and fast-paced campus," the "great assistance centers such as the Writing Center, minority centers, and the Career Center," and of course the "wonderful social opportunities," all of which "really contribute to the overall experience of an undergraduate." UI's stellar departments are myriad: Programs in creative writing, English, health sciences (bolstered by the presence of no fewer than three hospitals on campus), speech pathology and audiology, engineering, journalism, and pharmacology all earn students' raves, and that's just the tip of the iceberg. While the quality of teaching here "varies greatly amongst departments," "Almost all professors really do care about how each of their students does. They really stress their availability outside of class for all students to get help if it is needed." Ambitious students should note that "honors classes are available, and professors are open and excited about students who want to go above and beyond." Prospective students should be forewarned, however, that "as with any state-run organization, the school is plagued with bureaucratic process."

Life

"Life at Iowa can be whatever you make it," students at this massive university agree. "If you want to get wild and crazy on the weekends, you can." According to one undergrad, the "gazillion house parties or the trillion bars on campus" make the UI party scene "like a mini-Cancún." On the other hand, "If you like to lay low, you can hit the theater performances at Hatcher or play a few games of basketball," or "Catch a historically significant foreign film playing somewhere for free, or see important movers on the international stage giving speeches on the next big global issue." The point is, there's more to do here than party; as one student puts it, "Contrary to popular belief, not everyone on this campus drinks. There are many residence hall–sponsored activities like swing dances, dorm parties, barbecues, tug-of-war. [The school] tries to do something every weekend." One activity does unite the student body; nearly everyone here is "football crazy," with tailgates and the game both deemed "must-attend" events. Iowa City loves the football team as much as the students do, and students reciprocate by loving the city, which they describe as "the perfect college town" that offers "many social activities, restaurants, and coffee shops geared toward college students." Students also appreciate the fact that Iowa City "is a haven for Democrats, minorities, homosexuals, and others not generally accepted in the Midwest."

Student Body

"As far as the state of Iowa goes, this community is ethnically diverse and very welcoming of people with different religious viewpoints and sexual orientations," students at UI report, but they also remind us that nevertheless, "This school is located in Iowa, so most of the students are White and have Christian backgrounds." This "very liberal" school does, however, include its fair share of "hicks from Iowa and rich kids from Chicago," with some international students in the mix. With nearly 20,000 students, it's impossible to describe the typical UI student, but that didn't stop people from trying. One undergrad writes, "A typical student at the UI is pretty much an average young adult who likes to hang out, go to football games, and go to parties. There are some atypical students—those who are very religious, don't drink, or are punks. Even though they may be 'atypical,' there is still room for them here. Everyone finds a niche."

FINANCIAL AID: 319-335-1450 • E-MAIL: ADMISSIONS@UIOWA.EDU • WEBSITE: WWW.UIOWA.EDU

THE PRINCETON REVIEW SAYS

Admissions

Very important factors considered include: Class rank, academic GPA, rigor of secondary school record, standardized test scores. *Other factors considered include:* Recommendation(s), character/personal qualities, state residency, talent/ability, SAT or ACT required; ACT with Writing component recommended. TOEFL required of all international applicants. High school diploma is required and GED is accepted. *Academic units required:* 4 English, 3 mathematics, 3 science, 2 foreign language, 3 social studies. *Academic units recommended:* 4 mathematics, 4 foreign language.

Financial Aid

Students should submit: FAFSA, institution's own financial aid form. The Princeton Review suggests that all financial aid forms be submitted as soon as possible after January 1. *Need-based scholarships/grants offered:* Federal Pell, SEOG, state scholarships/grants, private scholarships, the school's own gift aid. *Loan aid offered:* Direct Subsidized Stafford, Direct Unsubsidized Stafford, Direct PLUS, Federal Perkins, Federal Nursing, state loans, college/university loans from institutional funds. Applicants will be notified of awards on a rolling basis beginning 3/15. Federal Work-Study Program available. Institutional employment available. Off-campus job opportunities are good.

The Inside Word

While the application process at University of Iowa is fairly formulaic and impersonal, candidates do have the luxury of knowing what to expect. Admission is automatically granted to applicants who meet secondary school course requirements and class rank and entrance exam minimums. The cut-offs are fairly high, and Iowa typically nets a strong crop of talented students. Out-of-state applicants, as well as candidates applying to the engineering school, face even tougher standards.

THE SCHOOL SAYS ". . ."

From The Admissions Office

"The University of Iowa has outstanding programs in the creative arts, notably the Iowa Writers' Workshop and the world-renowned International Writing Program. It also has strong programs in business, communication studies, journalism, English, engineering, political science, and psychology, and was the birthplace of the discipline of speech pathology and audiology. It offers excellent programs in the basic health sciences and health care programs, led by the top ranked College of Medicine and the closely associated University Hospitals and Clinics.

"The University of Iowa will accept either the new SAT or the old SAT (administered prior to March 2005 and without a Writing component), as well as the ACT with or without the Writing component."

SELECTIVITY

Admissions Rating	83
# of applicants	14,678
% of applicants accepted	83
% of acceptees attending	35
# accepting a place on wait list	140

FRESHMAN PROFILE

Range SAT Critical Reading	520–650
Range SAT Math	550–670
Range ACT Composite	23–27
Minimum paper TOEFL	600
Minimum computer TOEFL	250
Average HS GPA	3.56
% graduated top 10% of class	23
% graduated top 25% of class	54
% graduated top 50% of class	93

DEADLINES

Regular	
Priority	2/1
Deadline	4/1
Notification	rolling
Nonfall registration?	yes

APPLICANTS ALSO LOOK AT

AND OFTEN PREFER
University of Illinois at Urbana-Champaign
Northwestern University

AND SOMETIMES PREFER
Iowa State University
Drake University
University of Northern Iowa
Grinnell College
Indiana University at Bloomington

AND RARELY PREFER
Cornell College
Illinois State University
University of Missouri—Rolla

FINANCIAL FACTS

Financial Aid Rating	92
Annual in-state tuition	$5,548
Annual out-of-state tuition	$19,662
Room and board	$7,673
Required fees	$996
Books and supplies	$1,040
% frosh rec. need-based scholarship or grant aid	28
% UG rec. need-based scholarship or grant aid	30
% frosh rec. non-need-based scholarship or grant aid	24
% UG rec. non-need-based scholarship or grant aid	15
% frosh rec. need-based self-help aid	35
% UG rec. need-based self-help aid	43
% frosh rec. athletic scholarships	2
% UG rec. athletic scholarships	2
% frosh rec. any financial aid	80
% UG rec. any financial aid	82
% UG borrow to pay for school	61
Average cumulative indebtedness	$22,181

UNIVERSITY OF KANSAS

OFFICE OF ADMISSIONS & SCHOLARSHIPS, 1502 IOWA STREET, LAWRENCE, KS 66045 • ADMISSIONS: 785-864-3911 • FAX: 785-864-5017

CAMPUS LIFE

Quality of Life Rating	**88**
Fire Safety Rating	**74**
Green Rating	**82**
Type of school	public
Environment	city

STUDENTS

Total undergrad enrollment	20,474
% male/female	50/50
% from out of state	23
% live on campus	22
% in (# of) fraternities	13 (25)
% in (# of) sororities	18 (16)
% African American	4
% Asian	4
% Caucasian	81
% Hispanic	4
% Native American	1
% international	3
# of countries represented	114

SURVEY SAYS . . .
Great library
Athletic facilities are great
Great off-campus food
Everyone loves the Jayhawks
Student publications are popular
Lots of beer drinking

ACADEMICS

Academic Rating	**74**
Calendar	semester
Student/faculty ratio	19:1
Profs interesting rating	76
Profs accessible rating	77
% classes taught by TAs	18

MOST POPULAR MAJORS
psychology
biology/biological sciences
accounting

STUDENTS SAY ". . ."

Academics

"Strong in traditions, both sports and academics," the University of Kansas (KU to those in the know) is "paradise for sports fans, academicians, liberals, and partiers alike." Students stress that KU provides "the full college experience" through "many amazing research opportunities, supportive faculty, and strong academics, as well as a great social scene." KU boasts a wealth of solid programs, including an "amazing hands-on architecture program," a "fantastic journalism program," a highly reputed program in speech language and hearing, a "good nursing school," and solid science departments. As one student sees it, "My school can offer an Ivy League education to those who are willing to be the best they can be." No matter what discipline you pursue, "The price is amazing for everything that you receive. The buildings, the classrooms, the technology, the campus . . . and the location were all what I was looking for." While KU's class sizes "can be a bit overwhelming," professors "are interested in seeing their students succeed and make themselves readily available to students," and "discussions or labs help make [the large lectures] bearable." Those seeking a more intimate academic experience should consider the honors program; "The people who run it are all super-nice and helpful, and the honors classes themselves are much smaller and more discussion-based, which lets the students think more and become better friends."

Life

"Tradition is a big strength" of KU life. "Singing the alma mater and reciting the Rock Chalk chant before games and other events is awesome," students tell us. For many, "Life revolves around basketball from November to April." Reports one undergrad, "Going to games is great. I've never experienced anything like [it]. I love sitting in the student section. The energy radiating off of everyone is amazing. Camping out in line on the day of basketball games will be one of my greatest memories. You gotta love KU basketball." If you don't, though, you needn't despair, because "Lawrence offers a great downtown with bars, clubs, shops, coffeehouses, and music. There's always something to do, even if you're not 21." The town has "a big music scene, and bands like Pat Green, James Blunt, and Mat Kearney have played numerous shows. Smaller indie-rock bands come through as well. Liberty Hall downtown hosts concerts and projection movies, and the student union always brings in acts like Ben Folds or other celebrities." There's an active party scene on and off campus; according to one undergrad, "The majority of us bust our [butts] during the week, and party the weekend away. There are a lot of places for students to go on weekends to forget about how [crappy] their week was."

Student Body

KU students tell us there are "a lot of fraternity and sorority types at our school, and they're very active on (and off) campus," but there's also "a large number of alternative, indie, and minority students present, and they all fit into a niche as well. Overall, I would say it's a very pleasant coexistence between the two types of people," as "Most people are really easygoing and enjoy getting to know people who are different from them." Demographically, KU is made up of "pretty much plain-vanilla Midwestern college students." They're among the most liberal in the state, but, one student quips, "That isn't saying much, seeing as it is Kansas." However, "Most everyone here is very open-minded and willing to accept people for who they are." As one student puts it, "Nothing surprises me anymore. When I first came to KU it was interesting to see same-sex couples, rocker guys, and girls with their collars popped walking around the same campus. Now, it's just life."

FINANCIAL AID: 785-864-4700 • E-MAIL: ADM@KU.EDU • WEBSITE: WWW.KU.EDU

THE PRINCETON REVIEW SAYS

Admissions

Very important factors considered include: Academic GPA, Class rank, Rigor of secondary school record, Standardized test scores. *Academic units required:* 4 English, 3 math, 3 science, 3 history, 1 computer science/technology. *Academic units recommended:* 4 math, 2 foreign language.

Financial Aid

The Princeton Review suggests that all financial aid forms be submitted as soon as possible after January 1. Federal Work-Study Program available. Institutional employment available. Off-campus job opportunities are excellent.

The Inside Word

KU can process your application to its College of Liberal Arts and Sciences or its School of Engineering (architecture program excluded) in 48 hours. In-state students can be admitted to the College of Liberal Arts and Sciences if they achieve a 21/980 on the ACT/SAT (writing section excluded) or earn at least a 2.0 on the Kansas Board of Regents curriculum. Out-of-state students need a 24/1090 or at least a 2.5 on the board curriculum. No matter where you're from, a top-third high school class rank will do the trick. The School of Engineering requires a minimum 28/640 ACT/SAT Math section score for out-of-state students. In-state students need a minimum Math score of 22/540.

THE SCHOOL SAYS "..."

From The Admissions Office

"The University of Kansas has a long and distinguished tradition for academic excellence. Outstanding students from Kansas and across the nation are attracted to KU because of its strong academic reputation, beautiful campus, affordable cost of education, and contagious school spirit. KU provides students extraordinary opportunities in honors programs, research, internships, and study abroad. The university is located in Lawrence (40 minutes from Kansas City), a community of 80,000 regarded as one of the nation's best small cities for its arts scene, live music, and historic downtown.

"Students applying for Fall 2008 admission may provide scores from either version of the SAT, as well as the ACT. KU will look at the total score of the Math and the Critical Reading (Verbal) section of the exam for admission purposes."

SELECTIVITY
Admissions Rating	82
# of applicants	10,367
% of applicants accepted	92
% of acceptees attending	43

FRESHMAN PROFILE
Range ACT Composite	22–27
Average HS GPA	3.4
% graduated top 10% of class	28
% graduated top 25% of class	60
% graduated top 50% of class	90

DEADLINES
Regular	04/01
Nonfall registration?	Yes

FINANCIAL FACTS
Financial Aid Rating	74
Annual in-state tuition	$$5,844
Annual out-of-state tuition	$15,351
Room and board	$6,144
Required fees	$756
Books and supplies	$750
% frosh rec. any financial aid	59
% UG rec. any financial aid	50

UNIVERSITY OF KENTUCKY

100 FUNKHOUSER BUILDING, LEXINGTON, KY 40506 • ADMISSIONS: 859-257-2000 • FAX: 859-257-3823

CAMPUS LIFE

Quality of Life Rating	**70**
Fire Safety Rating	**84**
Green Rating	**60***
Type of school	public
Environment	city

STUDENTS

Total undergrad enrollment	18,960
% male/female	49/51
% from out of state	17
% live on campus	22
% in (# of) fraternities	15 (19)
% in (# of) sororities	19 (16)
% African American	5
% Asian	2
% Caucasian	88
% Hispanic	1
% international	1
# of countries represented	117

SURVEY SAYS . . .

Great computer facilities
Great library
Athletic facilities are great
Everyone loves the Wildcats
Student publications are popular
Lots of beer drinking

ACADEMICS

Academic Rating	**71**
Calendar	semester
Student/faculty ratio	17:1
Profs interesting rating	68
Profs accessible rating	63
% classes taught by TAs	20
Most common reg class size	20–29 students
Most common lab size	20–29 students

STUDENTS SAY ". . ."

Academics

The University of Kentucky in Lexington is "all about making a name for yourself by preparing for and getting involved in future career goals while having fun and enjoying what college is all about." "Making a name for yourself" here requires distinguishing yourself in a crowd of over 18,000 undergraduates; daunting as that sounds, students tell us it can be done. "Getting involved in future career goals" is easy enough, given the "great selection of courses and majors" available. Kentucky offers undergraduate degrees in 12 of its 19 divisions; choices include the College of Agriculture (with popular majors in animal science, agricultural economics, and hospitality management), the College of Business and Management, the College of Education, the College of Engineering, the College of Communications and Information Studies (advertising, journalism, and library science), and the College of Arts and Sciences (biology, history, and political science). Students here laud the "impressive teaching staff, dedicated to enhancing student knowledge and teaching students about the future." UK's brand-new library "is also quite amazing. It is the perfect place to go study because usually the dorms can be a bit too distracting." All told, go-getters willing to take initiative will find that UK offers "a safe and fun atmosphere where you have unlimited opportunities to get involved at a reasonable price."

Life

"Everyone is a Wildcat" at UK, because "UK has tremendous sports programs and big fans all around the United States." Men's basketball fans "are among the craziest in the nation," and students "would be football fanatics if our team would win a game every now and then." "Because UK is dry, most parties are held off campus," so social life for many revolves around the off-campus Greek houses where "There is always a party going on, but you have to be a part of a fraternity or sorority to really know about it and attend." Some students report that "there are a lot of nonalcoholic parties in the dorms that might be crazier than the alcoholic parties," although others advise, "It's better to live off campus because the residence halls are pretty bad (except for the new ones), the meal plan is awful, and everything off campus is a lot cheaper." Hometown Lexington "is a great city with much to do and lots of opportunities. It offers many different clubs, bars, and restaurants that college students can go to as well as horse racing. All of these venues have a 'College Day' where students get discounts." One sophomore warns, however, that "small-town students can become distracted by the lights of the city."

Student Body

"The typical UK student has a Southern accent, likes to party, and often shops at J. Crew," but, "As the undergraduate population is about 18,000, there are a lot of people who do not fit that description." True, one of the most common "types"—or at least the most conspicuous one—are the "beautiful people, the hot girls and guys who roam the campus and dress up to go to class." But for every "collar-popping, stuck-up frat boy" there is also "your typical country Kentucky boy, boots and all." What you won't find many of at UK are "liberals—they are few and far between—and the type of atypical student with wild hair colors or other style extremes." Most here "lean right politically, but generally the student body is apathetic." School spirit is rampant, so much so that "on an average day, one in three students will have some sort of UK clothing on."

FINANCIAL AID: 859-257-3172 • E-MAIL: ADMISSION@UKY.EDU • WEBSITE: WWW.UKY.EDU

THE PRINCETON REVIEW SAYS

Admissions

Very important factors considered include: Academic GPA, rigor of secondary school record, standardized test scores. *Other factors considered include:* Class rank, application essay, recommendation(s), alumni/ae relation, character/personal qualities, extracurricular activities, first generation, geographical residence, interview, racial/ethnic status, talent/ability, volunteer work, SAT or ACT required; TOEFL required of all international applicants. High school diploma is required and GED is accepted. *Academic units required:* 4 English, 3 mathematics, 3 science, 2 foreign language, 3 social studies, 5 academic electives, 2 Fine or Performing Arts (1), Health (.5), and Physical Ed. (.5). *Academic units recommended:* 4 English, 4 mathematics, 4 science, 2 foreign language, 3 social studies, 3 academic electives, 2 fine or performing arts (1), health (.5), and physical ed. (.5).

Financial Aid

Students should submit: FAFSA Regular filing deadline is 2/15. The Princeton Review suggests that all financial aid forms be submitted as soon as possible after January 1. *Need-based scholarships/grants offered:* Federal Pell, SEOG, state scholarships/grants, private scholarships, the school's own gift aid. *Loan aid offered:* Direct Subsidized Stafford, Direct Unsubsidized Stafford, Direct PLUS, FFEL Subsidized Stafford, FFEL Unsubsidized Stafford, FFEL PLUS, Federal Perkins, state loans, college/university loans from institutional funds. Applicants will be notified of awards on a rolling basis beginning 4/1. Federal Work-Study Program available.

The Inside Word

The University of Kentucky's admissions team is about as objective as they come. If you have the GPA, class rank, and test scores, you'll in all likelihood be welcomed into the Wildcat community. The university is continually looking to improve its selectivity, so hitting the books is a must if you want to be a serious contender.

THE SCHOOL SAYS "..."

From The Admissions Office

"The University of Kentucky offers you an outstanding learning environment and quality instruction through its excellent faculty. Of the 1,892 full-time faculty, 98 percent hold the doctorate degree or the highest degree in their field of study. Many are nationally and internationally known for their research, distinguished teaching, and scholarly service to Kentucky, the nation, and the world. UK's scholars (students, faculty, and alumni) have been honored by Nobel, Pulitzer, Rhodes, Fulbright, Guggenheim, and Grammy awards, and most recently the Metropolitan Opera and the Marshall Foundation. Yet, with a student/teacher ratio of only 17:1, UK faculty are accessible and willing to answer your questions and discuss your interests.

"UK will accept either version of the SAT. The new Writing sections of the ACT and SAT will not be used in the admission process. ACT and SAT score requirements will remain the same as the new score will not be figured into the total score used for admission consideration."

SELECTIVITY

Admissions Rating	79
# of applicants	10,024
% of applicants accepted	81
% of acceptees attending	52

FRESHMAN PROFILE

Range SAT Critical Reading	490–610
Range SAT Math	500–630
Range ACT Composite	21–26
Minimum paper TOEFL	527
Minimum computer TOEFL	197
Average HS GPA	3.48
% graduated top 10% of class	23
% graduated top 25% of class	50
% graduated top 50% of class	79

DEADLINES

Regular	
Priority	2/15
Deadline	2/15
Notification	rolling
Nonfall registration?	yes

APPLICANTS ALSO LOOK AT

AND OFTEN PREFER
Transylvania University
Centre College
Miami University
Indiana University—Bloomington

AND SOMETIMES PREFER
University of Tennessee—Knoxville
Western Kentucky University
Bellarmine University
Eastern Kentucky University
University of Louisville

AND RARELY PREFER
Purdue University—West Lafayette
University of Florida
University of Illinois at Urbana-Champaign
Florida State University
The Ohio State University—Columbus

FINANCIAL FACTS

Financial Aid Rating	85
Annual in-state tuition	$7,096
% frosh rec. need-based scholarship or grant aid	20
% UG rec. need-based scholarship or grant aid	24
% frosh rec. non-need-based scholarship or grant aid	35
% UG rec. non-need-based scholarship or grant aid	25
% frosh rec. need-based self-help aid	26
% UG rec. need-based self-help aid	29
% frosh rec. athletic scholarships	2
% UG rec. athletic scholarships	2
% frosh rec. any financial aid	40
% UG rec. any financial aid	38
% UG borrow to pay for school	67.6
Average cumulative indebtedness	$17,692

University of Louisiana at Lafayette

PO Drawer 41210, Lafayette, LA 70504 • Admissions: 337-482-6457 • Fax: 337-482-6195

STUDENTS SAY ". . ."

Academics

At the "medium-sized" University of Louisiana at Lafayette—in "the heart of Cajun country"—many students feel "under the shadow" of their mammoth cousin, LSU. We really don't know why. UL Lafayette offers "serious bang for your buck"; tremendously generous grant and scholarship programs and out-of-state fee waivers make UL Lafayette one of the best bargains in the country. Programs in "education, computer science, and engineering" are "ranked as some of the best in the nation." The nursing program is the "third largest" in the country and "one of the best" anywhere. "Seasoned" and "overwhelmingly helpful" professors are "friendly, fun" and "honestly interested in having you learn." "The experience has been absolutely wonderful academically," gushes a senior. "In over 120 hours of course study, I cannot remember hav[ing] one bad professor." Other students disagree; they remember a "couple of bad apples." A perennial complaint among students at UL Lafayette is that many professors from other countries "cannot be understood by the students." The administration is generally unpopular. "The bureaucracy is ridiculous," reports a general studies major. "The university is run like an out-of-date chicken farm," adds a finance major. "No one knows the answer to anything" and "Getting financial aid in a timely manner is a real problem." Students are generally very satisfied, though. "My overall college experience at University of Louisiana at Lafayette has been terrific," asserts a junior. "I would recommend this college to anyone."

Life

UL Lafayette's "beautiful campus" is "full of big trees and handsome Southern architecture." Unfortunately, "It always floods when it rains," some "lousy buildings" "need updating," and the parking situation is just "painful." Nevertheless, "School spirit is really high." "Football games are huge events," and Lafayette is, by all accounts, a "great" college town. "Believe me," swears a wide-eyed first-year student, "it is an experience." The Strip "is right by campus" and "lined with numerous bars and clubs." "Most people," however, "congregate downtown," where it's "almost like Bourbon Street in New Orleans." The local music scene is hopping, and festivals are frequent, including a very large International Music Festival and a gigantic Mardi Gras celebration. If partying isn't your bag, or if you get sick of it, Lafayette also offers an "abundance of coffee shops" and "numerous art venues." "There is so much history and culture in Louisiana" that, frankly, it's hard to "ever be bored or without something fun to do on any day of the week," and you can find "great food anywhere." "If you're looking for a good, inexpensive college education that is packed with good food, cold beer, and excitement, look no further than UL Lafayette."

Student Body

Students at UL Lafayette are "friendly and fun" and "always seem to be in a good mood." They have "Southern flair with a little bit of our Cajun cayenne," a marketing major quips. They're also "very strongly rooted in their religions"; in that regard, "Catholic conservatives" seem to predominate. Many "are from the surrounding area of Acadiana," "lower- to upper-middle class," and "receive some financial support from [their] parents." Many also "have part-time job[s]." Beyond that, "There are many different types of people" and "Everyone seems to get along together." One undergrad reports, "Our campus includes a very diverse group of students from various religious and racial backgrounds." There are also "a few oddballs" who "try to get themselves noticed by the way they dress and their eccentric hair." For the most part, however, "Everyone blends in." "No one really points out or harasses other students here at UL Lafayette, unless that student happens to be wearing LSU paraphernalia."

FINANCIAL AID: 337-482-6506 • E-MAIL: ADMISSIONS@LOUISIANA.EDU • WEBSITE: WWW.LOUISIANA.EDU

THE PRINCETON REVIEW SAYS

Admissions

Very important factors considered include: Class rank, academic GPA, rigor of secondary school record, standardized test scores. *Other factors considered include:* State residency, SAT or ACT required; TOEFL required of all international applicants. High school diploma is required and GED is accepted. *Academic units required:* 4 English, 4 mathematics, 3 science, 2 foreign language, 1 social studies, 2 history, 1 visual/performing arts, 1 computer science/literacy.

Financial Aid

Students should submit: FAFSA. The Princeton Review suggests that all financial aid forms be submitted as soon as possible after January 1. *Need-based scholarships/grants offered:* Federal Pell, SEOG, state scholarships/grants, private scholarships, the school's own gift aid, Federal Nursing Scholarships. *Loan aid offered:* FFEL Subsidized Stafford, FFEL Unsubsidized Stafford, FFEL PLUS, Federal Perkins, Federal Nursing Applicants will be notified of awards on a rolling basis beginning 4/1. Federal Work-Study Program available. Institutional employment available. Off-campus job opportunities are good.

The Inside Word

UL Lafayette is still a fallback school for many applicants. You are pretty much guaranteed admission if you carry an ACT score of at least 18 and complete a basic college-prep high school curriculum with a GPA of 2.5 or better. If your numbers are a little lower, you can submit an essay and some other credentials for possible admission through UL Lafayette's Admission by Committee. It should be noted, however, that Admission by Committee is limited to 7 percent of each incoming class.

THE SCHOOL SAYS "..."

From The Admissions Office

"The University of Louisiana at Lafayette offers students from throughout the United States and more than 90 countries strong academic training and personal enrichment opportunities in a friendly, comfortable, student-centered environment. UL Lafayette students are taught, mentored, and advised by some of the brightest and most accomplished faculty members in the United States. Although UL Lafayette offers more than 100 programs of study and the research opportunities, internship possibilities, and facilities of a major research-intensive university, average class size is approximately the same as that at many high schools and smaller higher education institutions.

"UL students receive a good deal of individual attention and support—both personal and academic—from faculty and staff.

"A wide range of cultural, recreational, and social activities are available on and off campus, including more than 150 campus organizations and clubs, NCAA Division I and intramural athletics, a state-of-the-art aquatic center, a thriving arts scene, a wide range of live music venues, shopping, a great variety of excellent restaurants, theaters, the second largest Mardi Gras in the nation, and an international music festival. In fact, *Utne Reader* magazine selected the city of Lafayette as Louisiana's 'Most Enlightened Town.'

"Our relatively low tuition and generous financial aid and scholarship programs, including an out-of-state tuition waiver for qualified students, make UL Lafayette one of the most affordable universities in the nation.

"Students who have completed the required college preparatory core curriculum in high school may qualify for admission on the basis of a combination of their high school cumulative grade point average and ACT or SAT scores. Writing scores are not required."

SELECTIVITY

Admissions Rating	74
# of applicants	7,203
% of applicants accepted	70
% of acceptees attending	55

FRESHMAN PROFILE

Range ACT Composite	20–24
Minimum paper TOEFL	525
Minimum computer TOEFL	195
Average HS GPA	3.2
% graduated top 10% of class	14
% graduated top 25% of class	39
% graduated top 50% of class	72

DEADLINES

Regular	
Priority	7/20
Nonfall registration?	yes

FINANCIAL FACTS

Financial Aid Rating	60*
Annual in-state tuition	$3,402
Annual out-of-state tuition	$9,582
Room and board	$3,820
Books and supplies	$1,200
% frosh rec. need-based scholarship or grant aid	46
% UG rec. need-based scholarship or grant aid	42
% frosh rec. non-need-based scholarship or grant aid	6
% UG rec. non-need-based scholarship or grant aid	4
% frosh rec. need-based self-help aid	20
% UG rec. need-based self-help aid	31
% frosh rec. athletic scholarships	2
% UG rec. athletic scholarships	2
% frosh rec. any financial aid	87
% UG rec. any financial aid	72

UNIVERSITY OF MAINE

5713 CHADBOURNE HALL, ORONO, ME 04469-5713 • ADMISSIONS: 207-581-1561 • FAX: 207-581-1213

CAMPUS LIFE

Quality of Life Rating	74
Fire Safety Rating	73
Green Rating	93
Type of school	public
Environment	village

STUDENTS

Total undergrad enrollment	8,777
% male/female	50/50
% from out of state	16
% live on campus	42
% in (# of) fraternities	NR (13)
% in (# of) sororities	NR (6)
% African American	1
% Asian	1
% Caucasian	94
% Hispanic	1
% Native American	2
% international	2
# of countries represented	67

SURVEY SAYS . . .
Great library
Athletic facilities are great
Everyone loves the Black Bears
Lots of beer drinking
Hard liquor is popular

ACADEMICS

Academic Rating	74
Calendar	semester
Student/faculty ratio	16:1
Profs interesting rating	68
Profs accessible rating	70
% classes taught by TAs	17
Most common reg class size	10–19 students
Most common lab size	10–19 students

MOST POPULAR MAJORS
education
engineering
business/commerce

STUDENTS SAY ". . ."

Academics

The University of Maine boasts "a phenomenal engineering school" and notable programs in ecology, marine science, and forestry. "The campus is beautiful," says a sophomore, "melding scenery, history, and modernity." "The resources available through the library are quite staggering." There are also some "very fancy new labs." "It can be disheartening to see the beauty and grand scale of the engineering and science buildings, and then walk back to the buildings where most of your classes are held and see the lack of basic upkeep," gripes a history major. The academic atmosphere here is "challenging but not overwhelming." "Classes range in size from 20-200." "Professors can vary noticeably." There are "some rather dull professors." There are also plenty of "intelligent, kind, realistic human beings" on the faculty who are "quite flexible about meeting with and accommodating students." Some students say the top brass is "reasonable," "decently efficient," and "personable." Others see "layers of administration" and "terrible" management.

Life

Prepare for "bitter, arctic-like cold" and "a lot of snow" if you attend UMaine. Prepare for "unhealthy" food, too. "Ninety percent of it is deep fried or covered in a dairy-based something," protests a famished junior. On the bright side, campus life is active. There are "tons of things to do." "Musicians, comedians, and other artists" perform frequently. Sports keep many students busy. "Intramurals are great." The recreation center is "state of the art" and "hugely popular." Naturally, "hockey is crazy." "The campus is usually buzzing on game day," and the arena is "generally packed." Students are probably "too obsessed with the Red Sox" as well. "The party scene isn't too shabby." All in all, "consuming large quantities of cheap beer" is pretty common. There's a decent Greek presence, and, for some students, the frat houses are "the place to go on the weekends." There are also "house parties" and "a few local bars." More intimate get-togethers happen, too. "There's a tremendous amount of small-scale social drinking," notes a junior. The "rural community" of Orono "maintains that remote appeal" but it's "boring." "There is a ton of natural beauty around," though. "The extensive wilderness between campus and Canada" provides hiking, kayaking, and hunting opportunities galore. "Ventures to Sugarloaf are abundant."

Student Body

"Most of the students are Maine natives" or New Englanders. To put it diplomatically, the "minority percentage reflects that of the state." To put it bluntly, "this school is almost all white." "The typical student at UMaine is one who loves the outdoors, embraces the cold, is not too concerned with fashion, and lives in North Face or Patagonia clothes," reflects a sophomore. However, students report that you can find "every type of white person imaginable" on this campus. "There are tons of unique styles and groups that mix together." You've got "Carhartt-wearing, wood-chopping, straight-from-the-sticks, true-blue Mainers." There are "hockey rowdies" and "obnoxious frat boys." "There are a lot of hippies" and people who "care about the environment." There are "rare, wild-looking characters" and nontraditional students as well. The atmosphere is "relaxed" and "laidback." "People are friendly up here." Some students tell us that "out-of-staters have a really hard time." Others disagree. "The in-state kids will totally accept you," promises a junior. "An out-of-stater can be distinguished from a Mainer fairly easily," explains a junior. "They can't drive, dress inappropriately for the weather, or wonder why school isn't cancelled during a blizzard. But we get used to them, and eventually, just maybe, by the time they graduate, part of them is Mainer, too."

FINANCIAL AID: 207-581-1324 • E-MAIL: UM-ADMIT@MAINE.EDU • WEBSITE: WWW.UMAINE.EDU

THE PRINCETON REVIEW SAYS

Admissions

Very important factors considered include: Class rank, academic GPA, rigor of secondary school record, standardized test scores. *Important factors considered include:* Application essay, recommendation(s). *Other factors considered include:* Character/personal qualities, extracurricular activities, geographical residence, interview, talent/ability, volunteer work, work experience. SAT or ACT required; High school diploma is required and GED is accepted. *Academic units required:* 4 English, 3 mathematics, 2 science, (2 science labs), 2 foreign language, 2 social studies, 4 academic electives, 1 PE for education majors. *Academic units recommended:* 4 English, 4 mathematics, 4 science, (3 science labs), 2 foreign language, 3 social studies, 1 history, 4 academic electives, 1 PE for education majors.

Financial Aid

Students should submit: FAFSA. The Princeton Review suggests that all financial aid forms be submitted by March 1. *Need-based scholarships/grants offered:* Federal Pell, SEOG, state scholarships/grants, private scholarships, the school's own gift aid. *Loan aid offered:* FFEL Subsidized Stafford, FFEL Unsubsidized Stafford, FFEL PLUS, Federal Perkins, state loans Applicants will be notified of awards on a rolling basis beginning 3/15. Federal Work-Study Program available. Institutional employment available. Off-campus job opportunities are good.

The Inside Word

The University of Maine is much smaller than most public flagship universities, and its admissions process reflects this; it is a much more personal approach than most others use. Candidates are reviewed carefully for fit with their choice of college and major, and the committee will contact students regarding a second choice if the first doesn't seem to be a good match. Prepare your application as if you are applying to a private university.

THE SCHOOL SAYS " . . ."

From The Admissions Office

"The University of Maine offers you the best of both worlds – the excitement, breadth and depth that are available at a land grant, sea grant, research university with the personal attention and community feel of a smaller college. Five academic colleges and an Honors College offer you the chance to belong to a supportive academic community, while providing the specialization, resources and opportunities for research, internships and scholarly activity you would expect at a major university. Academics are a priority at UMaine; most programs hold the highest level of accreditation possible, setting UMaine apart nationally.

"And at UMaine there is always something to do – there are over 200 clubs and student organizations, lots of volunteer opportunities, an active student government, a new multi-million dollar student recreation center with an busy intramural schedule and Division I varsity athletics to keep you busy. A special First Year Residence Experience (FYRE) will help support your transitions to college – this unique program includes special activities and theme living communities. It is located between the new Student Recreation Center and the newly renovated Hilltop dining complex. Check out our web page to learn more – or better yet - come visit us in person and see the campus for yourself!"

SELECTIVITY

Admissions Rating	78
# of applicants	6,958
% of applicants accepted	77
% of acceptees attending	36

FRESHMAN PROFILE

Range SAT Critical Reading	480–580
Range SAT Math	480–600
Range SAT Writing	470–570
Range ACT Composite	19–25
Average HS GPA	3.12
% graduated top 10% of class	21
% graduated top 25% of class	52
% graduated top 50% of class	86

DEADLINES

Early action	
Deadline	12/15
Notification	1/31
Regular	
Priority	2/1
Notification	rolling
Nonfall registration?	yes

FINANCIAL FACTS

Financial Aid Rating	76
Annual in-state tuition	$6,690
Annual out-of-state tuition	$18,960
Room and board	$7,484
Required fees	$1,790
Books and supplies	$600
% frosh rec. need-based scholarship or grant aid	53
% UG rec. need-based scholarship or grant aid	46
% frosh rec. non-need-based scholarship or grant aid	4
% UG rec. non-need-based scholarship or grant aid	3
% frosh rec. need-based self-help aid	52
% UG rec. need-based self-help aid	52
% frosh rec. any financial aid	76
% UG rec. any financial aid	93
% UG borrow to pay for school	76
Average cumulative indebtedness	$22,630

UNIVERSITY OF MARY WASHINGTON

1301 COLLEGE AVENUE, FREDERICKSBURG, VA 22401 • ADMISSIONS: 540-654-2000 • FAX: 540-654-1857

CAMPUS LIFE

Quality of Life Rating	77
Fire Safety Rating	73
Green Rating	83
Type of school	public
Environment	city

STUDENTS

Total undergrad enrollment	4,117
% male/female	34/66
% from out of state	22
% from public high school	76
% live on campus	61
% African American	3
% Asian	4
% Caucasian	68
% Hispanic	3
# of countries represented	28

SURVEY SAYS . . .

No one cheats
Athletic facilities are great
Students are friendly
Great off-campus food
Frats and sororities are unpopular
or nonexistent

ACADEMICS

Academic Rating	79
Calendar	semester
Student/faculty ratio	15:1
Profs interesting rating	89
Profs accessible rating	89
Most common	
reg class size	20–29 students
Most common	
lab size	20–29 students

MOST POPULAR MAJORS

business administration and
management
psychology
English language and literature

STUDENTS SAY ". . ."

Academics

The University of Mary Washington is a public bastion of the liberal arts in Virginia. It's "not too big and not too small," and it offers "a private school education at half the cost." Students here complain loudly about their "slow," "unfriendly," and "very unresponsive" administration. Financial aid is a perennial gripe, although the school has embarked on a capital campaign with scholarships as a major focus. "Sometimes, I feel students could do better than they do," wagers an English major. As long as students here don't have to deal with the staff, though, they're pretty happy. There are "great research opportunities." The academic experience is challenging and intimate. "This is an undergrad institution so the professors are here for the sole purpose of teaching," explains a psychology major. "I like the fact that not a single class it taught by a teaching assistant," adds an international affairs major. "Most middle- to upper-level courses have fewer than 20 students" and "smaller class sizes help create closer relationships with faculty." There are some "run of the mill" teachers, but, for the most part, "the professors at this school are absolutely amazing." "Each one has their own quirks that everyone loves." They are "usually quite approachable," too. "Professors greet their students by names semesters after having them in class," observes a Spanish major.

Life

The Internet connection and the food are "both terrible" bandwith is increasing for fall 2008, but Mary Washington's "beautiful" campus "feels homey." It's fun to "sit on the benches all around campus and just socialize." "The atmosphere of our school is its greatest strength," relates a junior. "You don't get lost here." "Everyone can find a niche with great friends." Intramural and intercollegiate sports are popular, but "school spirit (in the artificial, beer-chugging, football-watching, pennant-waving sense) is not required." There are school-sponsored events, though they tend to "vary in success." "You need to join a club or sport or else you will go insane or go home every weekend," advises a junior. Luckily, "it is extremely easy to get as involved as your heart desires." There's no official Greek scene, and alcohol and drug policies are "hard ass and zero tolerance." "The drinking scene is predominantly run by sports teams." "Fake fraternities" routinely throw parties as well. However, get-togethers are small (typically "between 20 and 40 people") and, on the whole, "this is not a party school." For a strong contingent of students, movies and relaxed dinners are very common. Off campus, Fredericksburg's Central Park shopping complex is a frequent destination. The "quaint" downtown area is "gorgeous to wander around," too. There are "some cool local bookstores and such," but, mostly, the surrounding area is "designed for the older tourist." "Town-gown relations are awful." Some students spend their weekends "traveling to other universities in Virginia." "It's an easy drive to the mountains, the beach, or D.C." as well.

Students

"A lot of people will complain that we are not ethically diverse," says one sophomore. "But I think that the fact that we have such a wide range of political, religious, and sexual backgrounds here makes up for [it]." Almost all of the students are white and from upper-middle or upper class backgrounds." "There is a strong influence of the preppy" here. However, "students freely mingle with each other without regard to social standing," and they are quick to point out that "there's no real cookie-cutter Mary Wash student." It's "an eclectic mix," they say. "There is your typical preppy Polo- and Sperry-wearing guy and Vera Bradley-carrying girl, but there are also a lot of other types of people." "There isn't a push to just wear designer clothing." "If you walk on campus you are more apt to notice the preppy Southern girls walking around, but once you're in class and living in the residence halls you notice that everyone is pretty different," says a senior. "I absolutely loathe the idea that ethnic diversity is the be-all, end-all of diversity," agrees a sophomore. "There are so many people from so many different social structures and outlooks—ranging from hardcore neocons to pansy liberals to militant anarchists to theater majors."

FINANCIAL AID: 800-468-5614 • E-MAIL: ADMIT@UMW.EDU • WEBSITE: WWW.UMW.EDU

THE PRINCETON REVIEW SAYS

Admissions

Very important factors considered include: Class rank, academic GPA, rigor of secondary school record, standardized test scores. *Important factors considered include:* Application essay, recommendation(s), character/personal qualities, extracurricular activities. *Other factors considered include:* Alumni/ae relation, first generation, racial/ethnic status, state residency, talent/ability, volunteer work, work experience. SAT Subject Tests recommended; SAT or ACT required; TOEFL required of all international applicants. High school diploma is required and GED is accepted. *Academic units required:* 4 English, 3 mathematics, 3 science, (3 science labs), 2 foreign language, 2 social studies, 1 history. *Academic units recommended:* 4 English, 4 mathematics, 4 science, (4 science labs), 4 foreign language, 2 social studies, 2 history.

Financial Aid

Students should submit: FAFSA, institution's own financial aid form. Regular filing deadline is 3/1. The Princeton Review suggests that all financial aid forms be submitted as soon as possible after January 1. *Need-based scholarships/grants offered:* Federal Pell, SEOG, state scholarships/grants, private scholarships, the school's own gift aid. *Loan aid offered:* FFEL Subsidized Stafford, FFEL Unsubsidized Stafford, FFEL PLUS, Federal Perkins Applicants will be notified of awards on or about 4/15. Federal Work-Study Program available. Institutional employment available. Off-campus job opportunities are good.

The Inside Word

It's hard to beat small, selective public colleges like Mary Washington for quality and cost. The admissions process is very selective and, with the exception of preferential treatment for Virginia residents, functions in virtually the same manner as small private college Admissions Committees do. Students who are interested need to focus on putting their best into all aspects of the application.

THE SCHOOL SAYS "..."

From The Admissions Office

"The University of Mary Washington has long been known for its commitment to providing a stellar undergraduate, liberal arts education. Our faculty are devoted to teaching – without teaching assistants – and are able to provide individualized attention to their students. An education at UMW, with multiple opportunities for student research and service learning, prepares graduates for outstanding careers or for entry into graduate school. Internship opportunities abound not only in Fredericksburg, but also an hour's drive away in either Washington, DC or Richmond, VA. A wide range of programs includes strong majors in political science/international affairs, English, biology, psychology, earth/environmental science, history, visual and performing arts, economics, and business. Also distinctive are historic preservation and a new concentration in creative writing. UMW's campus is one of the nation's most beautiful, with classic Jeffersonian architecture, spacious grounds, and a park-like character. Historic Fredericksburg's 40-square-block historic district is walking distance from campus. Several large, modern shopping and entertainment complexes are nearby. UMW provides a variety of residential options, from traditional residence halls to modern apartments. Currently under development is a new retail and garden apartment complex next to campus. More than 100 clubs and organizations are offered along with a top NCAA Division III athletic program. The University will soon reopen Lee Hall, an expanded facility providing enhanced student services, a new bookstore, and "Underground" snack bar/coffee house. UMW students are bright, multitalented, and involved. The University environment is friendly and welcoming, and UMW places great value on diversity within its student body."

SELECTIVITY

Admissions Rating	87
# of applicants	4,475
% of applicants accepted	80
% of acceptees attending	27
# accepting a place on wait list	235
% admitted from wait list	84

FRESHMAN PROFILE

Range SAT Critical Reading	560–660
Range SAT Math	530–630
Range SAT Writing	550–650
Range ACT Composite	23–27
Minimum paper TOEFL	580
Minimum computer TOEFL	230
Minimum web-based TOEFL	88
Average HS GPA	3.67
% graduated top 10% of class	30
% graduated top 25% of class	72
% graduated top 50% of class	98

DEADLINES

Early action	
Deadline	1/15
Regular	
Priority	1/15
Deadline	2/1
Notification	4/1
Nonfall registration?	yes

APPLICANTS ALSO LOOK AT AND OFTEN PREFER

University of Virginia
College of William and Mary

AND SOMETIMES PREFER

University of Richmond
James Madison University

FINANCIAL FACTS

Financial Aid Rating	62
Annual in-state tuition	$6,494
Annual out-of-state tuition	$16,968
Room and board	$6,606
Books and supplies	$900
% frosh rec. need-based scholarship or grant aid	13
% UG rec. need-based scholarship or grant aid	12
% frosh rec. non-need-based scholarship or grant aid	11
% UG rec. non-need-based scholarship or grant aid	6
% frosh rec. need-based self-help aid	18
% UG rec. need-based self-help aid	21
% frosh rec. any financial aid	57
% UG rec. any financial aid	59
% UG borrow to pay for school	57
Average cumulative indebtedness	$15,000

UNIVERSITY OF MARYLAND—BALTIMORE COUNTY

1000 HILLTOP CIRCLE, BALTIMORE, MD 21250 • ADMISSIONS: 410-455-2291 • FAX: 410-455-1094

CAMPUS LIFE

Quality of Life Rating	**69**
Fire Safety Rating	**85**
Green Rating	**76**
Type of school	public
Environment	metropolis

STUDENTS

Total undergrad enrollment	9,304
% male/female	54/46
% from out of state	7
% live on campus	34
% in (# of) fraternities	4 (9)
% in (# of) sororities	4 (8)
% African American	16
% Asian	21
% Caucasian	53
% Hispanic	4
% Native American	1
% international	4
# of countries represented	95

SURVEY SAYS . . .

Great computer facilities
Great library
Diverse student types on campus
Campus feels safe

ACADEMICS

Academic Rating	**75**
Calendar	4/1/4
Student/faculty ratio	18:1
Profs interesting rating	68
Profs accessible rating	67
% classes taught by TAs	2
Most common reg class size	10–19 students
Most common lab size	10–19 students

MOST POPULAR MAJORS

computer and information sciences
biology/biological sciences
psychology

STUDENTS SAY ". . ."

Academics

Students agree that University of Maryland—Baltimore County "is a great school for scientific and information technology people" that boasts "very good programs in biology and mechanical engineering." Undergrads here find themselves immersed in "a science-y environment with some good departments and some not-so-good, but if you find the right niche you'll do fantastically." Provided, that is, you can survive the "discouragingly difficult exams" and "very strict and/or too harsh grading of papers and exams" typically encountered in the school's trademark disciplines. Students of political science and government benefit from the fact that "The school is located near Baltimore and is a train ride from DC, which opens up internship and learning opportunities. (One political science professor takes kids to embassies related to the class he's teaching every semester; I've met the Iraqi and Indonesian ambassadors to the USA.)" Students in the liberal arts, on the other hand, complain that "the school has no concern for us. All money in the school only goes to the Science and Tech department," which explains the "amazing technology" undergrads brag about. "There's a lot of focus on research" at UMBC, so "The professors and the library are a great strength" here. Professors "are required to do research in their fields, so they are always up-to-date on that material that they teach. Even if they are mean or difficult, they all know what they are talking about." The library "has a great deal of research assistance and access to a consortium of millions of books."

Life

"For the most part, campus is quiet" because "people take studying seriously," and "during the weekend many students go home." Add the large commuter population and the school's proximity to some attractive social destinations (downtown Baltimore, DC, Columbia) and you begin to understand why "it may seem as if there's nothing going on" on the UMBC campus. Students assure us that, perceptions to the contrary, "someone is usually having a party or get together" on or around campus, most frequently in the apartment-style residences. Undergrads also enjoy about "200 clubs to join such as dancing, bike riding, football and even juggling" as well as "the game room or the Sports Zone if a person just wants to relax." Mostly, though, students find their fun away from school grounds. The school sponsors "shuttle buses to go to the clubs in Baltimore, so it's great that they promote safety in regard to drinking and driving." Fells Point, a bar district near Baltimore's Inner Harbor, is a popular destination, as is the University of Maryland's College Park campus. All in all, this is not a highly social campus; "Everybody really dances to his own beat here," we're told.

Student Body

"There is no typical student" on the "very diverse" UMBC campus. "Everyone varies, from preppy cheerleaders and jocks to antisocial art nerds to normal human beings to religious fanatics to animal rights activists to overachievers to underachievers to foreigners to truly gifted kids to how-did-they-pass-their-SATs kids to druggies to good people and everything in between." The campus is also "full of nontraditional students who are married/engaged, have kids, and work." The Asian population is so large at UMBC that "Some folks describe UMBC as 'U Must Be Chinese,' but the majority are Caucasians, with minority Black/African-Americans, and a noticeable number of Indian/Pakistani ethnic groups." The student body tends to form cliques along lines of background and academic field; this is hardly unusual for a predominantly commuter campus (only about one-third of students live on campus, over half of whom are freshmen).

UNIVERSITY OF MARYLAND—BALTIMORE COUNTY

FINANCIAL AID: 410-455-2387 • E-MAIL: ADMISSIONS@UMBC.EDU • WEBSITE: WWW.UMBC.EDU

THE PRINCETON REVIEW SAYS

Admissions

Very important factors considered include: Academic GPA, rigor of secondary school record, standardized test scores. *Important factors considered include:* Application essay, recommendation(s). *Other factors considered include:* Class rank, extracurricular activities, talent/ability, volunteer work, SAT required; SAT or ACT required; ACT required; ACT with Writing component recommended. TOEFL required of all international applicants. High school diploma is required and GED is accepted. *Academic units required:* 4 English, 3 mathematics, 3 science, 2 foreign language, 3 Social Studies & History. *Academic units recommended:* 4 science.

Financial Aid

Students should submit: FAFSA. The Princeton Review suggests that all financial aid forms be submitted as soon as possible after January 1. *Need-based scholarships/grants offered:* Federal Pell, SEOG, state scholarships/grants, private scholarships, the school's own gift aid. *Loan aid offered:* FFEL Subsidized Stafford, FFEL Unsubsidized Stafford, FFEL PLUS, Federal Perkins Applicants will be notified of awards on a rolling basis beginning 4/1. Federal Work-Study Program available. Institutional employment available. Off-campus job opportunities are excellent.

The Inside Word

UMBC is an Honors College within the University of Maryland system; after the College Park campus, it is perhaps the most prestigious state-run undergraduate institution in Maryland. Selectivity is somewhat hampered by the school's inability to accommodate residents; about 70 percent of students commute. Even so, the densely populated Baltimore metropolitan area gives the school plenty of top-flight candidates to choose from. Your high school transcript must show a challenging curriculum (and success in your most demanding courses) if you hope to attend this school.

THE SCHOOL SAYS "..."

From The Admissions Office

"When it comes to universities, a midsized school can be just right. Some students want the resources of a large community. Others are looking for the attention found at a smaller one. With an undergraduate population of over 9,000, UMBC can offer the best of both. There are always new people to meet and things to do—from Division I sports to more than 170 student clubs. As a research university, we offer an abundance of programs, technology, and opportunities for hands-on experiences. Yet we are small enough that students don't get lost in the shuffle. More than 80 percent of our classes have fewer than 40 students. Among public research universities, UMBC is recognized for its success in placing students in the most competitive graduate programs and careers. Of course, much of the success of UMBC has to do with the students themselves—highly motivated students who get involved in their education.

"Freshman applicants for Fall 2008 are strongly encouraged to take the new SAT or ACT; however, the Admissions Committee will consider scores from the old SAT or ACT if no new scores are available."

SELECTIVITY
Admissions Rating	85
# of applicants	5,836
% of applicants accepted	69
% of acceptees attending	36
# accepting a place on wait list	263
% admitted from wait list	48

FRESHMAN PROFILE
Range SAT Critical Reading	520–640
Range SAT Math	560–660
Range SAT Writing	520–630
Range ACT Composite	22–27
Minimum paper TOEFL	550
Minimum computer TOEFL	220
Minimum web-based TOEFL	80
Average HS GPA	3.6
% graduated top 10% of class	28.3
% graduated top 25% of class	58.6
% graduated top 50% of class	86.1

DEADLINES
Early action	
Deadline	11/1
Notification	12/15
Regular	
Priority	11/1
Deadline	2/1
Notification	rolling
Nonfall registration?	yes

APPLICANTS ALSO LOOK AT
AND OFTEN PREFER
Virginia Tech
Johns Hopkins University
AND SOMETIMES PREFER
Virginia Tech
Johns Hopkins University
University of Maryland—College Park
AND RARELY PREFER
Salisbury University
St. Mary's College of Maryland
Towson University

FINANCIAL FACTS
Financial Aid Rating	79
Annual in-state tuition	$8,707
% frosh rec. need-based scholarship or grant aid	39
% UG rec. need-based scholarship or grant aid	37
% frosh rec. non-need-based scholarship or grant aid	8
% UG rec. non-need-based scholarship or grant aid	4
% frosh rec. need-based self-help aid	41
% UG rec. need-based self-help aid	42
% frosh rec. athletic scholarships	6
% UG rec. athletic scholarships	5
% frosh rec. any financial aid	87
% UG rec. any financial aid	73
% UG borrow to pay for school	53
Average cumulative indebtedness	$20,572

UNIVERSITY OF MARYLAND—COLLEGE PARK

MITCHELL BUILDING, COLLEGE PARK, MD 20742-5235 • ADMISSIONS: 800-422-5867 • FAX: 301-314-9693

STUDENTS SAY ". . ."

Academics

The University of Maryland—College Park is a major research institution and students see this as a mixed blessing. Undergrads gain exposure to world-class scholars doing cutting-edge work in their fields. Unfortunately, some of those same professors would rather be doing their research or teaching graduate students instead of delivering an introductory lecture to freshmen. One student warns, "These professors are paid to research and told they have to teach. Many of them don't have teaching degrees and obviously have no idea how to teach." While the problem is most pronounced in the sciences and mathematics, it is by no means universal; even in the aforementioned areas, students report some "amazing" teachers among the duds. Still, most here note that, at UMD, "You are responsible for your own education. No one will hold your hand as they did in high school." Some believe this "prepares you for the real world. You are a number, but that make[s] you try harder to stand out." Those hoping for a warmer and fuzzier education need not abandon hope, provided they can gain admission to the "living-learning programs—i.e., Honors, College Park Scholars, [and] Civicus," which all "provide opportunities for smaller classes and meeting people." College Park's many outstanding programs include the "amazing journalism program" and strong departments in education, engineering, political science, criminology, and business.

Life

The Big Three of campus life at UMD are "Greek life," "bars and/or house parties," and "football games"—both "tailgating and attending." But with "tons of things to do" here, there's more than just "a lot of parties" at College Park. According to one student, the campus "is like its own little town. We have a movie theater, tons of dorms, a huge gym, athletic fields, convenience stores, many restaurants, a bowling alley—all on campus!" UMD students also enjoy hundreds of student groups and an active intramural scene. While a student could easily fill his or her hours with campus activities, the more adventurous take frequent advantage of the school's proximity to Washington, DC, which students confirm "is not a boring city—it has a fantastic nightlife and a great subway/metro system. It's easy to get around." The city of Baltimore is also easily reached by rail. It's not surprising that many here feel that UMD's "location is a big strength."

Student Body

"The great thing about a big public university is that there's no such thing as the typical student," explains a sophomore. "Lots of Jews, Catholics, African Americans, Muslims—it's a very nice melting pot," confirms a junior. UMD's College Park campus also hosts "a good mix of returning [i.e., nontraditional] students" who "seem to add to the environment." Undergrads here report that "it's common to see students of every race and background in a discussion class." When classes are finished, however, "Many students socialize and interact" only "within their 'clique,' whether it be religious, cultural, etc." While it is impossible to define a typical student on a campus this large, undergrads spot the following trends: Maryland students usually have "tons of Maryland shirts, sweatpants, and hoodies," "were in the top quarter of their high school," and "take classes seriously," but also "love to support the football and basketball teams. They party pretty hard on weekends, but buckle down when Sunday comes."

FINANCIAL AID: 301-314-9000 • E-MAIL: UM-ADMIT@UMD.EDU • WEBSITE: WWW.MARYLAND.EDU

THE PRINCETON REVIEW SAYS

Admissions

Very important factors considered include: Academic GPA, rigor of secondary school record, standardized test scores. *Important factors considered include:* Class rank, application essay, recommendation(s), first generation, state residency, talent/ability. *Other factors considered include:* Alumni/ae relation, character/personal qualities, extracurricular activities, geographical residence, racial/ethnic status, volunteer work, work experience. SAT or ACT required; ACT with Writing component required. TOEFL required of all international applicants. High school diploma is required and GED is accepted. *Academic units required:* 4 English, 3 mathematics, 3 science, (2 science labs), 2 foreign language, 3 social studies. *Academic units recommended:* 4 mathematics.

Financial Aid

Students should submit: FAFSA. The Princeton Review suggests that all financial aid forms be submitted as soon as possible after January 1. *Need-based scholarships/grants offered:* Federal Pell, SEOG, state scholarships/grants, private scholarships, the school's own gift aid. *Loan aid offered:* FFEL Subsidized Stafford, FFEL Unsubsidized Stafford, FFEL PLUS, Federal Perkins Applicants will be notified of awards on a rolling basis beginning 4/1. Federal Work-Study Program available. Institutional employment available. Off-campus job opportunities are good.

The Inside Word

Many state schools make admissions decisions based on little more than the high school transcript and standardized test scores. University of Maryland is not one of these schools; the College Park Admissions Office also considers (in descending order of importance): essay, extracurricular activities, counselor/teacher recommendations, and responses to its short-answer questions. Don't give any of these application components short shrift; admissions are competitive, and each needs to be strong in order for you to have a decent shot.

THE SCHOOL SAYS "..."

From The Admissions Office

"Commitment to excellence, to diversity, to learning—these are the hallmarks of a Maryland education. As the state's flagship campus and one of the nation's leading public universities, Maryland offers students and faculty the opportunity to come together to explore and create knowledge, to debate and discover our similarities and our differences, and to serve as a model of intellectual and cultural excellence for the state and the nation's capital. With leading programs in engineering, business, journalism, architecture, and the sciences, the university offers an outstanding educational value."

SELECTIVITY

Admissions Rating	94
# of applicants	24,176
% of applicants accepted	47
% of acceptees attending	37

FRESHMAN PROFILE

Range SAT Critical Reading	570–680
Range SAT Math	600–700
Minimum paper TOEFL	575
Minimum computer TOEFL	232
Average HS GPA	3.90
% graduated top 10% of class	56
% graduated top 25% of class	89
% graduated top 50% of class	99

DEADLINES

Early action	
Deadline	12/1
Notification	2/15
Regular	
Priority	12/1
Deadline	1/20
Notification	4/1
Nonfall registration?	yes

APPLICANTS ALSO LOOK AT
AND OFTEN PREFER
Cornell University
AND SOMETIMES PREFER
New York University
AND RARELY PREFER
University of Maryland—Baltimore County

FINANCIAL FACTS

Financial Aid Rating	68
Annual in-state tuition	$6,566
Annual out-of-state tuition	$20,805
Room and board	$8,854
Required fees	$1,403
Books and supplies	$1,025
% frosh rec. need-based scholarship or grant aid	29
% UG rec. need-based scholarship or grant aid	27
% frosh rec. non-need-based scholarship or grant aid	24
% UG rec. non-need-based scholarship or grant aid	14
% frosh rec. need-based self-help aid	23
% UG rec. need-based self-help aid	26
% frosh rec. athletic scholarships	1
% UG rec. athletic scholarships	1
% frosh rec. any financial aid	67.8
% UG rec. any financial aid	59.5
% UG borrow to pay for school	42
Average cumulative indebtedness	$18,958

UNIVERSITY OF MASSACHUSETTS AMHERST

UNIVERSITY ADMISSIONS CENTER, AMHERST, MA 01003-9291 • ADMISSIONS: 413-545-0222 • FAX: 413-545-4312

CAMPUS LIFE

Quality of Life Rating	**62**
Fire Safety Rating	**73**
Green Rating	**82**
Type of school	public
Environment	town

STUDENTS

Total undergrad enrollment	20,114
% male/female	50/50
% from out of state	20
% live on campus	60
% in (# of) fraternities	4 (19)
% in (# of) sororities	4 (15)
% African American	5
% Asian	8
% Caucasian	73
% Hispanic	4
% international	1
# of countries represented	28

SURVEY SAYS . . .

Class discussions are rare
Great computer facilities
Great library
Students aren't religious
Great off-campus food
Low cost of living
Student publications are popular
Lots of beer drinking
Hard liquor is popular

ACADEMICS

Academic Rating	**70**
Calendar	semester
Student/faculty ratio	17:1
Profs interesting rating	63
Profs accessible rating	62
% classes taught by TAs	14
Most common reg class size	10–19 students
Most common lab size	20–29 students

MOST POPULAR MAJORS

psychology
biological and physical sciences
English language and literature

STUDENTS SAY ". . ."

Academics

It's all about "finding out where you fit in" at the large University of Massachusetts Amherst, where students say the experience is "all what you make of it: If you want to party, there is one available to you almost every night. However, it is not difficult to get your work done and be successful." A pre-law student notes, "[You] can just slide by, [but] academics are challenging if [you] wants to get all A's or [are] taking honors courses." Academics are especially demanding in the engineering program, the hard sciences, the sports management program ("one of the oldest and best in the country"), and at the Isenberg School of Management. As at many big schools, "It is easy to not go to class because they are so large, although many teachers now use PRS [a handheld wireless interactive remote unit] which quizzes you and is a method of [taking] attendance during each class." Unlike many major research institutions, UMass Amherst has a surprising number of professors who "show a passion for teaching. I have yet to see a professor who just teaches for money," a sports management major reports. By all accounts, "More than half of the professors are awesome." Students agree that "UMass Amherst has countless opportunities for one to get involved and improve his or her leadership and responsibilities."

Life

"There is so much to do on campus here that you rarely have to leave the school to find something," students report, pointing out that, in addition to attending one of the school's ubiquitous sporting events, "You can go ice skating on campus, go to a play, see bands play, see a movie, etc." Are you sitting down? "Most of these things are also free of charge, or available for a reduced fee." When the weather permits, "Numerous people are outside doing some sort of activity, whether it's playing catch, playing a sport with a bunch of people, or just laying out in the sun. In the Southwest Residential area, there is a horseshoe that people call Southwest Beach because on nice days it is packed with hundreds of people." If you're into parties, "There is something going on every night of the week somewhere." However, "It is more than possible to stay in on a Friday night, do your laundry, and watch a movie with friends. Parties are available, but not required." To clarify: "Drinking is big here, but not totally out of control like some say. Off campus is an entirely different concept. The townhouses and off-campus apartments have been known to hold parties of over 1,200 people. Those can be a little intense." Hometown Amherst provides "great restaurants and shows." Northampton and Holyoke, both close by, are "good place[s] to go shopping."

Student Body

"There is no such thing as a typical student at UMass Amherst." An undergraduate population of over 20,000 makes that impossible; however, students do seem to fall into a few readily identified groups. There are "plenty of students who are here strictly for academics," "people who are here for the party scene," and "a lot of people who came here for academics but fell into the party scene." Most learn to balance fun and work; those who don't exit long before graduation. Students also "tend to fit the mold of their residence," undergrads tell us. One student writes, "Southwest houses students of mainstream culture. Students there can be seen wearing everything from UMass—Amherst sweats to couture. Students in Central (especially Upper Central) tend to be the 'hippie' or 'scene' type kid[s]. Northeast houses . . . the more reserved types. Orchard Hill typically houses the more quiet types as well. . . . The kids in Sylvan are those who couldn't get into their first-choice dorm and "spend their time . . . wishing that they lived somewhere else."

UNIVERSITY OF MASSACHUSETTS AMHERST

FINANCIAL AID: 413-545-0801 • E-MAIL: MAIL@ADMISSIONS.UMASS.EDU • WEBSITE: WWW.UMASS.EDU

THE PRINCETON REVIEW SAYS

Admissions

Very important factors considered include: Academic GPA, rigor of secondary school record. *Important factors considered include:* Class rank, standardized test scores. *Other factors considered include:* Application essay, recommendation(s), character/personal qualities, extracurricular activities, first generation, geographical residence, level of applicant's interest, state residency, talent/ability, volunteer work, work experience. SAT or ACT required. TOEFL required of all international applicants. High school diploma is required and GED is accepted. *Academic units required:* 4 English, 3 mathematics, 3 science, (2 science labs), 2 foreign language, 2 social studies, 2 academic electives.

Financial Aid

Students should submit: FAFSA. The Princeton Review suggests that all financial aid forms be submitted as soon as possible after January 1. *Need-based scholarships/grants offered:* Federal Pell, SEOG, ACG, SMART, state scholarships/grants, private scholarships, the school's own gift aid. *Loan aid offered:* Direct Subsidized Stafford, Direct Unsubsidized Stafford, Direct PLUS, Federal Perkins, state loans. Applicants will be notified of awards on a rolling basis beginning 4/1. Federal Work-Study Program available. Institutional employment available.

The Inside Word

University of Massachusetts Amherst requires applicants to identify a first-choice and a second-choice major; admissions standards are tougher in the school's most prestigious programs (such as engineering, business, communications and journalism, economics, computer science, and sports management). It is possible to be admitted for your second-choice major but not your first; it is also possible to be admitted as an "undeclared" student if you fail to gain admission via your chosen majors. You can transfer into either major later, although doing so will require you to excel in your freshman and sophomore classes.

THE SCHOOL SAYS "..."

From The Admissions Office

"The University of Massachusetts Amherst is the largest public university in New England, offering its students an almost limitless variety of academic programs and activities. Over 85 majors are offered, including a unique program called Bachelor's Degree with Individual Concentration (BDIC) in which students create their own program of study. (If you are a legal resident of Connecticut, Maine, New Hampshire, Rhode Island or Vermont, and the major you want at UMass Amherst is not available at your public college, you may qualify for reduced tuition through the New England Regional Student Program.)The outstanding full-time faculty of over 1,100 is the best in their fields and they take teaching seriously. Students can take courses through the honors program and sample classes at nearby Amherst, Hampshire, Mount Holyoke, and Smith Colleges at no extra charge. First-year students participate in the Residential First-Year Year Experience with opportunities to explore every possible interest through residential life. The extensive library system is the largest at any public institution in the Northeast. The Center for Student Development brings together more than 200 clubs and organizations, fraternities and sororities, multicultural and religious centers. The campus completes in NCAA Division I sports for men and women, with teams winning national recognition. Award-winning student-operated businesses, the largest college daily newspapér in the region, and an active student government provide hands-on experience. About 5,000 students a year participate in the intramural sports program. The picturesque New England Town of Amherst offers shopping and dining, and the ski slopes of western Massachusetts and southern Vermont are close by. SAT or ACT scores are required for admission to the university. The school takes a holistic view of the student's application package, and considers these scores as only part of the evaluation criteria. Additionally, any Advanced Placement, Honors, and SAT Subject Test scores are considered when reviewing each applicant. Increased applications in recent years have made admission more selective."

SELECTIVITY

Admissions Rating	83
# of applicants	27,138
% of applicants accepted	66
% of acceptees attending	24
# accepting a place on wait list	426
% admitted from wait list	54

FRESHMAN PROFILE

Range SAT Critical Reading	510–610
Range SAT Math	520–630
Minimum paper TOEFL	550
Minimum computer TOEFL	213
Average HS GPA	3.48
% graduated top 10% of class	22
% graduated top 25% of class	58
% graduated top 50% of class	94

DEADLINES

Early action	
Deadline	11/1
Notification	12/15
Regular	
Deadline	1/15
Notification	rolling
Nonfall registration?	yes

APPLICANTS ALSO LOOK AT

AND OFTEN PREFER
Boston College
Boston University
Tufts University

AND SOMETIMES PREFER
Northeastern University
University of Connecticut
Syracuse University

AND RARELY PREFER
University of Hartford
University of New Hampshire
University of Vermont
University of Rhode Island

FINANCIAL FACTS

Financial Aid Rating	72
Annual in-state tuition	$9,921
Books and supplies	$1,000
% frosh rec. need-based scholarship or grant aid	45
% UG rec. need-based scholarship or grant aid	39
% frosh rec. non-need-based scholarship or grant aid	4
% UG rec. non-need-based scholarship or grant aid	2
% frosh rec. need-based self-help aid	45
% UG rec. need-based self-help aid	46
% frosh rec. athletic scholarships	1
% UG rec. athletic scholarships	1
% frosh rec. any financial aid	84
% UG rec. any financial aid	78
% UG borrow to pay for school	56
Average cumulative indebtedness	$12,062

UNIVERSITY OF MIAMI

OFFICE OF ADMISSION, PO BOX 248025, CORAL GABLES, FL 33124-4616 • ADMISSIONS: 305-284-4323 • FAX: 305-284-2507

CAMPUS LIFE

Quality of Life Rating	96
Fire Safety Rating	84
Green Rating	86
Type of school	private
Environment	town

STUDENTS

Total undergrad enrollment	9,997
% male/female	46/54
% from out of state	74
% live on campus	45
% in (# of) fraternities	14 (14)
% in (# of) sororities	14 (10)
% African American	8
% Asian	5
% Caucasian	48
% Hispanic	23
% international	6

SURVEY SAYS . . .

Great library
Athletic facilities are great
Diverse student types on campus
Campus feels safe
Everyone loves the Hurricanes

ACADEMICS

Academic Rating	85
Calendar	semester
Student/faculty ratio	12:1
Profs interesting rating	78
Profs accessible rating	81
Most common reg class size	10–19 students
Most common lab size	10–19 students

STUDENTS SAY ". . ."

Academics

University of Miami students are convinced that their school offers "the perfect blend of academics, athletics, lifestyle, culture, and weather." You probably already know about the "beautiful campus, fabulous climate, and unyielding sense of school spirit" at Miami, but are you aware of "the world-class faculty and innumerable research and internship opportunities across disciplines"? "Academics are the sleeper at UM," undergrads here agree. This "perfect-sized school" offers "a great communication program" as well as solid programs in biology, marine science, film, and business. In all areas, students benefit from "amazing academic resources and a variety of learning tools. Also, internships, internships, internships! Most programs require them now," ensuring that "students of all different fields get hands-on opportunities to gain experience before going out into the 'real world.'" Undergrads also note that "thanks to a low student/teacher ratio in most classes, you can build a relationship with your professors, valuable for future graduate school applications and resume references." While "some students come here merely to party and enjoy the city," others "are extremely dedicated," and are well served by a school "that is working hard to increase the value of the degree for its students."

Life

"Studying doesn't seem like such a chore when you're sitting outside under the sun on a 70 degree day in January," UM undergrads agree, noting with glee that "while students elsewhere are wrapped in blankets trying to stay warm, students at the University of Miami are enjoying beautiful weather year-round." It also helps that "the campus is absolutely breathtaking. I swear, each day I walk to class I have to remind myself it's college, not a resort. It makes it a joy to get out of bed and get to class when you get to stroll past the fountains and under the sun into the air-conditioned environment of knowledge. With patio sets at each school and library, there's no excuse not to open a book. Here we study and enjoy the weather." When it's time to unwind, students hang out by "the lake in the middle of campus surrounded by palm trees" or work out in "the state-of-the-art gym." Hurricanes football is a big draw, and "football season is crazy, especially our week-long homecoming celebration." There are also "lots of free activities" offered by the school. For most students, though, "Social life is primarily focused off campus, at Coconut Grove and South Beach, each filled with clubs, bars, restaurants, shops, and movies."

Student Body

University of Miami has a reputation for being "a rich kid's school," and it's true that "you will see parking lots filled with Beemers and Escalades and shoulders slung with Balenciaga, Louis Vuitton, and Coach and eyes shaded by Versace, D&G, and Chanel glasses to name a few." But it's also true that "University of Miami is one of the most diverse colleges in the nation. One will find all types of ethnicities, religious and political faiths, as well as cultural backgrounds" here. The Hispanic and Latino communities are substantial, and there are "many international students." As one student puts it, "Miami is like living in a public-service announcement: beautiful setting, racially diverse people, [courses] available in other languages. The average student is upper-middle-class, is at least bilingual, studies during the week and goes out Thursday through Saturday, complains about the freezing weather on 65-degree days, and knows how to snag a private study room in the library and what clubs to go to in South Beach."

FINANCIAL AID: 305-284-5212 • WEBSITE: WWW.MIAMI.EDU/ADMISSIONS

THE PRINCETON REVIEW SAYS

Admissions

Very important factors considered include: Class rank, application essay, academic GPA, recommendation(s), rigor of secondary school record, standardized test scores, extracurricular activities. *Important factors considered include:* volunteer work. *Other factors considered include:* Alumni/ae relation, character/personal qualities, first generation, geographical residence, racial/ethnic status, talent/ability, work experience. SAT or ACT required; TOEFL required of all international applicants. High school diploma is required and GED is accepted. *Academic units recommended:* 4 English, 4 mathematics, 3 science, (2 science labs), 2 foreign language, 3 social studies, 2 history.

Financial Aid

Students should submit: FAFSA. The Princeton Review suggests that all financial aid forms be submitted as soon as possible after January 1. *Need-based scholarships/grants offered:* Federal Pell, SEOG, state scholarships/grants, private scholarships, the school's own gift aid, Federal Nursing Scholarships, Federal Academic Competitiveness Grant Federal SMART Grant. *Loan aid offered:* FFEL Subsidized Stafford, FFEL Unsubsidized Stafford, FFEL PLUS, Federal Perkins, Federal Nursing, college/university loans from institutional funds, Private Alternative Education Loans. Applicants will be notified of awards on a rolling basis beginning 3/1. Federal Work-Study Program available. Institutional employment available. Off-campus job opportunities are excellent.

The Inside Word

The University of Miami's campaign to overcome its reputation as a "football school" is an unqualified success. Each recent academic year has seen an increase in applications and UM's selectivity is on the rise. The school partially attributes this accomplishment to its alumni and gladly repays them by giving legacies a boost during the admissions process. Of course having a 'Cane for a parent isn't enough; students must demonstrate achievement in arduous classes, intellectual promise, and strong moral character.

THE SCHOOL SAYS "..."

From The Admissions Office

"The University of Miami in Coral Gables, Florida, is an innovative private research university in a location unlike any other in the country. Located 10 miles from the vibrant international city of Miami, UM's over 9,000 undergraduates come from every state and 114 nations, allowing people of many cultures to challenge and champion each other. Faculty work closely with students, and internships and research experiences are integral to academic life. Students work hard as community volunteers and exert leadership in a range of lively clubs and organizations, including the student-managed TV station, radio station, and newspaper.

"The University of Miami will accept the critical reading and math scores from the SAT, as well as the ACT with or without the Writing component."

SELECTIVITY

Admissions Rating	96
# of applicants	19,676
% of applicants accepted	38
% of acceptees attending	27
# of early decision applicants	811
% accepted early decision	47

FRESHMAN PROFILE

Range SAT Critical Reading	580–680
Range SAT Math	600–690
Range SAT Writing	560–650
Range ACT Composite	28–31
Minimum paper TOEFL	550
Minimum computer TOEFL	213
Average HS GPA	4.1
% graduated top 10% of class	65
% graduated top 25% of class	89
% graduated top 50% of class	98

DEADLINES

Early decision	
Deadline	11/1
Notification	12/15
Early action	
Deadline	11/1
Notification	2/1
Regular	
Deadline	1/15
Notification	4/15
Nonfall registration?	yes

APPLICANTS ALSO LOOK AT

AND OFTEN PREFER
Duke University

AND SOMETIMES PREFER
Vanderbilt University
New York University
University of Southern California
Boston University

AND RARELY PREFER
Florida State University

FINANCIAL FACTS

Financial Aid Rating	78
Annual tuition	$33,018
% frosh rec. need-based scholarship or grant aid	46
% UG rec. need-based scholarship or grant aid	46
% frosh rec. non-need-based scholarship or grant aid	16
% UG rec. non-need-based scholarship or grant aid	13
% frosh rec. need-based self-help aid	35
% UG rec. need-based self-help aid	39
% frosh rec. athletic scholarships	3
% UG rec. athletic scholarships	2
% UG borrow to pay for school	56
Average cumulative indebtedness	$23,576

UNIVERSITY OF MICHIGAN—ANN ARBOR

1220 STUDENT ACTIVITIES BUILDING, ANN ARBOR, MI 48109-1316 • ADMISSIONS: 734-764-7433 • FAX: 734-936-0740

CAMPUS LIFE

Quality of Life Rating	85
Fire Safety Rating	60*
Green Rating	83
Type of school	public
Environment	city

STUDENTS

Total undergrad enrollment	25,916
% male/female	50/50
% from out of state	32
% live on campus	63
% in (# of) fraternities	15 (38)
% in (# of) sororities	17 (23)
% African American	6
% Asian	12
% Caucasian	66
% Hispanic	5
% Native American	1
% international	5
# of countries represented	117

SURVEY SAYS . . .
Great library
Students love Ann Arbor, MI
Great off-campus food
Everyone loves the Wolverines
Student publications are popular
Lots of beer drinking

ACADEMICS

Academic Rating	83
Calendar	trimester
Student/faculty ratio	15:1
Profs interesting rating	65
Profs accessible rating	71
% classes taught by TAs	39
Most common reg class size	10–19 students
Most common lab size	20–29 students

MOST POPULAR MAJORS
psychology
business administration and management
English language and literature

STUDENTS SAY ". . ."

Academics

University of Michigan—Ann Arbor, the flagship school of the Michigan system, offers a great balance of two very different college worlds—the huge state school with amazing athletics and social scene, and a strong, competitive academic environment. More than one student refers to what a pleasure it is to "bleed Maize and Blue," and "U of M's student body is known for its advanced wave technique during football games, as well as during Orgo I lecture." The engineering program "is one of the best in the country and it shows," and like a lot of big name state schools, there are "plenty of research opportunities." Michigan has a lot of humbling entry-level "weed out courses" (such as Calculus I and Econ 101), which "can be tricky because so many people are taking them," affecting the curve. "If you are one of those people like me who in high school could study at the last minute and pull it off, you will be in for a rude awakening at Michigan," says a junior.

Though a lot of classes are taught by TA's (called GSI's here), as "professors are always doing research due to the 'publish or perish' mentality," students are actually quite satisfied with the level of teaching they receive. Professors are very approachable and "willing to talk outside of class" and "make students take a mature approach to their education and take care of themselves." The administration "is very willing to work with students to make sure that everyone is satisfied with important decisions," and every single department and Dean has a student advisory board." Though a few students report of getting lost in the shuffle, U of M is "a world for the self-motivated," and if you want help, ask and find it— "it won't come looking for you but is always available."

Life

In Ann Arbor, "the college defines the city it's in," and it's "an amazing town. It's small enough to feel homey, but it has everything you could ever need." Movie theaters, "amazing cultural performances from around the world," dancing, parties, "great food," comedy clubs, pep-rallies, shopping, and much more means "there is no excuse for 'I'm bored.'" With over a thousand student organizations (even a squirrel club!) at the U of M itself, "there is a club for everyone at our school no matter what you are interested in." Football Saturdays are events unto themselves, especially home games, where the vast majority of students pack into the Big House (Michigan Stadium) for the game. There's also a sizable Greek following on campus, and "a lot of people that aren't in the Greek system still go to Greek parties," but "it's not the give-all-end-all of the Michigan experience." Add in the town's notoriously "liberal marijuana laws," and students say that "when it's time to party, we party hard. When it's time to study, we study hard." With practically every option under the sun at the students' disposal, life can be fast-paced and party-oriented or quieter and more studious, "it really depends on the student."

Student Body

While a majority of students are in-state, there are still a very large percentage of out-of-staters. U of M's size makes it so that defining a typical student is somewhat difficult, but most everyone is some combination of "a drinker, a liberal, a studier." "Everyone can find a niche here," so the school "is as big as you want it to be." The school itself stresses ethnic diversity (even though "there are a lot of white kids"), but many students stress its lack of socioeconomic diversity is almost as important, in that the lack of scholarships mean that "the student-body is way too affluent."

FINANCIAL AID: 734-763-6600 • WEBSITE: WWW.ADMISSIONS.UMICH.EDU, WWW.FINAID.UMICH.EDU

THE PRINCETON REVIEW SAYS

Admissions

Very important factors considered include: Rigor of secondary school record. *Important factors considered include:* Application essay, academic GPA, recommendation(s), standardized test scores, character/personal qualities, first generation, state residency, talent/ability. *Other factors considered include:* Class rank, alumni/ae relation, extracurricular activities, geographical residence, level of applicant's interest, volunteer work, work experience. SAT or ACT required; TOEFL required of all international applicants. High school diploma is required and GED is accepted. *Academic units required:* 4 English, 3 mathematics, 3 science, 2 foreign language, 3 social studies. *Academic units recommended:* 4 English, 3 mathematics, 4 science, (1 science labs), 4 foreign language, 2 history, 2 visual/performing arts, 1 computer science, 1 academic elective.

Financial Aid

Students should submit: FAFSA, CSS/Financial Aid PROFILE, noncustodial PROFILE, Parent and Student 1040. Regular filing deadline is 4/30. The Princeton Review suggests that all financial aid forms be submitted as soon as possible after January 1. *Need-based scholarships/grants offered:* Federal Pell, SEOG, state scholarships/grants, private scholarships, the school's own gift aid, Federal Nursing Scholarships. *Loan aid offered:* Direct Subsidized Stafford, Direct Unsubsidized Stafford, Direct PLUS, Federal Perkins, Federal Nursing, state loans, college/university loans from institutional funds. , Health Professional student loans. Applicants will be notified of awards on a rolling basis beginning 3/15. Federal Work-Study Program available. Institutional employment available. Off-campus job opportunities are excellent.

The Inside Word

Making the cut at Michigan is tough—and it is getting even tougher for out-of-state applicants, though the university definitely wants them in large numbers. There are simply loads of applicants from outside the state. If being a Wolverine is high on your list of choices, make sure you're well prepared, and since Michigan admits on a rolling basis, apply early! Michigan establishes an enormous wait list each year. Controversies surrounding Michigan's approach to affirmative action have resulted in significant changes in the manner in which candidates are evaluated, with greater emphasis now given to aspects of candidates' backgrounds that are not quantified by grades and scores.

THE SCHOOL SAYS "..."

From The Admissions Office

"Michigan is a place of incredible possibility. Students shape that possibility according to their diverse interests, goals, energy, and initiative. Undergraduate education is in the academic spotlight at Michigan, offering more than 226 fields of study in 11 schools and colleges; more than 150 first-year seminars with 20 or fewer students taught by senior faculty; composition classes of 20 or fewer students; more than 1,200 first- and second-year students in undergraduate research partnerships with faculty; and numerous service learning programs linking academics with volunteerism. Some introductory courses have large lectures, but these are combined with labs or small group discussions where students get plenty of individualized attention. A Michigan degree is one of distinction and promise; graduates are successful in medical, law, and graduate schools all over the nation and world. A year after graduation, more than 95 percent of U-M alumni report that they are in the "next step" of their career—whether that is graduate or professional school, working, or volunteering.

"Students applying as freshmen for Summer 2008 or later will be required to submit the results from the new SAT or ACT (with Writing component). At this time, it has not been determined by the university how the Writing sub score will be integrated into the school's review process."

SELECTIVITY

Admissions Rating	96
# of applicants	27,474
% of applicants accepted	50
% of acceptees attending	43
# accepting a place on wait list	2,067

FRESHMAN PROFILE

Range SAT Critical Reading	590–690
Range SAT Math	630–730
Range ACT Composite	27–31
Minimum paper TOEFL	570
Minimum computer TOEFL	230
Average HS GPA	3.72
% graduated top 10% of class	92
% graduated top 25% of class	99
% graduated top 50% of class	100

DEADLINES

Early action	
Deadline	10/31
Notification	12/21
Regular	
Deadline	2/1
Notification	rolling
Nonfall registration?	yes

APPLICANTS ALSO LOOK AT

AND OFTEN PREFER
Harvard College
Duke University
Stanford University
Brown University
University of Pennsylvania

AND SOMETIMES PREFER
University of Notre Dame
New York University

AND RARELY PREFER
Penn State—University Park

FINANCIAL FACTS

Financial Aid Rating	91
Annual in-state tuition	$10,922
Annual out-of-state tuition	$32,211
Room and board	$8,190
Required fees	$189
Books and supplies	$1,020
% frosh rec. need-based scholarship or grant aid	22
% UG rec. need-based scholarship or grant aid	1090
% frosh rec. non-need-based scholarship or grant aid	46
% UG rec. non-need-based scholarship or grant aid	1310
% frosh rec. need-based self-help aid	48
% UG rec. need-based self-help aid	1930
% frosh rec. athletic scholarships	2
% UG rec. athletic scholarships	82
% frosh rec. any financial aid	48
% UG rec. any financial aid	46
% UG borrow to pay for school	46
Average cumulative indebtedness	$23,754

UNIVERSITY OF MINNESOTA—TWIN CITIES

240 WILLIAMSON HALL, 231 PILLSBURY DRIVE SOUTHEAST, MINNEAPOLIS, MN 55455-0213 • ADMISSIONS: 612-625-2008

CAMPUS LIFE
Quality of Life Rating	81
Fire Safety Rating	60*
Green Rating	91
Type of school	public
Environment	metropolis

STUDENTS
Total undergrad enrollment	28,703
% male/female	47/53
% from out of state	27
% live on campus	22
% in (# of) fraternities	NR (22)
% in (# of) sororities	NR (12)
% African American	5
% Asian	10
% Caucasian	78
% Hispanic	2
% Native American	1
% international	2

SURVEY SAYS . . .
Great library
Students love Minneapolis, MN
Great off-campus food
Student publications are popular
Lots of beer drinking

ACADEMICS
Academic Rating	75
Calendar	semester
Profs interesting rating	70
Profs accessible rating	69
Most common reg class size	10–19 students
Most common lab size	10–19 students

MOST POPULAR MAJORS
journalism
mechanical engineering
biology/biological sciences

STUDENTS SAY "..."

Academics

The University of Minnesota is an "insanely huge" "research institution" "in the heart of" the Twin Cities. You'll find a wealth of majors here. Business is "superb." Engineering is strong across the board. The U is also "a great place to study an obscure language" or virtually anything else you can imagine. There are more than 300 opportunities to work and study abroad. Local internships "and hands-on opportunities" are also ample. "The professors run the whole gamut." "There are some amazing ones and some really terrible ones," says a civil engineering major. Some faculty members are "brilliant" and "inspired people" who "enjoy teaching the material and getting to know the students personally." Other professors "are knowledgeable but not always great at conveying the concepts." "There are a few who can really be GPA wreckers," too. Lower-level classes are full of "massive crowds of students." The teaching assistants who "do the dirty work" are frequently "from foreign countries" and "have really thick accents," especially in the hard sciences. "As your progress into upper-division course, the lectures rarely eclipse 100," though, and you have more interaction with real professors. "The administration really seems to care about the students" and "the U is run very well for a university of its size." Also, advising can be "beyond terrible."

Life

The "beautiful," "very environmentally friendly" campus here is "spread over two cities and a river." Consequently, "the ease of getting around campus is not the greatest." Also, "frigid," "crazy winters" are perennial. "By January, all you can see of students is their eyes," observes a sophomore. "The rest of them are wrapped in coats, hats, and scarves." "The snow is great for outdoor fun like sledding and ice skating" but "don't come here if you can't handle the cold." Socially, "the U has everything, plain and simple." You can have a "totally different experience than someone else." "There's a group for just about every interest," and "there is always something to do, even on a random Tuesday night." The campus provides a variety of events and "always has something going on during the weekends." "Hockey games are always great" and sports are a "big thing." "Partying is very popular but there are also a lot of people who don't" participate. If you want to imbibe, though, "keggers," house parties, and frat blowouts are frequent. There's also quite a bit happening off campus. According to students here, "Minneapolis is one of the greatest places in the country." "The music scene is unreal." "Great art" and "gorgeous parks" abound. "Shopping at the Mall of America" is another favorite pastime. In some areas, "it is scary walking around at night," but the neighborhoods near campus are generally "very young and energetic" and public transportation is "readily available and cheap."

Student Body

"Students are generally from the Midwest somewhere." More often than not, they are "right out of suburbia" or from "small to medium-sized towns" in "Minnesota or Wisconsin." There are a lot of "tall," "blond," "pasty, white people" who "are 'Minnesota Nice.'" "The U of M is a human zoo," though. "It's a school that embraces diversity." "There are a lot of different ethnicities." Some people are "snooty." Others "grew up poor." Some are "bubbly." Some are "antisocial." Also, "there is a microcosm for just about every subculture imaginable." There are "the math nerds," the "frat boys," and "lots of hippies and artsy people." There's "a huge gay population." "Preppy, athletic, emo," and nontraditional students are also visible. Politically, "the conservatives add a good balance to the grand scheme of things," but the campus leans left. Some students are "very politically aware." "There always seems to be some group protesting or trying to convince me of something," notes one student. Not surprisingly, "there is a limited sense of community" at the U. "It is too easy to get lost in the mass of people here, wandering among so many faces without knowing one," laments a forlorn junior. Sooner or later, most everyone "is able to find their niche." After that, "most people stick to their cliques."

FAX: 612-626-1693 • FINANCIAL AID: 612-624-1665 • WEBSITE: ADMISSIONS.TC.UMN.EDU

THE PRINCETON REVIEW SAYS

Admissions

Very important factors considered include: Class rank, academic GPA, rigor of secondary school record, standardized test scores. *Other factors considered include:* Alumni/ae relation, character/personal qualities, extracurricular activities, first generation, geographical residence, racial/ethnic status, talent/ability, volunteer work, work experience. SAT or ACT required; ACT with Writing component required. High school diploma is required and GED is accepted. *Academic units required:* 4 English, 3 mathematics, 3 science, 2 foreign language, 3 social studies, 1 history.

Financial Aid

Students should submit: FAFSA, institution's own financial aid form. The Princeton Review suggests that all financial aid forms be submitted as soon as possible after January 1. *Need-based scholarships/grants offered:* Federal Pell, SEOG, state scholarships/grants, private scholarships, the school's own gift aid, Federal Nursing Scholarships. *Loan aid offered:* Direct Subsidized Stafford, Direct Unsubsidized Stafford, Direct PLUS, Federal Perkins, Federal Nursing, state loans, college/university loans from institutional funds. Federal Work-Study Program available. Institutional employment available.

The Inside Word

Despite what looks to be a fairly choosy admissions rate, it's the sheer volume of applicants that creates a selective situation at Minnesota. Only those with weak course selections and inconsistent academic records need to work up a sweat over getting admitted.

THE SCHOOL SAYS " . . ."

From The Admissions Office

"The University of Minnesota is one of the nation's top research universities. That means your college experience will be enhanced by world-renowned faculty, state-of-the-art learning facilities, and an unprecedented variety of options (such as 144 majors). 83% percent of our classes have fewer than 50 students, and our caring advisers will help you find the courses and opportunities that are right for you and your goals.

"Hands-on courses, volunteer opportunities, internships, and research opportunities are part of the U of M experience. You will find one of the nation's largest study abroad programs, with 300 opportunities in more than 60 countries. You will find historic architecture, and breathtaking views of the Minneapolis skyline right on campus. With a wealth of cultural, career, and recreational opportunities in the Twin Cities, there's no better place to earn your college degree! The Twin Cities are home to 20 Fortune 500 companies.

"The University of Minnesota is a world-class, Big Ten research university. We offer a fantastic education and prestigious degree at a competitive price. Residents of Minnesota benefit from in-state tuition. Minnesota residents may also qualify for the University of Minnesota Founders Free Tuition Program, which covers 100 percent of tuition and fees for eligible students. Details and eligibility requirements are at Founders.umn.edu.

"Residents of North Dakota, South Dakota, Wisconsin, or Manitoba qualify for special reciprocity tuition rates. Students from other states pay only in-state tuition rates plus $4,000 per year. Last year, we also awarded over $9 million in 4-year scholarship packages."

SELECTIVITY

Admissions Rating	89
# of applicants	26,097
% of applicants accepted	57
% of acceptees attending	36

FRESHMAN PROFILE

Range SAT Critical Reading	540–680
Range SAT Math	580–700
Range SAT Writing	530–660
Range ACT Composite	24–29
% graduated top 10% of class	44
% graduated top 25% of class	84
% graduated top 50% of class	98

DEADLINES

Priority	12/15
Nonfall registration?	yes

FINANCIAL FACTS

Financial Aid Rating	82
Annual in-state tuition	$9,598
Annual out-of-state tuition	$21,228
Room and board	$7,240
% frosh rec. need-based scholarship or grant aid	46
% UG rec. need-based scholarship or grant aid	44
% frosh rec. non-need-based scholarship or grant aid	18
% UG rec. non-need-based scholarship or grant aid	15
% frosh rec. need-based self-help aid	43
% UG rec. need-based self-help aid	43

UNIVERSITY OF MISSISSIPPI

145 MARTINDALE, UNIVERSITY, MS 38677 • ADMISSIONS: 662-915-7226 • FAX: 662-915-5869

CAMPUS LIFE
Quality of Life Rating	82
Fire Safety Rating	60*
Green Rating	60*
Type of school	public
Environment	village

STUDENTS
Total undergrad enrollment	12,597
% male/female	48/52
% from out of state	34
% from public high school	70
% live on campus	26
% in (# of) fraternities	NR (19)
% in (# of) sororities	NR (12)
% African American	13
% Asian	1
% Caucasian	82
% Hispanic	1
% international	1
# of countries represented	65

SURVEY SAYS . . .
Great library
Great off-campus food
Everyone loves the Ole Miss Rebels
Frats and sororities dominate social scene
Student publications are popular
Lots of beer drinking
Hard liquor is popular
(Almost) everyone smokes

ACADEMICS
Academic Rating	74
Calendar	semester
Student/faculty ratio	19:1
Profs interesting rating	70
Profs accessible rating	72
Most common reg class size	10–19 students
Most common lab size	20–29 students

MOST POPULAR MAJORS
elementary education and teaching
accounting
marketing/marketing management

STUDENTS SAY ". . ."

Academics

The University of Mississippi (or "Ole Miss," as it is familiarly known) is an institution "steeped in rich traditions" that its students praise for having "great people, a beautiful campus, and a hospitable community." Familial connections and affection for the school's past (which includes graduating "numerous senators and representatives, among them Trent Lott, Thad Cochran, and Roger Wicker") draw many to Ole Miss, but that doesn't mean the school is content to rest on its history. On the contrary, in recent years the school has taken major strides toward "making itself one of America's great public universities." The 1997 establishment of the Croft Institute for International Studies, "recently ranked the second best in the nation by the State Department in the areas of job placement," represents one such step. Another was the 1999 creation of the Lott Leadership Institute; together the two resources "provide unique and challenging fields of study that help distinguish Ole Miss academically." Solid programs in journalism, music, accounting, forensic chemistry, engineering, pharmacy, premedicine, and Southern studies help round out the academic picture. Those who can gain access to the Sally McDonnell Barkesdale Honors College should take advantage of the opportunity; the program "is so strongly supported by the administration and alumni that you can literally eat dinner with 14 other honor students and a visiting senator, and then the next day go talk with a visiting ambassador about opportunities for working with the State Department. Honors College students receive many perks, including the chance to go on a 'ventures' trip to a major city, paid for by the Honors College."

Life

Undergrads at Mississippi are generally a content lot. As one student happily exclaimed, "The school spirit and pride people have at Ole Miss is contagious." Indeed, many undergrads view the university as, "a great Southern school with amazing traditions and great standards that knows how to have a good time." Popular traditions include pregaming in The Grove, "a social setting jam-packed with friends and families all bound by the same values of hospitality and friendship." An "extremely popular" Greek system is another tradition that hasn't lost any steam; for many undergrads, "Most all activities outside of class or studying are centered on Greek life," which includes not only "an enormous amount of drinking and partying," but also "being among the most involved and active people on campus." Hometown Oxford "may be small, but there is always something to do. Oxford has some of the best restaurants in the South. Also, Oxford gets great live music, poetry readings, and famous authors frequently. Lake Sardis is also nearby. Many people go boating on free days."

Student Body

Ole Miss is home to more than 12,000 undergraduates, a size that makes generalizations about the entire population difficult and necessarily imprecise. That said, students here detect an undeniable presence of "students who are pretty wealthy and take pride in that"; this group is personified by the "preppy girl or boy wearing expensive labels and going to school to follow in his or her mom or dad's footsteps." Sums up one undergrad, "Ole Miss students are charming and very social; it is as if everyone has been raised attending cocktail parties and debutante balls forever. We are primarily conservative White Southerners who are unashamed of our Southern culture and heritage who flock to the Oxford campus. Those who fit this mold love Ole Miss; [others] seem to view the Southern elitism as 'snobbery.'" This perceived snobbery may be at least a partial result of the fact that the school is "not very diverse."

FINANCIAL AID: 662-915-7175 • E-MAIL: ADMISSIONS@OLEMISS.EDU • WEBSITE: WWW.OLEMISS.EDU

THE PRINCETON REVIEW SAYS

Admissions

Very important factors considered include: Academic GPA, rigor of secondary school record. *Important factors considered include:* Class rank, standardized test scores. *Other factors considered include:* Alumni/ae relation, state residency, talent/ability, TOEFL required of all international applicants. High school diploma is required and GED is accepted. *Academic units required:* 4 English, 3 mathematics, 3 science, (2 science labs), 1 foreign language, 1 social studies, 2 history, 1 academic elective. *Academic units recommended:* 4 mathematics, 4 science, 2 foreign language, 2 social studies.

Financial Aid

Students should submit: FAFSA. The Princeton Review suggests that all financial aid forms be submitted as soon as possible after January 1. *Need-based scholarships/grants offered:* Federal Pell, SEOG, state scholarships/grants, private scholarships, the school's own gift aid. *Loan aid offered:* FFEL Subsidized Stafford, FFEL Unsubsidized Stafford, FFEL PLUS, Federal Perkins, college/university loans from institutional funds. Applicants will be notified of awards on a rolling basis beginning 4/1. Federal Work-Study Program available. Institutional employment available. Off-campus job opportunities are good.

The Inside Word

While Ole Miss offers students tremendous educational opportunities, the university's admissions policies are less than strenuous. Applicants who demonstrate moderate success in college prep curricula will most likely secure admittance.

THE SCHOOL SAYS " . . ."

From The Admissions Office

"The flagship university of the state, The University of Mississippi, widely known as Ole Miss, offers extraordinary opportunities through more than 100 areas of study, including programs such as the Sally McDonnell Barksdale Honors College and the Croft Institute for International Studies. UM students are the only public university students in the state who have the opportunity to be tapped by the nation's oldest and most prestigious honor society, Phi Beta Kappa. Strong academic programs and a rich and varied campus life have helped Ole Miss graduate 24 Rhodes Scholars, and 11 Truman Scholars. Since 1998 alone, UM has produced five Goldwater Scholars, a Marshall Scholar, and four Fulbright Scholars.

"The campus is diverse; 32 percent come from other states and countries and 13 percent are African American. Recent significant campus improvements include the $25 million Gertrude Ford Performing Arts Center and the privately funded Paris-Yates Chapel and Peddle Bell Tower. UM ranks thirty-third in the nation among public universities for endowment per student. Ole Miss is home to 20 research centers, including the National Center for Justice and the Rule of Law, which provides training on investigating and prosecuting cybercrime; the William Winter Institute for Racial Reconciliation; and the National Center for Natural Products Research.

"The university is located in Oxford, consistently recognized as a great college town and as a center for writers and other artists. Like Ole Miss, Oxford is modest in size and large in the opportunities it provides residents, offering many of the advantages of a larger place in a friendly and open environment.

"Students applying for Fall 2008 will be allowed to take either version of the SAT and are not required to take the ACT Writing section. The university will not consider the writing section of either exam when evaluating students for admission, but certain specialty programs may request these scores."

SELECTIVITY
Admissions Rating	60*
# of applicants	7,946
% of applicants accepted	83
% of acceptees attending	37

FRESHMAN PROFILE
Range SAT Critical Reading	460–600
Range SAT Math	460–590
Range ACT Composite	20–28
Minimum paper TOEFL	550
Minimum computer TOEFL	213

DEADLINES
Regular	
Priority	6/15
Deadline	7/20
Notification	rolling
Nonfall registration?	yes

FINANCIAL FACTS
Financial Aid Rating	72
Annual tuition	$4,932
% frosh rec. need-based scholarship or grant aid	24
% UG rec. need-based scholarship or grant aid	26
% frosh rec. non-need-based scholarship or grant aid	26
% UG rec. non-need-based scholarship or grant aid	24
% frosh rec. need-based self-help aid	20
% UG rec. need-based self-help aid	28
% frosh rec. athletic scholarships	3
% UG rec. athletic scholarships	3
% frosh rec. any financial aid	69
% UG rec. any financial aid	72
% UG borrow to pay for school	41
Average cumulative indebtedness	$19,183

THE UNIVERSITY OF MONTANA—MISSOULA

101 LOMMASSON CENTER, MISSOULA, MT 59812 • ADMISSIONS: 406-243-6266 • FAX: 406-243-5711

CAMPUS LIFE

Quality of Life Rating	86
Fire Safety Rating	81
Green Rating	89
Type of school	public
Environment	city

STUDENTS

Total undergrad enrollment	11,572
% male/female	46/54
% from out of state	27
% from public high school	44
% live on campus	24
% in (# of) fraternities	6 (5)
% in (# of) sororities	6 (4)
% African American	1
% Asian	1
% Caucasian	84
% Hispanic	2
% Native American	4
% international	2
# of countries represented	74

SURVEY SAYS . . .

Athletic facilities are great
Students are friendly
Students love Missoula, MT
Great off-campus food
Students are happy
Everyone loves the Grizzlies
Lots of beer drinking
Hard liquor is popular

ACADEMICS

Academic Rating	70
Calendar	semester
Student/faculty ratio	19:1
Profs interesting rating	68
Profs accessible rating	64
% classes taught by TAs	9
Most common reg class size	20–29 students
Most common lab size	20–29 students

MOST POPULAR MAJORS

education
psychology
business administration and
management

STUDENTS SAY ". . ."

Academics

You can enjoy both "the outdoors and a great education" at The University of Montana—Missoula, a school that "is whatever you want it to be. It can be hiking and fishing, tailgating at Griz games and dancing at the Foresters' Ball, earning a great education and experiencing new cultures abroad, or it can be a little bit of everything." While "Some programs are better than others," there are many standouts, including forestry, journalism, business, anthropology, creative writing, pharmacy, physical therapy, music, and premedical programs. Class sizes "are very small for a state university" and the professors, who "come to Missoula to give up the city and enjoy the mountains and outdoors," are "available to students outside of class. They are amazing." Administrators are also accessible; they "maintain contact with the student body. For example, the Dean of the College of Arts and Sciences teaches a seminar class in which the president of the university attends a Q & A session with the students." Opportunities for "internships, TA positions, and work-study jobs are easy to find," leaving students feeling "very prepared to enter the job market." Top candidates should strongly consider the Davidson Honors College, where "Students have a great opportunity for interesting classes and an effective environment."

Life

"While students at UM are serious about school," partying "is also a big deal," as "Missoula students are known for throwing some pretty huge parties, and we sure do know how to have a good time." There's plenty to do besides party, though. Most students "have at least one extracurricular activity. Whether it is theater, intramural sports, or a job, UM students keep themselves busy. Sure, there is a good amount of partying that goes on, but there are also lots of alternatives for those who don't want to participate in such activities." Missoula "has beautiful outdoor recreation opportunities" that, for many, are the school's primary allure. One student explains, "With all of the rafting, rock climbing, hiking, skiing, and fishing, anyone who loves nature will love UM." There's also UM intercollegiate athletics, with a football team "that has made four national championship appearances in 10 years and has won its division 9 years out of 10. Yeah, I'd say we play some pretty good football! Not to mention both our men's and women's basketball teams reached the NCAA playoffs last year; that wasn't bad either." Musical and cultural opportunities around campus "are also outstanding, with concerts, plays, and galleries almost every night," and downtown Missoula "has great restaurants and local shopping. Missoula is like nowhere else in the world."

Student Body

There are "two major group types at Montana." One is the "Carhartt-wearing rancher or logger type." The other is "the hippie type." There are others here as well, and "The beautiful thing about The University of Montana is that there really is no 'typical' student. Walking through campus one would see first a student with dreadlocks down to [his or her] waist and amazing handmade clothing and a minute later see a student wearing dress pants and a button-up shirt. Both fit in to the school and town equally." Most here "enjoy the mountains and being in Montana and have found a place to call their own at The University of Montana." They are generally "easygoing and not trying to fit into a group. People mostly do whatever." The typical student also "probably owns a dog." Undergrads do note that "although we celebrate ethnic diversity, most of the population is White. What we lack in ethnic diversity we make up for in intellectual diversity." Much of the racial diversity that exists here "is achieved through the exchange program."

THE UNIVERSITY OF MONTANA—MISSOULA

FINANCIAL AID: 406-243-5373 • E-MAIL: ADMISS@UMONTANA.EDU • WEBSITE: WWW.UMT.EDU

THE PRINCETON REVIEW SAYS

Admissions

Very important factors considered include: Class rank, academic GPA, rigor of secondary school record, standardized test scores. *Important factors considered include:* Extracurricular activities, talent/ability. *Other factors considered include:* Application essay, recommendation(s), SAT or ACT required; TOEFL required of all international applicants. High school diploma is required and GED is accepted. *Academic units required:* 4 English, 3 mathematics, 2 science, (2 science labs), 3 social studies, 2 history, 2 academic electives, 2 Choice of two units in foreign language, computer science, visual/performing arts, or vocational education. *Academic units recommended:* 2 foreign language.

Financial Aid

Students should submit: FAFSA, UM Supplemental Information Sheet. The Princeton Review suggests that all financial aid forms be submitted as soon as possible after January 1. *Need-based scholarships/grants offered:* Federal Pell, SEOG, state scholarships/grants, private scholarships, the school's own gift aid. *Loan aid offered:* FFEL Subsidized Stafford, FFEL Unsubsidized Stafford, FFEL PLUS, Federal Perkins Applicants will be notified of awards on a rolling basis beginning 4/1. Federal Work-Study Program available. Institutional employment available. Off-campus job opportunities are good.

The Inside Word

The university operates on a rolling admissions basis, and the admissions game here is relatively straightforward: Decisions are based largely upon numbers. Applicants who enrolled in a college prep curriculum and earned average or better grades should be able to make the grade—especially if they apply earlier in the admissions cycle.

THE SCHOOL SAYS "..."

From The Admissions Office

"There's something special about this place. It's something different for each person. For some, it's the blend of academic quality and outdoor recreation. The University of Montana ranks fifth in the nation among public institutions for producing Rhodes scholars, and *Outside Magazine* lists Missoula in its 'Top Ten Amazing Places for Outdoor Recreation." For others, it's size—not too big, not too small. The University of Montana is a midsized university in the heart of the Rocky Mountains—accessible in both admission and tuition bills—that produces graduates considered among the best and brightest in the world. It is located in a community that could pass for a cozy college town or a bustling big city, depending on your point of view. There's a lot happening, but you won't get lost. People are friendly and diverse. They come from all over the world to study and learn and to live a good life. They come to a place to be inspired, a place where they feel comfortable yet challenged. Some never leave. Most never want to. For more information, go to http:admissions.umt.edu.

"The University of Montana has adjusted admission requirements to reflect the Writing portion of the SAT. The new admission requirements are available on the UM website.'"

SELECTIVITY
Admissions Rating	74
# of applicants	4,855
% of applicants accepted	96
% of acceptees attending	46

FRESHMAN PROFILE
Range SAT Critical Reading	480–600
Range SAT Math	480–600
Range SAT Writing	470–590
Range ACT Composite	20–25
Minimum paper TOEFL	500
Minimum computer TOEFL	173
Average HS GPA	3.26
% graduated top 10% of class	16
% graduated top 25% of class	40
% graduated top 50% of class	70

DEADLINES
Regular	
Priority	3/1
Notification	rolling
Nonfall registration?	yes

FINANCIAL FACTS
Financial Aid Rating	69
Annual in-state tuition	$5,336
% frosh rec. need-based scholarship or grant aid	33
% UG rec. need-based scholarship or grant aid	38
% frosh rec. non-need-based scholarship or grant aid	3
% UG rec. non-need-based scholarship or grant aid	1
% frosh rec. need-based self-help aid	42
% UG rec. need-based self-help aid	47
% frosh rec. athletic scholarships	3
% UG rec. athletic scholarships	3
% frosh rec. any financial aid	82
% UG rec. any financial aid	75
% UG borrow to pay for school	71
Average cumulative indebtedness	$15,876

UNIVERSITY OF NEBRASKA—LINCOLN

313 NORTH THIRTEENTH STREET, VAN BRUNT VISITORS CENTER, LINCOLN, NE 68588-0256 • ADMISSIONS: 402-472-2023

CAMPUS LIFE

Quality of Life Rating	**90**
Fire Safety Rating	**71**
Green Rating	**71**
Type of school	public
Environment	city

STUDENTS

Total undergrad enrollment	18,053
% male/female	54/46
% from out of state	17
% live on campus	41
% in (# of) fraternities	15 (27)
% in (# of) sororities	18 (18)
% African American	2
% Asian	3
% Caucasian	83
% Hispanic	3
% Native American	1
% international	3
# of countries represented	117

SURVEY SAYS . . .

Great library
Athletic facilities are great
Everyone loves the Cornhuskers
Intramural sports are popular

ACADEMICS

Academic Rating	**72**
Calendar	semester
Student/faculty ratio	19:1
Profs interesting rating	70
Profs accessible rating	75
% classes taught by TAs	18
Most common reg class size	20–29 students
Most common lab size	20–29 students

MOST POPULAR MAJORS

psychology
business administration and management
finance

STUDENTS SAY " . . . "

Academics

The University of Nebraska—Lincoln, "a big university" with a "small-town feel," attracts its 17,000-plus undergraduates with a mixture of "academic challenge, pioneering research, vast extracurricular opportunity, overwhelming school spirit, and the best people you'll ever meet, anywhere." Oh, yeah, "and great football." UNL is large enough to offer some pretty unique programs, including a "very good construction management program," biological systems engineering, food science, and "one of the best actuarial science programs in the nation." The school also shines in popular disciplines such as journalism, business, psychology, animal science, and engineering; among the most prestigious options here is the "highly selective J. D. Edwards Honor Program in Computer Science and Management, where students live and attend core classes together in business and computer science topics." In all areas, UNL strives to "provide the best possible educational and career opportunities— including excellent research opportunities and a great study abroad program—to a large student body while maintaining a low student/professor ratio," all "on a limited budget." As at many large schools, students say that you have to grind through lower-level classes but, once you reach the upper-level curricula, "Professors truly care about their students and their academic success. They make themselves available and encourage students to take advantage of office hours not just for homework help, but so they can get to know their students."

Life

"There is basically something going on every day, every night" at or around UNL; "You just have to find it." The campus "is literally three blocks from downtown, where bars line both sides of the streets," and "The old-fashioned downtown, called the Haymarket area, is within walking distance and has numerous restaurants." And when Lincoln seems a bit slow, students know they can "head to Omaha, which is only an hour away. Omaha has the Qwest Center, which brings in names like the Rolling Stones and Dave Matthews Band." Campus life "is obviously centered a lot on the athletic department. It is amazing to see how students and outside fans react to the athletes," observes one student. Intramural sports "or maybe just playing a game of Ultimate Frisbee" is also "a big part of the average college student's life." The Lied Center, located on campus, "is another major draw, with performances from major symphonies to *Stomp!* being the norm." Although "UNL is a dry campus," there is still "a vibrant off-campus party scene, and finding a party isn't too difficult." Participation in a "great Greek system" ensures that students are not only alerted to all the "great parties" but are also plugged into UNL's service community.

Student Body

"The typical Nebraska student has the good ol' Midwestern work ethic, is White," "is fairly conservative and concerned about doing well in school," and "prides himself or herself on being 'moral.'" Many "come from religious Christian backgrounds." Students "who hold liberal views have a tough time completely fitting in with certain groups," but fortunately, "At such a big school you can always find people who are like yourself." That's because "even though a large portion of students come from Nebraska high schools, we have many nontraditional, international, and minority students. You will definitely experience an atmosphere of diverse backgrounds at UNL." There is a noticeable divide on campus between "the stereotypical fraternity/sorority, partying-every-weekend kind of people," who appear to be in the majority, and the "significant minority of people who really take school seriously."

FAX: 402-472-0670 • FINANCIAL AID: 402-472-2030 • E-MAIL: NUHUSKER@UNL.EDU • WEBSITE: WWW.UNL.EDU

THE PRINCETON REVIEW SAYS

Admissions

Very important factors considered include: Class rank, standardized test scores. *Important factors considered include:* Rigor of secondary school record. *Other factors considered include:* Academic GPA, recommendation(s), first generation, talent/ability, SAT or ACT required; ACT recommended; High school diploma is required and GED is accepted. *Academic units required:* 4 English, 4 mathematics, 3 science, (1 science labs), 2 foreign language, 3 social studies. *Academic units recommended:* 1 history.

Financial Aid

Students should submit: FAFSA. The Princeton Review suggests that all financial aid forms be submitted as soon as possible after January 1. *Need-based scholarships/grants offered:* Federal Pell, SEOG, state scholarships/grants, private scholarships, the school's own gift aid. *Loan aid offered:* Direct Subsidized Stafford, Direct Unsubsidized Stafford, Direct PLUS, FFEL Subsidized Stafford, FFEL Unsubsidized Stafford, FFEL PLUS, Federal Perkins, college/university loans from institutional funds. Applicants will be notified of awards on a rolling basis beginning 4/1. Federal Work-Study Program available. Institutional employment available. Off-campus job opportunities are excellent.

The Inside Word

Admissions Officers at Nebraska concentrate on applicants' course selections, GPAs, and test scores. Students who have had some success in the classroom make strong candidates as potential future Huskers. A few programs, such as architecture and engineering, have stricter requirements, so applicants should investigate the requirements for their intended fields of study before applying.

THE SCHOOL SAYS ". . ."

From The Admissions Office

"The University of Nebraska—Lincoln offers one of today's most dynamic college experiences. The university has developed a national reputation for its substantial out-of-state scholarship program. As a result, more students nationwide are finding that the university, with its strength in undergraduate education, its tradition of student engagement, its lively campus atmosphere and its connection to downtown Lincoln, is uniquely suited to provide an enriching student experience. The university delivers on the promise of the friendliness of a private college with major university resources. It is no wonder alumni stay connected years after graduating and thousands of miles from campus.

"Established in 1869, the University of Nebraska—Lincoln has a rich tradition of excellence. Students join more than 200,000 alumni who have made their mark as industry leaders in business, engineering, the arts, journalism, education, and the sciences. A degree from Nebraska opens doors. UN—Lincoln graduates recently interviewed on campus with major national companies like Abercrombie & Fitch, the Central Intelligence Agency (CIA), IBM, Microsoft, Sprint, Target, and The Washington Post. Attending UN—Lincoln also means you will have built-in connections with 116 graduate degree programs, including those in University of Nebraska Law, Dental, and Medical Centers located either on campus or 50 miles east in Omaha.

"Freshmen students seeking admission should either be ranked in the upper one-half of their high school class, or have received an ACT composite score of 20 or higher or an SAT total score of 950 or higher (Critical Reading and Math only; Writing portion not considered)."

SELECTIVITY
Admissions Rating	78
# of applicants	9,598
% of applicants accepted	62
% of acceptees attending	71

FRESHMAN PROFILE
Range SAT Critical Reading	500–650
Range SAT Math	530–670
Range ACT Composite	22–28
% graduated top 10% of class	27
% graduated top 25% of class	53
% graduated top 50% of class	83

DEADLINES
Regular	
Priority	1/15
Deadline	5/1
Notification	rolling
Nonfall registration?	yes

FINANCIAL FACTS
Financial Aid Rating	80
Annual in-state tuition	$6,315
Books and supplies	$950
% frosh rec. need-based scholarship or grant aid	36
% UG rec. need-based scholarship or grant aid	33
% frosh rec. non-need-based scholarship or grant aid	5
% UG rec. non-need-based scholarship or grant aid	3
% frosh rec. need-based self-help aid	30
% UG rec. need-based self-help aid	34
% frosh rec. athletic scholarships	2
% UG rec. athletic scholarships	3
% frosh rec. any financial aid	41
% UG rec. any financial aid	36
% UG borrow to pay for school	61
Average cumulative indebtedness	$19,075

UNIVERSITY OF NEW HAMPSHIRE

FOUR GARRISON AVENUE, DURHAM, NH 03824 • ADMISSIONS: 603-862-1360 • FAX: 603-862-0077

STUDENTS SAY ". . ."

Academics

The benefits of going to a large, well-established state school such as the University of New Hampshire are exactly what one expects—its low in-state tuition, firmly established reputation, and place in the system allows it to offer "many resources to help students out in life." Located in tiny, beautiful Durham, the school "emphasizes research in every field, including non-science fields," and a lot of importance is placed "on the outdoors and the environment." The small town really fosters "lots of school spirit," and the laid-back denizens of UNH make it known that "having a good time" is a priority in their lives: "Weekends are for the Warriors."

Most professors "truly care" about the students' learning so that "you never feel like a number at the school but rather a respected student," and they "will get down and dirty when it comes to experiencing what they're teaching first-hand." Though there are definitely complaints that some can be "subpar," a student "just needs to posses the initiative to go to their office hours" and they're more than willing to help. Some of the general education classes "are HUGE," and TA's can be difficult to understand, but for the most part, students report that they've had a "good experience" and their academic career has been "very successful." The Honors program is particularly challenging (in a very positive way) and offers "great seminar/inquiry classes that have about fifteen students so you can really get in depth." Students universally pan the administration, claiming it "is a massive bureaucracy that gets little done," partially due to poor communication, or "the left hand has no idea what the right hand is doing." "The school is way more challenging than I thought it would be because the administration makes things harder than they need to be," says a sophomore.

Life

Located in a town just "fifteen minutes to the beach, one hour to the mountains, and one hour to Boston," the world is a Wildcat's oyster. Partying is big here, and the weekends are crazy; "Everyone goes out pretty much every Thursday, Friday, and Saturday night." The small number of bars in town "makes the age limit pretty well enforced," so there are few underage drinkers at the bars, which means they "go out to the frats or off-campus apartments." After a hard night out, "there are many late night convenience stores and food places to go to." In fact, it can be "difficult to find activities to do on the weekend that don't involve drinking," though UNH does a good job of bringing in "popular comedians, musicians, bands, political figures, etc.," and the school has tons of "amazing" a capella groups, so there is "almost always something to go see." Sports are also big here: "We love our hockey and football," says a student. Though there's a pretty big housing crunch, the oft-used athletic and recreational facilities here are both convenient and excellent, and since everything on this "beautiful" campus is only about ten minutes away, "you walk pretty much everywhere," though public transportation and school-provided buses run often. Students do a lot of socializing over meals at the "eight cafes or in any of the three dining halls"

Student Body

This being New Hampshire, people are "very politically and socially aware." Students here are mostly middle class and hail from New England (especially from New Hampshire, naturally), and a main point of contention among students is that there "is not a lot of ethnic/racial diversity," though the school is working on it. The size of UNH means that "even the most unique individual will find a group of friends if they look," and even the most atypical students "fit in perfectly well." Most of these "laid-back" and "easy to get along with" Wildcats party, and it can be "hard to find one that doesn't." "EVERYONE skis or snowboards," and in the cold weather "Uggs and North Face fleece jackets abound."

FINANCIAL AID: 603-862-3600 • E-MAIL: ADMISSIONS@UNH.EDU • WEBSITE: WWW.UNH.EDU

THE PRINCETON REVIEW SAYS

Admissions

Very important factors considered include: Class rank, academic GPA, rigor of secondary school record. *Important factors considered include:* Recommendation(s). *Other factors considered include:* Application essay, standardized test scores, alumni/ae relation, character/personal qualities, extracurricular activities, first generation, geographical residence, racial/ethnic status, state residency, talent/ability, volunteer work, work experience. SAT or ACT required; ACT with Writing component required. TOEFL required of all international applicants. High school diploma is required and GED is accepted. *Academic units required:* 4 English, 3 mathematics, 3 science, (2 science labs), 2 foreign language, 3 social studies. *Academic units recommended:* 4 English, 4 mathematics, 4 science, (3 science labs), 3 foreign language, 3 social studies, 1 academic elective.

Financial Aid

Students should submit: FAFSA. Regular filing deadline is 2/1. The Princeton Review suggests that all financial aid forms be submitted as soon as possible after January 1. *Need-based scholarships/grants offered:* Federal Pell, SEOG, state scholarships/grants, private scholarships, the school's own gift aid, Veterans Educational Benefits. *Loan aid offered:* FFEL Subsidized Stafford, FFEL Unsubsidized Stafford, FFEL PLUS, Federal Perkins, state loans, college/university loans from institutional funds. Applicants will be notified of awards on a rolling basis beginning 3/1. Federal Work-Study Program available. Institutional employment available. Off-campus job opportunities are excellent.

The Inside Word

New Hampshire's emphasis on academic accomplishment in the admissions process makes it clear that the Admissions Committee is looking for students who have taken high school seriously. Standardized tests take as much of a backseat here as is possible at a large public university.

THE SCHOOL SAYS "..."

From The Admissions Office

"The University of New Hampshire is an institution best defined by the students who take advantage of its opportunities. Enrolled students who are willing to engage in a high quality academic community in some meaningful way, who have a genuine interest in discovering or developing new ideas, and who believe in each person's obligation to improve the community they live in typify the most successful students at UNH. Undergraduate students practice these three basic values in a variety of ways: by undertaking their own, independent research projects, by collaborating in faculty research, and by participating in study abroad, residential communities, community service, and other cultural programs.

"University of New Hampshire will require all high school graduates to submit results from the new SAT or the ACT (with the Writing component). The Writing portions will not be used for admissions decisions during the first 2–3 admissions cycles. Students graduating from high school prior to 2006 can submit results from the 'old' SAT or ACT. The UNH admissions process does not require SAT Subject tests."

SELECTIVITY

Admissions Rating	81
# of applicants	14,382
% of applicants accepted	59
% of acceptees attending	31

FRESHMAN PROFILE

Range SAT Critical Reading	500–610
Range SAT Math	510–620
Minimum paper TOEFL	550
Minimum computer TOEFL	213
Minimum web-based TOEFL	80
% graduated top 10% of class	24
% graduated top 25% of class	66
% graduated top 50% of class	98

DEADLINES

Early action	
Deadline	11/1
Notification	1/1
Regular	
Deadline	2/1
Notification	4/15
Nonfall registration?	yes

APPLICANTS ALSO LOOK AT

AND OFTEN PREFER
University of Connecticut
University of Vermont
University of Massachusetts—Amherst

AND SOMETIMES PREFER
Northeastern University
Boston University
Providence College
University of Rhode Island

AND RARELY PREFER
Boston College
University of Maine
Syracuse University

FINANCIAL FACTS

Financial Aid Rating	74
Annual in-state tuition	$8,810
Annual out-of-state tuition	$21,770
Room and board	$8,168
Required fees	$2,260
Books and supplies	$1,400
% frosh rec. need-based scholarship or grant aid	55
% UG rec. need-based scholarship or grant aid	63
% frosh rec. non-need-based scholarship or grant aid	44
% UG rec. non-need-based scholarship or grant aid	40
% frosh rec. need-based self-help aid	54
% UG rec. need-based self-help aid	62
% frosh rec. athletic scholarships	2
% UG rec. athletic scholarships	2
% frosh rec. any financial aid	83
% UG rec. any financial aid	80
% UG borrow to pay for school	75
Average cumulative indebtedness	$25,145

UNIVERSITY OF NEW MEXICO

OFFICE OF ADMISSIONS, PO BOX 4895, ALBUQUERQUE, NM 87196-4895 • ADMISSIONS: 505-277-2446 • FAX: 505-277-6686

CAMPUS LIFE
Quality of Life Rating	**71**
Fire Safety Rating	**70**
Green Rating	**60***
Type of school	public
Environment	metropolis

STUDENTS
Total undergrad enrollment	18,330
% male/female	42/58
% from out of state	21
% live on campus	8
% in (# of) fraternities	3 (9)
% in (# of) sororities	3 (10)
% African American	3
% Asian	4
% Caucasian	46
% Hispanic	35
% Native American	6
% international	1
# of countries represented	102

SURVEY SAYS . . .
Great computer facilities
Great library
Diverse student types on campus
Great off-campus food
Everyone loves the Lobos
Student publications are popular
Lots of beer drinking
(Almost) everyone smokes

ACADEMICS
Academic Rating	**70**
Calendar	semester
Student/faculty ratio	20:1
Profs interesting rating	62
Profs accessible rating	61
Most common reg class size	20–29 students
Most common lab size	10–19 students

MOST POPULAR MAJORS
biology/biological sciences
psychology
business administration and management

STUDENTS SAY "..."

Academics

The University of New Mexico "offers a strong academic community with all of its many research opportunities [for] a bargain price," students at this large state university tell us. Excellent graduate programs in law, business, and medicine exert a trickle-down effect on the undergraduate divisions. Explains one undergrad, "We have one of the top 10 law schools and medical schools in the nation right now, and the undergraduate programs that lead into those schools want to make sure that at least some of their students get accepted and decide to attend one of these graduate programs." Students also praise UNM's offerings in pharmacy, psychology, architecture, anthropology, engineering, and sociology. With this many options, "Even if you don't know what you want, you are bound to find something that you love." Students may find that something through UNM's interesting freshman-year options, which include courses designed to get students up to speed in writing, math, and research skills; freshman learning communities, a pair of team-taught interdisciplinary classes; and freshman interest groups, theme-based seminars that allow students to delve a little deeper into one of their core curriculum requirements. For top-ranked students, UNM's University Honors Program places students in small, seminar-style classes with an intensive focus on writing and reading.

Life

"Campus life can be as full of activities as one wants it to be" at UNM. A large student population means there are always plenty of extracurricular options. Sizeable commuter and nontraditional populations, on the other hand, ensure that many students aren't interested in them, as they visit campus only to attend classes. Commuters do appreciate the university's addition of a new Student Union building, "with three floors that include a movie theater, pool tables, computer labs, art studios, tons of food options, and many ballrooms and conference rooms. Lots of students hang out in the SUB in between classes." For residents and those who live close by, "There is always something going on, whether it's a dance show, a movie on the field, a cultural event, a sporting event, or any other casual activity. There are also a lot of opportunities for community service projects and political activism." Everyone gets behind UNM's "amazing athletics," embraced as enthusiastically by the city of Albuquerque as by UNM students. Basketball has a huge fan base here, while football draws tailgaters regardless of the quality of the team. Because UNM's campus is officially dry, "Many students choose to go to local bars and downtown Albuquerque where there are many bars in one area" to socialize. Most students agree that there's much fun to be had in Albuquerque, "a fairly large city with frequent cultural activities (Zozobra, Balloon Fiesta, State Fair) that are really fun and interesting, especially if you are from out of state and haven't experienced them before."

Student Body

"UNM has students from all walks of life," which isn't so surprising given its undergraduate population of nearly 20,000. Many are nontraditional, are "roughly 25 years old, approach studies from a very practical perspective, and work a full-time job or close to it to pay for school." One undergrad observes, "Because of its many nontraditional students, the school can sometimes feel too old or too young. UNM needs to work on integrating all students and finding activities that allow all age groups to interact" (though any such efforts may be hampered by the fact that "most students are commuters, who are solely focused on earning their degree"). With "many Hispanic, Native American, Anglo, and other students," UNM is "extremely diverse." Notes one student, "There are so many different ethnicities here that racial discrimination really isn't an issue."

FINANCIAL AID: 505-277-2041 • E-MAIL: APPLY@UNM.EDU • WEBSITE: WWW.UNM.EDU

THE PRINCETON REVIEW SAYS

Admissions

Very important factors considered include: Academic GPA, rigor of secondary school record. *Important factors considered include:* Class rank, standardized test scores. *Other factors considered include:* Application essay, recommendation(s), character/personal qualities, extracurricular activities, first generation, volunteer work, work experience. SAT or ACT required; ACT with Writing component recommended. TOEFL required of all international applicants. High school diploma is required and GED is accepted. *Academic units required:* 4 English, 3 mathematics, 2 science, (1 science labs), 2 foreign language, 1 social studies, 1 history.

Financial Aid

Students should submit: FAFSA. The Princeton Review suggests that all financial aid forms be submitted as soon as possible after January 1. *Need-based scholarships/grants offered:* Federal Pell, SEOG, state scholarships/grants, private scholarships, the school's own gift aid, United Negro College Fund, Federal Nursing Scholarships. *Loan aid offered:* Direct Subsidized Stafford, Direct Unsubsidized Stafford, Direct PLUS, Federal Perkins, Federal Nursing, state loans, college/university loans from institutional funds. Applicants will be notified of awards on a rolling basis beginning 4/15. Federal Work-Study Program available.

The Inside Word

UNM's rolling admissions process is quite typical of large public universities. Consideration is based nearly entirely on courses, grades, and test scores, though recommendations can sometimes help a candidate. Solid average students should encounter no difficulty in gaining an offer of admission.

THE SCHOOL SAYS " . . ."

From The Admissions Office

"The University of New Mexico is a major research institution nestled in the heart of multicultural Albuquerque on one of the nation's most beautiful and unique campuses. Students learn in an environment graced by distinctive Southwestern architecture, beautiful plazas and fountains, spectacular art and a national arboretum . . . all within view of the 10,000-foot Sandia Mountains. At UNM, diversity is a way of learning with education enriched by a lively mix of students being taught by a world-class research faculty that includes a Nobel laureate, a MacArthur Fellow, and members of several national academies. UNM offers more than 225 degree programs and majors and has earned national recognition in dozens of disciplines, ranging from primary care medicine and clinical law to engineering, photography, Latin American history, and intercultural communications. Research and the quest for new knowledge fuels the university's commitment to an undergraduate education where students work side by side with many of the finest scholars in their fields.

"The university will continue to accept SAT or ACT scores, but does not require the Writing component at this time. The SAT Critical Reading portion will be used with the SAT Math to be considered in any admission decision based on formula. The use of ACT composite remains unchanged. These requirements are subject to change."

SELECTIVITY

Admissions Rating	78
# of applicants	7,134
% of applicants accepted	74
% of acceptees attending	59

FRESHMAN PROFILE

Range SAT Critical Reading	470–600
Range SAT Math	470–590
Range ACT Composite	19–25
Minimum paper TOEFL	520
Minimum computer TOEFL	190
Minimum web-based TOEFL	68
Average HS GPA	3.33
% graduated top 10% of class	21
% graduated top 25% of class	45
% graduated top 50% of class	79

DEADLINES

Regular	
Deadline	6/15
Nonfall registration?	yes

FINANCIAL FACTS

Financial Aid Rating	60*
Annual in-state tuition	$6,094
Annual out-of-state tuition	$19,923

UNIVERSITY OF NEW ORLEANS

AD 103, LAKEFRONT, NEW ORLEANS, LA 70148 • ADMISSIONS: 504-280-6595 • FAX: 504-280-5522

CAMPUS LIFE
Quality of Life Rating	64
Fire Safety Rating	60*
Green Rating	60*
Type of school	public
Environment	metropolis

STUDENTS
Total undergrad enrollment	8,653
% male/female	47/53
% from out of state	5
% from public high school	62
% live on campus	5
% in (# of) fraternities	1 (8)
% in (# of) sororities	1 (8)
% African American	20
% Asian	6
% Caucasian	60
% Hispanic	7
% Native American	1
% international	3
# of countries represented	85

SURVEY SAYS . . .
Large classes
Great computer facilities
Great library
Athletic facilities are great
Diverse student types on campus
Students get along with local community
(Almost) everyone smokes

ACADEMICS
Academic Rating	70
Calendar	semester
Student/faculty ratio	18:1
Profs interesting rating	66
Profs accessible rating	66
% classes taught by TAs	5
Most common reg class size	10–19 students

MOST POPULAR MAJORS
general studies
business administration and management
communication studies/speech
communication and rhetoric

STUDENTS SAY "..."

Academics

The University of New Orleans is "recovering at a snail's pace since Hurricane Katrina," but continues to provide "an equal opportunity for all people to get a superior education at an affordable price." You'll find a "diverse community of students" and "some of the best academics in the country." Classes are "challenging," "rewarding," and "offered at a variety of times, so it is easier for working students to attend class," but there are few bells and whistles. UNO "is geared to get students an education and doesn't fool around with extras." While "It is easy to get in" to UNO, it can be "hard to get out." "Classes are not easy." "UNO is for hard workers," a computer science major asserts. "It isn't an escalator for rich people to send their spoiled kids like the other schools in New Orleans." Faculty members are "accessible," "dedicated," and "extremely knowledgeable." They "have had extensive careers" and retain "good connections to the real world." Students note, however, that the bad professors are "really bad." Also, "since the hurricane," UNO has shut down "many programs," and many academic services "are only a fraction of what they were." UNO still excels in many areas including engineering and naval architecture. Business and hotel, restaurant, and tourism administration are strong as well. There is also a "great jazz program."

Life

"Hurricane Katrina has left our campus a mess," warns a junior. "UNO is getting back to normal, but it will be awhile before it will get better." "Areas of campus are still not rebuilt" and the campus was "a hideous sprawl" even before the storm. While "More people are living on campus" now, UNO remains "primarily a commuter campus." Students here are "almost completely focused on academics." Generally, when classes end, students "leave ASAP." "Job opportunities for college students are pretty good" and "Most students work either full- or part-time." "The overall experience at UNO is a very independent one," an English major reports. "There are clubs and organizations in which to be involved," but "It is hard to get people involved in extracurricular activities." "If you want a college life, you must join a fraternity or sorority or some type of group on campus," a business major ventures. On the plus side, UNO boasts a "world-class" gym, and, of course, the "amazing" city of New Orleans is still brimming "with a lot of opportunity." "It's New Orleans. My god!" exclaims a junior. The campus is "less than 10 minutes to the French Quarter." "There's so much to do" and the food "is unmatched anywhere." "We live in a city that is immersed in culture and entertainment, so fun is not too hard to find," says a senior. "You can find an open bar at any time of any day, but it isn't impossible to find a quiet spot and work out some math."

Student Body

UNO boasts "an eclectic assortment of students" who are "very serious" about academics, yet "very friendly." "Many different ethnic and social backgrounds" are represented here and it's definitely not "a regular 'all-American' college." "Because the school is a commuter school, the student population is made up mostly of local folks," observes an anthropology major. "But that doesn't stop the school from being extremely diverse." "Classmates range from high school grads to grandparents." "It's just a big gumbo of people," a sophomore writes. "The typical student" at UNO is probably "mid-20s, working full- or part-time while attending classes, [and] living off-campus in New Orleans." "I think the typical student at UNO is one who is excited to be in college, often entering or returning to college after spending some time in the workforce," a political science major reports. Many students are "married, have kids, and live in the suburbs" and many are "making a second or third try at college." In recent years, though, "the contingency of on-campus, fresh-out-of-high-schoolers" has grown by "leaps and bounds."

Financial Aid: 504-280-6603 • E-mail: admissions@uno.edu • Website: www.uno.edu

THE PRINCETON REVIEW SAYS

Admissions

Very important factors considered include: Class rank, academic GPA, rigor of secondary school record, standardized test scores. *Other factors considered include:* Recommendation(s), geographical residence, state residency, SAT or ACT required; TOEFL required of all international applicants. High school diploma is required and GED is accepted. *Academic units required:* 4 English, 3 mathematics, 3 science, 2 foreign language, 1 social studies, 2 history, 1 visual/performing arts, 1 math or science.

Financial Aid

Students should submit: FAFSA, institution's own financial aid form. The Princeton Review suggests that all financial aid forms be submitted as soon as possible after January 1. *Need-based scholarships/grants offered:* Federal Pell, SEOG, state scholarships/grants, private scholarships, the school's own gift aid. *Loan aid offered:* FFEL Subsidized Stafford, FFEL Unsubsidized Stafford, FFEL PLUS, Federal Perkins, college/university loans from institutional funds. Applicants will be notified of awards on a rolling basis beginning 4/20. Federal Work-Study Program available. Institutional employment available.

The Inside Word

Admission is straightforward here. Complete a basic college-bound high school curriculum with a GPA of at least 2.5, get at least an 18 on your ACT, or graduate in the top 25 percent of your high school class. Nontraditional students who don't want to pay the exorbitant prices of the more well-known private universities in New Orleans can find their niche at UNO; if you are 25 or older, the only requirement for admission is a legitimate high school diploma or a GED.

THE SCHOOL SAYS "..."

From The Admissions Office

"The University of New Orleans returned to its Lakefront campus in Spring 2006 with a full array of academic programs and an enhanced student life program, which includes a cybercafé, campus bar, first-run movies, and a host of exciting student activities. Damage from Hurricane Katrina was limited in scope, and campus facilities are expected to be fully operational for the Fall 2008 semester. A new residence hall, complete with private suite-style bedrooms, is expected to open in Fall 2007."

"The university will serve as a central player in the rebuilding of one of America's most unique and diverse cities. Many academic offerings will focus on the aftermath of the natural disaster and provide students with a living laboratory to address these issues across many disciplines. UNO embraces its mission by providing the best educational opportunities for undergraduate and graduate students, conducting world-class research, and serving a diverse and cultured community in critical areas. UNO's most outstanding offerings include a doctoral program in conservation biology, providing training in the most advanced molecular biological techniques; the largest U.S. undergraduate program in Naval Architecture and Marine Engineering; a leading jazz studies program; one of the top five film programs in the country; and the only graduate arts administration program in the Gulf South.

"UNO will use the total score from the Critical Reading/Verbal and Math subsections of both the old and new SAT or the composite score for the ACT. The Writing components of the ACT and SAT will be used for placement purposes, but not for admission purposes, at the current time."

SELECTIVITY
Admissions Rating	74
# of applicants	1,767
% of applicants accepted	81
% of acceptees attending	78

FRESHMAN PROFILE
Range SAT Critical Reading	470–610
Range SAT Math	480–620
Range SAT Writing	460–590
Range ACT Composite	20–24
Minimum paper TOEFL	525
Minimum computer TOEFL	195
Minimum web-based TOEFL	71
Average HS GPA	3.06
% graduated top 10% of class	12
% graduated top 25% of class	33
% graduated top 50% of class	65

DEADLINES
Regular	
Priority	7/1
Deadline	8/20
Notification	rolling
Nonfall registration?	yes

FINANCIAL FACTS
Financial Aid Rating	63
Annual in-state tuition	$3,292
Annual out-of-state tuition	$10,336
Room and board	$5,240
Required fees	$692
Books and supplies	$1,200
% frosh rec. need-based scholarship or grant aid	30
% UG rec. need-based scholarship or grant aid	29
% frosh rec. non-need-based scholarship or grant aid	25
% UG rec. non-need-based scholarship or grant aid	14
% frosh rec. need-based self-help aid	17
% UG rec. need-based self-help aid	26
% frosh rec. athletic scholarships	1
% UG rec. athletic scholarships	1
% UG borrow to pay for school	31
Average cumulative indebtedness	$24,657

THE UNIVERSITY OF NORTH CAROLINA AT ASHEVILLE

CPO #2210, 117 LIPINSKY HALL, ASHEVILLE, NC 28804-8510 • ADMISSIONS: 828-251-6481 • FAX: 828-251-6482

CAMPUS LIFE

Quality of Life Rating	92
Fire Safety Rating	82
Green Rating	85
Type of school	public
Environment	town

STUDENTS

Total undergrad enrollment	3,251
% male/female	42/58
% from out of state	14
% from public high school	87
% live on campus	33
% in (# of) fraternities	1 (1)
% in (# of) sororities	3 (2)
% African American	3
% Asian	1
% Caucasian	89
% Hispanic	2
% international	1
# of countries represented	16

SURVEY SAYS . . .

Small classes
No one cheats
Students are friendly
Students love Asheville, NC
Great off-campus food
Students are happy

ACADEMICS

Academic Rating	83
Calendar	semester
Student/faculty ratio	13:1
Profs interesting rating	89
Profs accessible rating	84
Most common reg class size	10–19 students
Most common lab size	10–19 students

MOST POPULAR MAJORS

English language and literature
psychology
business/commerce

STUDENTS SAY ". . ."

Academics

The centerpiece of any University of North Carolina at Asheville education is a core curriculum, known here as Integrative Liberal Studies (or ILS for short). ILS consumes a substantial portion of students' time; for many, it is the single most important reason for choosing to attend UNCA. ILS includes a number of introductory writing and humanities courses as well as Topical Clusters, which require students "to integrate the same topic through different disciplines, looking at one subject first from, for example, a natural science perspective, then studying it from a social science perspective." The curriculum also requires Intensives—that is, classes designed to strengthen basic academic skills (e.g., writing, research) while broadening students' intellectual horizons. The sum effect of ILS is to "put a lot of emphasis on thought, on thinking for yourself and deeper than most, and becoming involved in those things that are important to you." Offers one undergrad, "The liberal arts atmosphere allows a student to explore a number of different avenues for his or her future, and to decide, based on that exploration, what it is that he or she wants to do with his or her future. UNC Asheville is about finding yourself." Throughout ILS, major studies, and electives, UNCA undergrads enjoy "smaller classes that usually help with one-on-one assistance" and "dedicated professors who are passionate about their jobs." All of these assets "translate into a private liberal arts education at a public school price," undergrads happily note.

Life

North Carolina may be a red state, but it has its blue enclaves. Asheville, a "nice and progressive city," is certainly one of them. The community, students note, is an "artsy town nestled in the mountains" that hosts plenty of shows (including a big annual jam-band festival), "many wonderful restaurants, especially of the ethnic and vegetarian variety," and "lots of old-time music and contra dancing." The surrounding mountains provide "lots of outdoor recreation opportunities," with hiking, mountain biking, and kayaking among the most popular options. The area's many assets help compensate for the sense among some that "life on campus can get pretty routine at times." Then there are those who enthusiastically tout the merits of campus life; one such student writes, "Some people think it's boring, but I love it. There are basketball games, soccer games, and other sports. There are intramurals [in which] everyone is allowed to play. All the dorms have hall socials and study breaks with free food and games. There are parties for NFL games and other sports. Frisbee is a big thing on campus. A lot of people, including me, love to just hang out on the quad in the center of campus." And why not, since "the campus is beautiful, a great place to take your laptop out on the quad on a nice day and write a paper, or just take a walk in the botanical gardens."

Student Body

"There is a slogan that students made up that describes the student body perfectly" at UNCA, and that slogan is, "'Don't be bashful, it's Asheville.' Anything goes within the student body." One student observes, "Both UNCA and Asheville have a lot of 'atypical' people: a lot of hippies, punks, people with tattoos/piercings, artists, actors, musicians, and writers. It's sort of a running joke that you don't get your Asheville card unless you're some sort of oddball." The large hippie contingent brings "lots of activities such as dancing down at the drum circle on Friday nights." But hippies by no means dominate. The school is also home to "an increasing number of folks who lean toward 'prep'" as well as "your people who come from small mountain towns and who think that Asheville is a big city. They tend to be very religious." UNCA also has "many nontraditional [i.e., older] students." Even though UNCA "has a reputation of being very liberal, and there are many liberal students on campus," there are also "a lot of conservative students, as well." Undergrads assure us that "regardless of how students look, they are all very friendly, intelligent, and willing to speak to one another."

THE UNIVERSITY OF NORTH CAROLINA AT ASHEVILLE

FINANCIAL AID: 828-251-6535 • E-MAIL: ADMISSIONS@UNCA.EDU • WEBSITE: WWW.UNCA.EDU

THE PRINCETON REVIEW SAYS

Admissions

Very important factors considered include: Class rank, academic GPA, rigor of secondary school record. *Important factors considered include:* Application essay, recommendation(s), standardized test scores. *Other factors considered include:* Alumni/ae relation, extracurricular activities, first generation, geographical residence, interview, level of applicant's interest, racial/ethnic status, state residency, talent/ability, volunteer work, work experience. SAT or ACT required; ACT with Writing component required. TOEFL required of all international applicants. High school diploma is required and GED is not accepted. *Academic units required:* 4 English, 4 mathematics, 3 science, (1 science labs), 2 foreign language, 1 social studies, 1 history. *Academic units recommended:* 4 academic electives.

Financial Aid

Students should submit: FAFSA. The Princeton Review suggests that all financial aid forms be submitted as soon as possible after January 1. *Need-based scholarships/grants offered:* Federal Pell, SEOG, state scholarships/grants, private scholarships, the school's own gift aid. *Loan aid offered:* Direct Subsidized Stafford, Direct Unsubsidized Stafford, Direct PLUS, Federal Perkins, state loans, college/university loans from institutional funds. Applicants will be notified of awards on a rolling basis beginning 3/15. Federal Work-Study Program available. Institutional employment available. Off-campus job opportunities are good.

The Inside Word

UNC Asheville provides a sound public education in a small campus atmosphere and an increasing number of students are setting their sights on it each year. In kind, the school works diligently to create a diverse student body and thoroughly analyzes each application it receives. Although selectivity is rising, candidates who demonstrate reasonable academic success and a variety of extracurricular activities should be able to secure admittance.

THE SCHOOL SAYS "..."

From The Admissions Office

"If you want to learn how to think, how to analyze and solve problems on your own, and how to become your own best teacher, a broad-based liberal arts education is the key. UNC Asheville focuses on undergraduates, with a core curriculum covering humanities, language and culture, arts and ideas, and health and fitness. Students thrive in small classes, with a faculty dedicated first of all to teaching. The liberal arts emphasis develops discriminating thinkers, expert and creative communicators with a passion for learning. These are qualities you need for today's challenges and the changes of tomorrow.

"The University of North Carolina at Asheville will require the new SAT Reasoning Test. For students submitting an ACT score, the ACT with the Writing component is required."

SELECTIVITY

Admissions Rating	84
# of applicants	2,653
% of applicants accepted	76
% of acceptees attending	29

FRESHMAN PROFILE

Range SAT Critical Reading	540–640
Range SAT Math	520–620
Range SAT Writing	510–620
Range ACT Composite	22–26
Minimum paper TOEFL	550
Minimum computer TOEFL	213
Minimum web-based TOEFL	79
Average HS GPA	3.84
% graduated top 10% of class	19.5
% graduated top 25% of class	55.8
% graduated top 50% of class	96.8

DEADLINES

Early action	
Deadline	11/10
Notification	12/23
Regular	
Priority	11/10
Deadline	2/15
Notification	4/1
Nonfall registration?	yes

FINANCIAL FACTS

Financial Aid Rating	83
Annual in-state tuition	$2,307
Annual out-of-state tuition	$13,297
Room and board	$6,230
Required fees	$1,857
Books and supplies	$850
% frosh rec. need-based scholarship or grant aid	34
% UG rec. need-based scholarship or grant aid	36
% frosh rec. non-need-based scholarship or grant aid	5
% UG rec. non-need-based scholarship or grant aid	5
% frosh rec. need-based self-help aid	22
% UG rec. need-based self-help aid	32
% frosh rec. athletic scholarships	5
% UG rec. athletic scholarships	3
% frosh rec. any financial aid	62
% UG rec. any financial aid	58
% UG borrow to pay for school	48
Average cumulative indebtedness	$15,972

THE UNIVERSITY OF NORTH CAROLINA AT CHAPEL HILL

JACKSON HALL 153A, CAMPUS BOX #2200, CHAPEL HILL, NC 27599 • ADMISSIONS: 919-966-3621 • FAX: 919-962-3045

CAMPUS LIFE

Quality of Life Rating	95
Fire Safety Rating	87
Green Rating	96
Type of school	public
Environment	town

STUDENTS

Total undergrad enrollment	17,138
% male/female	41/59
% from out of state	17
% from public high school	82.7
% live on campus	46
% in (# of) fraternities	15 (32)
% in (# of) sororities	17 (22)
% African American	11
% Asian	7
% Caucasian	72
% Hispanic	4
% Native American	1
% international	1
# of countries represented	134

SURVEY SAYS . . .
Great library
Students love Chapel Hill, NC
Students are happy
Everyone loves the Tar Heels
Student publications are popular

ACADEMICS

Academic Rating	84
Calendar	semester
Profs interesting rating	79
Profs accessible rating	73
% classes taught by TAs	19
Most common reg class size	10–19 students
Most common lab size	10–19 students

MOST POPULAR MAJORS
biology/biological sciences
psychology
mass communication/media studies

STUDENTS SAY ". . ."

Academics
The University of North Carolina at Chapel Hill "is so well rounded," according to students who make their case by pointing to the "very highly recognized academics, sports, and quality students who are here to get a great education and have fun doing it." With a typically Southern approach, UNC "creates a very balanced atmosphere to live in. The workload isn't so overwhelming that you can't go out and do anything. . . . It makes for a good place to live because people aren't always stressed out." Undergrads report that "you won't find a better combination of quality, cost, and environment for any student specifically interested in undergraduate programs in business, journalism, or education," and that "the humanities and social sciences have a huge presence here" as well. The sciences aren't too shabby either; in fact, pretty much across the board "The academic life is very rigorous" and professors "are not only educated in their fields but have life experiences that add to the flavor of their courses." Many students warn that academic advising is a weak point; one student reports, "We have complicated requirements for majors and . . . sometimes students end up taking classes that don't count toward their major. Or, they end up not realizing they had to take a particular class until senior year." The constitution of the state of North Carolina keeps UNC's in-state tuition rates very low; some out-of-state students complain that the cost of this guarantee falls disproportionately to them.

Life
"UNC has a great nightlife" with plenty of options. Franklin Street, the main drag of Chapel Hill, runs along one side of the campus and "has tons of restaurants," "packed bars," and college-oriented shopping. "Students from Duke and NC State will often come party on Franklin Street" because it's the most student-friendly stretch in the Triangle. The campus offers "tons of clubs and organizations—more than 600—so there is plenty of stuff to do." The dorms "are wonderful, and there is always something going on," although "Dorm parties are hard to pull off on South Campus, where most of the freshmen live. Just about anything goes on North Campus, though." The active Greek scene also provides plenty of party options; GDIs note that "it's really easy to have a social life and be an independent." But what truly binds the campus are the Tar Heel athletic teams, with the men's basketball team paramount among them. One student reports, "People look forward to basketball season more than anything. The rivalries are intense" and the quality of play is excellent. The Atlantic Coast Conference is arguably the NCAA's strongest in basketball. Students also enjoy a "beautiful campus" and great weather; one student observes, "One of the most relaxing things to do is to sit outside on the grass in the quad studying in the 70 degree weather and sun in November."

Student Body
By state policy, native Tar Heels must make up 82 percent of each incoming undergraduate class at UNC, so "The typical student is a North Carolina resident." Out-of-state students "blend seamlessly into this mix, and are often the ones to take the helm of leadership opportunities." Undergraduates here "are very involved, whether it's in the Greek scene, the religious scene, playing intramural sports, or starting their own club. Philanthropic involvement is also high." Students typically "are academically oriented but aren't dominated by it. You can't 'feel' midterms in the air, as you can at other schools." You'll "find every stereotype represented here: The J. Crew snob, the polo shirt and sunglass-wearing frat boy, the emo/punk rocker, the Southern belle, etc." The most apparent stereotypes, though, are "the ones who look like they stepped out of the Carolina catalogue, sporting Carolina-blue laptop bags, polo shirts, and sneakers." UNC is liberal by Southern standards, although no one would ever confuse a UNC undergrad for a Reed College or Wesleyan University student.

The University of North Carolina at Chapel Hill

Financial Aid: 919-962-8396 • E-mail: unchelp@admissions.unc.edu • Website: www.unc.edu

THE PRINCETON REVIEW SAYS

Admissions

Very important factors considered include: Academic GPA, rigor of secondary school record, standardized test scores, class rank, application essay, character/personal qualities, extracurricular activities, recommendation(s), state residency, talent/ability. *Important factors considered include:* Alumni/ae relation, first generation, racial/ethnic status, volunteer work, work experience. SAT or ACT required; ACT with Writing component required. TOEFL required of all international applicants. High school diploma is required and GED is not accepted. *Academic units required:* 4 English, 4 mathematics, 3 science, (1 science labs), 2 foreign language, 2 social studies, 2 academic electives, 1 Included as Social Science-one must be U.S. History *Academic units recommended:* 4 English, 4 mathematics, 4 science, (1 science labs), 4 foreign language, 3 social studies.

Financial Aid

Students should submit: FAFSA, CSS/Financial Aid PROFILE The Princeton Review suggests that all financial aid forms be submitted as soon as possible after January 1. *Need-based scholarships/grants offered:* Federal Pell, SEOG, state scholarships/grants, private scholarships, the school's own gift aid. *Loan aid offered:* FFEL Subsidized Stafford, FFEL Unsubsidized Stafford, FFEL PLUS, Federal Perkins, state loans, college/university loans from institutional funds, Alternative Loans. Applicants will be notified of awards on a rolling basis beginning 3/15. Federal Work-Study Program available. Institutional employment available. Off-campus job opportunities are good.

The Inside Word

UNC's admissions process is highly selective. North Carolina students compete against other students from across the state for 82 percent of all spaces available in the freshman class; out-of-state students compete for the remaining 17 percent of the spaces. State residents will find the admissions standards high, and out-of-state applicants will find that it's one of the hardest offers of admission to come by in the country.

THE SCHOOL SAYS "..."

From The Admissions Office

"One of the leading research and teaching institutions in the world, UNC Chapel Hill offers first-rate faculty, innovative academic programs, and students who are smart, friendly, and committed to public service. Students take full advantage of extensive undergraduate research opportunities, a study abroad program with programs on every continent except Antarctica, and 600-plus clubs and organizations. We offer all this in Chapel Hill, one of the greatest and most welcoming college towns anywhere.

"Carolina's commitment to excellence, access, and affordability is reflected in premier scholarships, such as the prestigious Morehead and Robertson Scholarships, as well the Carolina Covenant, a national model that enables students from low-income families to graduate from Carolina debt-free. We invite you to visit—talk with our professors, attend a class, spend time with some students, and walk across the campus on which public education was born.

"All freshman applicants are required to submit an SAT or an ACT Writing component score. If students took the SAT or ACT before the Writing section was offered, the SAT with the writing section or ACT plus Writing score is still required. While test scores are important, our holistic review process includes other important factors such course work, grades, and extracurricular activities."

SELECTIVITY

Admissions Rating	97
# of applicants	20,090
% of applicants accepted	35
% of acceptees attending	56
# accepting a place on wait list	1,240
% admitted from wait list	18

FRESHMAN PROFILE

Range SAT Critical Reading	600–700
Range SAT Math	610–700
Range SAT Writing	590–690
Range ACT Composite	26–31
Minimum paper TOEFL	600
Minimum computer TOEFL	250
Average HS GPA	4.42
% graduated top 10% of class	76.45
% graduated top 25% of class	95.42
% graduated top 50% of class	98.77

DEADLINES

Early action	
Deadline	11/1
Notification	1/15
Regular	
Priority	1/15
Deadline	1/15
Nonfall registration?	no

APPLICANTS ALSO LOOK AT
AND SOMETIMES PREFER
University of Virginia
Duke University

AND RARELY PREFER
Wake Forest University
North Carolina State University

FINANCIAL FACTS

Financial Aid Rating	93
Annual in-state tuition	$3,705
Annual out-of-state tuition	$19,353
Room and board	$7,696
Required fees	$1,635
Books and supplies	$1,000
% frosh rec. need-based scholarship or grant aid	32
% UG rec. need-based scholarship or grant aid	32
% frosh rec. non-need-based scholarship or grant aid	15
% UG rec. non-need-based scholarship or grant aid	10
% frosh rec. need-based self-help aid	13
% UG rec. need-based self-help aid	18
% frosh rec. athletic scholarships	2
% UG rec. athletic scholarships	2
% frosh rec. any financial aid	63
% UG rec. any financial aid	58

THE UNIVERSITY OF NORTH CAROLINA AT GREENSBORO

1400 SPRING GARDEN STREET, GREENSBORO, NC 27402-6170 • ADMISSIONS: 336-334-5243 • FAX: 336-334-4180

CAMPUS LIFE

Quality of Life Rating	**84**
Fire Safety Rating	**70**
Green Rating	**60***
Type of school	public
Environment	city

STUDENTS

Total undergrad enrollment	13,245
% male/female	32/68
% from out of state	7
% live on campus	31
% in (# of) fraternities	NR (8)
% in (# of) sororities	NR (10)
% African American	21
% Asian	3
% Caucasian	66
% Hispanic	3
% international	1
# of countries represented	12

SURVEY SAYS . . .

Great computer facilities
Great library
Diverse student types on campus

ACADEMICS

Academic Rating	**74**
Calendar	semester
Student/faculty ratio	16:1
Profs interesting rating	76
Profs accessible rating	74
Most common reg class size	20–29 students
Most common lab size	20–29 students

MOST POPULAR MAJORS

nursing/registered nurse
(RN, ASN, BSN, MSN)
business administration and
management
biology/biological sciences

STUDENTS SAY ". . ."

Academics

Students describe The University of North Carolina at Greensboro as "about a half-and-half commuter school with great specialized programs and schools such as nursing, education, dance, and music." Undergrads here praise the "high quality of education at a significantly reduced rate, while having the smaller classes allowing closer bonds between faculty and students" than one could reasonably expect for the tuition charged. The key here is the faculty; "UNCG places a big emphasis on having great teachers. There are some duds, but overall, more of them are fantastic than anything else." The school excels in some off-the-beaten-path areas; programs in exercise and sports science, deaf education, and human development and family studies all receive enthusiastic praise from current students. Undergrads also love the "opportunities that are given to network with businesses and people outside of campus" and the "great internships" the school helps them find. Nontraditional students appreciate the "great support system for adult students." As the school's reputation continues to improve, some here worry that this "historically moderate-sized university where student well-being was the first priority . . . will change into a large research university where the focus is raising more and more money instead of concentrating on what is really best for students." One undeniable upside of the school's increased stature is that "you feel like you are respected in the community when you tell someone that you are a student at UNCG."

Life

UNCG is conveniently located "a mile from downtown and close to surrounding schools: Guilford College, NC A&T, Greensboro College, Elon, UNC, NC State." One student observes, "With six colleges around UNCG, a metropolis of 250,000-plus (1.1 million in the metro area), and access within a 3-hour drive to both beaches and mountains, there is always something to do." On campus "UNCG makes it easy for anyone and everyone to fit in and feel included. Through clubs, students have the ability to offer ideas and have them implemented. There's also intramural sports and free events." The high-profile arts programs on campus yield some wonderful cultural opportunities. "The Weatherspoon Museum of Art is amazing at showcasing the most modern American art and keeps this provincial little town on its toes," writes one artist. A performing arts student adds, "There are wonderful concerts and plays and lectures here. It's a great cultural center and you can always have something to do as long as you look for it." Intercollegiate athletics, students tell us, "are not as popular as they could be, even though they are often ranked nationally, or at least ranked in the conference." Many here feel the addition of a football team (the school has none) would change that; "It would really bring the school spirit up," opines one undergrad. The school's many commuters warn that "parking is horrendous. Prepare to get here an hour before class if you want to find a space on time."

Student Body

UNCG is a big school with "many people from all walks of life, social/cultural backgrounds, etc. The university promotes cultural diversity and acceptance and tolerance of people of different backgrounds." One student reports, "One minute you see a bunch of music majors talking about how much Bach has affected their life and the next minute, you see a bunch of sorority girls discussing the Gap. Mainly, I have observed that sorority girls stick together, jocks stick together, etc." Two in three students are female, and there is a widespread perception that "many of the males are either married or gay. The straight young chill male is a minority here." As at many state schools, "About half of the students at UNCG came here to party. The other half consists of hard-working students who are generally frustrated with the slacker mentality in a lot of our classes. This is less of a problem once you get past the intro-level lectures."

THE UNIVERSITY OF NORTH CAROLINA AT GREENSBORO

FINANCIAL AID: 336-334-5702 • E-MAIL: UNDERGRAD_ADMISSIONS@UNCG.EDU • WEBSITE: WWW.UNCG.EDU

THE PRINCETON REVIEW SAYS

Admissions

Very important factors considered include: Academic GPA, rigor of secondary school record. *Important factors considered include:* Standardized test scores. *Other factors considered include:* Recommendation(s), SAT or ACT required; ACT with Writing component required. High school diploma is required and GED is not accepted. *Academic units required:* 4 English, 4 mathematics, 3 science, (1 science labs), 2 foreign language, 2 social studies.

Financial Aid

Students should submit: FAFSA. The Princeton Review suggests that all financial aid forms be submitted as soon as possible after January 1. *Need-based scholarships/grants offered:* Federal Pell, SEOG, state scholarships/grants, private scholarships, the school's own gift aid. *Loan aid offered:* FFEL Subsidized Stafford, FFEL Unsubsidized Stafford, FFEL PLUS, Federal Perkins, college/university loans from institutional funds. Applicants will be notified of awards on a rolling basis beginning 3/15. Federal Work-Study Program available. Institutional employment available. Off-campus job opportunities are good.

The Inside Word

UNCG has yet to gain much attention outside of regional circles so, at least for the moment, gaining admission is not particularly difficult. The usual public university considerations apply; expect the Admissions Office to focus on grades and test scores, and not much else. Out-of-staters will find a much smoother path to admission here than at Chapel Hill and will still be within reasonable reach of internship and career possibilities in the Research Triangle.

THE SCHOOL SAYS "..."

From The Admissions Office

"UNCG is committed to helping students discover how they can make their mark in the world. Exceptional teaching and first-rate academic programs provide a solid learning foundation. Hands-on experiences in internships, leadership opportunities, and service-learning programs prepare students to take on the challenges of the twenty-first century. Students can broaden their experience by taking advantage of one of the most extensive and affordable study abroad programs in the country. The Lloyd International Honors College offers a genuinely unique opportunity for talented students in any major to benefit from an enriched and supportive intellectual life with a global perspective. UNCG's ideal size and supportive campus environment enable students to excel as individuals while discovering how they can have an impact on the larger community. Students get connected through more than 180 student organizations, intramural, club and intercollegiate sports, Greeks, outdoor adventures, residential colleges, and a friendly Southern city that quickly starts to feel like home.

"Freshmen applicants must submit at least one SAT or ACT score (including the Writing component)."

SELECTIVITY

Admissions Rating	82
# of applicants	8,856
% of applicants accepted	71
% of acceptees attending	39

FRESHMAN PROFILE

Range SAT Critical Reading	460–570
Range SAT Math	470–570
Range SAT Writing	450–550
Average HS GPA	3.57
% graduated top 10% of class	15
% graduated top 25% of class	45
% graduated top 50% of class	87

DEADLINES

Early action	
Deadline	1/15
Notification	4/1
Regular	
Deadline	3/1
Notification	rolling
Nonfall registration?	yes

FINANCIAL FACTS

Financial Aid Rating	72
Annual in-state tuition	$2,458
Annual out-of-state tuition	$13,726
Room and board	$6,151
Required fees	$1,571
Books and supplies	$1,812
% frosh rec. need-based scholarship or grant aid	33
% UG rec. need-based scholarship or grant aid	33
% frosh rec. non-need-based scholarship or grant aid	48
% UG rec. non-need-based scholarship or grant aid	44
% frosh rec. need-based self-help aid	40
% UG rec. need-based self-help aid	43
% frosh rec. athletic scholarships	1
% UG rec. athletic scholarships	1
% frosh rec. any financial aid	68
% UG rec. any financial aid	67
% UG borrow to pay for school	62
Average cumulative indebtedness	$16,708

UNIVERSITY OF NORTH DAKOTA

PO BOX 8135, GRAND FORKS, ND 58202 • ADMISSIONS: 800-225-5863 • FAX: 701-777-4857

CAMPUS LIFE

Quality of Life Rating	77
Fire Safety Rating	78
Green Rating	82
Type of school	public
Environment	town

STUDENTS

Total undergrad enrollment	10,085
% male/female	55/45
% from out of state	48
% live on campus	28
% in (# of) fraternities	8 (13)
% in (# of) sororities	8 (7)
% African American	1
% Asian	1
% Caucasian	89
% Hispanic	1
% Native American	3
% international	3
# of countries represented	67

SURVEY SAYS . . .
Great computer facilities
Great library
Athletic facilities are great
Students are friendly
Everyone loves the Fighting Sioux
Lots of beer drinking
Hard liquor is popular

ACADEMICS

Academic Rating	70
Calendar	semester
Student/faculty ratio	19:1
Profs interesting rating	66
Profs accessible rating	66
Most common reg class size	20–29 students
Most common lab size	10–19 students

MOST POPULAR MAJORS
psychology
airline/commercial/professional pilot
and flight crew
nursing/registered nurse
(RN, ASN, BSN, MSN)

STUDENTS SAY ". . ."

Academics
Outside of its home state, the University of North Dakota is best known for an aviation program that "is recognized as the best by most airlines and companies." Students note that "the aviation department is constantly changing and including advanced technology in the training. Most schools only teach you rules, while here at UND through the use of 360- and 260-degree sims [simulators], you get practical work experience. (The sims are designed to be exactly like what the FAA will use to train and evaluate you.)" But natives of the Peace Garden State (yes, that is North Dakota's official nickname) know that there's more to UND than flying and landing airplanes. There are also the "great programs in nursing, law, accounting, and forensic science," "the only meteorology program in the area," "a physical therapy program with a good reputation," and "an awesome honors program." In fact, "UND is just a great school to go to if you want lots of academic options." Students do, however, observe that "as with most public universities of this size, the classes are kind of hit or miss when it comes to the teaching skills of your professor. Some classes are excellent, others subpar. As far as class difficulty [is concerned], it is about as hit or miss as your professor." Large classes also provide students with a degree of "anonymity."

Life
"If you can stand the winter months, the University of North Dakota is a nice campus that is full of friendly people and good times," but prospective students should be forewarned that during the winter, "This seems like the coldest campus in the country." During the long winter, "The college hockey team is the biggest attraction. The hockey arena is one even NHL teams wish they could have. Hockey is everything around here." Otherwise, "Most people resort to indoor activities either at the gym, movies, bars, or clubs. During warmer months, many students go outside to play Ultimate Frisbee, baseball, football, and sand volleyball." All year round, students like to unwind with a beer or three: "A lot of people drink between two and four days out of the week," observes one respondent. Another remarks, "Grand Forks, North Dakota, offers a small-town atmosphere, as well as the small-town need for creativity when trying to find entertainment. The relative lack of entertainment perpetuates the use of alcohol. The proportion of fraternities and sororities per student is extremely high." Plenty of students tell us that they don't drink and still manage to occupy their time with "movies, hanging out with friends, camping, and hunting."

Student Body
According to one senior, "most UND students come from small towns and haven't been exposed to much." The aviation program counters the trend by "drawing in students from all 50 states and multiple countries." One undergrad notes, "If you're from out of state, everyone says, 'You're aviation, right?'" Because "this is Scandinavian country, many students are White, blonde, and have blue eyes." Most are "serious in terms of school, conservative in terms of politics, and somewhat religious." The typical student, we're told, is also "bundled in a wool parka freezing his or her butt off walking to class, grimacing in pain just because it is so cold."

FINANCIAL AID: 701-777-3121 • E-MAIL: ENROLLMENTSERVICES@MAIL.UND.EDU • WEBSITE: WWW.UND.EDU

THE PRINCETON REVIEW SAYS

Admissions

Very important factors considered include: Academic GPA, standardized test scores. *Other factors considered include:* Class rank, rigor of secondary school record, SAT or ACT required; High school diploma is required and GED is accepted. *Academic units required:* 4 English, 3 mathematics, 3 science, (3 science labs), 3 social studies. *Academic units recommended:* 1 foreign language.

Financial Aid

Students should submit: FAFSA, institution's own financial aid form. The Princeton Review suggests that all financial aid forms be submitted as soon as possible after January 1. *Need-based scholarships/grants offered:* Federal Pell, SEOG, state scholarships/grants, private scholarships, the school's own gift aid, Federal Nursing Scholarships. *Loan aid offered:* FFEL Subsidized Stafford, FFEL Unsubsidized Stafford, FFEL PLUS, Federal Perkins, Federal Nursing, Alternative Commercial Loans. Applicants will be notified of awards on a rolling basis beginning 5/15. Federal Work-Study Program available. Institutional employment available. Off-campus job opportunities are excellent.

The Inside Word

UND's loose admissions standards belie the national reputation it has earned. Akin to most state schools, it's all about meeting GPA and standardized test minimums. The lack of subjective criteria makes for a relatively painless application process, and a majority of students are admitted.

THE SCHOOL SAYS ". . ."

From The Admissions Office

"More than 10,000 students come to the University of North Dakota each year, from every state in the nation and more than 60 countries. They're impressed by our academic excellence, more than 190 programs, our dedication to the liberal arts mission, and alumni success record. Nearly all of the university's new students rank in the top half of their high school classes, with about half in the top quarter. As the oldest and most diversified institution of higher education in the Dakotas, Montana, Wyoming, and western Minnesota, UND is a comprehensive teaching and research university. Yet the university provides individual attention that may be missing at very large universities. UND graduates are highly regarded among prospective employers. Representatives from more than 200 regional and national companies recruit UND students every year. Our campus is approximately 98 percent accessible.

"Students applying for admission to UND are required to take either the ACT or SAT unless they are older than 25. The ACT Writing component is not a requirement for admission, and SAT results considered include only the Math and Verbal sections."

SELECTIVITY

Admissions Rating	78
# of applicants	3,783
% of applicants accepted	70
% of acceptees attending	70

FRESHMAN PROFILE

Range ACT Composite	20.5–25.5
Average HS GPA	3.36
% graduated top 10% of class	15
% graduated top 25% of class	38
% graduated top 50% of class	72

DEADLINES

Regular	
Notification	rolling
Nonfall registration?	yes

FINANCIAL FACTS

Financial Aid Rating	72
Annual in-state tuition	$5,025
Annual out-of-state tuition	$13,418
Room and board	$5,203
Required fees	$1,105
Books and supplies	$800
% frosh rec. need-based scholarship or grant aid	34
% UG rec. need-based scholarship or grant aid	30
% frosh rec. non-need-based scholarship or grant aid	9
% UG rec. non-need-based scholarship or grant aid	7
% frosh rec. need-based self-help aid	43
% UG rec. need-based self-help aid	45
% frosh rec. athletic scholarships	3
% UG rec. athletic scholarships	3
% frosh rec. any financial aid	70
% UG rec. any financial aid	73
% UG borrow to pay for school	65
Average cumulative indebtedness	$23,098

UNIVERSITY OF NOTRE DAME

220 Main Building, Notre Dame, IN 46556 • Admissions: 574-631-7505 • Fax: 574-631-8865

CAMPUS LIFE

Quality of Life Rating	**88**
Fire Safety Rating	**92**
Green Rating	**86**
Type of school	private
Affiliation	Roman Catholic
Environment	city

STUDENTS

Total undergrad enrollment	8,369
% male/female	53/47
% from out of state	92
% from public high school	50
% live on campus	76
% African American	4
% Asian	7
% Caucasian	76
% Hispanic	9
% Native American	1
% international	3
# of countries represented	98

SURVEY SAYS . . .

Lab facilities are great
Everyone loves the Fighting Irish
Intramural sports are popular
Frats and sororities are unpopular
or nonexistent

ACADEMICS

Academic Rating	**92**
Calendar	semester
Student/faculty ratio	13:1
Profs interesting rating	82
Profs accessible rating	93
% classes taught by TAs	7
Most common reg class size	10–19 students
Most common lab size	10–19 students

MOST POPULAR MAJORS
engineering
pre-medicine/pre-medical studies
business/commerce

STUDENTS SAY ". . ."

Academics

Notre Dame has many traditions, including a "devotion to undergraduate education" that you might not expect from a school with such an athletic reputation. Professors here are, by all accounts, "wonderful": "Not only are they invested in their students," they're "genuinely passionate about their field of study," "enthusiastic and animated in lectures," and "always willing to meet outside of class to give extra help." Wary that distance might breed academic disengagement, they ensure that "large lectures are broken down into smaller discussion groups once a week to help with class material and . . . give the class a personal touch." For its part, "The administration tries its best to stay on top of the students' wants and needs." They make it "extremely easy to get in touch with anyone." Like the professors, they try to make personal connections with students. For example, "Our president (a priest), as well as both of our present presidents emeritus, make[s] it a point to interact with the students in a variety of ways—teaching a class, saying mass in the dorms, etc." Overall, "while classes are difficult," "Students are competitive against one another," and "It's necessary to study hard and often, [but] there's also time to do other things."

Life

Life at Notre Dame is centered on two things: "residential life" and "sports." The "Dorms on campus provide the social structure" and supply undergrads with "tons of opportunities" "to get involved and have fun." "During the school week" students "study a lot, but on the weekends everyone seems to make up for the lack of partying during the week." The school "does not have any frats or sororities, but campus is not dry, and drinking/partying is permitted within the residence halls." The administration reportedly tries "to keep the parties on campus due to the fact that campus is such a safe place and they truly do care about our safety." In addition to dorm parties, "virtually every student plays some kind of sport [in] his/her residence hall, and the dorms are really competitive in the Interhall Sport System." Intercollegiate sports, to put it mildly, "are huge." "If someone is not interested in sports upon arrival, he or she will be by the time he or she leaves." "Everybody goes to the football games, and it's common to see 1,000 students at a home soccer game." Beyond residential life and sports, "religious activities," volunteering, "campus publications, student government, and academic clubs round out the rest of ND life."

Student Body

Undergrads at Notre Dame report that "the vast majority" of their peers are "very smart" "White kids from upper- to middle-class backgrounds from all over the country, especially the Midwest and Northeast." The typical student "is a type-A personality that studies a lot, yet is athletic and involved in the community. They are usually the outstanding seniors in their high schools," the "sort of people who can talk about the BCS rankings and Derrida in the same breath." Additionally, something like "85 percent of Notre Dame students earned a varsity letter in high school." "Not all are Catholic" here, though most are, and it seems that most undergrads "have some sort of spirituality present in their daily lives." "ND is slowly improving in diversity concerning economic backgrounds, with the university's policy to meet all demonstrated financial need." As things stand now, those who "don't tend to fit in with everyone else hang out in their own groups made up by others like them (based on ethnicity, sexual orientation, etc.)."

FINANCIAL AID: 574-631-6436 • E-MAIL: ADMISSIONS@ND.EDU • WEBSITE: WWW.ND.EDU

THE PRINCETON REVIEW SAYS

Admissions

Very important factors considered include: Rigor of secondary school record. *Important factors considered include:* Class rank, application essay, academic GPA, recommendation(s), standardized test scores, alumni/ae relation, character/personal qualities, extracurricular activities, talent/ability, volunteer work. *Other factors considered include:* First generation, level of applicant's interest, racial/ethnic status, religious affiliation/commitment, work experience. SAT or ACT required; TOEFL required of all international applicants. High school diploma is required and GED is not accepted. *Academic units required:* 4 English, 3 mathematics, 2 science, (2 science labs), 2 foreign language, 2 history, 3 academic electives. *Academic units recommended:* 4 English, 4 mathematics, 4 science, (2 science labs), 4 foreign language, 4 history.

Financial Aid

Students should submit: FAFSA, CSS/Financial Aid PROFILE, business/farm supplement, as may be requested on individual basis, signed Federal income tax return and W-2 forms, Student Federal income tax return. Regular filing deadline is 2/15. The Princeton Review suggests that all financial aid forms be submitted as soon as possible after January 1. *Need-based scholarships/grants offered:* Federal Pell, SEOG, private scholarships, the school's own gift aid, Federal ACG and SMART Grants. *Loan aid offered:* FFEL Subsidized Stafford, FFEL Unsubsidized Stafford, FFEL PLUS, Federal Perkins, Federal Nursing, Notre Dame Undergraduate Loan (NDUL). Applicants will be notified of awards on or about 4/1. Off-campus job opportunities are fair.

The Inside Word

Notre Dame is one of the most selective colleges in the country. Almost everyone who enrolls is in the top 10 percent of their graduating class and possesses test scores in the highest percentiles. But, as the student respondents suggest, strong academic ability isn't enough to get you in here. The school looks for students with other talents, and seems to have a predilection for athletic achievement. Legacy students get a leg up but are by no means assured of admission.

THE SCHOOL SAYS "..."

From The Admissions Office

"Notre Dame is a Catholic university, which means it offers unique opportunities for academic, ethical, spiritual, and social service development. The First Year of Studies program provides special assistance to our students as they make the adjustment from high school to college. The first-year curriculum includes many core requirements, while allowing students to explore several areas of possible future study. Each residence hall is home to students from all classes; most will live in the same hall for all their years on campus. An average of 93 percent of entering students will graduate within 5 years.

"The highest Critical Reading score and the highest Math score from either test will be accepted; the Writing component score is not required. The ACT is also accepted (with or without Writing component) in lieu of the SAT."

SELECTIVITY

Admissions Rating	98
# of applicants	14,503
% of applicants accepted	24
% of acceptees attending	56
# accepting a place on wait list	619
% admitted from wait list	29

FRESHMAN PROFILE

Range SAT Critical Reading	640–750
Range SAT Math	660–760
Range SAT Writing	630–720
Range ACT Composite	31–34
Minimum paper TOEFL	600
Minimum computer TOEFL	250
Minimum web-based TOEFL	100
% graduated top 10% of class	87
% graduated top 25% of class	97
% graduated top 50% of class	100

DEADLINES

Early action	
Deadline	11/1
Notification	12/20
Regular	
Deadline	12/31
Notification	4/10
Nonfall registration?	no

APPLICANTS ALSO LOOK AT

AND OFTEN PREFER
Stanford University
Princeton University

AND SOMETIMES PREFER
Duke University
Cornell University
Georgetown University
Northwestern University

AND RARELY PREFER
University of Michigan—Ann Arbor
University of Illinois at Urbana-Champaign

FINANCIAL FACTS

Financial Aid Rating	94
Annual tuition	$34,680
Room and board	$9,290
Required fees	$507
Books and supplies	$850
% frosh rec. need-based scholarship or grant aid	45
% UG rec. need-based scholarship or grant aid	44
% frosh rec. non-need-based scholarship or grant aid	32
% UG rec. non-need-based scholarship or grant aid	29
% frosh rec. need-based self-help aid	36
% UG rec. need-based self-help aid	41
% frosh rec. athletic scholarships	6
% UG rec. athletic scholarships	5
% UG borrow to pay for school	57
Average cumulative indebtedness	$27,569

UNIVERSITY OF OKLAHOMA

1000 ASP AVENUE, NORMAN, OK 73019-4076 • ADMISSIONS: 405-325-2252 • FAX: 405-325-7124

CAMPUS LIFE
Quality of Life Rating	**85**
Fire Safety Rating	**99**
Green Rating	**91**
Type of school	public
Environment	city

STUDENTS
Total undergrad enrollment	20,400
% male/female	49/51
% from out of state	25
% live on campus	28
% in (# of) fraternities	19 (24)
% in (# of) sororities	24 (16)
% African American	6
% Asian	6
% Caucasian	75
% Hispanic	4
% Native American	8
% international	2
# of countries represented	100

SURVEY SAYS . . .
Great library
Athletic facilities are great
Everyone loves the Sooners
Frats and sororities dominate
social scene
Lots of beer drinking

ACADEMICS
Academic Rating	**73**
Calendar	semester
Student/faculty ratio	18:1
Profs interesting rating	72
Profs accessible rating	75
% classes taught by TAs	21
Most common reg class size	10–19 students
Most common lab size	20–29 students

MOST POPULAR MAJORS
journalism
zoology/animal biology
management science

STUDENTS SAY "..."

Academics

The University of Oklahoma "prides itself on the leadership and ingenuity of its students," a number of whom credit the school's president, David Boren, with transforming OU "from well known in the state of Oklahoma to well known across the nation" in the past decade. Students call their academic experiences at OU "exceptional"—both in and out of the classroom. "We are encouraged to get not only a great academic base but also life experiences, through lab research, internships, and campus leadership positions." Not to be eclipsed by the famous meteorology department, the business and drama programs are starting to get attention as well. When it comes to teaching, some students see "a clear distinction between two types of professors: those who have been here forever and have tenure (they're boring and don't really 'teach'), and new professors, who have real-life experience and give students a feel for what the real world is like." More often than not, we read that the professors are "very helpful and knowledgeable." An economics student boasts that after e-mailing homework assignments to a calculus professor, she "received the answers back promptly." Undergrads wish the school would address the "definite need for more professors and more classes for the ever-growing number of students here at OU." A handful also gripes about having to jump through bureaucratic hoops; writes an all-too experienced senior: "There's a lot of standing in lines for everything." That said, many students find the administration members "available and helpful." Those in the honors program experience "a wonderful dynamic. It's nice to be at a big university but still get to take small, discussion-centered classes." One content sophomore writes, "I believe I am getting not only a great education, but also meeting people who make huge impressions in my life."

Life

To some, OU has a party school reputation, perhaps made possible by its "huge Greek population" (in total, OU offers 49 fraternities and sororities). A senior notes that "there are plenty of things to do on OU's campus besides partying," and students repeatedly point out that Greeks "work hard to co-program with various events and encourage members to attend activities out of their regular spectrum." For example, "In my sorority," writes one senior, "we have different groups come over for dinner and exchanges." This "ongoing process" of increasing interaction among all factions is starting to pay off in some campus wide participation. A senior recounts how OU started "a one-day community-service project called the Big Event that now [in its eighth year] attracts nearly one in every four students." The student union sponsors free new-release movies "just about every Friday night," and the Campus Activities Council organizes "free events like Homecoming, Howdy Week, pep rallies, and concert series (including the Dixie Chicks)." People call the town of Norman, 15 miles from Oklahoma City, "pretty bland to say the least," though it does have a museum, dollar theater, and popular 1950s-style diner. Of course, students and Norman locals come together in their undying love of Sooner football, packing the stadium to see the team and the talented marching band all through the fall.

Student Body

Most students hail from Oklahoma or Texas, and several comment that "you definitely feel the Bible Belt" at OU. Students describe typical classmates as "conservative"; however, in the words of a sophomore, "Most people here are not judgmental, at least openly, and tend to either ignore or respect foreign views and beliefs." In this welcoming group, "If you were to go to a football game by yourself and sit in the middle of the student section, everyone would give you a high five and yell along with you while you were there." One student observes a shift in his classmates: "People are still always talking about what they are doing that night; but surprisingly, students are starting to get more serious about school, which I think is really good."

FINANCIAL AID: 405-325-4521 • E-MAIL: ADMREC@OU.EDU • WEBSITE: WWW.OU.EDU

THE PRINCETON REVIEW SAYS

Admissions

Very important factors considered include: Class rank, academic GPA, rigor of secondary school record, standardized test scores. *Other factors considered include:* Application essay, recommendation(s), state residency, SAT or ACT required; TOEFL required of all international applicants. High school diploma is required and GED is accepted. *Academic units required:* 4 English, 3 mathematics, 2 science, (2 science labs), 2 social studies, 1 history, 3 academic electives. *Academic units recommended:* 2 foreign language, 1 computer science.

Financial Aid

Students should submit: FAFSA. The Princeton Review suggests that all financial aid forms be submitted as soon as possible after January 1. *Need-based scholarships/grants offered:* Federal Pell, SEOG, state scholarships/grants, private scholarships, the school's own gift aid, United Negro College Fund. *Loan aid offered:* FFEL Subsidized Stafford, FFEL Unsubsidized Stafford, FFEL PLUS, Federal Perkins, college/university loans from institutional funds. Applicants will be notified of awards on a rolling basis beginning 3/15. Federal Work-Study Program available. Institutional employment available. Off-campus job opportunities are excellent.

The Inside Word

It's plain from the approach of Oklahoma's evaluation process that candidates needn't put much energy into preparing supporting materials for their applications. This is one place that is going to get you a decision pronto—your numbers will call the shots.

THE SCHOOL SAYS "..."

From The Admissions Office

"Ask yourself some significant questions. What are your ambitions, goals, and dreams? Do you desire opportunity, and are you ready to accept challenge? What do you hope to gain from your educational experience? Are you looking for a university that will provide you with the tools, resources, and motivation to convert ambitions, opportunities, and challenges into meaningful achievement? To effectively answer these questions you must carefully seek out your options, look for direction, and make the right choice. The University of Oklahoma combines a unique mixture of academic excellence, varied social cultures, and a variety of campus activities to make your educational experience complete. At OU, comprehensive learning is our goal for your life. Not only do you receive a valuable classroom learning experience, but OU is also one of the finest research institutions in the United States. This allows OU students the opportunity to be a part of technology in progress. It's not just learning, it's discovery, invention, and dynamic creativity, a hands-on experience that allows you to be on the cutting edge of knowledge. Make the right choice and consider the University of Oklahoma!

"Both versions of the SAT (or ACT) will be used when considering freshman applicants for admission. The new Writing component of either test is not required of students and is not used in determining admission to the university. The student's best composite score from any one test will be used."

SELECTIVITY

Admissions Rating	84
# of applicants	8,768
% of applicants accepted	89
% of acceptees attending	50
# accepting a place on wait list	1,331
% admitted from wait list	90

FRESHMAN PROFILE

Range SAT Critical Reading	510–640
Range SAT Math	540–660
Range ACT Composite	23–28
Minimum paper TOEFL	550
Minimum computer TOEFL	213
Minimum web-based TOEFL	79
Average HS GPA	3.59
% graduated top 10% of class	33
% graduated top 25% of class	67
% graduated top 50% of class	93

DEADLINES

Regular	
Deadline	4/1
Nonfall registration?	yes

FINANCIAL FACTS

Financial Aid Rating	83
Annual in-state tuition	$2,609
Annual out-of-state tuition	$9,900
Room and board	$7,058
Required fees	$1,925
Books and supplies	$953
% frosh rec. need-based scholarship or grant aid	5
% UG rec. need-based scholarship or grant aid	14
% frosh rec. non-need-based scholarship or grant aid	38
% UG rec. non-need-based scholarship or grant aid	29
% frosh rec. need-based self-help aid	39
% UG rec. need-based self-help aid	38
% frosh rec. athletic scholarships	1
% UG rec. athletic scholarships	1
% frosh rec. any financial aid	80
% UG rec. any financial aid	73
% UG borrow to pay for school	47
Average cumulative indebtedness	$19,454

UNIVERSITY OF OREGON

1217 University of Oregon, Eugene, OR 97403-1217 • Admissions: 541-346-3201 • Fax: 541-346-5815

CAMPUS LIFE

Quality of Life Rating	**79**
Fire Safety Rating	**71**
Green Rating	**99**
Type of school	public
Environment	city

STUDENTS

Total undergrad enrollment	16,422
% male/female	48/52
% from out of state	28
% live on campus	21
% in (# of) fraternities	7 (13)
% in (# of) sororities	9 (9)
% African American	2
% Asian	6
% Caucasian	76
% Hispanic	4
% Native American	1
% international	5
# of countries represented	84

SURVEY SAYS . . .
Great library
Athletic facilities are great
Everyone loves the Ducks
Lots of beer drinking

ACADEMICS

Academic Rating	**72**
Calendar	quarter
Student/faculty ratio	18:1
Profs interesting rating	69
Profs accessible rating	74
% classes taught by TAs	16
Most common reg class size	20–29 students
Most common lab size	20–29 students

MOST POPULAR MAJORS
psychology
business/commerce
journalism

STUDENTS SAY "..."

Academics

Ask University of Oregon students what they like best about their school and a surprising number will mention intercollegiate athletics. Press them a bit harder, however, and they'll start to identify the school's many outstanding academic programs: a business school with "a great faculty" and "amazing facilities;" solid and popular foreign language programs, including robust offerings in Japanese and Chinese; an "esteemed" and "extremely challenging" journalism school; a "very strong program in psychology and neuroscience"; an architecture program that "is increasing in popularity"; and a music program that students tout as "one of the best in the country." The school also offers "a really strong study abroad program" that provides a "good outlet for all of the creative types at the university to pursue wild adventures or projects around the world," "tons of opportunities for internships," and "a whole world of unrecognized undergraduate lab research opportunities, which would give any student a foot in the door for a future in research." In other words, an ocean of opportunities awaits anyone here willing to seek it out; UO "is a place where you can get involved as deeply as you care to in social causes/politics, where you can become closely connected to your professors and their research, and where a sense of community (on campus and off) permeates your entire educational career." University of Oregon: come for the football and basketball, stay for the "incredible academics."

Life

"Life at UO is amazing all year round," undergrads report. In the fall "There is football, warm but crisp weather, and our campus is gorgeous." During the winter "There are basketball games and a lot of indoor parties." Spring and summer "are gorgeous" and the best time to enjoy the area's many outdoor opportunities, because "the rain keeps people inside during the fall and winter." Hometown Eugene "is great for the outdoors.... There are mountains to hike, rivers to float, and lakes to swim in all within 15 minutes. The coast is an hour away; the mountain is only an hour away (if you ski during the winter)." The school's Outdoor Program "has several trips each week. Depending on the season, they have rock climbing, snow excursions, white water rafting, and camping trips." The city is also great for cultural life; "The Hult Center and other venues host extensive arts and entertainment opportunities, including the annual Bach Festival, numerous other music festivals, art walks, the Saturday Market crafts fair—the list is extensive." Enthusiasm for sports permeates the campus, and "There's always a party going on" if that's what you're looking for. In short, "Whatever interests students hold, Eugene and the university usually have something going on that captures their attention."

Student Body

"There is a significant blend of students with different ethnicities, religious views, sexual orientations, and genders" at the University of Oregon, where students tend to be "laid back, environmentally conscious, and politically inclined...usually to the left." The population includes "more than its fair share of nerds, preps, theater kids, hippies, and maybe more pot smokers, but everyone seems to be super friendly, and most people just want to get along." The student body is "pretty white bread," though, partly in reflection of the state of Oregon's demographics (the state is 93 percent white). "If they lowered out-of-state costs, more people would attend who are from ethnically diverse cities," one student suggests. A "large Asian and Middle Eastern population" accounts for much of the racial diversity here.

FINANCIAL AID: 541-346-3211 • E-MAIL: UOADMIT@OREGON.UOREGON.EDU • WEBSITE: WWW.UOREGON.EDU

THE PRINCETON REVIEW SAYS

Admissions

Very important factors considered include: Academic GPA, rigor of secondary school record. *Other factors considered include:* Class rank, application essay, recommendation(s), standardized test scores, extracurricular activities, first generation, geographical residence, racial/ethnic status, state residency, talent/ability, volunteer work, work experience. SAT or ACT required; ACT with Writing component required. TOEFL required of all international applicants. High school diploma is required and GED is accepted. *Academic units required:* 4 English, 3 mathematics, 2 science, 2 foreign language, 3 social studies. *Academic units recommended:* (1 science labs), 2 additional units in required college preparatory areas recommended.

Financial Aid

Students should submit: FAFSA. The Princeton Review suggests that all financial aid forms be submitted as soon as possible after January 1. *Need-based scholarships/grants offered:* Federal Pell, SEOG, state scholarships/grants, private scholarships, the school's own gift aid. *Loan aid offered:* Direct Subsidized Stafford, Direct Unsubsidized Stafford, Direct PLUS, Federal Perkins, college/university loans from institutional funds. Applicants will be notified of awards on a rolling basis beginning 4/15. Federal Work-Study Program available. Institutional employment available. Off-campus job opportunities are good.

The Inside Word

Give your grades, rank, and serial number—sorry, make that test scores—and wait for the admissions office to crunch the numbers. A GPA of 3.00 in a college prep curriculum pretty much guarantees entry here; the school is willing to overlook substandard test scores for anyone meeting this threshold. Applicants whose personal circumstances may have hindered their academic achievement should inform the school, as the admissions office may show leniency in their cases.

THE SCHOOL SAYS "..."

From The Admissions Office

"At the UO, you'll be part of a community dedicated to making a difference in the world. Whether you want to change a community, a law, or one person's mind, the UO will provide you with the inspiration and resources you'll need to succeed. You'll attend classes alongside students from all 50 states, 4 U.S. territories, and 84 other countries, learn from people with diverse cultural, ethnic, and spiritual heritages, and have opportunities to participate in cutting-edge research and engage in intellectual dialog with renowned faculty. You'll graduate from the UO with the knowledge, experience, and research, writing, and critical thinking skills necessary to succeed in an increasingly global and diverse community. Set in a 295-acre arboretum, the UO is literally green. Both academic and outdoor programs will bring you into contact with forests, mountains, rivers, and lakes. The first facilities of their kind in the nation, the Green Chemistry Laboratory uses only nontoxic materials and the Tyler Instrumentation Center provides the full range of instruments needed in green chemistry. The Lillis Business Complex is the country's most environmentally friendly business school facility, and nationally recognized programs in sustainable business, architecture, and technology demonstrate the UO's ongoing commitment to the environment. With a student-teacher ratio of 18:1, average class size of 22 students, 273 academic programs, and more than 250 student organizations, you'll find that the UO is uniquely able to provide the advantages of a smaller liberal arts university in addition to all the resources of a major research institution. The early notification deadline for fall 2009 is November 1, 2008. The standard admission deadline for fall 2009 is January 15, 2009. To be eligible for freshman admission, you must have a high school GPA of at least 3.00, be a graduate of a standard or accredited high school, and submit SAT or ACT scores. A cumulative GPA of 3.25 or better on a 4.00 scale and completion of at least sixteen units of academic course work qualifies you for guaranteed admission."

SELECTIVITY

Admissions Rating	79
# of applicants	11,287
% of applicants accepted	87
% of acceptees attending	37

FRESHMAN PROFILE

Range SAT Critical Reading	486–606
Range SAT Math	496–611
Minimum paper TOEFL	500
Minimum computer TOEFL	173
Minimum web-based TOEFL	61
Average HS GPA	3.49
% graduated top 10% of class	23
% graduated top 25% of class	57
% graduated top 50% of class	91

DEADLINES

Early action	
Deadline	11/1
Notification	12/15
Regular	
Priority	11/1
Deadline	1/15
Notification	rolling
Nonfall registration?	yes

APPLICANTS ALSO LOOK AT

AND OFTEN PREFER
University of California—Berkeley
University of California—Santa Cruz
University of California—Santa Barbara
University of California—Davis

AND SOMETIMES PREFER
University of Puget Sound
University of Washington
Willamette University

AND RARELY PREFER
University of Colorado—Boulder
Oregon State University
University of Portland

FINANCIAL FACTS

Financial Aid Rating	69
Annual in-state tuition	$4,494
Annual out-of-state tuition	$17,250
Room and board	$7,849
Required fees	$1,542
Books and supplies	$1,050
% frosh rec. need-based scholarship or grant aid	15
% UG rec. need-based scholarship or grant aid	21
% frosh rec. non-need-based scholarship or grant aid	16
% UG rec. non-need-based scholarship or grant aid	11
% frosh rec. need-based self-help aid	27
% UG rec. need-based self-help aid	33
% UG rec. athletic scholarships	2
% frosh rec. any financial aid	62.7
% UG rec. any financial aid	56.7
% UG borrow to pay for school	.57
Average cumulative indebtedness	$18,728

UNIVERSITY OF THE PACIFIC

3601 PACIFIC AVENUE, STOCKTON, CA 95211 • ADMISSIONS: 209-946-2211 • FAX: 209-946-2413

STUDENTS SAY ". . ."

Academics

Many at University of the Pacific believe that "science is the driving force at Pacific" and that "accelerated programs in pharmacy and dentistry" are what bring many of the brightest students in the country here. "Many people who have been also accepted by other prestigious schools choose Pacific over these for the accelerated programs." This assessment correctly identifies Pacific's strengths in the sciences, but it doesn't give the rest of the university its due. Pacific's School of International Studies, for example, "is one of six in the nation—and the only one that requires undergraduates to go abroad." The Conservatory of Music is "great and very welcoming," the Sports Sciences Department offers a popular 5-year BA/MBA (as well as a unique sports management program), and the engineering program "provides individual attention and a successful co-op program that helps you to come out of college with experience in the real world." The school has a lot to offer in the way of programs, and in every area, "Pacific is completely for and about the students. You don't feel like you're just a number here. The professors learn your name (even in a lecture situation), and you have access to speak with any professor, dean, or even the president of the university." Furthermore, students proclaim, "You're guaranteed to get the classes you need to graduate in 4 years."

Life

"Student life on campus is good" at Pacific, with "over 120 clubs for student groups. We are [also] encouraged to start our own clubs if we feel that something is missing." Greek life "is pretty active and has a positive reputation." Partying is fairly widespread. "Despite the dry-campus policy, the Greeks get up to plenty of mischief," undergrads assure us. Hometown Stockton "may not exactly be the top destination of some students," but it's not as bad as some guidebooks make it out to be. In recent years, "Stockton has cleaned up downtown, adding new restaurants, a movie theater, and new bars and clubs. A new baseball park for the minor league Stockton Ports and a new arena for hockey, indoor soccer and arena football have just been built." Stockton also provides access to "many great nearby state parks," and is "not too far away from San Francisco." Pacific's sports teams, the Pacific Tigers, are "always very exciting to watch. Most of the students are very excited to see games and always bring a lot of school spirit."

Student Body

University of the Pacific "is a melting pot." "This is a pretty diverse campus, and most people here are very accepting of everyone." That said, the typical student, one undergrad tells us, "is from a higher-income household from Southern California or the Bay Area, clean cut, and dressed conservatively." There are, however, "plenty of atypical students," including "a large number of athletes, performance artists, musicians, artists, and engineers" to supplement "the largely professionally driven population." Outside of the high-profile programs, there are a number of students who "just want to have a good time," we're told. In fact, many feel that the campus splits between "those who are extremely motivated to achieve their academic and professional goals" and "those who are here to party and waste time until they become 'adults.'"

FINANCIAL AID: 209-946-2421 • E-MAIL: ADMISSIONS@PACIFIC.EDU • WEBSITE: WWW.PACIFIC.EDU

THE PRINCETON REVIEW SAYS

Admissions

Very important factors considered include: Rigor of secondary school record. *Important factors considered include:* Application essay, academic GPA, recommendation(s), standardized test scores, extracurricular activities, first generation. *Other factors considered include:* Class rank, alumni/ae relation, character/personal qualities, geographical residence, level of applicant's interest, talent/ability, volunteer work, work experience. SAT Subject Tests recommended; SAT or ACT required; SAT and SAT Subject Tests or ACT recommended; TOEFL required of all international applicants. High school diploma is required and GED is accepted. *Academic units recommended:* 4 English, 3 mathematics, (2 science labs), 2 foreign language, 3 social studies, 1 academic elective, 1 fine arts/performing arts.

Financial Aid

Students should submit: FAFSA. The Princeton Review suggests that all financial aid forms be submitted as soon as possible after January 1. *Need-based scholarships/grants offered:* Federal Pell, SEOG, state scholarships/grants, private scholarships, the school's own gift aid. *Loan aid offered:* Direct Subsidized Stafford, Direct Unsubsidized Stafford, Direct PLUS, FFEL Subsidized Stafford, FFEL Unsubsidized Stafford, FFEL PLUS, Federal Perkins, Direct Graduate/Professional PLUS Loans. Applicants will be notified of awards on a rolling basis beginning 3/15.

The Inside Word

Pacific wages a fierce battle for applicants amongst its California counterparts and this results in a deceptively high acceptance rate. While the Admissions Team considers a variety of factors, a challenging course load is most important. It is highly advantageous for interested students to enroll in honors and Advanced Placement classes.

THE SCHOOL SAYS "..."

From The Admissions Office

"One of the most concise ways of describing the University of the Pacific is that it is 'a major university in a small college package.' Our 3,400 undergraduates get the personal attention that you would expect at a small, residential college. But they also have the kinds of opportunities offered at much larger institutions, including more than 90 majors and programs; hundreds of student organizations; drama, dance, and musical productions; 16 NCAA Division I athletic teams; and two dozen club and intramural sports. We offer undergraduate major programs in the arts, sciences and humanities, business, education, engineering, international studies, music, pharmacy, and health sciences. Some of the unique aspects of our academic programs include the following: We have the only independent, coed, nonsectarian liberal arts and sciences college located between Los Angeles and central Oregon; we have the only undergraduate professional school of international studies in California—and it's the only one in the nation that actually requires you to study abroad; we have the only engineering program in the West that requires students to complete a year's worth of paid work experience as part of their degree; our Conservatory of Music focuses on performance but also offers majors in music management, music therapy, and music education; and we offer several accelerated programs in business, dentistry, dental hygiene, education, law, engineering, and pharmacy. Our beautiful New England–style main campus is located in Stockton (population: 289,800) and is within 2 hours or less of San Francisco, Santa Cruz, Yosemite National Park, and Lake Tahoe.

"SAT Subject Tests recommended: Mathematics, Chemistry (natural science majors only)."

SELECTIVITY
Admissions Rating	88
# of applicants	5,894
% of applicants accepted	59
% of acceptees attending	22
# accepting a place on wait list	30

FRESHMAN PROFILE
Range SAT Critical Reading	510–630
Range SAT Math	543–670
Range SAT Writing	510–630
Range ACT Composite	23–28
Minimum paper TOEFL	475
Minimum computer TOEFL	150
Average HS GPA	3.46
% graduated top 10% of class	41
% graduated top 25% of class	69.6
% graduated top 50% of class	93.8

DEADLINES
Early action	
Deadline	11/15
Notification	1/15
Regular	
Priority	1/15
Notification	3/15
Nonfall registration?	yes

APPLICANTS ALSO LOOK AT
AND SOMETIMES PREFER
University of Southern California
University of California—Berkeley
University of California—Los Angeles
California Polytechnic State University—San Luis Obispo
University of California—Davis

FINANCIAL FACTS
Financial Aid Rating	77
Annual tuition	$28,480
Room and board	$9,210
Required fees	$500
Books and supplies	$1,386
% frosh rec. need-based scholarship or grant aid	63
% UG rec. need-based scholarship or grant aid	64
% frosh rec. need-based self-help aid	59
% UG rec. need-based self-help aid	62
% frosh rec. athletic scholarships	3
% UG rec. athletic scholarships	4
% frosh rec. any financial aid	83
% UG rec. any financial aid	80

UNIVERSITY OF PENNSYLVANIA

ONE COLLEGE HALL, PHILADELPHIA, PA 19104 • ADMISSIONS: 215-898-7507 • FAX: 215-898-9670

CAMPUS LIFE
Quality of Life Rating	**88**
Fire Safety Rating	**71**
Green Rating	**93**
Type of school	private
Environment	metropolis

STUDENTS
Total undergrad enrollment	9,687
% male/female	51/49
% from out of state	81
% live on campus	64
% in (# of) fraternities	30 (32)
% in (# of) sororities	26 (16)
% African American	8
% Asian	17
% Caucasian	45
% Hispanic	6
% international	10
# of countries represented	111

SURVEY SAYS . . .
Great library
Athletic facilities are great
Great off-campus food
Students are happy
Student publications are popular
Lots of beer drinking
Hard liquor is popular

ACADEMICS
Academic Rating	**89**
Student/faculty ratio	6:1
Profs interesting rating	74
Profs accessible rating	80
% classes taught by TAs	5

MOST POPULAR MAJORS
business administration and management
finance
nursing/registered nurse
(RN, ASN, BSN, MSN)

STUDENTS SAY "..."

Academics
At the University of Pennsylvania, everyone shares an intellectual curiosity and top-notch resources, but doesn't "buy into the stigma of being an Ivy League school." Still, no one turns down the opportunity to rave about the school's strong academic reputation or the large alumni network, and students here are also "very passionate about what they do outside the classroom" and the opportunities presented to them through attending UPenn. The university is composed of four undergraduate schools (and "a library for pretty much any topic"), and students tend to focus on what they'll do with their degree pretty early on. Wharton, UPenn's "highly competitive undergraduate business school," creates a "tremendous pre-professional atmosphere" that keeps students competitive and somewhat stressed with their studies during the week, and this "career-oriented" attitude spills over into other factions of the university, leaving some desiring more grounds for creativity and less climbing over each other. "It's when individuals' grades are on the line when the claws come out," says a student.

Professors can "sometimes seem to be caught up more in their research than their classes," but "there are very few other institutions where you can take every one of your classes with a professor who is setting the bar for research in his or her field." If you are willing to put in the time and effort, your professors "will be happy to reciprocate." In general, the instructors here are "very challenging academically," and one student says that "some of them have been excellent, but all of them have at least been good." The administration is "very professional and efficient" and "truly interested in students' well being." "Academically, I have access to opportunities unparalleled elsewhere," says a student.

Life
Penn kids don't mind getting into intellectual conversations over dinner, but "partying is a much higher priority here than it is at other Ivy League schools." Many students schedule their classes so as to not have class on Fridays, making the weekend "officially" start on Thursday night, and frat parties and Center City bars and clubs are popular destinations. However, when it comes down to midterms and finals, "people get really serious and...buckle down and study." Between weekend jaunts to New York and Philadelphia itself ("a city large enough to answer the needs of any type of person"), students have plenty of access to restaurants, shopping, concerts, and sports games, as well as plain old "hanging out with hallmates playing Mario Kart." The school provides plenty of guest speakers, cultural events, clubs, and organizations for students to channel their energies, and seniors can even attend "Feb Club" in the month of February, which is essentially an event every night. It's a busy life at UPenn, and "people are constantly trying to think about how they can balance getting good grades academically and their weekend plans."

Student Body
This "determined" bunch is very career-oriented, "take their classes pretty seriously," leans to the left, and "personality-wise tends to be Type A." "There is always someone smarter than you are," says a Chemical Biomolecular Engineering major. Everyone has "a strong sense of personal style and his or her own credo," but no group deviates too far from the more mainstream stereotypes, and there's a definite lack of "emos" and hippies. There's "the Career-driven Wharton kid who will stab you in the back to get your interview slot" and "the Nursing kid who's practically non-existent," but on the whole, there is "tremendous school diversity," and whatever kind of person you are, "you will find a group of people like you."

FINANCIAL AID: 215-898-1988 • E-MAIL: INFO@ADMISSIONS.UGAO.UPENN.EDU • WEBSITE: WWW.UPENN.EDU

THE PRINCETON REVIEW SAYS

Admissions

Very important factors considered include: Rigor of secondary school record, Academic GPA, Recommendation(s), Talent/ability, Character/personal qualities. *Important factors considered include:* Standardized test scores, Application Essay, Extracurricular activities, First Generation. *Other factors considered include:* Class rank, Interview, Alumni/ae relation, Geographical residence, Racial/ethnic status. *Academic units recommended:*

Financial Aid

The Princeton Review suggests that all financial aid forms be submitted as soon as possible after January 1. Federal Work-Study Program available. Institutional employment available. Off-campus job opportunities are excellent.

The Inside Word

After a small decline four cycles ago, applications are once again climbing at Penn—the fifth increase in 6 years. The competition in the applicant pool is formidable. Applicants can safely assume that they need to be one of the strongest students in their graduating class in order to be successful.

THE SCHOOL SAYS "..."

From The Admissions Office

"The nation's first university, the University of Pennsylvania, had its beginnings in 1740, some 36 years before Thomas Jefferson, Benjamin Franklin (Penn's founder), and their fellow revolutionaries went public in Philadelphia with incendiary notions about life, liberty and the pursuit of happiness. Today, Penn continues in the spirit of the Founding Fathers, developing the intellectual, discussion-oriented seminars that comprise the majority of our course offerings, shaping innovative new courses of study, and allowing a remarkable degree of academic flexibility to its undergraduate students.

"Penn is situated on a green, tree-lined, 260-acre urban campus, four blocks west of the Schuylkill River in Philadelphia. The broad lawns that connect Penn's stately halls embody a philosophy of academic freedom within our undergraduate schools. Newly developed interdisciplinary programs fusing classical disciplines with practical, professional options enable Penn to define cutting-edge academia in and out of the classroom. Students are encouraged to partake in study and research that may extend into many of the graduate and professional schools. As part of our College House system, Penn's Faculty Masters engage students in academic and civic experience while leading residential programs that promote an environment where living and learning intersect around the clock.

"Penn students are part of a dynamic community that includes a traditional campus, a lively neighborhood, and a city rich in culture and diversity. Whether your interests include artistic performance, community involvement, student government, athletics, fraternities and sororities, or cultural and religious organizations, you'll find many different options. Most importantly, students at Penn find that their lives in and out of the classroom compliment each other and are full, interesting and busy. We invite you to visit Penn in Philadelphia. You'll enjoy the revolutionary spirit of the campus and city.

"Penn requires either the new SAT plus two SAT Subject Tests (in different fields) or the ACT. Scores from older versions of the SAT (pre-March 2005 version) and the ACT are acceptable. For the old SAT, scores must be submitted with the results of three SAT Subject Tests, one of which must be the writing test."

SELECTIVITY

Admissions Rating	99
# of applicants	22,645
% of applicants accepted	16
% of acceptees attending	66

FRESHMAN PROFILE

Range SAT Critical Reading	650–750
Range SAT Math	680–770
Range ACT Composite	29–33
Average HS GPA	3.8
% graduated top 10% of class	96
% graduated top 25% of class	99
% graduated top 50% of class	100

DEADLINES

Regular	
Priority	01/01
Nonfall registration?	No

APPLICANTS ALSO LOOK AT

AND OFTEN PREFER
Harvard College, Stanford University, Yale University

AND SOMETIMES PREFER
Brown University, Duke University

AND RARELY PREFER
Cornell University

FINANCIAL FACTS

Financial Aid Rating	96
Annual tuition	$35,916
Room and board	$10,621
Required fees	$3,925
Books and supplies	$1,043
% frosh rec. any financial aid	60
% UG rec. any financial aid	55

University of Pittsburgh—Pittsburgh Campus

4227 Fifth Avenue, First Floor, Alumni Hall, Pittsburgh, PA 15260 • Admissions: 412-624-7488 • Fax: 412-648-8815

STUDENTS SAY ". . ."

Academics

The University of Pittsburgh "is the perfect-sized institution," a place with "all the benefits of a large urban university, including research, internships, and lots of amazing experiences," but also small enough "that people truly have a chance to make a name for themselves on campus. You can't go five minutes without bumping into someone you know here." Many departments stand out; all medical fields benefit from the school's affiliation with the renowned research-oriented University of Pittsburgh Medical Center; and programs in dentistry, pharmacology, physical therapy, neuroscience, and biology are all considered outstanding. Programs in engineering, business, and the liberal arts are also noteworthy. Students appreciate the fact that "professors here are all very accessible and really want their students to learn and understand their courses. They are willing to work with the students to [help them] achieve better grades and enhance the learning experience." Opportunities to study abroad abound, and undergrads "can often find study-abroad programs that are cheaper for them than their tuition would have been."

Life

Pitt is located in Oakland, a "really nice location relative to downtown Pittsburgh and the surrounding neighborhoods." Thanks to "the school's arrangement" with the city of Pittsburgh, "every Pitt student gets free city busing," a perk that allows and encourages undergrads to explore the city. Further such encouragement comes in the form of PittArts, a program that "heavily subsidizes cultural events in the city. When Broadway shows come to Pittsburgh, you can get tickets for $10, a dinner at an Italian restaurant, and free transportation downtown. They also offer free lectures, operas, and symphonies." No wonder students tell us that "Pittsburgh is a college city, one that really caters to students. Bigger cities may offer more renowned acts coming through, or more famous museums, but in Pittsburgh we can actually afford to experience them!" The campus is also busy, with "many campus organizations," "free movies in the Union, student performances on campus, lectures (Maya Angelou came recently)"; these offer students lots of opportunities to socialize. Pitt athletics are also popular, with basketball and football drawing the biggest crowds. All of these options "make socializing easier and less alcohol-centric. While there is a lot of drinking on campus, it is just as easy and socially acceptable to sit down to coffee."

Student Body

A "very diverse population" of 16,796 undergraduates virtually guarantees that "everyone is bound to meet someone whom he or she would have never met staying in his or her hometown." The school has "over 450 organizations, and all those groups provide a place for students to come and be their own people in a group they feel comfortable with." Highly competitive admissions mean that "kids here are definitely intelligent and have a lot going for them." They're not just brainiacs, though—in fact, Pitt students "like to have a good time too, not just going out to parties. Many students really take advantage of the free admission to numerous museums and free city busing to visit the many neighborhoods of Pittsburgh." The most dedicated students here, our respondents report, can be found in the medical sciences (neuroscience, chemistry, and biology) as well as in some of the humanities (writing, literature, philosophy).

FINANCIAL AID: 412-624-7488 • E-MAIL: OAFA@PITT.EDU • WEBSITE: WWW.PITT.EDU

THE PRINCETON REVIEW SAYS

Admissions

Very important factors considered include: Academic GPA, rigor of secondary school record. *Important factors considered include:* Standardized test scores. *Other factors considered include:* Class rank, application essay, recommendation(s), character/personal qualities, extracurricular activities, first generation, geographical residence, level of applicant's interest, racial/ethnic status, talent/ability, volunteer work, work experience. SAT or ACT required; High school diploma is required and GED is not accepted. *Academic units required:* 4 English, 3 mathematics, 3 science, (3 science labs), 1 foreign language, 1 social studies, 4 academic electives. *Academic units recommended:* 4 mathematics, 4 science, 3 foreign language, 3 social studies, 2 history, 1 computer science.

Financial Aid

Students should submit: FAFSA, institution's own financial aid form. The Princeton Review suggests that all financial aid forms be submitted as soon as possible after January 1. *Need-based scholarships/grants offered:* Federal Pell, SEOG, state scholarships/grants, private scholarships, the school's own gift aid, Federal Nursing Scholarships. *Loan aid offered:* FFEL Subsidized Stafford, FFEL Unsubsidized Stafford, FFEL PLUS, Federal Perkins, Federal Nursing, college/university loans from institutional funds. Applicants will be notified of awards on a rolling basis beginning 3/15. Federal Work-Study Program available. Off-campus job opportunities are excellent.

The Inside Word

With the overwhelming number of applications Pitt receives, it's no wonder its Admissions Counselors rely on numbers. Comparable to its public university brethren, the school makes admit decisions based mostly on secondary school records and test scores. Applicants who provide transcripts laced with honors classes, Advanced Placement classes, and solid grades should be accepted.

THE SCHOOL SAYS "..."

From The Admissions Office

"The University of Pittsburgh is one of 62 members of the Association of American Universities, a prestigious group whose members include the major research universities of North America. There are nearly 400 degree programs available at the 16 Pittsburgh campus schools (two offering only undergraduate degree programs, four offering graduate degree programs, and ten offering both) and four regional campuses, allowing students a wide latitude of choices, both academically and in setting and style, size and pace of campus. Programs ranked nationally include philosophy, history and philosophy of science, chemistry, economics, English, history, physics, political science, and psychology. The University Center for International Studies is ranked one of the exemplary international programs in the country by the Council on Learning.

"Freshman applicants for Fall 2008 are required to submit SAT or ACT test results. All testing should preferably be completed by fall of your senior year for September admission. We strongly recommend that you take the SAT or ACT at least once as a junior and once as a senior."

SELECTIVITY
Admissions Rating	89
# of applicants	19,056
% of applicants accepted	56
% of acceptees attending	32
# accepting a place on wait list	310
% admitted from wait list	12

FRESHMAN PROFILE
Range SAT Critical Reading	570–670
Range SAT Math	580–670
Range ACT Composite	24–30
% graduated top 10% of class	48
% graduated top 25% of class	81
% graduated top 50% of class	98

DEADLINES
Regular	
Notification	rolling
Nonfall registration?	yes

FINANCIAL FACTS
Financial Aid Rating	77
Annual in-state tuition	$12,876
% frosh rec. need-based scholarship or grant aid	43
% UG rec. need-based scholarship or grant aid	40
% frosh rec. non-need-based scholarship or grant aid	25
% UG rec. non-need-based scholarship or grant aid	17
% frosh rec. need-based self-help aid	42
% UG rec. need-based self-help aid	44
% frosh rec. athletic scholarships	3
% UG rec. athletic scholarships	2

UNIVERSITY OF PUGET SOUND

1500 NORTH WARNER STREET, TACOMA, WA 98416-1062 • ADMISSIONS: 253-879-3211 • FAX: 253-879-3993

STUDENTS SAY ". . ."

Academics

Set "in the shadows of the Cascades" and just down the road from Washington State's Commencement Bay, the University of Puget Sound "offers a strong (and getting stronger) liberal arts education." A junior explains, "We are a very student-centered school," which means that teaching is top priority for this highly qualified faculty. Not only are professors "intelligent, well versed, [and] articulate," they're also concerned about the well-being of their students. "Many professors want to have conversations about what is going on in your life," writes a senior. "They make this school." So does the strong allotment of academic offerings. Students point to the Asian studies, biology, international political economy, and music offerings as the crème de la crème. You won't find the standard "huge lecture classes" at UPS; "Even intro-level lectures have maybe 30 people in them." Despite the friendly atmosphere in class, professors tend to set high expectations for their students. "Coasting by on natural ability doesn't work anymore," warns a senior. Opinions of the administration vary, but most find it to be "caring and supportive of the students. If you have an idea, they say go for it." Students are hoping that the new president of the university will help put the place on the map. As a psychology major puts it, "The university is academically strong, but needs to be recognized for that across the country, not just in the Pacific Northwest."

Life

Whether you're a city slicker or a rugged outdoorsman, UPS's location ensures you'll find something to satisfy your interests. Seattle is a short drive away and has everything from pro sports teams to world-class art exhibits. With beaches, the Sound, the Cascades, and the Olympic Rain Forest all nearby, outdoor enthusiasts are never at a loss for adventure. "Outdoor interests are really popular, [including] Ultimate Frisbee, soccer, biking, and hiking." "Athletics are huge," too, and with 21 varsity teams, 14 intramural sports, and three club sports, athletes have plenty of opportunities to flex their muscles. Sports aside, "There are tons of activities (presentations, volunteer opportunities, meetings, movies, talks, concerts, and clubs) every night of the week." In total, UPS offers about 75 student clubs, and "Most people are involved in a ton of groups." When they're not involved in parties, that is. "There are always plenty going on, either at Greek houses or in other nearby campus houses." But beware, warns an undergrad: "The administration can have a Gestapo-esque feel when it comes to parties and drinking on campus." Nonetheless, some students line up at the keg, while others fill the seats for the popular "one-dollar movies" on campus. Regardless of what you're doing, "If you're not doing anything in the evening, you're either lazy or antisocial . . . or dead."

Student Body

"There are three groups of students" at UPS, according to a senior: "(1) the preppies, (2) the hippies, (3) the Hawaiians." Among groups (1) and (2), you're likely to find "a lot of 'trustafarians' and rich kids." There's no doubt that liberalism rules the roost here, which causes one junior to note that "the least accepted student organization is, ironically, the Republican Majority." But political differences—or any differences, for that matter—don't cause irreparable rifts in this student body. According to a sophomore, "Everyone gets along extremely well, no matter what gender, religion, race, ethnicity, [or] social class. UPS has a great atmosphere that I sincerely appreciate." Another classmate adds, "Overall, students are accepting and curious about other beliefs. And students here are open-minded." They're open-hearted, as well. Many students reported participating in community service.

FINANCIAL AID: 800-396-7192 • E-MAIL: ADMISSION@UPS.EDU • WEBSITE: WWW.UPS.EDU

THE PRINCETON REVIEW SAYS

Admissions

Very important factors considered include: Academic GPA, rigor of secondary school record, standardized test scores. *Important factors considered include:* Application essay, recommendation(s), alumni/ae relation, character/personal qualities, extracurricular activities, racial/ethnic status, talent/ability. *Other factors considered include:* Class rank, first generation, interview, level of applicant's interest, volunteer work, work experience. SAT or ACT required; ACT with Writing component recommended. TOEFL required of all international applicants. High school diploma is required and GED is accepted. *Academic units recommended:* 4 English, 4 mathematics, 4 science, (4 science labs), 3 foreign language, 3 social studies, 3 history, 1 fine/visual/performing arts.

Financial Aid

Students should submit: FAFSA. The Princeton Review suggests that all financial aid forms be submitted as soon as possible after January 1. *Need-based scholarships/grants offered:* Federal Pell, SEOG, state scholarships/grants, private scholarships, the school's own gift aid. *Loan aid offered:* FFEL Subsidized Stafford, FFEL Unsubsidized Stafford, FFEL PLUS, Federal Perkins Applicants will be notified of awards on a rolling basis beginning 3/15. Federal Work-Study Program available. Institutional employment available. Off-campus job opportunities are excellent.

The Inside Word

The University of Puget Sound is on the right track with its willingness to supply students with detailed information about how the selection process works. If universities in general were more forthcoming about candidate evaluation, college admission wouldn't be the angst-ridden exercise that it is for so many students. All students are aware that their academic background is the primary consideration of every Admissions Committee. How they are considered as individuals remains mysterious. At Puget Sound, it is clear that people mean more to the university than its freshman profile and that candidates can count on a considerate and caring attitude before, during, and after the review process.

THE SCHOOL SAYS "..."

From The Admissions Office

"For over 100 years, students from many locations and backgrounds have chosen to join our community. It is a community committed to excellence—excellence in the classroom and excellence in student organizations and activities. Puget students are serious about rowing and writing, management and music, skiing and sciences, leadership and languages. At Puget Sound you'll be challenged—and helped—to perform at the peak of your ability.

"Applicants are required to submit the SAT or the ACT. For the foreseeable future, Puget Sound will record the SAT or ACT Writing component score, but will not require it as a part of a completed freshman admission application."

SELECTIVITY
Admissions Rating	90
# of applicants	5,273
% of applicants accepted	66
% of acceptees attending	18
# accepting a place on wait list	75
% admitted from wait list	7
# of early decision applicants	128
% accepted early decision	89

FRESHMAN PROFILE
Range SAT Critical Reading	570–690
Range SAT Math	550–660
Range SAT Writing	560–660
Range ACT Composite	25–30
Minimum paper TOEFL	550
Minimum computer TOEFL	213
Average HS GPA	3.54
% graduated top 10% of class	40
% graduated top 25% of class	69
% graduated top 50% of class	95

DEADLINES
Early decision I	
Deadline	11/15
Notification	12/15
Early decision II	
Deadline	1/2
Notification	2/15
Regular	
Priority	2/1
Deadline	2/1
Notification	4/1
Nonfall registration?	yes

APPLICANTS ALSO LOOK AT

AND OFTEN PREFER
Washington University in St. Louis
Pomona College

AND SOMETIMES PREFER
Lewis & Clark College
University of Washington

AND RARELY PREFER
Albertson College of Idaho
Whitworth College

FINANCIAL FACTS
Financial Aid Rating	80
Annual tuition	$32,060
Books and supplies	$1,000
% frosh rec. need-based scholarship or grant aid	60
% UG rec. need-based scholarship or grant aid	58
% frosh rec. non-need-based scholarship or grant aid	22
% UG rec. non-need-based scholarship or grant aid	26
% frosh rec. need-based self-help aid	45
% UG rec. need-based self-help aid	48
% frosh rec. any financial aid	86
% UG rec. any financial aid	88
% UG borrow to pay for school	60
Average cumulative indebtedness	$27,648

UNIVERSITY OF REDLANDS

1200 EAST COLTON AVENUE, REDLANDS, CA 92373 • ADMISSIONS: 909-335-4074 • FAX: 909-335-4089

STUDENTS SAY "..."

Academics

The University of Redlands is essentially two undergraduate programs in one. Through the College of Arts and Sciences (CAS), the majority of students follow a relatively conventional undergraduate curriculum, declaring majors and meeting the related requirements in order to graduate. About 200 students take a more independent approach through the Johnston Center for Integrative Studies, "where students who are accepted can create their own major with the help of their professors." These Johnston students write contracts for their courses and receive narrative evaluations of their work (rather than letter grades). This structure "allows students to learn in a way that is the most efficient for each individual." Because Johnston is a residential community, "Everyone works together to strengthen their education," much to the delight of participants. But regardless of the track they choose, Redlands undergrads enjoy a "personable, student-oriented" school that's "just small enough to have incredible personal attention, yet large enough to still see different people almost every day." Students also appreciate a study abroad program that "is strongly emphasized and encouraged. If there's anywhere in the world that you've had an interest in going—for a month or semester to a year—the University of Redlands is the perfect place to do it. Many students go to Austria because it's a wonderful program, and all your credits transfer when you come back." Redlands excels in a number of areas, including business, music, creative writing, and biology, but they don't do it without a bit of sweat. Undergrads warn, "The academics at Redlands are demanding; I find myself reading, writing, and studying with extremely high degrees of intensity."

Life

Redlands is close to a lot of great places, but the town of Redlands itself "isn't much," students say. A number of them use the nickname "Dead Lands" to sum up their attitude, and a freshman gripes that "we can't just go into town to read at a coffee shop because there is no town!" So while "There's not much to do if you don't have a car," for the automobile-enabled, "Everything is within an hour: the beach, LA, Palm Springs, and the mountains. Trips to the desert in Joshua Tree National Park are also common. Many people like to snowboard or ski in Big Bear in the winter." This nature-rich setting attracts outdoorsy types, and unsurprisingly Redlands "has a very involved outdoor activities group on campus that takes students kayaking, rock climbing and backpacking to destinations throughout the country." The Redlands campus "is beautiful for its Roman-style buildings and pillars, especially in the winter with the snow-capped mountains in the background," and it stays reasonably busy for a school of Redland's size. "Usually, there's something happening on campus, whether it's a philosophical discussion, a screening of a movie, karaoke night, or a basketball game." Still, "On weekends, most people end up drinking and going to parties," which the school frowns upon. Students wish the administration would be "a little more relaxed when it comes to party scenes. It seems like everyone is always getting in trouble. And even the frats have to be really careful and always have huge fines."

Student Body

Because of the CAS/Johnston academic fault line at Redlands, "The school is somewhat divided," with "ultra-liberal Johnston students who meander about the campus on long boards, leaving behind a perpetual smell of hemp and patchouli" on one side, and "more conservative Abercrombie-wearing NCAA athletes, Greeks, and California-skater types" on the other. The CAS student body also includes "math/science geeks, the philosophy brains, the artists and musicians, the business people, and the whimsical lit majors," about half of whom "regard the Johnston kids with complete suspicion and mistrust," in part because some of the Johnston kids seem to look down on the CAS majority. Johnston undergrads are known for being drawn to "a high-energy community of creativity, inhibition, and at times, spurts of college randomness. They are notorious for doing strange things!"

FINANCIAL AID: 909-335-4047 • E-MAIL: ADMISSIONS@REDLANDS.EDU • WEBSITE: WWW.REDLANDS.EDU

THE PRINCETON REVIEW SAYS

Admissions

Very important factors considered include: Academic GPA, recommendation(s), rigor of secondary school record, character/personal qualities, talent/ability. *Important factors considered include:* Application essay, standardized test scores. *Other factors considered include:* Alumni/ae relation, extracurricular activities, first generation, geographical residence, interview, racial/ethnic status, volunteer work, work experience. SAT or ACT required; ACT with Writing component recommended. TOEFL required of all international applicants. High school diploma is required and GED is accepted. *Academic units required:* 4 English, 3 mathematics, 2 science, (1 science labs), 2 foreign language, 2 social studies. *Academic units recommended:* 4 English, 4 mathematics, 3 science, (1 science labs), 3 foreign language, 2 social studies, 1 history.

Financial Aid

Students should submit: FAFSA, state aid form, GPA Verification form for California Residents.. The Princeton Review suggests that all financial aid forms be submitted as soon as possible after January 1. *Need-based scholarships/grants offered:* Federal Pell, SEOG, state scholarships/grants, private scholarships, the school's own gift aid. *Loan aid offered:* FFEL Subsidized Stafford, FFEL Unsubsidized Stafford, FFEL PLUS, Federal Perkins, college/university loans from institutional funds. Applicants will be notified of awards on a rolling basis beginning 2/28. Federal Work-Study Program available. Off-campus job opportunities are fair.

The Inside Word

The University of Redlands is a solid admit for any student with an above average high school record. Candidates who are interested in pursuing self-designed programs through the University's Johnston Center will find the admissions process to be distinctly more personal than it generally is; the center is interested in intellectually curious, self-motivated students and puts a lot of energy into identifying and recruiting them.

THE SCHOOL SAYS "..."

From The Admissions Office

"We've created an unusually blended curriculum of the liberal arts and pre-professional study because we think education is about learning how to think and learning how to do. For example, our environmental studies students have synthesized their study of computer science, sociology, biology, and economics to develop an actual resource management plan for the local mountain communities. Our creative writing program encourages internships with publishing or television production companies so that when our graduates send off their first novel, they can pay the rent as magazine writers. We educate managers, poets, environmental scientists, teachers, musicians, and speech therapists to be reflective about culture and society so that they can better understand and improve the world they'll enter upon graduation.

"First-year students applying for admission for Fall 2008 are required to submit the results of either the SAT or the ACT. We do not require the Writing section of either test. Students may also submit scores from the old SAT (prior to March 2005) or ACT and the student's best scores from either test will be used."

SELECTIVITY

Admissions Rating	88
# of applicants	3,607
% of applicants accepted	67
% of acceptees attending	25

FRESHMAN PROFILE

Range SAT Critical Reading	520–620
Range SAT Math	540–620
Range ACT Composite	22–26
Minimum paper TOEFL	550
Minimum computer TOEFL	213
Average HS GPA	3.58
% graduated top 10% of class	31
% graduated top 25% of class	70
% graduated top 50% of class	93

DEADLINES

Regular	
Priority	12/15
Deadline	4/1
Notification	rolling
Nonfall registration?	yes

APPLICANTS ALSO LOOK AT

AND OFTEN PREFER
Occidental College

AND SOMETIMES PREFER
Pitzer College
Whittier College
University of San Diego
Loyola Marymount University
Chapman University

AND RARELY PREFER
University of California—Riverside

FINANCIAL FACTS

Financial Aid Rating	87
Annual tuition	$30,626
Required fees	$300
% frosh rec. need-based scholarship or grant aid	29
% UG rec. need-based scholarship or grant aid	67
% frosh rec. need-based self-help aid	47
% UG rec. need-based self-help aid	54
% frosh rec. any financial aid	91
% UG rec. any financial aid	90
% UG borrow to pay for school	69
Average cumulative indebtedness	$28,656

UNIVERSITY OF RHODE ISLAND

14 UPPER COLLEGE ROAD, KINGSTON, RI 02881-1391 • ADMISSIONS: 401-874-7100 • FAX: 401-874-5523

CAMPUS LIFE
Quality of Life Rating	66
Fire Safety Rating	80
Green Rating	60*
Type of school	public
Environment	village

STUDENTS
Total undergrad enrollment	12,268
% male/female	44/56
% from out of state	39
% live on campus	45
% in (# of) fraternities	12 (11)
% in (# of) sororities	15 (9)
% African American	5
% Asian	2
% Caucasian	72
% Hispanic	5
# of countries represented	64

SURVEY SAYS . . .
Great library
Great off-campus food
Frats and sororities dominate
social scene
Student publications are popular
Lots of beer drinking
Hard liquor is popular
(Almost) everyone smokes

ACADEMICS
Academic Rating	70
Calendar	semester
Student/faculty ratio	19:1
Profs interesting rating	62
Profs accessible rating	62
Most common reg class size	20–29 students
Most common lab size	10–19 students

MOST POPULAR MAJORS
nursing/registered nurse
(RN, ASN, BSN, MSN)
communication studies/speech
communication and rhetoric
psychology
Pharm. D.

STUDENTS SAY "..."

Academics

The University of Rhode Island "is a pretty decent middle-sized school in a great location." Notable majors include "nursing, engineering, or anything science." The "excellent" pharmacy program at URI is competitive and nationally recognized. Many classes are "very rigorous." Others are "wicked easy." For both, "there are many resources available to get help." The faculty really runs the gamut. "There are some really good ones, but some are just awful." The good profs "genuinely care about teaching" and "willingly offer their time" outside of class. "All of my teachers have had considerable experience in their field and bring a lot to the classroom," says an impressed freshman. As for the bad professors, "there are some serious horror stories." Some students think the subpar professors "cancel class almost too much," some bemoan the lack of outside help and the brief periods of time that qualify as office hours, and some have a hard time understanding the accents of foreign professors. URI's administration receives similarly mixed reviews. "I have had very few problems with administration," says one student. "They are happy to sit down and talk with you about any concerns that you have and they will help solve your problems." Other students see "an ardent bureaucracy" "too obsessed with drinking policies to pay attention to what really matters." "These people are tools," remarks one student.

Life

"URI is a gorgeous school—especially in the fall—on a big hill." It's located in a "safe" and "rural" area. "Parking is horrible," though the university has recently opened 1,400 new student parking spaces and set a shuttle bus system into place so as to make pedestrian traffic safer. "Some of the dorm buildings are in very poor condition." For some students, URI is a "suitcase school." "A lot of students do go home on the weekends just because they live so close by." "If you get involved on campus you will love it," says a psychology major. "If not, you will want to transfer." Intramurals and varsity sports are popular. "Basketball is huge; so is hockey" "There are beautiful beaches right down the road from campus where you can surf, swim, or just sit and read," weather permitting. "Greek life is very popular, and if you live on campus it feels like everyone is part of it (but they're not)." The campus is ostensibly dry but the alcohol policy certainly "hasn't stopped URI students from getting wasted." "One thing I didn't know coming to URI was how much of the social life happens off campus," discloses an English major. Parties occur 15 minutes away— "down the line," as students here say. There are "raging house parties every single weekend" in Narragansett by the beach. Narragansett bars are popular, too. "If you are not 21, a fake ID is almost necessary." Students looking for more urban pursuits often travel 30 miles north to Providence.

Student Body

"The University of Rhode Island is an affordable option for in-state students." "Most out-of-state residents are from wealthy families or have scholarships." There are "a lot of generic college kids who go to college for the social aspect." "URI is mostly made up of guys that want to party and drive BMWs and girls that wear North Face jackets, Ugg boots, and big Dior sunglasses," stereotypes one student. Politically, it's a "pretty liberal" but mostly "apathetic" crowd. "However, if you search you can find some cool people who don't fit the mold." "There are many different students here," attests a nutrition major, "from jocks and jockettes to artists to frat boys and sorority girls." Ethnic diversity is not unreasonable but URI is cliquish. "People here do tend to hang out with people who are more similar to them." "Ethnicities mostly do not mix." Rhode Islanders often "stick to" high school friends.

UNIVERSITY OF RHODE ISLAND

FINANCIAL AID: 401-874-9500 • E-MAIL: URIADMIT@ETAL.URI.EDU • WEBSITE: WWW.URI.EDU/ADMISSIONS

THE PRINCETON REVIEW SAYS

Admissions

Very important factors considered include: Rigor of secondary school record. *Important factors considered include:* Class rank, application essay, academic GPA, standardized test scores. *Other factors considered include:* Recommendation(s), alumni/ae relation, character/personal qualities, extracurricular activities, first generation, geographical residence, level of applicant's interest, racial/ethnic status, state residency, talent/ability, volunteer work, work experienc SAT or ACT required; ACT with Writing component required. TOEFL required of all international applicants. High school diploma is required and GED is accepted. *Academic units required:* 4 English, 3 mathematics, 2 science, (1 science labs), 2 foreign language, 2 social studies, 5 academic electives.

Financial Aid

Students should submit: FAFSA. The Princeton Review suggests that all financial aid forms be submitted as soon as possible after January 1. *Need-based scholarships/grants offered:* Federal Pell, SEOG, state scholarships/grants, private scholarships, the school's own gift aid. *Loan aid offered:* Direct Subsidized Stafford, Direct Unsubsidized Stafford, Direct PLUS, Federal Perkins, Federal Nursing, state loans, college/university loans from institutional funds. Applicants will be notified of awards on a rolling basis beginning 3/31. Federal Work-Study Program available. Institutional employment available. Off-campus job opportunities are good.

The Inside Word

Any candidate with solid grades is likely to find the university's Admissions Committee to be welcoming. The yield of admits who enroll is low and the state's population small. Out-of-state students are attractive to URI because they are sorely needed to fill out the student body. Students who graduate in the top 10 percent of their class are good scholarship bets. If you are a resident of a New England state other then Rhode Island, you get a tuition discount, but only if you enroll in certain degree programs.

THE SCHOOL SAYS "..."

From The Admissions Office

"Outstanding freshman candidates for Fall 2009 admission with a minimum SAT score of 1200 (combined Critical Reading and Math) or ACT composite score of 25 who rank in the top quarter of their high school class are eligible to be considered for a Centennial Scholarship. These merit-based scholarships range up to full tuition and are renewable each semester if the student maintains full-time continuous enrollment and a 3.0 average or better. In order to be eligible for consideration, all application materials must be received in the Admission Office by the December 15, 2008 early action deadline. Applications are not considered complete until the application fee, completed application, official high school transcript, list of senior courses, personal essay, and SAT or ACT scores (sent directly from the testing agency) are received.

"If a student is awarded a Centennial Scholarship, and his or her residency status changes from out-of-state to regional or in-state, the amount of the award will be reduced to reflect the reduced tuition rate.

"The SAT Math and Critical Reading scores are used for admission evaluation and Centennial Scholarship consideration. The Writing score is not currently used for admission evaluation or Centennial Scholarship consideration."

SELECTIVITY
Admissions Rating	78
# of applicants	14,272
% of applicants accepted	79
% of acceptees attending	28

FRESHMAN PROFILE
Range SAT Critical Reading	490–590
Range SAT Math	500–600
Minimum web-based TOEFL	79
Average HS GPA	3.12
% graduated top 10% of class	12

DEADLINES
Early action	
Deadline	12/15
Notification	1/31
Regular	
Deadline	2/1
Notification	rolling
Nonfall registration?	yes

APPLICANTS ALSO LOOK AT
AND OFTEN PREFER
Northeastern University
University of Connecticut
University of Massachusetts—Amherst
AND SOMETIMES PREFER
Boston College
Providence College
Quinnipiac University
AND RARELY PREFER
Occidental College
University of Maryland—Baltimore County
Carnegie Mellon University

FINANCIAL FACTS
Financial Aid Rating	71
Annual in-state tuition	$6,440
Annual out-of-state tuition	$21,294
Room and board	$8,732
Required fees	$1,744
Books and supplies	$1,000
% frosh rec. need-based scholarship or grant aid	52
% UG rec. need-based scholarship or grant aid	53
% frosh rec. non-need-based scholarship or grant aid	7
% UG rec. non-need-based scholarship or grant aid	5
% frosh rec. need-based self-help aid	51
% UG rec. need-based self-help aid	52
% frosh rec. any financial aid	52
% UG rec. any financial aid	54
% UG borrow to pay for school	64
Average cumulative indebtedness	$21,125

UNIVERSITY OF RICHMOND

28 WESTHAMPTON WAY, RICHMOND, VA 23173 • ADMISSIONS: 804-289-8640 • FAX: 804-287-6003

CAMPUS LIFE

Quality of Life Rating	**85**
Fire Safety Rating	**70**
Green Rating	**88**
Type of school	private
Environment	metropolis

STUDENTS

Total undergrad enrollment	2,718
% male/female	51/49
% from out of state	84
% from public high school	62
% live on campus	92
% in (# of) fraternities	28 (5)
% in (# of) sororities	43 (8)
% African American	6
% Asian	4
% Caucasian	75
% Hispanic	3
% international	5
# of countries represented	70

SURVEY SAYS . . .

Small classes
No one cheats
Great off-campus food
Campus feels safe
Frats and sororities dominate social scene
Lots of beer drinking

ACADEMICS

Academic Rating	**93**
Calendar	semester
Student/faculty ratio	9:1
Profs interesting rating	91
Profs accessible rating	91
Most common reg class size	10–19 students
Most common lab size	10–19 students

MOST POPULAR MAJORS

business/commerce
English language and literature
political science and government

STUDENTS SAY ". . ."

Academics

With a strong liberal arts core that integrates a "great business school and equally strong leadership school" and "amazing and challenging premed programs," the University of Richmond serves well a student population that "knows that after college they will go to med, law, or grad school and end up with a high-paying job." Undergrads tell us that UR "is the perfect size. It's small enough where it's easy to get involved in lots of different things and to play a leadership role in that group. However, you always have plenty of options and are constantly meeting new people." The school "encourages undergraduate research, both in the sciences and in other fields, and most appealing is that students are often paid for their research," although the benefits to students' resumes aren't half bad either. Classes are "challenging, and the workload can be difficult," but "Professors tend to be understanding" and "really do care about their students." Undergrads love the academics, although many complain that the required writing-intensive, first-year course "is a pain that many students find annoying and pointless." Some here warn that due to the size of the school, "There are a limited number of classes offered. Especially in the less-popular departments, interesting classes that were in the catalogue were hardly offered and were almost impossible to get into for underclassmen." Support systems are strong; they include "academic advisors to ensure that the student is getting a quality education with opportunities to do internships and study abroad," "an effective Career Development Center," "speech, writing and academic skills centers (all excellent)," "free tutoring," and "a great alumni network."

Life

UR's coordinate system divides men and women into coordinate colleges: Richmond for men, Westhampton for women. Students dine and attend classes together and share some student organizations, but they function under separate governance systems, though some housing is co-ed. The benefits of this system include "great leadership opportunities for tons of men and women." "The week itself is intense with school work, but by the time the weekend arrives, everyone is ready to relax." The Greek houses help; students report that "the fraternity scene is central to the culture of the school, almost at the exclusion of every other weekend activity." Students might take greater advantage of their proximity to a big city except that "it is very difficult to go anywhere without a car because the university as well as the city has limited public transportation." One student explains, "This campus is located near a great city that many students never explore, outside of bars." Perhaps students stick so close to school because it's just so beautiful; everyone here agrees that "our campus is quite obviously one of the most gorgeous in the world. Everything from the lake and gazebo to the architecture of the buildings is breathtaking."

Student Body

UR, most students agree, "is extremely preppy, with a lot of very wealthy students. It is also very fraternity/sorority-oriented. If you aren't in one of those groups, it is definitely harder to find close friends because the school is so small." Harder, but not impossible; notes one outsider, "There is a decided proportion of students who don't fit this mold, who are easy to find and certainly fit in, but if you are one of this latter group, it may seem on occasion as though you are starring in 'Operation J. Crew Invasion.'" Most students "live, eat, study, and party on campus; they enjoy a sense of belonging here. Everyone you pass waves, nods, smiles or says 'hello,' even if you've never met them before. Walking to class can really put you in a good mood, no matter how late you were up cramming for a test."

FINANCIAL AID: 804-289-8438 • E-MAIL: ADMISSIONS@RICHMOND.EDU • WEBSITE: WWW.RICHMOND.EDU

THE PRINCETON REVIEW SAYS

Admissions

Very important factors considered include: Academic GPA, rigor of secondary school record. *Important factors considered include:* Class rank, application essay, standardized test scores, character/personal qualities, talent/ability. *Other factors considered include:* Recommendation(s), first generation, alumni/ae relation, extracurricular activities, geographical residence, racial/ethnic status, state residency, volunteer work, work experience. SAT or ACT required; TOEFL required of all non-native English speakers. High school diploma is required and GED is accepted. *Academic units required:* 4 English, 3 mathematics, 2 science, (2 science labs), 2 foreign language, 2 history. *Academic units recommended:* 4 English, 4 mathematics, 4 science, (4 science labs), 4 foreign language, 4 history.

Financial Aid

Students should submit: FAFSA, institution's own financial aid form. Regular filing deadline is 2/15. The Princeton Review suggests that all financial aid forms be submitted as soon as possible after January 1. *Need-based scholarships/grants offered:* Federal Pell, SEOG, state scholarships/grants, private scholarships, the school's own gift aid. *Loan aid offered:* Direct Subsidized Stafford, Direct Unsubsidized Stafford, Direct PLUS, Federal Perkins Applicants will be notified of awards on or about 4/1.

The Inside Word

While SAT Subject Tests are no longer required, the SAT Writing section has replaced this requisite and is considered equally important. There does appear to be an effort to look at the candidate's record carefully and thoroughly. Course of study, high school performance, and test scores are the most important parts of your application; however, Richmond also makes sure that all files are read at least two times before a final decision has been rendered.

THE SCHOOL SAYS "..."

From The Admissions Office

"The University of Richmond combines the characteristics of a small college with the dynamics of a large university. The unique size, beautiful suburban campus, and world-class facilities offer students an extraordinary mix of opportunities for personal growth and intellectual achievement. At Richmond, students are encouraged to engage themselves in their environment. Discussion and dialogue are the forefront of the academic experience, while research, internships, and international experiences are important components of students' co-curricular lives. The university is committed to providing undergraduate students with a rigorous academic experience, while integrating these studies with opportunities for experiential learning and promoting total individual development. The university also places a high value on diversity and believes in taking full advantage of the rich benefits of learning in a community of individuals from varied backgrounds. Service in the Richmond community is popular.

"The University of Richmond requires either the SAT or the ACT. We do not preference either test. We evaluate all three sections of the SAT (Critical Reading, Math, and Writing); the Writing section of the ACT is optional. If multiple tests are submitted, the Admission Committee considers those results which are most favorable to the applicant. We do not require or recommend SAT Subject Tests."

SELECTIVITY
Admissions Rating	95
# of applicants	6,649
% of applicants accepted	40
% of acceptees attending	31
# accepting a place on wait list	710
% admitted from wait list	9
# of early decision applicants	288
% accepted early decision	57

FRESHMAN PROFILE
Range SAT Critical Reading	590–690
Range SAT Math	610–690
Range SAT Writing	590–690
Range ACT Composite	27–31
Minimum paper TOEFL	550
Minimum computer TOEFL	213
% graduated top 10% of class	61.8
% graduated top 25% of class	88.7
% graduated top 50% of class	98.4

DEADLINES
Early decision	
Deadline	11/15
Notification	12/15
Regular	
Deadline	1/15
Notification	4/1
Nonfall registration?	no

APPLICANTS ALSO LOOK AT
AND OFTEN PREFER
University of Virginia
College of William and Mary
AND SOMETIMES PREFER
Vanderbilt University
Wake Forest University
Duke University
AND RARELY PREFER
Lafayette College
Bucknell University

FINANCIAL FACTS
Financial Aid Rating	95
Annual tuition	$38,850
Room and board	$8,200
Books and supplies	$1,050
% frosh rec. need-based scholarship or grant aid	43
% UG rec. need-based scholarship or grant aid	38
% frosh rec. non-need-based scholarship or grant aid	5
% UG rec. non-need-based scholarship or grant aid	4
% frosh rec. need-based self-help aid	37
% UG rec. need-based self-help aid	33
% frosh rec. athletic scholarships	6
% UG rec. athletic scholarships	7
% frosh rec. any financial aid	65
% UG rec. any financial aid	69
% UG borrow to pay for school	41
Average cumulative indebtedness	$19,214

UNIVERSITY OF SAN DIEGO

5998 ALCALA PARK, SAN DIEGO, CA 92110-2492 • ADMISSIONS: 619-260-4506 • FAX: 619-260-6836

STUDENTS SAY ". . ."

Academics

If you want "sun, surf, and professors who actually care about your work and your life," check out the University of San Diego. Everyone at this "relatively small" Catholic school must complete a demanding and "well-rounded" set of general education requirements. You won't get out of here without a heaping helping of English, math, science, foreign language, and, of course, religion. Beyond the core curriculum, the selection of majors is very good. The exceedingly popular business administration program is among the best in the country. Other popular and solid programs include communications, psychology, and accounting. "Academically, USD is challenging, but not ridiculously so." Classes are "comfortable" and small. "It's virtually impossible to get lost in the shuffle," and "it isn't like a state school where your teacher wouldn't notice that you're not there." Students avoid a few professors "like the plague" but the faculty as a whole is "magnificent" and "very passionate about teaching." "Their enthusiasm shows in the classroom," and they "practically beg for you to come visit them during office hours." "They make me feel like I matter to them," says an industrial engineering major. Views of management are more mixed. Some students tell us that the "very helpful" administration "takes care of things right away." Others contend that the staff is "overly politically correct," "cluttered, unorganized, helpless, and mad at you."

Life

"USD is studying in paradise." The "pristine, manicured" campus looks like "a resort" and "when it's 60 to 65 degrees and sunny in December, you tend to be happier." "School spirit is lackluster at best," but "clubs are big on campus and intramural sports are popular." The Greek scene looms large as well. If you seek spiritual growth, opportunities are ample. "You can be as involved or as uninvolved in the Catholic religion as you choose." Complaints include parking. "On bad days, it can take up to an hour" to find a spot. Still, as one senior warns, "having a car or a friend with one is a necessity." Also, USD's alcohol and drug policies are strict. The resident assistants in the dorms are often "too into their jobs," and campus security is a severe bunch. As a result, "partying on campus is nearly impossible." Students aren't too upset about any of this, though, because the real fun is at the beach. There's a genuine "beach culture atmosphere" here. Many upperclassmen live near the shore, and "most people go down to Mission Beach and Pacific Beach" for "day kegs," the bar scene, and parties galore. Students also tell us that the city of San Diego is "to die for." "You won't find a better spot for a school." "There are two state colleges within driving distance, so a lot of kids from each school intermingle at parties." "Padres and Chargers games are a fun way to hang out depending on cash flow or the season." And for really crazy nights, "there is always Tijuana."

Student Body

Ethnic diversity at USD is reasonably admirable. By far, Hispanics constitute the largest minority group. There are considerably more women than men. "The guys are very handsome." The women are "very hot." "There is a strong majority of Catholics," explains a first-year student, "but I don't get the impression that they tend to be deeply religious." There are "lots of Orange County kids" and "surfer dudes." "Most people are laidback," "down to earth," "outgoing, and friendly." They're "typical Southern Californians really." "I wouldn't say there are many wildly atypical students," observes a freshman. More than two-thirds of the students here receive financial aid, and "there are many students who are not wealthy." Others, however, "have a lot of money." Not for nothing is USD sarcastically called the "University of Spoiled Daughters." "The 'rich white girl' idea is a stereotype USD is working hard to break" but there is definitely a noticeable "flock of bleached blonde" "size zeros with BMW's" "dressed like they're on a runway." "Juicy sweats, Chanel shades, and name-brand handbags" are too common for some students' tastes. "The Ugg boot situation" is grave as well.

FINANCIAL AID: 619-260-4514 • E-MAIL: ADMISSIONS@SANDIEGO.EDU • WEBSITE: WWW.SANDIEGO.EDU/ADMISSIONS/UNDERGRADUATE

THE PRINCETON REVIEW SAYS

Admissions

Very important factors considered include: Academic GPA, rigor of secondary school record, standardized test scores. *Important factors considered include:* Class rank, application essay, recommendation(s), character/personal qualities, extracurricular activities, talent/ability, volunteer work. *Other factors considered include:* Alumni/ae relation, first generation, geographical residence, level of applicant's interest, racial/ethnic status, religious affiliation/commitment, work experience. SAT or ACT required; ACT with Writing component required. High school diploma is required and GED is accepted. *Academic units required:* 4 English, 3 mathematics, 3 science, (2 science labs), 2 foreign language, 3 social studies. *Academic units recommended:* 4 English, 4 mathematics, 4 science, (3 science labs), 3 foreign language, 4 social studies.

Financial Aid

Students should submit: FAFSA Regular filing deadline is 3/2. The Princeton Review suggests that all financial aid forms be submitted as soon as possible after January 1. *Need-based scholarships/grants offered:* Federal Pell, SEOG, state scholarships/grants, private scholarships, the school's own gift aid, Federal Nursing Scholarships. *Loan aid offered:* FFEL Subsidized Stafford, FFEL Unsubsidized Stafford, FFEL PLUS, Federal Perkins, college/university loans from institutional funds, non-federal loan programs. Applicants will be notified of awards on a rolling basis beginning 3/1. Federal Work-Study Program available. Institutional employment available. Off-campus job opportunities are good.

The Inside Word

The University of San Diego offers a broad liberal arts core, small classes, and close interaction between students and professors. The dazzling campus and an unbeatable location are just gravy. As such, admission here is competitive. Solid test scores and outstanding grades should be a given for applicants.

THE SCHOOL SAYS "..."

From The Admissions Office

"Looking at the University of San Diego is easy on the eyes. But really seeing our true character demands a little work.

"It is easy to focus on the obvious: the incredible beauty of the campus, the region's unparalleled climate and livability, long lists of recreational and co-curricular opportunities, the vitality of students walking through the central plaza, or even the obvious expressions of USD's Catholic character. But to focus on the superficial would be misleading.

"While the beach is nearby, USD is a serious academic institution. While the campus is stunning, the people make the difference. More than 10,000 candidates vie for 1,100 freshman openings. But to see the 'average' freshman as a 3.8 GPA or a 1220 SAT score would miss the person. Each is unique—selected on expressions of diversity, leadership, service, talent, and essential human character. Faculty, too, are rigorously screened. USD draws over 100 candidates for every faculty opening, and this screening goes well beyond their lists of publications or the names on their diplomas. To challenge and inspire, they bring innovative approaches to undergraduate research, experiential learning, and faculty mentoring. While often compared to much larger institutions, USD seeks to be recognized for undergraduate teaching and residential learning. In comparison to schools of similar character, USD's academic offerings are truly impressive; a small sample includes marine biology, environmental studies, Latino studies, communication studies, e-commerce, and professional programs in engineering, business, and education, each of which complements a rigorous liberal arts base. New facilities demonstrate this diversity, including a state-of-the-art science center, the Kroc Institute for Peace and Justice, and the Jenny Craig Sports Pavilion. Freshman applicants must submit scores from the new SAT or the ACT exam with Writing. Scores on the previous exams will not be considered. As always, these scores will be used in conjunction with many other factors; in particular, the student's grade point average, curriculum, extra curricular activities, and letters of recommendation."

SELECTIVITY

Admissions Rating	**92**
# of applicants	10,563
% of applicants accepted	48
% of acceptees attending	22
# accepting a place on wait list	419
% admitted from wait list	19

FRESHMAN PROFILE

Range SAT Critical Reading	530–630
Range SAT Math	550–650
Range SAT Writing	540–630
Range ACT Composite	24–28
Average HS GPA	3.76
% graduated top 10% of class	38
% graduated top 25% of class	74
% graduated top 50% of class	96

DEADLINES

Early action	
Deadline	11/15
Notification	1/31
Regular	
Priority	1/15
Deadline	3/1
Notification	4/15
Nonfall registration?	yes

FINANCIAL FACTS

Financial Aid Rating	**76**
Annual tuition	$34,000
Room and board	$11,870
Books and supplies	$1,566
% frosh rec. need-based scholarship or grant aid	42
% UG rec. need-based scholarship or grant aid	42
% frosh rec. non-need-based scholarship or grant aid	26
% UG rec. non-need-based scholarship or grant aid	20
% frosh rec. need-based self-help aid	30
% UG rec. need-based self-help aid	34
% frosh rec. athletic scholarships	3
% UG rec. athletic scholarships	2
% UG borrow to pay for school	38
Average cumulative indebtedness	$26,639

UNIVERSITY OF SAN FRANCISCO

2130 FULTON STREET, SAN FRANCISCO, CA 94117 • ADMISSIONS: 415-422-6563 • FAX: 415-422-2217

CAMPUS LIFE

Quality of Life Rating	86
Fire Safety Rating	60*
Green Rating	82
Type of school	private
Affiliation	Roman Catholic
Environment	metropolis

STUDENTS

Total undergrad enrollment	4,872
% male/female	36/64
% from out of state	24
% from public high school	52
% live on campus	48
% in (# of) fraternities	1 (4)
% in (# of) sororities	1 (4)
% African American	5
% Asian	23
% Caucasian	38
% Hispanic	14
% Native American	1
% international	7
# of countries represented	78

SURVEY SAYS . . .
Large classes
Great library
Athletic facilities are great
Diverse student types on campus
Students love San Francisco, CA
Great off-campus food
(Almost) everyone smokes

ACADEMICS

Academic Rating	83
Calendar	4/1/4
Student/faculty ratio	14:1
Profs interesting rating	83
Profs accessible rating	79
Most common reg class size	10–19 students
Most common lab size	10–19 students

MOST POPULAR MAJORS
psychology
nursing/registered nurse
(RN, ASN, BSN, MSN)
business/commerce

STUDENTS SAY ". . ."

Academics

The University of San Francisco is a smallish Jesuit school "in an urban setting" with a "very liberal" "social justice slant." Global awareness programs and seminars are routine, and a strong community-service ethic permeates the atmosphere. Class sizes are small, and students report that their academic experience is "intimate and intellectual." Some members of the faculty at USF "seem to just skate through the workday" and are "not necessarily the best teachers." On the whole, though, "the shining star of USF is its professors." They are "ridiculously generous with their time" and are "really the best reason" to enroll. Like at most Catholic schools, "you're required to take everything from English to philosophy to religion" here. "The core curriculum is a bitch," but it does expose you to considerable wisdom. Beyond all the mandatory coursework, USF offers a breadth of options typical of a much larger university. Highlights include the business school and "a very popular nursing program." Education is "also very strong," and there's a four-year Great Books program. Administratively, "the school is run quite well," but there are "disgruntled types who like to make things difficult." Also, "registration is frustrating at times," and advising can be hit or miss. "I've had great advisers who have guided me through registration over the years," says a math major, "but others aren't as lucky."

Life

"Housing is a catastrophe" at USF. Students feel "really crammed" and complain that the people in charge "just put people together with no thought to whether they are compatible." There's a nice gym, though, with a pool that "basically covers an entire city block." Socially, "there is no sense of community." "Student groups consist of only the hardcores," and "the lack of school spirit can be quite a downer." "Going to USF is definitely the nontraditional college experience because everyone is pretty much doing their own thing." "Drinking is prevalent" and students "smoke a lot of weed," but "there isn't a big party scene other than little get-togethers in the dorms." House parties are rare "and usually never work out." On-campus activities are sparse, "but who would go anyway?" USF is located "in the heart of San Francisco," and "there is always something going on" in this "vibrant," "distracting" city. Most students "go off-campus on the weekends to explore" and "have adventures." On sunny days, "the best place to be is either Golden Gate Park or the beach." "Stellar museums, numerous theaters, national landmarks, shopping, world-class dining, funky art houses," and pretty much anything else is readily available. "Getting around on the buses is super easy," and public transportation passes are built into the tuition price. "The university is totally integrated into the city, and those who come to USF new to San Francisco will leave feeling like they belong here," promises a senior.

Student Body

USF is home to "one of the most ethnically diverse schools in the country." The Asian and Latino populations are especially high, and there's a noticeable international contingent. According to many females, though, the ratio of women to men is "pitiful." It's "pretty hard to date or even hook up" if you are straight because "most guys are taken or gay." "Students tend to stick with a small, close-knit group of friends," but virtually everyone is "able to fit in easily in the USF community no matter how eccentric." Except possibly conservatives. Liberal politics pervade, and USF "may not be the place for more right-leaning students." Some students "dress in alternative or funky clothing" and are "experimental (with everything from sexuality and music to drugs)." "Many students are Catholic, but aren't necessarily strictly practicing." A lot of people smoke cigarettes. There are "science nerds," "hippies," and the occasional "shopping addict." Some students are "outspoken and outgoing." Others "have their iPods on *all the time*." "There are a lot of super-wealthy kids" from Southern California. Others are on scholarships and loans "and barely making it." "People are passionate. Some are lazy. A few are beautifully artistic. A bunch are athletic. A couple are phony. Some are damn smart. Others are pretty ignorant. But at least we got it all," muses a sophomore.

FINANCIAL AID: 415-422-6303 • E-MAIL: ADMISSION@USFCA.EDU • WEBSITE: WWW.USFCA.EDU

THE PRINCETON REVIEW SAYS

Admissions

Very important factors considered include: Academic GPA, recommendations, rigor of secondary school record, standardized test scores, character/personal qualities, first generation, alumni/ae relations, racial/ethnic status, volunteer work. *Important factors include:* Class rank, interview, extracurricular activities, talent/ability, work experience, level of interest. SAT or ACT required; ACT with Writing component required. TOEFL required of all international applicants. High school diploma is required and GED is accepted. *Academic units recommended:* 4 English, 3 mathematics, 2 science, (2 science labs), 2 foreign language, 3 social studies, 6 academic electives, 2 One chemistry and 1 biology or physics is required of nursing and science applicants.

Financial Aid

Students should submit: FAFSA, The Princeton Review suggests that all financial aid forms be submitted as soon as possible after January 1. *Need-based scholarships/grants offered:* Federal Pell, SEOG, state scholarships/grants, private scholarships, the school's own gift aid, Federal Nursing Scholarships. *Loan aid offered:* Direct Subsidized Stafford, Direct Unsubsidized Stafford, Direct PLUS, FFEL PLUS, Federal Perkins, Federal Nursing, college/university loans from institutional funds. Note: FFEL Loans are for Graduate students only. Applicants will be notified of awards on a rolling basis beginning 4/1. Federal Work-Study Program available. Institutional employment available. Off-campus job opportunities are excellent.

The Inside Word

The Admissions Committee at USF is not purely numbers focused. They'll evaluate your full picture here, using your academic strengths and weaknesses along with your personal character strengths, essays, and recommendations to assess your suitability for admission. It's matchmaking. If you fit well in the USF community, you'll be welcome.

THE SCHOOL SAYS " . . ."

From The Admissions Office

"The University of San Francisco has experienced a significant increase in applications for admission over the past 5 years. This has made the application evaluation process more challenging. Ultimately, it gives those who read the applications the opportunity to find applicants who can make the most of the university's academic opportunities, location in San Francisco, and its mission to educate minds and hearts to change the world. Community outreach and service to others, along with academic excellence are characteristics that help distinguish those offered admission.

"The university is in the middle of a complete administrative system upgrade. New housing software will provide the students with the capability to "compatibility match." Scheduled for completion in 2009."

"Applicants for Fall 2008 are required to take the new SAT Reasoning test (or the ACT with the Writing section). The Writing sections will be used for advising and placement purposes. SAT Subject Test scores will also be accepted. If scores from both the old and new SAT are submitted, the higher of the scores will be used."

SELECTIVITY

Admissions Rating	85
# of applicants	7,695
% of applicants accepted	67
% of acceptees attending	21

FRESHMAN PROFILE

Range SAT Critical Reading	510–620
Range SAT Math	520–620
Range SAT Writing	510–620
Range ACT Composite	22–27
Minimum paper TOEFL	550
Minimum computer TOEFL	213
Minimum web-based TOEFL	79
Average HS GPA	3.503
% graduated top 10% of class	25.8
% graduated top 25% of class	61.2
% graduated top 50% of class	91.4

DEADLINES

Early action	
Deadline	11/15
Notification	1/16
Regular	
Priority	1/15
Notification	4/1
Nonfall registration?	yes

APPLICANTS ALSO LOOK AT

AND OFTEN PREFER
University of Southern California
Stanford University
University of California—Berkeley
Santa Clara University
University of California—Davis

AND SOMETIMES PREFER
University of San Diego
University of California—Santa Cruz
University of California—Santa Barbara
Loyola Marymount University

AND RARELY PREFER
Fordham University
Boston College

FINANCIAL FACTS

Financial Aid Rating	70
Annual tuition	$33,160
Room and board	$11,130
Required fees	$340
Books and supplies	$950
% frosh rec. need-based scholarship or grant aid	48
% UG rec. need-based scholarship or grant aid	47
% frosh rec. non-need-based scholarship or grant aid	12
% UG rec. non-need-based scholarship or grant aid	9
% frosh rec. need-based self-help aid	50
% UG rec. need-based self-help aid	50
% frosh rec. athletic scholarships	3
% UG rec. athletic scholarships	3
% UG borrow to pay for school	63.7
Average cumulative indebtedness	$28,000

UNIVERSITY OF SCRANTON

800 LINDEN STREET, SCRANTON, PA 18510-4699 • ADMISSIONS: 570-941-7540 FAX: 570-941-5928

STUDENTS SAY ". . ."

Academics

With "an outstanding record for admission to graduate programs, not only in law and medicine but also in several other fields," the University of Scranton is a good fit for ambitious students seeking "a Jesuit school in every sense of the word. If you come here, expect to be challenged to become a better person, to develop a strong concern for the poor and marginalized, and to grow spiritually and intellectually." The school manages to accomplish this without "forcing religion upon you, which is nice." Undergraduates also approve of the mandatory liberal-arts-based curriculum that "forces you to learn about broader things than your own major." Strong majors here include "an amazing occupational therapy program, [an] excellent special education program," business, and biology. "This is a great place for premeds and other sciences," students agree. While the workload can be difficult, "a tutoring center provides free tutoring for any students who may need it, and also provides work-study positions for students who qualify to tutor." Need more help? Professors "are extremely accessible. They will go to any lengths to help you understand material and do well," while administrators "are here for the students, and show that every day inside and outside of the classroom." Community ties here are strong; as one student points out, "The Jesuits live in our dorms, creating an even greater sense of community, because we don't view them as just priests, we view them as real people who can relate on our level."

Life

"There is a whole range of activities to do on the weekends" at University of Scranton, including "frequent trips, dances, and movies that are screened for free." Students tell us that "the school and student organizations provide plenty of options, such as retreats, talent shows, and other various activities." There are also "many intramurals to become involved in, and the varsity sports (specifically the women's) are very successful." Furthermore, "Being a Jesuit school, social justice issues are huge. They are taught in the classroom, and students spend a lot of time volunteering." Hometown Scranton is big enough to provide "movie theaters, two malls, parks, a zoo, a bowling alley, and a skiing/snowboarding mountain." In short, there are plenty of choices for the non-partier at Scranton; the many we heard from in our survey reported busy extracurricular schedules. But those seeking a party won't be disappointed here, either. Scranton undergrads "party a lot, but they balance it with studying. Parties are chances to go out, see people, dance, and drink if you want." You "can find a party any time of day, seven days a week" here, usually with a keg tapped and pouring. Few here feel the party scene is out of hand, however; a typical student writes, "It's very different than at schools with Greek systems. It is a lot more laid-back, and all about everyone having a good time."

Students

While "the typical Scranton student is White, Catholic, and from the suburbs," students hasten to point out that "within this sameness, there is much diversity. There are people who couldn't care at all about religion, and there are people who are deeply religious. Even in the Catholic atmosphere of the school, the school only requires that you learn about Catholicism as it stands. Theology classes . . . are prefaced with the idea that 'You do not have to believe this!'" Undergrads here are generally "friendly and welcoming. Cliques are pretty much nonexistent, and anyone who would be classified as 'popular' is only considered so because they are extremely friendly, outgoing, and seek out friendships with as many people as possible." Students tend to be on the Abercrombie-preppy side, with lots of undergrads of Italian, Irish, and Polish descent.

UNIVERSITY OF SCRANTON

FINANCIAL AID: 570-941-7700 • E-MAIL: ADMISSIONS@SCRANTON.EDU • WEBSITE: WWW.SCRANTON.EDU

THE PRINCETON REVIEW SAYS

Admissions

Very important factors considered include: Class rank, academic GPA, rigor of secondary school record, standardized test scores. *Important factors considered include:* extracurricular activities. *Other factors considered include:* Application essay, recommendation(s), alumni/ae relation, character/personal qualities, interview, level of applicant's interest, talent/ability, volunteer work, work experience. SAT or ACT required; TOEFL required of all international applicants. High school diploma is required and GED is accepted. *Academic units required:* 4 English, 3 mathematics, 3 science, (1 science labs), 2 foreign language, 2 social studies, 2 history, 4 academic electives. *Academic units recommended:* 4 English, 4 mathematics, 3 science, (1 science labs), 2 foreign language, 3 social studies, 3 history, 4 academic electives.

Financial Aid

Students should submit: FAFSA. The Princeton Review suggests that all financial aid forms be submitted as soon as possible after January 1. *Need-based scholarships/grants offered:* Federal Pell, SEOG, state scholarships/grants, private scholarships, the school's own gift aid. *Loan aid offered:* FFEL Subsidized Stafford, FFEL Unsubsidized Stafford, FFEL PLUS, Federal Perkins, Federal Nursing Applicants will be notified of awards on a rolling basis beginning 3/15. Federal Work-Study Program available. Institutional employment available. Off-campus job opportunities are good.

The Inside Word

Admission to Scranton gets harder each year. A steady stream of smart kids from the Tristate Area keeps classes full and the admit rate low. Successful applicants will need solid grades and test scores. As with many religiously affiliated schools, students should be a good match philosophically as well.

THE SCHOOL SAYS "..."

From The Admissions Office

"A Jesuit institution in Pennsylvania's Pocono Northeast, the University of Scranton is known for its outstanding academics, state-of-the art campus, and exceptional sense of community. Founded in 1888, the university offers more than 80 undergraduate and graduate academic programs of study through four colleges and schools.

"For 13 consecutive years, *U.S. News & World Report* has named Scranton among the top-10 master's universities in the North. For the past 3 years, Scranton has also been among the 'Great Schools as a Great Price' in the 'Universities—Master's in the North' category. The Princeton Review included Scranton among *The Best 361 Colleges* in the nation for the past 5 years. For 4 consecutive years, *USA Today* included Scranton students on its 'All-U.S.A. College Academic Teams' list. In 2005, Scranton was the only college in Pennsylvania and the only Jesuit university to have a student named to the first academic team. In other national recognition, Kaplan counted Scranton among the nation's '369 Most Interesting Colleges' and was also listed among the 247 colleges in the nation included in the ninth edition of *Barron's Best Buys in College Education*.

"Known for the remarkable success of its graduates, Scranton is listed among the 'Top Producers' of Fulbright awards for American students in the October 20, 2006, issue of *The Chronicle of Higher Education*.

"Freshman applicants for Fall 2008 are required to take the SAT or ACT exam. The writing scores will not be considered in the admissions decision process. Students are encouraged to apply early for admission and can do so online with no application fee at Scranton.edu/apply."

SELECTIVITY

Admissions Rating	86
# of applicants	7,609
% of applicants accepted	66
% of acceptees attending	20
# accepting a place on wait list	481
% admitted from wait list	4

FRESHMAN PROFILE

Range SAT Critical Reading	510–600
Range SAT Math	520–620
Minimum paper TOEFL	500
Minimum computer TOEFL	173
Average HS GPA	3.36
% graduated top 10% of class	27
% graduated top 25% of class	63
% graduated top 50% of class	92

DEADLINES

Early action	
Deadline	11/15
Notification	12/15
Regular	
Deadline	3/1
Notification	rolling
Nonfall registration?	yes

APPLICANTS ALSO LOOK AT

AND OFTEN PREFER
University of Delaware
Fairfield University
Villanova University
Saint Joseph's University (PA)

AND SOMETIMES PREFER
Fordham University
Loyola College in Maryland
Penn State—University Park

FINANCIAL FACTS

Financial Aid Rating	70
Annual tuition	$27,604
% frosh rec. need-based scholarship or grant aid	67
% UG rec. need-based scholarship or grant aid	63
% frosh rec. non-need-based scholarship or grant aid	6
% UG rec. non-need-based scholarship or grant aid	4
% frosh rec. need-based self-help aid	59
% UG rec. need-based self-help aid	56
% frosh rec. any financial aid	85
% UG rec. any financial aid	82
% UG borrow to pay for school	76
Average cumulative indebtedness	$26,169

UNIVERSITY OF SOUTH CAROLINA—COLUMBIA

UNIVERSITY OF SOUTH CAROLINA, COLUMBIA, SC 29208 • ADMISSIONS: 803-777-7700 • FAX: 803-777-0101

CAMPUS LIFE

Quality of Life Rating	74
Fire Safety Rating	89
Green Rating	85
Type of school	public
Environment	city

STUDENTS

Total undergrad enrollment	18,497
% male/female	45/55
% from out of state	24
% live on campus	40
% in (# of) fraternities	14 (18)
% in (# of) sororities	15 (14)
% African American	12
% Asian	3
% Caucasian	72
% Hispanic	2
% international	1
# of countries represented	107

SURVEY SAYS . . .

Great library
Athletic facilities are great
Everyone loves the Fighting
Gamecocks
Frats and sororities dominate
social scene
Student publications are popular
Lots of beer drinking
Hard liquor is popular

ACADEMICS

Academic Rating	71
Profs interesting rating	67
Profs accessible rating	69
% classes taught by TAs	23

MOST POPULAR MAJORS

biology/biological sciences
experimental psychology
nursing/registered nurse
(RN, ASN, BSN, MSN)

STUDENTS SAY ". . ."

Academics

With a large in-state population and a proud football tradition, "The University of South Carolina is all about pride—in academics, athletics, and in life." Undergrads at this large research university embrace the entire USC experience, bragging of "an awesome mix of challenging academics and social activities." As at most large state universities, your academic experience at USC "is what you make of it. You can blow off your classes and get by, or you can dive in and try and learn as much as you want to." A few students warn that "most departments are more research oriented than education oriented. The philosophy is that research pays the bills, not the students, and therefore more emphasis should be placed on research." Even so, the academic experience is not an impersonal one; on the contrary, professors "will do everything they can to help you out with any problem, personal or academic. The people here are amazing. A stranger is as likely to be friendly and helpful as your best friend." Students tell us that USC excels in business, mathematics, nursing, education, technology, library service, journalism, psychology, and hotel, restaurant, and tourism management. One USC booster sums up: "The University of South Carolina offers the complete student experience: A variety of student organizations and student activities, a great nightlife in the state capital, challenging classes taught by great professors, and opportunities for research—all within a great environment on a beautiful campus."

Life

USC "is a fun place," especially for sports fans, as life here "mostly revolves around football and basketball. Everyone's always talking about the upcoming game or what next season is going to hold. There's a great sense of school pride." Undergrads proudly assert that "USC is probably the best college for tailgating. Football game days are so fun!" But students don't need a sporting event to have a good time; on the contrary, "Many people party every weekend (beginning Thursday nights)." When they do, "A lot of people hang out in Five Points"—which "offers many nightlife and dining options for college students"—"or the Vista"—which is similar to Five Points, but a bit more upscale. Aesthetes have plenty of options as well; on campus "The Koger Center for the Arts brings [in] great performers every year," while the city's Colonial Center "offers big concerts . . . from Elton John to Jimmy Buffett." Other Columbia highlights include "a very nice zoo" as well as plenty of options for hunting and fishing within 25 miles of the city. Beyond the immediate vicinity, "the mountains are an hour away and so is the beach. A weekend in Charleston, shopping in Charlotte, [and] going to the mountains in NC [North Carolina]" are excursions "you hear about every weekend (when there's not a football game going on)."

Student Body

With an undergraduate student body of over 18,000, USC is home to "so many different types of people . . . involved in so many different activities." When pressed to describe a typical student, undergrads identify "a fun-loving football fan who is a business student or a bio major," and explain that "most students are Southerners who come from a similar Christian, suburban background (although not all remain in that mindset)." However, students also report that USC is home to a "diverse minority and international communities" who "are becoming more and more recognized by the rest of the students." One undergrad sums up: "There isn't a typical student at USC, [but] there are different . . . group[s] that students could be classified into. There are the frat guys and the sorority girls; the good ol' boys who love to hunt and fish; the debutantes [who] are only here to get a MRS degree; the Northerners who came down to USC and had no idea what they were getting themselves into; and then there are the athletes, who pretty much interact only with other athletes."

UNIVERSITY OF SOUTH CAROLINA—COLUMBIA

FINANCIAL AID: 803-777-8134 • E-MAIL: ADMISSIONS-UGRAD@SC.EDU • WEBSITE: WWW.SC.EDU

THE PRINCETON REVIEW SAYS

Admissions

Very important factors considered include: Rigor of secondary school record, Standardized test scores. *Important factors considered include:* Academic GPA. *Other factors considered include:* Class rank, Application Essay, Recommendation(s), Extracurricular activities, Talent/ability, Character/personal qualities, Alumni/ae relation, State residency, Racial/ethnic status, Volunteer work, Work experience. *Academic units required:* TOEFL required of all international applicants.

Financial Aid

The Princeton Review suggests that all financial aid forms be submitted as soon as possible after January 1. Federal Work-Study Program available. Institutional employment available. Off-campus job opportunities are good.

The Inside Word

Students tell us that "the admissions process at USC is very fair. The school takes everything into consideration." This is good news for applicants with spotty high school transcripts or poor standardized test scores. Others need not worry—the school bulletin reports that applicants with a B average in college preparatory courses and SAT section scores between 550 and 600 "are normally competitive for admission."

THE SCHOOL SAYS ". . ."

From The Admissions Office

"In just 6 years, the number of annual undergraduate applicants to USC has doubled, making it more critical than ever for students to meet the university's priority application deadline. The University of South Carolina's national prominence in academics and research activities also has increased. USC is one of only 62 public research institutions to earn a designated status of 'very high research activity' by the Carnegie Foundation. As early as their freshman year, undergraduates are encouraged to compete for research grants. As South Carolina's flagship institution, USC offers more than 350 degree programs. Over 27,000 students seek baccalaureate, masters, or doctoral degrees. USC is known for its top-ranked academic programs, including its international business and exercise science programs—both rated number one nationally. Other notable programs include chemical and nuclear engineering; health education; hotel, restaurant, and tourism; marine science; law; medicine; nursing; and psychology, among others. USC is recognized for its pioneering efforts in freshman outreach. Its honors college is one of the nation's best, offering an Ivy League–caliber education at state college costs. USC offers student support in such areas as career development, disability services, pre-professional planning, and study abroad.

"On campus, students enjoy a state-of-the-art fitness center, an 18,000-seat arena, an 80,000-seat stadium, and nearly 300 student organizations. Off campus, South Carolina's world-famous beaches and the Blue Ridge Mountains are each less than a 3-hour drive away. The University of South Carolina is located in the state's capital city, making it a great place for internships and job opportunities.

"Because admissions criteria and deadlines are likely to change from year to year, it is important to check for the latest information at SC.edu/admissions.

"Applicants are required to take the Writing section of the SAT (or ACT) for any tests taken after March 2005. We will use the highest scores from either test for evaluation purposes."

SELECTIVITY

Admissions Rating	88
# of applicants	13,946
% of applicants accepted	63
% of acceptees attending	42

FRESHMAN PROFILE

Range SAT Critical Reading	520–620
Range SAT Math	540–640
Range ACT Composite 2	3–28
Average HS GPA	3.9
% graduated top 10% of class	29
% graduated top 25% of class	63
% graduated top 50% of class	93
Minimum paper TOEFL	570
Minimum computer TOEFL	230

DEADLINES

Regular	01/12
Priority	01/1
Nonfall registration?	Yes

APPLICANTS ALSO LOOK AT A ND OFTEN PREFER
University of North Carolina at Chapel Hill
AND SOMETIMES PREFER
Clemson University
AND RARELY PREFER
Wake Forest University

FINANCIAL FACTS

Financial Aid Rating	76
Annual in-state tuition	$8,346
% frosh rec. need-based scholarship or grant aid	19
% UG rec. need-based scholarship or grant aid	23
% frosh rec. non-need-based scholarship or grant aid	37
% UG rec. non-need-based scholarship or grant aid	27
% frosh rec. need-based self-help aid	33
% UG rec. need-based self-help aid	39
% frosh rec. athletic scholarships	3
% UG rec. athletic scholarships	3
% frosh rec. any financial aid	94
% UG rec. any financial aid	86
% UG borrow to pay for school	45
Average cumulative indebtedness	$21,129.00

THE UNIVERSITY OF SOUTH DAKOTA

414 EAST CLARK, VERMILLION, SD 57069 • ADMISSIONS: 605-677-5434 • FAX: 605-677-6323

CAMPUS LIFE

Quality of Life Rating	**68**
Fire Safety Rating	**91**
Green Rating	**73**
Type of school	public
Environment	village

STUDENTS

Total undergrad enrollment	6,844
% male/female	39/61
% from out of state	26
% from public high school	94
% live on campus	31
% in (# of) fraternities	17 (8)
% in (# of) sororities	9 (4)
% African American	2
% Asian	1
% Caucasian	93
% Hispanic	1
% Native American	2
% international	1
# of countries represented	30

SURVEY SAYS . . .

Small classes
Great computer facilities
Great library
Frats and sororities dominate
social scene
Lots of beer drinking
Hard liquor is popular
(Almost) everyone smokes

ACADEMICS

Academic Rating	**72**
Calendar	semester
Student/faculty ratio	14:1
Profs interesting rating	72
Profs accessible rating	68
% classes taught by TAs	4
Most common reg class size	20–29 students
Most common lab size	20–29 students

MOST POPULAR MAJORS

psychology
business/commerce
education

STUDENTS SAY ". . ."

Academics

For students interested in "career-centered" studies such as premedical studies, business, criminal justice, psychology, or "anything to do with numbers (e.g. accounting, math)," The University of South Dakota is "the perfect package," a place where "students excel in academics, attain strong social lives, get the advantage of small classroom one-on-one attention, and enjoy the benefits of Midwest hospitality." USD also boasts a highly regarded instrumental music department that features "one of the best music museums in the world." All this comes for "a very small price." As one student puts it, "USD is all about letting you explore your career options for the future without spending mass amounts of money." Professors here typically "know you as well as the other students in the class on a first-name basis. They always remind us where their office is and when we can contact them." And while students encounter the occasional prof who is "only in the college setting for the sake of doing research and could care less about teaching," even that isn't totally without an upside. As one student points out, "Virtually all professors in every department have research projects in addition to teaching, making it extremely easy for an interested student to participate in faculty research." All told, USD provides "a small-school feeling with great benefits that a big school can offer." Best of all, the school is "constantly improving." "There are a lot of building projects and remodeling going on right now, most of which should be done within the next year or so."

Life

Most folks agree that "There isn't a lot to do in Vermillion, but if you want to find things to do it is definitely possible." Options include "movie theaters, trips to Wal-Mart," and several bars. Students note that the area is "great for doing things outdoors" thanks to the "rivers and lakes nearby." The town itself is "very supportive of the students, at the beginning of the year, all the stores on Main Street come out and welcome us back with food and coupons. The community is very involved here." On the downside, "Housing in and around Vermillion is pretty crappy! If you are willing to pay a lot for a small space that you are going to be sharing, then that's great. You will love it here!" The same student advises to "Look at your options outside Vermillion before making your living choice. Living outside Vermillion will also help you get a better paying job and a nightlife!" Indeed, most students here ultimately conclude that the town is "lacking in things to do" and opt for entertainment options elsewhere. Fortunately, "Sioux City is only 30 minutes away, Sioux Falls is only 45, and Omaha is only two hours away. Getting out of town is often the only thing to do for fun in Vermillion if you're not into the partying scene." There is an active party scene on campus. "Lots of people drink because there is nothing else to do," says one student.

Student Body

The typical USD undergrad is "from the surrounding area and is here to go to school and have fun at the same time." The student body is "not diverse." "We all fit in because we are very similar," meaning that students "come from small towns and are into sports and meeting new people." They are also "a little more accustomed to sub-zero winds and having to drive two hours for a little entertainment" than their peers at other schools. The minority contingent includes "a healthy Native American population," as well as a scattering of students "of Asian and African descent." "All the different racial groups get along well." The great divide here, if there is one, is that "most of the students at USD fall into one of two groups: those who spend most of their time studying or those who spend quite a bit of time partying. A good majority of the students at USD are involved in campus activities."

FINANCIAL AID: 605-677-5446 • E-MAIL: ADMISS@USD.EDU • WEBSITE: WWW.USD.EDU

THE PRINCETON REVIEW SAYS

Admissions

Very important factors considered include: Class rank, academic GPA, rigor of secondary school record, standardized test scores. *Important factors considered include:* Alumni/ae relation. *Other factors considered include:* Application essay, recommendation(s), character/personal qualities, extracurricular activities, geographical residence, racial/ethnic status, state residency, talent/ability, volunteer work, work experience. SAT or ACT required; SAT and SAT Subject Tests or ACT required; TOEFL required of all international applicants. High school diploma is required and GED is accepted. *Academic units required:* 4 English, 3 mathematics, 3 science, (3 science labs), 3 social studies, 1 fine arts. *Academic units recommended:* 4 English, 4 mathematics, 4 science, (3 science labs), 2 foreign language, 3 social studies, 1 fine arts.

Financial Aid

Students should submit: FAFSA. The Princeton Review suggests that all financial aid forms be submitted as soon as possible after January 1. *Need-based scholarships/grants offered:* Federal Pell, SEOG, private scholarships, the school's own gift aid, Federal Nursing Scholarships. *Loan aid offered:* FFEL Subsidized Stafford, FFEL Unsubsidized Stafford, FFEL PLUS, Federal Perkins, Federal Nursing, college/university loans from institutional funds. Applicants will be notified of awards on a rolling basis beginning 3/1. Federal Work-Study Program available. Institutional employment available. Off-campus job opportunities are fair.

The Inside Word

Admissions at USD are pretty straightforward. Everyone who meets the admissions criteria is admitted. For entry in 2009, applicants must either achieve an ACT/SAT composite score of 21,990, or earn a high school GPA of 2.6, or rank in the upper 50 percent of their graduating class, and their high school curricula must meet certain minimum requirements.

THE SCHOOL SAYS "..."

From The Admissions Office

"The University of South Dakota is the perfect fit for students looking for a smart educational investment. The U is South Dakota's only designated liberal arts university and is consistently rated among the top doctoral institutions in the country. Annually, The U awards scholarships to more than 800 first-year students, and over 80 percent of U students receive some form of financial aid through grants, loans, and work-study jobs.

"U students earn the nation's most prestigious scholarships. Our quality of teaching and research prepares students to pursue their passions all over the world, at institutions such as Columbia, Johns Hopkins, The University of Chicago, and beyond. Fifty-nine U students have been awarded prestigious Fulbright, Rhodes, National Science Foundation, Boren, Truman, Udall, Gilman, and Goldwater scholarships and grants for graduate study. Personal attention from our award-winning faculty and our welcoming environment makes students feel right at home.

"As the flagship liberal arts institution in South Dakota, The University of South Dakota—founded in 1862—has long been regarded as a leader in the state and the region. Notable undergraduate and postgraduate alumni include journalist Ken Bode, author and former news anchor Tom Brokaw, writer and Emmy Award–winner Dorothy Cooper Foote, U.S. Senator Tim Johnson, *USA Today* Founder Al Neuharth, and U.S. Senator John Thune.

"Applicants for Fall 2009 are not required to take the new writing test for either SAT or ACT. USD recommends taking the ACT over the SAT. Students who wish to send their SAT scores will have their scores converted to ACT scores for placement and scholarship consideration."

SELECTIVITY

Admissions Rating	74
# of applicants	3,499
% of applicants accepted	80
% of acceptees attending	42

FRESHMAN PROFILE

Range SAT Critical Reading	420–540
Range SAT Math	490–590
Range ACT Composite	20–25
Minimum paper TOEFL	550
Minimum computer TOEFL	213
Average HS GPA	3.26
% graduated top 10% of class	14
% graduated top 25% of class	35
% graduated top 50% of class	69

DEADLINES

Notification	rolling
Nonfall registration?	yes

APPLICANTS ALSO LOOK AT

AND OFTEN PREFER
University of Nebraska—Lincoln
Minnesota State University—Mankato

AND SOMETIMES PREFER
South Dakota State University
Augustana College (SD)

AND RARELY PREFER
Northern State University
Dakota State University
Mount Marty College

FINANCIAL FACTS

Financial Aid Rating	85
Annual in-state tuition	$2,646
Annual out-of-state tuition	$3,966
Room and board	$5,442
Required fees	$5,827
Books and supplies	$900
% frosh rec. need-based scholarship or grant aid	24
% UG rec. need-based scholarship or grant aid	27
% frosh rec. non-need-based scholarship or grant aid	25
% UG rec. non-need-based scholarship or grant aid	18
% frosh rec. need-based self-help aid	51
% UG rec. need-based self-help aid	55
% frosh rec. athletic scholarships	8
% UG rec. athletic scholarships	6
% frosh rec. any financial aid	92
% UG rec. any financial aid	88
% UG borrow to pay for school	88
Average cumulative indebtedness	$22,781

UNIVERSITY OF SOUTH FLORIDA

4202 EAST FOWLER AVENUE, SVC-1036, TAMPA, FL 33620-9951 • ADMISSIONS: 813-974-3350 • FAX: 813-974-9689

STUDENTS SAY ". . ."

Academics

The University of South Florida is "an enormous and comprehensive research university" that is "growing out of control." To curb this trend, the Florida Board of Governors has frozen freshman enrollment at 2007 levels and directed public universities to reduce enrollment. "A huge range of majors" is available. The "amazing" honors college "is definitely something students should try to get into if possible." There's "a great nursing program." Premed, business, education, engineering, and environmental science are notable as well. "Everything seems to run fairly smoothly and is well organized" at USF, but the "distant" administration is "blissfully unaware of student opinions" and "hard to track down." Don't try calling anyone, "You end up in a permanent prompt loop." Lectures can be "very large," especially in introductory courses. Students report a "mix of good and bad professors." "It all comes down to the luck of the draw." Many professors are "very friendly," "down to earth," and "easily accessible." Other faculty members "are there mainly for research" and "just have no business teaching" or "struggle with the English language." "There are some professors who blow me away with how great they teach and explain material," observes an environmental science major, "but then there are others who blow me away because I hate them so much."

Life

USF has a handful of regional campuses, but the main one is in Tampa. It's very spread out and full of "open green spaces." The Tampa campus "could stand to be a little more aesthetically pleasing," though, and it "isn't located in the best neighborhood." "Campus security is a big issue." Also, USF is "a heavy commuter school," and "trying to park every day is hell." Socially, "it's not easy to just walk out and meet people" due to the mammoth size of this institution. However, "there are hundreds of campus activities to get involved in." "The school paper is awesome." Movies on the lawn are "tons of fun." "There is always something going on" at the student union. Busch Gardens—a theme park—is located just down the street from campus. Students here are "diehard Bulls football fans" in the fall and they "have a lot of school pride and spirit." There's also a decent smattering of Greek life. "USF students enjoy a party" and "large, loud, long" gatherings are abundant on Thursday nights and throughout the weekend. Many students also opt for the "world famous" club scene in Ybor City, a historic-district-turned-night-clubbing-district in Tampa's Latin Quarter. However, the overall caliber of the festivities here doesn't approach the scene at some other Florida schools. "I don't think we're a major party school," opines a senior.

Student Body

This campus is "full of Floridians," and "flip flops are a mandatory staple in any USF student's wardrobe." That's about all that unites the undergraduate population. "The thing about the University of South Florida is that there is no typical student." This is "a very diverse population of students by any standard." "We come from very different backgrounds and are headed in very different directions," says a senior. "Interests, talents, study habits, and hobbies vary greatly." "You've got the preps, the boozers, the druggies, the philosophers, the theater kids, etc." There are the "overachievers who like sit in circles and pat each other on the back." Other students "always wait until the last minute to complete assignments." "There is a large population of nontraditional and commuter students." A strong contingent works "at least part time." Many students "appear to be on a mission" and "just want to finish their school work and get out of here." There are "a lot of African Americans and significant Muslim, Hispanic, and international student minorities." "It is a beautiful thing to walk across campus and see so many different types of people," beams a sophomore. There is a lot of ethnic self-segregation, though. "It's awkward to see the group of black people hanging out in one corner while the Hispanics stand over there and the white kids sit at that table over there," observes a sophomore.

FINANCIAL AID: 813-974-4700 • WEBSITE: WWW.USF.EDU

THE PRINCETON REVIEW SAYS

Admissions

Very important factors considered include: Academic GPA, rigor of secondary school record, standardized test scores. *Important factors considered include:* Class rank, talent/ability. *Other factors considered include:* Application essay, recommendation(s), character/personal qualities, extracurricular activities, first generation, geographical residence, state residency, volunteer work, work experience. SAT or ACT required; ACT with Writing component required. TOEFL required of all non-native English speaking applicants. High school diploma is required and GED is accepted. *Academic units required:* 4 English, 3 mathematics, 3 science, (2 science labs), 2 foreign language, 3 social studies, 3 academic electives.

Financial Aid

Students should submit: FAFSA. The Princeton Review suggests that all financial aid forms be submitted as soon as possible after January 1. *Need-based scholarships/grants offered:* Federal Pell, SEOG, state scholarships/grants, the school's own gift aid. *Loan aid offered:* FFEL Subsidized Stafford, FFEL Unsubsidized Stafford, FFEL PLUS, Federal Perkins Applicants will be notified of awards on a rolling basis beginning 3/1. Federal Work-Study Program available. Institutional employment available. Off-campus job opportunities are excellent.

The Inside Word

A traditional college-prep high school course load is required for admission to USF. Beyond making sure that you complete all prerequisite classes, however, keep two other things in mind when applying to USF. First, admissions decisions are made on a rolling basis, so the earlier one applies, the better his or her chance of acceptance since there are more unfilled seats early in the admissions cycle. Second, Advanced Placement (AP) and International Baccalaureate (IB) classes are looked upon favorably in the Admissions Office here, so if your school offers them, load up on them and do well.

THE SCHOOL SAYS "..."

From The Admissions Office

"Located in the Tampa Bay area, USF is recognized as one of the nation's top metropolitan research universities.

"One of the most distinguishing features of USF is the Honors College. The college has a specially designed honors major, as well as a Research Scholars Program that is offered to students who have demonstrated excellent scholarship potential and who are interested in an intensive research experience. Admission to the Honors College and Research Scholars Program is based on university admissions requirements.

"As students begin the application process, they need to become familiar with USF's admission requirements. Admission is based on the strength of an applicant's high school background, including the degree of difficulty of courses selected, record of academic achievement, grade trends, and SAT or ACT scores. USF also takes into account the student's profile and special talents in and outside of the classroom.

"Students are encouraged to use academic electives to better enhance their preparation for entrance into a selected major. USF also encourages students with talent in music, art, dance, and theater to balance their high school experience with advanced courses in the visual and performing arts.

"It's always a great time to visit USF. Campus tours, information sessions, and tours of the residence halls are offered daily and most Saturday mornings from September through April. Reservations are strongly encouraged.

"Freshman and lower-level transfer applicants to USF who graduate from high school in 2006 or later are required to submit official results from either the SAT Reasoning Test or the ACT test with Writing."

SELECTIVITY
Admissions Rating	87
# of applicants	25,216
% of applicants accepted	50
% of acceptees attending	32

FRESHMAN PROFILE
Range SAT Critical Reading	500–600
Range SAT Math	510–610
Range SAT Writing	470–570
Range ACT Composite	22–26
Minimum paper TOEFL	550
Minimum computer TOEFL	213
Average HS GPA	3.66
% graduated top 10% of class	27
% graduated top 25% of class	63
% graduated top 50% of class	85

DEADLINES
Regular	
Priority	3/1
Deadline	4/15
Notification	rolling
Nonfall registration?	yes

APPLICANTS ALSO LOOK AT AND OFTEN PREFER
University of Florida

AND SOMETIMES PREFER
University of Central Florida
Florida State University

FINANCIAL FACTS
Financial Aid Rating	64
Annual in-state tuition	$3,383
Annual out-of-state tuition	$16,081
Room and board	$7,590
Required fees	$74
Books and supplies	$1,300
% frosh rec. any financial aid	56
% UG rec. any financial aid	50
% UG borrow to pay for school	53
Average cumulative indebtedness	$18,517

UNIVERSITY OF SOUTHERN CALIFORNIA

700 CHILDS WAY, LOS ANGELES, CA 90089-0911 • ADMISSIONS: 213-740-1111 • FAX: 213-740-6364

CAMPUS LIFE
Quality of Life Rating	78
Fire Safety Rating	96
Green Rating	82
Type of school	private
Environment	metropolis

STUDENTS
Total undergrad enrollment	16,091
% male/female	50/50
% from out of state	35
% from public high school	55
% live on campus	41
% in (# of) fraternities	21 (32)
% in (# of) sororities	24 (24)
% African American	6
% Asian	22
% Caucasian	48
% Hispanic	13
% Native American	1
% international	9
# of countries represented	133

SURVEY SAYS . . .
Great computer facilities
Great library
Students are happy
Everyone loves the Trojans
Frats and sororities dominate
social scene
Student publications are popular
Lots of beer drinking
Hard liquor is popular

ACADEMICS
Academic Rating	87
Calendar	semester
Student/faculty ratio	9:1
Profs interesting rating	78
Profs accessible rating	77
Most common reg class size	10–19 students
Most common lab size	20–29 students

MOST POPULAR MAJORS
communication studies/speech communication and rhetoric
business administration and
management
biology/biological sciences

STUDENTS SAY "..."

Academics
The University of Southern California boasts "a dynamic and culturally diverse campus located in a world-class city which is equally dynamic and culturally diverse." Everything related to cinema is "top notch." Among the other 150 or so majors here, programs in journalism, business, engineering, and architecture are particularly notable. The honors programs are "very good," too. One of the best perks about USC is its "large and enthusiastic alumni network." Becoming "part of the Trojan Family" is a great way to jumpstart your career because USC graduates love to hire other USC graduates. "Almost everyone talks about getting job offers based solely on going to USC." "The school seems to run very smoothly, with few administrative issues ever being problematic enough to reach the awareness of the USC student community," says an international relations major. The top brass "is a bit mysterious and heavy handed," though. Also, "they milk every dime they can get from you." Academically, some students call the general education courses "a complete waste of time." There are a few "real narcissists" on the faculty as well as some professors "who seem to just be there because they want to do research." Overall, though, students report that professors "make the subject matter come alive" and make themselves "very available" outside the classroom. "My academic experience at USC is fabulous," gushes an aerospace engineering major. "I would not choose any other school."

Life
Students at USC complain quite a bit about their "smelly, ugly" housing. Recreation facilities aren't much, either. "For such an athletic school, the student gym is embarrassing." Also, students stress the fact that the area around USC is "impoverished" and "notoriously unsafe." "People get mugged all the time." On campus, though, life is "vibrant." There are more than 600 student organizations. Theatrical and musical productions are "excellent." School spirit is "extreme" and "infectious." "Football games are huge." "There is absolutely nothing that can top watching our unbelievable football team throttle the competition," says a merciless sophomore. "Drinking is a big part of the social scene" as well. "We definitely have some of the sickest parties ever," claims an impressed freshman. "Greek life is very big" and, on the weekends, a strong contingent of students "religiously" visits "The Row, the street lined with all the fraternity and sorority houses." Students also have "the sprawling city of Los Angeles as their playground." It's an "eclectic place with both high and low culture and some of the best shopping in the world." "Hollywood clubs and downtown bars" are popular destinations. Art exhibits, concerts, and "hip restaurants" are everywhere. However, "you need a car." L.A. traffic may be "a buzz kill" but students report that it's considerably preferable to the "absolutely terrible" public transportation system.

Student Body
The one thing that unites everyone here is "tons of Trojan pride." USC students are also "intensely ambitious" and, while there are some "complete slackers," many students hit the books "harder then they let on." Otherwise, students insist that, "contrary to popular belief, USC has immense diversity." "The stereotypical USC student is a surfer fraternity bro or a tan, trendy sorority girl from the O.C." You'll find plenty of those. Many students are also "extremely good looking." Ethnic minorities and a high number of international students make up sizeable contingents of the undergraduate population as well. If you're gay, you shouldn't have any problems. "No one cares what your gender orientation is," says a first-year student. "The only important question is whether or not you can be hooked up with." There are "prissy L.A. types" and "spoiled" kids. In some circles, "family income and the brands of clothes you wear definitely matter." However, "though there are quite a few who come from mega wealth, there are also many who are here on a great deal of financial aid." There are "lots of nerds," too, and a smattering of "band geeks and film freaks." Most students don't stray too far from the mainstream, though. "You have to go out of your way to find funky people," advises a sophomore.

FINANCIAL AID: 213-740-1111 • E-MAIL: ADMITUSC@USC.EDU • WEBSITE: WWW.USC.EDU

THE PRINCETON REVIEW SAYS

Admissions

Very important factors considered include: Application essay, academic GPA, recommendation(s), rigor of secondary school record, standardized test scores. *Important factors considered include:* extracurricular activities, talent/ability. *Other factors considered include:* Class rank, alumni/ae relation, character/personal qualities, first generation, interview, racial/ethnic status, volunteer work, work experience. SAT or ACT required; ACT with Writing component required. TOEFL required of all international applicants. High school diploma is required and GED is not accepted. *Academic units required:* 4 English, 3 mathematics, 2 science, (2 science labs), 2 foreign language, 2 social studies, 3 academic electives. *Academic units recommended:* 4 English, 4 mathematics, 3 science, (3 science labs), 3 foreign language, 3 social studies, 3 academic electives.

Financial Aid

Students should submit: FAFSA, CSS/Financial Aid PROFILE, Parent and student Federal Income Tax form with all schedules and W-2s. USC Non-filing Forms for those not required to file. The Princeton Review suggests that all financial aid forms be submitted as soon as possible after January 1. *Need-based scholarships/grants offered:* Federal Pell, SEOG, state scholarships/grants, private scholarships, the school's own gift aid. *Loan aid offered:* FFEL Subsidized Stafford, FFEL Unsubsidized Stafford, FFEL PLUS, Federal Perkins, "Credit Ready" and Credit Based loans. Applicants will be notified of awards on a rolling basis beginning 3/15. Federal Work-Study Program available. Institutional employment available. Off-campus job opportunities are excellent.

The Inside Word

USC doesn't have the toughest admissions standards in California but it's up there. Your grades and test scores need to be outstanding to compete. Even if you are a borderline candidate, though, USC is certainly worth a shot. Few schools on the planet have a better alumni network and the "Trojan Family" really does create all kinds of opportunities for its members upon graduation.

THE SCHOOL SAYS "..."

From The Admissions Office

"One of the best ways to discover if USC is right for you is to walk around campus, talk to students, and get a feel for the area both as a place to study and a place to live. If you can't visit, we hold admission information programs around the country. Watch your mailbox for an invitation, or send us an e-mail if you're interested.

"Freshman applicants are required to submit a standardized Writing exam. We will accept either the new SAT or the ACT with its optional Writing section."

SELECTIVITY

Admissions Rating	98
# of applicants	33,760
% of applicants accepted	25
% of acceptees attending	35

FRESHMAN PROFILE

Range SAT Critical Reading	620–720
Range SAT Math	650–740
Range SAT Writing	640–720
Range ACT Composite	28–32
Average HS GPA	3.71
% graduated top 10% of class	86
% graduated top 25% of class	97
% graduated top 50% of class	100

DEADLINES

Regular	
Priority	12/10
Deadline	1/10
Notification	4/1
Nonfall registration?	yes

APPLICANTS ALSO LOOK AT

AND OFTEN PREFER
Harvard College
Duke University
Columbia University
Stanford University

AND SOMETIMES PREFER
Washington University in St. Louis
University of Virginia
Johns Hopkins University
University of California—Berkeley
Cornell University

AND RARELY PREFER
Emory University
Vanderbilt University
New York University

FINANCIAL FACTS

Financial Aid Rating	95
Annual tuition	$35,212
Room and board	$10,858
Required fees	$598
Books and supplies	$750
% frosh rec. need-based scholarship or grant aid	34
% UG rec. need-based scholarship or grant aid	38
% frosh rec. non-need-based scholarship or grant aid	22
% UG rec. non-need-based scholarship or grant aid	17
% frosh rec. need-based self-help aid	38
% UG rec. need-based self-help aid	41
% frosh rec. athletic scholarships	3
% UG rec. athletic scholarships	2
% frosh rec. any financial aid	72
% UG rec. any financial aid	69
% UG borrow to pay for school	53
Average cumulative indebtedness	$25,578

THE UNIVERSITY OF TENNESSEE AT KNOXVILLE

320 STUDENT SERVICE BUILDING, CIRCLE PARK DRIVE, KNOXVILLE, TN 37996-0230 • ADMISSIONS: 865-974-2184

STUDENTS SAY ". . ."

Academics

The University of Tennessee—Knoxville "offers something for everyone. If you want a party school, you get it; if you want great athletics, you get it, etc." It even offers "a great education at an affordable price," if that's what you're into, and many here are. They lap up the "opportunities for student growth in and outside of the classroom, whether it be introduction classes for majors one is interested in, study abroad opportunities, or on-campus support resources." UTK's recently inaugurated "Ready for the World" initiative encourages academic exploration; it "is about providing opportunities for intellectual growth both in the classrooms here in Knoxville and in the streets of foreign places… to make students 'ready for the world' in all aspects of life during a time of such globalization." As at most large state schools, "There's the good the bad and the ugly at UT, everything from teachers who will do anything to help you succeed to those that you only see in the classroom and leave before you do." Students warn of "The Big Orange Screw," a bureaucratic "mix up of financial, academic, and living all screwed together" to make students' lives more difficult. It includes "constant changes to the course catalogue to add general requirements to graduate" even though "we are already devoting half of our undergraduate hours trying to satisfy distribution requirements."

Life

For many at UT, "Life seems to revolve around two things: sports and partying." Sports "are a really big deal here," and "Football season is a way of life at UT. Even people who don't like football are involved on game day." Basketball is also quite popular (the Lady Vols took the national championship in 2006–07 and in 2007–08, while the men's team made it to the Sweet Sixteen), as is volleyball. The party scene is just as robust, and "revolves around The Strip, the main road through the campus area that is home to a plethora of bars and restaurants," and "For people who aren't of age, there are always house parties in The Fort, the main off-campus housing area located within walking distance of almost everything." Greek organizations are also a formidable presence on campus; one student reports that "Thursday is the beginning of the weekend to most people and usually includes a fraternity band party or sorority mixer/date party. Friday night includes bar hopping, Saturday all-day tailgating before a football game, and Sunday a day to catch up on sleep and schoolwork." While few here are fun averse, "Everyone knows when they need to crack down and study… Overall, it's all about time management and putting your studies ahead of your fun." There are even those who shun the party scene entirely; one student informs us that "There is a large number of students who don't party, even though most people think of the school as a party school."

Student Body

The typical student at UT "is usually dressed in comfortable clothes and shoes walking to class listening to an iPod." He or she is, in other words, your typical kid, which makes sense given that the undergraduate population is over 20,000 strong. It also makes sense that "everyone is able to find his or her own niche" in this population. Most conspicuous perhaps are the Greeks, who "are extremely exclusive" but are hardly the only ones; "The student body is pretty polarized," one student explains, with distinct social groups based on major, economic/religious/ethnic background, and organizational affiliation rarely interacting. "It is essentially high school all over again, only with more drama and alcohol," one student observes. Another clear divide among students exists between those "who come to party and get an education if that fits in" and those "who want to get an education and make a difference in the world."

THE UNIVERSITY OF TENNESSEE AT KNOXVILLE

FAX: 865-974-1182 • FINANCIAL AID: 865-974-3131 • E-MAIL: ADMISSIONS@UTK.EDU • WEBSITE: WWW.UTK.EDU

THE PRINCETON REVIEW SAYS

Admissions

Very important factors considered include: Academic GPA, rigor of secondary school record, standardized test scores. *Other factors considered include:* Class rank, application essay, recommendation(s), alumni/ae relation, character/personal qualities, extracurricular activities, first generation, geographical residence, level of applicant's interest, racial/ethnic status, state residency, talent/ability, SAT or ACT required; TOEFL required of all international applicants. High school diploma is required and GED is accepted. *Academic units required:* 4 English, 3 mathematics, 2 science, (1 science labs), 2 foreign language, 1 social studies, 1 history, 1 visual/performing arts.

Financial Aid

Students should submit: FAFSA. The Princeton Review suggests that all financial aid forms be submitted as soon as possible after January 1. *Need-based scholarships/grants offered:* Federal Pell, SEOG, state scholarships/grants, private scholarships, the school's own gift aid, Federal Nursing Scholarships. *Loan aid offered:* FFEL Subsidized Stafford, FFEL Unsubsidized Stafford, FFEL PLUS, Federal Perkins, college/university loans from institutional funds. Applicants will be notified of awards on a rolling basis beginning 3/15. Federal Work-Study Program available. Off-campus job opportunities are good.

The Inside Word

UTK must winnow through more than 12,000 freshman applications each year. That sort of volume doesn't allow for nuance; students with above-average high school GPA's (achieved in a reasonable college prep curriculum) and above-average standardized test scores pretty much all make the cut. The school considers peripherals—extracurriculars, essays, special talents—when deciding which marginal candidates to admit.

THE SCHOOL SAYS "..."

From The Admissions Office

"The University of Tennessee at Knoxville is the place where you belong if you're interested in outstanding resources and unlimited opportunities to foster your personal and academic growth. Nine colleges offer more than 110 majors to students from all 50 states and 106 foreign countries. More than 400 clubs and organizations on campus offer opportunities for fun, challenge, and service. UTK is a place where students take pride in belonging to a 200-year-old tradition and celebrate the excitement of 'the Volunteer spirit.' We invite you to explore the many advantages UTK has to offer.

"Freshman applicants to the University of Tennessee are required to submit ACT or SAT scores. The essay is not required."

SELECTIVITY

Admissions Rating	87
# of applicants	12,824
% of applicants accepted	71
% of acceptees attending	48

FRESHMAN PROFILE

Range SAT Critical Reading	520–630
Range SAT Math	530–640
Range ACT Composite	23–28
Minimum paper TOEFL	523
Minimum computer TOEFL	193
Minimum web-based TOEFL	70
Average HS GPA	3.61
% graduated top 10% of class	38.59
% graduated top 25% of class	68.5
% graduated top 50% of class	92.73

DEADLINES

Regular	12/1
Nonfall registration?	yes

APPLICANTS ALSO LOOK AT
AND SOMETIMES PREFER
University of South Carolina—Columbia
Vanderbilt University
Clemson University
AND RARELY PREFER
University of Mississippi
Virginia Tech
University of Alabama—Tuscaloosa

FINANCIAL FACTS

Financial Aid Rating	77
Annual in-state tuition	$5,376
Annual out-of-state tuition	$17,916
Room and board	$6,676
Required fees	$1,112
Books and supplies	$1,326
% frosh rec. need-based scholarship or grant aid	44
% UG rec. need-based scholarship or grant aid	37
% frosh rec. need-based self-help aid	23
% UG rec. need-based self-help aid	28
% frosh rec. athletic scholarships	2
% UG rec. athletic scholarships	2
% frosh rec. any financial aid	46
% UG rec. any financial aid	44
% UG borrow to pay for school	49
Average cumulative indebtedness	$19,341

THE UNIVERSITY OF TEXAS AT AUSTIN

PO BOX 8058, AUSTIN, TX 78713-8058 • ADMISSIONS: 512-475-7440 • FAX: 512-475-7475

CAMPUS LIFE

Quality of Life Rating	**88**
Fire Safety Rating	**60***
Green Rating	**60***
Type of school	public
Environment	metropolis

STUDENTS

Total undergrad enrollment	36,881
% male/female	48/52
% from out of state	5
% live on campus	20
% in (# of) fraternities	9 (26)
% in (# of) sororities	14 (22)
% African American	5
% Asian	17
% Caucasian	55
% Hispanic	18
% international	4
# of countries represented	127

SURVEY SAYS . . .
Great library
Athletic facilities are great
Students love Austin, TX
Everyone loves the Longhorns
Student publications are popular
Lots of beer drinking

ACADEMICS

Academic Rating	**75**
Calendar	semester
Student/faculty ratio	18:1
Profs interesting rating	69
Profs accessible rating	63
Most common reg class size	10–19 students
Most common lab size	10–19 students

MOST POPULAR MAJORS
biology/biological sciences
liberal arts and sciences/liberal studies
business/commerce

STUDENTS SAY "..."

Academics

Those who have the pleasure of spending four years on "the great forty acres" of The University of Texas at Austin will find the "perfect blend of challenging academics and a buzzing social atmosphere." Boasting around 50,000 students, this "gigantic mix-and-match campus" offers every imaginable opportunity to its wide range of students, and the general attitude that permeates the campus is a positive one. Though some students are daunted by the sheer size of the system, it means that everyone has the chance at the same resources. "Speaking up in class, attending office hours, and choosing a small department where you really get to know people are a must—they really 'shrink' your UT experience to a manageable size," says a senior. It's a large college, so don't expect anyone to hold your hand. "If you aren't 'old' enough to be able to take care of your own college stuff, I wouldn't go here," says a freshman nursing student. What the school sacrifices in intimacy, it makes up for in variety of courses, majors, living arrangements, and kinds of people. Students say that academically, you walk away with what you earn. "You have to put in a lot of time here outside the classroom or you really will fail," says a student. "You can make it into a great education or just a mediocre one," says another. Academic advising can be hit or miss, and it can be "hard to get into the classes that you want," especially with the oft-maligned registration process, but the classes themselves are helmed by "a lot of real experts with practical experience." The professors "are not only extremely competent in their various areas, but all show extreme self interest in the success of their students," and when numbers do play a factor in the amount of face time a teacher can put in, "the TAs are equipped to help students as much as possible, and are easily accessible." The "rigid" administration isn't as warmly received; as one can expect from a school this size, there is a lot of jumping through hoops and "waivers and requests and rubberstamps and red tape," though students report that if you do manage to find a friendly face in the system, they'll go to bat for you. In the end, there's a great love for the school and all its manifestations. "You would be hard pressed to find someone who doesn't see our longhorn insignia and not immediately associate it with UT," says a sophomore.

Life

The campus is extremely large, so "it's not uncommon to see first-year students walking around with a map for the first few weeks." Austin itself has quite the list of admirers, who love the "independent attitude" of the city, not to mention its live music, film festivals, "great outdoor attractions," "brilliant and hilarious shows at the Alamo Drafthouse," and "shopping on the Drag." "It is impossible to be bored. There is always something to do," says a junior. Football season is a huge deal at UT, and Saturdays in the fall are devoted entirely to watching the Longhorns play football, whether they are at home or away. Sororities and fraternities constitute the bulk of a lot of students' social lives, and "alcohol accompanies all sporting events, parties, and weekends in general." Whether you head downtown to the famous Sixth Street for the bar scene, tailgate on Game Day, or head to a campus blowout, "there's constantly someone somewhere having a good time." The school also has activities on tap, from "bowling or free movies at the Texas Union" to programs planned by RAs to frequent appearances by speakers such as Mo Rocca and the Dalai Lama.

Student Body

In a school this size, there is bound to be immense variety, and that's exactly what you'll find at UT. Other than the understandable Texan quotient, there's "a fairly substantial Greek population," a "big sports following," and then "hipsters, hippie co-op kids, Bible groups, a big musician community, bicycle kids, stoners, student government types, you name it." Basically, playing these numbers, a social group awaits pretty much anyone, and "even the so-called weirdoes will find people similar to them." As for fitting in, "whether you're a Taiwanese poker-playing lesbian or a Latino tap-dancing Buddhist, you're sure to find someone else who shares your interests!"

FINANCIAL AID: 512-475-6282 • WEBSITE: WWW.UTEXAS.EDU

THE PRINCETON REVIEW SAYS

Admissions

Very important factors considered include: Class rank, rigor of secondary school record. *Important factors considered include:* Application essay, standardized test scores, extracurricular activities, talent/ability, volunteer work, work experience. *Other factors considered include:* Academic GPA, recommendation(s), character/personal qualities, first generation, geographical residence, level of applicant's interest, racial/ethnic status, state residency, SAT or ACT required; ACT with Writing component required. High school diploma is required and GED is accepted. *Academic units required:* 4 English, 3 mathematics, 2 science, (2 science labs), 2 foreign language, 3 social studies, 1 academic elective, 1 fine arts. *Academic units recommended:* 4 English, 4 mathematics, 3 science, (3 science labs), 3 foreign language, 3 social studies, 1 academic elective, 1 fine arts.

Financial Aid

The Princeton Review suggests that all financial aid forms be submitted as soon as possible after January 1. Federal Work-Study Program available. Off-campus job opportunities are fair.

The Inside Word

Top faculty and super facilities draw a mega-sized applicant pool to UT, as does Longhorn football. Texas wants top athletes in each entering class, to be sure. But it also seeks students who are well qualified academically, and it gets loads of them. Both the university and Austin are thriving intellectual communities; Austin has the highest per capita book sales of any city in the United States. Many students continue on to grad school without ever leaving, which is understandable—it's hard to spend any time without developing an affinity for the school and the city.

THE SCHOOL SAYS "..."

From The Admissions Office

"For more than 120 years, students from all over the world have come to The University of Texas at Austin to obtain a first-class education. Recognized for research, teaching, and public service, the university boasts more than 130 undergraduate academic programs, more than 350 study-abroad programs, outstanding student services, cultural centers, and volunteer and leadership opportunities designed to prepare students to make a difference in the world. Along with its nationally ranked athletic programs, the university's spirit is enhanced by cultural, artistic, and scientific opportunities that help to make Austin one of the most inviting destinations in the country. The Performing Arts Center hosts plays, Austin's opera and symphony, and visiting musical and dance groups. Students access more than 8 million volumes in the university's 17 libraries and study prehistoric fossils at the Texas Memorial Museum, Renaissance and Baroque paintings in the Blanton Museum, original manuscripts at the Ransom Center, and life in the 1960s at the Lyndon B. Johnson Library and Museum.

"Each year the university enrolls about 50,000 students from richly varied ethnic and geographic backgrounds. Every day graduates contribute to the world community as volunteers, teachers, journalists, artists, engineers, business leaders, scientists, and lawyers. With world-renowned faculty, top-rated academic programs, successful alumni, and such an enticing location, it's no surprise that The University of Texas at Austin ranks among the best universities in the world.

"Freshman applicants must submit official scores from the new version of the SAT or the ACT with the optional Writing exam. SAT Subject Test scores are required only for applicants to the College of Engineering who need to submit scores to meet the Math Readiness Requirement."

SELECTIVITY	
Admissions Rating	92
# of applicants	27,237
% of applicants accepted	51
% of acceptees attending	54

FRESHMAN PROFILE	
Range SAT Critical Reading	540–670
Range SAT Math	570–700
Range SAT Writing	540–660
Range ACT Composite	23–29
% graduated top 10% of class	69.4
% graduated top 25% of class	93.5
% graduated top 50% of class	99.3

DEADLINES	
Regular	
Deadline	1/15
Nonfall registration?	yes

FINANCIAL FACTS	
Financial Aid Rating	91
Annual in-state tuition	$7,670
Annual out-of-state tuition	$24,544
Room and board	$8,576
Books and supplies	$800
% frosh rec. any financial aid	89
% UG rec. any financial aid	90

UNIVERSITY OF TORONTO

315 BLOOR STREET WEST, TORONTO, ON M5S1A3 • ADMISSIONS: 416-978-2190 • FAX: 416-978-7022

STUDENTS SAY ". . ."

Academics

One of Canada's premier universities, the University of Toronto offers world-class academic programs in a thriving, cosmopolitan setting. With faculty members "on the cutting edge of research in their fields," students agree, "The best of the best are teaching here, and it shows. You feel smarter every day just from listening to the lectures presented." The school capitalizes on its location in the center of Toronto: "The city and the university draw on each other in a variety of ways—clinical opportunities and research flow in both directions." On top of that, industrious undergrads tell us, "The libraries and other research facilities here are excellent and contribute much to the overall academic experience." With over 40,000 undergraduates, class sizes run large, especially in the first year. However, students reassure us that "after that, the class sizes drop off drastically to normally between 20 to 100 students," and "The teaching assistants and lab coordinators are really helpful and work with personal questions whenever necessary, so you're not left in the dark." Even so, those looking for an intimate and supportive academic environment might not find a good fit at U of T, as "The general attitude is one of professionalism, and very little mercy." A hearty sophomore declares, "The University of Toronto prepares its students for the real world—only the strong survive, and you're on your own to make things happen."

Life

When they aren't hitting the books, University of Toronto students enjoy life in "one of the coolest cities in North America." With an open campus that is fully integrated into the city's vibrant downtown, students benefit from the fact that "the Royal Ontario Museum is on campus, a ton of pubs and art galleries are within walking distance, and a nightlife to suit just about any type of person" can be found in Toronto. Many students also mention Toronto's art and cultural festivals, bustling ethnic markets, and extensive culinary options. A senior jokes, "It would be possible to eat at a different restaurant every day for the entire duration of my degree, and it's a challenge I only wish I could afford to take." When it comes to campus life, many students feel that the school's spirit and unity is negatively affected by the large number of commuter students who, "just run home after every class to study." Others insist that there are plenty of social and recreational opportunities for those willing to look. A junior elucidates, "Getting involved here takes some research in terms of navigating the over 300 clubs and endless academic/research opportunities, but once I did some searching, I found several places where I fit in well and have fun." For those who live on campus, sororities and fraternities help nurture social bonds, and "Most of the residential colleges have tons of events, from campus-wide capture the flag to movie nights" to "tons of intramural sports."

Student Body

At this large public school, the demographics on campus reflect those of surrounding Toronto, "one of the most diverse cities around." As one junior puts it, "Truly, one of the only things it can be said that all students here have in common is an excellent academic record prior to university. Beyond that, anything goes: There are huge variances in race, religion, sexual orientation, academic focus, postgraduate aspirations, socioeconomic background, disability, nationality, athleticism, and community involvement." A freshman chimes in, "On my floor alone there are kids from at least 10 different countries and, even with the different cultures, we have blended together to make a big family." Most students say it's relatively easy to find a social group among like-minded individuals, despite the school's impressive size and diversity. According to one senior, "Most students will find a niche where they feel comfortable; there's a place for everyone."

FINANCIAL AID: 416-978-2190 • E-MAIL: ADMISSIONS.HELP@UTORONTO.CA • WEBSITE: WWW.UTORONTO.CA

THE PRINCETON REVIEW SAYS

Admissions

Very important factors considered include: Class rank, rigor of secondary school record, standardized test scores, SAT Subject Tests required; SAT and SAT Subject Tests or ACT required; ACT with Writing component required. TOEFL required of all international applicants. High school diploma is required and GED is accepted.

Financial Aid

The Princeton Review suggests that all financial aid forms be submitted as soon as possible after January 1.

The Inside Word

The University of Toronto is one of Canada's premier public universities and one of the top research institutions in the world. Needless to say, gaining admission to the college is no easy feat. The process is rather objective, however, and applicants with solid numbers are likely candidates for acceptance. Candidates should be aware that qualifications vary from program to program; and as an international student you'll have more paperwork to file. U.S. students can apply for financial assistance from the U.S. Federal Family Education Program (FFELP). The University of Toronto is a recognized postsecondary institution for Federal Stafford Loans. All applicants are automatically considered for admission scholarships.

THE SCHOOL SAYS "..."

From The Admissions Office

"The University of Toronto is committed to being an internationally significant research university with undergraduate, graduate, and professional programs of study.

"Students educated at U.S. schools should present good scores on the SAT or ACT examinations. Students must present the Writing component for both tests. Applicants must also present at least three SAT Subject Tests scores or AP scores in subjects appropriate to their proposed area of study. Those seeking admission to science or business/commerce programs are strongly advised to complete AP Calculus AB or BC or IB Mathematics.

"Scores below 500 on any part of the SAT Reasoning or Subject Tests are not acceptable. While many of our programs require higher scores, students normally present scores of at least 1700 out of a possible 2400 on the SAT and 26 on the ACT."

SELECTIVITY	
Admissions Rating	**60***
# of applicants	62,983
% of applicants accepted	68
% of acceptees attending	30

FRESHMAN PROFILE	
Minimum paper TOEFL	600
Minimum computer TOEFL	250

DEADLINES	
Regular	
Deadline	3/1
Notification	rolling
Nonfall registration?	no

FINANCIAL FACTS	
Financial Aid Rating	**60***
Annual in-state tuition	$4,570
Annual out-of-state tuition	$17,640
Room and board	$9,000
Required fees	$1,000
Books and supplies	$1,050

THE UNIVERSITY OF TULSA

800 SOUTH TUCKER DRIVE, TULSA, OK 74104 • ADMISSIONS: 918-631-2307 • FAX: 918-631-5003

CAMPUS LIFE

Quality of Life Rating	**94**
Fire Safety Rating	**81**
Green Rating	**80**
Type of school	private
Affiliation	Presbyterian
Environment	metropolis

STUDENTS

Total undergrad enrollment	2,920
% male/female	52/48
% from out of state	34
% from public high school	77
% live on campus	68
% in (# of) fraternities	21 (7)
% in (# of) sororities	23 (9)
% African American	6
% Asian	3
% Caucasian	64
% Hispanic	4
% Native American	3
% international	11
# of countries represented	57

SURVEY SAYS . . .
Large classes
Great computer facilities
Athletic facilities are great
Students are friendly
Students are happy

ACADEMICS

Academic Rating	**86**
Calendar	semester
Student/faculty ratio	10:1
Profs interesting rating	89
Profs accessible rating	90
% classes taught by TAs	4
Most common reg class size	10–19 students
Most common lab size	10–19 students

MOST POPULAR MAJORS
management/marketing
petroleum engineering
psychology

STUDENTS SAY ". . ."

Academics
The University of Tulsa is a mid-size, private school that provides a superior learning environment and myriad academic opportunities to its 3,000 undergraduate students. Across disciplines, the academic experience is high quality and stimulating, incorporating "rigorous and invigorating lectures and well instructed lab periods." In addition to coursework, undergraduates benefit from unmatched "academic and professional opportunities reserved only for graduate students at other schools." A current student attests, "I had no trouble getting undergraduate research experience in biochemistry as early as sophomore year." Students rave about TU's outgoing professors, saying that "the faculty and staff at TU seem to take a personal interest in the students here. They are accessible and love to help students in any way possible, not only academically, but professionally and personally as well." How's this for involved? "I have even received a text message from a professor when I forgot to turn in a homework assignment," reports a sophomore. While course selection is occasionally limited by the school's size, "professors will frequently tailor independent study projects with students." When it comes to the administration, some students worry that they are too preoccupied with improving the college's rankings. Others insist that the administrative offices are just as student-friendly as the teaching staff. A sophomore shares, "I became involved in student government my third semester here, and I am so impressed by how accessible the administration is. The deans and president of the university really care about students."

Life
Student life at TU reflects the school's unequivocal emphasis on academics. Studious undergraduates agree that the University of Tulsa "is definitely not a big party school. Most of the students here are focused on studies." Nonetheless, there are plenty of opportunities for extracurricular involvement, and campus clubs range "from honor societies to multi-cultural groups to religious gatherings." The campus isn't too big, so students looking for leadership experience will be pleased to learn that "anyone can be involved and 'be someone' on campus." In addition to student clubs, "collegiate, intramural, and pick-up sports are really popular." About 20 percent of the campus is involved in a Greek organization, and "a lot of student life revolves strongly around sororities and fraternities." However, students reassure us that "even non-Greek students can visit the houses and hang out on a Friday night." If you don't feel like partying at fraternities, there's plenty more to do, on- and off-campus. A sophomore shares, "For fun my friends and I go bowling, explore the parks of Tulsa, watch movies, do arts and crafts, and go to the occasional party." While students readily admit that Tulsa isn't New York City, they appreciate the myriad pleasures of their manageable mid-size city, which boasts "some really great restaurants and coffee shops around TU and in historic Tulsa."

Student Body
Defined in broad strokes, most TU undergraduates hail from affluent, Christian families in the Midwest. However, TU students insist that, while there are some similarities within the campus community, they cannot be summed up so easily. In addition to the array of "jocks, computer geeks, fashionistas, 'good' students, loners, and partygoers," University of Tulsa has a "strong international community. Programs such as the petroleum engineering department attract a diverse international populace. One can hear five different languages simply walking to class!" Thanks, in part, to the international students, there is "a diverse religious life on campus (we even have a mosque!), several activist groups that meet on campus, and countless student organizations." No matter what your background, "the majority of students I know at TU are very open and accepting of everyone else, regardless of religion, race, sexual orientation, athletic ability, major, and Greek affiliation." In fact, it's easy to feel at home on the TU campus. A junior explains, "Because the campus is small, even if you don't know somebody's name, you normally recognize their face from somewhere; this leads to a great sense of community."

FINANCIAL AID: 918-631-2526 • E-MAIL: ADMISSION@UTULSA.EDU • WEBSITE: WWW.UTULSA.EDU

THE PRINCETON REVIEW SAYS

Admissions

Very important factors considered include: Class rank, academic GPA, rigor of secondary school record, standardized test scores, interview, level of applicant's interest. *Important factors considered include:* Application essay, recommendation(s), character/personal qualities, extracurricular activities, talent/ability. *Other factors considered include:* Alumni/ae relation, first generation, racial/ethnic status, volunteer work, work experience. SAT or ACT required; TOEFL required of all international applicants. High school diploma is required and GED is accepted. *Academic units recommended:* 4 English, 3 mathematics, 3 science, (2 science labs), 2 foreign language, 1 social studies, 2 history, 1 academic elective.

Financial Aid

Students should submit: FAFSA, institution's own financial aid form. The Princeton Review suggests that all financial aid forms be submitted as soon as possible after January 1. *Need-based scholarships/grants offered:* Federal Pell, SEOG, state scholarships/grants, private scholarships, the school's own gift aid. *Loan aid offered:* FFEL Subsidized Stafford, FFEL Unsubsidized Stafford, FFEL PLUS, Federal Perkins Applicants will be notified of awards on a rolling basis beginning 3/1. Federal Work-Study Program available. Institutional employment available. Off-campus job opportunities are good.

The Inside Word

TU is a university with solid academic offerings, a strong sense of community, lots of student-faculty interaction, and attainable admission standards. The school's commitment to undergrads is clear. One of TU's most impressive programs, The Tulsa Undergraduate Research Challenge (TURC), allows undergrads to complete research along with faculty.

THE SCHOOL SAYS "..."

From The Admissions Office

"The University of Tulsa is a private university with a comprehensive scope. Students choose from more than 80 majors offered through three undergraduate colleges—Arts and Sciences, Business Administration, and Engineering and Natural Sciences. Their curriculum can be customized with collaborative research, joint BS/MBA and BA/law degree programs, and an honors program, among other options. Professors are equally committed to teaching undergraduates and to scholarly research. This results in extraordinary individual achievement, as demonstrated by the nationally competitive scholarships TU students have won since 1995: 41 Goldwater scholars, 8 Truman scholars, 5 Udall scholars, and 4 Marshall scholars. Since 1994 campus life has benefited from more than $35 million in new student apartments and residence hall renovations. Over 160 registered clubs, organizations, special interest groups, and intramural and recreational sports exist on campus as well as 6 fraternities and 9 sororities. The 8,300-seat Reynolds Arena is home to the standout Golden Hurricane NCAA Division I men's basketball team, campus events, and concerts. A 40-acre sports complex includes a student fitness center and indoor tennis center that will host the 2008 NCAA Division I Men's and Women's tennis finals. An outdoor adventure freshman orientation program launches an entire first-year experience dedicated to developing students' full potential.

"Applicants for Fall 2008 term are required to submit the SAT or ACT. The Writing component is not required. For admission and scholarship consideration, the best composite score of submitted tests will be used."

SELECTIVITY
Admissions Rating	92
# of applicants	3,804
% of applicants accepted	51
% of acceptees attending	34
# accepting a place on wait list	150
% admitted from wait list	53

FRESHMAN PROFILE
Range SAT Critical Reading	560–700
Range SAT Math	580–700
Range ACT Composite	24–30
Minimum paper TOEFL	500
Minimum computer TOEFL	173
Minimum web-based TOEFL	61
Average HS GPA	3.8
% graduated top 10% of class	64
% graduated top 25% of class	81
% graduated top 50% of class	93

DEADLINES
Regular	
Priority	2/1
Notification	rolling
Nonfall registration?	yes

APPLICANTS ALSO LOOK AT
AND OFTEN PREFER
Saint Louis University
Oklahoma State University
Southern Methodist University
Texas Christian University
University of Oklahoma
AND SOMETIMES PREFER
Washington University in St. Louis
Tulane University
Baylor University
AND RARELY PREFER
University of Missouri—Columbia
University of Kansas

FINANCIAL FACTS
Financial Aid Rating	88
Annual tuition	$23,860
Room and board	$7,776
Required fees	$80
Books and supplies	$1,200
% frosh rec. need-based scholarship or grant aid	20
% UG rec. need-based scholarship or grant aid	22
% frosh rec. non-need-based scholarship or grant aid	48
% UG rec. non-need-based scholarship or grant aid	39
% frosh rec. need-based self-help aid	39
% UG rec. need-based self-help aid	38
% frosh rec. athletic scholarships	11
% UG rec. athletic scholarships	12
% frosh rec. any financial aid	91
% UG rec. any financial aid	90
% UG borrow to pay for school	54
Average cumulative indebtedness	$20,563

UNIVERSITY OF UTAH

201 SOUTH 1460 EAST, ROOM 250 S, SALT LAKE CITY, UT 84112 • ADMISSIONS: 801-581-7281 • FAX: 801-585-7864

CAMPUS LIFE
Quality of Life Rating	82
Fire Safety Rating	84
Green Rating	89
Type of school	public
Environment	metropolis

STUDENTS
Total undergrad enrollment	20,560
% male/female	55/45
% from out of state	17
% from public high school	93
% live on campus	8
% in (# of) fraternities	1 (9)
% in (# of) sororities	1 (7)
% African American	1
% Asian	6
% Caucasian	80
% Hispanic	5
% Native American	1
% international	3
# of countries represented	119

SURVEY SAYS . . .
Registration is a breeze
Great computer facilities
Great library
Students love Salt Lake City, UT
Great off-campus food
Campus feels safe
Students are happy
Everyone loves the Utes

ACADEMICS
Academic Rating	73
Calendar	semester
Student/faculty ratio	13:1
Profs interesting rating	73
Profs accessible rating	61
% classes taught by TAs	14
Most common	
reg class size	20–29 students
Most common	
lab size	10–19 students

MOST POPULAR MAJORS
economics
political science and government
communication, journalism, and
related programs

STUDENTS SAY ". . ."

Academics

Nestled amidst Salt Lake City's snowcapped mountains, the University of Utah is a large public school that offers extensive academic programs, ample research opportunities, and a surprisingly student-friendly atmosphere. No matter what your interests, you'll find like minds at U of U. "I have studied everything from Tai Chi/Yoga movement and stage combat to differential equations and linear algebra," says a junior. "The one thing that has remained consistent throughout is the appreciation and dedication that the people have for the topic that they are involved in." U of U is a research university that actually takes teaching seriously, and "every teacher that I've had shows incredible knowledge in their area, as well as personality and wit." "Classes are informative, challenging, and genuinely enjoyable." As is the case in many larger universities, "most general education courses are taught by grad students," whose teaching abilities can range from great to below average. "Ninety percent of my professors are fantastic; the ones that aren't are usually grad students," explains a junior. On this large campus, students have little contact with the school's administration and "there's definitely no hand-holding at the U of U—if you're unsure of your major or career plans, it's easy to slip through the cracks." However, students assure us that, "the administration puts student interests first whenever possible with a focus on keeping tuition low, creating a diverse environment, and providing opportunities and experience in order to prepare students to be productive citizens."

Life

While a large percentage of the undergraduate community at the University of Utah commutes to campus, there are still plenty of activities for the school's 2,000 resident students. There are many people "active in politics, environmental issues, and international issues," and, after hours, "the school holds different events throughout the year, such as Crimson Nights that feature activities such as bowling, crafts, games, food, and music." Socially, "Greek life is not as large as at other schools but is definitely a lot of fun and the best way to get to know more people your age." In addition, "during football season there are great tailgate parties with friends, drinks, and food." Right off campus, there are a range of great restaurants, and "the nightlife is hard to keep up with: There's always something good going on—whether it's at the bars and clubs downtown, or at small music venues." For outdoorsy types, U of U is a paradise. "We have all four seasons and some of the best outdoors in the nation," explains one student. "Killer snow, amazing hills, mountains, lakes, and streams." In this natural wonderland, "hiking, biking, boating, snow-skiing, and snowboarding are just a few of the hundreds of activities available to students."

Student Body

Located in Salt Lake City, hometown to the Church of Latter Day Saints, "a majority of students at the U of U are Mormon, but not a vast majority. There are plenty of social niches to fall into, and none of them are rigidly exclusive." A current student adds, "About half the student body is the typical Utah Mormon, and the other half is a mix of everything. The two halves usually stay separate but they get along." If you like a little cultural mix-up, U of U students agree that "there is more diversity here than in any other part of the state." However, out-of-state students are uncommon, and "those of us not from Utah are definitely in the minority." While there are a number of residential students, a very large percentage of students also chose to commute to school while living with their parents or family. In addition, "there are a lot of older students and a lot of married students." Academically, however, U of U undergraduates share a true dedication to studies, and are "independent, smart, and come to class ready to discuss ideas."

FINANCIAL AID: 801-581-6211 • E-MAIL: FAWIN1@SA.UTAH.EDU • WEBSITE: WWW.UTAH.EDU

THE PRINCETON REVIEW SAYS

Admissions

Very important factors considered include: Academic GPA, rigor of secondary school record, standardized test scores. *Important factors considered include:* talent/ability. *Other factors considered include:* Class rank, recommendation(s), extracurricular activities, interview, racial/ethnic status, SAT recommended; SAT or ACT required; SAT and SAT Subject Tests or ACT required; ACT recommended; TOEFL required of all international applicants. High school diploma is required and GED is accepted. *Academic units required:* 4 English, 2 mathematics, 3 science, (1 science labs), 2 foreign language, 1 history, 4 academic electives.

Financial Aid

Students should submit: FAFSA, institution's own financial aid form. The Princeton Review suggests that all financial aid forms be submitted as soon as possible after January 1. *Need-based scholarships/grants offered:* Federal Pell, SEOG, state scholarships/grants, private scholarships, the school's own gift aid, SMART and ACG Grants. *Loan aid offered:* FFEL Subsidized Stafford, FFEL Unsubsidized Stafford, FFEL PLUS, Federal Perkins, Federal Nursing, college/university loans from institutional funds, private alternative loans. Applicants will be notified of awards on a rolling basis beginning 4/15. Federal Work-Study Program available. Institutional employment available. Off-campus job opportunities are excellent.

The Inside Word

Utah is another state in which low numbers of high school grads keep selectivity down at its public flagship university. Admission is based primarily on the big three: Course selection, grades, and test scores; if you have a 3.0 GPA or better and average test scores, you're close to a sure bet for admission.

THE SCHOOL SAYS ". . ."

From The Admissions Office

"The University of Utah is a distinctive community of learning in the American West. Today's 28,000 students are from every state and 119 foreign countries. The U has research ties worldwide, with national standing among the top comprehensive research institutions. The U offers majors in 73 undergraduate and 94 graduate subjects. Nationally recognized honors and undergraduate research programs stimulate intellectual inquiry. Undergraduates collaborate with faculty on important investigations. The U's intercollegiate athletes compete in the NCAA Division I Mountain West Conference. The men's basketball team has been nationally ranked for several years, as have our women's gymnastics and skiing teams. The U's location in Salt Lake City provides easy access to the arts, theater, Utah Jazz basketball, and hockey. Utah's Great Outdoors—skiing, hiking, and five national parks—are nearby. The university was the site for the opening and closing ceremonies and the Athletes Village for the 2002 Winter Olympic Games.

"Residential Living has greatly expanded the opportunity for students to live on campus with a new and wide variety of housing. Heritage Commons, located in historic Fort Douglas on campus, consists of 21 newly constructed buildings, including three residence hall–style facilities, which accommodate more than 2,500 students.

"Applicants are required to submit ACT scores. SAT scores are also accepted, although ACT scores are preferred. Students are urged to take the ACT near the end of their junior year or early in the senior year of high school."

SELECTIVITY
Admissions Rating	79
# of applicants	7,123
% of applicants accepted	82
% of acceptees attending	47

FRESHMAN PROFILE
Range SAT Critical Reading	490–630
Range SAT Math	490–630
Range ACT Composite	21–27
Minimum paper TOEFL	500
Minimum computer TOEFL	173
Average HS GPA	3.53
% graduated top 10% of class	25.3
% graduated top 25% of class	48.7
% graduated top 50% of class	81.8

DEADLINES
Regular	
Priority	2/15
Deadline	4/1
Nonfall registration?	yes

FINANCIAL FACTS
Financial Aid Rating	65
Annual in-state tuition	$4,320
Annual out-of-state tuition	$14,944
Room and board	$5,778
Required fees	$717
Books and supplies	$1,080
% frosh rec. need-based scholarship or grant aid	21
% UG rec. need-based scholarship or grant aid	28
% frosh rec. non-need-based scholarship or grant aid	2
% UG rec. non-need-based scholarship or grant aid	1
% frosh rec. need-based self-help aid	19
% UG rec. need-based self-help aid	29
% frosh rec. any financial aid	28
% UG rec. any financial aid	38
% UG borrow to pay for school	41.2
Average cumulative indebtedness	$13,994

UNIVERSITY OF VERMONT

194 SOUTH PROSPECT STREET, BURLINGTON, VT 05401-3596 • ADMISSIONS: 802-656-3370 • FAX: 802-656-8611

CAMPUS LIFE

Quality of Life Rating	83
Fire Safety Rating	78
Green Rating	96
Type of school	public
Environment	city

STUDENTS

Total undergrad enrollment	9,454
% male/female	45/55
% from out of state	65
% from public high school	70
% live on campus	54
% in (# of) fraternities	6 (8)
% in (# of) sororities	5 (5)
% African American	1
% Asian	2
% Caucasian	93
% Hispanic	2
# of countries represented	46

SURVEY SAYS . . .

Students are friendly
Students love Burlington, VT
Great off-campus food
Lots of beer drinking
Hard liquor is popular

ACADEMICS

Academic Rating	76
Calendar	semester
Student/faculty ratio	16:1
Profs interesting rating	75
Profs accessible rating	77
% classes taught by TAs	2
Most common reg class size	10–19 students
Most common lab size	10–19 students

MOST POPULAR MAJORS

English language and literature
psychology
business administration and
management

STUDENTS SAY ". . ."

Academics

Quality of life issues are important to most University of Vermont undergrads; when discussing their reasons for choosing UVM, they're as likely to cite the "laid-back environment," the "proximity to skiing facilities," the "great parties," and their "amazing" hometown of Burlington as they are to mention the academics. But, students remind us, "That doesn't mean that there are not strong academics [at UVM]." On the contrary, UVM is made up of several well-established colleges and offers "a wide variety of majors." "You can jump around between majors, and then leave with a recognized diploma in hand for something you love to do." Students single out the business school, the "top-notch" education program, the Psychology Department, premedical sciences, and "the amazing animal science program" for praise, and are especially proud of The Rubenstein School of Natural Resources, home to UVM's environmental science majors; they tell us it "is a great college that feels like it's much smaller, [more] separate, and just cozier than the rest of the school." No matter which discipline, "You get out what you put in." "Teachers are readily available and are willing to help you do well in your classes. They encourage you to get help if you need it and are enthusiastic about what they teach. It's all there; you just have to take advantage of it." The size of the university, we're told, is just right; UVM is "a moderately large school," and it allows undergrads "to feel at home while still offering just about any activity possible."

Life

"UVM is known to be a party school," and "Even though the university has cracked down on drinking (they made it a dry campus this year), it hasn't actually changed much." Indeed, students tell us that one can find "a good balance of having fun and academics" at UVM, "but it's tough, because there's always a party going on somewhere." Students who want to dodge the party scene will find "There is always something" happening in Burlington. The town has "lots of wonderful restaurants, a few movie theaters, a rockin' music scene, several bars, some dancing, and various environmental and social activities downtown." "On campus, there is typically at least one university-sponsored event each night, including interesting lectures, movies, games, or social events." Students love outdoor activities: "When it snows, it's very popular to go to the ski resorts around here and ski or snowboard for the day. When it's still warm out, going to the waterfront and swimming in Lake Champlain is popular too." UVM is an intercollegiate hockey powerhouse, and "In the fall and winter, hockey games are huge social events." They're so popular "that you have to get tickets to them the Monday before the game, or they will be sold out!"

Student Body

There's a "great variety of students" at UVM "because it's a big university," undergrads report, but they also note that "students at UVM are mostly White" and that there's "a lot of money at this school." While the most prevalent UVM archetype is "the guitar-loving, earth-saving, relaxed hippie" who "care[s] strongly about the environment" and "social justice," the student body also includes "your athletic types, your artsy people, and a number of other groups" including "vocal LGBTQ and ALANA populations" who, "though they usually hang out in their own groups," "are also active in all sorts of clubs across campus." Not surprisingly, there are many "New England types," "potheads," and "snow bums." Students report they "pretty much get along well with everyone." They either come here loving the outdoors or learn to love the outdoors by the time they leave.

FINANCIAL AID: 802-656-3156 • E-MAIL: ADMISSIONS@UVM.EDU • WEBSITE: WWW.UVM.EDU

THE PRINCETON REVIEW SAYS

Admissions

Very important factors considered include: Rigor of secondary school record. *Important factors considered include:* Class rank, application essay, academic GPA, standardized test scores, character/personal qualities, state residency. *Other factors considered include:* Recommendation(s), alumni/ae relation, extracurricular activities, first generation, geographical residence, interview, level of applicant's interest, racial/ethnic status, talent/ability, volunteer work, work experience. SAT or ACT required; ACT with Writing component required. TOEFL required of all international applicants. High school diploma is required and GED is accepted. *Academic units required:* 4 English, 3 mathematics, 2 science, (1 science labs), 2 foreign language, 3 social studies.

Financial Aid

Students should submit: FAFSA. The Princeton Review suggests that all financial aid forms be submitted as soon as possible after January 1. *Need-based scholarships/grants offered:* Federal Pell, SEOG, state scholarships/grants, private scholarships, the school's own gift aid, Federal Nursing Scholarships. *Loan aid offered:* FFEL Subsidized Stafford, FFEL Unsubsidized Stafford, FFEL PLUS, Federal Perkins, Federal Nursing, college/university loans from institutional funds. Applicants will be notified of awards on a rolling basis beginning 3/15. Federal Work-Study Program available. Institutional employment available. Off-campus job opportunities are good.

The Inside Word

UVM is a very popular choice among out-of-state students, whom the school welcomes; over half the student body originates from outside of Vermont. While admissions standards are significantly more rigorous for out-of-staters, solid candidates (B-plus/A-minus average, about a 600 on each section of the SAT) should do fine here. The school assesses applications holistically, meaning students who are weak in one area may be able to make up for it with strengths or distinguishing skills and characteristics in other areas.

THE SCHOOL SAYS "..."

From The Admissions Office

"The University of Vermont blends the close faculty-student relationships most commonly found in a small liberal arts college with the dynamic exchange of knowledge associated with a research university. This is not surprising, because UVM is both. A comprehensive research university offering nearly 100 undergraduate majors and extensive offerings through its Graduate College and College of Medicine, UVM is one of the nation's premier public research universities. UVM prides itself on the richness of its undergraduate experience. Distinguished senior faculty teach introductory courses in their fields. They also advise not only juniors and seniors, but also first- and second-year students, and work collaboratively with undergraduates on research initiatives. Students find extensive opportunities to test classroom knowledge in field through practicums, academic internships, and community service. More than 100 student organizations (involving 80 percent of the student body), 20 Division I varsity teams, 15 intercollegiate club and 14 intramural sports programs, and a packed schedule of cultural events fill in where the classroom leaves off.

"Applicants for the entering class of Fall 2008 class and beyond are required to take the new version of the SAT, or the ACT with the Writing section, and must submit official test scores. SAT Subject Tests are neither required nor recommended for the admission application."

SELECTIVITY

Admissions Rating	83
# of applicants	18,814
% of applicants accepted	70
% of acceptees attending	19
# accepting a place on wait list	1,261

FRESHMAN PROFILE

Range SAT Critical Reading	540–630
Range SAT Math	540–640
Range SAT Writing	530–630
Range ACT Composite	23–28
Minimum paper TOEFL	550
Minimum computer TOEFL	213
% graduated top 10% of class	23
% graduated top 25% of class	61
% graduated top 50% of class	97

DEADLINES

Early action	
Deadline	11/1
Notification	12/15
Regular	
Deadline	1/15
Notification	3/31
Nonfall registration?	yes

FINANCIAL FACTS

Financial Aid Rating	74
Annual in-state tuition	$10,422
Annual out-of-state tuition	$26,306
Room and board	$8,024
Required fees	$1,632
Books and supplies	$936
% frosh rec. need-based scholarship or grant aid	50
% UG rec. need-based scholarship or grant aid	49
% frosh rec. non-need-based scholarship or grant aid	4
% UG rec. non-need-based scholarship or grant aid	3
% frosh rec. need-based self-help aid	45
% UG rec. need-based self-help aid	46
% frosh rec. athletic scholarships	2
% UG rec. athletic scholarships	1
% frosh rec. any financial aid	90
% UG rec. any financial aid	78
% UG borrow to pay for school	61
Average cumulative indebtedness	$23,567

UNIVERSITY OF VIRGINIA

OFFICE OF ADMISSION, PO BOX 400160, CHARLOTTESVILLE, VA 22906 • ADMISSIONS: 434-982-3200 • FAX: 434-924-3587

STUDENTS SAY ". . ."

Academics

It's all about balance at the University of Virginia: The balance "between public and private, large research university and small liberal arts college, tradition and progress, and work and play." Here at "Mr. Jefferson's University" the influence of the school's founder is paramount; the school "promotes a Jeffersonian spirit of learning in various aspects of student life," and this creates a cohesive community. In the spirit of one of democracy's greatest proponents, "a surprising amount of the school's administration is left to the students. For example, I think in the 1990s students lobbied for more study space, so Clemons Library was born. Also, honor code offenses and the like are handled by student-run bodies." Academically, UVA "demands a lot [from] students. Expectations of hard work—much less excellence—are high. If you do not study or do work outside of class, you will fall behind fast." In return for their hard work, undergrads gain access to "unlimited opportunity for hands-on experience. Study abroad and research opportunities are encouraged, and funding is always available. And you can tailor your courses to desired interests." Students particularly appreciate that these perks come at a public-school price. Standout programs include premedical study, business, politics, architecture (Jefferson's influence again!), environmental science, and biomedical engineering.

Life

Students at UVA are "very serious about academics and research, but also very much into extracurriculars and social life." Greek organizations "are huge at UVA," and Greek parties are the destination of choice for most freshmen and sophomores. Third- and fourth-years, on the other hand, "usually go to the bars located on the corner" when they want a little weekend rest and relaxation. There are also plenty of other options available; downtown Charlottesville "offers a wealth of opportunities, ranging from movies to concerts to shopping." Many students immerse themselves in student governance, which "permeates everything from the Resident Staff program to intramural sports to every club, publication, and organization. Students have the power to decide what gets done, and are challenged to make UVA a better place for having them as students." There's also UVA football, for which the campus basically grinds to a halt; one student explains, "Game day is devoted to dressing up, pre-game socializing, going to the game to socialize, and then after-game parties." Students also love to take advantage of the many options offered by the Shenandoah Valley, including "apple-picking at Carter's Mountain, hiking at Humpback Rock, and taking a Sunday drive around the beautiful surrounding county. Shenandoah National Park is only 30 minutes away from campus and offers a wealth of outdoor activities." UVA's grounds—please do not use the term "campus" here—are among the nation's loveliest.

Student Body

UVA is "a place where smart kids get together and are excited about learning. That doesn't mean it's a bunch of nerds, however. The intelligence of the average UVA student is masked under cheering at football games, drinking at parties, working out, and doing whatever else we find fun. Being smart is just an accepted fact here. We do our work [and] then go party." One undergrad remarks, "There is no typical student. The campus is big enough that there are lots of people you don't know, but you can [also] run into friends constantly. There's a strong Greek presence, so the typical student might be classified as preppy. There are a lot of average, blend-in type of students, as well, and lots of athletes." While one student warns potential undergrads not to "expect their lavish dream of collegiate social diversity to play out on UVA's campus," most agree that "because of the wide range of groups on grounds, all students are able to find their niche, and there are a lot of niches at UVA. You're pretty much guaranteed not to be the only person around who has a particular interest, hobby, or belief. That's the blessing of a big school."

FINANCIAL AID: 434-982-6000 • E-MAIL: UNDERGRADADMISSION@VIRGINIA.EDU • WEBSITE: WWW.VIRGINIA.EDU

THE PRINCETON REVIEW SAYS

Admissions

Very important factors considered include: Class rank, academic GPA, recommendation(s), rigor of secondary school record, alumni/ae relation, first generation, racial/ethnic status, state residency. *Important factors considered include:* Application essay, standardized test scores, character/personal qualities, extracurricular activities, talent/ability. *Other factors considered include:* geographical residence, volunteer work, work experience. Two SAT Subject Tests strongly recommended; SAT, or ACT with Writing component required. TOEFL required of all international applicants whose native language is not English. High school diploma is required and GED is accepted. *Academic units required:* 4 English, 4 mathematics, 2 science, 2 foreign language, 1 social studies. *Academic units recommended:* 5 mathematics, 4 science, 5 foreign language, 4 social studies.

Financial Aid

Students should submit: FAFSA, institution's own financial aid form. The Princeton Review suggests that all financial aid forms be submitted as soon as possible after January 1. *Need-based scholarships/grants offered:* Federal Pell, SEOG, state scholarships/grants, private scholarships, the school's own gift aid, Federal Nursing Scholarship. *Loan aid offered:* FFEL Subsidized Stafford Loans, FFEL Unsubsidized Stafford Loans, FFEL PLUS Loans, Federal Perkins, Federal Nursing, college/university loans from institutional funds, Alternative/Private Loans. Applicants will be notified of awards on or about 4/5. Federal Work-Study Program available. Institutional employment available.

The Inside Word

As one of the premier public universities in the country, UVA holds its applicants to high standards. While Admissions Officers don't set minimum requirements, all viable candidates have stellar academic records. Intellectual ability is imperative and prospective students are expected to have taken a rigorous course load in high school. Applicants should be aware that geographical location and legacies hold significant weight, as Virginia residents and children of alums are given preference.

THE SCHOOL SAYS "..."

From The Admissions Office

"Admission to competitive schools requires strong academic credentials. Students who stretch themselves and take rigorous courses (honors-level and Advanced Placement courses, when offered) are significantly more competitive than those who do not. Experienced Admission Officers know that most students are capable of presenting superb academic credentials, and the reality is that a very high percentage of those applying do so. Other considerations, then, come into play in important ways for academically strong candidates, as they must be seen as 'selective' well as academically competitive.

"SAT scores are preferred. The ACT test will also be accepted if the optional ACT Writing Test is also taken. It is strongly recommended that applicants take two SAT Subject Tests of the applicant's choice."

SELECTIVITY

Admissions Rating	97
# of applicants	17,798
% of applicants accepted	35
% of acceptees attending	52
# accepting a place on wait list	2,426
% admitted from wait list	7
# of early decision applicants	2,404
% accepted early decision	40

FRESHMAN PROFILE

Range SAT Critical Reading	590–700
Range SAT Math	610–720
Range SAT Writing	600–710
Average HS GPA	4.05
% graduated top 10% of class	87
% graduated top 25% of class	96
% graduated top 50% of class	99

DEADLINES

Regular	
Deadline	1/2
Notification	4/1
Nonfall registration?	no

APPLICANTS ALSO LOOK AT

AND OFTEN PREFER
College of William and Mary
Duke University

AND SOMETIMES PREFER
Penn State Lehigh Valley
Virginia Tech
Harvard College
Notre Dame College
Georgetown College
Cornell University
Yale University
University of North Carolina at Chapel Hill
Princeton University

FINANCIAL FACTS

Financial Aid Rating	94
Annual in-state tuition	$8,500
% frosh rec. need-based scholarship or grant aid	23
% UG rec. need-based scholarship or grant aid	21
% frosh rec. non-need-based scholarship or grant aid	13
% UG rec. non-need-based scholarship or grant aid	12
% frosh rec. need-based self-help aid	15
% UG rec. need-based self-help aid	18
% frosh rec. athletic scholarships	4
% UG rec. athletic scholarships	3
% frosh rec. any financial aid	55
% UG rec. any financial aid	47
% UG borrow to pay for school	33
Average cumulative indebtedness	$16,847

UNIVERSITY OF WASHINGTON

1410 NORTHEAST CAMPUS PARKWAY, 320 SCHMITZ BOX 355840, SEATTLE, WA 98195-5840 • ADMISSIONS: 206-543-9686

CAMPUS LIFE

Quality of Life Rating	**82**
Fire Safety Rating	**93**
Green Rating	**99**
Type of school	public
Environment	metropolis

STUDENTS

Total undergrad enrollment	26,509
% male/female	48/52
% from out of state	13
% live on campus	20
% in (# of) fraternities	6 (27)
% in (# of) sororities	5 (16)
% African American	3
% Asian	28
% Caucasian	53
% Hispanic	5
% Native American	1
% international	4
# of countries represented	107

SURVEY SAYS . . .

Great computer facilities
Great library
Athletic facilities are great
Students love Seattle, WA
Great off-campus food
Everyone loves the Huskies

ACADEMICS

Academic Rating	**78**
Calendar	quarter
Student/faculty ratio	12:1
Profs interesting rating	68
Profs accessible rating	70
Most common reg class size	20–29 students
Most common lab size	20–29 students

MOST POPULAR MAJORS

psychology
economics
political science and government

STUDENTS SAY "..."

Academics

Students find "a great combination of high-powered academics, an excellent social life, and a wide variety of courses, all in the midst of the exciting Seattle life" at the University of Washington, the state's flagship institution of higher learning. UW offers "a lot of really stellar programs and the best bang for the buck, especially for in-state students or those in the sciences." Indeed, science programs "are incredible. The research going on here is cutting-edge and the leaders of biomedical sciences, stem cell research, etc. are accessible to students." Undergrads warn, however, that science programs are extremely competitive, "high pressure," and "challenging," with "core classes taught in lectures that seat over 500 people," creating the sense that "professors don't seem to care too much whether you succeed." Pre-professional programs in business, law, nursing, medicine and engineering all earn high marks, although again with the caveat that the workload is tough and the hand holding nominal. As one student puts it, "The University of Washington provides every resource and opportunity for its students to succeed. You just have to take advantage of them. No one will do it for you." For those fortunate enough to get in, the Honors Program "creates a smaller community of highly motivated students…. It puts this school on top."

Life

UW students typically "have a good balance in their lives of education and fun." They "generally study hard and work in the libraries, but once the nighttime hits, they look forward to enjoying the night with their friends." Between the large university community and the surrounding city of Seattle, undergrads have a near-limitless selection of extracurricular choices. As one student explains, "There are tons of options for fun in Seattle. Going down to Pike's Market on a Saturday and eating your way through is always popular. There are tons of places to eat on 'The Ave,'" the shopping district that abuts campus, "and the UVillage shopping mall is a five minute walk from campus with chain-store comfort available. Intramural sports are big for activities, and going to undergraduate theater productions is never a disappointing experience. And during autumn or spring renting a canoe and paddling around lake Washington down by the stadium is fun." Husky football games "are amazing," and the Greek community "is very big" without dominating campus social life. In short, "The UW has anything you could want to do in your free time."

Student Body

"At such a large university, there is no 'typical' student," undergrads tell us, observing that "One can find just about any demographic here and there is a huge variety in personalities." There "are quite a lot of yuppies, but then again, it's Seattle," and by and large "the campus is ultraliberal. Most students care about the environment, are not religious, and are generally accepting of other diverse individuals." Otherwise, "You've got your stereotypes: you've got the Greeks, the street fashion pioneers, the various ethnic communities, the Oxford-looking grad students, etc." In terms of demographics, "The typical student at UW is white, middle class, and is from the Seattle area," but "There are a lot of African American students and a very large number of Asian students." All groups "seem to socialize with each other."

FAX: 206-685-3655 • FINANCIAL AID: 206-543-6101 • E-MAIL: ASKUWADM@U.WASHINGTON.EDU • WEBSITE: WWW.WASHINGTON.EDU

THE PRINCETON REVIEW SAYS

Admissions

Very important factors considered include: Application essay, academic GPA, rigor of secondary school record. *Important factors considered include:* Standardized test scores, character/personal qualities, extracurricular activities, first generation, talent/ability, volunteer work, work experience. *Other factors considered include:* State residency, SAT or ACT required; ACT with Writing component required. TOEFL required of all international applicants. High school diploma or equivalent is not required. *Academic units required:* 4 English, 3 mathematics, 2 science, (1 science labs), 2 foreign language, 3 social studies. *Academic units recommended:* 4 English, 4 mathematics, 3 science, (3 science labs), 3 foreign language, 4 social studies, 1 history, 1 visual/performing arts, 1 computer science.

Financial Aid

Students should submit: FAFSA. The Princeton Review suggests that all financial aid forms be submitted as soon as possible after January 1. *Need-based scholarships/grants offered:* Federal Pell, SEOG, state scholarships/grants, private scholarships, the school's own gift aid. *Loan aid offered:* Direct Subsidized Stafford, Direct Unsubsidized Stafford, Direct PLUS, Federal Perkins, Federal Nursing, college/university loans from institutional funds. Applicants will be notified of awards on or about 3/31. Federal Work-Study Program available. Institutional employment available. Off-campus job opportunities are excellent.

The Inside Word

In 2005, UW committed to a thorough review of all freshman applications, abandoning the previous process by which a formula was used to rank applicants according to high school GPA and standardized test scores. The new holistic approach allows admissions officers to take into account a student's background, the degree to which he or she has overcome personal adversity, and such intangibles as leadership quality and special skills. The move has so far resulted in increased racial and socioeconomic diversity, a result praised by some and criticized by others, who regard the new system as a poorly disguised affirmative action program.

THE SCHOOL SAYS "..."

From The Admissions Office

"Are you curious about everything, from comet dust to computer game design, salmon to Salman Rushdie, ancient Rome to the atmospherics of Mars? Do you seek the freedom to chart your own course—and work on breakthrough research? Are you ready to cheer on the Division I Huskies and spend your weekends sea kayaking? Would you like to walk to class on a 700-acre stunning, ivy-covered campus, yet be only 15 minutes from downtown Seattle? If the answers are yes, then the University of Washington may be the place for you. Offering more than 140 majors and 450 student organizations, the UW is looking for students who are both excited about the vast academic and social possibilities available to them and eager to contribute to the campus' cultural and intellectual life.

"We encourage you to take advantage of every opportunity in the application, especially the personal statement and activities summary, to tell us why Washington would be good fit for you and how you will contribute to the freshman class.

"Freshman applicants to the University of Washington are required to submit scores from either the new SAT or ACT (with the Writing component)."

SELECTIVITY

Admissions Rating	94
# of applicants	17,777
% of applicants accepted	65
% of acceptees attending	46
# accepting a place on wait list	773
% admitted from wait list	43

FRESHMAN PROFILE

Range SAT Critical Reading	530–650
Range SAT Math	560–670
Range SAT Writing	520–630
Range ACT Composite	23–29
Minimum paper TOEFL	537
Minimum computer TOEFL	207
Average HS GPA	3.69
% graduated top 10% of class	86
% graduated top 25% of class	11
% graduated top 50% of class	100

DEADLINES

Regular	
Deadline	1/15
Notification	rolling
Nonfall registration?	yes

APPLICANTS ALSO LOOK AT

AND OFTEN PREFER
University of Southern California
AND SOMETIMES PREFER
Western Washington University
Gonzaga University
AND RARELY PREFER
University of Colorado—Boulder
University of Puget Sound
Washington State University

FINANCIAL FACTS

Financial Aid Rating	76
Annual tuition	$6,385
% frosh rec. need-based scholarship or grant aid	22
% UG rec. need-based scholarship or grant aid	26
% frosh rec. non-need-based scholarship or grant aid	3
% UG rec. non-need-based scholarship or grant aid	3
% frosh rec. need-based self-help aid	25
% UG rec. need-based self-help aid	29
% frosh rec. athletic scholarships	2
% UG rec. athletic scholarships	2
% frosh rec. any financial aid	45
% UG rec. any financial aid	45
% UG borrow to pay for school	49
Average cumulative indebtedness	$16,100

UNIVERSITY OF WISCONSIN—MADISON

716 LANGDON STREET, MADISON, WI 53706-1481 • ADMISSIONS: 608-262-3961 • FAX: 608-262-7706

CAMPUS LIFE
Quality of Life Rating	**89**
Fire Safety Rating	**60***
Green Rating	**60***
Type of school	public
Environment	city

STUDENTS
Total undergrad enrollment	28,999
% male/female	47/53
% from out of state	32
% live on campus	24
% in (# of) fraternities	9 (26)
% in (# of) sororities	8 (11)
% African American	3
% Asian	6
% Caucasian	80
% Hispanic	3
% Native American	1
% international	4
# of countries represented	110

SURVEY SAYS . . .
Great library
Athletic facilities are great
Students love Madison, WI
Great off-campus food
Everyone loves the Badgers
Student publications are popular
Lots of beer drinking
Hard liquor is popular

ACADEMICS
Academic Rating	**80**
Calendar	semester
Student/faculty ratio	13:1
Profs interesting rating	71
Profs accessible rating	70
% classes taught by TAs	22
Most common reg class size	10–19 students
Most common lab size	20–29 students

MOST POPULAR MAJORS
political science and government
biology/biological sciences
psychology

STUDENTS SAY ". . ."

Academics
"The resources are phenomenal" at University of Wisconsin—Madison. "If you are proactive, you basically have the means and resources to pursue any academic or creative feat," promises a journalism major. "The liberal arts majors are fantastic." However, Madison is mostly known as "an amazing research institution," and the hard sciences and engineering programs get most of the pub. They iodized salt here, after all, and cultivated the first lab-based embryonic stem cells. The school of business is "excellent" as well and boasts "some of the best facilities on campus." "Overall the school runs surprisingly smoothly" but "red tape" sometimes "makes you want to kill someone." Courses can be large and "impersonal." Class sizes "plummet" after the intro courses but never get intimate. "Even as an upperclassman, I rarely see lectures with less than 100 people," observes a junior. The academic atmosphere is "challenging," though. Madison "definitely makes you earn your grades." "Some professors are amazing, and some suck." Also, "a lot of the classes for the undergrads are taught by teaching assistants who are not so good." "It becomes clear within the first few weeks which of your professors actually have lectures that are worthwhile for you to attend, which is probably about half," suggests a first-year student.

Life
UW—Madison's "reputation as a party school" is legendary. Halloween and the Mifflin Street Block Party are epic. "The weekend pretty much starts on Thursday night" as the streets of Madison "fill to the brim with drunk co-eds." There are house parties and frat parties galore. "Getting up at 9:00 A.M." to "bong a few beers for breakfast" before football games in the fall is common, and "nothing—absolutely nothing—can beat being in the student section at a Badger home football game." "The stadium is usually full" for hockey games, too. However, "no one looks at you differently if you choose not to drink" or attend sporting events. And, for everyone, "if you don't have a strong dedication to your education, you will slip up." Beyond the party and sports scene, UW is "energetic" and mammoth. "No one's going to hold your hand and point you to what it is you want." At the same time, whoever you are, "there is a group for you and a ton of activities for you." "Greek life is a big part of Madison." Two daily student newspapers "serve as the penultimate example of free speech in action." UW's lakefront campus provides "gorgeous" scenery. Many of the buildings "aren't that appealing," though, and some dorms are "absolutely horrible." Off-campus, "having the streets crawling with the homeless isn't so great," but Madison is teeming with culture, "live music," "late-night coffee shops," and "exceptional" chow from around the globe.

Student Body
Ethnic diversity at Madison is in the eye of the beholder. "If you're from a big city, it's pretty white," proposes a sophomore. "But, then again, I've met people here who had one black person in their high school and had never met a Jewish person." Without question, socioeconomic diversity flourishes. The majority of students are middle class Wisconsinites. "There is a prevalent rivalry between these students (sconnies) and the coasties who are generally wealthier and from the East or West Coast." "People from the Midwest think people from the coasts are stuck up. People from the coasts think people from the Midwest are hicks." Beyond that, it's impossible to generalize. "All types of people make up the student body here, ranging from the peace-preaching grass-root activist, to the protein-shake-a-day jock, to the overly privileged coastie, to the studious bookworm, to the computer geek," explains a first-year student. "There is a niche for everyone." "There are a lot of atypical students, but that is what makes UW—Madison so special," adds a senior. "Normal doesn't exist on this campus." Politically, "Madison is a hotbed for political and social debate." "Many people are passionate about many things and it provides a great opportunity to see things from others' points of view." You'll find conservatives but "leftwing, environmentally conscious nut jobs" who "stage protests" are more common.

UNIVERSITY OF WISCONSIN—MADISON

FINANCIAL AID: 608-262-3060 • E-MAIL: ONWISCONSIN@ADMISSIONS.WISC.EDU • WEBSITE: WWW.WISC.EDU

THE PRINCETON REVIEW SAYS

Admissions

Very important factors considered include: Class rank, academic GPA, rigor of secondary school record. *Important factors considered include:* Application essay, standardized test scores, state residency. *Other factors considered include:* Recommendation(s), alumni/ae relation, character/personal qualities, extracurricular activities, first generation, interview, level of applicant's interest, racial/ethnic status, talent/ability, volunteer work, work experience. SAT or ACT required; ACT with Writing component required. High school diploma is required and GED is accepted. *Academic units required:* 4 English, 3 mathematics, 3 science, 2 foreign language, 3 social studies, 2 academic electives. *Academic units recommended:* 4 English, 4 mathematics, 4 science, 4 foreign language, 4 social studies, 2 academic electives.

Financial Aid

Students should submit: FAFSA, institution's own financial aid form. The Princeton Review suggests that all financial aid forms be submitted as soon as possible after January 1. *Need-based scholarships/grants offered:* Federal Pell, SEOG, state scholarships/grants, private scholarships, the school's own gift aid. *Loan aid offered:* FFEL Subsidized Stafford, FFEL Unsubsidized Stafford, FFEL PLUS, Federal Perkins, Federal Nursing, state loans Applicants will be notified of awards on a rolling basis beginning 4/1. Federal Work-Study Program available. Institutional employment available. Off-campus job opportunities are excellent.

The Inside Word

Though it's not at the top tier of selectivity, Wisconsin has high expectations of its candidates. It's not quite entirely admission by formula; UW does look at each application individually, just not for very long.

THE SCHOOL SAYS "..."

From The Admissions Office

"UW—Madison is the university of choice for some of this country's (and the world's) best and brightest. Our freshman class has an average ACT score of 27.5 and an average SAT of 1260. Over half come from the top 10 percent of their high school class, and nearly 95 percent come from the top quarter.

"These factors combine to make admission to UW—Madison both competitive and selective. We consider academic record, course selection, strength of curriculum (honors, AP, IB, etc.), grade trend, class rank, results of the ACT and/or SAT, and non-academic factors. We do not have a prescribed minimum test score, GPA, or class rank criteria. Rather we admit the best and most well-prepared students—students who have challenged themselves and who will contribute to Wisconsin's strength and diversity—for the limited space available.

"Each application is personally reviewed by our admission counselors. Admission decisions are made within 6 weeks of the time when an applicant's admission file is complete. A complete file includes the application for admission, application fee, official high school transcript, and official test score report(s). Supplemental application materials may include a personal statement and letters of recommendation.

"We practice rolling admissions and applications are accepted beginning September 15. For full consideration for fall and summer terms, complete applications must be received by February 1. The deadline for the spring term is October 1. Applications received after these deadlines will be considered on a space-available basis.

"Starting in Fall 2008, all freshman applicants must submit results from either the new SAT or the ACT with the Writing component. Students who took either test before February 2005 must take at least one of the exams again in order to provide a Writing score and be eligible for admission."

SELECTIVITY

Admissions Rating	94
# of applicants	24,870
% of applicants accepted	56
% of acceptees attending	43

FRESHMAN PROFILE

Range SAT Critical Reading	550–670
Range SAT Math	620–710
Range SAT Writing	560–670
Range ACT Composite	26–30
Average HS GPA	3.77
% graduated top 10% of class	60
% graduated top 25% of class	93
% graduated top 50% of class	99

DEADLINES

Regular	
Priority	2/1
Deadline	2/1
Notification	rolling
Nonfall registration?	yes

FINANCIAL FACTS

Financial Aid Rating	72
Annual in-state tuition	$8,808
% frosh rec. need-based scholarship or grant aid	24
% UG rec. need-based scholarship or grant aid	26
% frosh rec. non-need-based scholarship or grant aid	17
% UG rec. non-need-based scholarship or grant aid	11
% frosh rec. need-based self-help aid	25
% UG rec. need-based self-help aid	29
% frosh rec. athletic scholarships	2
% UG rec. athletic scholarships	2
% UG borrow to pay for school	48
Average cumulative indebtedness	$21,018

UNIVERSITY OF WYOMING

DEPARTMENT 3435, 1000 EAST UNIVERSITY AVENUE, LARAMIE, WY 82071 • ADMISSIONS: 307-766-5160 • FAX: 307-766-4042

CAMPUS LIFE

Quality of Life Rating	**75**
Fire Safety Rating	**60***
Green Rating	**88**
Type of school	public
Environment	town

STUDENTS

Total undergrad enrollment	9,140
% male/female	48/52
% from out of state	28
% live on campus	21
% in (# of) fraternities	NR (8)
% in (# of) sororities	NR (6)
% African American	1
% Asian	1
% Caucasian	83
% Hispanic	3
% Native American	1
% international	2
# of countries represented	74

SURVEY SAYS . . .

Great computer facilities
Great library
Athletic facilities are great
Students are friendly
Everyone loves the Cowboys
Lots of beer drinking

ACADEMICS

Academic Rating	**75**
Calendar	semester
Student/faculty ratio	15:1
Profs interesting rating	73
Profs accessible rating	77
% classes taught by TAs	11
Most common reg class size	20–29 students
Most common lab size	20–29 students

MOST POPULAR MAJORS
elementary education and teaching
nursing/registered nurse
(RN, ASN, BSN, MSN)
psychology

STUDENTS SAY "..."

Academics
The University of Wyoming is "about getting a great education with an inexpensive price tag." A wide range of strong programs includes traditional fare (e.g., education, nursing, and majors across the arts and sciences) as well as majors aimed at more idiosyncratic populations (e.g., rangeland ecology and watershed management and agricultural economics). The engineering college is "a big draw" though future engineers here caution that you should expect to put in considerable "blood, sweat, and tears." UW's faculty truly runs the gamut. "Some of my teachers have the enthusiasm of people who have been truly inspired," says a first-year student. Others are "a bit dry." Still others are "just horrible teachers." "There are some of the best teachers in the country at the University of Wyoming," reports a sophomore. "There are also some of the worst." Overall, classes tend to be lectures and there is "little to no discussion." And while professors "are very much available for you" outside of class, you should expect "to make little effort" to get individual attention. Student opinion differs concerning the administration. Embittered students tell us that management is "one big, unorganized mess." Satisfied students call that the administration "very approachable." "They haven't done anything outrageous or heinous," reflects a senior. Most everyone seems to agree that "registering for classes is hell." "I am having a hard time getting into anything," vents a sophomore.

Life
"Parking is a joke," and "the surrounding area is very poorly lit," but "everything you would ever want to do is right on" UW's "stunningly beautiful" campus. School spirit is high. "Athletic events are electric and the hottest ticket in town." Football games in particular bring out a "rowdy crowd." The Friday Night Fever program "offers something different every Friday night for students for free." Intramurals are "very popular" as well and extracurricular activities are plentiful even if "not everyone chooses to participate." "Laramie is cold and doesn't have much," reports a junior, "so alcohol becomes a very good buddy." The bar scene can get "very crazy and hectic" Thursday through Saturday. "All the cowboys, athletes, and other students hang out in the same places, which is really fun." Beyond Laramie, UW's "proximity to mountains" makes for "spectacular" opportunities. "Most people enjoy winter sports like skiing and snowboarding." Rock climbing is big. "Fishing locally is great, and the fall is filled with hunting." Be warned, though, that it's "freakin' cold and windy" much of the time. "Students who don't tolerate cold well will be disappointed attending this school." Urban cities such as Fort Collins, Denver, and Cheyenne aren't impossibly far but "during the snowy season, Laramie can become sort of an island" because so many roads are closed.

Student Body
"Most of the students here are from Wyoming and the neighboring states." "These states are, in fact, quite ethnically monochromatic" but the few minority students at UW reportedly "assimilate well." The population "definitely has a small Wyoming feel." "There are many agriculture students." "There are the rancher students who like Coors Light, rodeo, tight Wranglers, and Copenhagen" but "it is a definite overstatement if anyone says that the majority of students are chewing, buckle-wearing cowboys." "There aren't as many hicks at UW as a person might think." The vast majority is "just normal college students who are interested in learning." These "outdoorsy" students describe themselves as "genuine," "independent," and "friendly and practical." They are "mostly laidback (except around finals) and unpretentious." They "have tons of pride in the state and the school," too. "There are very few loners and, if they are loners, it is by choice," asserts a first-year student. Politically, students are "more conservative." "Laramie is one of the most liberal cities in the state of Wyoming, but Wyoming is one of the most conservative states." Mostly, though, people are "generally libertarian in behavior" and political activity is minimal.

FINANCIAL AID: 307-766-2116 • E-MAIL: WHY-WYO@UWYO.EDU • WEBSITE: WWW.UWYO.EDU

THE PRINCETON REVIEW SAYS

Admissions

Very important factors considered include: Academic GPA, rigor of secondary school record, standardized test scores. *Important factors considered include:* Level of applicant's interest. *Other factors considered include:* Application essay, recommendation(s), character/personal qualities, extracurricular activities, interview, state residency, talent/ability, SAT or ACT required; TOEFL required of all international applicants. High school diploma is required and GED is accepted. *Academic units required:* 4 English, 3 mathematics, 3 science, (3 science labs), 3 Cultural Context Electives. *Academic units recommended:* 3 behavioral or social sciences, 3 visual or performing arts, 3 humanities or earth/space sciences.

Financial Aid

Students should submit: FAFSA. The Princeton Review suggests that all financial aid forms be submitted as soon as possible after January 1. *Need-based scholarships/grants offered:* Federal Pell, SEOG, state scholarships/grants, private scholarships, the school's own gift aid. *Loan aid offered:* FFEL Subsidized Stafford, FFEL Unsubsidized Stafford, FFEL PLUS, Federal Perkins Applicants will be notified of awards on a rolling basis beginning 3/1. Federal Work-Study Program available. Institutional employment available. Off-campus job opportunities are good.

The Inside Word

The admissions process at Wyoming is fairly formula-driven. State residents need a minimum 2.75 high school GPA to gain admission. Nonresidents have to have a 3.0 GPA. That and some solid test scores will open the door to the university.

THE SCHOOL SAYS "..."

From The Admissions Office

"The University of Wyoming and the town of Laramie are relatively small, affording students the opportunity to get the personal attention and develop a close rapport with their professors. They can easily make friends and find peers with similar interests and values. Over 200 student organizations offer students a great way to get involved and encourage growth and learning. Couple the small size with a great location, and you have a winning combination. Laramie sits between the Laramie and Snowy Range Mountains. There are numerous outdoor activities in which one can participate. Furthermore, the university works hard to attract other great cultural events. Major-label recording artists come to UW as well as some of today's great minds. In all, the University of Wyoming is a great place to be because of its wonderful blend of small town atmosphere with 'big city' activities.

"The University of Wyoming requires first-time, incoming freshmen to submit scores from either the ACT or SAT. The Writing component of the ACT and SAT is not required, but is reviewed if submitted. Scores from either the new or old SAT are accepted."

SELECTIVITY

Admissions Rating	88
# of applicants	3,371
% of applicants accepted	96
% of acceptees attending	49

FRESHMAN PROFILE

Range SAT Critical Reading	480–610
Range SAT Math	500–630
Range ACT Composite	21–26
Minimum paper TOEFL	525
Minimum computer TOEFL	197
Average HS GPA	3.459
% graduated top 10% of class	20.4
% graduated top 25% of class	49.5
% graduated top 50% of class	80.4

DEADLINES

Regular	
Priority	3/1
Deadline	8/10
Nonfall registration?	yes

FINANCIAL FACTS

Financial Aid Rating	73
Annual in-state tuition	$2,820
Annual out-of-state tuition	$10,230
% frosh rec. need-based scholarship or grant aid	23
% UG rec. need-based scholarship or grant aid	26
% frosh rec. non-need-based scholarship or grant aid	44
% UG rec. non-need-based scholarship or grant aid	37
% frosh rec. need-based self-help aid	40
% UG rec. need-based self-help aid	52
% frosh rec. athletic scholarships	5
% UG rec. athletic scholarships	5
% frosh rec. any financial aid	95
% UG rec. any financial aid	87
% UG borrow to pay for school	49
Average cumulative indebtedness	$16,005

URSINUS COLLEGE

URSINUS COLLEGE, ADMISSIONS OFFICE, COLLEGEVILLE, PA 19426 • ADMISSIONS: 610-409-3200 • FAX: 610-409-3662

CAMPUS LIFE
Quality of Life Rating	**85**
Fire Safety Rating	**89**
Green Rating	**91**
Type of school	private
Environment	metropolis

STUDENTS
Total undergrad enrollment	1,563
% male/female	48/52
% from out of state	39
% from public high school	61
% live on campus	95
% in (# of) fraternities	18 (7)
% in (# of) sororities	28 (7)
% African American	6
% Asian	5
% Caucasian	75
% Hispanic	3
% international	1
# of countries represented	13

SURVEY SAYS . . .
Large classes
Athletic facilities are great
Lots of beer drinking

ACADEMICS
Academic Rating	**91**
Calendar	semester
Student/faculty ratio	12:1
Profs interesting rating	85
Profs accessible rating	86
Most common reg class size	fewer than 10 students
Most common lab size	10–19 students

MOST POPULAR MAJORS
biology/biological sciences
psychology
economics

STUDENTS SAY "..."

Academics
Ursinus College, a small liberal arts school in aptly named Collegeville, Pennsylvania, offers a wide array of courses and "has the facilities of a much larger school." "I truly believe that Ursinus is a transformative experience," declares an international relations major. "If you embrace the liberal arts education, this is the institution to be at." "Academic rigor is demanding." A required pair of first-year courses called "the Common Intellectual Experience" "create a bonding experience for the students, and it gets them to think about some extremely important issues." Beyond that, students must complete a host of core requirements in addition to their majors. You'll "do your fair share of 10- to 15-page term papers; usually a couple per semester." "But it pays off in the end." The small size allows for "discussion-based classes" and professors "really try to get students involved." "Some professors are full of themselves," admits a neuroscience major. However, they are "great teachers and certainly know what they're talking about." "I have loved all of my professors," gushes a math major. "They've been friendly, helpful, and knowledgeable. They're eager to get students involved in research." Management is "accessible" as well. The "down-to-earth" administrators "are often seen about the campus attending lectures, concerts, and sporting events." Strong majors here include biology and chemistry. Ursinus boasts an impressive 90-plus percent acceptance rate with medical schools. Students also laud the economics and arts programs.

Life
Ursinus boasts "a very beautiful campus." Some of the older dorms cry out for refurbishing, though, and newer ones are "faintly reminiscent of a hospital." The food isn't great, either. "They stop carting out the good food after the second week," warns a biology major. Also, wireless Internet is spotty. Despite these complaints, students tell us they are extremely happy. "People overall love the school," says a freshman. Ursinus students are proud of their ability to have fun. "There are parties almost every night," especially Thursday through Saturday, as students "ruin their collective liver." The administration tries to crack down, but students persevere and the drinking scene remains rollicking. House parties or suite parties are options but the Greek system "rules campus life." "The keggers held by Greek organizations" are the most widely attended bashes. Not everyone drinks, of course, "not by a long shot." "The cool thing about Ursinus is that regardless of whether you drink or not, you can still go to the parties and have a great time." Some students warn that "Ursinus can be a little dull" if you insist on avoiding the party scene altogether. Others disagree. "There is an incredible availability of activities and clubs on campus," they say. Intramural and varsity athletics are also very popular. Students "love to go to all the food places in Collegeville" as well. It is "difficult" to get too far off campus without a car, though. (And first-year students can't have them.) While "there is no shame inherent in taking the bus" to Philadelphia, few students do.

Students
By and large, while ethnic diversity isn't terrible for a small liberal arts school, Ursinus is "homogenous." "Most people come from wealthier families" and grew up in the comfortable suburbs of "New Jersey, Pennsylvania, and New York." Ursinus students are "very hardworking" and "have similar values." Politically, there's a mildly liberal slant. "Most students on this campus are active and highly involved, although those who do not engage in clubs and activities do seem to find each other." The prototypical Ursinus student is a "somewhat clean-cut, friendly, occasionally drunk," "Hollister-clad, Ugg-wearing" prepster. "Different cliques are evident," though. There are "smart jocks and wonderfully weird nerds." There are "stereotypical frat boys." "There are many weirdoes and there are many average Joes." "Ursinus somehow seems to provide a safe and comfortable environment for people of all different interests," remarks one student.

URSINUS COLLEGE

FINANCIAL AID: 610-409-3600 • E-MAIL: ADMISSIONS@URSINUS.EDU • WEBSITE: WWW.URSINUS.EDU

THE PRINCETON REVIEW SAYS

Admissions

Very important factors considered include: Class rank, rigor of secondary school record, extracurricular activities. *Important factors considered include:* Application essay, academic GPA, recommendation(s), standardized test scores, alumni/ae relation, racial/ethnic status, talent/ability, volunteer work, work experience. *Other factors considered include:* Character/personal qualities, first generation, geographical residence, interview, level of applicant's interest, TOEFL required of all international applicants. High school diploma is required and GED is not accepted. *Academic units required:* 4 English, 3 mathematics, 1 science, (1 science labs), 2 foreign language, 1 social studies, 5 academic electives. *Academic units recommended:* 4 mathematics, 3 science, 4 foreign language, 3 social studies.

Financial Aid

Students should submit: FAFSA, institution's own financial aid form, CSS/Financial Aid PROFILE Regular filing deadline is 2/15. The Princeton Review suggests that all financial aid forms be submitted as soon as possible after January 1. *Need-based scholarships/grants offered:* Federal Pell, SEOG, state scholarships/grants, private scholarships, the school's own gift aid. *Loan aid offered:* FFEL Subsidized Stafford, FFEL Unsubsidized Stafford, FFEL PLUS, Federal Perkins, college/university loans from institutional funds, Ursinus Gate First Marblehead Loans. Applicants will be notified of awards on or about 3/15. Federal Work-Study Program available. Institutional employment available. Off-campus job opportunities are excellent.

The Inside Word

Grades, test scores, and class rank count for more than anything else, and unless you are academically inconsistent, you'll likely get good news. If you are hoping to snag a scholarship, it's really essential that you visit campus and get yourself interviewed. Students in the top 10 percent of their graduating classes aren't required to submit SAT score.

THE SCHOOL SAYS " . . ."

From The Admissions Office

"Located a half-hour from center-city Philadelphia, the college boasts a beautiful 168-acre campus that includes the Residential Village (renovated Victorian-style homes that decorate the Main Street and house our students) and the nationally recognized Berman Museum of Art. Ursinus is a member of the Centennial Conference, competing both in academics and in intercollegiate athletics with institutions such as Dickinson, Franklin & Marshall, Gettysburg, and Muhlenberg. The academic environment is enhanced with such fine programs as a chapter of Phi Beta Kappa, an early assurance program to medical school with the Medical College of Pennsylvania, and myriad student exchanges both at home and abroad. A heavy emphasis is placed on student research—an emphasis that can only be carried out with the one-on-one attention Ursinus students receive from their professors.

"Ursinus will continue to ask applicants for writing samples—both a series of application essays and a graded high school paper. Pending further examination, the Writing portion of the new SAT will not initially affect admissions decisions."

SELECTIVITY

Admissions Rating	89
# of applicants	5,141
% of applicants accepted	53
% of acceptees attending	17
# accepting a place on wait list	210
% admitted from wait list	29
# of early decision applicants	232
% accepted early decision	59

FRESHMAN PROFILE

Range SAT Critical Reading	550–660
Range SAT Math	560–660
Range SAT Writing	550–660
Range ACT Composite	22–29
Minimum paper TOEFL	500
Minimum computer TOEFL	173
% graduated top 10% of class	40
% graduated top 25% of class	74
% graduated top 50% of class	96

DEADLINES

Early decision	
Deadline	1/15
Notification	2/15
Early action	
Deadline	12/15
Notification	1/15
Regular	
Priority	2/15
Deadline	2/15
Notification	4/1
Nonfall registration?	yes

FINANCIAL FACTS

Financial Aid Rating	89
Annual tuition	$36,750
Room and board	$8,800
Required fees	$160
Books and supplies	$1,000
% frosh rec. need-based scholarship or grant aid	64
% UG rec. need-based scholarship or grant aid	68
% frosh rec. non-need-based scholarship or grant aid	13
% UG rec. non-need-based scholarship or grant aid	14
% frosh rec. need-based self-help aid	65
% UG rec. need-based self-help aid	70
% frosh rec. any financial aid	78
% UG rec. any financial aid	83
% UG borrow to pay for school	75
Average cumulative indebtedness	$18,509

VALPARAISO UNIVERSITY

KRETZMANN HALL, 1700 CHAPEL DRIVE, VALPARAISO, IN 46383 • ADMISSIONS: 219-464-5011 • FAX: 219-464-6898

STUDENTS SAY ". . ."

Academics
Valparaiso University, a small Lutheran university, "is a serious academic community with strong, but not forceful, religious background" that "prepares, motivates, and challenges tomorrow's leaders, engineers, nurses, and teachers while giving the opportunity for religious growth." Business, education, and engineering are the most popular majors, and are among Valpo's most celebrated departments. Other standout disciplines include nursing, music, theater ("the department involves touring professional directors a couple times a year, which speaks for itself" and "puts on great plays"), and one of the nation's largest meteorology programs (which "just erected a state-of-the-art Doppler radar, putting Valpo at the forefront for undergrad meteorology"). Undergrads here appreciate the breadth of excellent offerings as well as "the school's ability to integrate the liberal arts with a variety of majors... As a student I have been able to study engineering as well as hermeneutics, child development, and read classic texts ranging from Aristotle and Plato to Chuang Tzu and Derrida." Valpo operates under an honor code that students say, "creates an environment of trust and high moral responsibility." "People follow the honor code, especially because the punishments are strict, such as failing the class for a first offense," one student tells us. A few dissenters feel that "The honor code may reduce some cheating, but I don't think it comes near to eliminating it." Outstanding students may enroll in Christ College, an honors college, which they describe as "very intense but very rewarding."

Life
"There are several activities to choose from on Valparaiso's campus on a typical weekend, ranging from philanthropic dance parties at fraternity houses to music recitals to special guests speakers (to name just a few)," students tell us. Religious groups are active, and not just the Lutherans; the Catholic Church "is very active" here, offering "a student mass Sunday nights with a meal afterward, which is very nice" and "at least three events each week." Athletics are also popular; "We have Division I athletics, so it's fun to watch if you don't play, but Valpo also offers club sports (like Ultimate Frisbee) and intramurals for all student to participate in." The VU campus is officially dry, but that doesn't mean students don't drink; an aggressive campus police force means "There is lots of fear of getting arrested when drinking, but people do it anyway." Fraternity parties "have parties every Friday night," which helps to offset the perception that "the city of Valpo is horrible" because "there's not much to do" there. "If you can't entertain yourself, this is not the place for you," students warn. When they need big-city diversion, students will "hop on the train to go over to Chicago, an hour ride, for about $6, and get a CTA day pass for $4 (to ride Chicago's transit all day)." Another popular daytrip destination is the Indiana Dunes, which border Lake Michigan.

Student Body
The majority of Valpo students "are Caucasians who come from a well-off family, extremely religious Lutherans, and very conservative." One student estimates that "conservative, churchgoing studiers" make up about two-thirds of the student body. Most "come from somewhere in the Midwest," with many "from the Chicagoland area." The typical student is "here to learn. There are some that are just here for the party, but there are not many." Because "meteorology and engineering are large areas of study, there are some students who are 'nerdy,' but no one is left out of university activities." Valpo has "few minority students," and "it would be nice to have a little bit more diversity."

VALPARAISO UNIVERSITY

FINANCIAL AID: 219-464-5015 • E-MAIL: UNDERGRAD.ADMISSIONS@VALPO.EDU • WEBSITE: WWW.VALPO.EDU

THE PRINCETON REVIEW SAYS

Admissions
Very important factors considered include: Academic GPA, rigor of secondary school record. *Important factors considered include:* Class rank, standardized test scores, extracurricular activities, talent/ability. *Other factors considered include:* Application essay, recommendation(s), alumni/ae relation, character/personal qualities, first generation, interview, level of applicant's interest, racial/ethnic status, religious affiliation/commitment, volunteer work, work experience. SAT or ACT required; ACT with Writing component recommended. TOEFL required of all international applicants. High school diploma is required and GED is accepted. *Academic units required:* 4 English, 3 mathematics, 2 science, (2 science labs), 2 foreign language, 2 history, 3 academic electives. *Academic units recommended:* 4 English, 4 mathematics, 3 science, (3 science labs), 2 foreign language, 1 social studies, 2 history, 3 academic electives.

Financial Aid
Students should submit: FAFSA. The Princeton Review suggests that all financial aid forms be submitted as soon as possible after January 1. *Need-based scholarships/grants offered:* Federal Pell, SEOG, state scholarships/grants, private scholarships, the school's own gift aid. *Loan aid offered:* Direct Subsidized Stafford, Direct Unsubsidized Stafford, Direct PLUS, Federal Perkins, college/university loans from institutional funds. Applicants will be notified of awards on a rolling basis beginning 3/1. Federal Work-Study Program available. Institutional employment available. Off-campus job opportunities are good.

The Inside Word
Valparaiso's nearly 90 percent admit rate suggests a pretty generous admissions office. The figure is somewhat misleading; Valpo's applicant pool consists largely of students familiar enough with the school to know whether it's worth their while to apply here. In other words, the school doesn't receive a lot of 'reach' applications. Applicants indicating an interest in meteorology should expect a more rigorous review, as space in the program is limited.

THE SCHOOL SAYS "..."

From The Admissions Office
"Valpo provides students a blend of academic excellence, social experience, and spiritual exploration. The concern demonstrated by faculty and administration for the total well-being of students reflects a long history as a Lutheran-affiliated university."

SELECTIVITY	
Admissions Rating	85
# of applicants	3,475
% of applicants accepted	90
% of acceptees attending	23

FRESHMAN PROFILE	
Range SAT Critical Reading	490–610
Range SAT Math	500–640
Range SAT Writing	480–610
Range ACT Composite	22–28
Minimum paper TOEFL	550
Minimum computer TOEFL	213
Minimum web-based TOEFL	80
Average HS GPA	3.36
% graduated top 10% of class	28
% graduated top 25% of class	60
% graduated top 50% of class	89

DEADLINES	
Early action	
Deadline	11/1
Notification	12/1
Regular	
Priority	1/15
Deadline	8/15
Notification	rolling
Nonfall registration?	yes

APPLICANTS ALSO LOOK AT
AND OFTEN PREFER
Purdue University—West Lafayette
Indiana University—Bloomington
AND SOMETIMES PREFER
Butler University
Ball State University
AND RARELY PREFER
Marquette University
Bradley University
Loyola University—Chicago

FINANCIAL FACTS	
Financial Aid Rating	82
Annual tuition	$24,360
Room and board	$7,150
Required fees	$840
Books and supplies	$1,200
% frosh rec. need-based scholarship or grant aid	76
% UG rec. need-based scholarship or grant aid	68
% frosh rec. non-need-based scholarship or grant aid	12
% UG rec. non-need-based scholarship or grant aid	9
% frosh rec. need-based self-help aid	61
% UG rec. need-based self-help aid	57
% frosh rec. athletic scholarships	2
% UG rec. athletic scholarships	3
% frosh rec. any financial aid	98
% UG rec. any financial aid	96
% UG borrow to pay for school	73
Average cumulative indebtedness	$26,259

VANDERBILT UNIVERSITY

2305 WEST END AVENUE, NASHVILLE, TN 37203 • ADMISSIONS: 615-322-2561 • FAX: 615-343-7765

CAMPUS LIFE
Quality of Life Rating	**90**
Fire Safety Rating	**60***
Green Rating	**79**
Type of school	private
Environment	metropolis

STUDENTS
Total undergrad enrollment	6,330
% male/female	48/52
% from out of state	83
% from public high school	57
% live on campus	83
% in (# of) fraternities	34 (19)
% in (# of) sororities	50 (12)
% African American	8
% Asian	6
% Caucasian	67
% Hispanic	5
% international	2
# of countries represented	55

SURVEY SAYS . . .
Lab facilities are great
Students love Nashville, TN
Great off-campus food
Frats and sororities dominate
social scene
Student publications are popular
Lots of beer drinking

ACADEMICS
Academic Rating	**92**
Calendar	semester
Student/faculty ratio	9:1
Profs interesting rating	86
Profs accessible rating	83
Most common reg class size	10–19 students
Most common lab size	20–29 students

MOST POPULAR MAJORS
engineering science
psychology
sociology

STUDENTS SAY ". . ."

Academics

The word "balance" pops up a lot in students' descriptions of Vanderbilt University. Most often it's used to describe the amalgamation of "high academic standards" and "myriad" "social, service, and leadership opportunities" that characterizes so many students' experiences here. It is also used to describe the school's well-balanced mix of academic strengths; no surprise there, as Vandy excels in such diverse areas as premedicine, engineering, mathematics, sociology, psychology, and education. Sometimes the word refers to the balance between the "big city" benefits of Nashville—which include not only a world-class music scene but also "great opportunities for jobs, internships, [and] service"—and Vandy's "campus feel." In whatever context, students' numerous references to balance are a testimony to their comfort and satisfaction with the Vanderbilt experience. Undergrads here report a convivial atmosphere that takes away "a lot of the pressure" created by the "academically rigorous" curriculum. Professors "are generally good teachers who make themselves available through prompt responses to e-mail and through office hours," while administrators "are very accessible—you can see them in their office or spot them walking through campus." Fellow students "aren't competitive and are constantly helping each other."

Life

Vanderbilt's campus life is "stimulating, challenging, [and] fun." "There is always something going on," a sophomore reports. Greek life is "a very large part of Vanderbilt's social scene," as most "Fraternity parties are open to everyone." These parties "rival no other," and they "always have bands or themes or activities, so it's not just a crowd of people getting drunk." But there's more than the just the Greek scene for students to participate in; students tout "clubs for every interest, sports for every level of ability," and "student theater every night of the week." Students also tell us that "Christian and other religious organizations are a big part of Vanderbilt campus life" and that "service organizations are really important at Vanderbilt, and the majority of students are involved in volunteer work in the Nashville community." As for intercollegiate sports, "Attending sporting events is popular, though I wouldn't go so far as to say everyone is a devoted fan." Just about everyone has nice things to say about hometown Nashville. One student writes, "Nashville is a great place to live—there is always something going on. Centennial Park is right across the street; it's a great place to study, walk, or hang out. Downtown has an awesome party scene" that, of course, includes lots of live music. One student adds, "The weather is a pretty nice perk too."

Student Body

"Vanderbilt has come a long way from the stereotypical Southern, wealthy, White student," undergrads here assure us, noting that "there are students from all over the country." While there is "definitely still a strong presence of Polo-clad fraternity guys and sorority girls, the image of Vanderbilt has become so much more than that and now encompasses students from different ethnicities, religions, and geographical regions." Today, the glue that binds the student body is that "everyone is involved." It seems like every student has at least one passion that [he or she] pursue[s] actively on campus or off campus. Everyone is in at least one student organization. No one here is only about academics." Students also tend to be "religious," "very approachable, and friendly, [and] passionate about their studies."

FINANCIAL AID: 615-322-3591 • E-MAIL: ADMISSIONS@VANDERBILT.EDU • WEBSITE: WWW.VANDERBILT.EDU

THE PRINCETON REVIEW SAYS

Admissions

Very important factors considered include: Class rank, academic GPA, rigor of secondary school record, standardized test scores, extracurricular activities. *Important factors considered include:* Application essay, recommendation(s). *Other factors considered include:* Character/personal qualities, first generation, interview, racial/ethnic status, talent/ability, volunteer work, work experience. SAT Subject Tests recommended; SAT or ACT required; ACT with Writing component required. TOEFL required of all international applicants. High school diploma is required and GED is not accepted. *Academic units required:* 4 English, 3 mathematics, 2 science, (2 science labs), 2 foreign language, 2 social studies. *Academic units recommended:* 4 English, 4 mathematics, 4 science, (4 science labs), 4 foreign language, 4 social studies.

Financial Aid

Students should submit: FAFSA, CSS/Financial Aid PROFILE, noncustodial PROFILE. The Princeton Review suggests that all financial aid forms be submitted as soon as possible after January 1. *Need-based scholarships/grants offered:* Federal Pell, SEOG, state scholarships/grants, private scholarships, the school's own gift aid. *Loan aid offered:* FFEL Subsidized Stafford, FFEL Unsubsidized Stafford, FFEL PLUS, Federal Perkins, Federal Nursing, college/university loans from institutional funds, Undergrad Education Loan. Applicants will be notified of awards on or about 4/1. Federal Work-Study Program available. Institutional employment available.

The Inside Word

Vanderbilt received 25 percent more early decision applications for the 2006–2007 academic year than it did for the previous academic year, and as a result, competition has increased for those spaces. Still, if you consider early decision here (or anywhere, for that matter), remember that you will not learn about financial aid until long after you've received your binding decision.

THE SCHOOL SAYS "..."

From The Admissions Office

"Vanderbilt is one of a very small number of colleges that makes a dual promise: Applications are considered without regard for financial need (need-blind), and every admitted U.S. applicant's demonstrated financial need will be fully met. Early decision applicants who submit the CSS PROFILE at the time of application will be provided with a provisional award of need-based financial aid.

"Exceptional accomplishment and high promise in some field of intellectual endeavor are essential. The student's total academic and non-academic record is reviewed in conjunction with recommendations and personal essays. For students at the Blair School of Music, the audition is a prime consideration.

"Living on campus is a crucial element of the Vanderbilt experience. With the opening of the Commons fall 2008, all students will be expected to live on campus for four year. The Commons is Vanderbilt's new living-learning area for first-year students. The Commons includes five recently renovated and five newly constructed residence halls, which will allow the university to house all first year students in the same area of campus. Each residence hall (or "house") will also have a faculty member in residence, who will serve as a mentor to students and oversee programming for the house.

"The Vanderbilt undergraduate experience is often described as uniquely balanced. Students are encouraged to participate in a broad spectrum of campus organizations (over 350) among an increasingly diverse population including approximately 25 percent students of color in the class of 2010. This diversity is also evident from recent survey data which reveals that Vanderbilt first-year students self-identify almost equally as liberal, conservative, or moderate. Recent additions to campus include the Schulman Center for Jewish Life, a newly renovated Black Cultural Center, and the Studio Arts Building.

SELECTIVITY

Admissions Rating	98
# of applicants	12,189
% of applicants accepted	34
% of acceptees attending	39

FRESHMAN PROFILE

Range SAT Critical Reading	630–720
Range SAT Math	650–740
Range SAT Writing	630–710
Range ACT·Composite	28–32
Minimum paper TOEFL	570
Average HS GPA	4
% graduated top 10% of class	79
% graduated top 25% of class	95
% graduated top 50% of class	99

DEADLINES

Early decision II	
Deadline	1/3
Notification	2/15
Early decision	
Deadline	11/1
Notification	12/15
Regular	
Priority	1/3
Deadline	1/3
Notification	4/1
Nonfall registration?	no

APPLICANTS ALSO LOOK AT

AND OFTEN PREFER
Harvard College
Columbia University
Stanford University
Yale University

AND SOMETIMES PREFER
University of Virginia
Duke University
Northwestern University

AND RARELY PREFER
Washington University in St. Louis
Emory University

FINANCIAL FACTS

Financial Aid Rating	97
Annual tuition	$34,414
Books and supplies	$1,140
% frosh rec. need-based scholarship or grant aid	42
% UG rec. need-based scholarship or grant aid	38
% frosh rec. non-need-based scholarship or grant aid	27
% UG rec. non-need-based scholarship or grant aid	20
% frosh rec. need-based self-help aid	26
% UG rec. need-based self-help aid	26
% frosh rec. athletic scholarships	2
% UG rec. athletic scholarships	4
% UG borrow to pay for school	38
Average cumulative indebtedness	$19,429

VASSAR COLLEGE

124 RAYMOND AVENUE, POUGHKEEPSIE, NY 12604 • ADMISSIONS: 845-437-7300 • FAX: 845-437-7063

STUDENTS SAY ". . ."

Academics

Vassar College "is a great place to explore your options" because "There's no real core curriculum. All you need in the way of requirements are one quantitative class and one foreign language credit. Plus, one-quarter of your credits must be outside of your major." This approach, students agree, "really encourages students to think creatively and pursue whatever they're passionate about, whether that be medieval tapestries, neuroscience, or unicycles. Not having a core curriculum is great because it gives students the opportunity to delve into many different interests." So much academic freedom might be a license to goof off at some schools; here, however, students "are passionate learners who participate in both academic and extracurriculars with all their might." Most of these "smart hippies with books in hand discussing feminism and politics and last night" don't need curricular requirements to compel them to take challenging courses. Vassar excels in the visual and performing arts—the "Drama Department is huge" —as well as in English, psychology, history, life sciences, and natural sciences. In all disciplines, "Profs here are mostly great teachers, and they're teachers first. Since there are no grad students here, undergrads are the top priority, and it shows in the one-on-one interactions you have with your teachers."

Life

"Life is campus-centered" at Vassar, in large part because hometown Poughkeepsie "does not offer much in the way of entertainment. The campus provides most of the weekend activities." One undergrad observes, "It's unfortunate but not rare for people to graduate from Vassar knowing nothing about Poughkeepsie other than where the train station to New York City is." The sojourn to New York, alas, is a relatively "expensive endeavor for weekly entertainment; it's about $30 round-trip, and that doesn't include doing stuff once you get there." Fortunately, "There is a huge array of things to do every night on campus. Comedy shows, improv, an incredibly wide array of theater productions"—including "several shows a year and three student groups devoted to drama"—four comedy groups, five a cappella groups," and interesting lectures create numerous opportunities to get out of the dorms at night." Provided you "pay attention to all the events e-mails Vassar sends out, you can usually find something random, fun, and free to do on a slow afternoon or weekday night." Weekends, on the other hand, "are completely different. If you don't drink or like being in situations where drinking/recreational drugs are involved, you'll probably have a dead social life." It's "not a wild, enormous party scene like at a state school" here, but rather one that occurs "earlier in the night, and in smaller groups of people." Vassar's self-contained social scene illustrates "something called the 'Vassar Bubble,' which means that you see the same people every day. You are so cut off from the world that sometimes it's difficult to keep up with current events."

Student Body

"There are common labels that get placed on people at Vassar," including "'hippie,' 'hipster,' and 'pretentious,' and to a degree, the labels are accurate." Vassar is a comfortable respite for "indie-chic students who revel in obscurity, some socially awkward archetypes, and some prep school pin-ups with their collars popped. But the majority of kids on campus are a mix of these people, which is why we mesh pretty well despite the cliques that inevitably form." What nearly everyone shares is "an amazing talent or something that they passionately believe in" and "far-left politics, with no desire or intention to try to understand any political view even slightly left of center. Most of them are pretty nice people, though."

FINANCIAL AID: 845-437-5230 • E-MAIL: ADMISSIONS@VASSAR.EDU • WEBSITE: WWW.VASSAR.EDU

THE PRINCETON REVIEW SAYS

Admissions

Very important factors considered include: Rigor of secondary school record. *Important factors considered include:* Class rank, application essay, academic GPA, recommendation(s), standardized test scores, character/personal qualities, extracurricular activities. *Other factors considered include:* Alumni/ae relation, first generation, geographical residence, interview, level of applicant's interest, racial/ethnic status, talent/ability, volunteer work, work experience. SAT and SAT Subject Tests or ACT required; ACT with Writing component recommended. TOEFL required of all international applicants. High school diploma is required and GED is accepted. *Academic units required:* 4 English, 4 mathematics, 4 science, (3 science labs), 3 foreign language, 2 social studies, 2 history, 4 academic electives. *Academic units recommended:* 4 English, 4 mathematics, 4 science, (3 science labs), 4 foreign language, 4 social studies, 2 history.

Financial Aid

Students should submit: FAFSA, institution's own financial aid form, CSS/Financial Aid PROFILE, state aid form, noncustodial PROFILE, business/farm supplement. Regular filing deadline is 2/1. The Princeton Review suggests that all financial aid forms be submitted as soon as possible after January 1. *Need-based scholarships/grants offered:* Federal Pell, SEOG, state scholarships/grants, private scholarships, the school's own gift aid. *Loan aid offered:* FFEL Subsidized Stafford, FFEL Unsubsidized Stafford, FFEL PLUS, Federal Perkins, Loans for Non-citizens with need. Applicants will be notified of awards on or about 3/30. Federal Work-Study Program available. Institutional employment available. Off-campus job opportunities are fair.

The Inside Word

With acceptance rates hitting record lows, stellar academic credentials are a must for any serious Vassar candidate. Importantly, the college prides itself on selecting students that will add to the vitality of the campus; once Admissions Officers see that you meet their rigorous scholastic standards, they'll closely assess your personal essay, recommendations, and extracurricular activities. Indeed, demonstrating an intellectual curiosity that extends outside the classroom is as important as success within it.

THE SCHOOL SAYS "..."

From The Admissions Office

"Vassar presents a rich variety of social and cultural activities, clubs, sports, living arrangements, and regional attractions. Vassar is a vital, residential college community recognized for its respect for the rights and individuality of others.

"Candidates for admission to the Class of 2012 at Vassar must submit either the SAT Reasoning Test and two SAT Subject Tests taken in different subject fields, or the ACT exam (the optional ACT writing component is recommended)."

SELECTIVITY

Admissions Rating	97
# of applicants	6,393
% of applicants accepted	29
% of acceptees attending	37
# accepting a place on wait list	430
# of early decision applicants	534
% accepted early decision	48

FRESHMAN PROFILE

Range SAT Critical Reading	660–750
Range SAT Math	640–710
Range SAT Writing	650–740
Range ACT Composite	29–32
Minimum paper TOEFL	600
Minimum computer TOEFL	250
Average HS GPA	3.76
% graduated top 10% of class	69
% graduated top 25% of class	95
% graduated top 50% of class	100

DEADLINES

Early decision	
Deadline	11/15
Notification	12/15
Regular	
Deadline	1/1
Notification	4/1
Nonfall registration?	no

APPLICANTS ALSO LOOK AT

AND OFTEN PREFER
Yale University
Brown University

AND SOMETIMES PREFER
New York University
Wesleyan University

AND RARELY PREFER
Union College (NY)
Skidmore College

FINANCIAL FACTS

Financial Aid Rating	97
Annual tuition	$37,570
Room and board	$8,570
Required fees	$545
Books and supplies	$860
% frosh rec. need-based scholarship or grant aid	53
% UG rec. need-based scholarship or grant aid	51
% frosh rec. need-based self-help aid	53
% UG rec. need-based self-help aid	51
% frosh rec. any financial aid	54
% UG rec. any financial aid	52
% UG borrow to pay for school	54
Average cumulative indebtedness	$20,589

VILLANOVA UNIVERSITY

800 LANCASTER AVENUE, VILLANOVA, PA 19085-1672 • ADMISSIONS: 610-519-4000 • FAX: 610-519-6450

CAMPUS LIFE

Quality of Life Rating	99
Fire Safety Rating	89
Green Rating	81
Type of school	private
Affiliation	Roman Catholic
Environment	village

STUDENTS

Total undergrad enrollment	6,949
% male/female	49/51
% from out of state	71
% from public high school	56
% live on campus	72
% in (# of) fraternities	20 (9)
% in (# of) sororities	28 (9)
% African American	4
% Asian	6
% Caucasian	78
% Hispanic	6
% international	2

SURVEY SAYS . . .

Small classes
Career services are great
Students are friendly
Great off-campus food
Campus feels safe
Students are happy
Everyone loves the Wildcats

ACADEMICS

Academic Rating	88
Calendar	semester
Student/faculty ratio	13:1
Profs interesting rating	86
Profs accessible rating	92
Most common reg class size	10–19 students
Most common lab size	20–29 students

MOST POPULAR MAJORS

biological and physical sciences
nursing/registered nurse
(RN, ASN, BSN, MSN)
finance

STUDENTS SAY ". . ."

Academics

"An exceptional and well-known business program" with particular strengths in business attracts nearly a quarter of the undergraduate student body at Villanova University, a prestigious Augustinian school located in the suburbs of Philadelphia. "Employers look to employ Nova graduates" because they know they've studied with "professors who bring real-world experience to the classrooms" and have benefited from "an awesome internship program." Students here are not just business wonks; the school's "rigorous core curriculum" "emphasizes a solid foundation in liberal arts and creative thinking," thereby "developing the whole person through ethical learning." The ethical learning component here "goes far beyond the classroom," as "Participation in service programs (some of the largest in the country), involvement with extracurricular groups, and strong programs established by the university (such as learning communities), are a perfect complement to the excellent development that takes place inside the classroom." Engineering is another area in which Nova students enjoy "an incredible program" with "great facilities." Across the board, "Class sizes are small, and even in a bigger lecture atmosphere, groups are broken up once a week for discussion." Beyond this, "Villanova provides its students with a very high level of technology: access to wireless internet, webmail, and class websites."

Life

At Villanova, "You will work hard Sunday through Wednesday, have fun Thursday through Saturday, and on Sunday you will donate your time to a good cause." Academics, Nova athletics (especially men's basketball), and clubs keep students busy right up until Thursday evening, at which point "People are ready to party, so they either hop on the train to Philly, go to the local bars on the Main Line, or catch a ride to a fraternity party." (Because "There are no frat houses or team houses on campus," all parties "are off campus, and tickets often need to be purchased for as much as $30 the week before. Buses are taken to and from, or you have to know someone to get in. It is a huge hassle for an underclassman, but it's worth the effort.") For many, Sundays are dedicated to church and service. Semester breaks are often also devoted to service: "For fall, winter, and spring break our school runs trips to different parts of the world. Habitat for Humanity trips take place within the United States and allow students to build a house while interacting with the community, strengthening their faith, and creating amazing friendships. Mission trips travel outside of the United States to Mexico, South America, Africa, etc. These trips open the eyes and broaden the minds of those who go on them."

Student Body

"Villanova has the stereotype of White, preppy, private schooled, rich kids." It may be true that, at first glance, what one sees here is "a lot of outgoing, wealthy, well-kept, suburban students who look like they graced the cover of the newest J. Crew magazine and are currently shooting a Crest ad." It's worth noting, however, that "appearances are deceiving. There are plenty of people who do not fit this stereotype." Those schooled in the nuances of Villanova demographics tell us that "there are actually two typical types of students at Villanova. One type consists of preppy, White, rich kids. The other type of student is the one who's interested in community service. There are many students who care a great deal about others and will participate in any activity that allows them to do so." This student is quick to point out, however, that "this is not to say that these groups do not sometimes overlap."

FINANCIAL AID: 610-519-4010 • E-MAIL: GOTOVU@VILLANOVA.EDU • WEBSITE: WWW.VILLANOVA.EDU

THE PRINCETON REVIEW SAYS

Admissions

Very important factors considered include: Class rank, academic GPA, rigor of secondary school record, standardized test scores. *Important factors considered include:* Application essay, recommendation(s), extracurricular activities, talent/ability, volunteer work, work experience. SAT or ACT required; ACT with Writing component required. TOEFL required of all international applicants. High school diploma is required and GED is accepted. *Academic units required:* 4 English, 4 mathematics, 4 science, (2 science labs), 2 foreign language, 2 academic electives. *Academic units recommended:* 4 English, 4 mathematics, 4 science, (3 science labs), 4 foreign language, 2 academic electives.

Financial Aid

Students should submit: FAFSA, institution's own financial aid form. Regular filing deadline is 2/7. The Princeton Review suggests that all financial aid forms be submitted as soon as possible after January 1. *Need-based scholarships/grants offered:* Federal Pell, SEOG, state scholarships/grants, private scholarships, the school's own gift aid. *Loan aid offered:* FFEL Subsidized Stafford, FFEL Unsubsidized Stafford, FFEL PLUS, Federal Perkins, Federal Nursing Applicants will be notified of awards on or about 4/1. Federal Work-Study Program available. Institutional employment available. Off-campus job opportunities are excellent.

The Inside Word

While not as competitive as some of its Catholic brethren, Villanova's growing reputation makes it a strong choice for capable and accomplished students. The university gives equal weight to most facets of the application, and candidates are expected to do the same. Applicants should be aware that admissions criteria vary slightly among Villanova's schools. Students who opt to apply early action also must contend with more arduous standards.

THE SCHOOL SAYS ". . ."

From The Admissions Office

"The university is a community of persons of diverse professional, academic, and personal interests who in a spirit of collegiality cooperate to achieve their common goals and objectives in the transmission, the pursuit, and the discovery of knowledge. Villanova attempts to enroll students with diverse social, geographic, economic, and educational backgrounds. Villanova welcomes students who consider it desirable to study within the philosophical framework of Christian Humanism. Finally, this community seeks to reflect the spirit of St. Augustine by the cultivation of knowledge, by respect for individual differences, and by adherence to the principle that mutual love and respect should animate every aspect of university life."

—*Villanova University Mission Statement*

SELECTIVITY
Admissions Rating	95
# of applicants	15,088
% of applicants accepted	37
% of acceptees attending	28
# accepting a place on wait list	2,300
% admitted from wait list	10

FRESHMAN PROFILE
Range SAT Critical Reading	580–680
Range SAT Math	610–700
Range SAT Writing	590–680
Range ACT Composite	27–31
Minimum paper TOEFL	550
Minimum computer TOEFL	213
Average HS GPA	3.76
% graduated top 10% of class	54
% graduated top 25% of class	96
% graduated top 50% of class	98

DEADLINES
Early action	
Deadline	11/1
Notification	12/20
Regular	
Deadline	1/7
Notification	4/1
Nonfall registration?	no

APPLICANTS ALSO LOOK AT
AND OFTEN PREFER
University of Notre Dame
Georgetown University

AND SOMETIMES PREFER
Lehigh University
Bucknell University
Boston College

AND RARELY PREFER
University of Delaware
Drexel University
Loyola College in Maryland

FINANCIAL FACTS
Financial Aid Rating	71
Annual tuition	$34,320
Room and board	$9,810
Required fees	$300
Books and supplies	$950
% frosh rec. need-based scholarship or grant aid	43
% UG rec. need-based scholarship or grant aid	39
% frosh rec. non-need-based scholarship or grant aid	11
% UG rec. non-need-based scholarship or grant aid	11
% frosh rec. need-based self-help aid	45
% UG rec. need-based self-help aid	40
% frosh rec. athletic scholarships	2
% UG rec. athletic scholarships	2
% frosh rec. any financial aid	64
% UG rec. any financial aid	68
% UG borrow to pay for school	56
Average cumulative indebtedness	$28,107

VIRGINIA POLYTECHNIC INSTITUTE AND STATE UNIVERSITY (VIRGINIA TECH)

UNDERGRADUATE ADMISSIONS, 201 BURRUSS HALL, BLACKSBURG, VA 24061 • ADMISSIONS: 540-231-6267 • FAX: 540-231-3242

CAMPUS LIFE

Quality of Life Rating	**95**
Fire Safety Rating	**82**
Green Rating	**90**
Type of school	public
Environment	town

STUDENTS

Total undergrad enrollment	22,940
% male/female	58/42
% from out of state	25
% from public high school	95
% live on campus	39
% in (# of) fraternities	13 (31)
% in (# of) sororities	20 (12)
% African American	4
% Asian	7
% Caucasian	73
% Hispanic	3
% international	2
# of countries represented	65

SURVEY SAYS . . .

Athletic facilities are great
Great food on campus
Students are happy
Everyone loves the Hokies
Lots of beer drinking

ACADEMICS

Academic Rating	**77**
Calendar	semester
Student/faculty ratio	16:1
Profs interesting rating	75
Profs accessible rating	79
Most common reg class size	20–29 students
Most common lab size	20–29 students

MOST POPULAR MAJORS
engineering
biology/biological sciences

STUDENTS SAY ". . ."

Academics

Students at tech schools don't typically brag about their quality of life, but then again, Virginia Polytechnic Institute and State University, otherwise known as Virginia Tech, is not your typical tech school. Here, students happily discover that they don't have to forfeit "a variety of exciting extracurricular activities" that include "a football program that takes priority for all but the most dedicated students" in order "to achieve an excellent education." Programs in engineering, architecture, agricultural science, and forestry "are all national leaders in their areas" at VT, while the "outstanding" business program offers "top-notch access to occupations in the field through the efforts of the department." Throughout this large school, undergrads are "continually surprised by the genuine interest the faculty and instructors take in students and their education. Open office doors, beyond just the posted office hours, e-mail communication, and openness to accept undergraduate students in graduate course work and as researchers in labs demonstrate not only how committed VT teachers are, but also how optimistic they are of students' success." About one in five students here pursues engineering, a degree that "provides a mixture of practical and theoretical teaching in the classes, experimental labs, a design capstone" and "a cooperative education program that places great value on applying knowledge in the real world."

Life

Virginia Tech may be located "in the middle of nowhere," but students don't seem to mind, because "The people you meet and the cozy town of Blacksburg can be so much fun. Being part of the Hokie nation is really special." School spirit is high, driven by a football team that "is king in Blacksburg. It's hard not to be excited about football when you are tailgating with friends and seeing 60,000 people pack the stadium." While most students here struggle with heavy workloads, they still manage to enjoy themselves. "You can always find people outside playing volleyball or basketball, or using the drill field for games of pickup soccer and football" at Tech, and lots of students exploit the "perfect location for outdoor activities." According to one undergrad, "Within 30 minutes from campus, you can be hiking on the Appalachian Trail, floating down the New River, picnicking in the Jefferson National Forest, or listening to live old-time music at the Floyd Country Store on Friday nights." Shopping isn't quite as convenient: "The good local shopping is about 30 minutes away," students tell us. When it's time to kick loose, "Apartment parties are a big thing at Virginia Tech, and beer pong is almost as popular as football. There are plenty of party animals here, if that's your thing, but it's also pretty easy to find people who know how to have fun without getting drunk." Many of those people dedicate themselves to "the more than 500 student organizations on campus." When small-town life starts to feel to restrictive, "Roanoke is just down the road and offers malls and movie theaters."

Student Body

Virginia Tech's "large student body makes it easy to find many people that have the same interests and are able to become good friends." The unifying thread on campus is "that we are all proud Hokies. While everyone has their differences, we come together as a united campus. The students here are awesome!" There are, of course, "a lot of nerdy engineering boys" as well as "a corps of cadets" at VT, but "There are not many minority students on campus other than the international ones." The population shows a strong bias toward northern Virginia: "Some days it seems as if 25,000 kids from northern Virginia descended on a tiny mountain town," writes one student.

VIRGINIA POLYTECHNIC INSTITUTE AND STATE UNIVERSITY (VIRGINIA TECH)

FINANCIAL AID: 540-231-5179 • E-MAIL: VTADMISS@VT.EDU • WEBSITE: WWW.VT.EDU

THE PRINCETON REVIEW SAYS

Admissions

Very important factors considered include: Academic GPA, rigor of secondary school record, standardized test scores. *Other factors considered include:* Recommendation(s), alumni/ae relation, character/personal qualities, extracurricular activities, first generation, geographical residence, racial/ethnic status, state residency, talent/ability, volunteer work, work experience. SAT or ACT required; ACT with Writing component required. TOEFL required of all international applicants. High school diploma is required and GED is accepted. *Academic units required:* 4 English, 3 mathematics, 2 science, (2 science labs), 1 social studies, 1 history, 4 academic electives. *Academic units recommended:* 4 mathematics, 3 science, 3 foreign language.

Financial Aid

Students should submit: FAFSA, General Scholarship Application. The Princeton Review suggests that all financial aid forms be submitted as soon as possible after January 1. *Need-based scholarships/grants offered:* Federal Pell, SEOG, state scholarships/grants, private scholarships, the school's own gift aid, cadet scholarships/grants. *Loan aid offered:* Direct Subsidized Stafford, Direct Unsubsidized Stafford, Direct PLUS, Federal Perkins, college/university loans from institutional funds. Applicants will be notified of awards on a rolling basis beginning 3/30. Federal Work-Study Program available. Off-campus job opportunities are excellent.

The Inside Word

Students interested in Virginia state schools are advised to consider Tech. Although not as competitive as UVA or William & Mary, Tech is a well-regarded institution offering a great education at bargain prices. Admissions decisions tend to be based upon numbers and statistics. While there are no established cut-offs, the primary focus is on grades, strength of schedule, GPA, and test scores.

THE SCHOOL SAYS "..."

From The Admissions Office

"Virginia Tech offers the opportunities of a large research university in a small-town setting. Undergraduates choose from more than 70 majors in 7 colleges, including nationally ranked architecture, business, forestry, and engineering schools, as well as excellent computer science, biology, and communication studies, and architecture programs. Technology is a key focus, both in classes and in general. All first-year students are required to own a personal computer, each residence hall room has Ethernet connections, and every student is provided e-mail and Internet access. Faculty incorporate a wide variety of technology into class, utilizing chat rooms, online lecture notes, and multimedia presentations. The university offers cutting-edge facilities for classes and research, abundant opportunities for advanced study in the honors program, undergraduate research opportunities, study abroad, internships, and cooperative education. Students enjoy more than 600 organizations which offer something for everyone. Tech offers the best of both worlds—everything a large university can provide and a small-town atmosphere.

"Fall 2008 freshman applicants must take the new SAT or ACT with Writing section unless they are satisfied with SAT or ACT scores received prior to March 2005. We will use the highest scores from any SAT or ACT test scores submitted."

SELECTIVITY

Admissions Rating	89
# of applicants	19,429
% of applicants accepted	67
% of acceptees attending	39
# accepting a place on wait list	1,444
% admitted from wait list	4
# of early decision applicants	2,479
% accepted early decision	50

FRESHMAN PROFILE

Range SAT Critical Reading	530–630
Range SAT Math	570–670
Range SAT Writing	530–630
Minimum paper TOEFL	550
Minimum computer TOEFL	207
Average HS GPA	3.76
% graduated top 10% of class	39.8
% graduated top 25% of class	82.1
% graduated top 50% of class	97.3

DEADLINES

Early decision	
Deadline	11/1
Notification	12/15
Regular	
Deadline	1/15
Notification	4/1
Nonfall registration?	yes

APPLICANTS ALSO LOOK AT

AND OFTEN PREFER
University of Virginia
James Madison University

AND SOMETIMES PREFER
Virginia Commonwealth University

AND RARELY PREFER
College of William and Mary
University of North Carolina
at Chapel Hill

FINANCIAL FACTS

Financial Aid Rating	71
Annual in-state tuition	$7,937
Books and supplies	$1,067
% frosh rec. need-based scholarship or grant aid	30
% UG rec. need-based scholarship or grant aid	29
% frosh rec. non-need-based scholarship or grant aid	9
% UG rec. non-need-based scholarship or grant aid	6
% frosh rec. need-based self-help aid	26
% UG rec. need-based self-help aid	28
% frosh rec. athletic scholarships	2
% UG rec. athletic scholarships	2
% frosh rec. any financial aid	36
% UG rec. any financial aid	34
% UG borrow to pay for school	53
Average cumulative indebtedness	$20,209

WABASH COLLEGE

PO Box 352, 301 West Wabash Avenue, Crawfordsville, IN 47933 • Admissions: 765-361-6225 • Fax: 765-361-6437

CAMPUS LIFE
Quality of Life Rating	90
Fire Safety Rating	81
Green Rating	71
Type of school	private
Environment	village

STUDENTS
Total undergrad enrollment	910
% male/female	100/
% from out of state	24
% from public high school	91
% live on campus	91
% in (# of) fraternities	60 (10)
% African American	6
% Asian	2
% Caucasian	79
% Hispanic	5
% international	5
# of countries represented	21

SURVEY SAYS . . .
Large classes
Lab facilities are great
Great library
Athletic facilities are great
Career services are great
Everyone loves the Little Giants
Frats and sororities dominate
social scene
Lots of beer drinking

ACADEMICS
Academic Rating	95
Calendar	semester
Student/faculty ratio	10:1
Profs interesting rating	98
Profs accessible rating	99
Most common reg class size	10–19 students
Most common lab size	10–19 students

MOST POPULAR MAJORS
English language and literature
psychology
history

STUDENTS SAY ". . ."

Academics
There's only one rule at Wabash College, a small Indiana all men's school: "A Wabash man is to conduct himself as a gentleman both on- and off-campus." The administration typically takes a hands-off approach to enforcing this "Gentleman's Rule," meaning that "students are forced to take ownership over their experiences here, and be involved on campus." The young men here "have the freedom to make their own life choices and the freedom to face the real-life implications of those choices." While some feel this system fosters "an atmosphere that is hyper-masculine, overly conservative, sports-centric, sexist, and generally intolerant of diversity," the vast majority wouldn't have it any other way, telling us that it "molds average boys into successful men," in the same way that "when pressure is applied to common coal it can become a diamond." All agree that a Wabash education is top-notch, with a strong liberal arts focus that "educates men to think critically, act responsibly, lead effectively, and live humanely." Classes "are challenging, and through the course of four years [students learn] to love pushing [themselves] both in and out of the classroom to rise to the occasion." For those who can't handle the pressure, however, "the 'do-your-own-thing' approach means that you can crash and burn, because you're working without a net. If you really nosedive, professors will notice and step in, but a long slow spiral will continue unabated." Those who survive enjoy the benefit of "good alumni connections."

Life
"Wabash is stressful at times" because "the school is very tough academically and you get those weeks when it just keeps piling up." It's the sort of place where "students usually devote much of the week studying or attending campus-wide lectures or productions" and where "weekends are usually devoted to partying or visiting friends at other schools." Life is "very fraternity-oriented" with "some big fraternity parties after the football games" on weekends, and "if nothing is going on, you just relax and hang out with your brothers." The administration's laissez-faire governance "is usually great; people can actually do their own thing. If you want to build a trebuchet in your front lawn and launch paint cans over your fraternity, have fun. If you want to organize a communal bike program or a brewing club or a Tuvan throat-singing appreciation society, fine, here's a pile of cash." The drawback is that "the campus can also get pretty anarchic at times." "Get used to running belligerent drunks off your property, to taking your own measures against petty theft, and to hewing civilization out of chaos with bellowing and intimidation and a strong right arm. Thucydides would love it here."

Student Body
The typical Wabash student "is a loud, ruddy-cheeked Midwestern kid who in high school was a bit too brainy to fit in with the jocks and a bit too rowdy to fit in with the nerds" and "is smarter than other people think he is, but probably not quite as smart as he thinks he is." He tends to hit all three C's—Caucasian, Christian, and conservative—but students insist those outside the mainstream "have few problems fitting in." The archetypal student joins a fraternity; independents, we're told, "are much more diverse. There is no typical independent student because you have physics nerds, homosexuals, African Americans, international students from Asia, Europe, and South America, evangelical Christians, atheists, and the list goes on, all contained in the minority of an 900-person campus." Students warn that "open homosexuals, unfortunately, will not feel terribly welcome, although this area has shown recent improvement" in recent years, with "some fraternities [being] outspoken about welcoming homosexuals as members. Others are, to say the least, not."

FINANCIAL AID: 765-361-6370 • E-MAIL: ADMISSIONS@WABASH.EDU • WEBSITE: WWW.WABASH.EDU

THE PRINCETON REVIEW SAYS

Admissions

Very important factors considered include: Class rank, academic GPA, rigor of secondary school record. *Important factors considered include:* Recommendation(s), standardized test scores, character/personal qualities, extracurricular activities, interview, level of applicant's interest, talent/ability. *Other factors considered include:* Application essay, alumni/ae relation, first generation, geographical residence, racial/ethnic status, volunteer work, work experience. SAT or ACT required; TOEFL required of all international applicants. High school diploma is required and GED is accepted. *Academic units recommended:* 4 English, 4 mathematics, 2 science, (2 science labs), 2 foreign language, 2 social studies, 2 history.

Financial Aid

Students should submit: FAFSA, CSS/Financial Aid PROFILE, noncustodial PROFILE, Federal tax returns and W-2 statements. Regular filing deadline is 3/1. The Princeton Review suggests that all financial aid forms be submitted as soon as possible after January 1. *Need-based scholarships/grants offered:* Federal Pell, state scholarships/grants, private scholarships, the school's own gift aid. *Loan aid offered:* FFEL Subsidized Stafford, FFEL Unsubsidized Stafford, FFEL PLUS, college/university loans from institutional funds. Applicants will be notified of awards on or about 4/1. Institutional employment available. Off-campus job opportunities are good.

The Inside Word

Wabash is one of the few remaining all-male colleges in the country, and like the rest it has a small applicant pool. The pool is highly self-selected and the academic standards for admission, while selective, aren't especially demanding. Graduating is a whole other matter. Don't consider applying if you aren't ready to do the grueling work required for success here.

THE SCHOOL SAYS "..."

From The Admissions Office

"Wabash College is different—and distinctive—from other liberal arts colleges. Different in that Wabash is an outstanding college for men only. Distinctive in the quality and character of the faculty, in the demanding nature of the academic program, in the farsightedness and maturity of the men who enroll, and in the richness of the traditions that have evolved throughout its 174-year history, Wabash is preeminently a teaching institution, and fundamental to the learning experience is the way faculty and students talk to each other—with mutual respect for the expression of informed opinion. For example, students who collaborate with faculty on research projects are considered their peers in the research—an esteem not usually extended to undergraduates. The college takes pride in the sense of community that such a learning environment fosters. But perhaps the single most striking aspect of student life at Wabash is personal freedom. The college has only one rule: 'The student is expected to conduct himself at all times, both on and off the campus, as a gentleman and a responsible citizen.' Wabash College treats students as adults, and such treatment attracts responsible freshmen and fosters their independence and maturity.

"For students applying for admission into the Fall 2008 entering class, Wabash will accept either the new version of the SAT or the old version; the same policy applies for the ACT. Wabash will use the student's best scores from either examination, and will accept the SAT or ACT Writing portions in place of an essay. Wabash does not require SAT Subject Tests."

SELECTIVITY

Admissions Rating	89
# of applicants	1,419
% of applicants accepted	47
% of acceptees attending	37
# accepting a place on wait list	49
% admitted from wait list	22
# of early decision applicants	73
% accepted early decision	75

FRESHMAN PROFILE

Range SAT Critical Reading	520–630
Range SAT Math	540–660
Range SAT Writing	500–610
Range ACT Composite	21–27
Minimum paper TOEFL	550
Minimum computer TOEFL	213
Average HS GPA	3.6
% graduated top 10% of class	37
% graduated top 25% of class	70
% graduated top 50% of class	96

DEADLINES

Early decision	
Deadline	11/15
Notification	12/15
Early action	
Deadline	12/15
Notification	1/31
Regular	
Priority	12/15
Notification	rolling
Nonfall registration?	yes

APPLICANTS ALSO LOOK AT

AND OFTEN PREFER
Purdue University—West Lafayette
Indiana University—Bloomington

AND SOMETIMES PREFER
DePauw University
Butler University

AND RARELY PREFER
Franklin College

FINANCIAL FACTS

Financial Aid Rating	99
Annual tuition	$25,900
Room and board	$7,200
Required fees	$450
Books and supplies	$800
% frosh rec. need-based scholarship or grant aid	73
% UG rec. need-based scholarship or grant aid	70
% frosh rec. non-need-based scholarship or grant aid	13
% UG rec. non-need-based scholarship or grant aid	10
% frosh rec. need-based self-help aid	72
% UG rec. need-based self-help aid	69
% frosh rec. any financial aid	93
% UG rec. any financial aid	88
% UG borrow to pay for school	77
Average cumulative indebtedness	$21,497

WAGNER COLLEGE

One Campus Road, Staten Island, NY 10301-4495 • Admissions: 718-390-3411 • Fax: 718-390-3105

STUDENTS SAY ". . ."

Academics
Wagner College on Staten Island boasts one of the most pastoral campuses New York City has to offer. The college is also a pioneer in "practical liberal arts education." All students here must complete a pretty broad curriculum. Interdisciplinary courses for first-year students focus on a unifying theme and include about 30 hours of course-related fieldwork. Seniors must complete a thesis or a big project within their major. Also, "Wagner requires senior-year internships" and "most" students end up working somewhere pretty cool in Manhattan. Classes "never really exceed 30 people." Some students tell us that "this school is very strong academically." Others say that Wagner's coursework is "absolutely cake." The difficulty level really varies from class to class. There are "very personable" professors who "really know what they're talking about," and there are "terrible ones." "It all depends on who you get." Virtually the entire faculty is "constantly available," though. "The administration, up to the president, is very accessible and conscious of students' needs," relates a biology major. "You can generally walk in without an appointment and get whatever help you need." However, the "mean old women" in the bursar's office are a problem. Also, advising can be hit or miss. "Make sure you get a good adviser," counsels an arts administration major, "because mine blows."

Life
Some students at Wagner contend that "the dining hall is excellent." Others disagree. "The food here is terrible," gripes a sophomore. "I hate it." Critics also point out that "there are really no fast food places" near campus. "Some of the facilities are a little out of date," too. "Campus maintenance and upkeep would be my biggest complaint," suggests a first-year student. "If they fixed things like clogged drains and broken lights faster, it would be nice." Also, while it's unquestionably "safe" around campus, that's only because "the overprotective security feels like a Gestapo." On the plus side, students relish their "gorgeous" dorm-room views of the Lower Manhattan skyline. They also love their location. "Wagner represents a unique mix of big city and small town." "Rumors are atrocious and spread quickly," but, on the whole, it's "a friendly and small campus where you pretty much know everyone." "There's always a sporting event of some kind going on." The coffeehouse on campus "is a great place to meet new people and play a game of pool or hear great local bands." Otherwise, "Greek life and the theater program seem to dominate." "Parties are really not too extensive on campus but we get it done," says a sophomore. Local bars and clubs on Staten Island are popular for students who are 21 or who have solid fake ID's. When students tire of the local scene, there's always Manhattan. A free shuttle "runs to the ferry quite often" and "almost all of the students" take advantage frequently. "The city can sometimes be expensive," but "you're never bored."

Student Body
While there is clear and growing diversity in Wagner's numbers, one student notes there are "a lot of Staten Islanders and Jersey people." There are substantially more women than men here, and there's a decent gay population. As a result, "there just aren't that many guys who are actively pursuing girls." Overall, it's a "very cliquey" scene. There are "tanning princess types" and "spoiled rich kids" "who'd rather party than study." Other students "are your average go-to-class, hang-out-with-friends, and study kind of people." The biggest social divide is between thespians and jocks. "There are two main groups of students at Wagner," explains a senior. So expect some show tune humming mixed in with Sports Center recaps—and everything in between. Suprised? Didn't your mom tell ya New York City was a big melting pot?

FINANCIAL AID: 718-390-3183 • E-MAIL: ADMISSIONS@WAGNER.EDU • WEBSITE: WWW.WAGNER.EDU

THE PRINCETON REVIEW SAYS

Admissions

Very important factors considered include: Class rank, academic GPA, rigor of secondary school record. *Important factors considered include:* Application essay, recommendation(s), standardized test scores, extracurricular activities, interview. *Other factors considered include:* Character/personal qualities, geographical residence, level of applicant's interest, talent/ability, volunteer work, work experience. SAT or ACT required; TOEFL required of all international applicants. High school diploma is required and GED is accepted. *Academic units required:* 4 English, 3 mathematics, 2 science, (1 science labs), 2 foreign language, 1 social studies, 3 history, 6 academic electives.

Financial Aid

Students should submit: FAFSA, institution's own financial aid form, state aid form. The Princeton Review suggests that all financial aid forms be submitted as soon as possible after January 1. *Need-based scholarships/grants offered:* Federal Pell, SEOG, state scholarships/grants, private scholarships *Loan aid offered:* FFEL Subsidized Stafford, FFEL Unsubsidized Stafford, FFEL PLUS, Federal Perkins, Federal Nursing Applicants will be notified of awards on a rolling basis beginning 3/1. Federal Work-Study Program available. Institutional employment available. Off-campus job opportunities are good.

The Inside Word

As far as grades and test scores, the profile of the average freshman class at Wagner is solid but not spectacular. Don't take the application process too lightly, though. The admissions staff here is dedicated to finding the right students for their school. An interview is definitely a good idea.

THE SCHOOL SAYS "..."

From The Admissions Office

"At Wagner College, we attract and develop active learners and future leaders. Wagner College has received national acclaim (*Time* magazine, American Association of Colleges and Universities) for its innovative curriculum, The Wagner Plan for the Practical Liberal Arts. At Wagner, we capitalize on our unique geography; we are a traditional, scenic, residential campus, which happens to sit atop a hill on an island overlooking lower Manhattan. Our location allows us to offer a program that couples required off-campus experiences (experiential learning), with 'learning community' clusters of courses. This program begins in the first semester and continues through the senior capstone experience in the major. Fieldwork and internships, writing-intensive reflective tutorials, connected learning, 'reading, writing, and doing': At Wagner College our students truly discover 'the practical liberal arts in New York City.'

"Applicants for Fall 2008 are required to take the current version of the SAT, or the ACT with the Writing section."

SELECTIVITY

Admissions Rating	88
# of applicants	2,842
% of applicants accepted	60
% of acceptees attending	31
# accepting a place on wait list	72
% admitted from wait list	4
# of early decision applicants	130
% accepted early decision	59

FRESHMAN PROFILE

Range SAT Critical Reading	530–640
Range SAT Math	540–650
Range SAT Writing	530–640
Range ACT Composite	24–28
Minimum paper TOEFL	550
Minimum computer TOEFL	217
Average HS GPA	3.52
% graduated top 10% of class	18
% graduated top 25% of class	68
% graduated top 50% of class	92

DEADLINES

Early decision	
Deadline	1/1
Notification	2/1
Regular	
Priority	2/15
Deadline	3/1
Notification	3/1
Nonfall registration?	yes

APPLICANTS ALSO LOOK AT

AND OFTEN PREFER
New York University
Fairfield University

AND SOMETIMES PREFER
Hobart and William Smith Colleges
Fordham University

AND RARELY PREFER
Manhattan College
Marist College

FINANCIAL FACTS

Financial Aid Rating	84
Annual tuition	$29,400
Room and board	$8,900
Books and supplies	$725
% frosh rec. need-based scholarship or grant aid	62
% UG rec. need-based scholarship or grant aid	56
% frosh rec. non-need-based scholarship or grant aid	14
% UG rec. non-need-based scholarship or grant aid	11
% frosh rec. need-based self-help aid	48
% UG rec. need-based self-help aid	42
% frosh rec. athletic scholarships	5
% UG rec. athletic scholarships	5
% frosh rec. any financial aid	95
% UG rec. any financial aid	87
% UG borrow to pay for school	44
Average cumulative indebtedness	$35,717

WAKE FOREST UNIVERSITY

BOX 7305, REYNOLDA STATION, WINSTON-SALEM, NC 27109 • ADMISSIONS: 336-758-5201 • FAX: 336-758-4324

STUDENTS SAY " . . . "

Academics

"Our nickname, 'Work Forest,' applies," caution undergraduates at Wake Forest University, a private school that offers "the perfect combination of small college atmosphere with big university opportunities." "You have to put a lot of effort into your work" in this "tough atmosphere" where "The BS-ing that got you A's in high school will get you a C-minus at the most." Students agree, however, that although the workload is "sometimes excessive," it's worth it for the "incredible academic experience" and the "tremendous opportunities" it creates for a student body "anxious to get ahead in the world." Technology is another of the school's strengths; at Wake, "Each student is given a computer and printer at the beginning of their freshman and junior years, and technology aides are available in every dorm to assist students [with] computer or network problems." As for the workload, many here say it's tough but manageable and point out that "the administration and professors are accessible and willing to talk through difficult assignments or reevaluate things when given the students' perspectives." One undergrad sums it up perfectly: "Though everyone will find something to complain about, the truth is that Wake is amazing. Everyone has school spirit, everyone cares about the school, the professors care about the students, the campus is drop-dead gorgeous, and the people are just mad cool."

Life

"Frat parties are wildly popular" at Wake Forest; they occur "both on and off campus," and "are open to everyone." You "can find a party that serves alcohol pretty much any night of the week," although most students are too busy with schoolwork to maintain that type of social schedule. "When Wake students aren't partying or studying, sports are huge," as "Everyone goes out to football and basketball games. Intramurals are also very popular and some (such as flag football) are extremely competitive." Students are split over the appeal of Winston-Salem. Naysayers, who are in the majority, complain that "there isn't much to do in Winston-Salem other than the usual: mall, movies, clubs, and on-campus events. Most students aren't culturally interested in the activities that Winston-Salem has to offer. The town isn't for teenagers but for families." These students also feel that "it's unfortunate that the school is located in a residential area with no easily accessible commercial districts." Others insist that "Winston-Salem is a gold mine of opportunities . . . film festivals, art shows, theater performances, a great mall. Wake students always complain about Winston-Salem, but there is plenty of fun stuff to do if you look for it. And the downtown [area] is absolutely gorgeous." Quaint Reynolda Village, which is within walking distance of campus, offers some upscale shopping as well as an art museum.

Student Body

Wake has earned its reputation as a preppy haven; most students here seem to be "skinny, White, and conservative in [their] political views. They wear polos with popped collars—Vera Bradley bags, Sperry's, etc. roam the campus." One student observes, "Wake Forest can change your fashion style or habits because of the lack of variety. When I say 'variety' I don't mean the different colors of Ralph Lauren Polos." There is, however, "a growing and vocal liberal population." Left-leaning subgroups, "such as the gay and lesbian population, which is not only growing but finding better acceptance here," are expanding. There is even "a little more variety with respect to body shapes," and not everyone is rail thin on campus anymore. Racial minorities, however, "are still few and far between." Wake is home to "a small, very committed Christian population," but "most students are still sleeping in on Sunday mornings. Wake has a struck a strange balance between its Baptist heritage and the increasingly secular culture."

FINANCIAL AID: 336-758-5154 • E-MAIL: ADMISSIONS@WFU.EDU • WEBSITE: WWW.WFU.EDU

THE PRINCETON REVIEW SAYS

Admissions

Very important factors considered include: Class rank, application essay, academic GPA, rigor of secondary school record, standardized test scores, character/personal qualities. *Important factors considered include:* Recommendation(s), extracurricular activities, talent/ability. *Other factors considered include:* Alumni/ae relation, first generation, geographical residence, interview, level of applicant's interest, racial/ethnic status, religious affiliation/commitment, state residency, volunteer work, SAT or ACT required; ACT with Writing component required. TOEFL required of all international applicants. High school diploma is required and GED is accepted. *Academic units required:* 4 English, 3 mathematics, 1 science, 2 foreign language, 2 social studies. *Academic units recommended:* 4 English, 4 mathematics, 4 science, 4 foreign language, 4 social studies.

Financial Aid

Students should submit: FAFSA, CSS/Financial Aid PROFILE, state aid form, noncustodial PROFILE Regular filing deadline is 3/1. The Princeton Review suggests that all financial aid forms be submitted as soon as possible after January 1. *Need-based scholarships/grants offered:* Federal Pell, SEOG, state scholarships/grants, private scholarships, the school's own gift aid. *Loan aid offered:* FFEL Subsidized Stafford, FFEL Unsubsidized Stafford, FFEL PLUS, Federal Perkins, state loans, college/university loans from institutional funds, private alternative loans. Applicants will be notified of awards on a rolling basis beginning 4/1.

The Inside Word

Wake Forest's considerable application numbers afford Admissions Officers the opportunity to be rather selective. In particular, Admissions Officers remain diligent in their matchmaking efforts—finding students who are good fits for the school—and their hard work is rewarded by a high yield rate. Candidates will need to be impressive in all areas to gain admission, since all areas of their applications are considered carefully. A relatively large number of qualified students find themselves on Wake Forest's wait list.

THE SCHOOL SAYS "..."

From The Admissions Office

"Wake Forest University has been dedicated to the liberal arts for over a century and a half; this means education in the fundamental fields of human knowledge and achievement. It seeks to encourage habits of mind that ask why, that evaluate evidence, that are open to new ideas, that attempt to understand and appreciate the perspective of others, that accept complexity and grapple with it, that admit error, and that pursue truth.

"Wake Forest is among a small, elite group of American colleges and universities recognized for their outstanding academic quality. It offers small classes taught by full-time faculty—not graduate assistants—and a commitment to student interaction with those professors. Students are provided ThinkPad computers and color printer/scanner/copiers. Classrooms and residence halls are fully networked. Wake Forest maintains a need-blind admissions policy by which qualified students are admitted regardless of their financial circumstances.

"Applicants for Fall 2008 are required to submit scores from the SAT Reasoning Test and/or the ACT plus Writing. SAT Subject Tests are strongly recommended for students planning to apply for merit-based scholarships."

SELECTIVITY

Admissions Rating	95
# of applicants	7,341
% of applicants accepted	43
% of acceptees attending	36
# of early decision applicants	719
% accepted early decision	43

FRESHMAN PROFILE

Range SAT Critical Reading	610–690
Range SAT Math	630–710
Minimum paper TOEFL	600
Minimum computer TOEFL	250
% graduated top 10% of class	62
% graduated top 25% of class	88
% graduated top 50% of class	98

DEADLINES

Early decision	
Deadline	11/15
Notification	12/15
Regular	
Deadline	1/15
Notification	4/1
Nonfall registration?	yes

APPLICANTS ALSO LOOK AT AND SOMETIMES PREFER

Vanderbilt University
University of Virginia
Duke University
University of North Carolina at Chapel Hill

FINANCIAL FACTS

Financial Aid Rating	81
Annual tuition	$34,230
Room and board	$9,500
Required fees	$100
Books and supplies	$850
% frosh rec. need-based scholarship or grant aid	36
% UG rec. need-based scholarship or grant aid	34
% frosh rec. non-need-based scholarship or grant aid	26
% UG rec. non-need-based scholarship or grant aid	15
% frosh rec. need-based self-help aid	28
% UG rec. need-based self-help aid	29
% frosh rec. athletic scholarships	7
% UG rec. athletic scholarships	7
% UG borrow to pay for school	37
Average cumulative indebtedness	$20,655

WARREN WILSON COLLEGE

PO BOX 9000, ASHEVILLE, NC 28815-9000 • ADMISSIONS: 828-771-2073 • FAX: 828-298-1440

STUDENTS SAY ". . ."

Academics

The centerpiece of a Warren Wilson education is the Triad program, which "integrates work, service, and academics" by requiring all students to complete "15 hours of work every week on campus" and "100 hours of service before graduation" in addition to their course work. The goal is "to create students who look at the big picture, and see that there is a world outside of themselves." Students say it generally works: "Integrating work, service, and academics seems to bring about some sort of personal utopia," declares one undergrad. The work opportunities arise from the 1,100-acre campus, which includes a farm; students learn "blacksmithing, cooking, farming, being a writing tutor, maintaining the trails, and painting," but must also "be prepared to scrub toilets or wash dishes in the dining hall." One undergrad jokes, "WWC really stands for 'We Work Constantly.'" WWC's best academic programs piggyback on the Triad concept. "Programs in environmental education and sustainable agriculture are excellent," and "In science labs it's great to be able to walk outside and explore the campus or take a hike and find 90 percent of the plants and animals you were talking about in class." It's not all agriculture and technology, though; students tell us that "creative writing is an important program here." As is the case at many small schools, "Teachers are more than willing to meet you outside of class. They understand we have a life outside of the classroom, and they are willing to set up times to meet with you." Students appreciate the fact that their professors "are paid to teach. The school couldn't care less if they ever write a book. And there are no TAs."

Life

"Because of the work program, time is not as abundant here as it may be at other schools," WWC undergrads caution. The workload is substantial, as undergrads "run the campus. We do the landscaping, the cooking, the cleaning, the bike repair, the building, the gardening, and the farming. You can't be lazy here." Undergrads still manage to carve enough time out of their schedules to enjoy "excellent programs and activities such as fencing, dancing, climbing, hiking, camping, kayaking, herbal classes, and cooking." One student writes, "Many students have a surprisingly good-natured interest in dorky things like bird watching, contra dancing, and pot-lucks, a unanimous love of tubing down a flooded river," and "walking around the trails here and taking advantage of the campus beauty." As one student puts it, "When you first see the campus nestled in the mountains with the cows grazing in the field, it takes your breath away." Once a year, the school celebrates "Work Day," when students and staff come together to work on special projects (such as completing work on a farm), then gather at night for an evening of food and music." Nearby Asheville "is pretty awesome" for the occasional escape from campus. Some even consider it "the Paris of the mountains, with plenty of things to do downtown."

Student Body

The typical WWC undergrad "likes good organic wholesome food, a good local brew and bluegrass on a starry night, is health conscious but smokes hand-rolled cigarettes, dresses in work clothes but accessorizes, recycles, doesn't watch TV, and knows some botanical-ornithological basics." To put it more simply: "This place is a haven for hippies and very left-wing people." Other types pepper the student body, including "surfers, farmers, and punks, some people with dreadlocks, others with dyed hair. A small portion of the population has facial piercings and tattoos." But overall, "People here are just like people anywhere else. Yeah, there are the hippies, but just like any school there are a wide variety of personalities. If you are interested in this school in the first place, chances are you will fit right in."

FINANCIAL AID: 828-298-3325 • E-MAIL: ADMIT@WARREN-WILSON.EDU • WEBSITE: WWW.WARREN-WILSON.EDU

THE PRINCETON REVIEW SAYS

Admissions

Very important factors considered include: Application essay, rigor of secondary school record, standardized test scores, character/personal qualities, interview, volunteer work, work experience. *Important factors considered include:* Class rank, recommendation(s). *Other factors considered include:* Alumni/ae relation, extracurricular activities, state residency, talent/ability, SAT or ACT required; TOEFL required of all international applicants. High school diploma is required and GED is accepted. *Academic units required:* 4 English, 3 mathematics, 2 science, (2 science labs), 3 history. *Academic units recommended:* 2 foreign language.

Financial Aid

Students should submit: FAFSA, institution's own financial aid form. The Princeton Review suggests that all financial aid forms be submitted as soon as possible after January 1. *Need-based scholarships/grants offered:* Federal Pell, SEOG, state scholarships/grants, private scholarships, the school's own gift aid. *Loan aid offered:* FFEL Subsidized Stafford, FFEL Unsubsidized Stafford, FFEL PLUS, Federal Perkins, college/university loans from institutional funds. Applicants will be notified of awards on a rolling basis beginning 3/2.

The Inside Word

At Warren Wilson College, one's sense of social commitment is as vital to the admissions process as one's high school transcript—the college desires students who are actively engaged in their communities. Admissions Officers are interested in applicants who seek to make connections and understand how to apply what they learn in the classroom to outside projects and activities.

THE SCHOOL SAYS "..."

From The Admissions Office

"This book is *The Best 368 Colleges*, but Warren Wilson College may not be the best college for many students. There are 3,500 colleges in the U.S., and there is a best place for everyone. The 'best college' is one that has the right size, location, programs, and above all, the right feel for you, even if it is not listed here. Warren Wilson College may be the best choice if you think and act independently, actively participate in your education, and want a college that provides a sense of community. Your hands will get dirty here, your mind will be stretched, and you'll not be anonymous. If you are looking for the traditional college experience with football and frats and a campus-on-a-quad, this probably is not the right place. However, if you want to be a part of an academic community that works and serves together, this might be exactly what you are looking for.

"Students applying for Fall admission should provide results of the SAT or ACT."

SELECTIVITY

Admissions Rating	**84**
# of applicants	911
% of applicants accepted	75
% of acceptees attending	37
# of early decision applicants	86
% accepted early decision	90

FRESHMAN PROFILE

Range SAT Critical Reading	550–670
Range SAT Math	510–620
Range SAT Writing	530–630
Range ACT Composite	22–27
Minimum paper TOEFL	550
Average HS GPA	3.4
% graduated top 10% of class	22
% graduated top 25% of class	42
% graduated top 50% of class	83

DEADLINES

Early decision	
Deadline	11/15
Regular	
Deadline	2/28
Nonfall registration?	yes

APPLICANTS ALSO LOOK AT

AND OFTEN PREFER
Earlham College

AND SOMETIMES PREFER
The Evergreen State College

AND RARELY PREFER
Antioch College
Guilford College
Arizona State University at the Tempe campus

FINANCIAL FACTS

Financial Aid Rating	**71**
Annual tuition	$22,666
Room and board	$7,116
Required fees	$300
Books and supplies	$870
% frosh rec. need-based scholarship or grant aid	45
% UG rec. need-based scholarship or grant aid	48
% frosh rec. non-need-based scholarship or grant aid	20
% UG rec. non-need-based scholarship or grant aid	19
% frosh rec. need-based self-help aid	49
% UG rec. need-based self-help aid	42
% UG borrow to pay for school	35
Average cumulative indebtedness	$15,713

WASHINGTON COLLEGE

300 WASHINGTON AVENUE, CHESTERTOWN, MD 21620 • ADMISSIONS: 410-778-7700 • FAX: 410-778-7287

STUDENTS SAY " . . ."

Academics

Washington College is a small, private liberal arts college in eastern Maryland that is "steeped in history." It's the tenth oldest college in the United States. Undergraduate research is commonplace here, and internships are tremendous. Study abroad is "really big" and available in about two dozen destinations around the world. The creative writing program is "well respected." Other notable majors include business and theater. Course selection "isn't that great," but academics are "challenging." Some classes "have upwards of 50 people in them" but most are pretty intimate. Usually, "there is a great deal of individualized attention," and "there is no hiding in the back of the classroom." Washington College's "caring" professors are "ridiculously eager about their subjects." Most are "willing to meet outside of class or chat through e-mail" and "willing to go the extra mile." "My professors treat me as an individual and more than just the kid they have to grind the information into," relates an English major. Complaints include the library, which isn't much. Some students also grumble about tuition and call WAC "a money pit." The "ambitious" administration "does everything possible to keep students happy in most aspects of life," but the top brass can be "out of touch" and, sometimes, things "just don't run very smoothly."

Life

"The food on campus is usually not very good and sometimes difficult to eat." Also, some dorms are "falling apart," and a host of construction projects has made this campus look like a "war zone" lately. Some students say they like the way Washington College "combines colonial charm with modern facilities." Others disagree. "Concrete plus brick equals ugly," asserts a senior. Socially, WAC is "close-knit." "The general atmosphere is comfortable and laidback." "Pretty much everything happens on campus." "Numerous speakers and musical events" are frequent. There are "strong" athletic programs. Men's lacrosse is especially huge. Fraternities and sororities aren't overwhelming here but they are certainly noticeable. On the weekends, "parties are plentiful." "If you don't drink alcohol, this school isn't for you," advises a junior. The festivities around May Day get especially crazy. Off campus, "there really is nothing to do at all" in "sleepy," "remote," and "very rural" Chestertown. "Many old people live there." "The waterfront area of town is nice." If you want to, you can wakeboard, water ski, and sail to your heart's content. Otherwise, there are a few "little trinket and book shops," but that's about it. "The closet mall is 45 minutes" away. There's "a shuttle that runs to D.C. and Annapolis on the weekends," but "transportation is highly recommended." Many students with cars head to Baltimore and Philadelphia for day trips.

Student Body

"I find this school to be extremely diverse," indicates a first-year student. "Granted, we might have had four black kids in my high school." There's "a fun bunch" of international students and smattering of minorities but "Washington College, embodied in a human would be white." Some students "come from a rural way of life," and there are many middle-class students who "depend on fairly generous scholarships." However, a large contingent of students comes "from private high schools" in "wealthy suburbs" in "Jersey, Maryland, or Pennsylvania." "Most of us are pretty smart, go to class, and participate in extracurriculars," says a junior. There are "meathead athletes and musicians with tweed jackets." There also "tree huggers, rock climbers, wannabe rockers, dramatists, philosophers, future business leaders," and "your average goths and freaks." On the whole, though, the culture is very preppy. "It would be possible to believe that Polo sponsors our students because it is everywhere," explains a sophomore. "The kids are generic." "Cliques" are reportedly noticeable on this campus, and "boundaries are definitely defined." However, "there is a real sense of community" as well. "Everyone knows everyone," says a junior, "so it's very hard to be excluded."

FINANCIAL AID: 410-778-7214 • WEBSITE: HTTP://ADMISSIONS.WASHCOLL.EDU

THE PRINCETON REVIEW SAYS

Admissions

Very important factors considered include: Academic GPA, rigor of secondary school record, interview. *Important factors considered include:* Class rank, standardized test scores, level of applicant's interest. *Other factors considered include:* Application essay, recommendation(s), alumni/ae relation, character/personal qualities, extracurricular activities, first generation, geographical residence, racial/ethnic status, state residency, talent/ability, volunteer work, work experience. SAT or ACT required; High school diploma is required and GED is accepted. *Academic units required:* 4 English, 3 mathematics, 3 science, (2 science labs), 2 foreign language, 2 social studies, 2 history. *Academic units recommended:* 4 English, 4 mathematics, 4 science, (3 science labs), 4 foreign language, 4 social studies.

Financial Aid

Students should submit: FAFSA, institution's own financial aid form. The Princeton Review suggests that all financial aid forms be submitted as soon as possible after January 1. *Need-based scholarships/grants offered:* Federal Pell, SEOG, state scholarships/grants, private scholarships, the school's own gift aid. *Loan aid offered:* FFEL Subsidized Stafford, FFEL Unsubsidized Stafford, FFEL PLUS, Federal Perkins, college/university loans from institutional funds. Applicants will be notified of awards on a rolling basis beginning 3/15. Federal Work-Study Program available. Institutional employment available. Off-campus job opportunities are good.

The Inside Word

Though Washington's acceptance rate hovers just under 60 percent, the statistic belies the competitive nature of the applicants. Prospective students who view WC as one of their top choices should do themselves a favor and complete their application ahead of the prescribed deadline. Interviews are also highly recommended and those who decline the opportunity will be putting themselves at a disadvantage.

THE SCHOOL SAYS "..."

From The Admissions Office

"We tell our students, 'Your revolution starts here,' because the person who graduates from Washington College is not the same one who matriculated 4 years earlier, and because through your experiences here, you will be empowered and emboldened to change the world. Your education reflects the maxims of our founder, George Washington: The strength of America's democracy depends on the success of students like you to evolve as a critical and independent thinker, to persevere in the face of challenge, to assume the responsibilities and privileges of informed citizenship. That's where we come in, providing a truly personalized education that tests—and stretches—the limits of each student's talents and potentials. We reach beyond the classroom to create challenges and opportunities that expand your brainpower and creativity through collaborative research with faculty, through independent and self-directed study, and through the rigor of creating a senior project that demonstrates the power of a maturing intellect. All this happens in a wonderfully distinct setting—in historic Chestertown, on the Chester River, amid the ecological bounty of Maryland's Chesapeake Bay—that helps define who we are and that will shape your own college experience.

"Washington College requires either SAT or ACT scores. There is no minimum SAT/ACT cut-off score for admission. However, the middle 50 percent of accepted applicants have SAT scores in the 1050 to 1250 range. The average SAT (Critical Reading and Math) score for enrolled freshmen is 1150 (24 for ACT)."

SELECTIVITY

Admissions Rating	88
# of applicants	2,167
% of applicants accepted	64
% of acceptees attending	24
# accepting a place on wait list	218
% admitted from wait list	33
# of early decision applicants	40
% accepted early decision	75

FRESHMAN PROFILE

Range SAT Critical Reading	520–630
Range SAT Math	520–610
Range SAT Writing	520–610
Range ACT Composite	21–27
Average HS GPA	3.34
% graduated top 10% of class	32
% graduated top 25% of class	68
% graduated top 50% of class	92

DEADLINES

Early decision	
Deadline	11/1
Notification	12/1
Early action	
Deadline	11/15
Notification	12/15
Regular	
Priority	2/1
Deadline	3/1
Notification	rolling
Nonfall registration?	yes

FINANCIAL FACTS

Financial Aid Rating	89
Annual tuition	$33,385
Room and board	$7,180
Required fees	$620
Books and supplies	$1,000
% frosh rec. need-based scholarship or grant aid	36
% UG rec. need-based scholarship or grant aid	43
% frosh rec. non-need-based scholarship or grant aid	26
% UG rec. non-need-based scholarship or grant aid	32
% frosh rec. need-based self-help aid	27
% UG rec. need-based self-help aid	32
% frosh rec. any financial aid	79
% UG rec. any financial aid	85
% UG borrow to pay for school	60
Average cumulative indebtedness	$20,483

WASHINGTON & JEFFERSON COLLEGE

OFFICE OF ADMISSIONS, 60 SOUTH LINCOLN STREET, WASHINGTON, PA 15301 • ADMISSIONS: 888-W-AND-JAY OR 724-223-6025

CAMPUS LIFE

Quality of Life Rating	**72**
Fire Safety Rating	**85**
Green Rating	**85**
Type of school	private
Environment	village

STUDENTS

Total undergrad enrollment	1,514
% male/female	53/47
% from out of state	24
% from public high school	84
% live on campus	94
% in (# of) fraternities	30 (6)
% in (# of) sororities	33 (4)
% African American	3
% Asian	1
% Caucasian	89
% Hispanic	1
# of countries represented	7

SURVEY SAYS . . .

Small classes
Great computer facilities
Everyone loves the Presidents
Frats and sororities dominate
social scene
Lots of beer drinking
Hard liquor is popular

ACADEMICS

Academic Rating	**85**
Calendar	4/1/4
Student/faculty ratio	12:1
Profs interesting rating	86
Profs accessible rating	88
Most common reg class size	10–19 students
Most common lab size	10–19 students

MOST POPULAR MAJORS
business/commerce
English language and literature
psychology

STUDENTS SAY ". . ."

Academics

"High academic standards" and small class sizes, coupled with a student body made up of individuals "very serious about their education" leads to a lot of hard work and accountability for the undergrads of Washington & Jefferson College. While many choose the college for its strong programs in the sciences and the liberal arts, every major at W&J is reportedly difficult. The college's friendly professors, administrators, and staff, however, do their best to help students to succeed and "make you feel as comfy as possible." Despite the heavy workload, students describe W&J as a "fun, challenging, and nurturing environment" where students are truly mentored and supported by the faculty and staff. As one freshman writes, "The professors are amazing. They are always there whenever you are struggling, confused, or just want to talk. Even the administration is available to chat!" While the quality of the academic program is undisputed, some students gripe about the high costs of this private school. In particular, students tell us that "the Financial Aid Department needs some work." Commenting on this state of affairs, a freshman jokes that the college might consider changing its motto to "providing the best education possible for the most amount of money."

Life

When considering student life at W&J, a junior offers this 1980s analogy: "It's like a mullet: business in the front, party in the back." Indeed, students say that W&J is the place to go for both a "good education and a good time," as the friendly student body is as social as it is studious. On campus, "People are busy with sports, clubs, and fraternities/sororities"; athletics are also particularly popular with students. A sophomore writes, "Our school is all about education . . . and after education comes sports." During the weekend, the W&J campus comes alive with parties. "After a hard week of stressful classes, most of the people here drink," writes a student. However, undergraduates reassure us that there are "no crazy state school–style parties" at W&J, and most students prioritize books over booze. As one sophomore reports, "I like to drink and party on the weekends, but get my homework done during the week." Whether you like the W&J social life or not, you're stuck with it, as undergraduates are required to live on campus.

Student Body

On the whole, this small campus is home to "nice, studious, involved, and athletic" undergrads, most of whom take their education very seriously. Almost all students claim to be "hard workers" and generally describe their classmates as intelligent and motivated, but the similarities don't end there. A junior reports that "everyone is pretty typical—White, upper-middle-class American. We have very few minorities." Another confesses, "The majority of students are cookie-cutter images of each other. There is very little individuality on this campus." Even so, students claim that their classmates are generally accepting and friendly, even if there are very few students who don't fit in. A junior writes, "Everyone gets along no matter what they look like; a benefit to a small campus." In fact, students insist that W&J, "works like a small community; everyone helps everyone."

FAX : 724-223-6534 • FINANCIAL AID: 724-223-6019 • E-MAIL: ADMISSION@WASHJEFF.EDU • WEBSITE: WWW.WASHJEFF.EDU

THE PRINCETON REVIEW SAYS

Admissions

Very important factors considered include: Class rank, application essay, academic GPA, recommendation(s), rigor of secondary school record, interview. *Important factors considered include:* Standardized test scores, character/personal qualities, extracurricular activities. *Other factors considered include:* Alumni/ae relation, geographical residence, level of applicant's interest, racial/ethnic status, state residency, talent/ability, volunteer work, SAT or ACT required; TOEFL required of all international applicants. High school diploma is required and GED is accepted. *Academic units required:* 3 English, 3 mathematics, 2 foreign language, 1 history, 6 academic electives.

Financial Aid

Students should submit: FAFSA. The Princeton Review suggests that all financial aid forms be submitted as soon as possible after January 1. *Need-based scholarships/grants offered:* Federal Pell, SEOG, state scholarships/grants, private scholarships, the school's own gift aid, ACG and SMART Grants. *Loan aid offered:* FFEL Subsidized Stafford, FFEL Unsubsidized Stafford, FFEL PLUS, Federal Perkins, college/university loans from institutional funds. Applicants will be notified of awards on a rolling basis beginning 3/1. Federal Work-Study Program available. Institutional employment available. Off-campus job opportunities are good.

The Inside Word

In a reflection of the students they aim to admit, Washington & Jefferson College takes a well-rounded approach to admissions. Academic record, class rank, personal statement, and extracurricular activities are all thoroughly evaluated. Most prospective students work diligently to secure admittance. The lucky applicants who receive a fat letter in the mail are welcomed into a distinctive community that promises to broaden their horizons and prepare them for a successful future.

THE SCHOOL SAYS "..."

From The Admissions Office

"There is a palpable sense of momentum and energy at Washington & Jefferson. Enrollment has grown significantly over the past 5 years. Additional faculty members have been hired, and academic programs have been added and expanded to accommodate the increased enrollment. The student-centered teaching and learning community that has always distinguished W&J remains our top priority. It is no surprise that 100 percent of our graduates who took the bar exam passed in 2006, or that 90 percent of our graduates recommended for medical and law school are admitted. The college has added almost $75 million dollars in new facilities since 2002, including two new residence halls, ten theme-based residential houses, new athletic facilities, a state-of-the-art technology center, and the Howard J. Burnett Center, which houses our programs in accounting, business, economics, education, entrepreneurial studies, and modern languages. Construction on a new $30 million science facility is scheduled to begin within the next 2 years. Despite an almost fourfold increase in applications in this time, the Admission Staff remains committed to reviewing each application individually. Our students are balanced, goal oriented, active, engaged and involved and we look for evidence of these traits in prospective students. We encourage students to use every aspect of the application process to demonstrate that they possess these qualities. If you are looking to become part of an institution that is constantly changing for the better and that will be an even better place by the time you graduate, then we encourage you to consider W&J.

"Students applying for Fall 2009 must submit scores from the SAT (or ACT). It is not required that they take the new version of the SAT (or the ACT with the Writing section). We will allow students to submit scores from either version of the SAT (or ACT) and will use the student's best scores from either test."

SELECTIVITY

Admissions Rating	92
# of applicants	7,377
% of applicants accepted	34
% of acceptees attending	16
# accepting a place on wait list	98
% admitted from wait list	28
# of early decision applicants	12
% accepted early decision	50

FRESHMAN PROFILE

Range SAT Critical Reading	520–620
Range SAT Math	530–640
Range ACT Composite	23–27
Minimum paper TOEFL	500
Minimum computer TOEFL	267
Average HS GPA	3.46
% graduated top 10% of class	37
% graduated top 25% of class	76
% graduated top 50% of class	98

DEADLINES

Early decision	
Deadline	12/1
Notification	12/15
Early action	
Deadline	1/1
Notification	1/15
Regular	
Priority	1/15
Deadline	3/1
Notification	rolling
Nonfall registration?	yes

FINANCIAL FACTS

Financial Aid Rating	72
Annual tuition	$29,532
Books and supplies	$800
% frosh rec. need-based scholarship or grant aid	64
% UG rec. need-based scholarship or grant aid	62
% frosh rec. non-need-based scholarship or grant aid	69
% UG rec. non-need-based scholarship or grant aid	60
% frosh rec. need-based self-help aid	70
% UG rec. need-based self-help aid	64
% frosh rec. any financial aid	99
% UG rec. any financial aid	96
% UG borrow to pay for school	75
Average cumulative indebtedness	$20,000

WASHINGTON STATE UNIVERSITY

370 LIGHTY STUDENT SERVICES, PULLMAN, WA 99164-1067 • ADMISSIONS: 888-468-6978 • FAX: 509-335-4902

CAMPUS LIFE

Quality of Life Rating	71
Fire Safety Rating	82
Green Rating	96
Type of school	public
Environment	town

STUDENTS

Total undergrad enrollment	20,282
% male/female	48/52
% from out of state	10
% from public high school	99
% live on campus	35
% in (# of) fraternities	14 (24)
% in (# of) sororities	18 (14)
% African American	2
% Asian	6
% Caucasian	74
% Hispanic	5
% Native American	1
% international	3
# of countries represented	92

SURVEY SAYS . . .
Great library
Athletic facilities are great
Everyone loves the Cougars
Intramural sports are popular
Frats and sororities dominate
social scene
Lots of beer drinking
Hard liquor is popular

ACADEMICS

Academic Rating	70
Calendar	semester
Student/faculty ratio	14:1
Profs interesting rating	64
Profs accessible rating	67
% classes taught by TAs	8
Most common	
reg class size	10–19 students

MOST POPULAR MAJORS
marketing/marketing management
social sciences
journalism

STUDENTS SAY "..."

Academics

"A moderately large research university with some very good programs," Washington State University delivers quality and value in a pleasant small-town environment to Washington residents and out-of-state students alike. The Edward R. Murrow College of Communications is among WSU's major drawing cards; the university also boasts a veterinary program "that is one of the leading programs in the nation," a business school whose offerings include a "great MIS program," a "very good agriculture program," solid offerings in plant sciences, zoology, and molecular biosciences, and programs in material science and engineering in which "Students have good contact with professors." In fact, throughout the university professors are typically "extremely accessible and work very well with the students. My math professor even plays basketball with all the students at our state-of-the-art rec center every week." As at any school, "When you get a bad professor, look out, but fortunately the majority of professors at WSU are good and want you to do well." Even the administration, often the whipping boy of students at large state schools, earns mostly good marks; one undergrad writes, "The administration, the criticisms of some students notwithstanding, is actually working hard to improve the school's quality, which is noticeable and appreciated." Some even report sensing that "staff actually cares about you as a person, and not just as another random number who pays $20,000 a year. They care about my success, and I appreciate that."

Life

"The weekends are thriving" at WSU, where some head to small house parties while others beat a path to Greek Row, a popular destination. One student writes, "Every night of the weekend (and sometimes during the week) there is a party you can go to. . . . People over 21 go to one of the three bars near campus around 11:00 P.M. and can dance and drink the rest of the night. I love the party scene at WSU, it's a great way to meet friends and potential interests." Some contend that "if you don't like to party, options are a bit limited," but others point to a broad range of athletic events ("Student camaraderie is outstanding at basketball and football games!") and extracurriculars as alternate options. Hometown Pullman "is tiny, with only 27,000 people, of whom 20,000 are students." Many here relish the environment, pointing out that "it is such a small community, you know it is safe to walk around by yourself at night" and noting that "while some people complain about boredom here, they usually are not very social. With 16,000-plus undergraduates you have to lock yourself in your room to not find something to do."

Students

"It's hard to define a typical student" at WSU, as "There are a lot of students from rural areas of Washington and quite a few from suburban areas" along with what students say seems like a fair share of "rich White kids from Seattle." Students tell us that "it's definitely not a yuppie school. Most people are down to earth and lean a little conservative politically," but there's a substantial liberal population as well. Most important, "Most of these people are very tolerant, so there is no real worry about expressing your beliefs and being attacked for them." Minorities "are definitely outnumbered on campus, but the school has numerous cultural events to encourage diversity and to get everyone to interact. The largest ethnic groups on campus (after Caucasian) include Hawaiian, Asian, Hispanic, and African American." One minority student reports, "All in all, it's not hard to fit in here. Students are extraordinarily friendly, and the guys constantly open doors for the ladies, or vice versa. Little things like that indicate how fun, friendly, and welcoming people are here."

FINANCIAL AID: 509-335-9711 • E-MAIL: ADMISS2@WSU.EDU • WEBSITE: WWW.WSU.EDU

THE PRINCETON REVIEW SAYS

Admissions

Very important factors considered include: Academic GPA, standardized test scores. *Important factors considered include:* Personal statement, rigor of secondary school record. *Other factors considered include:* Recommendation(s), extracurricular activities, talent/ability, volunteer work, work experience. SAT or ACT required; TOEFL required of all international applicants. High school diploma is required and GED is accepted. *Academic units required:* 4 English, 3 mathematics, 2 science, (1 science labs), 2 foreign language, 3 social studies, 1 history, 1 visual/performing arts, 1 academic elective. *Academic units recommended:* Additional math and science courses.

Financial Aid

Students should submit: FAFSA. The Princeton Review suggests that all financial aid forms be submitted as soon as possible after January 1. *Need-based scholarships/grants offered:* Federal Pell, SEOG, ACG, SMART, tate scholarships/grants, private scholarships, the school's own gift aid (including university and department scholarships). *Loan aid offered:* FFEL Subsidized Stafford, FFEL Unsubsidized Stafford, FFEL PLUS, Federal Perkins, Federal Nursing Applicants will be notified of awards on a rolling basis beginning 4/1. Federal and State Work-Study Programs available. Institutional employment available. Off-campus job opportunities are good.

The Inside Word

The huge number of applications WSU must process each year should leave Admissions Officers little time to consider anything other than grades, quality of curriculum, and standardized test scores. Yet WSU also encourages applicants to submit a personal statement and, presumably, takes the time to read them. Herein lies your chance to make up for an inconsistent high school record or less-than-optimal test scores. Make the most of your opportunity.

THE SCHOOL SAYS "..."

From The Admissions Office

"At Washington State University, you work side by side with nationally renowned faculty who help you succeed. Many academic programs rank among the nation's best. Programs are designed to give you real-world experience through internships, community service, in-depth labs, and study-abroad experiences. Plus, many disciplines encourage you to participate in faculty research or conduct your own. If you have top grades and a passion for learning, the highly acclaimed Honors College challenges you with interdisciplinary studies, rich classroom discussions, and research opportunities.

"The campus forms the heart of a friendly college town where faculty and peers help you achieve your greatest potential. More than 200 campus organizations connect you with others who share your interests and empower you to build leadership skills. Year after year, employers return to campus seeking Washington State University graduates and regard them as the best prepared in the state.

"In addition to the Pullman campus, WSU has three nonresidential urban campuses in Spokane, the TriCities (Richland), and Vancouver.

"The priority date to apply for admission and the deadline to apply for scholarships is January 31. For your candidacy to be considered, you must complete the high school core curriculum and provide official scores from the new SAT or the ACT. We also urge you to deliver a strong personal statement (essay)."

SELECTIVITY

Admissions Rating	83
# of applicants	10,853
% of applicants accepted	76
% of acceptees attending	42

FRESHMAN PROFILE

Range SAT Critical Reading	490–600
Range SAT Math	510–610
Minimum paper TOEFL	520
Minimum computer TOEFL	190
Minimum web-based TOEFL	68
Average HS GPA	3.42
% graduated top 10% of class	36
% graduated top 25% of class	57
% graduated top 50% of class	86

DEADLINES

Regular	
Priority	1/31
Notification	rolling
Nonfall registration?	yes

FINANCIAL FACTS

Financial Aid Rating	71
Annual in-state tuition	$5,812
Annual out-of-state tuition	$16,126
Room and board	$7,316
Required fees	$1,054
Books and supplies	$912
% frosh rec. need-based scholarship or grant aid	25
% UG rec. need-based scholarship or grant aid	32
% frosh rec. non-need-based scholarship or grant aid	24
% UG rec. non-need-based scholarship or grant aid	16
% frosh rec. need-based self-help aid	36
% UG rec. need-based self-help aid	43
% frosh rec. athletic scholarships	3
% UG rec. athletic scholarships	2
% frosh rec. any financial aid	73
% UG rec. any financial aid	75

WASHINGTON UNIVERSITY IN ST. LOUIS

CAMPUS BOX 1089, ONE BROOKINGS DRIVE, ST. LOUIS, MO 63130-4899 • ADMISSIONS: 314-935-6000 • FAX: 314-935-4290

CAMPUS LIFE

Quality of Life Rating	99
Fire Safety Rating	87
Green Rating	60*
Type of school	private
Environment	city

STUDENTS

Total undergrad enrollment	6,467
% male/female	50/50
% from out of state	90
% from public high school	63
% live on campus	73
% in (# of) fraternities	25 (12)
% in (# of) sororities	25 (6)
% African American	10
% Asian	13
% Caucasian	61
% Hispanic	3
% international	4
# of countries represented	101

SURVEY SAYS . . .
Lab facilities are great
Great library
School is well run
Students are friendly
Great food on campus
Great off-campus food
Dorms are like palaces
Students are happy

ACADEMICS

Academic Rating	95
Calendar	semester
Student/faculty ratio	7:1
Profs interesting rating	83
Profs accessible rating	85
Most common reg class size	fewer than 10 students
Most common lab size	10–19 students

MOST POPULAR MAJORS
biology/biological sciences
psychology
finance

STUDENTS SAY "..."

Academics
"Rigorous but very rewarding," Washington University boasts a "strong" premed program, a "very intense" curriculum, and a "very, very stressful" academic atmosphere. "Teachers are tough," warns a biology major. "They have high expectations." "Architecture majors for instance, have so much work and that they go for days without sleeping," observes a junior. Overall, though, students at Wash U wouldn't have it any other way. "I've had an amazing time since my first day of class," declares an English major. However, students aren't without complaints. "Distribution requirements are complicated and difficult for students to understand." "The engineering professors are very poor teachers." However, "All of my professors have been brilliant," says a chemistry major. "My only problem with them is some of them are so smart that they can't even conceive how I don't understand an idea." Professors "really care though." They "love to talk to their students" and they are remarkably accessible. Management is a huge hit. "Administrators realize that their first priority should be the students." "This school is also very wealthy and therefore offers greater opportunities than some schools would be able to." "From building amazing new facilities to creating world class programs from scratch, it really feels like the sky is the limit."

Life
The food is "really amazing" on this "gorgeous campus." Dorms are reportedly fabulous, too. "Things are way too expensive," though. Outside of class, Wash U students hit the books hard. "The library is always incredibly crowded." "Campus involvement is big" as well and "no one social scene dominates the campus." "Wash U is a bit of a bubble," describes a senior, "When you're here, the school experience shapes your entire lifestyle. It's a pleasant world, but hard to divorce yourself from the happy beauty of the campus and take note of the greater world and its problems." "Not every weekend is buck wild" but, of course, debauchery does happen. Some students "seem to live this strange double life of intense studying and partying." "A lot of students go to parties at the fraternities." There is little pressure to drink, though. "If you just want to stay in and watch a movie or play board games with friends," it's not a problem. The eclectic area next to campus—fondly called "The Loop"—is "a great neighborhood to walk to for restaurants, boutiques, and bars," though sketchy neighborhoods are mere blocks away. "St. Louis is a great sports town, so there are always great baseball, football, and hockey games" and there is some culture here but much of the city "shuts down after about 1:00 A.M."

Student Body
"Some people may say the typical student is a Jew from Long Island, but really this is just a hyped-up stereotype," says a junior. East Coasters definitely have a presence at Wash U but Midwesterners predominate. The campus is "very ethnically diverse." However, "self-segregation is a big issue." "People who are very wealthy tend to hang out together," too. There is "a frantic premed culture" and, overall, the campus is "a little nerdy." "I hadn't seen so many hot geeks in one place until I came to Wash U," claims a first-year student. Jocks, punks, and goths are rare. "A lot of people look exactly the same. This isn't really the best place to explore your education or figure out what you want to do with your life," reflects a senior. "The typical student here has a plan and a goal they are working toward." These "overcommitted, fun-loving high-school all stars" are "pretty politically apathetic" but they have an array of other interests. "I think the thing that connects everyone is passion," suggests a sophomore. "Every student brings something different." "There are the students involved in way too many activities just for the sake of activities, the premeds, the counterculture and counter-counterculture art students, B-school partiers, intense architecture students, frat boys, sorority girls who promised themselves they would never join one, the ethnicity-obsessed, and then a huge melting pot of all of those mixed together."

FINANCIAL AID: 888-547-6670 • E-MAIL: ADMISSIONS@WUSTL.EDU • WEBSITE: WUSTL.EDU

THE PRINCETON REVIEW SAYS

Admissions

Very important factors considered include: Class rank, application essay, academic GPA, recommendation(s), rigor of secondary school record, standardized test scores, character/personal qualities, extracurricular activities, talent/ability, volunteer work, work experience. *Other factors considered include:* Alumni/ae relation, first generation, interview, level of applicant's interest, racial/ethnic status, SAT or ACT required; TOEFL required of all international applicants. High school diploma is required and GED is accepted. *Academic units recommended:* 4 English, 4 mathematics, 4 science, (4 science labs), 2 foreign language, 4 social studies, 4 history.

Financial Aid

Students should submit: FAFSA, CSS/Financial Aid PROFILE, noncustodial PROFILE, Student and parent 1040 tax return or signed waiver if there is no tax return. Regular filing deadline is 1/15. The Princeton Review suggests that all financial aid forms be submitted as soon as possible after January 1. *Need-based scholarships/grants offered:* Federal Pell, SEOG, state scholarships/grants, private scholarships, the school's own gift aid, United Negro College Fund, Federal Academic Competitiveness Grant, SMART Grant. *Loan aid offered:* FFEL Subsidized Stafford, FFEL Unsubsidized Stafford, FFEL PLUS, Federal Perkins, state loans, college/university loans from institutional funds. Applicants will be notified of awards on or about 4/1. Federal Work-Study Program available. Institutional employment available. Off-campus job opportunities are excellent.

The Inside Word

The fact that Washington U. doesn't have much play as a nationally respected car-window decal is about all that prevents it from being among the most selective universities. In every other respect—that is, in any way which really matters—this place is hard to beat and easily ranks as one of the best. No other university with as impressive a record of excellence across the board has a more accommodating admissions process. Not that it's easy to get in here, but lack of instant name recognition does affect Wash U's admission rate. Students with above-average academic records who are not quite Ivy material are the big winners. Marginal candidates with high financial need may find difficulty; the admissions process at Washington U. is not need-blind and may take into account candidates' ability to pay if they are not strong applicants.

THE SCHOOL SAYS "..."

From The Admissions Office

"Washington University in St. Louis is a research university that offers a unique environment for undergraduate students to learn and grow. Unparalleled curriculum flexibility and learning opportunities in a friendly and supportive community inspire undergraduates to explore their interests and develop new ones. Working with their advisors, undergraduates may choose a traditional single major, as many do. Others combine majors with minors, second majors, and pre-professional programs – all within their four-year undergraduate experience. We encourage our students to participate in internships, study abroad programs, research and scholarship, and over 200 clubs and organizations, rounding out Washington University's commitment to help each student identify and pursue his or her passion. Our students pursue their passions every day. Visit campus and ask them about their experiences. As part of this commitment to help our students, Washington University is working to eliminate need-based loans as part of its undergraduate financial aid awards to students from low-income families. This new initiative and its goal of helping families with the most need will not lessen our desire, responsibility, or ability to work with all families to ensure they have the financial resources they need. We remain committed to a flexible and independent approach to delivering financial aid to those who need it most. Applicants for Fall 2009 are required to submit scores from either the SAT or ACT test. Applicants who submit scores from the ACT test may submit with or without the Writing component."

SELECTIVITY

Admissions Rating	99
# of applicants	22,428
% of applicants accepted	17
% of acceptees attending	34

FRESHMAN PROFILE

Range SAT Critical Reading	680–750
Range SAT Math	690–780
Range ACT Composite	30–33
Minimum paper TOEFL	550
Minimum computer TOEFL	213
Minimum web-based TOEFL	79
% graduated top 10% of class	95
% graduated top 25% of class	100
% graduated top 50% of class	100

DEADLINES

Early decision	
Deadline	11/15
Notification	12/15
Regular	
Deadline	1/15
Notification	4/1
Nonfall registration?	no

APPLICANTS ALSO LOOK AT

AND OFTEN PREFER
Harvard College
Stanford University
Yale University
University of Pennsylvania

AND SOMETIMES PREFER
University of Chicago
Duke University
Cornell University
Northwestern University

AND RARELY PREFER
Tulane University
University of Michigan—Ann Arbor
Emory University
University of Rochester

FINANCIAL FACTS

Financial Aid Rating	99
Annual tuition	$36,200
Room and board	$11,636
Required fees	$1,048
Books and supplies	$1,220
% frosh rec. need-based scholarship or grant aid	38
% UG rec. need-based scholarship or grant aid	40
% frosh rec. non-need-based scholarship or grant aid	5
% UG rec. non-need-based scholarship or grant aid	3
% frosh rec. need-based self-help aid	29
% UG rec. need-based self-help aid	30
% frosh rec. any financial aid	39
% UG rec. any financial aid	41
% UG borrow to pay for school	41

WEBB INSTITUTE

298 CRESCENT BEACH ROAD, GLEN COVE, NY 11542 • ADMISSIONS: 516-671-2213 • FAX: 516-674-9838

STUDENTS SAY "..."

Academics

Webb Institute on Long Island is a ridiculously small school wholly dedicated to boats. If you feel destined to become one of "America's future ship designers and engineers," enroll here. Every student receives a four-year, full-tuition scholarship. The only costs are books and supplies, room and board, and personal expenses. Everyone majors in naval architecture and marine engineering. "There are no classes to choose," explains a junior. "The curriculum is set for all students." Webbies are exposed to a smattering of the liberal arts and a ton of advanced math and physics. Virtually every other course involves ship design. There's also a senior thesis and a "required internship program." In January and February, all students get real, paying jobs in the marine industry. Job prospects are phenomenal. Newly minted Webb graduates enjoy "a 100 percent placement rate in grad schools and careers." Coursework is "rigorous," but the academic atmosphere is very intimate. "A huge plus of Webb's small size is that everyone knows everyone," relates a junior. "You're not just another number." "The administration, professors, and students all work in the same building every day, every week." "The admiral can get carried away when he perceives a problem" but the faculty is "approachable," "always accessible," and "very dedicated to the school and students." "Professors have a great deal of respect for the students and work closely with us to accomplish our goals," says a sophomore. "If you're passionate about architecture and engineering, you cannot hope for a better learning environment."

Life

Webb has a "family-like atmosphere." It's "a tiny student body living, eating, sleeping, and learning ship design in a mansion" "in a residential area overlooking the beautiful Long Island Sound." There's an honor code "that is strictly adhered to by all students." Cheating and stealing just don't happen here. "You can leave your wallet lying in the reception room, and if someone doesn't return it to you just because they know what your wallet looks like compared to the other 90 wallets in the school, it will still be there the next day and even the next week." Life at Webb "revolves around course load and the attempts to find distractions from it." "We average about five to seven hours of homework per night," advises a freshman. "At the end of the semesters, life sucks due to a ton of projects." "People generally think about homework and spend most of their time discussing class assignments." When students find some down time, movies and unorganized sports are common. Not surprisingly, "many people turn to the water" for amusement as well. "Sailing is popular." "The school has a skiff and sailboats, which are frequently used during the warm months," says a sophomore. Annual whitewater rafting and ski trips are well attended. New York City is a little less than an hour away, and "a bunch of people venture into" Manhattan on the weekends. "A lot of spontaneous and off-the-wall things occur" too, and "a fair amount of partying goes on at least once a week." However, Webb is absolutely not a party school.

Student Body

The average Webbie is a "middleclass white male who enjoys engineering and sciences." "There are very few atypical students." "Everyone is motivated and works hard." Basically, you have your bookworms who "don't socialize as much" and your more social students who get their work done but also play sports and "have a good time." "The differences in these two groups are by far the most visible division within the student body." Camaraderie is reportedly easy due to the academic stress and Webb's small size. Everyone interacts with everyone else, regardless of background. With fewer than 100 students, it's "impossible to completely isolate yourself." "There are no social cliques, and everyone is included in anything they'd like to be included in." As at most engineering schools, the ratio between males and females is pretty severely lopsided here. "We want more women!" plead many students.

FINANCIAL AID: 516-671-2213 • E-MAIL: ADMISSIONS@WEBB-INSTITUTE.EDU • WEBSITE: WWW.WEBB-INSTITUTE.EDU

THE PRINCETON REVIEW SAYS

Admissions

Very important factors considered include: Class rank, academic GPA, rigor of secondary school record, standardized test scores, character/personal qualities, interview, level of applicant's interest. *Important factors considered include:* Recommendation(s), extracurricular activities. *Other factors considered include:* talent/ability, volunteer work, work experience. SAT required; SAT Subject Tests required; High school diploma is required and GED is not accepted. *Academic units required:* 4 English, 4 mathematics, 2 science, (2 science labs), 2 social studies, 4 academic electives.

Financial Aid

Students should submit: FAFSA Regular filing deadline is 7/1. The Princeton Review suggests that all financial aid forms be submitted as soon as possible after January 1. *Need-based scholarships/grants offered:* Federal Pell, state scholarships/grants, private scholarships, the school's own gift aid. *Loan aid offered:* FFEL Subsidized Stafford, FFEL Unsubsidized Stafford, FFEL PLUS Applicants will be notified of awards on or about 8/1. Off-campus job opportunities are fair.

The Inside Word

Let's not mince words; admission to Webb is mega-tough. Webb's Admissions Counselors are out to find the right kid for their curriculum—one that can survive the school's rigorous academics. The applicant pool is highly self-selected because of the focused program of study: naval architecture and marine engineering.

THE SCHOOL SAYS "..."

From The Admissions Office

"Webb, the only college in the country that specializes in the engineering field of naval architecture and marine engineering, seeks young men and women of all races from all over the country who are interested in receiving an excellent engineering education with a full-tuition scholarship. Students don't have to know anything about ships, they just have to be motivated to study how mechanical, civil, structural, and electrical engineering come together with the design elements that make up a ship and all its systems. Being small and private has its major advantages. Every applicant is special and the President will interview all entering students personally. The student/faculty ratio is 8:1, and since there are no teaching assistants, interaction with the faculty occurs daily in class and labs at a level not found at most other colleges. The college provides each student with a high-end laptop computer. The entire campus operates under the Student Organization's honor system that allows unsupervised exams and 24-hour access to the library, every classroom and laboratory, and the shop and gymnasium. Despite a total enrollment of between 70 and 80 students and a demanding workload, Webb manages to field six intercollegiate teams. Currently more than 60 percent of the members of the student body play on one or more intercollegiate teams. Work hard, play hard and the payoff is a job for every student upon graduation. The placement record of the college is 100 percent every year.

"Freshman applicants must take the new SAT. In addition, students may submit scores from the old SAT (before March 2005), and the best scores from either test will be used. We also require scores from two SAT Subject Tests: Math Level I or II and either Physics or Chemistry."

SELECTIVITY

Admissions Rating	98
# of applicants	95
% of applicants accepted	31
% of acceptees attending	79
# of early decision applicants	31
% accepted early decision	39

FRESHMAN PROFILE

Range SAT Critical Reading	620–700
Range SAT Math	680–740
Range SAT Writing	600–710
Average HS GPA	3.9
% graduated top 10% of class	83
% graduated top 25% of class	100
% graduated top 50% of class	100

DEADLINES

Early decision	
Deadline	10/15
Notification	12/15
Regular	
Priority	10/15
Deadline	2/15
Notification	rolling
Nonfall registration?	no

APPLICANTS ALSO LOOK AT

AND OFTEN PREFER
United States Naval Academy
United States Coast Guard Academy

AND SOMETIMES PREFER
Virginia Tech
The Cooper Union for the Advancement of Science and Art

AND RARELY PREFER
University of Michigan—Ann Arbor
State University of New York—Maritime College

FINANCIAL FACTS

Financial Aid Rating	85
Room and board	$9,500
Books and supplies	$750
% frosh rec. need-based scholarship or grant aid	8
% UG rec. need-based scholarship or grant aid	14
% frosh rec. non-need-based scholarship or grant aid	4
% UG rec. non-need-based scholarship or grant aid	10
% frosh rec. need-based self-help aid	21
% UG rec. need-based self-help aid	11
% frosh rec. any financial aid	25
% UG rec. any financial aid	20
% UG borrow to pay for school	20
Average cumulative indebtedness	$7,303

WELLESLEY COLLEGE

BOARD OF ADMISSION, 106 CENTRAL STREET, WELLESLEY, MA 02481-8203 • ADMISSIONS: 781-283-2270 • FAX: 781-283-3678

STUDENTS SAY ". . ."

Academics

Wellesley College, "a small liberal arts institution with the intimacy of a family and the academic excellence of a top-rank university," provides its "all-female" student body with "an excellent education to make women independent individuals" while "preparing ambitious women to succeed in the professional world." This elite school located just outside Boston offers "undergraduate research opportunities, close relationships with professors, a suburban environment," and much more. One student explains, "Wellesley has everything I was looking for. It was a small, liberal arts school in New England with small class sizes, excellent professors, and an amazing reputation. I also appreciated the culture within the student body, the dedicated alumnae network, and the academic challenge." "Class work is rigorous" at Wellesley as teachers here "have incredibly high expectations," "But there are lots of resources available to help you if you need it," not the least of which are professors who "hold a large amount of office hours and even provide you with their home phone numbers and cell phone numbers in case you have any questions, whether about the class, the assignment, or life. The dedication of the Wellesley community is what I find to be stand out about the school." Spending part of junior year abroad is a staple of a Wellesley education. One student reports that "over 50 percent of Wellesley students travel abroad." Indeed, at home or abroad Wellesley offers "unlimited opportunities" and "takes the steps necessary" to help young women "realize [their] potential."

Life

At Wellesley, "the focus is all on academics," especially during the week. "You won't see students partying here on weekdays! Instead, you'll find students attending lectures, or discussing the news or issues on campus and what homework they have." The school's "close-knit atmosphere and location" make for an "unbelievably rich" college experience. While it's true that "there are no males around, at least not to the degree that there would be on a co-ed campus," students see this as a benefit. A freshman says, "This simply makes me focus more on what I'm really at college for: To get the most out of the educational opportunities available to me. In class, I am able to focus wholeheartedly on the subject matter, which is sometimes more difficult to do if there's a cute guy sitting in the class with me who is looking at me or whom I like." When it's time to chill, "Students attend cultural shows and plays on campus but mostly head into Boston." Social connections in this city dictate that eventually "Everyone ends up knowing someone else who goes to school in Boston and from that person, develops an additional social network in the city. This gives students a much-needed break on weekends from the often stressful Wellesley environment."

Students

Students describe the typical Wellesley undergrad (aka "Wendy Wellesley") as "an overachiever balancing two majors, 10 extracurricular activities, and several volunteer jobs." She is "passionate, hardworking, and wants to have an impact on the world around her." One student notes that "strong personalities," "diverse" individuals, and a "large range of interests" do not "allow the existence of absolutely typical students." Though "trends do occur," the "common denominator" among students is their "commitment to academic excellence." Beyond these traits, "Students are extremely diverse—ethnically, geographically, and socioeconomically. Because students come from so many backgrounds, no students are truly in the minority, and it is therefore easy for anyone to fit in."

WELLESLEY COLLEGE

FINANCIAL AID: 781-283-2360 • E-MAIL: ADMISSION@WELLESLEY.EDU • WEBSITE: WWW.WELLESLEY.EDU

THE PRINCETON REVIEW SAYS

Admissions

Very important factors considered include: Application essay, academic GPA, recommendation(s), rigor of secondary school record, standardized test scores, character/personal qualities. *Important factors considered include:* Class rank, extracurricular activities. *Other factors considered include:* Alumni/ae relation, first generation, geographical residence, interview, level of applicant's interest, racial/ethnic status, state residency, talent/ability, volunteer work, work experience. SAT and SAT Subject Tests or ACT required; ACT with Writing component required. High school diploma or equivalent is not required. *Academic units recommended:* 4 English, 4 mathematics, 3 science, (2 science labs), 4 foreign language, 4 social studies, 4 history.

Financial Aid

Students should submit: FAFSA, institution's own financial aid form, CSS/Financial Aid PROFILE, noncustodial PROFILE, business/farm supplement, parents' and students' tax returns and W-2s. The Princeton Review suggests that all financial aid forms be submitted as soon as possible after January 1. *Need-based scholarships/grants offered:* Federal Pell, SEOG, state scholarships/grants, the school's own gift aid. *Loan aid offered:* FFEL Subsidized Stafford, FFEL Unsubsidized Stafford, FFEL PLUS, Federal Perkins, state loans, college/university loans from institutional funds. Applicants will be notified of awards on or about 4/1. Federal Work-Study Program available. Institutional employment available. Off-campus job opportunities are excellent.

The Inside Word

As the number of women's colleges diminishes—*The New York Times* recently reported that the U.S. now has only about 60 all-women's schools, down from over 300 in the 1960s—competition for admission to the remaining single-sex institutions stiffens. Wellesley has always been an elite institution, but it grows ever more so as its number of competitors for top women students shrinks. If you submit your application materials to Wellesley by November 1, the school will provide you with an early evaluation, giving you some idea of your chances for admission.

THE SCHOOL SAYS "..."

From The Admissions Office

"Ranked fourth among liberal arts and sciences colleges according to the 2006 *U.S. News & World Report* survey, and widely acknowledged as the nation's best women's college, Wellesley College provides students with numerous opportunities on campus and beyond. With a long-standing commitment to and established reputation for academic excellence, Wellesley offers more than 1,000 courses in 53 established majors and supports 180 clubs, organizations, and activities for its students. The college is easily accessible to Boston, a great city in which to meet other college students and to experience theater, art, sports, and entertainment. Considered one of the most diverse colleges in the nation, Wellesley students hail from 79 countries and all 50 states.

"As a community, we are looking for students who possess intellectual curiosity: the ability to think independently, ask challenging questions, and grapple with answers. Strong candidates demonstrate both academic achievement and an excitement for learning. They also display leadership, an appreciation for diverse perspectives, and an understanding of the college's mission to educate women who will make a difference in the world.

"SAT and SAT Subject Tests or ACT with Writing component required. Two SAT Subject Tests required, one of which should be quantitative (Math or Science). We strongly recommend that students planning to apply early decision complete the tests before the end of their junior year and no later than October of their senior year."

SELECTIVITY

Admissions Rating	97
# of applicants	4,017
% of applicants accepted	36
% of acceptees attending	41
# accepting a place on wait list	381
% admitted from wait list	3
# of early decision applicants	236
% accepted early decision	55

FRESHMAN PROFILE

Range SAT Critical Reading	660–750
Range SAT Math	640–730
Range SAT Writing	660–730
Range ACT Composite	29–32
% graduated top 10% of class	78
% graduated top 25% of class	98
% graduated top 50% of class	100

DEADLINES

Early decision	
Deadline	11/1
Notification	12/15
Regular	
Deadline	1/15
Notification	4/1
Nonfall registration?	no

FINANCIAL FACTS

Financial Aid Rating	98
Annual tuition	$34,994
% frosh rec. need-based scholarship or grant aid	53
% UG rec. need-based scholarship or grant aid	56
% frosh rec. need-based self-help aid	50
% UG rec. need-based self-help aid	53
% frosh rec. any financial aid	55
% UG rec. any financial aid	59
% UG borrow to pay for school	52
Average cumulative indebtedness	$11,902

WELLS COLLEGE

ROUTE 90, AURORA, NY 13026 • ADMISSIONS: 315-364-3264 • FAX: 315-364-3227

CAMPUS LIFE

Quality of Life Rating	**77**
Fire Safety Rating	**84**
Green Rating	**81**
Type of school	private
Environment	rural

STUDENTS

Total undergrad enrollment	544
% male/female	23/77
% from out of state	31
% from public high school	88
% live on campus	86
% African American	5
% Asian	2
% Caucasian	68
% Hispanic	4
% Native American	1
% international	2
# of countries represented	13

SURVEY SAYS . . .

Small classes
No one cheats
Students are friendly
Frats and sororities are unpopular
or nonexistent

ACADEMICS

Academic Rating	**88**
Calendar	semester
Student/faculty ratio	9:1
Profs interesting rating	94
Profs accessible rating	93
Most common	
reg class size	10–19 students

MOST POPULAR MAJORS

English language and literature
psychology
history

STUDENTS SAY ". . ."

Academics

Most Wells students enrolled expecting an education designed to "form a strong community and strong female leaders." Not surprisingly, the college's recent decision to admit men and the arrival of its first coed class have left the student body with mixed feelings toward the administration. "The deans and the president are not straightforward in their interaction[s] with students," writes a senior. "They say one thing but do another, with seemingly little interest as to the desires of the students." A more even-handed student tells us, "Although [the] administration has proven to be not fully trustworthy in the information conveyed to students regarding Wells going coed, they have been accessible for dialogue on the matter, as well as for personal concerns." Students unite in praise of the school's honor code, which rewards responsibility with freedom—"Students are allowed to take exams out of the classroom and leave it in the[ir] professor's office when they're done." They also enjoy "one-on-one relationships" with professors who "are often upset if you don't come to their office hours to bug them" and "will approach you after [class] if they think you did well or saw that you were unprepared." With "highly rigorous" academics, extensive study abroad opportunities, and a "very interesting and very rare" book arts center, we predict Wells will continue to attract students into its coed halls.

Life

The Wells existence "can be summarized in one word: isolation." Hometown Aurora mostly shuts down by 8:00 P.M. One student warns: "If you are from NYC, you may be culture shocked" when you find yourself spending "Friday and Saturday nights doing homework." Besides the farms and barns, "There's a bar where the entire senior class congregates on Fridays, a wickedly expensive inn, and a pizza place." Students tell us that at Wells "The most fun comes from the traditions: The Even/Odd rivalry, Junior Blast, Freshman Elves . . . these are really what give Wells its fabulous life." Civilization, meaning malls and other college students, lies 45 minutes away in Ithaca, but some people prefer to stay put, swimming in Cayuga Lake, sledding down Student Union hill, exploring the local cemetery, and involving themselves with campus organizations. Spontaneous games of "hallway soccer," "wine and Cheez-Its" parties, and trips to the 24-hour Wal-Mart are also common. Students emphasize the luxury of "the safe space we have here. You can walk back to your dorm across campus at 3:00 A.M. alone and your biggest worry is bumping into the campus skunk." However, that might not hold true during dining hours: "I was told I was going to get the 'freshman 15,'" a student writes. "Whoever said that never ate in my school's dining hall."

Student Body

With only about 470 undergrads, "Everyone knows everyone else" at Wells. So it's fortunate that, despite a lingering resentment over the administration's decision to go coed, most students are tolerant of their new male peers. One student explains, "There were a lot of protests over it [two years ago], but the people who were in those protests left that to [two years ago] and they treat the guys great." As a male student was elected freshman class president in 2005–2006, it would seem that male students have been fully integrated into the Wells community. One male student, however, offers a different perspective: "Guys have been discriminated against here, but that's [to be] expected. Over time this will fade. I think there is more anger at the girls who are here because of the guys than anger at the guys themselves!" Regardless of gender, Wells students are outspoken, with "politics, establishing fair trade with poor countries, [and] women's studies" common topics of conversation. The liberal students tend to dominate this discussion: "It's generally assumed that whoever goes to the school is either a feminist or a Democrat."

FINANCIAL AID: 315-364-3289 • E-MAIL: ADMISSIONS@WELLS.EDU • WEBSITE: WWW.WELLS.EDU

THE PRINCETON REVIEW SAYS

Admissions

Very important factors considered include: Academic GPA, recommendation(s), rigor of secondary school record, standardized test scores, extracurricular activities. *Important factors considered include:* Application essay, interview. *Other factors considered include:* Class rank, alumni/ae relation, character/personal qualities, level of applicant's interest, talent/ability, volunteer work, work experience. SAT or ACT required; TOEFL required of all international applicants. High school diploma is required and GED is accepted. *Academic units required:* 4 English, 3 mathematics, 2 science, (2 science labs), 1 social studies, 3 history, 2 academic electives. *Academic units recommended:* 4 mathematics, 3 science, (3 science labs), 2 foreign language, 2 social studies, 2 history, 3 academic electives, 2 music, art, computer science.

Financial Aid

Students should submit: FAFSA, CSS/Financial Aid Profile for Early Decision Applicants only. The Princeton Review suggests that all financial aid forms be submitted as soon as possible after January 1. *Need-based scholarships/grants offered:* Federal Pell, SEOG, state scholarships/grants, private scholarships, the school's own gift aid. *Loan aid offered:* FFEL Subsidized Stafford, FFEL Unsubsidized Stafford, FFEL PLUS, Federal Perkins Applicants will be notified of awards on a rolling basis beginning 3/1. Federal Work-Study Program available. Institutional employment available. Off-campus job opportunities are poor.

The Inside Word

Wells is engaged in that age-old admissions game called matchmaking. There are no minimums or cutoffs in the admissions process here. But don't be fooled by the high admit rate. The Admissions Committee will look closely at your academic accomplishments, but also gives attention to your essay, recommendations, and extracurricular pursuits. The committee also recommends an interview; we suggest taking them up on it.

THE SCHOOL SAYS "..."

From The Admissions Office

"Wells College believes the twenty-first century needs well-educated individuals with the ability, self-confidence, and vision to contribute to an ever-changing world. Wells offers an outstanding classroom experience and innovative liberal arts curriculum that prepares students for leadership in a variety of fields, including business, government, the arts, sciences, medicine, and education. By directly connecting the liberal arts curriculum to experience and career development through internships, off-campus study, study abroad, research with professors, and community service, each student has an ideal preparation for graduate and professional school as well as for the twenty-first century.

"Wells College requires freshman applicants to submit scores from the old or new SAT. Students may also choose to submit scores from the ACT (with or without the Writing component) in lieu of the SAT."

SELECTIVITY

Admissions Rating	85
# of applicants	1,148
% of applicants accepted	64
% of acceptees attending	24
# of early decision applicants	16
% accepted early decision	63

FRESHMAN PROFILE

Range SAT Critical Reading	510–640
Range SAT Math	490–590
Range ACT Composite	23–27
Minimum paper TOEFL	550
Minimum computer TOEFL	213
Average HS GPA	3.5
% graduated top 10% of class	25
% graduated top 25% of class	60
% graduated top 50% of class	92

DEADLINES

Early decision	
Deadline	12/15
Notification	1/15
Early action	
Deadline	12/15
Notification	2/1
Regular	
Priority	12/15
Deadline	3/1
Notification	4/1
Nonfall registration?	no

APPLICANTS ALSO LOOK AT

AND OFTEN PREFER
Hobart and William Smith Colleges
Mount Holyoke College

AND SOMETIMES PREFER
Hamilton College
Ithaca College

AND RARELY PREFER
Le Moyne College
Elmira College

FINANCIAL FACTS

Financial Aid Rating	75
Annual tuition	$17,580
Room and board	$8,420
Required fees	$1,900
Books and supplies	$800
% frosh rec. need-based scholarship or grant aid	71
% UG rec. need-based scholarship or grant aid	76
% frosh rec. non-need-based scholarship or grant aid	37
% UG rec. non-need-based scholarship or grant aid	34
% frosh rec. need-based self-help aid	71
% UG rec. need-based self-help aid	75
% frosh rec. any financial aid	71
% UG rec. any financial aid	76
% UG borrow to pay for school	77
Average cumulative indebtedness	$20,355

WESLEYAN COLLEGE

4760 FORSYTH ROAD, MACON, GA 31210-4462 • ADMISSIONS: 478-757-5206 • FAX: 912-757-4030 • 800-447-6610

CAMPUS LIFE

Quality of Life Rating	**89**
Fire Safety Rating	**60***
Green Rating	**83**
Type of school	private
Affiliation	Methodist
Environment	city

STUDENTS

Total undergrad enrollment	547
% male/female	/100
% from out of state	10
% from public high school	81
% live on campus	76
# of countries represented	22

SURVEY SAYS . . .
Small classes
No one cheats
Students are friendly
Diverse student types on campus
Different types of students interact
Campus feels safe

ACADEMICS

Academic Rating	**88**
Calendar	semester
Student/faculty ratio	7:1
Profs interesting rating	90
Profs accessible rating	90
Most common reg class size	fewer than 10 students
Most common lab size	fewer than 10 students

MOST POPULAR MAJORS
psychology
business administration, management and operations
teacher education, multiple levels

STUDENTS SAY ". . ."

Academics
"You may be tired and overwhelmed" by the workload at Wesleyan College, a tiny liberal arts school for women noted for "giving exceptional women exceptional education at an affordable price," but "You will love every minute here," especially if "participating in lots of traditions" appeals to you. Fewer than 600 women attend the school, which is "so small that classes are usually under 20 students and are only taught by professors, never by teaching assistants. Every class can be discussion based, and most are." Wesleyan professors "are all very down-to-earth and helpful. They're available when you need them, and they are always eager for everyone to participate in class discussions." That availability is important, because "The academics are pretty intense," a fact that makes it easy to fall behind. The intensity also means that students leave feeling "really prepared for whatever lies ahead." Fortunately, "The staff really helps the students, especially with easing them into their first year with facilities like the Academic and Writing Centers." Students single out the Departments of English, Music, and Business for praise. The administration, they say, is accessible but "doesn't always run efficiently."

Life
Campus life at Wesleyan College revolves around homework and sisterhood. The former is the result of academic rigor; the latter, a Wesleyan tradition in which "Each class has its own colors and its own mascot. We have class rivalries, but in a good way, and compete in class sports and other competitions." Sisterhood activities "are the main focus" of extracurricular life. Enrichment activities known as "convos" (short for "convocations") are also important; students are required to attend 10 per year. Otherwise, campus life is relatively quiet, with the peace occasionally punctuated by a "campus wide event like homecoming or the Spring Dance." Drinking and drugs are strictly prohibited on the campus, and "Being under the influence on campus is not taken lightly. There are parties, but they're underground." Students occasionally venture out to the clubs, movie theaters, and coffee shops off campus, but most agree that "there's not really a lot to do in Macon." Many also feel quite comfortable on campus, where the accommodations are top-notch. The "Dorms are very spacious and comfortable," and the grounds are "extremely beautiful and relaxing. It is nice to sit by the lake and watch the ducks." The only fly in the soup is the food, which is described by more than a few as "horrible." Adding insult to injury, some students gripe about dining hall hours; one writes: "The cafeteria is open for about an hour for each meal time, and that's it, although the school does work with students and departments that have scheduling problems. "

Student Body
For such a small student body, Wesleyan College has "an extremely diverse campus in terms of race, color, national origin, sexual orientation, musical tastes, and whatnot, and everybody fits in extraordinarily well." "Over 30 countries" are represented among the school's approximately 600 students, and the African American population here is substantial (at over 25 percent). All students enjoy "a great atmosphere of respect where we are able to learn about many different cultures, religions, and beliefs." Women here tend to keep busy. They "are usually on their way to their next activity. What you eventually realize here is that everyone has something in common with someone else. It could be classes, it could be a hobby, it could be a club, or it could be that you are roommates, but regardless, there is always someone to hang out with." Many are enthusiastic about the school's traditions; they are "into the sisterhood, the class cheers, the pep rallies, the works. Others, though, are totally uninterested in the sisterhood stuff and just focus on studies."

FINANCIAL AID: 800-447-6610 • E-MAIL: ADMISSION@WESLEYANCOLLEGE.EDU • WEBSITE: WWW.WESLEYANCOLLEGE.EDU

THE PRINCETON REVIEW SAYS

Admissions

Very important factors considered include: Rigor of secondary school record. *Important factors considered include:* Class rank, application essay, recommendation(s), standardized test scores, character/personal qualities, extracurricular activities, talent/ability, volunteer work. *Other factors considered include:* Alumni/ae relation, interview, work experience. SAT or ACT required; TOEFL required of all international applicants. High school diploma is required and GED is accepted. *Academic units required:* 4 English, 3 mathematics, 3 science, (2 science labs), 2 foreign language, 3 social studies. *Academic units recommended:* 4 English, 4 mathematics, 4 science, (3 science labs), 4 foreign language, 4 social studies, 2 academic electives.

Financial Aid

Students should submit: FAFSA, institution's own financial aid form, state aid form. Regular filing deadline is 6/30. The Princeton Review suggests that all financial aid forms be submitted as soon as possible after January 1. *Need-based scholarships/grants offered:* Federal Pell, SEOG, state scholarships/grants, private scholarships, the school's own gift aid. *Loan aid offered:* FFEL Subsidized Stafford, FFEL Unsubsidized Stafford, FFEL PLUS, Federal Perkins, college/university loans from institutional funds, CitiAssist, Wells FARGO,Collegiate Loans, Key Alternative Loans. Applicants will be notified of awards on a rolling basis beginning 3/1. Federal Work-Study Program available. Off-campus job opportunities are good.

The Inside Word

As a small school tucked away in Georgia, Wesleyan doesn't garner as large an applicant pool as a school of its caliber should. The college still manages to attract some talented students, however, and good candidates need to be academically competitive. A majority of students come from the region, so applicants who represent some geographic diversity might be at a slight advantage.

THE SCHOOL SAYS "..."

From The Admissions Office

"Mention the term 'women's college' and most people envision ivy-covered towers in the Northeastern U.S. However, Wesleyan College in Macon, Georgia was founded in 1836 as the first college in the world chartered to grant degrees to women. Today it is recognized as one of the nation's most diverse and affordable selective 4-year liberal arts colleges. Students value the college's tradition of service and rigorous academic program renowned for its quality. An exceptional faculty teaches classes in seminar style. A student/faculty ratio of 10:1 ensures that students are known by more than just a grade or a number. The acceptance rate of Wesleyan students into medical, law, business, and other graduate programs is exemplary.

"Undergraduate degrees are offered in 35 majors and 29 minors including self-designed majors and interdisciplinary programs, plus eight pre-professional programs that include seminary, engineering, medicine, pharmacy, veterinary medicine, health sciences, dental, and law. A $12.5 million science center added to the college's offerings for 2007. Master of Arts degrees in education and an accelerated Executive Master of Business Administration program enroll both men and women.

"Beyond the academic, Wesleyan offers a thriving residence life program, NCAA Division III athletics, championship IHSA equestrian program, and meaningful opportunities for community involvement and leadership. The college's beautiful 200-acre wooded campus, along with 30 historically significant buildings, is listed in the National Register of Historic Places as the Wesleyan College Historic District. Wesleyan is nestled in a northern suburb of Macon, the third largest city in the state.

"First-year applicants must take either the SAT or ACT."

SELECTIVITY
Admissions Rating	88
# of applicants	617
% of applicants accepted	49
% of acceptees attending	45
# of early decision applicants	64
% accepted early decision	47

FRESHMAN PROFILE
Range SAT Critical Reading	490–640
Range SAT Math	480–580
Range ACT Composite	19–25
Minimum paper TOEFL	550
Minimum computer TOEFL	213
Average HS GPA	3.5
% graduated top 10% of class	34
% graduated top 25% of class	57
% graduated top 50% of class	83

DEADLINES
Early decision	
Deadline	11/15
Notification	12/15
Early action	
Deadline	2/15
Notification	3/15
Regular	
Priority	5/1
Deadline	8/1
Notification	rolling
Nonfall registration?	yes

APPLICANTS ALSO LOOK AT
AND SOMETIMES PREFER
Agnes Scott College
Emory University
Mercer University—Macon
University of Georgia
AND RARELY PREFER
Rhodes College
Berry College
University of Florida
Florida State University

FINANCIAL FACTS
Financial Aid Rating	81
Annual tuition	$16,500
Room and board	$7,600
Books and supplies	$900
% frosh rec. need-based scholarship or grant aid	52
% UG rec. need-based scholarship or grant aid	63
% frosh rec. non-need-based scholarship or grant aid	14
% UG rec. non-need-based scholarship or grant aid	15
% frosh rec. need-based self-help aid	35
% UG rec. need-based self-help aid	43
% frosh rec. any financial aid	96
% UG rec. any financial aid	91
% UG borrow to pay for school	68
Average cumulative indebtedness	$11,883

WESLEYAN UNIVERSITY

STEWART M. REID HOUSE, 70 WYLLYS AVENUE, MIDDLETOWN, CT 06459-0265 • ADMISSIONS: 860-685-3000 • FAX: 860-685-3001

CAMPUS LIFE

Quality of Life Rating	**83**
Fire Safety Rating	**86**
Green Rating	**92**
Type of school	private
Environment	town

STUDENTS

Total undergrad enrollment	2,787
% male/female	50/50
% from out of state	92
% from public high school	57
% live on campus	99
% in (# of) fraternities	2 (9)
% in (# of) sororities	NR (4)
% African American	7
% Asian	11
% Caucasian	61
% Hispanic	8
% Native American	1
% international	6
# of countries represented	48

SURVEY SAYS . . .
No one cheats
Great computer facilities
Great library
Athletic facilities are great
Students are friendly

ACADEMICS

Academic Rating	**94**
Calendar	semester
Student/faculty ratio	9:1
Profs interesting rating	89
Profs accessible rating	83
Most common reg class size	10–19 students
Most common lab size	20–29 students

MOST POPULAR MAJORS
English language and literature
psychology
political science and government

STUDENTS SAY ". . ."

Academics

Students at Wesleyan University relish "the immense amount of freedom the school gives you," both in terms of curricular choices ("because of the lack of core curriculum, you can mold each semester however you want: lots of lecture, lots of discussion, a mix") and in extracurricular life (in other words, "Public Safety rarely bothers the students"). The latter may sound like a recipe for a nonstop party, but that's hardly the case at Wesleyan; students here don't see the school as a 24/7 kegger, but rather as "a playground for the most opinionated and social-norm-destroying students of our generation to debate issues that really matter to them." If that suggests a school entirely focused on humanities and social sciences, guess again; Wes "has one of the strongest science programs [of] any of the top liberal arts school[s]. One-quarter of the students major in a science. Since we're in a university, but have very few graduate students, there are tons of opportunities for students to get involved in research. As a sophomore, I was highly involved in a $5 million NIH grant. That's pretty unique and amazing." In all disciplines, "Professors are incredible. They are all as available as they could be to us and more willing to help than I ever expected college professors to be." Those who teach "upper level courses are ridiculously passionate about what they teach, and are usually doing research that is very relevant to their field. At Wesleyan, I always get the sense that I am surrounded by many brilliant minds." A "very active student body . . . frequently tries to make changes in the way that the school is run," and "The administration does a good job [of] working with students to ensure that we all have the most positive experience possible."

Life

The Wesleyan campus is a busy one, replete with club and intercollegiate athletics, frat and house parties, and lots of performances and lectures. One student explains, "The Wes social scene is very much what you want to make it. Want to party? We do have frats (though they're a super-small part of campus life) and house parties. Don't want to party? Go to a play, concert, movie, or just hang out. Not everyone here is partying." Indeed, "There is plenty to keep you occupied" at Wesleyan, including campus politics, as "On this campus there is always some issue being fought or demonstrated against." Students take a strong hand in driving campus life, as "Everything is mostly student-run." "If a Wes student wants something that doesn't currently exist on campus, [he or she] make[s] it happen." Hometown Middletown, while "clearly lacking the resources of a large city," "has lots of opportunities to get involved and feel like a member of the community for four years." A junior reports, "Main Street in Middletown has changed tremendously just in the three years I have been here. Lots of new restaurants, bars, and art galleries have opened."

Student Body

"Passionate" is a word that pops up frequently when Wesleyan undergrads describe their peers, as does "intelligent." In fact, Wesleyan is a magnet for kids who value intellect, not only as a means to good grades and a career, but also as an instrument of self-development. "Everyone is excited about something," undergrads report. Students here are engaged in campus life, meaning that "a lot of things on campus are student-run and a lot of learning takes place outside the classroom due to casual interaction between peers." Demographically speaking, there are "two main molds of a Wesleyan student: The preppy New England kid and the kid . . . that [is] some kind of mix between a hipster and a hippie. Outside of that it's an extremely diverse group of kids who come from all over and have a wide range of interests." Most students here "are liberal and 'alternative.'"

FINANCIAL AID: 860-685-2800 • E-MAIL: ADMISS@WESLEYAN.EDU • WEBSITE: WWW.WESLEYAN.EDU/

THE PRINCETON REVIEW SAYS

Admissions

Very important factors considered include: Rigor of secondary school record. *Important factors considered include:* Class rank, application essay, academic GPA, recommendation(s), standardized test scores, character/personal qualities, first generation, racial/ethnic status, talent/ability. *Other factors considered include:* Alumni/ae relation, extracurricular activities, geographical residence, interview, volunteer work, work experience. SAT and SAT Subject Tests or ACT required; ACT with Writing component recommended. TOEFL required of all international applicants. High school diploma or equivalent is not required. *Academic units recommended:* 4 English, 4 mathematics, 4 science, (3 science labs), 4 foreign language, 4 social studies.

Financial Aid

Students should submit: FAFSA, CSS/Financial Aid PROFILE, noncustodial PROFILE, business/farm supplement. Regular filing deadline is 2/15. The Princeton Review suggests that all financial aid forms be submitted as soon as possible after January 1. *Need-based scholarships/grants offered:* Federal Pell, SEOG, state scholarships/grants, private scholarships, the school's own gift aid. *Loan aid offered:* FFEL Subsidized Stafford, FFEL Unsubsidized Stafford, FFEL PLUS, Federal Perkins, college/university loans from institutional funds. Applicants will be notified of awards on or about 4/1. Federal Work-Study Program available. Institutional employment available. Off-campus job opportunities are good.

The Inside Word

You want the inside word on Wesleyan admissions? Read *The Gatekeepers: Inside the Admissions Process at a Premier College*, by Jacques Steinberg. The author spent an entire admissions season at the Wesleyan Admissions Office; his book is a wonderfully detailed description of the Wesleyan admissions process (which is quite similar to processes at other private, highly selective colleges and universities).

THE SCHOOL SAYS "..."

From The Admissions Office

"Wesleyan faculty believe in an education that is flexible and affords individual freedom and that a strong liberal arts education is the best foundation for success in any endeavor. The broad curriculum focuses on essential communication skills and analytical abilities through course content and teaching methodology, allowing students to pursue their intellectual interests with passion while honing those capabilities. As a result, Wesleyan students achieve a very personalized but broad education. Wesleyan's Dean of Admission and Financial Aid, Nancy Hargrave Meislahn, describes the qualities Wesleyan seeks in its students: 'Our very holistic process seeks to identify academically accomplished and intellectually curious students who can thrive in Wesleyan's rigorous and vibrant academic environment; we look for personal strengths, accomplishments, and potential for real contribution to our diverse community.'

"Applicants will meet standardized testing requirements one of two ways: by taking the new SAT plus two SAT Subject Tests of the student's choice, or by taking the old SAT plus three SAT Subject Tests (one of which must be Writing)."

SELECTIVITY

Admissions Rating	97
# of applicants	7,750
% of applicants accepted	27
% of acceptees attending	35
# accepting a place on wait list	441
% admitted from wait list	22
# of early decision applicants	665
% accepted early decision	43

FRESHMAN PROFILE

Range SAT Critical Reading	650–750
Range SAT Math	650–740
Range SAT Writing	650–740
Range ACT Composite	27–32
Minimum paper TOEFL	600
Minimum computer TOEFL	250
Minimum web-based TOEFL	100
Average HS GPA	3.77
% graduated top 10% of class	71
% graduated top 25% of class	93
% graduated top 50% of class	100

DEADLINES

Early decision	
Deadline	11/15
Notification	12/15
Regular	
Deadline	1/1
Notification	4/1
Nonfall registration?	no

APPLICANTS ALSO LOOK AT
AND OFTEN PREFER
Harvard College
Stanford University
Yale University
Brown University
AND SOMETIMES PREFER
Williams College
Princeton University
Swarthmore College
Bowdoin College
Amherst College
AND RARELY PREFER
Oberlin College
Brandeis University
Vassar College
Middlebury College

FINANCIAL FACTS

Financial Aid Rating	95
Annual tuition	$36,806
% frosh rec. need-based scholarship or grant aid	40
% UG rec. need-based scholarship or grant aid	43
% frosh rec. need-based self-help aid	44
% UG rec. need-based self-help aid	47
% frosh rec. any financial aid	43
% UG rec. any financial aid	44
% UG borrow to pay for school	45
Average cumulative indebtedness	$21,464

WEST VIRGINIA UNIVERSITY

ADMISSIONS OFFICE, PO BOX 6009, MORGANTOWN, WV 26506-6009 • ADMISSIONS: 304-293-2121 • FAX: 304-293-3080

CAMPUS LIFE

Quality of Life Rating	**86**
Fire Safety Rating	**86**
Green Rating	**87**
Type of school	public
Environment	town

STUDENTS

Total undergrad enrollment	21,145
% male/female	54/46
% from out of state	42
% live on campus	25
% in (# of) fraternities	7 (17)
% in (# of) sororities	8 (11)
% African American	3
% Asian	2
% Caucasian	90
% Hispanic	2
% international	2
# of countries represented	99

SURVEY SAYS . . .

Great computer facilities
Great library
Athletic facilities are great
Students are friendly
Students are happy
Everyone loves the WV
Mountaineers
Student publications are popular
Lots of beer drinking
Hard liquor is popular

ACADEMICS

Academic Rating	**67**
Calendar	semester
Student/faculty ratio	23:1
Profs interesting rating	66
Profs accessible rating	69
Most common reg class size	20–29 students
Most common lab size	30-39 students

MOST POPULAR MAJORS

engineering
health professions and
related clinical sciences
business/commerce

STUDENTS SAY ". . ."

Academics

"Awesome academics and great school spirit" (not always in that order) define the WVU experience for many undergraduates here. Whether they're bleeding blue and gold on game day, enjoying the "exceptional partying" around campus, or grinding their way through one of WVU's standout academic programs, Mountaineers constantly "take pride in our school and state." WVU excels in numerous academic areas, including engineering, premedicine, journalism, psychology, forensics, advertising, music, and athletic training; a number of recent facilities upgrades have helped make some of these programs even better. Students here tell us that, although "Professors have hundreds of students," they "are always willing and interested to meet their students individually," and that WVU "Administrators don't hide in their offices; they actively participate in school functions." Undergrads also appreciate "plenty of internship and research opportunities" as well as a "good co-op program." WVU's elite Honors College "is really a great strength" and "is amazing at working with [its] students."

Life

WVU's football program "is one of the best in the country, and every Saturday is a great day," because "the entire state converges on Mountaineer Field to witness some of the best in NCAA football." Students throw themselves completely into the games as well as the "amazing" tailgates. One student notes, "The unity that is created among athletics is unmatched." If your passion for sports is weak, however, there's no reason to despair: At WVU, "There is an organization for everyone. There's a Fall Fest where major bands such as O.A.R. and Cypress Hill play and the school offers food, soda/pop, and beer in a controlled environment. There is a full bowling alley, billiard hall, and arcade in the bottom floor of our Student Union building, along with a full food court. There is a state-of-the-art rec center that receives tremendous use." While there are plenty of beer- and booze-soaked parties for those who are so inclined, there's also an alcohol-free program each weekend called WV Up All Night "where there is fun stuff and movies and comedy shows and games and free food at the student center" (although some warn that many people "get drunk and then go there for the free food"). Other options include the "Christian groups on campus," which "provide fun, safe, and religious activities in place of partying." Hometown Morgantown earns high marks; students praise its "refreshing, slower pace of life" as well as "the 15 bars downtown that are no more than 80 feet from each other." Main Street offers shopping that "caters to many tastes and styles."

Student Body

"There isn't a 'typical student'" at this school of 20,000-plus undergrads, although it seems that "everyone wears gold and blue and fits in fine." Students here detect a "good mix of the country and the city" as well as "a large out-of-state population," and they tell us that "what makes it such a great school is how everyone meshes together." Minorities, however, mesh to a lesser extent; as one student observes, "WVU is 90 percent White, so ethnically diverse students stand out. It's not that they're singled out, but it's just easy to notice [them] around campus. However, there is no discrimination, and everyone gets along well from what I've seen." The student body includes "typical fraternity and sorority students, but there are also so many intellectuals and unique individuals that you see them no matter where you turn." Undergrads are generally "easygoing, friendly, and approachable" and are "involved in club sports, clubs, the arts, residential education, or the Morgantown community."

FINANCIAL AID: 304-293-5242 • E-MAIL: WVUADMISSIONS@ARC.WVU.EDU • WEBSITE: WWW.WVU.EDU

THE PRINCETON REVIEW SAYS

Admissions

Very important factors considered include: Academic GPA, standardized test scores. *Important factors considered include:* Level of applicant's interest, state residency. *Other factors considered include:* Recommendation(s), extracurricular activities, volunteer work, SAT or ACT required; TOEFL required of all international applicants. High school diploma is required and GED is accepted. *Academic units required:* 4 English, 4 mathematics, 3 science, (3 science labs), 2 foreign language, 3 social studies, 1 visual/performing arts.

Financial Aid

Students should submit: FAFSA, state aid form. Regular filing deadline is 3/1. The Princeton Review suggests that all financial aid forms be submitted as soon as possible after January 1. *Need-based scholarships/grants offered:* Federal Pell, SEOG, state scholarships/grants, private scholarships, the school's own gift aid. *Loan aid offered:* Direct Subsidized Stafford, Direct Unsubsidized Stafford, Direct PLUS, Federal Perkins, college/university loans from institutional funds. Applicants will be notified of awards on a rolling basis beginning 3/15. Federal Work-Study Program available. Institutional employment available. Off-campus job opportunities are good.

The Inside Word

While standards for general admission to WVU are not especially rigorous, you'll find admission to its premier programs to be quite competitive. Admission to the College of Business and Economics, for example, requires a high school GPA of at least 3.75 and an SAT Math score of at least 610. Programs in computer science, education, engineering, fine arts, forensics, journalism, medicine, and nursing all require fairly impressive credentials. If you are not admitted to the program of your choice, you may be able to transfer to it later if your grades are good enough, but it won't be easy.

THE SCHOOL SAYS "..."

From The Admissions Office

"From quality academic programs and outstanding, caring faculty to incredible new facilities and a campus environment that focuses on students' needs, WVU is a place where dreams can come true. The university's tradition of academic excellence attracts some of the region's best high school seniors. WVU has produced 25 Rhodes Scholars, 29 Goldwater Scholars, 18 Truman Scholars, 5 members of *USA Today*'s All-U.S.A. College Academic First Team, and 2 Udall Scholarship winners. Whether your goal is to be an aerospace engineer, reporter, physicist, athletic trainer, opera singer, forensic investigator, pharmacist, or CEO, WVU's 179 degree choices can make it happen. Unique student-centered initiatives include Operation Jump Start, which helps students experience true education extending beyond the classroom. Resident Faculty Leaders live next to the residence halls to mentor students, and WVU Up All Night provides a way to relax and have fun with free food and activities nearly every weekend. The Mountaineer Parents' Club connects more than 13,000 WVU families, and a parents' helpline (800-WVU-0096) leads to a full-time parent advocate. A new Student Recreation Center includes athletic courts, pools, weight/fitness equipment, and a 50-foot indoor climbing wall. Also, a brand-new life sciences building and completely renovated library complex just opened. With programs for studying abroad, a Center for Black Culture and Research, an Office of Disability Services, and a student body that comes from every WV county, 50 states, and 91 different countries, WVU encourages and nurtures diversity. More than $150 million in annual grant funding makes WVU a major research institution where undergraduates can participate. The main campus is one of the safest in the nation, and the area's natural beauty provides chances to ski, bike, hike, and go white-water rafting.

"All applicants beginning with the Fall 2007 class are required to take the new ACT Writing assessment as part of the ACT exam or take the new SAT exam to be considered for admission."

SELECTIVITY

Admissions Rating	76
# of applicants	13,634
% of applicants accepted	89
% of acceptees attending	39

FRESHMAN PROFILE

Range SAT Critical Reading	470–560
Range SAT Math	490–590
Range ACT Composite	21–26
Minimum paper TOEFL	550
Minimum computer TOEFL	173
Average HS GPA	3.3
% graduated top 10% of class	18
% graduated top 25% of class	43
% graduated top 50% of class	77

DEADLINES

Regular	
Priority	2/1
Deadline	8/1
Notification	rolling
Nonfall registration?	yes

APPLICANTS ALSO LOOK AT

AND OFTEN PREFER
Virginia Tech
Penn State—University Park
University of Pittsburgh—Pittsburgh Campus

AND SOMETIMES PREFER
University of Maryland—College Park
Marshall University
The Ohio State University—Columbus
James Madison University

AND RARELY PREFER
University of Delaware
Fairmont State College
Shepherd University

FINANCIAL FACTS

Financial Aid Rating	77
Annual in-state tuition	$4,722
% frosh rec. need-based scholarship or grant aid	19
% UG rec. need-based scholarship or grant aid	32
% frosh rec. non-need-based scholarship or grant aid	21
% UG rec. non-need-based scholarship or grant aid	30
% frosh rec. need-based self-help aid	21
% UG rec. need-based self-help aid	37
% frosh rec. athletic scholarships	1
% UG rec. athletic scholarships	1
% frosh rec. any financial aid	69
% UG rec. any financial aid	86

WESTMINSTER COLLEGE (PA)

319 SOUTH MARKET STREET, NEW WILMINGTON, PA 16172 • ADMISSIONS: 800-942-8033 • FAX: 724-946-7171

CAMPUS LIFE
Quality of Life Rating	**88**
Fire Safety Rating	**98**
Green Rating	**60***
Type of school	private
Affiliation	Presbyterian
Environment	village

STUDENTS
Total undergrad enrollment	1,387
% male/female	36/64
% from out of state	21
% from public high school	90
% live on campus	78
% in (# of) fraternities	33 (5)
% in (# of) sororities	34 (5)
% African American	3
% Caucasian	80
% Hispanic	1
# of countries represented	1

SURVEY SAYS . . .
Career services are great
Students are friendly
Frats and sororities dominate
social scene
Student government is popular

ACADEMICS
Academic Rating	**82**
Calendar	semester
Student/faculty ratio	12:1
Profs interesting rating	89
Profs accessible rating	87
Most common	
reg class size	10–19 students
Most common	
lab size	10–19 students

MOST POPULAR MAJORS
education
biology/biological sciences
business/commerce

STUDENTS SAY "..."

Academics
Students choose Westminster College, a small Presbyterian-affiliated liberal arts school north of Pittsburgh, for its cozy atmosphere and well-regarded pre-professional programs. Undergrads describe Westminster as "an extremely small school where everyone pretty much knows each other," where "professors are dedicated to helping students on all levels from the classroom and outside of class to calling them up on the weekends at home to discuss coursework," and where the community is like "a family bound together with blue and white pride and a love for the people who are currently attending and those that have moved on." Indeed, "Once you become a part of the Westminster tradition, it lasts for a lifetime!" The small class environment "creates opportunities and values diversified learning above focused, by-rote study," facilitated by a "very hands-on" approach from both faculty and administrators. Premedical studies excel here. Students warn that "being a biology major is much harder than some of the other majors, and even if you don't fail a class it is hard to graduate on time." However, this hard work pays off in Westminster's admit rate to medical schools, which is double the national average. Students also love the music, education, and public relations programs here. Other majors are "hit or miss...depending on the staff in the department." Where the school falls shortest, however, is in its facilities. Undergrads tell us that because Westminster is "a very old school that relies on alumni for donations, our building are terribly old and it shows" and that "the libraries are sub-par." Westminster has spent $36 million on renovations in the last few years, however, and current renovations to McGill Library will be complete in Fall 2008.

Life
Westminster has "a very active Greek life in which the majority of our student population is involved," and "students have integrated Greek life as a positive force and influence in their school careers with many opportunities for leadership roles and future connections leading up to a week-long "Greek Week."" Weekends usually "involve going to the fraternities," which "gets old after a while," but since the school is located "in a very small town located near an Amish community, there isn't much off-campus to do besides go to fraternity houses." On-campus alternatives include "weekly events with a musician, comedian, etc. Also, there are two free movies offered each weekend." As one student warns, "If you're into the bar scene, clubs, or big-city life, don't go to Westminster. You'll be disappointed. If you like things more laid-back and prefer a slow-paced life, Westminster is probably going to fit you pretty well." Aesthetes will also find much to enjoy, as "The campus is the most beautiful [place].... There are so many wide open spaces with pastures, barns, acres of land and the trees are gorgeous in the fall." Among intercollegiate athletics, "Football is a big thing on campus as well as basketball. Many students come out to support their fellow teammates and friends."

Student Body
"Westminster does not have a lot of diversity," as "most students are local," meaning that they tend to be "white and from a middle to upper middle class family." "Of course you have your various groups that have only been moderately refined since high school: the jocks, the gothic kids, the cheerleader types, the hippies that never bathe, etc., but the typical student here would have to be someone who is relatively laid back," explains one student. "They wear American Eagle jeans, vintage t-shirts, and flip-flops year round. They are moderately aware of the world around them, politically and environmentally. They play ultimate Frisbee and guitar, and have probably started or head some club on campus that is particular to their interests. In their free time they read poems, sing, practice an instrument, watch *Family Guy*, or catch up with some friends. Many on campus seem apathetic toward just about everything, but a surprising number actually take the responsibility and initiative to make a difference." Politically, the student body leans toward the "conservative."

FINANCIAL AID: 724-946-7102 • E-MAIL: ADMIS@WESTMINSTER.EDU • WEBSITE: WWW.WESTMINSTER.EDU

THE PRINCETON REVIEW SAYS

Admissions

Very important factors considered include: Rigor of secondary school record, standardized test scores, interview. *Important factors considered include:* Class rank, application essay, recommendation(s), character/personal qualities. *Other factors considered include:* Alumni/ae relation, extracurricular activities, racial/ethnic status, talent/ability, volunteer work, work experience. SAT or ACT required; TOEFL required of all international applicants. High school diploma is required and GED is accepted. *Academic units required:* 4 English, 3 mathematics, 2 science, (2 science labs), 2 foreign language, 2 social studies, 1 history, 3 academic electives.

Financial Aid

Students should submit: FAFSA, institution's own financial aid form, F. The Princeton Review suggests that all financial aid forms be submitted as soon as possible after January 1. *Need-based scholarships/grants offered:* Federal Pell, SEOG, state scholarships/grants, private scholarships, the school's own gift aid. *Loan aid offered:* FFEL Subsidized Stafford, FFEL Unsubsidized Stafford, FFEL PLUS, Federal Perkins, Resource Loans. Applicants will be notified of awards on a rolling basis beginning 11/1.

The Inside Word

Westminster College has grown increasingly more selective throughout the decade, the result of a 40+ percent increase in its applicant pool (without any corresponding increase in the size of its freshman class). The school is still less selective than most competitive undergraduate institutions, meaning those with less-than-stellar high school careers may find a home here. The school admits on a rolling basis. Apply early to improve your chances.

THE SCHOOL SAYS "..."

From The Admissions Office

"Since its founding, Westminster has been dedicated to a solid foundation in today's most crucial social, cultural, and ethical issues. Related to the Presbyterian Church (U.S.A.), Westminster is home to people of many faiths. Our students and faculty, tradition of campus, and small-town setting all contribute to an enlightening educational experience.

"For purposes of admission and merit scholarships Westminster College will evaluate applicants for Fall 2008 using the composite score of the Math and Critical Reading sections of the new SAT or the composite score of the ACT. Westminster will collect new Writing section scores and compare with national percentiles for possible inclusion in admission and scholarship criteria for the future."

SELECTIVITY
Admissions Rating	79
# of applicants	1,368
% of applicants accepted	71
% of acceptees attending	32

FRESHMAN PROFILE
Range SAT Critical Reading	480–592
Range SAT Math	480–590
Range ACT Composite	20–25
Minimum paper TOEFL	550
Minimum computer TOEFL	213
Average HS GPA	3.4
% graduated top 10% of class	20
% graduated top 25% of class	55
% graduated top 50% of class	87

DEADLINES
Early action	
Deadline	11/15
Notification	11/15
Regular	
Deadline	4/15
Notification	rolling
Nonfall registration?	no

APPLICANTS ALSO LOOK AT
AND SOMETIMES PREFER
Duquesne University
AND RARELY PREFER
Washington & Jefferson College
Thiel College
Allegheny College

FINANCIAL FACTS
Financial Aid Rating	62
Annual tuition	$25,900
Room and board	$8,110
Required fees	$1,100
Books and supplies	$1,000
% frosh rec. need-based scholarship or grant aid	81
% UG rec. need-based scholarship or grant aid	79
% frosh rec. non-need-based scholarship or grant aid	80
% UG rec. non-need-based scholarship or grant aid	71
% frosh rec. need-based self-help aid	68
% UG rec. need-based self-help aid	65
% UG borrow to pay for school	73
Average cumulative indebtedness	$17,930

WESTMINSTER COLLEGE (UT)

1840 SOUTH 1300 EAST, SALT LAKE CITY, UT 84105 • ADMISSIONS: 801-832-2200 • FAX: 801-832-3101

CAMPUS LIFE
Quality of Life Rating	**98**
Fire Safety Rating	**98**
Green Rating	**76**
Type of school	private
Environment	metropolis

STUDENTS
Total undergrad enrollment	2,020
% male/female	42/58
% from out of state	18
% from public high school	81
% live on campus	27
% African American	1
% Asian	3
% Caucasian	77
% Hispanic	6
% Native American	1
% international	2
# of countries represented	36

SURVEY SAYS . . .
Large classes
Great computer facilities
Great library
Athletic facilities are great
Students are happy
Frats and sororities are unpopular
or nonexistent

ACADEMICS
Academic Rating	**85**
Calendar	4/1/4
Student/faculty ratio	10:1
Profs interesting rating	97
Profs accessible rating	89
Most common reg class size	10–19 students
Most common lab size	fewer than 10 students

MOST POPULAR MAJORS
business/commerce
nursing/registered nurse
(RN, ASN, BSN, MSN)
psychology

STUDENTS SAY ". . ."

Academics
There is more than one Westminster College, so let's not get confused. This is the one in the heart of Salt Lake City that's "the only liberal arts college in Utah." "Small class sizes" and "personal attention" abound on this "beautiful campus." Pre-professional programs are strong, particularly in nursing, education, and business. Westminster also offers some of the coolest programs anywhere. During an intense May Term, students take unique courses, such as "Chemistry and Biology of Brewing," or study off campus. You can study aviation in Alaska, for example, or traditional Indian culture—in India. "The May Term trips are a great opportunity" to "learn more about a different country," a junior writes. A semester-long program called Winter at Westminster offers backcountry touring, clinics in bobsledding and Nordic jumping, and camping in a yurt. Back on campus, Westminster's "easily accessible" professors facilitate "fun and interactive" discussions. "All the professors know you on a first-name basis," explains one happy student. "They practically beg you to come to their office hours for help." Views of the administration are mixed. Some students see Westminster as "a well-oiled machine" and its administrators as "genuinely interested in how the students are doing and making sure that any problems are solved as quickly as possible." Other students call the administration "disconnected." "Our science and lab facilities are substandard," a senior writes, but the school broke ground for a $25 million science center in May 2008, and has spent almost $2 million in the past two years for new, state-of-the-art equipment.

Life
At Westminster, "Life on campus is very dramatic." "Everyone knows everyone else," and "Everyone is involved in everyone else's business." Fortunately, there are numerous reasons for undergrads to get out and about: "Many people are involved with extracurricular activities" and "leadership opportunities" are abundant. The ASWC (Associated Students of Westminster College) also sponsors "many activities each week," including stand-up comics and dances. In addition, "The Music and Theater Department[s] are very popular." Student opinion of the food ranges from "not great" to it "sucks"—"they fry everything." Off campus, "There is a lot to do" around the city and "the state of Utah." The college "is located in the heart of Sugarhouse," one of Salt Lake City's oldest neighborhoods. "Clothes stores, book stores, bars, and restaurants are all within walking distance." "For fun," students "go to a movie or out to dinner," or "bask in the aroma-rich atmospheres of the local coffee shops." While "Many students go to clubs and bars for fun," "This isn't a real big party school." "There is a segment of the student body population that will not party for religious reasons," notes a junior. "Proximity to the beautiful mountains" means that "outdoor activities" abound here. Westminster is only "minutes away from some pretty awesome ski resorts" so skiers and snowboarders can "maximize their time on the slopes." "Utah has the greatest snow on earth," avows a junior.

Students
"Westminster is not religiously affiliated" and many students here "are not religious at all." At the same time, "a large portion" of the student body is "religious and wholesome." "We're in Utah," explains a junior. When asked to describe a typical student, Westminster undergrads offer: "White, middle-class, from Utah, [and] fresh out of high school." "Most of the students are traditional students" but "There are many people over age 25" as well. The "self-motivated" students here are "very active (and liberal) politically" and "pretty studious." They "tend to be kind of preppy, but you can find hippies." There are "the children of the very rich who are just mediocre and the children of the very poor who are brilliant." "There are not many minorities on campus" and Westminster is "less diverse than the average university," but "more diverse, generally, than the rest of the state." Students from ethnic minorities who are here "seem to integrate well into the social groups on a friendly level."

FINANCIAL AID: 801-832-2500 • E-MAIL: ADMISSION@WESTMINSTERCOLLEGE.EDU • WEBSITE: WWW.WESTMINSTERCOLLEGE.EDU

THE PRINCETON REVIEW SAYS

Admissions

Very important factors considered include: Academic GPA, rigor of secondary school record. *Important factors considered include:* Class rank, application essay, standardized test scores, interview. *Other factors considered include:* Recommendation(s), alumni/ae relation, character/personal qualities, extracurricular activities, geographical residence, talent/ability, SAT or ACT required; ACT with Writing component recommended. TOEFL required of all international applicants. High school diploma is required and GED is accepted. *Academic units required:* 4 English, 2 mathematics, 3 science, 2 foreign language, 2 social studies, 1 history, 2 academic electives. *Academic units recommended:* 4 English, 3 mathematics, 3 science, 3 foreign language, 2 social studies, 1 history, 3 academic electives.

Financial Aid

Students should submit: FAFSA. The Princeton Review suggests that all financial aid forms be submitted as soon as possible after January 1. *Need-based scholarships/grants offered:* Federal Pell, SEOG, state scholarships/grants, private scholarships, the school's own gift aid, United Negro College Fund. *Loan aid offered:* FFEL Subsidized Stafford, FFEL Unsubsidized Stafford, FFEL PLUS, Federal Perkins Applicants will be notified of awards on a rolling basis beginning 3/15. Federal Work-Study Program available. Institutional employment available. Off-campus job opportunities are excellent.

The Inside Word

It's not spectacularly difficult to gain admission to Westminster, particularly if you have solid grades and have taken a reasonably broad college-prep curriculum; your high school grades are probably the single biggest admissions factor here; essays are also important. Your standardized test scores, on the other hand, don't need to be out of this world. While almost every student at Westminster is on some kind of scholarship, you should pay special attention to every facet of the application if you are gunning for a lot of free money.

THE SCHOOL SAYS "..."

From The Admissions Office

"Founded in 1875, Westminster College is a private, comprehensive, liberal arts college dedicated to students and their learning, and offers one of the most unique learning environments in the country. Located where the Rocky Mountains meet the vibrant city of Salt Lake, Westminster blends classroom learning with experiences derived from its unique location to help students develop skills and attributes critical for success in a rapidly changing world. Impassioned teaching and active learning are the hallmarks of the Westminster experience.

"Each application is read and reviewed individually by an Admissions Committee who takes into account both level of challenge in course work and grades received. Either the SAT or ACT exam is accepted. Writing ability will be assessed through the Writing sections of the SAT, ACT, application essays, and in some cases, other writing samples such as graded papers. For 2007–2008, the Writing section of the ACT is recommended but not required, and the Writing component of the SAT will be reviewed. However, only the Math and Critical Reading scores will be used for merit scholarship consideration for the 2007–2008 year.

"Westminster College has a rolling application deadline and will accept applications until the class is filled. To be eligible for the widest array of financial aid—and over 97 percent of freshmen receive some financial aid—April 15 is the priority consideration deadline for fall semester, and May 15 is the deadline for on-campus housing applications."

SELECTIVITY
Admissions Rating	82
# of applicants	1,146
% of applicants accepted	86
% of acceptees attending	46

FRESHMAN PROFILE
Range SAT Critical Reading	
490–632.5	
Range SAT Math	480–610
Range ACT Composite	21–27
Minimum paper TOEFL	550
Minimum computer TOEFL	213
Average HS GPA	3.521
% graduated top 10% of class	29
% graduated top 25% of class	56
% graduated top 50% of class	89

DEADLINES
Regular	
Notification	rolling
Nonfall registration?	yes

APPLICANTS ALSO LOOK AT
AND OFTEN PREFER
Utah State University
University of Utah
AND SOMETIMES PREFER
Brigham Young University (UT)
University of Puget Sound
Colorado College
Gonzaga University
AND RARELY PREFER
Lewis & Clark College

FINANCIAL FACTS
Financial Aid Rating	67
Annual tuition	$21,984
Room and board	$6,354
Required fees	$390
Books and supplies	$1,000
% frosh rec. need-based scholarship or grant aid	56
% UG rec. need-based scholarship or grant aid	58
% frosh rec. non-need-based scholarship or grant aid	11
% UG rec. non-need-based scholarship or grant aid	6
% frosh rec. need-based self-help aid	50
% UG rec. need-based self-help aid	53
% frosh rec. athletic scholarships	3
% UG rec. athletic scholarships	2
% frosh rec. any financial aid	97
% UG rec. any financial aid	86
% UG borrow to pay for school	59
Average cumulative indebtedness	$16,800

WHEATON COLLEGE (IL)

501 COLLEGE AVENUE, WHEATON, IL 60187 • ADMISSIONS: 630-752-5005 • FAX: 630-752-5285

STUDENTS SAY ". . ."

Academics

"As cheesy as it sounds, [Wheaton] really is about the integration of faith and learning," students assert, telling us that the school "is a close community of students with the same values and beliefs doing their best to learn and grow closer to each other and to God." With a "great theology program," "excellent ministry programs," and business and economics departments led by professors with "real-life experience [bringing] many real-life situations into the classroom," Wheaton "is probably the top Evangelical college in the nation," according to its undergraduates. They support their claim by describing the "many internship opportunities" available here and by pointing out that "In terms of resumes and formal instruction from professors, [Wheaton] students are well prepared for the business world or some of the best grad schools in the nation." Wheaton's "liberal arts focus causes [students] not to specialize completely but to be interested in everything and draw connections between completely different things," creating an environment in which "Wheaton students are very good at engaging with everything we are exposed to. We love to delight in and enjoy what is good and beautiful, whether that means the wonderful idioms of a spoken language, the counterintuitive nuances of quantum mechanics, or the pattern made by the icicles hanging from Williston [Hall]'s dormer windows." Although "the academics at Wheaton are superb," some departments suffer from under-funding. "Our science building, our music building, and our Internet capabilities are all extremely sub-par," students complain.

Life

Wheaton is located just west of Chicago, so "students have the entire world of Chicago open to them, which has everything you could want in a city," and because "there is a train station right on campus," the city is extremely accessible. Making matters even better, "The [area surrounding the campus] has a ton of little stores to explore and things to do." Wheaton's "rigorous course load" means that "school work consumes a large portion of [our time]," but students still make opportunities to "do very unusual things for fun, especially in winter when it is too cold to be outside, like pool, ping pong, darts, watching *The Office*, playing piano, movies (DVD's mainly), and when weather permits, Frisbee, volleyball, football, soccer, running, relaxing in the sun, and in general just talking with each other." What they don't do is "drink, smoke, or do drugs. Period. (Except for the occasional 21st birthday, and even then they don't get smashed.)" Whatever they're doing, "Whether it's playing games on the dorm floor, going into Chicago with friends, or getting involved in campus or church groups," "Life at Wheaton revolves around community." As one student explains, "The Christian stance makes for a feeling of community that permeates almost all of the events and even the classes. We're all like one big family, and the general congeniality of the students and the ease with which we can communicate with our teachers reinforces that feeling."

Student Body

The typical Wheaton undergrad "comes from a middle-class family, a strong Christian home, and excelled in their high school and scored highly on the SAT." Students tend to be "perfectionists…everyone wants to do the 'right' thing, so people stress a lot about grades, appearance, even making sure they have the right balance in their lives." Atypical students "probably [make up] 15 percent" of the student body; they include "those who are either here for athletic reasons or because their parents made them, and they don't follow the rules as much." Two conspicuous subpopulations here are the "conservies" (students of the conservatory) and homeschoolers; "The stereotype for these students is that they are socially awkward and are always practicing their instrument (conservies) or doing homework (homeschoolers)…The conservies all have each other…they hang out at the conservatory and talk about music. The homeschoolers eventually learn how to make friends and interact with people on a daily basis," although they are initially "socially awkward."

FINANCIAL AID: 630-752-5021 • E-MAIL: ADMISSIONS@WHEATON.EDU • WEBSITE: WWW.WHEATON.EDU

THE PRINCETON REVIEW SAYS

Admissions

Very important factors considered include: Application essay, academic GPA, recommendation(s), rigor of secondary school record, standardized test scores, character/personal qualities. *Important factors considered include:* Interview, level of applicant's interest, talent/ability. *Other factors considered include:* Class rank, alumni/ae relation, extracurricular activities, first generation, geographical residence, racial/ethnic status, religious affiliation/commitment, state residency, volunteer work, SAT or ACT required; ACT with Writing component required. TOEFL required of all international applicants. High school diploma is required and GED is accepted. *Academic units recommended:* 4 English, 4 mathematics, 4 science, 3 foreign language, 4 social studies.

Financial Aid

Students should submit: FAFSA, institution's own financial aid form. The Princeton Review suggests that all financial aid forms be submitted as soon as possible after January 1. *Need-based scholarships/grants offered:* Federal Pell, SEOG, state scholarships/grants, the school's own gift aid. *Loan aid offered:* FFEL Subsidized Stafford, FFEL Unsubsidized Stafford, FFEL PLUS, Federal Perkins Applicants will be notified of awards on a rolling basis beginning 3/1. Federal Work-Study Program available. Institutional employment available. Off-campus job opportunities are excellent.

The Inside Word

Admissions at Wheaton are highly competitive. Applicants must demonstrate strong academic skills and aptitude through schoolwork and testing. The applicant pool is small enough for admissions officers to consider each candidate very closely to ensure a good match between school and student. A sincere profession of faith, along with a letter of recommendation from a pastor, Bible study leader, or church official, is an essential part of any application.

THE SCHOOL SAYS "..."

From The Admissions Office

"At Wheaton, we're commited to being a community that fearlessly pursues truth, upholds an academically rigorous curriculum, and promotes virtue. The college takes seriously its impact on society. The influence of Wheaton is seen in fields ranging from government (the former speaker of the house) to sports (two NBA coaches) to business (the CEO of John Deere) to music (Metropolitan Opera National Competition winners) to education (over 40 college presidents) to global ministry (Billy Graham). Wheaton seeks students who want to make a difference and are passionate about their Christian faith and rigorous academic pursuit.

"Fall 2008 applicants are required to submit results from the new SAT, or ACT with Writing section. Wheaton will use the highest of these scores from either test in evaluating a student's application."

SELECTIVITY

Admissions Rating	95
# of applicants	2,160
% of applicants accepted	55
% of acceptees attending	49
# accepting a place on wait list	169
% admitted from wait list	54

FRESHMAN PROFILE

Range SAT Critical Reading	630–720
Range SAT Math	610–700
Range SAT Writing	610–710
Range ACT Composite	27–31
Minimum paper TOEFL	550
Minimum computer TOEFL	213
Average HS GPA	3.73
% graduated top 10% of class	56
% graduated top 25% of class	88
% graduated top 50% of class	98

DEADLINES

Early action	
Deadline	11/1
Notification	12/31
Regular	
Deadline	1/10
Notification	4/1
Nonfall registration?	no

APPLICANTS ALSO LOOK AT
AND SOMETIMES PREFER

Taylor University
Grove City College
Baylor University
Biola University
Westmont College

AND RARELY PREFER

Gordon College
Calvin College
Cedarville University

FINANCIAL FACTS

Financial Aid Rating	77
Annual tuition	$23,730
Room and board	$7,252
Books and supplies	$768
% frosh rec. need-based scholarship or grant aid	43
% UG rec. need-based scholarship or grant aid	39
% frosh rec. non-need-based scholarship or grant aid	21
% UG rec. non-need-based scholarship or grant aid	18
% frosh rec. need-based self-help aid	50
% UG rec. need-based self-help aid	45
% frosh rec. any financial aid	65
% UG rec. any financial aid	65.5
% UG borrow to pay for school	53
Average cumulative indebtedness	$20,087

WHEATON COLLEGE (MA)

OFFICE OF ADMISSION, NORTON, MA 02766 • ADMISSIONS: 508-286-8251 • FAX: 508-286-8271

CAMPUS LIFE

Quality of Life Rating	**67**
Fire Safety Rating	**83**
Green Rating	**86**
Type of school	private
Environment	village

STUDENTS

Total undergrad enrollment	1,551
% male/female	40/60
% from out of state	65
% from public high school	63
% live on campus	93
% African American	5
% Asian	3
% Caucasian	77
% Hispanic	3
% international	3
# of countries represented	39

SURVEY SAYS . . .

Large classes
Great library
*Frats and sororities are unpopular
or nonexistent*
Lots of beer drinking
Hard liquor is popular

ACADEMICS

Academic Rating	**92**
Calendar	semester
Student/faculty ratio	10:1
Profs interesting rating	88
Profs accessible rating	87
Most common reg class size	10–19 students
Most common lab size	10–19 students

MOST POPULAR MAJORS

psychology
English language and literature
economics

STUDENTS SAY " . . . "

Academics

A "small liberal arts school trying to break through and compete with the 'small Ivies' (Williams, Amherst, Colby etc.)," Wheaton College is "a true liberal arts college: People study what they are interested in for the sake of learning it and because it fascinates them" here. The school caters to students with eclectic interests through its Foundations requirements (which require at least one course in non-Western civilization) and its Connections curriculum (which requires students to take either two sets of two related courses or one set of three related courses across academic categories), leading students to crow that "Wheaton's curriculum is based on providing students with global awareness. It focuses on trying to get students to understand the dynamics of their own personal actions alongside that of those around the world." Undergrads also love the personal attention ("You can't get lost here—there's always someone you can talk to, your own age or a professor or administrator, if you're having problems. It's a really supportive and safe environment") and the "many opportunities to apply classroom knowledge outside of the class (whether through internships, research projects, fellowships, study abroad, etc.)." Many praise the school's new "absolutely amazing" Kollett Center, which houses "peer mentors, peer tutors for every subject, the academic advising office, and internship/career/job search Filene Center," "the most useful college center on the face of the planet...because they help with you in writing resumes, finding internships, and preparing for life after college." Wheaton students also benefit from "a really active" alumni network "willing to help in any way they can."

Life

"From Monday through Wednesday, people are reserved and very focused" on the Wheaton campus. Thursday "usually starts the weekend where upperclassmen will head to the bars," while on "Friday and Saturday, most of the school will socialize by drinking at one of the on-campus houses or in groups in the dorms." Students explain that "Because there are no frats, parties are held in houses (either on or off campus) or in dorm rooms." Observes one student, "It's actually a bit pathetic that that's the best they can do." There are also "college dances, which sometimes have free beer for those over 21," but many feel that "The dances are reminiscent of high school, and usually suck except for the free beer." There are also "tons of musical and theatrical performances, club events, lectures, and other great things going on" around campus. Even so, students concede that the campus "gets a little boring at times." Hometown Norton "is very, very, very (did I say very yet?) small," the sort of place where "the biggest decision is whether you want to walk to Walgreen or CVS," so students seeking off-campus diversion must travel further. That's why "A lot of students will go into Boston or Providence for a day on the weekends. Also, there are always home games or away games on the weekends, so many students attend one or the other."

Student Body

Wheaton "is made up of reasonably familiar subgroups. We have our jocks, and our über-nerds, slackers, and artists. There is, however, a large gray area, and most people don't limit themselves to one group." The predominant vibe is "a little bit preppy with a portion of hippie," with "the popped collar and pearls set" coexisting with "plenty of free spirits... Whether they choose to wear boat-shoes or Birks, they've got a place" here. Most students "are well-balanced...academically serious, but school is not the only activity in their lives." They "seem to generally be liberal, but everyone is so apathetic toward current events that it is difficult to inspire student activism." Undergrads estimate that "35 percent of us are varsity athletes"; more than a few of the remaining 65 percent "do not like [the athletes] and feel like they get preferential treatment just because they are athletes."

FINANCIAL AID: 508-286-8232 • E-MAIL: ADMISSION@WHEATONCOLLEGE.EDU • WEBSITE: WWW.WHEATONCOLLEGE.EDU

THE PRINCETON REVIEW SAYS

Admissions

Very important factors considered include: Application essay, academic GPA, rigor of secondary school record, character/personal qualities, extracurricular activities, first generation, talent/ability. *Important factors considered include:* Class rank, recommendation(s), alumni/ae relation, interview, volunteer work, work experience. *Other factors considered include:* Standardized test scores, geographical residence, level of applicant's interest, racial/ethnic status, state residency, TOEFL required of all international applicants. High school diploma is required and GED is accepted. *Academic units recommended:* 4 English, 4 mathematics, 3 science, (2 science labs), 4 foreign language, 3 social studies, 2 history.

Financial Aid

Students should submit: FAFSA, CSS/Financial Aid PROFILE, noncustodial PROFILE, business/farm supplement, Parent and Student Federal Tax Returns and W-2s. Regular filing deadline is 2/1. The Princeton Review suggests that all financial aid forms be submitted as soon as possible after January 1. *Need-based scholarships/grants offered:* Federal Pell, SEOG, state scholarships/grants, private scholarships, the school's own gift aid. *Loan aid offered:* FFEL Subsidized Stafford, FFEL Unsubsidized Stafford, FFEL PLUS, Federal Perkins Applicants will be notified of awards on or about 4/1. Federal Work-Study Program available. Institutional employment available. Off-campus job opportunities are good.

The Inside Word

Wheaton gives applicants the option of not submitting standardized test scores. The school also invites applicants to submit optional personal academic portfolios, collections of completed schoolwork that demonstrates talents the applicant wants to highlight. All applicants should seriously consider this option; for those who do not submit test scores, an academic portfolio is practically imperative, both as an indicator of the applicant's seriousness about Wheaton and as evidence of academic excellence (evidence that standardized test scores might otherwise provide).

THE SCHOOL SAYS "..."

From The Admissions Office

"What makes for a 'best college'? Is it merely the hard-to-define notions of prestige or image? We don't think so. We think what makes college 'best' and best for you is a school that will make you a first-rate thinker and writer, a pragmatic professional in your work, and an ethical practitioner in your life. To get you to all these places, Wheaton takes advantage of its great combinations: a beautiful, secluded New England campus combined with access to Boston and Providence; a high quality, classic liberal arts and sciences curriculum combined with award-winning internship, job, and community-service programs; and a campus that respects your individuality in the context of the larger community. What's the 'best' outcome of a Wheaton education? A start on life that combines meaningful work, significant relationships, and a commitment to your local and global community. Far more than for what they've studied or for what they've gone on to do for a living, we're most proud of Wheaton graduates for who they become.

"Wheaton does not require students to submit the results of any standardized testing. The only exception is the TOEFL for students for whom English is a second language. Students who choose to submit standardized testing may use results from the historic SAT, its revised version, or from the ACT."

SELECTIVITY

Admissions Rating	93
# of applicants	3,833
% of applicants accepted	37
% of acceptees attending	30
# accepting a place on wait list	283
% admitted from wait list	6
# of early decision applicants	259
% accepted early decision	75

FRESHMAN PROFILE

Range SAT Critical Reading	580–670
Range SAT Math	560–650
Range ACT Composite	25–28
Minimum paper TOEFL	580
Minimum computer TOEFL	243
Average HS GPA	3.5
% graduated top 10% of class	44
% graduated top 25% of class	70
% graduated top 50% of class	94

DEADLINES

Early decision	
Deadline	11/1
Notification	12/15
Regular	
Deadline	1/15
Notification	4/1
Nonfall registration?	yes

APPLICANTS ALSO LOOK AT

AND OFTEN PREFER
Connecticut College
Bates College

AND SOMETIMES PREFER
Hamilton College
University of Vermont
Skidmore College

AND RARELY PREFER
Brandeis University
Clark University
Boston University

FINANCIAL FACTS

Financial Aid Rating	89
Annual tuition	$36,430
Room and board	$8,640
Required fees	$260
Books and supplies	$940
% frosh rec. need-based scholarship or grant aid	51
% UG rec. need-based scholarship or grant aid	47
% frosh rec. need-based self-help aid	53
% UG rec. need-based self-help aid	48
% frosh rec. any financial aid	70
% UG rec. any financial aid	64
% UG borrow to pay for school	58
Average cumulative indebtedness	$23,222

WHITMAN COLLEGE

345 BOYER AVENUE, WALLA WALLA, WA 99362-2083 • ADMISSIONS: 509-527-5176 • FAX: 509-527-4967

STUDENTS SAY ". . ."

Academics

If learning can be both rigorous and laid-back at the same time, it happens at Whitman College in Walla Walla, Washington. The "challenging" academics here are coupled with a "relaxed attitude" in order to give students "the best education possible without sacrificing all the fun one expects of college." Populated mainly by "intelligent, ambitious liberals with far-reaching goals," this somewhat idealistic school seeks to build critical thinking skills through "an earnest discourse about 'life, the universe, and everything.'" So that no one starts off with a blank slate, all first-year students are required to take a course referred to as "Core" which offers a survey of Western thought, starting with The Odyssey, working through Socrates, Plato, Augustine, up through Marx, Voltaire, and other thinkers who shaped modern thought. Distribution requirements ensure that all students get a breadth of courses, and a lack of TA's ensures that they get all the attention they need. Although there's always a dud or two in the mix, professors are "genuinely brilliant and interesting people" and "love to spend time with students outside of class," whether it be for academic help or just conversation. "It is not uncommon to have potlucks, classes, or movie night over at your professor's house with your class," says one student.

On the administrative side of things, bureaucracy and red tape are kept to a minimum in this chill environment through "effortless use of the 'system,'" and the administration gets raves all around for its devotion to "maintaining quality student life," which is something of a rarity. "I have never heard of ANY college being as supportive as this place has been to me in just the past two years," says a student. "Whitman's president gave me a ride to campus one semester after I met him at the airport," says another. As one can imagine, all these things come together to form a student body that's "happy, well-balanced, and well-cared-for."

Life

Most people stay on campus for their fun, "especially first-years," and throughout this "bubble" the "sense of closeness and comradeship is very evident through attendance at student-run concerts, art shows, etc." Everything is within ten minutes' walking distance. Academics take precedence for almost everyone, but "most students find time to party on the weekends" at the frats, due to a "lenient and fair" alcohol policy. Thanks to the Campus Activities Board, "there's almost always something fun going on, whether or not a person chooses to drink," such as Drive-In Movie Night and Casino Night. With "four beautiful seasons," outdoor activities are also very popular, thanks to "a great gear rental program that gets people outside hiking, biking, kayaking, and rock climbing," and "Frisbees are everywhere when it's warm." In fact, there's so much going on that "if someone says they are bored, students laugh and wish they could relate."

Student Body

It's a sociable bunch at Whitman, where most students "are interested in trying new things and meeting new people" and "everyone seems to have a weird interest or talent or passion." The quirky Whitties "usually have a strong opinion about SOMETHING," and one freshman refers to her classmates as ""cool nerds." As with many northwestern schools, diversity here is pretty low, but the school at least puts up a fight for getting more than the typical "mid- to upper-class and white" contingent. Everyone here is pretty outdoorsy and environmentally aware ("to the point where you almost feel guilty for printing an assignment"), and leans far enough to the left to tip over; there's also not much of a religious quotient to the student body, and those that are find themselves "subtly looked down upon."

FINANCIAL AID: 509-527-5178 • E-MAIL: ADMISSION@WHITMAN.EDU • WEBSITE: WWW.WHITMAN.EDU

THE PRINCETON REVIEW SAYS

Admissions

Very important factors considered include: Rigor of secondary school record, Application essay, academic GPA, application essay, character/personal qualities. *Important factors considered include:* Standardized test scores, extracurricular activities, racial/ethnic status, talent/ability. *Other factors considered include:* Alumni/ae relation, first generation, geographical residence, interview, volunteer work, work experience. SAT or ACT required; ACT with Writing component required. TOEFL required of all international applicants. High school diploma is required and GED is accepted. *Academic units recommended:* 4 English, 4 mathematics, 3 science, (2 science labs), 2 foreign language, 2 social studies, 2 history, 1 arts.

Financial Aid

Students should submit: FAFSA, CSS/Financial Aid PROFILE. Regular filing deadline is 2/1. The Princeton Review suggests that all financial aid forms be submitted as soon as possible after January 1. *Need-based scholarships/grants offered:* Federal Pell, SEOG, state scholarships/grants, private scholarships, the school's own gift aid. *Loan aid offered:* FFEL Subsidized Stafford, FFEL Unsubsidized Stafford, FFEL PLUS, Federal Perkins, state loans, Alternative student loans. Applicants will be notified of awards after each round of admission notification. Federal Work-Study Program available. Institutional employment available.

The Inside Word

Whitman's Admissions Committee is to be applauded; any admissions process that emphasizes essays and extracurriculars over the SAT has truly gotten it right. The college cares much more about who you are and what you have to offer if you enroll than it does about what your numbers will do for the freshman academic profile. Whitman is a mega-sleeper. Educators all over the country know it as an excellent institution, and the college's alums support it at one of the highest rates of giving at any college in the nation. Student seeking a top-quality liberal arts college owe it to themselves to take a look.

THE SCHOOL SAYS ". . ."

From The Admissions Office

"Whitman is a place that encourages you to explore past the boundaries of disciplines because learning and living don't always fall neatly into tidy little compartments. Many students choose Whitman specifically because they're interested in a particular career such as business or engineering but want the well-rounded preparation that only a liberal arts education provides. Signatures of Whitman include Cove (first-year program), senior exams, semester in the West, and Fellowships.

"Applicants for Fall 2009 are required to take the new SAT or ACT with Writing section. For students who take the SAT or ACT more than once, Whitman will combine the best sub scores."

SELECTIVITY

Admissions Rating	95
# of applicants	2,892
% of applicants accepted	48
% of acceptees attending	29
# accepting a place on wait list	116
% admitted from wait list	19
# of early decision applicants	160
% accepted early decision	73

FRESHMAN PROFILE

Range SAT Critical Reading	620–730
Range SAT Math	620–700
Range SAT Writing	610–700
Range ACT Composite	27–32
Minimum paper TOEFL	560
Minimum computer TOEFL	220
Average HS GPA	3.77
% graduated top 10% of class	61
% graduated top 25% of class	91
% graduated top 50% of class	99

DEADLINES

Early decision	
Deadline	11/15
Notification	12/21
Regular	
Priority	11/15
Deadline	1/15
Notification	4/1
Nonfall registration?	yes

APPLICANTS ALSO LOOK AT

AND OFTEN PREFER
Pomona College
Carleton College
Stanford University

AND SOMETIMES PREFER
Macalester College
Colorado College

AND RARELY PREFER
Lewis & Clark College
University of Puget Sound

FINANCIAL FACTS

Financial Aid Rating	88
Annual tuition	$32,670
Room and board	$8,310
Required fees	$310
Books and supplies	$1,400
% frosh rec. need-based scholarship or grant aid	48
% UG rec. need-based scholarship or grant aid	44
% frosh rec. non-need-based scholarship or grant aid	6
% UG rec. non-need-based scholarship or grant aid	4
% frosh rec. need-based self-help aid	43
% UG rec. need-based self-help aid	44
% frosh rec. any financial aid	70
% UG rec. any financial aid	74
% UG borrow to pay for school	53
Average cumulative indebtedness	$15,811

WHITTIER COLLEGE

13406 PHILADELPHIA STREET, PO BOX 634, WHITTIER, CA 90608 • ADMISSIONS: 562-907-4238 • FAX: 562-907-4870

CAMPUS LIFE

Quality of Life Rating	69
Fire Safety Rating	83
Green Rating	83
Type of school	private
Environment	city

STUDENTS

Total undergrad enrollment	1,257
% male/female	45/55
% from out of state	27
% live on campus	60
% in (# of) fraternities	14 (4)
% in (# of) sororities	20 (5)
% African American	3
% Asian	8
% Caucasian	46
% Hispanic	30
% Native American	1
% international	2
# of countries represented	17

SURVEY SAYS . . .

Large classes
Great library
Lots of beer drinking
Hard liquor is popular
(Almost) everyone smokes

ACADEMICS

Academic Rating	84
Calendar	4/1/4
Student/faculty ratio	13:1
Profs interesting rating	87
Profs accessible rating	92
Most common reg class size	10–19 students
Most common lab size	10–19 students

MOST POPULAR MAJORS

business/commerce
biology/biological sciences
psychology

STUDENTS SAY "..."

Academics

Whittier College in California provides the quintessential liberal arts education by placing a strong focus on writing and maintaining a wide breadth and depth of knowledge within the humanities. With just 1,300 students enrolled, Whittier offers a small school experience, meaning "there aren't always a ton of choices, but the sense of community and the personal attention mostly makes up for it." "The academic experience all depends on how much work you put in," says a student, and the potential for greatness is there for those who want it. However, while everyone agrees that the academics are solid as a rock, many do express dissatisfaction with the overall quality of life, citing ancient facilities, difficulty getting into desired classes, and poor housing and meal plan options as some of the sore spots.

Higher up, students say that the school's administration "leaves much to be desired," alluding to a lack of communication between different divisions ("trying to pay tuition and get financial aid to work out is like chewing on broken glass") and uneven distribution of resources between different areas of campus life. However, one would be hard pressed to find better professors. They're here "because they love to teach and it shows"; all do most of the teaching themselves rather than "foisting it off onto a TA," which means that teachers and students have the opportunity to be peers and "defy typical 'college classroom' norms." Most classes are very small and are structured around discussion rather than straight lectures, and the instructors "keep the busywork to a minimum, basing your grade on a handful of papers, a midterm, and a final." "Really, the professors MAKE Whittier College," sums up a senior.

Life

The location of the campus is favorable due to the ease with which one is able to "travel to the posh LA scene, the beach, or to relax in Orange County." Uptown Whittier isn't really a college town, but it does offer a "number of different restaurants," as well as a movie theater, street fairs, and coffee shops. The school itself has only one dining hall, and the food there "is awful and open only limited hours, though this was a temporary situation, and new dining facilities are expected to open for fall 2008." The college provides "a variety of dances, movie nights, athletic events, theatrical events, and guest entertainers/speakers to keep students moderately occupied," and students organizations and clubs help pass the rest of the time. "Even in January, there are days when we can lay out and sunbathe outside the dorms," says a junior. Though a lot of in-staters choose to go home on weekends, there is a "large chunk" of the school population involved in societies (Whittier's version of sororities or fraternities), and after class, "almost everyone is constantly in party mode." Many students "get the impression that people become bored easily here," and resort to drinking and marijuana, both of which are very prevalent at Whittier.

Student Body

Diversity is the name of the game at Whittier, and nearly a third of the campus is Hispanic, often the first generation in their family to attend college. International students are also well-represented, as are those hailing from Hawaii. Such a mixed pot makes for a lot of melting, and most students don't have any problems finding a niche, choosing to "stay with their clubs, majors, sports teams, and other such groupings," though mingling between defined groups is somewhat rare. Many students are here because of financial aid or scholarship, which makes some sad that their classmates "look forward to a night out at the nearby Radisson hotel for 'thirsty Thursdays' rather than an awesome discussion in their $800-a-day, ten student class." It's a small campus, so by the time you're a senior, "you know pretty much everyone on campus," which most think is "a fabulous thing."

FINANCIAL AID: 562-907-4285 • E-MAIL: ADMISSION@WHITTIER.EDU • WEBSITE: WWW.WHITTIER.EDU

THE PRINCETON REVIEW SAYS

Admissions

Very important factors considered include: Application essay, rigor of secondary school record. *Important factors considered include:* Academic GPA, recommendation(s), standardized test scores, character/personal qualities, extracurricular activities, interview, talent/ability, volunteer work. *Other factors considered include:* Class rank, alumni/ae relation, first generation, geographical residence, racial/ethnic status, state residency, work experience. SAT or ACT required; ACT with Writing component required. TOEFL required of all international applicants. High school diploma is required and GED is accepted. *Academic units required:* 3 English, 2 mathematics, 1 science, (1 science labs), 2 foreign language, 1 social studies. *Academic units recommended:* 4 English, 3 mathematics, 2 science, 3 foreign language, 2 social studies.

Financial Aid

Students should submit: FAFSA, CSS/Financial Aid PROFILE Regular filing deadline is 6/30. The Princeton Review suggests that all financial aid forms be submitted as soon as possible after January 1. *Need-based scholarships/grants offered:* Federal Pell, SEOG, state scholarships/grants, private scholarships, the school's own gift aid. *Loan aid offered:* Direct PLUS, FFEL Subsidized Stafford, FFEL Unsubsidized Stafford, FFEL PLUS, Federal Perkins, Alternative Financing Loans. Applicants will be notified of awards on a rolling basis beginning 2/15. Federal Work-Study Program available. Off-campus job opportunities are good.

The Inside Word

While the relatively high admissions rate for a private college may indicate otherwise, the Admissions Committee at Whittier subjects each candidate to very close scrutiny and their interest in making good solid matches between candidates and the college is paramount. If Whittier is high on your list, make sure you put forth a serious effort to demonstrate what you want out of the college and what you'll bring to the table in return.

THE SCHOOL SAYS "..."

From The Admissions Office

"Faculty and students at Whittier share a love of learning and delight in the life of the mind. They join in understanding the value of the intellectual quest, the use of reason, and a respect for values. They seek knowledge of their own culture and the informed appreciation of other traditions, and they explore the interrelatedness of knowledge and the connections among disciplines. An extraordinary community emerges from teachers and students representing a variety of academic pursuits, individuals who have come together at Whittier in the belief that study within the liberal arts forms the best foundation for rewarding endeavor throughout a lifetime.

"Freshman applicants for Fall 2008 must take the new SAT (or the ACT with the Writing component). In addition, students may submit scores from the old SAT (before March 2005) or ACT, and we will use their best scores from either test."

SELECTIVITY

Admissions Rating	84
# of applicants	2,196
% of applicants accepted	67
% of acceptees attending	20

FRESHMAN PROFILE

Range SAT Critical Reading	480–600
Range SAT Math	480–602
Range SAT Writing	480–590
Range ACT Composite	20–27
Minimum paper TOEFL	550
Minimum computer TOEFL	230
Average HS GPA	3.11
% graduated top 10% of class	34
% graduated top 25% of class	45
% graduated top 50% of class	89

DEADLINES

Early action	
Deadline	12/1
Notification	12/30
Regular	
Priority	2/1
Notification	rolling
Nonfall registration?	yes

APPLICANTS ALSO LOOK AT

AND OFTEN PREFER
University of Redlands
Occidental College

AND SOMETIMES PREFER
Pitzer College
Loyola Marymount University

AND RARELY PREFER
Claremont McKenna College
Chapman University

FINANCIAL FACTS

Financial Aid Rating	84
Annual tuition	$31,950
Room and board	$9,050
Required fees	$520
Books and supplies	$1,566
% frosh rec. need-based scholarship or grant aid	54
% UG rec. need-based scholarship or grant aid	55
% frosh rec. non-need-based scholarship or grant aid	39
% UG rec. non-need-based scholarship or grant aid	45
% frosh rec. need-based self-help aid	59
% UG rec. need-based self-help aid	64
% frosh rec. any financial aid	92
% UG rec. any financial aid	89
% UG borrow to pay for school	73
Average cumulative indebtedness	$31,179

WILLAMETTE UNIVERSITY

900 STATE STREET, SALEM, OR 97301 • ADMISSIONS: 503-370-6303 • FAX: 503-375-5363

STUDENTS SAY ". . ."

Academics

Willamette University is an "academically rigorous," intimate, and "seriously gorgeous" liberal arts school in Oregon. "Outstanding" academic programs include the sciences, a "great focus" on the arts, a popular Japanese Studies Program, and "a highly acclaimed political science program." Across the board, undergrads report "a lot of school work" which includes a first-year seminar and a senior project. On the plus side, "Small class sizes allow lots of discussion and personal attention" and undergraduate research opportunities allow students to work with faculty members on the kinds of projects reserved for grad students at most other schools. Willamette is also "very accommodating for double majors." Professors are, "for the most part, super interesting and exciting." "The really good professors make every single class really enjoyable," are "very involved with students' lives," and are "very responsive to the needs of students." A politics major beams: "I'm only a freshman and I've already had dinner at a professor's house, just like the 'spiel' said." Administrators "seem to slack off in a lot of ways" but, ultimately, they "will help you out with whatever you'd like to pursue." "If you want to start something on campus, there is usually a way."

Life

"The overall ambience" at Willamette is "relaxed and inviting." Students here describe their school as "an oasis of enlightenment" surrounded by a "sketchy" "cultural wasteland" (Salem, Oregon). Intercollegiate and intramural sports are hugely popular here, and the "incredibly strong" track and cross-country programs are especially noteworthy. Quite often "You'll see students reading or relaxing on campus by the stream, or in the [quad]." "Some of the most fun I have is just hanging out with people at random places on campus," adds a sophomore. Willamette does, however, "gear up every now and again for campus activities like our music festival or for a sit-in," explains an anthropology major. While "There are several events that are sponsored by Greeks," frats don't dominate. "If you're in one and know people in them, they're great. If you aren't, then you don't really care." A junior takes a more concerned position: "One of the biggest drawbacks to our school is that the party scene is not very good. The administration is very restrictive with Greek parties, off-campus parties, and other sorts of parties that students try to have." By all accounts, however, "access to outdoor activities" is fantastic. Willamette is "two hours from the coast" and "two hours from the mountains." Also, "it's only a 45-minute drive over to Portland" and "a ton of cultural stuff."

Student Body

Undergrads report "a lot of rich kids" at Willamette, and portray "the typical student" as "White," suburban, and "from the Northwest, most likely Oregon." Many students, however, receive "sweet" financial aid packages, and an excellent scholarship program "attracts students from a huge variety of backgrounds." Still, "There are not that many ethnic minorities." Asian students make up the largest minority here, and a fair number hail from Japan "as Willamette has a program with the Tokyo International University." Students at Willamette rate their "interesting, intelligent, genuine, [and] community-oriented" peers as "pretty hard workers" and say "There's a social group for almost everyone—jocks, preps, partiers, nerds; you name it." There are also "outdoorsy" types and "a lot of musicians" here. Conflict between groups is very minimal. "Everyone is accepting . . . so it's not intimidating to meet random people." Politically, Willamette is "extremely liberal." There are plenty of "politically left-wing people who love granola and Howard Dean," though, interestingly, few "real hippies."

WILLAMETTE UNIVERSITY

FINANCIAL AID: 503-370-6273 • E-MAIL: LIBARTS@WILLAMETTE.EDU • WEBSITE: WWW.WILLAMETTE.EDU

THE PRINCETON REVIEW SAYS

Admissions

Very important factors considered include: Class rank, application essay, academic GPA, rigor of secondary school record, standardized test scores. *Important factors considered include:* Recommendation(s), alumni/ae relation, character/personal qualities, interview. *Other factors considered include:* Extracurricular activities, first generation, geographical residence, racial/ethnic status, talent/ability, volunteer work, work experience. SAT or ACT required; ACT with Writing component required. TOEFL required of all international applicants. High school diploma is required and GED is accepted. *Academic units recommended:* 4 English, 4 mathematics, 3 science, (3 science labs), 3 foreign language, 1 social studies, 2 history.

Financial Aid

Students should submit: FAFSA, CSS/Financial Aid PROFILE. CSS PROFILE only required for Early Action applicants (to be filed by 12/01). Regular filing deadline is 2/1. The Princeton Review suggests that all financial aid forms be submitted as soon as possible after January 1. *Need-based scholarships/grants offered:* Federal Pell, SEOG, state scholarships/grants, private scholarships, the school's own gift aid. *Loan aid offered:* FFEL Subsidized Stafford, FFEL Unsubsidized Stafford, FFEL PLUS, Federal Perkins, state loans, Private loans. Applicants will be notified of awards on or about 4/1. Federal Work-Study Program available. Institutional employment available. Off-campus job opportunities are good.

The Inside Word

Willamette is a bit of safety school for the Northwest. Although almost 50 percent of the students here graduated in the top 10 percent of their high school classes, test scores are within range for a lot of applicants. The admissions process is pretty standard for a small liberal arts college. Extracurriculars, recommendations, and essays are helpful but, more than likely, your grades will determine your fate.

THE SCHOOL SAYS "..."

From The Admissions Office

"The interactions between great teachers and great students are at the heart of the Willamette University experience. Considering that 8 of the past 16 Oregon Professors of the Year (selected by the Council for Advancement and Support of Education) come from our campus, it is no surprise that student surveys overwhelmingly praise 'the quality of education' and 'interactions with faculty' as satisfying attributes of the Willamette experience. To further enhance the strength of the faculty and the opportunities for student-faculty interaction, Willamette is adding 25 new faculty positions over the next 5 years.

"The accomplishments of Willamette graduates help put the quality of the education in perspective. In the past decade, nearly 90 of our students have been awarded competitive, national scholarships and fellowships, including Trumans, Fulbrights, Goldwaters and Watsons. With 20 Peace Corps volunteers currently serving, Willamette ranks in the top 10 for small colleges and universities with the most alumni volunteers.

Recent "on-campus developments include the opening of Kaneko Commons, the first of four residential commons that will transform campus living organizations. Kaneko, much anticipated by the Campus Sustainability Council, was our first LEED-certified 'green' building."

SELECTIVITY

Admissions Rating	90
# of applicants	2,983
% of applicants accepted	77
% of acceptees attending	19
# accepting a place on wait list	136
% admitted from wait list	9

FRESHMAN PROFILE

Range SAT Critical Reading	570–690
Range SAT Math	550–660
Range SAT Writing	550–660
Range ACT Composite	25–29
Minimum paper TOEFL	550
Minimum computer TOEFL	213
Average HS GPA	3.68
% graduated top 10% of class	47
% graduated top 25% of class	76
% graduated top 50% of class	96

DEADLINES

Early action	
Deadline	12/1
Notification	1/15
Regular	
Priority	2/1
Notification	4/1
Nonfall registration?	yes

APPLICANTS ALSO LOOK AT

AND OFTEN PREFER
Whitman College

AND SOMETIMES PREFER
Occidental College
Lewis & Clark College
University of Puget Sound
University of Washington
Santa Clara University
Colorado College

AND RARELY PREFER
University of Oregon

FINANCIAL FACTS

Financial Aid Rating	84
Annual tuition	$28,416
Room and board	$7,000
Required fees	$170
Books and supplies	$800
% frosh rec. need-based scholarship or grant aid	66
% UG rec. need-based scholarship or grant aid	62
% frosh rec. non-need-based scholarship or grant aid	27
% UG rec. non-need-based scholarship or grant aid	15
% frosh rec. need-based self-help aid	57
% UG rec. need-based self-help aid	56
% frosh rec. any financial aid	92
% UG rec. any financial aid	92
% UG borrow to pay for school	79
Average cumulative indebtedness	$18,756

WILLIAM JEWELL COLLEGE

500 COLLEGE HILL, LIBERTY, MO 64068 • ADMISSIONS: 816-415-7511 • FAX: 816-415-5040 • 888-2-JEWELL

CAMPUS LIFE

Quality of Life Rating	**89**
Fire Safety Rating	**79**
Green Rating	**65**
Type of school	private
Environment	town

STUDENTS

Total undergrad enrollment	1,329
% male/female	40/60
% from out of state	29
% live on campus	62
% in (# of) fraternities	31 (4)
% in (# of) sororities	34 (4)
% African American	4
% Asian	1
% Caucasian	88
% Hispanic	3
% Native American	2
# of countries represented	2

SURVEY SAYS . . .

No one cheats
Students are friendly
*Students get along with
local community*
Students love Liberty, MO
Great off-campus food
*Frats and sororities dominate
social scene*
Very little drug use

ACADEMICS

Academic Rating	**88**
Calendar	semester
Student/faculty ratio	11:1
Profs interesting rating	90
Profs accessible rating	86
Most common reg class size	fewer than 10 students
Most common lab size	10–19 students

MOST POPULAR MAJORS

psychology
nursing/registered nurse
(RN, ASN, BSN, MSN)
business/commerce

STUDENTS SAY ". . ."

Academics

William Jewell College is a historically Baptist bastion of the liberal arts and sciences with a solidly pre-professional bent that offers "strong academics, a personal atmosphere, and a close-knit community." "I love the one-on-one interaction with professors," beams a business major. "I love the small class sizes." Nursing, music, and education are among the notable programs here. A broad core curriculum includes lots of hands-on learning. The "extremely intense" Oxbridge Honors Program subjects students to English tutorial-style instruction and a year of study in England. There are study abroad opportunities in over 30 other places far-flung as well. Some students call the professors "hit or miss." Others say the faculty is "a generally gifted bunch." "The professors are invested in their students' success and are always there to help," says an accounting major. Some students tell us that management "has its moments of idiocy." "The administration is completely ignorant of what's going on and live in their self-made marketing paradise," charges a philosophy major. "The financial aid office is hell," adds an international relations major. Other students don't see the problem. "The administration is always asking for your opinion," notes a nursing major. "The president is accessible and visible on campus, calling students by name on the Quad."

Life

"Jewell's technology is way behind" and the Internet connection is reportedly "horrendous." "The cafeteria is awful" and "The school isn't known for fancy dorm rooms," either. "The actual college life is wonderful," though. "Everyone here is involved in a lot of activities." "The Greek system is our greatest strength," says a proud frat member. "Going Greek on this campus really helps a first-year get into college life in a healthy, safe way." Independent students aren't as thrilled by the frat scene and mention that relations between Greeks and everyone else is "a tense, frustrating thing." Whatever the case, the fraternities and sororities largely dominate social life, and William Jewell is "not a good place to go if you want to have a social life but don't want to be Greek." Also, unlike at other schools, the Greeks here don't really party on the weekends, or any other time. In fact, "there usually aren't parties" at all. "It is evident that William Jewell is a religious school," imparts a senior. "The worst thing you can find on our campus is a can of beer." "In this town, you have to have a fake ID to be able to get alcohol," advises a junior. Students frequently head to nearby Kansas City to shop and occasionally hit the bars and dance clubs. Also, the nationally recognized Harriman-Jewell Series arranges student tickets to a sweeping and really amazing array of performing arts events to Kansas City.

Student Body

"There are days when I would like to be somewhere else because of the lack of diversity," ponders a senior. "The school is taking drastic steps to bring in minorities," swears a sophomore. In the meantime, declares one student, "it is exhausting hearing about all the ways that Jewell is not diverse and all the ways Jewell is trying to become diverse." Jewell's population is largely "from the Midwest" and "middleclass" (though some students are certainly "well to do"). They are mostly "studious" "hard workers who have an interest in their education." "There are very few atypical students" but, at the same time, "there are a lot of odd kids here." People of all types "all are welcomed and fit in." "The social setup is no different than high school. There are the preppy kids, the jocks, the drama freaks, the band geeks, nerds, punks, etc.," observes a senior. "The only real difference is that they all get along and work together much better at college." You'll find some secular liberals here but the majority of Jewell's students range from "Christian and conservative" to "moderately religious Christian."

FINANCIAL AID: 888-2-JEWELL • E-MAIL: ADMISSION@WILLIAM.JEWELL.EDU • WEBSITE: WWW.JEWELL.EDU

THE PRINCETON REVIEW SAYS

Admissions

Very important factors considered include: Rigor of secondary school record. *Important factors considered include:* Class rank, academic GPA, recommendation(s), standardized test scores. *Other factors considered include:* Application essay, alumni/ae relation, character/personal qualities, extracurricular activities, first generation, talent/ability, volunteer work, work experience. SAT or ACT required; ACT with Writing component recommended. High school diploma is required and GED is accepted. *Academic units required:* 4 English, 3 mathematics, 3 science, (1 science labs), 2 foreign language, 3 social studies. *Academic units recommended:* 4 English, 4 mathematics, 3 science, (1 science labs), 3 foreign language, 3 social studies, 2 academic electives.

Financial Aid

Students should submit: FAFSA. The Princeton Review suggests that all financial aid forms be submitted as soon as possible after January 1. *Need-based scholarships/grants offered:* Federal Pell, SEOG, state scholarships/grants, the school's own gift aid. *Loan aid offered:* FFEL Subsidized Stafford, FFEL Unsubsidized Stafford, FFEL PLUS, Federal Perkins, Federal Nursing, Non-Federal Private Loans. Applicants will be notified of awards on a rolling basis beginning 2/15. Federal Work-Study Program available. Institutional employment available. Off-campus job opportunities are excellent.

The Inside Word

Admission to William Jewell requires the usual suspects: solid grades and test scores. The college is competitive, but admission is not out of reach for the average student. Once admitted, undergrads benefit from William Jewell's leading efforts in experiential learning.

THE SCHOOL SAYS "..."

From The Admissions Office

"'Founded in 1849, William Jewell College continues to earn a solid reputation as one of mid-America's most consistently honored and academically challenging private colleges. With its academic culture and focus on student achievement, the college promises students an outstanding liberal arts education that cultivates leadership, service, and spiritual growth within a community inspired by Christian ideals and committed to open, rigorous intellectual pursuits.

"William Jewell students consistently earn high-profile national recognition. The college's Debate Team captured the National Parliamentary Tournament of Excellence championship in 2007, defeating top-seeded University of California-Berkeley to win the national team title. In 2006 and 2007, the college claimed a Fulbright Scholar, a Goldwater Scholar, two Rhodes Scholar national finalists, a Truman Scholar, a National Institute of Health Fellow, a George J. Mitchell Scholarship, a Council of Independent Colleges American Graduate Fellowship finalist and a Point Foundation Scholar.

"Distinctive programs are the hallmark of the William Jewell experience. The internationally recognized Oxbridge Honors Program combines British tutorial methods of instruction with opportunities for a year of study in Oxford or Cambridge. The new Applied Critical Thought and Inquiry major (ACT-In) allows most students to graduate with a second major by completing the liberal arts core plus three applied learning experiences. Jewell's new Nonprofit Leadership major is one of only 13 undergraduate programs nationwide. The Harriman-Jewell Series is considered the Midwest's premier presenting program in the performing arts. The Pryor Leadership Studies Program includes course work, community service projects and internships that help students enhance their leadership skills in a variety of settings.

"Jewell students enjoy all the amenities of a small-town campus setting with big-city access. Just 20 minutes from downtown Kansas City, the 200-acre campus is perched above the historic town of Liberty among the rolling hills of western Missouri. Enrollment stands at approximately 1,200 full-time students."

SELECTIVITY

Admissions Rating	87
# of applicants	990
% of applicants accepted	92
% of acceptees attending	32

FRESHMAN PROFILE

Range SAT Critical Reading	530–650
Range SAT Math	500–650
Range ACT Composite	22–28
Average HS GPA	3.62
% graduated top 10% of class	28
% graduated top 25% of class	62
% graduated top 50% of class	88

DEADLINES

Regular	
Priority	12/1
Deadline	8/15
Notification	rolling
Nonfall registration?	yes

FINANCIAL FACTS

Financial Aid Rating	81
Annual tuition	$23,000
Room and board	$6,130
Required fees	$300
Books and supplies	$1,000
% frosh rec. need-based scholarship or grant aid	72
% UG rec. need-based scholarship or grant aid	66
% frosh rec. need-based self-help aid	45
% UG rec. need-based self-help aid	47
% frosh rec. athletic scholarships	11
% UG rec. athletic scholarships	12
% frosh rec. any financial aid	99
% UG rec. any financial aid	98
% UG borrow to pay for school	71
Average cumulative indebtedness	$24,240

WILLIAMS COLLEGE

33 STETSON COURT, WILLIAMSTOWN, MA 01267 • ADMISSIONS: 413-597-2211 • FAX: 413-597-4052

CAMPUS LIFE

Quality of Life Rating	91
Fire Safety Rating	60*
Green Rating	60*
Type of school	private
Environment	village

STUDENTS

Total undergrad enrollment	1,962
% male/female	50/50
% from out of state	86
% from public high school	58
% live on campus	93
% African American	10
% Asian	11
% Caucasian	64
% Hispanic	9
% international	7
# of countries represented	61

SURVEY SAYS . . .

Lab facilities are great
Campus feels safe
Everyone loves the Ephs
Frats and sororities are unpopular
or nonexistent
Lots of beer drinking

ACADEMICS

Academic Rating	98
Calendar	4/1/4
Student/faculty ratio	7:1
Profs interesting rating	94
Profs accessible rating	99
Most common reg class size	fewer than 10 students
Most common lab size	10–19 students

MOST POPULAR MAJORS

economics
visual and performing arts
English language and literature/
letters

STUDENTS SAY "..."

Academics

Williams College is a small bastion of the liberal arts "with a fantastic academic reputation." Administrators sometimes "ignore student consensus in their misguided efforts to improve campus life" but they are "incredibly compassionate and accessible" and red tape is virtually unheard of. Financial aid is outrageous. Absolute, "full-ride" assistance with no loans is available to any student who needs it. "Williams students tend to spend a lot of time complaining about how much work they have" but they say the academic experience is "absolutely incomparable." Classes are "small" and "intense." "The facilities are absolutely top notch in almost everything." Research opportunities are plentiful. A one-month January term offers study abroad programs and a host of short pass/fail courses that are "a college student's dream come true." "The hard science departments are incredible." Economics, art history, and English are equally outstanding. Despite the occasional professor "who should not even be teaching at the high school level," the faculty at Williams is one of the best. Most professors "jump at every opportunity to help you love their subject." "They're here because they want to interact with undergrads." "If you complain about a Williams education then you would complain about education anywhere," wagers an economics major.

Life

Students at Williams enjoy a "stunning campus." "The Berkshire mountains are in the background every day as you walk to class" and opportunities for outdoor activity are numerous. The location is in "the boonies," though, and the surrounding "one-horse college town" is "quaint" at best. "There is no nearby place to buy necessities that is not ridiculously overpriced." Student life happens almost exclusively on campus. Dorm rooms are "large" and "well above par" but the housing system is "very weird." While some students like it, there is a general consensus that its creators "should be slapped and sent back to Amherst." Entertainment options include "lots of" performances, plays, and lectures. Some students are "obsessed with a capella groups." Intramurals are popular, especially broomball ("a sacred tradition involving a hockey rink, sneakers, a rubber ball, and paddles"). Intercollegiate sports are "a huge part of the social scene." For many students, the various varsity teams "are the basic social blocks at Williams." "Everyone for the most part gets along, but the sports teams seem to band together," expplains a sophomore. Booze-laden parties" "and general disorder on weekends" are common. "A lot of people spend their lives between homework and practice and then just get completely smashed on weekends." Nothing gets out of hand, though. "We know how to unwind without being stupid," says a sophomore.

Student Body

The student population at Williams is not the most humble. They describe themselves as "interesting and beautiful" "geniuses of varying interests." They're "quirky, passionate, zany, and fun." They're "athletically awesome." They're "freakishly unique" and at the same time "cookie-cutter amazing." Ethnic diversity is stellar and you'll find all kinds of different students here including "the goth students," "nerdier students," "a ladle of environmentally conscious pseudo-vegetarians," and a few "west coast hippies." However, "a typical student looks like a rich white kid" who grew up "playing field hockey just outside Boston" and spends summers "vacationing on the Cape." Sporty students abound. "There definitely is segregation between the artsy kids and the athlete types but there is also a significant amount of crossover." "Williams is a place where normal social labels tend not to apply," report a junior. "Everyone here got in for a reason. So that football player in your theater class has amazing insight on Chekhov and that outspoken environmental activist also specializes in improv comedy."

FINANCIAL AID: 413-597-4181 • E-MAIL: ADMISSION@WILLIAMS.EDU • WEBSITE: WWW.WILLIAMS.EDU

THE PRINCETON REVIEW SAYS

Admissions

Very important factors considered include: Application essay, academic GPA, recommendation(s), rigor of secondary school record, standardized test scores. *Important factors considered include:* Class rank, extracurricular activities, talent/ability. *Other factors considered include:* Alumni/ae relation, character/personal qualities, first generation, racial/ethnic status, volunteer work, work experience. SAT or ACT required; SAT and SAT Subject Tests or ACT required; ACT with Writing component required. High school diploma or equivalent is not required. *Academic units recommended:* 4 English, 4 mathematics, 3 science, (3 science labs), 4 foreign language, 3 social studies.

Financial Aid

Students should submit: FAFSA, CSS/Financial Aid PROFILE, noncustodial PROFILE, business/farm supplement, Parent and Student federal taxes and W-2s. Regular filing deadline is 2/1. The Princeton Review suggests that all financial aid forms be submitted as soon as possible after January 1. *Need-based scholarships/grants offered:* Federal Pell, SEOG, state scholarships/grants, private scholarships, the school's own gift aid. *Loan aid offered:* Direct Subsidized Stafford, Direct Unsubsidized Stafford, Direct PLUS, Federal Perkins, college/university loans from institutional funds. Applicants will be notified of awards on or about 4/1. Federal Work-Study Program available. Institutional employment available.

The Inside Word

As is typical of highly selective colleges, at Williams high grades and test scores work more as qualifiers than to determine admissibility. Beyond a strong record of achievement, evidence of intellectual curiosity, noteworthy non-academic talents, and a noncollege family background are some aspects of a candidate's application that might make for an offer of admission. But there are no guarantees—the evaluation process here is rigorous. The Admissions Committee (the entire Admissions Staff) discusses each candidate in comparison to the entire applicant pool. The pool is divided alphabetically for individual reading; after weak candidates are eliminated, those who remain undergo additional evaluations by different members of the staff. Admission decisions must be confirmed by the agreement of a plurality of the committee. Such close scrutiny demands a well-prepared candidate and application.

THE SCHOOL SAYS "..."

From The Admissions Office

"Special course offerings at Williams include Oxford-style tutorials, where students (in teams of two) research and defend ideas, engaging in weekly debate with a faculty tutor. Annually 30 Williams students devote a full year to the tutorial method of study at Oxford; half of Williams students pursue overseas education. Four weeks of Winter Study each January provide time for individualized projects, research, and novel fields of study. Students compete in 32 Division III athletic teams, perform in 25 musical groups, stage 10 theatrical productions, and volunteer in 30 service organizations. The college receives several million dollars annually for undergraduate science research and equipment. The town offers two distinguished art museums, and 2,200 forest acres—complete with a treetop canopy walkway—for environmental research and recreation.

"Students are required to submit either the SAT or the ACT including the optional Writing section. Applicants should also submit scores from any two SAT Subject Tests."

SELECTIVITY

Admissions Rating	99
# of applicants	7,500
% of applicants accepted	18
% of acceptees attending	45
# accepting a place on wait list	682
% admitted from wait list	10
# of early decision applicants	537
% accepted early decision	40

FRESHMAN PROFILE

Range SAT Critical Reading	670–760
Range SAT Math	670–760
Range ACT Composite	29–33
% graduated top 10% of class	89
% graduated top 25% of class	100
% graduated top 50% of class	100

DEADLINES

Early decision	
Deadline	11/10
Notification	12/15
Regular	
Deadline	1/1
Notification	4/1
Nonfall registration?	no

APPLICANTS ALSO LOOK AT
AND OFTEN PREFER
Harvard College
Stanford University
Massachusetts Institute of Technology
Yale University
Princeton University
AND RARELY PREFER
Amherst College
Carleton College
Haverford College
Middlebury College
Colgate University

FINANCIAL FACTS

Financial Aid Rating	98
Annual tuition	$35,438
Room and board	$9,470
Required fees	$232
Books and supplies	$800
% frosh rec. need-based scholarship or grant aid	51
% UG rec. need-based scholarship or grant aid	46
% frosh rec. need-based self-help aid	51
% UG rec. need-based self-help aid	47
% frosh rec. any financial aid	51
% UG rec. any financial aid	47
% UG borrow to pay for school	45
Average cumulative indebtedness	$9,727

WITTENBERG UNIVERSITY

PO Box 720, Springfield, OH 45501 • Admissions: 800-677-7558 • Fax: 937-327-6379

STUDENTS SAY ". . ."

Academics

A little liberal arts school located in Springfield, Ohio, this "quaint college campus that values traditions" has multiple students talking about "discovering your own personal light" and spreading it to others (echoing the sentiment of Wittenberg's motto). The "small community atmosphere" means that nothing much goes unnoticed, so it's a good thing that students are pretty happy here. Teachers at Wittenberg are warmly revered, with students applauding their availability and their attitude toward understanding "how students learn and tailor their lessons to each individual student." "They want to know about you as a person, your goals, and then they help you achieve them. "If one day, I do not speak in class discussion, my professor will pull me aside after class and ask if everything is going OK in my life, and ask if I need to talk about anything," says a senior. "I often find myself calling my family and friends to recite the amazing stories a professor just told in class," says another senior. Though a few students complain about the facilities needing to be updated, the school offers plenty of resources, such as the Writing Center, Math Workshop, and Language Center. As far as the administration goes, the majority are happy with what they've got, but a couple of students feel "there is a disconnect when talking about student life and what actually goes on around campus as far as drinking, partying, and social issues/needs," and those in charge are neutralizing the social aspects of the school. The "engaging" president is so tied into the students "he even lived in a residence hall when he first became president to get a view of 'true' college life."

Life

Most students stay on campus on the weekends, but trips to Columbus or Dayton offer quick escapes. The on-campus weekend fun quite often involves "successful athletics" and/or drinking; "House parties are common" and "typically you can walk down the street and go into five or so houses, no questions asked." For those that prefer to stay dry, "you do not have to party to have fun because there are so many other things always going on" in terms of campus activities (such as "movies in the hollow, concert series, academic speakers, and philanthropy events") and student organizations. In fact, there are so many extracurriculars offered that "it's a must to get involved." The food on campus "can not be worse," which is a problem as "it's hard to get off campus to get food if you do not have a car."

Student Body

Naturally, there are "plenty of students from Ohio and the Midwest" who are "white, New-England-like, athletic or active, outgoing, and fun," and quite a few people mention that they wouldn't mind seeing the student body diversified through out-of-state and international recruiting. Though "there aren't a lot of atypical students," the school "has embraced diversity so the minority students fit right in." The cozy atmosphere means "everyone generally ends up knowing each other," which lends itself to an overall amiability, and "it seems that most students can strike up a conversation with anyone and are very welcoming." Most people don't seclude themselves to one group of friends, and "although there are cliques, there's a lot of meshing between them."

FINANCIAL AID: 800-677-7558 • E-MAIL: ADMISSION@WITTENBERG.EDU • WEBSITE: WWW.WITTENBERG.EDU

THE PRINCETON REVIEW SAYS

Admissions

Very important factors considered include: Class rank, application essay, academic GPA, recommendation(s), rigor of secondary school record, interview. *Important factors considered include:* Character/personal qualities, extracurricular activities, talent/ability, volunteer work. *Other factors considered include:* Standardized test scores, alumni/ae relation, work experience. TOEFL required of all international applicants. High school diploma is required and GED is not accepted. *Academic units required:* 4 English, 3 mathematics, 3 science, (2 science labs), 2 foreign language, 2 history. *Academic units recommended:* 4 English, 4 mathematics, 5 science, (2 science labs), 3 foreign language, 3 history.

Financial Aid

Students should submit: FAFSA. The Princeton Review suggests that all financial aid forms be submitted as soon as possible after January 1. *Need-based scholarships/grants offered:* Federal Pell, SEOG, state scholarships/grants, private scholarships, the school's own gift aid. *Loan aid offered:* FFEL Subsidized Stafford, FFEL Unsubsidized Stafford, FFEL PLUS, Federal Perkins, college/university loans from institutional funds, Private "alternative" loans. Applicants will be notified of awards on a rolling basis beginning 3/1. Federal Work-Study Program available. Institutional employment available. Off-campus job opportunities are excellent.

The Inside Word

Wittenberg's applicant pool is small but quite solid coming off of a couple of strong years. Students who haven't successfully reached an above-average academic level in high school will meet with little success in the admissions process. Candidate evaluation is thorough and personal; applicants should devote serious attention to all aspects of their candidacy.

THE SCHOOL SAYS " . . ."

From The Admissions Office

"At Wittenberg, we believe that helping you to achieve symmetry demands a special environment, a setting where you can refine your definition of self yet gain exposure to the varied kinds of knowledge, people, views, activities, options, and ideas that add richness to our lives. Wittenberg is a university where students are able to thrive in a small campus environment with many opportunities for intellectual and personal growth in and out of the classroom. Campus life is as diverse as the interests of our students. Wittenberg attracts students from all over the United States and from many other countries. Historically, the university has been committed to geographical, educational, cultural, and religious diversity. With their varied backgrounds and interests, Wittenberg students have helped initiate many of the more than 125 student organizations that are active on campus. The students will be the first to tell you there's never a lack of things to do on or near the campus any day of the week, if you're willing to get involved.

"Wittenberg University requires freshman applicants to submit scores from the old or new SAT. Students may also choose to submit scores from the ACT (with or without the Writing component) in lieu of the SAT."

SELECTIVITY

Admissions Rating	79
# of applicants	2,887
% of applicants accepted	73
% of acceptees attending	26
# of early decision applicants	48
% accepted early decision	56

FRESHMAN PROFILE

Range SAT Critical Reading	490–610
Range SAT Math	500–559
Range ACT Composite	22–27
Minimum paper TOEFL	550
Minimum computer TOEFL	213
Average HS GPA	3.41
% graduated top 10% of class	29
% graduated top 25% of class	50
% graduated top 50% of class	81

DEADLINES

Early decision	
Deadline	11/15
Notification	1/1
Early action	
Deadline	12/1
Notification	1/1
Regular	
Priority	3/15
Notification	rolling
Nonfall registration?	yes

APPLICANTS ALSO LOOK AT
AND SOMETIMES PREFER
The College of Wooster
Denison University
Ohio Wesleyan University
The Ohio State University—Columbus
AND RARELY PREFER
Ohio Northern University
Capital University
Gettysburg College

FINANCIAL FACTS

Financial Aid Rating	82
Annual tuition	$32,936
Room and board	$8,314
Required fees	$300
Books and supplies	$800
% frosh rec. need-based scholarship or grant aid	77
% UG rec. need-based scholarship or grant aid	73
% frosh rec. need-based self-help aid	76
% UG rec. need-based self-help aid	69
% frosh rec. any financial aid	99
% UG rec. any financial aid	99
% UG borrow to pay for school	88
Average cumulative indebtedness	$25,568

WOFFORD COLLEGE

429 NORTH CHURCH STREET, SPARTANBURG, SC 29303-3663 • ADMISSIONS: 864-597-4130 • FAX: 864-597-4147

STUDENTS SAY ". . ."

Academics

"A great tradition of academic excellence, a good social life, and a community that lasts far beyond graduation" all draw students to Wofford College, a small Southern liberal arts school with "an outstanding biology program" that produces "a high percentage of students accepted into medical and dental school." Pre-law tracks, theology, and business are also reportedly quite strong here. In all areas, "Academics are very, very rigorous," but while "The workload here is heavy most of the time," Wofford never loses sight of its goal to provide "a well-balanced experience that stresses academics and a good, well-rounded education" that includes "community involvement and having fun." Great instructors help; students tell us that "the entire faculty at Wofford College is devoted to helping each and every student succeed. The professors are extremely willing to meet outside of class in order to answer any questions." In addition, Wofford "has a peer tutoring program that is extremely helpful. The program is free to students, and tutors are paid by the school. In short, if ever you find that you're having trouble, there's always someone who can help you get it sorted out." Sums up one undergrad, "Wofford College is a place to call home, where the course work is challenging but enjoyable, and you are known by a name, face, and personality rather than just an ID number."

Life

Imagine the idealized campus of a small, elite Southern college, and you'll have a pretty good mental picture of Wofford, whose campus "looks like a picture out of a movie!" The country club–like setting "is pristine, the grass is green, the buildings are maintained, and trash is something you rarely see." Sports are huge here; Wofford is a Division I school with 17 teams, meaning a good portion of the school's 1,100 students are involved in competitive sports teams. Even bigger, though, is Greek life; students agree that the Greek houses are "the center of campus, not only for the social scene but also as the leaders in the classroom and on-campus organizations." Undergrads warn that "on the weekends, the partying can be pretty intense as people relieve stress from their workload during the week. However, there also are lots of activities for nondrinkers. We have several theaters, a mall, many restaurants, free movie rentals from the library, and other colleges hosting events." Hometown Spartanburg "is a relatively small town that has all the basic stores you could ever need and tons of college appropriate restaurants, but only a select handful of nice places to eat." The school is "situated in an awkward area of Spartanburg. There isn't really anything near to it (within walking distance) except, of course, for the Krispy Kreme. Thank God for Krispy Kreme!" As a result, "We usually go to Greenville (25 minutes away) for most concerts and shopping."

Student Body

There is a definite "Wofford type," students tend to agree. One explains, "The typical student is a preppy kid from South Carolina who drives an SUV, likes music from Alabama to Jimmy Buffet, is a member of a sorority or fraternity, and dreams of being added onto George W. Bush's family tree." He or she is "serious about life and success," was "exceptionally gifted in high school in some area (academics or athletics usually)," and "is looking for a professional degree to use in order to continue on with education or get a job." There are, of course, students who don't fit the mold, however. One such student claims, "At first it can be difficult to acclimate, but being different, it becomes more apparent who is similarly minded, and there is a sort of 'force de resistance' among the atypical students." The school is making things easier for those outside the norm with its living-learning communities, such as "the race relations group and the arts LLC," both of which have promoted better-integrated campus community interactions.

FINANCIAL AID: 864-597-4160 • E-MAIL: ADMISSIONS@WOFFORD.EDU • WEBSITE: WWW.WOFFORD.EDU

THE PRINCETON REVIEW SAYS

Admissions

Very important factors considered include: Academic GPA, rigor of secondary school record. *Important factors considered include:* Class rank, application essay, standardized test scores, character/personal qualities, extracurricular activities, racial/ethnic status, talent/ability, volunteer work. *Other factors considered include:* Recommendation(s), alumni/ae relation, first generation, geographical residence, interview, work experience. SAT or ACT required; ACT with Writing component required. TOEFL required of all international applicants. High school diploma is required and GED is accepted. *Academic units recommended:* 4 English, 4 mathematics, 3 science, (3 science labs), 3 foreign language, 2 social studies, 1 history, 1 visual/performing arts, 1 computer science, 1 academic elective.

Financial Aid

Students should submit: FAFSA. The Princeton Review suggests that all financial aid forms be submitted as soon as possible after January 1. *Need-based scholarships/grants offered:* Federal Pell, SEOG, state scholarships/grants, the school's own gift aid. *Loan aid offered:* FFEL Subsidized Stafford, FFEL Unsubsidized Stafford, FFEL PLUS, Federal Perkins Applicants will be notified of awards on or about 3/31. Federal Work-Study Program available. Institutional employment available. Off-campus job opportunities are good.

The Inside Word

Wofford College distinguishes itself by providing students with an extremely supportive environment. This concern extends to the applications it receives, each of which is given careful consideration. Students who have earned decent grades in challenging courses will find themselves with an opportunity to attend a school that is gaining a reputation as one of the South's premier liberal arts colleges.

THE SCHOOL SAYS "..."

From The Admissions Office

"Approaching the end of his first year in office in the spring of 2001, Wofford President Benjamin Dunlap (a Rhodes scholar and Harvard PhD) asked the faculty, 'If you had the assurance of sufficient time and institutional support to teach the sort of course you've always dreamed of, what would you do?' In response, using grants from the Andrew Mellon and National Science Foundations, Wofford faculty created approximately 50 new courses and almost a dozen new interdisciplinary course sequences. Some of the new courses are 'learning communities,' the prototype for which was fashioned by a biologist and an English professor on 'the nature and culture of water.' A Spanish language course is taught in conjunction with a Latin American and Caribbean history course and a sociology course featuring fieldwork in the local Hispanic community. Handsomely appointed rooms suitable for meetings, meals, and seminars have been included in an ongoing series of major building projects and renovations to forge even closer relationships between faculty and students. Blessed with a Phi Beta Kappa academic tradition, a nationally ranked program of studies abroad, and an economy of scale that encourages innovation and collaboration among faculty and students, Wofford is positioning itself among the national leaders in redefining the liberal arts. More importantly, however, the college community is vigorously pursuing a goal of educating young leaders who can make connections, cross boundaries, and negotiate a world no longer neatly divided into categories of endeavor.

"Wofford College requires freshman applicants to submit scores from either the old or new SAT. Students may also choose to submit scores from the ACT in lieu of the SAT."

SELECTIVITY
Admissions Rating	91
# of applicants	2,354
% of applicants accepted	53
% of acceptees attending	31
# accepting a place on wait list	58
% admitted from wait list	5
# of early decision applicants	523
% accepted early decision	87

FRESHMAN PROFILE
Range SAT Critical Reading	560–680
Range SAT Math	570–680
Range SAT Writing	560–660
Range ACT Composite	22–27
Minimum paper TOEFL	550
Minimum computer TOEFL	213
Average HS GPA	4.05
% graduated top 10% of class	58
% graduated top 25% of class	87
% graduated top 50% of class	97

DEADLINES
Early decision	
Deadline	11/15
Notification	12/1
Regular	
Deadline	2/1
Notification	3/15
Nonfall registration?	yes

APPLICANTS ALSO LOOK AT
AND OFTEN PREFER
Wake Forest University
AND SOMETIMES PREFER
Furman University
AND RARELY PREFER
University of South Carolina—Columbia
Clemson University

FINANCIAL FACTS
Financial Aid Rating	87
Annual tuition	$27,830
Room and board	$7,705
Books and supplies	$907
% frosh rec. need-based scholarship or grant aid	43
% UG rec. need-based scholarship or grant aid	47
% frosh rec. non-need-based scholarship or grant aid	25
% UG rec. non-need-based scholarship or grant aid	24
% frosh rec. need-based self-help aid	21
% UG rec. need-based self-help aid	25
% frosh rec. athletic scholarships	14
% UG rec. athletic scholarships	14
% UG borrow to pay for school	51
Average cumulative indebtedness	$17,635

WORCESTER POLYTECHNIC INSTITUTE

100 INSTITUTE ROAD, WORCESTER, MA 01609 • ADMISSIONS: 508-831-5286 • FAX: 508-831-5875

STUDENTS SAY ". . ."

Academics

Worcester Polytechnic Institute, students boast, "is revolutionary with its approach to teaching," employing a "project-based curriculum that stresses the importance of both theory and practice." Students here must complete three projects, "one relating to the humanities, one relating to the impact of technology on society, and a final senior project" that is typically a "group project done in cooperation with industry; i.e., not an 'academic' project." The Project Enhanced Curriculum ensures that students get "real-world industry experience before getting into the real world by applying what you learn in the classroom into projects." Students typically travel abroad to complete at least one of their projects, allowing them to "help another community on the other side of the world." As yet another added bonus, "The projects program looks excellent on your resume." Students also love WPI's quarterly academic calendar. One writes, "If I don't like a class but have to get through it, it's only 7 weeks. If I love the material, I can get out in 7 weeks and jump onto the next class!" Students warn that "the terms are pretty intense and go by so quickly that there is little room for error" but add that "it is very easy to get in touch with the professors after class, and they are very willing to help." A lenient grading system—"You can only receive an A, B, C, or an NR"—reduces the pressure somewhat, although it does little to mitigate the "immense workload." Independent students are especially well suited to WPI, which "fosters a can-do attitude that allows students to pave their own ways, create their own degree programs, and arrange their own degree requirement projects."

Life

"During the week [at WPI], most of the attention is focused on school activities, whether it's homework, clubs, or other extracurriculars," while "on the weekends, people try to relax after the week that has just ended and prepare themselves for the upcoming week." The campus enjoys "a strong sense of community, probably because of the campus set-up. The campus is on a hill, so we are separate from the city, and we are our own community with its own issues, and we deal with issues as a whole." Students tell us that "the Greek life on campus holds a big presence, and it is hard to find other activities to occupy your free time without at least socializing with members of the Greek community." Of the intercollegiate sports, "Basketball is big. The men's team made it to the NCAA Division III national tournament in 2005 and 2006." Because "Worcester isn't the greatest town," students tend to stick close to campus for fun, although "We also make trips to Boston and other better cities," including Hartford and Providence.

Student Body

The WPI student body spans two extremes, from "the students who do not come out of their room and are very nerdy," and those who "are very involved and meet everyone and fit in." One student writes, "WPI is an experiment in social interactions the likes of which the world rarely sees. For every typical frat guy and girl, there's a computer nerd or D&D guru who could write this entire response in COBOL coding for you." Nearly everyone here was "an atypical high school student" who "did very well in high school" while also being "really good in X (where X is a sport, club president, highly active student)." Finally, the "One thing that binds everyone at WPI is their love for technology. Within that major division of technology-loving people, the campus is filled with diverse students."

FINANCIAL AID: 508-831-5469 • E-MAIL: ADMISSIONS@WPI.EDU • WEBSITE: WWW.WPI.EDU

THE PRINCETON REVIEW SAYS

Admissions

Very important factors considered include: Academic GPA, rigor of secondary school record. *Important factors considered include:* Class rank, application essay, recommendation(s), standardized test scores, character/personal qualities, extracurricular activities. *Other factors considered include:* Alumni/ae relation, geographical residence, interview, level of applicant's interest, racial/ethnic status, talent/ability, volunteer work, work experience. SAT or ACT required; TOEFL required of all international applicants. High school diploma is required and GED is accepted. *Academic units required:* 4 English, 4 mathematics, 2 science, (2 science labs). *Academic units recommended:* 4 science, 2 foreign language, 2 social studies, 1 history.

Financial Aid

Students should submit: FAFSA, CSS/Financial Aid PROFILE, noncustodial PROFILE, Parent's and copy of student's prior year Federal Tax Return. Regular filing deadline is 2/1. The Princeton Review suggests that all financial aid forms be submitted as soon as possible after January 1. *Need-based scholarships/grants offered:* Federal Pell, SEOG, state scholarships/grants, private scholarships, the school's own gift aid. *Loan aid offered:* FFEL Subsidized Stafford, FFEL Unsubsidized Stafford, FFEL PLUS, Federal Perkins, state loans, college/university loans from institutional funds. Applicants will be notified of awards on or about 4/1. Federal Work-Study Program available. Institutional employment available. Off-campus job opportunities are good.

The Inside Word

WPI's high admission rate is the result of a self-selecting applicant pool; very few people bother to apply here if they don't think they have a good chance of getting in. The relatively low rate of acceptees attending tells you that WPI is a 'safety' or backup choice for students hoping to get into MIT, CalTech, RPI, Case Western, and other top tech schools.

THE SCHOOL SAYS "..."

From The Admissions Office

"Projects and research enrich WPI's academic program. WPI believes that in these times simply passing courses and accumulating theoretical knowledge is not enough to truly educate tomorrow's leaders. Tomorrow's professionals ought to be involved in project work that prepares them today for future challenges. Projects at WPI come as close to professional experience as a college program can possibly achieve. In fact, WPI works with more than 200 companies, government agencies, and private organizations each year. These groups provide opportunities where students get a chance to work in real, professional settings. Students gain invaluable experience in planning, coordinating team efforts, meeting deadlines, writing proposals and reports, making oral presentations, doing cost analyses, and making decisions.

"Applicants for Fall 2008 are required to take either the new SAT or the ACT (the Writing section is optional). We will allow students to submit scores from the old SAT (prior to March 2005) or ACT as well, and will use the student's best scores from either test. Science and Math SAT Subject Tests are recommended."

SELECTIVITY

Admissions Rating	**93**
# of applicants	4,931
% of applicants accepted	67
% of acceptees attending	24
# accepting a place on wait list	174
% admitted from wait list	16

FRESHMAN PROFILE

Range SAT Critical Reading	560–670
Range SAT Math	640–720
Range SAT Writing	550–640
Range ACT Composite	25–30
Minimum paper TOEFL	550
Minimum computer TOEFL	213
Minimum web-based TOEFL	79
Average HS GPA	3.7
% graduated top 10% of class	53
% graduated top 25% of class	83
% graduated top 50% of class	99

DEADLINES

Early action	
Deadline	1/1
Notification	12/15
Regular	
Deadline	2/1
Notification	4/1
Nonfall registration?	yes

APPLICANTS ALSO LOOK AT

AND OFTEN PREFER
Cornell University
Massachusetts Institute of Technology

AND SOMETIMES PREFER
Carnegie Mellon University
Boston University
Tufts University
Rensselaer Polytechnic Institute

AND RARELY PREFER
Northeastern University
University of Connecticut
University of Massachusetts—Amherst

FINANCIAL FACTS

Financial Aid Rating	**77**
Annual tuition	$34,830
Comprehensive fee	$45,240
Books and supplies	$1,000
% frosh rec. need-based scholarship or grant aid	76
% UG rec. need-based scholarship or grant aid	67
% frosh rec. non-need-based scholarship or grant aid	23
% UG rec. non-need-based scholarship or grant aid	16
% frosh rec. need-based self-help aid	51
% UG rec. need-based self-help aid	54
% frosh rec. any financial aid	96
% UG rec. any financial aid	94
% UG borrow to pay for school	82.4
Average cumulative indebtedness	$34,409

XAVIER UNIVERSITY OF LOUISIANA

ONE DREXEL DRIVE, BOX 132, NEW ORLEANS, LA 70125-1098 • ADMISSIONS: 504-520-7388 • FAX: 504-520-7941

CAMPUS LIFE

Quality of Life Rating	**65**
Fire Safety Rating	**60***
Green Rating	**60***
Type of school	private
Affiliation	Roman Catholic
Environment	metropolis

STUDENTS

Total undergrad enrollment	2,316
% male/female	28/72
% from out of state	43
% from public high school	81
% live on campus	43
% in (# of) fraternities	NR (4)
% in (# of) sororities	1 (4)
% African American	75
% Asian	7
% Caucasian	2
% Hispanic	1
% international	3
# of countries represented	8

SURVEY SAYS . . .

Large classes
Lab facilities are great
Great computer facilities
Great library
Great off-campus food
Frats and sororities dominate
social scene
Student government is popular
Very little drug use

ACADEMICS

Academic Rating	**77**
Calendar	semester
Student/faculty ratio	15:1
Profs interesting rating	81
Profs accessible rating	83
Most common	
reg class size	20–29 students
Most common	
lab size	20–29 students

MOST POPULAR MAJORS

psychology
pre-medicine/pre-medical studies
pre-pharmacy studies

Academics

Located in New Orleans, Louisiana, "Xavier University is a historically black, Catholic University that promotes learning, leadership, and service." On a national level, "Xavier's strength is its life sciences and pharmacy programs," and the school holds the claim-to-fame of being "number one in placing African Americans into medical school." However, "what people don't know is that every academic program is great" at Xavier. A freshman attests, "Being a History major, I know first hand that the liberal arts professors are the best you can find." No matter what your discipline, XU professors are intimately involved in the learning experience, and "if a student shows that they are in a classroom to learn, they will go out of their way to make sure that he or she understands the material." On top of that, there are plenty of resources to help the struggling student, and "Xavier takes good care of their science majors by providing tutoring centers for each area and requiring that we attend drill sessions every week." The downside to the XU college experience is that "Xavier focuses so much on academics that it is easy to get stressed." However, students agree that the rigorous coursework is well worth the investment. A current student shares, "The course load is difficult so, while your final grade may not be one that you like, if you put in the time and worked hard, you finish knowing the material."

Life

While they are an outgoing and friendly bunch, Xavier students say there isn't much time for goofing off or going out at their serious school. A sophomore explains, "There are things on campus, but it is definitely not a party school. I think that most students appreciate this aspect though, because that's what they expected when they chose Xavier." Socializing can actually be a bit academic at times, as participation in study groups is "heavily promoted by the school." In addition to being academically prudent, study groups can be "a good way to meet other students." On campus, "the University Center is also an area where many students can be found in between classes and where most activities occur. Because the school is so small, it is not hard to meet people and most have the same interests." Despite the demands of coursework, students say it is possible to achieve a balanced lifestyle. A senior tells us, "It is hard to juggle school, work, and play, but with some discipline it can be done." When it comes to social activities, "Greek life is extremely popular and many students strive to be a part of different groups." However, students admit that the administrative rules on campus—such as the nightly curfew in the dorms and strict alcohol policy—can be a bit "old-fashioned." As a result, many students look for their entertainment off-campus. "Many people go to the movies, clubs, or house parties," and, thanks to the school's New Orleans location, "Bourbon Street is also a major attraction for the college students."

Student Body

United by a common desire for success, Xavier students describe their classmates as "very focused and goal-oriented." Fortunately, their interest in success does not translate into competitiveness, as most Xaverites are also "friendly and easy to get along with." When it comes to demographics, students explain, "Because Xavier is a historically black university, the majority of the student body is African-American. The student population is about 75 percent Black, 9 percent white and Asian, and 16 percent other races (roughly)." As is the trend at universities nationwide, the school is majority female, and about 72 percent of undergraduates are women. Xavier is Catholic-affiliated; however, a wide range of religions are represented in the campus community, and "less than half of the school's population is Catholic." Generally speaking, XU students make a good mix, and life at Xavier "seems like a huge community of all different kinds of people working together." Socially, students admit that "everyone has their cliques." However, on the whole, "acceptance and equality permeates throughout the entire student, faculty, and staff population."

FINANCIAL AID: 504-520-7517 • E-MAIL: APPLY@XULA.EDU • WEBSITE: WWW.XULA.EDU

THE PRINCETON REVIEW SAYS

Admissions

Very important factors considered include: Academic GPA, recommendation(s), rigor of secondary school record, standardized test scores. *Important factors considered include:* Class rank. *Other factors considered include:* Application essay, alumni/ae relation, character/personal qualities, extracurricular activities, interview, talent/ability, volunteer work, work experience. SAT or ACT required; TOEFL required of all international applicants. High school diploma is required and GED is accepted. *Academic units required:* 4 English, 2 mathematics, 1 science, 1 social studies, 8 academic electives. *Academic units recommended:* 4 mathematics, 3 science, 1 foreign language, 1 history.

Financial Aid

Students should submit: FAFSA. The Princeton Review suggests that all financial aid forms be submitted as soon as possible after January 1. *Need-based scholarships/grants offered:* Federal Pell, SEOG, state scholarships/grants, private scholarships, the school's own gift aid, United Negro College Fund. *Loan aid offered:* Direct Subsidized Stafford, Direct Unsubsidized Stafford, Direct PLUS, FFEL Subsidized Stafford, FFEL Unsubsidized Stafford, FFEL PLUS, Federal Perkins Applicants will be notified of awards on a rolling basis beginning 4/1. Federal Work-Study Program available. Institutional employment available. Off-campus job opportunities are good.

Inside Word

This school is a prestigious pipeline for those committed to a career in both natural and hard sciences. Xavier is best known for its identity as a Catholic institution with a predominantly African American student body and its reputation as a great premed school.

THE SCHOOL SAYS "..."

From The Admissions Office

A Message FROM THE SGA president:

"It is my pleasure to invite you to a college experience that will change and enhance your life. Xavier alumni are known for being exceptional doctors, lawyers, educators, business leaders, journalists, and the like.

"As a graduating Biology major, I know Xavier has prepared me for my career in medicine while nurturing me academically and socially. That remains true, despite our campus enduring the devastation of Hurricane Katrina in 2005.

"Since our campus reopened in January 2006, the Xavier family has grown stronger. With hardship often comes an opportunity to rise to greater heights. In its own way, Hurricane Katrina may have added to the character of our people and enhanced the very principles upon which this university was founded.

"St. Katharine Drexel clearly understood when she founded Xavier, the necessity to provide minority students with a quality education and the skills needed to become leaders in their communities. Her vision was to help build a more just and humane society. What better time than now to become a part of the rebuilding of one of America's most unique cities, New Orleans.

"Higher education is not only about gaining intellectual knowledge, but acquiring social and community skills as well. At Xavier we offer a wide array of clubs, organizations and teams to suit the needs and interests of the student body.

"If SGA can be of service to you please feel free to e-mail me at sgapres@xula.edu or sga@xula.edu.

Sincerely,

Reuben Battley, 2007–2008 SGA President"

SELECTIVITY

Admissions Rating	76
# of applicants	3,074
% of applicants accepted	59
% of acceptees attending	36

FRESHMAN PROFILE

Range SAT Critical Reading	400–520
Range SAT Math	400–550
Range SAT Writing	410–510
Range ACT Composite	18–23
Minimum paper TOEFL	550
Average HS GPA	3.1
% graduated top 10% of class	25
% graduated top 25% of class	49
% graduated top 50% of class	76

DEADLINES

Early action	
Deadline	1/15
Notification	2/15
Regular	
Priority	3/1
Deadline	7/1
Notification	rolling
Nonfall registration?	yes

FINANCIAL FACTS

Financial Aid Rating	70
Annual tuition	$13,700
Room and board	$6,975
Required fees	$1,000
Books and supplies	$1,200
% frosh rec. need-based scholarship or grant aid	69
% UG rec. need-based scholarship or grant aid	56
% frosh rec. non-need-based scholarship or grant aid	55
% UG rec. non-need-based scholarship or grant aid	43
% frosh rec. need-based self-help aid	73
% UG rec. need-based self-help aid	70
% frosh rec. athletic scholarships	3
% UG rec. athletic scholarships	3
% frosh rec. any financial aid	84
% UG rec. any financial aid	87
% UG borrow to pay for school	73
Average cumulative indebtedness	$41,742

XAVIER UNIVERSITY (OH)

3800 VICTORY PARKWAY, CINCINNATI, OH 45207-5311 • ADMISSIONS: 513-745-3301 • FAX: 513-745-4319

CAMPUS LIFE

Quality of Life Rating	85
Fire Safety Rating	68
Green Rating	73
Type of school	private
Affiliation	Roman Catholic-Jesuit
Environment	metropolis

STUDENTS

Total undergrad enrollment	3,814
% male/female	44/56
% from out of state	40
% from public high school	46
% live on campus	46
% African American	11
% Asian	3
% Caucasian	80
% Hispanic	3
% international	1
# of countries represented	42

SURVEY SAYS . . .

Students are friendly
Everyone loves the Musketeers
Frats and sororities are unpopular
or nonexistent

ACADEMICS

Academic Rating	80
Student/faculty ratio	12:1
Profs interesting rating	80
Profs accessible rating	86

MOST POPULAR MAJORS

marketing/marketing management
liberal arts and sciences/
liberal studies
nursing/registered nurse
(RN, ASN, BSN, MSN)

STUDENTS SAY ". . ."

Academics

Xavier University, a medium-sized Jesuit institution "in the heart of Cincinnati," instills "a real sense of community and social conscience" while still "giving students the needed skills to succeed in all of their life endeavors." Xavier even tosses in a broad liberal arts education for good measure, courtesy of a core curriculum and distribution requirements that include lots of theology, philosophy, English, history, and foreign language. But it's business that many students—one in four, to be more precise—major in here; undergrads tout the "great entrepreneurship program" and XU's "great record" for placing accounting students in graduate schools. XU's nursing program is also "very strong," with "an excellent" "pass rate on the NCLEX," and the education program earns similar plaudits. In all areas, XU offers "relatively small" classes, "which can make it hard when it's time for registration, but when you're in class it's great." Academics are "challenging, but the teachers and administration help make the transition [from high school] smooth and are there whenever you need their help." "Academically, it is nearly impossible to fail," a freshman adds. "There are always tutoring centers and help [is] available for any subject, whenever you need it." The school also "excels at real-world placement. If you want an internship, just ask. There's even a team of people here whose only job is to find internships and co-ops for students." Undergrads also appreciate their classmates' low-key approach; they "care, but are very laid-back in classes."

Life

"Xavier University has a little bit of everything: service projects, strong academics, social events, religious events, weekend trips, and lots of other activities to get involved in." A good number of the aforementioned activities "are put on by [the] Student Activities Council and by student government." Many Xavier students "go to the sporting events," with a heavy focus on the men's basketball team, which "is obviously a huge deal here" (the team was the 2005–2006 Atlantic 10 champion). Students say XU parties "usually don't get too out of control. I've never really heard or experienced any . . . of the typical bad college party experiences," a sophomore reports. They also tell us that "there are few bars around (mainly only one, for upper classmen) so people generally party at houses." Big city living lures some students off campus; Cincinnati "is a great city to go out in—there are areas such as Mt. Adams and Newport that provide entertainment and dining for both college-aged students and young professionals."

Student Body

"I'd say 95 percent of the students at this school are friendly and always willing to meet new people or help you if you have a problem," writes one student, expressing a commonly held perception of Xavier undergrads. Students "spend a lot of time with varieties of people—not just a "clique" or single group of people—[so] it is fairly easy to get to know a large percentage of your classmates, especially the peers in your graduating class." In terms of demographics, "Lots of kids come from suburban areas and went to Catholic schools, so there is a large population of wealthy, religious students." Adding some ethnic diversity are "significant populations of minority students (Black, Asian, international, etc.) who each have [a] strong voice on campus." Alternative culture is hardly found here; one student notes, "It's rare to find a kid with a mohawk unless the rugby team shaved his head. Most kids are clean-cut." An accounting and finance major adds, "There are no real emo/goth kids at this school (thank God)." However, a weekend degree program and night classes draw a substantial nontraditional population to the school.

FINANCIAL AID: 513-745-3142 • E-MAIL: XUADMIT@XAVIER.EDU • WEBSITE: WWW.XAVIER.EDU

THE PRINCETON REVIEW SAYS

Admissions

Very important factors considered include: Rigor of secondary school record. *Important factors considered include:* Class rank, Academic GPA, Standardized test scores, Application Essay, Recommendation(s), Character/personal qualities. *Other factors considered include:* Volunteer work, Work experience, Level of applicant's interest, First Generation, Alumni/ae relation, Extracurricular activity, Talent/ability. *Academic units recommended:* TOEFL required of all international applicants.

Financial Aid

The Princeton Review suggests that all financial aid forms be submitted as soon as possible after January 1. Federal Work-Study Program available. Institutional employment available. Off-campus job opportunities are excellent.

The Inside Word

Above-average students should encounter little difficulty in gaining admission to Xavier. Others may be able to finagle their way in with some elbow grease, credible demonstrations of commitment to academics and Jesuit ideals of service, and a Catholic approach to academics.

THE SCHOOL SAYS ". . ."

From The Admissions Office

"Founded in 1831, Xavier University is the fourth oldest of the 28 Jesuit colleges and universities in the United States. The Jesuit tradition is evident in the university's core curriculum, degree programs and involvement opportunities. Xavier is home to 6,600 total students; 3,800 degree-seeking undergraduates. The student population represents more than 34 states and 50 foreign countries.

"Xavier offers 69 academic majors and concentrations and 42 minors in the Colleges of Arts and Sciences; Business; and Social Sciences, Health, and Education. Most popular majors include business, communication arts, education, psychology, biology, sport management/marketing, and pre-professional study. Other programs of note include University Scholars; Honors AB; Philosophy, Politics, and the Public; Army ROTC, study abroad, academic service-learning, and service fellowship.

"There are over 100 academic clubs, social and service organizations, and recreational sports activities on campus. Students participate in groups such as student government, campus ministry, performing arts, and intramural sports. Xavier is a member of the Division I Atlantic 10 Conference and fields teams in men's and women's basketball, cross-country, track, golf, soccer, swimming, and tennis, as well as men's baseball and women's volleyball.

"Xavier is situated on more than 148 acres in a residential area of Cincinnati, Ohio. The face of Xavier has continued to change with the planned addition of a technology-based learning commons, renovated library and classroom buildings, a new building for the Williams College of Business, a new retail and residential complex, and a new student recreation facility. The additions are part of a $200 million capital campaign and will begin being built in 2008.

"Applicants must submit results from the SAT or ACT. Xavier will accept results from the old or new SAT/ACT and the student's best score(s) from either test will be used. The Writing portion of the SAT/ACT is not required and will not be used in admission and scholarship decisions."

SELECTIVITY

Admissions Rating	87
# of applicants	5,649
% of applicants accepted	73
% of acceptees attending	21

FRESHMAN PROFILE

Range SAT Critical Reading	520–640
Range SAT Math	530–640
Range ACT Composite	23–29
Average HS GPA	3.6
% graduated top 10% of class	29
% graduated top 25% of class	61
% graduated top 50% of class	86
Minimum paper TOEFL	530
Minimum computer TOEFL	197
Minimum web-based TOEFL	71

DEADLINES

Regular	02/01
Nonfall registration?	Yes

APPLICANTS ALSO LOOK AT

AND OFTEN PREFER
University of Notre Dame
AND SOMETIMES PREFER
University of Dayton
Miami University
The Ohio State University—Columbus
AND RARELY PREFER
University of Cincinnati

FINANCIAL FACTS

Financial Aid Rating	77
Annual tuition	$24,600
% frosh rec. need-based scholarship or grant aid	55
% UG rec. need-based scholarship or grant aid	51
% frosh rec. non-need-based scholarship or grant aid	55
% UG rec. non-need-based scholarship or grant aid	51
% frosh rec. need-based self-help aid	43
% UG rec. need-based self-help aid	41
% frosh rec. athletic scholarships	5
% UG rec. athletic scholarships	4
% frosh rec. any financial aid	96
% UG rec. any financial aid	99
% UG borrow to pay for school	63
Average cumulative indebtedness	$24,769

YALE UNIVERSITY

PO BOX 208234, NEW HAVEN, CT 06520-8234 • ADMISSIONS: 203-432-9316 • FAX: 203-432-9392

STUDENTS SAY " . . ."

Academics
Listening to Yale students wax rhapsodic about their school, one can be forgiven for wondering whether they aren't actually describing the Platonic form of the university. By their own account, students here benefit not only from "amazing academics and extensive resources" that provide "phenomenal in- and out-of-class education," but also from participation in "a student body that is committed to learning and to each other." Unlike some other prestigious prominent research universities, Yale "places unparalleled focus on undergraduate education," requiring all professors to teach at least one undergraduate course each year "so [you know] the professors actually love teaching, because if they just wanted to do their research, they could have easily gone elsewhere." A residential college system further personalizes the experience. Each residential college "has a Dean and a Master, each of which is only responsible for 300 to 500 students, so administrative attention is highly specialized and widely available." Students further enjoy access to "a seemingly never-ending supply of resources (they really just love throwing money at us)" that includes "the 12 million volumes in our libraries." In short, "The opportunities are truly endless." "The experiences that you have here and the people that you meet will change your life and strengthen your dreams," says ones student. Looking for the flip side to all this? "If the weather were a bit nicer, that would be excellent," one student offers. Guess that will have to do.

Life
Yale is, of course, extremely challenging academically, but students assure us that "Aside from the stress of midterms and finals, life at Yale is relatively carefree." Work doesn't keep undergrads from participating in "a huge variety of activities for fun. There are over 300 student groups, including singing, dancing, juggling fire, theater...the list goes on. Because of all of these groups, there are shows on-campus all the time, which are a lot of fun and usually free or less than $5. On top of that, there are parties and events on-campus and off-campus, as well as many subsidized trips to New York City and Boston." Many here "are politically active (or at least politically aware)" and "a very large number of students either volunteer or try to get involved in some sort of organization to make a difference in the world." When the weekend comes around, "There are always parties to go to, whether at the frats or in rooms, but there's definitely no pressure to drink if you don't want to. A good friend of mine pledged a frat without drinking and that's definitely not unheard of (but still not common)." The relationship between Yale and the city of New Haven "sometimes leaves a little to be desired, but overall it's a great place to be for four years."

Student Body
A typical Yalie is "tough to define because so much of what makes Yale special is the unique convergence of different students to form one cohesive entity. Nonetheless, the one common characteristic of Yale students is passion—each Yalie is driven and dedicated to what he or she loves most, and it creates a palpable atmosphere of enthusiasm on campus." True enough, the student body represents a wide variety of ethnic, religious, economic, and academic backgrounds, but they all "thrive on learning, whether it be in a class, from a book, or from a conversation with a new friend." Students here also "tend to do a lot." "Everyone has many activities that they are a part of, which in turn fosters the closely connected feel of the campus." Undergrads tend to lean to the left politically, but for "those whose political views aren't as liberal as the rest of the campus...there are several campus organizations that cater to them."

YALE UNIVERSITY

FINANCIAL AID: 203-432-2700 • E-MAIL: UNDERGRADUATE.ADMISSIONS@YALE.EDU • WEBSITE: WWW.YALE.EDU/ADMIT

THE PRINCETON REVIEW SAYS

Admissions

Very important factors considered include: Class rank, application essay, academic GPA, recommendation(s), rigor of secondary school record, standardized test scores, character/personal qualities, extracurricular activities, talent/ability. *Other factors considered include:* Alumni/ae relation, first generation, geographical residence, interview, level of applicant's interest, racial/ethnic status, state residency, volunteer work, work experience. SAT and SAT Subject Tests or ACT Writing component required. TOEFL required of all international applicants. High school diploma or equivalent is not required.

Financial Aid

Students should submit: FAFSA, CSS/Financial Aid PROFILE, noncustodial PROFILE, business/farm supplement, Parent Tax returns. Regular filing deadline is 3/1. The Princeton Review suggests that all financial aid forms be submitted as soon as possible after January 1. *Need-based scholarships/grants offered:* Federal Pell, SEOG, state scholarships/grants, private scholarships, the school's own gift aid, United Negro College Fund. *Loan aid offered:* FFEL Subsidized Stafford, FFEL Unsubsidized Stafford, FFEL PLUS, Federal Perkins, state loans, college/university loans from institutional funds. Applicants will be notified of awards on or about 4/1.

The Inside Word

Yale estimates that over three-quarters of all its applicants are qualified to attend the university, but less than ten percent get in. That adds up to a lot of broken hearts among kids who, if admitted, could probably handle the academic program. With so many qualified applicants to choose from, Yale can winnow to build an incoming class that is balanced in terms of income level, racial/ethnic background, geographic origin, and academic interest. For all but the most qualified, getting in typically hinges on offering just what an admissions officer is looking for to fill a specific slot. Legacies (descendents of Yale grads) gain some advantage—they're admitted at a 30 percent rate.

THE SCHOOL SAYS "..."

From The Admissions Office

"The most important questions the Admissions Committee must resolve are 'Who is likely to make the most of Yale's resources?' and 'Who will contribute significantly to the Yale community?' These questions suggest an approach to evaluating applicants that is more complex than whether Yale would rather admit well-rounded people or those with specialized talents. In selecting a class of 1,300 from over 20,000 applicants, the Admissions Committee looks for academic ability and achievement combined with such personal characteristics as motivation, curiosity, energy, and leadership ability. The nature of these qualities is such that there is no simple profile of grades, scores, interests, and activities that will assure admission. Diversity within the student population is important, and the Admissions Committee selects a class of able and contributing individuals from a variety of backgrounds and with a broad range of interests and skills.

"Applicants for the entering class of Fall 2009 may take either version of the SAT. In addition, applicants will be required to take two SAT Subject Tests of their choice. Applicants may take the ACT, with the Writing component, as an alternative to the SAT and SAT Subject Tests."

SELECTIVITY

Admissions Rating	99
# of applicants	19,323
% of applicants accepted	9
% of acceptees attending	71

FRESHMAN PROFILE

Range SAT Critical Reading	700–800
Range SAT Math	700–790
Range ACT Composite	30–34
Minimum paper TOEFL	600
Minimum computer TOEFL	250
% graduated top 10% of class	97
% graduated top 25% of class	100
% graduated top 50% of class	100

DEADLINES

Early action	
Deadline	11/1
Notification	12/15
Regular	
Deadline	12/31
Notification	4/1
Nonfall registration?	no

FINANCIAL FACTS

Financial Aid Rating	96
Annual tuition	$34,530
Room and board	$10,470
Books and supplies	$2,700
% frosh rec. need-based scholarship or grant aid	42
% UG rec. need-based scholarship or grant aid	42
% frosh rec. need-based self-help aid	43
% UG rec. need-based self-help aid	43
% UG borrow to pay for school	32
Average cumulative indebtedness	$13,344

PART 4

"COW TIPPING IS DEFINITELY PASSÉ HERE."

Our survey has seven questions that allow students to answer in narrative form. We tell students that we don't care *what* they write: If it is "witty, informative, or accurate," we try to get it into this book. We use all the informative and accurate essays to write the "Students Speak Out" sections; below are excerpts from the wittiest, pithiest, and most outrageous narrative responses to our open-ended questions.

LITERARY ALLUSIONS...

"To study at this school is to have infinite control over your destiny: You can crouch in your room like Gregor Samsa transformed into a dung beetle, or you can plunge into the infinite sea of faces that each year flood OSU like a tidal wave."

—A.W., Ohio State University

"'Prosperity unbruised cannot endure a single blow, but a man who has been at constant feud with misfortunes develops a skin calloused by time . . . and even if he falls he can carry the fight upon one knee.' —Seneca on Providence."

— Matthew D., University of Connecticut

"Very definitely a love/hate relationship here. This is the level of hell that Dante missed."

—Amy P., Caltech

"The Deep Springs Experience is like working in an atrophy factory. Much of what you do in labor and government is fixing, improving, or replacing what came before you. No matter what frame of reference you use—daily, monthly, or yearly—you still feel like Sisyphus. The joy and value comes in building your muscles on so many different rocks."

—Whet M., Deep Springs College

"Lewd quotes on the bathroom walls, at least, come from great authors."

—Matt J., Simon's Rock College of Bard

FOOD...

"In the cafeteria, the chocolate milk is cheap and delicious. It is also always satisfying. Plus, Seattle University doesn't have my dad, who was always drunk. This is good."

—Anonymous Freshman, Seattle University

"When students first arrive, they call the Observatory Hill Dining Facility 'O-Hill.' They soon learn to call it 'O-Hell,' because the food here is beyond revolting."

— Greg F., University of Virginia

"If I had known that I'd be rooming with roaches and poisoned by the cafeteria staff I would have gone to Wayne State. I really can't complain, though, because I have met my husband here, like my mom did 20 years before."

— M.L.P., Fisk University

"If you're looking for gray skies, a gray campus, and gray food, then Albany is the place to be!"

— Michele G., SUNY—UNiversity at Albany

"You should mention Lil', the lady who has worked in the dining hall for 50 years and who everyone loves. She plays the spoons all the time and runs around."

— Aaron R., Tufts University

HOMETOWN...

"In my experience New York is a place that allows people to be anyone they want to be. You can wear a zebra-striped bikini in the middle of winter on a snow-covered street here, and people would hardly look twice"

—Sophomore, Barnard College

"Change the name of UC—Irvine to UC—Newport Beach and we would have more girls."

— Pat M., UC—Irvine

"As this school is located in a tiny Texas town, a favorite activity is called 'rolling.' Rolling entails piling into a car with many drinks and driving the backcountry roads. Very slowly."

— Anonymous, Southwestern University

"Connecticut is a cute state. It's a great place to go to school, but I wouldn't want to live here."

— Claire S., NJ native, Fairfield University

"Socially, the surrounding area is so dead that the Denny's closes at night."

— Thomas R., UC—Riverside

"The local liquor stores and towing companies make a lot of money."

— Katherine R., University of Rhode Island

"Davis is boring; you need a lot of drugs."

—Anonymous, UC—Davis

"It is definitely important to have a car, as the population of Canton frequently matches our winter temperature. 'Canton gray,' our perennial sky color, is one Crayola missed."

— Daniel R., St. Lawrence University

"Montreal is the sh*@!"

—Elizabeth R., McGill University

"Fredericksburg is boring if one is not amused by the simple pleasures of existence such as breathing, sleep, and other things."

—Rich W., Mary Washington College

SECURITY...

"Campus security is made up of a bunch of midget high school dropouts with Napoleonic complexes who can spot a beer can from a mile away."

—Anonymous, UC—San Diego

"Public safety here is a joke. The public safety officers are like the Keystone Kops on Thorazine."

—Anonymous, Bryn Mawr College

"For fun we try to ski around campus on the snow, but campus safety must feel that we should be smoking weed because they allow that more than outdoor activities."

—Male Junior, Clarkson University

"No doors are locked here—none—but you have to notice the doorknob."

—Female Senior, Simon's Rock College of Bard

"If you're thinking of applying to MIT, go ahead. Because, believe it or not, most people here are at least as stupid as you are."

—Patrick L., MIT

"The typical student is mostly an easygoing, skirt-wearing, intelligent, procrastinating kid. Although, there [are] of course, many many many variations on this. Not all kids wear skirts. Not all the boys in skirts are straight. Not all the girls in skirts are straight. 'Everybody here looks like Jesus!' was a pretty accurate description from an outsider."

—Amy P., New College of Florida

"Students here mostly get along, and since it is a business school we all have a common goal of being rich."

—Female Sophomore, Babson College

"People who go to school here are all pretty good looking, especially the women. It should be renamed UKB, the University of Ken and Barbie."

—Tony H., Arizona State University

"Wesleyan is not only the 'diversity university' but also the 'controversy university,' the 'fight adversity university,' and the 'if we keep trying we might have some unity' university. We satisfy all types."

—John P., Wesleyan University

"Mt. Holyoke students are friendly and respectful with the exception of the occasions when the entire campus gets PMS."

—Abigail K., Mount Holyoke College

"My roommate's a complete jerk so I spend most of my nights sleeping in the backseat of my truck."

—Ronald G., Arizona State University

"Girls over 5'8", watch out—for some reason, guys here have munchkin blood in them or something."

—Robyn A., Tufts University

"A school can be defined by its graffiti and its level of cleverness. Three-quarters of our school graffiti is pro- or anti- a specific fraternity, with the other one-quarter devoted to homophobic or misogynist theories."

—Matthew E., College of William & Mary

"This is a great university if you're not studying sciences involving animal research, politics, teacher education (certification), or anything that offends any long-haired leftist who's a vegetarian."

—Brock M., University of Oregon

"Most of my peers are narrow-minded morons who seem to live in the 50s. Because of this constant annoyance, the rest of us have a camaraderie that allows us to see how the other half lives."

—Gary A., Louisiana State University

"Everyone here is too smart for their [sic] own good. As one upper-level executive in the Houston area put it, 'The students at Rice know how to make it rain, but they don't know to come in out of it.'"

—John B., Rice University

"Bates is so diverse! Yesterday I met somebody from Connecticut!"

—Ellen H., Bates College

"Most are either Bible-thumping, goodie-goodie, White, stuck-up, right-wing, straight-A losers or work-hard, play-harder and party-hardy, willing-to-try-anything cool people."

—Male Sophomore, Colorado School of Mines

"We have this typical student stereotype we call 'Wendy Wellesley.' Wendy takes copious notes, is a devoted member of 10 organizations, always has an internship, goes over the page limit on every assignment, takes six classes, goes to all the office hours, triple majors, and is basically diligent, overcommitted, extroverted, overachieving, and energetic (but without a sense of humor or ability to relax)."

—R.D., Wellesley College

"I am constantly impressed with the creativity of hell-raisers on campus. One day I walked past the Manor House to find a dozen plastic babies climbing all over the roof! Right before Parents' Weekend, some people hung up signs saying 'Princeton Review reports: "LC students ignore herpes on a regular basis." Please visit the health clinic!'"

—Anonymous, Lewis & Clark College

"Diversity in the female population means different shades of hair color . . . we often joke that Burberry is SMU Sorority Camouflage."

—Male Senior,
Southern Methodist University

ADMINISTRATION...

"The only thing the administration does well is tasks involving what Kenneth Boulding would call 'suboptimization.' Give them something that really doesn't need doing, and it will be accomplished efficiently."

—Dana T.,
University of Minnesota—Twin Cities

"Our Business Office may be the smoothest-running machine since the Pinto!"

—Robert C., University of Dallas

"Despite the best efforts of the administration to provide TCNJ students with an inefficient, cold-hearted, red-tape-infested, snafu-riddled Soviet-style administrative bureaucracy, The College of New Jersey is a pretty decent place to go for a fairly reasonable amount of money."

—Anonymous,
The College of New Jersey

"Our advisors are amazing as well. I have been on a first-name basis with mine since our first e-mail (when I'm not calling her 'the Goddess')."

—Female Freshman, American University

"Administration is like the stock market, you invest time and money, sometimes you get a return, other times you don't."

—J.W.R., Albertson College of Idaho

"Columbia is like a fruit truck. It picks up varied and exotic fruits and deposits them rotten at their destination."

—Paul L., Columbia University

"The University of Minnesota is a huge black hole of knowledge. It sucks things into it from far and wide, compressing to the essence. Unfortunately, it is very hard to get anything out of a black hole. What I have managed to eke out has been both rewarding and depressing."

—James McDonald,
University of Minnesota

"The strangest incident I've ever had in class was when one of my journalism profs burnt our tests in the microwave. But he decided to give everyone in the class an A, instead of retesting."

—Ashlea K., Ohio University

"Boulder is the world in a nutshell, served with alfalfa sprouts."

—Glenn H.,
University of Colorado—Boulder

"Going to Northwestern is like having a beautiful girlfriend who treats you like crap."

—Jonathan J. G., Northwestern University

"Unless you are totally committed to science, do not come. Caltech has as much breadth as a Russian grocery store."

—Daniel S., Caltech

"Life at school is an oxymoron."

—Dave G., UC—Davis

"One other thing I love about NYU: online registration! God bless the NYU Registrar!"

—Timothy A., New York University

"Vassar is like a sexual disease: Once you've accepted it, it's great, but when you realize you've got another three years to put up with it, you go see a medical adviser immediately."

—Henry R., Vassar College

"I feel that this school is a maze with snakes and bulls. If you live with a raised fist or a raised phallus, it is easy. If you are earthly, bound to do nothing, come."

—Anonymous, University of Oregon

"Getting an education from MIT is like getting a drink from a firehose."

—Juan G., MIT

"My life here is as the torrential rains of Dhamer upon the Yaktong Valley. I bleat like a llama shedding out of season."

—Ronald M., James Madison University

"Intro classes have the consistency of Cheez Whiz: They go down easy, they taste horrible, and they are not good for you."

—Pat T., University of Vermont

"This school was founded by Jesuits . . . . However, I believe that it has been hijacked by yuppie prisses."

—Anonymous,
Loyola Marymount University

SEX, DRUGS, ROCK & ROLL...

"This school is no good for people who like art, music, and Sonic Youth. 'Society is a hole.' There's a quote by Sonic Youth."

—Meghan S., Lake Forest College

"The university tries to offer activities as an alternative to alcohol on the weekends. Those are not heavily attended. The weekends are for drinking."

—Maura G., Ohio University

"Beam, Bud, beer, babes—the four essential B's."

—"Jim Beam," Wittenberg University

"William & Mary: where you can drink beer and have sex in the same place your forefathers did."

—Adam L., College of William & Mary

"Yeah, there aren't any guys, but who doesn't like doing homework on a Saturday night?"

—Nicole C., Wellesley College

"The dances here are a riot because I love watching nerds and intellectuals dance."

—Male Senior, Columbia University

"For such a small school there is a surprising amount of on-campus activities such as academic speakers, weekend concerts, speed-dating nights, and good sex talks."

—Junior, Colorado College

"The typical Hampshire student is queer—perhaps not in actual sexual orientation, but definitely in attitude."

—Freshman, Hampshire College

"Any campus attempt to provide drug-free entertainment shuts down at 10:20 P.M. to allow plenty of time to be drunk. The general campus motto is 'If you weren't wasted, the night was.'"

—Junior, Lehigh University

"Drug use here is extremely prevalent. People smoke pot everywhere, even outdoors."

—Freshman, New College of Florida

SCHOOL VS. THE "REAL WORLD"...

"College is the best time of your life. Never again will you be surrounded by people the same age as you, free from grown-ups and the threat of working in the real world. Your parents give you money when you ask for it, and all you have to do is learn!"

—Jennifer F., Syracuse University

"Real-life experience in such concepts— alienation, depression, suppression, isolationism, edge of racial tension, apathy, etc.—before the 'real world.'"

—Anonymous, NYU

SCHOOLS THAT ARE ALL THAT AND A BAG OF CHIPS

"For the first time in my life I am allowed to think for myself. . . . This is an environment where one can proclaim in class that Socrates is a bastard and, if able to support the statement, be respected for it."

—Female Freshman,
Simon's Rock College of Bard

"Best ever, dude! Nobody complains if I leave the toilet seat up."

—Derek L., Deep Springs College

"We play dodge ball at recess and think what it would be like if we could fly."

—Joseph W., Beloit College

"The students here are as diverse as their views and backgrounds. My friends are mostly thespians and lesbians, and they rock!"

—Female Junior, Bennington College

IN CASE YOU WERE WONDERING...

$Drexel = (Content[good] - Schedule[finals] - Tuition)^{[sum(geeks)/sum(jocks)]} + [avg_{i,j}(sqrt[(geekPos[i] - jockPos[j]).x^2 + (geekPos[i] - jockPos[j]).y^2]) - 200ft] = 8.5/10$

—Male Junior, Drexel University

"There's about 15 too many classes along the lines of 'Talking Heads: The Politics of Cabbage in Nineteenth Century Guam.'"

—Sarah G., Bennington College

"Classes are hard to get. Usually you have to cheat and just add the class, telling them you are a graduating senior. I've done that for the last three years and it works!"

—Anonymous, UC—Davis

"I am a hermit who enjoys Ramen noodles and skin flicks. In the winter, I sit in a yoga position by a patch of ice on the sidewalk and mock people as they fall. I often bend spoons with my mind."

—Junior,
Indiana University of Pennsylvania

"When I'm not trying to free Mumia, experience non-gender orgasm/trans-gender interpretive dance, contracting any number of venereal diseases, or trying to be hopelessly unique, I obsess to no end in trying to reconcile my existentialist beliefs with paying $30,000 a year to attend this socially legitimizing institution."

—Katherine S., Bard College

"Those who oppose the Dark Lord will be crushed, but those who are its friend will receive rewards beyond the dreams of avarice."

—Anonymous, Sarah Lawrence College

"There is a real problem with moles on this campus; no one is willing to talk about them."

—Alexander D., Bates College

"Bates College is a phallocentric, logocentric, Greco-Roman, linear-rational, ethnocentric, homophobic, patriarchal institution. How's that for a list of catchwords?"

—Stephen H., Bates College

"To begin, there's an apartment complex on a main road in my college city, and one of the apartments has put up a sign a few times this year that reads 'Honk for a drink.' So anytime someone drives by and honks his/her horn, the guys on the balcony take a swig of beer. I have also heard a story of a guy who turned 21 here, and his buddies had a beer tube made that went from the third floor apartments down to the ground filled with beer for the guy to drink. . . . Someone like me would never survive an ordeal like that, given my stature. Also, because Interstate 81 cuts through our campus, many drunk girls, especially on homecoming, enjoy giving the truck drivers a little peep show either day or night. . . . One of the great things about our school, though, is that we have a bus service called 'Ride with Len.' This man had a relative die from a drunk driver, and so on the weekends he takes to driving a huge bus around our town to take college kids to their prospective [sic] places safely. He has gotten so popular that more buses and drivers have been added. So I'd say that although many people drink here, they drink responsibly."

—Anonymous, James Madison University

CONFUSED PEOPLE...

"A crust of bread is better than nothing. Nothing is better than true love. There-fore, by the transitive property, a crust of bread is better than true love."

—Jason G., Gettysburg College

"Bentley College has fulfilled all and more of my expectations than I ever imagined."

— Dawn T., Bentley College

"Everyone seems to be really into political correctness, but in the wake of the recent Supreme Court decision, I don't see that lasting very long."

—John R., Birmingham-Southern College

On the academics/administration: "They think they know a lot but they actually don't know anything, but some of them know that, so they know everything."

—Male Junior, College of the Atlantic

PART 5

INDEXES

INDEPENDENT COUNSELING

There are currently two professional organizations for independent counselors that require professional credential review: Independent Educational Consultants Association (IECA) and National Association for College Admission Counseling (NACAC). Counselors affiliated with both groups provide varied and detailed services to students and families exploring future educational opportunities. Should you consider seeking the services of an independent counselor, I encourage you to visit both the IECA and NACAC websites for up-to-date information and listings.

Sincerely,

Robert Franek

Lead Author, *The Best 368 Colleges*

VP—Publisher

The Princeton Review

IECA—The Independent Educational Consultants Association is a national non-profit professional association of independent consultants.

www.iecaonline.com

NACAC—The National Association for College Admission Counseling is an organization of 9,000 global professionals dedicated to serving students as they make choices in pursuing postsecondary education.

www.nacacnet.org

INDEX OF SCHOOLS

INDEX OF SCHOOLS BY LOCATION

INDEX OF SCHOOLS BY COST

Price categories are based on current tuition (out-of-state tuition for public schools) and do not include fees, room, board, transportation, or other expenses.

LESS THAN $15,000

Robert Franek is a graduate of Drew University and vice president and publisher for The Princeton Review. He has proudly been a part of the company for five years. Robert comes to The Princeton Review with an extensive admissions background. In addition, he owns a walking tour business, leading historically driven, yet not boring, walking tours of his favorite town, New York City!

Tom Meltzer is a graduate of Columbia University. He has taught for The Princeton Review since 1986 and is the author or coauthor of seven Princeton Review titles, the most recent of which is *Illustrated Word Smart*, which Tom cowrote with his wife, Lisa. He is also a professional musician and songwriter. A native of Baltimore, Tom now lives in Hillsborough, North Carolina.

Christopher Maier is a graduate of Dickinson College. During the past five years, he's lived variously in New York City, coastal Maine, western Oregon, central Pennsylvania, and eastern England. Now he's at an oasis somewhere in the Midwestern cornfields—the University of Illinois—where he's earning his MFA in fiction. Aside from writing for magazines, newspapers, and The Princeton Review, he's worked as a radio disc jockey, a helping hand in a bakery, and a laborer on a highway construction crew. He's trying to avoid highway construction these days.

Carson Brown graduated from Stanford University in 1998, and after getting paid too much for working for various Internet companies for several years, sold her BMW and moved to Mexico. She has now overstayed her welcome south of the border and is returning to San Francisco to be responsible and further her career working as a writer and editor.

Julie Doherty is a freelance writer, web designer, and preschool teacher. She lives in Mexico City.

Andrew Friedman graduated in 2003 from Stanford University, where he was a President's Scholar. He lives in New York City.

Counselor Order Form

The Princeton Review

NAME:_____ TITLE:_____

Company or School Name:_____

Billing Address:_____ City:_____ State:_____ Zip Code:_____

Shipping Address: (If different from billing)_____

City:_____ State:_____ Zip Code:_____

Phone:_____ Fax:_____ Email Address:_____

BILLING INFORMATION: *Check one of the following*

❏ Enclosed a check for the sum of:_____

❏ Please send me a bill with a Purchase Order #_____

❏ Please charge my credit card for the sum of:_____

Credit Card # and type:_____ Expiration Date:_____

Name on the Card:_____ Signature:_____ Date:_____

ORDERING INSTRUCTIONS:

The Essential Package includes 1 of each book listed in the Essential Package column. There is no limit to the quantity you may order.

		Essential Package	Single Books	Your Price	Total Price
Your Educator DISCOUNT		30%	15%	15%	
Essential Package Price		**$163**			**$163**
TITLE	**ISBN**	**Quantity**	**Quantity**		
The Best 368 Colleges, 2009 edition	9780375748722	Included		$18.66	
Complete Book of Colleges, 2009 edition	9780375428746	Included		$22.91	
Guide to College Visits, 2009 edition	9780375766008	Included		$18.12	
The Best Northeastern Colleges, 2009 edition	9780375428739	Included		$14.41	
Guide to College Majors, 2008 edition	9780375766374	Included		$17.85	
College Essays that Made a Difference	9780375428760	Included		$11.86	
Parents' Guide to College Life	9780375764943	Included		$11.86	
The K&W Guide to Colleges for Students with Learning Disabilities and A.D.D., 9th edition	9780375766336	Included		$22.95	
Guiding Teens with Learning Disabilities	9780375764967	Included		$19.51	
Paying for College Without Going Broke (with foreword by former President Bill Clinton)	9780375428838	Included		$17.00	
The Gay and Lesbian Guide to College Life	9780375766237	Included		$11.86	
College Navigator	9780375765834	Included		$11.01	
The Road to College	9780375766176	Included		$11.86	
SUB-TOTAL Books					$

Don't Forget Shipping & Handling

Books: $2.95 for 1, $9.95 for 2 or more

Total (Books and Shipping and Handling)

$_____

Please fax this order form to
      attn: Adam Davis, 212-874-1754
or mail to
      The Princeton Review attn: Adam Davis
      2315 Broadway, New York, NY 10024
Please call or Email with questions
      212-874-8282 x1440 or TPRBooks@Review.com

Paying For College 101

It's not a long shot to bet that you're reading this book because you're thinking of going to college. We're near psychic, right?! The odds are also good that you understand if you want to get into the college of your choice, you need the grades and the scores, and you need to demonstrate the things you dig outside the four walls of your classroom.

Positioning yourself for college admissions is not gambling; it's an investment. You've been investing your time and effort to be the best candidate for your prospective colleges and now, you've invested a little bit of money—right now by buying and reading this book! We applaud you for it!

But what else do you need to know to go to college?

If you answered, How am I going to pay for it? Then you're not alone and you're solidly on the right track to figuring it out. We think we can help.

Your college education is an investment in your future, and paying for college is a big part of that investment. In the next pages you'll find lots of basic information on that big scary subject -- financial aid. While we tried to stick to "need to know" nuggets, the information you'll read about here is powerful because it diffuses frenzy around the aid process and equips you with the knowledge to navigate the process as an educated consumer. We ask that you take a little bit of time right now to learn about what it takes to afford yourself an excellent education.

WHAT ARE THE COSTS INVOLVED?

The first thing that comes to mind when you think about how much it costs to go to school is tuition, right? Well, tuition may be the first thing, but don't make the mistake of thinking that's it. The total cost of a year at college involves more than just the tuition amount that the school lists.

Let's break it down:

- Tuition and fees
- Room and board
- Books and supplies
- Personal expenses
- Travel expenses

All of these things together make up the total cost of attendance (COA) for a year at a particular college. So your tuition might be $20,000, but add on room and board, the cost of books, lab fees, not to mention the cost of travel back and forth for breaks, and miscellaneous personal expenses (you will need to buy toothpaste occasionally), and your COA could be as much as $30,000—that's a big difference.

According to a study by The College Board, during the 2006-2007 school year, the cost of attending a four-year private college for that year averaged approximately $30,367. The same study found that the total cost of attending a public university for that year was, on average, $12,796.

Paying for college is hard, yes; just about everyone needs some kind of financial assistance. More than 17 million students attend college each year—and only 20 percent manage to pay for it without some kind of financial aid package. That means almost 14 million students receive help.

Check out the Tuition Cost Calculator
PrincetonReview.com/college/finance/tcc

WHATS IN A FINANCIAL AID PACKAGE?

A typical financial aid package contains money, from the school, federal government, or state, in various forms: grants, scholarships, work-study programs, and loans.

Grants

Grants are essentially gifts—free money given to you by the federal government, state agencies, and an individual college. They are usually need-based, and you are not required to pay them back.

Some states have grant programs established specifically to help financially needy students, usually to attend schools within that state. Different states have different standards and application requirements.

Check out the Aid Comparison Calculator
PrincetonReview.com/college/finance/acc/calc.asp

Scholarships

Scholarships are also free money, but unlike grants, they are merit-based. Some are also based on your financial need; others are based on different qualifications, and are often need-blind.

Scholarships can be based on anything: academic achievement or test scores (the National Merit Scholarship is a well-known one), athletic achievements, musical or artistic talent, religious affiliations or ethnicity, and so on.

They don't have to come from colleges, either. Corporations, churches, volunteer organizations, unions, advocacy groups, and many other organizations offer merit-based, need-based, or simply existence-based scholarships.

When considering outside scholarships, make sure you know how the college(s) you're applying to treat them. Some schools (but not all!) will count any money you receive from outside sources as income, and reduce the amount of any aid package accordingly.

Check out the Scholarship Search page
PrincetonReview.com/college/finance

Work-Study Programs

The federal government subsidizes a nationwide program that provides part-time, on-campus jobs to students who need financial aid to attend school. Work-study participants can work in academic departments, deans' offices, libraries, and so on. You get a paycheck, like you would at any job, and you can spend the money however you like—but it's meant for tuition, books, and food.

My Family Doesn't Have $30,000 Lying Around!

You and your family are not alone. In many cases, a school's financial aid package doesn't cover all of your costs, and you might not have the resources to make up the difference. When a school doesn't offer enough in the way of aid to cover the cost of attendance, many families turn to loans.

Let's start with the biggest source of student loans—the federal government.

Last year the federal government gave more than $86 billion in student aid.

Federal student aid is intended to bridge the gap between what college costs and what you and your family can actually afford to pay. The government does this in two ways: It makes money available to colleges, which then, through their financial aid offices, make the money available to students in the form of aid packages; and it helps students get affordable loans themselves, through guarantees to loan lenders and other ways (which we'll discuss in a minute).

How Does the Government Decide How Much to Give Me?

When you're applying for financial aid, you'll be filling out a lot of forms. The most important of those forms will be the Free Application for Federal Student Aid (FAFSA). Basically, the FAFSA will want to know the following information:

- Your parents' available income
- Your parents' available assets
- Your available income
- Your available assets

The federal government will take all this information and apply a complex formula to determine what your family's expected contribution should be.

For help filling out the FAFSA, check out MyRichUncle's easy-to-use FAFSA-Assistant tool at MyRichUncle.com/TPR

What Is This "Expected Contribution"?

This is how much of your and your family's income and assets the government thinks you can afford to put toward the cost of attending college. This amount is called the Expected Family Contribution, or EFC.

Your financial need (i.e., the money you need in order to attend college) is defined as the difference between the school's total cost of attendance (tuition, room and board, books, etc.) and your expected family contribution. Or, to put it another way:

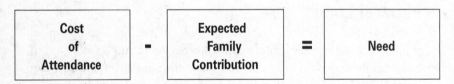

Chances are you don't have a lot of assets—you probably don't own a house, or even a car, you might not have any stocks or bonds—or do you? Did your parents or grandparents give you any bond certificates? Did they ever give you any stocks, or sign over any of their assets into your name? These are all things the financial aid people will look at when assessing your need.

When you are accepted to a college, the school's financial aid office will then put together an aid package that, hopefully, will make up this difference and cover the cost of your need.

What Do You Mean, "Hopefully"?

The idea is that your EFC will be the same for every school, regardless of the cost of the school. This means that if your EFC is determined to be $9,500, that is the amount you would be expected to pay if you go to State U., where the COA is $14,000, or if you go to Private U., where the COA is $37,000. Ideally, the school will then provide you with a financial aid package that makes up the difference—$4,500 in the case of State U., $27,500 for Private U.

Ideally?

Yes, in a perfect world, where a school offers to meet 100% of your need, you and your family would pay no more than your EFC, and your EFC would always be exactly what you and your family believe you can afford.

In reality, this doesn't happen nearly as often as we'd like. Some schools have larger endowments for financial aid and can meet your need 100%. Other schools may not.

When that happens, you and your family may want to investigate student loans.

LOANS

The federal government and private commercial lenders offer educational loans to students. Federally-guaranteed loans are usually the "first resort" for borrowers because many are subsidized by the federal government and offer capped interest rates. Private loans, on the other hand, have fewer restrictions or borrowing limits, but may have higher interest rates and more stringent credit-based qualification process—but not always, as we'll see later on.

Federal Loans

For many students seeking financial aid, the Stafford loan is the typical place to start. The federal Stafford loan program features a low capped interest rate and yearly caps on the maximum amount a student can borrow. Stafford loans can either be subsidized (the government pays the interest while you're in school) or unsubsidized (you are responsible for the interest that accrues while in school). Most students who get Stafford loans will end up with a combination of the two. Stafford loans do not have to be repaid until you've graduated or dropped below part-time status.

Here's the thing you might not know about Stafford loans:

Many people assumed that the government sets the rate on student loans, and that that rate is locked in stone. That's not true. The government merely sets the maximum rate lenders can charge (which is 6.8% as of 2007). Lenders are free to charge less than that if they want to.

Historically, however, most lenders have charged the maximum rate because Stafford loans are distributed via colleges' financial aid offices, which maintain preferred lender lists of a limited number of lenders to choose from. Reduced numbers of lenders meant little competition for borrowers, which meant the lenders had very little incentive to offer more competitive rates.

In the last few years, though, a lot has changed. More students now know that they are not required to take a loan from a lender on a preferred lender list. And there are more lenders now willing to compete on price. It's vital that you, as the person making this important and, frankly, expensive investment in your future, educate yourself fully as to all your options when it comes to student loans.

Know Your Rights

You have the right to shop for and secure the best rates possible for your student loans. You have the right to choose the lending institution you prefer. You do not have to use the lenders recommended by your college. All your college must do—and all it is legally allowed to do—is to certify for the lending institution of your choice that you are indeed enrolled and the amount you are eligible to receive.

Private Loans

Student loans from private lenders can make it possible to cover the costs of higher education when other sources of funding have been exhausted.

When you apply for a private loan, the lending institution will check your credit score and determine your capacity to pay back the money you borrow. For individuals whose credit history is less than positive, or if you have no credit history, lenders may require a co-borrower: a creditworthy individual—often a parent—who also agrees to be accountable to the terms of the loan. While private loans do have annual borrowing limits, they are usually higher than government loans, around $40,000; they also have higher interest rates and have floating rate caps, not fixed as in federal loans.

Let's say you have no credit history or a creditworthy co-borrower. You might consider Preprime™: an underwriting methodology pioneered by MyRichUncle. Instead of focusing solely on credit history, MyRichUncle with its Preprime™ option, also takes into account academic performance, student behavior, and other factors that can indicate that a student will be a responsible borrower. www.myrichuncle.com/PreprimeLoans.aspx

Do Your Research

All student loan lenders are not created equal, so investigate all your options, and look for lenders that are offering loans at rates less than the federally mandated maximum (remember, that's 6.1% for subsidized Staffords, and 6.8% for unsubsidized as of July 2008).

One lending institution that's been in the news lately is MyRichUncle. MyRichUncle offers federal loans, including subsidized and unsubsidized Stafford loans and private loans. However, MyRichUncle has remembered that the government sets the maximum interest rate for Stafford loans, and has chosen to discount the rate upon repayment. Those discounts will not disappear, like they may with other lenders, unless you default on the loan.

So, Why MyRichUncle?

Well, we here at The Princeton Review think it's important that you have all the information when you're figuring out how to pay for college, and we think MyRichUncle is doing something different—and helpful—with their approach to student loans.

They know that getting a student loan can be a complicated and intimidating process. They believe, as does The Princeton Review, that students should have access to the best education even if they don't yet have a credit history, or at least an opportunity to prove they can be credit-worthy borrowers. They also believe student loan debt can be a serious problem so your loans should be about getting the tools necessary for the best education possible that will position you for the most opportunities when you graduate.

Something else to remember: Your student loan will, ultimately, be your responsibility. When you enter into a loan agreement, you're entering into a long-term relationship with your lender—10 to 15 years, on average. The right student loan, from the right lender, can help you avoid years of unnecessary fees and payments.

THE BOTTOM LINE

College is expensive, period. But if you're reading this book, you're already invested in getting the best education that you can. You owe it to yourself and your future to invest just as much in learning about all your financial options—and opportunities—as well.

Here's a tip: *don't default.* If you ever feel that you are going to be unable to pay off your loans, contact your lender immediately. They will be happy to help you figure out a way to repay your loans, as long as you are upfront and honest with them about the difficulties you may be having.

MyRichUncle was featured in *FastCompany* magazine's Fast 50 and *BusinessWeek*'s Top Tech Entrepreneurs. MyRichUncle and its parent company, MRU Holdings, are financed by a number of leading investment banks and venture capitalists, including subsidiaries of Merrill Lynch, Lehman Brothers, and Battery Ventures For more information, check out

MY RICH UNCLE
STUDENT LOANS

IS THIS BOOK JUST LIKE YOUR COURSE?

Since the book came out, many students and teachers have asked us, "Is this book just like your course?" The short answer is no.

It isn't easy to raise SAT scores. Our course is more than 50 hours long and requires class participation, quizzes, homework, four practice examinations, and possibly additional tutoring.

We like to think that this book is fun, informative, and well written, but no book can capture the magic of our instructors and course structure. Each Princeton Review instructor has attended a top college and has excelled on the SAT. Moreover, each of our instructors undergoes rigorous training.

While this book contains many of the techniques we teach in our course, some of our techniques are too difficult to include in a book without a trained and experienced Princeton Review teacher to explain and demonstrate them. Moreover, this book is written for the average student. Each class in our course is tailored so that we can gear our techniques to each student's level.

We're Flattered, But…

Some tutors and schools use this book to run their own "Princeton Review course." While we are flattered, we are also concerned.

It has taken us many years of teaching tens of thousands of students across the country to develop our SAT program, and we're still learning. Many teachers think that our course is simply a collection of techniques that can be taught by anyone. It isn't that easy.

We train each Princeton Review instructor for many hours for every hour he or she will teach class. Each of the instructors is monitored, evaluated, and supervised throughout the course.

Another concern is that many of our techniques conflict with traditional math and English techniques as taught in high school. For example, in the Math section, we tell our students to avoid setting up algebraic equations. Can you imagine your math teacher telling you that? And in the Critical Reading section, we tell our students not to read the passage too carefully. Can you imagine your English teacher telling you that?

While we also teach traditional math and English in our course, some teachers may not completely agree with some of our approaches.

Beware of Princeton Review Clones

We have nothing against people who use our techniques, but we do object to tutors or high schools who claim to "teach The Princeton Review method." If you want to find out whether your teacher has been trained by The Princeton Review or whether you're taking an official Princeton Review course, call us toll-free at 1-800-2REVIEW.

If You'd Like More Information

Princeton Review sites are in hundreds of cities around the country. For the office nearest you, call 1-800-2REVIEW.

stimate your (or your child's) college degree will cost, including four years of tuition,
, fees, books and other expenses? (Choose one.)

$100,000

$100,000

$75,000

$50,000

$25,000

ary will financial aid (education loans, scholarships or grants) be to pay for your (your
ege education? (Choose one.)

ely

what

all

ur biggest concern about applying to or attending college? (Choose one.)

t get into first-choice college

get into first-choice college, but won't have sufficient funds/financial aid to attend

get into a college I (my child) want(s) to attend, but will take on major loan debt to do so

attend a college I (my child) may not be happy about

uld you gauge your stress level about the college application process? (Choose one.)

ry High

gh

verage

ow

ery Low

ly, how far from home would you like the college you (your child) attends to be? (Choose one.)

to 250 miles

250 to 500 miles

500 to 1,000 miles

1,000 miles or more

en it comes to choosing which college you (or your child) will attend, which of the following do you
nk it is most likely to be? (Choose one.)

College with best academic reputation

College with best program for my (my child's) career interests

College that will be the most affordable

College that will be the best overall fit

onal: What advice would you give to college applicants or parents of applicants going through this
erience next year?

AP Exams

Cracking the AP Biology Exam, 2008 Edition
978-0-375-76640-4 • $18.00/C$22.00

Cracking the AP Calculus AB & BC Exams, 2008 Edition
978-0-375-76641-1 • $19.00/C$23.00

Cracking the AP Chemistry Exam, 2008 Edition
978-0-375-76642-8 • $18.00/C$22.00

Cracking the AP Computer Science A & AB Exams, 2006–2007 Edition
978-0-375-76528-5 • $19.00/C$27.00

Cracking the AP Economics Macro & Micro Exams, 2008 Edition
978-0-375-42841-8 • $18.00/C$22.00

Cracking the AP English Language & Composition Exam, 2008 Edition
978-0-375-42842-5 • $18.00/C$21.00

Cracking the AP English Literature Exam, 2008 Edition
978-0-375-42843-2 • $18.00/C$22.00

Cracking the AP Environmental Science Exam, 2008 Edition
978-0-375-42844-9 • $18.00/C$22.00

Cracking the AP European History Exam, 2008 Edition
978-0-375-42845-6 • $18.00/C$22.00

Cracking the AP Physics B Exam, 2008 Edition
978-0-375-42846-3 • $18.00/C$21.00

Cracking the AP Physics C Exam, 2008 Edition
978-0-375-42854-8 • $18.00/C$21.00

Cracking the AP Psychology Exam, 2008 Edition
978-0-375-42847-0 • $18.00/C$22.00

Cracking the AP Spanish Exam, 2006–2007 Edition
978-0-375-76530-8 • $17.00/C$24.00

Cracking the AP Statistics Exam, 2008 Edition
978-0-375-42849-4 • $19.00/C$23.00

Cracking the AP U.S. Government & Politics Exam, 2008 Edition
978-0-375-42850-0 • $18.00/C$22.00

Cracking the AP U.S. History Exam, 2008 Edition
978-0-375-42851-7 • $18.00/C$21.00

Cracking the AP World History Exam, 2008 Edition
978-0-375-42852-4 • $18.00/C$22.00

SAT Subject Tests

Cracking the SAT Biology E/M Subject Test, 2007–2008 Edition
978-0-375-76588-9 • $19.00/C$25.00

Cracking the SAT Chemistry Subject Test, 2007–2008 Edition
978-0-375-76589-6 • $18.00/C$22.00

Cracking the SAT French Subject Test, 2007–2008 Edition
978-0-375-76590-2 • $18.00/C$22.00

Cracking the SAT Literature Subject Test, 2007–2008 Edition
978-0-375-76592-6 • $18.00/C$22.00

Cracking the SAT Math 1 and 2 Subject Tests, 2007–2008 Edition
978-0-375-76593-3 • $19.00/C$25.00

Cracking the SAT Physics Subject Test, 2007–2008 Edition
978-0-375-76594-0 • $19.00/C$25.00

Cracking the SAT Spanish Subject Test, 2007–2008 Edition
978-0-375-76595-7 • $18.00/C$22.00

Cracking the SAT U.S. & World History Subject Tests, 2007–2008 Edition
978-0-375-76591-9 • $19.00/C$25.00

WE KNOW APPLYING TO COLLEGES IS STRESSFUL.
Why Not Win $1,000 for It?

Participate in our 2009 "College Hopes & Worries Survey."

You might win our college scholarship prize.

The Princeton Review has conducted this survey of high school students applying to colleges and parents of applicants since 2002. Why? We're curious to know what concerns you the most about your application experiences and what your dream college would be.

Our survey has just 10 questions – way shorter than any college app. You can zip through it in less than three minutes. Plus, in addition to our $1,000 scholarship prize we'll give to one lucky participant chosen at random, we'll give another 25 participants (also chosen at random) a free copy of one of our college-related guidebooks. They can chose from either our *Paying for College without Going Broke*, our *Guide to College Majors*, or our *Parents' Guide to College Life*. In March, about the time you'll (hopefully) be receiving those college acceptance and financial aid award letters, we'll post the findings on our site and inform the scholarship winner and book winners. For more information, see "OFFICIAL RULES" below.

We know how exciting and how stressful college applications can be. We hope the college info on our site and in our books helps you find (and get in to!) the college best for you. We wish you great success in your applications and your college years ahead.

Official Rules:

Princeton Review 2009 "College Hopes & Worries Survey" Prize Sweepstakes

NO PURCHASE NECESSARY. OPEN TO RESIDENTS OF THE 50 UNITED STATES (AND D.C.) 13 YEARS OF AGE AND OLDER ONLY

1. HOW TO ENTER: To enter via the Internet, visit www.princetonreview.com/go/survey. You may also fax your completed questionnaire to: Robert Franek, 212-874-1754. LIMIT ONE ENTRY PER PERSON, EMAIL ADDRESS OR PHONE/FAX NUMBER. All on-line or faxed entries must be received by 11:59 p.m. EDT on March 7, 2009. To enter without Internet access or answering the questionnaire, handwrite your name, complete address and phone number on a postcard and mail to: The Princeton Review, 2009 College Hopes & Worries Survey c/o Robert Franek, 2315 Broadway, New York NY, 10024-4332. Mail-in entries must be received by March 14, 2008. Not responsible for lost, late or misdirected mail.

2. ELIGIBILITY: Open to residents of the 50 United States and D.C., 13 years of age and older, except for employees of The Princeton Review, Inc. ("Sponsor"), its affiliates, subsidiaries and agencies (collectively "Promotion Parties"), and members of their immediate family or persons living in the same household. Void where prohibited.

3. RANDOM DRAWINGS: A random drawing will be held on or about March 31, 2009. Odds of winning will depend upon the number of eligible entries received. Winner will be notified by e-mail/mail and/or telephone, at Sponsor's option and will be required to sign and return any required Affidavit of Eligibility, Release of Liability and Publicity Release within seven (7) days of attempted delivery or prize will be forfeited and an alternate winner may be selected. The return of any prize or prize notification as undeliverable may result in disqualification and an alternate winner may be selected.

4. PRIZES: One (1) Grand Prize: $1,000.00 Scholarship, awarded as a check. Twenty-Five (25) First Prizes: winners choice of one of the following Princeton Review books: Paying for College without Going Broke, Guide to College Majors, or Parents' Guide to College Life. Approximate Retail Value: $19.00. Total prize value: $1475.00. Limit one prize per family/household. All prizes will be awarded.

5. GENERAL RULES: All income taxes resulting from acceptance of prize are the responsibility of winner. By entering sweepstakes, entrant accepts and agrees to these Official Rules and the decisions of Sponsor, which shall be final in all matters. By accepting prize, winner agrees to hold Promotion Parties, their affiliates, directors, officers, employees and assigns harmless against any and all claims and liability arising out of use of prize. Acceptance also constitutes permission to the Promotion Parties to use winner's name and likeness for marketing purposes without further compensation or right of approval, unless prohibited by law. Promotion Parties are not responsible for lost or late mail, or for technical, hardware or software malfunctions, lost or unavailable network connections, or failed, incorrect, inaccurate, incomplete, garbled or delayed electronic communications whether caused by the sender or by any of the equipment or programming associated with or utilized in this sweepstakes, or by any human error which may occur in the processing of the entries in this sweepstakes. If, in the Sponsor's opinion, there is any suspected evidence of tampering with any portion of the promotion, or if technical difficulties compromise the integrity of the promotion, the Sponsor reserves the right to modify or terminate the sweepstakes in a manner deemed reasonable by the Sponsor, at the Sponsor's sole discretion. In the event a dispute arises as to the identity of a potentially winning online entrant, entries made by internet will be declared made by the name on the online entry form. All federal and state laws apply.

6. WINNERS LIST: For the names of the winners, available after May 1, 2009 send a self-addressed, stamped (#10) envelope to: The Princeton Review, 2009 College Hopes & Worries Survey Contest Winners, c/o Robert Franek, 2315 Broadway, New York, NY, 10024-4332

SPONSOR: The Princeton Review, Inc., New York, NY 10024.

The Princeton Review
College Hopes &
www.PrincetonReview.com

Snail mail to Robert Franek, The Princeton Review, 231
or fax to Robert Franek, 212-874-1754 or fill out online a

Name _____

Address (optional) _____

City / State / Zip _____

Daytime phone _____

E-mail address _____

I am ____ a parent of a student ____ a student applying to at

____ Spring or Fall 2009 ____ Spring or Fall 2010 ____ Later

1. What would be your "dream" college? What college would you mos attend) if chance of being accepted or cost were not an issue?"

_____

2. How many colleges will you (your child) apply to?

____ 1 to 4

____ 5 to 8

____ 9 to 12

____ 13 or more

3. How would you rate the information and support you've received from guidance counselor to help you through your (your child's) college application

____ Outstanding

____ Very good

____ Adequate

____ Fair

____ Poor

4. What has been, or do you think will be the toughest part of your (your child's) c experience? (Choose one.)

____ Research: getting info on colleges, visiting them, and winnowing a list of sch

____ Admission and placement tests: taking and scoring well on the SAT, ACT, or A

____ Preparing application packages: meeting requirements, completing forms, and in on time

____ The anxious wait for acceptance/aid award letters and decision of which college

5. What do you room & board

____ More tha

____ $75,000 t

____ $50,000

____ $25,000

____ Less tha

6. How necess child's) col

____ Extrem

____ Very

____ Some

____ Not a

7. What's Y

____ Won

____ Will

____ Will

____ Wil

8. How w

____ Ve

____ Hi

____ A

____ L

____ V

9. Idea

10. W th

Opt exp

AP Exams

**Cracking the AP Biology Exam,
2008 Edition**
978-0-375-76640-4 • $18.00/C$22.00

**Cracking the AP Calculus AB & BC Exams,
2008 Edition**
978-0-375-76641-1 • $19.00/C$23.00

**Cracking the AP Chemistry Exam,
2008 Edition**
978-0-375-76642-8 • $18.00/C$22.00

**Cracking the AP Computer Science A & AB
Exams, 2006–2007 Edition**
978-0-375-76528-5 • $19.00/C$27.00

**Cracking the AP Economics Macro & Micro
Exams, 2008 Edition**
978-0-375-42841-8 • $18.00/C$22.00

**Cracking the AP English Language &
Composition Exam, 2008 Edition**
978-0-375-42842-5 • $18.00/C$21.00

**Cracking the AP English Literature Exam,
2008 Edition**
978-0-375-42843-2 • $18.00/C$22.00

**Cracking the AP Environmental
Science Exam, 2008 Edition**
978-0-375-42844-9 • $18.00/C$22.00

**Cracking the AP European History Exam,
2008 Edition**
978-0-375-42845-6 • $18.00/C$22.00

**Cracking the AP Physics B Exam,
2008 Edition**
978-0-375-42846-3 • $18.00/C$21.00

**Cracking the AP Physics C Exam,
2008 Edition**
978-0-375-42854-8 • $18.00/C$21.00

**Cracking the AP Psychology Exam,
2008 Edition**
978-0-375-42847-0 • $18.00/C$22.00

**Cracking the AP Spanish Exam,
2006–2007 Edition**
978-0-375-76530-8 • $17.00/C$24.00

**Cracking the AP Statistics Exam,
2008 Edition**
978-0-375-42849-4 • $19.00/C$23.00

**Cracking the AP U.S. Government
& Politics Exam, 2008 Edition**
978-0-375-42850-0 • $18.00/C$22.00

**Cracking the AP U.S. History Exam,
2008 Edition**
978-0-375-42851-7 • $18.00/C$21.00

**Cracking the AP World History Exam,
2008 Edition**
978-0-375-42852-4 • $18.00/C$22.00

SAT Subject Tests

**Cracking the SAT Biology E/M
Subject Test, 2007–2008 Edition**
978-0-375-76588-9 • $19.00/C$25.00

**Cracking the SAT Chemistry Subject Test,
2007–2008 Edition**
978-0-375-76589-6 • $18.00/C$22.00

**Cracking the SAT French Subject Test,
2007–2008 Edition**
978-0-375-76590-2 • $18.00/C$22.00

**Cracking the SAT Literature Subject Test,
2007–2008 Edition**
978-0-375-76592-6 • $18.00/C$22.00

**Cracking the SAT Math 1 and 2
Subject Tests, 2007–2008 Edition**
978-0-375-76593-3 • $19.00/C$25.00

**Cracking the SAT Physics Subject Test, 2007–
2008 Edition**
978-0-375-76594-0 • $19.00/C$25.00

**Cracking the SAT Spanish Subject Test, 2007–
2008 Edition**
978-0-375-76595-7 • $18.00/C$22.00

**Cracking the SAT U.S. & World History Sub-
ject Tests, 2007–2008 Edition**
978-0-375-76591-9 • $19.00/C$25.00

WE KNOW APPLYING TO COLLEGES IS STRESSFUL.

Why Not Win $1,000 for It?

Participate in our 2009 "College Hopes & Worries Survey."

You might win our college scholarship prize.

The Princeton Review has conducted this survey of high school students applying to colleges and parents of applicants since 2002. Why? We're curious to know what concerns you the most about your application experiences and what your dream college would be.

Our survey has just 10 questions – way shorter than any college app. You can zip through it in less than three minutes. Plus, in addition to our $1,000 scholarship prize we'll give to one lucky participant chosen at random, we'll give another 25 participants (also chosen at random) a free copy of one of our college-related guidebooks. They can chose from either our *Paying for College without Going Broke*, our *Guide to College Majors*, or our *Parents' Guide to College Life*. In March, about the time you'll (hopefully) be receiving those college acceptance and financial aid award letters, we'll post the findings on our site and inform the scholarship winner and book winners. For more information, see "OFFICIAL RULES" below.

We know how exciting and how stressful college applications can be. We hope the college info on our site and in our books helps you find (and get in to!) the college best for you. We wish you great success in your applications and your college years ahead.

Official Rules:

Princeton Review 2009 "College Hopes & Worries Survey" Prize Sweepstakes

NO PURCHASE NECESSARY. OPEN TO RESIDENTS OF THE 50 UNITED STATES (AND D.C.) 13 YEARS OF AGE AND OLDER ONLY

1. HOW TO ENTER: To enter via the Internet, visit www.princetonreview.com/go/survey. You may also fax your completed questionnaire to: Robert Franek, 212-874-1754. LIMIT ONE ENTRY PER PERSON, EMAIL ADDRESS OR PHONE/FAX NUMBER. All on-line or faxed entries must be received by 11:59 p.m. EDT on March 7, 2009. To enter without Internet access or answering the questionnaire, handwrite your name, complete address and phone number on a postcard and mail to: The Princeton Review, 2009 College Hopes & Worries Survey c/o Robert Franek, 2315 Broadway, New York NY, 10024-4332. Mail-in entries must be received by March 14, 2008. Not responsible for lost, late or misdirected mail.

2. ELIGIBILITY: Open to residents of the 50 United States and D.C., 13 years of age and older, except for employees of The Princeton Review, Inc. ("Sponsor"), its affiliates, subsidiaries and agencies (collectively "Promotion Parties"), and members of their immediate family or persons living in the same household. Void where prohibited.

3. RANDOM DRAWINGS: A random drawing will be held on or about March 31, 2009. Odds of winning will depend upon the number of eligible entries received. Winner will be notified by e-mail/mail and/or telephone, at Sponsor's option and will be required to sign and return any required Affidavit of Eligibility, Release of Liability and Publicity Release within seven (7) days of attempted delivery or prize will be forfeited and an alternate winner may be selected. The return of any prize or prize notification as undeliverable may result in disqualification and an alternate winner may be selected.

4. PRIZES: One (1) Grand Prize: $1,000.00 Scholarship, awarded as a check. Twenty-Five (25) First Prizes: winners choice of one of the following Princeton Review books: Paying for College without Going Broke, Guide to College Majors, or Parents' Guide to College Life. Approximate Retail Value: $19.00. Total prize value: $1475.00. Limit one prize per family/household. All prizes will be awarded.

5. GENERAL RULES: All income taxes resulting from acceptance of prize are the responsibility of winner. By entering sweepstakes, entrant accepts and agrees to these Official Rules and the decisions of Sponsor, which shall be final in all matters. By accepting prize, winner agrees to hold Promotion Parties, their affiliates, directors, officers, employees and assigns harmless against any and all claims and liability arising out of use of prize. Acceptance also constitutes permission to the Promotion Parties to use winner's name and likeness for marketing purposes without further compensation or right of approval, unless prohibited by law. Promotion Parties are not responsible for lost or late mail, or for technical, hardware or software malfunctions, lost or unavailable network connections, or failed, incorrect, inaccurate, incomplete, garbled or delayed electronic communications whether caused by the sender or by any of the equipment or programming associated with or utilized in this sweepstakes, or by any human error which may occur in the processing of the entries in this sweepstakes. If, in the Sponsor's opinion, there is any suspected evidence of tampering with any portion of the promotion, or if technical difficulties compromise the integrity of the promotion, the Sponsor reserves the right to modify or terminate the sweepstakes in a manner deemed reasonable by the Sponsor, at the Sponsor's sole discretion. In the event a dispute arises as to the identity of a potentially winning online entrant, entries made by internet will be declared made by the name on the online entry form. All federal and state laws apply.

6. WINNERS LIST: For the names of the winners, available after May 1, 2009 send a self-addressed, stamped (#10) envelope to: The Princeton Review, 2009 College Hopes & Worries Survey Contest Winners, c/o Robert Franek, 2315 Broadway, New York, NY, 10024-4332

SPONSOR: The Princeton Review, Inc., New York, NY 10024.

College Hopes & Worries Survey 2008

Snail mail to Robert Franek, The Princeton Review, 2315 Broadway, New York, NY 10024
or fax to Robert Franek, 212-874-1754 or fill out online at PrincetonReview.com/go/survey

Name _____

Address (optional) _____

City / State / Zip _____

Daytime phone _____

E-mail address _____

I am ____ a parent of a student   ____ a student applying to attend college beginning in

____ Spring or Fall 2009 ____ Spring or Fall 2010 ____ Later (indicate year:_____).

1   What would be your "dream" college? What college would you most like to attend (or see your child attend) if chance of being accepted or cost were not an issue?"

_____

2   How many colleges will you (your child) apply to?

____ 1 to 4

____ 5 to 8

____ 9 to 12

____ 13 or more

3   How would you rate the information and support you've received from your (your child's) school guidance counselor to help you through your (your child's) college application experience? (Choose one.)

____ Outstanding

____ Very good

____ Adequate

____ Fair

____ Poor

4   What has been, or do you think will be the toughest part of your (your child's) college application experience? (Choose one.)

____ Research: getting info on colleges, visiting them, and winnowing a list of schools to apply to

____ Admission and placement tests: taking and scoring well on the SAT, ACT, or APs

____ Preparing application packages: meeting requirements, completing forms, and getting everything in on time

____ The anxious wait for acceptance/aid award letters and decision of which college to attend

5   What do you estimate your (or your child's) college degree will cost, including four years of tuition, room & board, fees, books and other expenses? (Choose one.)

_____ More than $100,000

_____ $75,000 to $100,000

_____ $50,000 to $75,000

_____ $25,000 to $50,000

_____ Less tha $25,000

6   How necessary will financial aid (education loans, scholarships or grants) be to pay for your (your child's) college education? (Choose one.)

_____ Extremely

_____ Very

_____ Somewhat

_____ Not at all

7   What's your biggest concern about applying to or attending college? (Choose one.)

_____ Won't get into first-choice college

_____ Will get into first-choice college, but won't have sufficient funds/financial aid to attend

_____ Will get into a college I (my child) want(s) to attend, but will take on major loan debt to do so

_____ Will attend a college I (my child) may not be happy about

8   How would you gauge your stress level about the college application process? (Choose one.)

_____ Very High

_____ High

_____ Average

_____ Low

_____ Very Low

9   Ideally, how far from home would you like the college you (your child) attends to be? (Choose one.)

_____ 0 to 250 miles

_____ 250 to 500 miles

_____ 500 to 1,000 miles

_____ 1,000 miles or more

10 When it comes to choosing which college you (or your child) will attend, which of the following do you think it is most likely to be? (Choose one.)

_____ College with best academic reputation

_____ College with best program for my (my child's) career interests

_____ College that will be the most affordable

_____ College that will be the best overall fit

Optional: What advice would you give to college applicants or parents of applicants going through this experience next year?

_____

_____